The Relative Importance of the National Debt

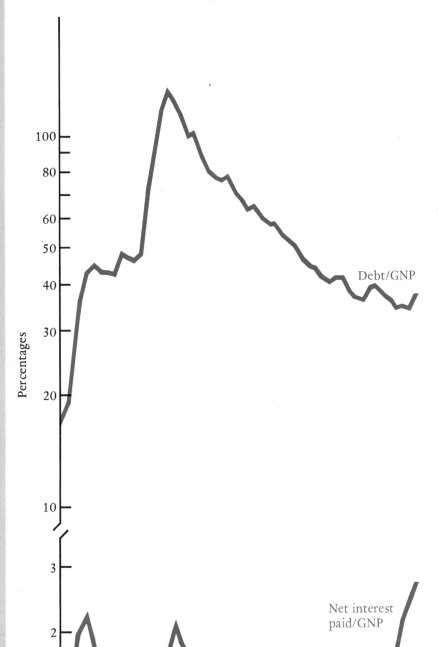

The national debt has not reached alarming proportions in relation to GNP. Stated as a proportion of the country's national income, the national debt rose dramatically during the slide into the Great Depression, 1929–1933, but not much during the New Deal. It rose dramatically again during World War II, but since then the trend has been steadily downward. Net interest payments on the national debt have been a rising proportion of GNP since 1973. The different trends in debt and debt servicing between 1973 and 1981 are accounted for by the rising cost of servicing the debt due to rising interest rates.

ECONOMICS

ECONOMICS
SEVENTH EDITION

Richard G. Lipsey
QUEEN'S UNIVERSITY

Peter O. Steiner
THE UNIVERSITY OF MICHIGAN

Douglas D. Purvis
QUEEN'S UNIVERSITY

HARPER & ROW, PUBLISHERS, New York
Cambridge, Philadelphia, San Francisco,
London, Mexico City, São Paulo, Sydney

1817

Sponsoring Editor: David Forgione
Development Editor: Mary Lou Mosher
Project Editor: Nora Helfgott
Interior Designer: Helen Iranyi
Production Assistant: Debi Forrest Bochner
Compositor: Ruttle, Shaw & Wetherill, Inc.
Printer and Binder: Kingsport Press
Art Studio: J&R Art Services, Inc.

Economics, Seventh Edition

Library of Congress Cataloging in Publication Data

Lipsey, Richard G., 1928-
  Economics.

  Includes index.
  1. Economics. I. Steiner, Peter Otto, 1922-
II. Purvis, Douglas D. III. Title.
HB171.5.L733 1984   330   83–22605

ISBN 0-06-043927-0
Harper International Edition
ISBN 0-06-350425-1

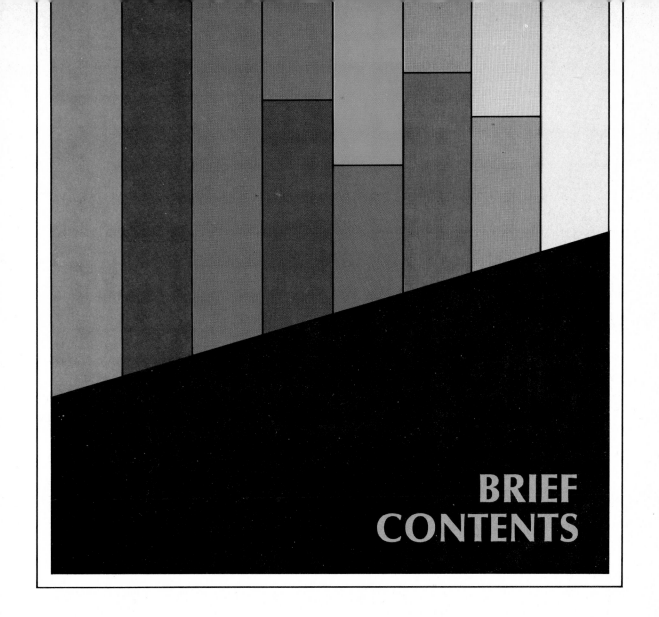

BRIEF CONTENTS

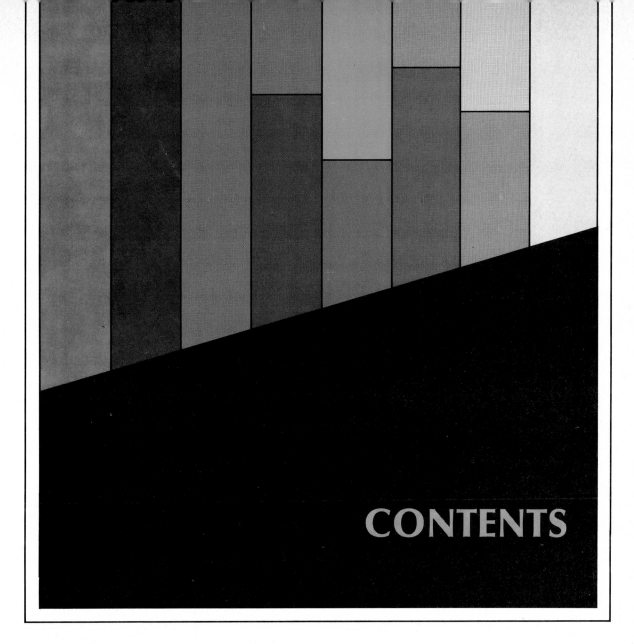

CONTENTS

PREFACE

Our basic motivation in writing *Economics* always has been, and in this seventh edition still is, to provide a book that reflects the enormous changes in economics over the last 40 years. Economics is always changing, but in the last few decades there has been a change of such importance that we do ourselves and our students a great disservice if we neglect it. During this period economics has moved very rapidly toward becoming a science. We apply the term *science* neither to praise nor to castigate

economics, but to describe its movement toward the characteristic that distinguishes any science: the systematic confrontation of theory with observation.

The quotation from Lord William Beveridge on page xxxiii of this book is our text—in the preacher's sense of that word. Beveridge was scolding the profession in 1937, but things since then have clearly changed for the better. Today most of us agree that economics is not a stage on which we parade our pet theories and ask to have them admired solely for their elegance or their conclusions, nor is it a container in which we collect quantities of unrelated institutional and statistical material about the economy. Economists are pushing back the frontiers of ignorance about the economic environment in order both to understand it and to control it. But new problems and new phenomena continually challenge our existing knowledge. Economists are therefore continually concerned with the relations among theory, institutions, and facts and must regard every theory as subject to empirical challenge.

A second major theme of this book concerns the relations between economic theory and economic policy. An appreciation of these relations is not new to economics. Indeed, many nineteenth-century economists expressed the modern view that although economic theory can show us some of the consequences of our actions, it can never show us what we ought to do. What is new today is the realization of how little can be said about policy on the basis of the purely qualitative theories, and the resulting successful application of the quantitative revolution of the last 40 years to matters of policy. Four decades of systematic observations have provided us with a much better idea of how things are related to one another quantitatively, and this knowledge has greatly increased the economist's power to say sensible and relevant things about public policy. This is not to deny that there are still great areas where economists' knowledge is painfully sparse, as the current debates about how to cope with the twin problems of unemployment and inflation, and on the relative efficacy of monetary and fiscal policy, remind us.

The third major feature of the book relates to the way we view modern students. We have tried in several different ways to be as honest with them as is possible within the confines of an introductory textbook. No subject worth studying is always easy, and we have not glossed over hard points just because they are hard. We have tried to follow Einstein's advice: make things as simple as possible, but not simpler. We do not approve of slipping particularly hard bits of analysis past students without letting them see what is happening and what has been assumed, nor do we approve of teaching them things they will have to unlearn if they go on in economics (a practice sometimes justified on the grounds that it is important to get to the big issues quickly).

Every student who continues in economics soon learns that, although economics has many triumphs to its credit, there are areas where present knowledge is woefully inadequate. It is sometimes argued that in an elementary course such inadequacies should be played down or altogether suppressed so that beginning students will not lose faith in their subject. We reject this view. Both student education and our subject depend upon careful criticism.

Effective criticism of existing ideas is the springboard to progress in science, and we believe that an introduction to economics should also introduce students to methods for testing, criticizing, and evaluating the present state of the subject. We do not accept the notion that if you suggest the possibility of criticism to students, they will make hasty and confused criticisms. Students will always make criticisms and evaluations of their courses, and their criticisms are much more likely to be informed and relevant if they are given both practice and instruction in how to go about challenging in an effective, constructive manner what they have been taught rather than reverting to mere dogmatic assertion of error or irrelevance.

MAJOR REVISIONS IN THIS EDITION

This revision is one of the most comprehensive we have undertaken since the second edition. Users of the sixth edition will want to check the details of the new table of contents carefully. The most basic change is the revision of the presentation of macroeconomic theory and policy, as described in detail below. But other major changes have been made throughout the book. We believe our treatment is now more up-to-date, more relevant to contemporary issues, and easier for students. Only time—and your letters—will tell us if we are right.

Changes in Microeconomics

Major changes have occurred, but roughly the same chapter structure remains. These changes include the following:

1. We have incorporated important new empirical knowledge about topics such as causes of the American productivity decline (Chapter 13), the impact of minimum wages (Chapter 21), and the effectiveness of transfer payments in alleviating poverty (Chapter 23).

2. We have provided a background for an evaluation of the impact of the Reagan Administration's sharp changes in direction with respect to areas such as regulation (Chapter 18), poverty (Chapter 23), social insurance (Chapter 23), and urban problems (Chapter 25).

3. We have provided some *micro*economic theoretical underpinnings for the *macro*economic controversy about how firms and markets respond to fluctuations in aggregate demand and whether or not labor markets clear. Issues of price flexibility (Chapter 16) and the existence of involuntary unemployment (Chapter 21) are newly discussed.

4. We have addressed sharply changing world conditions that require substantial rewriting to update the discussion of OPEC (Chapter 17) and agriculture (Chapter 8).

Beyond this, as with every revision, there are new topics or new approaches to exposition that have been suggested to us or that simply seem timely to introduce. We have expanded the discussion of efficiency and inefficiency, and the case for and against relying on the free market to allocate resources and distribute income. This change affects, and we think improves, our whole treatment of microeconomics, but especially Chapters 14, 15, and 24. We have eliminated the sixth edition's Chapter 10 ("Demand Theory in Action"), which many of you told us you did not have time to cover, but retained some of its empirical findings on demand elasticities to enliven the previously theoretical Chapter 6. We have reorganized the demand (household choice) material so as to make it easier to choose *either* marginal utility *or* indifference curve approaches. And we have put agriculture into a separate chapter so you can give it greater attention or skip it. Among the new material are discussions of the likelihood of destructive competition, predatory practices, moral hazard, principal-agent issues, and the value of oil in the ground. As always, we have read every paragraph, and reviewed every figure and table to see if we could make our book more accessible, more interesting, and more meaningful to students.

Changes in Macroeconomics

Virtually every chapter in macroeconomics has been extensively revised. In addition, there is one new chapter (Chapter 30), as well as important structural changes. Parts Seven, Eight, and Nine have been rewritten to develop more fully aggregate demand (*AD*) and aggregate supply (*AS*) curves as the central framework of macro analysis. The basic approach taken in the sixth edition has been retained, but with considerable changes. Specifically, the treatment of the *AS* curve has been totally rethought; the new Chapter 30 "Changes in National Income II: The Role of Aggregate Supply" is devoted to its role. All the other "core" macro chapters have been thoroughly revised to incorporate fully the *AD/AS* approach.

In more detail, the most important changes are:

1. The empirical and policy issues treated in Chapter 38 of the sixth edition have been integrated throughout Chapters 26–38 of the seventh edition.

2. Now Chapter 26 not only describes the key macro variables but also discusses how and why these variables matter in economic welfare and economic policy.

3. Chapter 27 now offers *three* approaches to accounting for national income—the output, expenditure, and income approaches—to give both a more complete and a clearer discussion than was possible using only two approaches.

4. Chapter 30 is new. It treats in detail the factors influencing the slope of the *AS* curve and the forces that cause the *AS* curve to shift. The

distinction, important for most of the remaining chapters, between the short-run aggregate supply curves (*SRAS*) and long-run aggregate supply curves (*LRAS*) is met and carefully explained.

5. The theoretical sections of Chapters 31, 32, 33, and 34 have been rewritten to incorporate more fully the *AS/AD* apparatus. In addition, Chapter 32 contains a new section on the economics of budget deficits.

6. The treatment of money has been reorganized. Chapters 32 and 33 from the sixth edition have been shortened and combined into one chapter, Chapter 33, that contains detailed discussions of recent deregulation of the banking system and the changing definitions of key monetary aggregates. Chapter 34 treats the role of money in macroeconomics and develops in detail the monetary adjustment mechanism underlying the slope of the *AD* curve. Chapter 35 on monetary policy now includes a discussion of the targets and instruments framework, and of the recent monetary policy focus on controlling monetary aggregates and disinflation.

7. Part Nine now includes separate chapters on inflation (Chapter 36) and unemployment (Chapter 37). Inflation is discussed in terms of the *AD/AS* model; the Phillips curve discussion appears in an appendix. Economic growth is included in this part (Chapter 38), reflecting our belief that issues of growth and productivity are again at the forefront of economic debate. Chapter 39 covers recent macroeconomic controversies, including full treatment of rational expectations and the new Classical economics.

Changes in International Economics and Comparative Systems

Chapter 40, "The Gains from Trade," gives more emphasis to gains made possible from exploiting returns to scale. Chapter 41 includes a discussion of the apparent failure of the most recent meeting of the GATT, and of the sources of growing world-wide pressure for increased protectionism. Chapter 43 has been rewritten to focus on recent experience

with flexible exchange rates; the discussion of the collapse of the gold standard and of the adjustable-peg Bretton Woods system has been moved to an appendix. Chapter 45 includes, for the first time, a discussion of the economic development of China.

TEACHING AIDS

Tag lines and captions for figures and tables. The boldface tag line below or next to the figure or table indicates succinctly the central conclusion intended by the illustration; the lightface caption provides information needed to reach that conclusion. Titles, tag lines, and captions are, with the figure or table, a self-contained set, and many students find them a useful device for reviewing.

Boxes. The material in "boxes" contains examples or materials that are relevant extensions of the text narrative but need not be read in sequence. The boxes are all optional. *Some* contain further theoretical material that some instructors like to cover while others like to omit. Others contain illustrations and applications of the points covered in the text. The basic principle is that the material is all optional although much of it is, we hope, interesting. The boxes give instructors easy flexibility in expanding or contracting the coverage of specific chapters.

End-of-chapter material. Each chapter contains a Summary, a list of Topics for Review, and a set of Discussion Questions. The questions are particularly useful for class discussion or for "quiz sections." They are answered in the Instructor's Manual.

Mathematical notes. Mathematical notes to the body of the text are collected in a self-contained section at the end of the book. Since mathematical notation and derivation is not required to understand the principles of economics, but is helpful in more advanced work, this seems to us to be a sensible arrangement. It provides clues to the uses of mathematics for the increasing numbers of students who come to beginning economics with some background in math, without encumbering the text with notes that may appear formidable to those who find mathematics arcane or frightening. Students with a mathematical background have many times told us they find the notes helpful.

Glossary. The glossary covers widely used definitions of economic terms. Because some users treat micro- and macroeconomics in that order, and others in reverse order, words in the glossary are printed in boldface type when they are first mentioned in *either half* of the text.

Endpapers. Inside the front cover are two figures; one represents the relative importance of the national debt, and the other represents the changing form of major federal expenditures. Inside the back cover is a list of the most commonly used abbreviations in the text and a set of useful data from the U.S. economy.

Supplements

Our book is accompanied by a workbook, *Study Guide and Problems*, prepared by Professor Dascomb R. Forbush and Professor Frederic C. Menz. The workbook is designed to be used either in the classroom or by the students working on their own.

An *Instructor's Manual*, prepared by us, and a *Test Bank*, prepared under our supervision, are available to instructors adopting the book. The Test Bank is also available in a computerized form; contact the publisher for details.

USING THE BOOK

This textbook reflects to some extent the way its authors teach their own basic courses. Needs of students differ; some want to have material that goes beyond the average class level, but others have gaps in their backgrounds. To accommodate the former, we have included more material than we would assign to every student. Also, because there are many different kinds of first-year economics courses in colleges and universities, we have in-

cluded more material than normally would be included in any single course. Requests and suggestions from users of previous editions have prompted us to include some additional alternative material.

Although teachers can best design their own courses, it may be helpful if we indicate certain views of our own as to how this book *might* be adapted to different courses.

Sequence

Because the choice of order between macro and micro is partly a personal one, it cannot be decided solely by objective criteria. We believe that in the 1980s there are good reasons for preferring the micro-macro order. Whereas in the immediate post-World War II years, the major emphasis was on the development of both the theory and the policy implications of Keynesian economics, the thrust over the last 20 years has been to examine the micro underpinnings of macro functions and to erect macroeconomics on a firmer base of micro behavioral relations. Virtually every current macro controversy to which one wishes to draw a student's attention turns on some micro underpinning. For "micro-firsters" this poses no problem. For "macro-firsters" it is often hard to explain what is at issue.

Changes have occurred not only in economic theory but in the problems that excite students. Although macroeconomic problems such as inflation and unemployment are still of great concern, many of the problems that students find most challenging today—the plight of the cities, poverty, pollution, and managing wage and price controls— are microeconomic in character. The micro-macro order, moreover, reflects the historical evolution of the subject. A century of classical and neoclassical development of microeconomics preceded the Keynesian development of macroeconomics.

For those who prefer the macro-micro order and who wish to reverse the order of our book, we have attempted to make reversibility virtually painless. The overview chapter that ends Part One has been built up to provide an improved base on which to build either the microeconomics of Part Two or the macroeconomics of Part Seven. Chapter 5 should be assigned after Chapter 4, even in macro-first courses. Where further microeconomic concepts are required—as in the macro investment chapter—we have added brief sections to make the treatment self-contained, while providing review material for those who have been through the microeconomic section.

One-Semester Courses

Thorough coverage of the bulk of the book supposes a two-semester course in economics. A great many first courses in economics are only one semester (or equivalent) in length and our book can be easily adapted to such courses. Suggestions for use of this book for such courses are given on pages xxix–xxx. We recognize that for any one-semester course a choice must be made among emphases. Most one-semester survey courses necessarily give some coverage to theory and to policy, to micro- and to macroeconomics, but the relative weights vary. Instructors will wish to choose the topics to be included or excluded and to vary the order to suit their own preferences.

ACKNOWLEDGMENTS

So many teachers, colleagues, students, and friends contributed to the original book and to its continuing revision that it is impossible for us to acknowledge our debts to all of them individually. Hundreds of users, both teachers and students, have written us with specific suggested improvements, and much of the credit for the fact that the book has become more teachable belongs to them. We can no longer list them individually but we thank them all, most sincerely. A few individuals provided reviews of the sixth edition that were most helpful in preparing the present edition. These are Gerald M. Miller, Miami University of Ohio; Michael Perelman, California State University, Chico; Joseph J. Seneca, Rutgers University; R. Charles Vars, Jr., Oregon State University; and Jeffrey Wolcowitz, Harvard University. When revising the macro half of the book, we benefitted greatly from several critical readings of early drafts of new chapters. Those who provided such reviews were Christine Augustyniak, College of the Holy Cross, Worcester; James T. Campen, University of Massachusetts, Boston; Hugh Hayakawa, University of Georgia; Taka Ito, University of Minnesota; James Price, Syracuse University; Bernard Saffran, Swarthmore College; and William C. Wood, University of Virginia.

We owe special thanks to Robert Dernberger and Robert Summers for detailed suggestions for revision of particular chapters in their areas of specialty.

The new edition has benefitted greatly from the research assistance of Murray Frank, John Kari Kari, Judith Roberts, and David Steiner. Frederick Menz, Dascomb Forbush, Douglas Auld, and Kenneth Grant, who contributed to the supplements, have all contributed to this edition as well.

Dorothy Edwards, Evelyn Chipps, and especially Ellen McKay and Dorothy O'Reilly coped with mountains of manuscript with extraordinary skill and patience under difficult circumstances. Weidenfeld and Nicholson generously gave permission to use material first prepared for the sixth edition of *An Introduction to Positive Economics* by R. G. Lipsey.

Finally, we thank Patricia Owen Steiner whose eagle eye and voracious reading have contributed to the illustrative examples and end-of-chapter questions in this edition, as in every edition since the second. We dedicate this seventh edition to her.

Richard G. Lipsey
Peter O. Steiner
Douglas D. Purvis

SUGGESTED OUTLINE FOR A ONE-SEMESTER COURSE[1]

Basic Core Chapters for Courses Covering Both Micro and Macro

[1] A full semester course can cover not more than 25 full chapters. The core consists of about 18 chapters. Selections from other chapters, as listed below or according to the instructor's own preferences, can produce courses with various emphases.

Chapters That Can Be Added to Give Different Emphases to Different Courses[2]

[2] Chapters shown with an * are particularly appropriate for courses with a heavy policy orientation. Chapters not listed here or in the core seem to us to be of lower priority in a one-semester course.

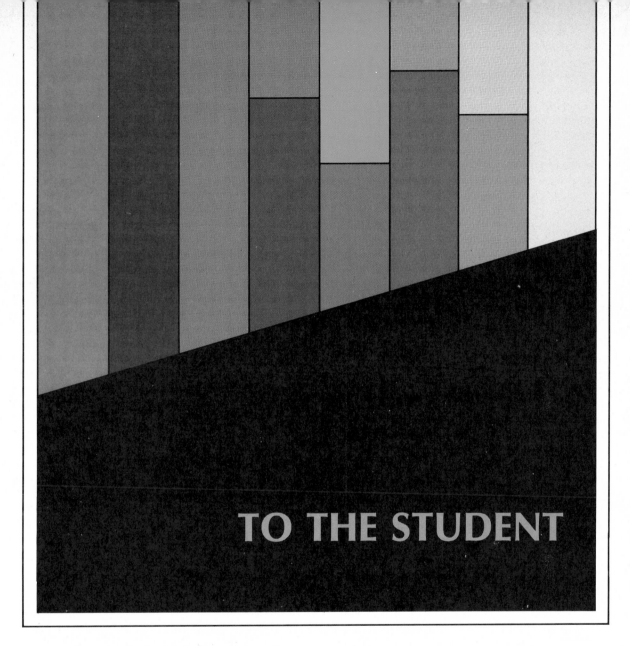

TO THE STUDENT

A good course in economics will give you insight into how an economy functions and into some currently debated policy issues. Like all rewarding subjects, economics will not be mastered without effort. A book on economics must be worked at. It cannot be read like a novel.

Each of you must develop an individual technique for studying, but the following suggestions may prove helpful. It is usually a good idea to read a chapter quickly in order to get the general run of the argument. At this first reading you may want to skip the "boxes" of text material and any footnotes. Then, after reading the Topics for Review and the Discussion Questions, reread the chapter more slowly, making sure that you understand each step of the argument. With respect to the figures and tables, be sure you understand how the conclusions stated in the brief tag lines with each table or figure have been reached. You should be prepared to spend time on difficult sections; occasionally, you may spend an hour on only a few pages. Paper and a pencil are indispensable equipment in your reading. It is best to follow a difficult argument by building your own diagram while the argument unfolds rather than by relying on the finished diagram as it appears in the book. It is often helpful to invent numerical examples to illustrate general propositions. The end-of-chapter questions require you to apply what you have studied. We advise you to outline answers to some of the questions. In short, you should seek to understand economics, not to memorize it.

After you have read each part in detail, reread it quickly from beginning to end. It is often difficult to understand why certain things are done when they are viewed as isolated points, but when you reread a whole part, much that did not seem relevant or entirely comprehensible will fall into place in the analysis.

We call your attention to the glossary at the end of the book. Any time you run into a concept that seems vaguely familiar but is not clear to you, check the glossary. The chances are that it will be there, and its definition will remind you of what you once understood. If you are still in doubt, check the index entry to find where the concept is discussed more fully. Incidentally, the glossary, along with the captions that accompany figures and tables and the end-of-chapter summaries, may prove very helpful when reviewing for examinations.

The bracketed colored numbers in the text itself refer to a series of 54 mathematical notes that are found starting on page 954. For those of you who like mathematics or prefer mathematical argument to verbal or geometric exposition, these may prove useful. Others may ignore them.

We hope that you will find the book rewarding and stimulating. Students who used earlier editions made some of the most helpful suggestions for revision, and we hope you will carry on the tradition. If you are moved to write to us, please do.

EINSTEIN STARTED FROM FACTS

The Morley-Michelson measurements of light, the movements of the planet Mercury, the unexplained aberrancies of the moon from its predicted place. Einstein went back to facts or told others where they should go to confirm or to reject his theory—by observation of stellar positions during a total eclipse. . . .

. . . It is not necessary, of course, for the verification of a new theory to be done personally by its propounder. Theoretical reasoning from facts is as essential a part of economic science as of other sciences, and in a wise division of labour there is room, in economics, as elsewhere, for the theoretician pure and simple, for one who leaves the technical business of verification to those who have acquired a special technique of observation. No one demanded of Einstein that he should visit the South Seas in person, and look through a telescope; but he told others what he expected them to see, if they looked, and he was prepared to stand or fall by the result. It is the duty of the propounder of every new theory, if he has not himself the equipment for observation, to indicate where verification of his theory is to be sought in facts—what may be expected to happen or to have happened if his theory is true, what will not happen if it is false.

[Now consider by way of contrast the behaviour of the participants in a current controversy in economics.] . . . None of them takes the point that the truth or falsehood of . . . [a] theory cannot be established except by appeal to facts; none of them tests it by facts himself. The distinguishing mark of economic science, as illustrated by this debate, is that it is a science in which verification of generalisations by reference to facts is neglected as irrelevant.

. . . I do not see how . . . [members of the public who survey the controversy] can avoid the conclusion that economics is not a science concerned with phenomena, but a survival of medieval logic, and that economists are persons who earn their livings by taking in one another's definitions for mangling. . . .

I know that in speaking thus I make enemies. I challenge a tradition of a hundred years of political economy, in which facts have been treated, not as controls of theory, but as illustrations. I shall be told that in the Social Sciences verification can never be clean enough to be decisive. I may be told that, in these sciences, observation has been tried and has failed, has led to shapeless accumulations of facts which themselves lead nowhere. I do not believe for a moment that this charge of barrenness of past enquiries can be sustained; to make it is to ignore many achievements of the past and to decry much solid work that is being done at this School and elsewhere. But if the charge of barrenness of realistic economics in the past were justified completely, that would not be a reason for giving up observation and verification. It would only be a reason for making our observations more exact and more numerous. If, in the Social Sciences, we cannot yet run or fly, we ought to be content to walk, or to creep on all fours as infants. . . . For economic and political theorising not based on facts and not controlled by facts assuredly does lead nowhere. . . .

There can be no science of society till the facts about society are available. Till 130 years ago we had no census, no knowledge even of the numbers and growth of the people; till fifteen years ago we had no comprehensive records about unemployment even in this country, and other countries are still where we were a generation or more ago; social statistics of every kind—about trade, wages, consumption—are everywhere in their infancy. . . .

From Copernicus to Newton is 150 years. Today, 150 years from the *Wealth of Nations*, we have not found, and should not expect to find, the Newton of economics. If we have traveled as far as Tycho Brahe we may be content. Tycho was both a theorist and an observer. As a theorist, he believed to his last day in the year 1601 that the planets went round the sun and that the sun and the stars went round the earth as the fixed centre of the universe. As an observer, he made with infinite patience and integrity thousands of records of the stars and planets; upon these records Kepler, in due course, based his laws and brought the truth to light. If we will take Tycho Brahe for our example, we may find encouragement also. It matters little how wrong we are with our theories, if we are honest and careful with our observations.

Extracts from Lord William Beveridge's farewell address as Director of the London School of Economics, June 24, 1937. Published in POLITICA, September, 1937.

PART ONE
THE NATURE
OF ECONOMICS

1 THE ECONOMIC PROBLEM

Many of the world's most compelling problems are economic. The dominant problem of the 1930s was the massive unemployment of workers and resources known as the Great Depression. The wartime economy of the 1940s solved that problem but created new ones, especially the question of how quickly to reallocate scarce resources between military and civilian needs. By the 1950s inflation was becoming a major problem in many countries. It is still with us. Much attention in the latter half of the 1960s was devoted to trying to combat a slowdown in the pace of economic growth. The central problems of the 1970s were the rising cost of energy—oil prices increased tenfold over the decade—and the emergence of the disturbing combination of high unemployment *and* high rates of inflation. Problems change from decade to decade, yet there are always problems.

Of course, not all of the world's serious problems are primarily economic. Political, biological, social, cultural, and philosophic issues often predominate. But no matter how "noneconomic" a particular problem may seem, it will almost always have a significant economic dimension.

The crises that lead to wars often have economic roots. Nations fight for oil and rice and land to live on, although the rhetoric of their leaders evokes God and Glory and the Fatherland. Arabs and Israelis fight for a homeland, to be sure, but also for pastures and farms and water and transportation routes.

A population explosion threatens to overrun the globe as a result of humanity's spectacular ability to reduce its mortality rates much faster than its birthrates. The current rate of world population growth is 2.2 persons a second, or about 70 million persons per year. The causes are mainly biological, medical, and cultural, but the economic consequences are steady pressures on the available supplies of natural resources and agricultural land. Unless the human race can find ways to increase its food supply as fast as its numbers, increasing millions face starvation.

Race is not primarily an economic phenomenon, but the problem of racial discrimination has important economic effects on individuals and on the economy. It means untapped human talent. It means a waste of social resources. It means children growing up undernourished, undereducated, unqualified for good jobs, and hostile to an alien world.

ECONOMIC PROBLEMS OF THE MID EIGHTIES

Every new decade the United States confronts a somewhat different set of economic issues than those of the previous decade. Here are a few issues that are getting lots of attention in the mid 1980s.

Unemployment and Inflation

In 1978 Congress enacted the Humphrey-Hawkins Full Employment and Balanced Growth Act, which officially established full employment and

stable prices as twin goals of economic policy. Reasonable as that may sound as a policy goal, the fact is that we have seldom had both full employment and completely stable prices at the same time, and so far in the eighties we have had neither. At the end of 1982 unemployment stood at about 10 percent of the labor force, and prices had risen at an annual rate of greater than 6 percent. The Humphrey-Hawkins bill had specified 4 percent unemployment and 3 percent inflation by 1983 as attainable medium-term goals. Most economists today wonder whether achieving these levels will ever be possible, given our present economic and political systems.

How did the existence, unprecedented before the 1970s, of both "too high" unemployment and "too high" inflation arise, and how can it be eliminated? Are zero unemployment and zero inflation reasonable *long-run* goals? What is an "acceptable" level of unemployment? After the prolonged recession of the early eighties, can we be sure that we will never again experience the trauma of the 1930s, when up to a quarter of all those who sought work were unable to find it?

What is an "acceptable" amount of inflation? Why do prices in some countries rise 30 percent or 40 percent a year while in others they rise at a rate of 5 percent or 6 percent? Why did inflation accelerate dramatically over most of the world in the early 1970s? Can a country control inflation?

These questions concern the stability of the economy and the causes and consequences of depression and inflation. They also concern the ability of people, individually or through governments, to control and change their economic environment.

Productivity and Growth

Not very long ago Americans prided themselves on having the highest standard of living in the world and a rate of growth in the per capita output of goods and services that doubled living standards every generation. This happened most recently between 1946 and 1970. Between 1970 and 1975 the annual rate of growth dropped to half that of the

1946–1970 period, and from 1975 to 1980 it dropped to a third. From 1979 to 1982 there was no growth at all. As a result of these trends, America is no longer the world's richest country. A generation ago few Americans would have believed this possible.

What causes such a loss of momentum in the economy? Is it the uncertain state of today's economy? Is it the burden of high taxes on both individuals and businesses? Is it the heavy drain imposed on the economy by the government's regulation of business in more and more ways to provide cleaner, safer working conditions, bigger unemployment benefits, and more generous pensions and medical care?

Can we find ways to reverse the slowdown in our nation's economic growth? Do we *want* another century of rapid growth and industrialization? Without the automobile, the airplane, and electricity, ours would be a different and less comfortable world. But because of them air pollution has become not only a major inconvenience but may also be dangerously warming the earth's climate. Is large-scale pollution the inevitable companion of economic growth? If it is, how much growth do we really want? If it is not, how can we achieve growth with less pollution?

These questions concern the use, and abuse, of society's resources. They involve understanding why markets sometimes fail to work satisfactorily and how to deal with such failures. They also involve understanding why government intervention sometimes works and sometimes fails.

Government and the Individual

Poverty is a dominant problem in the world. It is still a major problem in America even though the average American continues to be among the richest individuals in the world. How can poverty survive in the midst of relative plenty? Who are the poor, and what makes them so? Does poverty take care of itself as average income rises? Can poverty ever be eliminated in the United States? Can it be eliminated in the world? Is a more equal distribution of income a desirable or attainable national goal? Do governmental policies improve or impair the lot of those who are poor? What remedial action should the government take and what should it leave to the private sector?

Do we, as John Kenneth Galbraith charges, allocate too little to government expenditure for such valuable things as health and education while growing sated on frivolous, privately produced goods such as electric can openers? Or, as charged by Milton Friedman, do we instead invite the government to do badly many things that private groups could do well? Do we, as some "supply-side" economists charge, create *dis*incentives to productive labor by imposing high tax rates to pay for all those governmental expenditures while providing a "welfare net" that saps people's initiative even as it protects them from economic hardship?

These questions concern the distribution of the nation's income and the government's role in altering that distribution.

Government Deficits and the National Debt

Almost everyone running for public office these days calls for a balanced budget, but no president or Congress seems able to achieve it. President Reagan, who made balanced budgets a cornerstone of his campaign, has run up the biggest deficits in American history. Does it really matter? If so, why? The national debt in 1982 was over 1.2 *trillion* dollars. Does such a number threaten national bankruptcy, or is it well within reasonable bounds? Since politicians apparently cannot balance the federal budget on their own, should we have a constitutional amendment that compels them to do so?

These questions concern the government's fiscal operations, regarding both the financing of its own activities and its impact on the private economy.

Money Supply, Banks, and International Finance

We all depend on money. Banks have a great deal to say about how easy or hard it is to borrow. Are their policies too tight, too easy, or too unpredictable for the economic health of the nation?

In our interdependent world, can monetary crises in Mexico, Poland, or Zaire threaten our economic welfare? Mexico alone has foreign debts totaling $81 billion, of which $28 billion was due to be repaid to private banks within one year. If (as seems quite possible) countries with huge foreign debts default on their loans from U.S. banks, would it (in the absence of massive government assistance) trigger a chain of bank failures like those that ushered in the Great Depression of the 1930s. If this happens should the government bail out banks that made unsound loans when dollars from oil producers were pouring into their banks in the 1970s, or should it let them pay the penalty for errors they made in trying to turn a quick profit?

These questions concern the functioning and stability of our monetary system, which is a peculiar mixture of private and public institutions whose actions vitally affect the economy.

Energy

Energy is vital to an industrial economy. Over the last 200 years, America's energy output has grown and with it our demand for the earth's limited fossil fuels. The amount of energy used in the United States doubled between 1950 and 1970. It reached a peak in 1973 and has declined slightly since.

Throughout most of American history, the increase in energy consumption caused no serious problems because new supplies were discovered as rapidly as old ones were exhausted. In the middle of the 1960s a dramatic change occurred. Although historically America's consumption of energy had grown at a slightly less rapid rate than its production of energy, since 1965 it has become a substantial net importer; in the late 1970s we imported one-quarter of our consumption.

The United States, with one-twentieth of the world's population, uses a third of the world's energy. Are we cured of our addiction to petroleum, or is the present easing of the energy crisis only apparent, due more to temporarily improved supplies than to our learning to live with less? Are the world's supplies of oil and gas adequate to its demands for energy? If so, is the United States' non-self-sufficiency in oil and gas only a problem in trade, transportation, or foreign policy? Can nuclear or solar energy render oil and gas as unnecessary as oil and gas rendered whale oil? Should the government ration energy, or will the free market effectively prevent an energy disaster?

These questions concern our ability to discover and bring to market the basic resources we need, to find substitutes for depleted resources, and to adapt to scarcities by changing our techniques of production. They also concern the roles of the free price system and of government intervention in the workings of our market economy.

WHAT IS ECONOMICS?

We have listed a few of today's important issues on which economic analysis is designed to shed light. One way to define the scope of economics is to say that it is the social science that deals with such problems. Fifty years ago such all-embracing definitions were popular. Perhaps the best known was Alfred Marshall's: "Economics is a study of mankind in the ordinary business of life." Because economic problems have certain common features, one may, by looking at them, arrive at a more penetrating definition.

The problems of economics arise out of the use of scarce resources to satisfy unlimited human wants. Scarcity is inevitable and is central to economic problems.

What are society's resources? Why is scarcity inevitable? What are the consequences of scarcity?

Resources and Commodities

A society's resources consist of the free gifts of nature, such as land, forests, and minerals; human resources, both mental and physical; and all sorts of manufactured aids to further production, such as tools, machinery, and buildings. Economists call such resources **factors of production**[1] because they are used to *produce* those things that people desire. The things produced are called **commodities.** Commodities may be divided into goods and services. **Goods** are tangible (e.g., cars or shoes), and **services** are intangible (e.g., haircuts or education). Notice the implication of positive value contained in the terms *goods* and *services.* (Compare the terms *bads* and *disservices.*)

Goods and services are the means by which people seek to satisfy some of their wants. The act of making goods and services is called **production,** and the act of using them to satisfy wants is called **consumption.** For most people in most societies goods are not regarded as desirable in themselves; few people want to pile them up endlessly in warehouses, never to be consumed. They are valued because people want the services they provide. An automobile, for example, helps to satisfy its owner's desires for transportation, mobility, and possibly status.

Scarcity

For practical purposes, human wants may be regarded as limitless. An occasional individual may "have everything," but our capacity to generate new wants as fast as old ones are satisfied is well known to psychologists. For the overwhelming preponderance of the world's 4 billion human beings, *scarcity* is real and ever present. In relation to our desires (for more and better food, clothing, housing, schooling, vacations, entertainment, etc.), existing resources are woefully inadequate; there are enough to produce only a small fraction of the goods and services that we want.

Is not America rich enough that scarcity is nearly banished? After all, we have been characterized as the affluent society. Whatever affluence may mean, it does not end the problem of scarcity. Most households that spend $50,000 a year (a princely amount by worldwide standards) have no trouble spending it on things that seem useful to

[1] The definitions of the terms in **boldface** type are gathered together in the glossary at the end of the book.

them. Yet it would take more than twice the present output of the American economy to produce enough to allow all American households to consume that amount.

Choice

Because resources are scarce, all societies face the problem of deciding what to produce and how to divide it among their members. Societies differ in who makes the choices and how they are made, but the need to choose is common to all.

Just as scarcity implies the need for choice, so choice implies the existence of cost.

Opportunity Cost

A decision to have more of one thing requires a decision to have less of something else. It is this fact that makes the first decision costly. We offer first a trivial example and then one that vitally affects all of us; both examples involve precisely the same fundamental principles.

Consider the choice that must be made by a small boy who has 10¢ to spend and who is determined to spend it all on candy. For him there are only two kinds of candy in the world: gumdrops, which sell for 1¢ each, and chocolates, which sell for 2¢. The boy would like to buy 10 gumdrops and 10 chocolates, but he knows (or will soon discover) that this is not possible. (In technical language, it is not an *attainable combination* given his scarce resources.) There are, however, several attainable combinations that he might buy: 8 gumdrops and 1 chocolate, 4 gumdrops and 3 chocolates, 2 gumdrops and 1 chocolate, and so on. Some of these combinations leave him with money unspent, and he is not interested in them. Only six combinations (as shown in Figure 1-1) are both attainable and use all his money.

After careful thought, the boy has almost decided to buy 6 gumdrops and 2 chocolates, but at the last moment he decides that he simply must have 3 chocolates. What will it cost him to get this extra chocolate? One answer to this question is 2 gumdrops. To get the extra chocolate he must sac-

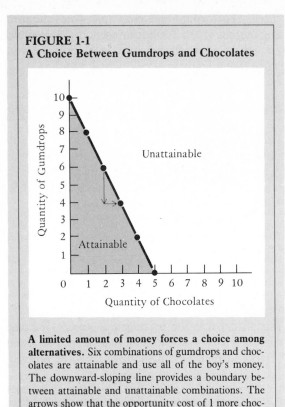

FIGURE 1-1
A Choice Between Gumdrops and Chocolates

A limited amount of money forces a choice among alternatives. Six combinations of gumdrops and chocolates are attainable and use all of the boy's money. The downward-sloping line provides a boundary between attainable and unattainable combinations. The arrows show that the opportunity cost of 1 more chocolate is 2 gumdrops. In this example, the opportunity cost is constant and therefore the boundary is a straight line.

rifice 2 gumdrops, as is seen in Figure 1-1. Economists would describe his sacrifice of 2 gumdrops to obtain the third chocolate as its **opportunity cost.**

Another answer is that the cost of the third chocolate is 2¢, but given the boy's budget and his intentions, this answer is less revealing than the first one. Where the real choice is between more of this and more of that, the cost of "this" is fruitfully looked at as what you must sacrifice of "that." The idea of opportunity cost is one of the central insights of economics.

Every time one is forced by scarcity to make a choice, one is incurring opportunity costs. These costs are measured in terms of foregone alternatives.

Production Possibilities

Although the previous example concerned a minor consumption decision, the essential nature of the decision is the same whatever the choice being considered.

Exactly the same problems arise, for example, in the important social choice between military and nonmilitary goods—between swords and plowshares. Throughout the 1960s and 1970s, about 7 percent of the American gross national product was spent for defense. The American government made a choice as to the relative amounts of the production of goods for civilian consumption and the production of arms. Such a choice is similar in form to the one facing the boy deciding what candies to buy with his dime. It is not possible to produce an unlimited quantity of both arms and civilian goods. If we have full employment of resources and we wish to produce more arms, then we must produce less of all other goods, thereby reducing the quantity of goods available to satisfy civilian wants. The opportunity cost of more arms is foregone civilian goods, and somehow a choice must be made.

The choice is illustrated in Figure 1-2. Because resources are limited, some combinations—those that would require more than the total available supply of resources for their production—cannot be obtained. The downward-sloping curve on the graph divides the combinations that can be obtained from those that cannot be obtained. Points to the right of this curve cannot be obtained because there are not enough resources; points to the left of the curve can be obtained without using all of the available resources; and points on the curve can just be obtained if all the available resources are used. The curve is called the **production possibility boundary.** It slopes downward because, when all resources are being used, to get more of one kind of goods, some of the other kind must be sacrificed.

A production possibility boundary illustrates three concepts: scarcity, choice, and opportunity cost. Scarcity is implied by the unattainable combinations above the boundary; choice, by the need to choose among the attainable points; opportunity cost, by the downward slope of the boundary.

The production possibility boundary in Figure 1-2 is drawn *concave* downward, showing that more and more civilian goods must be given up to achieve equal successive increases in military goods. This shape implies that the opportunity cost grows larger and larger as we increase the amount of arms produced. (Drawn as a straight line, as in Figure 1-1, the curve implies that the opportunity cost of each good stays constant, no matter how much of it is produced.) As we shall see, there are reasons to believe that the rising opportunity cost case applies to many important choices.[2]

Types of Economic Problems

Modern economies involve thousands of complex production and consumption activities. While the complexity is important, many basic decisions that must be made are not very different from those made in a primitive economy in which people work with few tools and barter with their neighbors. Nor do capitalist, socialist, and communist economies differ in their need to solve the same basic problems, though they do differ, of course, in how they solve these problems. Most problems studied by economists fall within six areas.

1. What Goods and Services Are Being Produced and in What Quantities?

This question concerns the allocation of scarce resources among alternative uses, called **resource allocation.** Any economy must have some mechanism for making decisions on the problem of resource allocation.

How are choices made between points such as *a* and *b* in Figure 1-2? In free-market economies, most decisions about the allocation of resources are made through the price system. In other systems, more of the decisions are made by central planners. Economists are interested in the consequences of

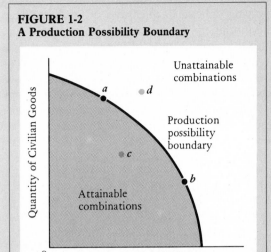

FIGURE 1-2
A Production Possibility Boundary

The downward-sloping boundary shows the combinations that are just attainable when all of the society's resources are efficiently employed. The quantity of military goods produced is measured along the horizontal axis, the quantity of civilian goods along the vertical axis. Thus any point on the diagram indicates some amount of each kind of good produced. The production possibility boundary separates the attainable combinations of goods such as *a*, *b*, and *c* from unattainable combinations such as *d*. It slopes downward because resources are scarce: More of one good can be produced only if resources are freed by producing less of the other goods. Points *a* and *b* represent efficient combinations that use all of the society's resources. Point *c* represents either inefficient use of resources or failure to use all the available resources.

different kinds of decision making on resource allocation.

2. By What Methods Are Goods and Services Produced?

Generally, there is more than one technically possible way in which a commodity can be made. Agricultural commodities, for example, can be produced by taking a small quantity of land and applying to it large quantities of fertilizer, labor, and

[2] The importance of scarcity, choice, and opportunity cost has led many to define economics as the problem of allocating scarce resources among alternative and competing ends. The issues emphasized by this definition are very important, but, as will be seen in the next section, there are other, equally important issues in economics that the definition does not stress.

machinery or by using a large quantity of land and applying only small quantities of fertilizer, labor, and machinery. Either method can be used to produce the same quantity of some crop.

Which alternative method should be adopted? A common criterion is the avoidance of inefficient methods. Any scheme of production that uses all of society's resources but produces inefficiently leads to an output combination that falls *inside* the production possibility boundary (at a point such as *c* in Figure 1-2). It would be possible to get more of either (or both) goods by using more efficient methods of production. Because resources are scarce, efficient methods of production are desirable. Economists are interested in distinguishing between efficient and inefficient methods, in determining how the choice of efficient methods can be assured, and in learning why inefficient methods are sometimes chosen.

3. How Is the Supply of Goods Allocated Among the Members of the Society?

Economists want to know what determines how a nation's total income is distributed among the population. Everyone knows it is not distributed equally. What determines the distribution of income among such groups as landowners, laborers, and capitalists? Or among other groups such as farmers, union members, blacks, and the poor? Economists are interested also in the consequences of government policies designed to change the distribution of income by using devices such as progressive income taxes, farm price supports, and programs of social insurance.

These first three questions fall within **microeconomics,** which concerns the allocation of resources and the distribution of income as they are affected by the workings of the price system and by some government policies.

4. Are the Country's Resources Being Fully Utilized, or Are Some Lying Idle?

It may seem strange that this question needs to be asked at all. Surely, if resources are so scarce

that there are not enough of them to produce all urgently required goods, then available resources will not be left idle. Yet one of the most disturbing characteristics of free-market economies is that such waste sometimes occurs. Unemployed workers would like to have jobs, the factories in which they could work are available, the managers and owners would like to be able to operate their factories, raw materials are available in abundance, and the goods that could be produced by these resources are needed by individuals in the community. But for some reason nothing happens. Unemployment forces the economy *inside* its production possibility boundary, at a point such as *c* in Figure 1-2.

Unemployment of resources is thus similar to an inefficient use of them (discussed above) in that both lead to production inside the full-employment production possibility boundary. They are not the same problem, however, and the remedies are very different.

5. Is Purchasing Power Being Eroded Because of Inflation?

The world's economies have often experienced periods of prolonged and rapid changes in price levels. Over the long swing of history, price levels have sometimes risen and sometimes fallen. In recent decades, however, the course of prices has almost always been upward. The seventies saw a period of accelerating inflation in the United States and in most of the world.

Inflation reduces the purchasing power of money and savings. It is closely related to the amount of money in the economy. Money is the invention of human beings, not of nature, and the amount in existence can be controlled by them. Economists ask many questions about the causes and consequences of changes in the quantity of money and the effects of such changes on the price level. They also ask about other causes of inflation.

6. Is the Economy's Capacity to Produce Goods Growing over Time?

Productive capacity grows rapidly in some countries and slowly in others, and in some countries it

FIGURE 1-3
The Effect of Economic Growth on the Production Possibility Boundary

Production possibility boundary after growth

Quantity of Civilian Goods

Production possibility boundary before growth

0

Quantity of Military Goods

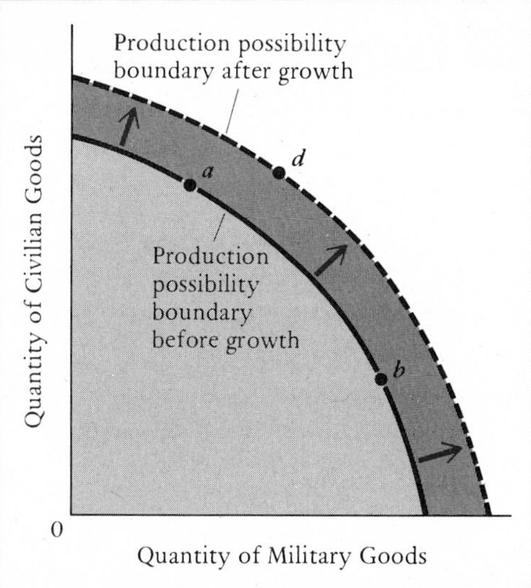

Economic growth shifts the boundary outward and makes it possible to produce more of all commodities. Before growth in productive capacity, points *a* and *b* were on the production possibility boundary and point *d* was an unattainable combination. After growth, point *d* and many other previously unattainable combinations are attainable, as shown by the dark shaded band.

actually declines. Generally the most rapid growth in productive capacity has occurred in those countries that already have relatively high standards of living. As a result, living standards diverge more and more between the "have" and the "have-not" countries. Growth in productive capacity can be represented in a production possibility diagram as a pushing outward of the boundary, as shown in Figure 1-3. If the economy's capacity to produce goods and services is growing, combinations that are unattainable today will become attainable tomorrow. Clearly, in an economy in which not nearly enough can be produced to satisfy all wants, growth will be important because growth makes it possible to have more of all goods. But growth is

not free. What are the ways in which growth occurs and what are its costs?

Questions 4 to 6 fall within **macroeconomics,** the study of the determination of economic aggregates such as total output, total employment, the price level, and the rate of economic growth.

Economics: A Working Definition

The six-way classification just discussed does not embrace all the things that interest economists. Additional topics such as the problems of international trade or comparative economic systems might be included in one or more of those categories, or they might be treated separately. Similarly, the theory of economic policy might be regarded as affecting all of the problem areas mentioned, or it might be treated separately.

Economics, broadly defined, concerns:

1. The ways in which a society uses its resources and distributes the fruits of production to individuals and groups in the society.
2. The ways in which production and distribution change over time.
3. The efficiency of economic systems in getting the most from the resources at their command.

ECONOMIC ANALYSIS AND ECONOMIC POLICY

Economics helps in understanding and predicting many aspects of human behavior. People, by nature curious about their environment, want to predict this behavior in order that they may control their environment and adapt it to their needs.

The Pervasiveness of Policy Decisions

Governments derive their authority to form and carry out policy from their police power—indeed, the words *policy* and *police* come from the Greek word for state, *politeia*. Some governments lean toward a policy of laissez faire, or non-interference, others toward a policy of attempting strict control over every facet of the economy. All governments have economic policies. Even the decision not to act but to let nature take its course is a policy decision. Whether to rely on marketplace decision making or to replace it is as much a policy decision as is a government's decision to tax cigarettes.

Every year thousands of economic policy decisions are made by local, state, and federal governments. Most of them are never seriously debated. Nor is every facet of existing policy debated anew each year; indeed, many policy decisions now in force (such as giving unions the right to organize) were made decades ago. Only a few policy issues attract attention and become the subject of earnest and heated argument in a particular year.

The Economists' Roles in Economic Policy

Any policy action has two aspects: the goals (or ends) that the decision makers are attempting to achieve and the means by which the desired ends are to be achieved. Economists do not establish goals, but they are often involved in helping to resolve conflicts among competing goals, in forging the links between goals and the means available to achieve them, and in evaluating policy proposals.

Defining Conflicts of Policy

Governments have many goals. A particular policy that serves one goal may hinder another and have no effect on yet a third. Unemployment compensation, for example, may promote justice by protecting unemployed families from debilitating hardships; at the same time it may hinder the quickness with which labor moves from labor-surplus to labor-scarce occupations, thereby decreasing efficient use of resources. Moreover, it will have no effect one way or the other on air pollution.

Economics has a large role to play in defining goal conflicts by identifying the effects, indirect as well as direct, of a proposed policy. Raising the minimum wage may seem extremely desirable to people who believe that the lowest-paid workers are not earning enough income to maintain a decent standard of living. But if that policy results in some workers being laid off and becoming unemployed, the benefits to those who get higher wages must be balanced by the costs of the extra unemployment.

Proposing Policies

It is frequently the role of the economist to suggest policies. Given a statement of objectives, economic analysis can be used to invent or publicize proposed policies that will achieve these objectives. Economists in and out of government have had a major impact on policy.

The Employment Act of 1946 created a Council of Economic Advisers to advise the president on the state of the economy and on how the goal of full employment could best be achieved. The Humphrey-Hawkins Act expanded the responsibility of the Council to formulate policies for achieving reasonable price stability along with increased employment, decreased unemployment, and more rapid growth. By 1984, forty professional economists had served as members of the three-person Council, and hundreds had served on the professional staff. (A list of past and present Council members is always contained in the Council's annual report.) The chairman in 1983 was Martin Feldstein; his distinguished predecessors include Arthur Burns, Walter Heller, Paul McCracken, Gardner Ackley, Alan Greenspan, the late Arthur Okun, Charles Schultze, and Murray Weidenbaum.

Other economists play major policy roles in the cabinet, on regulatory commissions and boards, and in many executive departments and administrative agencies. Congress, too, utilizes economic advisers such as Alice Rivlin, until recently director of the influential Congressional Budget Office.

Nor is it necessary to be in government to affect government policy. Dozens of economists have had significant influence on economic policy from the sidelines. Milton Friedman, Paul Samuelson, James Tobin, Otto Eckstein, and Lawrence Klein are prominent among those whose widely reported statements influence policy decisions. John Kenneth Galbraith has had an enormous effect on public opinion about economic matters with his best-selling books, and Leonard Silk writes an influential column for the *New York Times*.

Forming and Evaluating Policies

Economists must frequently determine whether a particular policy proposal—which may or may not have originated with them—is the best way to meet a particular problem. While each issue has its own special characteristics, there are also common concerns. Five main questions need to be asked in every case: (1) What are the policy goals? (2) Do the proposed means achieve those goals? (3) What costs are directly imposed? (4) Do the proposed means have adverse side effects? (5) Are there better alternative means?

Consider an example. In anticipation of a possible war in the Middle East and a sudden decrease in availability of gasoline, a team of economists is asked to evaluate a proposal that the federal government institute rationing of gasoline by issuing coupons to every registered automobile owner. Each dated coupon permits the holder to purchase a specific number of gallons of gasoline during a specific week. How might the economists go about evaluating this proposal?

The economists would start by asking what goals gasoline rationing is meant to achieve. They are told that its purpose is, first, to limit total purchases of gasoline to a specific number of gallons per week and, second, to do so in a way that shares the reduction in gasoline supply equitably among all drivers.

Given these goals, the economists would next ask how well the proposal meets them. If the authorities can effectively enforce the rule that gasoline not be sold without coupons, the quantity of coupons will asssure that no more than that number of gallons will be sold. This amount will be an upper limit, not the actual quantity, because it takes *both* money and coupons to get gasoline. Some users will not want to buy their full allotment of gasoline; others will want to buy more than they are allowed.

The number of coupons issued that will actually be used may be hard to predict. It will certainly be less than the total number issued if there is no legal way to transfer surplus coupons from those who would not use them to those who want extra coupons. While the coupons are not transferable, there may nevertheless be an illegal trade in the coupons unless the government takes severe measures to prevent it.

The economists may well conclude that the proposal can achieve its first objective, to control the quantity of gasoline actually sold. Examining the second objective, however, they may find that issuing coupons to *owners* does not achieve equal treatment of *drivers*. Some persons own two or more cars; others own no car and depend on borrowed or rented cars. Moreover, some persons must drive long distances to and from work, while others need not. The rationing plan tends to impose equal mileage, not equal sacrifice of mileage, on coupon receivers. Thus, it imposes a greater sacrifice on people who need to drive above average distances and a lesser sacrifice on people who drive below average distances. The same allotment of gallons per week may seem generous to a retired couple living in Rhode Island and ridiculously small to a ranching couple in Wyoming.

On the basis of this much analysis, the economists are likely to report that the plan does not meet its second objective. They will urge rejection or modification of the proposal. They will also point out that a revised allocation plan, based on demonstrated needs plus a small free-driving allowance, would correct the deficiency. Let us suppose that a number of modifications in the plan have been made and that the economists have concluded it will fulfill its basic purposes.

The economists will now ask how costly the plan would be to put into effect and enforce. They would estimate the direct costs of printing and distributing the coupons, of developing and running an allocation system, of establishing a means to hear the inevitable appeals from outraged citizens, of policing the use of coupons, and of enforcing the nontransferability of coupons. The total estimated costs would be reported to the policy-makers. If the costs seemed too large relative to

WHY ECONOMISTS DISAGREE

Economists and economics have never been as visible, audible and publicized as they are now. Nor have the disagreements and divergent forecasts within the profession ever been as rife.

One consequence of this babble of prophecy is that the repute of economics and its practitioners has fallen to one of its lowest points in the 200 years since publication of *The Wealth of Nations*. The reason is simply that the testimony of professional economists is offered on almost any side of each major economic-policy issue.

This quote is from a column in *Newsweek*. The author, Charles Wolf, Jr., suggests four reasons for the disagreement among economists: (1) Different economists use different benchmarks: Inflation is *down* compared with last year but *up* compared with the 1950s. (2) Economists fail to make it clear to their listeners whether they are talking short run or long run: tax cuts will stimulate consumption in the short run and investment in the long run. (3) Economists fail to acknowledge the full extent of their ignorance. (4) Different economists have different values, and these normative views play a large part in their public discussions.

There is surely some truth in each of these assessments. But there is a fifth and even more important reason: the public's *demand for disagreement*. Assume that all economists were in fact agreed on some proposition, for example, that unions are not a major cause of inflation. This view would be unpalatable to some individuals. Those who are hostile to unions, for instance, would like to blame inflation on them and would be looking for an intellectual champion. Fame and fortune would await the economist who espoused their cause, and a champion would soon be found.

This fact assures that there will not be unanimity among economists on any issue over which the public or policymakers are split. This forces anyone wanting to know the profession's opinion on a given issue to form a judgment by first determining what proportion of the profession supports it and how much weight to give to a particular view.

Disagreement does exist but can also be exaggerated. Media coverage is a major source of exaggeration. When the media cover an issue, they naturally wish to give both sides of it. Normally, the public will hear one or two economists for each side of a debate, regardless of whether the profession is divided right down the middle or is nearly unanimous in its support of one side. Thus the public will not know that in one case a reporter could have chosen from dozens of economists to present each side while in a second case the reporter had to spend three days trying to locate someone willing to take a particular side because nearly all economists contacted thought it was wrong. On many issues, the profession overwhelmingly supports one side. In their desire to show both sides of the case, however, the media present the public with the appearance of a profession equally split over all matters.

Thus, anyone seeking to discredit economists' advice by showing that they disagree will have no trouble supporting his or her case. But those who wish to know if there is a majority view or even a strong consensus will find one on a surprisingly large number of issues. Of course, there are also genuine disagreements among economists on many issues, especially those that involve recent and incompletely understood events, and there will always be controversies at the frontiers of current research. But there is no evidence to suggest that disagreements among economists are more common now than in the past.

the benefits, the entire plan might be dropped right there. But suppose the costs, although large, seem to be small enough to be offset by the benefits of the gasoline rationing scheme.

Next the economists might search for ways in which this policy serves or conflicts with other goals. Does it serve the public interest by encouraging production of more efficient cars? Does it work against the public interest by encouraging crime in the form of the counterfeiting or theft of ration coupons or the bribing of officials who allocate coupons? Does it fail to prevent some people from using gasoline frivolously while it forces others to curtail vital activities? There are a host of similar questions to be asked.

Ideally, the existence and importance of each side effect must be estimated. When a policy action helps to achieve one goal but hinders the attainment of others, it is necessary to establish trade-offs among them. Usually there will be some rate at which people will be willing to trade a loss in one direction for a gain in another. Let us suppose that if this were the end of the matter, the economists and policymakers would conclude that, all things considered, the gasoline rationing plan is better than nothing and deserves further study.

The final step for the economists is to consider whether modifications of the plan, or alternatives to it, will achieve the goals equally well but at lower cost or less sacrifice in terms of setbacks to other policy objectives. They may well consider, for example, whether allowing the coupons to be sold legally will lead to fairer, more efficient gasoline usage, less crime, and smaller enforcement costs. Another proposal they may consider is to discourage gas consumption by an extra $1 per gallon gasoline tax, combined with a series of money grants to poorer people who must drive as part of their work.

This final step is very important. It compares a particular feasible proposal not only against a "do nothing" approach but also against other feasible proposals.

At any stage of their investigation, the economists may conclude that gasoline rationing is not the most effective means of achieving the policy-

makers' objectives. (In fact many economists have reached that conclusion.) But suppose that the team of economists concludes that gasoline rationing *does* achieve the desired goals, that the direct costs and undesirable effects in other directions are judged (by the policymakers) to be less important than the desirable effects in achieving the stated policy goals, and that there are no other practicable measures that would better achieve the goals? The team will then conclude that there is a strong case in favor of the proposal.

Do the views—and prejudices—of the investigators have a great deal to do with the outcome of their investigation? A particular group of economists may have strong views on the specific measure it is attempting to assess. If the economists do not like the measure, they are likely to be relentless in identifying costs and searching out possible unwanted effects and somewhat less than thorough in discovering effects that help to achieve the desired goals. It is important though difficult to guard against an unconscious bias of this sort. Fortunately, there are likely to be others with different biases. One advantage of publishing evaluations and submitting them to review and discussion is that it provides opportunities for those with different biases to discover arguments and evidence originally overlooked. The box on page 14 explores some of the reasons for the frequent disagreements among economists.

Economic and Political Objectives

Actual policymaking is more complicated than the previous discussion suggests, and a few of the many reasons policy issues get settled in a less systematic fashion deserve mention.

Decisions on interrelated issues of policy are made by many different bodies. Congress passes laws, the Supreme Court interprets laws, the administration decides which laws to enforce with vigor and which to soft-pedal. The Treasury and the Federal Reserve System influence monetary factors, and a host of other agencies and semi-autonomous bodies determine actions in respect to different aspects of policy goals. Because of the multiplicity of decision makers, it would be truly amazing if fully consistent behavior resulted. The majority of Americans believe that there are advantages to this separation of responsibilities, but one of its consequences is that inconsistent decisions will be made.

Furthermore, in a system such as ours, inconsistent decisions may result from political compromises between two or more interested groups, factions, or agencies. Such compromises are common in Congress, between Congress and the executive branch, and among executive departments.

Another problem arises from the fact that in a democracy legislators and political officials have as important goals their own and their president's reelection. This means, for example, that any measure that imposes large costs and few benefits obvious to the electorate over the next few years is unlikely to find favor, no matter how large the long-term benefits are. There is a strong bias toward myopia in an elective system. Although much of this bias stems from shortsightedness and selfishness, some of it reflects genuine uncertainty about the future. The further into the future the economist calculates, the wider the margin of possible error. It is not surprising that politicians who must worry about the next election often tend to worry less about the long-term effects of their actions. "After all," they may argue, "who can tell what will happen 20 years hence?"

These problems of political decision making are what George Bernard Shaw had in mind when he said that the only strong argument in favor of democracy is that all of its alternatives are even worse.

SUMMARY

1. Economic problems are among the important concerns of every generation. A common feature of such problems is that they concern the use of limited resources to satisfy virtually unlimited human wants.

2. Scarcity is a fundamental problem faced by all economies. Not enough resources are available to produce all the goods and services that people would like to consume. Scarcity makes it necessary to choose. All societies must have a mechanism for deciding what commodities will be produced and in what quantities.

3. The concept of opportunity cost emphasizes the problem of scarcity and choice by measuring the cost of obtaining a unit of one commodity in terms of the number of units of other commodities that could have been obtained instead.

4. Six basic questions faced by all economies are: What commodities are being produced and in what quantities? By what methods are the commodities produced, and are those methods efficient? Who gets the commodities that are produced and in what quantities? Are the society's resources being fully utilized? What is happening to the purchasing power of money and savings? Is the economy's capacity to produce growing over time or remaining static?

5. Not all economies resolve these questions in the same ways or equally satisfactorily. Economists study how these questions are answered in various societies and the consequences of using one method rather than another to provide answers.

6. Governments, in varying degree, choose to intervene in the functioning of the economy. In so doing, they pursue economic policies.

7. It is necessary to distinguish between certain ends that are being sought and the means by which they will be achieved. Economics does not allow a "scientific" choice between alternative ends: It does not tell which of competing goals should be adopted. Economic analysis can help to determine whether a particular measure contributes to stated goals and at what cost.

8. One of the main reasons particular policies will always be subject to debate and disagreement is that most policies that are effective in bringing us closer to some goals take us further away from others. This leads to policy conflicts, and it is necessary to judge how much of one objective is to be sacrificed to get more of another.

TOPICS FOR REVIEW

Scarcity and the need for choice
Choice and opportunity cost
Production possibility boundary
Resource allocation
Unemployed resources
Growth in productive capacity
Steps in evaluating economic policies
Conflicts of policies

DISCUSSION QUESTIONS

1. What does each of the following quotations tell you about the policy conflicts perceived by the person making the statement and about how he or she has resolved them?

    a. "We've got so many people out of work, and we've got so much unused industrial capacity, that I think if we carefully target employment opportunities around the country, we can decrease unemployment substantially before we start becoming equally concerned about inflation."

    b. Russell Baker, commenting on the decision of Nantucket Island residents to approve a Holiday Inn to cater to oil drillers: "Economics compels us all to turn things into slums. Although it will be too bad, it will be absolutely justifiable. An economic necessity. Another step down the ladder to paradise."

    c. "Considering our limited energy resources and the growing demand for electricity, the United States really has no choice but to use all of its possible domestic energy sources, including nuclear energy. Despite possible environmental and safety hazards, nuclear power is a necessity."

    d. The king of Saudi Arabia: "Increasing oil production in order to lower oil prices would be the most damaging thing that could happen to humanity. Experts say that if oil consumption continues to increase as it has, oil reserves will dry up by the end of this century."

2. What is the difference between scarcity and poverty? If everyone in the world had enough to eat, could we say that food was no longer scarce?

3. Consider the right to free speech in political campaigns. Suppose that the Flat Earth Society, the Socialist party, and the Republican party all demand equal time on network television in a presidential election. What economic questions are involved? Can there be freedom of speech without free access to the scarce resources needed to make one's speech heard?

4. The United States entered World War II with substantial unemployment of resources and gradually moved to full employment of available resources. Contrast the opportunity costs of fighting the war under these circumstances with the opportunity costs for an economy already at full employment.

5. Evidence accumulates that the use of chemical fertilizers, which increases agricultural production greatly, causes damage to water quality. Show the choice involved between more food and cleaner water in using such fertilizers. Use a production possibility curve with agricultural output on the vertical axis and water quality on the horizontal axis. In what ways does this production possibility curve reflect scarcity, choice, and opportunity cost? How would an improved fertilizer that increased agricultural output without further worsening water quality affect the curve? Suppose a pollution-free fertilizer were developed; would this mean there would no longer be any opportunity cost in using it?

6. Does the United States government have a policy on old-age pensions? Did it have one before the Social Security Act was passed in 1935? Is there any defined issue on which the government can be said not to have a policy? Why or why not?

7. What goals might lead people to prefer allocating gas by coupon rather than letting price rise? What goals might lead to a preference for having such coupons salable rather than nontransferable? What factual questions might bear on each decision?

2 ECONOMICS AS A SOCIAL SCIENCE

Economics is generally regarded as a social science. What exactly does it mean to be scientific? Can economics ever hope to be "scientific" in its study of those aspects of human behavior with which it is concerned? The first step in answering these questions is to be able to distinguish between positive and normative statements. The ability to make this distinction has been one of the reasons for the success of science in the last 300 years.

The Distinction Between Positive and Normative

The success of modern science rests partly on the ability of scientists to separate their views on *what does happen* from their views on *what they would like to happen*. For example, until the nineteenth century virtually all people living under the general influence of Christianity, Judaism, or Muhammadanism believed that the earth was only a few thousand years old. About 200 years ago, evidence began to accumulate that some existing rocks were millions or even billions of years old. Most people found this hard to accept: it forced them to rethink their religious beliefs and abandon those that were based on a literal reading of the Bible or the Koran. Many wanted the evidence to be wrong; they wanted rocks to be only a few thousand years old. Nevertheless, the evidence accumulated until today virtually everyone accepts that the earth is neither thousands, nor millions, but 4 or 5 billion years old. This advance in our knowledge came because the question "How old are observable rocks?" could be separated from the feelings of scientists (many of them devoutly religious) about the age they would have liked the rocks to be. Distinguishing what *is* from what we would *like* the facts to show depends on recognizing the difference between positive and normative statements.

Positive statements concern what is, was, or will be. **Normative statements** concern what one believes ought to be.

Positive statements, assertions, or theories may be simple or complex, but they are basically about matters of fact.

Disagreements over positive statements are appropriately settled by an appeal to the facts.

Normative statements, because they concern what ought to be, are inextricably bound up with philosophical, cultural, and religious systems. A normative statement is one that makes, or is based on, a value judgment—a judgment about what is good and what is bad.

Disagreements over normative statements cannot be settled merely by an appeal to facts.

The Distinction Illustrated

The statement "It is impossible to break up atoms" is a positive statement that can quite definitely be (and of course has been) refuted by empirical observations, while the statement "Scientists ought not to break up atoms" is a normative statement that involves ethical judgments. The questions "What government policies will reduce unemployment?" and "What policies will prevent inflation?" are positive ones, while the question "Ought we to be more concerned about unemployment than about inflation?" is a normative one. The statement "A government deficit will reduce unemployment but cause an increase in prices" is a very simple hypothesis in positive economics, a hypothesis that can be tested by an appeal to empirical observation, while the statement "Because unemployment ought to matter more than inflation, a government deficit is sound policy" is a normative hypothesis that cannot be settled solely by an appeal to observation.

The Importance of the Distinction

If we think something ought to be done, we can deduce other things that, if we wish to be consistent, ought to be done; but we can deduce nothing about what is done (i.e., is true). Similarly, if we know that two things are true, we can deduce other things that must be true, but we can deduce nothing about what is desirable (i.e., *ought* to be).

It is logically impossible to deduce normative statements from only positive statements or positive statements from only normative ones.

First, consider an example involving a normative statement. Suppose I believe that (1) as a moral principle I ought to be charitable to all human beings. Then if I am told that (2) the inhabitants of China, while not Christians, are human beings, it follows that (3) therefore I ought to be charitable toward Chinese. From (1) and (2) a normative rule has been deduced about how I ought to behave in a particular case. However, no positive statement about how I *do* behave can be deduced from (1) and (2).

Now suppose that someone else comes along and says, "You ought not to be charitable toward the Chinese because my moral principles dictate that you should be charitable only toward Christians." If an argument arises about whether to be charitable toward the Chinese, this argument will turn on value judgments about how we ought to behave.

These are questions on which reasonable people sometimes have to agree to disagree. If both sides insist on holding to their views on charity, even if both are perfectly reasonable, there is no civilized way of forcing either to admit error.

Second, consider an example involving only positive statements. Assume I say that (1) capital punishment is a strong disincentive to murder and that (2) the Chinese abolished capital punishment after the Revolution, so that (3) therefore (unless some major additional development offsets this result) the number of murders must have risen in China since the Revolution. The two factual statements, (1) and (2), and the deduction that follows from them are all positive statements. Nothing can be deduced about the moral desirability of abolishing capital punishment from statements (1) and (2), even if they are factually correct.

Now suppose you say, "The number of murders has not risen in China since the Revolution; in fact, the number has fallen." If you hold to this view, you must deny one or the other of the first two positive statements, or you must show that some other change occurred which offset the predicted increase in murders. You could deny statement (1) by saying, for example, that capital punishment is actually an incentive to commit murder. You could deny statement (2) by saying, for example, that, although the Chinese pretended to abolish capital punishment as a propaganda move, they in fact retained it after the Revolution. Or you could show, for example, that a government policy removing firearms from the population was enormously effective over this same period. In each case the disagreement is over factual statements. If enough facts were gathered, and if both parties were reasonable, one party could be forced to admit being wrong.

The distinction between positive and normative allows us to keep our views on how we would like the world to work separate from our views on how the world actually does work. We may be interested in both. It can only obscure the truth, however, if we let our views on what we would like to be bias our investigations of what actually is. It is for this reason that the separation of the positive from the normative is one of the foundation stones of

science and that scientific inquiry, as it is normally understood, is usually confined to positive questions.

Limits on the Distinction

While the distinction between positive and normative is useful, it is not the be-all and end-all of scientific analysis for several reasons.

The classification is not exhaustive. The classifications *positive* and *normative* do not cover all statements that can be made. For example, there is an important class, called *analytic statements*, whose truth or falsehood depends only on the rules of logic. Thus the sentence "*If* all men are immortal *and if* you are a man, *then* you are immortal" is a true analytic statement. It tells us that *if* two things are true, *then* a third thing must be true. The truth of this *statement* is not dependent on whether or not its individual parts are in fact true. Indeed the sentence "All men are immortal" is a positive statement which has been decisively refuted. Yet no amount of empirical evidence on the mortality of men can upset the truth of the "if-then" sentence quoted above. Analytic statements—which proceed by logical analysis—play an important role in scientific work and form the basis for much of our ability to theorize.

Not all positive statements are testable. A positive statement asserts something about the universe. It may be empirically true or false in the sense that what it asserts may or may not be true of the universe. If it is true, it adds to our knowledge of what can and cannot happen. Many positive statements are refutable: if they are wrong this can be ascertained (within a margin for error of observation) by checking them against data. For example, the positive statement that the earth is less than 5,000 years old was tested and refuted by a mass of evidence which had been accumulated in the nineteenth century. The statement "Angels exist and frequently visit the earth in visible form" is, however, also a positive statement. It asserts something about the universe. But we could never refute this statement with evidence because, no matter how hard we searched, believers could argue that we did not look in the right places or in the right way, or that angels do not reveal themselves to nonbelievers, or any one of a host of other alibis. Thus statements that could conceivably be refuted by evidence if they are wrong are a subclass of positive statements; other positive statements are irrefutable. Scientifically, positive statements that are not testable are not of very much interest.

The distinction is not unerringly applied. Because the positive-normative distinction helps the advancement of knowledge, it does not follow that all scientists automatically and unerringly apply it. Scientists are human beings. Many have strongly held values, and they may let their value judgments get in the way of their assessment of evidence. For example, many scientists are not prepared to consider evidence that there may be differences in intelligence among races because as good liberals they feel that all races ought to be equal. Nonetheless, the desire to separate *what is* from *what we would like to be* is a guiding light, an ideal, of science. The ability to do so, albeit imperfectly, is attested to by the acceptance, first by scientists and then by the general public, of many ideas that were initially extremely unpalatable—ideas such as the extreme age of the earth and the theory of evolution.

Positive and Normative Statements in Economics

Economics, like other sciences, is concerned with questions, statements, and hypotheses that could conceivably be shown to be wrong (that is, false) by actual observations of the world. It is not necessary to show them to be either consistent or inconsistent with the facts tomorrow or the next day; it is only necessary to be able to imagine evidence that could show them to be wrong. Other questions, including normative ones, cannot be settled by a mere appeal to empirical observation. Of course, this does not mean that they are unimportant. Such questions as "Should we subsidize higher education?" and "Should we send food to Afghanistan?" must be decided by means other than a simple appeal to facts. In democratic prac-

tice, such questions are usually settled by voting on them.

This does not mean that economists nor anyone else need confine their discussions to positive, testable statements. Economists can usefully hold or discuss value judgments as long as they do not confuse such judgments with evaluations of positive statements.

Moreover, having grasped the distinction between positive and normative, we should be careful not to turn it into an inquiry-stopping, dogmatic rule. From the fact that positive economics does not include normative questions (because its tools are inappropriate to them) it does *not* follow that students of positive economics must stop their inquiries as soon as someone says the word *ought*. Consider the statement "It is my value judgment that we *ought to have* rent control because controls are *good*." It is quite in order for a practitioner of positive economics to ask "Why?" It may then be argued that controls have certain consequences, and it is these consequences that are judged to be good. But the statements about the consequences of rent control will be positive, testable statements.

Thus the pursuit of what appears to be a normative statement will often turn up positive hypotheses on which the *ought* conclusion depends. For example, there are probably relatively few people who believe that government control of industry is in itself good or bad. Their advocacy or opposition will be based on certain beliefs about relations that can be stated as positive rather than normative hypotheses. For example: "Government control reduces (increases) efficiency, changes (does not change) the distribution of income, leads (does not lead) to an increase of state control in other spheres." A careful study of this emotive subject would reveal enough positive economic questions to keep a research team of economists occupied for many years.

The Scientific Approach

Very roughly, the scientific approach, or the scientific method as it is sometimes called, consists of relating questions to evidence. When presented with a controversial issue, scientists will ask what the evidence is both for and against it. They may then take a stand on the issue, with more or less conviction depending on the weight of the evidence. If there is little or no evidence, scientists will say that at present it is impossible to take a stand. They will then set about searching for relevant evidence. If they find that the issue is framed in terms that make it impossible to gather evidence for or against it, they will then usually try to recast the question so that it can be answered by an appeal to the evidence. This approach to a problem is what sets scientific inquiries off from other inquiries.

In some fields, the scientist, having reframed the question, is able to generate observations that will provide evidence for or against the hypothesis. Experimental sciences such as chemistry and some branches of psychology have an advantage because it is possible for them to produce relevant evidence through controlled laboratory experiments. Other sciences such as astronomy and economics cannot do this. They must wait for natural events to produce observations that may be used as evidence in testing their theories, or they must rely on nonlaboratory experiments that are not fully controlled. An example of the latter is the space probe programs of recent years, which have added greatly to astronomers' knowledge about the universe.

The ease or difficulty with which one can collect evidence does not determine whether a subject is scientific or nonscientific.

How scientific inquiry proceeds and the ease with which it can be pursued do, however, differ substantially between fields in which laboratory experiment is possible and those in which it is not. Some of these differences will be discussed in Chapter 3. Until then we shall consider general problems more or less common to all sciences.

Is Human Behavior Predictable?

It is possible to conduct a scientific study in the field of human behavior? When considering whether it is possible to make a scientific study of such subjects as the causes of unemployment and the consequences of a large national debt, it is sometimes argued that natural sciences deal with inanimate matter that is subject to natural "laws" while the social sciences deal with human beings who have free will and therefore cannot be made the subject of natural laws.

Natural Versus Social Sciences

The notion that natural and social sciences differ fundamentally in their ability to predict implies that inanimate matter will show stable responses to certain stimuli but animate matter will not. For example, if you put a match to a dry piece of paper, the paper will burn, whereas if you subject human beings to torture, some will break down and do what you want them to do and others will not. Even more confusing, the same individual may react differently to torture at different times.

Does human behavior show sufficiently stable responses to factors influencing it to be predictable within an acceptable margin of error? This is a positive question that can be settled only by an appeal to evidence and not by *a priori* speculation. (*A priori* may be defined as the use of knowledge that is prior to actual experience.) The question itself might concern either the behavior of groups or that of isolated individuals.

Group Behavior Versus Individual Behavior

It is a matter of simple observation that when a group of individuals is considered, they do not behave capriciously but instead display stable responses to various forces that act on them. The warmer the weather, for example, the more people visit the beach and the higher the sales of ice cream and Coca-Cola. It may be hard to say when or why one individual will buy an ice cream cone or a Coke, but a stable response pattern from a large group of individuals can be seen: The higher the temperature, the greater the sales of these two products at the beach.

There are many situations in which group behavior can be predicted accurately without certain knowledge of individual behavior. No social scientist can predict, for example, when an apparently healthy individual is going to die, but death rates for large groups are stable enough to make life insurance a profitable business. This would not be so if group behavior were capricious. Although social scientists cannot predict what particular individuals will be killed in auto accidents in the next holiday weekend, they can come very close to knowing the total number who will die. The more objectively measurable data they have (for example, the state of the weather on the days in question and the trend in gasoline prices), the more closely they will be able to predict total deaths.

The well-known fact that pollsters usually do a good job of predicting elections on the basis of sample surveys provides evidence that human attitudes do not change capriciously. If group behavior were truly capricious, there would be no point in trying to predict anything on the basis of sample surveys. The fact that 80 percent of the voters sampled said they intended to vote for a certain candidate would give no information about the probable outcome of the election. Today's information would commonly be reversed tomorrow.

The difference between predicting individual and group behavior is illustrated by the fact that economists can predict with fair accuracy what households as a group will do when their take-home pay is increased. Some individuals may do surprising and unpredictable things, but the total response of all households to a permanent change in tax rates that leaves more money in their hands is predictable within quite a narrow margin of error. This stability in the response of households' spending to a change in their available income is the basis of economists' ability to predict successfully the outcome of major revisions in the tax laws.

This does not mean that people never change their minds or that future events can be foretold by a casual study of the past. People sometimes think in terms of a simple dichotomy: Either there are historical laws apparent to the casual observer or there is random behavior. They observe a prophet predicting that some change will take place in the future merely because it took place in the past. Upon seeing the prophet make an utterly mistaken prophecy, they conclude that, because the

prophet cannot prophesy, human behavior is random and thus unamenable to scientific study. The stability discussed here is a stable response to causal factors (e.g., next time it gets warm, ice cream sales will rise) and not merely inertia (e.g., ice cream sales will go on rising in the future because they have risen in the past).

The "Law" of Large Numbers

Successful predictions about the behavior of large groups are made possible by the statistical "law" of large numbers. Broadly speaking, this law asserts that random movements of many individual items tend to offset one another. This law is based on one of the most beautiful constants of behavior in the whole of science, natural and social, and yet it can be derived from the fact that human beings make errors! The law is based on the *normal curve of error*, which is encountered in elementary statistics.

What is implied by this law? Ask any one person to measure the length of a room and it will be almost impossible to predict in advance what sort of error of measurement he or she will make. Dozens of things will affect the accuracy of the measurement and, furthermore, the person may make one error today and quite a different one tomorrow. But ask a thousand people to measure the length of the same room, and it can be predicted within a very small margin just how this *group* will make its errors. It can be asserted with confidence that more people will make small errors than will make large errors, that the larger the error, the fewer will be the number making it, that roughly the same number of people will overstate as will understate the distance, and that the average error of all individuals will be zero.

If a common cause should act on each member of the group, it is possible to predict the average behavior of the group even though any one member may act in a surprising fashion. If, for example, each of the thousand individuals is given a tape measure that understates "actual" distances, it can be expected that, on the average, the group will understate the length of the room. It is, of course, quite possible that one member, who had in the past been consistently undermeasuring distance because of psychological depression, will now overmeasure the distance because the state of his health has changed. But some other event may happen to another individual that will turn her from an overmeasurer into an undermeasurer. Individuals may act strangely for inexplicable reasons. But the group's behavior, when the inaccurate tape is substituted for the accurate one, will be predictable precisely because the odd things that one individual does will tend to cancel out the odd things some other individual does.

Irregularities in individual behavior tend to cancel one another out, so that the regularities tend to show up in repeated observations.

The Nature of Scientific Theories

There is abundant evidence of stable response patterns in human behavior. Some regularity between two or more things is observed, and we ask why this should be so. A *theory* attempts to explain why. Once we have a theory, we are able to predict as yet unobserved events. For example, national income theory predicts that an increase in the government's budget deficit will increase the rate of inflation. The simple theory of market behavior predicts that, under specified conditions, the introduction of a tax on a commodity will be accompanied by an increase in the price of the commodity but that the price increase will be less than the amount of the tax. It also lets us predict that if there is a partial failure of the potato crop, the total receipts earned by potato farmers will rise!

Theories are used in explaining observed phenomena. A successful theory enables us to predict the consequences of various occurrences.

The Pervasiveness of Theories

Observations concern consequences of events. Any explanation whatsoever of how these events are linked together is a theoretical construction. Theories are used to impose order on these observations, to explain how what is seen is linked to-

gether. Without theories there would be only a shapeless mass of meaningless observations.

The choice is not between theory and observation but between better or worse theories to explain observations.

In a particular case we might see an increase in interest rates followed by a reduction in borrowing by corporations. The practical person may think the link is obvious, and indeed in some sense it may be, but nonetheless it requires a theoretical construction. Before these two events can be linked together, it is necessary to have a theory of what the corporate managers are trying to do and how they try to do it, plus the assumption that the managers know what behavior will achieve their goals.

True in Theory but Not in Practice

Misunderstanding about the place of theories in scientific explanation gives rise to many misconceptions. One of these is illustrated by the phrase "True in theory but not in practice." The next time you hear someone say this (or, indeed, the next time you say it yourself) you should immediately reply, "All right then, tell me what does happen in practice." Usually you will not be told mere facts, but you will be given an alternative theory—a different explanation of the facts. The speaker should have said, "The theory in question provides a poor explanation of the facts" (that is, it is contradicted by some factual observations); "I have a different theory that does a much better job."

What Is a Theory and How Is It Tested?

A theory consists of (1) a set of definitions that clearly define the *variables* to be used, (2) a set of *assumptions* that outline the conditions under which the theory is to apply, (3) one or more *hypotheses* about the relationships of variables, and (4) *predictions* that are deduced from the assumptions of the theory and can be tested against actual empirical observations.

KINDS OF VARIABLES

Endogenous and Exogenous Variables

Endogenous variables are those that are explained within a theory. **Exogenous variables** are those that influence the endogenous variables but are themselves determined by considerations outside of the theory. Consider the theory that the price of apples in Seattle on a particular day is a function of several things, one of which was the weather in Wenatchee, Washington, during the previous apple-growing season. We can safely assume that the state of the weather is not determined by economic conditions. The price of apples in this case is an endogenous variable—something determined within the framework of the theory. The state of the weather in Wenatchee is an exogenous variable; changes in it influence prices because they affect the supply of apples, but the weather is uninfluenced by these prices.

Other words are sometimes used for the same distinction. One frequently used pair is *induced* for endogenous and *autonomous* for exogenous.

Stock and Flow Variables

A distinction between variables that is important in economics is that between stocks and flows. A flow variable has a time dimension; it is so much per unit of time. The quantity of grade A large eggs purchased in Cleveland is a flow variable. No useful information is conveyed if we are told that purchases were 2,000 dozen eggs unless we are also told over what period of time these purchases occurred. Two thousand dozen per hour would indicate an active market in eggs, while 2,000 dozen per week would indicate a sluggish market. A stock variable has no time dimension; it is just so much. Thus, if the egg producers' cooperative has 2 million dozen eggs in warehouses around the country, the quantity is a stock. All those eggs are there at one time. The stock variable is just a number, not a rate of flow of so much *per day* or *per month*.

Economic theories use both flow variables and stock variables, and it takes a little practice to keep them straight. The amount of income earned is a flow; there is so much per year or per month or per hour. The amount of a household's expenditure is also a flow—so much spent per week or per month. The amount of money in a bank account or a miser's hoard (earned, perhaps, in the past, but unspent) is a stock—just so many thousands of dollars. What of the interest earned by the miser who puts money into a savings bank? It is a flow. The key test is always whether a time dimension is required to give the variable significant meaning.

Variables

Theories are concerned with how various things are related to one another. If we know how two things are related, then we know how one of them will change as the other changes. The things that we relate to one another are called variables. A **variable** is some magnitude that can take on different possible values. Variables are the basic elements of theories, and each one needs to be carefully defined.

Price is an example of an important economic variable. The price of a commodity is the amount of money that must be given up to purchase one unit of that commodity. To define a price we must first define the commodity to which it attaches. Such a commodity might be one dozen grade A large eggs. We could then inquire into the price of such eggs sold in, say, supermarkets in Fargo, North Dakota. This would define the variable. The particular values taken on by the variable might be $.98 on July 1, 1984, $1.02 on July 8, 1984, and $.99 on July 15, 1984.

There are many distinctions between kinds of

variables; two of the most important are discussed in the box on page 25.

Assumptions

Assumptions are essential to theorizing. Students are often greatly concerned about the justification of assumptions, particularly if they seem unrealistic. Suppose an economic theory starts out: "Assume that there is no government." Surely, says the reader, this assumption is totally unrealistic, and I cannot therefore take seriously anything that comes out of the theory. But this assumption may merely be the economist's way of saying that, whatever the government does, even whether it exists, *is irrelevant for the purposes of this particular theory.*

Now, put this way, the statement becomes an empirical assertion. The only way to test it is to see if the predictions that follow from the theory do or do not fit the facts that the theory is trying to explain. If they do, then the theorist was correct in the assumption that the government could be ignored for the particular purposes at hand. In this case the criticism that the theory is unrealistic because there really is a government is completely beside the point.

Another important use of an apparently unrealistic assumption may be to outline the set of conditions under which a theory is meant to hold. Consider a theory that assumes the government has a balanced budget. This may mean that the theorist intends that theory to apply only when there is a balanced budget; it may *not* mean that the size of the government's budget surplus or deficit is irrelevant to the theory.

An assumption may mean many different things. When you encounter an assumption in economic theory, ask yourself whether it is being used to convey the idea that (1) the world actually behaves as assumed, (2) the factor under consideration is irrelevant to the theory, (3) the theory only holds when the condition specified in the assumption actually holds, or (4) a convenient fiction is being introduced to simplify some quite complex piece of behavior. An assumption that meets any one of these criteria may be useful.

Usually it is not appropriate to criticize the simplifying assumptions of a theory only on the grounds that they are unrealistic. All theory is an abstraction from reality. If it were not, it would merely duplicate the world and would add nothing to our understanding of it. A good theory abstracts in a useful and significant way; a poor theory does not. If we believe that the theorist has assumed away something important for the problem at hand, then we must believe, and try to show, that the conclusions of the theory are contradicted by the facts.

Hypotheses

Relations among variables. The critical step in theorizing is formulating hypotheses. A hypothesis is a statement about how two or more variables are related to each other. For example, it is a basic hypothesis of economics that the quantity produced of any commodity depends, among other things, upon its price. Thus, the two variables, the price of eggs and the quantity of eggs produced, are related to each other according to an economic hypothesis.

Functional relations. [1]   A **function,** or a functional relation, is a formal expression of a relation among variables.

The particular hypothesis that the quantity of eggs produced is related to the price of eggs is an example of a functional relation in economics. In its most general form, it merely says that quantity produced is related to price. A more specific hypothesis may be that as the price of eggs falls, the quantity produced will also fall. In other words, in this hypothesis price and quantity vary *positively* with each other. In the case of many hypotheses of this kind, economists can be even more specific about the nature of the functional relation. On the basis of detailed factual studies, economists often have a pretty good idea of by *how much* quantity

---

[1] The appendixes for each chapter appear starting on page 887. The appendix to this chapter (page 889) gives a more detailed discussion of functional relations.

produced will change as a result of specified changes in price—that is, they can predict magnitude as well as direction.

Predictions

A scientific prediction is not the same thing as a prophecy.

A scientific prediction is a conditional statement that takes the form: *If* you do this, *then* such and such will follow.

If hydrogen and oxygen are mixed under specified conditions, *then* water will be the result. *If* the government has a large budget deficit, *then* the rate of inflation will increase. It is most important to realize that this prediction is very different from the statement: "I prophesy that in two years' time there will be a large increase in inflation because I believe the government will decide to have a large budget deficit." The government's decision to have a budget deficit or surplus in two years' time will be the outcome of many complex factors, emotions, objective circumstances, chance occurrences, and so on, few of which can be predicted by the economist. If the economist's prophecy about the level of inflation turns out to be wrong because in two years' time the government does not have a large deficit, then all that has been learned is that the economist is not a good guesser about the behavior of the government. However, *if* the government does have a large deficit (in two years' time or at any other time) and *then* the amount of inflation does not increase, a conditional scientific prediction in economic theory has been contradicted.

Testing Theories

A theory is tested by confronting its predictions with evidence. It is necessary to discover if certain events are followed by the consequences predicted by the theory. For example, is an increase in the government's budget deficit followed by an increase in inflation?

Generally, theories tend to be abandoned when they are no longer useful. And theories cease to be useful when they cannot predict the consequences

of actions in which one is interested better than the next best alternative. When a theory consistently fails to predict better than the available alternatives, it is either modified or replaced. Figure 2-1 summarizes the discussion of theories.

Economics As a Developing Science

Economics is like other sciences in at least two respects. First, there are many observations of the world for which there are, at the moment, no fully satisfactory theoretical explanations. Second, there are many predictions that no one has yet satisfactorily tested. Serious students of economics must not expect to find a set of answers to all their questions as they progress in their study. Very often they must expect to encounter nothing more than a set of problems that provides an agenda for further research. Even when they do find answers to problems, they should accept these answers as tentative and ask even of the most time-honored theory, "What observations would be in conflict with this theory?"

Economics is still a young science. On the one hand, economists know a good deal about the behavior of the economy. On the other hand, many problems are almost untouched. Students who decide to specialize in economics may find themselves, only a few years from now, publishing a theory to account for some of the problems mentioned in this book; or they may end up making a set of observations that will upset some venerable theory described in these pages.

A final word of warning: Having counseled a constructive disrespect for the authority of accepted theory, it is necessary to warn against adopting an approach that is too cavalier. No respect attaches to the person who says, "This theory is for the birds; it is *obviously* wrong." This is too cheap. To criticize a theory effectively on empirical grounds, one must demonstrate, by a carefully made set of observations, that some aspect of the theory is contradicted by the facts. This is a task worth attempting, but it is seldom easily accomplished.

FIGURE 2-1
The Interaction of Deduction and Measurement in Theorizing

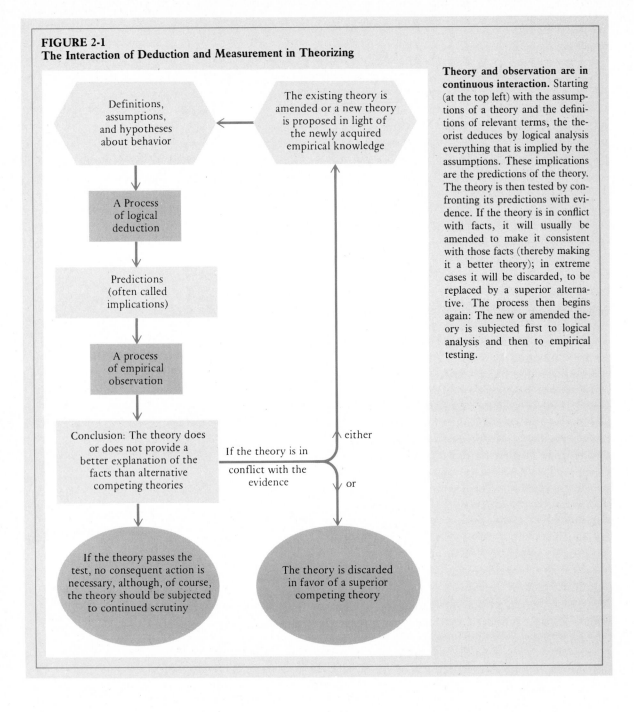

Theory and observation are in continuous interaction. Starting (at the top left) with the assumptions of a theory and the definitions of relevant terms, the theorist deduces by logical analysis everything that is implied by the assumptions. These implications are the predictions of the theory. The theory is then tested by confronting its predictions with evidence. If the theory is in conflict with facts, it will usually be amended to make it consistent with those facts (thereby making it a better theory); in extreme cases it will be discarded, to be replaced by a superior alternative. The process then begins again: The new or amended theory is subjected first to logical analysis and then to empirical testing.

SUMMARY

1. It is possible, and fruitful, to distinguish between positive and normative statements. Positive statements concern what is, was, or will be, while normative statements concern what ought to be. Disagreements over positive statements are appropriately settled by an appeal to the facts. Disagreements over normative statements can never be settled by a mere appeal to factual evidence.

2. The success of scientific inquiry depends on separating positive questions about the way the world works from normative questions about how one would like the world to work. The scientific approach involves formulating positive questions precisely enough so that they can be settled by an appeal to evidence and then finding means of gathering or producing the necessary evidence.

3. Some people feel that although natural phenomena can be subject to scientific inquiry and "laws" of behavior, human phenomena cannot. The evidence, however, is otherwise. Social scientists have observed many regular and stable human behavior patterns, and these form the basis for successful predictions of how people will behave under certain conditions.

4. The fact that people sometimes act strangely, even capriciously, does not destroy the possibility of a scientific study of group behavior. Indeed, the odd and inexplicable things that one person does will tend to cancel out the odd and inexplicable things that another person does. Observation of group behavior often discloses fairly stable and predictable responses to things that exert a significant influence on the members of the group.

5. Observations reveal only sequences of events. Theories are designed to give meaning and coherence to these events. Theories thus pervade all attempts to explain events. A theory consists of a set of definitions of the variables to be employed, a set of assumptions giving the conditions under which the theory is meant to apply, and a set of hypotheses about how things behave. Any theory has certain logical implications that must be true if the theory is true.

6. A theory provides predictions of the type "*if* one event occurs, *then* another event will also occur." An important method of testing theories is to confront their predictions with evidence. When theories fail to predict better than the available alternatives, theories tend to be rejected. The progress of any science lies in finding better explanations of events than are now available. Thus, in any developing science, one must expect to discard present theories and replace them with demonstrably superior alternatives. Such a process improves the quality of the explanations.

7. The important concept of a functional relation is discussed in more detail in the appendix to this chapter, which begins on page 889.

TOPICS FOR REVIEW

Positive and normative statements

Testable statements

The law of large numbers and the predictability of human behavior

The roles of variables, assumptions, and predictions in theorizing

Endogenous and exogenous variables

Stock and flow variables

Functional relations

Prediction versus prophecy

The scientific approach

DISCUSSION QUESTIONS

1. A baby doesn't "know" of the theory of gravity, yet in walking and eating the child soon learns to use its principles. Distinguish between behavior and causation of behavior. Does a business executive or a farmer have to understand economic theory to behave in a pattern consistent with economic theory?

2. "If human behavior were completely capricious and unpredictable, life insurance could not be a profitable business." Explain. Can you think of any businesses that do *not* depend on predictable human behavior?

3. Write five statements about inflation. (It does not matter whether the statements are correct, but you should confine yourself to those you think might be correct.) Classify each statement as positive or normative. If your list contains only one type of statement, try to add a sixth statement of the other type. Check the validity of your positive statements as well as you can against the data given in this text (see *Inflation* in the index). If you are not yet satisfied of their validity, outline how you would go about completing the test of your statements.

4. Each of the following unrealistic assumptions is sometimes made. See if you can visualize situations in which each of them might be useful.
   a. The earth is a plane.
   b. There are no differences between men and women.
   c. There is no tomorrow.
   d. People are wholly selfish.

5. "The following theory of wage determination proceeds on the assumption that labor unions do not exist." Of what use can such a theory be in the United States today?

6. What may first appear to be untestable statements can often be reworded so that they can be tested by an appeal to evidence. How might you do that with respect to each of the following assertions?
   a. The American economic system is the best in the world.
   b. The provision of free medical care for more and more people will inevitably end in socialized medicine for all, and socialized medicine will destroy our standards of medical practice by destroying the doctor's incentive to do his or her job well.
   c. Robotics ought to be outlawed, because it will destroy the future of the working classes.
   d. Inflation is ruining the standard of living of the American worker and destroying the integrity of the family.

3 THE ROLE OF STATISTICAL ANALYSIS

In this chapter we look at two very different problems in statistics. We study first the important statistical tool of index numbers, which are used throughout economics and occur constantly in this book. You cannot read far in a newspaper or a news magazine without encountering important index numbers such as the Consumer Price Index, measures of productivity growth, and indexes of industrial output. Then we discuss some very general questions concerning the use of theory to measure and test economic relationships.

INDEX NUMBERS

Economists frequently seek simple answers to questions such as "How much have prices risen this year?" or "Has the quantity of industrial production increased this year, and, if so, by how much?" There is no perfectly satisfactory answer to the first question because all prices do not move together, nor to the second because one cannot simply add up tons of steel, pieces of furniture, and gallons of gasoline to get a meaningful total. Yet these are not foolish questions. There *are* trends in prices and production, and thus there are real phenomena to describe. It is of no help to someone who asks about price changes over some period to be given a list of 4,682 individual prices and told, "See for yourself, they varied."

Index numbers are statistical measures that are used to give a concise summary answer to the inherently complex questions of the kind just suggested. An **index number** measures the percentage change in some broad average since some base period. As such it points to overall tendencies or general drifts, not to specific single facts. The two most important kinds of index numbers are price indexes and production indexes.

Calculating an Index Number of Prices[1]

A **price index** shows the average percentage change that has occurred in some group of prices over some period of time. The point in time from which the change is measured is called the **base year** (or **base period**), while the point in time to which the change is measured is called the **given year** (or **given period**). Several elements are involved in the definition of index numbers.

First, what group of prices should be used? This depends on the index. The **Consumer Price Index,** known affectionately as the **CPI,** covers prices of commodities commonly bought by households. Changes in the CPI are meant to measure changes in the typical household's "cost of living." The

Producer Price Index (formerly the wholesale price index) measures a different group of commodities commonly bought and sold by wholesalers. The "national income deflator" is a price index that covers virtually all of the goods and services produced in the economy; it includes not only the prices of consumer goods and services bought by households but the prices of capital goods such as plant and machinery bought by firms.

Second, what kind of average should be used? If all prices were to change in the same proportion, this would not be an important question. A 10 percent rise in each and every price covered means an average rise of 10 percent no matter how much importance we give to each price change when calculating the average. But what if—as is almost always the case—different prices change differently? Now it does matter how much importance we give to each price change. A rise of 50 percent in the price of caviar is surely much less important to the average consumer than a rise of 40 percent in the price of bread. And this in turn is surely less important than a rise of 30 percent in the cost of housing. Why? The reason is that the typical household spends less on caviar than on bread and less on bread than on housing.

In calculating any price index, statisticians seek to *weight* each price according to its importance. Let us see how this is done for the CPI. Government statisticians survey periodically a group of households to discover how they spend their incomes. The average bundle of goods bought is calculated, and the quantities in this bundle become the weights attached to the prices. In this way the average price change heavily weights commodities on which consumers spend a lot and lightly weights commodities on which consumers spend only a little. The procedure is illustrated in Table 3-1.

The statisticians then calculate the average change. This is done by comparing the cost of purchasing the typical bundle of commodities in the base year with that of purchasing it in the given year. The given year cost is expressed as a percentage of the base year cost, and this figure is the index number of the new period. Thus, a CPI of 110 means that the cost of purchasing the "repre-

---

[1] There are index numbers of prices, of outputs, of productivity ratios, and of many other things. In this section we shall look only at index numbers of prices, but the principles of averaging and weighting are similar for other index numbers. In the next section calculation of a quantity index is briefly discussed.

TABLE 3–1 THE CALCULATION OF A PRICE INDEX COVERING THREE COMMODITIES

Commodity	Quantity in fixed bundle	Base year 1980		Given year 1984	
		Price in 1980	Value in 1980	Price in 1984	Value in 1984
A	500 units	$1.00	$ 500	$2.00	$1,000
B	200 units	5.00	1,000	7.00	1,400
C	50 units	2.00	100	9.60	480
			1,600		2,880

$$\text{Index value } 1980 = \frac{1,600}{1,600} \times 100 = 100$$

$$\text{Index value } 1984 = \frac{2,880}{1,600} \times 100 = 180$$

A price index shows the ratio of the costs of purchasing a fixed bundle of goods between two years (multiplied by 100). The cost of purchasing the fixed bundle is calculated at the prices ruling in each year. The index for year 1984 is the cost of purchasing that bundle in 1984 expressed as a percentage of the cost of purchasing the *same* bundle in the base year (which is 1980 in this example). The price index is thus always 100 in the base year. The index of 180 means that prices have risen on average by 80 percent between the base year and the year in question. This average weights price changes by their *importance* in the average household's budget in the base year.

sentative" bundle of goods is 110 percent of what it was in the base year.

A price index number for a given year tells the ratio of the cost of purchasing a bundle of commodities in that year to the cost of purchasing the *same* bundle in the base year multiplied by 100 [1][2]

The percentage *change* in the cost of purchasing the bundle is thus the index number minus 100. An index number of 110 indicates a percentage increase in prices of 10 percent over those ruling in the base year.

Some Difficulties with Price Index Numbers

An index number is meant to reflect the broad trend in prices rather than the details. This means that although the information it gives may be extremely valuable, it must be interpreted with care. Here are three of the many reasons why care is required.

[2] Notes giving mathematical demonstrations of the concepts presented in the text are designated by colored reference numbers. These notes can be found beginning on page 954.

First, the weights in the index refer to an average bundle of goods. This average, although "typical" of what is consumed in the nation, will not be typical of what each household consumes. The rich, the poor, the young, the old, the single, the married, the urban, and the rural household will typically consume different bundles. An increase in air fares, for example, will raise the cost of living of a middle income traveler while leaving that of a poor stay-at-home unaffected. In the example shown in Table 3-1, the cost of living would have risen by 100 percent, 40 percent, and 380 percent respectively for three different families, one of whom consumed only commodity A, one only commodity B, and one only commodity C. The index in the table shows, however, that the cost of living went up by 80 percent for a family that consumed all three goods in the relative quantities indicated.

The more an individual household's consumption pattern diverges from that of the typical pattern used to weight prices in the price index, the less well the price index will reflect the average change in prices relevant to that household.

To assess the importance of this problem, separate indexes are calculated for different sub-groups. For example, since January 1980, there has been both an "all-urban" CPI and a separate index for "urban wage and clerical workers." These indexes differ because the typical consumption pattern of wage and clerical workers differs from that of other urban dwellers.

Second, households usually alter their consumption patterns in response to price changes. A price index that shows changes in the cost of purchasing a fixed bundle of goods does not allow for this. For example, a typical cost of living index for middle income families at the turn of the century would have given heavy weight to the cost of maids and laundresses. A doubling of servants' wages in 1900 would have greatly increased the middle-class cost of living. Today it would have little effect, for the rising cost of labor has long since caused middle income families to cease to employ full-time servants. A household that has dispensed altogether with a commodity whose price is rising rapidly does not have its cost of living rise as fast as a household that continues to consume that commodity in an undiminished quantity.

A fixed-weight price index tends to overstate cost of living changes because it does not allow for changes in consumption patterns that shift expenditure away from commodities whose prices rise most and toward those whose prices rise least.

Third, as time goes by, new commodities enter the typical consumption bundle and old ones leave. A cost of living index in 1890 would have had a large item for horse-drawn carriages but no allowance at all for automobiles and gasoline.

A fixed-weight index makes no allowance for the rise of new products nor for the declining importance of old in the typical household's consumption bundle.

The longer the period of time that passes, the less some fixed consumption bundle will be typical of current consumption patterns. For this reason the Bureau of Labor Statistics (BLS), the government body responsible for the CPI, makes a new survey of household expenditure patterns about once every 10 years and revises the weights. The base period is then usually changed to be near the year in which the new set of commodity weights was calculated. At the end of 1982, using 1972 weights, the CPI stood at 292.4 (1967 = 100). This meant that the cost of purchasing the bundle of goods bought by a typical household in 1972 had risen 192.4 percent in the intervening 10 years. Ten years is a long time for fixed-weights to be used, and during 1982 the BLS was busy estimating a new set of weights preparatory to shifting the weighting year of the CPI to some year in the early 1980s.

Index Numbers of Physical Outputs

There are many output indexes, and the Federal Reserve Board's Index of Industrial Production is one of the leading economic indicators. This index stood at 125.8 in June 1974 but had fallen to 110.0 in March 1975. By July 1981 the cyclical peak of 153.9 had been reached. By October 1982 the index had fallen to 136.3. In each case, 1967 was the base period (for which the index was 100). This means that whatever the index measured was 25.8 percent higher in June 1974 than in the base period, but fell 15.8 points (approximately 13 percent) in the next three months. By 1981 it was 53.9 percent above its value in the 1967 base period. To the extent that the index is meaningful, it measures both the growth of the American economy in the period 1967–1981, a recession between mid 1974 and early 1975, and another recession after July 1981. But what exactly does the index measure?

Like the price indexes discussed above, it is an average of the changes in thousands of individual items. It is not hard to measure the change in production of tons of steel from month to month or year to year, nor that of tires or television sets. It is somewhat harder to measure the quantity of printing, of furniture, and of aircraft because the unit of output is less well defined; but these too can be approximated.

The compilers of the Index of Industrial Production first compute indexes of the change in quantity of output for individual industries and then combine them into an overall index by using the value of output in each industry as a weighting

TABLE 3–2 THE CALCULATION OF A QUANTITY INDEX

	Output		Quantity relative	Value of output (billions of dollars)	
	1982 (Q_0)	1983 (Q_1)	Q_1/Q_0	V_0	$\frac{Q_1}{Q_0} \times V_0$
Industry A	40,000 tons	50,000 tons	1.25	$10	$12.5
Industry B	200,000 yards	300,000 yards	1.50	2	3.0
Total				$12	$15.5
Index value (1982 = 100)				100	129.2

This quantity index weights quantity changes by the relative importance of the quantities in the base year. The increase in quantity in each industry is shown in the "quantity relative" column, Q_1/Q_0. Industry A is more important than industry B, as is shown by V_0, the values of outputs in year zero. Thus industry A gets greater weight in computing the price index. The total value of output in 1982 was $12 billion. The last column shows the increase in value of output caused by the increase in quantity, assuming that prices and relative importance of the two commodities did not change. This computed value is $15.5 billion for 1983. The index for 1983 is: 15.5/12.0 × 100 = 129.2.

device. Table 3-2 illustrates in simplified form the kind of computation that would be required for a two-industry world. The final computation shows that the index has increased by 29.2 percent between 1982 and 1983. This is the weighted average of the 25 percent increase in the production of industry A and the 50 percent increase in that of industry B. Nothing tangible increased by 29.2 percent. Yet this average reflects the fact that both industries expanded output and that industry A was in the aggregate five times as important as industry B. The procedure used in Table 3-2 can be extended to include thousands of commodities, and this leads to an overall index of physical production. Compilers of index numbers of physical output face many practical problems—which products to include, how to adjust for changes in quality of production, and which values to use as weights.

The Accuracy and Significance of Index Numbers

Index numbers of either price or output are by their very nature crude approximations. Given the changing nature of goods and products over time (a 1967 car was different from a 1981 car) and the changing relative importance of different commodities (the role of food in consumers' total budgets is declining and that of services is rising), any fixed bundle of commodities becomes out of date very quickly. But if an important trend of prices or production is under way, there is need to measure it approximately.

It would be foolish to make very much of the fact that the Consumer Price Index rose from 292.2 to 292.8 between July and August 1982 (1967 = 100), for an index number is the average of many changes. Some prices rose and others fell; some rose a lot, others very little, and so on. When the net change is so small, it may not mean very much by itself. This result, however, taken in conjunction with similar monthly increases throughout that year and the next, revealed a major slowdown in the inflationary trend.

Index numbers are useful, then, as general indicators. Yet people often become mesmerized by them and treat them as though they had an accuracy that their compilers do not claim for them. Being aware of their limitations should not lead one to neglect numbers for the useful information they do show: average changes over time.

MEASUREMENT AND TESTING OF ECONOMIC RELATIONS

It is one thing for economists to theorize that two variables are related to each other; it is quite another for them to be able to say *how* these variables are related. Economists might generalize on the basis of a casual observation that when households receive more income, they are likely to buy more of most commodities. But precisely how much will the consumption of a particular commodity rise as household incomes rise? Are there exceptions to the rule that the purchase of a commodity rises as income rises? For estimating precise magnitudes and for testing general rules or hypotheses, common sense, intuition, and casual observation do not take us very far. More systematic statistical analysis is required.

Statistical analysis is used to test the hypothesis that two things are related and, when they are, to estimate the numerical values of the function that describes the relation.

In practice, the same data can be used simultaneously to test whether a relationship exists and, when it does exist, to provide a measure of it.

Techniques for Testing Theories

The techniques used to test theories differ considerably between those disciplines that can use laboratory methods and those that cannot.

Laboratory Sciences

In some sciences all the observations required for testing theories can be obtained from controlled experiments made under laboratory conditions. In these experiments all the factors that are thought to affect the outcome of the process being studied are held constant. These factors are then varied one by one and the influence of each variation observed.

Suppose chemists have a theory predicting that the rate at which a substance burns is a function of (1) the rate at which oxygen is made available during the process of combustion and (2) the chemical properties of the substance. To test this theory they may take many identical pieces of a substance and burn them, varying the amount of available oxygen in each case. This procedure will show how combustion varies with the quantity of oxygen supplied. They may then take a number of substances with different chemical compositions and burn them, using identical amounts of oxygen in each case. This procedure will show how combustion varies with chemical composition.

Being able to conduct such experiments, scientists are never forced to use data in which both chemical composition and the quantity of oxygen vary at once. Laboratory conditions serve to hold other factors constant and to produce data for situations in which factors can be varied one at a time.

Nonlaboratory Sciences

In many sciences factors cannot be isolated individually in laboratory experiments. In these sciences observations can be used to establish relationships and to test theories, even though they show what happens when several causes operate at the same time. Testing is more difficult where laboratory methods cannot be used, but not only is it possible, it is frequently done.

In a situation in which many influences vary at once, data must be used carefully. If only two men are studied and it is found that the one with the better nutritional standards during youth has the poorer adult health record, this finding would not disprove the hypothesis that a good diet contributes to better health. It might well be that some other factor has exerted an overwhelming influence. The less healthy man may have lived most of his adult life in a disease-ridden area, while the healthier man may have lived in a relatively healthy place. A single exception does not disprove the hypothesis that two variables are related as long as we admit that other variables can also influence the outcome. But if thousands of people are studied with respect to childhood diet and adult health record, we can expect individual irregularities to cancel out and an underlying regularity to show up.

Contrast this strategy of basing decisions on a large number of observations with the practice in much ordinary conversation of acting as though a single contrary case disproved a theory. Notice how often one person advances a possible relation (e.g., between legal education and some facet of character) and someone else "refutes" this theory by citing a single counterexample (e.g., "Ralph Nader went to law school and did not turn out like that"). This "refutation" errs in focusing on one individual's behavior, which may well be unpredictable, instead of an overall pattern of behavior that is predictable.

The Statistical Testing of Economic Theories: An Example

Economics is a nonlaboratory science. It is rarely possible to conduct controlled experiments with the economy. However, millions of *uncontrolled experiments* are going on every day. Households are deciding what to purchase given changing prices and incomes; firms are deciding what to produce and how to produce it; and the government is involved in the economy by its various taxes, subsidies, and controls. Because all these activities can be observed and recorded, a mass of data is continually produced by the economy.

The variables that interest economists, such as the volume of unemployment, the price of wheat, and the share of income going to wage earners, are generally influenced by many factors, all of which vary simultaneously. If economists are to test their theories about relations among variables in the economy, they must use statistical techniques designed for situations in which other things cannot be held constant.

How then do we proceed? To illustrate how data may be used to test theories even while other things are not held constant, we take the very simple and intuitively plausible hypothesis that the federal income taxes paid by American families increase as their incomes increase. To begin with, observations must be made of family income and tax payments. It is not practical to do so for all American families, so a small number (called a **sample**) must be stud-

ied on the assumption that they are typical of the entire group.

The Sample

We start by picking a sample of three families and recording their incomes and taxes paid. The results, shown in Table 3-3, may lead us to wonder whether the hypothesis is wrong, but before we jump to that conclusion we note that "by chance" the three families selected may not be typical of all the families in the country. Tax payments, we know, are influenced by factors other than income. Possibly these other factors just happen to dominate in these three cases.

Increasing the number of families in the sample may reduce the chances of consistently picking untypical families. Suppose the next sample checked is larger: it consists of 100 families selected from among our friends and acquaintances. A statistician points out, however, that the new group is a *biased* sample, for it contains families from only a limited geographical area, probably with only a limited occupational range, and very possibly with similar incomes. (Since we are now testing how income tax payments vary as income varies, this last point is likely to have serious consequences.) As a result of these limitations, it is unlikely that this sample of friends and acquaintances will be representative of all families in the United States, the group in which we are interested.

TABLE 3–3 THREE OBSERVATIONS ON FAMILY INCOME AND FEDERAL INCOME TAX PAYMENTS IN 1979

Family	Family income	Federal income tax payments
1	$14,327	$2,137
2	36,743	1,844
3	42,364	997

These three observations suggest that tax payments go down as income rises, but a sample of three is too small to be reliable. Each family studied has both a level of family income and an amount of tax payments in each year.

The statistician advises us to take a random sample of families in the United States. A **random sample** is chosen according to a rigidly defined set of conditions guaranteeing among other things that every family in which we are interested has an equal chance of being selected. Choosing the sample in a random fashion has two important consequences.

First, it reduces the chance that the sample will be unrepresentative of all families. Second, and more important, it allows us to calculate just how likely it is that the sample is unrepresentative in any given aspect by any stated amount. This second result is important because it allows us to make statements about the probability that the behavior of all families in the United States will differ by any quantitative amount from that of families in the sample.

The reason for the predictability of random samples is that such samples are chosen by chance, and chance events are predictable.

That chance events are predictable may sound surprising. But if you pick a card from a deck of ordinary playing cards, how likely is it that you will pick a heart? An ace? An ace of hearts? You play a game in which you pick a card and win if it is a heart and lose if it is anything else; a friend offers you $5 if you win against $1 if you lose. Who will make money if the game is played a large number of times? The same game is played again, but now you get $3 if you win and pay $1 if you lose. Who will make money over a large number of draws? If you know the answers to these questions (we will bet that most of you do), you must believe that chance events are in some sense predictable.

To analyze the hypothesis being tested, we have chosen for illustration a random sample of 212 families from data collected by the Survey Research Center of the University of Michigan. (How representative the sample is of all relevant families can be checked by comparing characteristics of the families in it with results that are known to hold for American families in general, e.g., how many have two cars or how many have two members who have completed four years of college.) Once the

TABLE 3–4 FEDERAL TAX PAYMENTS CROSS-CLASSIFIED BY FAMILY INCOME

Annual family income	Average income tax payment	Number of families in sample
Less than $10,000	$ 70	38
$ 10,000–19,999	893	76
20,000–29,999	2,470	42
30,000–39,999	4,205	28
40,000–99,999	7,755	28
100,000 or more	—	none

Tax payments tend to increase as family income increases. The data on 212 families are grouped into the income classes shown in the first column. The average tax payment for families in each income group is calculated and listed in the second column. When we read down this second column, we find an unbroken rise in tax payments. This cross-classification reduces 212 individual observations to a mere 5. More (or less) detail could have been preserved by varying the size of the income classes used in the first column.

sample is chosen and checked for representativeness, the information required from it is collected. In this case, the information desired is the income of each family and the federal income tax it pays.

Graphic and Tabular Analysis of the Data

There are several ways in which the data may be used to evaluate the hypothesis.

Scatter diagram. One is the **scatter diagram.**[3] Figure 3-1 is a scatter diagram that relates family income to federal income tax payments. The pattern of the dots suggests that there is a strong tendency for tax payments to be higher when family income is higher. It thus supports the hypothesis.

There is some scattering of the dots because the relationship is not "perfect"; in other words, there is some variation in tax payments that cannot be associated with variations in family income. These

[3] The appendix to this chapter outlines the elements of graphs and the graphical analysis of economic data. If you find graphical analysis baffling, you might read this appendix now.

unexplained variations in tax payments occur mainly for two reasons. First, factors other than income influence tax payments, and some of these other factors will undoubtedly have varied among the families in the sample. Second, there will inevitably be some errors in measurement. For example, a family might have incorrectly reported its tax payments to the person who collected our data.

Cross-classification table. A cross-classification table provides another way to examine the hypothesis that tax payments vary directly with income. Table 3-4 cross-classifies families by their income and their average tax payments. At the loss of considerable detail, the table makes clear the general tendency for tax payments to rise as income rises.

Regression Analysis

While both the scatter diagram and the cross-classification table reflect the general relationship between federal income tax payments and family income, neither concisely characterizes what the precise relationship is. **Regression analysis,** a widely used technique, provides quantitative measures of what the relationship between two variables is and how closely it holds. Regression analysis may be used if certain conditions are fulfilled.[4] Regression analysis employs a **regression equation** that represents the best estimate of the *average* relationship between the variables being tested. Such an equation can be used to describe the tendency for higher family income to be associated with higher tax payments.[5]

A measure of how closely the relationship holds can be obtained by calculating the percentage of the variance in federal tax payments that can be accounted for by variations in household income.[6] This measure is called the **coefficient of determi-**

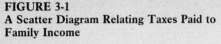

FIGURE 3-1
A Scatter Diagram Relating Taxes Paid to Family Income

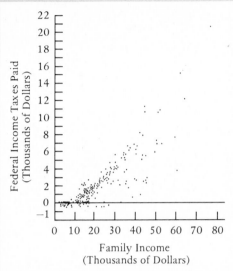

The scatter pattern shows a clear tendency for taxes paid to rise with family income. Family income is measured along the horizontal axis, and federal income taxes are paid along the vertical axis. Each dot represents a single family in the sample and is located on the graph according to the family's income and taxes paid. The dots fall mainly within a narrow, rising band, suggesting the existence of a systematic relationship between income and taxes paid. But they do not fall along a single line, which suggests that things other than family income affect taxes paid. The data are for 1979. (Negative amounts of tax liability arise because of such things as capital losses that may be carried forward.)

---

[4] The detailed discussion of techniques and conditions is left to courses in statistics and econometrics.
[5] The equation of a straight line fitted to the data shown in Figure 3-1 is $T = -1,924 + 0.19Y$, where T is taxes paid and Y is income in thousands of dollars per year. The equation shows that for every increase of $1,000 in family income, taxes paid tend to increase by $190.
[6] *Variance* is a precise statistical measure of the amount of variability (dispersion) in a set of data.

nation (r^2). For our sample $r^2 = 0.734$. It indicates in this case that 73.4 percent of the variance in tax payments can be "explained" by associating it with variations in family incomes.

A *significance test* can be applied to determine the odds that the relation discovered in the sample does not exist for the whole population but has arisen by chance because the families selected happen not to be representative of the entire set of American families. It turns out that in this example there is less than one chance in 1 million that the rising pattern of dots shown in Figure 3-1 would have been observed if there were no increasing relation between income and tax payments for U.S. families. Since this chance is very small, we conclude that the hypothesis that these two variables—tax payments and family income—are positively related is correct. Statistically the relationship is said to be *significant*.

Extending the Analysis to Three Variables

The scatter diagram and the regression equation show that *all* the variation in income tax payments cannot be accounted for by observed variations in family income. If it could, all the dots would lie on a line, and r^2 would equal 1.0. Since they do not, some other factors must influence tax payments. What could make one family with an income of $12,000 pay 20 percent more in income taxes than another family with the same income?

One reason is difference in family size, for American tax laws provide for exemptions based on the number of family members. (There will be other reasons too, such as differences in itemized deductions for medical expenses or charitable donations.) We anticipate that family size will be an important second reason. The survey also collected data on family size, which we now use.

There are now *three* observations for each of the 212 families: annual income, federal income tax payments, and family size. How should these data be handled? Unfortunately, the scatter diagram technique is not available because the relation between three data series cannot conveniently be shown on a two-dimensional graph.

The data may, however, be grouped once again. This time we are testing two variables that are thought to influence tax payments, and the data have to be cross-classified in a more complicated manner, as shown in Table 3-5.

The device of cross-classification shown in Table 3-5 demonstrates clearly how we hold one variable roughly constant while allowing another to vary. Reading across each row, we see that income is held constant within a specified range and family

TABLE 3-5 FEDERAL INCOME TAXES PAID CROSS-CLASSIFIED BY FAMILY INCOME AND FAMILY SIZE

Annual family income	Number of family members		
	3 or less	4 or 5	6 or more
$ 0–9,999	$ 26	$ 142	$ 175
10,000–19,999	1,028	995	507
20,000–29,999	2,950	2,491	935
30,000–39,999	5,349	3,802	2,372
40,000–99,999	9,459	8,624	4,193
100,000 or more	none in the sample		

Tax payments tend to vary positively with family income and negatively with family size. Each row in the table shows the effect of family size on tax payments for a given level of income. For example, reading across the second row shows that families with incomes between $10,000 and $20,000 paid an average of $1,028 if their family had less than 4 members, $995 if their family had 4 or 5 members, and $507 if their family had 6 or more members. The declining numbers across each row show that for each income group tax payments tend to decline as family size increases. Each column on the table shows the effect of income on tax payments for a given family size. The increase in taxes paid as we move down each column shows that tax payments increase with family income.

size is varied; reading down each column, we see that size of family is held constant within a specified range and income is varied.

To estimate a numerical relation among family income, family size, and tax payments, **multiple regression analysis** is used.[7] This type of analysis allows estimation of both the separate and joint effects on tax payments of variations in family size and variations in income by fitting to the data an equation that "best" describes them. It also permits the measurement of the proportion of the total

[7] Details must be left to a course in statistics. The regression equation for our example is $T = -733 + .197Y - 344F$, where F is the number of family members. On average, an additional family member decreases taxes paid by $344. R^2, the coefficient of determination in multiple regression analysis, is .774. Comparison with the previous $r^2 = .734$ shows that adding family size to the analysis increased the percentage of variance explained from 73.4 percent to 77.4 percent.

variation in tax payments that can be explained by associating it with variations both in income and family size. Finally, it permits the use of significance tests to determine how likely it is that the relations found in the sample are the result of chance and thus do not reveal an underlying relationship for all U.S. families. Chance plays a role because by bad luck an unrepresentative sample of families might have been chosen.

Evaluating the Evidence

Statistical techniques can help to measure the nature and strength of economic relationships and show how probable it is that a certain result has occurred by chance. What they cannot do is prove that a hypothesis is either true or false. Nor can they tell us unambiguously when a hypothesis should be accepted or rejected.

Can a Hypothesis Be Proven True or False?

Most hypotheses in economics are universal. They say that whenever certain specified conditions are fulfilled, cause X will always produce effect Y. Such universal hypotheses cannot be proven correct with 100 percent certainty. No matter how many observations are collected that agree with the hypothesis, there is always some chance that a long series of untypical observations has been made or that there have been systematic errors of observation. After all, the mass of well-documented evidence accumulated several centuries ago on the existence of the power of witches is no longer accepted, even though it fully satisfied most contemporary observers. The existence of observational errors—even on a vast scale—has been shown to be possible, although (one fervently hopes) it is not very frequent. Observations that disagree with the theory may begin to accumulate, and after some time a theory that looked nearly certain may begin to look rather shaky.

By the same token a universal hypothesis can never be proven false with 100 percent certainty. Even when current observations consistently con-

flict with the theory, it is still possible that a large number of untypical cases or systematic errors of observation has been selected. For instance, evidence was once gathered "disproving" the hypothesis that high income taxes tend to discourage work. More recent research suggests that economists may have been wrong to reject the theory that high taxes tend to discourage work. As a result of measurement errors and bad experimental design, the conflicting evidence may not have been as decisive as was once thought.

There is no absolute certainty in any knowledge. No doubt some of the things we now think true will eventually turn out to be false, and some of the things we currently think false will eventually turn out to be true. Yet while we can never be certain, we can assess the balance of evidence.

Some hypotheses are so unlikely to be true, given current evidence, that for all practical purposes we may regard them as false. Other hypotheses are so unlikely to be false, given current evidence, that for all practical purposes we may regard them as true.

This kind of practical decision must always be regarded as tentative. Every once in a while we will discover that we have to change our mind: Something that looked right will begin to look doubtful, or something that looked wrong will begin to look possible.

The Decision to Reject or Accept

In general, a hypothesis can never be proven or refuted conclusively, no matter how many observations are made. Nonetheless, since decisions have to be made, it is necessary to accept some hypotheses (to act as if they were proven) and reject some hypotheses (to act as if they were refuted). Just as a jury can make two kinds of errors (finding an innocent person guilty or letting a guilty person go free) so can statistical decision makers make two kinds of errors. They can reject hypotheses that are true, and they can accept hypotheses that are false. Luckily, like a jury, they can also make correct decisions—and indeed they expect to do so most of the time.

Although the possibility of error cannot be eliminated in statistics, it can be controlled.

The method of control is to decide in advance how large a risk to take of accepting a hypothesis that is in fact false.[8] Conventionally in statistics this risk is often set at 5 percent or 1 percent. When the 5 percent cutoff point is used, we will accept the hypothesis if the results that appear to establish it could have happened by chance no more than 1 time in 20. Using the 1 percent decision rule gives the hypothesis a sterner test. A hypothesis is accepted only if the results that appear to establish it could have happened by chance no more than 1 time in 100.

Consider the hypothesis that a certain coin is "loaded," favoring heads over tails. The coin is flipped 100 times and comes up heads 53 times. While this result is not inconsistent with the hypothesis, such an unbalanced result could happen by chance more than 22 percent of the time. Thus the hypothesis of a head-biassed coin would not be accepted using either a 1 percent or a 5 percent cutoff. Had the experiment produced 65 heads and 35 tails, a result that would occur by chance less than 1 percent of the time, we would (given a 1 percent or a 5 percent cutoff) accept the hypothesis of a loaded coin.[9]

When action must be taken, some rule of thumb is necessary. But it is important to understand, first, that no one can ever be *certain* about being right in rejecting any hypothesis and, second, that there is nothing magical about arbitrary cutoff points. Some cutoff point must be used whenever decisions have to be made.

Finally, recall that the rejection of a hypothesis is seldom the end of inquiry. Decisions can be reversed should new evidence come to light. Often the result of a statisical test of a theory is to suggest a new hypothesis that "fits the facts" better than the old one. Indeed, in some cases just looking at a scatter diagram or making a regression analysis uncovers apparent relations that no one anticipated and leads economists to formulate a new hypothesis.

SUMMARY

1. Index numbers are summary measures that give the average percentage change in a set of related items between a "base" year and another "given" year.

2. The Consumer Price Index (CPI) measures the percentage change in the cost of purchasing a typical bundle of commodities since the base year. It is thus a measure of the average change in prices in which each price is weighted by the importance of that commodity in the typical consumption bundle.

3. Some problems with index numbers are (1) the weights on which they are based are broad averages that do not reflect each individual's expenditure pattern, (2) the fixed weights make no allowance for changes in consumption patterns that occur in response to price changes, and (3) the fixed weights cannot allow for important new products, the decline of old ones, and changes in the quality of commodities that continue to be bought. For these and other reasons the weights are revised periodically.

4. Index numbers measure broad trends, and therefore not too much importance should be given to small changes unless they persist. Index numbers provide very valuable summary information—provided it is understood that they are only meant to reflect major changes for broad aggregates.

5. Theories are tested by checking their predictions against actual evidence. In some sciences, these tests can be conducted under laboratory conditions where only one thing changes at a time. In other sciences, testing must be done using the data produced by the world of ordinary events, where many factors are changing all at once. Modern statistical analysis is designed to test hypotheses

---

[8] Return to the jury analogy: Our notion of a person being innocent unless the jury is persuaded of guilt "beyond a reasonable doubt" rests on our wishing to take only a small risk of accepting the hypothesis of guilt if the person being tried is in fact innocent.

[9] The actual statistical testing process is more complex than this example suggests but must be left to a course in statistics.

where many variables are changing at once.

6. Sample data are often used in testing economic hypotheses. If the sample is random, the probability of the measured characteristics of the sample being misleading (because of the unlucky choice of a nonrepresentative sample) can be calculated.

7. Scatter diagrams or simple cross-classification tables are devices for exploring the presence of systematic relationships between two variables. Regression analysis permits more specific measures of the relationship: what it is, how closely it holds, and whether or not it is "significant."

8. Hypotheses involving several variables require more sophisticated statistical techniques such as the use of complex cross-classification tables and multiple regression analysis, each of which attempts to identify the separate and joint effects of several variables on one another.

9. While statistical tests allow us to assess the probability that what we observe is consistent with a particular hypothesis, they never allow determination of the truth or falsity of a hypothesis beyond any doubt. Because it is often necessary to act as though certain hypotheses are true and others false, decision rules may be required. Two frequently used cutoff points are 5 percent and 1 percent.

10. Methods of graphing economic observations are discussed in more detail in the appendix to this chapter.

TOPICS FOR REVIEW

Price index numbers
Base years and given years
The need for weights in index numbers
Problems with fixed-weight indexes calculated over long time periods
The twofold role of statistical analysis: measurement and testing
Scatter diagrams
Cross-classification tables
The difference between proving a hypothesis true and accepting the hypothesis
The difference between proving a hypothesis false and rejecting the hypothesis

DISCUSSION QUESTIONS

1. According to a senior vice-president of Mellon Bank: "When it comes to forecasting the economy, the stock market has as good a record—if not better—than most economists." Can this hypothesis be tested? If so, how? If not, why not?

2. In the seventies the cost of automobile insurance rose sharply. The American Automobile Association said its increase was due not (as some charged) to the passage by many states of no-fault insurance laws but to the inflation in the cost of parts used in repairing cars. How might the AAA's hypothesis be tested?

3. "The simplest way to see that capital punishment is a strong deterrent to murder is to ask yourself whether you might be more inclined to commit murder if you knew in advance that you ran no risk of ending in the electric chair, the gas chamber, or on the gallows." Comment on the methodology of social investigation implied by this statement. What alternative approach would you suggest?

4. Since 1979, when the data used in Figure 3-1 were collected, federal tax laws have changed, lowering the tax rates that apply to higher incomes. How would you expect this development to change a scatter diagram of income and tax payments? Would you expect it to change the regression results? Do these changes lead you to reject the conclusions of the analysis of the 1979 data?

5. There are hundreds of eyewitnesses to the existence of flying saucers and other UFOs. There are films and eyewitness accounts of Nessie, the Loch Ness monster. Are you persuaded of their existence? If not, what would it take to persuade you? If so, what would it take to make you change your mind?

6. Relate the role of the "law" of large numbers (see Chapter 2) to the statistical idea that one can test hypotheses by using average relationships based on random samples.

7. A classic example of biased sampling was the attempt made by the *Literary Digest* in 1936 to predict the result of the presidential election. The magazine forecast a substantial Republican victory, and its subsequent demise has been attributed to this error. (Franklin D. Roosevelt won every state but Maine and Vermont from Republican Alfred Landon, and the political platitude, "As Maine goes, so goes the nation" was reworded "As Maine goes, so goes Vermont.") The *Literary Digest* poll was based on a random sample of names in telephone directories. Can you spot a potential flaw in this sample? Remember that this happened in 1936. Would the same bias have existed if the survey had been made in 1984? By 1948 the selection of the sample was much more sophisticated, but the Roper polls

predicted Dewey over Truman by such a substantial margin that polling was discontinued after September 30. Truman, of course, won the election. What was the nature of the sampling error this time?

8. Look up in the *Economic Report of the President* the behavior of the major categories of the CPI over the last two years. Compare the rise in the costs of living of someone who spent most of his income on food and someone who spent her income in proportion to the overall CPI weights.

What commodity groups would have heavy weights in the budget of a person whose cost of living had risen much less than the average? What about the budget of a person whose cost of living had risen much more than the average?

9. Housing costs play a big role in the CPI. With rising interest rates, housing costs have risen sharply. Why? Should a family that owns its own home "free and clear" have its cost of living based on an index that neglects changes in mortgage interest rates?

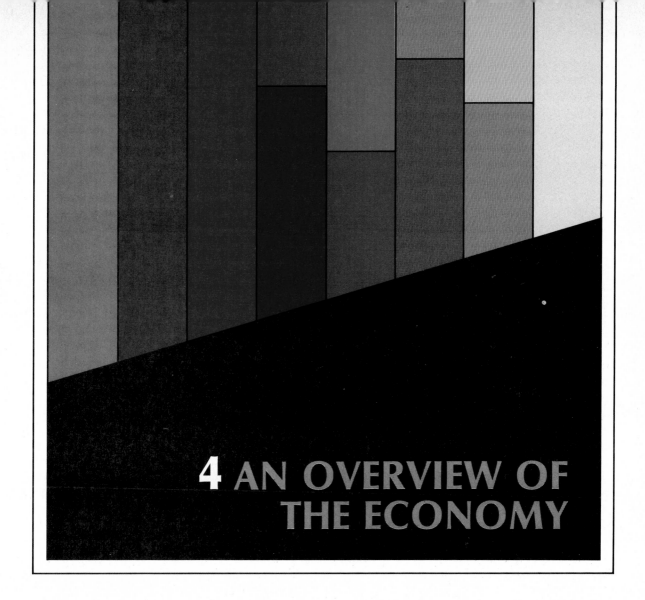

4 AN OVERVIEW OF THE ECONOMY

THE EVOLUTION
OF MARKET ECONOMIES

The central economic problem of our times—choice under conditions of scarcity—has been with us a mere 8,000 years or 10,000 years, little more than an instant in the millions of years in which humanoid creatures have been on earth. It began with the original agricultural revolution, when human beings first found it possible to stay in one place and survive. Gradually abandoning their no-madic life of hunting and food gathering, people settled down to tend crops that they had learned to plant and animals that they had learned to domesticate. All societies since that time have faced the problem of choice under conditions of scarcity.

Surplus, Specialization, and Trade

Along with permanent settlement, the agricultural revolution brought surplus production. Farmers could produce substantially more than they needed to survive. The agricultural surplus allowed the creation of new occupations and thus new economic and social classes such as artisans, soldiers, priests, and government officials. Freed from having to grow their own food, these new classes turned their talents to performing specialized services and producing goods other than food. They also produced more than they themselves needed, so they traded the excess to obtain whatever they required.

The allocation of different jobs to different people is called **specialization of labor.** Specialization has proven extraordinarily efficient compared with self-sufficiency for at least two reasons. First, individual talents and abilities differ, and specialization allows each person to do the job he or she can do relatively best, while leaving everything else to be done by others. People not only do their thing; they do their own best thing. Second, a person who concentrates on one activity becomes better at it than could a jack-of-all-trades.

The exchange of goods and services in early societies commonly took place by simple mutual agreement among neighbors. In the course of time, however, trading became centered in particular gathering places called markets. Today we use the term **market economy** to refer to a society in which people specialize in productive activities and meet most of their material wants through exchanges voluntarily agreed upon by the contracting parties.

Specialization must be accompanied by trade. People who produce only one thing must trade most of it to obtain all the other things they require.

The earliest market economies depended on **barter,** the trading of goods directly for other goods. But barter can be a very costly process in terms of time spent searching out satisfactory exchanges. *Money* evolved to make trade easier. It eliminates the inconvenience of barter by allowing the two sides of the barter transaction to be separated. If a farmer has wheat and wants a hammer, he does not have to search for an individual who has a hammer and wants wheat. He merely has to find someone who wants wheat. The farmer takes money in exchange, then finds another person who

wishes to trade a hammer and swaps the money for the hammer.

By eliminating the need for barter, money greatly facilitates trade and specialization.

Factor Services and Division of Labor

Market transactions in early economies mainly involved goods and services for consumption. Producers specialized in making a commodity and then traded it for the other products they needed. The labor services required to make the product would usually be provided by the makers themselves, by apprentices learning to be craftsmen, or by slaves. Over the last several hundred years, many technical advances in methods of production have made it efficient to organize agriculture and industry on a very large scale. These technical developments have made use of what is called the **division of labor,** which is a further step in the specialization of labor. This term refers to specialization within the production process of a particular commodity. The labor involved is divided into a series of repetitive tasks, and each individual does a single task that may be just one of hundreds of tasks necessary to produce the commodity. Today it is possible for an individual to work on a production line without knowing what commodity emerges at the end of that line!

To gain the advantages of the division of labor it became necessary to organize production in large and expensive factories. With this development workers lost their status as craftsmen (or peasants) and became members of the working class, wholly dependent on their ability to sell their labor to factory (or farm) owners and lacking a plot of land to fall back on for subsistence in times of need. The day of small craftsmen who made and sold their own goods was over. Today's typical workers do not earn their incomes by selling commodities they personally have produced; rather they sell their labor services to firms and receive money wages in return. They have increasingly become

THE DIVISION OF LABOR

Adam Smith began *The Wealth of Nations* with a long study of the division of labor. Among other things, he had this to say.

> The greatest improvements in the productive powers of labour . . . have been the effects of the division of labour.
>
> To take an example . . . the trade of the pinmaker; a workman not educated to this business (which the division of labour has rendered a distinct trade), nor acquainted with the use of the machinery employed in it could scarce, perhaps, with his utmost industry, make one pin in a day, and certainly could not make twenty. But in the way in which this business is now carried on . . . it is divided into a number of branches. . . . One man draws out the wire, another straightens it, a third cuts it, a fourth points it, a fifth grinds it at the top for receiving the head; to make the head requires two or three distinct operations; to put it on, is a peculiar business, to whiten the pins is another; it is even a trade by itself to put them into the paper; and the important business of making a pin is, in this manner, divided into about eighteen distinct operations, which, in some manufactories, are all performed by distinct hands, though in others the same man will sometimes perform two or three of them.

Smith observes that even in smallish factories, where the division of labor is exploited only in part, output is as high as 4,800 pins per person per day!

Later Smith discusses the general importance of the division of labor and the forces that limit its application.

> Each animal is still obliged to support and defend itself, separately and independently, and derives no sort of advantage from that variety of talents with which nature has distinguished its fellows. Among men, on the contrary, the most dissimilar geniuses are of use to one another; the different produces of their respective talents, by the general disposition to truck, barter, and exchange, being brought, as it were, into a common stock, where every man may purchase whatever part of the produce of other men's talents he has occasion for.
>
> As it is the power of exchanging that gives occasion to the division of labour, so the extent of this division must always be limited by the extent of that power, or, in other words, by the extent of the market. When the market is very small, no person can have any encouragement to dedicate himself entirely to one employment for want [i.e., lack] of the power to exchange all that surplus part of the produce of his own labour, which is over and above his own consumption, for such parts of the produce of other men's labour as he has occasion for.

Smith notes that there is no point in specializing to produce a large quantity of pins, or anything else, unless there are enough persons making other commodities to provide a market for all the pins that are produced. Thus, the larger the market, the greater the scope for the division of labor and the higher the resulting opportunities for efficient production.

cogs in a machine that they do not fully understand or control.

Markets and the Allocation of Resources

The term **resource allocation** refers to the way in which the available factors of production are distributed among the various uses to which they might be put. There are not enough resources to produce all the goods and services that could be consumed. It is therefore necessary to allocate the available resources among their various possible uses and in so doing to choose what to produce and what not to produce. In a market economy, millions of consumers decide what commodities to buy and in what quantities; a vast number of firms produce these commodities and buy the factor services that are needed to make them; and millions of factor owners decide to whom they will sell these services. These individual decisions collectively determine the economy's allocation of resources.

In a market economy, the allocation of resources is the outcome of countless independent decisions made by consumers and producers, all acting through the medium of markets.

Our main objective in this chapter is to provide an overview of this market mechanism.

THE DECISION MAKERS

Economics is about the behavior of people. Much that we observe in the world and that economists assume in their theories can be traced back to decisions made by individuals. There are millions of individuals in most economies. To make a systematic study of their behavior more manageable, we categorize them into three important groups: households, firms, and the government (central authorities).[1] These groups are economic theory's cast of characters, and the stage on which their play is enacted is the market.

Households

A **household** is defined as all the people who live under one roof and who make, or are subject to others making for them, joint financial decisions. Economic theory gives households a number of attributes.

First, economists assume that each household makes consistent decisions, as though it were composed of a single individual. Thus economists ignore many interesting problems of how the household reaches its decisions. Family conflicts and the moral and legal problems concerning parental con-

trol over minors are dealt with by other social sciences.[2] These problems are avoided in economics by the assumption that the household is the basic decision-making atom of consumption behavior.

Second, economists assume that each household is consistently attempting to achieve some goal when it makes choices. In demand theory we assume that the goal of the household is the maximization of its *satisfaction* or *well-being* or *utility*, as the concept is variously called. The household tries to do this within the limitations of its available resources.

Third, economists assume that households are the principal owners of factors of production. They sell the services of these factors to firms and receive their incomes in return. It is assumed that in making these decisions on how much to sell and to whom to sell it, each household seeks to maximize its utility.

Firms

A **firm** is defined as the unit that employs factors of production to produce commodities that it sells to other firms, to households, or to the central authorities (defined below). For obvious reasons a firm is often called a *producer*. Economic theory gives firms several attributes.

First, economists assume that each firm makes consistent decisions, as though it were composed of a single individual. Thus economic theory ignores the internal problems of who reaches particular decisions and how they are reached. In doing this, economists assume that the firm's internal organization is irrelevant to its decisions. This allows them to treat the firm as the atom of behavior on the production or supply side of commodity markets, just as the household is treated as the atom of behavior on the consumption or demand side.

---

[1] Although in basic economic theory we can get away with three sets of decision makers, it is worth noting that there are others. Probably the most important are such nonprofit organizations as private universities and hospitals, charities such as the American Cancer Society, and funding organizations such as the Ford Foundation. These bodies are responsible for allocating some of the economy's resources.

[2] In academic work, as elsewhere, a division of labor is useful. However, it is important to remember that when economists speak of *the* consumer or *the* individual, they are in fact referring to the group of individuals composing the household. Thus, for example, the commonly heard phrase *consumer sovereignty* really means *household sovereignty*.

Second, economists assume that most firms make their decisions with a single goal in mind: to make as much profit as possible. This goal of *profit maximization* is analogous to the household's goal of utility maximization.

Third, economists assume that in their role as producers, firms are the principal users of the services of factors of production. In markets where factor services are bought and sold, the roles of firms and households are thus reversed from what they are in commodity markets: In factor markets firms do the buying and households do the selling.

Government (Central Authorities)

The term **government** is used in economics in a very broad sense to include all public officials, agencies, government bodies, and other organizations belonging to or under the direct control of governments. State and local governments, as well as the federal government, are included. In the United States, the term *government* includes the president, the Federal Reserve System, the city council, commissions and regulatory bodies, the legislature, and the police force, among others. Sometimes this broad concept of government is referred to by the more descriptive term **central authorities.** It is not important to draw up a comprehensive list, but one should have in mind a general idea of the organizations that have legal and political power to exert control over individual decision makers and over markets.

It is *not* a basic assumption of economics that the government always acts in a consistent fashion or as though it were a single individual. Three important reasons for this may be mentioned here. First, the mayor of Los Angeles, a Utah state legislator, and a United States senator from Maine represent different constituencies, and therefore they may express different and conflicting views and objectives.

Second, individual public servants, whether elected or appointed, have personal objectives (such as staying in office, achieving higher office, power, prestige, and personal aggrandizement) as well as public service objectives. Although the balance of importance given to the two types of objectives will vary among persons and among types of office, both will almost always have some importance. It would be a rare senator, for example, who would vote against a measure that slightly reduced the "public good" if this vote almost guaranteed his defeat at the next election. ("After all," he could reason, "if I am defeated, I won't be around to vote against *really* bad measures.")

Third, the whole system of checks and balances is designed to set one part of the government against another part, thereby producing the characteristic American pluralism in government. (Here American practice differs sharply from that of most of the rest of the English-speaking world, whose governments are based on the British parliamentary system that was not designed to produce pluralism.)

MARKETS AND ECONOMIES

We have seen that households, firms, and the government are the main actors in the economic drama. Their action takes place in individual markets.

Markets

The word *market* originally designated a place where goods were traded. The Fulton Fish Market in New York is a world-famous modern example of markets in the everyday sense, and most cities have produce markets where fresh produce is brought early in the morning and promptly sold. Much early economic theory attempted to explain price behavior in just such markets. Why, for example, can you sometimes obtain tremendous bargains at the end of the day and at other times get what you want only at prices that appear exorbitant in relation to prices quoted only a few hours before?

As theories of market behavior were developed, they were extended to cover commodities such as wheat. Wheat produced anywhere in the world can be purchased almost anywhere else in the world, and the price of a given grade of wheat tends to be nearly uniform the world over. When we talk about the wheat market, the concept of a market has been extended well beyond the idea of a single place to which the producer, the storekeeper, and the home-maker go to sell and buy.

For present purposes, a **market** is satisfactorily defined as an area over which buyers and sellers negotiate the exchange of a well-defined commodity. Economists distinguish two broad types of markets: **product markets,** in which firms sell their outputs of goods and services, and **factor markets,** in which households sell the services of the factors of production they control.

Economies

An **economy** is rather loosely defined as a set of interrelated production and consumption activities. It may refer to this activity in a region of one country (*the economy of New England*), in a country (*the American economy*), or in a group of countries (*the economy of Western Europe*). In any economy the allocation of resources is determined by the production, sales, and purchase decisions made by firms, households, and the government.

A **free-market economy** is an economy in which the decisions of individual households and firms (as distinct from the government) exert the major influence over the allocation of resources.[3]

The opposite of a free-market economy is a **command economy,** in which the major decisions about the allocation of resources are made by the government and in which firms and households produce and consume only as they are ordered.

The terms *free-market* and *command economy* are

---

[3] Free-market economies are sometimes called *capitalist economies*; in fact, the term *capitalist* often is used as a synonym for *free market*. In Marxist literature, *capitalist* refers to the private ownership of the factor of production, called *capital*. But it is possible to be capitalist in Marx's sense of the word and yet have overwhelming public intervention into markets. Thus, *capitalist* (private ownership of capital) does not mean the same as *free* (uncontrolled) *market*. For most purposes of modern economies, it is who controls the markets rather than who owns the capital that is the important matter.

used to describe tendencies that are apparent, even though no real economies rely solely on either free markets or commands. Thus in practice all economies are **mixed economies** in the sense that some decisions are made by firms and households and some by the government.

Sectors of an Economy

Parts of an economy are usually referred to as **sectors** of that economy. For example, the agricultural sector is the part of the economy that produces agricultural commodities.

Market and Nonmarket Sectors

Producers make commodities. Consumers use them. Commodities may pass from one group to the other in two ways: they may be sold by producers and bought by consumers through markets, or they may be given away.

When commodities are bought and sold, producers must cover their costs with the revenue they obtain from selling the product. We call this production *marketed production*, and we refer to this part of the country's activity as belonging to the **market sector.**

When the product is given away, the costs of production must be covered from some source other than sales revenue. We call this production *nonmarketed production*, and we refer to this part of the country's activity as belonging to the **nonmarket sector.** In the case of private charities, the money required to pay for factor services may be raised from the public by voluntary contributions. In the case of production by the government—which accounts for the bulk of nonmarketed production—the money is provided from government revenue, which in turn comes mainly from taxes.

Whenever a government enterprise *sells* its output, its production is in the market sector. But much state output is in the nonmarket sector by the very nature of the product provided. For example, one could hardly expect the criminal to pay the judge for providing the service of criminal justice. Other products are in the nonmarket sector because governments have decided that there are advantages to removing them from the market sector. This is the case, for example, with most of American education. Public policy places it in the nonmarket sector even though much of it could be provided by the market sector.

The Public and Private Sectors

The productive activity of a country is often divided in a different way than between market and nonmarket sectors. In this alternative division, the **private sector** refers to all production that is in private hands and the **public sector** refers to all production that is in public hands. The distinction between the two sectors depends on the legal distinction of ownership. In the private sector, the organization that does the producing is owned by households or other firms; in the public sector, it is owned by the state. The public sector includes all production of goods and services by the government plus all production by government-operated industries that is sold to consumers through ordinary markets.

The distinction between market and nonmarket sectors is economic: it depends on whether or not the costs of producing commodities are recovered by selling them to their users. The distinction between the private and the public sectors is legal: it depends on whether the producing organizations are privately or publicly owned.

MICRO- AND MACROECONOMICS

An Overview of Microeconomics

Early economists observed the market economy with wonder. They saw that most commodities were made by a large number of independent producers and yet in approximately the quantities that people wanted to purchase them. Natural disasters aside, there were neither vast surpluses nor severe shortages of products. They also saw that in spite of the ever-changing requirements in terms of geographical, industrial, and occupational patterns, most laborers were able to sell their services to employers most of the time.

How does the market produce this order in the absence of conscious coordination by the government? It is one thing to have the same good produced year in and year out when people's wants and incomes do not change; it is quite another thing to have production adjusting continually to changing wants, incomes, and techniques of production. Yet this relatively smooth adjustment is accomplished by the market—albeit with occasional, and sometimes serious, interruptions.

The great discovery of eighteenth century economists was that the price system is a social control mechanism.

Adam Smith, in his classic *The Wealth of Nations*, published in 1776, spoke of the price system as "the invisible hand." It allows decision making to be centralized under the control of millions of individual producers and consumers but nonetheless to be coordinated. Two examples may help to illustrate how this coordination occurs.

A Change in Demand

For the first example, assume that households wish to purchase more of some commodity than previously. To see the market's reaction to such a change, imagine a situation in which farmers find it equally profitable to produce either of two crops, carrots or brussels sprouts, and so are willing to produce some of both commodities, thereby satisfying the demands of households who wish to consume both. Now imagine that consumers develop a greatly increased desire for brussels sprouts and a diminished desire for carrots. This change might have occurred because of the discovery of hitherto unsuspected nutritive or curative powers of brussels sprouts, or it might have been the result of a successful advertising campaign on the part of the association of brussels sprout producers: "Eat brussels sprouts; they're grown *above* ground." Whatever the reason, there has been a major shift toward sprouts and away from carrots.

What will be the effects of this shift? When consumers buy more brussels sprouts and fewer carrots, a shortage of brussels sprouts and a glut of carrots develop. To unload their surplus stocks of carrots, merchants reduce the price of carrots—

in the belief that it is better to sell them at a reduced price than not to sell them at all. Sellers of brussels sprouts, however, find that they are unable to satisfy all their customers' demands for that product. Sprouts have become a scarce commodity, so the merchants charge more for them. As the price rises, fewer people are willing and able to purchase sprouts. Thus making them more expensive limits the demand for them to the available supply.

Farmers see a rise in the price of brussels sprouts and a fall in the price of carrots. Brussels sprout production has become more profitable than in the past: the costs of producing sprouts remain unchanged at the same time that their market price has risen. Similarly, carrot production will be less profitable than in the past because costs are unchanged but the price has fallen. Attracted by high profits in brussels sprouts and deterred by low profits or potential losses in carrots, farmers expand the production of sprouts and curtail the production of carrots. Thus the change in consumers' tastes, working through the price system, causes a reallocation of resources—land and labor—out of carrot production and into brussels sprout production.

As the production of carrots declines, the glut of carrots on the market diminishes and their price begins to rise. On the other hand, the expansion in brussels sprout production reduces the shortage and the price begins to fall. These price movements will continue until it no longer pays farmers to contract carrot production and to expand brussels sprout production. When the dust settles, the price of sprouts is higher than it was originally but lower than it was when the shortage sent the price soaring before output could be adjusted; and the price of carrots is lower than it was originally but higher than when the initial glut sent the price tumbling before output could be adjusted.

The reaction of the market to a change in demand leads to a transfer of resources. Carrot producers reduce their production; they will therefore be laying off workers and generally demanding fewer factors of production. Brussels sprout producers expand production; they will therefore be hiring workers and generally increasing their demand for factors of production.

Labor can probably switch from carrot to sprout production without much difficulty. Certain types of land, however, may be better suited for growing one crop rather than the other. When farmers increase their sprout production, their demands for those factors especially suited to sprout production also increase—and this creates a shortage of these resources and a consequent rise in their prices. Meanwhile, with carrot production falling, the demand for land and other factors of production especially suited to carrot growing is reduced. A surplus results, and the prices of these factors are forced down.

Thus factors particularly suited to sprout production will earn more and will obtain a higher share of total national income than before. Factors particularly suited to carrot production, however, will earn less and will obtain a smaller share of the total national income than before.

Changes of this kind will be studied more fully later; the important thing to notice now is how a change in demand initiated by a change in consumers' tastes causes a reallocation of resources in the direction required to cater to the new set of tastes.

A Change in Supply

For a second example, consider a change originating with producers. Begin as before by imagining a situation in which farmers find it equally profitable to produce either sprouts or carrots and in which consumers are willing to buy, at prevailing market prices, the quantities of these two commodities that are being produced. Now imagine that, at existing prices, farmers become more willing to produce sprouts than in the past and less willing to produce carrots. This shift might be caused, for example, by a change in the costs of producing the two goods—a rise in carrot costs and a fall in sprout costs that would raise the profitability of sprout production and lower that of carrot production.

What will happen now? For a short time, nothing at all; the existing supply of sprouts and carrots on the market is the result of decisions made by farmers at some time in the past. But farmers now begin to plant fewer carrots and more sprouts, and soon the quantities on the market begin to change. The quantity of sprouts available for sale rises, and the quantity of carrots falls. A shortage of carrots and a glut of sprouts results. The price of carrots consequently rises, and the price of sprouts falls. This provides the incentive for two types of adjustments. First, households will buy fewer carrots and more sprouts. Second, farmers will move back into carrot production and out of sprout production.

This example began with a situation in which there was a shortage of carrots that caused the price of carrots to rise. The rise in the price of carrots removed the shortage in two ways: it reduced the quantity of carrots demanded and it increased the quantity offered for sale (in response to the rise in the profitability of carrot production). Remember that there was also a surplus of brussels sprouts that caused the price to fall. The fall in price removed the surplus in two ways: it encouraged the consumers to buy more of this commodity and it reduced the quantity of sprouts produced and offered for sale (in response to a fall in the profitability of sprout production).

These examples illustrate a general point:

The price system is a mechanism that coordinates individual, decentralized decisions.

The existence of such a control mechanism is beyond dispute. How well it works in comparison with alternative coordinating systems has been in serious dispute for over a hundred years. It remains today a major unsettled social question.

Micro- and Macroeconomics Compared

All economic analysis depends on some aggregation of individual behavior and on some attention to the interdependence of different aspects of the economy. Micro- and macroeconomics differ in the particular questions each asks. In particular, they differ critically in the level of aggregation used.

Microeconomics deals with the determination of prices and quantities in individual markets and with the relations among these markets. Thus it looks at the details of the market economy. It asks, for example, how much labor is employed in the fast food industry and why the amount is increasing. It asks about the causes and consequences of wages being higher in one industry, occupation, or region than in another. It asks about the determinants of the output of brussels sprouts, pocket calculators, automobiles, and Kentucky Fried Chicken. It asks, too, about the prices of these things, why some prices go up and others down. Microeconomics looks in detail at the decision making processes of households and firms preparing to choose from thousands of individual products. When it speaks of demand (and supply), it means demand for (and supply of) McDonalds' hamburgers, or television sets, or carpenters. To be sure, even microeconomics involves some aggregation. It does not ask how many times *you* go to the movies each month, but rather wonders about the market demand for movies.

At this level of aggregation—the level of individual products and occupations—economists interested in microeconomics analyze how the levels of outputs and inputs respond to any of a series of exogenous shocks that impinge upon a particular market. Such shocks may be caused by events in other markets, by governmental policy, or by external events. Economists ask how a new innovation, a government subsidy, or a drought will affect the production of beet sugar, and the employment of farm workers.

In contrast, macroeconomists focus their attention on much broader aggregates. They look at such things as the total number of people employed and unemployed, at the average level of prices and how it changes over time, at aggregate national output, and aggregate consumption. Macroeconomics asks what determines these aggregates and how they change in response to changing conditions. Whereas microeconomics looks at demand and supply with regard to particular commodities, macroeconomics looks at *aggregate* demand and *aggregate* supply.

The Circular Flow in Micro- and Macroeconomics

Microeconomic Flows Between Firms and Households

The black portion of Figure 4-1 focuses on firms, households, and two sets of markets, factor markets and product markets, through which the decisions of firms and households are coordinated. Consider households first. The members of households want commodities to keep them fed, clothed, housed, entertained, healthy, and secure; they also want commodities to educate, edify, beautify, stupefy, and otherwise amuse them. Households have, in varying amounts, resources with which to attempt to satisfy these wants. But not all their wants can be satisfied with the resources available. Households are forced, therefore, to make choices as to what goods and services to buy in product markets that offer them myriad ways to spend their incomes.

The signals to which households respond are product-market prices; for each given set of prices, households make a set of choices. In so doing they also, in the aggregate, affect those prices. The prices also serve as signals to firms of what goods *they* may profitably provide. Given technology and the cost of factors, firms must choose among the products they might produce and sell, among the ways of producing them, and among the various quantities (and qualities) they can supply. By so doing, the firms too affect prices.

Firms must buy factors of production. The quantities demanded depend on the firms' production decisions, which in turn depend on consumers' demands. The demands for factors will in turn affect the prices of labor, managerial skill, raw materials, buildings, machinery, use of capital, land, and all other factors. The households who are owners of factors (or who possess the skills that can provide the factor services) respond to factor prices and make *their* choices about where to offer their services. These choices determine factor supplies

and affect factor prices. Payments by firms to factor owners provide the owners of the factors with incomes. The recipients of these incomes are households whose members want commodities to keep them fed, clothed, housed, entertained. We have now come full circle!

The action of the drama involves firms and households inextricably bound up with each other. Payments flow from households to firms through product markets and back to households again through factor markets.

Macroeconomic Flows Between Sectors

The idea of payments flowing from households to firms and back to households in a closed circle, as shown in the black portion of Figure 4-1, is the starting point of macroeconomics. The money spent by firms to purchase factor services becomes income to the households who sell the factor services, and the money spent by households to buy the goods produced by firms becomes the receipts of the firms. If the economy consisted only of households and firms, if households spent *all* the income they received on buying goods and services produced by firms, and if firms distributed *all* their receipts to households either by purchasing factor services or by distributing profits to their owners, then the circular flow would be very simple indeed. Everything that households received would be passed on to firms, and everything that firms received would be passed on to households. The circular flow would be a completely closed system, and macroeconomics would involve little more than measuring the amount of the flow.

However, there are reasons why the circular flow is not a completely closed system. First, neither households nor firms spend all of their income and receipts on purchasing goods and services from the other. Households, for example, have to pay income and other taxes to the government and some of their after-tax income is saved and deposited in financial institutions. Only what is left becomes the receipts of firms. Furthermore, not all of the receipts of firms are paid out to factors; some are

FIGURE 4-1
The Circular Flow of Expenditures and Income

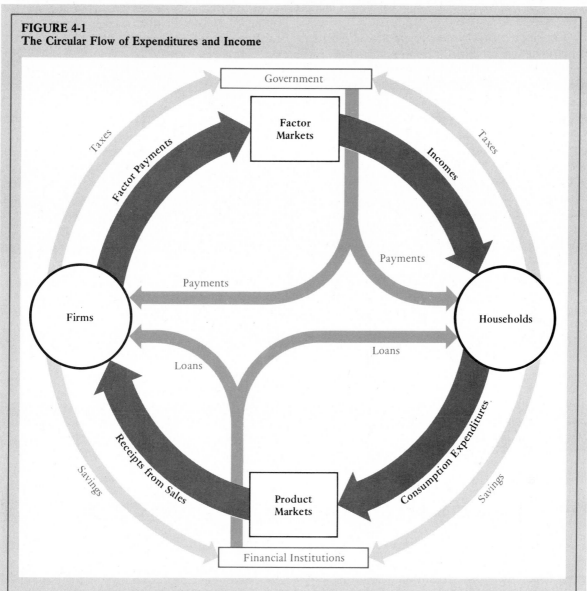

The interaction of firms and households in product and factor markets generates a flow of expenditure and income. These flows are also influenced by other institutions such as governments and the financial system. Factor services are sold by households through factor markets, which leads to a flow of income from firms to households. Commodities are sold by firms through product markets, which leads to a flow of receipts from households to firms. If these primary flows, shown by the dark gray shaded arrows, were the only flows, the circular flow would be a closed system. But other institutions, such as governments and financial institutions, play roles. For example, governments may inject funds in the form of government payments to households and firms, and banks may inject funds in the form of loans to households and firms for investment expenditures. Such *injections* are illustrated by the dark color arrows. Similarly, governments may withdraw funds in the form of taxes, and financial institutions may do so by accepting funds that households and firms wish to save. Such *withdrawals* are illustrated by the light color arrows.

paid to the government in the form of business taxes, and some are saved by the firms.

A second reason why the circular flow of income is not a completely closed system is that firms receive receipts that do not arise from the spending of households, and households receive income that does not arise from the spending of firms. When the government spends money on goods and services that are produced by firms, for example, receipts are created that do not arise directly out of the expenditure of private households. When the government hires the services of civil servants, mine inspectors, road builders, and other workers, the income it creates for households does not arise directly out of the spending of firms. Similarly, when the government makes welfare or social security payments to individuals (or other kinds of "transfer payments"), the income it creates for households does not arise from firms. If some firms purchase machines and equipment (say, out of funds borrowed from banks), the receipts received by the other firms that manufacture the equipment and by the households that supply the required factor services do not arise directly out of household spending. If firms receive subsidies (or other transfer payments) from the government, this too creates receipts for firms that do not arise from household spending.

There is a circular flow of payments from households to firms and back to households, but not all incomes and receipts are passed on and some arise from other units. Thus the circular flow is not a simple, closed system.

The *colored* boxes and arrows in Figure 4-1 suggest some of these additional elements to the circular flow. They are critically important to macroeconomics. It should be intuitively clear from this discussion that the size of the total incomes received by households and firms depends not only on their total purchases from one another but also on what they receive from other sources of spending. Macroeconomics studies the determinants of all these flows of spending. Why they are the size they are and why they change are important ques-

tions, for the flows themselves determine the total output produced, the total income earned, and the total amount of employment available.

An Overview of Macroeconomics

Macroeconomics is concerned with the determinants and behavior of *aggregate demand* and *aggregate supply.* We can aggregate all the buyers of the nation's output in one group and all the producers and sellers of the nation's output in a second group. We can then observe their purchases and sales. Afterward, the value of what buyers buy must of course equal the value of what sellers sell. But previous to the exchange, the value of what buyers would like to buy (at going prices) may not equal the value of what sellers would like to sell (at those same prices). The value of desired purchases is called **aggregate demand** and the value of desired sales is called **aggregate supply.** Explaining why these are what they are and why they change are among the major problems of macroeconomics. The consequences of such changes may be very great for an economy.

Major changes in aggregate demand are called *demand shocks* while major changes in aggregate supply are called *supply shocks.* When these shocks occur there will be important changes in the broad averages and aggregates that are the concern of macroeconomics, including total output, total employment, and the average levels of prices and wages. But such changes need not go on unaffected by governmental policies. Government actions (which may sometimes be the *cause* of demand or supply shocks) may also be used in an attempt to cushion those shocks or change their effect. These policies too are among the concerns of macroeconomics.

Both microeconomics and macroeconomics deal with important economic considerations, but they examine different aspects of the same economy. Whichever is studied first, it is important to remember that micro- and macroeconomics are complementary, not competing, theories and that both are needed for a full understanding of the functioning of a modern economy.

SUMMARY

1. This chapter provides an overview of the workings of the market economy. All modern economies are based on the specialization and division of labor, which necessitate the exchange of goods and services. Exchange takes place in markets and is facilitated by the use of money. Much of economics is devoted to a study of how free markets work to coordinate millions of individual, decentralized decisions.

2. In economic theory, three kinds of decision-makers—households, firms, and the government—interact in markets. It is assumed that households seek to maximize their satisfaction (to the best of their ability) and that firms seek to maximize their profits but that the government may have multiple objectives.

3. A market is defined, for the present, as an area over which buyers and sellers negotiate the exchange of a well-defined commodity. A free-market economy is one in which the allocation of resources is determined by the production, sales, and purchase decisions made by firms and households acting in response to such market signals as prices and profits.

4. Subdivisions of an economy are called sectors. Economies are commonly divided into market and nonmarket sectors and into public and private sectors. These divisions cut across each other; the first is based on the economic distinction of how costs are covered, and the second is based on a legal distinction of ownership.

5. It is common to distinguish microeconomics and macroeconomics. Microeconomics deals with the determination of prices and quantities in individual markets and the relations among those markets. In a general way it is concerned with the price system, which provides a set of signals that reflects changes in demand and supply and to which producers and consumers can react in an individual but nonetheless coordinated manner.

6. The microeconomic interactions between households and firms through markets may be illustrated in a circular flow diagram that traces money flows between households and firms. These flows are the starting point for studying the circular flows of aggregate income that are key elements of macroeconomics.

7. A key difference between micro- and macroeconomics is in the level of aggregation to which attention is directed. Microeconomics looks at prices and quantities in individual markets and how they respond to various shocks that impinge on those markets. Macroeconomics looks at broader aggregates such as aggregate consumption, employment and unemployment, and the rate of change of the price level.

8. Macroeconomic flows are complex because not all income received by households is spent for the output of firms and some receipts of firms are not paid out to households. Also, some payments to firms do not result from the spending of households and some payments to households do not result from the spending of firms. The flows of expenditure in the economy determine total output, total income, and total employment.

9. The questions asked in micro- and macroeconomics may differ, but they are complementary parts of economic theory. They study different aspects of a single economic system, and both are needed for an understanding of the whole.

TOPICS FOR REVIEW

Specialization and the division of labor
Economic decision makers
Markets and market economies
Market and nonmarket sectors
The private and public sectors

The price system as a social control mechanism
Linkages between firms and households
The circular flow of income in micro- and macroeconomics
The relation between microeconomics and macroeconomics

DISCUSSION QUESTIONS

1. Suggest some examples of specialization and division of labor among people you know.
2. There is a greater variety of specialists and specialty stores in large cities than in small cities having populations with the same average income. Explain this in economic terms.
3. Define the household of which you are a member. Consider your household's income last year. What proportion of it came from the sale of factor services to firms? Identify the other sources of income. Approximately what proportion of the expenditures by your household became income for firms?
4. "It is not from the benevolence of the butcher, the brewer, or the baker that we expect our dinner, but from their regard to their self-interest. We address ourselves, not to their humanity, but to their self-love, and never talk to them of our necessities, but of their advantages, not to their humanity, but to their self-love, and never talk to them out of our necessities, but of their advantages." Do you agree with this quotation from *The Wealth of Nations?* How are "their self-love" and "our dinner" related to the price system? What are assumed to be the motives of firms and of households?
5. Trace the effect of a sharp change in consumer demand away from cigarettes and toward chewing gum as a result of continuing reports linking smoking with lung cancer and heart disease. Can producers of cigarettes do anything to prevent their loss of profits?
6. Make a list of decision makers in the U.S. economy today that do not fit into the categories of firm, household, and government. Are you sure that the concept of a firm will not stretch sufficiently to cover some of the items on your list?
7. Consider a major baby boom such as occurred following World War II. Trace out some significant microeconomic and macroeconomic effects of such a boom. Is there a clear line between them in every case?
8. Can you visualize one $20 bill being used in transactions that create $200 of income in one month? If so, how? If not, why not? Can you visualize it not being used in any transactions that create income in one month? If so, how? If not, why not? Do your answers imply that money and income are unrelated?
9. Which, if any, of the arrows in Figure 4-1 do each of the following affect in the first instance?
   a. Households increase their consumption expenditures by reducing saving.
   b. The government lowers income-tax rates.
   c. In view of a recession, firms decide to postpone production of some new products.
   d. Consumers like the 1987 model American cars and borrow money from the banking system to buy them in record numbers.
   e. The E.T. fad dies out as consumers shift their expenditures to other items.

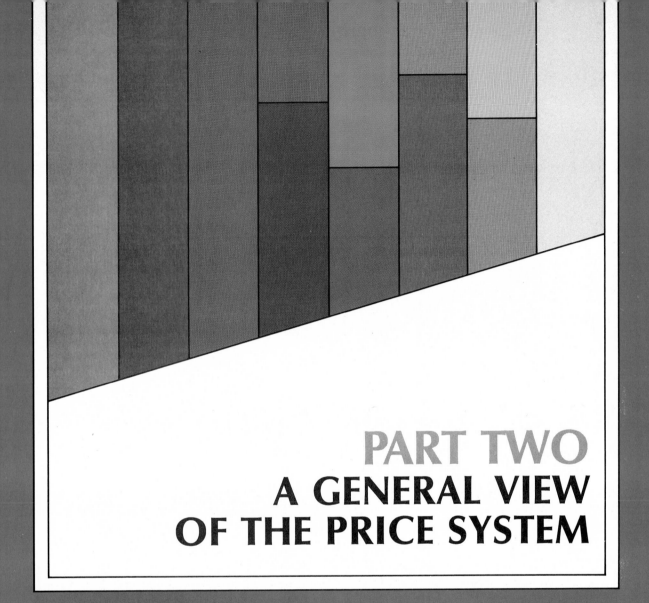

PART TWO
A GENERAL VIEW
OF THE PRICE SYSTEM

5 DEMAND, SUPPLY, AND PRICE

Some people believe that economics begins and ends with the "law" of supply and demand. It is, of course, too much to hope for "economics in one lesson." (An unkind critic of a book with that title remarked that the author needed a second lesson.) Still, the so-called laws of supply and demand are an important beginning in the attempt to answer vital questions about the workings of a market system.

A first step is to understand what determines the demands for commodities and the supplies of them. Then we can see how supply and demand operate together to determine price and how the price system as a whole allows the economy to reallocate resources in response to changes in demand and in supply. Supply and demand prove to be helpful concepts in discussing both the price system's successes and its failures. They also can be used to discuss the consequences of particular forms of government intervention such as price controls, minimum-wage laws, and sales taxes.

THE BASIC THEORY OF DEMAND

The American consumer spent about $2.0 trillion on goods and services in 1982. What was it spent on, and why? Table 5-1 shows the composition of this expenditure and how it has changed over nearly 30 years. Economists ask many questions about the pattern of consumer expenditure: Why is it what it is at any moment of time? Why does it change in the way it does? Why did the fraction of total consumer expenditure for food decline from more than one-third in 1910 to only one-fifth by 1982? Why did U.S. consumers allocate a negligible percentage of their total expenditure to automobiles in 1920, 4 percent in 1929, only 2 per-

cent in 1932, 7 percent in 1972, and less than 6 percent in 1982? Why do Americans now heat their homes with electricity, oil, and natural gas when 30 years ago they used coal? How have they reacted to the large changes in fuel prices that occurred in the late 1970s and early 1980s? Why do people who build houses in Norway and the American West rarely use brick, while it is commonly used in England and the eastern United States? Why have the maid and the washerwoman been increasingly replaced by the vacuum cleaner and the washing machine?

THE NATURE OF QUANTITY DEMANDED

The total amount of a commodity that all households wish to purchase is called the **quantity demanded** of that commodity.[1] It is important to notice three things about this concept. First, quantity demanded is a *desired* quantity. It is how much households are willing to purchase, given the price of the commodity, other prices, their incomes, tastes, and so on. This may be a different amount than households actually succeed in purchasing. If sufficient quantities are not available, the amount households wish to purchase may exceed the amount they actually do purchase. To distinguish these two concepts, the term *quantity demanded* is used to refer to desired purchases, and phrases such as **quantity actually bought** or **quantity exchanged** are used to refer to actual purchases.

Second, *desired* does not refer to idle dreams or future possibilities but to effective demands—that is, to the amounts people are willing to *buy* given the price they must pay for the commodity. For persons intending to spend $100 this year on a commodity whose price is $20, the quantity demanded is 5 units even though they would prefer

TABLE 5–1 COMPOSITION OF PERSONAL CONSUMPTION EXPENDITURES, 1955 AND 1982 (Percentages)

	1955	1982
Durable goods	15.2	12.3
Motor vehicles and parts	7.0	5.4
Furniture and household equipment	6.4	4.7
Other	1.8	2.2
Nondurable goods	48.5	38.7
Food	26.5	20.2
Clothing and shoes	9.1	6.0
Gasoline and oil	3.4	4.8
Other	9.5	7.7
Services	36.3	49.0
Housing and household operation	19.0	23.8
Other	17.3	25.2
Total	100.0	100.0

Source: Economic Report of the President, 1983.

The declining relative importance of food, clothing, and durables, and the rising importance of gasoline and oil and services of all kinds stand out.

---

[1] In this chapter we concentrate on the demand of *all* households for commodities. Of course, what all households do is only the sum of what each individual household does, and in Chapter 9 we shall study the behavior of individual households in greater detail.

to consume much more if only they did not have to pay for it.

Third, quantity demanded refers to a continuous *flow* of purchases. It must therefore be expressed as so much per period of time: 1 million oranges *per day*, 7 million *per week*, or 365 million *per year*. If you were told, for example, that the quantity of new television sets demanded (at current prices) in the United States was 500,000, this would mean nothing until you were also told the period of time involved. Five hundred thousand television sets demanded *per day* would be an enormous rate of demand; 500,000 *per year* would be a very small rate. (The important distinction between stocks and flows is discussed in the box on page 25.)

What Determines Quantity Demanded?

How much of some commodity will all households be willing to buy per month? This amount will be influenced by a number of variables. The following are the most important. [2]

1. The commodity's own price.
2. The prices of related commodities.
3. Average household income.
4. Tastes.
5. The distribution of income among households.
6. The size of the population.

This list of variables that influence the quantity of a commodity demanded is even longer than it looks, for *many* prices are covered under the second point. We can neither develop a simple theory nor understand the separate influence of each variable if we start by trying to consider what happens when everything changes at once.

Fortunately, there is an easier way: We can consider the influence of the variables one at a time. To do this, we hold all but one of them constant. Then we let that one selected variable vary and study how it affects quantity demanded. We can do the same for each of the other variables in turn, and in this way we can come to understand the

importance of each.[2] Once this is done, we can aggregate the separate influences of two or more variables to discover what would happen if several things changed at the same time—as they often do in practice.

Holding all other influencing variables constant is often described by the words "other things being equal" or by the equivalent Latin phrase, *ceteris paribus*. When economists speak of the influence of the price of wheat on the quantity of wheat demanded *ceteris paribus*, they refer to what a change in the price of wheat would do to the quantity demanded if all other factors that influence the demand for wheat did not change.

Demand and Price

We are interested in developing a theory of how commodities get priced. Thus we are necessarily interested in the influence on quantity demanded of each commodity's own price. We begin by holding all other influences constant and asking: How do we expect the quantity of a commodity demanded to vary as its own price varies?

A basic economic hypothesis is that the lower the price of a commodity, the larger the quantity that will be demanded, other things being equal.

Why might this be so? Commodities are used to satisfy desires and needs, and there is almost always more than one commodity that will satisfy any given desire or need. Such commodities compete with one another for the purchasers' attention. Hunger may be satisfied by meat or vegetables, a desire for green vegetables by broccoli or spinach. The need to keep warm at night may be satisfied by several woollen blankets or one electric blanket, or for that matter by a sheet and a lot of oil burned

---

[2] A relation in which many variables—in this case average income, population, tastes, and many prices—influence a single variable—in this case quantity demanded—is called a *multivariate* relation. The technique of studying the effect of each of the influencing variables one at a time, while holding the other variables constant, is common in science and mathematics. Indeed, it is such a common procedure that there is a mathematical concept, the partial derivative, explicitly designed to accomplish this task.

in the furnace. The desire for a vacation may be satisfied by a trip to the seashore or to the mountains, the need to get there by different airlines, a bus, a car, even a train. And so it goes: Name any general desire or need, and there will be at least two and often dozens of different commodities that will satisfy it. Even something so basic as the body's need for fluid may be satisfied by drinking water, tea, coffee, Coke, Dr. Pepper, lemonade, beer, and so on.

We can now see what happens if we hold income, tastes, population, and the prices of all other commodities constant and vary only the price of one commodity. As that price goes up, the commodity becomes an increasingly expensive way to satisfy a want. Some households will stop buying it altogether; others will buy smaller amounts; still others will continue to buy the same quantity. Because many households will switch wholly or partially to other commodities to satisfy the same want, it follows that less will be bought of any commodity whose price has risen. As meat becomes more expensive, for example, households may switch to some extent to meat substitutes; they may also forego meat at some meals and eat less meat at others. As carrots get increasingly expensive, people may switch to brussels sprouts or broccoli to satisfy their desire for vegetables.

Alternatively, a fall in a commodity's price makes it a cheaper method of satisfying a want. Purchasers as a whole will buy more of it. Consequently, they will buy less of similar commodities whose prices have not fallen and which as a result have become expensive *relative to* the commodity in question. As pocket calculators have fallen in price over the last 15 or 20 years, more and more of them have been purchased. When a bumper tomato harvest drives prices down, shoppers switch to tomatoes and cut their purchases of many other vegetables that now look relatively more expensive.

The Demand Schedule and the Demand Curve

How can the relationship between quantity demanded and price be portrayed? One method is to use a **demand schedule.** This is a numerical tab-

TABLE 5-2 A DEMAND SCHEDULE FOR CARROTS

	Price per ton p	Quantity demanded when average household income is $20,000 per year (thousands of tons per months) D
U	$ 20	110.0
V	40	90.0
W	60	77.5
X	80	67.5
Y	100	62.5
Z	120	60.0

The table shows the quantity of carrots that would be demanded at various prices, *ceteris paribus*. Consider, for example, row *W*, which indicates that if the price of carrots were $60 per ton, consumers would desire to purchase 77,500 tons of carrots per month, given the values of other variables that may affect quantity demanded (such as average household income).

ulation showing the quantity that is demanded at selected prices.

Table 5-2 is a hypothetical demand schedule for carrots. It lists the quantity of carrots that would be demanded at various prices on the assumption that average household income is fixed at $20,000 (and that tastes and all other prices do not change.) The table gives the quantities demanded for six selected prices, but actually a separate quantity would be demanded at each possible price from one cent to several hundreds of dollars.

A second method of showing the relation between quantity demanded and price is to draw a graph. The six price-quantity combinations shown in Table 5-2 are plotted on the graph shown in Figure 5-1, which has price on the vertical axis and quantity on the horizontal axis. The smooth curve drawn through these points is called a **demand curve.** It shows the quantity of carrots that purchasers would like to buy at each price. The curve slopes downward to the right, which indicates that the quantity demanded increases as the price falls.

A single point on the demand curve indicates a single price-quantity combination. Notice that while any point on the demand curve represents a

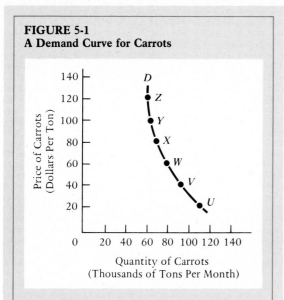

FIGURE 5-1
A Demand Curve for Carrots

This demand curve relates quantity of carrots demanded to their price; its downward slope indicates that quantity demanded increases as price falls. The six points correspond to the price-quantity combinations shown in Table 5-2. Each row in the table defines a point on the demand curve. The smooth curve drawn through all of the points and labeled *D* is the demand curve.

specific quantity demanded, the demand curve as a whole shows more.

The whole demand curve represents the complete relation between quantity demanded and price, other things being equal.

When economists speak of the conditions of demand in a particular market as being given or known, they are referring not just to the particular quantity being demanded at the moment (i.e., not just to a particular point on the demand curve) but to the entire demand curve—to the complete functional relation whereby desired purchases are related to all the possible alternative prices of the commodity.

Thus the term **demand** refers to the entire relation between price and quantity (as shown, for example, by the schedule in Table 5-2 or the curve in Figure 5-1). In contrast, a single point on a

demand schedule or curve is the *quantity demanded* at that point (for example, at point *W* in Figure 5-1, 77,500 tons of carrots a month are demanded at a price of $60 a ton).

Shifts in the Demand Curve

The demand schedule is drawn up, and the demand curve plotted, on the assumption of *ceteris paribus*. But what if other things change, as surely they must? What, for example, if households find themselves with more income? If households spend their extra income, they will buy additional quantities of commodities *even though prices have not changed*.

But if households increase their purchases of any one commodity whose price has not changed, the purchases cannot be represented on the original demand curve. When they are represented on a new demand curve, the new curve must be to the right of the old curve. Thus the rise in household income has shifted the demand curve to the right. This illustrates the operation of an important general rule.

A demand curve is drawn on the assumption that everything except the commodity's own price is held constant. A change in any of the variables previously held constant will shift the demand curve to a new position.

A demand curve can shift in many ways; two of them are particularly important. If more is bought at *each* price, the demand curve shifts right so that each price corresponds to a higher quantity than it did before. If less is bought at *each* price, the demand curve shifts left so that each price corresponds to a lower quantity than it did before.

The influence of changes in variables other than price may now be studied by determining how changes in each variable shift the demand curve. Any change will shift the demand curve to the right if it increases the amount people wish to buy, other things remaining equal, and to the left if it decreases the amount households wish to buy, other things remaining equal.

Average household income. If the income of the average household increases, households can be expected to purchase more of most commodities

TABLE 5–3 TWO ALTERNATIVE DEMAND SCHEDULES FOR CARROTS

Price per ton p	Quantity demanded when average household income is $20,000 per year (thousands of tons per month) D_0		Quantity demanded when average income is $24,000 per year (thousands of tons per months) D_1	
$ 20	110.0	U	140.0	U'
40	90.0	V	116.0	V'
60	77.5	W	100.8	W'
80	67.5	X	87.5	X'
100	62.5	Y	81.3	Y'
120	60.0	Z	78.0	Z'

An increase in average income increases the quantity demanded at each price. When average income rises from $20,000 to $24,000 per year, quantity demanded at a price of $60 per ton rises from 77,500 tons per month to 100,800 tons per month. A similar rise occurs at every other price. Thus the demand schedule relating columns p and D_0 is replaced by one relating columns p and D_1. The graphical representations of these two functions are labeled D_0 and D_1 in Figure 5-2.

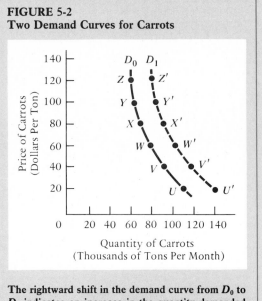

FIGURE 5-2
Two Demand Curves for Carrots

The rightward shift in the demand curve from D_0 to D_1 indicates an increase in the quantity demanded at each price. The lettered points correspond to those in Table 5-3. A rightward shift in the demand curve indicates an increase in demand in the sense that more is demanded at each price and that a higher price is paid for each quantity.

even though commodity prices remain the same.[3] Considering all households, we expect that no matter what price we pick, more of any commodity will be demanded than was previously demanded at the same price. This shift is illustrated in Table 5-3 and Figure 5-2.

A rise in average household income shifts the demand curve for most commodities to the right. This indicates that more will be demanded at each possible price.

Other prices. We saw that the downward slope of a commodity's demand curve occurs because the lower its price, the cheaper the commodity is, relative to other commodities that can satisfy the same needs or desires. Those other commodities are called **substitutes.** Another way to accomplish the same change in relative cheapness is for the price of the substitute commodity to rise. For example,

carrots can be made cheap relative to cabbage either by lowering the price of carrots or by raising the price of cabbage. Either change will tend to increase the amount of carrots households are prepared to buy.

A rise in the price of a substitute for a commodity shifts the demand curve for the commodity to the right. More will be purchased at each price.

For example, a rise in the price of a substitute for carrots could shift the demand curve for carrots from D_0 to D_1 in Figure 5-2.

Another class of commodities is called **complements.** These are commodities that tend to be used jointly with each other. Cars and gasoline are complements; so are golf clubs and golf balls, electric stoves and electricity, an airplane trip to Vail and lift tickets on the mountain. Since complements

[3] Such commodities are called *normal goods*. For commodities called *inferior goods*, the amount purchased falls as income rises. These concepts are defined and discussed in Chapter 6.

tend to be consumed together, a fall in the price of either will increase the demand for both.

A fall in the price of a complementary commodity will shift a commodity's demand curve to the right. More will be purchased at each price.

For example, a fall in the price of airplane trips to Vail will lead to a rise in the demand for lift tickets at Vail even though their price is unchanged.

Tastes. Tastes have a large effect on people's desired purchases. A change in tastes may be long lasting, such as the shift from fountain pens to ball-point pens or from slide rules to pocket calculators. Or it may be a short-lived fad such as the craze for hula hoops or Billy Beer. In either case a change in tastes in favor of a commodity shifts the demand curve to the right. More will be bought at each price.

Distribution of income. If a constant total of income is redistributed among the population, demands may change. If, for example, the government increases the deductions that may be taken for children on income tax returns and compensates by raising basic tax rates, income will be transferred from childless persons to heads of large families. Demand for commodities more heavily bought by the childless will decline, while demand for commodities bought by those with large families will increase.

A change in the distribution of income will shift to the right the demand curves for commodities bought most by those gaining income. On the other hand, it will shift to the left the demand curves for commodities bought most by people losing income.

Population. Population growth does not by itself create new demand. The additional people must have purchasing power before demand is changed. Extra people of working age, however, usually means extra output, and if they produce, they will earn income. When this happens, the demand for all the commodities purchased by the new income earners will rise. Thus it is usually (although not always) true that:

A rise in population will shift the demand curves for

commodities to the right, indicating that more will be bought at each price.

These shifts are summarized in Figure 5-3 and its caption.

Movements Along the Demand Curve Versus Shifts of the Whole Curve

Suppose you read in today's newspaper that the rising price of housing has caused a declining demand as people have found ways of economizing

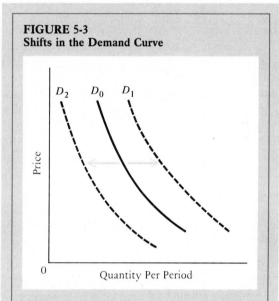

FIGURE 5-3
Shifts in the Demand Curve

A shift in the demand curve from D_0 to D_1 indicates an increase in demand; a shift from D_0 to D_2 indicates a decrease in demand. An increase in demand means that more is demanded at each price. Such a rightward shift can be caused by a rise in income, a rise in the price of a substitute, a fall in the price of a complement, a change in tastes that favors the commodity, an increase in population, or a redistribution of income toward groups who favor the commodity.

A decrease in demand means that less is demanded at each price. Such a leftward shift can be caused by a fall in income, a fall in the price of a substitute, a rise in the price of a complement, a change in tastes that disfavors the commodity, a decrease in population, or a redistribution of income away from groups who favor the commodity.

on their use of housing. Then tomorrow you read that the rising price of housing has been caused by a rising demand for housing. The two statements appear to contradict each other. The first associates a rising price with a declining demand, the second associates a rising price with a rising demand. How can both statements be true? The answer is that they refer to different things. The first describes a movement along a demand curve in response to a change in price; the second describes a shift in the whole demand curve. Using the words *declining demand* and *rising demand* in each case can only cause confusion.

Consider first the statement that less is being bought because it has become more expensive. This refers to a movement along a given demand curve, and reflects a change between two specific quantities being bought, one before the price rose and one afterward. Any one point on a demand curve represents a specific amount being bought at a specified price. It represents, therefore, a particular quantity demanded. A movement along a demand curve is referred to as a change in the quantity demanded. [3]

A movement down a demand curve is called an *increase* (or a rise) in the quantity demanded; a movement up the demand curve is called a *decrease* (or a fall) in the quantity demanded.

Now consider the shift in demand. We have seen that *demand* refers to the whole demand curve. Economists reserve the term **change in demand** to describe a shift in the whole curve—that is, a change in the amount that will be bought at *every* price.

An *increase in demand* means that the whole demand curve has shifted to the right; a *fall in demand* means that the whole demand curve has shifted to the left.

To illustrate this terminology, look again at Table 5-3. When average income is $20,000, an increase in price from $60 to $80 decreases the *quantity demanded* from 77.5 to 67.5 thousand tons a month. An increase in average income from $20,000 to $24,000 increases *demand* from D_0 to D_1.

THE BASIC THEORY OF SUPPLY

America's private sector produced goods and services worth nearly $3 trillion in 1981. A broad classification of *what* was produced is given in Table 5-4. Economists have as many questions to ask about production and its changing composition as they do about consumption. The percentages shown in Table 5-4 reflect some of the changes in 26 years. Even more dramatic changes are visible in more detailed data.

For example, the increase in output of the chemical industries was almost 16 times that of the primary metals industries, 7 times that of mining industries, and 3 times that of the petroleum industry in the quarter century since 1955. Economists want to know why. Why did the aluminum industry grow faster than the steel industry? Why, even within a single industry, did some firms prosper and grow, others hold their own, and still others decline and fail? Why and how do firms and industries come into being? All these questions and many others are aspects of a single question: *What*

TABLE 5–4 **COMPOSITION OF NATIONAL PRODUCT BY INDUSTRY OF ORIGIN, 1955 AND 1981** (Percentages)

Industry group[a]	1955	1981
Manufacturing	33.5	24.8
Mining and construction	8.6	9.8
Agriculture, forestry, fisheries	5.5	3.3
Transport utilities	9.8	10.1
Wholesale and retail trade	18.3	18.2
Finance, insurance, real estate	13.8	17.2
Other services	9.4	14.9
Other	1.1	1.7
	100.0	100.0

Source: Economic Report of the President, 1983.
[a] Excluding government and government enterprises.

Over a generation manufacturing, agriculture, forestry, and fisheries have all declined in relative importance while services have become more important.

determines the quantities of commodities that will be produced and offered for sale?

Full discussion of these questions of supply will come later (in Part Four). For now it is enough to develop the basic relation between the price of a commodity and the quantity that will be produced and offered for sale by firms, and to understand what forces lead to shifts in this relationship.

The Nature of Quantity Supplied

The amount of a commodity that firms wish to sell is the **quantity supplied** of that commodity. This is the amount that firms are willing to offer for sale; it is not necessarily the amount they succeed in selling. The term **quantity actually sold** or **quantity exchanged** indicates what they actually succeed in selling. Quantity supplied is a flow; it is so much per unit of time, per day, per week, or per year.

Notice that while we use different terms (quantity demanded and quantity supplied) to distinguish desired purchases from desired sales, we use the same term, *quantity exchanged*, to describe actual purchases and actual sales. This reflects an important fact of life: although households may desire to purchase an amount that differs from what sellers desire to sell, they cannot succeed in buying what someone else does not sell. A purchase and a sale are merely two sides of the same transaction. Looked at from the buyer's side, there is a purchase; looked at from the seller's side, there is a sale.

Since desired purchases do not have to equal desired sales, different terms are needed to describe the two separate amounts. But because the quantity actually purchased must be the same amount as the quantity actually sold, both can be described by a single term, *quantity exchanged*.

What Determines Quantity Supplied?

How much of a commodity will firms be willing to produce and offer for sale? The amount will be influenced by a number of variables. The following are the most important: [4]

1. The commodity's own price.
2. The prices of other commodities.
3. The costs of factors of production.
4. The goals of the firm.
5. The state of technology.

The situation is the same here as it is on the demand side. The list of influencing variables is long, and we will not get far if we try to discover what happens when they all change at the same time. So again we use the very convenient *ceteris paribus* technique to study the influence of the variables one at a time.

Supply and Price

Since we want to develop a theory of how commodities get priced, we are necessarily interested in the influence on quantity supplied of a commodity's own price. We start by holding all other influences constant and asking: How do we expect the quantity of a commodity supplied to vary with its own price?

A basic economic hypothesis is that for many commodities the higher their price, the larger the quantity that will be supplied, other things being equal.

Why might this be so? It is because the profits that can be earned from producing a commodity are almost certain to increase if the price of that commodity rises while the costs of factors used to produce it remain unchanged. Furthermore, if the prices of other commodities remain unchanged, the profits that can be earned by producing them will be unchanged, and as a result there will be a rise in *relative* profitability of producing the commodity whose price has risen. This will make firms, which are in business to earn profits, wish to produce more of the commodity whose price has risen and less of other commodities.

Notice, however, the qualifying word *many* in the hypothesis stated above. It is used because, as we shall see in Part Four, there are exceptions to

TABLE 5–5 **A SUPPLY SCHEDULE FOR CARROTS**

	Price per ton p	Quantity supplied (thousands of tons per month) S
u	$ 20	5.0
v	40	46.0
w	60	77.5
x	80	100.0
y	100	115.0
z	120	122.5

The table shows the quantities that producers wish to sell at various prices, *certeris paribus*. For example, row y indicates that if the price were $100 per ton, producers would wish to sell 115,000 tons of carrots per month.

FIGURE 5-4
A Supply Curve for Carrots

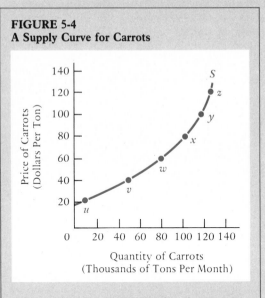

This supply curve relates quantity of carrots supplied to their price; its upward slope indicates that quantity supplied increases as price increases. The six points correspond to the price-quantity combinations shown in Table 5-5. Each row in the table defines a point on the supply curve. The smooth curve drawn through all of the points and labeled S is the supply curve.

this rule. Although the rule states the usual case, a rise in price (*ceteris paribus*) is not always necessary to call forth an increase in quantity in the case of all commodities.

The Supply Schedule and the Supply Curve

The general relationship just discussed can be illustrated by a supply schedule that shows the quantities that producers would wish to sell at alternative prices of the commodity. A **supply schedule** is analogous to a demand schedule: the former shows what producers would be willing to sell, while the latter shows what households would be willing to buy at alternative prices of the commodity. Table 5-5 presents a hypothetical supply schedule for carrots.

A **supply curve,** the graphic representation of the supply schedule, is illustrated in Figure 5-4. Once again, while each point on the supply curve represents a specific price-quantity combination, the whole curve shows more.

The whole supply curve represents the complete relation between quantity supplied and price, other things being equal.

When economists speak of the conditions of supply as being given or known, they refer not just to the particular quantity being supplied at the moment (that is, not to just a particular point on the supply curve) but to the entire supply curve, to the complete functional relation by which desired sales are related to all possible alternative prices of the commodity.

Supply refers to the entire relation between supply and price. A single point on the supply schedule or curve refers to the *quantity supplied* at that price.

Shifts in the Supply Curve

A shift in the supply curve means that at each price a different quantity will be supplied than previously. An increase in the quantity supplied at

TABLE 5–6 TWO ALTERNATIVE SUPPLY SCHEDULES FOR CARROTS

Price per ton p	Quantity supplied before cost-saving innovation (thousands of tons per month) S_0		Quantity supplied after the innovation (thousands of tons per month) S_1	
$ 20	5.0	u	28.0	u'
40	46.0	v	76.0	v'
60	77.5	w	102.0	w'
80	100.0	x	120.0	x'
100	115.0	y	132.0	y'
120	122.5	z	140.0	z'

A cost-saving innovation increases the quantity supplied at each price. As a result of the cost-saving innovation, quantity supplied at $100 per ton rises from 115,000 to 132,000 tons per month. A similar rise occurs at every price. Thus, the supply schedule relating p and S_0 is replaced by one relating p and S_1.

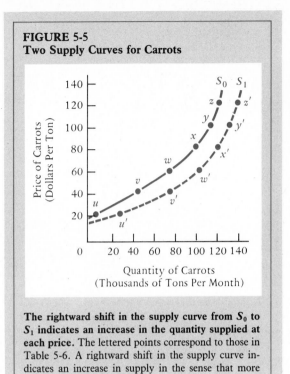

FIGURE 5-5
Two Supply Curves for Carrots

The rightward shift in the supply curve from S_0 to S_1 indicates an increase in the quantity supplied at each price. The lettered points correspond to those in Table 5-6. A rightward shift in the supply curve indicates an increase in supply in the sense that more carrots are supplied at each price.

each price is shown in Table 5-6 and graphed in Figure 5-5. This change appears as a rightward shift in the supply curve. In contrast, a decrease in the quantity supplied at each price would appear as a leftward shift. A shift in the supply curve must be the result of a change in one of the factors that influence the quantity supplied other than the commodity's own price. The major possible causes of such shifts are summarized in the caption of Figure 5-6 and are considered briefly below.

For supply, as for demand, there is an important general rule.

A change in any of the variables (other than the commodity's own price) that affect the amount of a commodity that firms are willing to produce and offer for sale will shift the whole supply curve for that commodity.

Other prices. Commodities may be substitutes or complements in production as well as in consumption. Land that grows wheat can also grow corn, or it can be used to raise hogs. Suppose the price of corn falls and as a result corn is less profitable to produce. Some farmers will shift from corn to wheat production. Thus a fall in the price of corn may shift the supply curve of wheat to the right, indicating that at each price of wheat more will be supplied than before.

Since commodities are alternative outputs for producers, a fall in the price of one commodity may shift the supply curve of another to the right.

Prices of factors of production. The price paid for a factor of production is a cost to a firm that uses it. A change in factor prices changes the quantity that producers will be willing to offer for sale because it changes costs and hence profits. Just as profits are increased by an *increase* in the commodity's price, factor costs remaining constant, so are they increased by a fall in factor prices, the price of the commodity remaining constant. A rise in factor prices reduces the profitability of a commodity at any given price of that commodity. The initial profitability can be restored only if the price of the commodity rises.

FIGURE 5-6
Shifts in the Supply Curve

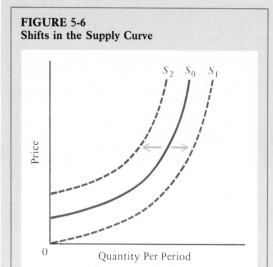

A shift in the supply curve from S_0 to S_1 indicates an increase in supply; a shift from S_0 to S_2 indicates a decrease in supply. An increase in supply means that more is supplied at each price. Such a rightward shift can be caused by certain changes in producers' goals, improvements in technology, decreases in the prices of other commodities, or decreases in the prices of factors of production that are important in producing the commodity.

A decrease in supply means that less is supplied at each price. Such a leftward shift can be caused by certain changes in producers' goals, increases in the prices of other commodities, or increases in the prices of factors of production that are important in producing the commodity.

A rise in the costs of factors of production shifts to the left the supply curve of a commodity that uses that factor, indicating that less will be supplied at any given price.

The goals of the firm. In elementary economic theory, the firm is assumed to have the single goal of profit maximization. Firms might, however, have other goals either in addition to or as substitutes for profit maximization. If the firm worries about risk, it will pursue safer lines of activity even though they promise lower probable profits. If the firm values size, it may produce and sell more than the profit-maximizing quantities. If it worries

about its image in society, it may forsake highly profitable activities (such as the production of dioxin) when there is major public disapproval. However, as long as the firm prefers more profits to less, it will respond to changes in the profitabilities of alternative lines of action, and supply curves will slope upward.

A change in the importance that firms give to other goals will shift the supply curve one way or the other, indicating a changed willingness to supply the quantity at any given price and hence a changed level of profitability.

Technology. At any time, what is produced and how it is produced depends on what is known. Over time knowledge changes; so do the quantities of individual commodities supplied. The enormous increase in production per worker that has been going on in industrial societies for about 200 years is largely due to improved methods of production. Yet the Industrial Revolution is more than a historical event; it is a present reality. Discoveries in chemistry have led to lower costs of production of well-established products, such as paints, and to a large variety of new products made of plastics and synthetic fibers. The invention of transistors and silicon chips has revolutionized production in television, high-fidelity equipment, computers, and guidance-control systems.

Any technological change that decreases production costs will increase the profits that can be earned at any given price of the commodity. Since increased profitability tends to lead to increased production, this change will shift the supply curve to the right, indicating an increased willingness to produce the commodity and offer it for sale at each possible price.

**Movements Along the Supply Curve
Versus Shifts of the Whole Curve**

As with demand, it is important to distinguish movements along supply curves from shifts of the whole curve. The term **change in supply** is reserved for a shift of the whole supply curve. This means a change in the quantity supplied at each price of the commodity. A movement along the supply curve indicates a *change in the quantity supplied* in response to a change in the price of the commodity. Thus an *increase in supply* means that the whole supply curve has shifted to the right; an *increase in the quantity supplied* means a movement upward to the right along a given supply curve.

THE DETERMINATION OF PRICE BY DEMAND AND SUPPLY

So far demand and supply have been considered separately. The next question is: How do the two forces interact to determine price in a competitive market? The theory that answers this question is called **price theory.** (In developing this theory we shall continue, until the final section of this chapter, with the simplifying assumption that all forces that might influence demand or supply, other than the commodity's own price, are held constant.)

Table 5-7 brings together the demand and supply schedules from Tables 5-2 and 5-5. The quantities of carrots demanded and supplied at each price may now be compared (see column 4 of Table 5-7).

There is only one price, $60 a ton, at which the quantity of carrots demanded equals the quantity supplied. At prices of less than $60 a ton there is a shortage of carrots because the quantity demanded exceeds the quantity supplied. This is often called a situation of **excess demand** or, what is the same thing, one of deficient supply. At prices greater than $60 a ton, there is a surplus of carrots because the quantity supplied exceeds the quantity demanded. This is called a situation of **excess supply** or one of deficient demand.

To discuss the determination of market price, suppose first that the price is $100 a ton. At this price, 115,000 tons would be offered for sale, but only 62,500 tons would be demanded. There would be an excess supply of 52,500 tons a month. We assume that sellers will then cut their prices to get rid of this surplus and that purchasers, observing the stock of unsold carrots, will offer less for what they are prepared to buy.

The tendency for buyers to offer, and sellers to ask for, lower prices when there is excess supply implies a downward pressure on price.

Next consider the price of $20 a ton. At this price, there is excess demand. The 5,000 tons produced each month are snapped up very quickly, and 105,000 tons of desired purchases cannot be made. Rivalry between would-be purchasers may lead to their offering more than the prevailing price to outbid other purchasers. Also, perceiving that

TABLE 5–7 DEMAND AND SUPPLY SCHEDULES FOR CARROTS AND EQUILIBRIUM PRICE

(1) Price per ton p	(2) Quantity demanded (thousands of tons per month) D	(3) Quantity supplied (thousands of tons per month) S	(4) Excess demand (+) Excess supply (−) (thousands of tons per month) D − S
$ 20	110.0	5.0	+ 105.0
40	90.0	46.0	+ 44.0
60	77.5	77.5	0.0
80	67.5	100.0	− 32.5
100	62.5	115.0	− 52.5
120	60.0	122.5	− 62.5

Equilibrium occurs where quantity demanded equals quantity supplied—where there is neither excess demand nor excess supply. These schedules are those of Tables 5–2 and 5–5. The equilibrium price is $60. For lower prices, there is excess demand; for higher prices there is excess supply.

they could have sold their available supplies many times over, sellers may begin to ask a higher price for the quantities that they do have to sell.

The tendency for buyers to offer, and sellers to ask for, higher prices when there is excess demand implies an upward pressure on price.

Finally, consider a price of $60. At this price, producers wish to sell 77,500 tons a month and purchasers wish to buy that quantity. There is neither a shortage nor a surplus of carrots. There are no unsatisfied buyers to bid the price up, nor are there unsatisfied sellers to force the price down. Once the price of $60 has been reached, therefore, there will be no tendency for it to change.

An equilibrium implies a state of rest, or balance, between opposing forces. The **equilibrium price** is the one toward which the actual market price will tend. It will persist once established, unless it is disturbed by some change in market conditions.

The price at which the quantity demanded equals the quantity supplied is called the equilibrium price.

Any other price is called a **disequilibrium price:** quantity demanded does not equal quantity supplied, and price will be changing. A market that exhibits excess demand or excess supply is said to be in a state of **disequilibrium.**

When the market is in equilibrium, quantity demanded equals quantity supplied. Anything that must be true if equilibrium is to be obtained is called an **equilibrium condition.** In the competitive market, the equality of quantity demanded and quantity supplied is an equilibrium condition. [5]

This same story is told in graphic terms in Figure 5-7. The price of $60 is the equilibrium price because there is neither excess supply nor excess demand. All other prices are disequilibrium prices, and if they occur, the market will not be in a state of rest. At prices below the equilibrium, there will be shortages and rising prices; at prices above the equilibrium, there will be surpluses and falling prices.

The quantities demanded and supplied at any price can be read off the two curves, while the

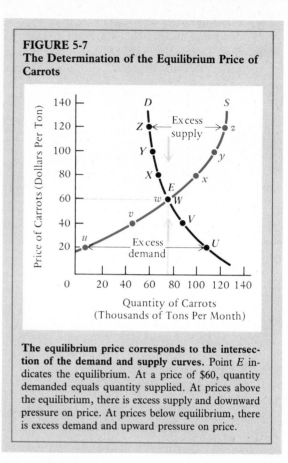

FIGURE 5-7
The Determination of the Equilibrium Price of Carrots

The equilibrium price corresponds to the intersection of the demand and supply curves. Point E indicates the equilibrium. At a price of $60, quantity demanded equals quantity supplied. At prices above the equilibrium, there is excess supply and downward pressure on price. At prices below equilibrium, there is excess demand and upward pressure on price.

magnitude of the shortage or surplus is shown by the horizontal distance between the curves at each price. The figure makes it clear that the equilibrium price occurs where the demand and supply curves intersect. Below that price there will be a shortage and hence an upward pressure on the existing price. Above it there will be a surplus and hence a downward pressure on price. These pressures are represented by the vertical arrows in the figure.

The "Laws" of Supply and Demand

Changes in any of the variables other than price that influence quantity demanded or supplied will cause a shift in either the supply curve or the demand curve (or both). There are four possible

SUPPLY AND DEMAND: WHAT REALLY HAPPENS

"The theory of supply and demand is neat enough," said the skeptic, "but tell me what really happens."

"What really happens," said the economist, "is that first, demand curves slope downward; second, supply curves slope upward; third, prices rise in response to excess demand; and fourth, prices fall in response to excess supply."

"But that's theory," insists the skeptic. "What about reality?"

"That is reality as well," said the economist. "Show me," said the skeptic.

The economist produced the following passages from recent articles in the *New York Times*.

Increased demand for macadamia nuts causes price to rise above competing nuts. Major producer now plans to double the size of its orchards during the next five years.

*   *   *

The ghost town of de Lamar, Idaho, is a mute witness to the recent unprofitability of silver mining. But now silver is stirring again. Prices rose between 1970 and 1979 from $1.30 an ounce to about $50.00, making it economical to begin mining again. De Lamar is now coming back in production at a rate that is expected soon to make it the third largest silver producer in the U.S.

*   *   *

Last summer, Rhode Island officials reopened the northern third of Narragansett Bay, a 9,500-acre fishing ground that had been closed since 1978 because of pollution. Suddenly clam prices dropped, thanks to an underwater population explosion that had transformed the Narragansett area into a clam harvester's dream.

*   *   *

The effects of [the first year of] deregulation of the nation's airlines were spectacular: cuts in air fares of up to 70 percent in some cases, record passenger jam-ups at the airports, and a spectacular increase in the average load factor [the proportion of occupied seats on the average commercial flight].

*   *   *

Today's surplus of oil—the oil glut—has come as something of a relief to a nation with plenty of other problems on its mind. Instead of outraged motorists waiting in line to buy gasoline, there are price wars.

It is no coincidence that the glut and the recession are occurring at the same time.

As industrial production stagnates, so too must the demand for energy. With that demand wavering and supplies of petroleum holding steady, the short-term glut emerges.

*   *   *

The skeptic's response is not recorded, but you will have no trouble telling which clippings illustrate which of the economist's four statements about "what really happens."

---

shifts: (1) a rise in demand (a rightward shift in the demand curve); (2) a fall in demand (a leftward shift in the demand curve); (3) a rise in supply (a rightward shift in the supply curve); and (4) a fall in supply (a leftward shift in the supply curve).

To analyze the effects of any of these shifts we use the method known as **comparative statics.**[4]

[4] The term *statics* is used because we are not concerned about the actual path by which the market goes from the first equilibrium position to the second. Analysis of that path would be described as dynamic analysis.

We start from a position of equilibrium and then introduce the change to be studied. The new equilibrium position is determined and *compared* with the original one. The differences between the two positions of equilibrium must result from changes in the data that were introduced—for everything else has been held constant.

The four shifts give rise to effects that embody the four so-called laws of supply and demand. Each of the four laws describes what happens when an initial position of equilibrium is disturbed by an

FIGURE 5-8
The "Laws" of Supply and Demand

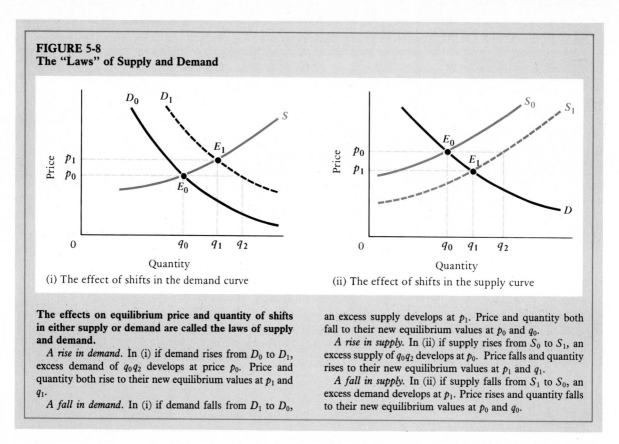

(i) The effect of shifts in the demand curve   (ii) The effect of shifts in the supply curve

The effects on equilibrium price and quantity of shifts in either supply or demand are called the laws of supply and demand.

A rise in demand. In (i) if demand rises from D_0 to D_1, excess demand of q_0q_2 develops at price p_0. Price and quantity both rise to their new equilibrium values at p_1 and q_1.

A fall in demand. In (i) if demand falls from D_1 to D_0, an excess supply develops at p_1. Price and quantity both fall to their new equilibrium values at p_0 and q_0.

A rise in supply. In (ii) if supply rises from S_0 to S_1, an excess supply of q_0q_2 develops at p_0. Price falls and quantity rises to their new equilibrium values at p_1 and q_1.

A fall in supply. In (ii) if supply falls from S_1 to S_0, an excess demand develops at p_1. Price rises and quantity falls to their new equilibrium values at p_0 and q_0.

exogenous event that shifts one of the curves and destroys the equilibrium at the original price and quantity. The shift then causes adjustments (or endogenous changes) that establish a new position of equilibrium.[5]

Figure 5-8, which illustrates the four laws of supply and demand, generalizes our specific discussion about carrots. Previously, we had given the axes specific labels, but from here on we will simplify. Because it is intended to apply to any commodity, the horizontal axis is simply labeled *Quantity*. This should be understood to mean quantity per period in whatever units output is conventionally described. *Price* should be understood to mean the price measured as dollars per unit of quantity for the same commodity.

The laws of supply and demand are

1. A rise in demand causes an increase in both the equilibrium price and the equilibrium quantity exchanged.
2. A fall in demand causes a decrease in both the equilibrium price and the equilibrium quantity exchanged.
3. A rise in supply causes a decrease in the equilibrium price and an increase in the equilibrium quantity exchanged.
4. A fall in supply causes an increase in the equilibrium price and a decrease in the equilibrium quantity exchanged.

In this chapter we have studied many forces that can cause demand or supply curves to shift. These

---

[5] The detailed argument in each case follows that of pages 73–74 and Figure 5-7 as to what happens when supply does not equal demand. Be sure you understand the market *behavior* that gives rise to each of the four "laws" summarized here.

LAWS, PREDICTIONS, HYPOTHESES

In what sense can the four propositions developed for supply and demand be called laws? They are not like acts passed by Congress, interpreted by courts, and enforced by the police; they cannot be repealed if people do not like their effects. Nor are they like the laws of Moses, revealed to man by the voice of God. Are they natural laws similar to Newton's law of gravity? In labeling them *laws*, classical economists clearly had in mind Newton's laws as analogies.

The term *law* is used in science to describe a theory that has stood up to substantial testing. A law of this kind is not something that has been proven to be true for all times and all circumstances, nor is it regarded as immutable. As observations accumulate, laws may often be modified or the range of phenomena to which they apply may be restricted or redefined. Einstein's theory of relativity, for one example, forced such amendments and restrictions on Newton's laws.

The "laws" of supply and demand have stood up well to many empirical tests, but no one believes that they explain all market behavior. Indeed, the range of markets over which they seem to meet the test of providing accurate predictions is now much smaller than it was 80 years ago. It is possible—though most economists would think it unlikely—that at some future time they would no longer apply to any real markets. They are thus laws in the sense that they predict certain kinds of behavior in certain situations and the predicted behavior occurs sufficiently often to lead people to continue to have confidence in the predictions of the theory. They are not laws—any more than are the laws of natural science—that are beyond being challenged by present or future observations that may cast their predictions in doubt. Nor is it a heresy to question their applicability to any particular situation.

Laws, then, are hypotheses that have led to predictions that seem to account for observed behavior. They are theories that—in some circumstances at least—have survived attempts to refute them and have proven useful. It is possible, in economics as in the natural sciences, to be impressed both with the "laws" we do have and with their limitations: to be impressed, that is, both with the power of what we know and with the magnitude of what we have yet to understand.

were summarized in Figures 5-3 and 5-6. By combining this analysis with the four "laws" of supply and demand, we can link many real-world events that cause demand or supply curves to shift with changes in market prices and quantities.

The theory of the determination of price by demand and supply is beautiful in its simplicity. Yet, as we shall see, it is powerful in its wide range of applications.[6]

[6] The laws of supply and demand apply in competitive markets where a supply curve exists and slopes upward. As we shall see later, not all markets satisfy these conditions.

The Theory of Price in an Inflationary World

Up to now we have developed the theory of the prices of individual commodities under the assumption that all other prices remained constant. Does this mean that the theory is inapplicable to an inflationary world when virtually all prices are rising? Fortunately the answer is no.

The key lies in what are called *relative prices*. We have mentioned several times that what matters for demand and supply is the price of the commodity in question relative to the prices of other commodities. A **relative price** measures the price of the specific commodity relative to other prices.

In an inflationary world we are often interested in the price of a given commodity as it relates to the average price of all other commodities. If, during a period when the general price level rose by 40 percent, the price of oranges rose by 60 percent, then the price of oranges rose relative to the price level as a whole. Oranges became *relatively* expensive. However, if oranges had risen in price by only 30 percent when the general price level rose by 40 percent, then the relative price of oranges would have fallen. Although the money price of oranges rose substantially, oranges became *relatively* cheap.

In Lewis Carroll's famous story *Through the Looking Glass*, Alice finds a country where you have to run in order to stay still. So it is with inflation. A commodity's price must rise as fast as the general level of prices just to keep its relative price constant.

It has been convenient in this chapter to analyze a change in a particular price in the context of a constant price level. The analysis is easily extended to an inflationary period by remembering that any force that raises the price of one commodity when other prices remain constant will, given general inflation, raise the price of that commodity faster than the price level is rising. For example, a change in tastes in favor of carrots that would raise their price by 20 percent when other prices were constant, would raise their price by 32 percent if at the same time the general price level goes up by 10 percent.[7] In each case the price of carrots rises 20 percent *relative to the average of all prices.*

In price theory, whenever we talk of a change in the price of one commodity we mean a change relative to other prices.

If the price level is constant, this change requires only that the money price of the commodity in question should rise. If the price level is itself rising, this change requires that the money price of

the commodity in question should rise faster than the price level.

SUMMARY

1. The amount of a commodity that households wish to purchase is called the *quantity demanded*. It is a flow expressed as so much per period of time. This quantity is determined by the commodity's own price, the prices of related commodities, average household income, tastes, the distribution of income among households, and the size of the population.

2. Quantity demanded is assumed to increase as the price of the commodity falls, *ceteris paribus.* The relationship between quantity demanded and price is represented graphically by a demand curve that shows how much will be demanded at each market price. A movement along a demand curve indicates a change in the quantity demanded in response to a change in the price of the commodity.

3. The demand curve shifts to the right (an increase in demand) if average income rises, if the price of a substitute rises, if the price of a complement falls, if population rises, or if there is a change in tastes in favor of the product. The opposite changes shift the demand curve to the left (a decrease in demand). A shift in a demand curve represents a change in the quantity demanded at each price and is referred to as a *change in demand.*

4. The amount of a commodity that firms wish to sell is called the *quantity supplied*. It is a flow expressed as so much per period of time. This quantity depends on the commodity's own price, the prices of other commodities, the costs of factors of production, the goals of the firm, and the state of technology.

5. Quantity supplied is assumed to increase as the price of the commodity increases, *ceteris paribus.* A movement along a supply curve indicates a change in the quantity supplied in response to a change in price.

---

[7] In the first case the price level is 100 and an index of carrot prices rises from 100 to 120 (100 × 1.2 = 120). In the second case the index of the price level becomes 110 and the index of carrot prices must rise to 132 (110 × 1.2 = 132).

6. The supply curve shifts to the right (an increase in supply) if the prices of other commodities fall, if the costs of producing the commodity fall, or if, for any reason, producers become more willing to produce the commodity. The opposite changes shift the supply curve to the left (a decrease in supply). A shift in the supply curve indicates a change in the quantity supplied at each price and is referred to as a *change in supply*.

7. The equilibrium price is the one at which the quantity demanded equals the quantity supplied. At any price below the equilibrium there will be excess demand, while at any price above the equilibrium there will be excess supply. Graphically, equilibrium occurs where demand and supply curves intersect.

8. Price is assumed to rise when there is a shortage and to fall when there is a surplus. Thus the actual market price will be pushed toward the equilibrium price, and when it is reached, there will be neither shortage nor surplus and price will not change until either the supply curve or the demand curve shifts.

9. Using the method of comparative statics, the effects of a shift in either demand or supply can be determined. A rise in demand raises both equilibrium price and quantity; a fall in demand lowers both. A rise in supply raises equilibrium quantity but lowers equilibrium price; a fall in supply lowers equilibrium quantity but raises equilibrium price. These are the so-called laws of supply and demand.

10. Price theory is most simply explained against a backdrop of a constant price level. Price changes discussed in the theory are changes *relative to* the average level of all prices. In an inflationary period, a rise in the relative price of one commodity means that its price rises by more than does the price level; a fall in its relative price means that its price rises by less than does the price level.

TOPICS FOR REVIEW

Quantity demanded and quantity exchanged
Demand schedules and demand curves
Quantity supplied and quantity exchanged
Supply schedules and supply curves
Movements along a curve and shifts in the curve
Changes in quantity demanded and changes in demand
Changes in quantity supplied and changes in supply
Equilibrium, equilibrium price, and disequilibrium
The determination of equilibrium
Comparative static analysis
The "laws" of supply and demand
Relative price

DISCUSSION QUESTIONS

1. What shifts in demand or supply curves would produce the following results? (Assume that only one of the two curves has shifted.)
   a. The price of pocket calculators has fallen over the last few years and the quantity exchanged has risen greatly.
   b. As the American standard of living rose over the past three decades, both the prices and the consumption of prime cuts of beef rose steadily.
   c. A leading department store is offering $1.20 for 100 pennies.
   d. Summer sublets in Ann Arbor, Michigan, are at rents of 50 percent or less of the regular rental.
   e. Because the "preppy look" is in, the sale of jeans has declined.
   f. Federal safety and antipollution regulations decrease the sales of American car manufacturers.
   g. "Gourmet food market grows as affluent shoppers indulge."
2. Recently the Department of Agriculture predicted bumper crops of corn and wheat. But its chief economist, Don Paarlberg, warned consumers not to expect prices to decrease since the costs of production were rising and foreign demand for American crops was increasing. "The classic pattern of supply and demand won't work this time," Mr. Paarlberg said. Discuss his observation.
3. Explain each of the following in terms of changes in supply and demand.
   a. DuPont increased the price of synthetic fibers, although it acknowledged demand was weak.
   b. "Master Charge has replaced sugar-daddy," a Beverly Hills furrier said, explaining the rise in sales of mink coats.
   c. The Edsel was a lemon when produced in 1958–1960 but is now a best-seller among cars of its vintage.
   d. The decision not to deploy the MX missile in western Utah signaled the collapse in land prices in that area.

4. Suppose that video recorder producers find that they are selling more video recorders at the same price than they did two years ago. Is this a shift of the demand curve or a movement along the curve? Suggest at least four reasons why this rise in sales at an unchanged price might occur.

5. What would be the effect on the equilibrium price and quantity of marijuana if its sale were legalized? What would be the effect on the equilibrium prices of gold and paper if all the world's banks sold off their gold supplies and replaced them with paper certificates that were officially accepted as reserves?

6. The relative price of a color television set has dropped drastically over time. Would you explain this falling price in terms of demand or supply changes? What factors are likely to have caused the demand or supply shifts that did occur?

7. Classify the effect of each of the following as (a) a decrease in the demand for fish, (b) a decrease in the quantity of fish demanded, or (c) other. Illustrate each diagrammatically.
   a. The government of Iceland bars fishermen of other nations from its waters.
   b. People buy less fish because of a rise in fish prices.
   c. The Roman Catholic Church relaxes its ban on eating meat on Fridays.
   d. The price of beef falls and as a result households buy more beef and less fish.
   e. In the interests of training marine personnel for national defense, the U.S. government decides to subsidize the American fishing industry.
   f. It is discovered that eating fish is better for one's health than eating meat.

8. "The effect of price changes often eludes analysis. For example, two of the food groups that have shown absolute decreases in consumption per capita—flour and potatoes—have also shown decreases in price relative to the prices of all goods. Consumption of meat per capita has been rising in the face of an increase in relative prices." Do the changes elude your analysis? How would you reword this statement to make clear what you think did happen?

9. Predict the effect on price of at least one commodity of each of the following:
   a. Winter snowfall is at record high in Colorado, but drought continues in New England ski areas.
   b. A recession decreases employment in Detroit automobile factories.
   c. The French grape harvest is the smallest in 20 years.
   d. The state of New York cancels permission for citizens to cut firewood in state parks.

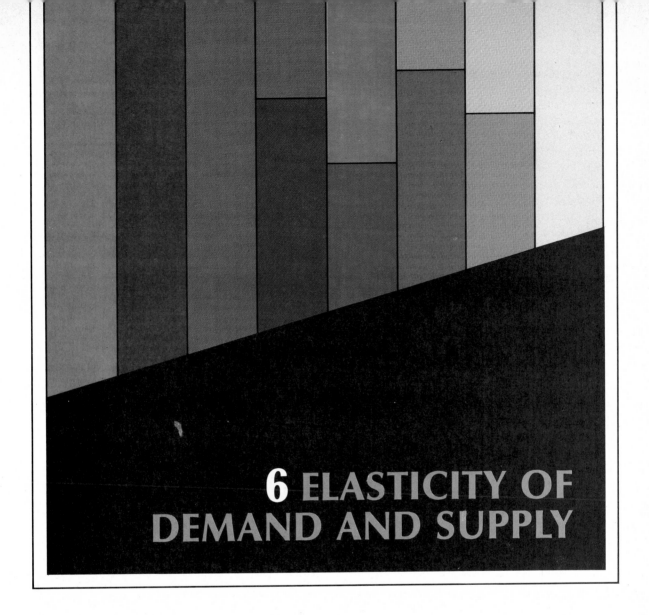

6 ELASTICITY OF DEMAND AND SUPPLY

The laws of supply and demand predict the *direction* of changes in price and quantity in response to various shifts in demand and supply. But very often it is not enough to know merely whether quantity rises or falls in response to a change in price; it is also important to know by how much.

When flood damage led to major destruction of the onion crop, onion prices rose generally. In Hartford, Connecticut, they rose 42 percent in one week. Not surprisingly, consumption fell. In this case, the press reported that many consumers stopped using onions altogether and substituted onion salt, sauerkraut, cabbage, and other products. Other consumers still bought onions but in reduced quantities. Overall consumption was down sharply. Were aggregate dollar sales of onions (price *times* quantity) higher or lower? The data above do not tell, but this is the sort of information that may matter a good deal. A government concerned with the effect of a partial crop failure on farm income will not be satisfied with being told that food prices will rise and quantities consumed will fall; it will need to know by approximately how much they will rise and fall if it is to assess the effects on farmers.

In 1982 the New York City Opera, faced with a growing deficit, *cut* its ticket prices by 20 percent, hoping to attract more customers. At the same time, the New York Transit Authority *raised* subway fares to reduce its growing deficit. Was one of these two opposite approaches to reducing a deficit necessarily wrong? The answer, as we shall see, is no.

Measuring and describing the extent of the responsiveness of quantities to changes in prices and other variables is often essential if we are to understand the significance of these changes. This is what the concept of elasticity seeks to do.

PRICE ELASTICITY OF DEMAND

Suppose there is a fall in the supply of a farm crop, that is, a leftward shift in the supply curve. The two parts of Figure 6-1 show the same leftward shift. Because the demand curves are different, the effects on equilibrium price and quantity are different.

The difference may have great policy significance. Consider what would happen if the government persuaded farmers to produce more of a certain crop. (It might, for example, pay a subsidy to

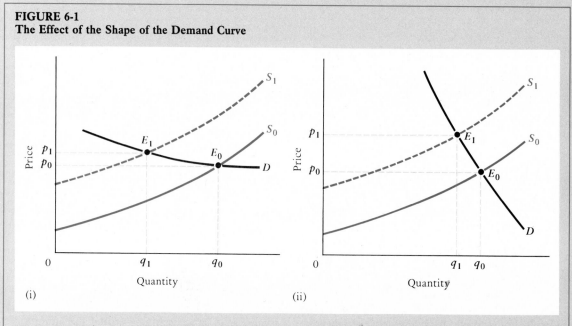

FIGURE 6-1
The Effect of the Shape of the Demand Curve

(i)

(ii)

The flatter the demand curve, the less the change in price and the greater the change in quantity. Both parts of the figure show the same leftward shift in the supply curve. In each part, initial equilibrium is at price p_0 and output q_0 and the new equilibrium is at p_1 and q_1. In (i) the effect of the shift in supply from S_0 to S_1 is a slight rise in the price and a large decrease in quantity. In (ii) the effect of the identical shift in the supply curve from S_0 to S_1 is a large increase in the price and a relatively small decrease in quantity.

farmers for growing this crop.) If the government is successful, then at every possible price of the product there will be an increase in the quantity that farmers would be willing to produce. Thus the whole supply curve of the product would shift to the right. This may be visualized in both parts of Figure 6-1 by assuming that the supply curve shifts from S_1 to S_0.

Figure 6-1(i) illustrates a case in which the quantity that consumers demand is very sensitive to price changes. The extra production brings down price, but because the quantity demanded is very responsive, only a small change in price is necessary to restore equilibrium. The effect of the government's policy, therefore, is to achieve a large increase in the production and sales of this commodity and only a small decrease in price.

Figure 6-1(ii) shows a case in which the quantity demanded is quite unresponsive to price changes. As before, the increase in supply at the original price causes a surplus that brings the price down. But this time the quantity demanded by consumers does not increase very much in response to the fall in price. Thus the price continues to drop until, discouraged by lower and lower prices, farmers reduce the quantity supplied very nearly to the level attained before they received the increased incentive to produce. The effect of the government's policy is to bring about a large fall in the price and only a small increase in the quantity produced and sold.

In comparing the cases diagrammed in Figure 6-1, it can be seen that the government's policy has exactly the same effectiveness as far as farmers' willingness to supply the commodity is concerned (the supply curve shifts are identical). But the effects on the equilibrium price and quantity are very different because of the different degrees to which the quantity demanded by consumers responds to price changes. If the purpose of the policy is to increase the quantity of this commodity produced and consumed, then the policy will be a great success when the demand curve is similar to the one shown in Figure 6-1(i), but it will be a failure when the demand curve is similar to the one shown in Figure 6-1(ii). If, however, the main purpose of the policy is to achieve a large reduction in the price of the commodity, the policy will be a failure when demand is as shown in (i) but it will be a great success when demand is as shown in (ii).

A shift in supply can have very different effects, depending on the shape of the demand curve.

Price Elasticity: A Measure of the Responsiveness of Quantity Demanded to Price Changes

When considering the responsiveness of the quantity demanded to changes in price, we may wish to make statements such as "The demand for carrots was more responsive to price changes 10 years ago than it is today" or "The demand for meat responds more to price changes than does the demand for green vegetables." In order to make such comparisons, a measure of the degree to which quantity demanded responds to changes in price is required.

In the previous examples it was possible to compare the geometrical steepness of the two demand curves in Figure 6-1 because the curves were both drawn on the same scale. Thus, for any given price change, the quantity changes more on the flatter curve than it does on the steeper one. However, it can be very misleading to inspect a *single* curve and to conclude from its general appearance something about the degree of responsiveness of quantity demanded to price changes. You can make a curve appear as steep or as flat as you like by changing the scales. For example, a curve that looks steep when the horizontal scale is 1 inch = 100 units will look much flatter when the horizontal scale is 1 inch = 1 unit if the same vertical scale is used in each case.

Instead of gaining a vague general impression from the shape of demand curves, one could note the actual change in quantity demanded in response to a certain price change. But it would still be impossible to compare degrees of responsiveness for different commodities.

TABLE 6–1 PRICE REDUCTIONS AND CORRESPONDING INCREASES IN QUANTITY DEMANDED

Commodity	Reduction in price	Increase in quantity demanded
Beef	$.20 per pound	7,500 pounds
Men's shirts	.20 per shirt	5,000 shirts
Radios	.20 per radio	100 radios

Assume that we have the information shown in Table 6-1. Should we conclude that the demand for radios is not so responsive to price changes as the demand for beef? After all, price cuts of $.20 cause quite a large increase in the quantity of beef demanded but only a small increase in radios.

There are two problems here. First, a reduction of price of $.20 will be a large price cut for a low-priced commodity and an insignificant price cut for a high-priced commodity. The price reductions listed in Table 6-1 represent very different fractions of the total prices. Actually it is more revealing to know the percentage change in the prices of the various commodities. Second, by an analogous argument, knowing the quantity by which demand changes is not very revealing unless the level of demand is also known. An increase of 7,500 pounds is quite a significant reaction of demand if the quantity formerly bought was 15,000 pounds, but it is only a drop in the bucket if the quantity formerly demanded was 10 million pounds.

Table 6-2 shows the original and new levels of price and quantity. Changes in price and quantity

expressed as percentages of the average prices and quantities are shown in the first two columns of Table 6-3.[1] **Elasticity of demand,** the measure of responsiveness of quantity demanded to price changes, is symbolized by the Greek letter eta, η. It is defined as: [6]

$$\eta = \frac{\text{percentage change in quantity demanded}}{\text{percentage change in price}}$$

This concept is frequently called **demand elasticity** or, when it is necessary to distinguish this measure of elasticity from other related concepts, *price elasticity of demand* since the variable causing the change in quantity demanded is the commodity's own price.

Interpreting Numerical Values of Elasticity of Demand

Because demand curves slope downward, an *increase* in price is associated with a *decrease* in quantity demanded and vice versa. Since the percentage changes in price and quantity have opposite signs,

[1] The use of averages is designed to avoid the ambiguity caused by the fact that, for example, the $.20 change in the price of beef is a different percentage of the original price, $1.70, than it is of the new price, $1.50 (11.8 percent versus 13.3 percent). We want the elasticity of demand between any two points (A and B) to be independent of whether we move from A to B or from B to A; as a result, using either "original" prices and quantities or "new" prices and quantities would be less satisfactory than using averages. In this illustration, $.20 is unambiguously 12.5 percent of $1.60 and applies to a price increase from $1.50 to $1.70, as well as to the decrease discussed in the text. Further discussion is found in the appendix to this chapter, which begins on page 901.

TABLE 6–2 PRICE AND QUANTITY INFORMATION UNDERLYING DATA OF TABLE 6–1

Commodity	Unit	Original price	New price	Average price	Original quantity	New quantity	Average quantity
Beef	per pound	$ 1.70	$ 1.50	$ 1.60	116,250	123,750	120,000
Men's shirts	per shirt	8.10	7.90	8.00	197,500	202,500	200,000
Radios	per radio	40.10	39.90	40.00	9,950	10,050	10,000

These data provide the appropriate context of the data given in Table 6–1. The table relates the $.20 per unit price reduction of each commodity to the actual prices and quantities demanded.

TABLE 6–4 THE CHANGES IN TOTAL REVENUE
(TOTAL EXPENDITURE) FOR THE EXAMPLE OF TABLE 6–2

Commodity	Price × quantity (original prices and quantities)	Price × quantity (new prices and quantities)	Change in revenue (expenditure)	Elasticity of demand from Table 6–3
Beef	$ 197,625	$ 185,625	− $12,000	0.5
Men's shirts	1,599,750	1,599,750	0	1.0
Radios	398,995	400,995	+ 2,000	2.0

Whether revenue increases or decreases in response to a price cut depends on whether demand is elastic or inelastic. The $197,625 figure is the product of the orig- inal price of beef ($1.70) and the original quantity (116,250 pounds). The $185,625 is the product of the new price ($1.50) and quantity (123,750), and so on.

Consider two real examples. When a bumper potato crop in the United States sent prices down 50 percent, quantity sold increased only 15 percent and potato farmers found their revenues falling sharply. Demand was clearly inelastic. When, some years ago, Salt Lake's transit authority cut its bus fares from $.25 to $.15 for the average journey, the volume of passenger traffic increased from 4.4 mil- lion to 14 million journeys within two years and revenues rose sharply. Demand was clearly elastic.

What Determines Elasticity of Demand?

Table 6-5 shows some measured elasticities of de- mand. Evidently they can vary considerably. The main determinant of elasticity is the availability of substitutes. Some commodities, such as margarine, cabbage, lamb, and Fords, have quite close sub- stitutes—butter, other green vegetables, beef, and similar makes of cars. A change in the price of these commodities, *the prices of the substitutes re- maining constant*, can be expected to cause much substitution—a fall in price leading consumers to buy more of the commodity and less of the substi- tutes, and a rise in price leading consumers to buy less of the commodity and more of the substitutes. Other, more broadly defined commodities, such as all foods, all clothing, cigarettes, and gasoline, have few if any satisfactory substitutes. A rise in their

TABLE 6–5 ESTIMATED PRICE ELASTICITIES OF DEMAND IN THE UNITED STATES[a] (Selected Commodities)

Inelastic demand (less than unity)	
Potatoes	0.3
Sugar	0.3
Public transportation	0.4
All foods	0.4
Cigarettes	0.5
Gasoline	0.6
All clothing	0.6
Consumer durables	0.8
Demand of approximately unit elasticity[b]	
Beef	
Beer	
Marijuana	
Elastic demand (greater than unity)	
Furniture	1.2
Electricity	1.3
Lamb and mutton (U.K.)	1.5
Automobiles	2.1
Millinery	3.0

[a] For the United States except where noted.
[b] Greater than 0.9 and less than 1.1.

The wide range of price elasticities is illustrated by these selected measures. These elasticities, from var- ious studies, are representative of literally hundreds of existing estimates. Explanations of some of the differ- ences are discussed in the text.

price can be expected to cause a smaller fall in quantity demanded than would be the case if close substitutes were available.

A commodity with close substitutes tends to have an elastic demand, one with no close substitutes an inelastic demand. The closer the substitutes for a commodity, the greater the elasticity of demand.

Closeness of substitutes—and thus measured elasticity—depends both on how the commodity is defined and on the time period.

Definition of the Commodity

Food is a necessity of life. Thus for food taken as a whole demand is inelastic over a large price range. It does not follow, however, that any one food, such as white bread or beef, is a necessity in the same sense. Therefore individual foods can have quite elastic demands and they frequently do.

Durable goods provide a similar example. Durables as a whole are less elastic than individual kinds of durable goods. For example, when the price of television sets rises, many households may replace their lawnmower or their vacuum cleaner instead of buying that extra television set. Thus, while their purchases of television sets fall, their total purchases of durables do not.

Because most specific manufactured goods have close substitutes, studies show they tend to have price-elastic demand. Millinery, for example, has been estimated to have an elasticity of 3.0. In contrast, clothing in general tends to be inelastic.

Any one of a group of related products will tend to have an elastic demand, even though the demand for the group as a whole may be inelastic.

Long-Run and Short-Run Elasticity of Demand

Because it takes time to develop satisfactory substitutes, a demand that is inelastic in the short run may prove elastic when enough time has passed. For example, when the Tennessee Valley Authority (TVA) brought cheap electric power to the rural South in the 1930s, very few households were wired for electricity. The initial measurements showed demand for electricity to be very inelastic. Some commentators even argued that it was foolish to invest so much money in bringing cheap electricity to the South because people did not buy it even at low prices. But gradually households became electrified and purchased appliances, and new industries moved into the area to take advantage of TVA's cheap electric power. As this occurred, measured elasticity steadily increased.

Gasoline provides a similar, more recent example. Traditionally gasoline was thought to be highly inelastic because of the absence of satisfactory substitutes. But the very large price increases of gasoline over the 1970s have led to the development of smaller, more fuel-efficient cars and to less driving. The most recent estimates of elasticity of demand for gasoline have risen from around 0.6 to around unity. Given another decade in which to develop substitutes, gasoline demand may prove elastic, a fact that worries some oil producers a good deal.

The degree of response to a price change, and thus the measured price elasticity of demand, will tend to be greater the longer the time span considered.

Short-Run and Long-Run Demand Curves

Because the elasticity of demand for a commodity changes over time as consumers adjust their habits and substitutes are developed, the demand curve also changes; hence an important distinction can be made between short-run and long-run demand curves. Every demand curve shows the response of consumer demand to a change in price. For such commodities as cornflakes and pillowcases, the full response occurs quickly and there is little reason to worry about longer term effects. But other commodities are typically used in connection with highly durable appliances or machines. A change in price of, say, electricity and gasoline may not have its major effect until the stock of appliances and machines using these commodities has been adjusted. This adjustment may take a long time to occur.

FIGURE 6-4
Short- and Long-Run Demand Curves

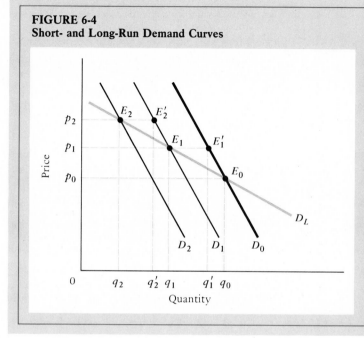

The long-run demand curve is more elastic than the short-run curves. D_L is a long-run demand curve. Suppose consumers are fully adjusted to price p_0. Equilibrium is then at E_0, with quantity demanded q_0. Now suppose price rises to p_1. In the short run, consumers will react along the short-run demand curve D_0 and reduce consumption to q_1'. Once time has permitted the full range of adjustments to price p_1, however, a new equilibrium at E_1 will be reached with quantity q_1, leading to a new short-run demand curve D_1. A further rise in price to p_2 would lead first to a short-run equilibrium at E_2' but eventually to a new long-run equilibrium at E_2. The screened long-run demand curve is more elastic than the short-run curves.

For commodities whose substitutes are developed over a period of time, it is helpful to identify two kinds of demand curve. A *short-run demand curve* shows the response of quantity demanded to a change in price for a given structure of the durable goods that use the commodity and for the existing sets of substitute commodities. A different short-run demand curve will exist for each such structure.

The *long-run demand curve* shows the response of quantity demanded to a change in price after enough time has passed to assure that all adjustments to the changed price have occurred. The relation between long-run and short-run demand curves is shown in Figure 6-4. The principal conclusion, already suggested in the discussion of elasticity, is:

The long-run demand curve for a commodity will tend to be substantially more elastic than any of the short-run demand curves.

The importance of this distinction will be evident in the chapters that follow.

INCOME AND CROSS-ELASTICITY OF DEMAND

The Concept of Income Elasticity

One of the most important determinants of demand is the income of the potential customers. When the Food and Agricultural Organization of the United Nations (the FAO) wants to estimate the future demand for some crop, it needs to know by how much world income will grow and how much of that additional income will be spent on the particular foodstuff. For example, as a nation gets richer, its consumption patterns change, with relatively more being spent on meat and relatively less on staples such as rice and potatoes.

The responsiveness of demand to changes in income is termed **income elasticity of demand** and may be symbolized η_Y.

$$\eta_Y = \frac{\text{percentage change in quantity demanded}}{\text{percentage change in income}}$$

For most goods, increases in income lead to increases in demand and income elasticity will be positive. These are called **normal goods**. Goods for which consumption decreases in response to a rise in income have negative income elasticities and are called **inferior goods**.

The income elasticity of normal goods may be less than unity (inelastic) or greater than unity (elastic), depending on whether (say) a 10 percent increase in income leads to less than or more than a 10 percent increase in the quantity demanded. Not surprisingly, different commodities have different income elasticities (see Table 6-6).

The reaction of demand to changes in income is extremely important. We know that in most West-

ern economies economic growth has caused the level of income to double every 20 to 30 years over a sustained period of at least a century. This rise in income is shared to some extent by most households in the country. As they find their incomes increasing, they increase their demands for most commodities. But the demands for some commodities such as food and basic clothing will not increase very much as incomes rise while the demands for other commodities increase rapidly as incomes rise. In developing countries such as Ireland and Mexico, the demand for durable goods is increasing most rapidly as household incomes rise, while in the United States it is the demand for services that is rising most rapidly. The uneven impact of the growth of income on the demands for different commodities has very important effects on the economy and groups in it, and these will be studied at several different points in this book, beginning with the discussion of agriculture in Chapter 8.

The Determinants of Income Elasticity

The variations in income elasticities shown in Table 6-6 suggest that the more basic or staple a commodity, the lower is its income elasticity. Food as a whole has an income elasticity of 0.2, consumer durables of 1.8. In the United States pork and such starchy roots as potatoes are inferior goods; their quantity consumed falls as income rises.

Does the distinction between luxuries and necessities explain differences in income elasticities? The table suggests that it does. The case of meals eaten away from home is one example; such meals are almost always more expensive, calorie for calorie, than meals prepared at home. It would thus be expected that at lower ranges of income restaurant meals would be regarded as an expensive luxury, but the demand for them would expand substantially as households became richer. This is in fact what happens.

Does this mean that the market demand for the foodstuffs that appear on restaurant menus will also have high income elasticities? Generally the answer

---

TABLE 6–6 ESTIMATED INCOME ELASTICITIES OF DEMAND[a] (Selected Commodities)

Inferior goods (negative income elasticities)	
Whole milk	−0.5
Pig products	−0.2
Starchy roots	−0.2
Inelastic normal goods (0.0 to 1.0)	
Coffee	0.0
Wine (France)	0.1
All food	0.2
Poultry	0.3
Cheese	0.4
Beef	0.5
Housing	0.6
Cigarettes	0.8
Elastic normal goods (greater than 1.0)	
Gasoline	1.1
Wine	1.4
Cream (U.K.)	1.7
Wine (Canada)	1.8
Consumer durables	1.8
Poultry (Sri Lanka)	2.0
Restaurant meals (U.K.)	2.4

[a] For the United States except where noted.

Income elasticities vary widely across commodities and sometimes across countries. The basic source of food estimates by country is the FAO, but many individual studies have been made. Explanations of some of the differences are discussed in the text.

is no; when a household eats out rather than preparing meals at home, the main change is not in what is eaten but in who prepares it. The additional expenditure on "food" goes mainly to pay cooks and waiters and to yield a return on the restaurateur's capital. Thus, when a household expands its expenditure on restaurant food by 2.4 percent in response to a 1 percent rise in its income, most of the extra expenditure on "food" goes to workers in service industries; little, if any, finds its way into the pockets of farmers. Here is a striking example of the general tendency for households to spend a higher proportion of their incomes on services as their incomes rise.

The revealing relationship shown in Table 6-6 between whole milk, cheese, and cream suggests that as incomes rise people tend to change the form of the milk products they consume—less whole milk, more cheese, and more cream. (Ice cream, not included in the FAO data, had a high income elasticity for American consumers in measurements of three or four decades ago. Today the income elasticity is lower. To an earlier generation ice cream was a special treat; at current American income levels and prices, ice cream has become a staple.)

The more basic an item in the consumption pattern of households, the lower its income elasticity.

So far we have focused on differences in income elasticities among commodities. However, income elasticities for a single commodity also vary with the level of a household's income. When incomes are very low, households may eat virtually no meat and consume lots of starchy foods such as bread and potatoes; at higher levels, they may eat the cheaper cuts of meat and more green vegetables along with their bread and potatoes; at yet higher levels they are likely to eat more (and more expensive) meat, to substitute frozen for canned vegetables, and to eat a greater variety of foods. In this sequence the income elasticity of hamburger may be high at low levels of income but decrease as income rises and steak replaces hamburger. Different commodities will show different patterns. Po-

tatoes are likely to exhibit low income elasticity while steak proves to be income-elastic over a wide range of income.[2]

What is true of individuals is also true of countries. Empirical studies show that for different countries at comparable stages of economic development, income elasticities are similiar. But the countries of the world are at various stages of economic development and so have widely different income elasticities for the same products. Notice in Table 6-6 the different income elasticity of poultry in the United States, where it is a standard item of consumption, and in Sri Lanka, where it is a luxury.

Graphic Representation of Income Elasticities

Increases in income shift an ordinary demand curve to the right for a normal good and to the left for an inferior good. Figure 6-5 shows a different kind of graph, an **income-consumption curve** that resembles the ordinary demand curve in one respect: it shows the relation of quantity demanded to *one* variable, *ceteris paribus*. The variable, however, is not price but household income. (An increase in the price of the commodity, incomes remaining constant, would shift downward the curves shown in Figure 6-5.)

The figure shows three different patterns of income elasticity. Goods that consumers regard as necessities will have high income elasticities at low levels of income but show low income elasticities beyond some level. The obvious reason is that as incomes rise it becomes possible for households to devote a smaller proportion of their income to meeting basic needs and a larger proportion to buying things they have always wanted but could not afford. Some of these necessities may even become inferior goods. So-called luxury goods will not tend to be purchased at low levels of income

[2] It is common to use the terms *income-elastic* and *income-inelastic* to refer to income elasticities of greater or less than unity. See the box on page 93.

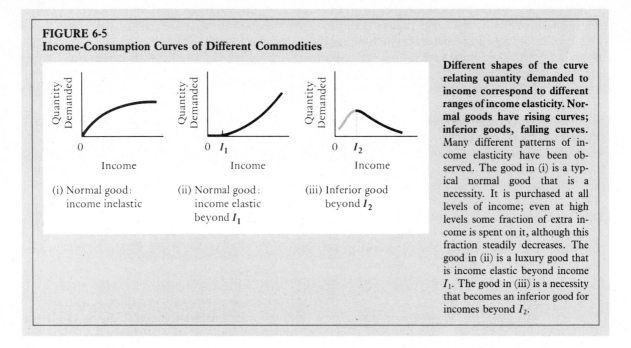

FIGURE 6-5
Income-Consumption Curves of Different Commodities

(i) Normal good:
income inelastic

(ii) Normal good:
income elastic
beyond I_1

(iii) Inferior good
beyond I_2

Different shapes of the curve relating quantity demanded to income correspond to different ranges of income elasticity. Normal goods have rising curves; inferior goods, falling curves. Many different patterns of income elasticity have been observed. The good in (i) is a typical normal good that is a necessity. It is purchased at all levels of income; even at high levels some fraction of extra income is spent on it, although this fraction steadily decreases. The good in (ii) is a luxury good that is income elastic beyond income I_1. The good in (iii) is a necessity that becomes an inferior good for incomes beyond I_2.

but will have high income elasticities once incomes rise enough to permit households to sample the better things of life available to them.[3]

Cross-Elasticity of Demand

The responsiveness of demand to changes in the prices of other commodities is called **cross-elasticity of demand**. It is often denoted η_X and defined as

$$\eta_x = \frac{\text{percentage change in quantity demanded of one good, } X}{\text{percentage change in price of another good, } Y}$$

[3] In Figure 6-5, in contrast to the ordinary demand curve, quantity demanded is on the vertical axis. This follows the usual practice of putting the to-be-explained variable (called the *dependent variable*) on the vertical axis and the explanatory variable (called the *independent variable*) on the horizontal axis. It is the ordinary demand curve that has the axes "backward." This practice dates to Alfred Marshall's *Principles of Economics* (1890), the classic that is one of the foundation stones of modern price theory. [8] For better or worse, Marshall's scheme is now used by everybody—although mathematicians never fail to wonder at this further example of the odd ways of economists.

Cross-elasticity can vary from minus infinity to plus infinity. Complementary commodities will have negative cross-elasticities. Cars and gasoline, for example, are complements. A large rise in the price of gasoline will lead (as it has in America) to a decline in the demand for cars as some people decide to do without a car and others decide not to buy a second (or third) car. Substitute commodities have positive cross-elasticities. Cars and public transport are substitutes. A large rise in the price of cars (relative to public transport) would lead to a rise in the demand for public transport as some people shifted from cars to public transport.

Measures of cross-elasticity sometimes prove helpful in defining whether producers of similar products are in competition with each other. Glass bottles and tin cans have a high cross-elasticity of demand. The producer of bottles is thus in competition with the producer of cans. If the bottle company raises its price, it will lose substantial sales to the can producer. Men's shoes and women's shoes have a low cross-elasticity. Thus a producer of men's shoes is not in close competition with a

TERMINOLOGY OF ELASTICITY

Terminology	Symbol	Numerical measure of elasticity	Verbal description
A. Price elasticity of demand [supply]	$\eta[\eta_S]$		
Perfectly or completely inelastic.		Zero	Quantity demanded [supplied] does not change as price changes
Inelastic		Greater than zero, but less than one	Quantity demanded [supplied] changes by a smaller percentage than does price
Unit elasticity		One	Quantity demanded [supplied] changes by exactly the same percentage as does price
Elastic		Greater than one, but less than infinity	Quantity demanded [supplied] changes by a larger percentage than does price
Perfectly, completely, or infinitely elastic		Infinity	Purchasers [sellers] are prepared to buy [sell] all they can at some price and none at all at an even slightly higher [lower] price
B. Income elasticity of demand	η_Y		
Inferior good		Negative	Quantity demanded decreases as income increases
Normal good		Positive	Quantity demanded increases as income increases:
Income-inelastic		Greater than zero, less than one	less than in proportion to income increase
Income-elastic		Greater than one	more than in proportion to income increase
C. Cross-elasticity of demand	η_X		
Substitute		Positive	Price increase of a substitute leads to an increase in quantity demanded of this good (and less of the substitute)
Complement		Negative	Price increase of a complement leads to a decrease in quantity demanded of this good (as well as less of the complement)

producer of women's shoes. If the former raises its price, it will not lose many sales to the latter. This kind of knowledge has been extremely important in antitrust cases where the issue was whether a firm in one industry was or was not in active competition with firms in another industry. Indeed, many of the most interesting studies of cross-elasticity have been made during antitrust inquiries to determine whether specific products are substitutes (see Chapter 18, page 307). Whether cellophane and Saran Wrap, or aluminum cable and copper cable, are or are not substitutes may determine questions of monopoly under the law. The positive or negative sign and the size of cross-elasticities tell us whether or not goods are substitutes.

SUPPLY ELASTICITY

The concept of elasticity can be applied to supply as well as to demand. Just as elasticity of demand measures the response of quantity demanded to changes in any of the forces that influence it, so elasticity of supply measures the response of quantity supplied to changes in any of the forces that influence it. We will focus on the commodity's own price as a factor influencing supply.

Elasticity of supply measures the responsiveness of the quantity supplied to a change in the commodity's own price. It is denoted η_s and defined as

$$\eta_s = \frac{\text{percentage change in quantity supplied}}{\text{percentage change in price}}$$

The supply curves considered in this chapter all have positive slopes: An increase in price causes an increase in quantity sold. Such supply curves all have positive elasticities.

There are important special cases. If the supply curve is vertical—the quantitiy supplied does not change as price changes—elasticity of supply is zero. This would be the case, for example, if suppliers produced a given quantity and dumped it on the market for whatever it would bring. A horizontal supply curve has an infinitely high elasticity of supply: A small drop in price would reduce the

quantity producers are willing to supply from an indefinitely large amount to zero. Between these two extremes elasticity of supply will vary with the shape of the supply curve.[4]

What Determines Elasticity of Supply?

Supply elasticities are very important for many problems in economics. We shall discuss them only briefly here for two reasons. First, much of the treatment of demand elasticity carries over to supply elasticity and does not need repeating. For example, the ease of substitution can vary in production as well as in consumption. If the price of a commodity rises, how much more can be produced profitably? This depends in part on whether it is easy to shift from the production of other commodities to the one whose price has risen. If agricultural land and labor can be readily shifted from one crop to another, the supply of any one crop will be more elastic than if they can not. Here also, as with demand, length of time for response is critical. It may be difficult to change quantities supplied in response to a price increase in a matter of weeks or months but easy to do so over a period of years. An obvious example concerns the planting cycle of crops. Also, new oil fields can be discovered, wells drilled, and pipelines built over a period of years, but not in a few months. Thus elasticity of oil supply is much greater over five years than over one year.

The second reason for brevity of treatment is that supply elasticity depends to a great extent on how costs behave as output is varied, an issue that will be treated at length in Part Three. If costs of production rise rapidly as output rises, then the stimulus to expand production in response to a price rise will quickly be choked off by increases in costs. In this case supply will tend to be rather inelastic. If, however, costs rise only slowly as production increases, a rise in price that raises profits

[4] Steepness, which is related to absolute rather than percentage changes, is *not* always a reliable guide. As is shown in the appendix to this chapter, any upward-sloping straight line passing through the origin has an elasticity of $+1.0$ over its entire range.

will call forth a large increase in quantity supplied before the rise in costs puts a halt to the expansion in output. In this case supply will tend to be rather elastic.

SUMMARY

1. Elasticity of demand (also called *price elasticity*) is a measure of the extent to which the quantity demanded of a commodity responds to a change in its price. We define it as the percentage change in quantity divided by the percentage change in price that brought it about. Elasticity is here defined to be a positive number that varies from zero to infinity.

2. When the numerical measure of elasticity is less than 1, demand is *inelastic*. This means that the percentage change in quantity is less than the percentage change in price that brought it about. When the numerical measure exceeds unity, demand is *elastic*. This means that the percentage change in quantity is greater than the percentage change in price that brought it about.

3. Elasticity and total revenue of sellers are related in this way: If elasticity is less than unity, a fall in price lowers total revenue; if elasticity is greater than unity, a fall in price raises total revenue; and if elasticity is unity, total revenue does not change as price changes.

4. The main determinant of the price elasticity of demand is the availability of substitutes for the commodity. The more and better the substitutes, the higher the elasticity. The price elasticity of a commodity group tends to be higher the more narrowly it is defined and the more adequate are its substitutes. Any one of a group of close substitutes will tend to have an elastic demand even though the group as a whole has a highly inelastic demand.

5. Elasticity of demand tends to be greater the longer the time over which adjustment occurs. Items that have few substitutes in the short run may develop ample substitutes when consumers have time to adapt.

6. Income elasticity is the percentage change in quantity demanded divided by the percentage change in income that brought it about. It tends to be lower the more basic, or staple, is the commodity. Thus luxuries tend to have higher income elasticities than necessities. The income elasticity of demand for a commodity may well change as income varies. For example, a commodity that has a high income elasticity at a low income (because increases in income bring it within reach of the typical household) may have a low or negative income elasticity at higher incomes (because with further rises in incomes it can be replaced by a superior substitute).

7. Cross-elasticity is the percentage change in quantity demanded divided by the percentage change in the price of some other commodity that brought it about. It is used to define commodities that are substitutes for one another (positive cross-elasticity) and commodities that complement one another (negative cross-elasticity).

8. Elasticity of supply is an important concept in economics. It measures the ratio of the percentage change in the quantity supplied of a commodity to the percentage change in its price. It is the analogue on the supply side to the elasticity of demand.

9. An appendix to this chapter, for students with some mathematical background, extends the analysis.

TOPICS FOR REVIEW

Elasticity of demand
Significance of elastic and inelastic demands
The difference between inelastic and perfectly inelastic
The relation between demand elasticity and total expenditure
Income elasticity of demand
Short-run and long-run demand curves
The difference between income-elastic and income-inelastic
Normal goods and inferior goods
Cross-elasticity of demand
Substitutes and complements
Elasticity of supply

DISCUSSION QUESTIONS

1. From the following quotations what (if anything) can you conclude about elasticity of demand?
   a. "Good weather resulted in record corn harvests and sent corn prices tumbling. For many corn farmers the result has been calamitous."
   b. "Ridership always went up when bus fares came down, but the increased patronage never was enough to prevent a decrease in overall revenue."
   c. "When the Cincinatti Telephone Company started charging for directory assistance calls, the number of [such] calls dropped 80 percent."
   d. "The 30 percent increase in postal rates has led us [The Narrangansett Electric Co.] to have 60 percent of our bills hand delivered instead of mailed."
   e. "Coffee to me is an essential—you've gotta have it no matter what the price."

2. What would you predict about the relative price elasticity of demand of (a) food, (b) meat, (c) beef, (d) chuck roast, (e) Safeway chuck roast? What would you predict about their relative income elasticities?

3. "Avocados have a very limited market, not greatly affected by price until the price falls to less than $.12 a pound. Then they are much demanded by manufacturers of dog food." Interpret this statement in terms of price elasticity.

4. "Video games have proven the big surprise of the 1980s in sales appeal. But per capita sales are much lower in Puerto Rico than the U.S., lower in Mississippi and Arkansas than in Illinois and Texas. Manufacturers are puzzled by the big differences." Can you offer an explanation in terms of elasticity?

5. What elasticity measure or measures would be useful in answering the following questions?
   a. Will cheaper transport into the central city help keep downtown shopping centers profitable?
   b. Will raising the bulk-rate postage rate increase or decrease the postal deficit?
   c. Are producers of toothpaste and mouthwash in competition with each other?
   d. What effect will falling gasoline prices have on the sale of cars that use diesel fuel?
   e. Why do rising interest rates hurt the sales of houses and of art that is purchased as an investment?

6. Interpret the following statements in terms of the relevant elasticity concept:
   a. "As fuel for tractors has gotten more expensive, many farmers have shifted from plowing their fields to no-till farming. No-till acreage increased from 30 million acres in 1972 to 95 million acres in 1982."
   b. "Fertilizer makers brace for dismal year as farm slump is projected."
   c. "When farmers are hurting, small towns feel the pain."

7. It has been observed recently that obesity is a more frequent medical problem for the relatively poor than for the middle-income classes. Can you use the theory of demand to shed light on this observation?

8. Suggest commodities that you think might have the following patterns of elasticity of demand.
   a. high income elasticity, high price elasticity
   b. high income elasticity, low price elasticity
   c. low income elasticity, low price elasticity
   d. low income elasticity, high price elasticity

9. Look at Table 6-5. Can you suggest why cigarettes and gasoline are inelastic but electricity is elastic? Why is furniture more elastic than all consumer goods taken together?

10. Look at Table 6-6. Can you suggest why gasoline is more income elastic than cigarettes or housing? Or why coffee is more income inelastic than beef?

11. In 1983 the new United States Football League was playing to half empty stadiums. The Michigan Panthers averaged 22,250 people at its regular season games. When the team made the playoffs, its owner Alfred Taubman *lowered* ticket prices about 30 percent and drew a crowd of over 60,000 to the Silverdome, near Detroit. "This crowd gave us a hint," said the Panthers' general manager. "We will sit down and take that turnout into consideration. I think tickets for Panther games will be cheaper next season."

    What does this tell us about price elasticity of demand? Does the fact that Detroit was suffering from 25 percent unemployment at the time have any relevance in evaluating the experience?

7 SUPPLY AND DEMAND IN ACTION I: PRICE CONTROLS, RENT CONTROLS, AND THE VOLUNTEER ARMY

The laws of supply and demand and the concepts of elasticity of demand and supply have immediate application to many real-world problems. In this chapter and the next, we apply these basic concepts and the method of comparative statics, first encountered on page 75. The method, you will recall, is to start from a position of equilibrium in the market and then introduce the change to be studied—for example, a shift to the left of the supply curve. Then we determine the new equilibrium position and compare it with the original one. The differences between the two positions of equilibrium (higher price, lower quantities actually exchanged) can be attributed to the change introduced for that is the only change that has been allowed to occur.

In this chapter we apply supply and demand analysis to situations in which the government has set either minimum or maximum prices. We then examine two case studies in some detail: rent controls, and the choice between a draft and a volunteer army. In Chapter 8 we examine a third case study: agriculture and U.S. policies toward it. At the end of Chapter 8 (pages 130–132) we draw some general conclusions about resource allocation and government intervention in markets.

THE THEORY OF FLOOR PRICES AND CEILING PRICES

In a free market, price tends to move toward its equilibrium value, where the quantities demanded and supplied are equal. Some government price controls are designed to hold the market price below equilibrium. In so doing they cause quantity demanded to exceed quantity supplied at the controlled price, creating shortages. Other government policies are designed to hold prices above equilibrium. In so doing they cause quantity supplied to exceed quantity demanded at the controlled price, creating surpluses. The consequences of these shortages or surpluses must then be dealt with.

Quantity Exchanged at Non-Equilibrium Prices

In competitive markets, price tends to change whenever quantity supplied does not equal quantity demanded. Thus price will move toward its equilibrium value, where there are neither unsatisfied suppliers nor unsatisfied demanders. However, price controls may hold price at a disequilibrium value. When this happens, what determines the quantity actually traded on the market? A moment's thought will show that any voluntary market transaction requires both a willing buyer and a willing seller. This means that if quantity demanded is less than quantity supplied, the former will determine the amount actually exchanged and the rest of the quantity supplied will remain in the hands of the unsuccessful sellers. On the other hand, if quantity demanded exceeds quantity supplied, the latter will determine the amount actually traded and the rest of the quantity demanded will represent desired purchases of unsuccessful buyers.

At any disequilibrium price, quantity exchanged is determined by the *lesser* of quantity demanded or quantity supplied.

This is shown graphically in Figure 7-1. Quantity exchanged at any price is determined by the curve *on the left* at that price—that is, the demand curve above, and the supply curve below, the equilibrium price.

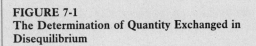

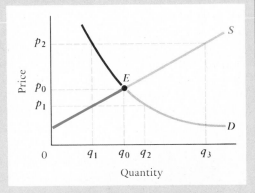

FIGURE 7-1
The Determination of Quantity Exchanged in Disequilibrium

In disequilibrium, quantity exchanged is determined by the *lesser* of quantity demanded or quantity supplied. At p_0 the market is in equilibrium, with quantity demanded equal to quantity supplied at q_0. For prices below p_0, such as p_1, the quantity exchanged will be determined by the supply curve. For example, the quantity q_1 will be exchanged at the disequilibrium price p_1 in spite of the excess demand of q_1q_2. For prices above p_0, such as p_2, the quantity exchanged will be given by the demand curve. For example, the quantity exchanged will be only q_1 at the price p_2 in spite of the excess supply of q_1q_3. Thus the darker portions of the S and D curves show the whole set of actual quantities exchanged at different prices.

Floor Prices

The government sometimes establishes a minimum or **floor price** for a good or service. Minimum wages for labor and guaranteed prices for certain agricultural commodities are well-known examples. If the floor price is set at or below the equilibrium price, it will have no effect because equilibrium will still be attainable and will not be inconsistent with the floor price set by law. If, however, the floor price is above the equilibrium price, it is said to be binding or "effective." We shall deal with situations in which it is binding.

Sometimes floor prices are simply rules that make it illegal to sell the commodity below the prescribed price. That is the case with the minimum wage, which is examined in some detail in Chapter 21. Sometimes floor prices are established by the government's announcing that it will guarantee a certain price, if necessary by buying the product itself at that price. For a long time our government bought gold at a guaranteed price of $35 an ounce. Such guarantees are also a feature of much of American agricultural policy, examined in detail in Chapter 8.

No matter what the mechanism, the key result of floor prices is always the same, as is illustrated in Figure 7-2:

Whenever price is maintained above the free-market level, the quantity that suppliers wish to sell will exceed the quantity buyers wish to purchase. Either an unsold surplus will exist or someone must step in and buy the excess production.

The consequences of excess supply will of course differ from commodity to commodity. If the commodity is labor which is subject to a minimum wage, excess supply translates into people without jobs. If the commodity is wheat, and more is produced than can be sold, the surplus wheat must accumulate in grain elevators or government warehouses. These consequences may or may not be "worth it" in terms of the other goals achieved. But the consequences are inevitable whenever the floor price is set above the market clearing equilibrium price, and nothing further is done.

Why might the government wish to incur these consequences? The answer lies in the fact that those who actually succeed in selling their commodities at the floor price are better off than if they had to accept the lower equilibrium price. Workers and farmers are among those who have persuaded the government to help them raise the prices of what they sell by establishing minimum prices.

Ceiling Prices

It is common in wartime, and increasingly frequent in peacetime, for the government to fix the *maximum prices* at which certain goods and services may be sold. Price controls on oil, natural gas, and

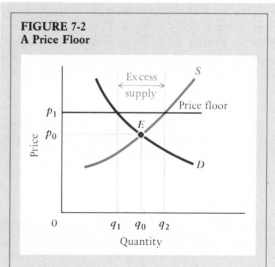

FIGURE 7-2
A Price Floor

If a price floor is above the equilibrium price, quantity supplied will exceed quantity demanded. The free-market equilibrium is at E, with price p_0 and quantity q_0. If the government makes it illegal for the price to fall below p_1, it has established an effective price floor. Quantity supplied will exceed quantity demanded by $q_1 q_2$. If the government does nothing, this excess supply will be in private hands and will either go to waste or accumulate in inventories. If the government buys the excess supply, sellers will get rid of the full quantity they wish to produce, q_2, but the government will have the quantity $q_1 q_2$ to store or dispose of.

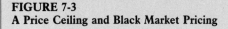

FIGURE 7-3
A Price Ceiling and Black Market Pricing

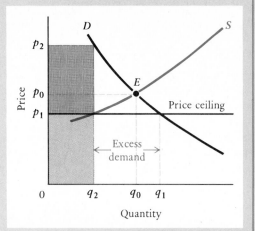

A ceiling price below the equilibrium price causes
excess demand and invites a black market. Equilibrium price is at p_0. If a price ceiling is set at p_1, the
quantity demanded will rise to q_1 and the quantity
supplied will fall to q_2. Quantity actually exchanged
will be q_2. Although excess demand is q_2q_1, price may
not legally rise to restore equilibrium. If all the available supply of q_2 were sold on a black market, price
to consumers would rise to p_2, with black marketeers
earning receipts shown by the shaded areas. The dark
shaded area shows the profit of those who buy at the
ceiling price and sell at the black market price.

rental housing have been features of the U.S. scene
for some or all of the time since World War II.
Indeed, in the face of continuing inflation there are
many who call for price controls in America to
prevent the hardships imposed on consumers by
continuing rises in the prices of many commodities.
Although frequently referred to as fixed or "frozen" prices, most price controls actually specify
the highest permissible price, often called the **ceiling price**, that producers may legally charge. Once
again we shall confine our attention to situations in
which the ceiling price is binding, that is, below
the free-market equilibrium price. This means that
the free-market price must be reduced. The forced
reduction will cause a fall in the quantity supplied,
an increase in the quantity demanded, and a short-

age of the commodity (see Figure 7-3). A first
prediction of the effect of price control in a competitive market is

Ceiling prices lead to excess demand for the commodity, and the quantity exchanged will fall below its equilibrium amount.

In inflationary situations, price controls often
take the form of "freezing" prices at current free-
market levels. At the moment of imposition the
price control is not effective, but as inflation occurs
the free-market price rises, and thus the controlled
price becomes an effective ceiling price.

Allocating a Commodity
in Short Supply

What happens to the excess demand produced
by establishing ceiling prices? The free market
eliminates excess demand by allowing price to rise,
thereby allocating the available supply among
would-be purchasers. Since this does not happen,
some other method of allocation must be adopted.
Experience shows that certain alternatives are
likely.

If stores sell their available supplies on a first-
come, first-served basis, people will rush to those
stores that are said to have stocks of any commodity
in short supply. In Europe during World War II,
the word—even the rumor—that a shop was selling
supplies of a scarce commodity could cause a local
stampede. Buyers often spent hours in line, waiting
to get into the shop, and supplies were usually
exhausted long before all were served. Standing in
lines is a way of life in many command economies
today.

A different system will develop if storekeepers
individually decide who will get the scarce commodities. Goods may be kept "under the counter"
and sold only to regular customers. This happened
in 1978, during periods of gasoline shortages, as
some gas station operators sold only to their regular
customers. When sellers decide to whom they will
(and will not) sell scarce supplies, allocation is by
sellers' preferences. If the government dislikes the
distribution that results from sellers' preferences,
it can do at least two things.

First, it can pass laws requiring suppliers to sell on a first-come, first-served basis. Some legislation of this type exists in the United States. To the extent that it is effective it leads to allocation according to willingness to stand in line. These laws are not easily enforceable, and there is little doubt that some available supplies are sold to favored customers according to sellers' preferences.

Second and more drastic, the government can ration the commodity. To do so, it prints only enough coupons to match the available supplies and then distributes the coupons to purchasers, who will need both money and ration coupons to buy the commodity. The coupons may be distributed equally among the population or on the basis of age, family status, occupation, or any other criterion.

Rationing substitutes the government's preferences for the seller's preferences in allocating a price-controlled commodity.

Coupon rationing appeals to many people because other schemes, such as first-come, first-served or allocation by sellers' preferences, may appear arbitrary or capricious and thus unfair.

Black Markets

Ceiling prices, with or without rationing, usually give rise to black markets. In a **black market** goods are sold (illegally) at prices above the legal maximum price. Most products have many retailers, and although it may be easy to police the producers, it is often impossible to control effectively the price at which retailers sell to the general public.

Suppose the government can control producers but not retailers. Production remains at the level consistent with the maximum permitted price because the producers receive the controlled price for their product. At the retail level, however, the opportunity for a black market arises because purchasers are willing to pay more than the ceiling price for the limited amounts of the commodity that are available. The theory of supply and demand leads to this prediction:

The potential for a black market always exists when binding ceiling prices are imposed because it will pay someone to buy at the controlled price and sell at the black-market price.

Figure 7-3 illustrates the limiting case in which all the available supply is sold on a black market. The development of such a market depends on there being a few people willing to risk heavy penalties by running a black-market supply organization and a reasonably large number of persons prepared to purchase goods illegally on such a market. This case is extreme because there are honest people in every society and because governments ordinarily have considerable power to enforce their price laws. Usually some, not all, of a price-controlled commodity is sold at a black-market price. (It is a revealing comment on human nature that there are few known cases in which binding price ceilings were not accompanied by the growth of a black market.)

Does the existence of a black market mean that the goals sought by imposing ceiling prices have been thwarted? This question can be answered only when we know what the government hopes to achieve with its ceiling price. Governments might be interested mainly in (1) restricting production (perhaps to release resources for war production), (2) keeping prices down, or (3) satisfying notions of equity in the consumption of a commodity that is temporarily unusually scarce. When ceiling prices are accompanied by a black market, the first objective, but not the second and third, is achieved. The second objective is frustrated to the extent that goods find their way onto the black market. If equity is the goal, effective ceiling prices on manufacturers plus an extensive black market at the retail level will produce the worst possible results. There will be less to go around than if there were no controls, and the available quantities will tend to go to those with the most money or the least social conscience.

The Experience with Ceiling Prices

There is evidence to confirm all these predictions about ceiling prices. Practically all belligerent countries in World War I and World War II put ceilings on prices of certain key items made exceptionally scarce by wartime requirements. These ceilings were always followed first by shortages, second by either the introduction of rationing or the growth of some alternative method of allocation such as sellers' preferences, and third by the rise of a black market. Establishing ceiling prices was more effective in limiting consumption than in controlling prices, although ceilings did restrain price increases because the patriotic response of many people to wartime controls led them to do without rather than to patronize the black market.

A more comprehensive kind of ceiling price control is sometimes attempted in peacetime in an effort to curb inflation. A freeze is put on virtually all prices. But if there is general excess demand, this kind of policy is sure to fail unless something is done to attack the causes of the excess of demand over supply. Price freezes sometimes work for a while, but eventually the backlog of purchasing power bursts out somewhere, and black markets follow. Pressure builds up on the government to remove the controls. Only after prices rise do supplies increase. This happened in the United States after the Nixon administration imposed a price freeze in 1971, and it has happened throughout the world whenever general ceiling prices have been imposed.

RENT CONTROLS: A CASE STUDY OF CEILING PRICE CONTROL

A widespread, growing use of ceiling prices in North America today relates to the rental of houses and apartments for private occupancy. Rent controls have been used the world over, with similar consequences: the creation of severe housing shortages, private allocation systems, and black markets. For example, to make up the difference between the controlled rent and the free-market rent, the landlord may charge the new tenant a grossly inflated sum for a few shabby sticks of furniture. Alternatively, landlords may ration in accordance with their own preferences for tenants and discriminate against students, families with young children, or on some other basis.

Controls have existed in New York City, London, Paris, and many other large cities at least since World War II. In Sweden and Britain, where rent controls on unfurnished apartments have existed for decades, housing shortages are endemic except in neighborhoods where population is declining. Whole areas of London are full of abandoned, rotting houses that would have lasted for centuries but which, at controlled rentals, did not even pay the owner the cost of upkeep. When British controls were extended to furnished apartments in 1973, the supply of such accommodations dried up, at least until loopholes were found in the law. When rent controls were initiated in Rome in 1978, a housing shortage developed virtually overnight. This kind of rent control-induced shortage led University of Chicago Professors George Stigler and Milton Friedman to point to the conflict between "ceilings" and "roofs."

Rent controls are spreading in the United States. Economic theory makes a number of predictions that are useful in understanding the current American experience with rent controls and in predicting the consequences.

The Theory of Ceiling Prices Applied to Rent Controls

Rent controls are just a special case of ceiling prices. Controls are usually imposed to freeze rents at their current level at a time when equilibrium rents are rising either because demand is shifting rightward (due to forces such as rising population and income) or because supply is shifting leftward (due to forces such as rising costs). Soon rents are being held below the free-market equilibrium level and excess demand appears. Figure 7-3 can be applied to rent controls. The following predictions about rent controls are simply applications to housing of results that apply to any commodity subject to binding ceiling prices.

1. There will be a housing shortage in the sense that quantity demanded will exceed quantity supplied.

2. The actual quantity of accommodation will be less than if free-market rents had been charged.
3. The shortage will lead to alternative allocation schemes. Landlords may allocate by sellers' preferences, or the government may intervene. In the housing market, government intervention usually takes the form of security-of-tenure laws, which protect the tenant from eviction and thus give existing tenants priority over potential new tenants.
4. Black markets will appear. Landlords may require large lump-sum entrance fees from new tenants. In general, the larger the housing shortage, the bigger the sum required. In the absence of security-of-tenure laws, landlords may force tenants out when their leases expire, and they may even try to evict them to extract a large entrance fee from new tenants.

Special Aspects of the Housing Market

Housing has unusual attributes that make the analysis of rent controls somewhat special. The most important is the nature of the commodity itself. So far in this book we have mainly considered markets for commodities that are consumed soon after they are purchased. But housing is an example of a **durable good,** a good that yields its services only gradually over an extended period of time. Once built, an apartment can last for decades or even centuries, yielding its valuable services continuously over that time. Thus the supply of rental accommodation depends on the *stock* of rental housing available, and in any year it is composed mainly of buildings built in prior years. The stock is added to by conversions of housing from other uses and construction of new buildings, and it is diminished by conversions to other uses and demolition or abandonment of existing buildings whose economic life is over. The stock usually changes slowly from year to year.

These considerations mean we can draw more than one supply curve for rental accommodation, depending on how much time is allowed for reactions to occur to any given level of rents. We shall distinguish just two such curves. The *long-run supply curve* relates rents to the quantity of rental accommodation that will be supplied after sufficient time has passed for all adjustments to be made. The *short-run supply curve* relates rents to quantity supplied when only a short time—say, a few months—is allowed for adjustments to be made in response to a change in rents. We shall assume that in the short run very few new conversions and very little new construction can occur. As we saw in Chapter 6, elasticity of supply is likely to be greater in the long run than in the short run.

The Long-Run Supply Curve

Among the many suppliers of rental accommodations are large investment companies and individuals with modest savings invested in one or two small apartments. There is a large potential source of supply, for it is relatively easy to build a new apartment or to convert an existing house and offer its units for rent. If the expected return from investing in new apartments rises significantly above the return on comparable other investments, there will be a flow of investment funds into the building of new apartments. However, if the return from apartments falls significantly below that obtainable on comparable investments, funds will go elsewhere. The construction of new apartments will fall off and possibly stop altogether. Old apartments will not be replaced as they wear out, so the quantity available will fall drastically. Therefore the long-run supply curve of apartments is highly elastic.

The Short-Run Supply Curve

Now consider the supply response over a few months. What if rents rise? Even though it immediately becomes profitable to invest in new apartments, it may well take years for land to be obtained, plans drawn up, and construction completed. Thus a long time may pass between the decision to create more apartments and the occupancy by tenants of the new apartments built in response to market signals. Of course, some existing housing can be more quickly converted to rental uses, but in many cases even this will take more than a few months.

What if rents fall? New construction will fall off, which will surely decrease the supply at some time in the future. It will, however, pay the owners of existing apartments with no attractive alternative use of their rental units to rent them for whatever they will earn, providing that the rentals at least cover current out-of-pocket costs such as taxes and heating. Some rental housing can be abandoned or converted to other uses, but, again, this will not usually happen very quickly.

Thus the short-run supply curve that relates rentals to the quantity supplied tends to be quite inelastic at the level of the quantity currently supplied. The longer the time horizon, the less inelastic it will be. For the very short run, however, it is likely to be almost completely inelastic.

Supply Response to Changes in Rents

If rents rise due to a housing shortage, what will the supply response be? In the short run, the quantity will remain more or less the same because the short-run supply curve is inelastic. For a while existing landlords will make **windfall profits,** profits that bear no relation to current or historical costs. Yet these profits are the spur to the long-run allocation of resources. New construction will begin, and after a year or two new rental units will begin to come onto the market. The quantity will continue to expand until a new point on the long-run supply curve has been attained. At that point all windfall profits have been eliminated.

If rents decrease, the quantity supplied will also remain more or less unchanged because of the inelastic short-run supply curve. Firms that were breaking even will now suffer windfall losses. As the profitability of supplying rental accommodations falls, new construction will be curtailed. But it will take time before the stock of rental housing shrinks to its new point on the long-run supply curve. Only then will it again pay to maintain the stock of rental housing.

Short-run windfall profits or losses provide the signals that bring about long-run supply adjustments in a free market.

Because houses are durable, they will not quickly disappear. But owners of rental properties can speed the shrinkage in various ways. Some apartments can be withdrawn from the rental market and sold to owner-occupiers more or less on an "as is" basis. Others can be converted into cooperatives or condominiums. Other apartments occupy land with valuable alternative uses. If rents fall far enough, it will pay to demolish those apartments and use the land for something else. (Of course, it requires a substantial and long-lasting fall in rents before demolition costs are worth incurring.)

Many existing apartment buildings and other rental accommodations have no real alternative uses and will continue to serve as apartments until they are abandoned as useless. Yet the useful life of an apartment depends on how well it is maintained. In general, the less spent on maintenance and repairs, the shorter the structure's effective life. The lower the rents, the less will it pay landlords to spend on upkeep, and thus the faster the apartment will "wear out."

If rental revenues fall below the minimum costs of operation (which include taxes and heating), the owner may simply abandon the apartment. Although this may sound extreme, it has happened repeatedly in North America and Europe. When it happens, a stock of housing that might have lasted decades or even centuries is dissipated within a few years.

The special features of the housing market lead to an important additional prediction about rent controls.

Because the long-run supply curve of rental housing is highly elastic, rent controls that hold rents below their free-market levels for an extended period will inevitably lead to a large reduction in the quantity of rental housing available.

This prediction is illustrated in Figure 7-4.

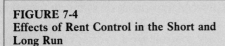

FIGURE 7-4
Effects of Rent Control in the Short and Long Run

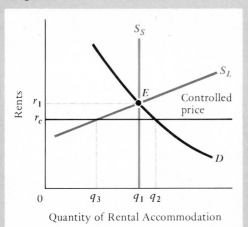

Quantity of Rental Accommodation

Rent control causes housing shortages that worsen as time passes. The controlled rent, r_c, is below the equilibrium rent r_1. The short-run supply of housing is shown by the inelastic curve S_S. Thus quantity supplied remains at q_1 in the short run, and the housing shortage is q_1q_2. Over time the quantity supplied shrinks, as shown by the long-run supply curve S_L. In long-run equilibrium there are only q_3 units of rental accommodation, far fewer than when controls were instituted. Since the long-run supply is quite elastic, the housing shortage of q_3q_2 that occurs after supply has fully adjusted ends up being much larger than the initial shortage of q_1q_2.

The Demand for Rental Housing

There are many reasons to expect the demand for apartments and other forms of rental housing to be quite elastic. As the relative price of rental accommodation in an area rises, each of the following will occur:

1. Some people will stop renting and buy instead.
2. Some will move to where rental housing is cheaper.
3. Some will economize on the amount of housing they consume by renting smaller, cheaper ac-

commodations (or renting out to others a room or two in their present accommodations).
4. Some will double up and others will not "undouble" (for example, young adults will not move out of parental homes as quickly as they might otherwise do).

Such occurrences contribute to a substantial elasticity of the demand for rental housing: increases in rents will sharply decrease the quantity demanded.

Rent controls prevent such increases in rents from occurring. Thus, even while the supply of rental housing is shrinking for the reasons discussed above, the signal to economize on rental accommodation is *not* given through rising rentals. The housing shortage grows as the stock of rental accommodation shrinks while nothing decreases the quantity demanded.

When Rent Controls May Work: Short-Term Shortages

Pressure for rent controls seems to arise in response to rapidly rising rents for housing. The case for controlling rising rentals is strongest when the shortages causing the increasing rents are temporary.

Sometimes there is a temporary influx of population into an area. Possibly an army camp is established in wartime, or a pipeline or a power complex is being built, and many workers are required for the time being even though few will remain behind. When the temporary workers flood in, market rents will rise. New construction of apartments will not occur, however, because investors recognize the rise in demand and rentals as temporary. In this case, rent control may stop existing owners from gaining windfall profits, with few harmful supply effects since a long-run supply response is not expected in any case. After the boom is over, demand will fall and free-market rents will return to the controlled level (their original level). Controls may then be removed with little further effect. This is illustrated in Figure 7-5.

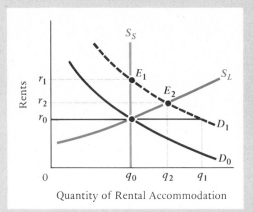

FIGURE 7-5
Rent Controls in Response to Increasing Demand

Rents: r_1, r_2, r_0

S_S, E_1, E_2, S_L, D_1, D_0

0 q_0 q_2 q_1

Quantity of Rental Accommodation

Rent controls prevent a temporary skyrocketing of rents when demand rises but also prevent the long-term supply adjustment to demand increases.

Temporary demand fluctuations. The short-run supply curve S_S applies. In the free market a temporary rise in demand from D_0 to D_1 and then back to D_0 will change rents from r_0 to r_1 and then back to r_0. Rent control would hold rents at r_0 throughout; there would be a housing shortage due to excess demand of q_0q_1 as long as demand was D_1, but rent control would not affect the quantity of housing available.

Permanent changes in demand. The long-run supply curve S_L applies. A permanent rise in demand from D_0 to D_1 will cause free-market rents to rise temporarily from r_0 to r_1 and then to fall to r_2 as the quantity of accommodation supplied grows from q_0 to q_2. Controlling the rent at r_0 to prevent windfall profits produces a permanent housing shortage of q_0q_1.

Even when rent controls have no long-run adverse effect, there will be some disadvantages. At controlled rents there will be a severe housing shortage but no incentive to existing tenants to economize on housing and no incentive for potential suppliers to improvise by finding ways of providing extra short-run accommodation. If rents rise on the free market, existing tenants will economize and some tenants and owners will find it profitable to rent out rooms. Even though the supply of permanent apartments does not change, the supply of casual temporary accommodation (mobile homes,

for example) will increase. Such reactions are induced by the signal of rising rents but inhibited by controls.

Temporary controls are also disadvantageous because political pressures to make them permanent may prove irresistible. During World War II, many American cities imposed rent controls because of temporary shortages. Most cities removed controls after the war to allow the housing supply to expand when factors of production were again available for construction. Some cities, among them New York, kept the controls, thus inhibiting the adjustments in supply that were needed to eliminate the shortages.

When Rent Controls Fail: Long-Term Shortages

Long-Run Increases in Demand

What if the rise in demand for rental accommodation is not temporary? An example is provided by the sun belt states, where in-migration is increasing the population rapidly, creating severe local housing shortages and forcing up rents. Such increases in rentals give the signal that apartments are very profitable investments. A consequent building boom will lead to increases in the quantity supplied, and it will continue as long as windfall profits can be earned.

If rent controls are imposed in the face of such long-term increases in demand, they will prevent short-run windfalls, but they will also prevent the needed long-run construction boom from occurring. Thus controls will convert a temporary shortage into a permanent one. This too is illustrated in Figure 7-5.

Inflation in Housing Costs

Rent controls also fail when they are introduced to protect tenants from rent increases in an inflationary world. Inflation raises both the costs of construction of new housing and the costs of operating and maintaining existing housing. As we saw in Chapter 5, a rise in costs shifts the supply curve upward and to the left. If inflation raises the

THE CLAMOR FOR RENT CONTROL

In the face of the predicted and observed consequences, why does rent control persist and even grow? The answer is largely that the primary victims of rent control do not identify themselves as such, while the primary beneficiaries do.

Whatever the overall effects of rent control, existing tenants who can stay in their present locations will benefit from it. Existing tenants know that rent controls hold down the cost of housing. (The only risk to them comes if landlords allow their apartment buildings to deteriorate.) Thus existing tenants constitute an important political constituency for rent controls.

Many renting families live on incomes that are small, fixed, and being eroded steadily by inflation. Renters include a disproportionate fraction of the aged, the unemployed, welfare recipients, and members of minority groups. They also include many students. A high percentage of these groups are paying at least half their money incomes to a landlord (who seems never to be in view except to collect the rent), and these groups are truly being squeezed by the rising costs of everything. (Of course not all existing renters are poor, nor landlords rich.)

If the beneficiaries of rent control are existing tenants, who are the victims? The housing shortage hurts those who will want rental housing that will not be there in the future. The elderly couple who fight to keep rent control on the apartment they occupy are behaving wholly in their own best interest. But they are making life more difficult for the next generation of aged couples, many of whom will not find housing of the same quality if rent controls are kept. The welfare family protected today will have a hard time finding housing if it moves when the opportunity for a job arises or when its present apartment house is abandoned. Minority groups generally will find that their members are hurt in the long run by the steadily shrinking quantity and quality of available rental housing.

Why do so many people favor rent controls when control-induced shortages will make it more difficult for them to find a suitable apartment? The answer, when it is not an ideological dislike of landlords, seems to be that they do not recognize the link between the lower rents they will pay—if they are lucky enough to find a rent controlled apartment where they want it—and the *decreased chance* of finding such an apartment. If they knew that rent control was the reason they had to wait so long and search so hard to find accommodation, they might prefer to pay the free-market rent. But they do not know this—and once "in," they will be protected by rent controls.

Thus the call for rent control comes both from existing tenants, who gain at the expense of those who do not have secured leases in rental housing, and from potential tenants, who underestimate the adverse effects on *them* of the rent control-induced housing shortage. In contrast, the *articulate* opposition is the much smaller (and less sympathetic) group of landlords. The silent victims, who are the future unsuccessful searchers for rental units, may never realize the causal link between rent controls and the housing shortage from which they suffer.

That many individuals are either selfish or myopic in calling for rent control is understandable. That their leaders and public representatives do not appreciate and weigh the long-term consequences is less comprehensible except in very political terms. Economic theory predicts and worldwide experience confirms that rent controls create shortages, that shortages do not benefit the population as a whole, that the real costs of providing housing do not diminish when controls are imposed, and that when the private market does not provide housing, either tenants will bear the cost by doubling up or doing without or public taxes will have to be raised to provide public housing. Perhaps the politicians are myopic too, judging next month's election (and hence today's constituency) to be more important than the adverse, long-run future effects.

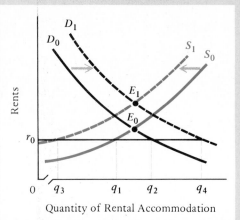

FIGURE 7-6
An Ever-growing Housing Shortage

In a growing, inflation-prone economy, rent control will cause the housing shortage to worsen year by year. In a growing economy the demand curve is continually shifting rightward as more people with higher real incomes demand more housing. In an inflationary economy the supply curve is continually shifting leftward because construction, maintenance, and operating costs are rising. Such shifts, when combined with rent control, cause the housing shortage to grow over time. For example, when the curves are D_0 and S_0, rent control at r_0 is accompanied by a housing shortage of q_1q_2. When the curves have shifted to D_1 and S_1, however, the same controlled rent causes an overall housing shortage of q_3q_4.

costs of providing rental housing above the rents received, it does not pay landlords to maintain buildings. As a result they become dilapidated. Eventually as landlords find rental revenue falling short of minimum unavoidable costs, they will actually abandon their buildings. This has happened in many places including New York City. Large areas of the city have suffered this fate, becoming ghost neighborhoods until either the city takes over and becomes a slumlord, or instead tears down the abandoned housing.

Fixed rent controls in an economy that is experiencing a steady inflation will produce a housing shortage that grows over time. If inflation is com-

bined with growth in demand, the growth in the housing shortage becomes very large (see Figure 7-6).

Of course the housing shortage does not need to grow if the controlled rent is allowed to rise as fast as the equilibrium rent. But the usual *purpose* of controls is to hold rents down in the face of rapid increases in costs and demand. As a result, controlled rents have been allowed to rise over the years much less fast than the rate of inflation. Thus the housing shortage in fact grows over the years, although not as fast as it would if controlled rents were *never* changed.

The Alternatives to Rent Controls

Most rent controls in the United States today are not responses to short-term shortages but are meant to protect the average tenant against both profiteering by landlords in the face of severe local shortages and the steadily rising cost of housing, the result of inflation and economic growth. From Cambridge, Massachusetts, to Santa Monica, California, many cities have adopted rent controls, and others are considering them.

Advocates of starting or keeping rent controls often say that construction costs are now too high to erect buildings that offer apartments at rents that middle-class people can afford. Suppose this to be true. How could this problem be handled?

One possibility is to control rents below the cost of new building, with the inevitable consequence of a shortage of rental housing that grows as the stock of rental accommodation wears out and is not replaced.

An alternative is for government to step in with public housing and fill the gap between total demand and private supply. Subsidized public housing will then be financed at the taxpayers' expense (since the high costs of housing must be paid by someone).

A third possibility is to let rents rise on the free market sufficiently to cover costs. If "middle-class people" (and others) really decide they cannot afford these apartments and will not rent them, then the building of apartments will cease. It is more likely, however, in light of past consumer behavior, that agonizing choices will be made to spend a higher proportion of total income on housing and/or to economize on housing.

The costs of providing additional housing cannot be voted out of existence; they can only be transferred from one set of persons to another.

Several European countries have been through the whole process of imposing rent controls to protect tenants and ending up with excess demand and an increasingly expensive program of subsidized public housing. In the face of other public needs, they are now trying to give more scope to private markets for housing, but policies of rent controls are always politically popular. Only time will tell how far the United States is to travel the same path. Economics cannot tell society which hard choice to make, but it can show what the choices are. The greatest danger is that the long-run costs will be neglected in making the choice.

THE VOLUNTEER ARMY VERSUS THE DRAFT

A volunteer army enlists only those who choose voluntarily to be soldiers. But, as with any civilian occupation, the main method of adjusting quantity supplied to quantity demanded is by altering the market price. Thus the volunteer army is a price-system army—one in which soldiers' pay and non-monetary rewards are adjusted until the required army is obtained. In contrast, the **draft** uses legal compulsion to raise an army of requisite size. By various means, certain individuals are chosen for service, and the legal power of the state is used to force service from all who are not willing to face the penalties for refusing to serve.

From 1940 to 1973, the United States relied heavily on "selective service" to provide enough recruits to supplement volunteers and to fill the requirements of the American armed services. The draft was never popular with those who might be called, but it was not until the end of American ground participation in the Vietnam War that the draft was ended and the armed forces became composed entirely of volunteers. The shift to a volunteer army was accompanied by a near doubling of entry level pay and allowances, an increase that made soldiers' earnings comparable to those of relatively unskilled civilians of the same age group.

In 1980 registration for the draft was again reintroduced, and the possibility that the draft will again be used sometime during the 1980s cannot be dismissed. What difference could it make? The simple theory of supply and demand sheds a good deal of light on this question.

The two most important kinds of drafts are the **lottery draft,** in which the government selects by chance from the eligible pool of potential draftees, and the **exemption draft,** in which the government grants exemptions on the basis of such attributes as age, health, occupation, and family status.

Effects of Alternative Methods

Some people enjoy the military life, possibly because they have martial temperaments or because they are otherwise suited to the autocratic structure and discipline of the military organization. Thus, if wages for military service were exactly equal to wages for civilian occupations requiring similar amounts of education, training, and physical condition, some persons would choose military careers. For others, a preference for civilian occupations might be overcome by various premiums in military pay. Indeed, the higher the level of military pay, the larger the number of volunteers. The supply curve of volunteers for military service is upward-sloping, even though for some individuals abhorrence of the army and of wars may mean that no level of pay would induce them to serve voluntarily.

Suppose that at any moment the nation's military requirements can be represented by a wholly inelastic demand curve. This reflects the assumption that the size of the required army is set by Congress on the basis of considerations other than the level of military pay. If at the going wage rate the military cannot enlist enough recruits, it will have to induce extra men and women to serve by

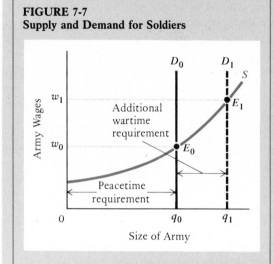

FIGURE 7-7
Supply and Demand for Soldiers

Increases in army wage rates and the draft are alternative means of raising an army of a given size. Suppose the going army wage rate is w_0 and D_0 and S are the demand for and supply of soldiers. A volunteer army of size q_0 will be recruited. Now let demand shift to D_1 because of the outbreak of war. We assume the supply curve does not change. To induce an additional q_0q_1 soldiers to serve, the wage rate must rise to w_1 or q_0q_1 soldiers must be drafted, with the wage rate held at w_0.

raising military pay or compel them to serve by law. This is true in both peacetime and wartime, and thus the theory is the same. As a practical matter, however, the problems are likely to be much more severe in war because the size of the extra group of recruits required is usually very large and the supply curve is likely to be quite inelastic at the quantities required to staff a wartime army. No major war has been fought in modern times with an all-volunteer army. These assumptions about the supply and demand for soldiers are illustrated in Figure 7-7.

Who Serves?

In the volunteer army, those who serve will be those who are the least reluctant to do so. Unless

there is a great wave of patriotic enlistment, it is unlikely that many nuclear physicists or successful lawyers will volunteer, or that many others with high-paying civilian jobs will do so. It is also unlikely that many rich people or their children will choose to enlist. One might reasonably expect the army to be recruited mainly from the poor, the undereducated, and the unemployed. These are the people with the lowest opportunity costs, so they are the most likely to be attracted by the steady pay, educational potential, and job security that goes with the army. Volunteer armies, past and present, have generally been composed of this sort of recruit. The only exceptions are major, "popular" wars where patriotic fervor assures a large representative group of volunteers.

The lottery draft (if it is a true lottery) will select a random cross section of people with respect to such attributes as education, occupation, and wealth. The pianist, the plumber, the plutocrat, and the physicist all have an equal chance of service. This system provides equal treatment that is readily understood by everyone, but it has other consequences. It will cause a much greater reduction in the value of civilian output than other methods. Moreover, it does not allow the government to establish its own priorities and to designate certain groups of individuals as too valuable in the civilian economy to be released into the army.

The exemption draft permits the government to establish exemptions based on some criteria of value to the civilian economy. To minimize the loss in civilian production, the authorities might exempt people with the highest earnings and draft only those with the lowest earnings. Most people would reject such an income-based exemption system on grounds of equity, but it is interesting to observe that it would produce broadly the same sort of army as would the volunteer system. An exemption draft more usually exempts on some criteria of social desirability, or the value to the nation of an individual's occupation, rather than on the basis of income. A physicist may be exempted because his services are regarded as essential to the war effort or to the general national interest; a baseball superstar may not be exempted even though the money value of his civilian services is very high, vastly higher than the physicist's.

When the required army is so large that the number of allowable exemptions must be small—for example, in a war such as World War II or in a small, embattled country such as Israel—general agreement on who should be exempted is probably easily reached. When the required army is smaller—for example, in the Vietnam War—and many more exemptions are possible, there is room for considerable conflict. Should women be drafted? Should graduate students in physics, economics, and German literature receive exemptions? Because their protests are thought by the authorities to be of negative social value, should the social revolutionary and the antiwar demonstrator lose the exemptions to which they would otherwise be entitled?

There is plenty of room for genuine disagreement over which social values should be used, as well as for actual abuse when exemptions are denied or removed as a punishment levied without normal legal processes and against which there is little chance of appeal. Generally, the greater the range of exemptions allowed and the greater the disagreement in society over the use of the armed forces, the more the difficulties of the exemption draft can be expected to increase.

A volunteer army will be much less representative of the population as a whole than an army raised by a lottery draft. An exemption draft will be intermediate between them.

Who Pays?

The various systems affect the total bill and who must pay it, as is analyzed in Figure 7-8.

In the volunteer army the extra soldiers are attracted by an increase in pay. The total wage bill rises, and the taxpayer pays the cost. Much of the extra pay goes to new recruits, but some of it goes to people who would have served in any case. They benefit from the reluctance of their fellow citizens to serve. Thus the total extra cost is borne by taxpayers, but only part of it is received by the new volunteers.

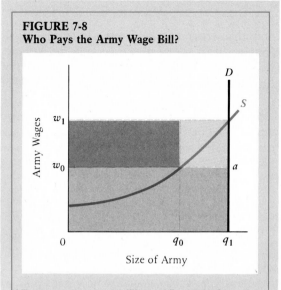

FIGURE 7-8
Who Pays the Army Wage Bill?

Taxpayers lose and willing soldiers gain from the volunteer army; draftees lose and taxpayers gain from the draft. With wage rate w_0, if the army is increased in size from q_0 to q_1 using the draft, the total wage payments are as indicated by the light gray shaded area ($w_0 a q_1 0$). An army of size q_1 can be recruited by offering the wage rate w_1. The total wage bill then rises to the entire shaded area. Of this, the color-shaded area represents payments to the new recruits in excess of the amount that would have been paid to draftees. The dark gray shaded area represents a windfall to soldiers already in the army. They receive a wage increase not needed to cause them to serve.

In the draft all soldiers are paid the basic army wage. The taxpayer pays much less, but (by compulsion) an army of the same size is raised. The difference in cost is paid by the draftees in the form of lost civilian opportunities and lost freedom of choice. Depending on who the draftees are, how they react to army life, and what their alternatives for employment may be, the cost may be very small or very large.

A volunteer army benefits financially those who would have volunteered even with a draft; it also benefits all who would have been forced to serve against their will. But it is more expensive to taxpayers.

Evaluation of Alternatives

More than economics is involved in evaluating alternative plans; there are, especially in wartime, issues of equity, of equal exposure to risk, and of patriotism. But economic differences in terms of who serves, who pays, and who ends up doing something he or she would prefer not to do are also important. The predictions we have reached can help in understanding the normative issues even though they cannot settle the debate on which system is best.

Who Should Pay?

What affects who should pay? In the volunteer army it is the general taxpayer who pays the full cost. Because the services of the army are supposed to be for the public good, some regard this as wholly appropriate. But others ask why a relatively low-income taxpayer should have to pay the cost of raising soldiers' wages because the children of the wealthy do not choose to serve.

In either the lottery or the exemption draft of young men, the unwilling draftee bears a good part of the cost of his service by virtue of being unlucky enough to be drafted or to lack the skills that would have led to exemption. (Note that these skills may themselves be related to wealth or economic status: the son of wealthy white parents is more likely to be a doctor, a student, or a scientist than is the son of poor blacks.) Because there are poor and rich among draftees, among taxpayers, and to a lesser extent among volunteers, the purely distributional issues of how to raise an army are complex.

Who is the primary beneficiary of an exemption from service? When an individual serves in the army against his will, he may be regarded as discharging a personal obligation to his country or providing a public service—or both. When a congressman or a concert pianist is allowed to avoid military service, who is the big gainer? If he is the gainer, perhaps he should pay; if you are, perhaps you should pay. People differ in their views as to who really benefits and on whether this should affect who should pay.

The issues clearly depend on competing values: on equity of treatment, on the desired composition of a citizen army, on the efficient use of human resources, and on the justice of alternative ways of paying the cost. Economic analysis can sharpen the debate by making clear which schemes have which effects. It can also identify important quantitative magnitudes. One example is whether or not the volunteer army involves a large cost to the taxpayer and a large premium to the already willing soldier; the amounts depend on the *slope* of the supply curve. If the supply curve is very steep, it will take a large increase in wages to attract volunteers, and the areas above w_0a in Figure 7-8 will loom large. If the supply curve is very flat, a small wage increase will suffice, and the extra costs will be small.

The evidence of the recent peacetime volunteer army suggests that the supply curve is moderately elastic (elasticity about unity) at least in the face of a generally depressed economy. Armed forces' salaries and bonuses were increased by an aggregate of about 25 percent in 1981 and 1982, making them fully competitive with civilian pay for similar education and skill qualifications. Both new enlistments and reenlistments increased roughly in proportion to the pay increases and each of the services achieved or exceeded its enlistment goals.

Who Should Serve?

One of the hot issues of a renewed draft would surely be whether women should be included. However that issue is decided, a person who feels strongly that military service should be an overriding and equal obligation of all, independent of taste, wealth, talent, or temperament, will probably prefer the lottery draft. Similarly, for one who wants the army to represent as wide a cross section of the society as possible so that the places and the manner in which the army is used are a subject of serious concern to all groups in the nation, the lottery draft is most likely to be satisfactory.

This does not change the fact that the lottery draft involves both compulsion and a higher loss in the value of civilian output than any other system. The exemption draft provides less equal treatment of individuals and a less representative army than the lottery draft, but it allows scope to exempt from service those whose civilian talents are regarded by the government as especially important. Thus it may avoid certain inefficiencies in the use of personnel, but those with no special merit (in the eyes of the authorities) cannot avoid service by reason of mere wealth.

If efficiency and lack of compulsion are given great weight as goals, the volunteer army becomes attractive. It does not use people of high earning power, and so avoids certain evident inefficiencies. It provides less compulsion than other schemes. The volunteer army compels only by economic pressures. It leads, however, to an unrepresentative military, with a predominance of poorer, relatively uneducated people. It is racially different, too, with a larger percentage of blacks and other minority groups. For those who believe the army will be more responsive to civilian influences if it is a cross section of the population, this unrepresentativeness is a major disadvantage.

SUMMARY

1. The elementary theory of supply, demand, and price provides powerful tools for analyzing and understanding some real-world problems and policies. This chapter and the next one illustrates a few of them.

2. Floor prices that hold the price of a commodity above its equilibrium price cause surpluses of the good or service whose price is kept high. Either the potential seller is left with a good or a service that cannot be sold, or the government must step in and buy the surplus. While there may be reasons for establishing floor prices, these are inevitable consequences.

3. Ceiling prices that are binding cause shortages and provide a strong incentive for black marketeers to buy at the controlled price and sell at the higher free-market price.

4. Rent controls are a persistent and spreading form of price ceiling. The major effect of rent control is a shortage of rental accommodation that gets worse due to a slow but inexorable decline in the quantity of rental housing.

5. Rent controls can be an effective response to temporary situations in which there is a ban on building or a transitory increase in demand. They will almost surely fail when they are introduced as a response to a long-run increase in demand or to inflation in the costs of providing rental housing.

6. The volunteer army, the lottery draft, and the exemption draft are alternative ways to raise an army of given size. Differences among these systems can be analyzed using the tools of demand and supply.

7. The volunteer army will produce an army of persons with the lowest opportunity cost in civilian life. This will tend to weight the army heavily with the poor, the undereducated, and the unemployed. The exemption draft excludes the groups the government wishes to exclude and produces a cross section of the rest. The lottery draft selects a cross section of the whole population and is likely to have soldiers with a higher average civilian opportunity cost than any of the other systems.

8. The cost to the taxpayer is highest in the volunteer army. In the lottery or exemption drafts, draftees pay much of the cost in lost civilian opportunities. With the volunteer army, those who were willing to serve in any event are paid more than is necessary to have them serve; they benefit from the reluctance of others to serve.

TOPICS FOR REVIEW

Comparative statics
Floor prices and ceiling prices
Allocation by sellers' preferences, rationing, and black markets
Windfall profits and their allocative function
Short-run and long-run supply curves
Alternative methods of raising an army
Benefits and costs of a volunteer army

DISCUSSION QUESTIONS

1. "When a controlled item is vital to everyone, it is easier to start controlling the price than to stop controlling it. Such controls are popular with consumers, regardless of their uneconomic consequences. In this respect oil price controls resemble rent controls." Explain why it may be inefficient to have such controls, why they may be popular, and why, if they are popular, the government might nevertheless choose to decontrol prices.

2. If there is an opportunity for a black market with ceiling prices, is there a similar opportunity with floor prices?

3. When in the mid 1970s there was a shortage of natural gas, the columnist William Safire called it "the unnatural shortage of natural gas." He wrote: "Be angry at the real villains: the Washington-knows-best Congressmen, the self-anointed consumer 'protectors' and the regulatory bureaucracy. They thought they could protect the consumer by breaking the laws of supply and demand, and as a result have made a classic case against government intervention." From these remarks what do you judge the policy to have been? Could *producers* have created the shortage of natural gas? If so, how? How would you define a "shortage"? Is there a useful distinction between a "natural shortage" and an "unnatural shortage"?

4. Medical and hospital care in Britain is provided free to individuals by the National Health Service, with the costs paid by taxation. Some British doctors complain that patients want "too much" medical care; patients complain that they have to wait "too long" in doctors' offices for the care they get, and months or years for needed operations. Use the theory of supply and demand to discuss these complaints. Would you expect a private (pay) medical market to grow up alongside the National Health Service? Would you expect the government to welcome or discourage such a second service? Can you reconcile your analysis with the fact that polls always show the National Health Service to be very popular in the population at large?

5. The Yarvard Law School, in Princetown, has 1,000 qualified applicants for 200 places in the first-year class. It is debating a number of alternative admission criteria: (a) a lottery, (b) date of initial application, (c) LSAT score, (d) recommendations from alumni, (e) place of residence of applicant. An economist on the faculty determined that if the tuition level is doubled, the excess demand will disappear. Argue for (or against) using the tuition rate to replace each of the other suggested criteria.

6. It is sometimes asserted that the rising costs of construction are putting housing out of the reach of ordinary citizens. Who bears the heaviest cost when rentals are kept down by (a) rent controls, (b) a subsidy to tenants equal to some fraction of their rent payments, and (c) low-cost public housing.

7. In England rents are set by public bodies that are instructed to fix fair rents without regard for local conditions of demand and supply. What might this mean? Analyze some of the effects of this policy on the workings of local housing markets.

8. In the case of each of the following alternative major objectives, what method to increase the size of the army might be favored?
   a. to minimize the cost to the taxpayer
   b. to have an army that is broadly representative of the whole society
   c. to minimize the loss in value of civilian output
   d. to give the individual maximum freedom of choice as to whether to serve
   e. to use service in the army as a sanction against behavior disapproved of by the authorities

9. How might each of the following affect the willingness of Congress to utilize the volunteer army.
   a. the size of the armed forces required
   b. the state of patriotism among the nation's youth
   c. the level of unemployment in the economy
   d. evidence of a taxpayers' revolt

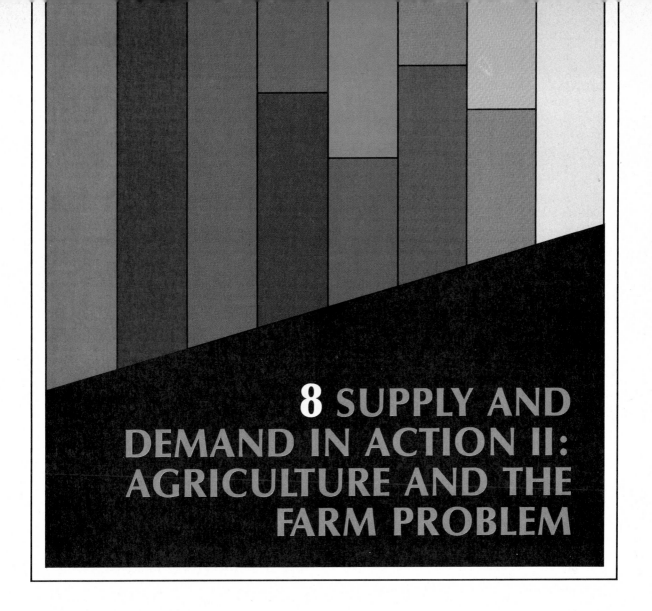

8 SUPPLY AND DEMAND IN ACTION II: AGRICULTURE AND THE FARM PROBLEM

For nearly 80 years the "farm problem" has challenged and troubled U.S. policymakers. It is really two quite different problems. The first is long-term. Until very recently and to some extent still today, the average income and prosperity level of those living and working on farms has been well below that found in most other sectors of the economy. Farmers believe that they are entitled to more nearly equal incomes, and many of their claims are summed up in a demand for "parity." Economics can help us understand what caused these generally lower farm incomes, and what are some of the consequences of trying to raise them.

The second farm problem is short-term but recurring. It is one of highly fluctuating incomes, of boom and bust cycles caused by unavoidable changes in weather and other elements that affect crop yields. Farmers want help in stabilizing their incomes in the face of these uncertainties. The laws of supply and demand help us to understand the causes of fluctuating incomes, and to see the possibilities in (and drawbacks of) policies designed to mitigate the fluctuations.

Government policy has attacked both the long- and short-term problems. Much of government farm policy has been nominally directed toward stability, but stability at a *higher* average level of income has also been sought.

The Importance of the Farm Problem

Today only about 6 million people—less than 3 percent of the American population—live on farms, and even for that group less than 40 percent of their income comes from farm sources. Why then has farming and the farm problem loomed so large in American politics and economic policy?

The answer is partly historical. Farmers have not always been so few in number. Farmers in 1910 were 35 percent of the American population, and as recently as 1969 were over 5 percent. More importantly, the declining proportion of farmers has not been matched by a comparable decline in their political influence.

Ninety-eight percent of all farms in 1980 were family farms with an average size of 450 acres; the other 2 percent were corporate farms, some with more than 100,000 acres under cultivation. While that 2 percent accounts for over a third of all farm output, family farmers—and those who make their living supplying farmers—constitute the dominant political force in 16 or 17 states. They elect one-third of the 100 U.S. senators. The farm bloc remains a potent political influence in Congress.

American farm problems are important not only because of the importance of farmers in American life but also because American agriculture is critical to the world's food supply. Although traditionally regarded as a manufacturing nation, the United States now provides two-thirds of all grain and soybeans exported in world trade. American agriculture is the regular supplier to hundreds of millions of people outside the United States and the

buffer against crop failure for more than 3 billion others. People around the globe depend for their very survival on America's remaining one of the world's greatest granaries.

LONG-TERM TRENDS: HIGH PRODUCTIVITY AND LOWER INCOME

The historical record of farm incomes is shown in Figure 8-1. At least until the 1970s farmers lagged behind the rest of the American population in material prosperity. Even during the 1970s farm employment was 4 percent of national employment, but income earned by farmers from farming was only about 1.5 percent of personal income. Because farm families often earn non–farm income as well—by having one member work in town, for example—they were not as badly off as these statistics suggest. Moreover, because the costs of living are lower in rural areas and because farm families consume a good deal of home-grown food, money incomes do not tell the whole story. Nonetheless, the average farm family in America has achieved, on average, a lower level of material prosperity than the average urban family.

Surprisingly, the gap in farm incomes is not a product of low productivity, or poor and depleted soils, but of the reverse. American agriculture is, and has long been, one of the most rapidly innovative industries in the entire world. New seeds, new crops, new mechanical methods, cloning, computerization, and a host of other new methods have led to rising production per worker and per acre. Since 1900 the output per worker in agriculture has increased tenfold. Between 1967 and 1980 alone it doubled. (In contrast, productivity in American manufacturing increased by only 16 percent between 1967 and 1980.)

Rising productivity in agriculture allows more people to be fed by the same number of workers. The results have been spectacular. Rough estimates of the number of people who can be fed per worker employed on the land are 59 in the United States,

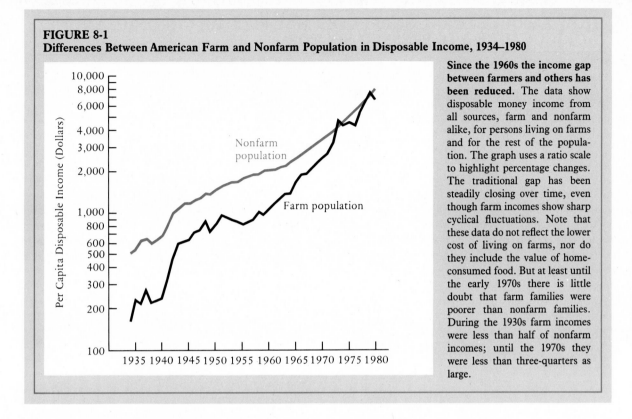

FIGURE 8-1
Differences Between American Farm and Nonfarm Population in Disposable Income, 1934–1980

Since the 1960s the income gap between farmers and others has been reduced. The data show disposable money income from all sources, farm and nonfarm alike, for persons living on farms and for the rest of the population. The graph uses a ratio scale to highlight percentage changes. The traditional gap has been steadily closing over time, even though farm incomes show sharp cyclical fluctuations. Note that these data do not reflect the lower cost of living on farms, nor do they include the value of home-consumed food. But at least until the early 1970s there is little doubt that farm families were poorer than nonfarm families. During the 1930s farm incomes were less than half of nonfarm incomes; until the 1970s they were less than three-quarters as large.

19 in Western Europe, 14 in Japan, and 10 in the Soviet Union, with all other countries bringing the world *average* down to just over 5! Rapid productivity growth means that American agricultural output can grow faster than that of any other large producing nation. Therein lies the hope, and the problem, for American agriculture.

Large output leads to great prosperity only if the output can be profitably sold. The historical problem for American agriculture is that its production capability has increased faster than its markets.

Lagging Domestic Demand

For most of the last century, the average American family has steadily earned more income and enjoyed an increasing standard of living. How do households wish to consume their extra income? The relevant measure, we have seen, is income elasticity of demand. At the levels of income existing in the United States and other advanced industrial nations, most foodstuffs have low income elasticities because most people are already well fed. When these people get extra income, they tend to spend much of it on consumers' durables, entertainment, and travel. Thus, as incomes grow, the demand for agricultural goods tends to increase relatively slowly.

If productivity is expanding uniformly among industries, the demands for goods with low income elasticities will be expanding more slowly than output. In such industries excess supplies will develop, prices and profits will be depressed, and resources will be induced to move elsewhere. Exactly the reverse will happen for industries pro-

HOW AGRICULTURAL SURPLUSES MAY BECOME CHRONIC, AND AGRICULTURE A DEPRESSED SECTOR

Imagine a simplified economy that has only two sectors, agriculture and services. Over a 20-year period, assume that national income doubles. The income elasticity of demand is assumed to be 0.5 in agriculture and 1.5 in services. Thus, if relative prices stay the same, quantity demanded will increase by 50 percent in agriculture and by 150 percent in services. If productivity growth is the same in both sectors, this will require a substantial shift of resources from agriculture to services to satisfy the changed demands. (See case 1 in the table below.) If productivity growth is higher in the agricultural sector than in the service sector, the size of the required resource shift needed to avoid surpluses or shortages will be much greater. (See case 2 in the table below.) In the table, to illustrate the pressures on each sector we have assumed that resources actually did move from one sector to the other.

How does the market respond to these pressures? Because output is expanding faster than demand in the agricultural sector, prices will fall and incomes of producers will fall. In response to falling farm prices, demand for farm labor and the other factors of production used in agriculture will decline, as will the earnings of these factors. At the same time, exactly the opposite tendencies will be observed in service industries. Here demand is expanding faster than output; prices will rise, incomes and profits of producers will rise, and there will be a large demand for the factors of production used in service industries. So the price of these factors, and consequently the incomes that they earn, will be bid upward. In short, services will be a buoyant sector and agriculture a depressed sector. Now if resources move freely, there will be a continuing flow of labor (and land and other factors of production) from agriculture to services. But if resources move too slowly, there will be a continuing depression in agriculture and chronic surpluses, while the service sector will be buoyant with chronic scarcities.

A NUMERICAL EXAMPLE OF SHIFTING DEMANDS FOR RESOURCES

	Case 1: Productivity the same in each sector		Case 2: Productivity greater in agriculture	
	Agriculture	Services	Agriculture	Services
1. Production = quantity demanded, beginning of period	100	100	100	100
2. Assumed growth in output due to productivity	100	100	150	50
3. Production, end of period	200	200	250	150
4. Assumed income elasticity	0.5	1.5	0.5	1.5
5. Quantity demanded when income doubles and prices remain unchanged	150	250	150	250
6. Surplus (shortage)	50	(50)	100	(100)

ducing goods with high income elasticities. Demands will expand faster than supplies, prices and profits will tend to rise, and resources will move into the industries producing these goods.

When productivity is growing more rapidly in a sector with low-income elasticities, the build-up of surplus productive capacity can be rapid. The way it works for a simplified economy is shown in the box.

The steady, rapid growth of agricultural productivity reflects the increasing application of factors other than land and simple labor to farms. Farming is increasingly a vast, capital-intensive, corporate activity. Mechanization, large-scale production, and computerized analysis of day-to-day decisions are common. Many a modern American farmer has a college degree, even a postgraduate degree in business administration, and spends more time in the office analyzing computer printouts than in the fields. In some ways large-scale modern farming resembles an automobile assembly line more than it does the traditional small and often poor family farm. By the end of the decade, more than half of farm output will be produced on giant farms.

The continuing pace of these changes is reflected in the fact that between 1970 and 1980 total American farm production increased by nearly 30 percent while farm labor input *decreased* by 3.2 percent per year, machinery use increased 2.5 percent per year, and use of chemicals increased by 4.3 percent per year.

The innovations in agriculture that make possible the increase in output with the use of less labor have been encouraged by a long American tradition of government-financed research, agricultural assistance services in every state, and government programs designed to keep farm prices and incomes high even when production is increasing faster than demand. If steadily rising productivity is not to mean excess supply of agricultural products and thus falling prices and falling incomes for farmers, either resources must move out of the surplus sector or new sources of demand must be found, or both.

Supply Response

The magnitude of the supply response required if domestic demand is to absorb production is easily shown. In 1929 there were 12.8 million people employed on farms. The output they produced in 1929 could be produced today by 1.7 million people! If resources had not been reallocated out of farming, there would have been enormous increases in output which could hardly have been sold within the United States at any price. Fortunately, resources did move: actual employment on farms was 3.7 million in 1980.

The movement out of farming has not, however, been quite as fast as required. Adjusting for both productivity increases and population increases, about 3 million farmers in 1980 could have supplied every American with the same output of agricultural goods as each American consumed in 1929. This number is 700,000 fewer farmers than we had in 1980. Since per capita consumption of all agricultural products had not risen sharply, there were necessarily excess supplies of farm products to meet domestic needs. Either foreign demand had to be counted on to absorb them, or farmers faced chronic oversupply.

In a competitive economy, pain is the spur to those who live and work in a sector with surplus production, especially when resources move slowly in response to depressed incomes. It is the prospect of low incomes that forces people to think of doing something else. But pain is not always enough. It may be easy for the farmer's son or daughter to move to the city, but it may be quite difficult for the farmer and the farmer's parents, who are set in their ways or limited in their skills, to make the same move. As a result, resources may move too slowly to avoid depressed-industry conditions.

This is not uniquely an agricultural problem. The same kind of problem will bother any industry in which the growth in demand proves less rapid than the growth in supply from the resources trapped in that industry. Many economists believe we are now witnessing this phenomenon in American manufacturing industries such as steel and automobiles. If so they may be plagued over the next decade by some of the same problems from which agriculture has suffered.

Mitigating the Problem of Long-Term Oversupply

Export Demand

Until the 1970s foreign demand was not very important to American farmers. American exports were heavily industrial and other nations served as breadbaskets for the world. In the 1960s only about 14 percent of America's agricultural output was sold abroad. By 1980 the figure was 30 percent.

While dramatic events, such as the massive sales of wheat to the Soviet Union in 1972 and the normalization of trade relations with China, with its 1 billion population, have underlined America's expanding role as a food exporter, this expansion has come about gradually. Its underlying causes have been the enormous growth in the world's population and rising incomes in many underdeveloped countries. These countries are at a stage of development where income elasticities of demand for wheat, dairy products, and meat are relatively high; thus, they are prepared to spend a good fraction of their increased income on them.

Agricultural exports increased by an average of 20 percent per year during the seventies, and in 1981 they stood at over $43 billion. Just at a time when American manufactures seemed expensive in world markets, American farm products became relatively cheaper. Drought and hunger in many countries of Asia and Africa have led these countries to increase food imports, providing relief from excess supplies of many American farm products.

Much of this growth in foreign demand did not just happen. It has been carefully cultivated by such government agencies as the Foreign Agricultural Service, which has sought new markets and provided technical and financial assistance to other countries that can be taught to buy and process American agricultural output. Much of the growth, too, has been financed by economic aid to less-developed countries.

Government Intervention to Eliminate Excess Supply

Because farmers are people—and voters—the government tends to respond to their cries for help in overcoming the consequences of excess supply instead of allowing the free market to do so via low prices and low incomes. Through a variety of programs dating from 1929 to the present, the government has bought surplus farm products from farmers at a guaranteed price above the free-market level. Such programs solve the surplus problem for the individual farmer, but they do not do so for the nation, for surplus commodities accumulate in government warehouses.

Eventually, if agricultural surpluses persist, the stored crops would have to be destroyed, dumped on the market for what they would bring, or otherwise disposed of at a fraction of their cost. If the crops are thrown on the market and allowed to depress the price, then the original purpose in purchasing them—to stabilize prices and raise farm incomes—is defeated. If the crops are destroyed or allowed to rot, the efforts of a large quantity of the country's scarce factors of production (the land, labor, and capital that went into producing the stored goods) will have been completely wasted.

Destroying crops is a vexing moral problem when millions are starving, but if the stored crops are not to depress the price, they must be kept off the market. Giving crops away to those who would not otherwise buy them is sometimes attempted but is hard to achieve.

When support schemes begin to produce ever-larger surpluses, often the next step is to try to limit each farmer's production. Quotas may be assigned to individual farmers and penalties imposed for exceeding the quotas. Or, as has been done in the past, bonuses may be paid for leaving the land idle and for plowing crops under. Such measures waste resources because the desired output could be produced with fewer resources and the remain-

LET THEM EAT CHEESE

Surplus commodities have been accumulating in government warehouses for over 30 years, but every once in a while some aspect of the program catches the public imagination. In December 1981, President Reagan announced a distribution of some surplus cheese to the needy. The commentators had a field day, as the following excerpts suggest.

Russell Baker in the *New York Times*:
I was surprised to hear that the Reagan Administration was giving free cheese to the poor. The credo of the Reagan people, if I've heard them right, is "There is no free lunch." I always assumed this included the cheese course.

What bothers me is their giving it away to the poor. This is against everything President Reagan stands for. How are you going to put any backbone into the poor so they'll get out and take care of themselves if you give them free cheese?

Time Magazine:
Free the cheese! Consumer groups have been beaming that message at the White House in petitions and telegrams for a month, and last week Ronald Reagan agreed to do just that. In an Oval Office ceremony, during which he signed an $11 billion farm price-support bill, the President announced that the Government will give away 30 million lbs. of surplus cheese to states for distribution to the needy. Explained Reagan: "At a time when American families are under increasing financial pressure, their Government cannot sit by and watch millions of pounds of food turn to waste."

As Reagan noted in signing the farm bill last week, "surpluses will continue to pile up" because the Government must keep on buying dairy products at prices that are currently higher than commercial buyers will pay.

Other suggestions for disposing of the surplus range from dumping the cheese in the sea to staging bring-your-own-wine-and-crackers parties at warehouses. Reagan hinted last week that some of the cheese might be sold abroad, at a loss to the Government. The all-too-obvious solution, of course, would be to lower price-support levels until dairy farmers are no longer tempted to produce more cheese than they can sell commercially. But that would be a lot to ask of politicians. The new farm bill actually increases present price-support levels over four years. Meanwhile, the Government is left with a stockpile that is a mess . . . oh, all right, no matter how you slice it.

Newsweek:
The scene conjured up images of the Great Depression. Thousands of poor people, including pensioners and young mothers with infants swaddled in blankets against the biting chill, stood in line for hours outside Washington's First Rising Mount Zion Baptist Church recently to receive their share of the 30 million pounds of surplus government-owned cheese that President Reagan has agreed to give away to America's poor. . . . But that still represents only a fraction of the 637 million pounds of cheese currently in storage—a glut caused in part by a 33-year-old Federal farm-price-support policy that critics say actually encourages farmers to produce more than the market can bear.

Farmers . . . defend price supports as a necessary cushion against the fluctuations of the market. "Price-support legislation, assures farmers a fair return on basic crops." Critics say that subsidies do more than that: "The support system in this country, . . . allows farmers to produce a product knowing they can sell it even though there isn't a market demand for it." But the powerful farm bloc has successfully defeated Reagan Administration efforts to cut dairy subsidies beyond last year's level, which was set as a better-than-nothing compromise that has done little to ease the current glut in subsidized foodstuffs.

ing resources used to produce other goods. All they dispense with is the visible symbol of trouble, the accumulating surpluses.

Schemes that try to solve the long-run farm problem without creating new markets or inducing resources to shift to other more productive uses may actually conflict in the long run with the goal of raising farmers' incomes. If the artificially profitable and stable market provides a stimulus for research and development that further increases productivity in the farm sector, it will shift the supply curve to the right, creating a further excess of quantity supplied over quantity demanded.

Has the Long-Term Problem Been Solved?

Look again at Figure 8-1. Over the last decade the income disadvantage of American farmers seems to have been largely eliminated. A main cause of the boom was the increase in export demand already discussed. Indeed, government-held crop inventories were suddenly in demand, and what seemed like unlimited supplies of some commodities were quickly sold off.

No sooner had some commentators relegated the farm problem to economic history than American agriculture suffered two bad years in 1980 and 1981. A worldwide recession sharply reduced foreign demand for our surplus products. This fall in demand was made even worse by the fact that the American dollar became more and more expensive during these years. At the same time, rising interest rates and fuel costs raised costs of production in farming and meant that any drop in prices threatened large losses to farmers squeezed by rising costs. Farmers were hurting once again, and their clamor for government relief became more insistent. In December 1981 President Reagan signed into law a new four-year farm bill that was remarkably similar to earlier bills and provided for renewed government price supports and purchases.

At this time it is unclear whether the long-term problem in American agriculture has been solved. On the one hand, rapid productivity growth combined with an ever-increasing world demand for food, might spell the beginning of a new era of prosperity for American farmers. On the other hand, to translate this increase in supply into prosperity for farmers depends in part on American costs remaining competitive and in part on the rest of the world's being able to earn the purchasing power to turn its *need* for agricultural goods into an effective *demand* for them.

SHORT-TERM FLUCTUATIONS

Short-term price volatility is typical of many agricultural markets. Why do such fluctuations occur? What is their effect on farmers' well-being, and what can or should be done about them?

Farm crops are subject to variations in output because of many factors completely beyond farmers' control. Some variation is simply a matter of season, but pests, floods, and lack of rain can drastically reduce farm output, and exceptionally favorable conditions can cause production greatly to exceed expectations. By now you should not be surprised to hear that such unplanned fluctuations in output cause fluctuations in farm prices and in farmers' incomes. But there are some surprises in how it all works out.

Consider some examples. The winter and spring of 1976 were mild and warm, and the good weather generated bumper fruit crops in California, where more than half of America's fruit—and virtually the entire crop for canning—is grown. At prevailing prices the state director of food and agriculture predicted 100,000 tons of unsold peaches, 50,000 tons of unsold pears, and large surpluses of apricots, cherries, and nectarines. California's canneries would take the surplus but only at sharply reduced prices, prices that meant lower incomes for fruit growers. While growers cursed a bountiful nature, consumers stood to benefit.

In 1981 the American peanut crop dropped from 2 million tons to 1.1 million tons due to drought. Prices of peanuts rose from $455 to $1,510 a ton. Peanut butter became scarce in supermarkets, and its price soared. Peanut farmers in Plains, Georgia, and elsewhere prospered. Some complained that if only the drought and government acreage restrictions had not reduced the size of their crops, they would *really* have made some money for a change. (We will soon see why they were wrong.)

Or consider an even more complex chain of effects. When bad weather destroyed 80 percent of the U.S. soybean crop in a year when most other grains were also in short supply, a series of indirect but predictable results occurred. Soybeans are a primary ingredient of chicken feed for the mass-production broiler chicken industry. The decrease in supply of soybeans (a leftward shift of the supply curve) caused the price of soybeans to triple in two months. Chicken farmers found the cost of soybeans rising so fast that it did not pay to continue feeding baby chicks. Millions were simply killed, and many more millions were not allowed to hatch. This led to a decrease in the supply of chickens (a leftward shift in the supply curve of chickens) and a rise in the price of chickens to households.

Fluctuating Supply with Inelastic Demands

Because demand curves slope downward, variations in farm output placed on the market cause price fluctuations in the opposite direction to crop sizes. A bumper crop sends prices down, a small crop sends them up. The price change will be larger, the less elastic the demand curve. (See Figure 8-2).

For products with inelastic demands, fluctuations in their prices will be large in response to unplanned changes in production.

What are the effects on the receipts of farmers? If the commodity in question has an elasticity of demand less than unity, farmers' receipts will vary inversely with quantity supplied.

If demands are inelastic, good harvests will bring reductions in total farm receipts and bad harvests will bring increases.

FIGURE 8-2
The Effect on Price of Unplanned Variations in Output Depends on Elasticity of Demand

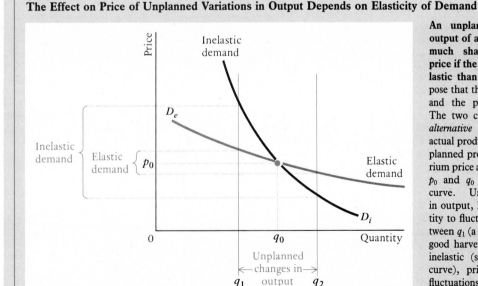

An unplanned fluctuation in output of a given size leads to a much sharper fluctuation in price if the demand curve is inelastic than if it is elastic. Suppose that the expected price is p_0 and the planned output is q_0 The two curves D_i and D_e are *alternative* demand curves. If actual production always equaled planned production, the equilibrium price and quantity would be p_0 and q_0 with either demand curve. Unplanned variations in output, however, cause quantity to fluctuate year by year between q_1 (a bad harvest) and q_2 (a good harvest). When demand is inelastic (shown by the heavy curve), prices will show large fluctuations. When demand is elastic (shown by the screened curve), price fluctuations will be much smaller.

Most farm products do have inelastic demands. When nature is bountiful and produces a bumper crop, farmers' receipts dwindle; when nature is moderately unkind and output falls unexpectedly, their receipts rise. The interests of the farmer and the consumer are exactly opposed in such cases. This conflict is dramatically illustrated every time a partial crop failure sends food prices soaring but raises farm incomes, and whenever a bumper crop that brings relief to consumers nevertheless evokes a cry for help from the farm belt, where incomes are shrinking.

Cyclical Fluctuations in Prices and Incomes

As the tide of business activity ebbs and flows, demand curves for all commodities rise and fall. The effects on prices and outputs depend on the elasticity of *supply*. Industrial products typically have rather elastic supply curves, so shifts in demand cause fairly large changes in outputs but only small changes in prices. Agricultural commodities typically have rather inelastic supply curves because land, labor, and machinery devoted to agricultural uses is not quickly transferred to nonagricultural uses when demand falls nor quickly returned to agriculture when demand rises.

Given an inelastic supply curve for agricultural products as a whole, farm prices, farm receipts, and farm income will be very sensitive to demand shifts, as Figure 8-3(i) illustrates. A sharp drop in demand (a leftward shift of the demand curve) will cause hardship among those whose income depends on farm crops.

To the public (and to many in Congress) the economic plight of farmers during the Great Depression seemed to be caused by the great fall in prices, which was caused by the fall in demand for commodities with an inelastic supply curve. The notion of **price parity**, the ratio of the prices farmers received for things they sold to the prices they paid for things they bought, was invoked to measure their hardship. As a result, programs were proposed to restore price parity to farmers.

But this appealing diagnosis is incomplete. It is income earned and wages received, not prices, that

determines how much people have to spend. As Figure 8-3(ii) shows, a very elastic supply curve can be as much a curse as a very inelastic one in the face of a decrease in demand! The loss in receipts in this case is due primarily to a decline in *quantity* sold rather than to a decline in *price*, but that does not make it less painful, as the experience in the United States during the Great Depression shows.

Agriculture and industry both suffered in the Great Depression but with different symptoms: farmers via low prices, as in Figure 8-3(i), and industry via low production and high unemployment of workers and resources, as in Figure 8-3(ii).

From 1929 to 1932, agricultural output fell 1 percent while prices fell 56 percent, leaving revenues at about 44 percent of their 1929 levels. Over the same period, manufacturing prices fell only 30 percent but output fell 47 percent, leaving revenues at only 37 percent of their 1929 levels.[1] While farmers clamored for the government to do something about prices, industry and industrial workers clamored for the government to act to overcome unemployment of people and underemployment of factories.

Agricultural Stabilization in Theory

Governments throughout the world intervene in agricultural markets in attempts to stabilize agricultural prices and incomes in the face of short-term and uncontrollable fluctuations in supply and cyclical fluctuations in demand.

Because income stabilization and price stabilization are not the same, there has been confusion about what is intended by programs designed to achieve *orderly agricultural marketing* or *farm parity*—phrases used in American legislation. We shall consider several types of plans.

---

[1] It is revenues, not profits, that are relevant to this comparison. Farmers' income is not simply farm profits, for the wages paid to farm labor are also incomes attributable to farming. Similarly, the revenues earned in industry provide the wages and salaries of workers as well as the profits of business people.

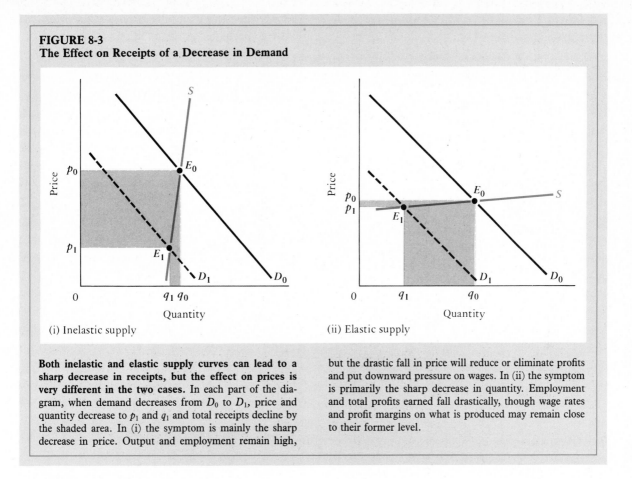

FIGURE 8-3
The Effect on Receipts of a Decrease in Demand

(i) Inelastic supply

(ii) Elastic supply

Both inelastic and elastic supply curves can lead to a sharp decrease in receipts, but the effect on prices is very different in the two cases. In each part of the diagram, when demand decreases from D_0 to D_1, price and quantity decrease to p_1 and q_1 and total receipts decline by the shaded area. In (i) the symptom is mainly the sharp decrease in price. Output and employment remain high, but the drastic fall in price will reduce or eliminate profits and put downward pressure on wages. In (ii) the symptom is primarily the sharp decrease in quantity. Employment and total profits earned fall drastically, though wage rates and profit margins on what is produced may remain close to their former level.

Suppose the supply curve in each case refers to planned (or average) production per year, but actual production fluctuates around that level. In a free market, as we have seen, this causes both prices and farmers' receipts to fluctuate widely from year to year.

The Ever-Normal Granary

One method of preventing fluctuations in prices and gross receipts is for individual farmers to form a producers' association that tries to stabilize—to keep "ever normal"—the supply *actually coming onto the market* in spite of variations in production. It does this by storing a crop, say grain, in years of above average production and selling out of its storage elevators in years of below average production.

Since one farmer's production is an insignificant part of total production, there is no point in an individual farmer's holding some production off the market in an effort to prevent a fall in price in a year of bumper crops. But if all farmers get together and agree to vary the supply coming onto the market, then, collectively, they can have a major effect on price. The appropriate policy is shown in Figure 8-4.

Since revenues accrue to the producers when the goods are actually sold on the market, total revenues can be stabilized by keeping sales constant at the equilibrium output even though production varies. This can be accomplished by add-

FIGURE 8-4
Stabilizing Sales Despite Variable Production:
The Ever-normal Granary

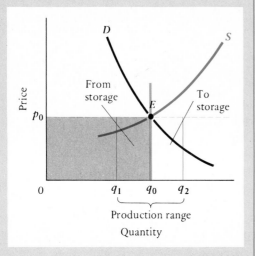

The **ever-normal granary scheme stabilizes the quantity sold by farmers even though actual production varies.** The planned supply curve is S; p_0 and q_0 are the equilibrium price and quantity, respectively. Actual production varies between q_1 and q_2. When production is q_2 the producers' association sells q_0 and stores q_0q_2. When production is q_1 it still sells q_0, supplementing the current production by selling q_1q_0 from its stored crops. Producers' revenue is stabilized at $p_0 \times q_0$ (the shaded area) every year.

ing to or subtracting from inventories the excesses or shortages of production.

The fully successful ever-normal granary stabilizes both prices and revenues of producers.

The costs of this plan are those of providing storage and organizing and administering the program.

Government Price Supports at the Equilibrium Price

Because there are many difficulties in organizing and administering private stabilization programs such as the ever-normal granary, can government

do the same thing and do it more efficiently? The answer (perhaps surprisingly) is no.

Suppose the government, instead of the producers' association, enters the market, buying in the market and adding to its own stocks when there is a surplus and selling in the market—thereby reducing its stocks—when there is a shortage. If it had enough grain elevators and warehouses, and if its support price were set at a realistic level, the government could stabilize prices indefinitely. But, as Figure 8-5 illustrates, it would not succeed in stabilizing farmers' revenues and incomes, for farmers would find their revenues high with a bumper crop and low with a poor crop.

FIGURE 8-5
Government Price Supports at the Equilibrium Price

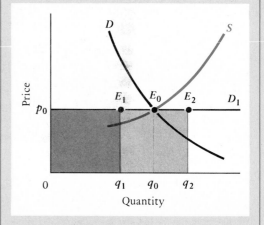

Government price supports at the equilibrium price stabilize prices (not quantities sold by farmers) and do not accumulate surpluses but cause revenues to vary directly with production. Actual production varies around the equilibrium level of q_0. When production is q_2 the government buys q_0q_2 and stores it. When production is q_1 the government sells q_1q_0 from storage. The quantity sold to the public is always q_0, and this stabilizes price at p_0. The government policy converts the demand curve facing farmers to D_1. If q_0 is average production, there is no trend toward the accumulation of storage crops.

Farmers' revenue varies from p_0q_1 (the darker shaded area) when production is q_1 to p_0q_2 (the entire shaded area) when production is q_2.

Government price supports at the equilibrium price would not stabilize revenues. They would, however, reverse the pattern of revenue fluctuation of a crop with inelastic demand and a fluctuating supply.

In effect, the government policy imposes a demand curve that is perfectly elastic at the support price. This stabilizes price, but it does not stabilize receipts to producers.

Government Stabilization of Farmers' Revenues by Open Market Purchases and Sales

Obviously there must be a government buying and selling policy that will stabilize farmers' receipts. What are its characteristics? As has been seen, too much price stability causes receipts to vary directly with production and too little price stability causes receipts to vary inversely with production. It appears that the government should aim at some intermediate degree of price stability. If the government allows prices to vary in inverse proportion to variations in production, then receipts will be stabilized. A 10 percent rise in production should be met by a 10 percent fall in price, and a 10 percent fall in production by a 10 percent rise in price.

To stabilize farmers' receipts, the government must make the demand curve facing the farmers one of unit elasticity. It must buy in periods of high output and sell in periods of low output, but only enough to let prices change in inverse proportion to farmers' output.

Government Price Supports Above the Free-Market Equilibrium Level

To avoid long-term problems, the government policy just described should allow prices to average the free-market level. In practice, however, stabilization plans involving price supports usually set prices above the average free-market equilibrium level. This is due to the fact that stabilization is not the only goal; there is also a desire to assure farmers a standard of living comparable with that of city dwellers. This involves attempting to *raise* farm incomes in addition to stabilizing them.

Here too the government buys in periods of high

output and sells in periods of low output, but on average it buys much more than it sells. The consequences are what one would expect from the theory of floor prices discussed in Chapter 7. As we saw there, such a policy inevitably leads to the accumulation of inventories of unsold product in government warehouses. (See Figure 7-2 on page 99.) As an incidental result, agricultural support programs will surely show a deficit, for goods will have been purchased that cannot be sold except at a loss. This deficit means that taxpayers generally will be paying farmers for producing goods that no one is willing to purchase at prices that come near to covering costs.

FIFTY YEARS OF AMERICAN FARM POLICY

The American experience in trying to help the large, often poor, and always politically influential farm population illustrates the theory just developed. In particular, it shows the twin difficulties of surplus production and slow resource reallocation out of agricultural production.

Before World War II

The first serious government intervention in agricultural markets was in 1929, when the Federal Farm Board was set up to buy and sell farm produce to promote "orderly agricultural marketing." The Board's operations failed when its attempt to support prices led to the accumulation of large stocks and a rapid exhaustion of available funds.

The Roosevelt administration (1933–1945) had learned the lesson that unless output can be restricted, holding prices above the market level requires unending injections of federal money to buy crops that can never be sold. It could not, however, politically or morally abandon the farmers, who were among the earliest victims of the Great Depression. The primary objective of New Deal farm policy was to achieve some form of parity between farmers' incomes and other incomes in the nation. It was hoped (rather naively) that income parity could be achieved by legislating for price parity. The relative prices of the agricultural crops farmers sold and the manufactured goods farmers bought were to be restored to what they were in the period just before World War I, 25 years earlier. Since farm prices had fallen relative to the prices of manufactured goods, this meant that they were to be supported by the government at levels well above their free-market equilibrium levels.

A prominent feature of the New Deal program was designed to prevent the buildup of surplus output by paying farmers *not to produce* as well as paying them for what they did produce. The farm program also imposed acreage restrictions and marketing quotas on individual farmers.

But supported prices and guaranteed sales, government-financed research, and government loans for farm improvements were an enormous incentive to productivity, and output per acre and output per worker soared. Thus total output was not held down in spite of acreage limitations, and the federal costs for buying the resulting surplus crops or storing and eventually destroying them—or selling them abroad at low prices—remained at a very high level.

From the Mid 1940s to the 1970s

After World War II farm policy was modified but not basically changed. In the 1950s the notion of parity with pre-World War I relative prices was finally dropped, and the base for parity was made the average of prices ruling during the previous 10 years. Moreover actual prices were allowed to fall to a certain fraction of parity prices before the full price support was given. While this modification allowed a decline in relative prices over time, the permitted decline could occur only slowly, and at the same time the effects of even these small price changes were weakened by additional measures that gave further assistance to farmers. The details are unimportant; what matters is that by subsidizing farmers, the government reduced the incentive to shift resources out of farming and encouraged further research and development.

Meanwhile, the so-called soil bank and other programs continued to pay farmers not to produce commodities that consumers would not buy at the prevailing prices. By the end of the sixties, the federal government was paying about $3 billion per year to farmers for leaving 233 million acres unplanted. This acreage could have been used to increase grain output (say) by roughly 20 percent to 25 percent. But that would have either depressed prices or added to the 100 million tons already in storage.

The Decade of the Seventies

Quite unexpectedly, dramatic shifts on the demand side changed the entire farm outlook during the first half of the 1970s. Rising world population, growing world income, and some massive crop failures around the world created the specter of a worldwide food shortage, leading to hunger and starvation. Decreases in the value of the dollar relative to many other currencies, along with productivity gains, made American farm products cheaper abroad. The increasing demand for wheat, cotton, soybeans, and livestock depleted stored reserves and in some cases led to shortages.

The combination of rising demand and increasing productivity led to sharp rises in farm incomes. Productivity increases led to improved acreage yields, and at the same time total acreage planted *increased* from 230 million acres in 1970 to 300 million in 1980. Needless to say, this rising prosperity slowed down the outflow of resources from farming, although there was still a decrease in the number of farmers, as farms grew in size and substituted machinery for labor.

This period of prosperity gave the federal government a chance to modify some agricultural support programs that had proven so troublesome in the past. The modifications were relatively minor, however, and continued to provide substantial income supports. Under the revised programs, the government makes direct cash payments to farmers only when market prices fall below government-set "target prices" that are designed to cover most but not all production costs. These payments do not guarantee farmers a "reasonable" profit, as did many earlier schemes, but they do shield them from large losses. And they leave the crops in the farmers' hands, to be sold when the farmers wish.

WHAT PRICE PARITY?

In the spring of 1979, thousands of farmers drove their tractors to Washington, D.C., to demand "parity." Farmers were demanding prices that would have restored the relative price of farm and manufactured products to 90 percent of what it was in the period before World War I, despite enormous increases in the relative productivity of agriculture. While we can all endorse the concept of just and equitable treatment, there are important costs to using parity as an economic rule of thumb.

Price Parity

Price parity in effect freezes relative prices.

To freeze relative prices at levels existing at any one time prevents the price system from allocating resources in response to changes in tastes and incomes on the demand side and to costs and availabilities on the supply side.

If the prices of calculators or computers had been frozen relative to the price of slide rules as of 1960, none of us would be using calculators or computers today. Society progresses by substituting newer, cheaper products for more expensive ones, not by keeping relative prices the same forever. Yet parity implies keeping the relationship fixed.

Income Parity

Since freezing prices is not an efficient way to protect farmers' income, why not provide *income* parity instead? This could be done by paying an appropriate sum to those whose income falls below the level of parity.

Much the same problems would occur as with freezing prices. Falling demands for some commodity or service need to be met by reduction of supply. Changing relative incomes signal resources to move from one occupation to another. By freezing relative incomes, the government would not only eliminate the incentive to use resources efficiently but would also reduce incentives for owners or workers to move resources from poorer to better uses. It would be more efficient to subsidize people to change occupations or producers to change products than to subsidize them to stay where they are not needed and to produce products that are not profitably marketed.

Price Parity As Bankruptcy Protection

The farmers' march of 1979 was undertaken because farmers felt that the combination of high interest rates and low prices for their output threatened their ability to pay off investments made five or six years earlier, when the optimistic farm outlook led them to invest in newer and bigger machinery.

Throughout history, new products and new techniques have led to investment resulting from the need to install new productive capacity. Investment booms often tended to go too far as investors rushed to get rich quick. Some investments would prove unprofitable, and many investors would lose their money. After this "shakeout" the remaining investment would be "here to stay."

In the late 1970s, then, farmers were suffering from an age-old problem: too much investment in new technologies during boom times. Only their reaction to it was novel. Present-day farmers expected the government to protect their investment from the losses they saw looming.

Well, why not? Once again the problem lies in the inefficiency caused. If people know the government will bail them out if they overinvest in some industry, they will tend to do so. If demand turns out to be unexpectedly strong, they will earn the profits; if it turns out to be unexpectedly weak, the government will pay the bill. While those investing can't lose, society is sure to lose if people overinvest in the industry. It's just a question of who pays for it.

The unrelieved prosperity of the first part of the decade was replaced by a more typical cyclical pattern in the last half. In 1974 the world entered the most serious economic recession since the 1930s. Hard times hit every sector of the economy. Buoyant international demand and declining export surpluses elsewhere in the world, however, shielded U.S. agriculture from a repetition of the 1930s. But for farmers who had incurred a heavy debt to expand and mechanize rapidly during the early 1970s, even a mild decline threatened disaster. Between 1974 and 1978, prices *paid* by farmers rose by 31 percent but prices received by them rose only 9 percent. When the market ceased to expand as fast as expected, farmers facing rising costs found it difficult to keep up the payments on their loans. They marched on Washington for higher support prices to protect their investments. A general economic recovery of 1978 stilled much of their demand for extra help—but only temporarily.

The overall experience of the 1970s showed that large-scale agriculture is still subject to the old cyclical problems even though the underlying trend seemed to point in the direction of greater average prosperity.

Prospects for American Farm Policy in the 1980s

The worldwide recession that began in 1980 revived farmers' demands for protection from the age-old fluctuations in their income. Although the Reagan administration had come to office committed to letting the market, not the federal government, regulate agriculture, political realities dictated otherwise. The Agriculture and Food Act of 1981 is remarkably similar to its predecessors. Minimum target prices for wheat, corn, cotton, and rice remain and may be raised by the secretary of agriculture as deemed appropriate. Special programs for dairy products, peanuts, soybeans, sugar, and wool were continued in slightly modified form.

The support programs of the 1980s seem designed to avoid some of the excesses of earlier programs and are less likely than past ones to produce an endless accumulation of unsold and unsalable surpluses in government warehouses. However, pressure groups are still with us, and on some occasions they succeed in getting supports at above free-market levels. When Congress gives in to their demands, the problem of government surpluses reemerges virtually overnight.

A current example concerns dairy products. Despite enormous stockpiles, the government continues to buy about two-thirds of all the powdered milk, 30 percent of the butter, and 20 percent of the cheese produced in the United States. Dairy farmers, not surprisingly, have responded to the continuing subsidies. In 1982 the number of milk cows on U.S. dairy farms *increased* by 79,000 and milk production per cow increased by nearly 2 percent, thus increasing the quantities that the government must buy. Yet an attempt to reduce dairy farm supports was soundly defeated in the Senate.

Although most economists and many politicians believe that our historical farm policies have proven expensive and wasteful, and have impeded some overdue long-run adjustments required by changing tastes and technology, the prospects for major changes are not bright. A major reduction of farm subsidization seems to require a sustained period of agricultural prosperity (as we had at the beginning of the 1970s) *and* a national mood favoring deregulation, decreased federal expenditure, and restoration of a free-market environment (as was evidenced in the 1980 election). Apparently either one alone is not sufficient. The decade of the 1980s shows signs of being business as usual at the Department of Agriculture.

SOME GENERAL LESSONS ABOUT RESOURCE ALLOCATION

In Chapters 7 and 8 we have examined several examples of government intervention in markets that might have been left unregulated. Public debate about the desirability of more or less intervention is lively today, both with respect to deregulation in areas of existing regulation and with respect to imposing wage and price controls to cope with the ever-rising prices in our inflationary economy. Our discussion suggests three widely applicable lessons.

1. Costs May Be Shifted, But They Cannot Be Avoided

Production, whether in response to free-market signals or to government controls, uses resources; thus it involves costs to members of society. The average standard of living depends on the amounts of resources available to the economy and the efficiency with which these resources are used. *It follows that costs are real* and are incurred no matter who provides the goods. Rent controls, subsidies to agriculture, or using the draft to recruit an army can change the share of the costs paid by particular individuals or groups—lowering the share for some and raising the share for others—but they cannot make the costs go away.

Different ways of *allocating* the costs may also affect the total amount of resources used, and thus the amount of costs incurred. Controls that keep prices and profits of some commodity below free-market levels will lead to increased quantities demanded and decreased quantities supplied. Unless government steps in to provide additional supplies, fewer resources will be allocated to producing the commodity. If government chooses to supply all the demand at the controlled prices, more resources will be allocated to it, which means fewer resources will be devoted to other kinds of goods and services.

2. The Price System Is a Decentralized Control System That Encourages Economical Use of Resources

Commodities and resources are scarce, and thus they must be rationed. The price system allocates commodities via a set of prices that adjust so as to equate the amount consumers wish to buy with the amount producers wish to sell. The price system also allocates resources among the many goods and services that could be produced.

The price system is decentralized. Producers and consumers see and respond to prices over which they have no control but which signal relative scarcities. Prices that are high and rising (relative to other prices) provide an incentive to purchasers to economize on the commodity. They may choose to satisfy the want in question with substitutes whose prices have not risen so much (because they are less costly to provide) or to satisfy less of that want by shifting expenditure to the satisfaction of other wants.

On the supply side, rising prices tend to produce rising profits. High profits attract further resources into production. Short-term windfall profits that bear no relation to current costs repeatedly occur in market economies; they cause resources to move into those industries having profits until profits fall to levels that can be earned elsewhere in the economy.

Falling prices and falling profits provide the opposite motivations. Purchasers are inclined to buy more; sellers are inclined to produce less and to move resources out of the industry and into more profitable undertakings.

The price system responds to need for change in the allocation of resources, say, in response to an external event such as the loss of a source of a raw material, or the outbreak of a war. Changing relative prices and profits signal the need for change to which consumers and producers respond.

3. Government Intervention Affects Resource Allocation and Requires Alternative Allocation Mechanisms

Governments intervene in the price system, sometimes to satisfy generally agreed social goods, and sometimes to help politically influential self-interest groups. Government intervention involves changing the allocation of resources the price system would achieve. Whether or not the intervention is justified by social values, there are always costs of intervention to be set against the gains.

Interventions have allocative consequences because they inhibit the free-market allocative mechanism. Some controls, such as rent controls, prevent prices from rising (in response, say, to an increase in demand with no change in supply). If the price is held down, the signal is not given to consumers to economize on a commodity that is in short supply. On the supply side, when prices and profits are prevented from rising, the profit signals that would attract new resources into the industry are never given. The shortage continues, and the movements of demand and supply that would resolve it are not set in motion.

Other controls, such as agricultural price supports, prevent prices from falling (in response, say, to an increase in supply with no increase in demand). This leads to excess supply, and the signal is not given to producers to produce less, or to buyers to increase their purchases. Surpluses continue, and the movements of demand and supply that would eliminate them are not set in motion.

Intervention typically requires alternative allocative mechanisms. During times of shortages, allocation will be by sellers' preferences, by first-come first-served, or by some system of government rationing. During periods of surplus, there will be unsold supplies unless the state buys and stores the surpluses. Since long-run changes in demand and costs do not induce resource reallocations through private decisions, the state will have to step in. It will have to force resources out of industries where prices are held too high, as it tried to do in agriculture in the 1950s and 1960s, and into industries where prices are held too low, as it can do, for example, by providing public housing or using its power to draft young people for military service.

Intervention almost always has both benefits and costs. Positive economics cannot answer the questions of whether a particular intervention with free markets is desirable, but it can clarify the issues by identifying what are the benefits and costs, and who will enjoy or bear them. In doing so it can identify the competing values involved. These matters will be discussed in detail in Chapter 24.

SUMMARY

1. The elementary theory of supply, demand, and price provides powerful tools for analyzing and understanding some real-world problems and policies. The chapter illustrates this with respect to agricultural policies.

2. Historically, average farm incomes in America have lagged well behind those of the rest of the population despite the fact that farm products are vital to our economy. The long-term problems of agriculture arise from a high rate of productivity growth on the supply side and a low income elasticity on the demand side. This means that, unless many resources are being transferred out of agriculture, quantity supplied will increase faster than quantity demanded year after year.

3. Although the number of farmers has decreased, it has not done so quite as fast as would be required to keep domestic demand and supply in balance without incurring sharply falling prices.

4. During the 1970s, a sharp rise in demand for American farm products by foreign nations at least temporarily relieved the long-standing supply surplus and led to a burst of prosperity that showed signs of eliminating the income gap of farmers relative to the rest of the population. Whether export demand will provide a long-term solution for chronic surpluses remains to be seen. Foreign nations will have to have sufficient purchasing power, and American prices will have to remain competitive in world markets. Neither is certain.

5. Agricultural prices and incomes tend to be depressed because of chronic surpluses in agricultural markets. If the tendency is not counteracted, hardships would result whose political and social consequences no American political party has been willing to accept because of the political clout of the farm bloc in Congress. Thus national policy has devised various schemes to protect farm incomes, including buying farmers' output at above free-market prices, limiting production and acreage by quotas, paying farmers bonuses for leaving crops unproduced, subsidizing farmers to store their crops, and insuring farmers against catastrophic losses.

6. The efforts of the government to maintain farm income at a level that compares favorably with incomes earned elsewhere tends to inhibit the reallocation mechanism and thus to increase farm surpluses above what they would otherwise be. These efforts also lead to the government's accumulating surpluses, a problem for which it has no satisfactory solution.

7. In addition to the long-term problems, agricultural commodities are subject to wide fluctuations in crop yields and market prices, and these often lead to fluctuations of producers' incomes. This is because of year-to-year unplanned fluctuations in supplies combined with inelastic demands and because of cyclical fluctuations in demands combined with inelastic supplies. Where demand is inelastic, large crops tend to be associated with low total receipts and small crops with high total receipts.

8. A key element in farm policy has been the attempt to decrease the fluctuations in farm income that accompany the unavoidable fluctuations in market supply and demand. Fluctuations in farmers' gross receipts can be reduced by a producer's association that stores crops unsold when output is high and sells from inventories when output is low, or by appropriate government purchases and sales in the open market.

9. The history of American farm policy from 1930 on shows that price stabilization schemes inevitably tend to involve stabilization at above average free-market equilibrium levels, with resulting surpluses. To avoid these surpluses plans have been adopted to restrict farmers' output. More recently, some progress has been realized toward stimulating foreign demand. But there is no indication of a fundamental change in farm policy nor of a solution to the failures and inefficiencies that have characterized it under every administration.

10. Some general lessons about resource allocation are that (1) costs may be shifted but they cannot be avoided; (2) the price system is a decentralized control system that encourages economical use of resources; and (3) government intervention affects resource allocation and requires alternative allocation mechanisms.

TOPICS FOR REVIEW

High productivity as a cause of low farm incomes
Income elasticity, productivity, and need for resource transfers
Importance of export demand
Price supports at and above the level of free-market equilibrium
Price stabilization versus income stabilization
Price parity and income parity

DISCUSSION QUESTIONS

1. "This year the weather smiled on us, God smiled on us and we made a crop," says Don Marble, a grain and cotton farmer in South Plains, Texas. "But just as we made a crop, the economic situation changed." This quotation brings to mind the old saying: "If you are a farmer, the weather is always bad." Discuss the sense in which this saying might be true.

2. "This ought to be a time of rejoicing in the vineyards of California. The crop of wine grapes has rarely been richer, the harvest is nearly complete, and Americans are drinking more California wine than ever before." Why then were there falling profits and a record number of bankruptcies in the industry?

3. The Kenya Meat Commission (KMC) decided it was undemocratic to allow meat prices to be out of the reach of the ordinary citizen. It decided to freeze meat prices. Six months later, in a press interview, the managing commissioner of the KMC made each of the following statements.
   a. "The price of almost everything in Kenya has gone up, but we have not increased the price of meat. The price of meat in this country is still the lowest in the world."
   b. "Cattle are scarce in the country, but I do not know why."
   c. "People are eating too much beef, and unless they di-

versify their eating habits and eat other foodstuffs the shortage of beef will continue."

Do the facts alleged make sense, given KMC's policy?

4. Gerhard Schramm, a hog farmer from Albert City, Iowa, expanded the family hog facilities in late 1979 to accommodate as many as 15,000 baby pigs a year. At its peak, the family business provided work for three of the Schramms' sons, two sons-in-law, and two daughters-in-law. The Schramms had figured on paying 9½ percent interest to finance their hog buildings, but owing to a general rise in market interest rates, they ended up paying closer to 17 percent, Mrs. Schramm recalls. Then two years ago, corn prices climbed $1 a bushel, vastly increasing their feed costs. And hog prices, which had been $50 per hundred pounds when the Schramms decided to expand, dropped below $30. Early last year, they realized they couldn't continue. They managed to sell the hog buildings last summer, but at "a very big loss."

What, if anything, ought the government do to help the Schramms and people like them?

5. Discuss the following comments about foreign demand for American farm products.

   a. Agriculture Secretary Block: "If only each Chinese would eat one doughnut a day . . ."

   b. "Foreign demand has helped with the long-run problem of American farm policy, but it promises to increase the fluctuations in farm incomes."

   c. "As long as there are hungry Americans, we ought not sell food to the Russians."

6. Three million acres of American farmland are being converted each year to other uses (out of about 540 million acres available in 1982). The American Farmland Trust calls this "one of the most critical problems facing our country and the world today." It has appealed to the public for contributions on the ground that "steps need to be taken immediately to preserve the prime agricultural land on which the food you eat is now grown."

Discuss whether this is a critical problem, and if it is, whether the free market can be expected to solve it.

7. Congressman Stangeland (R–Minn.), supporting government policies that restricted imports of sugar and helped keep sugar prices high: "I vehemently disagree with the notion that our government should be more concerned with the welfare of other countries' economies than with the financial condition of our domestic sugarbeet growers and our farm sector." How might critics of the policy reply to the congressman?

8. What do the following quotes tell you about the politics of farm policy?

   a. Farmer Peter de Gravelles, Jr., of Franklin, Louisiana, an ardent supporter of President Reagan's free enterprise philosophy: "I am not asking the government to guarantee me a profit for my sugar cane: I just wanted a safety net so that I would not go bankrupt in bad years like this one."

   b. "The whole Agriculture Committee is biased toward agricultural interests," said Representative George E. Brown, Jr., of California, a senior Democrat on the panel. "We're not evil or anything, just a little one-sided."

PART THREE
CONSUMPTION, PRODUCTION, AND COST

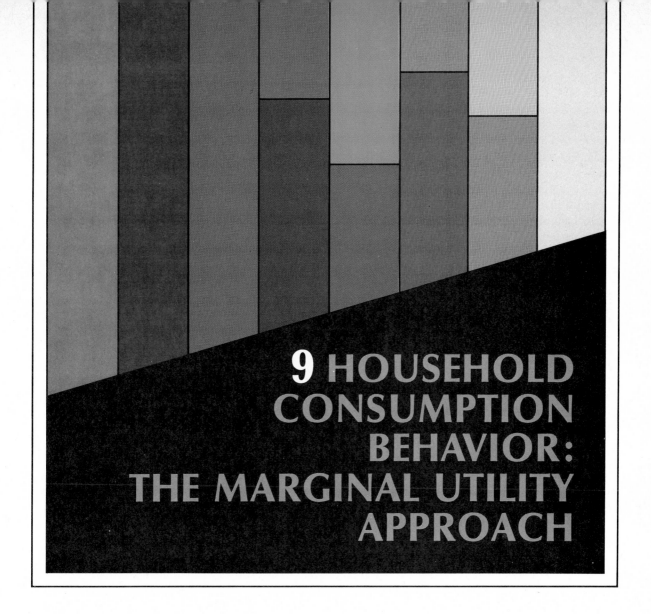

9 HOUSEHOLD CONSUMPTION BEHAVIOR: THE MARGINAL UTILITY APPROACH

Explaining household behavior has interested economists from the earliest times. In this chapter and the next we explore two approaches, each of which offers somewhat different insights.

Early economists, struggling with the problem of what determines the relative prices of commodities, encountered what they came to call the **paradox of value:** Necessary commodities such as water have prices that are low compared with the prices of luxury commodities such as diamonds.

Water is necessary to our existence, these economists of some 200 years ago argued, while diamonds are frivolous and could disappear from the face of the earth tomorrow without causing any real upset. Does it not seem odd, then, that water is so cheap and diamonds are so expensive? It took a long time for economists to resolve this apparent paradox, so it is not surprising that even today the confusion persists in many quarters and clouds some current policy discussions.

We have already met one answer: It is supply and demand, not "necessity" or "luxury," that determine price in any competitive market. The equilibrium price that equates supply and demand is relatively low for water and relatively high for diamonds. But why is the demand for a necessity not enough to assure that its price will be high? After all, water is essential to life itself.

To address this fundamental question, we must now go behind the market demand curve, which is the aggregate of all households' desired purchases at each possible price, and consider the behavior and motivation of individual households. This involves looking first at the relation between the market demand curve and the demand curves of individual households, then at individual behavior.

Market demand curves tell how much is demanded by all purchasers. For example, in Figure 5-1 (see page 65) the market demand for carrots was 90,000 tons when the price was $40 per ton. This 90,000 tons is the sum of the quantities demanded by millions of different households. It may be made up of 4 pounds for the McDaniels, 7 pounds for the Gonzaleses, 1.5 pounds for the Wilsons, and so on. The demand curve for carrots also tells us that when the price rises to $60, aggregate quantity demanded falls to 77,500 tons per month. This quantity too can be traced back to individual households. The McDaniels might buy only 3 pounds, the Gonzaleses 6.5 pounds, and the Wilsons perhaps none at all. Notice that we have now described two points, not only on the market demand curve but on the demand curves of each of these households.

Aggregate behavior is merely the sum of the behavior of individual households. The market demand is the horizontal sum of the demand curves of the individual households.

It is the *horizontal* sum because we wish to add quantities demanded at a given price, and quantities are measured in the horizontal direction on a conventional demand curve graph. This process is illustrated in Figure 9-1.

MARGINAL UTILITY THEORY

Marginal and Total Utility

The satisfaction someone receives from consuming commodities is called his or her **utility.** The total utility obtained from consuming some commodity can be distinguished from the marginal utility of consuming one unit more or one unit less of it.

Total utility refers to the total satisfaction from consuming some commodity. **Marginal utility** refers to the change in satisfaction resulting from consuming a little more or a little less of the commodity. Thus, for example, the total utility of consuming 10 units of any commodity is the total satisfaction that those 10 units provide. The marginal utility of the tenth unit consumed is the satisfaction added by the consumption of that unit—or, in other words, the difference in total utility between consuming 9 units and consuming 10 units:[1]

The significance of this distinction can be seen by considering two questions: (1) If you had to give up consuming one of the following commodities completely, which would you choose: water or the movies? (2) If you had to choose between one of the following, which would you pick: increasing your water consumption by 35 gallons a month (the amount required for an average bath) or attending one more movie a month?

In (1) you are comparing the value you place on your total consumption of water with the value you place on all your attendances at the movies. You are comparing the *total utility* of your water consumption with the *total utility* of your movie attendances. There is little doubt that everyone would answer (1) in the same way, revealing that the total utility derived from consuming water exceeds the total utility derived from attending the movies.

---

[1] Here and elsewhere in elementary economics it is common to use interchangeably two concepts that mathematicians distinguish. Technically, *incremental* utility is measured over a discrete interval, such as from 9 to 10, while marginal utility is a rate of change measured over an infinitesimal interval. But common usage applies the word *marginal* when the last unit is involved, even if a one-unit change is not infinitesimal. [9]

FIGURE 9-1
The Relation Between Household and Market Demand Curves

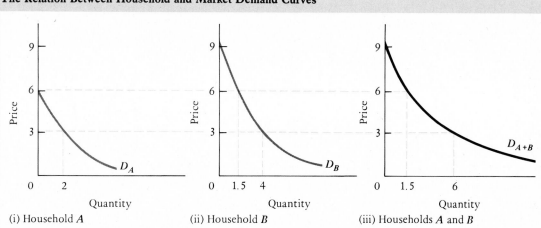

(i) Household *A*　　(ii) Household *B*　　(iii) Households *A* and *B*

An aggregate demand curve is the horizontal sum of the individual demand curves of all households in the market. The figure illustrates aggregation over only two households. At a price of $3, household *A* purchases 2 units and household *B* purchases 4 units; thus together they purchase 6 units. No matter how many households are involved the process is the same.

In (2) you are comparing the value you place on a small addition to your water consumption with the value you place on a small addition to your movie attendances. You are comparing your *marginal utility* of water with your *marginal utility* of movies. The response to choice (2) is far less predictable than the response to choice (1).

Some might select the extra movie; others might decide they have seen all the movies they can stand (marginal utility of another visit to the movies, *zero*) and would select the extra water. Furthermore, their choice would depend on whether it was made at a time when water was plentiful, so that they had more or less all the water they wanted (marginal utility of a little more water, *low*), or when water was scarce, so that they might put quite a high value on obtaining a little more water (marginal utility of a little more water, *high*).

Choices of type (1) are encountered much less commonly than are choices of type (2). If our income rises a little, we have to decide to have some more of one thing or another. When we find that we are overspending, or when our income falls, we have to decide what to cut down on, to have a little less of this or a little less of that.

Real choices are rarely conditioned by total utilities; it is marginal utilities that are relevant to choices concerning a little more or a little less.

The Hypothesis of Diminishing Marginal Utility

The basic hypothesis of utility theory, sometimes called the *law of diminishing marginal utility,* is

The utility that any household derives from successive units of a particular commodity will diminish as total consumption of the commodity increases, the consumption of all other commodities being held constant.

Consider further the case of water. Some minimum quantity is essential to sustain life, and a person would, if necessary, give up all his or her income to obtain that quantity of water. Thus, the marginal utility of that much water is extremely high. More than this bare minimum will be drunk, but the marginal utility of successive glasses of water drunk over a period will decline steadily.

Evidence for this hypothesis will be considered later, but you can convince yourself that it is at least reasonable by asking yourself a few questions. How much money would induce you to cut your consumption of water by one glass per week? The answer is, very little. How much would induce you to cut it by a second glass? By a third glass? To only one glass consumed per week? The answer to the last question is, quite a bit. The fewer glasses you are consuming already, the higher the marginal utility of one more or one less glass of water.

But water has many uses other than for drinking. A fairly high marginal utility will be attached to some minimum quantity for bathing, but much more than this minimum will only be used for more frequent baths and for having a water level in the tub higher than is absolutely necessary. The last weekly gallon used for bathing is likely to have a low marginal utility. Again, some small quantity of water is necessary for tooth brushing, but many people leave the water running while they brush. They can hardly pretend that the water going down the drain between wetting and rinsing the brush has a high utility. When all the extravagant uses of water by the modern consumer are considered, it is certain that the marginal utility of the last, say, 30 percent of all units consumed is very low, even though the total utility of *all* the units consumed is extremely high.

Utility Schedules and Graphs

Assuming that utility can be measured, it is possible to illustrate the hypothesis. The schedule in Table 9-1 is hypothetical. It merely illustrates the assumptions that have been made about utility. The table shows that total utility rises as the number of movies attended each month rises. Every-

thing else being equal, the more movies the household attends each month the more satisfaction it gets—at least over the range shown in the table. But the marginal utility of each additional movie per month is less than that of the previous one (even though each movie adds something to the household's satisfaction). The marginal utility schedule declines as quantity consumed rises. [10] The same data are shown graphically in the two parts of Figure 9-2.

Can marginal utility reach zero? With many commodities there is some maximum consumption after which additional units give no additional utility. If the individual were forced to consume more, the additional units would actually reduce his or her total utility.

TABLE 9–1 **TOTAL AND MARGINAL UTILITY SCHEDULES**

Number of movies attended (per month)	Total utility	Marginal utility
0	0	
1	30	30
2	50	20
3	65	15
4	75	10
5	83	8
6	89	6
7	93	4
8	96	3
9	98	2
10	99	1

Total utility rises but marginal utility declines as this household's consumption increases. The marginal utility of 20, shown as the second entry in the last column, arises because total utility increased from 30 to 50—a difference of 20—with attendance at the second movie. Technically this is "incremental utility" over the interval from 1 to 2 units. To indicate that the marginal utility is associated with the change from one rate of movie attendances to another, the figures are recorded between the rows. When plotting marginal utility on a graph, it is plotted at the midpoint of the interval over which it is computed.

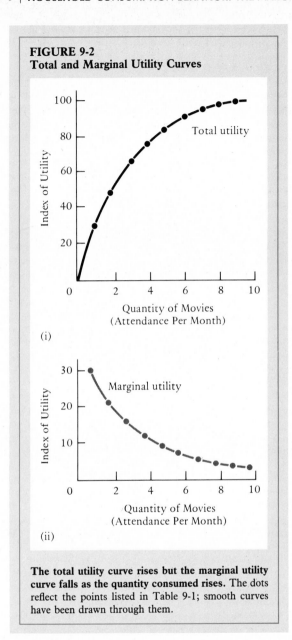

FIGURE 9-2
Total and Marginal Utility Curves

(i)

(ii)

The total utility curve rises but the marginal utility curve falls as the quantity consumed rises. The dots reflect the points listed in Table 9-1; smooth curves have been drawn through them.

Cigarettes are an obvious example. Even for heavy smokers, long before consumption has reached the point of chain-smoking from the second of awakening to the moment of falling asleep, smoking an additional cigarette would cease to add to utility and would begin to subtract from it. At that point additional cigarettes would have a negative marginal utility or, as it is sometimes called, a marginal *disutility*. The same is true of many other commodities such as food, alcoholic beverages, and most recreation. (Although a few fanatics might be happy to play golf from sunup to sunset seven days a week for the rest of their lives, most people would not.)

Maximizing Utility

A basic assumption of the economic theory of household behavior is that households consistently follow a particular rule.

The members of a household are assumed to maximize their total utility.

This is one way of saying that the members of households try to make themselves as well off as they possibly can in the circumstances in which they find themselves. Sometimes this assumption is taken to mean that households are narrowly selfish and have no charitable motives. Not so; if, for example, the household derives utility from giving its money away to others, this can be incorporated into the analysis. The marginal utility it gets from a dollar given away can be compared with the marginal utility it gets from a dollar spent on itself.

The Equilibrium of a Household

How can a household adjust its expenditure so as to maximize the total utility of its members? Should it go to the point at which the marginal utility of each commodity is the same, that is, the point at which it would value equally the last unit of each commodity consumed? This would make sense only if each commodity had the same price per unit. But if a household must spend $3 to buy an additional unit of one commodity and only $1 for a unit of another, the first commodity would represent a poor use of its money if the marginal utility of each were equal: It would be spending $3 to get satisfaction that it could have acquired for only $1.

The household maximizing its utility will allocate its expenditure among commodities so that the utility of the last dollar spent on each is equal.

Imagine that the household is in a position in which the utility of the last dollar spent on carrots yields three times the utility of the last dollar spent on brussels sprouts. In this case, total utility can be increased by switching a dollar of expenditure from sprouts to carrots and gaining the difference between the utilities of a dollar spent on each.

The utility-maximizing household will continue to switch its expenditure from sprouts to carrots as long as a dollar spent on carrots yields more utility than a dollar spent on sprouts. But this switching reduces the quantity of sprouts consumed and, given the law of diminishing marginal utility, raises the marginal utility of sprouts; at the same time, it increases the quantity of carrots consumed and thereby lowers the marginal utility of carrots. Eventually, the marginal utilities will have changed enough so that the utility of a dollar spent on carrots is just equal to the utility of a dollar spent on sprouts.

At this point there is nothing to be gained by a further switch of expenditure from sprouts to carrots. If the household persisted in reallocating its expenditure, it would further reduce the marginal utility of carrots (by consuming more of them) and raise the marginal utility of sprouts (by consuming less of them). Total utility would then be lower because the utility of a dollar spent on sprouts would now exceed the utility of a dollar spent on carrots.

Let us now leave carrots and sprouts and deal with commodities in general. Denote the marginal utility of the last unit of X by MU_x and its price by p_x. Let MU_y and p_y refer to a second commodity. The marginal utility per dollar of X will be MU_x/p_x. For example, if the last unit adds 30 units to utility and costs \$2, then its marginal utility per dollar is $30/2 = 15$.

The condition required for a household to maximize its utility is, for any pair of commodities,

$$\frac{MU_x}{p_x} = \frac{MU_y}{p_y} \qquad [1]$$

This says that the household will allocate its expenditure so that the utility gained from the last dollar spent on each commodity is equal.

This is the fundamental equation of the utility theory of demand. Each household demands each good (for example, movie attendance) up to the point at which the marginal utility per dollar spent on it is the same as the marginal utility of a dollar spent on another good (for example, water). When this condition is met, the household cannot shift a dollar of expenditure from one commodity to another and increase its utility.

An Alternative Interpretation of Household Equilibrium

It is possible to rearrange the terms in Equation [1] to gain an additional insight into household behavior.

$$\frac{MU_x}{MU_y} = \frac{p_x}{p_y} \qquad [2]$$

The right-hand side of this equation is given to the household by the market; it states the *relative* price of the two goods. It is determined by the market and is outside the control of the individual household, which reacts to these market prices but is powerless to change them. The left-hand side concerns the ability of the goods to add to the household's satisfaction; it is within the control of the household. In determining the quantities of different goods it buys, the household determines also their marginal utilities. (If you have difficulty seeing why, look again at Figure 9-2(ii).)

If the two sides of Equation [2] are not equal, the household can increase its total satisfaction by rearranging its purchases. Assume, for example, that the price of a unit of X is twice the price of a unit of Y, ($p_x/p_y = 2$), while the marginal utility of a unit of X is three times that of a unit of Y, ($MU_x/MU_y = 3$). It will now pay the household to buy more X and less Y. If, for example, it reduces its purchases of Y by two units, it will free enough purchasing power to buy a unit of X. Since one new unit of X bought yields 1.5 times the satisfaction of two units of Y foregone, this switch is worth making. What about a further switch of

X for Y? As the household buys more X and less Y, the marginal utility of X will fall and the marginal utility of Y will rise. The\household will go on rearranging its purchases—reducing Y consumption and increasing X consumption—until, in this example, the marginal utility of X is only twice that of Y. At this point there is no further room to increase total satisfaction by rearranging purchases between the two commodities.

Now consider what the household is doing. It is faced with a set of prices that it cannot change. The household responds to these prices, and maximizes its satisfaction, by adjusting the things it can change—the quantities of the various goods it purchases—until Equation [2] is satisfied for all pairs of commodities.

This sort of equation—one side representing the choices the outside world gives decision makers and the other side representing the effect of those choices on their welfare—recurs in economics again and again. It reflects the equilibrium position reached when decision makers have made the best adjustment they can to the external forces that limit their choices.

When all households are fully adjusted to a given set of market prices, each and every household will have identical ratios of its marginal utilities for each pair of goods. This is because each household faces the same set of market prices. Of course a rich household may consume more of each commodity than will a poor household. The rich and the poor households (and every other household) will, however, adjust their *relative* purchases of each commodity so that the relative marginal utilities are the same for each household. Thus, if the price of X is twice the price of Y, each household will purchase X and Y to the point at which the household's marginal utility of X is twice its marginal utility of Y.

The Derivation of the Household's Demand Curve

To derive the household's demand curve for a commodity, it is only necessary to ask what happens when there is a change in the price of that commodity. To do this for candy, take Equation [2] and let X stand for candy and Y for all other commodities. Assume that candy involves a small proportion of the consumer's total expenditure. If total expenditure on candy rises from $1 a month to $2 in response to a 10 percent fall in the price of candy, this represents a large increase in candy consumption, and the marginal utility of candy must fall. But the extra dollar spent on candy may mean only 1¢ less spent on each of a hundred different commodities, and this reduction in the consumption of each of them is so small that it will have a negligible effect on their marginal utilities.

What will happen if, with all other prices constant, the price of candy rises? The household that started from a position of equilibrium will now find itself in a position in which[2]

$$\frac{MU \text{ of candy}}{MU \text{ of } Y} < \frac{\text{price of candy}}{\text{price of } Y} \qquad [3]$$

To restore equilibrium, it must buy less candy, thereby raising its marginal utility until once again Equation [2] is satisfied (where X is candy). The common sense of this is that the marginal utility of candy *per dollar* falls when its price rises. The household began with the utility of the last dollar spent on candy equal to the utility of the last dollar spent on all other goods, but the rise in candy prices changes this. The household buys less candy (and more of other goods) until the marginal utility of candy rises enough to make the utility of a dollar spent on candy the same as it was originally. Thus, if candy prices have doubled, the quantity purchased must be reduced until the marginal utility of candy has doubled.

This analysis leads to the basic prediction of demand theory.

A rise in the price of a commodity (with income and the prices of all other commodities held constant) will lead to a decrease in the quantity of the commodity demanded by each household.

---

[2] The inequality sign ($<$) always points to the smaller of two magnitudes. When the price of candy rises, the right-hand side of Equation [2] increases. Until the household adjusts its consumption patterns, the left-hand side will stay the same. Thus Equation [2] is replaced by Inequality [3].

If this prediction is valid for each household, it is also true for all households taken together. Thus, the theory predicts a downward-sloping market demand curve.

USING MARGINAL UTILITY THEORY

Consumers' Surplus

Assume that you would be willing to pay as much as $100 a month for the amount of a commodity you consume rather than do without it. Further, assume that you actually buy the commodity for $60 instead of $100. What a bargain! You have paid $40 less than the top figure you were willing to pay. Yet this sort of bargain is not rare; it occurs every day in any economy where prices do the rationing. Indeed it is so common that the $40 "saved" in this example has a name: *consumers' surplus*. A precise definition will come later; in the meantime, let us see how this surplus arises.

Consumers' surplus is a direct consequence of diminishing marginal utility. To illustrate the connection, suppose we have collected the information shown in Table 9-2 on the basis of an interview with Mrs. Schwartz. Our first question is, If you were getting no milk at all, how much would you be willing to pay for one glass per week? With no hesitation, she replies, $3. We then ask, If you had already consumed that one glass, how much would you pay for a second glass per week? After a bit of thought she answers, $1.50. Adding one glass per week with each question, we discover that she would be willing to pay $1 to get a third glass per week and $.80, $.60, $.50, $.40, $.30, $.25, and $.20 for successive glasses from the fourth to the tenth glasses per week. The information shows that she puts progressively lower valuations on each additional glass of milk, and this illustrates the general concept of diminishing marginal utility.

But Mrs. Schwartz does not have to pay a different price for each glass of milk she consumes each week. Instead she finds that she can buy all the milk she wants at the prevailing market price.

Suppose the price is $.30. She will buy eight glasses per week (one each weekday and two on Sunday) because she values the eighth glass just at the market price while valuing all earlier glasses at higher amounts. Because she values the first glass at $3 but gets it for $.30, she makes a "profit" of $2.70 on that glass. Between her $1.50 valuation of the second glass and what she has to pay for it she clears a "profit" of $1.20. She clears $.70 on the third glass, and so on. These "profit" amounts are called her consumers' surpluses on each glass. They are shown in column 3 of the table; the total surplus is $5.70 per week.

While other consumers would put different numerical values into Table 9-2, diminishing marginal utility implies that the figures in column 2 would be declining for each consumer. Since a consumer will go on buying further units until the value he or she places on the last unit equals the market price, it follows that there will be a consumers' surplus on every unit consumed except the last one.

In general, **consumers' surplus** is the difference between the total value consumers place on all the units consumed of some commodity and the payment they must make to purchase that amount of that commodity. The total value placed by each consumer on the total consumption of some commodity can be estimated in at least two ways: The valuation that the consumer places on each successive unit may be summed; or the consumer may be asked how much he or she would pay to consume the amount in question if the alternative were to have none of the commodity.[3]

The data in columns 1 and 2 of Table 9-2 give Mrs. Schwartz's demand curve for milk. It is her demand curve because she will go on buying glasses

---

[3] This is only an approximation, but it is good enough for our purposes. More advanced theory shows that the calculations presented here ignore an "income effect." As a result, they slightly overestimate consumers' surplus. Although it is sometimes necessary to correct for this bias, no amount of refinement upsets the general result that we establish here: When consumers can buy all units they require at a single market price, they pay for the quantity consumed much less than they would be willing to pay if faced with the choice between that amount and nothing.

TABLE 9–2 CONSUMERS' SURPLUS ON MILK CONSUMPTION BY ONE CONSUMER

(1) Glasses of milk consumed per week	(2) Amount the consumer would pay to get this glass	(3) Consumers' surplus if milk costs $.30 per glass
First	$3.00	$2.70
Second	1.50	1.20
Third	1.00	0.70
Fourth	0.80	0.50
Fifth	0.60	0.30
Sixth	0.50	0.20
Seventh	0.40	0.10
Eighth	0.30	0.00
Ninth	0.25	—
Tenth	0.20	—

Consumers' surplus on each unit consumed is the difference between the market price and the maximum price the consumer would pay to obtain that unit. The table shows the value that a single consumer, Mrs. Schwartz, puts on successive glasses of milk consumed each week. Because marginal utility declines, she would pay successively lower amounts for each additional unit consumed. As long as she would be willing to pay more than the market price for any unit, she will buy that unit and obtain a consumers' surplus on it. The marginal unit is the one valued just at the market price and on which no consumers' surplus is earned.

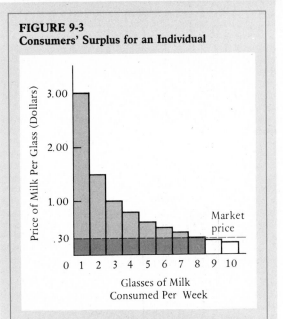

FIGURE 9-3
Consumers' Surplus for an Individual

Glasses of Milk Consumed Per Week

Consumers' surplus is the sum of the extra valuations placed on each unit over and above the market price paid for each. This figure is based on the data in Table 9-2. Mrs. Schwartz will pay the dark shaded area for the eight glasses of milk she will consume per week when the market price is 30¢ a glass. The total value she places on these eight glasses is the entire shaded area. Hence her consumers' surplus is the light shaded area.

of milk as long as she values each glass at least as much as the market price she must pay for it. When the market price is $3 per glass, she will buy only one glass; when it is $1.50, she will buy two glasses—and so on. The total valuation is the area below her demand curve, and consumers' surplus is that part of the area that lies above the price line. This is shown in Figure 9-3. Figure 9-4 shows that the same relation holds for the smooth market demand curve that indicates the total amount all consumers would buy at each price.

The Paradox of Value Revisited

We saw at the beginning of this chapter that early economists found it paradoxical that the market often valued necessary commodities such as water

much lower than it valued such luxuries as diamonds. To restate the "paradox," they distinguished a commodity's *value in use* (its total utility) and its *value in exchange* (its total market value, that is, price *times* quantity).[4] It seemed reasonable to them that commodities with high use values should have high market values. A precise statement of what they expected is this: For any two commodities, the ratio of their values in exchange

[4] The total utilities of two commodities cannot be simply related to their relative market *prices*, since the latter can be made anything we want by choosing the units appropriately. For example, one barrel of diamonds is expensive relative to one barrel of water, but a one-carat diamond is cheap relative to one reservoir full of water.

DOES DEMAND THEORY REQUIRE HOUSEHOLDS TO BE PERFECTLY RATIONAL?

We have deduced that if households wished to maximize their utility, they would vary their consumption patterns so that relative marginal utilities would be exactly proportional to relative market prices.

It is tempting to dismiss this theory out of hand with the objection that it is unrealistic to pretend that households always act with such mechanical consistency. After all, most of us know people who occasionally buy strawberries in spite of, or even because of, a rise in their price, or who spend a week's pay on a binge or a frivolous purchase that they afterward regret.

To judge such an observation, it is helpful to distinguish three possible uses of demand theory. The first use is to study the aggregate behavior of all households—as illustrated, for example, by the market demand curve for a product. The second use is to make statements about an individual household's probable actions. The third use is to make statements about what each household will certainly do.

Now consider a firm that is wondering about the effect on its sales of a price increase. Clearly, the first use of demand theory is what interests the firm. It does not care what every last household will do, nor really, does it care what *you* will do. It wants to know whether in the aggregate, and by how much, its sales will decrease if it raises prices.

This aggregate use of demand theory is the most common in economics. It depends on having knowledge of the shapes of relevant market demand curves. It does not, however, require that we know the behavior of each individual household. The second use of demand theory, though much less common than the first, is occasionally important; it is sometimes desirable to be able to say what a single household (or a group of households) will probably do. The third use is by far the least important, for it is rarely necessary, possible, or even interesting to try to state categorically what each household will certainly do.

The criticisms cited in the second paragraph of this box apply only to the third use of demand theory. The observations referred to refute only the prediction that *all* households *always* behave as assumed by the theory. To predict the existence of a relatively stable downward-sloping market demand curve (the first use), or to predict what an individual household will probably do (the second use), we do *not* require that *all* households behave as is assumed by the theory all of the time. Consider two illustrations.

First, some households may always behave in a manner not assumed by the theory. Households whose members are mental defectives or have serious emotional disturbances are obvious possibilities. The inconsistent or erratic behavior of such households will not cause market demand curves to depart from their downward slope, provided these households account for a minority of total purchasers of any product. Their erratic behavior will be swamped by the normal behavior of the majority of households.

Second, an occasional irrationality or inconsistency on the part of every household will not upset the downward slope of the market demand curve so long as these isolated inconsistencies do not occur at the same time in all households. As long as such inconsistencies are unrelated across households, occurring now in one and now in another, their effect will be offset by the normal behavior of the majority of households.

The downward slope of the demand curve requires only that at any moment of time most households are behaving as assumed by the theory. This is compatible with inconsistent behavior on the part of some households all of the time and on the part of all households some of the time.

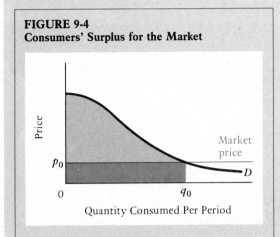

FIGURE 9-4
Consumers' Surplus for the Market

Price (vertical axis)

p_0

Market price

D

0   q_0

Quantity Consumed Per Period

Total consumers' surplus is the area under the demand curve and above the price line. The demand curve shows the amount consumers would pay for each unit of the commodity if they had to buy their units one at a time. The area under the demand curve shows the total valuation consumers place on all units consumed. For example, the total value that consumers place on q_0 units is the entire shaded area under the demand curve up to q_0. At a market price of p_0 the amount paid for q_0 units is the dark shaded area. Hence consumers' surplus is the light shaded area.

should conform to the ratio of their values in use. In the case of water and diamonds, this led to the *incorrect* prediction that

$$\frac{p \times q \text{ of diamonds}}{p \times q \text{ of water}} = \frac{\text{total utility of diamonds}}{\text{total utility of water}} \quad [4]$$

The paradox of value was resolved when later economists discovered that Equation [4] was inconsistent with the assumption that households are utility maximizers. The reason is that utility-maximizing behavior relates *marginal* utilities to prices (as shown in Equation [2]), not total utilities to total values purchased (as hypothesized in Equation [4]).

Thus, for example, the fact that air is free means that people will use it until its marginal utility is zero. However, its zero value in exchange does not preclude its having a high value in use (total utility). To understand the case of water and dia-

monds, remember that water is cheap because there is enough of it that people consume it to the point at which its *marginal* utility is very low; they are not prepared to pay a high price to obtain a little more of it. Diamonds are expensive because they are scarce (the owners of diamond mines keep diamonds scarce by limiting output), and those who buy them have to stop at a point where marginal utility is still high; they are prepared to pay a high price for an additional diamond.

Elasticity of Demand: Necessities and Luxuries

Closely related to the paradox of value is the idea of relating elasticities to total utilities. It is possible to define necessities and luxuries in terms of total utilities. Certain commodities, called *luxuries*, have low total utilities; they can be dispensed with altogether if circumstances require. Other commodities, called *necessities*, are essential to life; they have high total utilities because certain minimum quantities of them are essential indeed.

So far so good. Error often creeps in, however, when people try to use commonsense knowledge about luxuries and necessities to predict demand elasticities and to dispense with the need for measurement. They argue that since luxuries can easily be given up, they will have highly elastic demands: when their prices rise, households can stop purchasing them. On the other hand, necessities ought to have almost completely inelastic demands because when prices rise, households have no choice but to continue to buy them.

If it worked, this approach would save us time; we would have to determine only whether a particular commodity was a necessity or a luxury to be able to predict its elasticity of demand. But elasticity of demand depends on marginal utilities, not total utilities.

Demand theory leads to the prediction that when the price of a commodity—say, eggs—rises, the household will reduce its purchase of eggs enough to increase its *marginal* utility to the point where the marginal utility per dollar spent on eggs is the same as for other commodities whose prices

WHAT DO ATTITUDE SURVEYS MEASURE?

Consider a type of survey that is popular both in the daily newspapers and in sociology and political science. These surveys take the form of asking such questions as:

Do you like the Republicans more than the Democrats?

In deciding to live in area A rather than area B, what factors influenced your choice? List the following in order of importance: neighbors, schools, closeness to swimming area, price and quality of housing available, play areas for children, general amenities.

In choosing a university, what factors were important to you? List in order of importance: environment, academic excellence, residential facilities, parents' opinion, school opinion, athletic facilities, tuition.

You should be able to add other examples to this list (which was drawn from real cases). *All of the above survey questions, and most of those you will be able to add, attempt to measure total rather than marginal utilities.* The total value being asked about includes the consumers' surplus. There is of course nothing illegal or immoral about this. People are free to measure anything that interests them, and in some cases knowledge of total utilities may be of practical value. But in many cases, actual behavior will be determined by marginal utilities, and anyone who attempts to predict such behavior from a (correct) knowledge of total utilities will be hopelessly in error.

Where the behavior being predicted involves an either-or decision, such as a vote for the Democratic or the Republican candidate, the total utility that is attached to each choice will indeed be what matters because the voters are choosing one or the other. But where the decision is marginal, between a little more and a little less, total utility is not what will determine behavior.

A recent newspaper poll in a large midwestern city showed that two-thirds of the city's voters rated its excellent school system as one of its important assets. Yet in a subsequent election the voters turned down a school bond issue. Is this irrational behavior, as the newspaper editorials charged? Does it show a biased sample in the poll? It demonstrates neither. The poll measured the people's assessment of the total utility derived from the school system (high), while the bond issue vote depended on the people's assessment of the marginal utility of a little more money spent on the school system (low). There is nothing contradictory in anyone's feeling that the total utility of the city's fine school system is very large but that the city has other needs that have a higher marginal utility than further money spent on school construction.

A recent survey showed—paradoxically, it claimed—that many Americans are getting more pleasure from their families just at the time that they are electing to have smaller families. There is nothing paradoxical about a shift in tastes that increases the marginal utility of the first two or three children and reduces the marginal utility of each further child. Nor is there any paradox in a parent's getting a high total utility from the total time spent with the children but assigning a low marginal utility to the prospect of spending a little additional time with them each evening.

did not rise. But will the reduction in quantity required to raise the marginal utility be a little or a lot? This depends on the shape of the marginal utility curve in the range that is relevant. If the marginal utility curve is flat, a large change in quantity is required and demand will be elastic. If the curve is steep, a small change will suffice and demand will be inelastic. Figure 9-5 presents two possible responses to a doubling in price. It leads to these important conclusions:

The response of quantity demanded to a change in price (i.e., the elasticity of demand) depends on the marginal utility over the relevant range and has no necessary relation to the total utility of the good.

Free Goods, Scarce Goods, and Freely Provided Goods

A **free good** is one for which the quantity supplied exceeds the quantity demanded at a price of zero. Such goods will therefore not command positive prices in a free-market system. Since a household's total utility can always be increased by its consuming more of any good having positive marginal utility, it follows that free goods will be consumed up to the point at which their marginal utilities are zero. Private firms have no incentive to produce free goods, but such goods may exist in nature. At some times in some places, air, water, salt, sand, and wild fruit have been free goods. Note that a good may be free at one time or place but not at another. But when a good is naturally free, the amount supplied by nature is so plentiful that every household can consume it to the point of zero marginal utility without exhausting the available supply.

There is no allocative reason to charge a price for a free good, for there is no reason to limit consumption.

A **scarce good** is one for which the quantity demanded exceeds the quantity supplied at a price of zero. Such goods will therefore command positive prices in a free-market system. Most goods are scarce goods. If all such goods had zero prices, the total amount that people would want to consume would greatly exceed the amount that could be

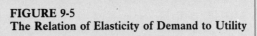

FIGURE 9-5
The Relation of Elasticity of Demand to Utility

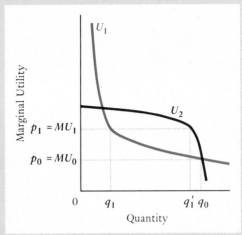

Elasticity of demand is determined by marginal utilities in the relevant range, not total utilities. Consider two different marginal utility curves for a commodity, U_1 and U_2. Suppose price is p_0. Given either utility curve the household consumes the quantity q_0, where the last unit consumed has a marginal utility of MU_0. When the price doubles to p_1, the household must cut its consumption. The marginal utility required to achieve a new equilibrium doubles to MU_1. If the black line U_2 is the household's marginal utility curve, consumption only falls to q_1' and the household will have a very inelastic demand curve for the product. If, however, the colored line U_1 is the household's marginal utility curve, consumption falls to q_1 and the household will have a very elastic demand curve. Although the shape of the marginal utility curve in the relevant range is thus important, its shape outside of this range is irrelevant. But total utility depends upon the whole area under the curve. Depending on what happens between 0 and q_1, the colored curve can show more or less total utility. Thus total utility has no influence on the household's behavior when it seeks to raise marginal utility from MU_0 to MU_1.

produced by all the economy's resources. Thus goods are scarce in relation to households' desires for what can be produced.

The price system is one way of allocating scarce resources among competing uses in a way that permits households to maximize their utility, given the fact of scarcity.

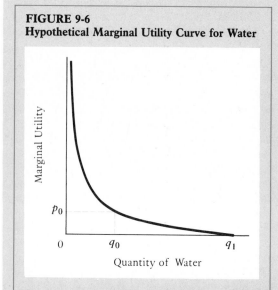

FIGURE 9-6
Hypothetical Marginal Utility Curve for Water

The imposition of a modest price may greatly reduce the quantity of water consumed without causing a large total sacrifice in the utility derived from water consumption. Suppose water is a scarce commodity, not a free good. If water is priced at p_0, consumers will consume q_0 units per month. Lowering the price to zero would increase the consumption to q_1. Much of the water that a household would consume at a zero price has a very low marginal utility.

Sometimes a scarce good is freely provided to consumers by the government. Whatever the merits of a particular free distribution, the economic consequences are clear. Households will treat it as free-to-them and consume to the point of zero marginal utility. This point is illustrated in Figure 9-6. Since even the last units require resources to produce, the government is in this situation using scarce resources to produce some units of the good which have low marginal utilities.

"Just" Prices

The emotional reaction to goods is often a response to their total utilities rather than to their marginal

utilities. We often hear an argument such as this: Water is a necessity of life of critical importance to rich and poor; it is wrong, therefore, to make people pay for so necessary a commodity. The government, so goes the argument, should freely provide such goods.

Such a policy will yield predictable results. If, for example, water is provided free instead of at a modest cost, the extra consumption that will occur will be for many uses that yield a relatively low utility (such as letting the water run while brushing teeth). The relevant question when deciding between a zero price and a modest price for water is not "Is water so necessary that we do not want to deprive anyone of *all* of it?" but rather "Are the marginal uses of water such that we do not want to discourage anyone from using water for these purposes?" Clearly, the two questions can be given different answers.

Evidence about the consumption of water at various prices suggests that the marginal utility curve for water is shaped like the curve in Figure 9-6. The difference between providing water free and charging a modest price for it may mean a great deal in the quantity of water consumed. The additional water is costly to provide, and its provision requires scarce resources that could have been used to produce other things. If the utility of the commodities foregone is higher than the utility of the extra water consumed, then people are worse off as a result of receiving water free. A charge for water would release resources from water production to produce goods that yield a higher utility. Of course, some minimum quantity of water could be provided free to every household, but the effects of this would be very different from those of making water generally free.

Similar considerations apply to food, medical services, and a host of other commodities that are necessities of life but also have numerous low utility uses which will be encouraged if the commodity is scarce but is provided very cheap or free.

The box on page 148 provides a very different example of the distinction between marginal and total utility.

Used Car Prices:
The Problem of "Lemons"

It is common for people to regard the huge loss of value of a new car in the first year as a sign that American consumers are overly style conscious and will always pay a big premium for the latest in anything. Professor George Akerlof of the University of California suggests a different explanation based upon the proposition that the utility expected to be received from a *purchased* one-year-old car will be lower than that of the average one-year-old car. Consider his theory.

Any particular model year of automobiles will include a certain proportion of "lemons"—cars that have one or more serious defects. Purchasers of new cars of a certain year and model take a chance on their car's turning out to be a lemon. Those who are unlucky and get a lemon are more likely to resell their car then those who are lucky and get a quality car. Hence in the used car market there will be a disproportionately large number of lemons for sale. Similarly, not all cars are driven in the same manner. Those that are driven long distances or under bad conditions are much more likely to be traded in or sold used than those that are driven on good roads and in moderate amounts.

Thus buyers of used cars are right to be suspicious of why the car is for sale, while salespeople are quick to invent reasons ("It was owned by a little old lady who only drove it on Sundays"). Because it is very difficult to identify a lemon, or a badly used car, before buying it, the purchaser will be prepared to buy a used car only at a price low enough to offset the increased probability that it is of poor quality.

These are wholly sensible consumer responses to uncertainty and may explain why one-year-old cars typically sell for a discount much larger than can be explained by the physical depreciation that occurs in one year in the average car of that model. The large discount reflects the lower utility the purchaser can expect from a used car because of the higher probability that it will be a lemon.

SUMMARY

1. Market demand curves reflect the aggregate of the consumption behavior of the millions of households in the economy.

2. Marginal utility theory distinguishes between the total utility gained from the consumption of all units of some commodity and the marginal utility resulting from the consumption of one more unit of the commodity.

3. The basic assumption made in utility theory about a household's tastes is that the utility the household derives from the consumption of successive units of a commodity per period of time will diminish as the consumption of that commodity increases.

4. The household maximizes its utility and thus reaches equilibrium when the utility derived from the last dollar spent on each commodity is equal. Another way of putting this is that the marginal utilities derived from the last unit of each commodity consumed will be proportional to their prices.

5. Consumers' surplus arises when a household can purchase every unit of a commodity at a price equal to the value that it places on the last unit purchased. Diminishing marginal utility implies that the household places a higher value on all other units purchased and hence that all but the last unit purchased will yield a consumers' surplus.

6. It is vital to distinguish between total and marginal utilities because most choices are related to marginal utilities and cannot be predicted from a knowledge of total utilities. The paradox of value involved a confusion between total and marginal utilities. Knowing whether a good is a necessity or a luxury will perhaps allow us to determine its total utility but will tell us nothing about its marginal utility. Yet it is marginal utility that is required for defining elasticity and understanding market behavior.

TOPICS FOR REVIEW

The paradox of value
Market demand and individual household demand curves
Total utility versus marginal utility
The hypothesis of diminishing marginal utility
Conditions for maximizing utility
The interpretation of $MU_x/MU_y = p_x/p_y$
Consumers' surplus

DISCUSSION QUESTIONS

1. Why is market demand the *horizontal* sum of individual demand curves? Is the vertical sum different? What would a vertical sum of individual demand curves show? Can you imagine any use of vertical summation of demand curves?
2. Which of the choices implied below involve a consideration of marginal utilities and which total utilities?
   a. The State Legislature debates whether 17-year-olds should be given the vote.
   b. A diet calls for precisely 1,200 calories per day.
   c. My doctor says I must give up smoking and drinking or else accept an increased chance of heart attack.
   d. When Armand Hammer decided to buy the Rembrandt painting *Juno* for a record $3.25 million, he called it the "crown jewel of my collection."
   e. I enjoyed my golf game today, but I was so tired that I decided to stop at the seventeenth hole.
3. Explain the transactions described in the following quotations in terms of the utility of the commodity. Interpret "worthless" and "priceless" as used here.
   a. "Bob Koppang has made a business of selling jars of shredded U.S. currency. The money is worthless, and

yet he's sold 53,000 jars already and has orders for 40,000 more—at $5.00 a jar. Each jar contains about $10,000 in shredded bills."
   b. "Leonardo da Vinci's priceless painting *Genevra de' Benci* was sold to the National Gallery of Art for $5 million."
4. The *New York Times* called it the great liver crisis. Chopped liver is a delicacy on the table, particularly the kosher table, but in the late 1970s it was a glut on the market. Prices had sunk to a 20-year low as supplies had risen to an all-time high due to a very high cattle slaughter. What do the following quotations from the *Times'* story tell you about the marginal and total utility of liver?
   a. "Grade A-1 liver is being used for cats and dogs instead of people. It's unheard of, it's a waste," says the manager of Kosher King Meat Products. "Even Israel is drowning in chopped liver."
   b. "They're falling all over their feet to sell to me," said the president of Mrs. Weinberg's Kosher Chopped Liver Co., which uses 3,500 pounds of liver daily. "I've been offered prices so low I can't believe them."
   c. "The nature of people being what they are, even though they like a good bargain, they're not going to eat something that doesn't agree with their taste."
5. John Ehrlichman, after leaving government service but before serving a prison sentence, was quoted as saying: "When I get to be king of the world, everybody is going to have four or five hours every day just for themselves, and the world will be a better place." What does this tell you about Mr. Ehrlichman's utility schedule? Under what circumstances would the world be a better place if someone made it obligatory for everyone to have several hours "just for themselves"?
6. "A survey shows that most people prefer butter to margarine." What exactly might this mean? Supposing it to be true, can you acccount for the facts that many people buy some of both butter and margarine each month and that in total more pounds of margarine are sold than pounds of butter?

10 HOUSEHOLD CONSUMPTION BEHAVIOR: BUDGET LINES AND THE INDIFFERENCE CURVE APPROACH

The marginal utility approach to household behavior discussed in Chapter 9 came first historically. It is still valued because of the great insights that the concept of marginal utility opened up. With the publication in 1939 of Sir John R. Hicks' classic *Value and Capital,* an alternative approach often called indifference curve analysis became popular in English-language economics.[1] This is not a com-

[1] Hicks, whose career has been spent mainly at Oxford, was the first British recipient of the Nobel prize in economics for the contributions to economics that he made in *Value and Capital* and elsewhere. He did not invent indifference curve analysis; he took over, popularized, and extended the use of a concept developed by the great Italian economist Vilfredo Pareto in the first decade of this century. As is so often true in science, it is not the discoverer or the inventor but the one who makes the timely and insightful application who has the major impact. Thus it was Hicks, not Pareto, who led to the almost universal use of indifference analysis by economists in the 1940s and 1950s. Pareto in his time was following "hints" given in 1896 by the American economist Irving Fisher and in a slim volume published in 1886 by the Italian engineer Giovanni Antonelli. Such is the history of ideas.

peting theory but a slightly different way of looking at choices by households. Its major innovation was to dispense with the notion of a *measurable* concept of utility that is required by marginal utility theory.

THE BUDGET LINE

Consider a household faced with the choice between only two goods, food (*F*) and clothing (*C*). (Such choices between two goods reveal everything necessary for elementary theory.) Assume that the household has a certain money income, say $120 a week, and that the prices for food and clothing are fixed at the outset at $4 a unit for food and $2 a unit for clothing. The household does not save; its only choice is in deciding how much of its $120 to spend on food and how much to spend on clothing.

The household's problem is illustrated by the line *ab* in Figure 10-1, which shows the combinations of food and clothing available to it. The household could spend all its income on clothing and obtain 60*C* and no *F* per week. Or it could decide to have 1*F* each week, at a cost of $4, and only 58*C*. It could also go to the other extreme and purchase only food, buying 30*F* and no *C*.

When all the points indicating combinations that are available to the household if it spends all its income are joined, the result is called the household's **budget line.** (It is also sometimes called an *isocost line* since all points on the line represent bundles of goods with the same total cost of purchase.)

Among the important properties of the budget line are the following. (You should check enough examples against Figure 10-1 to satisfy yourself that they are true.)

1. Points on the budget line represent bundles of commodities that exactly use up the household's income. (Try, for example, the point 20*C* and 20*F*.)
2. Points between the budget line and the origin represent bundles of commodities that use up less than the household's income. (Try, for example, the point 20*C* and 10*F*.)

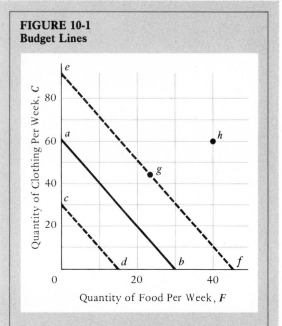

**FIGURE 10-1
Budget Lines**

The budget line shows the quantities of goods available to a household given its money income and the prices of the goods it buys. Any point indicates a combination (or *bundle*) of so much food and so much clothing. Point *h*, for example, indicates 60 units of clothing and 40 units of food per week. With an income of $120 a week and prices of $4 for food and $2 for clothing, the household's budget line is *ab*. This line shows all the combinations of *F* and *C* available to a household spending that income at those prices. Neither combination *g* nor *h* is attainable.

An increase in money income from $120 to $180, with money prices of *F* and *C* constant, shifts the budget line outward to the parallel line *ef*. At this level of income, combination *g* is attainable. A decrease in money income to $60 shifts the budget line to *cd*.

3. Points above the budget line represent combinations of commodities costing more to purchase than the household's present income. (Try, for example, the point 30*C* and 40*F*.)

The budget line shows all combinations of commodities that are available to the household given its money income and the prices of the goods that it purchases, if it spends all its income on them.

Shifts in the Budget Line

Changes in Money Income

What happens to the budget line when money income changes? If the household's money income is halved from $120 to $60 per week, prices being unchanged, then the amount of goods it can buy will also be halved. If it spends all its income on clothing, it will now get $30C$ and no F (point c in Figure 10-1; if it spends all its income on food, it will get $15F$ and no C (point d). All possible combinations now open to the household appear on budget line cd, which is closer to the origin than the original budget line.

If the household's income rises to $180, it will be able to buy more of both commodities than it could previously. The budget line shifts outward. If the household buys only clothing, it can have $90C$; if it buys only food, it can have $45F$; if it divides its income equally between the two goods, it can have $45C$ and $22.5F$.

Variations in the household's money income, with prices constant, shift the budget line parallel to itself.

Proportional Changes in Prices of Both Goods

Changing both prices in the same proportion shifts the budget line parallel to itself in the same way that a money income change shifted it. Doubling both prices with money income constant halves the amount of goods that can be purchased and thus has exactly the same effect on the household's budget line as halving money income with money prices constant. In both cases the household's original budget line is shifted inward.

It is now apparent that it is possible to have exactly offsetting changes in prices and money incomes. Such a situation leaves the real choices available to the household unchanged.

A change in money income and a *proportional* change of the same amount in all money prices leaves the position of the budget line unchanged.

The **indexing** of money values is an arrangement that automatically increases them as the average level of all prices rises during an inflation. For example, when money wages are indexed, they are increased in proportion to increases in the price level. The purpose of indexing is to accomplish the offsetting changes analyzed in the preceding paragraph. Prices rise, shifting inward the budget line for a constant money income. Indexing then raises incomes in proportion to the price rise. This shifts the budget line back to its original position and leaves the purchasing power of wages unaffected by the inflation.

Changes in Relative Prices

Absolute price or *money price* or merely *price* of a commodity means the amount of money that must be spent to acquire one unit of the commodity. A **relative price** is the ratio of two absolute prices. The statement "the price of F is $2" refers to an absolute price; "the price of F is twice the price of C" refers to a relative price.

A change in a relative price can be accomplished either by changing both of the absolute prices in different proportions or by holding one price constant and changing the other. It is useful for our purposes to do the latter. The effects of such a change are shown in Figure 10-2. The basic conclusion that emerges is this:

A change in relative prices—such as occurs when one price changes while the other price remains constant—changes the slope of the budget line.

The economic significance of the slope of the budget line for food and clothing (which we have just seen to be related to the relative prices of the two commodities) is that it reflects the opportunity cost of food in terms of clothing. To increase food consumption with expenditure constant, one must move along the budget line, consuming less clothing. Suppose the price of food (p_F) is $2 and the price of clothing (p_C) is $1. With income fixed, it is necessary to forego the purchase of two units of clothing to acquire one unit extra of food. The opportunity cost of food in terms of clothing is thus two units of clothing. But it can also be stated as p_F/p_C, which is the relative price. Notice that

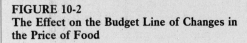

FIGURE 10-2
The Effect on the Budget Line of Changes in
the Price of Food

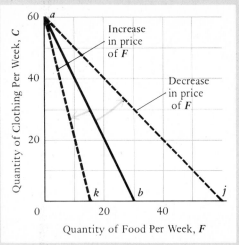

A change in the price of one commodity changes
relative prices and thus changes the slope of the
budget line. The original budget line *ab* arose from a
money income of $120, with units of *C* priced at $2
and units of *F* at $4. A fall in the price of *F* to $2
doubles the quantity of *F* obtainable for any given
quantity of *C* purchased and pivots the budget line
outward to *aj*. A rise in the price of *F* to $8 reduces
the quantity of *F* obtainable and pivots the budget
line inward to *ak*.

is, the quantity of goods and services that can be
purchased with its money income.

If money prices remain constant, any change in
money income will cause a corresponding change
in real income. If the household's money income
rises by 10 percent (say from $10,000 to $11,000),
the household can if it wishes buy 10 percent more
of all commodities—its real income has also risen
by 10 percent.

If prices change, however, real and money incomes will not change in the same proportion—
indeed, they can easily change in opposite directions. Consider a situation in which all money
prices rise by 10 percent. If money income falls,
or rises by any amount less than 10 percent, real
income falls. If money income also rises by 10
percent, real income will be unchanged. Only if
money income rises by more than 10 percent will
real income also rise.

Changes in real income are shown graphically
by shifts in the budget line. When the budget line
in Figure 10-1 shifts outward, away from the origin, real income rises. When the line shifts inward,
toward the origin, real income falls.

If we are interested in the household's potential
standard of living, we are interested in its ability
to purchase goods and services; this is appropriately measured by real income, not by money income.

INDIFFERENCE CURVE ANALYSIS

What the household does is determined by both
what it can do and what it would like to do. The
budget line shows what the household *can do;* the
choices that it can make given its money income
and the prices of the commodities that it buys.
What the household *wants to do* is determined by
its tastes.

An Indifference Curve

Take an imaginary household and give it some
quantity of each of the two goods, say 18 units of
clothing and 10 units of food. (A consumption
pattern for a household that contains quantities of

this relative price ($p_F = 2p_C$) is consistent with an
infinite number of absolute prices. If $p_F = \$40$ and
$p_C = \$20$, it still takes the sacrifice of two units of
clothing to acquire one unit of food. This shows
that it is relative, not absolute, prices that determine opportunity cost. The general conclusion is
that the opportunity cost of *F* in terms of *C* is
measured by the slope of the budget line or (the
equivalent) by the relative price ratio. [11]

Real and Money Income

A household's **money income** is its income measured in money units, so many dollars and cents
per week or per year. A household's **real income**
is the purchasing power of its money income, that

two or more distinct goods is called a *bundle* or a *combination* of goods.) Now offer the household an alternative bundle of goods, say 13 units of clothing and 15 units of food. This alternative has 5 fewer units of clothing and 5 more units of food than the first one. Whether the household prefers this bundle depends on the relative valuation that it places on 5 more units of food and 5 fewer units of clothing. If it values the extra food more than the foregone clothing, it will prefer the new bundle to the original one. If it values the food less than the clothing, it will prefer the original bundle.

There is a third alternative: If the household values the extra food the same as it values the foregone clothing, it would gain equal satisfaction from the two alternative bundles of food and clothing. In this case, the household is said to be indifferent between the two bundles.

Assume that after much trial and error a number of bundles have been identified, each of which gives equal satisfaction. These are shown in Table 10-1.

There will of course be combinations of the two commodities other than those enumerated in the table that will give the same level of satisfaction to the household. All of these combinations are shown in Figure 10-3 by the smooth curve that passes through the points plotted from the table. This curve is an indifference curve. In general, an **indifference curve** shows all combinations of goods that yield the same satisfaction to the household.

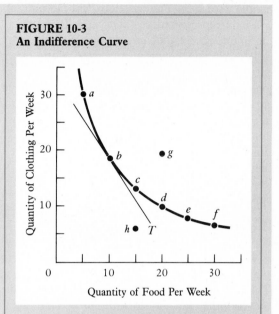

**FIGURE 10-3
An Indifference Curve**

This indifference curve shows combinations of food and clothing that yield equal satisfaction and among which the household is indifferent. Points *a* to *f* are plotted from Table 10-1. The smooth curve through them is an indifference curve; each combination on it gives equal satisfaction to the household. Point *g* above the line is a preferred combination to any point on the line; point *h* below the line is an inferior combination to any point on the line. The slope of the line *T* gives the marginal rate of substitution at point *b*. Moving down the curve from *b* to *f*, the slope flattens, showing that the more food and the less clothing the household has, the less willing it will be to sacrifice further clothing to get more food.

TABLE 10-1 ALTERNATIVE BUNDLES GIVING A HOUSEHOLD EQUAL SATISFACTION

Bundle	Clothing	Food
a	30	5
b	18	10
c	13	15
d	10	20
e	8	25
f	7	30

These bundles all lie on a single indifference curve. Since all of these bundles of food and clothing give equal satisfaction, the household is "indifferent" among them.

A household is *indifferent* between the combinations indicated by any two points on one indifference curve.

Any points above and to the right of the curve show combinations of food and clothing that the household would prefer to combinations indicated by points on the curve. Consider, for example, the combination of 20 food and 18 clothing, which is represented by point *g* in the figure. Although it may not be obvious that this bundle must be preferred to bundle *a* (which has more clothing but less food), it is obvious that it will be preferred to bundle c because there is both less clothing and less food represented at c than at g. Inspection of the graph shows that *any* point above the curve will be obviously superior to *some* points on the curve in the sense that it will contain both more food and more clothing than those points on the curve. But since all points on the curve are equal in the household's eyes, the point above the curve must be superior to *all* points on the curve. By a similar argument, points below and to the left of the curve represent bundles of goods that are inferior to bundles represented by points on the curve.

The Marginal Rate of Substitution

How much clothing would the household be prepared to give up to get one more unit of food? The answer to this question measures what is called the marginal rate of substitution of clothing for food. The **marginal rate of substitution (MRS)** is the amount of one commodity a consumer would be prepared to give up to get one more unit of another commodity. The first basic assumption of indifference theory is that the algebraic value of the MRS is always negative. This means that to gain a positive change in its consumption of one commodity, the household is prepared to incur a negative change in its consumption of a second.

Graphically the negative marginal rate of substitution is shown by the downward slope of all indifference curves. (See for example the curve in Figure 10-3.)

The Hypothesis of Diminishing Marginal Rate of Substitution

The second basic assumption of indifference theory is that the marginal rate of substitution between any two commodities depends on the amounts of the commodities currently being consumed by the household. Consider a case where the household has a lot of clothing and only a little food: Common sense suggests that the household might be willing to give up quite a bit of its plentiful clothing to get one unit more of very scarce food. Now consider a case where the household has

only a little clothing and quite a lot of food: Common sense suggests that the household would be willing to give up only a small amount of its scarce clothing to get one more unit of already plentiful food.

This example illustrates the hypothesis of the **diminishing marginal rate of substitution**. In terms of our clothing-food example, the hypothesis states that the less clothing and the more food the household has already, the smaller will be the amount of clothing it will be willing to give up to get one further unit of food.

The hypothesis says that the marginal rate of substitution changes systematically as the amounts of two commodities presently consumed vary. Take any two commodities, A and B. The more A and the less B the household currently has, the less B will it be willing to give up to get a further unit of A. The graphical expression of this hypothesis is that the slope of any indifference curve becomes flatter as the household moves downward to the right along the curve. [12] In Figure 10-3 a movement downward to the right means that less clothing and more food is being consumed. The decreasing steepness of the curve means that less and less clothing need be sacrificed to get one further unit of food.

The hypothesis is illustrated in Table 10-2, which is based on the example of food and clothing in Table 10-1. The last column of the table shows the rate at which the household is prepared to sacrifice units of clothing per unit of food obtained. At first the household will sacrifice 2.4 units of clothing to get 1 unit more of food, but as its consumption of clothing diminishes and that of food increases, the household becomes less and less willing to sacrifice further clothing for more food.[2]

---

[2] Movements between widely separated points on the indifference curve have been examined. In terms of a very small movement from any of the points on the curve, the rate at which the household will give up clothing to get food is shown by the slope of the tangent to the curve at that point. The slope of the line T, which is a tangent to the curve at point b in Figure 10-3, may thus be thought of as the slope of the curve at that precise point. It tells us the rate at which the household will sacrifice clothing per unit of food obtained when it is currently consuming 18 clothing and 10 food (the coordinates of point b).

TABLE 10–2 **THE MARGINAL RATE OF SUBSTITUTION BETWEEN CLOTHING AND FOOD**

Movement	(1) Change in clothing	(2) Change in food	(3) Marginal rate of substitution (1) ÷ (2)
From a to b	−12	5	−2.4
From b to c	− 5	5	−1.0
From c to d	− 3	5	− .6
From d to e	− 2	5	− .4
From e to f	− 1	5	− .2

The marginal rate of substitution of clothing for food declines as the quantity of food increases. This table is based on Table 10-1. When the household moves from a to b, it gives up 12 units of clothing and gains 5 units of food; it remains at the same level of overall satisfaction. The household at point a was prepared to sacrifice 12 clothing for 5 food (i.e., $^{12}/_5 = 2.4$ units of clothing per unit of food obtained). When the household moves from b to c, it sacrifices 5 clothing units for 5 food units (a rate of substitution of 1 unit of clothing for each unit of food).

The Indifference Map

So far we have constructed only a single indifference curve. However, there must be a similar curve through other points in Figure 10-3. Starting at any point, such as g, there will be other combinations that will yield equal satisfaction to the household and, if the points indicating all of these combinations are connected, they will form another indifference curve. This exercise can be repeated as many times as we wish, and as many indifference curves as we wish can be generated. The farther any indifference curve is from the origin, the higher will be the level of satisfaction given by any of the combinations of goods indicated by points on the curve.

A set of indifference curves is called an **indifference map,** an example of which is shown in Figure 10-4. It specifies the household's tastes by showing its rate of substitution between the two commodities for every level of current consump-

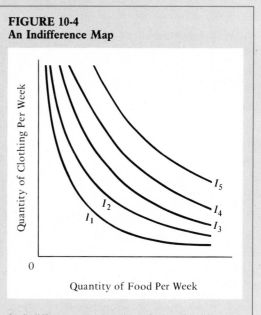

**FIGURE 10-4
An Indifference Map**

Quantity of Clothing Per Week (vertical axis)
Quantity of Food Per Week (horizontal axis)

I_5, I_4, I_3, I_2, I_1

An indifference map consists of a set of indifference curves. All points on a particular curve indicate alternative combinations of food and clothing that give the household equal satisfaction. The further the curve from the origin, the higher the level of satisfaction it represents. Thus I_5 is a higher indifference curve than I_4 and represents a higher level of satisfaction.

tion of these commodities. When economists say that a household's tastes are *given,* they do not mean that the household's current consumption pattern is given; rather, they mean that the household's entire indifference map is given.

The Equilibrium of the Household

Indifference maps describe the preferences of households. Budget lines describe the possibilities open to the household. To predict what households will actually do, both of these sets of information must be put together. This is done in Figure 10-5. The household's budget line is shown in the figure by the straight line, while its tastes are shown by its indifference map (a few of whose curves are shown in the figure). Any point on the budget line

FIGURE 10-5
The Equilibrium of a Household

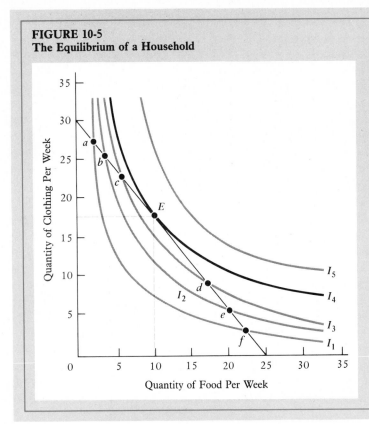

Equilibrium occurs at *E*, where an indifference curve is tangent to the budget line. The household has an income of $750 a week and faces prices of $25 a unit for clothing and $30 a unit for food. A combination of *C* and *F* indicated by point *a* is attainable, but by moving along the budget line higher indifference curves can be reached. The same is true at *b* and *c*. At *E*, however, where an indifference curve is tangent to the budget line, it is impossible to reach a higher curve by moving along the budget line. If the household did alter its consumption bundle by moving from *E* to *c* or *d*, for example, it would move to the lower indifference curve *I₃* and thus to a lower level of satisfaction.

is attainable. But which point will actually be chosen by the household that is interested in maximizing its satisfactions?

Since the household wishes to maximize its satisfactions, it wishes to reach its highest attainable indifference curve. Inspection of the figure shows that if the household purchases any bundle on its budget line at a point cut by an indifference curve, a higher indifference curve can be reached. Only when the bundle purchased is one where an indifference curve is tangent to the budget line is it impossible for the household to alter its purchases and reach a higher curve.

The household's satisfaction is maximized at the point at which an indifference curve is tangent to its budget line.

At such a tangency position, the slope of the in-

difference curve (the marginal rate of substitution of the goods in the household's preferences) is the same as the slope of the budget line (the relative prices of the goods in the market). The common sense of this result is that if the household values goods at a different rate than the market does, there is room for profitable exchange. The household can give up some of the good it values relatively less than the market and take in return some more of the good it values relatively higher than the market does. When the household is prepared to swap goods at the same rate as they can be traded on the market, there is no further opportunity for it to raise its satisfaction by substituting one commodity for the other.

The household is presented with market information (prices) that it cannot itself change. It adjusts to these prices by choosing a bundle of goods such that, at the margin, its own subjective evaluation of the goods conforms with the evaluations given by market prices.

The Reaction of the Household to a Change in Income

We have seen that a change in income leads to parallel shifts of the budget line—inward toward the origin when income falls and outward away from the origin when income rises. For each level of income there will be an equilibrium position at which an indifference curve is tangent to the relevant budget line. Each such equilibrium position means that the household is doing as well as it possibly can for that level of income. If we move the budget line through all possible levels of income, and if we join up all the points of equilibrium, we will trace out what is called an **income-consumption line,** an example of which is shown in Figure 10-6. This line shows how consumption bundles change as income changes, with relative prices held constant. It differs from the income-consumption curve for a single commodity studied in Chapter 6 (see page 92), which graphed the consumption of a single commodity against the level of income.

The Reaction of a Household to a Change in Price

We already know that a change in the relative price of the two goods changes the slope of the budget line. If the price of food is varied continuously, each price will have an equilibrium position. Connecting these positions traces out a **price-consumption line,** as is shown in Figure 10-7. Notice that as the relative price of food and clothing changes, the relative quantities of food and clothing purchased also change. In particular, as the price of food falls the household buys more food.[3]

[3] There is a rarely encountered but theoretically possible exception to this rule, a Giffen good, that is described in the last part of this chapter.

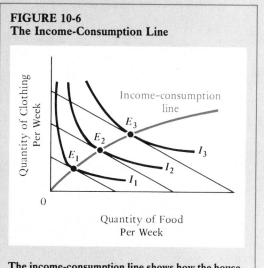

FIGURE 10-6
The Income-Consumption Line

Income-consumption line

E_3

E_2

E_1

I_3

I_2

I_1

Quantity of Clothing Per Week

0

Quantity of Food Per Week

The income-consumption line shows how the household's purchases react to a change in income with relative prices held constant. Increases in income shift the budget line out parallel to itself, moving the equilibrium from E_1 to E_2 to E_3. By joining up all the points of equilibrium, an income-consumption line is traced out.

Derivation of Demand Curves

If food and clothing were the only two commodities purchased by households, we could derive a demand curve for food from the price-consumption line of Figure 10-7. On an indifference map, that line represents how the quantity of food demanded varied as the price of food changed, with the price of clothing unchanged. To use indifference theory to derive the kind of demand curve introduced in Chapter 5, however, it is necessary to depart from the world of two commodities that we have used so far in this chapter.

What happens to the household's demand for some commodity, say carrots, as the price of that commodity changes, *all other prices being held constant?* In Figure 10-8 a new type of indifference map is plotted in which the quantity of carrots is represented on the horizontal axis and the value of all other goods consumed is represented on the

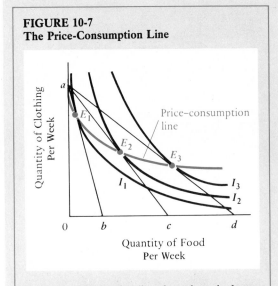

FIGURE 10-7
The Price-Consumption Line

The price-consumption line shows how the household's purchases react to a change in one price with money income and other prices held constant. Decreases in the price of food (with money income and the price of clothing constant) pivot the budget line from ab to ac to ad. The equilibrium position moves from E_1 to E_2 to E_3. By joining up all the points of equilibrium, a price-consumption line is traced out.

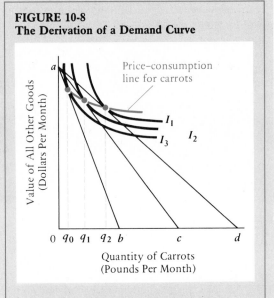

FIGURE 10-8
The Derivation of a Demand Curve

Every point on the price-consumption line corresponds to both a price of the commodity and a quantity of the commodity demanded; this is the information required for a demand curve. The household has $\$a$ of income; if it buys no carrots, it can consume $\$a$ worth of all other goods. For each price of carrots there is a single budget line. As the price of carrots falls, the budget line pivots from ab to ac to ad, and the quantity of carrots demanded rises from q_0 to q_1 to q_2. This leads to a downward-sloping demand curve for carrots.

vertical axis. We have in effect used "everything but carrots" as the second commodity. The indifference curves give the rate at which the household is prepared to swap carrots for money (which allows it to buy all other goods) at each level of consumption of carrots and of other goods. Given the money price of carrots and the household's income, a budget line can be obtained showing all those combinations of carrots and other goods that the household can consume for its given level of money income and the given price of carrots. Now assume a change in the money price of carrots. By joining the points of equilibrium, we can trace a price-consumption line between carrots and all other commodities in the same way that such a line was traced for food and clothing in Figure 10-7.

Figure 10-8 is similar to Figure 10-7, but notice

two differences. First, the axes are labeled differently, and second, the price-consumption line in Figure 10-8 is crowded into the upper part of the diagram, indicating that whatever the price of carrots, the household does not spend a large part of its income on them. Every point on the price-consumption line corresponds to one price and one quantity of carrots demanded. In the figure, the quantity of carrots consumed increases as their price falls. These pairs of price-quantity values can be transferred to a new figure, whose axes represent price of carrots and quantity of carrots, and used to plot a conventional downward-sloping demand curve.

The Slope of the Demand Curve[4]

The price-consumption line in Figure 10-8 slopes down to the right as price decreases, indicating that quantity of carrots demanded increases. But, as a little experimentation will show you, one can draw indifference curves in such a way that, in response to a decrease in price, the quantity demanded remains unchanged—that is, the demand would be perfectly inelastic. It is even possible that in response to a decrease in price, less is actually consumed rather than more. This possibility, which means that a commodity might have an upward-sloping demand curve, has been discussed at length in demand theory. A good with such a demand curve is called a **Giffen good,** after the Victorian economist who is thought to have observed such a case. The conditions that would bring this situation about are not often found in the real world, but we can deepen our understanding of the economic theory of demand by seeing what they are.

Income and Substitution Effects

A fall in the price of a commodity can lead a household to increase purchases of it for two different reasons. First, because its relative price has fallen, people will tend to substitute the commodity for other, more expensive goods, even if the household's total purchasing power remains unchanged. This is called the **substitution effect.** Second, a fall in the price of one commodity with all other prices constant has the effect of a rise in income by making it possible for the household to have more of all goods. This is a second incentive to increase quantity consumed and is called the **income effect** of a price change.

We illustrate these two effects graphically in Figure 10-9, which is similar to Figure 10-8 but examined under a magnifying glass. Points E_0 and E_2 are on the price-consumption line for carrots. The increase in quantity of carrots demanded is the result of both a substitution and an income effect. Figure 10-9 separates the two effects. We can think of this separation as occurring in the following way. The substitution effect is defined by sliding the budget line around a fixed indifference curve until it is tangent at the slope that represents the lower price. This leads to a move from point E_0 to an imaginary equilibrium point such as E_1. The income effect is then defined by a parallel shift of the budget line that is required to move from E_1 to the actual new equilibrium point, E_2. The move from E_1 to E_2 is as if the household's income is increased with no change in price from an initial position of E_1.

In Figure 10-9 income and substitution effects are in the same direction, both tending to increase quantity demanded in response to a decrease in price. Is this necessarily the case? The answer is no. While it follows from the convex shape of indifference curves that the substitution effect is always in the same direction, income effects can be in either direction. The direction depends on the distinction we drew earlier between normal and inferior goods.

The Slope of the Demand Curve for a Normal Good

For a normal good, an increase in real income due to a decrease in the price of the commodity leads to its increased consumption, reinforcing the substitution effect. Because quantity demanded increases, the demand curve slopes downward.

The Slope of the Demand Curve for an Inferior Good

Figure 10-10 shows indifference curves for an inferior good. The income effect is negative in each part of the diagram. This follows from the nature of an inferior good: as income rises, less of the good is consumed. In each case the substitution effect serves to increase the quantity demanded as price decreases and is offset to some degree by the negative income effect. The final result depends

---

[4] The remainder of this chapter may be omitted without loss of continuity.

FIGURE 10-9
The Income Effect and the Substitution Effect in Indifference Theory

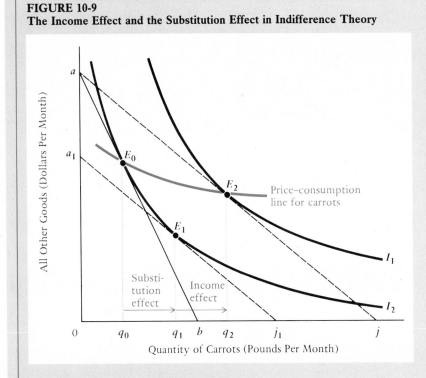

The substitution effect is defined by sliding the budget line around a fixed indifference curve; the income effect is defined by a parallel shift of the budget line. The original budget line is at ab and a fall in the price of carrots takes it to aj. The original equilibrium is at E_0 with q_0 of carrots consumed and the final equilibrium is at E_2 with q_2 of carrots consumed. To remove the income effect, imagine reducing the household's income until it is just able to attain its original indifference curve by shifting the line aj to a parallel line nearer the origin until it just touches the indifference curve that passes through E_0. The intermediate point E_1 divides the quantity change into a substitution effect q_0q_1 and an income effect q_1q_2. It can also be defined by sliding the original budget line ab around the indifference curve until its slope reflects the new relative prices.

upon the relative strengths of the two effects. In 10-10(i) the negative income effect only partially offsets the substitution effect and thus quantity demanded increases as a result of the price decrease, though not as much as for a normal good. This is the typical pattern for inferior goods, and it too leads to downward-sloping demand curves, often relatively inelastic ones.

In 10-10(ii) the negative income effect actually outweighs the substitution effect and thus leads to an upward-sloping demand curve. This is the Giffen case. For this to happen the good must be inferior. But that is not enough; the change in price must have a negative income effect *strong enough* to offset the substitution effect. A combination of circumstances that makes this possible is not often

expected, and therefore an upward-sloping market demand curve is at most an infrequent exception to the general prediction that demand curves will slope downward.

The Shape of Market Demand Curves

Empirically, economists tend to accept the so-called **law of demand** that asserts that the price of a product and the quantity demanded in the market vary inversely with each other. Criticisms of the law of demand have taken various forms, focusing on the Giffen good, the conspicuous consumption good, and (by far the most important) the good whose demand is perfectly inelastic. Let us consider each of these in turn.

FIGURE 10-10
Income and Substitution Effects for Inferior Goods

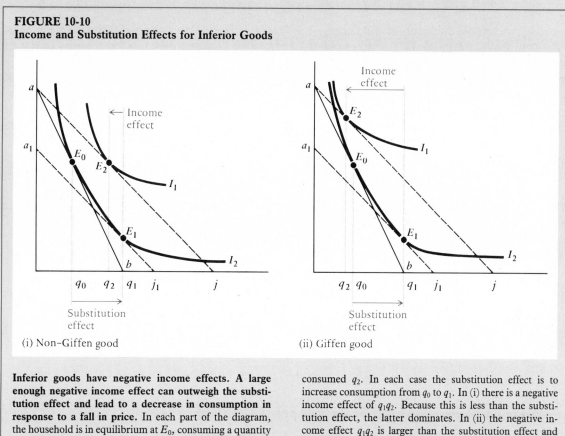

(i) Non–Giffen good

(ii) Giffen good

Inferior goods have negative income effects. A large enough negative income effect can outweigh the substitution effect and lead to a decrease in consumption in response to a fall in price. In each part of the diagram, the household is in equilibrium at E_0, consuming a quantity of carrots q_0. Now the price decreases and the budget line shifts to aj, with a new equilibrium at E_2 and quantity

consumed q_2. In each case the substitution effect is to increase consumption from q_0 to q_1. In (i) there is a negative income effect of q_1q_2. Because this is less than the substitution effect, the latter dominates. In (ii) the negative income effect q_1q_2 is larger than the substitution effect and quantity consumed actually decreases. This is the so-called Giffen case.

The Giffen Good

Great interest was attached to Giffen's apparent refutation of the law of demand. He is supposed to have observed that during the nineteenth century a rise in the price of imported wheat led to an increase in the price of bread but that the consumption of bread by the British working class increased.

While there is some doubt that what Giffen asserted really occurred, it is certainly possible. Suppose that bread is the diet staple of a great many people and that its price rises sharply. This may be

expected to compel larger expenditures on bread, further impoverishing many households to the point where they are forced to substitute bread (even though it is more expensive) for other more luxurious forms of nourishment. While possible, the fact is that such cases are all but unknown in the real world.

Conspicuous Consumption Goods

Thorstein Veblen in *The Theory of the Leisure Class* (1899) suggested that some commodities were consumed not for their intrinsic qualities but because they carried a snob appeal. The more expensive such a commodity became, the *greater* might be its ability to confer status on its purchaser.

This too is possible. Elizabeth Taylor and Joe Namath may buy diamonds, not because they particularly like diamonds per se but because they wish to show off their wealth in an ostentatious but socially acceptable way. They are assumed to value diamonds precisely because they are expensive; thus a fall in price might lead them to stop buying diamonds and to switch to a more satisfactory object of conspicuous consumption. People of this sort will have upward-sloping *individual* demand curves for diamonds. They may also behave in the same way with respect to luxury cars: they may buy them *because* they are expensive.

However, no one has ever observed statistically an upward-sloping *market* demand curve for commodities such as diamonds or luxury cars. The reason for this, notwithstanding the snob appeal of certain goods, is easy to discover. Consideration of the countless lower-income consumers who would be glad to buy diamonds or Cadillacs if only they were sufficiently inexpensive suggests that upward-sloping demand curves for a few individual wealthy households are much more likely than is an upward-sloping market demand curve for the same commodity.

Perfectly Inelastic Demand Curves

Even if demand curves do not slope *upward to the right* as the previous cases have suggested, the substantial insight provided by the law of demand would be diminished if there were many important commodities for which changes in price had virtually no effect on quantity demanded.

It is surprising how often the assumption of a vertical demand curve is implicit. A common response of urban bus or subway systems to financial difficulties is to propose a percentage fare increase equal to the percentage their deficit is of their revenues. Even professors are not immune: At a meeting of the American Association of University Professors, a motion was introduced "to raise annual dues by 20 percent, in order to raise revenues by 20 percent"—in spite of the empirical evidence that a previous increase in dues had led (as the theory would predict) to a significant drop in membership.

It was once widely argued that the demand for gasoline was virtually perfectly inelastic—on the ground that people who had paid thousands of dollars for cars would never balk at a few pennies extra for gas. The events of recent years have proven how wrong that argument was: Higher gas prices led to smaller cars, to more car pools, to more economical driving speeds, and to less pleasure driving. Falling gas prices in the early 1980s have led to a reversal of these trends.

As we have seen, a mass of accumulated evidence suggests that most demand curves do in fact slope downward to an appreciable degree.

For practical purposes, the hypothesis of the downward-sloping demand curve can be regarded as conforming with the evidence.

SUMMARY

1. Indifference curves and indifference theory provide an alternative way of studying household consumption behavior. The basic constructs of indifference curve analysis are the budget line and the indifference map.

2. The budget line shows all combinations of commodities that are available to the household given its money income and the prices of the goods that it purchases, if it spends all its income on them.

3. Variations in the household's money income shift the budget line parallel to itself. Changes in relative prices change the slope of the budget line.

4. While the budget line describes what the household *can* purchase, indifference curves describe the household's tastes and, therefore, refer to what it would *like* to do. A single indifference curve joins combinations of commodities that give the household equal satisfaction and among which it is therefore indifferent. An indifference map is a set of indifference curves.

5. The basic hypothesis about tastes is that of a diminishing marginal rate of substitution. This hypothesis states that the less of one good and the more of another that the household has, the less willing it will be to give up some of the first good to get a further unit of the second. Graphically this means indifference curves are downward-sloping and convex to the origin.

6. The household achieves an equilibrium that maximizes its satisfactions given its budget line at the point at which an indifference curve is tangent to its budget line.

7. The income-consumption line shows how quantity consumed changes as income changes with relative prices constant.

8. The price-consumption line shows how quantity consumed changes as relative prices change. When prices change, the household will consume relatively more of the commodity whose relative price falls and relatively less of the commodity whose relative price rises. The price-consumption line between one commodity and all other commodities contains the same information as an ordinary demand curve. Transferring the price-quantity pairs to a diagram whose axes represent price and quantity leads to a conventional demand curve.

9. The effect of a change in price of one commodity, all other prices and money income constant, not only changes relative prices but also real incomes. A price decrease can affect consumption both through the substitution effect that depends upon relative prices and the income effect.

10. Demand curves for normal goods slope downward because both income and substitution effects work in the same direction, a decrease in price leading to increased consumption.

11. For an inferior good, a decrease in price leads to more consumption via the substitution effect and less consumption via the income effect. In the extreme case of a Giffen good, the negative income effect actually more than offsets the substitution effect, and the consumption of the commodity could decrease as a result of a price decrease. This is a theoretical possibility without much empirical support.

12. The so-called law of demand leads to the prediction that the market demand curve for a commodity will slope downward and to the right except in very special circumstances. A great accumulation of empirical evidence supports the law of demand.

TOPICS FOR REVIEW

The budget line
Real income and money income
Indifference curves and indifference maps
The marginal rate of substitution
The tangency of the budget line and an indifference curve
The price-consumption and income-consumption lines
Income effect and substitution effect
Giffen goods, conspicuous consumption goods, and goods with perfectly inelastic demands
The law of demand

DISCUSSION QUESTIONS

1. Is a household relatively better off if its money income is decreased by 10 percent or if the prices of all the goods it buys are increased by 10 percent? Does it matter in answering this question whether the household spends all its income?

2. Some people do not care about the difference between two similar products. To see what effect this would have on their behavior, draw a typical indifference curve of a man who values white and whole wheat bread identically. Show his consumption equilibrium position when the price of white bread is held constant at $1.00 a loaf while that of whole wheat changes from $.80 to $1.00 to $1.20. How does this behavior differ from that of a household that likes both kinds of bread but has a diminishing marginal rate of substitution between white and whole wheat bread.

3. Between 1977 and 1982 the after-tax money incomes of American households rose by 65.3 percent while the CPI rose by 59.3 percent. What happened to real incomes?

4. When no-frills houses came on the market, they were regarded as a response to high prices. But they have captured

more of the market than expected. Some builders estimate they may ultimately constitute 80 percent of all houses sold. Suggest alternative explanations of this unexpected success. A leading builder says, "It's just like people driving smaller cars and drinking beer instead of Scotch." Is it also like students wearing running shoes instead of sneakers, or today's parents having fewer children than their parents did? Which of these things represent changes in taste, and which represent responses to changes in prices or incomes? If you don't know, what economic data would be useful in answering the question?

5. A reliable newspaper reports that synthetic motor oil is gaining in sales despite its high price relative to natural oil. What can account for a synthetic oil's selling at $4.95 a quart when the best conventional oils were readily available at about $1.50?

6. Answer question 6 on page 152 (in Chapter 9), using indifference curve analysis.

11 THE FIRM, PRODUCTION, AND COST

Ask almost anyone you know to name 10 American business firms. The odds are overwhelming that the list will include some of these firms: General Motors Corporation, U.S. Steel, General Electric, American Telephone & Telegraph, Dow Chemical, Standard Oil, Du Pont, the Bank of America, United Airlines, the Prudential Insurance Company, and the National Broadcasting Company. Drive around Ypsilanti, Michigan, and note at random 10 firms that come into view. They will likely include an A & P supermarket, Richardson's Pharmacy, a Shell service station, Schaeffer's Hardware Store, Haabs, and the First National Bank of Ypsilanti. Drive through Iowa or Nebraska and look around you: Every farm is a business firm as well as a home.

Firms develop and survive because they are efficient institutions for organizing resources to produce goods and services and for organizing their sale and distribution. While General Motors,

Haabs, and the Iowa farm are all *firms,* what do they have in common? It is not hard to count ways in which they are different. But insight can also be gained in treating them all under a single heading. This is what economic theory does. Economists usually assume that the firm's behavior can be understood in terms of a common motivation. Whether the firm is Ma and Pa's Bar and Grill or the Ford Motor Company and whether a particular decision is made by the board of directors, the third vice-president in charge of advertising, or the owner-manager is regarded as irrelevant to predicting what decisions are made.

Before studying how the firm is treated in economic theory, we shall examine more closely the firm in America today, to see from what we are abstracting. Criticisms that the theory neglects differences among firms will be considered in Chapter 19.

THE ORGANIZATION OF PRODUCTION

Proprietorships, Partnerships, and Corporations

There are three major forms of business organization: the single proprietorship, the partnership, and the corporation. In the **single proprietorship,** a single owner makes all decisions and is personally responsible for everything done by the business. In the **partnership,** there are two or more joint owners. Either may make binding decisions, and each partner is personally responsible for everything done by the business. In the **corporation,** the firm legally has an entity of its own. The owners (the stockholders) are not each personally responsible for everything that is done by the buiness. Owners elect a board of directors who hire managers to run the firm under the board's supervision.

In the United States today, there are about 7 million single proprietorships (not counting farms), 1 million partnerships, and nearly 2 million corporations.

Corporations account for more than two-thirds of the nation's privately produced income.

In manufacturing, transportation, public utilities, and finance, corporations do almost all of the nation's business. In trade and construction, they do about half the total business. Only in agriculure and in services (such as hair styling, medicine, and accounting) is the corporation relatively unimportant, yet even here its share of the business is steadily rising.

The Proprietorship and the Partnership: Advantages and Disadvantages

The major advantage of the single proprietorship is that the owner can readily maintain full control over the firm. The owner is the Boss. The disadvantages are, first, that the size of the firm is limited by the capital the owner can personally raise and, second, that the owner is personally responsible in law for all debts of the firm.

The ordinary (or general) partnership overcomes to some extent the first disadvantage of the proprietorship but not the second. Ten partners may be able to finance a much bigger enterprise than could one owner, but they are still subject to unlimited liability. Each partner is fully liable for all the debts of the firm. This liability is independent of the amount of money a particular partner may have invested in the firm. If a tenth partner makes $1,000 available (or $100, or nothing, for that matter) when joining a firm that subsequently goes bankrupt with debts of $100,000, this individual, and each of the other nine partners, is fully liable for the $100,000. If none of the other partners has salable personal assets, while the tenth partner has a house, a car, furniture, and some investments, he or she may lose all personal possessions so that the debts of the partnership can be cleared.

Obviously, people with substantial personal assets will be unwilling to enter a partnership unless they have complete trust in the other partners and a full knowledge of all the obligations of the firm. This need for trust is compounded because each partner usually has full power to sign contracts that bind the firm in its ordinary lines of business. One partner's fortune is at the mercy of every other partner's judgment. As a direct consequence of this authority and of the fact of unlimited liability, it is difficult to raise money through a partnership from persons who wish to invest but not be active in the business. Investors may be willing to put up $1,000 but unwilling to jeopardize their entire fortune; if, however, a person joins a partnership in order to do the former, he or she may also do the latter.

A further disadvantage of an ordinary partnership is that any time a partner dies or resigns the partnership agreement must be redrawn. This may make it difficult to have as a partner someone who is not genuinely interested and involved in the business but who wants to invest in it. For such a partner may decide at any time to liquidate his or her interest and so dissolve the partnership.

The **limited partnership** is designed to avoid some of these difficulties. General partners continue to have unlimited authority and unlimited liability, but there will also be limited partners. The limited partner's liability is restricted to the amount that he or she has invested in the firm. Such partners do not participate in the management of the firm or engage in agreements on behalf of the partnership. In effect, the limited partnership permits some division of the functions of decision making, provision of capital, and risk taking.

In most respects, this division of responsibility is more effectively achieved through the corporation. But there are certain professions in which general partnership is traditional. These include law, medicine, and (until recently) brokerage. Partnerships survive in these fields partly because each depends heavily on a relationship of trust with its clients, and the partners' unlimited liability for one another's actions is thought to enhance public confidence in the firm.

The Corporation: Advantages and Disadvantages

The corporation is regarded in law as an entity separate from the individuals who own it. It can enter into contracts, it can sue and be sued, it can own property, it can contract debts, and it can generally incur obligations that are the legal obligations of the corporation *but not of its owners*. This means that the corporation can enter into contracts in its own right and that its liability to adhere to such contracts can be enforced by suing the corporation, but not by suing the owners. The right of the corporation to be sued may not seem to be an advantage, but it is, because it makes it possible for others to enter into enforceable contracts with the corporation.

Although some corporations are very small or are owned by just a few stockholders who also manage the business, the most important type of corporation is one that sells shares to the general public. The company raises the funds it needs for the business by the sale of stock, and the shareholders become the company's owners. They are entitled to share in corporate profits. Profits when paid out, are called **dividends. Undistributed profits** also belong to the owners, but they are usually reinvested in the firm's operations. If the corporation is liquidated, shareholders split up any assets that remain after all debts are paid.

Diffuse ownership of corporate shares usually means that the owners cannot all be managers. Stockholders, who are entitled to one vote for each share they own, elect a board of directors. The board defines general policy and hires senior managers who are supposed to translate this general policy into detailed decisions.

Should the company go bankrupt, the personal liability of any one shareholder is limited to whatever money that shareholder has actually invested in the firm. This is called **limited liability.**

From a shareholder's viewpoint, the most important aspect of the corporation is limited liability.

The corporation's advantage is that it can raise capital from a large number of individuals, each of whom shares in the firms profits but has no liability for corporate action beyond risking the loss of the amount invested. Thus, investors know their exact maximum risk and may simply collect dividends without needing to know anything about policy or operation of the firm that they own collectively. Because shares are easily transferred from one person to another, a corporation has a continuity of life unaffected by frequent changes in the identity of its owners.

From the individual owner's point of view, there are disadvantages in investing in a corporation.

First, the owner may have little to say about the management of the firm. For example, if those who hold a majority of the shares decide that the corporation should not pay dividends, an individual investor cannot compel the payment of "his" or "her" share of the earnings. Second, the income of the corporation is taxed twice. The corporation is today taxed on its income at a rate of 46 percent before dividends are paid. Dividends are paid out of the after-tax income. Then individual stockholders are also taxed on any dividends paid to them. This "double taxation" of corporate income is viewed by some as clearly unfair and discriminatory; others see it as the price to be paid for the advantage of incorporation. Judging fom the continuing importance of the corporation in the United States, despite a corporate tax rate that has long been around 50 percent, the price has not been prohibitive.

The Rise of the Modern Corporation

The corporate form of organization is employed today wherever large enterprises are found. The principal reason is that it has decisive advantages over any other form in raising the vast sums of capital required for major enterprises. Historically, wherever and whenever large accumulations of capital in a single firm were required, the limited liability company developed. The corporate form has spread even to the service industries and agriculture, as firms in these industries grew to the point where they needed a lot of capital to function effectively.

Although historians have found roots of the corporation in Roman law and in the medieval guild system, the direct predecessor of the modern corporation was the English chartered company of the sixteenth century. The Muscovy Company, granted a charter in 1555, the East India Company, first chartered in 1600, and the Hudson's Bay Company, chartered in 1609 and still going strong in Canada 375 years later, are famous early examples of joint-stock ventures with limited liability. These companies were granted charters by the Crown so that English merchants could trade with particular re-

gions. Their special needs for many investors to finance a ship that would not return with its cargo for years—if it returned at all—made this *exceptional* form of organization seem desirable.

In the next three centuries, the trading company's critical needs (e.g., large capital requirements and the need to diversify risk) were seen to exist in other fields, and charters were granted in the fields of insurance, turnpikes and canals, and banking, as well as foreign trade. The Industrial Revolution, which made the large firm efficient, extended the needs for large amounts of capital committed over long periods of time to many more fields, and, during the nineteenth century, the demand for a general rather than a special privilege of incorporation became strong. General laws permitting incorporation with limited liability, *as a matter of right rather than special grant of privilege*, became common in England and in the United States during the late nineteenth century.

Today incorporation is relatively routine, although it is subject to a variety of state laws. Moderate fees are charged for the privilege of incorporation, and competition among the states for the incorporation fees has served to liberalize the conditions for incorporation throughout the country. Delaware is an example of a small state that at one time had a highly disproportionate share of incorporations because of its permissive laws. In insurance, Connecticut took the lead; most insurance companies founded before 1930 have Connecticut charters.

The Firm in Economic Theory

IBM and Alice's Restaurant certainly make decisions in different ways. Indeed, within a single large corporation not all decisions are made by the same people or in the same way. Nor are all decisions equally important. To take an example, someone at IBM decided to introduce a small computer in 1981. Someone else decided to call it the IBM personal computer and market it for home use. Someone else decided how and where to produce it. Someone else decided its price. Someone else decided how best to promote its sales. The

DIFFERENT KINDS OF FIRMS

In economic theory the firm is defined as the unit that makes decisions with respect to the production and sale of commodities. This single definition covers a variety of business organizations from the single proprietorship to the corporation, and a variety of business sizes from the unshaven inventor operating in his garage and financed by whatever he can extract from a reluctant bank manager to vast undertakings with tens of thousands of shareholders and creditors. We know that in large firms, decisions are actually made by many different individuals. We can nonetheless regard the firm as a single consistent decision making unit because of the assumption that all decisions are made to achieve the common goal of maximizing the firm's profits.

Whether a decision is made by a small independent proprietor, a plant manager, or a board of directors, that person or group is the firm for the purpose of that decision. This is a truly heroic assumption; it amounts to saying that for purposes of predicting those aspects of their behavior that interest us, we can treat a farm, a corner grocery, a department store, a small law

partnership, General Motors, and a giant multinational corporation, all under the umbrella of a single theory of the behavior of the firm. If this turns out to be even partially correct, it will prove enormously valuable in revealing some unity of behavior where to the casual observer there is only bewildering diversity.

You should not be surprised, therefore, if at first encounter the theory appears rather abstract and out of touch with reality. To generalize over such a wide variety of behavior, the theory must ignore many features with which we are most familiar and which distinguish the farmer from the grocer and each of them from the Exxon Corporation. Any theory that generalizes over a wide variety of apparently diverse behavior necessarily has this characteristic because it ignores those factors that are most obvious to us and which create in our minds the appearance of diversity. If it were not possible to do this, it would be necessary to have dozens of different theories, one for each type of firm. The task of learning economics would then be much more complex than it now is!

common aspect of these decisions is that all were in pursuit of the same goal—the manufacture and sale of successful computers and related products to earn profits for the owners of IBM.

Economic theory assumes that the same principles underlie each decision made within a firm and that the decision is uninfluenced by who makes it. The assumption that all firms are the same is further discussed in the box.

Motivation: Profit Maximization

It is assumed that the firm makes decisions in such a way that its profits will be as large as possible. In technical language, it is assumed that the

firm *maximizes its profits*. The concept of profits requires careful definition, which will be given later in this chapter. For now we may treat it in the everyday sense of the difference between the value of the firm's sales and the costs to firm of producing what is sold.

The assumption of profit maximization provides a principle by which a firm's decisions can be predicted.

Economists predict the firm's behavior in regard to the choices open to it by studying the effect that making each of the choices would have on the firm's profits. They then predict that from these alternatives the firm will select the one that produces the largest profits.

At this point you may well ask if it is sensible to build an elaborate theory on such a simple assumption about the motives of business people. Of course some business people are inspired by motives other than an overwhelming desire to make as much money as possible. Cases in which they use their positions to seek political influence or pursue charitable objectives are not difficult to document.

This theory does not say, however, that profit is the *only* factor that influences business people. It says only that profits are so important that a theory that assumes profit maximization to be the business firm's sole motive will produce predictions that are substantially correct.

Why is this assumption made? First, it is necessary to make *some* assumption about what motivates decision makers if the theory is to predict how they will act. Second, a great many of the predictions of theories based on this assumption have been confirmed by observation. Third, there is no general agreement that an alternative assumption has yet been shown to yield substantially better results. However, the assumption has been criticized, and alternatives have been suggested (see Chapter 19).

Factors of Production

The firm is in business to make profits. It attempts to do this by producing and selling commodities. Production is roughly like a sausage machine. Certain elements, such as raw materials and the services of capital and labor, are fed in at one end, and a product emerges at the other. The materials and factor services used in the production process are called **inputs,** and the products that emerge are called **outputs.** One way of looking at the process is to regard the inputs as being combined to produce the output. Another equally useful way is to regard the inputs as being used up, or sacrificed, to gain the output.

Each distinct input into the production process can be regarded as a factor of production. Literally hundreds of inputs enter into the output of a spe-

cific good. Among the inputs entering into automobile production are, to name only a few, sheet steel, rubber, spark plugs, electricity, machinists, cost accountants, fork-lift operators, managers, and painters. These inputs can be grouped into four broad classes: (1) those that are inputs to the automobile manufacturer but outputs to some other manufacturer, such as spark plugs, electricity, and sheet steel; (2) those that are provided directly by nature, such as land; (3) those are provided directly by households, such as labor; and (4) those that are provided by the machines used for manufacturing automobiles.

The first class of inputs is made up of goods produced by other firms. These products appear as inputs only because the stages of production are divided among different firms so that, at any one stage, a firm is using as inputs goods produced by other firms. If these products are traced back to the firm that provided them, it will be found that they were produced with the same four types of inputs.

Eventually, however, if these products are traced back to their sources, all production can be accounted for by the services of only three kinds of inputs, which are often called the *basic factors of production.* All the gifts nature, such as land and raw materials, the economist calls **land.** All physical and mental efforts provided by people are called **labor** services. All machines and other production equipment are grouped in a category called **capital,** defined as man-made aids to further production.

Extensive use of capital—the services of machines and other capital goods—is one distinguishing feature of modern as opposed to primitive production. Instead of making consumer goods directly with only the aid of simple natural tools, productive effort goes into the manufacture of tools, machines, and other goods that are desired not in themselves but as aids to making further goods. The use of capital goods renders the production processes *roundabout.* Instead of making what is wanted directly, a roundabout process first makes tools that will subsequently be used to make what is finally wanted.

TECHNOLOGICAL VERSUS ECONOMIC EFFICIENCY: AN EXAMPLE

Suppose, given the state of technology, there are only four known ways to produce 100 widgits per month:

	Quantity of inputs received	
	Capital	Labor
Method A	6	200
Method B	10	250
Method C	10	150
Method D	40	50

Method B is technologically inefficient because it uses more of both inputs than does method A. It thus wastes 4 units of capital and 50 units of labor. Among the other three methods, method A uses the least capital, but it is the most labor-using.* Method D conserves labor but uses much more capital. Method C is intermediate between them. (If you are tempted to consider method D technologically most effi-

* There is yet a third concept of efficiency, "engineering efficiency," in which least use of a particular factor is involved. When engineers speak of the efficiency of an engine, they may mean how much of the fuel it turns into power. Similarly, a maker of labor-saving machines might consider method D the most efficient because it uses the least amount of labor.

cient because it uses only 90 units of all resources, think again.)

Methods A, C, and D are all technologically efficient because no one of them uses more of both resources than either of the others.

Which one is the least costly—that is, is economically efficient? We cannot tell without knowing the costs of capital and of labor. Economic efficiency depends on factor prices. Consider the three cases shown in the table below. As we move from case I to II to III, a unit of labor becomes increasingly expensive *relative to* a unit of capital.

Method A is economically efficient when labor is cheap relative to capital. Method C becomes efficient when labor gets somewhat more expensive relative to capital. Finally, when labor gets very expensive relative to capital, method D, which uses least labor per unit of capital, becomes economically efficient.

To test your understanding, answer these questions:

1. Can a technologically *inefficient* method ever be economically efficient?
2. Is there a set of factor prices for which *both* method C and method D will be economically efficient?

	Factor prices per unit		Total cost of factors		
	Capital	Labor	Method A	Method C	Method D
Case I	$50	$3	$ 900	$950	$2,150
Case II	20	5	1,120	950	1,050
Case III	15	5	1,090	900	850

Economic Efficiency

Firms must decide not only what and how much to produce but by what method goods will be produced. In general, there is more than one way to

produce a given product. Indeed, if this were not the case there would be no need for firms to face the decision of *how* to produce. It is possible to produce agricultural commodities by farming a small quantity of land, combining a great deal of labor and capital with each acre of land, as is done in Belgium; it is also possible to produce the same commodities by farming a great deal of land, using only a small amount of labor and capital per acre of land, as is done in Australia.

What does it mean to ask which process is best? One meaning of *best* is the process that uses the fewest inputs for producing a given output, or, in other words, the one that is technically most efficient. **Technological efficiency** measures use of inputs in physical terms; **economic efficiency** measures use in terms of costs.[1] An example distinguishing the concepts is shown in the box on page 175.

The economically most efficient method is the one that costs the least. Economic efficiency depends on factor prices *and* on technological efficiency.

COST AND PROFIT TO THE FIRM

The Meaning and Measurement of Cost

Economic efficiency has been defined in terms of cost. But what is cost? **Cost,** to the producing firm, is the *value* of the factors of production used in producing its output.

Notice the use of the word *value* in the definition. A given output produced by a given technique, say 6,000 cars produced each week by American Motors with its present production methods, will have a given set of inputs associated with it—so many working hours of various types of laborers, supervisors, managers, and technicians, so many tons of steel, glass, and aluminum, so much electric light and other services, and so many hours of the time of various machines. To know the cost of this diverse set of factor inputs, the value of each in money terms must be calculated. The sum of these separate costs is the total cost to American Motors of producing 6,000 cars

per week. "Costing" may be very easy or very difficult.

Purpose in Assigning Costs

Economists' interest in costs is a direct consequence of the notion that factor services are scarce and, as a result, valuable. Thus, in using them up to produce outputs, the firm uses things that have value. From the point of view of a profit-maximizing firm, the profit from production consists of the difference between the value of the outputs and the value of the inputs. Knowing costs, then, is a precondition to knowing profits, and knowing profits is necessary to understanding behavior. An economist might discuss this behavior for several reasons: (1) to *describe* actual behavior of a firm, (2) to *predict* how the firm's behavior will respond to specified changes in the conditions it faces, (3) to *help* the firm make the best decisions it can in achieving its goals, and (4) to *evaluate* how well firms use scarce resources.

The same measure of cost need not be correct for all of these purposes. For example, if the firm happens to be misinformed about the value of some resource, it will behave according to that misinformation. In describing or predicting the firm's behavior, economists should use the information the firm actually uses, even if the economist knows it is incorrect. But in helping the firm to achieve its goals, economists should substitute the correct information.

Economists use a well-established definition of costs in solving problems of the kind cited in items 3 and 4 of the above list. If business people use the same definition and have the same information, the economist's definition will be appropriate for problems of types 1 and 2 as well. This will be assumed for the moment.

Opportunity Cost

Although the details of economic costing vary, they are governed by a common principle that is sometimes called *user cost* but is more commonly called *opportunity cost*.

[1] Efficiency plays an important role in economic discussions. We shall discuss it at greater length in Chapter 14.

OPPORTUNITY COST MORE GENERALLY

Opportunity cost plays a vital role in economic analysis, but it is also a fundamental principle that applies to a wide range of situations. It is one of the great insights of economics. Consider some examples:

■ George Bernard Shaw, on reaching his 90th birthday, was asked how he liked being 90. He is reputed to have said, "It's fine, when you consider the alternative."

■ Llewelyn Formed likes to hear both Dan Rather and John Chancellor. If he finally settles on Chancellor, what is the opportunity cost of this decision?

■ Link Heartthrob, a 31-year-old bachelor, is thinking about marrying at last. But, although he thinks Miss Piggy is a lovely girl, he figures that if he marries her, he will give up the chance of wedded bliss with another girl he may meet next year. So he decides to wait a while. What additional information do you require to determine the opportunity cost of the decision?

■ Serge Ginn, M.D., complains that now that

he is earning large fees he can no longer afford to take the time for a vacation trip to Europe. In what way does it make sense to say that the opportunity cost of his vacation depends upon his fees?

■ Retired General William Russ, who is married to a very wealthy woman, has decided to contribute $5,000 to a political candidate he likes very much. His lawyer points out to him that since he is in the 50 percent tax bracket, and since political contributions are not deductible from his income, the real cost of his contribution is the same as giving an extra $10,000 to his favorite charity, the Gen. Russ Foundation. Is the opportunity cost of the political contribution $5,000 or $10,000?

■ Hard-Luck Harry loses $100 a week in a dice game. He knows the game is crooked but plays anyway because, as he says, "it's the only game in town." A reform mayor is elected and shuts down all gambling establishments. What is the opportunity cost to Harry?

The cost of using something in a particular venture is the benefit foregone (or opportunity lost) by not using it in its best alternative use.

An old Chinese merchants' proverb says: "Where there is no gain, the loss is obvious." The economic sense of this proverb is that the merchant who shows no gain has wasted time—time that could have been used in some other venture. The merchant has neglected the opportunity cost of his time.

What is given up *is* the cost of what is done. One of the problems in evaluating costs is that different people (or groups) may see or care about different alternatives. Jones sees the alternative to

watching television on a Saturday afternoon as playing golf; his wife regards the alternative as a family outing. For the present, analysis will be limited to cost as seen by the firm. In Chapter 24 other points of view will be considered. (The box considers opportunity cost more generally.)

The Measurement of Opportunity Cost by the Firm

In principle, measuring opportunity cost is easy. The firm must assign to each factor of production it has used a monetary value equal to what it has sacrificed to use the factor. Applying this principle to specific cases, however, reveals some tough problems.

Purchased and Hired Factors

Assigning costs is a straightforward process when factors purchased in one period are used up in the same period and where the price the firm pays is set on a competitive market by the forces of supply and demand. Many raw material and intermediate-product purchases fall into this category. From the point of view of the firm purchasing in a competitive market, if it pays $110 per ton for coal delivered to its factory, it has sacrificed its claims to whatever else $110 can buy, and thus the purchase price is a reasonable measure of the opportunity cost to it of using one ton of coal.

For hired factors of production, where the rental price is the full price, the situation is identical. Borrowed money is paid for by payment of **interest**. An **interest rate** is the money price paid to use $1 for one year. Interest payments measure the opportunity cost of borrowed funds. Most labor services are hired and the cost includes the wages paid. It also includes the employer's contribution to social security, to pension funds, to unemployment and disability insurance, and to other fringe benefits.

Imputed Costs

Cost must also be assessed for factors of production that the firm uses but neither purchases nor hires for current use. Since no payment is made to anyone outside the firm, these costs are not so obvious. They are called **imputed costs.** If the most profitable lines of production are to be discovered, the opportunity cost of these factors should be reckoned at values that reflect what the firm might earn from the factors if it shifted them to their next best use. The remaining examples all involve imputed costs.

Using the firm's own money. Consider a firm that uses $100,000 of its own money that it could instead have loaned out at a rate of 14 percent per year.

Thus, $14,000 (at least) should be deducted from the firm's revenue as the cost of funds used in production. If, to continue the example, the firm makes only $6,000 over all other costs, then one should say not that the firm made a profit of $6,000 by producing but that it lost $8,000. For if it had closed down completely and merely loaned out its money to someone else, it could have earned $14,000.

The cost of money may be higher than this if the best alternative use of the money could yield more than the market interest rate. Many firms cannot obtain nearly as much money as they would wish by borrowing. If a firm is rationed in the amount of funds it can borrow, it will place a high value on the funds that it does have. In these circumstances, the firm must look at the other ventures it might have undertaken to assign opportunity cost because its inability to raise all the capital it wants means that it will be unable to do all the things it wants. Many business firms operate with "cut-off rates of return" that approximate the opportunity cost of money to the firm. They are chosen to approximate the return on projects that the firm cannot undertake because it lacks sufficient funds.[2]

Costs of durable assets. The costs of using assets owned by the firm, such as buildings, equipment, and machinery, consist of the cost of the money tied up in them and a charge, called **depreciation,** for the loss in value of the asset because of its use in production. Depreciation includes both the loss in value due to physical wear and tear and that due to obsolescence. The economic cost of owning an asset for a year is the loss in value of the asset during the year.

---

[2] Empirical studies of certain American manufacturing industries suggest that the opportunity cost of money is substantially higher than the rate of interest on bonds and long-term loans. An accurate figure may well be as high as 35 percent. The fact that it is so high helps explain why many firms are anxious to retain a major portion of their profits and why many stockholders (who do not have similar personal investment opportunities) are willing to have corporations pay dividends that are substantially less than earnings and reinvest the remainder to earn their internal rate of return.

Accountants use several conventional methods of depreciation based on the price originally paid for the asset. One of the most common is *straight-line depreciation*, in which the same amount of historical cost is deducted in every year of useful life of the asset. While historical costs are often useful approximations, they may in some cases differ seriously from the depreciation required by the opportunity cost principle. Consider two examples of the possible error involved.

Assets that may be resold. A women buys a $6,000 automobile that she intends to use for six years. She may think that, using straight-line depreciation, this will cost her $1,000 per year. But if after one year the value of her car on the used car market is $4,000, it has cost her $2,000 to use the car during the first year. Why should she charge herself $2,000 depreciation during the first year? After all, *she* does not intend to sell the car for six years. The answer is that one of the purchaser's alternatives was to buy a one-year-old car and operate it for five years. Indeed, that is the very position she is in after the first year. Whether she likes it or not, she has paid $2,000 for the use of the car during the first year of its life. If the market had valued her car at $5,500 after one year (instead of $4,000), the depreciation would have been only $500.

Sunk costs. In the previous example, an active used-asset market was considered. At the other extreme, consider an asset that has no alternative use. This is sometimes described as the case of "sunk" costs. Assume that a firm has a set of machines it purchased some time ago for $100,000. These machines should last 10 years and the firm's accountant calculates the depreciation costs of these machines by the straightline method at $10,000 per year. Assume also that the machines can be used to make one product and nothing else. Suppose too that they are installed in the firm's plant, they cannot be leased to any other firm, and their scrap value is negligible. In other words, the machines have no value except to this firm in its current operation. Assume that if the machines are used to produce this product, the cost of all other factors utilized will amount to $25,000, while the goods produced can be sold for $29,000.

Now, if the accountant's depreciation "costs" of running the machines are added in, the total cost of operation comes to $35,000; with revenues at $29,000, this makes an annual loss of $6,000 per year. It appears that the goods should not be made!

The fallacy in this argument lies in adding in a charge based on the sunk cost of the machines as one of the costs of current operation. The machines have no alternative uses whatsoever. *Clearly their opportunity cost is zero.* The total costs of producing this line of goods is thus only $25,000 per year (assuming all other costs have been correctly assessed), and the line of production shows an annual profit of $4,000, not a loss of $6,000.

To see why the second calculation leads to the correct decision, notice that if the firm decides this line of production is unprofitable and does not continue it, it will have no money to pay out and no revenue received on this account. If the firm takes the economist's advice and pursues the line of production, it will pay out $25,000 and receive $29,000, thus making it $4,000 per year richer than if it had not done so. Clearly, production is worth undertaking. The amount the firm happened to have paid out for the machines in the past has no bearing whatever on deciding the correct use of the machines once they are installed on the premises.

Bygones are bygones. Because they involve neither current nor future costs, sunk costs should have no influence on deciding what is currently the most profitable thing to do.

The "bygones are bygones" principle extends well beyond economics and is often ignored in poker, in war, and perhaps in love. Because you have invested heavily in a poker hand, a battle, or a courtship does not mean you should stick with it if the prospects of winning become very small. At every moment of decision, you should be concerned with how benefits from this time forward compare with current and future costs.

Risk taking. One difficult problem in imputing costs concerns the evaluation of the service of risk taking. Business enterprise is often a risky affair. The risk is borne by the owners of the firm who, if the enterprise fails, may lose the money they have invested in the firm. The owners will not take these risks unless they receive a remuneration in return. They expect a return that exceeds what they could have obtained by investing their money in a virtually riskless manner, say, by buying a government bond.

Risk taking is necessary to production and thus has a cost. It is a service that must be provided if the firm is to carry on production, and it must be paid for by the firm. If a firm does not yield a return sufficient to compensate for the risks involved, the firm will not be able to persuade people to contribute money to it in return for a part ownership in the firm.

Investors demand a higher return on a risky venture than on a sure one because, in addition to having their capital used, they take the chance of never getting it back.

Suppose, in investing $100,000 in a class of risky ventures, a businesswoman expects that most of the ventures will be successful but some will fail. In fact, she expects about $10,000 worth to be a total loss. (She does not know which specific projects will be the losers, of course.) Suppose further that she requires a 20 percent return on her total investment. To earn a $20,000 profit and recover the $10,000 expected loss, she needs to earn a $30,000 profit on the $90,000 of successful investment. This is a rate of return of 33⅓ percent. She charges 20 percent for the use of the capital, 13⅓ percent for the risk she takes.

Patents, trademarks, and other special advantages. Suppose a firm owns a valuable patent or a highly desirable location, or produces a popular brand-name product such as Coca-Cola, Chevrolet, or Marlboro. Each of these involves an opportunity cost to the firm in production (even if it was acquired free) because if the firm does not choose to use the special advantage itself, it could sell or lease it to others. Typically, the value of these advantages will differ from their historical cost. Indeed, typically several alternative uses will be open to the owner. The opportunity cost in any one is the value foregone in the *best* alternative use.

Profits: Their Meaning and Significance

Profits, although often defined loosely in everyday usage, may be given a series of more precise definitions. **Economic profits** on goods sold are defined as the difference between revenues received from the sale and the opportunity cost of the resources used to make them. (If costs are greater than revenues, such "negative profits" are called *losses*.)

This definition includes in costs (and thus excludes from profits) the imputed returns to capital and to risk taking. This use of the words "profit" and "loss" gives specialized definitions to words that are in everyday use. They are, therefore, a potential source of confusion to the student who runs into other uses of the same words. Table 11-1 may help clarify the definitions.

Some economists, while following substantially the same definitions, label as **normal profits** the imputed returns to capital and risk taking just necessary to prevent the owners from withdrawing from the industry. These normal profits are of

TABLE 11–1 THE CALCULATION OF ECONOMIC PROFITS: AN EXAMPLE

Gross revenue from sales	$1,000
Less: direct cost of goods sold (materials, labor, electricity, etc.)	650
"Gross profits" (or "contributions to overhead")	350
Less: indirect costs (depreciation, overhead, management salaries, etc.)	140
"Net profits" before income taxes	210
Less: imputed charges for own capital used and for risk taking } = "normal profits"	100
Economic profits before income taxes	110
Less: income taxes payable	100
Economic profits after income taxes	$ 10

The main difference between "economic profits" and the usual everyday definition of profits is the subtraction of imputed charges for use of capital owned by the firm and for risk taking. Income tax is levied on whatever definition of profits the taxing authorities choose, usually closely related to "net profits."

course, what has been defined as the opportunity costs of risk taking and capital. Whatever they are called, they are costs that have to be covered if the firm is to stay in operation in the long run.

Other Definitions of Profits

Business firms define profits as the excess of revenues over the costs with which accountants provide them. We explore in the appendix to this chapter some of the differences between accountants' and economists' views of business transactions. Some of these differences affect the meaning of profits. Accountants do not include as costs charges for risk taking and use of owners' own capital, and thus these items are recorded by businesses as part of their profits. When a businessman says he *needs* profits of such and such an amount to stay in business, he is making sense within his definition, for his "profits" must be large enough to pay for those factors of production that he uses but that the accounting profession does not include as costs.

The economist would express the same notion by saying that the business needs to cover *all* its costs, including those not employed in accounting conventions. If the firm is covering all its costs (in the sense that we have defined costs), then it could not do better by using its resources in any other line of activity than the one currently being followed. Indeed, it would probably do worse in most other lines of activity.

A situation in which revenues equal costs (economic profits of zero) is a satisfactory one—because all factors, hidden was well as visible, are being rewarded at least as well as in their *best* alternative uses.

With zero profits then, in the economist's sense of that concept, you can do no better, although you might do worse. To reverse the Chinese proverb cited earlier, "Where there is no loss compared to the best alternative use of every factor, the gain is obvious."

The income tax authorities have yet another definition of profits, which is implicit in the thousands of rules as to what may and may not be included

as a deduction from revenue in arriving at taxable income. In some cases, the taxing authorities allow more for cost than the accountant recommends; in other cases, they allow less.

It is important to be clear about different meanings of the term *profits* not only to avoid fruitless semantic arguments but because a theory that predicts that certain behavior is a function of profits defined in one way will not necessarily predict behavior accurately, given some other definition. For example, if economists predict that new firms will seek to enter an industry whenever profits are earned, this prediction will frequently be wrong if the accountants' definition is used to determine profits. The definition of profits as an excess over all opportunity costs is for many purposes the most useful, but in order to apply it to business behavior or to tax policy, appropriate adjustments must be made. And to apply accounting or tax data to particular theories, the data must be rectified.

Profits and Resource Allocation

When resources are valued by the opportunity cost principle, their costs show how much these resources would earn if used in their best alternative uses. If there is an industry in which all firms' revenues exceed opportunity costs, all the firms in the industry will be earning profits. Thus, the owners of factors of production will want to move resources into this industry because the earnings potentially available to them are greater there than in alternative uses of the resources. If in some other industry firms are incurring losses, some or all of this industry's resources are more highly valued in other uses, and owners of the resources will want to move them to those other uses.

Economic profits and losses play a crucial signaling role in the workings of a free-market system.

Profits in an industry are the signal that resources can profitably be moved into the industry. Losses are the signal that the resources can profitably be moved elsewhere. Only if there are zero economic profits is there no incentive for resources to move into or out of an industry.

SUMMARY

1. The firm is the economic unit that produces and sells commodities. The economist's definition of the firm abstracts from real-life differences in size and form of organization of firms.

2. The single proprietorship, the partnership, and the corporation are the major forms of business organization in the United States today. The corporation is by far the most common business wherever large-scale production is required. The corporation is recognized as a legal entity; its owners, or shareholders, have a liability that is limited to the amount of money they have actually invested in the organization. Corporate ownership is readily transferred by sale of shares in organized securities markets.

3. Economic theory assumes that the same principles underlie each decision made within the firm and that the actual decision is uninfluenced by who makes it. The key behavioral assumption is that the firm seeks to maximize its profit.

4. Production consists of transforming inputs (or factors of production) into outputs (or goods and services). It is often convenient to divide factors of production into categories. One common classification is land, labor, and capital. Land includes all primary products, labor means all human services, and capital denotes all man-made aids to further production. An outstanding feature of modern production is the use of capital goods and roundabout methods of production.

5. Because there is more than one way to engage in production, the firm must decide *how* to produce. Efficiency is a measure of the relative amount of input necessary to produce a given output. Technological efficiency evaluates units of input in physical terms. Economic efficiency evaluates them in terms of costs.

6. The opportunity cost of using a resource is the value of that resource in its best alternative use. If the opportunity cost of using a resource in one way is less than or equal to the gain from using the

resource in this way, there is no superior way of using it.

7. Measuring opportunity cost to the firm requires some difficult imputations in cases involving resources not purchased or hired for current use. Among these imputed costs are those for use of owners' money, depreciation, risk taking, and any special advantages that the firm may possess.

8. A firm maximizing profits, defined as the difference between revenue and opportunity cost, is making the best allocation of the resources under its control, according to the firm's evaluation of its alternatives.

9. Profits and losses provide important signals concerning the reallocation of resources. Profits earned in an industry provide a signal that more resources can profitably move into the industry. Losses show that some resources have more profitable uses elsewhere and serve as a signal for them to move out of that industry.

10. The appendix to this chapter introduces balance sheets and profit and loss statements and uses them to discuss some of the differences between the concept of profits used by accountants and that used by economists.

TOPICS FOR REVIEW

The firm in theory and in the U.S. economy
The role of profit maximization
Single proprietorship, partnership, and corporation
Advantages of the corporation
Factors of production
Economic efficiency
Opportunity costs
Economic and other definitions of profits
Profits and resource allocation

DISCUSSION QUESTIONS

1. Many modern firms go through stages of being in turn a single proprietorship, a partnership, and a corporation. Can you suggest why such an evolution might be sensible? If you were to start a business, which form would you choose? Why?

2. Can the economic theory of the firm be of any help in analyzing the productive decisions of such nonprofit organizations as governments, churches, and colleges? What, if any, role does the notion of opportunity cost play for them?

3. In *The Engineers and the Price System,* Thorstein Veblen argued that businessmen who made decisions about financing, pricing, and the like were largely superfluous to the operation of a business. In his view, knowledge of the technology would be sufficient to ensure efficient operation of firms. Discuss Veblen's contention.

4. "There is no such thing as a free lunch." Can anything be costless? Gas stations have traditionally provided free services, including windshield cleaning, air pumps for tire inflation, and road maps. Now, many sell road maps and have discontinued free services. Indeed, self-service stations are becoming increasingly popular with motorists who like the lower gas prices of those stations. Under what conditions will profit-maximizing behavior lead to the coexistence of full-service and self-service gas stations? What would determine the proportions in which each occurred?

5. What is the opportunity cost of
   a. a politician's being fined $10,000 and sent to prison for one year
   b. lending $500 to a friend
   c. not permitting a $116-million electric power dam to be built because it would destroy the snail darter, a rare 3-inch-long fish found only in that particular river
   d. towing icebergs to Saudi Arabia to provide drinking water at the cost of $.50 per cubic meter

6. You are a manufacturer and invent something that can increase your profits. You patent the invention. The total cost of developing and patenting your invention is $1,000. General Industries offers you $100,000 for the exclusive rights to use your patent. You say no, preferring to use it yourself. What is your cost of using the patent in your own business?

7. Is straight-line depreciation an appropriate method of assessing the annual cost to the typical American household of using a passenger automobile? Some firms that use trucks allocate the cost on a per-mile basis. Why might this method be more nearly appropriate for trucks than for automobiles owned by households?

8. Having bought a used car from Smiling Sam for $900, you drive it two days and it stops. You now find that it requires an extra $500 before it will run. Assuming that the car is not worth $1,400 fixed, should you make the repairs?

9. "The higher the opportunity cost, the poorer the investment." Do you agree with this statement? If you do not, how could you formulate the maxim so that you did agree?

10. "To meet the 1981 standard of 3.4 grams of carbon monoxide per mile driven, General Motors has calculated that it will cost $100 million and prolong 200 lives by one year each, thus costing $500,000 per year of extra life. Human lives are precious, which is why it is so sad to note another use of that money. It has been estimated that the installation of special cardiac-care units in ambulances could prevent premature deaths each year at an average cost of only $200 for each year of extra life."

    Assume the facts in this quotation are correct. If the money spent on carbon monoxide control would have been spent on cardiac care units instead, what is the opportunity cost of the carbon monoxide requirement? If the money would not have been so spent but simply reduced automobile companies' costs, what is the opportunity cost? In either case, do the facts tell us whether the regulation of carbon monoxide to the 3.4 gram level is desirable or undesirable?

11. Which concept of profits is implied in the following quotations:
    a. "Profits are necessary if firms are to stay in business."
    b. "Profits are signals for firms to expand production and investment."
    c. "Increased depreciation lowers profits and thus benefits the company's owners."

12 PRODUCTION AND COST IN THE SHORT RUN

Of the four domestic automobile manufacturers, General Motors is year-in and year-out more profitable than Ford, and Ford more profitable than Chrysler and American Motors. The prices charged for comparable models are approximately the same, but the profits *per automobile* are very different. A good part of the reason lies in the very different levels of output. General Motors has about a 60 percent share of the four companies' aggregate sales, Ford a 25 percent share, Chrysler a 12 percent share, and American Motors Corporation only about a 3 percent share. American Motors with dollar sales of nearly $3 billion may not sound like a small company, but for the automobile industry it is because the costs of making and selling cars decline sharply with increases in volume of cars sold. Thus the smaller companies are at a big disadvantage relative to GM even if they are every bit as imaginative in design, management, and salesmanship. Over the past 40 years several once-profitable smaller producers, among them Packard, Crosley, Studebaker, and Kaiser-Frazer, were unable to increase their volume and found that costs had become greater than revenues. They left the industry after suffering heavy losses. This experience illustrates one very important aspect of the theory of cost of production: Cost of production per unit may be very different for different levels of output.

A different aspect of the theory of costs relates to factor prices. When rising chicken feed prices reached the point at which it cost more to feed chickens as they grew than they sold for when fully grown, chicken farmers shut down temporarily. Similarly, during a period when price controls were in effect, meat packers were squeezed between the legal maximum price at which they could sell and the rising cost of the livestock they bought. Some of them suspended production.

In the previous chapter we defined costs of production. The next steps in this chapter are to see how and why costs vary with the level of production and how they are affected by changes in factor prices.

REAL CHOICES OPEN TO THE FIRM

Consider a firm producing a single product in a number of different plants. If its rate of sales has fallen off, should production be reduced correspondingly? Or should production be held at the old rate and the unsold amounts stored up against an anticipated future rise in sales? If production is to be reduced, should a single plant be closed or should all plants be operated fewer hours per week? If demand increases sharply and unexpectedly, how can more production be squeezed out of the existing facilities?

All these matters concern how best to use *existing* plant and equipment. They also involve time periods too short to build new plants or to install more equipment. The decisions made will be implemented quickly: A plant can be shut down on a week's notice, overtime can be increased tomorrow, and new production workers can be added as soon as they can be hired and trained.

More weighty decisions must be made when managers do long-range planning. Should the firm adopt a highly automated process that will greatly reduce its wage bill, even though it must borrow large sums of money to buy the equipment? Or should it continue to build new plants that use the same techniques it is now using? Should it build new plants in an area where labor is plentiful, but that is distant from its sources of raw materials? These matters concern what a firm should do when it is changing or replacing its plant and equipment. Such decisions may take a long time to put into effect.

In the above examples, managers make decisions from known possibilities. Large firms also have research and development (R&D) staffs whose job it is to discover new methods of production. But the firm must decide how much money to devote to R&D and in what areas the payoff for new development will be largest. If, for example, a shortage of a particular labor skill or raw material is anticipated, the research staff can be told to try to find ways to economize on that input or even eliminate it from the production process.

Time Horizons for Decision Making

To reduce to manageable proportions the decisions firms are constantly making, economists organize the decisions into three theoretical groups: (1) How best to employ existing plant and equipment (the *short run*). (2) What new plant and equipment and production processes to select, given the framework of known technical possibilities (the *long run*). (3) What to do about encouraging the invention of new techniques (the *very long run*). In using these periods, economists abstract from the more complicated nature of real decisions and focus on the key factors that restrict the range of choice in each set of decisions.

The Short Run

Short-run decisions are those made when the quantity of some inputs cannot be varied. The firm cannot get more of the **fixed factors** than it has on hand, and it is committed to make any money payments that are associated with these fixed factors.[1] Factors that can be varied in the short run are called **variable factors.**

In the short run, what matters is that at least one significant factor is fixed. The factor is fixed in the sense that while the firm may or may not use all that it has, it cannot get more for the duration of the short run. The fixed factor is usually an element of capital (such as plant and equipment), but it might be land, the services of management, or even the supply of skilled labor.

The short run does not correspond to a definite number of months or years. In some industries, it may extend over many years; in others it may be only a matter of months or even weeks. Furthermore, it may last a different period of time when an industry is expanding than when it is contracting.

In the electric power industry, for example, it takes three or more years to acquire and install a steam-turbine generator. An unforeseen increase in demand will involve a long period during which the extra demand must be met as best it can with the existing capital equipment. Once installed, this equipment has a very long life, and a decrease in demand leaves the firm committed, possibly for decades, to all the costs of this equipment that do not vary with output.

In contrast, a machine shop can acquire new equipment or sell existing equipment in a very few weeks, so the short run is correspondingly short. An increase in demand will have to be met with the existing stock of capital for only a brief time, after which it will be possible to adjust the stock of equipment to the level made desirable by the higher demand.

---

[1] Sometimes it is physically impossible to increase the quantity of a fixed factor in a short time. For instance, there is no way to build a hydroelectric dam or a nuclear power plant in a few months. Other times it might be physically possible, but prohibitively expensive, to increase the quantity. For example, a suit-manufacturing firm could conceivably rent a building, buy and install new sewing machines, and hire a trained labor force in a few days if money were no consideration. Economists regard prohibitive cost along with physical impossibility as a source of fixed factors.

The Long Run

Long-run decisions are those made when the inputs of all factors of production may be varied but the basic technology of production is unchanged. Again, the long run does not correspond to a specific period of time.

The special importance of the long run in production theory is that it corresponds to the situation facing the firm when it is planning to go into business, to expand the scale of its operations, to branch out into new products or new areas, or to modernize, replace, or reorganize its method of production.

The firm's *planning decisions* characteristically are made with fixed technical possibilities but with freedom to choose from a variety of production processes that will use factor inputs in different proportions.

The Very Long Run

Unlike the short and long run, the **very long run** concerns the opportunities arising from changing technology. A central characteristic of modern industrial society has been the continuously changing technology that leads to new and improved products and new and improved production methods. Some of these technological advances arise from within the firm as part of its own research and development efforts. For example, much of the innovation in cameras and films has been due to the efforts of the Kodak and Polaroid companies. Firms in certain other industries may merely adopt technological changes developed elsewhere. For example, the transistor and the electronic chip have revolutionized dozens of industries that had nothing to do with developing them in the first place. The firm must regularly decide how much to spend in its efforts to change its technology either by developing new techniques or adapting techniques developed by others.

Connecting the Runs: The Production Function

Although it is convenient to treat production decisions in stages, they are interrelated. The plant built today (a long-run decision) affects tomorrow's short-run decisions. Similarly, an alternative to coping with a plant of inadequate size by running overtime shifts (a short-run expedient) is constructing a new wing (a long-run decision) or searching for a new technique of production (a very-long-run decision).

The various "runs" are simply different aspects of the same basic problem: getting output from inputs efficiently. They differ in terms of what the firm is able to change.

The relation between factor services used as inputs into the production process and the quantity of output obtained is called the **production function.** A simplified production function in which there are only two factors of production, labor and capital, will be considered here, but the conclusions apply equally when there are many factors. The variation of output and cost under the assumption that one of the two factors is fixed is examined in this chapter. (Capital is taken to be the fixed factor and labor the variable one.) The long-run situation in which both factors can be varied is covered in the next chapter.

TABLE 12–1 **THE VARIATION OF OUTPUT WITH CAPITAL FIXED AND LABOR VARIABLE**

(1) Quantity of labor (L)	(2) Total product (TP)	(3) Average product (AP)	(4) Marginal product (MP)
0	0	—	
1	15	15.0	15
2	34	17.0	19
3	48	16.0	14
4	60	15.0	12
5	62	12.4	2

The relation of output to changes in the quantity of labor can be looked at in three different ways. Capital is assumed to be fixed at four units. As the quantity of labor increases, the rate of output (the total product) increases. Average product increases at first and then declines. The same is true of marginal product.

Marginal product is shown between the lines because it refers to the *change* in output from one level of labor input to another. When graphing the schedule, *MP*s of this kind shold be plotted at the midpoint of the interval. Thus, graphically, the marginal product of 12 would be plotted to correspond to quantity of labor of 3.5.

SHORT-RUN CHOICES

Total, Average, and Marginal Products

Assume that a firm starts with a fixed amount of capital (say four units) and contemplates applying various amounts of labor to it. Table 12-1 shows three different ways of looking at how output varies with the quantity of the variable factor. As a first step, some terms need to be defined.

1. **Total product** (*TP*) means the total amount produced during a given period of time by all the factors of production employed. If the inputs of all but one factor are held constant, total product will change as more or less of the variable factor is used. This variation is shown in columns 1 and 2 of Table 12-1, which gives a total product schedule. Figure 12-1(i) shows such a schedule graphically. (The shape of the curve will be discussed shortly.)

2. **Average product** (*AP*) is merely the total product per unit of the variable factor, labor. The number of units of labor will be denoted by *L*.

$$AP = \frac{TP}{L}$$

It is shown in column 3 of Table 12-1. Notice that as more of the variable factor is used, average product first rises and then falls. The level of output (34 units in the example) where average product reaches a maximum is called the **point of diminishing average productivity.**

3. **Marginal product** (*MP*), sometimes called **incremental product,** is the change in total product resulting from the use of 1 unit more of the variable factor. [13]

$$MP = \frac{\Delta TP}{\Delta L}$$

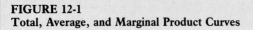

FIGURE 12-1
Total, Average, and Marginal Product Curves

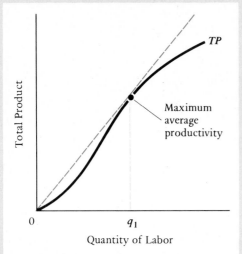

(i) Total product curve

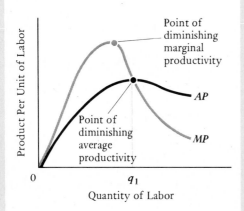

(ii) Average and marginal product curves

TP, AP, and MP curves often have the shapes shown here. (i) The total product curve shows the total product steadily rising, first at an increasing rate, then at a decreasing rate. This causes both the average and the marginal product curves in (ii) to rise at first and then decline. The point of maximum average product (also called the point of diminishing average productivity) is q_1 where TP is tangent to the ray from the origin. At this point $MP = AP$.

Computed values of marginal product are shown in column 4 of Table 12-1.[2] The figures in this column are placed between the other lines of the table to stress that the concept refers to the *change* in output caused by the *change* in quantity of the variable factor. For example, the increase in labor from 3 to 4 units ($\Delta L = 1$) raises output by 12 from 48 to 60 ($\Delta TP = 12$). Thus the MP equals 12, and it is recorded between 3 and 4 units of labor. Note that the MP in the example rises and then falls. The level of output at which marginal product reaches a maximum is called the **point of diminishing marginal productivity.**

Figure 12-1(ii) plots average product and marginal product curves. Although three different schedules are shown in Table 12-1 and three different curves are shown in Figure 12-1, they are all aspects of the same single relationship that is described by the production function. As we vary the quantity of labor, with capital fixed, output changes. Sometimes it is interesting to look at the total increase in output, sometimes at the average increase, and sometimes at the marginal increase.

Finally, bear in mind that the schedules of Table 12-1 and the curves of Figure 12-1 all assume a specified quantity of the fixed factor. If the quantity of capital had been, say, 6 or 10 instead of the 4 units that were assumed, there would be a different set of total product, average product, and marginal product curves. The reason for this is that if any specified amount of labor has more capital to work with, it can produce more output—that is, its total product will be greater.

The Shape of the Marginal and Average Product Curves

The Law of Diminishing Returns

The variations in output that result from applying more or less of a variable factor to a given

---

[2] ΔL is read "a change in the quantity of labor." For the definition of marginal product, we want a 1-unit change in labor, that is, $\Delta L = 1$.

quantity of a fixed factor are the subject of a famous economic hypothesis. Usually it is called the **law of diminishing returns.**

The hypothesis states that if increasing amounts of a variable factor are applied to a given amount of a fixed factor, eventually a situation will be reached in which each additional unit of the variable factor adds less to total product than did the previous unit.

The common sense of diminishing marginal product is that the fixed factor limits the amount of additional output that can be realized by adding more of the variable factor. The hypothesis of diminishing returns predicts only that sooner or later the *MP* curve will decline. It is conceivable that marginal returns might diminish from the outset, so that the first unit of labor contributes most to total production and each successive unit contributes less than the previous unit. (This is the case in what is known as the Cobb-Douglas production function.) It is also possible for the marginal product to rise at first and decline later. Thus, what is called the law of diminishing marginal returns might more accurately be described as the law of *eventually* diminishing marginal returns. The reason for such a rise and decline is clear when seen in the context of the organization of production.

Consider the use of a variable number of workers in a manufacturing operation. If there is only one worker, that worker must do all the tasks, shifting from one to another and becoming competent in each. As a second, third, and subsequent workers are added, it is often possible to break the tasks into a large number of separate jobs, with each laborer specializing in one job and becoming expert at it. This process is called the *division of labor.* If additional workers permit more and more efficient divisions of labor, marginal product will rise. This may go on for some time, but (according to the hypothesis of diminishing returns) the scope for such economies must eventually disappear and sooner or later the marginal products of additional workers must decline. When this happens each additional worker will increase total output by less than the previous worker increased it. This sort of

case is the one illustrated in Figure 12-1, where marginal product rises at first and then declines.

Eventually, marginal product may reach zero and became negative. It is not hard to see why, when you consider the extreme case where there are so many workers in a limited space that additional workers simply get in the way.

The hypothesis is usually described in terms of diminishing marginal returns, but it can equally well be stated in terms of diminishing average returns. The law of diminishing *average* returns states that if increasing quantities of a variable factor are applied to a given quantity of fixed factors, the average product of the variable factor will eventually decrease. [14]

The Significance of the Law of Diminishing Returns

There is a great deal of empirical confirmation of both diminishing marginal and diminishing average returns. Some examples are illustrated in the box on page 190. One might wish that it were not so. The consequence of diminishing returns is easily seen in a simple example. If the law were not true, there would be no reason to fear that the world population explosion will bring with it a food crisis. If the marginal product of additional workers applied to a fixed quantity of land were constant, then world food production could be expanded in proportion to the population merely by keeping a constant fraction of the population on farms. But with fixed techniques, the hypothesis of diminishing returns predicts an inexorable decline in the marginal product of each additional laborer because an expanding population has a fixed world supply of agricultural land. Thus, unless there is a continual improvement in the techniques of production, continuous population growth will bring with it, according to the hypothesis of diminishing returns, declining average living standards and eventually widespread famine.

This was the gloomy prediction of the early nineteenth century English economist Thomas Malthus. No wonder economics was popularly known at the time as the dismal science!

DIMINISHING RETURNS

In each of the following examples, you should be able to identify the variable factor and the fixed factor or factors, as well as the "product" that is subject to diminishing returns.

■ Experimenters with chemical fertilizers at the Rothampsted Experimental Station, an agricultural research institute in Hertfordshire, England, in 1921 applied different amounts of a particular fertilizer to 10 apparently identical quarter-acre plots of land. For one such test, using identical seed grain, the results were

Plot	Fertilizer dose	Yield index*
1	15	104.2
2	30	110.4
3	45	118.0
4	60	125.3
5	75	130.2
6	90	132.4
7	105	131.9
8	120	132.3
9	135	132.5
10	150	132.8

*Yield without fertilizer = 100

You may find it useful to compute the average and marginal product of fertilizer and identify the (approximate) points of diminishing average and marginal productivity.

■ When Southern California Edison was required by the State of California to modify its Mojave power plant to reduce the amount of fly ash emitted into the atmosphere, it discovered that a series of filters applied to the smokestacks could do the job. A single filter eliminated half the discharge. Five filters in series reduced the fly ash discharge to the 3 percent allowed by law. When a state senator proposed a new standard that would permit no more than 1 percent fly ash emission, the company brought in experts who testified that such a requirement (if it could be met) would require at least 15 filters per stack and would triple the cost.

■ Idaho's Salmon River, a noted sport fishing river, has become the center of a thriving, well-promoted tourist trade. As the fishing pressure in the Salmon River has increased, the total number of fish caught has steadily increased, but the number of fish per person fishing has decreased and the average hours fished for each fish caught has increased. The average weight of the fish caught has remained the same.

■ An oldtime Texas rancher interviewed in a television documentary, *The New Dust Bowl?*, denied vehemently that there was a serious water problem in his state: "The water's there, just like it's always been. Get yourself a rig and start drilling. Either you'll hit oil, in which case you'll forget about water, or you'll find water. I've been doing it for 30 years. Used to hit water at 12 to 18 feet; now it's more like 70 to 80 feet, but it's there just the same."

■ Gallup, Roper, and all other pollsters, as well as all students of statistics, know that you can use a sample to estimate characteristics of a very large population. Even a relatively small sample can provide a useful estimate—at a tiny fraction of the cost of a complete enumeration of the population. However, sample estimates are subject to *sampling error*. If, for example, 38 percent of a sample approves of a certain policy, the percentage of the population that approves of it is likely to be close to 38 percent, but it might well be anywhere from 36 to 40 percent. The theory of statistics shows that the size of the expected sampling error can always be reduced by increasing the sample size. The 4 percent interval (in the example above) could be cut in half—to 2 percent—by *quadrupling* the sample size. That is, if the original sample had been 400, a new sample of 1,600 would halve the expected error. To reduce the interval to 1 percent, the new sample would have to be quadrupled again—to 6,400. In other words, there are diminishing marginal returns to sample size.

THE BATTING AVERAGE OF PETE ROSE: MARGINAL AND LIFETIME

The relationship between the concepts of marginal and average measures is very general. An illuminating example comes from the *Baseball Encyclopedia*. The table gives the batting average (number of hits—output—divided by official times at bat—input) of Pete Rose over his illustrious career in the National League, during which he has set all kinds of hitting records. For each year column 1 gives his batting average for his whole major-league career on opening day of the season. Thus it shows his lifetime average at that time. Columns 2 and 3 give the data needed to compute his batting average for the current, or "marginal," year. This is given in column 4.

Whenever his current year average is below his lifetime-to-date average, the latter falls (although it may be necessary to calculate to four decimal places to see it.) See, for example, 1971, 1974, and 1980. Whenever his current year average is above the lifetime average, the latter rises. This is true whether the marginal itself is rising or falling. For example, in the years 1975, 1976, and 1977, Rose raised his lifetime batting average because each was an above-average year. In some of those years (e.g., 1976), he was improving on the previous year (marginal rising); in others (e.g., 1977), he was doing worse than the previous year (marginal falling).

If the average is to rise, all that matters is that the marginal is above the average; if the average is to fall, all that matters is that the marginal is below the average.

	(1) Lifetime average on opening day	(2) Hits during year	(3) Official at bats during year	(4) Batting average during year
1963	.000	170	623	.273
1964	.273	139	516	.269
1965	.271	209	670	.312
1966	.286	205	654	.313
1967	.294	176	585	.301
1968	.295	210	626	.335
1969	.302	218	627	.348
1970	.3085	205	649	.316
1971	.3095	192	632	.304
1972	.3088	198	645	.307
1973	.3087	230	680	.338
1974	.312	185	652	.284
1975	.309	210	662	.317
1976	.3098	215	665	.323
1977	.3108	204	655	.311
1978	.3109	198	655	.302
1979	.3103	208	628	.331
1980	.3115	185	655	.282
1981	.3099	140	431	.325
1982	.3104	172	634	.271
1983	.3084			

The Relation Between Marginal and Average Curves

Notice that in Figure 12-1(ii) the *MP* curve cuts the *AP* curve at the latter's maximum point. Although the relation between marginal and average curves is a mathematical one and not a matter of economics, it is important to understand how these curves are related. [15]

The average product curve slopes upward as long as the marginal product curve is above it; it makes no difference whether the marginal curve is itself sloping upward or downward. The common sense of this relation is that if an additional worker is to raise the average product of all workers, his or her output must be greater than the average output of all other workers. It is immaterial whether the new worker's contribution to output is greater or less than the contribution of the worker hired immediately before; all that matters is that his or her contribution to output exceeds the average output of *all* workers hired previously. (The relation between marginal and average measures is further illustrated in the box about Pete Rose).

TABLE 12–2 THE VARIATION OF COSTS WITH CAPITAL FIXED AND LABOR VARIABLE

(1) Labor (L)	(2) Output (q)	Total cost ($)			Marginal cost ($ per unit)	Average cost ($ per unit)		
		(3) Fixed (TFC)	(4) Variable (TVC)	(5) Total (TC)	(6) (MC)	(7) Fixed (AFC)	(8) Variable (AVC)	(9) Total (ATC)
0	0	100	0	100		—	—	—
					0.67			
1	15	100	10	110		6.67	0.67	7.33
					0.53			
2	34	100	20	120		2.94	0.59	3.53
					0.71			
3	48	100	30	130		2.08	0.62	2.71
					0.83			
4	60	100	40	140		1.67	0.67	2.33
					5.00			
5	62	100	50	150		1.61	0.81	2.42

The relation of cost to level of output can be looked at in several different ways. These cost curves are computed from the product curves of Table 12–1, given the price of capital of $25 per unit and the price of labor of $10 per unit. Marginal cost (in column 6) is shown between the lines of total cost because it refers to the *change* in cost divided by the *change* in output that brought it about. For example, the MC of $.71 is the $10 increase in total cost (from $120 to $130) divided by the 14-unit increase in output (from 34 to 48). For graphical purposes, marginal costs should be plotted midway in the interval over which they are computed. The MC of $.71 would be plotted at output 41.

Short-Run Variations in Cost

We now shift our attention from the firm's production function to its costs. We consider firms that are not in a position to influence the prices of the factors of production they employ. These firms must pay the going market price for all factors.[3] Given the prices paid for factors and the physical returns summarized by the product curves, the costs of different levels of output can be calculated.

Cost Concepts Defined

The following brief definitions of several cost concepts are closely related to the product concepts just introduced.

1. **Total cost (TC)** means the total cost of producing any given level of output. Total cost is divided into two parts, total fixed costs (*TFC*) and total variable costs (*TVC*). **Fixed costs** are those that do not vary with output; they will be the same if output is 1 unit or 1 million units. These costs

are also referred to as *overhead costs* or *unavoidable costs*. All costs that vary directly with output, rising as more is produced and falling as less is produced, are called **variable costs.** In the example of Table 12-1, since labor was the variable factor of production, the wage bill is a variable cost. Variable costs are often referred to as *direct costs* or *avoidable costs.*

2. **Average total cost (ATC),** also called **average cost (AC),** is the total cost of producing any given output divided by the number of units produced, or the cost per unit. ATC may be divided into **average fixed costs (AFC)** and **average variable costs (AVC)** in the same way that total costs were divided.

Although average *variable* costs may rise or fall as production is increased (depending on whether output rises more rapidly or more slowly than total variable costs), it is clear that average fixed costs decline continuously as output increases. A doubling of output always leads to a halving of fixed costs per unit of output. This is a process popularly known as *spreading one's overhead.*

3. **Marginal cost (MC),** sometimes called **incremental cost,** is the increase in total cost resulting from raising the rate of production by one unit. Because fixed costs do not vary with output, marginal fixed costs are always zero. Therefore mar-

---

[3] The important problems that arise when the firm is in a position to influence the prices it pays for its factors of production are considered in Chapter 21.

FIGURE 12-2
Total, Average, and Marginal Cost Curves

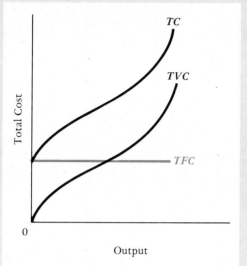

(i) Total cost curves

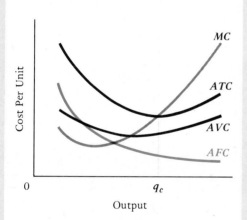

(ii) Marginal and average cost curves

TC, AC, and MC curves often have the shapes shown here. (i) Total fixed cost does not vary with output. Total variable cost and the total of all costs ($TC = TVC + TFC$) rise with output, first at a decreasing rate, then at an increasing rate. The total cost curves in (i) give rise to the average and marginal curves in (ii). AFC declines as output increases. AVC and ATC fall and then rise as output increases. MC does the same, intersecting ATC and AVC at their minimum points. Capacity output is q_c, the minimum point on the ATC curve.

ginal costs are necessarily marginal variable costs, and a change in fixed costs will leave marginal costs unaffected. For example, the marginal cost of producing a few more potatoes by farming a given amount of land more intensively is the same, whatever the rent paid for the fixed amount of land. [16]

These three measures of cost are simply different ways of looking at a single phenomenon. They are mathematically interrelated.

Short-Run Cost Curves

Take the production relationships in Table 12-1. Assume that the price of labor is $10 per unit and the price of capital is $25 per unit. The cost schedules computed for these values are shown in Table 12-2.[4]

Figure 12-2 plots cost curves that are similar in shape to those arising from the data in Table 12-2. Notice that the marginal cost curve cuts the ATC and AVC curves at their lowest points. This is another example of the relation (discussed above) between a marginal and an average curve. The ATC curve, for example, slopes downward as long as the marginal cost curve is below it; it makes no difference whether the marginal cost curve is itself sloping upward or downward.

Short-run average variable cost. In Figure 12-2 the average variable cost curve reaches a minimum and then rises. With fixed factor prices, when average product per worker is a maximum, average variable cost is a minimum. [17] The common sense of this proposition is that each additional worker adds the same amount to cost but a different amount to output, and when output per worker is rising, the cost per unit of output must be falling—and vice versa.

The hypothesis of eventually diminishing average productivity implies eventually increasing average variable costs.

---

[4] If you do not see where any of the numbers come from, review Table 12-1 and the definitions of cost just given.

Short-run average total cost curve. Short-run *ATC* curves are often drawn U-shaped. This reflects the assumptions that (1) average productivity is increasing when output is low but (2) at some level of output average productivity begins to fall fast enough to cause average variable costs to increase faster than average fixed costs fall. When this happens, *ATC* increases.

Marginal cost curves. In Figure 12-2 the marginal cost curve is shown as a declining curve that reaches a minimum and then rises. This is the mirror image of the usual shape of the marginal product curve. The reason is clear. With a fixed price per unit of the variable factor, if extra units of the variable factor produce increasing quantities of output (marginal *product* rising), the cost per unit of extra output must be falling (marginal *cost* falling). If marginal product is falling, marginal cost will be rising. Thus, the hypothesis of eventually diminishing marginal product implies eventually increasing marginal cost. [18]

The Definition of Capacity

The output that corresponds to the minimum short-run average total cost is often called by economists and business people the **capacity** of the firm. Capacity in this sense is not an upper limit on what can be produced. Instead it is the largest output that can be produced without encountering rising average costs per unit. In Figure 12-2(ii) capacity output is q_c units, but higher outputs can be achieved, provided the firm is willing to accept the higher perunit costs that accompany output "above capacity." A firm producing with **excess capacity** is producing at an output smaller than the point of minimum average total cost.

The technical definition gives the word *capacity* a meaning different from that in everyday speech, but the concept proves useful, and in any case it is widely used in economic and business discussions.

A Family of Short-Run Cost Curves

A short-run cost curve shows how costs vary with output for a given quantity of the fixed factor—say, a given size of plant.

There is a different short-run cost curve for each given quantity of the fixed factor.

A small plant for manufacturing nuts and bolts will have its own short-run cost curve. A medium-size plant and a very large plant will each have its own short-run cost curve. If a firm expands and replaces its small plant with a medium-size plant, it will move from one short-run cost curve to another. This change from one plant size to another is a long-run change. How short-run cost curves of plants of different size are related to each other is studied in the next chapter.

SUMMARY

1. The firm's production decisions can be classified into three groups: (a) how best to employ existing plant and equipment (the short run); (b) what new plant and equipment and production processes to select, given the framework of known technical possibilities (the long run); and (c) what to do about encouraging, or merely adapting to, the invention of new techniques (the very long run).

2. The short run involves decisions in which one or more factors of production are fixed. The long run involves decisions in which all factors are variable but in which technology is unchanged. In the very long run, technology can change.

3. The production function describes the ways in which different inputs may be combined to produce different quantities of output. Short-run and long-run situations can be interpreted as implying different kinds of constraints on the production function. In the short run, the firm is constrained to use no more than a given quantity of some fixed factor; in the long run, it is constrained only by the available techniques of production.

4. The theory of short-run behavior depends on the productivity of variable factors when applied to fixed factors. The concepts of total, average, and marginal product represent alternative ways of looking at the relation between output and the quantity of the variable factor of production.

5. The hypothesis, or "law," of eventually diminishing returns asserts that if increasing quantities of a variable factor are applied to a given quantity of fixed factors, the marginal and the average product of the variable factor will eventually decrease. This hypothesis leads directly to implications of rising marginal and average costs.

6. Given physical productivity schedules and the costs per unit of factors, it is a simple matter of arithmetic to develop the whole family of short-run cost curves.

7. Short-run average total cost curves are drawn as U-shaped to reflect the expectation that average productivity increases for small outputs but eventually declines sufficiently rapidly to offset advantages of spreading overheads. The output corresponding to the minimum point of a short-run average total cost curve is called the plant's capacity.

8. There is a whole family of short-run cost curves, one for each quantity of the fixed factor.

TOPICS FOR REVIEW

Short run, long run, and very long run
Marginal and average productivity
The law of diminishing returns
The relation between marginal and average curves
The relation between productivity and cost
Marginal cost and average cost
Capacity and excess capacity

DISCUSSION QUESTIONS

1. Is the short run the same number of months for increasing output as for decreasing it? Must the short run in industry A be the same length for all firms in the industry? Under what circumstances might the short run actually involve a longer time span than even the very long run?
2. How would the following factors increase or reduce the relative importance of short-run decisions for management?

   a. a guaranteed annual employment contract of at least 48 40-hour weeks of work for all employees
   b. a major economic depression during which there is substantial unemployment of labor and in which equipment is being used at well below capacity levels of production
   c. a speeding up of delivery dates for new easy-to-install equipment

3. A leading American general argued against saturation bombing of German targets in World War II. He said that "after the first waves of bombers, diminishing returns set in." Was he using the term as economists define it?
4. Indicate whether each of the following conforms to the hypothesis of diminishing returns; and if so, whether it refers to marginal or average returns, or both.

   a. "The bigger they are, the harder they fall."
   b. As more and more of the population receive smallpox vaccinations, the reductions in the smallpox disease rate for each additional 100,000 vaccinations become smaller.
   c. For the seventh year in a row, the average depth of drilling required to hit oil in Texas increased.
   d. Five workers produce twice as much today as 10 workers did 40 years ago.

5. Consider the education of a human being as a process of production. Regard years of schooling as one variable factor of production. What are the other factors? What factors are fixed? At what point would you expect diminishing productivity to set in? For an Einstein, would it set in during his lifetime?
6. Suppose that each of the following news items is correct. Discuss each in terms of its effects on the level of average total cost.

   a. The U.S. Office of Education reports that the increasing level of education of our youth has led both to higher productivity and to increases in the general level of wages.
   b. During the winter of 1977 many factories were forced by fuel shortages to reduce production and to operate at levels of production far below capacity.
   c. For the third year in a row, the Post Office's production exceeded its capacity.
   d. NASA reports that the space program has led to development of electronic devices that have brought innovations to many industries.

7. "Because overhead costs are fixed, increasing production lowers costs. Thus small business is sure to be inefficient. This is a dilemma of modern society, which values both smallness *and* efficiency." Discuss.

13 PRODUCTION, SUBSTITUTION, AND PRODUCTIVITY INCREASES: COST IN THE LONG AND VERY LONG RUN

Analyzing the short-run behavior of the firm helps us understand how markets work to allocate resources, but it cannot show us why standards of living have risen throughout much of the world. Only an analysis of much longer run phenomena can do this. In this chapter we first look at the firm's long-run behavior, when it is free to vary all factors of production. Should the firm use a great deal of capital and only a small amount of labor? Or should it use less capital and more labor? What do these decisions mean in terms of the firm's costs?

In the second part of the chapter, we examine the improvements in technology and productivity that have been dramatically increasing output and incomes in the United States for more than 100 years but more recently have shown signs of slowing down. The causes of this rapid growth and the present slowdown are subject to debate. What do we know about them?

THE LONG RUN: NO FIXED FACTORS[1]

In the long run all factors can be varied. When this is the case, there are alternative ways of achieving the same total output, and it is necessary to choose among them. The long run is concerned with firms' planning how to design their plant and equipment for maximum profits.

The hypothesis of profit maximization provides a simple rule for doing this: Any firm that is trying to maximize its profits should select the method that produces output at the lowest possible cost. This implication of the hypothesis of profit maximization is called the implication of **cost minimization.**

From the alternatives open to it, the firm chooses the least costly ways of achieving any specific output.

If there is a stable, required output rate, and if the costs of factors are known, that is all there is to it. In other words, the firm selects the economically efficient way of producing any level of output.

These long-run planning decisions are important because today's variable factors are tomorrow's fixed factors. A firm deciding on a new steel mill and the machinery to go into it will choose among many alternatives. But once installed, that equipment is fixed for a long time. If the firm makes a wrong choice now, its survival may be threatened; if it estimates shrewdly, it may reward both owners and foresighted managers with large profits and bonuses.

Long-run decisions are among the most difficult and important the firm makes. They are difficult because the firm must anticipate what methods of production will be efficient not only today but in the years ahead, when costs of labor and raw ma-

terials may have changed. The decisions are difficult, too, because the firm must estimate how much output it will want to be producing. Is the industry of which it is a part growing or declining? Is it going to increase or decrease its share of the market? Will new products emerge to render its buggy whips less useful than an extrapolation of past sales suggests?

Conditions for Cost Minimization

What should a firm do to make its costs as low as possible? The firm does not have the least costly method of production if it is possible to substitute one factor for another so as to keep its output constant while reducing its total cost.

This idea can be stated more formally: The firm should substitute one factor (for example, capital) for another factor (for example, labor) as long as the marginal product of the one factor *per dollar expended on it* is greater than the marginal product of the other factor *per dollar expended on it*. The firm cannot have minimized its costs as long as these two magnitudes are unequal. Using K to represent capital, L labor, and p the price of a unit of the factor, the necessary condition of cost minimization may be stated:

$$\frac{MP_K}{p_K} = \frac{MP_L}{p_L} \qquad [1]$$

This equation is analogous to the condition for the utility-maximizing household, given on page 142, in which the household equated the marginal utility per dollar of two goods.[2]

To see why this equation needs to be satisfied if costs of production are to be minimized, suppose that the left-hand side of Equation [1] is equal to 10, showing that the last dollar spent on capital produced 10 units of output, while the right-hand side is equal to 4, showing that the last dollar spent

---

[1] The analysis in this section is based on marginal productivity analysis. An alternative analysis of long-run decision making based on isoquants is often used. We present it in the appendix to this chapter, which begins on page 913. Isoquant analysis is related to marginal productivity analysis in the same way that indifference curve analysis (Chapter 10) is related to marginal utility analysis (Chapter 9).

[2] In the appendix to this chapter the condition is given a graphic analysis similar to that given household behavior in Chapter 10.

on labor added only 4 units to output. In such a case, the firm, by using $2.50 less of labor, would reduce output by 10 units. But it could regain that lost output by spending $1 more on capital.[3] Making such a substitution of capital for labor would leave output unchanged and reduce cost by $1.50. Thus the original position was not the cost-minimizing one.

Whenever the two sides of Equation [1] are not equal, there are factor substitutions that will reduce costs.

By rearranging the terms in Equation [1] we can look at the cost-minimizing condition a bit differently.

$$\frac{MP_K}{MP_L} = \frac{p_K}{p_L} \qquad [2]$$

The ratio of the marginal products on the left-hand side compares the contribution to output of the last unit of capital and the last unit of labor. If the ratio is 4, this means one unit more of capital will add 4 times as much to output as one unit more of labor. The right-hand side shows how the cost of one unit more of capital compares to the cost of one unit more of labor. If it is also 4, it does not pay the firm to substitute capital for labor or vice versa. But suppose the right-hand side is 2. Capital, although twice as expensive, is 4 times as productive. It will pay the firm to switch to a method of production that uses more capital and less labor. If, however, the right-hand side is 6 (or *any* number more than 4), it will pay to substitute labor for capital.

This formulation shows how the firm can adjust the elements over which it has control (the quantities of factors used, and thus the marginal products of the factors) to the prices or opportunity costs of the factors given to it by the market. A precisely analogous adjustment process is involved when households adjust their consumption of

---

[3] The argument in the previous two sentences assumes that the marginal products do not change when expenditure is changed by a few dollars.

goods to the market prices of those goods (see pages 142–143).

The Principle of Substitution

Suppose that a firm is producing where the cost-minimizing conditions shown in Equations [1] or [2] are met but that the cost of labor increases while the cost of capital remains unchanged. As we have just seen, the least-cost method of producing any output will now use less labor and more capital than was required to produce the same output before the factor prices changed. The prediction called the **principle of substitution** follows from the assumption that firms try to minimize their costs.

Methods of production will change if the relative prices of factors change. Relatively more of the cheaper factor and relatively less of the more expensive one will be used.

The principle of substitution may be readily illustrated. As construction workers' wages have risen sharply relative to the wages of factory labor and the cost of machinery, many home builders have shifted from on-site construction to panelization. Panelization is a method of building standardized modules so that the wiring, plumbing, insulation, and painting are done at the factory. The bulk of the work is performed by machinery and by assembly line workers, whose wages are only half those of on-site construction workers.

The principle of substitution plays a central role in the allocation of resources in a market economy since it relates to the way the individual firm will respond to changes in relative factor prices. Such changes in relative factor prices are caused by the changing relative scarcity of factors to the economy as a whole. The individual firm is thus motivated to use less of factors that have become scarcer to the economy.

Consider another example. One country has a great deal of land and a small population. Here the price of land will be low while, because labor is in short supply, the wage rate will be high. Producers of agricultural goods will tend to make lavish use of the cheap land while economizing on expensive labor; thus a production process will be adopted that utilizes a low ratio of labor to land.

A second country is small in area and has a large population. Here the demand for land will be high relative to its supply, and land will be relatively expensive while labor will be relatively cheap. Firms producing agricultural goods will tend to economize on land by using a great deal of labor per unit of land; thus, a productive process will be adopted that uses a high ratio of labor to land.

Similar decisions will be made with respect to the relative scarcity of any factor. If capital is scarce relative to other factors, it will be expensive; firms following their own self-interest will use it sparingly. If capital is plentiful relative to other factors, it will be cheap. Firms will adopt production processes that make lavish use of capital.

Once again we see that the price system is an automatic control system. No single firm needs to be aware of national factor surpluses and scarcities. Prices determined in the competitive market tend to reflect them, and individual firms that never look beyond their own private profit are nonetheless led to economize on factors that are scarce to the nation as a whole. Thus, the price system leads profit-maximizing firms to take account of the nation's relative factor scarcities when deciding which of the possible methods of production to adopt.

This discussion suggests why methods of producing the same commodity differ among countries. In the United States, where labor is highly skilled and very expensive, a large-scale farmer may use elaborate machinery to economize on labor. In China, where labor is abundant and capital scarce, a much less mechanized method of production is appropriate. The Western engineer who believes that the Chinese lag behind Westerners because they are using methods long dismissed in the West as inefficient may be missing the truth about economic efficiency in the use of resources. The notion that to aid underdeveloped countries we have only to export Western "know-how" is misleading.

Cost Curves in the Long Run

There is a best (least-cost) method of producing each level of output when all factors are free to be varied. In general, this method will not be the same for different levels of output. If factor prices are given, a minimum cost can be found for each possible level of output and, if this minimum achievable cost is expressed as an amount per unit of output, we can obtain the long-run average cost of producing each level of output. When this information is plotted on a graph, the result is called a **long-run average cost curve (LRAC)**. Figure 13-1 shows such a curve.

This long-run average cost curve is determined by the technology of the industry (which is assumed to be fixed) and by the prices of the factors of production. It is a "boundary" in the sense that points below the curve are unattainable, points above the curve are attainable, and points on the curve are also attainable if sufficient time elapses for all factors to be adjusted. Indeed, points above the *LRAC* curve may represent the best that can be done in the short run when all factors are not freely variable.

The LRAC curve divides the cost levels that are attainable with known technology and given factor prices from those that are unattainable.

The Shape of the Long-Run Average Cost Curve

The long-run average cost curve shown in Figure 13-1 falls at first and then rises. This curve is often described as U-shaped, although "saucer-shaped" might be more accurate.

Decreasing costs. Over the range of output from zero to q_m the firm has falling long-run average costs. An expansion of output results in a reduction of costs per unit of output once enough time has elapsed to allow adjustments in the techniques of production. Since the prices of factors are assumed to be constant, the reason for the decline in costs per unit must be that output increases faster than inputs as the scale of the firm's

FIGURE 13-1
A Long-Run Average Cost Curve

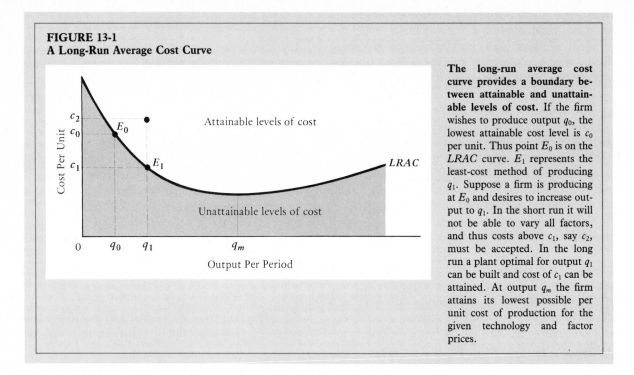

The long-run average cost curve provides a boundary between attainable and unattainable levels of cost. If the firm wishes to produce output q_0, the lowest attainable cost level is c_0 per unit. Thus point E_0 is on the *LRAC* curve. E_1 represents the least-cost method of producing q_1. Suppose a firm is producing at E_0 and desires to increase output to q_1. In the short run it will not be able to vary all factors, and thus costs above c_1, say c_2, must be accepted. In the long run a plant optimal for output q_1 can be built and cost of c_1 can be attained. At output q_m the firm attains its lowest possible per unit cost of production for the given technology and factor prices.

production expands. Over this range of output the firm is often said to enjoy long-run **increasing returns.**[4]

Increasing returns may arise as a result of increased opportunities for specialization of tasks made possible by the division of labor even with no substitution of one factor of production for another. Or they may arise because of factor substitution. Even the most casual observation of the differences in production technique used in large-size and small-size plants shows the differences in factor proportions. These differences arise because large, specialized equipment is useful only when the volume of output that the firm can sell justifies its employment.

For example, assembly line techniques, body-stamping machinery, and multiple-boring engine-block machines in automobile production are eco-nomically efficient only when individual operations are repeated thousands of times. Using elaborate harvesting equipment (which combines many individual tasks that would otherwise be done by hand and by tractor) provides the least-cost method of production on a big farm but not on a few acres.

Typically, as the level of planned output increases, capital is substituted for labor and complex machines for simpler machines. Robotics is a contemporary example. Electronic devices can handle huge volumes of operations very quickly, but unless the level of production requires very large numbers of operations, it does not make sense to use robotics or other forms of automation.

Increasing costs. Over the range of outputs greater than q_m the firm encounters rising costs. An expansion in production, even after sufficient time has elapsed for all adjustments to be made, will be accompanied by a rise in average costs per unit of output. If costs per unit of input are constant, this rise in costs must be the result of an expansion in output less than in proportion to the

---

[4] Economists shift back and forth between speaking in physical terms (i.e., increasing *returns* to production) and cost terms (i.e., decreasing *costs* of production). Thus, the same firm may be spoken of as having decreasing costs or enjoying increasing returns.

expansion in inputs. Such a firm is said to suffer long-run **decreasing returns**.[5] Decreasing returns imply that the firm suffers some diseconomy of scale. As its scale of operations increases, diseconomies, say of management, are encountered that increase its per unit costs of production.

At output q_m in Figure 13-1 the firm has reached its lowest possible long-run costs per unit of output. While every point on the $LRAC$ is efficient in the sense that *that output* is not attainable at a lower cost per unit (given current technology and factor prices), the output q_m is efficient in a second sense: no other output can be produced at so low a cost. Under certain conditions, called those of *perfect competition*, each firm in equilibrium will produce at the minimum point on its $LRAC$. (See Chapter 14 and its appendix for a full discussion of this proposition.)

Constant returns. In Figure 13-1 the firm's long-run average costs fall to output q_m and rise thereafter. Another possibility should be noted: The firm's $LRAC$ curve might have a flat portion over a range of output around q_m. With such a flat portion, the firm would be encountering constant costs over the relevant range of output. This would mean that the firm's average costs per unit of output were not changing as its output changed. Since factor prices are assumed to be fixed, this must mean that the firm's output is increasing exactly as fast as its inputs are increasing. Such a firm is said to be encountering **constant returns.**

The Relation Between Long-Run and Short-Run Costs

The various short-run cost curves mentioned at the conclusion of Chapter 12 and the long-run curve studied in this chapter are all derived from the

same production function. Each assumes given prices for all factor inputs. In the long run, all factors can be varied; in the short run, some must remain fixed. The long-run average cost curve ($LRAC$) shows the lowest cost of producing any output when all factors are variable. The short-run average cost curve ($SRAC$) shows the lowest cost of producing any output when one or more factors is not free to vary.

The short-run cost curve cannot fall below the long-run curve because the $LRAC$ curve represents the *lowest* attainable costs for every output. It might be the same curve if precisely the same-size plant was the best for any level of output. But that is not likely. The usual situation is that as the level of output is increased, a larger plant makes it possible to lower unit costs. Thus, a larger plant is required to achieve the lowest attainable costs. This is shown in Figure 13-2.

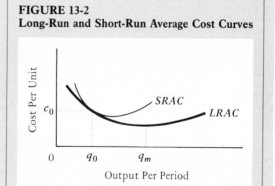

FIGURE 13-2
Long-Run and Short-Run Average Cost Curves

The short-run average cost curve is tangent to the long-run curve at the output for which the quantity of the fixed factors is optimal. If output is varied around q_0 units with plant and equipment fixed at the optimal level for producing q_0, costs will follow the short-run cost curve. Whereas $SRAC$ and $LRAC$ are at the same level for output q_0 where the fixed plant is optimal for that level, for all other outputs there is too little or too much of the fixed factor and $SRAC$ lies above $LRAC$. If some output other than q_0 is to be sustained, costs can be reduced to the level of the long-run curve when sufficient time has elapsed to adjust the fixed factors.

[5] Long-run decreasing returns differ from the short-run diminishing returns that we encountered earlier. In the short run, at least one factor is fixed and the law of diminishing returns ensures that returns to the variable factor will eventually diminish. In the long run, all factors are variable and it is possible that physically diminishing returns would never be encountered—at least as long as it was genuinely possible to increase inputs of all factors.

FIGURE 13-3
The Envelope Relation Between the Long-Run Average Cost Curve and All the Short-Run Average Cost Curves

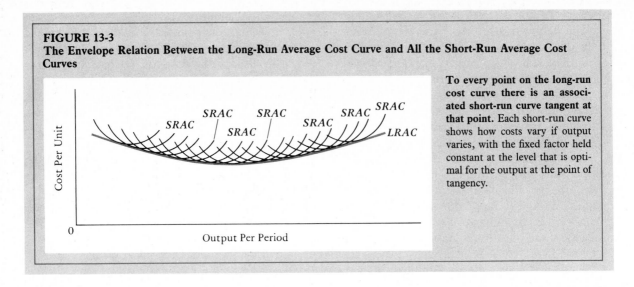

To every point on the long-run cost curve there is an associated short-run curve tangent at that point. Each short-run curve shows how costs vary if output varies, with the fixed factor held constant at the level that is optimal for the output at the point of tangency.

We saw at the end of Chapter 12 that a *SRAC* curve such as that in Figure 13-2 is one of many such curves. Each curve shows how costs vary as output is varied from a base output, holding some factors fixed at the quantities most appropriate to the base output (see Figure 13-3). The long-run curve is sometimes called an **envelope curve** because it encloses the whole family of short-run curves. Each short-run cost curve is tangent to (touches) the long-run curve at the level of output for which the quantity of the fixed factor is optimal and lies above it for all other levels of output.

Shifts in Cost Curves

The cost curves derived so far show how cost varies with output, given constant factor prices and fixed technology. Changes in either technological knowledge or factor prices will cause the entire family of short-run and long-run cost curves to shift. Loss of existing technological knowledge is rare, so technological change normally works in only one direction, to shift cost curves downward. Improved ways of making existing commodities will mean that lower-cost methods of production become available. (Technological change is discussed in the next section of this chapter.)

Factor price changes can exert an influence in either direction. If a firm has to pay more for any factor that it uses, the cost of producing each level of output will rise; if the firm has to pay less, costs will fall.

A rise in factor prices shifts the family of short-run and long-run cost curves upward. A fall in factor prices or a technological advance shifts the entire family of cost curves downward.

Although factor prices usually change gradually, they sometimes rise suddenly and drastically. This was the case in the 1970s. One reason was the sharp general inflation that beset the American economy; a second reason was the sudden and dramatic increase in energy prices that was triggered by the rise in the price of oil following the emergence of OPEC as an effective cartel.

Oil prices quadrupled within a year and had increased tenfold by the end of the decade. The effect was to shift upward the cost curves of all users. The size of the shift varied from product to product, depending on how important particular inputs were to total production. Oil price increases had some effects on almost all industries, and they had a major effect on such industries as synthetic rubber, plastics, and airlines.

THE VERY LONG RUN

The Importance and Relevance of Technical Change

The decrease in cost levels that can be achieved by choosing wisely among available factors of production, known techniques, and alternative levels of output is necessarily limited, since a firm can never utilize more than 100 percent of what is currently available. But improvements by invention and innovation are potentially limitless. For this reason, the long-term struggle to get more from the world's limited resources is critically linked to discovery.

Changes in technology are to a major degree *endogenous* responses to changing economic signals. That is, they are responses to the same things that induce the substitution of one factor for another with a given technology. In our discussion of long-run demand curves in Chapter 6, we looked at just such technological changes in response to rising relative prices when we spoke of the development of smaller, more fuel-efficient cars in the wake of rising gasoline prices. Similarly, much of the move to substitute capital for labor in American industry in response to rising wage rates has taken the form of developing labor-saving methods of production.

Three sets of changes tend to dominate the production function in the very long run. All are related to technology, broadly defined. First is the change in the techniques available for producing existing products. Over an average lifetime in the twentieth century, such changes have been dramatic. About the same amount of coal is produced today as 50 years ago, but the number of coal miners is less than one-tenth of what it was then. Seventy years ago roads and railways were built by gangs of workers using buckets, spades, and draft horses. Today bulldozers, steam shovels, giant trucks, and other specialized equipment have completely banished the workhorse from construction sites and to a great extent have displaced the pick-and-shovel worker.

Second is the change in available goods and services. Television, polio vaccine, nylon, and many current consumer products did not exist two generations ago. Other products are so changed that the only connection they have with the "same" commodity produced in the past is the name. A 1981 Ford automobile is very different from a 1931 Ford. Modern jets are revolutionary compared with the DC–3, which itself barely resembled Lindbergh's *Spirit of St. Louis.*

Third, improvements in such intangibles as health and education raise the quality of labor services. Today's managers and workers are healthier and better educated than their grandparents. Even unskilled workers today tend to be literate and competent in arithmetic, and their managers are apt to be trained in modern scientific methods of business control and computer science.

Technological changes like these have been vital to the economic life of the industrialized countries. Recently, however, there has been evidence of a major slowdown in the rate of technological change. To understand both the historical growth and the recent slowdown we must first understand the forces that affect technological change.[6]

The Nature and Significance of Productivity

Economics used to be known as the dismal science because some of its predictions were dismal. Basically, classical economists predicted that in the long run population would continue to expand and the pressure of more and more people on the world's limited resources would cause a decline in output per person. Human history would see more and more people living less and less well, with the surplus population that could not be supported dying off from hunger and disease.

This prediction has proven wrong for the industrial countries for two main reasons. First, the population has not expanded as rapidly as foreseen by early economists writing before birth control techniques were widely known. Second, pure knowledge and its applied techniques have ex-

---

[6] The theory of economic growth is discussed in more detail in Chapters 38 and 44. This is a brief introduction.

panded so rapidly during the last 150 years that our ability to squeeze more out of limited resources has expanded faster than the population.

To measure the extent of technological change, economists utilize the notion of **productivity**, defined as a measure of output per unit of resource input. This concept highlights society's ability to get more and better output from the basic resources of the economy. One widely used measure of productivity is output *per hour* of labor.[7] The rate of increase in productivity provides a measure of the progress caused by technical change.

It is growth in productivity that permits increases in output per person and thus contributes to rising standards of living.

Productivity increases are a powerful force for increasing living standards. Our great-grandparents would have regarded today's standard of living in most industrialized countries as unattainable. An apparently modest rate of increase in productivity of 2 percent per year leads to a doubling of output per hour of labor every 35 years. Productivity in the United States increased at a rate greater than this in every decade from 1900 to 1970.

In other countries the growth rate has been even higher. Since World War II productivity in Germany has increased at 5 percent per year, doubling output every 14 years, and in Japan it has increased at more than 9 percent per year—a rate that doubles output per hour of labor approximately every 8 years! In many countries, including the United States, productivity growth at a stable rate came to be taken for granted as an automatic source of ever-increasing living standards.

Then, abruptly, after 1965 productivity increases dropped sharply below their historic trends. This drop happened worldwide to some degree but was particularly acute in the United States and Canada. Indeed, from 1976 to 1980 American nonagricultural productivity did not increase at all. If this should prove to be permanent, the consequences will be severe. Lower productivity growth combined with a stable level of employment leads to a lower rate of increase of real output. Combined with declining employment, it may actually contribute to declining output per person. Declining productivity growth means that living standards rise more slowly or actually decline.

Decreases in rates of productivity growth also contribute to inflation. If productivity increases at 3 percent per year, all factor prices, and profits too, can increase 3 percent per year on average without leading to product price increases. But the same factor price increases become inflationary once productivity growth falls below that rate.

In the rest of this chapter we shall examine the major sources of increasing productivity and the most widely held explanations of why productivity growth has slowed.

Major Sources of Increasing Productivity

Productivity is increased by anything that increases output while maintaining the number of hours worked or that decreases the hours required to attain the same output. Here are the major historical sources of productivity increase.

Substitution of Capital for Labor

In manufacturing, transportation, communications, mining, and agriculture, capital has been substituted for labor to a major extent. This substitution can be measured by the **capital-labor ratio**, which determines changes in the amount of capital per worker. The capital-labor ratio increased steadily over the 100 years from 1870 to 1970. Increases in the capital-labor ratio are accompanied by increasing productivity.

Three reasons for this substitution can be identified. First, the price of labor rose relative to capital goods. Second, more productive machines were developed to replace older ones. Third, the opportunity provided by both population growth and growth in demand enabled businessmen to utilize more capital and thus take advantage of economies of scale.

---

[7] It is the measure we shall use. Other possible measures include output *per worker* and output *per person*.

When a country starts to industrialize, labor is generally employed in labor-intensive, low productivity industries. This starting point gives great scope for developing capital-intensive industries and shifting labor into them. As the shift happens, productivity rises. But as a country becomes industrialized, there is less scope for further gains since much less labor is left working with little capital.

Energy Substitution

Related to the substitution of capital for labor has been the increasing reliance on inanimate energy for production. Energy to plow fields, to turn machines, to move goods, to provide heat, and to transform natural resources is a major determinant of the productive power of an economy. In 1900 more than half of all energy requirements in the United States was supplied by human beings, horses, mules, and oxen. By 1980 human and animal power provided less than 10 percent of all energy; they have been replaced by coal, oil, gas, nuclear, and water power.

Improved Characteristics of Factors of Production

Labor. While an "hour of work" is a readily measurable unit of human labor effort and thus a convenient yardstick for measuring productivity, the tasks a human being can do in one hour vary greatly. An individual's contribution to the level of output in a single hour will depend on his or her health, education, and training. Over the last 100 years the level of "human capital" investment in the population, and consequently in the work force, has steadily increased, contributing to increases in the productivity of labor.

Are these human investment opportunities being exhausted? It is true that most of the population is now literate. But the opportunities for further education and training, in computer use for example, still seem large.

Materials. The quality of materials, from fabrics to metals, has improved over time. For ex-

ample, the type and quality of metals has changed: steel replaces iron and aluminum substitutes for steel in a process of change that makes a statistical category such as "primary metals" seem unsatisfactory and obsolete. Even for a given category—say, "steel"—today's product is lighter, stronger, and more flexible than the product manufactured only 15 years ago.

Management. Productivity can increase with the improvement of managerial skills. Better organization of production will in itself account for increases in productivity. New ideas improve efficiency when applied to new products or processes. An assembly line can be made more efficient even with no change in the quantity, quality, or proportions of factors.

Invention and Innovation

Invention is the discovery of something new, such as a production technique or a product. **Innovation** is the introduction of an invention into use. Invention is thus a necessary pre-condition to innovation.

Invention. Invention is cumulative; a useful invention is adopted, a useless one discarded. The cumulative impact of many small, useful inventions may be fully as great or greater than that of the occasional dramatic invention such as the steam engine, the cotton gin, or the sewing machine. Indeed, none of these famous inventions represented a single act of creative inspiration. Each depended on the contributions of prior inventors. The backlog of past inventions constitutes society's technical knowledge, and in turn that backlog feeds innovation.

Invention was once thought to be mainly a random process, done by crackpots and mad scientists working in garages or basements. We now know better. Invention is frequently an economic activity that is produced on demand. The development of the atomic bomb in the 1940s is only one very dramatic example of this fact. Major changes in the store of technical knowledge are the result of expenditures on research and development (R&D) by private firms, by the government, and by scholars and scientists in research institutions.

Money can buy invention. In the United States in 1982, about $70 billion was devoted to R&D expenditures, of which roughly 40 percent was expended by the federal government, 40 percent by private industry, and the rest by universities and other institutions. Among the corporate research centers are such giants as AT&T's Bell Labs (with 17,000 employees) and the research centers of IBM and General Electric in New York and Texas Instruments in Texas. Most major industrial companies have research and development centers or divisions, and hundreds of small, private R&D firms do contract research. Approximately 2 percent to 3 percent of gross business sales revenue is spent on R&D, although the percentage varies enormously from industry to industry and from year to year.

Current evidence indicates that productivity growth is to a significant degree a response to expenditures on R&D. Those countries, particularly Germany and Japan, that have stepped up such expenditures have experienced much higher levels of productivity growth than those countries (the United States, Canada, and the United Kingdom) that have let such expenditures lag. Similarly, industries that are major R&D spenders (chemicals, electrical equipment, air transport) have maintained productivity growth much better than others that engage in very little R&D (steel and construction). Some sectors that do little R&D, such as coal mining and farming, may buy their equipment, fertilizer, and seed from industries that do a great deal and thus achieve gains in productivity. These sectors buy R&D in the price they pay for inputs.

Innovation. Innovation depends upon a steady supply of new inventions, but it must take a key additional step: introduction into use. New methods, machines, materials, and products are introduced not "because they are there" but because (and when) it appears *profitable* to introduce them. Productivity growth may rise or decline as the profit incentives to innovate are strong or weak.

Profit incentives in turn are affected by many aspects of the economic climate, among them the rate of growth of the economy, the level of capacity utilization, the cost and availability of money for investment, and all sorts of government policies from taxes to regulations.

Reasons for the Decline in Productivity Growth

Table 13-1 shows the dramatic decline in U.S. productivity performance. The sharp contrast between the years 1950–1965 and the years 1965–1980 with respect to total productivity is even more dramatic when attention is focused on the nonagricultural sectors of the U.S. economy. Not sur-

TABLE 13–1 PRODUCTIVITY INCREASES IN THE UNITED STATES, 1950–1980 (Annual Percentage Rate of Change of Output Per Hour)

Period	Farm Productivity	Nonfarm Productivity	Total Productivity
1950–1955	5.47	2.22	2.95
1955–1960	4.96	1.85	2.42
1960–1965	4.85	3.51	3.85
1950–1965	5.10	2.53	3.08
1965–1970	6.36	1.53	1.97
1970–1975	3.47	1.24	1.35
1975–1980	4.07	0.89	1.13
1965–1980	4.63	1.22	1.48
1950–1980	4.86	1.87	2.29

The historical rate of growth of productivity of about 3 percent per year has declined sharply since 1965. Growth in output per hour declined from about 3 percent per year from 1950 to 1965 to only about 1.5 percent per year average over the next 15 years. The last 5 years of the period 1975–1980 showed the sharpest decline. Excluding agriculture, where productivity growth has remained strong, the decline in recent years is very sharp. In 1979–1980 and again in 1980–1981, nonfarm productivity actually declined.

prisingly there is some disagreement about the various causes of the decline and their relative importance, but it is possible to identify major contributing forces.

Sharply Rising Energy Costs

Cheap energy fueled American productivity growth for a century. As we shall see in Chapter 17, OPEC changed that situation abruptly in the early 1970s. Energy, instead of being plentiful and cheap, became scarce and expensive. Just as falling energy costs meant rising productivity, rising energy costs may be expected to slow productivity increases. If energy is again to be a source of increasing productivity, new and cheaper fuels must be discovered.

In the long run, rising energy prices may bring about substitution of new capital in the form of energy-economizing devices. In the short run, however, rising energy prices have slowed the installation and use of energy-using machinery. This in turn has slowed the substitution of machinery for labor that has always been an important source of productivity increases. In the year 1973–1974, the year of the big oil shortages, manufacturing productivity in the United States actually fell by 5 percent, the largest decline recorded in American productivity statistics in 40 years.

Declining Growth in Aggregate Output

When productivity declines, so does growth in output. But output growth can slow for reasons other than productivity, and such slowdowns can reinforce productivity declines. The end of the postwar baby boom is one of a number of forces currently decreasing growth in output. When relatively few industries and firms are expanding, less investment will take place. A growing industry often has profitable opportunities for investment in additional machines as well as machines geared to a larger scale of output. Every time a firm seeks new investment it is likely to look at the latest, most modern technology available. The introduc-

tion of that technology leads to productivity increases.

An economy that has stopped growing cannot adapt easily to the changing skill requirements of its labor force. It is much harder to retrain existing workers than to educate and train new entrants into the labor force with the new skills they will need. Moreover, the lack of job and promotion opportunities in new occupations may discourage young people from acquiring the fresh skills needed for productivity growth.

Shifts in Demand and the Composition of Output

Industries and sectors of the economy differ greatly from one another in what is called their *technological base,* that is, in the opportunities they provide for increasing productivity. It is much harder for social workers to increase their output (cases handled per year) than it is for airline pilots to increase their output (passenger miles flown per year). This has nothing to do with the skill or dedication of the social worker compared with that of the pilot; it concerns the nature of their tasks and the tools at their disposal. The social worker has no counterpart to the bigger, faster plane that increases the pilot's productivity.

The productivity level of the economy is the weighted average of the levels of productivity of each of its sectors. Aggregate productivity can fall even though the level of productivity in each individual sector remains unchanged.

The same is true of *growth* in productivity. Suppose, for example, that the economy has only two sectors. In "manufacturing" productivity grows by 5 percent per year; in "services" it grows by 1 percent per year. If each sector produces one-half of total output, total productivity growth will be 3 percent per year. But if services become 75 percent of the total and manufacturing 25 percent, the aggregate productivity increase will fall to 2 percent.

There is little doubt that some of the earlier rise and recent decrease in productivity growth in the

United States reflects shifts in the demand for goods. In 1948 the *level* of agricultural productivity was just 40 percent of the national average.[8] Thus every worker moving from agriculture to industry increased productivity. From 1948 to 1965, 8 percent of the total number of hours worked shifted from agriculture to industry, thus contributing to a major increase in national average productivity. By the mid 1970s this source of productivity gain had virtually ceased.

Similarly, there has been a major shift from manufacturing to services. Many of the commodities we increasingly consume have a low technological base and low productivity. These include such items as fast-food hamburgers, and services designed to provide such amenities as garbage collection, clean air, police protection, and libraries. In the same way, demands for safety and for medical and hospital care have increased relative to demands for copper, manufactured goods, and transportation. The resulting shifts of labor from sectors with relatively high levels of productivity to those with much lower levels has automatically decreased average productivity. If, in addition, the growing sectors are services which have less scope for increasing productivity, the growth of productivity over time will surely decrease.

Shifts in the Size and Composition of the Labor Force

One of the dramatic demographic and sociological shifts of the last two decades has been the remarkable change in the composition of the labor force. Not only has the baby boom generation come of age, with young people entering the labor force in ever-increasing numbers, but women of all ages are increasingly in the labor market. Between 1960 and 1980 the percentage of the labor force consisting of persons under 25 years old rose from 16

---

[8] We are now talking about the level of productivity in different sectors, not the *rate of growth* of productivity. Farm productivity, which we see in Table 13-1 has increased much faster than nonfarm productivity, is still below the latter in level.

percent to 22 percent, and females (of all ages) increased from 34 percent to 43 percent of the labor force. The growth in the numbers of youth and women in the labor force has lowered the capital-labor ratio and thus tended to decrease productivity. New workers, whoever they are, necessarily have less work experience and less job-specific training than existing labor force members. Until they acquire experience, their presence tends to lower average productivity.

Policies Designed to Control Inflation

Many recent policies designed to control inflation have also discouraged investment. This is true of tight-money policies that have driven up interest rates, and it is true of policies that have allowed recessions to continue as a way of cooling off an inflationary economy. Investment expenditures are highly sensitive to both the cost of capital and the level of economic activity.

Those policies that discourage investment worsen the capital-labor ratio and depress productivity growth. High interest rates do so by raising the cost of capital relative to labor. As to recessions, productivity always falls off during cyclical slumps. One important reason is that in recessions new investment tends to fall sharply as expansion is postponed. Firms with excess capacity not only delay expansion, they postpone replacing existing equipment as it wears out. Since new investment is a main source of introducing innovations, postponing investment directly harms productivity growth. Another reason is that bottlenecks in production are infrequent when there is general slack in the economy. Bottlenecks trigger both the substitution of one input for another and the invention of substitutes for scarce items. With excess capacity, firms tend to try to increase demand rather than to reduce costs.

The failure of the U.S. economy to achieve anything like full utilization of its capacity during the period 1973–1983 added a cyclical damper to productivity growth that accentuated the effects of the slowdown in economic growth.

The Institutional Climate

The profits from innovation depend, among other things, on tax laws and regulatory requirements. If innovators are allowed to reap large gains from successful innovations, they will more likely take the risks of innovating. Innovation can be encouraged by investment tax credits, strong patent laws, low tax rates, government subsidies, and government-assisted R&D. It can be discouraged by regulatory burdens such as environmental impact statements, safety regulation, and the hassles and delays involved in meeting government requirements. Many regulatory commissions limit entry into fields in which an innovative firm might otherwise see a chance to make a profit.

A different aspect of the institutional climate arises from the desire of the citizens of a relatively rich country to protect workers and firms from the harsh forces of economic competition. The rigors of the marketplace may force productivity improvements because they are essential to survival; protecting firms may remove these incentives. Foreign competition that threatens domestic firms may spur them to adopt more efficient techniques; restrictions on that competition may remove the need and thus the incentive for such innovations.

Many believe that the institutional climate in the United States became increasingly hostile to private innovation in the sixties and seventies and that high taxes, government regulation, and economic protection all added to the forces inhibiting innovation and growth. These factors may partly explain the decline in R&D expenditures as a percent of national income from 2.9 percent in 1965 to about 2.3 percent in 1980.

How Much Productivity Growth Do We Want?

Some observers saw in 1982 signs that the dismal productivity performance of the previous decade was about to be reversed. Professor John Kendrick of George Washington University, a leading authority on productivity, confidently forecast "the coming rebound in productivity" partly as a result of America's adapting to higher energy prices, changing labor force composition and composition of output, and partly as a result of the more supportive climate of the Reagan administration. Others, such as Professor Lester Thurow of M.I.T., believed that without a major change in attitudes, the policies required to discourage consumption and encourage investment will not occur, and until they do, productivity will not rebound. Time will tell which group of economists is right.

There remains an important question about social values. Progress, as measured by productivity growth, is no longer an unquestioned overriding goal of society. Progress has come to mean growth, and growth has meant industrialization. Applied to the economy as a whole, industrialization and its accompanying changes in productivity have vastly increased our material well-being and permitted ever more people to escape the ravages of hunger and poverty. Clearly, we do not wish to remain permanently an economy whose productivity growth is absent or very low. But not all the slowdown in productivity growth is unwanted. The shift to the provision of services with high income elasticities but low productivity levels is the most obvious example. The population evidently does not want more manufactured goods if it means less police protection, or more food at the cost of less recreation, even though such shifts would increase productivity growth.

Moreover, growth in productivity has often been accompanied by increased pollution and more industrial accidents. Nothing is without its cost. In the case of growth this fact is increasingly being recognized. The gasoline engine, the steel mill, the jet airplane, DDT, plastics, and the skyscraper with its hundreds of thousands of electric lights are the artifacts of our progress over the last century. Many believe that they have lowered the quality of life even while raising the standard of living.

Just as members of a society can benefit (at some stage in economic development) from more luxuries and fewer basic necessities, so too may they benefit from more amenities and lower productivity growth. To the extent that they can, a slower rate of productivity growth may reflect a better life, not a worse one.

SUMMARY

1. There are no fixed factors in the long run. The profit-maximizing firm chooses, from the alternatives open to it, the least costly way of achieving any specific output. A long-run cost curve represents the boundary between attainable and unattainable levels of cost for the given technology.

2. The principle of substitution says that efficient production will substitute cheaper factors for more expensive ones. If the relative prices of factors change, relatively more of cheaper factors and relatively less of more expensive ones will be used. An alternative development of the theory of production in the long run, using isoquants, appears in the appendix to this chapter.

3. The shape of the long-run cost curve depends on the relationship of inputs to outputs as the whole scale of a firm's operations changes. Increasing, constant, and decreasing returns lead to decreasing, constant, and increasing long-run average costs.

4. The relation between long-run and short-run cost curves is shown in Figures 13-2 and 13-3. Every "long-run" cost corresponds to *some* quantity of each factor and is thus on some short-run cost curve. The short-run cost curve shows how costs vary when that particular quantity of a fixed factor is used to produce outputs greater than or less than those for which it is optimal.

5. Cost curves shift upward or downward in response to changes in the prices of factors or the introduction of changed technology. Increases in factor prices shift the cost curves upward. Decreases in factor prices or technological advances

that make it possible to produce the same amount of output with lower quantities of all inputs shift cost curves downward.

6. Over extended periods, the most important influence on costs of production and the standard of living has been the increases in output made possible by new technology and reflected in increasing productivity. These considerations involve the so-called very long run.

7. Major sources of productivity growth in industrializing countries include the substitution of capital for labor (an increasing capital-labor ratio); increased energy use; improvements in factors of production such as improved health, the education and training of labor, improved materials, and better organization of production; and invention and innovation.

8. Behind improvements in productivity lie invention and innovation. Invention—the discovery of new methods—occurs in many ways, but research and development expenditures play a major role. Changes in the level and type of R&D can be traced in an economy's productivity record.

9. Innovation requires invention and also profitable opportunities for the introduction of available knowledge. The economic climate (its growth and level of capacity utilization), the institutional climate, and the differences in technological possibilities in sectors where demand is growing and declining all affect the opportunities for innovation.

10. The slowdown in productivity growth in the United States during the 1970s, with its consequent reduction in the average growth rate of living standards, has been due to a combination of circumstances including sharply rising energy costs, declining growth in aggregate output, shifts in demand from higher productivity to lower productivity activities, shifts in the size and composition of the labor force, factors decreasing the level of investment, and a less encouraging institutional climate.

11. Not all of the slowdown in measured productivity growth represents a worsening of the quality of life. Material progress leads both to more goods and services per person and to opportunities for better living. Yet progress of this kind is not an unmixed blessing; pollution of the environment accompanies growth, and an increased number of injuries and accidents occur.

TOPICS FOR REVIEW

The implication of cost minimization
The interpretation of $MP_K/MP_L = p_K/p_L$ and of
   $MP_K/P_K = MP_L/P_L$
The principle of substitution
Increasing, decreasing, and constant returns
The envelope curve
The distinction between production and productivity
The level of productivity and the rate of growth of productivity
Sources of increasing productivity
Invention and innovation
Determinants of innovation
Causes of the slowdown in growth of productivity

DISCUSSION QUESTIONS

1. Why does the profit-maximizing firm choose the least costly way of producing any given output? Might a non-profit-maximizing organization such as a university or a church or a government intentionally choose a method of production other than the least costly one? Might an ordinary business corporation do so intentionally?

2. In Dacca, Bangladesh, where gasoline costs $3 a gallon and labor is typically paid less than 20¢ an hour, Abdul Khan pedals a bicycle-ricksha (pedicab) for his living. It's exhausting work that is coming under increasing attack by those who feel it is an inhumane practice. "We really want to get rid of them and move to motorized taxis, but I'm afraid it will take a long, long time," says the Bangladesh information officer. Ricksha drivers earn $2 a day, which is more than a skilled worker gets in Dacca. Explain the use of pedicabs in Dacca but not in New York or Tokyo. Comment on the information officer's statement.

3. Use the principle of substitution to predict the effect of each of the following:
   a. During the 1960s, salaries of professors rose much more rapidly than those of teaching assistants. During the 1970s, salaries of teaching assistants rose more than those of professors.
   b. The cost of land in big cities increases more than the cost of high-rise construction.
   c. Gold leaf is produced by pounding gold with a hammer. The thinner it is, the more valuable. The price of gold is set on a world market, but the price of labor varies among countries.
   d. OPEC keeps oil prices increasing faster than prices of most other raw materials.
   e. Wages of textile workers and shoe machinery operators rise more in New England than in South Carolina.

4. The long-run average cost curve can be thought of as consisting of points from each of a number of short-run average cost curves. Explain in what sense any point on the long-run curve is also on some short-run curve. What is the meaning of a move from one point on a long-run cost curve to another point on the same curve? Contrast this with a movement along a short-run curve.

5. The director of federal energy programs urged the American people to make necessary "long-run adjustments to the energy shortage by reducing energy input per unit of output." How exactly might this be done? Is this use of *long-run* the economists' use of that concept?

6. Israel, a small country, imports the "insides" of its automobiles but manufactures the bodies. If this makes economic sense, what does it tell us about cost conditions of automobile manufacture?

7. Name five important modern products that were not available when you were in grade school. Make a list of major products that you think have increased their sales at least tenfold in the last 30 years. Check your judgment by consulting the *Statistical Abstract of the United States, Business Statistics* (biennial of the U.S. Department of Commerce) or similar sources. Consider to what extent the growth in each series may reflect product or process innovation.

8. Each of the following is a means of increasing productivity. Discuss which groups within the society might oppose each one.
   a. a labor-saving invention that permits all goods to be manufactured with less labor than before
   b. a rapidly increasing growth of population in the economy

c. removal of all government production safety rules

d. a reduction in corporate income taxes

e. discovery of a new, cheap substitute for oil

9. Mobil Oil chairman Rawleigh Warner, Jr., has said, "Our government has adopted a gratuitously hostile attitude. Industry has been compelled to spend more and more of its research dollars to comply with environmental, health and safety regulations—and to move away from longer-term efforts aimed at major scientific advance." Suppose this is true. Is it necessarily a sign that government policies are misguided?

10. Which of the following might be expected to affect the rate of productivity growth? In each case indicate the direction and the mechanism of the change.

a. increases in interest rates

b. decreased control of strip mining

c. increased production of agricultural commodities with a corresponding decrease in manufacturing output

PART FOUR
MARKETS AND PRICING

14 PRICING IN COMPETITIVE MARKETS

Is Goodyear in competition with Goodrich? Does Macy's compete with Gimbels? Is the farmer from Wheatland, Iowa, in competition with a wheat farmer from North Platte, Nebraska? In the ordinary meaning of the noun *competition* and the verb *compete*, the answers to the first two questions are plainly yes, and the answer to the third question is probably no.

Goodyear and Goodrich both advertise extensively to persuade tire buyers to buy *their* product.

Goodrich has even been known to confuse the issue by asking: See that blimp up there? It's theirs, not ours. If you want Goodrich tires you'll just have to remember Goodrich." Everyone knows that Macy's and Gimbels watch each other like hawks and that swarms of comparison shoppers check their respective prices and qualities every day. But nothing the Iowa farmer can do will affect either the sales or the profits of the Nebraska farmer.

FIRM BEHAVIOR
AND MARKET STRUCTURE

To sort out the questions of who is competing with whom and in what sense, it is useful to distinguish between the behavior of individual firms and the type of market in which the firms operate. The concept of competitive behavior is quite distinct from the concept of competitive market structure. The degree of *competitive behavior* refers to the degree to which individual firms actively compete with one another.

Economists use the term *market structure* to refer to the market type. The degree of *competitiveness of the market structure* refers to the extent to which individual firms lack power over that market—power to influence the price or other terms on which their product is sold. In everyday use, *competition* usually refers only to competitive behavior; economists, however, are interested both in the competitive behavior of individual firms and in competitive market structures.

Goodrich and Goodyear certainly engage in competitive (i.e., rivalrous) behavior. It is also true that both individually and together they have some power over the market. Either firm could raise its prices and still continue to sell tires; each has the power to decide—within limits set by buyers' tastes and the prices of competing tires—what price consumers will pay for its own product.

The Iowa and the Nebraska wheat farmers do not engage in active competitive behavior with each other. They operate, however, in a market over which they have no power. Neither has significant power to change the market price for its wheat by altering its behavior.

At one extreme of competitive market structures, economists use a theory in which no single firm has any market power. There are so many firms that each must accept the price set by the forces of market demand and supply. In this theory of the *perfectly competitive market structure* there is no need for individual firms to behave competitively with respect to one another since none has any power over the market. One firm's ability to sell its product does not depend on the behavior of any other firm. The apparent paradox that interfirm competition does not occur in perfectly competitive markets is resolved when we recognize the distinction between interfirm competitive *behavior* and the competitive *structure* of the market in which the firm operates.

The theory of the perfectly competitive market structure applies directly to a number of real-world markets. It also provides a benchmark for comparison with other market structures in which there are so few firms that each has some significant market power.

The Significance of Market Structure

Although market demand curves and cost curves of individual firms are the basic elements of the theory of product pricing, they are not themselves sufficient to provide a theory of price. Hypotheses are needed that tell how these elements interact and finally come together in the market. At the outset we need to define two basic concepts, the market and the industry.

From the point of view of a household, the **market** consists of those firms from which it can buy a well-defined product; from the point of view of a firm, the market consists of those buyers to whom it can sell a well-defined product. A group of firms that sells a well-defined product, or closely related set of products, is said to constitute an **industry.** The market demand curve is the demand curve for an industry's product.[1]

Consider a firm that produces a specific product for sale in a particular market and competes for customers with other firms in the same industry. If a profit-maximizing firm knows the demand curve it faces, it knows the price it could charge for each rate of sales and thus knows its potential revenues. If it also knows its costs, the firm can readily discover the profits that would be associated with any rate of output and can choose the rate that maximizes its profits. But what if the firm knows its costs and only the *market* demand curve

---

[1] An industry typically sells many different products and sells in many markets. For our elementary treatment, we shall focus attention on the single-product firm and the market in which that product is sold.

for its product? It does not know what its own sales would be. In other words, the firm does not know its *own* demand curve. In order to determine what fraction of the total market demand will be met by other sellers, it needs to know how other firms will respond to its change in price. If it reduces its price by 10 percent, will other sellers leave their prices unchanged or will they also reduce them? If they reduce their prices, will they do so by less than 10 percent, by exactly 10 percent, or by more than 10 percent? Obviously, each possible outcome will have a different effect on the firm's sales and thus on its revenues and profits.

The answers to questions about the relation of a firm's demand curve to the market demand curve depend on such variables as the number of sellers in the market and the similarity of their products. For example, if there are only two large firms in an industry, each may be expected to meet most price cuts that the other makes; but if there are 5,000 small firms, a price cut by one may go unmatched. If two firms are producing identical products, they may be expected to behave differently with respect to each other than if they were producing similar but not identical products.

The central hypothesis of industrial organization economics is that firm behavior and performance will be affected by the characteristics of the markets in which the firm operates.

Market structure is defined as those characteristics of market organization that affect firms' behavior and performance. The number of sellers and the nature of the product are the most significant dimensions of market structure. There are others as well, such as the ease of entering the industry, the nature and size of the purchasers of the firm's products, and the firm's ability to influence demand by advertising. To reduce these aspects to manageable proportions, economists have focused on a few theoretical market structures that they believe represent a high proportion of the cases actually encountered in market societies. In this chapter and the next two, we shall look at four market structures: perfect competition, monopoly, monopolistic competition, and oligopoly.

Before considering any of these market structures, it is useful to deal with the rules of behavior common to all firms that seek to maximize their profits.

Behavioral Rules for the Profit-Maximizing Firm[2]

The firm always has the option of producing nothing. If it produces nothing, it will have an operating loss equal to its fixed costs. If it decides to produce, it will add the variable cost of production to its fixed costs, and the receipts from the sale of its product to its revenue. Therefore, if there is some level of output for which revenue exceeds variable cost, it will pay the firm to produce; if, however, revenue is less than variable cost at every level of output, the firm will actually lose more by producing than by not producing.

Rule 1. A firm should not produce at all if the average revenue from selling its product does not equal or exceed the average variable cost of producing it. [19]

If a firm decides that, according to rule 1, production is worth undertaking, it must decide how much to produce. Common sense dictates that on a unit-by-unit basis, if any unit of production adds more to revenue than it does to cost, that unit will increase profits; if it adds more to cost than to revenue, it will decrease profits. If the firm is in a position where a further unit of production will increase profits, it should expand output; if it is in a position where the last unit of production decreased profits, it should contract output. The notion of the change in cost brought about by an additional unit is, of course, marginal cost (*MC*). A parallel concept, **marginal revenue (*MR*)**, may be defined as the change in total revenue resulting from the sale of one additional unit.

A second rule may now be stated formally:

Rule 2. Assuming that it pays the firm to produce at all, it will be profitable for the firm to expand output whenever marginal revenue is greater than marginal cost; expansion should thus continue until marginal revenue equals marginal cost. [20]

[2] Formal proofs of the propositions discussed in the text are given in the Mathematical Notes.

These two rules can be restated as three necessary conditions for a firm's maximizing its profits. It must be producing at a level of output where (1) price is at least as great as average variable cost, (2) marginal revenue equals marginal cost, and (3) the marginal cost curve cuts the marginal revenue curve from below.[3] [21]

These rules apply to all profit-maximizing firms whatever the market structure in which they operate. The rules refer to each firm's cost and its own revenues. Before we can apply the rules we need to consider particular market structures in order to provide links between the demand curve for an industry's product and the demand curves—and thus the revenue curves—facing individual firms.

THE ELEMENTS OF THE THEORY OF PERFECT COMPETITION

The Assumptions of Perfect Competition

The theory of **perfect competition** is built on two critical assumptions, one about the behavior of the individual firm and one about the nature of the industry in which it operates.

The *firm* is assumed to be a **price taker;** that is, the firm is assumed to act as though it can alter its rate of production and sales within any feasible range without such action having a significant effect on the price of the product it sells. Thus, the firm must passively accept whatever price happens to be ruling on the market.

The *industry* is assumed to be characterized by

freedom of entry and exit; that is, any new firm is free to set up production if it so wishes, and any existing firm is free to cease production and leave the industry. Existing firms cannot bar the entry of new firms, and there are no legal prohibitions on entry or exit.

The ultimate test of the theory based on these assumptions will be the usefulness of its predictions, but because students are often bothered by the first assumption, it is worth examining whether it is in any way reasonable. To see what is involved in the assumption of price taking, contrast the demands for the products of an automobile manufacturer and a wheat farmer.

An automobile manufacturer. General Motors is aware that it has market power. If it substantially increases its prices, sales will fall off; if it lowers prices substantially, it will sell more of its products. If GM decides on a large increase in production that is not a response to a known or anticipated rise in demand, it will have to reduce prices in order to sell the extra output. The automobile manufacturing firm is *not* a price taker. The quantity that it is able to sell will depend on the price it charges, but it does not have to accept passively whatever price is set by the market. In other words, the firm manufacturing automobiles is faced with a downward-sloping demand curve for its product. It may select any price-quantity combination consistent with that demand curve.

A wheat farmer. In contrast, an individual firm producing wheat is just one of a very large number of firms all growing the same product; one firm's contribution to the total production of wheat will be a tiny drop in an extremely large bucket. Ordinarily, the firm will assume that it has no effect on price and will think of its own demand curve as being horizontal. Of course, the firm can have *some* effect on price, but a straightforward calculation will show that the effect is small enough that the firm can justifiably neglect it.

The market elasticity of demand for wheat is approximately 0.25. This means that if the quantity of wheat supplied in the world increased by 1 percent, the price would have to fall by 4 percent to

---

[3] The third condition is designed to distinguish between profit-maximizing and profit-minimizing positions. Consider a situation in which *MC* cuts *MR* from above: For outputs to the left of the intersection marginal cost exceeds marginal revenue, which indicates that these units reduce profits and thus that profits could be increased by *reducing* output. For outputs to the right of the intersection marginal revenue exceeds marginal cost, which indicates that these units increase profits and thus that profits could be increased by *increasing* output. The intersection must thus represent minimum profits.

induce the world's wheat buyers to purchase the whole crop. Even huge farms produce a very small fraction of the total crop. In a recent year an extremely large Canadian wheat farm produced about 50,000 tons, only about 1/4,000 of the world production of 200 million tons. Suppose a large wheat farm increased its production by 20,000 tons, say from 40,000 to 60,000 tons. This would be a big percentage increase in its own production but an increase of only 1/100 of 1 percent in world production. Table 14-1 shows that this increase would lead to a decrease in the world price of 4/100 of 1 percent (4¢ in $100) and give the firm an elasticity of demand of 1,000! This is a very high elasticity of demand; the farm would have to increase its output 1,000 percent to bring about a 1 percent decrease in the price of wheat. Because the firm's output cannot be varied this much, it is not sur-

prising that the firm regards the price of wheat to be unaffected by any change in output that it could conceivably make.

It is only a slight simplification to say that the firm is unable to influence the world price of wheat and that it is able to sell all that it can produce at the going world price. In other words, the firm is faced with a perfectly elastic demand curve for its product—it is a price taker.

The difference between firms producing wheat and firms producing automobiles is one of degree of market power. The wheat firm, as an insignificant part of the whole market, has no power to influence the world price of wheat. But the automobile firm does have power to influence the price of automobiles because its own production represents a significant part of the total supply of automobiles.

TABLE 14–1 THE CALCULATION OF A FIRM'S ELASTICITY OF DEMAND (η_F) FROM MARKET ELASTICITY OF DEMAND (η_M)

Given
$\eta_M = 0.25$
World output $= 200$ million tons
Firm's output increases from 40,000 to 60,000 tons, a 40% increase over the average quantity of 50,000 tons

Step 1. Find the percentage change in world price:

$$\eta_M = -\frac{\text{percentage change in world output}}{\text{percentage change in world price}}$$

$$\text{Percentage change in world price} = -\frac{\text{percentage change in world output}}{\eta_M}$$

$$= -\frac{\text{$\frac{1}{100}$ of 1\%}}{0.25}$$

$$= -\text{$\frac{4}{100}$ of 1\%}$$

Step 2. Compute the firm's elasticity of demand:

$$\eta_F = -\frac{\text{percentage change in firm's output}}{\text{percentage change in world price}}$$

$$= -\frac{+40\%}{-\frac{4}{100}\text{ of 1\%}} = +1,000$$

Because even a large change in output to the firm is a minute change in world wheat production, the effect on world price is very small. Thus the firm's elasticity of demand is high. This table relies on the concept of elasticity of demand developed in Chapter 6. Step 1 shows that a 40 percent increase in the firm's output leads to

only a tiny decrease in the world's price. Thus, as step 2 shows, the firm's elasticity of demand is very high: 1,000.

The arithmetic is not important, but understanding why the wheat farm will be a price taker in these circumstances is vital.

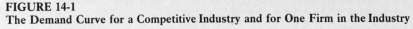

FIGURE 14-1
The Demand Curve for a Competitive Industry and for One Firm in the Industry

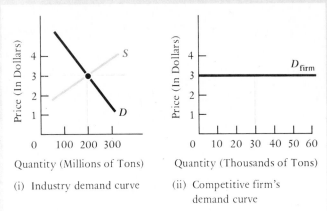

(i) Industry demand curve

(ii) Competitive firm's
demand curve

The industry's demand curve is downward-sloping; the firm's demand curve is virtually horizontal. Notice the difference in the quantities shown on the horizontal scale in each part of the figure. The competitive industry is assumed to be operating at a level where price is equal to $3, producing approximately 200 million tons. The firm takes the market price as given to it and considers producing up to 60 thousand tons. The firm's demand curve in (ii) appears horizontal because of the change in the quantity scale compared to (i). The firm's output variation has only a tiny effect on industry output. If one plotted the industry demand curve from 199,970 thousand tons to 200,030 thousand tons on the scale used in (ii), the D curve would appear virtually horizontal.

Demand and Revenue Curves for the Perfectly Competitive Firm

One must be careful not to confuse the individual firm's demand curve under perfect competition with the market demand curve for the product. The market demand curve is downward-sloping for the reasons discussed in Chapters 9 and 10. A consequence, as we saw, is that a rightward shift of the supply curve will lead to a fall in market price, other things being equal.

The demand curve facing a single firm in perfect competition is horizontal because variations in its production *over the range that we need to consider for all practical purposes* will have such a small effect on price that the effect can safely be assumed to be zero. Of course, if the single firm increased its production by a vast amount, a thousandfold say, this might well cause a significant increase in supply and the firm would be unable to sell all it produced at the going price. The horizontal (perfectly elastic) demand curve does not mean that the firm could actually sell an infinite amount at the going price; rather, that the variations in production *that it will normally be practicable for the firm to make* will leave price virtually unaffected. Figure

14-1 contrasts the demand curve for a competitive industry and for a single firm in that industry.

Total, Average, and Marginal Revenue Curves

The notions of total, average, and marginal revenue are the demand counterparts of the notions of total, average, and marginal cost that we considered in Chapter 12. We focus now on the receipts to a seller from the sale of a product.

Total revenue (TR) is the total amount received by the seller. If q units are sold at p dollars each, $TR = p \cdot q$. (The dot between p and q is a "times" sign, frequently used instead of $p \times q$, to avoid confusion with variables labeled x.)

Average revenue (AR) is the amount of revenue *per unit* sold: This is the price of the product.

Marginal revenue (**MR**), sometimes called incremental revenue, has already been defined. It is the change in total revenue resulting from the sale of an additional unit of the commodity. [22]

Calculations of these revenue concepts for a price-taking firm are illustrated in Table 14-2. The table shows that as long as the firm's output does not affect the price of the product it sells, both average and marginal revenue will be equal to price at all levels of output. Thus, graphically (as is shown in Figure 14-2), average revenue and marginal revenue are both horizontal lines at the level of market price. Since the firm can sell any quantity it wishes at this price, the same horizontal line is also the *firm's* demand curve.

If the market price is unaffected by variations in the firm's output, then the firm's demand curve, the average revenue curve, and the marginal revenue curve coincide in the same horizontal line.

Total revenue, of course, does vary with output; since price is constant, it follows that total revenue rises in direct proportion to output.

SHORT-RUN EQUILIBRIUM: FIRM AND INDUSTRY

Equilibrium Output of a Firm in Perfect Competition

The firm in perfect competition is a price taker and can adjust to varying market conditions only by changing the quantity it produces. In the short run it has fixed factors, and the only way to vary its output is by using more or less of those factors that it can vary. Thus, the firm's short-run cost curves are relevant to its output decision.

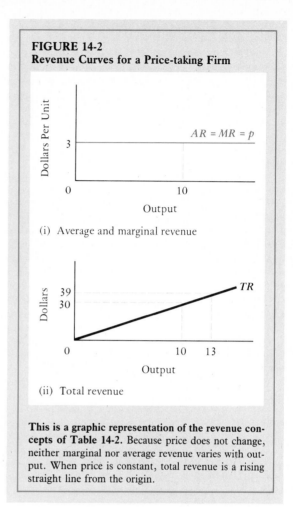

FIGURE 14-2
Revenue Curves for a Price-taking Firm

(i) Average and marginal revenue

(ii) Total revenue

This is a graphic representation of the revenue concepts of Table 14-2. Because price does not change, neither marginal nor average revenue varies with output. When price is constant, total revenue is a rising straight line from the origin.

TABLE 14–2 **REVENUE CONCEPTS FOR A PRICE-TAKING FIRM**

Price p	Quantity q	$TR = p \times q$	$AR = TR/q$	$MR = \Delta TR/\Delta q$
$3.00	10	$30.00	$3.00	
3.00	11	33.00	3.00	$3.00
3.00	12	36.00	3.00	3.00
3.00	13	39.00	3.00	3.00

When price is fixed, $AR = MR = p$. Marginal revenue is shown between the lines because it represents the change in total revenue (e.g., from $33 to $36) in reponse to a change in quantity (from 11 to 12 units),

$MR = \dfrac{36-33}{12-11} = \$3$ per unit

We saw earlier that any profit-maximizing firm will seek to produce at a level of output where marginal cost equals marginal revenue. In the immediately preceding section we saw that a perfectly competitive firm's demand and marginal revenue curves coincide in the same horizontal line whose height represents the price of the product.

For a perfectly competitive firm, price equals marginal revenue.

It follows immediately that a perfectly competitive firm will equate its marginal cost of production to the market price of its product (as long as price exceeds average variable cost).

The market determines the highest price at which the firm can sell its product. The firm picks the quantity of output that maximizes its profits. This is the output for which $p = MC$. When the firm is maximizing profits, it has no incentive to change its output. Therefore, unless prices or costs change, the firm will continue producing this output because it is doing as well as it can do, given the situation. The firm is said to be in **short-run equilibrium,** which is illustrated in Figure 14-3.

The perfectly competitive firm is a mere quantity adjuster. It pursues its goal of profit maximization by increasing or decreasing quantity until it equates its short-run marginal cost with the prevailing price of its product—a price that is given to it by the market.

The market price to which the perfectly competitive firm responds is itself set by the forces of demand and supply. The individual firm, by ad-

justing quantity produced to whatever price is ruling on the market, helps to determine market supply. The link between the behavior of the firm and the behavior of the competitive market is provided by the market supply curve.

Short-Run Supply Curves

A supply curve shows the relation between the quantity supplied and price. For any given price we need to ask what quantity will be supplied. This question may be answered by supposing that a price is specified and then determining how much each firm will choose to supply. Then a different price is supposed and quantity supplied again determined—and so on, until all possible prices have been considered.

The Supply Curve of One Firm

Figure 14-4(i) shows a firm's marginal cost curve with four alternative levels of price. Each such price line is the firm's demand curve *if* the market price is at that level. The firm's marginal cost curve gives the marginal cost corresponding to each level of output. We require a supply curve that shows the quantity the firm will supply at every price. For prices below *AVC*, the firm will supply zero units (rule 1). For prices above *AVC*, the firm will equate price and marginal cost (rule 2 modified by the proposition that $MR = p$ in perfect competition). From this it follows that

In perfect competition the firm's supply curve has the identical shape as the firm's marginal cost curve above AVC.

The Supply Curve of an Industry

Figure 14-5 illustrates the derivation of an industry supply curve for an example of only two firms. The general result is that

In perfect competition the industry supply curve is the horizontal sum of the marginal cost curves (above the level of average variable cost) of all firms in the industry.

FIGURE 14-3
The Equilibrium of a Competitive Firm

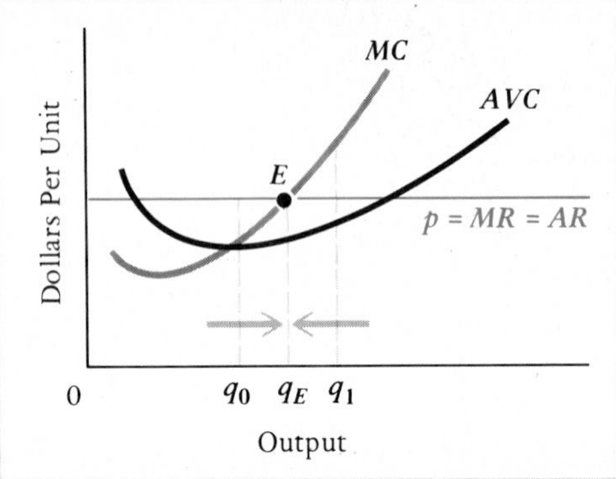

The firm chooses the output for which $p = MC$ above the level of *AVC*. When $p = MC$ as at q_E, the firm would decrease its profits if it either increased or decreased its output. At any point left of q_E, say q_0, price is greater than the marginal cost, and it pays to increase output (as indicated by the left-hand arrow). At any point to the right of q_E, say q_1, price is less than the marginal cost, and it pays to reduce output (as indicated by the right-hand arrow). The equilibrium output for the firm is q_E.

FIGURE 14-4
Deriving the Supply Curve for a Price-taking Firm

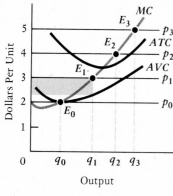

(i) *MC* and *AVC* curves

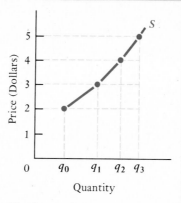

(ii) The supply curve

For a price-taking firm, the supply curve has the same shape as its *MC* curve above the level of *AVC*. As prices rise from \$2 to \$3 to \$4 to \$5, the firm wishes to increase its production from q_0 to q_1 to q_2 to q_3. For prices below \$2, output would be zero because the firm is better off if it shuts down. The point E_0, where price equals *AVC*, is the shutdown point. If price were \$3, the firm would produce output q_1 rather than zero because it would be making a contribution to fixed costs, as shown by the shaded rectangle. The firm's supply curve is shown in (ii).

FIGURE 14-5
The Derivation of an Industry Supply Curve

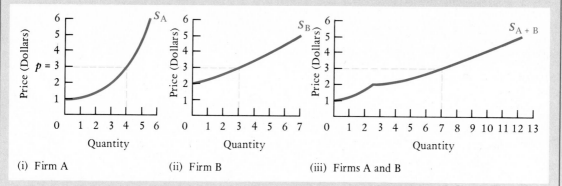

(i) Firm A

(ii) Firm B

(iii) Firms A and B

The industry supply curve is the horizontal sum of the supply curves of each of the firms in the industry. At a price of \$3, firm A would supply four units and firm B would supply three units. Together, as shown in (iii), they would supply seven units. If there are hundreds of firms, the process is the same: Each firm's supply curve (which is derived in the manner shown in Figure 14-4) shows what

the firm will produce at any given price *p*. The industry supply curve relates the price to the sum of the quantities produced by each firm. In this example, because firm B does not enter the market at prices below \$2, the supply curve $S_{A + B}$ is identical to S_A up to price \$2 and is the sum of $S_A + S_B$ above \$2.

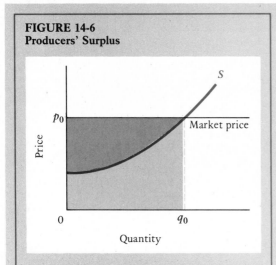

**FIGURE 14-6
Producers' Surplus**

Total producers' surplus is the area above the supply curve and under the price line. The short-run supply curve shows the amount producers would have to be paid to produce each unit of output. The area under the supply curve (the light shaded area) shows the minimum amount—their total variable costs—they would require if forced to sell their units one by one. If the market price is p_0 and q_0 is sold, producers receive the price p_0 for all units; graphically this is shown by both the light and dark shaded areas. The dark shaded area is the producers' surplus and represents the excess of revenue over variable costs received by producers.

The reason for this is that each firm's marginal cost curve tells us how much that firm will supply at any given market price, and the industry supply curve is the sum of what each firm will supply at each market price.

This supply curve, based on the short-run marginal cost curves of the firms in the industry, is the industry's **short-run supply curve.**

Producers' Surplus

In Chapter 9 we defined the concept of consumers' surplus in connection with a downward-sloping demand curve. (See Figure 9-4 and the discussion in the text accompanying it.) There is a precisely corresponding concept of producers' surplus in connection with an upward-sloping short-run supply curve. **Producers' surplus** is the difference between the amount producers are paid for all units sold of a commodity and the aggregate minimum amount they would have required to produce each successive unit. The supply curve shows the price required to produce each unit of output. As Figure 14-6 illustrates, in a competitive market with a rising supply curve all units except the last one produced receive a price greater than the amount required to produce them in the short run. The sum of these excesses of price over supply-price constitutes the producers' surplus; graphically, it is the area above the supply curve and below the market price line at the level of output actually sold. This represents the amount by which total revenues received exceed total *variable* cost. It is available to meet depreciation and other fixed costs and to provide a return to invested capital.

The Determination of Short-Run Equilibrium Price

The short-run supply curve and the demand curve for the industry's product together determine the market price. (This happens in the manner analyzed in Chapter 5.) Although no one firm can influence market price significantly, the collective actions of all firms in the industry (as shown by the industry supply curve) and the collective actions of households (as shown by the industry's demand curve) together determine market price at the point where the demand and supply curves intersect.

At the equilibrium market price each firm is producing and selling a quantity for which its marginal cost equals the market price. No firm is motivated to change its output in the short run. Since total quantity demanded equals total quantity supplied, there is no reason for market price to change in the short run; the market and all the firms in the industry are in short-run equilibrium.

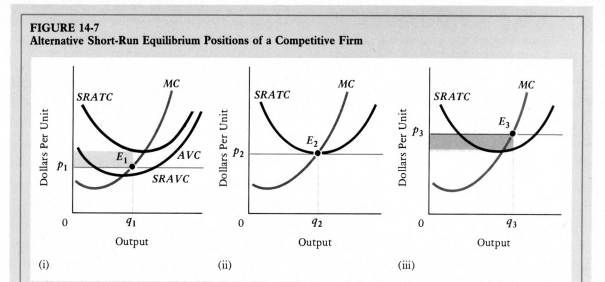

FIGURE 14-7
Alternative Short-Run Equilibrium Positions of a Competitive Firm

(i)   (ii)   (iii)

When it is in short-run equilibrium, a competitive firm may be suffering losses, breaking even, or making profits. The diagrams show a firm with given costs faced with three alternative prices p_1, p_2, and p_3. In each part of the diagram, E is the point at which $MC = MR$ = price. Since in all three cases price exceeds AVC, the firm is in short-run equilibrium.

In (i) price is p_1 and the firm is suffering losses, shown by the color shaded area, because price is below average total cost. Since price exceeds average variable cost, it pays the firm to keep producing, but it does *not* pay it to replace its capital equipment as the capital wears out.

In (ii) price is p_2 and the firm is just covering its total costs. It does pay the firm to replace its capital as it wears out since it is covering full opportunity cost of its capital.

In (iii) price is p_3 and the firm is earning profits, shown by the gray shaded area, in excess of all its costs.

Short-Run Profitability of the Firm

Although we know that when the industry is in short-run equilibrium the competitive firm is maximizing its profits, we do not know *how large* these profits are. It is one thing to know that a firm is doing as well as it can in particular circumstances; it is another to know how well it is doing.

Figure 14-7 shows three possible positions for a firm in short-run equilibrium. In all cases, the firm is maximizing its profits by producing where $p = MC$, but in (i) the firm is making losses, in (ii) it is just covering all costs, and in (iii) it is making profits in excess of all costs. In (i) it might be better to say that the firm is minimizing its losses rather than maximizing its profits, but both statements mean the same thing. The firm is doing as well as it can, given its costs and prices.

LONG-RUN EQUILIBRIUM

While Figure 14-7 shows three possible short-run equilibrium positions for the profit-maximizing firm in perfect competition, not all of them are possible equilibrium positions in the long run.

The Effect of Entry and Exit

The key to long-run equilibrium under perfect competition is entry and exit. We have seen that when firms are in *short-run* equilibrium, they may

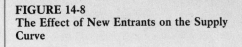

FIGURE 14-8
The Effect of New Entrants on the Supply Curve

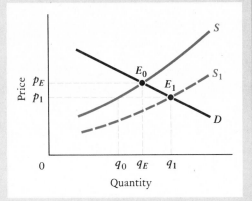

New entrants shift the supply curve to the right and lower the equilibrium price. Initial equilibrium is at E_0. If the supply curve shifts to S_1 by virtue of entry, the equilibrium price must fall to p_1 while output rises to q_1. At this price before entry, only q_0 would have been produced. The extra output is supplied by the new productive capacity.

being earned by existing firms. Suppose that in response to high profits for 100 existing firms, 20 new firms enter. The market supply curve that formerly added up the outputs of 100 firms now must add up the outputs of 120 firms. At any price, more will be supplied because there are more suppliers.

This shift in the short-run supply curve, with an unchanged market demand curve, means that the previous equilibrium price will no longer prevail. The shift in supply will cause the equilibrium price to fall, and both new and old firms will have to adjust their output to this new price. This is illustrated in Figure 14-8. New firms will continue to enter and price will continue to fall until all firms in the industry are just covering their total costs. Firms will then be in the position of the firm in Figure 14-7(ii), which is called a *zero-profit equilibrium*.

Profits in a competitive industry are a signal for the entry of new capital; the industry will expand, forcing price down until the profits fall to zero.

If the firms in the industry are in the position of the firm in Figure 14-7(i), they are suffering losses. They are covering their variable costs, but the return on their capital is less than the opportunity cost of this capital; the firms are not covering their total costs. This is a signal for the exit of firms. As plant and equipment are discarded, they will not be replaced. As a result, the industry's short-run supply curve shifts left and market price rises. Firms will continue to exit and price will continue to rise until the remaining firms can cover their total costs—that is, until they are all in the zero-profit equilibrium illustrated in Figure 14-7(ii). Exit then ceases.

Losses in a competitive industry are a signal for the exit of capital; the industry will contract, driving price up until the remaining firms are covering their total costs.

In all of this we see profits serving their function of allocating resources among the industries of the economy.

be making profits or losses or just breaking even. Since costs include the opportunity cost of capital, firms that are just breaking even are doing as well as they could if they invested their capital elsewhere. Thus there will be no incentive for existing firms to leave the industry; neither will there be an incentive for new firms to enter the industry, for capital can earn the same return elsewhere in the economy. If, however, existing firms are earning profits over all costs, including the opportunity cost of capital, new capital will enter the industry to share in these profits. If existing firms are making losses, capital will leave the industry because a better return can be obtained elsewhere in the economy. Let us consider the process in a little more detail.

If all firms in the competitive industry are in the position of the firm in Figure 14-7(iii), new firms will enter the industry, attracted by the profits

The Level of Cost at Equilibrium

An industry is nothing more than a collection of firms; for an industry to be in long-run equilibrium, each firm must be in long-run equilibrium. It follows that when a perfectly competitive industry is in long-run equilibrium, all firms in the industry will be selling at a price equal to minimum average total cost—that is, they must be in zero-profit equilibrium, as in Figure 14-7(ii). This result plays an important role in the appeal that perfect competition has had to economists, as we shall see. (Further discussion of the level of cost in long-run equilibrium will be found in the appendix to this chapter.)

The theory can now be used to help understand two commonly observed situations.

The Long-Run Response of a Perfectly Competitive Industry to a Change in Technology

Consider an industry in long-run equilibrium. Since the industry is in equilibrium, each firm must be in zero-profit equilibrium. Now assume that some technological development lowers the cost curves of newly built plants. Since price is just equal to the average total cost for the old plants, new plants will now be able to earn profits, and more of them will now be built. But this expansion in capacity shifts the short-run supply curve to the right and drives price down. The expansion in capacity and the fall in price will continue until price is equal to the *SRATC* of the *new* plants. At this price, old plants will not be covering their long-run costs. As long as price exceeds their average variable cost, however, such plants will continue in production. As the outmoded plants wear out, they will gradually disappear. Eventually a new long-run equilibrium will be established in which all plants use the new technology.

What happens in a competitive industry in which technological change occurs not as a single isolated event but more or less continuously? Plants built in any one year will tend to have lower costs than plants built in any previous year.[4] This is a common occurrence; it is illustrated in Figure 14-9.

Industries subject to continuous technological change have a number of interesting characteristics. One is that plants of different ages and different levels of efficiency will exist side by side. This characteristic is dramatically illustrated by the variety of vintages of steam turbine generators found in any long-established electric utility. Critics who observe the continued use of older, less efficient plants and urge that "something be done to eliminate these wasteful practices" miss the point of economic efficiency. If the plant is already there, the plant can be profitably operated as long as it can do anything more than cover its variable costs. As long as a plant can produce goods that are valued by consumers at an amount above the value of the resources currently used up for their production (variable costs), the value of society's total output is increased by using that plant to produce goods.

A second characteristic of such an industry is that price will be governed by *the minimum ATC of the most efficient plants*. Entry will continue until plants of the latest vintage are just expected to earn normal profits over their lifetimes. The benefits of the new technology are passed on to consumers because all units of the commodity, whether produced by new or old plants, are sold at a price that is related solely to the *ATC* of the new plants. Owners of older plants find their returns over variable costs falling steadily as more and more efficient plants drive the price of the product down.

A third characteristic is that old plants will be discarded (or "mothballed") when the price falls below their *AVC*. This may occur well before the plants are physically worn out. In industries with continuous technical progress, capital is usually discarded because it is *economically obsolete*, not

---

[4] This statement refers to real resource costs, which tend to fall due to technological change. Of course, in times of general inflation, *money* costs of plants may well be rising. In the comparisons made here, we are assuming that costs have been adjusted for changes in the general price level.

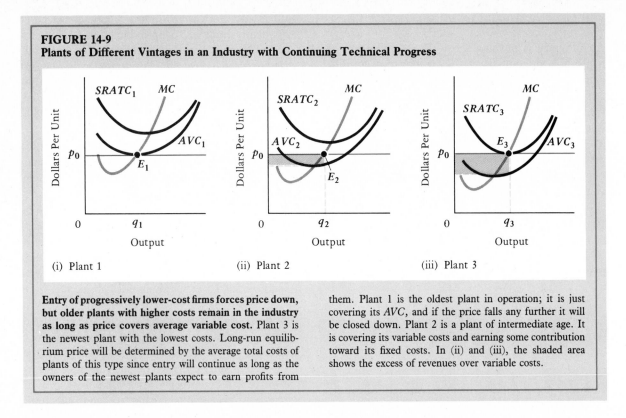

FIGURE 14-9
Plants of Different Vintages in an Industry with Continuing Technical Progress

(i) Plant 1   (ii) Plant 2   (iii) Plant 3

Entry of progressively lower-cost firms forces price down, but older plants with higher costs remain in the industry as long as price covers average variable cost. Plant 3 is the newest plant with the lowest costs. Long-run equilibrium price will be determined by the average total costs of plants of this type since entry will continue as long as the owners of the newest plants expect to earn profits from them. Plant 1 is the oldest plant in operation; it is just covering its AVC, and if the price falls any further it will be closed down. Plant 2 is a plant of intermediate age. It is covering its variable costs and earning some contribution toward its fixed costs. In (ii) and (iii), the shaded area shows the excess of revenues over variable costs.

because it has physically worn out. Old capital is obsolete when its average variable cost exceeds the average total cost of new capital.

Industries That Are Declining Due to a Steady Decrease in Demand

What happens when a competitive industry in long-run equilibrium begins to suffer losses due to a permanent and continuing decrease in the demand for its products? As demand declines, price falls and firms that were previously covering ATC are not now able to do so. They find themselves in the position shown in Figure 14-7(i). Firms earn losses instead of breaking even, and the signal for exit of capital is given. But exit takes time. The economically correct response to a steadily declining demand is not to replace old equipment but to continue to operate with existing equipment as long as the firm can cover its variable costs of production.

Gradually, equipment will break down and not be repaired or replaced. The capacity of the industry will shrink, slowly at first. If demand keeps declining, capacity must keep shrinking.

Declining industries typically present a sorry sight to the observer. Revenues are below long-run total costs, and as a result new equipment is not brought in to replace old equipment as it wears out. The average age of equipment in use thus rises steadily. The untrained observer seeing the industry's very real plight is likely to blame it on the antiquated equipment in use.

The antiquated equipment in a declining industry is the effect rather than the cause of the industry's decline.

It would not usually make sense for firms to modernize in the face of steadily falling demand even when new, improved equipment is available. To do so would increase the industry's capacity and its output, thereby making its overall plight still worse. Price would fall even more rapidly, adding further to the losses of existing firms.

A striking example of the confusion of cause and effect in a declining industry occurred during the debate over the nationalization of the coal industry in Great Britain in the period between the two world wars.

The view that public control was needed to save an industry from the dead hand of third-rate, unenterprising private owners was commonly held about the British coal industry and was undoubtedly a factor leading to its nationalization in 1946.

The late Sir Roy Harrod, a leading British economist from the 1920s to the 1960s, shocked many by taking the opposite view, arguing that the rundown state of the coal industry in South Wales and Yorkshire represented the correct response of the owners to the signals of the market.

Economic efficiency does not consist in always introducing the most up-to-date equipment that an engineer can think of but rather in the correct adaptation of the amount of new capital sunk to the earning capacity of the old asset. In not introducing new equipment, the managements may have been wise, not only from the point of view of their own interest, but from that of national interest, which requires the most profitable application of available capital . . . it is right that as much should be extracted from the inferior mines as can be done by old-fashioned methods [i.e., with equipment already installed], and that they should gradually go out of action.[5]

The general point that Professor Harrod makes is extremely important. It is in the public and the private interest that what appear to be antiquated methods be employed in declining industries. Capital resources are scarce; to install new plant and equipment in a genuinely declining industry is to use the nation's scarce resources of new capital where they will not lead to the largest possible increases in the value of output.

[5] Roy Harrod, *The British Economy* (New York: McGraw-Hill, 1963), page 54.

THE APPEAL OF PERFECT COMPETITION

The theory of perfect competition shows that profit-maximizing price-taking firms, responding to prices set by the impersonal forces of supply and demand, will be motivated to provide all commodities for which total revenues are equal to or greater than total costs. They will be motivated to produce every unit for which price is greater than marginal cost, and they will thus expand production up to the point where price equals marginal cost. The entry and exit of firms will, in long-run equilibrium, push prices to the level of minimum average total costs—that is, to the lowest level attainable for the given technology and factor prices.

Consider an economy in which every industry operates as a perfectly competitive industry. For the nineteenth century liberal economists, such a world was more than a theoretical model, it was a most attractive ideal. One of them, Bascom, glowingly characterized such an economic system as "more provocative of virtue than virtue herself." The appeal of a competitive economy has both noneconomic and economic aspects.

The Noneconomic Appeal of Competition

In a perfectly competitive economy, there are many firms and many households. Each is a price taker, responding as it sees fit, freely and without coercion, to signals sent to it by the market. For one who believes in the freedom of individuals to make decisions and who distrusts all power groups, the perfectly competitive model is almost too good to be true. No single firm and no single consumer has any power over the market. Individual consumers and producers are passive quantity adjusters who respond to market signals.

Yet the impersonal force of the market produces an appropriate response to all changes. If tastes change, for example, prices will change, and the allocation of resources will change in the appropriate direction. Throughout the entire process, no one will have any power over anyone else. Dozens of firms will react to the same price changes, and if one firm refuses to react, there will be countless other profit-maximizing firms eager to make the appropriate changes.

Because the market mechanism works, it is not necessary for the government to intervene. Market reactions, not public policies, will eliminate shortages or surpluses. There is no need for government regulatory agencies or bureaucrats to make arbitrary decisions about who may produce what, how to produce it, or how much it is permissible to charge for the product. If there are no government officials to make such decisions, there will be no one to bribe to make one decision rather than another.

In the impersonal decision-making world of perfect competition, neither private firms nor public officials wield economic power. The market mechanisms, like an invisible hand, determines the allocation of resources among competing uses.

It is a noble model: no one has power over anyone, and yet the system behaves in a systematic and purposeful way. Many will feel that it is a pity that it corresponds so imperfectly to economic reality as we know it today. Not surprisingly, some people still cling tenaciously to the belief that the perfectly competitive model describes the world in which we live; so many problems would disappear if only it did.

The Economic Appeal of Perfect Competition: Efficiency

The Concept of Inefficiency

Resources are scarce relative to the wants of society's members, so it is desirable not to waste the resources we have. The most obvious way to waste resources is not to use them at all. When labor is unemployed and factories lie idle (as occurs in serious depressions), their potential current output is lost. If these resources could be reemployed,

total output would be increased and hence everyone could be made better off.

But full employment of resources by itself is not enough to prevent the waste of resources. Even when resources are being fully used, they may be used inefficiently.

Let us look at three possible sources of inefficiency in resource use.

1. If firms do not use the least costly method of producing their chosen outputs, they will waste resources. By adopting the least costly method, they will free resources to be used to make other commodities. For example, in a firm that achieves its monthly production of 30,000 pairs of shoes at a resource cost of $400,000 when it could be done at a cost of only $350,000, resources are being used inefficiently. If the lower cost method were used, $50,000 worth of other commodities could be produced each month by transferring the resources saved to their best alternative use.

2. If some firms are too large and others too small, each will not be producing at the lowest point on its long-run average cost curve. Thus any given level of the industry's production will use more resources than is necessary.

3. If too much of one product and too little of another is produced, resources are also being used inefficiently. To take an extreme example, say that so many shoes were produced that their *marginal* utility was zero while the marginal utility of coats remained high at the current level of output. Since no one places any value on the last pair of shoes produced, while someone does place a high value on an additional coat, no one will be made worse off by reducing the output of shoes, yet someone will be made better off by using the resources to increase the production of coats.

These examples suggest that we must refine our ideas of the waste of resources beyond the simple notion of ensuring that all resources are used. Economists define rather precisely what is meant by efficiency and inefficiency in resource use.

Resources are said to be used *inefficiently* when it would be *possible* by using them differently to make at least one household better off without making any household worse off. Conversely, resources are said to be used *efficiently* when it is impossible by using them differently to make any one household better off without making at least one other household worse off.

Inefficiency in the use of resources implies that we can help someone without hurting someone else. Efficiency implies that we cannot. When resources are already being used efficiently, we can only make one household better off at the cost of making another household worse off.

Efficiency in the use of resources is often called **Pareto-efficiency** or **Pareto-optimality** in honor of the great Italian economist Vilfredo Pareto (1848–1923), who pioneered in the study of efficiency.

So much for the meaning of efficiency; now how do we achieve it? The three sources of inefficiency numbered above suggest important conditions that must be fulfilled if economic efficiency is to be attained.

Productive Efficiency

The first condition of economic efficiency is that whatever output is produced must be produced at the lowest possible cost of production. This condition is defined as **productive efficiency.** It implies, first, that every firm be producing at the cost level shown on its long-run average cost curve. If this condition is not met, there is (by definition) a less costly way for that firm to produce. It further implies that industry output be produced as cheaply as possible. If one firm is producing "too little" output—that is, producing along the downward-sloping part of its *LRAC* curve—and another firm is producing "too much" output—that is, producing more than is required to achieve the minimum level of average total cost, then industry costs can be decreased by having the first firm produce more and the second firm produce less. If in equilibrium all firms are producing at the minimum points of their long-run average cost curves, both implications of productive efficiency have been met. As we saw above, a perfectly competitive industry in long-run equilibrium meets these conditions.

A competitive industry in long-run equilibrium satisfies the condition of productive efficiency. The product is produced as cheaply as possible.

Allocative Efficiency

Productive efficiency avoids the first two sources of inefficiency mentioned above. The third source concerns the appropriate mix of products. Resources must be allocated among various goods, and they are not being used efficiently when they are being used to produce products that no one wants. **Allocative efficiency** obtains when it is impossible to change the allocation of resources in such a way as to make someone better off without making someone else worse off.

What is the right mix? How many shoes and how many coats should be produced for allocative efficiency? The answer is that (under certain conditions that we shall specify later) the allocation of resources to any one commodity is efficient when its price is equal to its marginal cost of production, that is, $p = MC$.

This rather subtle condition has been one of the most influential ideas in the whole of economics. To understand it, we need to remind ourselves of two points established earlier: First, the price of any commodity indicates the value that each household places on the last unit of the commodity that it consumes (per period); second, marginal cost indicates the value that the resources used to produce the marginal unit of output would have in their best alternative uses.

The first proposition follows directly from marginal utility theory (see page 142). A household will go on increasing its rate of consumption of a commodity until the *marginal* valuation that it puts on the commodity is equal to its price. The household gets a consumers' surplus on all units but the marginal unit because it values them more than the price it has to pay. On the marginal unit, however, it only "breaks even" because the valuation placed on it is just equal to its price.

The second proposition follows from the nature of opportunity cost (see pages 176–178). The marginal cost of producing some commodity is the opportunity cost of the resources used. Opportunity cost reflects the value of the resources in their best alternative uses.

To see how these propositions fit together, assume that shoes sell for $30 a pair but have a marginal production cost of $40. If one less pair of shoes were produced, the value that households place on the pair of shoes not produced would be $30. But by the meaning of opportunity cost, the resources that would have been used to produce that pair of shoes could instead produce other goods (say a coat) valued at $40. If society can give up something its members value at $30 and get in return something its members value at $40, the original allocation of resources is inefficient. Someone can be made better off, and no one need be worse off. This is easy to see when the same household gives up the shoes and gets the coat. But it follows even when different households are involved, for the gaining household could compensate the losing household and still come out ahead.

Assume next that shoe production is cut back until the price of a pair of shoes rises from $30 to $35 while its marginal cost falls from $40 to $35. The efficiency condition is now fulfilled in shoe production because $p = MC = \$35$. Now if one less pair of shoes were produced, $35 worth of shoes would be sacrificed while at most $35 worth of other commodities could be produced with the freed resources. In this situation the allocation of resources to shoe production is efficient because it is not possible to change it and make someone better off without making someone else worse off. If one household were to sacrifice the pair of shoes, it would give up goods worth $35 and would then have to get all of the new production of the alternative commodity produced just to break even. It cannot gain without making another household worse off. The same argument can be repeated for every commodity, and it leads to this conclusion:

The allocation of resources among commodities is efficient when for each commodity price equals marginal cost.

Allocative efficiency is thus satisfied when $p = MC$ in all industries. This is given a graphical interpretation in the box. For every industry in perfect competition, $p = MC$ in equilibrium. Thus:

Universal perfect competition fulfills the condition for allocative efficiency by ensuring that price equals marginal cost in every industry.

Some Words of Warning About the Efficiency of Perfect Competition

An economy that consisted of perfectly competitive industries would in equilibrium achieve allocative efficiency. Further, if the costs for each such industry were the lowest costs attainable, the economy would also achieve productive efficiency in the production of every commodity. This is because the forces of competition push equilibrium price to the level where $p = MC = ATC$.

Before jumping to the conclusion that perfect competition is the best of all possible worlds and that government policy ought to do everything possible to achieve it, we must consider certain qualifications. Four will be mentioned here, to be developed in later chapters.

Costs may be higher under perfect competition than under alternative market structures. In a competitive industry, production occurs at the lowest level of cost attainable by the competitive firm. But it is possible, for example, that firms in a perfectly competitive industry may not innovate as rapidly as firms in another industry structure, and thus the cost of producing the competitive output will not be as low as it might be.

This matter is discussed more fully in Chapters 15, 16, and 18.

Perfect competition may not pertain simultaneously everywhere in the economy. Our argument about allocative efficiency rested on $p = MC$ everywhere in the economy. But there are many industries in which price does not and cannot equal marginal cost. (The reasons will be explored in Chapter 18.) In such a world there is no general presumption of what the effect will be of prices equaling marginal costs *somewhere* in the economy.

A GRAPHIC INTERPRETATION OF ALLOCATIVE EFFICIENCY

Consider a competitive industry where forces of demand and supply establish a competitive price. Because the industry supply curve represents the sum of the marginal cost curves of the firms in the industry, the market clearing price is one at which $p = MC$. In the figure, such a price is shown as p^*, and the corresponding output is q^*. For every unit produced up to this output, the value consumers would be willing to pay (as shown by the demand curve) is greater than the opportunity cost of the resources used to produce it (as shown by the $S = MC$ curve).

Consider the gray shaded areas. The light gray shaded area between the demand curve and the price line is what we have defined as the *consumers' surplus* associated with output q^* (see pages 145–146). The dark gray shaded area above the supply curve and below the price line is the *producers' surplus* associated with the output q^*.

Allocative efficiency is achieved when the *sum* of the surpluses is maximized. This occurs at the output q^*, where $p = MC$. For any output less than q^*, such as q_1, a slight increase is output toward q^* would lead to an addition to both consumers' and producers' surplus. This is because at the level of output q_1 consumers' valuation of the commodity (shown by the demand curve) exceeds the opportunity cost of producing it (shown by the supply curve). For any output greater than q^*, such as q_2, this is not the case. For every unit beyond q^*, the demand curve (what consumers would pay) is below the supply curve (what producers must be paid). Extra units beyond q^* would subtract from both producers' and consumers' surpluses. The color shaded area shows how much is lost when output is increased from q^* to q_2.

Producers' plus consumers' surplus is maximized *only* at output q^*, which is thus the only output that is allocatively efficient. If some invisible authority wanted producers to "maximize the sum of producers' and consumers' surplus," it would instruct producers to produce every unit up to q^*. The perfectly competitive market price, p^*, provides exactly that signal!

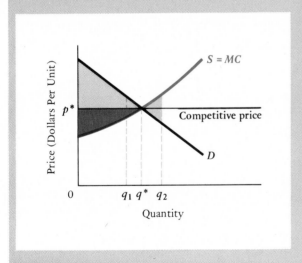

Thus, if price does not equal marginal cost in industry A, the fact that $p = MC$ in industry B may not lead to allocative efficiency.

This proposition illustrates what is known as the "theory of the second best": We may know how to identify the best of all possible worlds (from the limited point of view of the optimum we are discussing), but we may have a harder task when attempting to rank two situations in the very imperfect world in which we live.

Private costs may be poor measures of society's costs. Producing a good up to the point at which the price just equals the *firm's* marginal cost is efficient from society's point of view only if the firm's private costs reflect the opportunity costs to society of using the resources elsewhere. As we shall see in Chapter 24, this is often not the case because of what are called *externalities*. For example, if the competitive firm uses resources it does not pay for (such as the clean air around its factories), it may produce too much output and too much pollution to be efficient. It does so because *its* own marginal costs fail to include the value that members of society place on some of the resources (clean air) the firm uses up.

Efficiency is not the only goal. A competitive economy distributes output as well as produces it. A freely functioning competitive economy might produce a distribution of income consisting of one millionaire and 999 paupers. Such an economy may be more efficient than an economy with 1,000 persons of roughly equal income. Before one can speak of a competitive economy as being "virtuous," one must consider goals other than efficiency. This matter is discussed further in Chapter 24.

SUMMARY

1. Market behavior is concerned with whether and how individual firms compete against one another; market structure is concerned with the type of market firms operate in. Market structure affects the degree of power that individual firms have to influence such market variables as the price of the product. Under the market structure known as perfect competition, individual firms are powerless to influence market price. Therefore they do not have any incentive to indulge in competitive behavior against their fellow producers in the same industry.

2. A profit-maximizing firm will produce at a level of output where (a) price is at least as great as average variable cost, (b) marginal cost equals marginal revenue, and (c) the marginal cost curve cuts the marginal revenue curve from below.

3. The two critical assumptions of the theory of perfect competition are that firms are price takers and that the industry displays freedom of entry and

exit. A firm that is a price taker will adjust to different market conditions by varying its output.

4. The perfectly competitive firm's short-run supply curve is the same shape as its MC curve above AVC. The perfectly competitive industry's short-run supply curve is the horizontal sum of its firms' supply curves (i.e., the horizontal sum of the firms' marginal cost curves).

5. When perfectly competitive firms are in short-run equilibrium, they must, if they are producing at all, be covering their variable costs. But they may be making losses (price less than average total cost), making profits (price greater than average total cost), or just covering all costs (price equal to average total cost).

6. In the long run, profits or losses will lead to the entry or exit of capital from the industry. Entry of new firms or exit of existing firms will push a competitive industry to a long-run zero-profit equilibrium and move production to the level of minimum average total cost. Long-run equilibrium is discussed at greater length in the appendix to this chapter.

7. The long-run response of a growing, perfectly competitive industry to steadily changing technology is the gradual replacement of less efficient plants and machines by more efficient ones. Older machines will be utilized as long as price exceeds $AVC;$ only when price falls below AVC will they be discarded and replaced by newer, more modern ones. The long-run response of a declining industry will be to continue to satisfy the remaining demand from its existing machinery as long as price exceeds AVC. Despite the appearance of being antiquated, this is the correct response in the face of steadily falling demand.

8. The great appeal of the theory of perfect competition as a means of organizing production has both noneconomic and economic elements. The noneconomic appeal lies in the decentralized decision making of myriad firms and households. No individual exercises power over the market. At the same time, it is not necessary for the government to intervene to determine resource allocation and

prices; thus, there is no need for government agencies to exercise arbitrary or bureaucratic power.

9. The economic appeal of a world of perfect competition arises from the fact that, under certain conditions, it exhibits both productive and allocative efficiency. Productive efficiency is achieved because the same forces that lead to long-run equilibrium lead to production at the lowest attainable cost. Allocative efficiency is achieved because in competitive equilibrium, price equals marginal cost for every product. If this condition is met in all industries, no shift of resources can increase the satisfaction of any household without decreasing it for some other household. Other terms for allocative efficiency are *Pareto-optimality* and *Pareto-efficiency.*

10. The efficiency of perfect competition should be understood yet interpreted with caution. Four qualifications to its being "ideal" are: (a) costs may be higher under perfect competition than under alternative market structures; (b) perfect competition will not pertain simultaneously everywhere in the economy; (c) private costs may be poor measures of society's costs; (d) efficiency is not the only goal of the members of society. Because of the first three, competitive equilibrium in a particular industry may not even be efficient. Because of the fourth, even an efficient competitive equilibrium may be regarded as less than ideal in its results.

TOPICS FOR REVIEW

Competitive behavior and competitive market structure
Behavioral rules for the profit-maximizing firm
Price taking and a horizontal demand curve
Average revenue, marginal revenue, and price under perfect
  competition
The relation of the industry supply curve to firms' marginal
  cost curves
Producers' surplus
Role of entry and exit in achieving equilibrium
Short-run and long-run equilibrium of firms and industries
Productive and allocative efficiency
Pareto-optimality (and Pareto-efficiency)

DISCUSSION QUESTIONS

1. Consider the suppliers of the following commodities. What are the elements of market structure that you might want to invoke to account for differences in their market behavior? Could any of these be characterized as perfectly competitive industries?
   a. television broadcasting
   b. automobiles
   c. sand and gravel
   d. medical services
   e. mortgage loans
   f. retail fruits and vegetables
   g. soybeans

2. Which of the following observed facts about an industry are inconsistent with its being a perfectly competitive industry?
   a. Different firms use different methods of production.
   b. There is extensive advertising of the industry's product by a trade association.
   c. Individual firms devote 5 percent of sales receipts to advertising their own product brand.
   d. There are 24 firms in the industry.
   e. The largest firm in the industry makes 40 percent of the sales and the next largest firm makes 20 percent, but the products are identical and there are 61 other firms.
   f. All firms made large profits in 1980.

3. In which of the following sectors of the American economy might you expect to find competitive behavior? In which might you expect to find industries that were classified as operating under perfectly competitive market structures?
   a. manufacturing
   b. agriculture
   c. transportation and public utilities
   d. wholesale and retail trade
   e. criminal activity

4. In the 1930s the U.S. coal industry was characterized by easy entry and price taking. Because of large fixed costs in mine shafts and fixed equipment, however, exit was slow. With declining demand, many firms were barely covering their variable costs but not their total costs. As a result of a series of mine accidents, the federal government began to enforce mine safety standards, which forced most firms to invest in new capital if they were to remain in production. What predictions would competitive theory make about market behavior and the quantity of coal produced? Would coal miners approve or disapprove of the new enforcement program?

5. Suppose entry into an industry is not artificially restricted

but takes time because of the need to build plants, acquire know-how, and establish a marketing organization. Can such an industry be characterized as perfectly competitive? Does ease of entry imply ease of exit, and vice versa?

6. What, if anything, does each one of the following tell you about ease of entry or exit in an industry?

a. Profits have been very high for two decades.

b. No new firms have entered the industry for 20 years.

c. The average age of the firms in a 40-year-old industry is less than seven years.

d. Most existing firms are using obsolete equipment alongside newer, more modern equipment.

e. Profits are low or negative; many firms are still producing, but from steadily aging equipment.

7. In the 1970s grain prices in the United States rose substantially relative to other agricultural products. Explain how each of the following may have contributed to this result; then consider how a perfectly competitive grain industry might be expected to react in the long run.

a. crop failures caused by unusually bad weather around the world in several years

b. rising demand for beef and chickens because of rising population and rising per capita income

c. great scarcities in fishmeal, a substitute for grain in animal diets, because of a mysterious decline in the anchovy harvest off Peru

d. increased Soviet purchases of grain from the United States

15 PRICING IN MONOPOLY MARKETS

Is AT&T a monopoly? How about IBM, U.S. Steel, the National Football League, or the Coca-Cola Company? Just as the word *competition* has both an everyday meaning and a more specialized technical one, so too does the word *monopoly*. Monopoly, as economists use the concept, is a market structure that leads to certain predicted kinds of market behavior.

The word *monopoly* comes from the Greek words *monos polein*, which mean "alone to sell." It is convenient for now to think of **monopoly** as the situation in which the output of an entire industry is controlled by a single seller. This seller will be called the monopolist. Later in this chapter we will define monopoly in a less restrictive way.

A MONOPOLIST SELLING AT A SINGLE PRICE

Consider first an industry producing a single product in which a monopolist sets a price and supplies

TABLE 15–1 THE RELATION OF AVERAGE REVENUE AND MARGINAL REVENUE: A NUMERICAL ILLUSTRATION

Price $p = AR$	Quantity q	$TR = p \times q$	$MR = \Delta TR/\Delta q$
$9.10	9	$81.90	
9.00	10	90.00	$8.10
8.90	11	97.90	7.90

Marginal revenue is less than price because price must be lowered to sell an extra unit. A monopolist can choose either the price or the quantity to be sold. But choosing one determines the other. In this example, to increase sales from 10 to 11 units, it is necessary to reduce the price on all units sold from $9 to $8.90. The extra unit sold brings in $8.90, but the firm sacrifices $.10 on each of the 10 units that it could have sold at $9 had it not wanted to increase sales. The net addition to revenue is the $8.90 minus $.10 times 10 units, or $1, making $7.90 altogether. Thus the marginal revenue resulting from the increase in sales by 1 unit is $7.90, which is less than the price at which the units are sold.

Marginal revenue is shown displaced by half a line to emphasize that it represents the effect on revenue of the *change* in output.

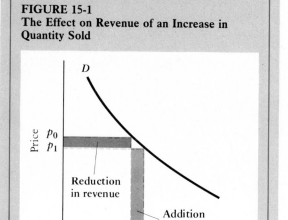

FIGURE 15-1
The Effect on Revenue of an Increase in Quantity Sold

For a downward-sloping demand curve, marginal revenue is less than price. A reduction of price from p_0 to p_1 increases sales by one unit from q_0 to q_1 units. The revenue from the extra unit sold (i.e., its price) is shown as the lighter shaded area. But to sell this unit, it is necessary to reduce the price on each of the q_0 units previously sold. The loss in revenue is shown as the darker shaded area. Marginal revenue of the extra unit is equal to the *difference* between the two areas.

the entire quantity that buyers wish to purchase at that price. In contrast to the competitive firm, the monopolist is a price setter, not a price taker. The monopolistic firm faces a downward-sloping demand curve and can pick any price-quantity combination on the demand curve. The monopolist is sometimes said to be able to *administer* its price. This means that unlike the perfect competitor, it can and usually does select its own price.

The Monopolist's Revenue Curves

Because the monopolistic firm is assumed to be the only producer of a particular product, its demand curve is identical with the demand curve for that product. The market demand curve, which shows the aggregate quantity that buyers will purchase at every price, also shows the quantity that the monopolist will be able to sell at any price it sets. Given the market demand curve, the monopolist's

average revenue and marginal revenue curves can be readily deduced.

When the seller charges a single price for all units sold, average revenue per unit is identical with price. Thus, the market demand curve is also the average revenue curve for the monopolist. But marginal revenue is less than price because the monopolist has to lower the price that it charges on *all* units in order to sell an *extra* unit. [23] This is an important difference from the case of perfect competition; it is explored numerically in Table 15-1 and graphically in Figure 15-1.

Figure 15-2 illustrates the average and marginal

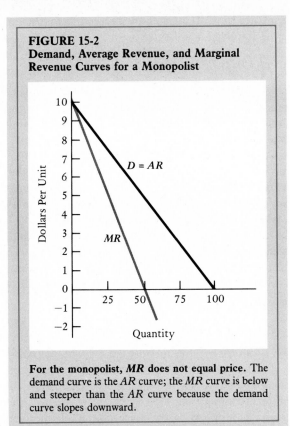

FIGURE 15-2
Demand, Average Revenue, and Marginal Revenue Curves for a Monopolist

For the monopolist, *MR* does not equal price. The demand curve is the *AR* curve; the *MR* curve is below and steeper than the *AR* curve because the demand curve slopes downward.

revenue rises as quantity increases, and hence the total revenue curve is upward-sloping. Because total revenue is increasing as quantity is increasing, marginal revenue must be positive. Next consider

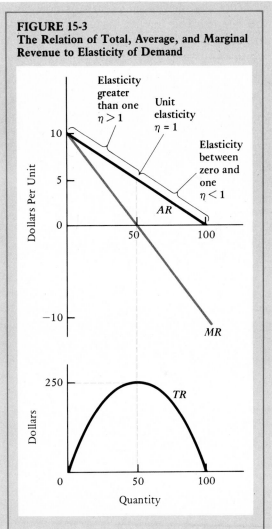

FIGURE 15-3
The Relation of Total, Average, and Marginal Revenue to Elasticity of Demand

When *TR* is rising, *MR* is greater than zero and elasticity is greater than unity. In this example, for outputs from 0 to 50, marginal revenue is positive, elasticity is greater than unity, and total revenue is rising. For outputs from 50 to 100, marginal revenue is negative, elasticity is less than unity, and total revenue is falling.

revenue curves for a monopolist, based on a downward-sloping straight-line demand curve.[1]

Marginal Revenue, Total Revenue, and Elasticity of Demand

A demand curve represents a single relationship between quantity and price, but there are many different ways of looking at this relationship.

Figure 15-3 shows how total revenue and elasticity of demand (η) are related to *AR* and *MR*. Consider first that part of the demand curve where elasticity is greater than one. This means that total

---

[1] It is helpful (for sketching revenue curves, etc.) to remember that if the demand curve is a downward-sloping straight line, the *MR* curve also slopes downward and is twice as steep. Its price intercept (where $q = 0$) is the same as that of the demand curve, and it cuts the quantity axis (where $p = 0$) at just half the output that the demand curve does. [24]

the point at which elasticity of demand is exactly unity. Here total revenue remains constant as quantity sold increases. This implies that marginal revenue is zero. Consider finally the part of the demand curve where elasticity is less than one. This means that total revenue falls as quantity increases, and hence the total revenue curve is now downward-sloping. This implies that marginal revenue is negative. Marginal revenue thus goes from positive to negative as the demand curve goes from elastic to inelastic, or (what is the same thing) as the total revenue curve stops rising, reaches its maximum, and begins to fall. (The relation between elasticity and total revenue was examined in Chapter 6.)

This relationship has an immediate and important implication. Since marginal cost is greater than zero, the profit-maximizing monopoly (which produces where MR equals MC) will produce where MR is positive, that is, where demand is elastic.

A profit-maximizing monopolist will never push its sales of a commodity into the range over which the commodity's demand curve becomes inelastic.

The common sense of this is that if demand is inelastic, marginal revenue is negative. Thus the monopolist can both increase revenue and reduce cost by reducing its sales.

Profit Maximization in a Monopolized Market

To describe the profit-maximizing position of a monopolist, we need only bring together information about the monopolist's revenues and its costs and apply the rules developed in Chapter 14.

The monopolist produces an output such that marginal revenue equals marginal cost. The price corresponding to that output is given by its demand curve.

This profit-maximizing position is shown in each part of Figure 15-4.

Note for future reference a key respect in which this monopolistic equilibrium differs from that of a firm in perfect competition. While a competitive firm produces at an output where $p = MC$, the monopolistic firm produces at an output where p

is greater than MC. Later we shall return to discuss some implications of this.

The Profits of a Monopolist

The fact that a profit-maximizing monopolist produces at an output where $MR = MC$ says nothing about how large profits will be—or even whether there will be monopoly profits. Profits may exist, as shown in Figure 15-4(i), and indeed they may persist for a long time because as long as the firm retains its monopoly, entry of new firms does not push price down to the level of average total cost.

But, as Figure 15-4(ii) shows, the profit-maximizing monopolist may break even or suffer losses. Nothing guarantees that a monopolist will make profits, and if it cannot eliminate its losses, the firm will eventually fail.

A Monopolist's Supply Curve?

In describing the monopolist's profit-maximizing behavior, we did not introduce the concept of a supply curve, as we did in the discussion of perfect competition. A supply curve relates the quantity supplied to the price offered. In perfect competition, the industry short-run supply curve is known as soon as the marginal cost curves of the individual firms are known. This is because the profit-maximizing firms equate marginal cost to price. Given marginal costs, it is possible to know how much will be produced at each price.

In monopoly there is no unique relation between market price and quantity supplied.

Like all profit-maximizing firms, a monopolistic firm equates marginal cost with marginal revenue; but, unlike firms in perfect competition, for the monopolist marginal revenue does not equal price. Because the monopolist does *not* equate marginal cost to price, it is possible for different demand conditions to give rise to the same output but to differing prices.[2]

---

[2] In order to know the amount produced at any given price, it is necessary to know something about the shape and position of the marginal revenue curve in addition to knowing the marginal cost curve. This means that there is not a supply curve independent of the demand curve for the monopolist's product.

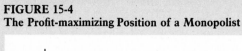

FIGURE 15-4
The Profit-maximizing Position of a Monopolist

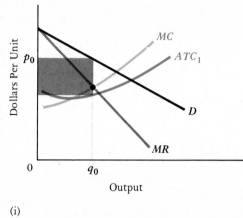

(i)

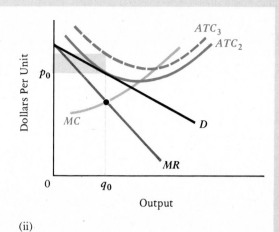

(ii)

Profit-maximizing output is q_0, where $MR = MC$; price is above MC at that output. The rules for profit maximization require $MR = MC$ and $p > AVC$. (AVC is not shown in the diagram, but it would be below ATC.) This happens at output q_0. Whether or not there are profits depends on the position of the ATC curve. In (i) where average total cost is ATC_1, there are profits, as shown by the dark gray shaded area. In (ii) where average total cost is ATC_2, profits are zero. If average total costs rose to ATC_3, the monopolist would suffer losses, as shown by the color shaded area in (ii).

Equilibrium of the Firm and Industry

When a monopolist is the only producer in an industry, there is no need for separate theories of the firm and the industry, as is necessary with perfect competition. The monopolist *is* the industry. Thus the profit-maximizing position of the firm shown in Figure 15-4 is the short-run equilibrium of the industry.

In a monopolized industry, as in a perfectly competitive one, profits provide an incentive for new firms to enter. If such entry occurs, the equilibrium position will change and the firm will no longer be a monopolist. **Barriers to entry** are impediments to the entry of new firms into an industry.

If monopoly is to persist in the long run, there must be barriers to the entry of other firms into an industry.

Barriers may come about in many ways. Patent laws, for instance, may create and perpetuate monopolies by conferring on the patent holder the sole right to produce a particular commodity. A firm may be granted a charter or a franchise that prohibits competition by law. Monopolies may also arise because of economies of scale. The established firm that is able to produce at a lower cost than any new, small competitor may well retain a monopoly through a cost advantage.

A monopoly may also be perpetuated by force or by threat. Potential competitors can be intimidated by threats ranging from sabotage to a price war in which the established monopoly has sufficient financial resources to ensure victory.

It is the barriers to entry in one form or another that allow a monopolist to earn profits that persist in the long run. In perfect competition, an equilibrium in which firms earn profits can occur in the short run but cannot last longer than it takes for entry to force prices down to the level of average total cost. Because of barriers to entry, the short-run profitable equilibrium of a monopolist can continue indefinitely.

The Inefficiency of Monopoly

In Chapter 14 we saw that (subject to certain qualifications) perfect competition produces efficient results. By leading firms to produce at levels of output at which $p = MC$ and $p = ATC$, it satisfies conditions of both productive and allocative efficiency. It also leads to production at the minimum point on the ATC curve, the lowest attainable cost of production.

Productive Efficiency

The output of a monopolized industry will in general be different from that of a competitive industry. A monopolist, just like any other firm, will wish to produce its profit-maximizing output at the lowest cost *for that output.* Thus it will be motivated to achieve productive efficiency for that output. Since there is only one firm, the issue of allocating that output efficiently among the firms does not arise.

Allocative Inefficiency
(Price Greater than *MC*)

While productively efficient, the monopolist will produce the "wrong" output from the standpoint of efficiency. As we have seen, the monopolist chooses an output at which the price charged is greater than marginal cost. This violates the conditions for allocative efficiency discussed on page 231. When price equals marginal cost, consumers pay for the last unit purchased an amount just equal to the opportunity cost of producing that unit. But at a monopoly price and output, price is greater than marginal cost. Thus consumers pay for the last unit an amount that exceeds the opportunity cost of producing it. Consumers would be prepared to buy additional units for an amount greater than the cost of producing these units. Recall that opportunity cost is the market value consumers would receive if the resources were used in their best alternative use. Some consumers could be made better off, and none worse off, by shifting extra resources into production of this commodity. In other words, allocative efficiency could be improved by increasing production of the product. This is illustrated graphically in the box.

The monopoly output is not allocatively efficient; equivalently, it is not Pareto-optimal.

The Inefficiency of Monopoly: A Warning

Just as the conclusion that perfect competition is efficient was subject to some words of warning (see page 232), so too are the conclusions about the inefficiency of monopoly. The detailed comparison of monopoly and competition we defer to Chapter 18, but a preview is in order. Much of the case against monopoly depends on the monopoly's having the same costs as a competitive industry yet producing allocatively inefficient quantities. This assumption has been called into question in the very long run. For example, if monopolists engage in more innovation than would firms in a competitive industry, the cost curves of the industry may shift downward enough to create productive efficiencies in the very long run that will more than offset any allocative inefficiency. (The important question of the influence of market structure on innovation is discussed in Chapter 18.)

THE NATURE AND EXTENT OF MONOPOLY POWER

The *theory* of monopoly just developed assumes that the monopolist is unconcerned about competition. It is, however, difficult to imagine a firm without *any* competition. A firm may have a complete monopoly on a particular product at a given moment, but every product has some present or potential substitutes for the services it provides. Some products have fairly close substitutes, and even a single seller producing such a product will have close rivals. Other products may have no existing close substitute, but new products may be developed that will compete with it. For these reasons it is useful to recognize monopoly power as a variable that can be relatively slight or nearly complete, rather than as an attribute which either does or does not exist.

Monopoly power exists to the extent that a firm is insulated from loss of customers to other sellers.

THE ALLOCATIVE INEFFICIENCY OF MONOPOLY: A GRAPHIC INTERPRETATION

In the box on page 233, we gave a graphic interpretation of allocative efficiency. That analysis can be extended here, with reference to the figure below.

The output q^* represents the allocatively efficient output where $p = MC$. The monopolist restricts output to q_M in order to charge price p_M, which maximizes the monopolist's profits. At that output, consumers put a value of p_M on the last unit produced, but the resources used to produce that last unit have a lower value, MC_M, in their best alternative uses. Every unit between q_M and q^* would cost less to produce than the value consumers place on it. The two *gray* shaded areas (the triangle *adc*) represent a so-called *deadweight loss* due to the allocative inefficiency of monopoly.

To understand why this occurs, we must consider the matter from the point of view both of the monopolist and of the consumers. The monopolist restricts output. As a result price, p_M, is greater than marginal cost. The monopolist gains (at the expense of consumers) by raising price and restricting output. *But the monopolist's gain is smaller than consumers' losses.*

First consider the effect on the producer of raising the price from p^* to p_M. On the first q_M units there is a big increase in the producer's profits, shown by the color shaded rectangle (p^*p_Mab). To be sure, the producer loses some profits on the sales from q_M to q^*. These lost profits are shown by the dark gray shaded area (*bcd*). The net gain to the producer is the colored rectangle *minus* the dark gray shaded triangle.

Now consider consumers. Their loss of consumers' surplus is the colored rectangle *plus* the light gray shaded triangle *abc*. The colored rectangle is a pure redistribution from consumers to the monopolist. It reflects extra payments by consumers on the first q_M units. Such a redistribution does not affect allocative efficiency.

But the two shaded areas are losses to one group that are not gains to the other group. They are the deadweight losses.

The monopolist, by restricting output and raising price above the competitive level, gains a larger share of a smaller "pie." The deadweight loss arises because of the decrease in the size of the pie caused by not producing units that consumers value above the opportunity cost of production.

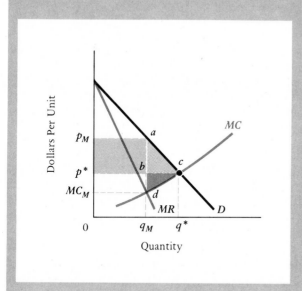

Monopoly Power As a Variable

How is the extent of monopoly power to be defined? The mere fact that a firm's demand curve slopes downward means that if the firm raises its price, it will lose some sales. But there may be limits on the firm's power over price other than the slope of the market demand curve. Any producer who is facing a downward-sloping demand curve could choose the price quantity combination (where

$MR = MC$ that appears to maximize its profits. *But this price might not turn out to be the long-run profit-maximizing price* because the choice of a particular price-quantity combination may itself lead to changes in the behavior of other firms that in turn *shift* the original firm's demand curve. If, for example, a firm raises its price and (as an indirect result) its demand curve shifts to the left, its sales and profits will be less than the firm would have expected on the basis of the original demand curve.

Consider an example. The Coca-Cola Company is the sole producer of Coca-Cola and faces a downward-sloping demand curve. But the Coca-Cola Company is not a complete monopolist. To see why, suppose that the demand curve for Coke shows that if the price is cut by 20 percent *and* if all other soft drink suppliers keep their prices at their present levels, sales of Coke will increase by 50 percent. This would almost surely result in an increase in the company's profits. Since the Coca-Cola Company is unquestionably free to cut price by 20 percent, why does it not do so? The answer is that if it did, other soft drink prices would not remain unchanged—and the company knows this. The very action of reducing prices would almost surely cause sellers of other soft drinks to reduce *their* prices. If they did so, Coca-Cola's sales would not increase as much as its demand curve predicts based on the assumption of no changes in others' prices. Sales would not increase by 50 percent; instead they might increase by (say) only 10 percent. In such an event the company's profits would decrease rather than increase. Thus the Coca-Cola Company, while it has a monopoly of Coca-Cola sales, does not have a monopoly of soft drink sales, although it may well have some market power.

The larger the *shifts* in a demand curve that are induced by a firm's changing its price, the less is that firm's monopoly power. Such shifts have two main sources. The first (as in the Coca-Cola example) is the price reactions of existing producers of substitute products. The second is the entry of new firms that succeed in capturing part of the sales that the monopolist included in "its" demand curve. Such shifts in the demand curve, from either cause, limit the market power of the firm and reduce its profits.

Since no firm is perfectly insulated from all competition for all time, total monopoly power does not exist. Monopoly power is a variable.

It matters a good deal that monopoly power is measured in terms of "more" or "less" rather than "you have it" or "you don't." One consequence is that a monopoly over a single product does not necessarily confer a high degree of monopoly power. A single producer of a product (e.g., Coke) with many close substitutes may have less monopoly power than either of two firms that produce a product (e.g., soap) with few close substitutes. A second consequence is that (while it is usually true that more competitors mean more competition) it is not *necessarily* true that effective monopoly power increases as the number of firms in an industry decreases. For example, less monopoly power may be exercised in an industry where only 2 or 3 firms compete vigorously than in an industry where 8 or 10 firms cooperate with each other. Such firms could agree among themselves to set a common price and/or to share the market and act in exactly the same way as if they were a single-firm monopoly. Such behavior is known as **collusion**.

Measuring Monopoly Power

In order to use the theory of monopoly, we must be able to define monopolistic markets. Furthermore, it is a matter of public policy that uncontrolled monopoly power is undesirable. Government agencies such as the Department of Justice and the Federal Trade Commission, which enforce these policies, and the judges who decide the cases, must know where monopoly power exists if they are to control or eliminate it.

Measuring monopoly power is not easy. Ideally, prices, outputs, and profits of firms in any industry should be compared with what they would be if all firms were under unified (monopoly) control and were fully insulated from entry. But such a hypothetical comparison does not lend itself to measurement.

Concentration Ratios

In practice, two alternative measures are widely used. The first of these is the **concentration ratio,** which shows the fraction of total market sales controlled by the largest group of sellers. Common types of concentration ratios cite the share of total market sales made by the largest four or eight firms. How well concentration ratios measure effective monopoly power is a matter of substantial debate among economists.

A first problem is to define the market with reasonable accuracy. For one example, concentration ratios in national cement sales are low, but they understate the market power of cement companies because heavy transportation costs divide the cement *industry* into a series of regional *markets*, in each of which there are relatively few firms. (We shall discuss problems of market definition further in Chapter 18.)

A second problem is the interpretation of concentration ratios. Are they adequate proxies for the intensity of competition? Clearly, market share is one measure of the *potential* power to control supply and set price. The inclusion in concentration ratios of the market shares of several firms rests on the possibility that large firms will, in one way or another, adopt a common price–output policy that is no different from the policy they would adopt if they were in fact under unified management.

Such common behavior may occur with or without an actual agreement to collude. If no agreement actually occurs, lawyers speak of **conscious parallel action** and economists of **tacit collusion** when referring to the noncollusive parallel behavior that results. Concentration ratios measure the *actual* exercise of monopoly power only if collusion—whether overt or tacit—occurs.

High concentration ratios may be necessary for the exercise of monopoly power, but they are not sufficient. They tend to show the potential for monopoly power but not necessarily the actuality.

Profits as a Measure of Monopoly Power

Many economists, following the lead of Professor Joe S. Bain, use profit rates as a measure of monopoly power. By *high profits*, these economists mean returns sufficiently in excess of all opportunity costs that potential new entrants desire to enter the industry. Persistently high profits, so goes the logic, are indirect evidence that neither rivalry among sellers nor entry of new firms prevents existing firms from pricing as if they were monopolists.

Using profits in this way requires care because, as we have seen (page 181), profits as reported in firms' income statements are not pure profits over opportunity cost. In particular, allowance must be made for differences in risk and in required payments for the use of owners' capital.

While neither concentration ratios nor profit rates are ideal measures of the degree of market power that a firm, or group of firms, actually exercises, both are of value and are widely used. In fact, concentration ratios and high profit rates are themselves correlated. Because of this, alternative classifications of markets and industries, according to their monopoly power measured in these two ways, do not differ much from one another. In spite of the difficult problems of measuring monopoly power, the theory of monopoly is widely used by economists and policymakers.

PRICE DISCRIMINATION

Raw milk is often sold at one price when it is to go into fluid milk but at a lower price when it is to be used to make ice cream or cheese. Doctors usually charge for their services according to the incomes of their patients. Movie theaters may have lower admission prices for children than for adults. Railroads charge different rates per ton mile for different products. Electric companies sell electricity more cheaply for industrial than for home use. State universities charge out-of-state students higher tuition than residents. Japanese steel companies sell steel more cheaply in the United States than in Japan.

Such price differences could never persist under perfect competition. Yet many of these examples have existed for decades. Persistent price differences clearly require the exercise of some monopoly power because the seller is exerting influence over the price at which its product is sold. Why should a firm want to sell some units of output at a price well below the price it gets for other units? Why, in other words, does it practice price discrimination?

Price discrimination occurs when a producer sells different units of a specific commodity to buyers at two or more different prices, for reasons not associated with differences in cost. Not all price differences represent price discrimination. Quantity discounts, differences between wholesale and retail prices, and prices that vary with the time of day or the season of the year are not generally considered price discrimination because the same physical product sold at a different time or place or in different quantities may have different costs. If an electric power company has unused capacity at certain times of day, it may be cheaper to provide service at those hours than at peak demand hours. If the price differences reflect cost differences, they are nondiscriminatory. However, when price differences rest merely on different buyers' valuations of the same product, they are discriminatory. It does not cost a movie theater operator less to fill a seat with a child than an adult, but it may pay to let the children in at a discriminatory low price if few of them would attend at the full adult fare.

Why Price Discrimination Pays

Persistent price discrimination comes about either because different buyers may be willing to pay different amounts for the same commodity or because one buyer may be willing to pay different amounts for different units of the same commodity. (You should now review the discussion of consumers' surplus on pages 145–146.) The basic point about price discrimination is that in either of these circumstances sellers may be able to capture some of the consumers' surplus that would otherwise go to buyers.

Discrimination Among Units Sold to One Buyer

Look back to Table 9-2 on page 146, which showed the consumer's surplus received by one consumer if she bought eight glasses of milk at a single price. If the seller could sell her each glass separately, it could capture this consumer's surplus. In the example, it would sell the first unit for $3, the second for $1.50, the third for $1, and so on until the eighth was sold for $.30. The seller would get total revenues of $8.10 rather than the $2.40 received by selling at the single price. In this example, the seller has been able to discriminate perfectly and extract every bit of the consumer's surplus.

Of course, such perfect price discrimination may not be possible. But suppose the firm could charge two different prices, one for the first four units sold, and one for the next four sold. If it sold the first four for $.80 and the next four for $.30, it would receive $4.40—less than if it could discriminate perfectly but more than it would receive from sale at any single price.

Discrimination Among Buyers

Think of the demand curve in a market containing individual buyers, each of whom has indicated the price he or she is prepared to pay for a single unit. Suppose for simplicity that there are only four buyers, the first of whom is prepared to pay any price up to $4, the second $3, the third $2, and the fourth $1. Suppose the product has a marginal cost of production of $1 per unit for all units. If the seller is limited to a single price, it will maximize its profits by charging $3, sell two units, and earn profits of $4. If the seller can discriminate between units, it could charge the first buyer $4, and the second $3—thus increasing profits from the first two units to $5. Moreover, it could also sell the third unit for $2, and the fourth unit for $1. Its revenues and its profits would increase.

Price Discrimination More Generally

Demand curves slope downward because different units are valued differently, either by one individual owing to diminishing marginal utility or by different individuals. That fact, combined with a single price, gives rise to consumers' surplus.

The ability to charge multiple prices gives a seller the opportunity to capture some (or, in the extreme, all) of the consumers' surplus.

In general, the more prices that can be charged, the greater the seller's ability to increase its revenue at the expense of consumers. This is illustrated in Figure 15-5.

It follows, for any given output, that if a seller is able to price discriminate according to buyers' willingness to pay, it can increase revenues received, (and thus also its profits) from the sale of those units. [25] But price discrimination is not always possible, even if there are no legal barriers to its use.

When Is Price Discrimination Possible?

Discrimination among units of output sold to the same buyer requires that the seller be able to keep track of the units a buyer consumes each period. Thus the tenth unit purchased by a given buyer in a given month can be sold at a different price than the fifth unit *only* if the seller can keep track of who buys what. This can be done by the electric company through its meter readings or by the magazine publishing firm's distinguishing between renewals and new subscriptions. It may also be done by establishments' giving a certificate or coupon providing, for example, a reduced price car wash for a return visit.

Discrimination among buyers is only possible if the goods cannot be resold by the buyer who faces the low price to the buyer who faces the high price.

FIGURE 15-5
Price Discrimination

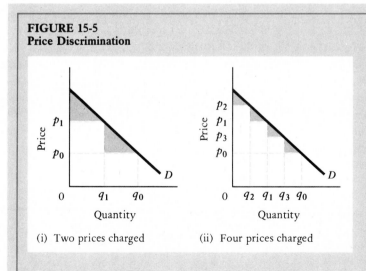

(i) Two prices charged

(ii) Four prices charged

Multiple prices permit a seller to capture buyers' consumers' surplus. Suppose in either diagram that if a single price were charged, it would be the price p_0. Quantity q_0 would be sold, and consumers' surplus would be the entire area above p_0 and below the demand curve. In (i) two prices are charged: p_1 for the first q_1 units and p_0 for other units. Consumers' surplus is reduced to the two shaded areas and the seller's revenue increased accordingly. In (ii) four prices are charged: p_2 for the first q_2 units, p_1 for the units between q_2 and q_1, and so on. Producers' revenues are increased and consumers' surplus further reduced to the shaded areas. At the extreme, if a different price could be charged for each unit, producers could extract every bit of the consumers' surplus, and the price discrimination would be perfect.

However much the local butcher might like to charge the banker's wife twice as much for hamburger as he charges the taxi driver, he cannot succeed in doing so. Madame Banker can always shop for meat in the supermarket, where her husband's occupation is not known. Even if the butcher and the supermarket agreed to charge her twice as much, she could hire the taxi driver to shop for her. The surgeon, however, may succeed in discriminating (if all reputable surgeons will do the same) because it will not do the banker's wife much good to hire the taxi driver to have her operations for her.

Price discrimination is possible only if the seller can distinguish individual units bought by a single buyer or separate buyers into classes such that resale among classes is impossible.

Ability to prevent resale tends to be associated with the character of the product or the ability to classify buyers into readily identifiable groups. Services are less easily resold than goods; goods that require installation by the manufacturer (e.g., heavy equipment) are less easily resold than movable goods such as household appliances. An interesting example of nonresalability occurs in the case of plate glass. Small pieces sell much more cheaply per square foot than bigger pieces, but the person who needs glass for a $6' \times 10'$ picture window cannot use four pieces of $3' \times 5'$ glass. Transportation costs, tariff barriers, and import quotas separate classes of buyers geographically and may make discrimination possible.

It is, of course, not enough to be able to separate buyers or units into separate classes. The seller must be able to control the supply to each group. This is what makes price discrimination an aspect of the theory of monopoly.[3]

----

[3] For price discrimination to be profitable, the different groups must have different degrees of willingness to pay. The hypothesis of diminishing marginal utility (see page 139) would lead to the prediction that different valuations are placed by an individual on different units, and differences in income and tastes would lead to the prediction that different subgroups will have different elasticities of demand for a given commodity. Thus, the potential for profitable price discrimination is usually present.

The Effects of Price Discrimination

The positive consequences of price discrimination are summarized in two propositions.

1. For any given level of output, the most profitable system of discriminatory prices will provide higher total revenue to the firm than the profit-maximizing single price.

This proposition was illustrated graphically in Figure 15-5. All it requires is a downward-sloping demand curve. To see that this is reasonable, remember that a monopolist with the power to discriminate *could* produce exactly the same quantity as a single-price monopolist and charge everyone the same price. Therefore, it need never get *less* revenue, and it can do better if it can raise the price on even one unit sold.

2. Output under monopolistic discrimination will generally be larger than under single-price monopoly.

To see that this is reasonable, remember that a single-price monopolist stops selling at an output where price is greater than MC. Suppose the monopolist is able to sell additional units without reducing the price on all earlier units. Since price is greater than MC on some units not yet sold, it will be profitable to lower the price a bit and sell additional units. It follows that when a firm can price its product unit by unit, it will pay it to produce more than if it were limited to a single price.

Another way to look at the same phenomenon is to remember that a monopolistic firm which must charge a single price produces less than the perfectly competitive industry because it is aware that by producing and selling more it drives down the price against itself. Price discrimination allows it to avoid this disincentive. To the extent that the firm can sell its output in separate blocks, it can sell another block without spoiling the market for the block already being sold. In the case of *perfect* price discrimination, where every unit of output is sold at a different price, the profit-maximizing firm will produce every unit for which the price charged can be greater than or equal to its marginal cost.

It will, therefore, produce the same output as the firm in perfect competition.

The Normative Aspects of Price Discrimination

The predicted combination of higher average revenue and higher output does not in itself have any *normative* significance. It will typically lead to a different distribution of income and a different level of output than when the seller is limited to a single price. The ability of the discriminating monopolist to capture some of the consumers' surplus will seem undesirable to consumers but not to the monopolist. How outsiders view the transfer may depend on who gains and who loses. For instance, when railroads discriminated against small farmers, the results aroused public anger; when doctors discriminate by giving low-priced service to poor patients, it is taken to be necessary since the poor would not be able to afford medical care if doctors charged all their patients the same fees.

Price discrimination, we have seen, tends to lead to larger output than is produced by a single-price monopoly. Thus price discrimination tends to *decrease* the allocative inefficiency of monopoly. Indeed, under perfect price discrimination the monopolist produces up to the point where price equals marginal cost and thus achieves allocative efficiency.

The fact that price discrimination may actually improve efficiency may seem paradoxical, for price discrimination has a bad reputation among economists and lawyers. To many people *discrimination* has odious connotations. Laws make certain kinds of price discrimination illegal. But was discrimination by airlines in giving students lower standby fares really bad? Some further examples are explored in the box on page 250.

There are two quite separate questions involved in evaluating a particular example of price discrimination. First is whether it increases the available *sum* of producers' and consumers' surplus. This is the question of allocative efficiency. Second is who gets whatever surplus is available. This is a question of distribution. Economists can identify both kinds of effects, and the desirability of each can be debated. Whether an individual judges price discrimination as "evil" depends on the details of the particular example as well as on personal value judgments. Very often it is the income redistribution caused by price discrimination that accounts for the strong emotional reactions to price discrimination. When it transfers income from poor to rich, price discrimination may seem bad even if it increases efficiency; when it transfers income from rich to poor, it may seem good for distributional reasons.

Price Discrimination: Systematic and Unsystematic

The discussion so far has been concerned with systematic and persistent price discrimination. Systematic price discrimination most often consists of classifying buyers according to their age, location, industry, income, or the use they intend to make of the product, and then charging different prices for the different "classes" of buyers. It may also take other forms, such as charging more for the first unit bought than for subsequent units, or vice versa.

Another sort of price discrimination is common. Any firm that occasionally gives a favorite customer a few cents off, or shaves its price to land a new account, is also engaged in price discrimination. If these practices are used irregularly, they are called *unsystematic discrimination*. Such discrimination is not really part of the price structure, and we have ignored it here. This does not mean that it is unimportant; on the contrary, unsystematic price discrimination plays a major role in the dynamic process by which prices change in response to changed conditions of supply and demand.

The causes and consequences of systematic price discrimination are very different from those of unsystematic price discrimination.

The law, however, is generally unable to distinguish between the two kinds of price discrimination and so hits at both. Legislation, motivated solely by a desire to attack systematic discrimina-

IS PRICE DISCRIMINATION BAD?

The consequences of price discrimination differ from case to case. No matter what an individual's values are, he or she is almost bound to evaluate individual cases differently.

Secret rebates. A very large oil-refining firm agrees to ship its product to market on a given railroad, provided that the railroad gives the firm a secret rebate on the transportation cost and does not give a similar concession to rival refiners. The railroad agrees and is thereby charging discriminatory prices. This rebate gives the large oil company a cost advantage that it uses to drive its rivals out of business or to force them into a merger on dictated terms. (John D. Rockefeller was accused of using such tactics in the early years of the Standard Oil Company.)

Use of product. When the Aluminum Company of America had a virtual monopoly on the production of aluminum ingots, it sold both the raw ingots and aluminum cable made from the ingots. At one time ALCOA sold cable at a price 20 percent *below* its price for ingots. (Of course, the cable price was above ALCOA's cost of pro-

ducing cable.) It did so because users of cable could substitute copper cable, but many users of ingot had no substitute for aluminum. In return for its "bargain price" for cable, ALCOA made the purchasers of cable agree to use it only for transmission purposes. (Without such an agreement, any demander of aluminum might have bought cable and melted it down.)

Covering costs. A product that many people want to purchase has a demand and cost structure such that there is no single price at which a producing firm can cover total cost. However, if the firm is allowed to charge discriminatory prices, it will be willing to produce the product and it may make a profit. This is illustrated in the figure.

Because *ATC* is everywhere higher than the demand curve, no single price would lead to revenues equal to costs. A price-discriminating monopolist may be able to cover cost. The total cost of output *q* is the area $0cbq$. The maximum revenue attainable at any output by perfect discrimination is the area under the demand curve. For output *q* that area, shown as gray shaded, exceeds total cost since the gray shaded triangle *cda* is greater than the color shaded triangle *abe*.

Equitable fares. For many years, British railways were not allowed to discriminate among passengers in different regions. To prevent discrimination, a fixed fare per passenger mile was specified and charged on all lines, whatever their passenger traffic and whatever the elasticity of demand for the services of the particular line. In the interest of economy, branch lines that could not cover costs closed down. Some lines stopped operating even though their users preferred rail transport to any alternatives and the strength of their preference was such that they would have willingly paid a price sufficient for the line to yield a profit. But the lines were closed because it was thought inequitable to discriminate against the passengers of these lines. (The policy was eventually dropped.)

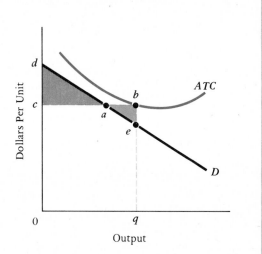

tion, may have unforeseen and possibly undesired effects on unsystematic discrimination. Because unsystematic price discrimination is important for the working of competition, prohibiting it may aid the maintenance of monopoly power.

SUMMARY

1. Our analysis of monopoly begins with two simplifying assumptions: first, that an entire industry is supplied by a single seller, called a monopolist; second, that the monopolist sets a single price and supplies the entire quantity that buyers wish to purchase at that price.

2. Under these circumstances, the monopolist's own demand curve is identical with the market demand curve for the product. The market demand curve is the monopolist's average revenue curve. The marginal revenue resulting from the sale of another unit by a monopolist will always be less than the price obtained for that unit.

3. When the monopolist is maximizing profits (i.e., producing where $MR = MC$), marginal revenue will be positive, and thus elasticity of demand will be greater than unity. The amount of profits that a monopolist earns is not predicted by the theory. The amount may be large, small, zero, or negative in the short run, depending on the relation of demand and cost.

4. The presence of profits in a monopolized industry provides the same incentive to entry as it does in perfect competition. Therefore, for monopoly profits to persist in the long run, there must be effective barriers to entry. Such barriers include patent laws, charters or franchises, economies of scale, and coercive tactics.

5. Monopolists producing where $MR = MC$ and with price greater than MC do not achieve the allocative efficiency associated with perfect competition. In restricting output the monopolist does not produce the output that maximizes the sum of consumers' and producers' surplus. While monop-

olists will chose the lowest cost for producing a particular output, there is no assurance in equilibrium that the output produced is that for which ATC is a minimum.

6. There is no such thing as a complete monopoly. Monopoly power is limited by the presence of existing substitute products, by the development of new products, and by the possibility of entry of new firms.

7. Monopoly power exists to the extent that a firm is insulated from loss of customers to other sellers. The degree of monopoly power may best be thought of as a quantitative variable. Two widely used measures of the degree of monopoly power are concentration ratios and the comparison of profits in one industry with those earned in other industries of similar risk and invested capital.

8. Price discrimination occurs when different units of the same commodity are sold for different prices, for reasons not associated with differences in costs. Different buyers may be charged different prices, or the same buyer may be charged different prices on different units of the commodity purchased. A successful price discriminator captures some of the consumers' surplus that would exist at a single price.

9. The conditions under which a seller can succeed in charging discriminatory prices are, first, that it can control the supply of the product offered to particular buyers and, second, that it can prevent the resale of the commodity from one buyer to another.

10. Commodities that are likely to meet the conditions for price discrimination include services, equipment requiring installation by the manufacturer, and commodities whose buyers can be isolated geographically by transport costs or international trade barriers.

11. Two predictions about price discrimination are (a) for any given level of output, the best system of discriminatory prices will provide higher total revenue to the firm than the best single price, and (b) output will usually be larger than under a single-price monopoly. As a result of (b), the allocative inefficiency of monopoly tends to decrease.

12. The consequences of price discrimination can differ from case to case. Price discrimination affects the distribution of income, the quantities produced, and the allocation of resources. Any individual is almost certain to evaluate individual cases differently, whatever his or her personal set of values. Further, there are important differences in the effects of systematic and unsystematic price discrimination.

TOPICS FOR REVIEW

The relationship of price and *MR* for a monopolist
The relationships among *MR, TR,* and elasticity
Allocative inefficiency of monopoly
Measures of monopoly power
Price discrimination
Conditions that make price discrimination both possible and profitable

DISCUSSION QUESTIONS

1. Suppose that only one professor teaches economics at your school. Would you say this professor is a monopolist who can exact any "price" from students in the form of readings assigned, tests given, and material covered? Suppose that two additional professors are hired; has the original professor's monopoly power been decreased?

2. Imagine a monopoly firm with fixed costs but no variable or marginal costs—for example, a firm owning a spring of water that produces indefinitely, once certain pipes are installed, in an area where no other source of water is available. What would be the firm's profit-maximizing price? What elasticity of demand would you expect at that price? Would this seem to be an appropriate pricing policy if the water monopoly were municipally owned? Suppose now that entry becomes easy because of the discovery of many additional springs. What price behavior would you

expect to occur? What price equilibrium would be predicted?

3. Each of the following has some "monopoly power": Xerox Corporation, Pepsi-Cola Company, Mobil Oil, OPEC, and AT&T. In each case, what do you think is the basis of the monopoly power? How might you decide which of the organizations listed has the greatest degree of monopoly power?

4. Which of these industries—licorice candy, copper wire, outboard motors, coal, local newspapers—would you most like to monopolize? Why? Does your answer depend on several factors or just one or two? Which would you as a consumer least like to have monopolized by someone else? If your answers are different in the two cases, explain why.

5. A movie exhibitor, Aristotle Murphy, owns movie theaters in two Indiana towns of roughly the same size, 50 miles apart. In Monopolia he owns the only chain of theaters; in Competitia there is no theater chain, and he is but one of a number of independent operators. Would you expect movie prices to be higher in Monopolia than in Competitia in the short run? In the long run? If differences occurred in his prices, would Mr. Murphy be discriminating in price?

6. Airline rates to Europe are higher in summer than in winter. Canadian railroads charge lower fares during the week than on weekends. Electricity companies charge consumers lower rates, the more electricity they use. Are these all examples of price discrimination? What additional information would you like to have before answering?

7. Discuss whether each of the following represents price discrimination. In your view, which are the most socially harmful?

   a. Standby fares on airlines that are a fraction of the full fare

   b. Standby fares, as above, available only to bona fide students under 22 years of age

   c. First class fares that are 50 percent greater than tourist fares, recognizing that two first class seats use the space of three tourist seats

   d. Negotiated discounts from list price, where sales personnel are authorized to bargain hard and get as much in each transaction as the traffic will bear

   e. Higher tuition for out-of-state students at state-supported colleges and universities

   f. Higher tuition for law students than for history students

16 INDUSTRIAL ORGANIZATION AND THEORIES OF IMPERFECT COMPETITION

Texaco, Shell, and Mobil are three of the "major" oil companies. They are not, singly or collectively, monopolists, nor are they firms in perfect competition. Yet they are typical of many real firms in our economy. Similar comments apply to the Coca-Cola and Pepsi-Cola companies. Do the two basic theories of pricing behavior we have studied—perfect competition and monopoly—have any relevance to their behavior?

The essential features of perfect competition are that each firm sells a product sufficiently similar to those sold by its numerous competitors that no one firm has any power to influence price (firms are price takers) and that the industry exhibits freedom of entry and exit. The essential features of monopoly are blockaded entry and a demand curve that is substantially the same for the firm and for the industry. Do the theories of perfect competition and monopoly provide a sufficient basis for predictions about price and market behavior in the real economy? Sixty years ago, most economists would have said yes; today most would say no.

This chapter looks first at some statistics to see how well the assumptions about monopoly and competition *describe* the American economy. This is not the whole of the matter, for it is the method of science to abstract from the full complexity of reality, and it might well be that descriptively unrealistic models were analytically adequate to make predictions that were confirmed by observations. If this were true, one would be able to predict the behavior of all American industries by classifying each as competitive or monopolistic *for purposes of predicting responses.* Many economists believe that although the models of monopoly and perfect competition are clearly useful, there is a need for other models as well. This chapter suggests some of them.

STRUCTURE OF THE AMERICAN ECONOMY

Our first task is to analyze how well the models of perfect competition and monopoly describe American firms and industries.

Two Groupings of American Industries

It is relatively easy to divide much of American industry into two broad groups, those with a large number of relatively small firms and those with a few relatively large firms. If these two groups are described by the two market forms we have studied so far, then perfect competition would characterize the first group and monopoly would characterize the second.

Sectors with Many Small Firms

Between 40 and 50 percent of the economy's national product is produced by industries made up of a large number of small firms. This includes most agricultural production, most services (travel agents, lawyers, plumbers, television technicians, etc.), most retail trade (stores, gas stations, etc.), most wholesale trade, most construction, and industries whose major business is exchange (real estate agents, stockbrokers, etc.).[1]

The competitive model, with the addition of government intervention where necessary, does quite well in describing many of these industries. This is obviously so where the business of the industry is exchange rather than production. Foreign exchange markets and stock exchanges are notable examples. Agriculture also fits fairly well in most ways; the individual farmer is clearly a price taker, entry into farming is easy, and exit is possible though not in fact very rapid. Many basic raw materials such as iron ore, tin, and copper are sold on world markets where prices fluctuate continually in response to changes in demand and supply.

Some other industries, however, do not seem to be described by the perfectly competitive model even though they contain many firms. In the retail trades and services, for example, most firms have some influence over prices. The local grocery, supermarket, discount house, and department store not only consider weekend specials and periodic sales important to business success, they spend a good deal of money advertising them. Moreover, each store in these industries has a unique location that may give it some local monopoly power over nearby customers. In wholesaling, the sales representative is regarded as a key figure—which would not be true if the firm could sell all it wished at a given market price. We are, as Professor R. L. Bishop has observed "a race of eager sellers and coy buyers, with purchasing agents getting the Christmas presents from the salesmen rather than the other way around."

The first group of industries therefore contains some that are clearly described by the model of perfect competition and many others that are not.

Sectors with a Few Large Firms

About 50 percent of the national product is produced by industries dominated by a few large

---

[1] Although, as we saw in Chapter 8, the size of American farms has increased dramatically in recent years, even the largest farm is small in relation to total market demand. Thus, even the largest farmer is a price taker, not a price setter.

firms. The names of these firms are part of the average citizen's vocabulary. In this category fall most transportation firms (e.g., the Penn Central Railroad, the Santa Fe Railroad, United Airlines, American Airlines, Greyhound), communications (AT&T, NBC, CBS, Western Union), public utilities (American Electric Power, Consolidated Edison), and much of the largest sector of the American economy, the manufacturing sector.

A casual look at the manufacturing sector can be misleading if one does not distinguish between products and firms. In some manufacturing industries there are many differentiated products produced by only a few firms. In soaps and detergents, for example, a vast variety of products is produced by a mere two firms, Lever Brothers and Procter & Gamble. Similar circumstances exist in chemicals, breakfast foods, cigarettes, and numerous other industries where many more or less competing products are in each case produced by a very few firms. Clearly these industries are not perfectly competitive. Yet neither do they appear to be monopolies, for the few firms typically compete energetically against one another.

Few American industries are easily characterized as monopolies. Many railway companies once enjoyed monopolies of service over rural areas (although seldom between major cities, which were normally served by several companies). In this century, however, both airlines and trucking have provided intense competition to the railroads. In manufacturing, examples of single-firm monopoly outside the regulated areas are few. The Aluminum Company of America was the sole producer of primary aluminum in the United States from 1893 until World War II. ALCOA and a few other companies have been described with reasonable accuracy as monopolies. The United Shoe Machinery Company had a monopoly on certain types of shoe machinery until antitrust decrees limited its exercise of monopoly power. The National Cash Register Company, the International Nickel Company, the Climax Molybdenum Company, and International Business Machines all had control, at one time or another, over more than 90 percent of the output of the industries in which they operated.

Monopolies exist in certain utility industries such as power and light, telephone communication, and postal services. Even here, however, the monopoly sometimes exists only because of government regulation. For example, if a legal monopoly were not enforced by the government, postal and parcel delivery services would be fiercely competitive. In other cases a monopoly that seemed quite unassailable has not persisted. Technological breakthroughs have made voice communication an industry with significant competition in contrast to the one-time monopoly of AT&T.

Monopoly and perfect competition do not *describe* much of the American economy. Many industries with numerous firms depart from some of the conditions of perfect competition; most industries with no more than a few firms depart from the conditions of monopoly.

Patterns of Concentration in Manufacturing

Let us take a closer look at American manufacturing. Table 16-1 shows current four-firm concentration ratios in selected industries that together account for about 40 percent of all manufacturing shipments. Notice that, descriptively, few of these industries fit either of the models studied so far. Among the high-concentration industries such as automobiles, aluminum, and cereals, the very high concentration is achieved by three or four firms in apparently vigorous rivalry with one another. That these firms have appreciable market power is undoubted; that they may be described by the monopoly model is questionable. The competitive model conceivably fits the two or three industries at the bottom of the list, but even here there are doubts.

For women's clothing, manufacturers have some control over price, contrary to the conditions of perfect competition, because of style and fashion. Metal stamping firms, print shops, and soft drink bottlers, while very numerous nationally, operate in small regional and local markets in which a small number of sellers, in direct rivalry with one another, do not regard themselves as price takers.

Table 16-2 shows that in nearly three-quarters of manufacturing industries, the four largest firms

TABLE 16–1 **CONCENTRATION RATIOS IN SELECTED MANUFACTURING INDUSTRIES, 1977**

Industry	Four-firm concentration ratio
Automotive	
Vehicles	93
Parts	62
Office machines	60
Tires and tubes	70
Soaps and detergents	59
Aircraft	
Planes	59
Engines and parts	74
Aluminum	
Primary	76
Rolling and drawing mills	81
Radio and television	
Sets	51
Equipment	20
Steel mills and blast furnaces	45
Chemicals	
Organic industrial	38
Plastics	22
Pharmaceutical	24
Machinery	
Farm	46
Construction	47
Metal stamping	9
Nonferrous wire	40
Petroleum refining	30
Foods	
Cereals	89
Bread and cake	33
Fluid milk	18
Canned fruit and vegetables	22
Soft drinks	15
Forest products	
Paper mills	23
Pulp mills	26
Clothes	
Men's and boy's suits and coats	21
Women's and misses' dresses	8
Fur goods	11
Commercial printing, lithography	6

Source: U.S. Department of Commerce, *1977 Census of Manufactures,* 1981.

Concentration ratios vary greatly among manufacturing industries. These data, from the 1977 census of manufactures, show the share of the industries' shipments accounted for by the four largest firms.

control between 20 and 80 percent of the value of shipments. Such industries are not monopolies because there are several firms in the industry, and these firms engage in rivalrous behavior. Residents even of small towns will find more than one drugstore, garage, barber, and dress shop competing for their patronage. Similarly, manufacturers of computers, television sets, and chemicals belong to industries in which there are several close domestic rivals (and often foreign competitors). But neither are these firms in perfectly competitive markets. Often there are only a few major rival firms in an industry, but even when there are many, *they are not price takers.* Virtually all consumers' goods are differentiated commodities. Any one firm will typically have several lines of a product that differ more or less from each other and from competing lines produced by other firms. There is no market setting a single price for razor blades, or television sets, that equates overall demand to overall supply. Instead, it is in the nature of such products that *sellers must state a price at which they are willing to sell.* (Of course, a certain amount of "haggling" is possible, particularly at the retail level, but this is

TABLE 16–2 **MANUFACTURING INDUSTRIES, CLASSIFIED BY 1977 CONCENTRATION RATIOS**

Concentration ratio (percentage)	Number of industries listed by the census	Percentage of value of total shipments of all manufacturing industries
80–100	22	8
60–79	49	12
40–59	123	23
20–39	165	38
Less than 20	86	19
Total	445	100

Source: U.S. Department of Commerce, *1977 Census of Manufactures,* 1981.

Notice the importance measured both in numbers and in value of shipments of industries in the three middle groups. These data were computed from the 1977 census of manufactures. The concentration ratios are those for the four largest firms in each industry.

usually within well-defined limits set by the price initially quoted by the seller.)

Rivalrous behavior among firms that are not price takers immediately takes us out of the domain of either perfect competition or monopoly. We thus require additional market structures if we wish to explain the behavior.

The Importance of Administered Prices

We have seen that most American businesses do not correspond to the firm in perfect competition. In perfect competition, firms face a market price that they are quite unable to influence, and they adjust their quantities to that price. In perfect competition firms are price takers and quantity adjusters. Changes in market conditions are signaled to firms by changes in the market prices that they face.

In all other market structures, firms face downward-sloping demand curves and thus know that they have a choice of price for their product. A monopolist faces a downward-sloping demand curve because its product must compete with other products for consumer expenditure, and it chooses its price accordingly. More generally, most firms have a choice of price because they sell differentiated products. Each firm may have several lines of the one general product, and few firms have products that are identical. Although the products produced by various firms in an industry may be close substitutes for each other, they are seldom perfect substitutes, as in perfect competition. In such situations, firms have some control over their prices; they must decide on a price to quote for each of their product lines. If they are unsatisfied with their price–output position, they can change their quote, but quote a price they must. In such circumstances, we say that the firm administers its price. The term **administered prices** refers to prices that are set by the decisions of individual firms rather than by impersonal market forces.

When a firm sets its price, the amount that it sells is determined by its demand curve. Changes in market conditions change the amount that can be sold at its administered price. The changed con-

ditions may or may not lead the firm to change the price that it charges.

With market structures other than perfect competition, firms set their prices and then let demand determine their sales. Changes in market conditions are signaled to the firm by changes in the quantity it can sell at its administered price.

The inadequacy of the perfect competition and monopoly models in dealing with much of American industry has led to intense study of two further kinds of market structure, called *monopolistic competition* and *oligopoly*.

COMPETITIVE MARKET STRUCTURE: IMPERFECT COMPETITION AMONG THE MANY

Before the 1930s economists mainly studied the two polar market structures of perfect competition and monopoly. Then in the 1930s dissatisfaction with these two extremes led to the development of a theory of a new market structure called **monopolistic competition.** The theory was developed in two classic books, one by the British economist Joan Robinson, the other by the American economist Edward Chamberlin.

The market envisaged in the new theory was similar to perfect competition in that there were many firms with freedom of entry and exit. But it differed in one important respect: Each firm had some power over price because each sold a product that was differentiated significantly from those of its competitors. One firm's soap might be similar to another firm's soap, but it differed in chemical composition, color, smell, softness, brand name, and a host of other characteristics that mattered to customers. This is the phenomenon of **product differentiation.** It implies that each firm has a certain degree of local monopoly power over its own product. This is the "monopolistic" part of the theory. The monopoly power is severely restricted, however, by the presence of similar products sold by competing firms and by free entry and exit. This is the "competition" part of the theory.

From a theoretical point of view, the major difference between monopolistic and perfect competition lies in the assumptions of homogeneous and differentiated products. Firms in perfect competition sell a **homogeneous product,** which from a practical point of view means a product similar enough across the industry so that no one firm has any power over price. Firms in monopolistic competition sell a **differentiated product,** which from a practical point of view means a group of commodities similar enough to be called a product but dissimilar enough that the producer of each has some power over its own price.

The theory of monopolistic competition was extremely important as a step in the development of models of intermediate market structures. Its main prediction is outlined below.[2]

The Excess Capacity Theorem

There are two major characteristics of monopolistic competition. First, each firm is not a price taker. Instead, each firm faces a downward-sloping demand curve. But the curve is rather elastic because similar products sold by other firms provide many close substitutes. The downward slope of the demand curve provides the potential for monopoly profits in the short run.

Second, freedom of entry and exit forces profits to zero in the long run. If profits are being earned by existing firms in the industry, new firms will enter. Their entry will mean that the demand for the product must be shared among more brands. Thus the demand curve for any one firm's brand will shift left. Entry continues until profits fall to zero. Thus average revenue must equal average cost at some level of output but exceed it at none. Together these requirements imply that when a monopolistically competitive industry is in long-run equilibrium, its firms will be producing where

[2] The discussion here refers to large-group monopolistic competition, which exercised economists' imaginations in the decades after Chamberlin's and Robinson's writings. Small-group monopolistic competition is discussed in the next section on oligopoly.

their demand curves are tangent to (i.e., just touching at one point) their average total cost curves.

Two curves that are tangent at a point have the same slope at that point. If a downward-sloping demand curve is to be tangent to the average total cost curve, the latter must also be downward-sloping at the point of tangency. In such a situation, each firm is producing an output less than the one for which its *ATC* reaches its minimum point.

The zero-profit equilibrium of a monopolistically competitive firm occurs at an output less than the one at which average total cost is a minimum.

This prediction is known as the **excess capacity theorem**. It is an implication of the assumptions of downward-sloping demand curves and free entry. To recapitulate: Free entry pushes firms to the point at which the demand curve is tangent to the average total cost curve. The demand curve slopes downward because buyers are supposed to think in such terms as, "I *prefer* Del Monte peaches"; "I *trust* Mr. Green, even if he is a little more expensive"; and "Isn't that the brand Joe DiMaggio uses?" But if the demand curve slopes downward, it must be tangent to the average total cost in its declining portion. This prediction is illustrated in Figure 16-1.

The excess capacity theorem aroused passionate debate. It seemed to say that industries selling differentiated products are inefficient because they have excess capacity in long-run equilibrium and thus have a level of costs of production that is higher than necessary.

The modern conclusion, however, is that the "excess capacity" of monopolistic competition does not necessarily indicate inefficiency.

Monopolistic competition produces a wider range of products but less cheaply than perfect competition.

With differentiated products there is a choice available to consumers among several brands. Clearly, people have different tastes; some prefer one differentiated product and some prefer another. For example, each brand of breakfast food or video game has its sincere devotees. This creates a trade-off—from the point of view of consumer

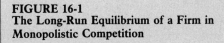

FIGURE 16-1
The Long-Run Equilibrium of a Firm in Monopolistic Competition

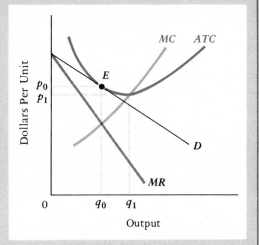

A monopolistically competitive firm in equilibrium has zero profits and excess capacity. Equilibrium is at point E where $MC = MR$ and where the demand curve is tangent to ATC. This results from free entry of firms with closely similar products. Price is p_0 and quantity q_0. Price is greater and quantity is less than the purely competitive equilibrium price and quantity (p_1 and q_1). At equilibrium, the monopolistically competitive firm has excess capacity of q_0q_1.

The Relevance of Monopolistic Competition

Perhaps the major blow that the theories of Robinson and Chamberlin suffered was the slow realization that monopolistically competitive industries were rarely, if ever, found in the economy. At first look this claim may sound surprising.

Although there are many industries in which a large number of slightly differentiated products compete for the buyers' attention, in most such cases the industries have only a few firms, each of which sells a large number of products. Consider the soap and detergent industry. Among the well-known brands currently on sale in the United States are Cheer, Dash, Duz, Gain, Oxydol, Tide, Dreft, Ivory Snow, Ivory Liquid, Joy, Cascade, Camay, Lava, Safeguard, Zest, Mr. Clean, Top Job, Spic and Span, Comet, and Samson. Surely this is impressive differentiation among a large number of products. This list of products might appear to provide a perfect example of monopolistic competition. But *every one* of the products named above is manufactured by a single company, Proctor & Gamble, which, with Lever Brothers, dominates sales of soaps, cleansers, and detergents in America. Clearly, such industries are not the large-group case envisaged by the framers of the theory of monopolistic competition. Today, product differentiation occurs mainly where a small group rather than a large group of firms compete with each other.[3]

The Lasting Contribution of Monopolistic Competition

Looking back, we see that the original theory of monopolistic competition contributed at least two

welfare—between producing more products to better satisfy diverse tastes and producing any given set of products at the lowest possible cost. Under these conditions, consumers' satisfactions are not maximized by increasing production of one or two brands of a product until each is produced at its least-cost point. Instead, the number of differentiated products must be increased until the gain from adding one more equals the loss from having to produce each existing product at a higher cost (because less of each is produced). For this reason, among others, the charge that monopolistic competition would lead to a waste of resources is no longer accepted as necessarily, or even probably, true.

[3] At first sight retailing may appear to be closer to the conditions of monopolistic competition than is manufacturing. Certainly every city has a very large number of retailers selling any one commodity. The problem is that they are differentiated from each other mainly by their geographical location, each firm having only a few competing close neighbors. Thus a model of interlocking oligopolies, with every firm in close competition with only a few neighbors, seems to be a better model for retailing than the large-group monopolistic competition model, in which every firm competes directly with a large number of other firms.

important things to the development of economics. At the time that it was first developed, perfect competition was under attack for the lack of realism of its assumptions. The theory of monopolistic competition recognized the facts of product differentiation, the ability of firms to influence prices, and the presence of advertising. The incorporation of these factors into a new theory encouraged economists to consider the question of their effects on the operation of the price system.

A second major contribution of the theory is that many economists have been profoundly influenced by it. It rekindled economists' interest in such important things as how and when firms took each other's reactions into account, what made for easy or restricted entry, and the significance to competition of different products that were roughly similar to one another.

The Modern Theory of Monopolistic Competition

Today it is the small-group case of differentiated oligopoly rather than the large-group case of monopolistic competition that seems relevant. In the last half of the 1970s there was a great outburst of theorizing about all aspects of product differentiation.[4]

This modern theory is the direct descendant of the earlier theories of monopolistic competition. The focus remains on product differentiation and on industrial structures thought to describe the nature of the modern economy. The new theory is consistent with the famous propositions of Chamberlin and Robinson that it pays firms to differentiate their products, to advertise heavily, and to engage in other forms of nonprice competition. These are characteristics to be found in the world but not in perfect competition. Most of the modern theory of product differentiation relates to indus-

tries with a small number of firms. This is the theory of oligopoly.

COMPETITION AMONG THE FEW: THE THEORY OF OLIGOPOLY

Manufacturing industries are often characterized by small groups of firms rather than large groups.[5] **Oligopoly** is a market structure in which there are relatively few firms that have enough market power that they may not be regarded as price takers (as in perfect competition) but are subject to enough rivalry that they cannot consider the market demand curve as their own. In most of these cases entry is neither perfectly easy nor wholly blockaded. In many industries, a small number of firms—between three and a dozen—tend to dominate the industry, and newcomers find it hard to establish themselves.

While the American automobile industry is a somewhat extreme example of this, its experience is revealing. Today three large firms and one much smaller firm constitute the industry. At least one of them is struggling to survive. No one has successfully entered the industry in the more than 50 years since the Dodge brothers split with Ford and started making their own cars. Henry Kaiser attempted to enter in 1946. His Kaiser-Frazer came on the market, but despite the postwar boom in car sales the company suffered staggering losses and quietly withdrew in 1953. Recently, foreign automobile firms have been setting up plants in the United States. These are not new entrants into the world's automobile industry, however, but merely new plants being set up by old established firms.

What makes the automobile industry unusual is the absence of a "competitive fringe." The cigarette industry is similar—there are only 8 firms in the entire industry. In contrast, there are 192 petroleum refiners, but the 142 smallest firms together

---

[4] It is one of those regrettable facts of life that the theory that studies market structures where a *small* number of firms compete to sell a large number of differentiated products has also taken the name **monopolistic competition.** The term now refers to any industry in which more than one firm sells differentiated products.

[5] Oligopolies may be present even in nationally unconcentrated industries such as cement. A national concentration ratio is relevant where there is one national market. But if transport costs split the country into numerous regional markets, each one may contain a small number of oligopolistic firms.

account for only 6 percent of value of output. There are 121 tire and tube manufacturing companies, of which the 100 smallest supply in aggregate less than 3 percent of the market. Oligopoly is not inconsistent with a large number of small sellers when the "big few" dominate the decision making in the industry.

Typically in oligopolistic industries, prices are administered and products differentiated, and the intensity and nature of rivalrous behavior varies greatly from industry to industry and from one period of time to another. This variety has invited extensive theoretical speculation and empirical study. Two important facts have been established and their significance debated. First, in oligopolistic industries, short-run cost curves are very flat rather than U-shaped. Second, oligopolistic prices change relatively infrequently; they are sometimes said to be "sticky."

Short-Run Costs in Oligopoly

Saucer-shaped Average Variable and Marginal Cost Curves

Ever since economists began measuring manufacturing firms' costs, they have reported very flat variable short-run cost curves. By now, the evidence is overwhelming that in manufacturing, and in some other industries, cost curves are shaped like the curve shown in Figure 16-2, with a long, flat, middle portion and sharply rising sections at each end. (This "saucer" shape is to be compared with the traditional U-shaped cost curve shown in Figure 12-2 on page 193.) For such a cost curve, there is a large range of output over which average variable costs do not vary with the level of output. Over that range marginal costs are equal to average variable costs, and they too are constant per unit of output. [26]

Given a flat-bottomed cost curve, the nature of capacity output as we previously defined it becomes very much less useful because there is a wide range of output for which average cost is approximately minimized. It is now useful to distinguish between capacity output (as defined on page 194) where *ATC* is a minimum and **normal capacity output,**

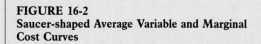

FIGURE 16-2
Saucer-shaped Average Variable and Marginal Cost Curves

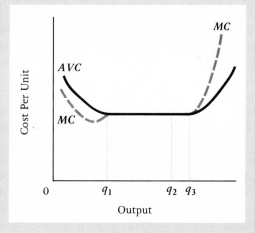

When *AVC* is horizontal, marginal costs coincide with average variable costs and are likewise constant per unit of output. It is possible to design a plant that achieves roughly constant variable and marginal costs over a large range of output. Such a curve is shown here. While average variable costs decrease for outputs up to q_1 and increase beyond q_3, they are constant over the large range q_1 to q_3. The level of output q_2 is normal capacity output, which is the average output the firm hopes to achieve. This is less than the level of output at which either *AVC* or *ATC* is a minimum. With this cost curve, the firm can vary production over the whole interval from q_1 to q_3 and have constant marginal costs per unit.

a somewhat lower level (such as q_2 in Figure 16-2) that the firm hopes to maintain on average.[6] The margin between normal capacity output and capacity output is available to meet unexpected, seasonal,

[6] There are really three different levels of capacity output that are sometimes talked about. In terms of Figure 16-2, there is first the level, q_2, which we call *normal capacity output*. Second, there is the higher level, q_3, where marginal and average *variable* costs turn sharply upward. Third, there is the still higher output (not shown) where *ATC* is a minimum. Since average fixed costs decline steadily, average total cost is declining over the whole horizontal range of the flat *AVC* curve. All of this is confusing. Business people almost always use the concept of normal capacity. You can usually tell what economists mean from the context.

or cyclical peaks in demand. The firm expects to use it in periods of peak demand but not in periods of average or slack demand.

Explaining the Saucer-shaped Curves

As evidence accumulated that the saucer-shaped curve was common, the question arose as to why. The answer is that firms designed plants that yielded this result. They did so on purpose, so that they could accommodate the inevitable seasonal and cyclical swings in demand for their product. As Professor George Stigler (the 1982 Nobel Laureate in Economics) was the first to point out, a firm faced with the two possible AVC curves, such as those shown in Figure 16-3, might well prefer to build a plant that resulted in the flat-bottomed one if it anticipated widely fluctuating demand. On average, the saucer-shaped curve would lead to

lower costs, even though at normal capacity output, the U-shaped cost curve dips below it.

How does it happen that the firm has a choice of the shape of its short-run average cost curve? Consider again the law of diminishing returns first encountered on page 188. The U-shaped short-run cost curve envisaged applying a variable amount of one factor, say labor, to a fixed amount of a second factor, say capital. Thus, as output is varied, factor proportions are necessarily varied. The argument for a U-shaped curve rested on first applying too low a ratio of the variable factor to the fixed factor. As production is increased, more of the variable factor is used and a more efficient combination with the fixed factor achieved. Once the optimal combination is achieved, further units of the variable factor lead to too high a ratio and rising average variable costs. Only one quantity of labor led to the precisely optimal factor proportions. This argument assumed that all of the fixed factor must be used all of the time; in other words, that the fixed factor be *indivisible*.

While a plant can be built that way, it may also be built so that the fixed factor is in fact *divisible*. Even though the firm's plant and equipment may be fixed in the short run, so that no more is available, it may well be possible to utilize less than all the fixed capital.

Consider as a simple example a "factory" that consists of 10 sewing machines in a shed, each with a productive capacity of 20 units per day when operated for 1 shift by 1 operator. If 200 units per day are required, then all 10 machines are operated on a normal shift. If demand falls to 180, then 1 operator can be laid off. But there is no need to have the 9 remaining operators dashing about trying to work 10 machines. Clearly, 1 machine can be "laid off" as well, and the ratio of *employed* labor to *employed* machines held constant. Production can go from 20 to 40 to 60 all the way to 200 without any change in factor proportions of factors in use. In this case we would expect the factory to have constant marginal costs from 20 to 200 units and only then to encounter rising costs, as production must be expanded by overtime and other means of combining more labor with the maximum supply of 10 machines.

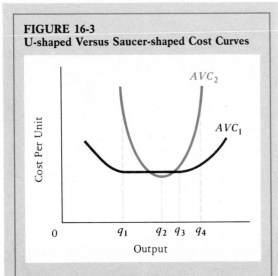

FIGURE 16-3
U-shaped Versus Saucer-shaped Cost Curves

A firm anticipating fluctuating output may choose a plant with a flat-bottomed cost curve. AVC_1 and AVC_2 are alternatives based on how a plant is designed and built. While the colored AVC_2 curve achieves lower unit costs than does the black AVC_1 if output is very close to q_2, it is much less adaptable to either higher or lower outputs. If the firm could count on producing q_2 every period, it would prefer the plant yielding AVC_2. But if it anticipated outputs ranging from q_1 to q_4, it might well prefer AVC_1.

In such a case the fixed factor is divisible. Since some of it may go unemployed, there is now no need to depart from the most efficient ratio of labor used to capital used as production is decreased. Thus, average variable costs can be constant over a large range, up to the point at which all the fixed factor is used.

The possibility of designing plants in which physical capital is divisible, combined with the advantage of doing so in an economy in which demand for a firm's product varies greatly from period to period, appears to account for the observed empirical fact of flat-bottomed plant cost curves. A similar situation can occur when a firm has many plants. For example, a plywood manufacturer with 10 or more plants chooses to cut its output by temporarily closing one or more plants while operating the rest at normal capacity output. In this case, too, the firm's short-run variable costs tend to be constant over a wide range of output.

Sticky Prices

One of the most striking contrasts between perfectly competitive and oligopolistic markets concerns the behavior of prices. In perfect competition prices change daily, even hourly, in response to changes in demand and supply. Oligopolistic prices change less frequently. Manufacturers of radios, automobiles, television sets, and men's suits do not change their prices with anything like the frequency that prices change in markets for basic materials or stocks and bonds. If you price a man's suit or a woman's skirt today in your local store, chances are that the price will be the same when you return to the store tomorrow. Of course, prices do change, but in oligopolistic industries prices usually change by relatively large amounts at discrete intervals in time. Book publishers and appliance manufacturers, for example, typically announce list prices for their products and change them infrequently.

The basic empirical finding is as follows:

Oligopolistic firms do not alter their prices every time demand shifts. Instead, they fix prices and let quantity sold do the adjusting in the short term.

This phenomenon is often referred to as the *stickiness* of oligopolistic prices. Before considering possible explanations of why prices may be sticky, it is important to recognize that they often do change.

When Oligopolistic Prices Do Change

Oligopolistic prices ordinarily change when there are major changes in costs of production. Rises in raw material prices or wage rates are passed on fairly quickly by rises in product prices.[7] Also, major reductions in costs, as when a new product such as the home computer is being developed, are usually followed by steady and major reductions in prices. This is because of the rivalry among oligopolistic firms: if one firm fails to cut price when costs fall, another firm will do so, seeking thereby to increase its market share.

Major unexpected shifts in demand also typically lead to price adjustments in oligopolistic prices. If an industry finds itself faced with an apparently permanent and unexpected downward shift in demand, it will often cut its prices in an attempt to retain its market until longer-term adjustments can be made. For example, the American car industry was faced with declining demand in the early 1980s due to its lag in developing small, fuel-efficient cars that were competitive with Japanese imports. It offered big rebates that slashed prices to levels that could not be maintained in the long run.

When Prices Are Sticky

The rigidity of oligopolistic prices lies not in the situations considered above. Instead, it lies mainly in *predictable* cyclical and seasonal shifts in demand. The ebb and flow of business activity is well known to firms, even if its precise course cannot be predicted in advance. Oligopolistic firms hold

[7] Oligopolistic pricing may, however, convert more or less continuous changes in input prices into discrete changes in output prices. Say that inflation is steadily raising the prices of industrial raw materials as determined in perfectly competitive markets. Firms find it expensive to change list prices every day or every week. They will therefore make discrete jumps in their output prices every few months, first getting output prices ahead of input prices, then slowly falling behind until a further adjustment of output prices is necessary.

THE KINKED DEMAND CURVE

An explanation of oligopolistic price stickiness was developed in the 1930s by the economist Paul Sweezy. This theory predicts price stickiness in the face of significant shifts both in demand and in costs.

Professor Sweezy's explanation was based on a novel demand curve for the oligopolist firm. Each oligopolist conjectures that its rivals will match any price decreases it makes but will not follow it in any price increases. If the firm raises its price and no one follows, it will lose market share and its sales will fall off rapidly; its demand curve will be very flat. If the firm lowers

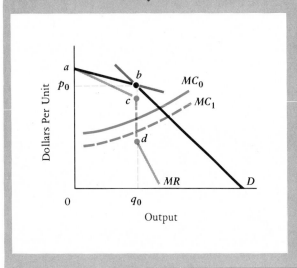

its price and everyone follows, it will not gain market share and its sales will expand only in proportion to the expansion in the industry's sales. The demand curve for price cuts will thus be steeper than the demand curve for price increases. The resulting **kinked demand curve** is shown in the figure.

The black curve abD is the firm's perception of its own demand curve. The corresponding marginal revenue curve is the discontinuous curve $acdMR$. [27] A shift in marginal cost from MC_0 to MC_1 changes neither the price nor the output that maximizes profits.

With the kinked demand curve there is an interval over which the firm's profit-maximizing price will be unchanged despite changing economic conditions. This theory predicts that prices will be inflexible in response to changes in costs anywhere in the interval from c to d.

This ingenious theory survives in many textbooks to this day. It has, however, almost no supporting evidence. Its two main deficiencies are first, while it predicts a tendency for a price, once set, to be maintained, it says nothing about what price is set initially. Second, it predicts price stickiness not only in the case of fluctuating demand but also in the face of sharp shifts in costs. This latter prediction is repeatedly contradicted by empirical evidence.

their prices fairly constant in the face of normal fluctuations in demand. These fluctuations thus cause output to vary while prices stay relatively stable.

Explaining Sticky Prices

Numerous theories have been offered to explain the stickiness of oligopolistic prices. An early interpretation stems from the pioneering work of two Oxford economists, Robert Hall and Charles Hitch. Their view was that businessmen were conventional creatures of habit who were clearly not profit maximizers. They calculated their full costs at normal capacity and then added a conventional markup to determine price. They then sold whatever they could at that price. Thus, demand fluctuations caused quantity rather than price fluctuations. This view of the conventional markup successfully explained the observed oligopolistic price stickiness but did not explain the observed fact that markups varied from time to time. We shall look at it more closely in Chapter 19. A second early explanation, much embraced a generation ago but now largely abandoned, is the so-called theory of the kinked demand curve, described in the box.

Most economists today believe that two forces account for the stickiness of oligopolistic prices. First, flat short-run average cost curves are frequently found for oligopolistic firms. Second, there are high costs of changing administered prices—including the costs of printing new list prices for the many products of a typical multiproduct firm, the costs of notifying all customers, the accounting and billing difficulty of keeping track of frequently changing prices, and the loss of customer and retailer loyalty due to the uncertainty caused by frequent changes in prices.

The theory spelled out. This explanation of sticky prices is illustrated in Figure 16-4. Firms make their decisions in stages. They estimate their *normal demand curve,* which is the average of what they can expect to sell at each price over booms and slumps. Having built a plant consistent with this demand and the expected fluctuations in output, they then pick as their "normal price" the profit-maximizing price for their normal demand curve. Short-run fluctuations in demand are then met by holding price constant and varying output. This avoids all the costs involved in repeated change in prices.

The behavior just described is profit-maximizing behavior. Because the cost of changing prices is high, often the best thing a firm can do is to set

FIGURE 16-4
A Theory of Sticky Prices in the Face of Fluctuating Demand

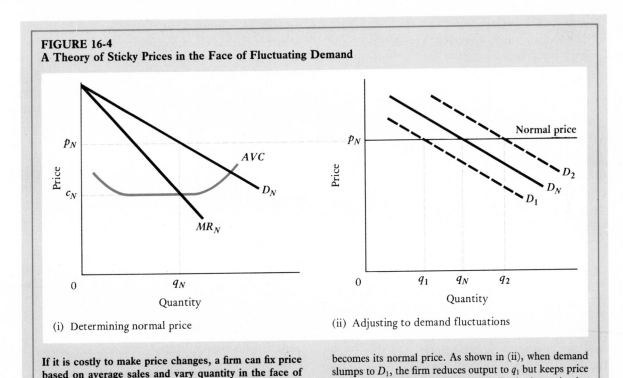

(i) Determining normal price

(ii) Adjusting to demand fluctuations

If it is costly to make price changes, a firm can fix price based on average sales and vary quantity in the face of fluctuating demand. In (i) the firm with normal capacity q_N and a normal (average) demand curve D_N sets p_N as the profit-maximizing price, where $MR = MC$. This price becomes its normal price. As shown in (ii), when demand slumps to D_1, the firm reduces output to q_1 but keeps price unchanged. When demand peaks at D_2, it also maintains prices and increases output to q_2.

the price that maximizes profits for average demand and then adjust output rather than price as demand varies over the cycle.

Implications of the theory. The behavior described has a number of other important implications.

1. As long as output remains within a range where the average cost curve is flat, the price charged tends to be a relatively fixed markup over cost. Thus the notion of a normal price is consistent with "normal markups" of the sort that led Hall and Hitch to their theory of sticky prices.
2. Cyclical fluctuations in demand are met by quantity adjustments rather than price adjustments.
3. Cost changes in either an upward or a downward direction are passed on through price changes (although possibly with a lag because oligopolistic firms find it costly to make continuous price changes).
4. Oligopolistic firms receive signals from the economy just as do perfectly competitive firms. But the form the signals take is different. While market changes are signaled to perfect competitors by a price change, oligopolies receive their signals about changes in market conditions from a change in their volume of sales.

The second and the third implications are especially important when we study some current controversies in macroeconomics. We shall return to them in Chapter 39.

Longer-Run Theories of Oligopoly Behavior

The discussion above concentrated on the short-run pricing decisions of oligopolistic firms. We now consider how these prices are set, and this raises the most critical aspect of oligopoly: firms know that they have identifiable rivals whose behavior they cannot afford to neglect. If Macy's watches Gimbels, so too does Gimbels watch Macy's.

An oligopolistic firm's price and output decisions depend on how it *thinks* its competitors will react to its moves, and the outcome of its policy depends on how they *do* in fact react. Under these circumstances there is no simple set of rules for the equilibrium either of the firm or of the small group of firms that constitutes the industry. Neither is there a set of simple predictions about how the firms will react, either individually or collectively, to changes in such things as taxes, costs, and market demand.[8]

In the face of this complexity, economists have sometimes proposed simplifying models, and sometimes turned to empirical findings to suggest generalizations. We shall look at examples of each.

Cournot-Nash Equilibrium

A pathbreaking attack on the oligopoly problem occurred as long ago as 1838 in the work of the French economist A. A. Cournot. He dealt with the special case of an industry containing only two firms, called a **duopoly.** The two firms sold an identical product. Cournot assumed that each firm chose its profit-maximizing output on the assumption that the other firm would hold its own output constant. He then showed that if each firm in turn adjusted to the last move made by its competitor (on the assumption that the competitor would make no further move), a stable equilibrium would be reached in which the market was divided between the two firms in a definite way. Each firm would charge the same price as the other, and that price would be higher than the perfectly competitive price but lower than the price a monopolist would charge. This finding established oligopoly as a truly intermediate case between perfect competition and monopoly.

---

[8] It is often said that, under these circumstances, price and output are *indeterminate*. Such a statement is misleading since the price and output do, of course, get determined somehow. What is meant, however, is that, under oligopoly, price and output are not uniquely determined by the same factors as in large-group cases. In small-group cases an additional set of factors—competitors' real and imagined reactions to each other's behavior—contributes to the determination of price and output.

Firms in the situation analyzed by Cournot will raise price and lower output when costs rise, and they will usually raise price and raise output when demand increases. Thus changes in price and quantity are in the same direction as under perfect competition, though the magnitude of the changes will be different.

The equilibrium Cournot analyzed has survived in modern theorizing. It is now called a **Nash equilibrium** or a **Cournot-Nash equilibrium.** It is the equilibrium that results when each firm makes its decisions on the assumption that all other firms' behavior will be unchanged.

Nash equilibria can be determined for many oligopolistic situations. Their properties can be compared with the equilibria that would result from perfect competition and from monopoly (usually, higher prices and lower output than under competition; lower prices and higher output than under monopoly). The price-quantity differences can also be studied when equilibrium changes under the impact of shifts in input costs or demand for the industry's output.

To many economists the Cournot-Nash assumption that each firm takes its rival's behavior as given seems simply wrong in a great many small-group situations. The Ford Motor Company knows (or quickly learns) that if it slashes the prices of some of its cars, GM, Chrysler, and American Motors will react by adjusting their prices on comparable cars. Similar considerations apply when General Mills considers changing the advertising for one of its breakfast cereals or Lever Brothers the prices of its soaps.

Thus not only must an oligopolistic firm be concerned with how *buyers* of its products will react to changes it makes, it must anticipate how each of a few identified rival *sellers* will react.

Conjectural Variations

Economists dealing with oligopoly next broadened the Cournot approach by assuming that each firm recognized its interdependence with its rivals and made its decisions subject to what are called *conjectural variations.* A firm making, say, a price decision conjectures what variations its choice would induce its rivals to make in their prices and takes those variations into account in its decisions.

One problem with this approach is that a wide range of conjectural variations is possible. For example, firm A might assume that whatever price it sets, its rivals will set the same price. Or it might assume that its rivals will undercut any price it charges. Equilibrium can be shown to exist for many conjectural variations. Unfortunately there is almost no end to the possible patterns of conjectural variation or the range of outcomes that is possible. Unless one knows that one set of conjectural variations is the way firms "really think," one cannot predict actual behavior.

Additional Problems for Industries Producing Differentiated Products

All the difficulties mentioned above arise even for oligopolists selling homogeneous products. Another set of oligopoly problems arises when firms sell differentiated products. For example, one brand of cigarettes sold by the American Tobacco Company differs not only from all other brands sold by that company but from all brands sold by competing companies. With differentiated products, each product is distinct from every other product, and firms can use quality changes, advertising, and multiple products as competitive weapons. This added complexity means that (so far as pure theory is concerned) almost anything is possible under conditions of oligopoly. This is not very helpful in dealing with real-world situations.

Empirically Based Approaches to Oligopolistic Behavior

Because the oligopoly problem is so complex, some economists have sought to build a theory from observations of the behavior of oligopolistic firms. These economists believe that we need to begin with detailed knowledge of the actual behavior of such firms. The knowledge is then used to narrow the range of theoretically possible cases by selecting those that actually occur.

In this section we shall describe one major empirically based hypothesis about oligopoly behavior and then describe briefly a number of subsidiary hypotheses concerning forces that pull in opposite directions.

The Hypothesis of Qualified Joint Profit Maximization

While explicit collusion is illegal in the United States, why cannot a small group of firms that recognize their interdependence simply act in a common manner? Such tacit collusion has been called *quasi-agreement* by Professor William Fellner. If all firms behave as though they were branches of a single firm, they can achieve the ends of a monopolist by adopting price and output policies that will maximize their *collective* (joint) *profits*. Every firm is interested, however, in *its own* profits, not the industry's profits, and it may pay one firm to depart from the joint profit-maximizing position, if, by so doing, it can increase its share of the profits.

The hypothesis of qualified joint profit maximization thus rests on the notion that a firm in an oligopolistic industry responds to *two* sets of influences.

Any oligopolistic firm wants to cooperate with its rivals to maximize their joint profits; it also wants to receive as large a share of the profits as possible.

Consider the conflicting pressures on an oligopolistic firm when it chooses its price. First, if firms in a group recognize that they are interdependent and face a downward-sloping demand curve, they will recognize that their joint profits depend on the price that each of them charges. This pulls each firm to cooperate with its rivals in charging the same price that a single firm would charge if it monopolized the industry.

Second, despite this pull, an aggressive seller may hope to gain more than its rivals by being the first to cut price below the monopoly level. But if it does this, other firms may follow and the total profits earned in the industry will fall as prices are pushed below their joint profit-maximizing level.

A firm that initiates such a price-cutting strategy must balance what it expects to gain by securing a larger *share* of the profits against what it expects to lose because there will be a smaller total of profits to go around.

The hypothesis of qualified joint profit maximization is that the relative strength of the two tendencies (toward and away from joint profit maximization) varies from industry to industry in a systematic way that may be associated with observable characteristics of firms, markets, and products.

Let us consider some examples.

Some Specific Hypotheses About Oligopolistic Behavior

1. The tendency toward joint maximization is greater for small numbers of sellers than for larger numbers. Here the argument concerns both ability and motivation. When there are few firms, they will know that there is no chance that any one of them can gain sales without inducing retaliation by its rivals. At the same time, a smaller number of firms can tacitly coordinate their policies with less difficulty than a larger number.

2. The tendency toward joint maximization is greater for producers of very similar products than for producers of sharply differentiated products. The argument here is that the more nearly identical the products of sellers, the closer will be the direct rivalry for customers and the less the ability of one firm to gain a decisive advantage over its rivals. Thus, other things being equal, such sellers will prefer joint efforts to achieve a larger pie to individual attempts to take customers away from each other.

3. The tendency toward joint maximization is greater in a growing than in a contracting industry. The argument here is that when demand is growing, firms can utilize their capacity fully without resorting to attempts to "steal" their rivals' customers. In contrast, when firms have excess capacity, they are tempted to give discounts or secret price concessions in order to pick up customers. Eventually their rivals will retaliate, and large price cuts may become general.

4. The tendency toward joint maximization is greater when the industry contains a dominant firm rather than a set of more or less equal competitors. A dominant firm may become a **price leader,** which is a firm that sets the industry's price while all other firms fall into line. If a dominant firm knows that it really is a price leader, it can set the monopoly price, confident that all other firms will follow it. Indeed the dominant firm may be able to gain a disproportionate share of the industry's profits by setting an output that all other firms accept as given. But even if a dominant firm is not automatically a price leader, other firms may look to it for judgment about market conditions, and its decisions become a tentative focus for quasi-agreement.

5. Tacit price fixing to maximize joint profits will cause nonprice competition that will take the industry away from its joint maximizing position. The argument here is that when firms seek to suppress their basic rivalry by agreeing, tacitly or explicitly, not to engage in price competition, rivalry will break out in other forms. Firms then seek to maintain or increase their market shares through massive advertising, quality changes, the establishment of new products, bonuses, give-aways, and a host of other schemes for gaining at the expense of their rivals while leaving the list prices of products unchanged.

6. The tendency toward joint profit maximizing is greater, the greater are the barriers to entry of new firms. The high profits of existing firms will attract new entrants, who will drive down price and reduce profits. The greater the barriers to entry, the less this will occur. Thus the greater the entry barriers, the closer the profits of existing firms can be to their joint maximizing level. Such barriers to entry may be natural or created by the firm. Perhaps the most important empirical observation about actual oligopoly behavior is the critical importance of what Professor Joe S. Bain called the *condition of entry.* It is worth a closer look.

Barriers to Entry

Suppose firms in an oligopolistic industry succeed in raising prices above long-run average total costs so that economic profits are earned. Why do these profits not cause further firms to enter the industry? Why does entry not continue until the extra output forces price down to the level where only the opportunity cost of capital is being earned (i.e., economic profits are zero)?

The answer lies in *barriers to entry,* which are anything that puts new firms that wish to enter an industry at a significant competitive disadvantage relative to existing firms in the industry. Barriers are of three sorts: natural barriers, barriers created by the firms already in the industry, and barriers created by government policy. We discuss the first two in this chapter.

Natural Barriers

Natural barriers to entry may result from an interaction between market size—as shown by the market demand curve—and economies of scale—as shown by the firm's long-run average total cost curve (*LRATC*).

One type of natural barrier depends on the shape of the *LRATC* curve and in particular on what is called **minimum efficient scale (*MES*).** This term refers to the smallest size firm that can reap all the available economies of large scale.

Suppose the technology of an industry is such that the typical firm's *MES* is 10,000 units a week at an *ATC* of $10 per unit and that at a price of $10 the total quantity demanded is 30,000 units per week. Clearly there is room for no more than three plants of efficient size—and hence three firms at most will serve this market. The industry will naturally tend to be oligopolistic. Even if these firms tacitly agree to reduce output to 9,000 units each and raise price, there is not room for an additional firm.

Natural barriers to entry occur when the output at which *MES* is achieved is large relative to total demand.

Under these circumstances a small number of existing firms may earn profits without inducing a further firm to enter the market.

A second type of natural cost barrier occurs when there are **absolute cost advantages.** This means that existing firms have average cost curves that are significantly lower over their entire range than those of potential new entrants. Among possible sources of such an advantage are control of crucial patents or resources, knowledge that comes only from "learning by doing" in the industry, and established credit ratings that permit advantageous purchasing and borrowing. Each of these may be regarded as only a temporary disadvantage of new firms, which, given time, might develop their own know-how, patents, and satisfactory credit ratings.

This kind of barrier, however, makes it possible for existing firms to charge a price such that although existing firms earn profits, new entrants may face losses for some time after entry. This price is known as a **limit price.** The early losses, which persist until the new firms' *ATC*s fall to the level of the going price, can make entry seem sufficiently unprofitable—in spite of the expectation of later profits—to prevent entry.

Firm-created Barriers to Entry

If natural entry barriers do not exist, oligopolistic firms can earn long-run economic profits only if they can create barriers that prevent their profits from attracting new entrants into the industry. Product proliferation and brand-image advertising can be used to create substantial barriers to entry where natural barriers are weak.

To the extent that these practices raise entry barriers, they allow existing firms to move in the direction of joint profit maximization without fear of a flood of new entrants attracted by the high profits.

Brand proliferation. Many products have several characteristics, each of which can be varied over a wide range. Thus there is room for a large number of similar products, each with a somewhat different mix of characteristics. Consider the many different kinds of breakfast cereals or cars. The multiplicity of brands is in part a response to consumers' tastes. If you doubt this, try to persuade a sports car addict to switch to a standard four-door sedan, or try to get a lover of Granola to switch to Sugar Puffs, or try to make all the members of one family eat the same cereal every day of the week.

Product proliferation can also serve as a barrier to entry. Because there are some economies of scale in producing every differentiated product, an infinite variety cannot be provided. Even though a small group of consumers could be found who would prefer each of 10,000 different breakfast cereals, their demands would not be large enough to cover the costs of production. Thus there is room in the market for perhaps only 50 or 60 brands rather than a few thousand. By producing many kinds of cars, cereals, or soaps and adding new ones whenever demand either increases or shifts toward a different mix of characteristics, existing firms can make it more difficult for new firms selling a differentiated product to enter the industry.

Having many differentiated products confers other advantages on existing firms. If the product is one in which consumers switch brands frequently, then increasing the number of brands sold by existing firms will reduce the expected sales of a new entrant. Say that an industry contains three large firms, each selling one brand of cigarettes, and say that 30 percent of all smokers choose brands in a random fashion each year. If a new firm enters the industry, it can expect to pick up 25 percent of these smokers (it has one brand out of a total of four available brands). This would give it 7.5 percent (25 percent of 30 percent) of the total market the first year merely as a result of picking up its share of the random switchers, and it would keep increasing its share year by year thereafter.[9] If, however, the existing three firms had five brands each, there would be fifteen brands already available and a new small firm selling one new brand could expect to pick up only one-sixteenth of the

_____

[9] Because it is smaller than its rivals, it will lose fewer customers to them by random switching than it will gain from them.

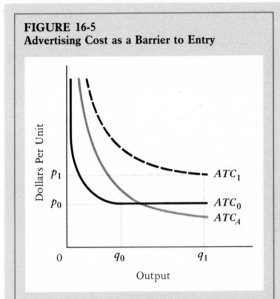

FIGURE 16-5
Advertising Cost as a Barrier to Entry

Large advertising costs can increase the *MES* of production and thereby increase entry barriers. The ATC_0 curve shows that the *MES* without advertising is at q_0. The curve ATC_A shows that advertising cost per unit falls as output rises. Advertising increases total cost to ATC_1 and raises *MES* to q_1. Advertising has given a scale advantage to large sellers and has thus created a barrier to entry.

brand switchers, giving it less than 2 percent of the total market the first year, and its gains in subsequent years would also be less.

The fact that brand proliferation creates entry barriers helps explain an apparent paradox of everyday industrial life: the fact that one firm sells multiple brands of the same product, which often compete directly against one another. The soap and cigarette industries provide classic examples of this behavior.

Advertising. The heavy levels of advertising in differentiated oligopolistic industries are also to be understood in part on the basis of entry barriers. Suppose there are few scale economies so that a new firm can reach minimum costs at an output that is low relative to total industry output. Thus

there are only weak natural barriers to entry. (This is the case, for example, in the cigarette and soap industries.) Existing firms can create entry barriers by imposing fixed costs on new entrants. These fixed costs raise the *MES* of all firms, including new entrants.

Advertising is one such policy. Where there is much effective brand-image advertising, a new firm will have to spend a great deal on advertising its product in order to bring it to the public's attention. If the firm's sales are small, advertising costs *per unit sold* will be very large. Only when sales are large, so that the advertising costs can be spread over a large number of units, will costs per unit be brought down to a level low enough that they will not confer a significant competitive disadvantage on the new firm.

Figure 16-5 illustrates how heavy advertising can shift the cost curves of a firm with a low *MES* to make it one with a high *MES*. In essence, what happens is that a scale advantage of advertising is added to a low *MES* of production with the result that the overall *MES* is raised. Thus a new entrant who must both produce and advertise finds itself at a substantial cost disadvantage relative to its established rivals.

A firm with no natural entry barriers may be able to create them by use of nonprice competition. Advertising of course does things other than create barriers to entry. Among them, it may perform the useful function of informing buyers about their alternatives, thereby making markets work more smoothly. Indeed, a new firm may find that advertising is essential, even when existing firms do not advertise at all, simply to call attention to its entry into an industry where it is unknown.

Two further kinds of firm-created barriers to entry are considered in the box on page 272.

Oligopoly and Resource Allocation

Firms in oligopolistic markets (as well as monopolies) administer their prices. The market signaling system works slightly differently when prices are determined by the market than when they are

DISCOURAGING ENTRY: PREDATORY PRICING AND PREEMPTIVE EXPANSION

In addition to natural barriers to entry of new firms and barriers created by nonprice competition, there are other ways of discouraging potential entrants. Some are plainly illegal, such as hiring thugs to "persuade" potential rivals to stay away. This method is not uncommon in industries that are controlled by criminals. Others are more genteel—and if they are illegal it is under antitrust laws, not as ordinary crimes. Consider two.

Predatory Pricing

A firm that is considering entry will not do so if faced with certain losses after entry. One way existing firms can create such a situation is to cut prices to—or below—cost whenever entry occurs and keep them there until the entrant goes bankrupt. The existing firms sacrifice profits while doing so, but they send a discouraging message to future as well as present potential rivals.

There is much controversy concerning predatory pricing. Some economists argue that pricing policies that appear to be predatory can be explained by other motives and that existing firms only hurt themselves when they engage in such practices instead of reaching an accommodation with new entrants. Others argue that predatory pricing seems to have been observed and that it is in the long-run interests of existing firms to punish new entrants even when it is costly to do so in the short run.

Whatever the outcome of this debate among economists, the courts have taken the position that predatory pricing does occur. A number of firms have been convicted of using it in restraint of trade.

Preemptive Expansion

Suppose three firms are in an expanding market. Suppose also that the industry demand curve is shifting outward at a rate such that there will be room for each of three existing firms to open one more plant operating at *MES* every four years, beginning in 1985. If the firms were not worried about entry, each would build a new plant in 1985, 1989, and so on. But faced with this strategy, a new firm could build a plant in 1984 or 1988, and so on—and thus be in possession of a market when the new plant became profitable a year later. The investment in fixed capital represents a commitment to the market. The first three new plants that get built will have preempted the new part of the market, and it will not pay anyone else to build yet another plant because four new plants would all lose money.

In order to prevent this from happening, existing firms will be tempted to build their new plants long before the demand expands enough for them to be operated at a profit. Once the plant is built, it will not pay a new firm to build a further plant, and the existing firms will remain in possession of the market when demand expands sufficiently to allow the new plant to cover its costs. Existing firms may well be in a much stronger position to expand in anticipation of future demand than potential new firms. This type of entry-preventing strategy—building new capacity to serve an expanding market before it is needed—has been alleged to occur in several oligopoly and monopoly situations.

administered. Changes in the market conditions for both inputs and outputs are signaled to the perfectly competitive firm by changes in the *prices* of its inputs and its outputs. Changes in the market conditions for inputs are signaled to the oligopolist by changes in the prices of its inputs. Changes in the market conditions for the oligopolist's product are typically signaled, however, by a change in sales at the administered price.

The oligopolist that administers its price gets a signal when the demand for its product changes, the signal taking the form of a variation in its sales.

Rises in costs of inputs will shift cost curves upward, and oligopolistic firms will be led—if the shift is not reversed—to raise price and lower output. Rises in demand will cause the sales of oligopolistic firms to rise. Firms will then respond by increasing output, thereby increasing the quantities of society's resources that are allocated to producing that commodity.

The market system reallocates resources in response to changes in demand and costs in roughly the same way under oligopoly as it does under perfect competition.

Although the market system allocates resources under oligopoly in a manner that is qualitatively similar to what happens under perfect competition, the actual allocation is not likely to be the same. Generally, oligopolistic industries will earn profits and will charge prices that exceed marginal cost (because the firms face downward-sloping demand curves and will equate marginal cost to marginal revenue, not to price). In this respect oligopoly is similar to monopoly.

There is a wide range of oligopolistic behavior. Some oligopolies succeed in coming close to the sort of joint profit maximization that would characterize monopoly. Others compete so intensely among themselves that they approximate competitive prices and outputs. The allocative consequences vary accordingly.

In some respects, oligopolistic industries differ from either perfect competition or monopoly: they may exhibit more price rigidity, more advertising, and more product differentiation. There may also be some tendency for more nonprice competition than consumers want.

Oligopoly is an important market structure in today's economy because there are many industries where the *MES* is simply too large to support a perfectly competitive market. Oligopoly will not, in general, achieve the optimal allocative efficiency of perfect competition. Rivalrous oligopoly, however, may produce more satisfactory results than monopoly. The defense of oligopoly as a market form is that it may be the best of the available alternatives where the *MES* is large. The challenge to public policy is to keep oligopolists competing. Public policies that have this objective are discussed in Chapter 18.

SUMMARY

1. A review of the structure of the American economy shows that while there are both large-firm and small-firm sectors, most of the industries involved do not conform descriptively to the models of either perfect competition or monopoly. Firms are not price takers, but engage in rivalrous behavior. Understanding their behavior requires additional forms of market structure.

2. In market structures other than perfect competition, firms tend to administer prices and accept the quantities they can sell at those prices. Changes in market conditions are signaled not by the prices they receive but by the quantities they can sell.

3. Monopolistic competition is a market structure in which firms sell a differentiated product. Large-group monopolistic competition does not seem to apply to a significant number of industries in today's world. The theory was, however, extremely important in the development of economics, and the term is used today to deal with the theory of markets involving differentiated products.

4. Differentiated products abound, but generally they are produced in industries that contain a small number of firms each one of which sells many such products. This is small-group oligopoly.

5. The basic characteristics of oligopoly are (a) the firms in an industry are sufficiently few so that they recognize they are interdependent; (b) anything that one firm does will probably lead to a reaction by rival sellers; (c) typically, entry is neither perfectly free nor entirely blockaded.

6. A key empirical finding about oligopolistic industries is that short-run cost curves tend to be very flat over a substantial range of output. This reflects the decision of firms to build plants capable of being operated over a range of outputs at roughly constant marginal cost to keep average costs low in the face of fluctuating output.

7. A second important empirical finding is the relative stickiness of oligopoly prices in response to seasonal and cyclical fluctuations in output. This stickiness results from a combination of the flat short-run cost curves and the costs involved in changing administered prices frequently. While prices are changed when the firms' costs change, or in response to permanent shifts in demand, oligopolistic firms find it profitable to accept output fluctuations while keeping prices fixed, as demand fluctuates around normal levels.

8. Turning to longer range considerations, there is no simple set of predictions about the outcome of oligopolistic situations. Everything depends on the strategies adopted by the various rivals. Therefore, instead of a single theory, there are many possible patterns of behavior to understand, explain, and predict. A very general hypothesis of qualified joint profit maximization says that firms which recognize that they are rivals will be motivated by two sets of opposing forces, one set moving them toward joint profit maximization and the other moving them away from it.

9. In order to suggest how observable variables such as size and number of sellers, nature of the product, and conditions of demand may influence the two sets of opposing forces, six specific hypotheses are suggested. The list is illustrative of a much larger list that might be provided.

10. Oligopolies persist because of barriers to entry, which may be natural or created. Natural barriers include large minimum efficient scales and absolute cost advantages. Firm-created barriers include advertising and brand proliferation.

11. Under oligopoly the price system works to reallocate resources in response to changes in demand and costs in qualitatively the same way as it does under perfect competition. Oligopoly may not be as efficient as perfect competition, but it is responsive to major changes in economic conditions.

TOPICS FOR REVIEW

Concentration ratios
Administered prices
Product differentiation
Saucer-shaped short-run average costs
Sticky prices
Conjectural variations
Barriers to entry
Minimum efficient scale

DISCUSSION QUESTIONS

1. Is the consumer benefited by lower prices, by higher quality, by more product variety, by advertising? If trade-offs are necessary (more of one means less of another), how would you evaluate their relative importance with respect to the following products?
   a. vitamin pills
   b. beer
   c. cement
   d. bath soap
   e. women's dresses
   f. television programs
   g. prescription drugs
2. White sidewall tires cost about $1 per tire more to manufacture than black sidewall tires, and they lower somewhat the durability of tires. At the retail level the extra cost of a white sidewall tire is at least $5 per tire. Yet 70 percent of all passenger car tires manufactured in the United States in 1983 were the white sidewalls. What, if anything, do these facts tell you about the market structure of the manufacture, distribution, or marketing of automobile tires? If white sidewalls are found to be somewhat more likely to suffer blowouts, should their use be prohibited by law?

3. It is sometimes said that there are more drugstores and gasoline stations than are needed. In what sense might that be correct? Does the consumer gain anything from this plethora of retail outlets? How would you determine the optimal number of movie theaters or gasoline stations in a city of 100,000 people?

4. Are any of the following industries monopolistically competitive? Explain your answer.
   a. textbook publishing (fact: there are over 50 elementary economics textbooks in use somewhere in the United States this year)
   b. college education
   c. cigarette manufacture
   d. restaurant operation
   e. automobile retailing

5. It has been estimated that if automobile companies did not change models for 10 years, the cost of production would be reduced by approximately 30 percent. In view of this fact, why are there annual model changes? Which, if any, of the reasons you have suggested depend on the industry's being oligopolistic? Should frequent model changes be forbidden by law?

6. Compare and contrast the effects on the automobile and the wheat industries of each of the following.
   a. the effect of a large rise in demand on quantity sold
   b. the effect of a large rise in costs on price
   c. the effect on price of a temporary cut in supplies coming to market due to a three-month rail strike
   d. the effect on price and quantity sold of a rush of cheap foreign imports
   e. the effects of a large rise in the price of one of the industry's important imports

In the light of your answers discuss general ways in which oligopolistic industries fulfill the same general functions as do perfectly competitive industries.

7. Some analysts of the beer industry believe that the big national companies are going to get bigger and the smaller companies will disappear relatively rapidly. Their reasoning is that big national brewers have decisive advantages over local and regional brewers. What are these analysts assuming about the cost conditions in the beer industry? Is this assumption consistent with the report by *Fortune* which indicated that a small regional brewery has higher labor productivity than the newest but larger plant of Anheuser Busch? If the efficient size of *plant* in the industry is small, might there be reasons to expect multiplant firms to predominate?

8. Many people in advertising have thought that economists, with their emphasis on efficiency in the allocation of resources, have not been duly appreciative of the role of advertising in influencing consumer preferences. What roles does economic analysis give to advertising? Which are regarded as improving resource allocation and which as worsening it?

9. Does the relative stickiness of oligopoly prices mean that oligopolists are not profit maximizers? Suppose it could be shown that oligopolists changed prices less frequently than did monopolists faced with the same fluctuations of demand. What interpretation would you suggest?

17 PRICE THEORY IN ACTION: BOYCOTTS, CARTELS, OPEC, AND THE POWER OF COMPETITION

Price theory helps us to understand and to make predictions about things that are reported in the newspapers every day: the effect of a grain shortage on the price of chicken feed, for example, or the increased use of car pools and smaller cars when gasoline became hard to find and its price rose. In this chapter we apply price theory to some real-world situations. In the first section the effects of boycotts are examined. In the following section the theories of monopoly and perfect competition are used to study how producers in competitive industries often try, through collective action, to obtain monopolistic profits but fail to do so perfectly. In the third section we examine the successes and limits of OPEC, once described as the world's most successful cartel.

BOYCOTTS AND THEIR EFFECT ON MARKET PRICE

A **boycott** is defined by the dictionary as the process of "engaging in a concerted refusal to have anything to do with something or someone." Boycotts for political, social, and economic ends are familiar. Blacks in the early years of the civil rights movement boycotted segregated buses; President Carter called for a boycott of the 1980 Moscow Olympic Games in order to express American concern over Soviet aggression in Afghanistan.

Many boycotts are intended to have their effect through economic harm imposed on the targets. Some women's groups urged convention boycotts of states that did not ratify the Equal Rights Amendment in order to hurt the industries of those states and thus generate political support for their cause. Consumers have been urged to boycott grapes and lettuce by farm unions seeking to put pressure on the producers who were their employers. A meat boycott in the mid 1970s was designed to bring down the price of meat. In 1980 automobile workers urged a boycott of foreign-made automobiles in an effort to force Japanese manufacturers to use American assembly plants, rather than ship completed cars assembled by Japanese workers in Japan.

There are also sellers' boycotts. When producers of milk or cattle or oil attempt to withhold their products from the market, they too are trying, through a concerted refusal to sell, to influence market results.

A boycott is an attempt to shift to the left the demand or supply curve of a product. If successful, a buyers' boycott will shift the demand curve, a sellers' boycott will shift the supply curve.

A Buyers' Boycott

Consider, as an example of a strictly economic boycott, an organized attempt of consumers' groups to "do something" about the very high and rapidly rising price of meat. With rising meat prices, boycotts are talked about every couple of years; such a boycott was actually attempted in 1973.

The background to the 1973 meat boycott was the rising trend in meat consumption, which led to a steady rightward shift of the demand curve for meat. Quantity supplied was also increasing, but as meat production rose, the costs of factors of production also rose. The rising costs led to rising prices. For a while all this occurred gradually, with average meat prices rising by 2 percent to 5 percent per year. Then, in 1972, the pace of price changes suddenly accelerated. A worldwide grain shortage caused the price of cattle feed to escalate, shifting up costs (and supply curves) of cattle and meat production.

Continuing rightward shifts in the demand curve, combined with a sharp leftward shift of the supply curve, are predicted to lead to sharply rising prices. This is precisely what happened. Prices of meat increased at a rate of 5 percent *a month* between December 1972 and the following March. They were a major contributing factor as food prices rose at a rate unprecedented in the memories of most Americans.

A meat boycott was organized in response. Americans were urged not to buy meat, starting the first week in April, in order to force prices down. On April 2, the boycott began. The *New York Times* applauded the action editorially on April 3:

Never underestimate the power of the embattled consumer. . . . Millions of Americans are seeking—almost spontaneously—to impose their own discipline on the marketplace by refusing to buy steak, chops or other cuts of meat at the present wildly inflated prices.

Consider this boycott in terms of the competitive theory of supply and demand. See Figure 17-1. Suppose first that housewives reduced permanently their purchases of meat and supply curves remained the same. The decrease in demand would lead to a leftward shift in the demand curve and a decrease in price. This is what the boycott leaders wanted. The effect would last as long as the new level of demand and the old supply curve applied.

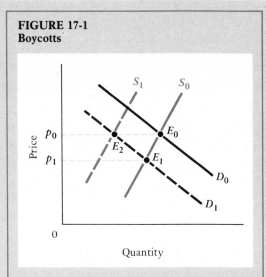

FIGURE 17-1
Boycotts

A buyers' boycott shifts the demand curve leftward;
a sellers' boycott shifts the supply curve leftward.
Buyers' boycott. With equilibrium at E_0, a buyers' boycott shifts the demand curve from D_0 to D_1, and price
falls from p_0 to p_1. When the boycott ends, unless
people's tastes have changed, demand returns to D_0,
and prices will again rise to p_0.
Sellers' boycott. With equilibrium at E_1, a shift in
the supply curve to S_1 will cause price to rise from p_1
back to p_0. When the boycott ends, unless producers
have changed their production plans, price falls back
to p_1.
Buyers' and sellers' boycott. With equilibrium at E_0,
suppose buyers impose a boycott and sellers retaliate.
Demand and supply shift to D_1 and S_1. Equilibrium
shifts from E_0 to E_2. It is quantity exchanged, not
price, that is greatly changed.

But while boycotts are easily started, they are less
easily sustained. What would happen if, after
prices fell, consumers ended their boycott and re-
sumed their purchasing at the old rate? Demand
would increase, and prices would go back up.

A temporary consumers' boycott can bring temporary
price reductions. For a permanent effect on price, the
boycott must produce a permanent reduction in demand.

The 1973 buyers' boycott of meat did not even
produce very large short-run price reductions be-

cause meat producers countered with a sellers' boycott.

A Sellers' Boycott

If sellers withhold part of their supply, the supply
curve will shift to the left and price will rise for as
long as the smaller supply is provided. This too is
shown in Figure 17-1.

In responding to the buyers' boycott of 1973,
many cattle ranchers expected the consumers' boycott to be short-lived. They held cattle off the
market in anticipation of the end of the boycott
and urged other ranchers to do the same. They did
not want to sell, at a low price, cattle that could
be kept on the ranch for a few extra weeks and
sold later at a higher price.

This temporary withholding of meat (which was
in effect a sellers' boycott) shifted the supply curve
to the left.

Indeed, within two weeks the reduction in supply was large enough to offset the reduction in
demand and to restore prices to their pre-boycott
levels. In the short run, the boycott and withholding led to a decrease in both demand and supply
and no reduction in price. Whatever the psychological benefits to either party, neither had gained.
While the boycott lasted, ranchers sold and households ate less meat than they had before the boycott.

Boycotts are attempts, usually sporadic, to limit
the quantity purchased or sold of a product. Monopolists seek a limited but long-term reduction in
quantities produced in order to raise prices above
competitive levels. Thus a sellers' boycott is similar
to monopoly output restriction in that each is an
attempt to move up and to the left along the market
demand curve by restricting supply.

PROBLEMS IN ATTEMPTS
TO MONOPOLIZE COMPETITIVE
INDUSTRIES

Sellers of goods and services often seek collective
action to raise what they consider excessively low

prices. Cocoa producers in west Africa, wheat producers in the United States and Canada, the Organization of Petroleum Exporting Countries (OPEC), coffee growers in Brazil, taxi drivers in many cities, and labor unions throughout the world have all sought to obtain, through collective action, some of the benefits of departing from perfectly competitive situations. Basically they have sought to form organizations to regulate the price and output of the goods or services they supply.

The motive behind this drive for monopoly power is easy to understand. The equilibrium position of a perfectly competitive industry is one in which a restriction of output and a consequent increase in price will always increase the profits of all producers. This is particularly obvious when (as is so often the case with agricultural goods) the demand for the product is inelastic at the equilibrium price; then marginal revenue is negative. Because marginal cost is positive, since it surely costs something to produce every extra unit, a reduction in output will not only raise the total revenues of producers, it will also reduce total costs.

It is equally true that the industry's profits can always be increased, even if demand is elastic at the competitive equilibrium price. At such an equilibrium, each firm is producing where marginal cost equals price. Because the market demand curve slopes downward, the industry's marginal revenue is less than price—and thus less than marginal cost. Therefore, in competitive equilibrium, the last unit sold necessarily contributes more to the industry's costs than to its revenue.

In a perfectly competitive industry, profits will increase if the producers enter into an effective agreement to restrict output.

The big "if" is the ability to form and maintain an *effective* agreement. A **cartel** is an organization of producers designed to eliminate competition among its members, usually by restricting output. OPEC is the best known cartel of modern times, and for a time it was the most effective. It was successful because (1) it could prevent large-scale cheating, (2) it was supported by a large fraction of the world's oil producers, (3) its product had an

inelastic demand in the short term, and (4) entry of new large-scale competitors into oil production was difficult.

That each of these conditions was important to OPEC's success is illustrated in the following sections, where we see what happens when these conditions are *not* met. Then we will return to a closer examination of OPEC itself.

Cheating: The Instability of Cartels

A **producers' cooperative** or co-op is a joint selling organization for a group of producers. Such a co-op often acts as a cartel and attempts to reduce the output of a commodity by getting each producing firm to agree to restrict its output. While there is an incentive under perfect competition for all producers to enter into such an agreement, there is also an incentive for each producer to violate it.

To see how this would happen, consider a producers' cooperative that raises prices by cutting production. Suppose that every firm except one restricts its output. That one firm will be doubly well off in that it can sell its original output at the new, higher price received by all other firms that have restricted their production. But the same is true for *each* firm.

A co-op organized mainly to restrict output is subject to competing pressures, illustrated in Figure 17-2. Each of the firms is better off if the co-op is formed and is effective; but each firm is even better off if every other firm plays ball while only it does not. Yet if everyone cheats (or stays out of the co-op), everyone will be worse off.

Cartels tend to be unstable because of the incentives for individual producers to violate output quotas.

The history of schemes to raise farm incomes by limiting crops bears ample testimony to the accuracy of this prediction. Crop restriction agreements often break down, and prices fall, as individuals exceed their quotas. The great bitterness and occasional violence that is sometimes exhibited by members of crop restriction plans against non-

FIGURE 17-2
Cheating: The Dilemma of a Cartel Member

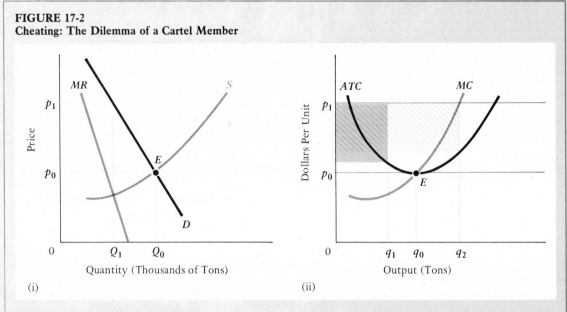

(i)

(ii)

All producers benefit when they restrict output; any one producer will benefit even more if others reduce output but it does not. Market conditions are represented in (i), conditions for an individual producer in (ii). (Note the change of scale.) Before the cartel is formed, the market is in competitive equilibrium at price p_0 and output Q_0, and the individual producer is producing output q_0 and just covering costs. A cartel is formed and reduces industry output to Q_1 by persuading each producer to produce only

q_1. This output, where supply equals marginal revenue, maximizes joint profits with price p_1. The individual producer earns profits shown by the shaded area.

Once price is raised to p_1, however, the individual producer would like to increase output to q_2 and thus earn the profits shown in the diagonally striped area. But if all producers try to increase their outputs, price will fall back toward p_0.

members and members who cheat is readily understandable.

Partial Participation: The Need to Control Industry Output

The previous discussion revealed the need to police the activities of members of any output-restricting scheme. Another well-documented case shows the problems that occur when the producers' organization covers only a small fraction of the total output in the industry.

In the late 1960s there were 72,000 dairy farmers in Wisconsin, of whom about 4,300 were members

of a militant group known as the National Farmers Organization. The NFO members controlled about 6 percent of the milk produced in the state. Angry about low milk prices and recognizing the inelasticity of the market demand curve, the NFO in 1967 proposed to withhold milk from the market. By dumping it in rivers, fields, and roads, they hoped to dramatize the plight of the dairy farmer and raise the price of milk by 20 percent. The elasticity of demand for milk is approximately 0.5; to achieve a 20 percent price increase would require a reduction in quantity sold of about 10 percent.

The NFO urged all farmers, whether members or not, to join them, but only members withheld supplies, and they withheld *all* their milk. During a three-week period, member farmers removed about 6 percent of the total usually supplied. If this withholding action had had the full effect predicted by the theory, given the elasticity of demand of 0.5, it would have raised prices by 12 percent and *benefited only the farmers who were continuing to produce,* not those who were dumping their milk. The participants lost an average of $400 each in the action. The action failed because the total response was too small and too unevenly shared.

Just as in the meat boycott, any increase in price would have persisted only as long as reduction in flow continued. Withholding milk for a week or three weeks and then resuming full production would at most drive prices up only until supply increased and brought them down.

A monopoly would seek to decrease the supply as a long-term policy. For a cartel to achieve the same results requires a long-term withholding. This could benefit the withholders only if a great majority of producers shared both in the withholding and in the production of what was sent to market. When the NFO failed to enlist the general support of milk producers, its attempt to raise the incomes of its members was doomed to fail.

Controlling New Competition: Restriction of Output in the Long Run

Even complete control over the output of existing producers of a given product will not be enough to sustain monopoly profits if new supplies of (or substitutes for) the cartel's product enter the market in response to the early success of the cartel. In the short run, a cartel or monopoly can restrict output, change prices far in excess of costs, and thus earn exceptional profits. But profits are the "carrot" of the free enterprise system, and no monopolist is immune to potential competition from those who want their share of the consumer's dollar. Consider some examples.

Competition from New Products

Keuffel & Esser had by the 1960s achieved a dominant position in the manufacture and sale of slide rules, an essential tool of the engineer and the applied scientist. Its dominant position and highly profitable operations were wiped out, not by a better slide rule, but by the pocket calculator. When first introduced in the early 1970s, pocket calculators were relatively expensive, often costing over $100. They were also relatively crude in their capabilities. Nonetheless they proved popular; sales and profits rose, and firms rushed to enter the lucrative new field. Competition led simultaneously to product improvement and price reduction. Today calculators that perform basic calculations can be bought for a few dollars, and sophisticated scientific and programmable pocket calculators can be bought for under $50. Few of today's college students have heard of Keuffel & Esser, but most know about Texas Instruments.

Similarly, during the 1980s, minicomputers for home and office are showing signs of sweeping away the markets of many currently important products and services. For instance, in-store computers are being used to answer customer questions and decrease the need for sales people. One day computers may even displace the college textbook.

Erosion of a Patent Monopoly

The very great power of the incentive to share in a monopoly profit, whether created by a successful cartel or in some other way, can be illustrated by the case of ball-point pens, where a legal monopoly was created by patent. A patent is designed to give its owner 17 years of protection from competition for an invention. That is the purpose, but it does not always work out that way.

In 1945, Milton Reynolds acquired a U.S. patent on a new type of pen that wrote with a ball bearing rather then a conventional nib. He formed the Reynolds International Pen Company, capitalized at $26,000, and began production on October 6, 1945.

The Reynolds pen was introduced with a good deal of fanfare by Gimbels, which guaranteed that the pen would write for two years without refilling. The price was set at $12.50 (the maximum price allowed by the wartime Office of Price Administration). Gimbels sold 10,000 pens on October 29, 1945, the first day they were on sale. In the early stages of production, the cost of production was estimated to be around $.80 per pen.

The Reynolds International Pen Company quickly expanded production. By early 1946 it employed more than 800 people in its factory and was producing 30,000 pens per day. By March 1946 it had $3 million in the bank.

Macy's, Gimbels' traditional rival, introduced an imported ball-point pen from South America. Its price was $19.98 (production costs unknown).

The heavy sales quickly elicited a response from other pen manufacturers. Eversharp introduced its first model in April, priced at $15. In July 1946 *Fortune* magazine reported that Sheaffer was planning to put out a pen at $15, and Eversharp announced its plan to produce a "retractable" model priced at $25. Reynolds introduced a new model but kept the price at $12.50. Costs were estimated at $.60 per pen.

The first signs of trouble emerged. The Ball Point Pen Company of Hollywood put a $9.95 model on the market, and a manufacturer named David Kahn announced plans to introduce a pen selling for less than $3. *Fortune* reported fears of an impending price war in view of the growing number of manufacturers and the low cost of production. In October, Reynolds introduced a new model, priced at $3.85, that cost about $.30 to produce.

By Christmas 1946 approximately 100 manufacturers were in production, some of them selling pens for as little as $2.98. By February 1947 Gimbels was selling a ball-point pen made by the Continental Pen Company for $.98. Reynolds introduced a new model priced to sell at $1.69, but Gimbels sold it for $.88 in a price war with Macy's. Reynolds felt betrayed by Gimbels. Reynolds introduced a new model listed at $.98. By this time, ball-point pens had become economy rather than luxury items but were still highly profitable.

In mid 1948 ball-point pens were selling for as little as $.39 and costing about $.10 to produce. In 1951 prices of $.25 were common. Within six years the power of the monopoly was gone forever. Ever since then the market has been saturated with a wide variety of models and prices of pens ranging from $.19 up. Their manufacture is only ordinarily profitable.

Control of Entry and Profits

The general lesson of the previous examples is concisely stated:

Unless producers can control entry, they cannot succeed in keeping earnings above the competitive level in the long run.

Another example is discussed in the box.

Of course there can still be very strong incentives to gain monopoly power and profits, even if the effort is sure to fail eventually. The lag between an original monopoly and its subsequent erosion by competition may be long enough to insure very large profits to the monopolist. It is estimated, for example, that Milton Reynolds earned profits as high as $500,000 *in a single month*—about 20 times his original investment, and Keuffel & Esser's founders were richly rewarded for their efforts. OPEC, as we shall see, amassed enormous profits for its members before its power began to be seriously eroded.

OPEC: CASE STUDY OF A CARTEL

In 1970 regular gasoline in Ann Arbor, Michigan, was selling for 29.9¢ a gallon. An enterprising shopper could almost always find a station within 30 miles where the price was in the low twenties owing to a local price war. American automobile manufacturers sold about 10 million new cars that year, mostly big fancy ones. Volkswagens and foreign sports cars (and other imports), while not unknown, especially on the two coasts, amounted to only 5 percent of the total cars sold in the United States.

Early in the 1980s regular gasoline in Ann Arbor, Michigan, was fluctuating between $1.20 and $1.49 a gallon. (Some of this increase since 1970 reflected inflation, but gasoline prices increased at nearly double the inflation rate over the 1970s.) There were many fewer gas stations than in 1970,

THE PRICE OF HAIRCUTS AND THE PROFITS OF BARBERS

Assume that there are many barber shops and freedom of entry into barbering: anyone who qualifies can set up as a barber. Assume that the going price for haircuts is $5 and that at this price all barbers believe their income is too low. The barbers hold a meeting and decide to form a trade association. They agree on the following points: First, all barbers in the city must join the association and abide by its rules; second, any new barbers who meet certain professional qualifications will be required to join the association before they are allowed to practice their trade; third, the association will recommend a price for haircuts that no barber shall undercut.

The barbers intend to raise the price of haircuts in order to raise their incomes. You are called in as a consulting economist to advise them of the probable success of their plan. Suppose you are persuaded that the organization does have the requisite strength to enforce a price rise to, say, $7. What are your predictions about the consequences?

You now need to distinguish between the short-run and the long-run effects of an increase in the price of haircuts. In the short run the number of barbers is fixed. Thus, in the short run, the answer depends only on the elasticity of the demand for haircuts.

If the demand elasticity is less than 1, total expenditure on haircuts will rise and so will the incomes of barbers; if demand elasticity exceeds 1, the barbers' revenues will fall. Thus you need some empirical knowledge about the elasticity of demand for haircuts.

Suppose on the basis of the best available evidence you estimate the elasticity of demand over the relevant price range to be 0.45. You then predict that barbers will be successful in raising incomes in the short run. A 40 percent rise in price will be met by an 18 percent fall in business, so the total revenue of the typical barber will rise by about 15 percent.*

Now what about the long run? If barbers were just covering costs before the price change, they will now be earning profits. Barbering will become an attractive trade relative to others requiring equal skill and training, and there will be a flow of barbers into the industry. As the number of barbers rises, the same amount of business must be shared among more and more barbers, so the typical barber will find business—and thus profits—decreasing. Profits may also be squeezed from another direction. With fewer customers coming their way, barbers may compete against one another for the limited number of customers. The association does not allow them to compete through price cuts, but they can compete in service. They may spruce up their shops, offer their customers expensive magazines to read, and so forth. This kind of competition will raise operating costs.

These changes will continue until barbers are just covering their opportunity costs, at which time the attraction for new entrants will vanish. The industry will settle down in a new long-run equilibrium in which individual barbers make incomes only as large as they did before the price rise. There will be more barbers than there were in the original situation, but each barber will be working for a smaller fraction of the day and will be idle for a larger fraction (the industry will have excess capacity). Barbers may prefer this situation; they will have more leisure. Customers may or may not prefer it: They will have shorter waits even at peak periods, and they will get to read a wide choice of magazines, but they will pay more for haircuts.

But you were hired to report to the barbers with respect to the effect on their incomes, not the effect on their leisure. The report that you finally present will thus say. "You will succeed in the short run (because you face a demand curve that is inelastic), but your plan is bound to be self-defeating in the long run unless you are able to prevent the entry of new barbers.

---

* Let p and q be the price and quantity before the price increase. Total revenue after the increase is $TR = (1.40p)(.82q) = 1.148pq$.

and there were few if any price wars. American automobiles were selling at the rate of only about 7 million cars per year, even with big discounts thrown in. American cars were smaller and more fuel-efficient than the gas guzzlers of a decade earlier, and all the American auto companies were having a hard time. Foreign imports, mostly from Japan, accounted for over 25 percent of U.S. sales.

One key to the explanation of these facts about the automobile industry is the changing price of gasoline and the economy's adaptations to it. These factors can be understood largely in terms of the theories of supply and demand, competition and monopoly, with some government intervention thrown in. What happened?

Before OPEC: Energy Binge

During the half century before 1973, Americans increased their consumption of energy at an annual rate of about 5 percent—enough to double consumption every 14 years. That energy came increasingly from oil and gas, the use of which soared. Indeed, just between 1970 and 1973 U.S. oil consumption increased from about 15 million barrels per day to about 17.5 million barrels per day. Much of the long-term surge in energy consumption resulted from the growing use of the mass-produced automobile, which, like Hollywood movies, became a distinctively American contribution to the twentieth century. Automobiles became the symbol of the American dream. As American households became richer they tended to buy larger numbers of ever faster, bigger, and more lavishly equipped cars—to say nothing of trailers, vans, and recreational vehicles. Year by year the demand for gasoline to power their internal combustion engines rose. Yet the price of gasoline remained low, so low that throughout this period the cost of fuel remained a trivial part of the cost of owning and operating a car.

This epoch of ever-increasing demand at a constant price is analyzed in Figure 17-3. The long-run supply curve seemed to be almost perfectly elastic at a low price. For every barrel of oil pro-

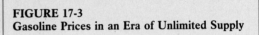

FIGURE 17-3
Gasoline Prices in an Era of Unlimited Supply

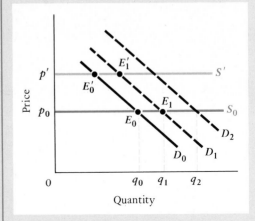

With a horizontal long-run supply curve, demand can increase year by year with no increase in price. S_0 is a long-run supply curve that is perfectly elastic at price p_0. Suppose S_0 applies to the United States in the early 1970s. The various demand curves refer to different years; each year as gasoline consumption increases the demand curve shifts rightward from D_0 to D_1 to D_2 and so on. There is no gasoline shortage on the horizon. The U.S. equilibrium in year 0 is E_0, and it is expected to shift to E_1 in year 1, with larger consumption but no increase in price above p_0.

The screened supply curve S' is also perfectly elastic—at a higher price, p'. Suppose it reflects the supply in European countries that have levied a high tax on gasoline. For the same set of demand curves, equilibrium consumption is much lower in European countries than in America, yet there too it increases year by year, with no increase in price, as shown by E_0' and E_1'.

duced, another was discovered. Although everyone knew this could not go on forever, a rising supply price was far in the future. Indeed, the enormous quantities of oil being discovered and produced in the Middle East so threatened the profitability of American oil producers that the U.S. government imposed quotas that limited the imports of cheap foreign oil. At the same time, the government also gave tax incentives to American oil companies to find and produce more oil.

The fact that the demand curve shifted rightward year after year was not a cause for alarm; indeed, the reverse was true: Energy fueled the increasing productivity that led to ever-rising material standards of living. America rode the crest of a wave of prosperity based upon cheap and plentiful oil.

Americans traveling abroad were amused by the small, cramped cars they saw and rented, and they were appalled by the high cost of gasoline. The high prices abroad were due to very high taxes on gasoline and led to lower gasoline consumption. Europeans drove smaller cars, waited until they reached a higher level of income before buying a car (or buying a second car), and relied more on bicycles and public transportation. The European situation during this period is also shown in Figure 17-3.

OPEC's Embargo

Although not all U.S. oil came from abroad, a virtually horizontal supply curve of the sort shown in Figure 17-3 was due to the willingness of oil exporters in the Middle East to supply as much oil as the United States and European countries wanted at a fixed price. What would happen if and when the oil exporters changed their minds?

The world found out in 1973, when, in conjunction with the Arab-Israeli war, members of OPEC placed an embargo on exports of Mideast oil. The United States and other oil importers suddenly had to rely on much more limited non-OPEC sources. They discovered that supply from these sources was not perfectly elastic. The change in shape of the supply curve due to OPEC is illustrated in Figure 17-4.

The theory of supply and demand leads to two clear predictions: a sharp rise in gasoline prices due to the upward shift of the supply curve, and a significant reduction in consumption as households adjusted to the new price level. These predictions rest on two assumptions, neither of which was correct in 1974: first, that price was free to rise in response to the embargo-induced scarcity; second,

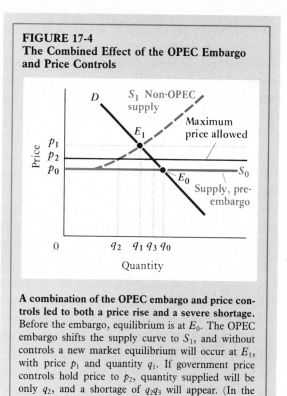

FIGURE 17-4
The Combined Effect of the OPEC Embargo and Price Controls

A combination of the OPEC embargo and price controls led to both a price rise and a severe shortage. Before the embargo, equilibrium is at E_0. The OPEC embargo shifts the supply curve to S_1, and without controls a new market equilibrium will occur at E_1, with price p_1 and quantity q_1. If government price controls hold price to p_2, quantity supplied will be only q_2, and a shortage of q_2q_3 will appear. (In the short run, before quantity demanded could be reduced to q_3, an even greater shortage would exist.)

that consumers would reduce consumption rapidly in response to any price increase that occurred.

Gasoline Price Controls

It happened that, at the time of the OPEC embargo, the federal government was setting maximum prices for gasoline. General price and wage controls had been imposed by the Nixon administration in 1971. Most items had been decontrolled by the time of the embargo, but not gasoline. The result was predictable: a sudden, sharp gas shortage at the controlled prices. This too is illustrated in Figure 17-4. Long lines developed at gas stations, and the stations eventually ran out of gas and closed down.

When price does not allocate limited supplies,

there is always a need for alternative allocation schemes. Many gas stations would sell only to regular customers. Others sold only a few gallons at a time, thereby increasing the customer's time spent in line. Others exacted hidden prices by selling gas in large quantities only to those who bought tires, batteries, or windshield wipers (at very inflated prices). Travelers spent endless hours searching for gas or sitting in lines. The government was urged to allocate gasoline on a fair and equitable basis, both to dealers and, by issuing ration coupons, to consumers.

While the government did not adopt gasoline rationing, it took some steps. It permitted some price rises, and it attempted to allocate gasoline to the hardest hit areas. It imposed lower speed limits, and it exhorted people to form car pools. Some state governments imposed rationing through odd-even day sales and by closing stations on Sundays. These expedients helped reduce waiting lines. But even after prices had been allowed to rise to what approximated new equilibrium levels, the shortages continued. Why?

Price Increases and Demand Adjustments

In response to a sharp rise in the price of gasoline, households and firms would be expected to consume less of it, as the demand curve shows. Yet price rises had less effect on consumption than suggested by a downward-sloping demand curve such as D in Figure 17-4. The reason is that it takes time to achieve adjustments in quantity demanded in response to a rise in price. The demand curve shown in Figure 17-4 is a demand curve that shows quantity demanded after consumers have had time to adjust; it is the long-run demand curve we first met in Chapter 6.

For example, if they had expected gasoline to cost $1.50 a gallon, the suburban Smith family would not have built their life-style around two cars that gave only 12 and 15 miles to the gallon. They might not have moved to a location where a 20-mile commute to work and the ferrying of children to school, lessons, doctor's appointments, and parties were required daily. And they certainly

would not have bought a fancy recreational vehicle for family vacations. But having done all those things, the Smiths were stuck and had to make the best of it. They began to use their cars more sparingly, but it would have been silly to leave them in the garage and take taxis. (The *variable* cost of using the family car was less than the *total* cost of a taxi ride.) They tried to sell the RV, but the few people who answered their ad in the local paper were willing to pay only a small fraction of the price the Smiths thought was fair.

As we saw in Chapter 6, the longer the period of time for adjustment, the greater the possibility of substituting away from commodities whose relative price is rising. Thus, in general, the longer the period of time, the more elastic the demand curve will be.

While such adjustments to the high price of gasoline quickly began to occur, they did not happen overnight. Thus the initial shortage of gasoline was even greater than that shown in Figure 17-4 and added to the sense of panic caused by the embargo.

Within months, producers and distributors of small, fuel-saving cars, such as American Motors and Volkswagen, found demand for their products rising; other automobile manufacturers found large cars not selling. The latter stopped production and laid off workers while they strained to shift production into their relatively few plants suitable for producing small cars. Used-car dealers found that their big cars would not sell but their small cars were being snapped up at existing prices—so they changed the structure of their prices.

The adjustment to smaller, more efficient cars continued into the 1980s. As it occurred, the price of gasoline began to fall. Measured in constant 1981 dollars, a gallon of gasoline cost $.79 in 1971. Its price rose to $.96 by 1974 and would have risen further but for some governmental controls. From that point on, however, an easing of demand was felt and price gradually fell to $.87 by the beginning of 1979 (when a new round of OPEC price increases went into effect).

We can capture the spirit of the adjustment by recalling the distinction made in Chapter 6 between a relatively elastic long-run demand curve and a relatively inelastic short-run curve. The short-run demand curve for gasoline proved much less elastic than the long-run curve. Such an inelastic demand curve would lead to shortages in the short run even if price jumped at once to the new long-run equilibrium price. Not only would the Smiths have to pay the new and "outrageous" higher price, they could not even then be sure of getting gas at that price!

As time passed, however, the demand curve became more elastic. With a more elastic demand curve, there was no shortage: quantity demanded was reduced until it equaled quantity supplied.

OPEC As a Successful Cartel

The oil embargo created a shortage of oil in the United States, but it did not lead to profits for the oil-producing countries. As we have seen, a sellers' boycott (which is what the embargo was) does not generate revenues for those who withhold their supply. But the experience showed the oil exporters how dependent Americans (and others) were on their product, and how willing they were to pay more for gasoline.

Oil exporters in Saudi Arabia, Kuwait, and Iran could increase profits by restricting output and raising price, just as others can who cartelize a previously competitive industry. The sons of the sheiks had attended the Harvard Business School and learned all about monopolies and cartels. After the embargo, the oil-producing countries did not return to unlimited supply but instead adopted a regime of carefully controlled supply. Producing a limited supply, combined with the ever-rising demand for oil, will keep prices high. See Figure 17-5. By taking into account how much non-OPEC oil is produced, the members of OPEC could determine how much they should produce to maximize their own profits.

Once or twice a year, OPEC members meet to survey world supply and demand and to set prices. This implies that they also set output quotas for their members, for the high prices can be main-

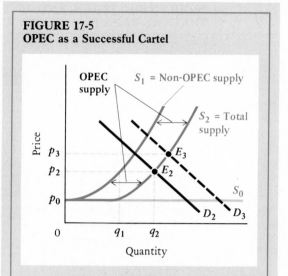

FIGURE 17-5
OPEC as a Successful Cartel

Given a sharply rising non-OPEC supply curve of oil, the members of OPEC can determine equilibrium prices by choosing their contribution to total supply. The curve S_1 represents the non-OPEC supply of the product. If OPEC were prepared to supply unlimited quantities at p_0 the supply curve would be S_0 and the situation shown in Figure 17-3 would be restored. But by fixing its production, OPEC can determine the new total (OPEC + non-OPEC) supply curve S_2. OPEC can, for given demand curves and non-OPEC supplies, pick a price (such as p_2) and determine what quantity to supply ($q_1 q_2$) to make that the equilibrium price. If demand is increasing, as from D_2 to D_3, the same OPEC supply will lead the price to increase from p_2 to p_3.

tained only if excess production is avoided. As long as the demand curve for oil remained relatively inelastic and did not shift to the left, and as long as non-OPEC oil did not greatly increase in supply, the OPEC cartel was in a position to make a killing. For much of the 1970s it did just that. The price of a barrel of Saudi Arabian crude oil, which was $5 in 1971 (prices expressed in 1981 constant dollars), was increased to about $19 a barrel by 1974 in the first of two rounds of massive price increases. This level of real prices fell slightly until 1979, when a temporary cut-off of Iranian oil supplies led OPEC members to a further series of major

TABLE 17–1 **PRODUCTION, PRICES, AND REVENUES OF A CARTEL THAT CAN RAISE PRICES ONLY BY RESTRICTING OUTPUT**

Year	Cartel production (millions of barrels per day)	Price per barrel received by cartel members (in 1981 dollars)	Revenue per day (millions of 1981 dollars)	Profit per day if cost is constant at $5 per barrel (millions of 1981 dollars)
1971	32	$ 6	$192	$ 32
1975	29	19	551	446
1980	21	33	693	688
1983[a]	16	33	528	448

[a] Estimated

Whether output restriction to maintain high prices pays in terms of profits depends on the required size of the output restriction necessary to maintain the price increase. This table is a simplified representation of OPEC's prices, output levels, and profits from 1971 to 1983. All dollar figures are in constant 1981 dollars. Cost is assumed to be $5 per barrel. The success of the cartel in the 1970s is reflected in its ability to raise price greatly with only moderate output restriction. After 1980 increased supplies of non-OPEC oil and reduced demand required continuing decreases in production merely to maintain high prices. As a result, revenue and profit to cartel members began to fall.

price increases that pushed prices to $33 a barrel by 1981.

Price increases of these magnitudes required output limitation. OPEC's production capacity is estimated at about 34 million barrels per day. In order to maintain prices at the levels reached by the first (1973–1974) boost in prices, it was necessary to hold production down to 28 million to 29 million barrels per day. To achieve the 1981 level of prices, production had to be decreased to roughly 21 million barrels per day. By December 1982 output was limited to 18.5 million barrels per day. Yet further reductions in OPEC's production have subsequently been required merely to maintain prices at that level. The reasons why ever-decreasing quotas were both necessary and ultimately hard to achieve will be discussed in the next section.

During the 1970s, however, OPEC was a very successful cartel. It prevented cheating, it had the participation of a large fraction of the world's producers, and it was not overwhelmed by new competition. It succeeded in reducing output, raising prices, and increasing revenues. Since costs per unit were roughly constant, this led to huge increases in profits. The first three lines of Table 17-1 show how this occurred.

OPEC: A Cartel in Trouble?

When the 13 member nations of OPEC met in Geneva in January 1983, they faced falling prices, an oil glut, and great internal dissension regarding the lowering of the oil production quotas that had been adopted only two months before. Those quotas limited aggregate production to 18.5 million barrels per day. It was estimated that a reduction to 17.5 million barrels per day would be necessary to prevent further slippage in prices. At that level of production, only about half the available capacity would be utilized, and the revenues that had risen so rapidly in the 1970s would continue to fall. While in 1983 OPEC members were still way ahead of where they had been before 1973, the apparent need to keep reducing output could only spell trouble for the future.

Why did OPEC's members need to adopt more and more rigid output limitations merely to maintain a given price? Economic theory predicts that

THE OPPORTUNITY COST OF OIL IN THE GROUND

The price of oil affects how much of it is produced and consumed today and also how much will be produced and consumed over the next 50 years. Not only oil producers but also oil consumers have to worry about the relation of current consumption to the world's reserves. Conservation is a particularly important issue because oil is a nonrenewable resource. The current price of oil must reflect not only the direct costs of extracting and refining it but also the cost of oil foregone in the future. For example, suppose that oil were available "free" in the sense of having a zero cost of extraction and refining but that it was also available only in a fixed amount. Use of some oil today would still involve a cost to society because it would result in less oil being available for use in the future.

For efficient allocation of the world's resources, the world price of oil must accurately reflect its opportunity cost, not just its cost of extraction. Thus the high prices that lead to high profits for today's oil producers play an efficiency as well as a monopoly role.

But what is the "right" price? If set too low, irreplaceable oil supplies will be squandered, and our heirs will suffer from an energy shortage. If set too high, high-cost substitutes for oil will be developed, and we will find that we have invested enormous sums in meeting an "energy shortage" that never really existed.

Because of the potential (but not yet actual) availability of nuclear and solar energy in vast quantities, the problem of the "right" price for oil today is difficult and subtle. Therefore, the great controversy surrounding it is not surprising. Given the fact that no one can be certain about when, or at what cost, substitutes for oil will render the world's oil supplies unneeded, there is no reason to believe that either competition or monopoly or government fiat will lead to what (after the fact) proves to have been the price that just covers the opportunity cost of oil consumed today.

There are those, even in oil-consuming countries, who believe that OPEC has done the world a great favor by forcing conservation on an energy-mad society. There are others who feel that the current price is far above the real opportunity cost and thus is imposing a great and unneeded burden on the current generation. Only time will tell who is right.

this would result either if demand for OPEC's output declined or if non-OPEC supplies increased. Both were occurring in the early 1980s.

Declining Demand

The demand curve for oil shifted to the left. This was partly the result of a decrease in incomes caused by the worldwide economic slowdown (which in turn was at least partly the result of rising energy prices!). It also reflected the change in tastes that had resulted from recognizing the existence of an energy crisis. Further, it reflected the substitution of other fuels, both coal and natural gas, for oil. In the United States oil consumption *decreased* by about 5 percent per year from 1978 to 1982, thus reversing the historical trend. While some of the decrease was recession-related and thus temporary, a good part reflected a long-run shift in the demand curve.

This leftward shift in the short-run demand curve—reflecting the greater elasticity of demand of oil products in the long run—was slow at first but has speeded up as consumers have had more time to adjust their consumption habits. Cars have become progressively smaller and more fuel-efficient and have been driven fewer miles; houses have been better insulated so that less fuel is required to achieve the same temperatures; consumers have made do in homes that are not so well heated. With oil products at relatively higher prices, consumers wished to purchase less. This they could do increasingly as time passed, for they could find other ways to meet their needs.

Increasing Alternative Sources of Supply

The high prices and high profits achieved by the OPEC cartel spurred major additions to the world's oil supply by non-OPEC suppliers. This was, in effect, new entry. In 1973 OPEC had produced more than 70 percent of the world's oil; 10 years later it produced less than 50 percent. North Sea oil, Mexican oil, Soviet oil, and increased American and Canadian production gradually replaced output that had been withdrawn from the market by OPEC. Higher prices made it economical to drill for oil that would have been uneconomical to produce at lower prices and to produce more from existing reserves. This is discussed more fully in the box. In the United States this production trend was greatly speeded by the relaxation of price con-

trols on oil and gas. As domestic output increased, imported oil fell from nearly 50 percent of all oil consumed in the United States in 1978 to less than one third by 1982. As the supply of non-OPEC oil increased, the amount of OPEC production that was consistent with maintaining a given total supply shrank.

The combined effect of decreasing demand and increasing supplies is illustrated in Figure 17-6. The shrinking market for OPEC oil at the high OPEC price necessitated ever stiffer production limitations if the cartel was to maintain its prices. This created increasing problems.

Problems of a Monopolist

Assume, for the moment, that OPEC is a single sovereign country choosing to maximize its profits from sale of its oil. It would face important and difficult choices of strategy. Should it seek to maintain prices while accepting the shrinking share of the market required to do that? Or should it allow prices to fall in order to discourage non-OPEC production (which is generally much higher in cost)

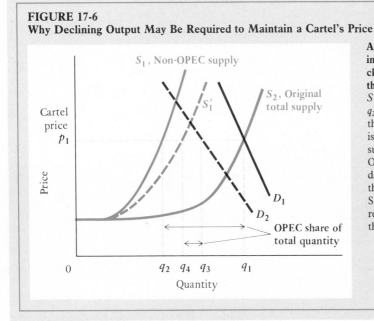

FIGURE 17-6
Why Declining Output May Be Required to Maintain a Cartel's Price

As demand declines and non-OPEC oil supply increases, OPEC members must accept declining production if they wish to maintain the cartel price. Total supply is S_2, of which S_1 is from non-OPEC sources and the quantity q_2q_1 from OPEC. Demand is originally D_1, and the cartel price p_1 prevails. Total quantity sold is q_1, of which the cartel's share is q_2q_1. Now suppose demand decreases to D_2 and non-OPEC supply increases to S_1', as shown by the dashed lines. If the cartel wishes to maintain the price at p_1, it must limit total supply to q_3. Since non-OPEC supply will be q_4, this means restricting its own supply to q_4q_3, much less than before the shifts occurred.

and also to slow down the shift away from oil consumption?

These would be difficult choices because all sorts of uncertainties must be faced. Oil not produced now will still be there later. In that sense, delayed production is not as bad as if the oil just disappeared. But will owning oil reserves 50 years hence promise wealth beyond the wildest dreams of avarice because oil is then so scarce, or will oil then be a valueless product of quaint historical interest whose one-time functions have been taken over by solar or nuclear fuels? If an oil monopolist believes that oil will be valuable in the future, it will be more willing to restrict production now and save oil for the future. If it believes that anything not produced now will soon be valueless, the incentive is strong to produce and sell oil now while there is still a market.

The problem for an oil monopolist is not merely one of guessing the future but also of affecting it. The higher the price it charges consumers for using oil today, the greater will be their incentive to find permanent substitutes for it. One does not have to be a monopolist to consider this a real problem. Oil producers with vast reserves, such as Saudi Arabia, are aware of what has happened to the market for oil in the last decade. They have seen the substitution of other fuels, such as coal, natural gas, and (to a small degree) nuclear fuels, for oil. They are equally aware of the potential threat from the increased use of nuclear fuels, from the so-called synthetic fuels, and possibly from solar energy. Nor is that the only kind of substitution that threatens them. Consumers can substitute insulation of houses for heating oil; smaller, more fuel-efficient cars for gasoline; and natural products for oil-based plastics. There is every evidence that these considerations weigh heavily on the government of Saudi Arabia.

OPEC: Internal Disagreements

OPEC is, of course, not a monopolist, nor is it under the control of a single country. Its members are 13 different countries with vastly different needs, goals, and oil reserves. Saudi Arabia has huge reserves, a small population, and a high per capita income. It wants to preserve the role of oil in the future and to discourage both the development of oil substitutes and the use of high-cost oil from other sources. It is willing to forego short-run monopoly profits in favor of lower prices and larger production so that there will be fewer incentives for the substitution of other products for Middle Eastern oil. Iran, which also has large oil reserves, was fighting a war with Iraq and urgently needed cash. Libya, Nigeria, Algeria, and Venezuela have smaller reserves, but they too have a great need for immediate cash. They care less about the market for oil 40 years hence than does Saudi Arabia since higher prices mean higher profits now. Yet unless they can all agree, the cartel will run into trouble. In early 1983 it appeared that the trouble had arrived.

Further, even if they subsequently agree on an appropriate total production quota, how can they agree on each country's share? Should Saudi Arabia, with over 40 percent of OPEC's oil reserves and 30 percent of its production capacity but only 3 percent of its population, be allowed 40 percent, 30 percent, or 3 percent of the total? Saudi Arabia wants the highest number; everyone else in OPEC wants it to have the lowest one. The key to OPEC's survival is Saudi Arabia; it must limit its output greatly if price is to be kept high, and it has gained greatly from OPEC's ability to raise price. But it has the most to lose as OPEC loses market share to other suppliers of oil and as oil loses its dominance as the world's energy source. Other nations cannot simply outvote Saudi Arabia in OPEC meetings, for OPEC cannot survive if Saudi Arabia leaves the cartel. But Saudi Arabia also needs the other OPEC members. It is the largest single source of oil reserves, but the other nations could supply all of the world's needs at present levels of consumption.

These are the traditional problems of cartels. OPEC did well to keep them in the background for much of the seventies. The problems are becoming more pressing, however, as OPEC's customers become more self-reliant.

As long as the rest of the world depends on

OPEC oil to meet a significant fraction of its energy needs, OPEC can manipulate its contribution to total world supply to serve its own best interests. The problems of OPEC will continue as long as the world's energy consumers find other sources of supply or reduce their demands. But if consumers react to a reduction of oil prices by a new energy binge, they will again be an easy target for OPEC or a different cartel.

SUMMARY

1. This chapter illustrates the use of price theory to understand important real-world events. It is not the examples that matter but the use of economic tools in achieving an understanding of why things happen.

2. A boycott in which some purchasers refuse to purchase a product sold in a competitive market reduces demand and, as long as it lasts, exerts downward pressure on price. This effect can be offset by a sellers' response—organized or spontaneous—in which supplies are withheld from the market. In either case, when the boycott ends, the effect on price is reversed. Unless a boycott leads to a permanent change in supply or demand, it does not have a permanent effect on price.

3. Groups supplying goods or services under conditions that approximate those of competitive equilibrium have a strong incentive to organize to restrict output. The reason is that their collective profits will surely increase, since the last units being produced have marginal costs in excess of marginal revenues.

4. To achieve and retain the benefits of monopolization requires more than just agreeing to restrict output. An effective cartel must be able to police and enforce its output quotas because it is in any one producer's interest to cheat. It must also cover most of the output of the industry, control the entry of new producers, and be insulated from too many close substitutes for the product it produces.

5. The OPEC cartel proved remarkably successful during the 1970s in raising the prices of oil above the previous, approximately competitive, level. At the time, OPEC included a large fraction of the world's oil-exporting countries, and it succeeded in a concerted effort to raise prices and to limit the output so that the high prices would stick. Its success was due partly to political unity among the Arab states, partly to the fact that neither demand nor alternative sources of supply can change quickly, and partly to governmental policies of price control in the United States that slowed down such adjustments.

6. In the era before OPEC, demand for oil products rose steadily in response to low prices and a highly elastic long-run supply. OPEC changed the supply situation overnight, by means of an embargo (a sellers' boycott). The embargo, combined with government price controls, led to shortages, long lines, and the clamor for government allocation—all predicted by the theory of a price fixed below the equilibrium level.

7. Following the embargo, OPEC limited the supply of oil through a cartel output restriction strategy that converted a horizontal supply curve to a steeply rising one. Throughout the 1970s, OPEC managed the price of oil and received enormous monopoly profits from its sales.

8. OPEC's ability to control the oil market has been weakened as oil-consuming countries have decreased their reliance on oil and as non-OPEC sources of energy supply have steadily expanded. In the early 1980s, OPEC nations found it necessary to accept ever stiffer reductions in their production to maintain their prices. This has generated increasing tensions within the cartel.

9. All producers, monopolists as well as members of cartels, are the potential victims of new competition from other existing producers, from new entrants, or from new products. Competition is motivated by high profits and must be prevented if high prices are to be maintained. The longer the time period, the greater the threat from new producers or new products.

TOPICS FOR REVIEW

Buyers' boycott and sellers' boycott
Long-run effects of a temporary boycott
The motive for output restriction in a competitive industry
Why cartels may fail to raise profits
Why cartels may succeed in the short run and not survive in the long run
Substitutes for the product of a monopolist
Long-run and short-run demand curves

DISCUSSION QUESTIONS

1. There is no law against consumer boycotts. When coffee prices soared in the mid 1970s, each of the following statements was made. Comment on them in terms of the theory of boycotts.

   a. Elinor Guggenheimer (New York City commissioner of consumer affairs): "We've heard all about the cold weather in Brazil and the damaged coffee trees. What we haven't heard is any valid explanation of why the consumer should be forced to bear the impact of this frost. We're going to ask supermarkets and restaurants to stress coffee alternatives, tea and soup. If enough people don't drink coffee, at some point prices will have to be turned around."

   b. William Safire (columnist): "Let the boycott go forward, not only to cut the price, but to put the cartelniks of OPEC on notice: When challenged to economic war, even a little one, the American public is willing to make sacrifices. An effective coffee boycott would send a message to monopolists of oil."

   c. Coffee importer: "The U.S. customer is not the prime factor in the coffee market. The 43 coffee-producing nations couldn't care less if Americans drink coffee, because other people will. Americans can spite themselves, and hurt *me,* but they won't touch Brazil."

2. Technological advances of the 1950s dramatically boosted chicken and egg production in the United States. Petaluma, California, became the center of a booming industry. The Petaluma egg producers tried unsuccessfully and persistently to restrict supply by forming voluntary associations. Why do you think these associations did not succeed? In the 1970s the California State Marketing Board did what the private associations failed to do: It compelled cutbacks in production. Why do you suppose it did so, and why was it more successful than the voluntary associations?

3. Profit-making blood banks account for about 10 percent of all blood used in transfusions in the United States. They buy blood from commercial donors and sell blood to hospitals. The blood business has proven highly profitable for decades. Can you think of reasons why provision of this product has proven more than normally profitable? (There has been no evidence of a price-fixing agreement among blood suppliers.) Incidentally, discuss whether or not competition ought to be permitted in blood supply.

4. Use price theory in discussing the following news stories.

   a. The analysis sent out by a leading stock brokerage firm: "Prices of digital watches are following the pattern of pocket calculators—down 25 percent a year. This is just what we expected; it is normal. Expect squeezed profit margins and some bankruptcies."

   b. Donald Hollister, inventor of a new long-lasting light bulb that won't burn out for at least 10 years: "Even if this catches on, I expect to do well, but not to make a million dollars. The idea is too simple." (By the way, would you expect Mr. Hollister's patent to be as valuable as the exclusive rights to manufacture E.T. dolls? Why or why not?)

   c. Newspaper report from Greensville, South Carolina, about the growth of "gut row": "It's a bit mind boggling to see so many fast-food restaurants in one place. All the national chains are there—Burger King, McDonald's, Shakey's Pizza—and you have your choice of chicken, seafood, barbecue or even native favorites like sausage biscuits. It's great for the family, but nobody's making any money."

   d. From *Small Business Newsletter:* "Electronic games, and the arcades that supply them, are highly profitable today, but are loaded with hazard for the small businessman. Think twice before buying a franchise."

5. What bearing does each of the following facts have on the ability of OPEC to keep raising the price of oil?

   a. Between 1973 and 1981, OPEC's share of the world oil supply decreased from over 70 percent to under 50 percent.

   b. "Saudi Arabia's interest lies in extending the life span of oil to the longest possible period," said Sheik Yamani.

   c. The Soviet Union, in order to earn Western currency to pay for grain, increases its oil exports to the West and becomes the world's second largest exporter.

   d. The Iran-Iraq war greatly decreased oil production in the Mideast.

6. Comment on the following statements about OPEC:

   a. The Japanese minister of trade and industry, Komoto, responding to an OPEC price increase, said, "An outrageous act that ignores economic principles and is therefore regrettable.''

   b. Saudia Arabian oil trader Sylaiman Olayan: "We must allow oil buyers to plan their future spending costs for energy intelligently."

   c. William Brown, Hudson Institute in 1982: "OPEC is 100% dead. There is nothing to save them."

   d. Sheik Yamani of Saudi Arabia: "OPEC exists to lower prices as well as to raise them."

7. Which of the following groups stand to gain, and which to lose, if OPEC oil prices fall in real terms over the decade of the 1980s.

   a. American consumers

   b. coal miners in the United States

   c. people who have invested in companies developing synthetic fuels

   d. Indonesia, an oil-exporting country with small oil reserves and a large population

   e. U.S. wildcat drillers

   f. Saudi Arabia

8. "The 1970s proved to the world that there are very available substitutes for gasoline, among them bicycles, car pools, moving closer to work, cable TV, and Japanese cars." Discuss whether, and if so how, each of these is a substitute for gasoline.

18 MONOPOLY VERSUS COMPETITION

Monopoly has been regarded with suspicion for a very long time. Even today in some quarters it takes a large share of the blame for inflation, for the energy shortage, for discrimination in employment, and for inequalities in income. It is widely believed that modern economic theory has *proved* that monopoly allows the powerful producer to exploit the consumer, while the competitive system always works to the consumer's advantage. In *The Wealth of Nations* (1776), Adam Smith—the foun-

der of classical economics—developed a ringing attack on monopolies and monopolists. Since then, most economists have criticized monopoly and advocated freer competition. In Chapters 14 and 15 we saw that perfect competition has appealing features and that it is efficient in ways that monopoly is not.

But competition is not always welcomed either. Protection of firms from competition occurs in many guises. Protection of U.S. firms from foreign competition; protection of small firms from bigger, more efficient rivals; protection of firms generally from "unfair" competition; and protection of firms in depressed industries from destructive or cut-throat competition—all are part of the American scene.

Is a preference for competition and a distrust of monopoly justified? Can competition be too intense for the public good? This chapter carries further the comparison of monopoly and competition in terms of their predicted effects, then looks at the principal policies for dealing with monopoly and competition in the United States.

Throughout the discussion we speak of *monopoly* in the sense of monopoly power, not merely of the single firm. Similarly we speak of *competition* to refer to competitive behavior, whether in the market structure known as perfect competition or more generally.

COMPARISONS BETWEEN MONOPOLY AND COMPETITION

A number of interesting questions can be asked concerning the differences between monopolistic and competitive industries. For example, we may ask whether a change in market structure affects the level of cost, or whether monopoly provides greater incentives to innovate, or what conditions are most conducive to destructive competition. We shall examine each of these, but first we shall look at the essence of the "case against monopoly."

The Monopolization of a Competitive Industry with No Change in Costs

The classical case against monopoly is to a great extent based on this prediction:

If a perfectly competitive industry should be monopolized, and if the cost curves of all productive units are unaffected by this change, the price will rise and the quantity produced will fall.

Assume that a competitive industry is monopolized as the result of a single firm's buying out all

the individual producers and operating each one as an independent plant. Further assume that cost curves are not affected by this change. This means that the marginal costs will be the same to the monopolist as to the competitive industry.

When the industry is monopolized, it becomes profitable to drive price up by restricting output for precisely the same reasons it pays a producers' co-op to do so (see page 279). As long as neither market demand nor costs change, it will always pay the monopolist who charges a single price to restrict output below, and to raise price above, their perfectly competitive levels (see Figure 18-1).

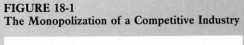

FIGURE 18-1
The Monopolization of a Competitive Industry

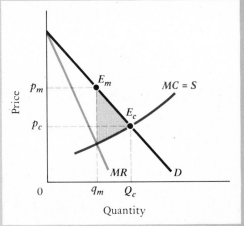

When a competitive industry is monopolized, output falls and price rises and a deadweight loss occurs. The competitive industry's supply curve and the monopolist's marginal cost curve are identical. The industry faces demand curve D. A competitive industry would produce Q_c at price p_c. The monopolist reduces output to q_m because units between q_m and Q_c add more to its cost than to its revenue. The shaded area shows that consumers are willing to pay more for each unit of lost output than its marginal cost of production. This deadweight loss of monopolization is a source of allocative inefficiency. It is the sum of the consumers' and producers' surpluses lost by reducing output from Q_c to q_m.

The consequences of this change in equilibrium price and quantity were presented in Chapters 14 and 15: (1) at competitive but not monopolistic equilibrium, the level of average cost is necessarily the lowest attainable, given the technology of the society, and (2) at competitive but not monopolistic equilibrium, $p = MC$, and thus allocative efficiency is achieved.

Under these circumstances, the monopolization of a competitive industry surely introduces allocative inefficiency, and it may lead to productive inefficiency. Notwithstanding, the question of monopoly *versus* competition continues to be hotly debated because most modern economists are aware that costs are not unaffected by market structure.

The Effect of Market Structure on Cost

What if costs are not the same for monopolist as for the competitive industry? Costs may be affected when an industry is monopolized or when a large number of small firms is replaced by a small number of large firms. If any savings occur from combining numerous competing groups into a single integrated operation, the costs of producing any given level of output will be lower than they were previously. If cost reductions are large enough, output will be increased and price will be lowered as a result of the replacement of a perfectly competitive industry by a firm with monopoly power. This may occur in two very different ways.

Advantages of Large Scale

The cost advantage of having 1 railroad between two points rather than 50 railroads (or 1 water company in a city, or 1 telephone system in a country) is obvious. In such situations, it would be inefficient to have a large number of firms each producing a small output at a high cost per unit. If such a situation existed, any firm that grew bigger than its rivals would soon find itself in a position to cut price below its rivals' costs and monopolize the industry. This situation is called **natural monopoly.** It exists where the size of the market allows at most one firm of efficient size.

Natural monopoly is just the extreme version of a much more common situation in industrialized countries in which advantages of scale will make perfect competition wholly unattainable because there is room for only a small number of firms of efficient size.

Today the effective choice is usually not between monopoly and perfect competition but between more or less oligopoly.

Whenever there are long-run advantages of large-scale production, of marketing and distribution, of learning by doing, or of innovation or invention, the minimum efficient scale (*MES*) of firms will tend to be large.

When *MES* is large, it is likely that productive efficiency will be improved, rather than worsened, by a shift from competition to a more concentrated market structure.

Lower Levels of Cost of Producing a Given Output

Even if there are no advantages of large-scale *plants*, large *firms* may be able to achieve economies, and thus lower costs, by multiproduct production and associated large-scale distribution, national advertising, and large-scale purchasing. Such economies have been described as **economies of scope** rather than of scale.

If the change in market structure shifts marginal costs downward, it is possible for output to be increased and price to be lowered as a result of the monopolization of a perfectly competitive industry. Such a situation is illustrated in Figure 18-2.

Saying that monopoly *may* lead to lower costs does not mean that departures from competition *must* lead to lower costs. A large firm that is protected from competition by an entry barrier may reduce the efficiency of production and so shift marginal and average cost curves upward. In such a case (compared with the competitive industry) monopolization will certainly raise price and lower output.

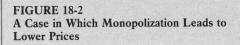

FIGURE 18-2
A Case in Which Monopolization Leads to Lower Prices

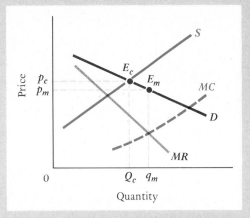

If monopolization lowers costs sufficiently, it may lead to greater output and lower price than competition. D and S are the demand and supply curves of a competitive industry that is in equilibrium at E_c with p_c and Q_c. If costs are unaffected by monopolization, S will become the monopolist's marginal cost curve and the monopolist will restrict output and raise price. However, if the monopolization reduces costs to MC, the equilibrium will be at E_m, with p_m less than p_c and q_m greater than Q_c.

Innovation Under a Monopoly

A monopolist can always increase its profits if it can reduce costs. And because it is able to prevent the entry of new firms into the industry, the additional profits will persist into the long run. Thus, from the standpoint of maximizing profits, the monopolist has both a short-run and a long-run incentive to reduce costs by innovation.

Innovation requires research and development, and that costs money. The monopolistic firm may have an advantage over the competitive firm in that funds for research and development are more readily available to it. In the first place, it may have profits to invest in such ventures even though credit is tight. In the second place, tax laws that permit writing off business expenses may make research and development relatively cheap.

Some critics of monopoly concede that innovation occurs but argue that monopolists engage in the wrong kinds of innovation. Monopolists may be expected to give special attention to kinds of innovation that increase or preserve the barriers to entry of potential competitors, as well as undertaking innovations that reduce costs to consumers in the long run.

Thus the key empirical question is, in what circumstances do large firms in less competitive market structures achieve lower levels of cost than an industry composed of large numbers of small firms? Much of the answer depends on how market structure affects the rate of innovation.[1]

The Incentive to Innovate

Firms in any market structure have an incentive to innovate in order to find a cost-saving process or a more popular new product. There has been extended debate over which kinds of market structure are most conducive to innovation.

[1] At this time we suggest you read again the discussion of invention and innovation on pages 205–206.

Innovation Under Competition

The firm in perfect competition has the same profit incentive to innovate as the monopolist, but only in the short run, not in the long run. In the short run, a reduction in costs will allow the firm that was just covering costs to earn profits. In the long run, however, the profits will disappear. Existing firms will copy the cost-saving innovation, new firms motivated by the existence of profits will enter the industry using the new techniques, and the profits of the innovator will eventually disappear.

The effectiveness of profits as an incentive to reduce costs for a firm will depend on the magnitude of the extra profits and the length of time they persist.

If it takes only a few months for existing firms and new entrants to copy and install any new invention, then the innovating firm's profits will be above normal for only a short time and the extra profits actually earned may not be sufficient to compensate for the risks and the costs of developing the new innovation. In such cases the direct incentive to innovate will be absent from a competitive industry. Alternatively, if it takes several years for other firms to copy and install the cost-saving innovation, then the profits earned over these years by the innovating firm might be more than sufficient to compensate for all costs and risks and might yield a handsome profit as well. In this case the incentive to innovate is present in a competitive industry.

The Greater Incentive to Innovate?

Might competition be *more* conducive to innovation than monopoly? Some think so. A monopolist who does not innovate may be missing larger profits, yet it can still have some long-run profits. But, the argument runs, if the competitive firm does not innovate, some of its competitors are likely to do so and it will find itself in a position in which it cannot even keep up with its competitors, thus incurring losses and eventual bankruptcy.

A very different view was that of the distinguished Austrian (and later American) economist Joseph A. Schumpeter. In brief, his argument was that only the incentive of profits leads entrepreneurs to take the great risks involved in innovation and that monopoly power is much more important than competition in providing the climate under which innovation occurs. The profits of the monopolist provide the incentive for other people to try to get their share. This might involve imitating the monopolist's product (thereby eroding the monopoly market) or trying to come up with a new product that would better serve the underlying wants that make the monopolist rich. As a result no monopoly will last forever; it will not even last very long if it fails to innovate and to anticipate its future competition. Schumpeter called the process of one monopoly being replaced by another *the*

process of creative destruction. In *Capitalism, Socialism and Democracy* (1942) he said:

What we have got to accept is that it has come to be the most powerful engine of that progress and in particular of the long-run expansion of total output not only in spite of, but to a considerable extent through, this strategy which looks so restrictive when viewed in the individual case and from the individual point of time. In this respect, perfect competition is not only impossible but inferior, and has no title to being set up as a model of ideal efficiency. It is hence a mistake to base the theory of government regulation of industry on the principle that big business should be made to work as the respective industry would work in perfect competition.

Innovation Under Oligopoly

Many students of industrial organization have theorized that intermediate market structures, such as oligopoly, might lead to more innovation than either competitive or monopolistic industries. They argue that the oligopolist is faced with clear and present competition from existing rivals and cannot afford the more relaxed life of the monopolist who might choose not to maximize profits. At the same time, however, the oligopolist expects to keep a good share of the profits it earns because of the barriers to entry and its ability to avoid excessive price competition with existing rivals.

The empirical evidence is broadly consistent with this hypothesis. Professor Jesse Markham of Harvard University concluded a survey of empirical findings by saying

If technological change and innovational activity are, as we generally assume, in some important way a product of organized R&D activities financed and executed by business companies, it is clear that the welfare payoffs that flow from them can to some measurable extent be traced to the doorsteps of large firms operating in oligopolistic markets.

Everyday observation provides some confirmation of this finding. Leading U.S. firms that operate in highly concentrated industries, such as Kodak, IBM, du Pont, Western Electric, Xerox, General Electric, and Minnesota Mining & Manufacturing, have been highly innovative over many years.

While Schumpeter's hypothesis, applied to oligopoly, has substantial credibility, it is also true that the relationship is far from perfect. Some highly oligopolistic American industries, such as steel, appear to have lagged far behind their foreign competitors. Evidently the long, sustained absence of competition led them to become complacent and relatively inefficient. (A Schumpeterian might respond that the result is due to such things as tariff protection and other *governmental* impediments to creative destruction.)

Patents and the Incentive to Innovate

Economists who believe that competitive market structures best serve consumers by assuring them low prices, but who worry about the possible lack of incentives to innovate under competition, believe that other institutions, such as the patent laws, can provide the necessary incentives.

Patent laws confer a temporary monopoly on the use of an invention. The intent of the patent laws is to lengthen the short-run period during which whoever controls the invention can earn supernormal profits as a reward for inventing it. Once the patent expires—and sometimes even before, as we saw in the case of ball-point pens—other firms can copy the invention and, if there are no other barriers to entry, production will expand until profits fall to normal. There is little doubt that without patent laws, many inventions would be copied sooner and the original innovators would not earn as much extra revenue to compensate them for the costs and risks of development. Thus patents do increase the rewards to invention. Just how much actual extra invention occurs is a subject of substantial debate.

Because patented items *can* be imitated, the real advantage of patents to the competitive firm should not be exaggerated. Some have argued that patents may be of even greater advantage to a monopolistic than to a competitive firm. A monopolist, so goes the argument, has the resources to develop, patent, and "keep on the shelf" processes that might enable a potential competitor to challenge its position.

The Incentive to Engage in Destructive Competition

Competition, when it works well, leads to prices at the level of minimum attainable long-run average total costs. Firms generate revenues just sufficient to maintain their capital stock and to replace it as it wears out. As we saw in Chapter 14, in the short run with overall excess capacity, firms may find it profitable to operate with prices below *LRAC* as long as price exceeds average *variable* cost. This provides a signal for resources to leave the industry, and when they have done so, an equilibrium is achieved, with the remaining firms covering average total costs.

Circumstances could arise, however, that would cause a chronic *long-run* tendency for firms to engage in excessive competition and result in prices that do not recover total costs in the long-run. Such a situation is often described as *destructive competition*, or sometimes as *cutthroat competition*.

Destructive competition requires that long-lived capital investments play a big part in the total cost picture. For example, airlines, coal mining companies, and steamship lines often find that their average total costs are primarily fixed costs arising from large initial capital investments. In any short-run period, depreciation costs can be ignored (under the bygones are bygones principle). Over the life of the equipment, however, unless sufficient funds are earned to replace capital as it wears out, the industry will surely shrink. In such circumstances, *too much* competition could conceivably occur. It would cause severe difficulties for an industry that could survive under less competitive conditions.

To see how this can happen, consider a simplified example in which marginal costs are zero and all costs are for the purchase of fixed capital equipment. The capital costs $100,000 and lasts 10 years. At full capacity output, the firm's capital can produce 10,000 units of output per year. The firm must earn $10,000 a year—an average of $1 per unit for 10,000 units—if it is to cover its capital costs. A single-firm monopolist (we assume) finds that it pays to sell its capacity output of 10,000 units for $3 per unit. It does so, and earns profits of $20,000 over full (capital) cost. Attracted by the high profits, a second and third firm enter, each with a plant costing $100,000 and a capacity of 10,000 units of output per year. They offer to sell at $3, and each captures one-third of the market.

Although each firm covers its costs by selling 3,333 units per year at the $3 price, all three firms now find they have excess capacity, for they are sharing the original monopolist's market. Since marginal costs are zero, one of them reasons, "Why not cut prices a bit and sell all my potential output?" He cuts price to $2.90 and at first greatly increases his sales. His rivals, however, lose customers and they retaliate. Price falls to $2.50, then to $2. Each firm gains some sales, since market quantity demanded increases, but each firm still has excess capacity. A price war develops and does not stop until price has been driven down to the price at which each seller is at full capacity. Say that price is $.40. Each of the sellers is doing better than shutting down, since revenue of $.40 a unit for 10,000 units ($4,000) exceeds the nonexistent variable costs. But none of the firms is earning enough to cover its full costs over the lifetime of its plant.

If this situation continues, after 10 years each will have earned only $40,000, not enough to cover the capital costs of $100,000 every 10 years. Eventually, two of the three firms will leave the industry. The survivor can then replace its plant, charge the monopoly price of $3 a unit, and earn profits if no one else enters. But this will invite entry, and we are back at the beginning again.[2]

The example just discussed is extreme in that it assumed the variable costs were zero. But there are many industries in which the difference between variable costs, which must be covered by current operations, and total costs, which must be covered in the long run, is very large. Airlines are perhaps a prime example. Once an airline owns a fleet of wide-bodied planes, extra passengers can be carried at very low marginal cost. Even flying extra flights with the same number of planes (although it re-

quires extra gasoline, pilots, and others) is far less costly than adding planes to the fleet. The gap between total costs and variable costs combines with excess capacity to create conditions in which sellers are tempted on the one hand to collude and on the other to engage in price cutting to fill their planes.

Successful collusion will lead to prices above the competitive level; uncontrolled price competition may lead to a chronic tendency for prices well below the competitive level. Policymakers face a dilemma. A monopolist would restrict output and raise price above the long-run competitive level. But replacing monopoly with unbridled competition might not work. Myopic, short-run competitive behavior would drive price down to variable cost and lead to a situation in which no firm could stay in the industry long. The industry then would suffer from chronic destructive competition. This view of destructive competition, especially in oligopolistic industries with more than three or four firms, was prevalent in the 1930s, when excess capacity was the general rule. It led to some direct legislative attempts to exempt price stabilization activities from antitrust control and to many regulatory agencies' changing their behavior, as we shall see.

Later generations of economists have been more skeptical about the occurrence of destructive competition. They do not deny occasional price wars but believe that such situations tend to self-correct fairly rapidly. However, many businessmen and regulators are not persuaded by the economists' arguments. Whether conditions for chronic destructive competition occur frequently is an extremely important unresolved empirical question. Those who believe that they do, support government regulation to limit competition or advocate a tolerant attitude toward price stabilizing activities. Those who believe that firms need no such protection (on the ground that they can learn to avoid destructive competition) tend to advocate leaving the market alone except to implement antitrust activities that discourage collusion or price fixing. Much of the current debate about more or less regulation and deregulation turns on this issue.

[2] The example is based on the model of the nineteenth century French mathematician Joseph Bertrand.

ANTITRUST POLICY AS PROTECTION AGAINST MONOPOLY POWER

The theory of monopoly leads to three principal predictions. (1) Where monopoly power exists in an industry, it will lead to a restriction of the flow of resources into the industry and thus to the employment of fewer resources than would be used under competitive conditions. (2) Consequently firms with monopoly power will be able to charge higher prices and will be able to earn profits in excess of opportunity costs. (3) Their owners will command a larger share of the national income than they would under conditions of competition. In short, an economy characterized by firms with monopoly power will lead to a different allocation of resources and a different distribution of income than will an economy composed largely of competitive industries.

Antitrust laws attempt to prohibit the acquisition or exercise of monopoly power by business firms.

The first American antitrust law, the Sherman Antitrust Act, was passed in 1890, in an era when economists believed that perfect competition both produced ideal results and was the feasible alternative to monopoly. American antitrust laws prohibit: monopoly; attempts to monopolize; and contracts, combinations, and conspiracies in restraint of trade. They give the courts the power to stop such practices and to dissolve into a number of independent companies a company that has violated the law.

The Nature of Antitrust Policy

The dominant theme of antitrust policy has been to foster competition against those who would seek to restrain trade.[3]

Anticompetitive results and monopoly power may be achieved or perpetuated in many ways:

1. By firms conspiring among themselves (colluding) to restrict output or raise prices, or otherwise failing to compete with one another
2. By firms adopting practices "in restraint of trade," such as contracts that bind a purchaser to buy all its supplies from a single seller
3. By a firm's employing "predatory" practices against rival sellers in an effort to force them into bankruptcy, "good behavior," or merger
4. By a merger of existing firms into a new and larger firm
5. By one firm's acquiring control of other firms through purchasing their stock or acquiring their physical assets
6. By a firm's finding monopoly "thrust upon it" (in the words of the distinguished American jurist Learned Hand) either by its natural efficiency as a single producer or by successful innovation

Each of the first five ways has been the object of antitrust legislation. Such practices may be either criminal or civil offenses. In criminal law, a firm found guilty may be fined and its officers may be fined and/or sentenced to jail.

In civil cases, a firm found in violation of the law may be required by the court to abandon certain practices, or it may be forced to dissolve itself into a number of separate companies. In the legal phrase, a firm found violating the law must *cleanse itself* of its violation in a manner prescribed by the court. In private cases, a firm may be obliged to pay injured parties an amount up to three times the amount of damages caused by the violation. *Treble damages* were designed to provide a substantial incentive to private firms to root out violations of the law that might escape the notice of government prosecutors.

Who Establishes Our Antitrust Policies?

Antitrust laws prohibit certain forms of activity. Since they are laws, they are enforced in the courts, and enforcement in the main follows the usual legal

---

[3] There are also noneconomic motives for dealing with the "monopoly problem." Many people fear the political influence of those who have substantial economic power.

procedures.[4] The overall effect of antitrust policy at any time rests on three things: the nature of the laws themselves, the courts' interpretation of them, and the vigor with which prosecutions are brought by the government and by private plaintiffs. All three have changed over time, and as a result the overall antitrust climate has changed.

Principal Laws Promoting Competition[5]

The Sherman Antitrust Act (1890) was enacted in response to the great growth in the size of firms during the last half of the nineteenth century. Section 1 of the act declared illegal every contract, combination, or conspiracy in restraint of trade. Section 2 made it illegal to monopolize or to attempt to monopolize. It also prohibited conspiracies or combinations that resulted in monopolization. The language of the Sherman Act was strong, but it was vague. It was some time before the courts defined the act's scope more specifically.

The Clayton Antitrust Act (1914) was an attempt to be more precise and to strengthen the powers of the antitrust prosecutors by allowing them to strike at potentially anticompetitive practices "in their incipiency." It also identified certain practices as illegal "where the effect may be substantially to lessen competition." Its most important provisions were Section 7, applying to acquisition of stock in a competing company; Section 2, limiting the practice of price discrimination; and Section 3, regulating exclusive dealing and tying contracts. (A tying contract requires a buyer to purchase other items in order to purchase the item it wants.) An important provision in the Clayton

Antitrust Act specifically exempted collective bargaining by labor unions from the antitrust provisions.

Although the Clayton Act made it sometimes illegal to take control of another firm by purchasing its *stock*, the act neglected to prohibit taking control by purchasing the firm's *assets*. Thus, although it dealt with the trust, or "loose-knit" combination of competitors, it neglected the merger, or "close-knit" combination. In 1950 this loophole was closed by passage of the Celler-Kefauver Act, which applied the same provisions to asset acquisitions as had previously applied only to acquisitions of stock.

Variation in Judicial Interpretation

The rule of reason. The first important series of antitrust prosecutions occurred at the beginning of the twentieth century. Two major decisions were issued in 1911 when, in forcing the Standard Oil Company and the American Tobacco Company to divest themselves of a large share of their holdings of other companies, the Supreme Court enunciated the "rule of reason." Not all trusts, but only *unreasonable* combinations in restraint of trade, merited conviction under the Sherman Act.

The rule of reason received a narrow interpretation for 25 years. In the famous *U.S. Steel* case (1920), the Court found that the company had not violated the law, even though it found that the organizers of the company had *intended* to monopolize the industry, and even though the company had earlier conspired to fix prices. The Court held that U.S. Steel had not succeeded in *achieving* a monopoly (indeed, its vain attempts at price fixing proved that!). The fact that it was a big company controlling half the industry and with potential monopoly power was, the Court ruled, beside the point. The decision said in part, "The law does not make mere size an offense. It . . . requires overt acts."

In related decisions, the Court not only reiterated that mere size was not an offense but added that neither was the existence of unexerted monopoly power, no matter how impressive that power.

---

[4] Under Federal antitrust law, government cases originate either within the antitrust division of the Department of Justice or within procedures of the Federal Trade Commission (FTC). Many cases never go to trial because they are settled by agreement between the Department of Justice or the FTC and the companies. Justice Department and private cases go to trial before federal district courts. FTC cases are heard first by the Commission. In all cases appeal is to the appropriate Circuit Court of Appeals and then to the Supreme Court. Supreme Court decisions, here as elsewhere, stand until modified by other decisions of this highest court.

[5] The principal antitrust provisions are quoted in the box on page 304.

PRINCIPAL ANTITRUST PROVISIONS

Sherman Antitrust Act (26 Stat 209, 1890, as amended)

§1. Every contract, combination in the form of trust or otherwise, or conspiracy, in restraint of trade or commerce among the several States, or with foreign nations, is hereby declared to be illegal. . . . Every person who shall make any contract or engage in any combination or conspiracy shall be deemed guilty of a felony and on conviction thereof, shall be punished by a fine not exceeding one million dollars if a corporation, or, if any other person, one hundred thousand dollars, or by imprisonment not exceeding three years, or by both . . . in the discretion of the Court.

§2. Every person who shall monopolize, or attempt to monopolize, or combine or conspire with any other person or persons, to monopolize any part of the trade or commerce among the several States, or with foreign nations, shall be deemed guilty of a felony . . .

§8. That the word "person," or "persons," wherever used in this act shall be deemed to include corporations. . . .

Clayton Antitrust Act (38 Stat 730, 1914, as amended)

§2. (Including Robinson-Patman Amendments, 1948).

(a) That it shall be unlawful for any person engaged in commerce, in the course of such commerce, either directly or indirectly, to discriminate in price between different purchasers of commodities of like grade and quality . . . where the effect of such discrimination may be substantially to lessen competition or tend to create a monopoly in any line of commerce. . . . *Provided*, That nothing herein contained shall prevent differentials which make only due allowance for differences in the cost . . . resulting from the differing methods or quantities in which such commodities are . . . sold or delivered. . . .

§3. That it shall be unlawful for any person engaged in commerce, in the course of such commerce, to lease or make a sale or contract . . . on the condition, agreement, or understanding that the lessee or purchaser thereof shall not use or deal in the . . . commodities of a competitor . . . where the effect of such . . . agreement . . . may be to substantially lessen competition or tend to create a monopoly in any line of commerce.

§4. Any person who shall be injured in his business or property by reason of anything forbidden in the antitrust laws may sue therefor . . . and shall recover threefold the damages by him sustained, and the cost of suit, including a reasonable attorney's fee . . . .

§7. (As amended by Celler-Kefauver Act of 1950.)

That no corporation engaged in commerce shall acquire . . . the whole or any part . . . of another corporation engaged also in commerce, where in any line of commerce in any section of the country, the effect of such acquisition may be substantially to lessen competition, or to tend to create a monopoly. . . .

§16. That any person, firm, corporation, or association shall be entitled to sue and have injunctive relief, in any court of the United States having jurisdiction over the parties, as against threatened loss or damage by a violation of the antitrust laws. . . .

Federal Trade Commission Act (38 Stat 717, 1914, as amended)

§5. (a)

(1) Unfair methods of competition . . . and unfair or deceptive acts or practices in or affecting commerce, are hereby declared unlawful.

(6) The Commission is hereby empowered and directed to prevent . . . using unfair methods . . . or deceptive acts or practices in commerce.

§5. (1)

Any person . . . who violates an order of the commission to cease and desist . . . shall pay a civil penalty of not more than $10,000 for each violation . . . each day of continuance . . . shall be deemed a separate offense.

These decisions reflected the business-oriented mood of the country during the 1920s, a mood shared by a highly conservative Supreme Court. Under this interpretation, which lasted until World War II, the antitrust laws were virtually unenforceable so far as attacks on the structure of heavily concentrated industries were concerned.

A new Sherman Act? A sharp break in this situation occurred in a series of cases prosecuted in the late 1930s, which reached the Court both before and just after World War II. A landmark decision in *United States* v. *Socony-Vacuum Oil Co.* (1940) enunciated a strong rule against price fixing: "Under the Sherman Act a combination formed for the purpose and with the effect of raising, depressing, fixing, pegging or stabilizing the price of a commodity in interstate commerce is illegal *per se.*" Thus where price fixing was concerned, no test of reasonableness or sound social purpose would be applied.

An even more basic attack on the rule of reason was enunciated in the Aluminum Company of America (ALCOA) case decided in 1945. The decision reversed the U.S. Steel and International Harvester decisions and found ALCOA to be an illegal monopoly even though it had engaged in no unreasonable behavior. The decision suggested that beyond some point mere size would in itself be an offense if the defendants had not done everything possible to avoid becoming dominant. This reversal was possible because the mood of the country—and the composition of its courts—had changed sharply.

This case and others led some people to speak of the "new Sherman Act." Subsequent decisions have modified the strongly anti-big-business aspects of the ALCOA case, but the retreat from ALCOA has stopped well short of the Harvester and U.S. Steel decisions. The conduct of firms with massive market power, such as IBM, Kodak, and AT&T, is closely scrutinized to distinguish between competitive and monopolistic behavior.

The Warren Court. The modification of Section 7 of the Clayton Act in 1950, together with the onset of the Warren Court—so named for its chief

justice, Earl Warren, a former Republican governor of California—ushered in a period of virtually unbroken triumphs for the government in its antitrust cases. Justice Potter Stewart, a frequent dissenter, wryly remarked that the only principle he could discern in the Court's decisions was that "the government always wins."

In particular, the Warren Court's antitrust decisions greatly restricted the ability of large corporations to merge, even when their market shares were relatively small. For example, in the Von's Grocery case (1965), a merger of two supermarkets was ruled illegal even though the merged firms would have had only a 7.5 percent share of the local (Los Angeles) market. The merger of Brown Shoe Company with a chain of retail stores (Kinney) was found illegal even though Kinney sold less than 2 percent of the nation's shoes and Brown supplied only 8 percent of Kinney's needs. In other areas as well, the Warren Court was highly critical of any business practice that might appear to restrain trade.

The Burger Court. The Warren Court has been replaced by the Burger Court, four of its nine members having been appointed by President Nixon and one each by Presidents Ford and Reagan. This Court's views on antitrust matters are much more tolerant of business practices that involve some limitations on trade, so long as they are normal business practices. In particular, this Court has been reluctant to expand the list of actions that are illegal per se. While the pendulum has swung back toward a pro-business attitude, the present judicial stance is much more balanced than that of the years before World War II.

Periods of Vigorous Prosecution

Courts, whatever their predilections, decide only those cases that come before them. Whether to prosecute, and which cases to prosecute, is largely decided by the antitrust division, whose head is a presidential appointee.

When the Sherman Act was passed in 1890, it was adopted with little discussion and attracted remarkably little attention. It was not until President Theodore Roosevelt set up the antitrust division in the Department of Justice in 1903 that "trustbusting" became important. His administration initiated the series of major prosecutions that led to the Standard Oil, American Tobacco, and U.S. Steel decisions.

The rule of reason, World War I, and a sharply conservative turn in American attitudes during the 1920s and then the trauma of the Great Depression accompanied 25 years of unaggressive antitrust, from 1912 to 1937. The appointment of Thurman Arnold in 1937 to the leadership of the antitrust division marked the beginning of a most vigorous period of antitrust activity. The fruits of this activity included the ALCOA and Socony-Vacuum decisions.

Antitrust policy was pushed to the sidelines by the overriding problems of World War II, the postwar readjustment, and the Korean War. It did not begin to re-emerge until the 1950s. A relatively vigorous antitrust policy was pursued during the Eisenhower, Kennedy, and Johnson administrations. It reached a climax in the mid sixties in the decisions of the Warren Court.

Although the Nixon, Ford, Carter, and Reagan administrations have been more conservative, antitrust prosecutions by the antitrust division, by the FTC, and by private plaintiffs have remained fairly active. In recent years both the courts and the prosecutors have resisted an even more vigorous antitrust enforcement policy. Indeed the 1980s seem likely to be a relatively quiet period in antitrust innovation.

But the political and legal climate can change quickly. Many antitrust specialists expected the 1980s to be a pathbreaking decade because the Justice Department was vigorously engaged in trying major monopolization cases against two American corporate giants—IBM and AT&T—and the FTC was testing a novel theory of "shared monopoly" by bringing cases against Kellogg and the other cereal manufacturers. It seemed likely that all three cases would eventually reach the Supreme Court and lead to a series of precedent-creating decisions. The expectation proved wrong. The cereals' case was dismissed by the FTC, and

the IBM and AT&T cases have been settled, thus depriving the Burger Court of a major opportunity to reinterpret the law of monopoly.

The Success of Antitrust Policy Against Monopoly

Economists do not generally agree on how much the *structure* of American industry has been influenced by decades of antitrust policy. American industry remains highly concentrated (see Chapter 16), but empirical studies show no tendency for the concentration either to increase or to decrease drastically. Would the pattern be very different if there had been no antitrust laws, or if the existing laws had been more vigorously enforced? We do not know for sure.

Many economists and antitrust lawyers believe that U.S. antitrust laws have been quite successful in inhibiting price fixing and certain restrictive practices. At the same time, the laws have done little to alter the basic structure of the economy. Whether this constitutes a signal success or a brave failure depends on one's diagnosis of the health of the American market system. Here people disagree sharply. The role of economic analysis in antitrust is discussed briefly in the box.

PUBLIC UTILITY REGULATION OF NATURAL MONOPOLY

Natural monopoly arises because of economies of scale (as was discussed on page 297). Policymakers have not wanted to compel the maintenance of a large number of small, inefficient producers when a single firm would be much more efficient; neither have they wanted to give a monopolist the opportunity to restrict output, raise price, and appropriate as profits the gains available by virtue of large-scale production.

The public utility concept grew out of the recognition by economists that when there are major economies of large-scale production, protection of the public interest by competition is impractical, if not impossible.

ECONOMICS AND ANTITRUST LAW

Economic concepts such as competition, monopoly, and markets lie at the heart of antitrust policy. Economists are employed in the Justice Department, by the Federal Trade Commission, and by lawyers for private companies. Market definition, for example, plays a critical role in antitrust merger litigation: Section 7 of the Clayton Act requires evaluation of a merger by asking whether "in any line of commerce, in any section of the country the effect of such acquisition may be substantially to lessen competition or to tend to create a monopoly."

"Line of commerce" and "section of the country" involve product and geographic market definitions because competition occurs only within sensibly defined markets. A great many antitrust cases have turned on market definition, and some have even utilized such economic concepts as cross-elasticity of demand.

Here are a few questions the courts have asked and answered: Is cellophane in the same market as wax paper, Saran wrap, and other flexible wrapping materials? (Yes, said the Supreme Court.) Are glass jars and tin cans in the same market? (Yes, said the Supreme Court.) Are insulated aluminum and copper cable in the same market? (Yes, said the District Court; no, said the Supreme Court.) Are New York and Philadelphia banks in the same market and thus in competition with one another? (No, said the courts in 1963.) Do different grades of coal in Illinois constitute an economic market? (No, said the District Court, in part because it found the relevant market to be energy. The Supreme Court did not reverse the decision.) Even though courts decide these matters, the matters themselves involve economic questions, and economic studies or witnesses were introduced by both parties in each of these litigations.

But while antitrust policies use economic theory and economic expertise, our antitrust laws ignore certain distinctions that economists think are important. In particular, the role of big business, even monopoly, in promoting dynamic advances, as argued by Professor Schumpeter, has many adherents yet is largely ignored by antitrust policies. Some decisions have protected smaller competitors against larger, more efficient rivals. The distinction between injury to *competition* and injury to *competitors* has not always been made clearly by the courts. Finally, the courts have had a difficult time in coming to grips with oligopoly. Should it be regarded favorably because it is much more competitive than monopoly—or unfavorably because it is much less competitive than perfect competition?

Economists themselves are divided as to whether these distinctions are important. Some believe that public policy ought to be based on things such as size and market share, without regard for actual conduct or performance. Others offer their own "rule of reason," called *workable competition*. They argue that the real choice is between more or less oligopoly and that the positive effects of a given market share, or merger, on prices, on profits, and on costs should be determined in each individual case. This seems so reasonable; why do some people object? They object because they believe that workable competition will lead to endless studies and no action. Because economists do not speak with a unified voice on such matters, it is perhaps not surprising that the basic nature of the antitrust program continues to be set by the lawyers.

One possible response to this dilemma is for government to assume ownership of the single firm and instruct (or delegate to) the managers of the *nationalized* industry how much to produce and what price to charge, in each case being guided by the national interest. Many countries have done precisely that with telephone and railroad services, among others. The characteristic American response since the late nineteenth century, when the modern regulatory commissions first appeared, has been to allow private enterprise but to regulate its behavior.

Public utility regulation gives to appropriate public authorities (usually specially constituted regulatory commissions such as the Interstate Commerce Commission and the Wisconsin Public Utilities Commission) control over the price and quantity of service provided by a natural monopoly, with the object of achieving the efficiency of a single seller without the output restriction of the monopolist.

In return for giving a company a franchise or license to be the sole producer, the public utility regulators reserve the right to regulate its behavior.

Regulation of this kind began with the establishment of the Interstate Commerce Commission (ICC) in 1887. Its primary function was to regulate railroad rates. Public utility regulation subsequently spread to other forms of transportation (airlines and pipelines) as well as to the standard utilities: telephone, electricity, water, and gas.

Although regulatory commissions were first created to deal with natural monopoly problems, most regulatory activity is no longer of that kind, including much of the regulatory activity of agencies such as the ICC. In the discussion that follows, we are concerned only with natural monopoly regulation.

The Theory of Natural Monopoly Regulation

The dilemma of natural monopoly is illustrated in Figure 18-3. To achieve low costs, a single large

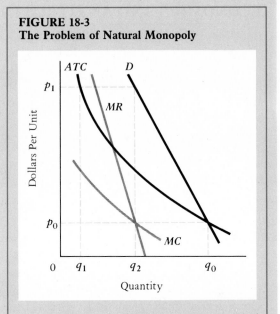

FIGURE 18-3
The Problem of Natural Monopoly

Cost conditions in a situation of natural monopoly are such that a single firm is needed to achieve the economies of scale, but a monopolist finds it profitable to restrict output to maximize profits. Because *ATC* declines sharply, efficiency is served by having a single firm. Clearly, one firm producing at q_0 would be more efficient than several firms each producing q_1 at a cost of p_1 per unit. But an unregulated monopoly would restrict output to q_2 and charge price p_1, thereby depriving consumers of the advantages of large-scale production.

producer is necessary, but an unregulated profit-maximizing monopoly would restrict output, raise price, and fail to provide the large volume of output at a low price that the technology makes possible.

What price should a regulatory commission permit? It might wish to set price equal to marginal cost (the way it would be in perfect competition), but such a price and quantity would surely lead to losses, for marginal cost is necessarily below average cost when average cost is falling. This is illustrated in Figure 18-4. Such a pricing scheme would require a continuing subsidy of the resulting losses.

An alternative is to permit the company to charge a price that allows it to cover all its costs

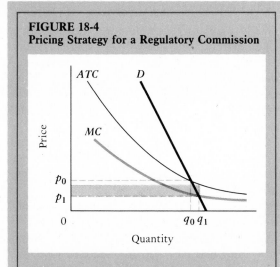

FIGURE 18-4
Pricing Strategy for a Regulatory Commission

Average cost pricing is the goal of regulatory commissions, which seek the lowest prices possible without losses for natural monopolies. Although perfect competition leads to production where price equals marginal costs, here the price cannot be set at p_1, where demand equals marginal cost, because the firm would necessarily suffer losses (the shaded area). Price p_0 covers all costs (including the opportunity cost of capital). The corresponding output q_0 achieves most of the cost advantages of large-scale output.

and earn a fair return on its investment. In essence, this is the objective of most regulatory commissions with regard to pricing in natural monopoly situations. The theory is extraordinarily simple. The problems of putting the theory into practice are difficult.

Problems of Implementing the Theory

Regulation has aimed at setting prices high enough to permit firms to cover all their costs yet low enough to achieve the large sales required to reap the scale economies that characterize natural monopoly situations. If a regulatory commission knew exactly what the demand curve and the cost curves looked like, it could simply pick the point on the demand curve that corresponded to the lowest price that covered average total costs. But precise demand and cost information is seldom available. In its absence commissions have tended to judge prices according to the level of profits they produce. Generally, having set prices, regulatory agencies permit price increases when profits fall below "fair" levels and require price reductions if profits exceed such levels.

While it is true that if the appropriate price is charged, economic profits will be zero, the reverse is not necessarily true. Profits can be zero because of inefficient operation or misleading accounting, as well as pricing at the lowest attainable level of average cost. Thus commissions that rely on profits as their guide to pricing must monitor a number of other aspects of the regulated firm's behavior.

The Definition of Costs

If a company is to be allowed to charge a price determined as "cost plus a fair profit" (as the regulators say), and if that price is below the profit-maximizing one, it is clearly in the firm's interest to exaggerate reported costs if it can. One major activity of regulatory commissions has been to define rules of allowable costing. Cost supervision is an important activity of public utility regulation for another reason as well. Without it, managers of the regulated industries might have little incentive to be efficient and might simply let costs drift upward.

The Rate Base

Average total cost includes an appropriate rate of return on the capital invested in the business. Suppose it is agreed that a firm should be allowed to earn a rate of return of 11 percent on its capital. The **rate of return** is defined as the ratio of profits to invested capital. What is the value of the capital to which 11 percent is to be applied? The allowable amount is called the **rate base.** There has been no more controversial area than this in public utility regulation. Should the original cost or the reproduction cost of the firm's assets be used? It does not make much difference unless prices are changing, but in the inflationary situation of the last 35 years, reproduction cost is uniformly higher than original costs and thus leads to higher bases, higher permitted profits, and higher rates to users. If the major concern is to generate earnings to buy replacement equipment, reproduction cost is appropriate. If the major concern is to generate profits to compensate past capital investments, original cost may be appropriate. Regulatory commissions (and the courts) have vacillated on this issue.

The precise nature of regulatory rules is important because the rules affect the incentives of those regulated. Economists Harvey Averch and Leland Johnson have shown that a regulated utility has a lesser incentive to resist high capital costs than an unregulated one and that in some circumstances it pays the unregulated utility to buy relatively unproductive equipment. This is true because if profits depend on the rate base, it often pays the firm to increase its rate base. Thus the notion of "necessary and prudent investments" enters into regulatory rules. This tendency for one regulation to lead to a need for yet further regulation has been called the *tar-baby effect,* after a fictional creature made of tar that overcame an attacker by enmeshing it.

A Fair Return

The permitted rate of return that is implicit in the theory of public utility regulation is the opportunity cost of the owners' capital, with allowances for risk. Regulatory commissions have paid some attention to overall earnings rates in the economy, and the level of permitted earnings has changed slightly over time. But "fairness" and tradition have played a much larger role than considerations of opportunity cost, and regulatory commissions have been slow to adjust permitted rates of return to changing market conditions. For decades permitted rates of return of 6 to 9 percent were employed. But when market interest rates soared to double-digit figures during the late 1970s, the traditional levels were not sufficient to induce new investment. Yet regulatory commissions have been reluctant to permit the large increases in prices that would result from sharp increases in the permitted rate of return.

The Curtailment of Service

While regulatory commissions regulate prices with an eye on profits, they do not guarantee profits. Because profits are not guaranteed, a regulated utility in a declining industry may have a serious problem. If it is failing to make profits equal to the permitted rate, it may apply for permission to increase its prices, but if its demand is elastic, a rise in rates will lead to a reduction in revenues and may reduce profits. Privately owned urban transit systems and passenger rail lines have proven unprofitable because of secularly declining demand as people shifted to substitutes: private cars and airplanes. Given elastic demand curves, when transport companies raise fares (hoping to increase revenues), they find they only lose more customers to other means of transport.

At this point a local bus company, for example, may look to its costs to see how it can avoid losses. Often it finds that some parts of its service (such as routes to outlying neighborhoods) no longer cover the variable costs of providing them, and it proposes to the regulatory authority that this service be dropped. Often the regulators say no. The reason is that they see other considerations in abandoning the bus service (such as increased congestion in the downtown area as even more people used their own cars) that loom large to the regulators but not to the bus company.

The regulators want the regulated company to "cross-subsidize" the less popular routes with profits from the more popular routes; at the same time, they do not want to force the company into bankruptcy. Thus, each time a curtailment of service is proposed, regulators must make the difficult determination of whether the company is merely trying to increase its profits and is shirking its public service responsibility or whether it is truly in trouble.

The Success of Natural Monopoly Regulation

The moral of the public utility experience is that what looks like a simple and straightforward theory of regulating natural monopoly turns out in practice to be highly complex. In large part this is because regulated companies adapt their behavior to the rules that are imposed on them—and thus begins a chain of adaptation and change by regulators and regulated that produces a complex and cumbersome apparatus. Moreover, the need for due process in decisions that affect property rights has made procedures and decisions legalistic and resource-using. The costs of regulation include more than the costs of running regulatory commissions and the costs imposed on the courts by seemingly endless appeals. Regulatory costs are also imposed on businesses that must strive to comply with paperwork.

Many people believe that, as long as competition is not possible, there are benefits to traditional public utility regulation. But there is debate even about that. Some, including Professor George Stigler of the University of Chicago, argue that the evidence shows that the levels of prices, quantities, and profits are about the same under public utility regulation as they would have been without it; they even go so far as to suggest that unregulated monopoly would have performed better. If that is so, we incur costs, but not benefits, from public utility regulation.

The more common basis of disenchantment with public utility regulatory commissions is that they have changed their function. They have largely abandoned protection of the consumer from natural monopoly and have become protectors of firms *from* competition.

PROTECTION *AGAINST* COMPETITION IN ANTITRUST AND PUBLIC UTILITY REGULATION

While the main thrust of antitrust policy and the original purpose of the regulatory commissions was the protection of *competition*, a parallel and for a time growing aspect of public policy in these areas was a shift to protection of *competitors* against the rigors of competition. To understand both the overall nature of American competition policy and the current movement toward deregulation, it is necessary to review its protectionist aspects.

The "Deviant Theme" in Antitrust[6]

"Antitrust" was given two meanings from its earliest days. One was anti-monopoly, and the other anti-big firm. Some of the supporters of the original Sherman Act saw its purposes as the protection of small independent businessmen from the tyranny of markets in which large corporations were coming to play such a big role. When the Sherman Act was not so interpreted, they rallied behind passage of the Federal Trade Commission Act (1914), which legislated against "unfair methods of competition." From at least that time until the 1970s, when Justices Black and Douglas left the Supreme Court, the populist view had its voice on the Court, and that view often was protectionist in its effect. In 1918, in *Chicago Board of Trade,* the court supported overnight restrictions on price competition in order to let traders enjoy a more tranquil life. In *Appalachian Coals* (1933), effective output restriction to prevent distress price cutting was allowed by small coal producers devastated by the Great Depression. In *Von's Grocery* (1965), cited earlier, the underlying concern was the plight of the small "Ma and Pa" grocery stores that were being displaced by the ever-growing presence of the chain stores.

Perhaps the easiest way to understand this protectionist theme within antimonopoly policy is to notice that the distributive aspects of monopoly have been at least as important to public policy-makers as the allocative inefficiencies that so concern economists. In the industrial sectors of the economy, corporate managers and stockholders are typically of above average income. Thus the higher salaries and higher dividends of corporate monopoly tend to lead to a more unequal distribution of income. Monopoly power, when exercised by those

---

[6] Professor (now Judge) Robert Bork uses this phrase to contrast these decisions to the main, pro-competition thrust of antitrust.

who are relatively poor rather than relatively rich, has frequently been supported rather than opposed by the government. For example, the efforts of farmers to increase farm income have not only been approved but actively promoted by public policies of crop restriction, price supports, and exemption of producers' cooperatives from antitrust laws. Labor unions are also exempt from antitrust prosecutions, and the efforts of unions to achieve some degree of monopoly power over the supply of labor were also supported actively by those public policies that encouraged the growth of unions.

During the 1930s the protectionist theme—once an occasional, minority voice—became the central thrust of American policy toward industry. Despite the fears of business about Franklin Roosevelt's radicalism, no administration before or since has given such encouragement to policies in restraint of trade! Roosevelt's first administration (1933–1937) was so concerned with stemming the Great Depression that under the National Recovery Administration it fostered industry councils that were encouraged to fix prices and limit outputs in an attempt to restore stability to demoralized markets.

Legislation of the same period included the Guffey Coal Act and the Connally "Hot Oil" Act, designed to provide emergency relief against excessive competition in coal and petroleum. It also included passage of the Robinson-Patman Act (1936), which greatly limited price cutting where the results might be classified as discriminatory, and the Miller-Tydings Act (1937), which allowed manufacturers to establish and enforce minimum prices for their products in the name of "fair trade." These laws were used to prevent aggressive price competition by chain stores and by discount houses. Their most telling aspect, as anticompetitive statutes, is that most prosecutions under them have been brought by competitors (not customers) of the firms charged with violations.

Many aspects of this protectionist period survive in legal opinions that are still valid today. To many economists, they fail to distinguish between acts that injure competition (such as price fixing) and acts that injure competitors (such as cutting prices below the level of an inefficient firm's costs).

At least temporarily, protectionism in antitrust is on the wane. The Fair Trade laws have been repealed, and both Congress and the courts have restricted the FTC's ability to impose limitations on unfair competitive practices. Moreover, the Reagan administration's appointees to the Antitrust Division seem determined to pursue price fixing and downplay prosecution of other practices that, while apparently restrictive, may actually be pro-competitive. At the same time, this backing away from explicitly protectionist attitudes has been accompanied by a general decrease in antitrust prosecutions.

The Protectionist Policies of the Regulatory Commissions

In antitrust, pro-competitive and anti-competitive tendencies have existed side by side. In public utility regulation, it is often argued, protection of the regulated has replaced protection of the consumer.

There seems little doubt that originally the ICC regulated railroad rates in order to keep them down. By the 1930s, however, the ICC had become concerned by the depressed economic condition of the railroads, the potentially destructive competition among them, and the emerging vigorous competition from trucks and barges. The ICC became the protector of the railroads, permitting them to establish minimum rates for freight of different classes, allowing price discrimination, and encouraging other restrictive practices. Moreover, it became a leading advocate of bringing motor carriers under the regulatory umbrella.

Restricting entry into trucking and setting minimum rates for trucks can only be seen as protectionist. The trucking industry has never exhibited natural monopoly attributes. The only reason for regulating the large interstate carriers was to control their competition with the railroads.

One of the problems with protectionist regulation is illustrated by the motor carrier experience. The big interstate carriers were limited in where they could go and how *low* a price they could quote. As a result, they became targets for small, unregulated truckers who could cut rates and thus draw away customers without fear of retaliation. To eliminate the rate competition, regulation was extended to small truckers.

Nor is the transportation experience unique. When the Federal Communications Commission (FCC) began regulating telephone communications, AT&T was a natural monopolist, at least with respect to its need to create a nation-wide network of telephone wires. With the development of microwave relay stations and then of satellite communication, competition in message transmission became possible, and (given AT&T's rate structure as approved by the FCC) highly profitable. The FCC sought to prevent such competition and bring AT&T's potential competitors under its regulation, and until limited first by the courts and more recently by Congress, it did so.

Finally, consider airline regulation. When the Civil Aeronautics Board (CAB) began regulating airline routes and fares, there was arguably so little demand that competition could not have been effective, for flying was not yet a standard way of travel. By the mid sixties, however, the regulation was plainly protectionist and designed to shield the major carriers from excessive competition, on the ground that such competition might ruin the industry and even invite cost-cutting practices that endangered public safety.

These are not the only examples, nor has all regulation turned protectionist. But they suggest why by the late 1970s both Jimmy Carter and Ronald Reagan could be arguing for *deregulation* in the name of increasing competition in the United States. (It is perhaps ironic that at the same time pressure was increasing for protection of U.S. industries from foreign competition.)

What accounted for the turn toward protectionism by regulatory commissions whose original charge was protection of consumers from natural monopolists? One thesis is that the regulatory commissions were gradually captured by those they were supposed to regulate. Another is that the protectionist policies of the 1930s really reflected the public's mood and a genuine fear of destructive competition. The depression of the 1930s deeply affected a whole generation. It shook public con-

fidence in many long-held beliefs, including the "received wisdom" that competition was in the public's interest. Faith in competition was greatly shaken by bank and business failures and by the massive unemployment of workers and factories. With the emergence of a new generation for whom the Great Depression is an episode in past history, not a continuing nightmare, some degree of faith in competition is returning. But it is fragile, as was demonstrated anew by the calls for more protectionism during the recession of 1981–1983.

The Prospects for Regulation and Deregulation

Deregulation was a key issue in the 1980 election campaign. The recent deregulation of airline rates and routes and the imminent complete deregulation of motor carriers are examples of a movement that will be a major source of political debate for years to come.

More is involved in the movement for deregulation than just reversing the protectionist policies of regulatory commissions such as the ICC and FCC. It concerns, more basically, the whole question of how much interference with private decisionmaking is desirable. Much of the regulation that is targeted for review is "social regulation" that is concerned with protection of consumers, not from high prices or monopolistic exploitation, but from other kinds of hazards. The targets of this deregulation include the Food and Drug Administration (FDA), the Securities and Exchange Commission (SEC), the Environmental Protection Agency (EPA), and the Occupational Safety and Health Administration (OSHA). These agencies protect consumers from health hazards, fraud, pollution, and occupational and product dangers rather than from excessive prices.

The debate about this kind of regulation concerns "externalities," and the case for and against it will be discussed in Chapter 24. It asks questions such as "Are the benefits of pollution control and occupational safety rules worth the costs they impose?" Many people think they are; many others think not. The question sounds like a factual one, but alleged benefits and costs are difficult—if not impossible—to measure with any precision. Thus, much of the debate is ideological, notwithstanding its expression in terms of dollar estimates of benefits and costs. Are the accidents avoided by industrial safety standards worth the extra expenditures they require? Victims of such accidents may answer differently from those who are required to pay more for products because those products are produced under safer working conditions.

What about deregulation applied to natural monopoly regulation? There seems in 1984 to be a remarkable consensus that such regulation has failed to live up to the expectations held for it. Perhaps the most widely held view is that regulation, even when effective at first, becomes too rigid and unresponsive to change and as a result fails to recognize and to permit such competition as is possible. Given changing technology, yesterday's natural monopoly of a single railroad may become but one mode of transportation in a competitive transportation industry. Wire telephone communications are no longer unique, given radio and satellites. Even the Post Office is not the only way to send written messages and parcels from one place to another. Thus, the scope of natural monopoly regulation keeps changing. But regulators tend to cling to, and in some cases are legally committed to, rules and assumptions that may no longer fit the world they are regulating.

As to the fear of catastrophic, destructive competition, it has faded greatly since its heyday in the 1930s. If belief in destructive competition survives today, it is mostly in the fear of *foreign* competition with traditional American industries. Indeed, the view is widespread that the regulation of American industries is an important barrier to their competition in what are increasingly world markets.

Changes in regulation in some form or another seem likely to continue over the next decade in response to this growing consensus. Some favor rapid deregulation and reliance on market forces. Others believe that the deficiencies lie in the structure of regulation and that changing the way regulation is carried out will improve matters. Still others think that the failures of regulation require nationalization or new legislation defining a novel approach to what regulators should do.

Which of many proposed directions for regulatory reform will be followed is unclear at this stage. The deregulation of airlines has been accomplished, and that of motor carriers is underway. As of this date Congress has decreased the regulatory authority of the ICC and the FTC. The breakup of AT&T as a result of the 1982 settlement of its long-standing antitrust case will pave the way for much less regulation of its activities, and it is now free to compete in areas where it was previously excluded.

But the movement favoring deregulation is not without opposition. Many regulatory activities, from banking to nuclear energy to pipelines, have powerful political support in Congress. Moreover, many industries subject to regulation are staunchly resisting deregulation.

Will the experience with deregulation quickly resolve the key factual questions about whether the free market works better than regulation? The answer is probably no. One cannot quickly undo the effects of decades of regulation and move to a long-run unregulated equilibrium. Industries such as the airlines developed under regulation and made long-term investments on the expectation that regulatory rules would continue in effect. After 30 or 40 years of regulation, all the decision makers in the industry were geared toward a regulatory rather than a free-market environment. When, suddenly, the environment changed, all sorts of transitional problems occurred, as was to be expected, and these may take years to work themselves out.

The experience with airline deregulation suggests why it is difficult to evaluate results. Starting in 1978, the Civil Aeronautics Board (CAB) removed regulations on airline rate making and on protecting individual airline routes. The initial responses seemed almost miraculous: tumbling air fares, supersaver discounts, increased air service on popular routes, increased passenger travel, and a boom in the industry. But a year later fares were *up* 25 to 40 percent over the regulated levels, some of the major carriers were having severe financial troubles—one of them, Braniff, went bankrupt—service to certain locations had been curtailed, and the euphoria of a year earlier was gone. Some new carriers have established themselves, others had not. Fares between certain cities are much lower than they would have been, others are higher.

But it will be years before enough experience exists to permit a definitive evaluation of the benefits and costs of airline deregulation. Without hard evidence, one can find assertions on each side. To the president of United Airlines the answer was that while fares had risen, they had risen much less than would have been the case with regulation—that is, deregulation was a success. To the senior vice-president of American Airlines, deregulation was raising costs and thus prices by encouraging excess capacity on most routes. In his view deregulation was an expensive failure.

SUMMARY

1. The economist's traditional dislike of monopoly is based on the proposition that if costs, demand, and products are unchanged, the monopolization of a previously competitive industry will lead to a rise in price and a decline in output. In such circumstances, monopoly will lead to allocative inefficiency and may lead to productive inefficiency.

2. Levels of cost are not independent of market structures. If there are advantages of large scale in production, distribution, marketing, or purchasing, the minimum efficient size of the firm may be too large to be compatible with conditions of perfect competition. In such cases a shift from competition to a more concentrated market structure—oligopoly or monopoly—may lead to lower costs and increased efficiency. Because costs are not independent of market structure, the prima facie case in favor of competition and against concentration of market power is weakened. Most economists believe that substantial competition is compatible with efficient operation of American industry and that it is desirable to foster at least that amount of competition.

3. A major issue in the evaluation of different market structures concerns the incentive provided for invention and innovation. Joseph Schumpeter believed that the incentive to innovate was so much greater under monopoly that monopoly was to be preferred to perfect competition. While few modern economists go that far, the empirical evidence suggests that technological change and innovation can to a measurable extent be traced to the efforts of large firms in oligopolistic industries.

4. Another issue in the evaluation of market structures concerns the possibility of chronic excessive competition, in which industries characterized by heavy fixed investments will, if unregulated, be led into price wars that threaten the survival of an industry that could survive under less competitive conditions. While this possibility surely exists, many economists are highly skeptical about whether it is sufficiently likely to warrant all of the protectionism it has spawned.

5. The policy implications of the classical view of monopoly and competition led American legislators of the late nineteenth century in two directions: public utility regulation to deal with natural monopoly and antitrust laws to deal with other kinds of monopoly.

6. The basic tool of antitrust policy is the series of laws that seeks to eliminate practices that lead to monopoly. The overall effect of antitrust policy at any time rests on three things: the nature of the laws themselves, the attitude and interpretation of the courts, and the vigor with which prosecutions are brought by the government and by private plaintiffs. Antitrust policy is an ever-present aspect of the American industrial landscape. Most observers believe that antitrust laws have been more nearly successful in inhibiting restrictive practices than in altering the basic structure of the economy.

7. The original philosophy of public utility regulation was to grant a monopoly where necessary to achieve the advantages of large-scale production but to prevent the monopolist from restricting output and raising price. The most common regulatory approach has been to regulate prices. This is done by watching profits: allowing price increases only if necessary to permit the regulated utility to earn a fair return on its capital and requiring price decreases if profits rise above the approved level.

8. Implementation of this straightforward theory encounters difficulties because any set of rules becomes a set of signals that induces patterns of response from those regulated. Thus it has been necessary for regulators to define carefully "proper" costs, how the costs should be measured, the appropriate rate base, what constitute "necessary and prudent" additions to capital equipment, and what constitutes a fair return. They have also been forced to determine when and whether utilities can discontinue providing services to groups in the community. Natural utility regulation appears to most observers not to have been an unqualified success. To some, this is because the regulators have not made much difference. To others, it is because regulators have tended to shift their focus from protection of consumers to protection of the firms being regulated.

9. Protection of firms *from* competition has been a parallel theme with protection *of* competition itself from the earliest days of antitrust and public utility regulation. During the Great Depression, it emerged as a dominant theme, and some believe that it has permanently transformed the regulatory environment.

10. The entire regulatory apparatus has come under close scrutiny in recent years. A first step toward deregulation was the passage in 1978 of the Airline Deregulation Act, which will gradually phase out of existence the Civil Aeronautics Board, which has controlled both rates and routes. A second step was the 1980 passage of a bill to deregulate motor carriers. How far the deregulation movement will go is sure to be a major political issue of the rest of the 1980s.

TOPICS FOR REVIEW

Effects of monopolizing a competitive industry
Competition and allocative efficiency
The effect of market structure on costs
Destructive competition
Purposes of antitrust legislation
Natural monopoly
Difficulties of public utility regulation
Protection of competition versus protection of competitors
Deregulation

DISCUSSION QUESTIONS

1. Consider an innovation that lowers the marginal cost of production by the same amount in each of two industries, one of which is perfectly competitive, the other a single-firm monopoly. Show that prices will fall in each industry but that prices and quantities will change less in monopoly than in competition as a response to a change in marginal costs.

2. "I think there are some people, in and out of government, who get a little confused and associate bigness with badness. Success alone is now evidence enough to warrant intensive scrutiny by the government to determine how the success can be remedied—as if it were some sort of disease. The age of Orwell's doublethink, prophesied for 1984, has come early. For now, to win is to lose. The real losers are the consumers. They lose the advantages of free competition; new and better products, lower prices and wider choices." Comment on these views of a leading GM executive.

3. Economists Armen Alchian and Reuben Kessel have advanced the hypothesis that monopolists choose to satisfy more of their nonmonetary aims than do perfect competitors. Consider three aims:
   a. exercising the prejudices of the monopolists against certain racial minorities
   b. enjoying a good life with big expense accounts
   c. promoting their political philosophies by advertising and broadcasting

   What theoretical arguments could support the Alchian-Kessel hypothesis? Would the same arguments apply to oligopolists?

4. Evaluate the wisdom of having the antitrust division use profits as a measure of monopoly power in deciding whether to prosecute a case. Would such a rule be expected to affect the behavior of firms with high profits? In what ways might any changes be socially beneficial and in what ways socially costly?

5. Price fixing agreements are (with some specific exemptions) violations of the antitrust laws. Consider the effects of the following. In what way, if at all, should they be viewed as being similar to price fixing agreements?

a. a manufacturer "recommending" minimum prices to its dealers

b. manufacturers publishing product price lists that are changed only every three months

c. a trade association that publishes "average industry total costs of production" every month

6. The Department of Justice merger guidelines permit a "failing company" defense to an otherwise illegal acquisition but reject an "efficiency" defense. Thus a merger that keeps a failing and presumably inefficient firm in business is permitted, but one that achieves a more efficient level of production is not. What arguments can you develop that support or oppose this policy?

7. Under what circumstances should some aspect of market structure or market conduct be treated as *illegal per se*— that is, without considering the effect in the particular case?

8. It is often asserted that when a regulatory agency such as a public utilities commission is established, it will ultimately become controlled by the people it was intended to regulate. This argument raises the question of who regulates the regulators. Can you identify why this might happen? How might the integrity of regulatory boards be protected?

9. "In a competitive market the least-cost production techniques are revealed by entry and exit, while in public utility regulation they are revealed by commission rate hearings. It is easier to fool the commission than the market. Therefore, wherever possible, competition should be permitted." Discuss.

19 WHO RUNS THE FIRM AND FOR WHAT ENDS?

Once upon a time most Americans had great faith in the ability of private firms to produce the goods and services on which the nation's prosperity was founded. America had the highest living standard in the world, and it seemed to be living proof that American-style private capitalism not only worked, it worked much better than any known alternative.

Today the public's perception seems to have changed. Many American firms are floundering, apparently unable to meet foreign competition. Attitude surveys show that private firms no longer enjoy the public's full confidence. Many people question both the morality of business behavior and the ability of business to act as the prime mover of a successful free enterprise system. Today, many Americans are in the anomalous position of believing in the free-market private enterprise system in general while harboring deep suspicions about whether our major corporations can or will make it work.

Important questions are involved here. Does the continuing success of the American economy depend on the initiative of healthy, independent, private firms? Does it depend instead on increased public scrutiny and control of the behavior of these firms? Does it require subsidization or protection of our firms from foreign competition? Is the economy's apparent failure to perform as well in the past decade as it did in previous decades due to a failure of private firms? Or is it perhaps due to increasing government interference with their activities?

What light does the theory we have studied so far shed on these important questions? In economic theory firms are users of factors of production and producers of commodities. They face cost and demand curves that are largely determined by forces beyond their control. They seek to maximize their profits by keeping their costs as low as possible and producing to satisfy consumers' demands. They care only about profits, and their decisions are uninfluenced by their internal structure. Thus they contribute to our high living standards by producing, as cheaply as possible, goods that satisfy consumers' demands.

An important body of criticism disputes this standard theory of the firm. It says instead that actual firms have the power to control their market conditions and that they use that power. They manipulate demand by advertising, and they are not under heavy competitive pressure to produce efficiently by holding costs down. Firms, the critics continue, do not even seek to maximize profits. Instead they seek other goals that are determined by their internal structure, and these goals often cause them to behave in ways that are socially undesirable. If true, such criticisms would support the views that firms hinder rather than advance consumer welfare and that they need to be forced by government or by the cold winds of foreign competition to act in the social interest.

In past chapters we studied the traditional view that firms, seeking private profits, serve the inter-ests of consumers. In the present chapter we will study some criticisms of that view. We begin with those that strike at the very core of the standard microeconomic theory.

DO FIRMS MANIPULATE THE MARKET?

In conventional theory, demand curves depend decisively on consumers' tastes and incomes and are to a significant degree independent of the actions of firms. Firms are assumed to be in business to make money, which they do by producing and selling the goods and services that consumers want. The successful firm is the one that best satisfies consumers' demands, while the firm that consistently does not do this will eventually fail. The ultimate source of all profits is consumers' desires. (Even monopoly profits depend on consumers' willingness to buy the product that the monopolist controls.) The need for firms to respond to consumers' desires is an important part of any argument for the free enterprise system. If firms did not so respond, there would be little justification in allowing them to exert major influences on the allocation of the country's resources.

The Hypothesis That Firms Control the Market

A very different hypothesis was given its most prominent expression by John Kenneth Galbraith and consumer advocate Ralph Nader. In this view it is *not* consumers' real wants that create the market signals that in turn provide the profit opportunities that motivate business behavior. Instead, large corporations have great power to create and manipulate demand. Firms must plan and invest for an uncertain future, and the profitability of the enormous investments that they make is threatened by the unpredictability of events. Firms try to make the future less unpredictable by actively manipulating market demand and by co-opting government agencies that are supposed to control their activities.

Manipulation of Demand

The most important source of unpredictable events that may jeopardize corporate investments is unexpected shifts in market demand curves. To guard against the effects of unexpected declines in demand, corporations spend vast amounts on advertising that allows them to sell what they want to produce rather than what consumers want to buy. At the same time, corporations decide not to produce products that consumers would like to buy. This reduces the risks inherent in investing in wholly new and untried products and avoids the possibility that successful new products might spoil the market for an existing product.

According to this hypothesis, we consumers are the victims of the corporations; we are pushed around at their whim, persuaded to buy things we do not really want, and denied products we would like to have. In short we are brainwashed ciphers with artificially created wants, and we have no real autonomy with respect to our own consumption.

Corruption of Public Authorities

A second threat to the long-range plans and investments of corporations comes from uncontrollable and often unpredictable changes in the nature of government interference with the freedom of the corporation. This political threat is met by co-opting or corrupting the members of Congress, who pass laws affecting corporations, and the government agencies that are supposed to be regulating them. Corporation managers, according to the theory, indirectly subvert public institutions, from universities to regulatory agencies.

Government, instead of regulating business and protecting the public interest, has become the servant of the corporation. It supplies the corporate sector with such essential inputs as educated, trained, healthy, socially secure workers. Government also serves the giant corporation through policies concerning tariffs, import quotas, tax rules, subsidies, and research and development. These policies protect the industrial establishment from competitive pressures and reinforce its dominance and profitability.

Corruption of Our Value System

The managers of modern firms have great power. The corporations they manage earn large profits that can be reinvested to further the achievement of the values of the ruling group; a group that Galbraith calls the *technostructure*. The values of this "ruling class" emphasize industrial production, rapid growth, and materialistic aspirations at the expense of the better things of life (such as cultural and aesthetic values) and the quality of the environment.

More important, the industrial managers join with the military in a military-industrial complex that utilizes, trains, and elevates the technicians to positions of power and prestige not only in industry but in the armed services, in the defense establishment, and in the highest positions of government. In so doing, the corporations and their managers threaten to dominate if not subvert our foreign policies as well as our domestic policies.

The New Industrial State

The foregoing is an outline of what Galbraith calls the *New Industrial State*.[1] If Galbraith's theories of the behavior of modern corporations were substantially correct, we would have to make major revisions in our ideas of how free-market economies work.

According to the concept of the New Industrial State, the largest corporations (1) tend to dominate the economy, (2) largely control market demand rather than being controlled by it, (3) co-opt government processes

---

[1] These views did not originate with the publication in 1967 of Galbraith's book by that title nor with the formation of "Nader's Raiders." Much earlier James Burnham wrote *The Managerial Revolution* and Robert Brady sounded an alarm in *Business as a System of Power*. Thorstein Veblen had predicted the technocratic takeover of society in *The Engineers and the Price System* in 1921, and Karl Marx predicted the subversion of the government bureaucrat by the businessman more than a century ago.

instead of being constrained by them, and (4) utilize their substantial discretionary power against the interests of society.

The Evidence for the Hypothesis

Superficially, many facts of the American economy lend support to Galbraith's hypothesis. Corporations do account for nearly three-quarters of all business done in the United States today, and large corporations dominate the corporate sector. There are nearly 250,000 manufacturing corporations, but only 1 percent of them have assets of $25 million or more. These largest corporations hold 87 percent of all manufacturing assets. It takes fewer than 600 corporations to account for 75 percent of the total assets of manufacturing.

The giant corporations are well known: General Motors, Exxon, Dow Chemical, U.S. Steel, Sears Roebuck, General Electric, and so on. Many are highly profitable, and most are so widely owned that managers, rather than stockholders, exercise effective control. If power comes with size, a "few" people—several thousand strategically placed executives of a few hundred leading corporations—have great power over economic affairs. Moreover, these people are primarily white, male, wealthy, and politically conservative.

As for political influence, individual corporations and trade associations have lobbyists and exercise whatever persuasion they can. The law firms that represent them annually hire the cream of the crop of skilled young advocates. Executives of many of these corporations serve on public commissions and frequently take important government positions. They make large contributions to political campaigns. Political influence is exercised at all levels of government—Congress, the Executive branch, regulatory commissions, the courts, and state and local governments.

The political activities of corporations are not confined to the United States. In the 1970s the Lockheed Corporation was implicated in scandals involving million-dollar bribes to secure foreign orders. The list of persons involved included (among many others) a former Japanese prime minister, the husband of the ruling queen of the Netherlands, and several former Italian Christian Democratic cabinet ministers. There is no doubt that corporations have succeeded in corrupting governments at the highest levels (or at least in harnessing the corruption that was already there) and have achieved through political channels results they might never have achieved in the marketplace.

The great corporations, along with many smaller firms, spend vast amounts on advertising—as the hypothesis predicts. In 1982 total advertising expenditure accounted for approximately 2½ percent of the value of the contribution of the private sector to the GNP. These expenditures are obviously designed to influence consumers' demand, and there is little doubt that if firms such as Lever Brothers, Gulf Oil, Schlitz, and IBM were to cut their advertising, they would lose sales to their competitors.

It is also true that much environment pollution is associated with industries that consist of well-known large firms. If automobiles, electric power, steel, oil, industrial chemicals, detergents, and paper are the primary sources of our pollution, surely Ford, Consolidated Edison, Bethlehem Steel, Texaco, Monsanto, Procter & Gamble, and International Paper are significantly to blame. Each of these is among the 100 largest nonfinancial corporations.

Doubts About the Hypothesis

Sensitivity to Market Pressures

Even the largest, most powerful industries are not immune to market pressures. Ford's Edsel was a classic example of the market's rejecting a product. The penetration of small foreign cars into the American market forced the automobile industry into first the compact car and then the still cheaper subcompacts. In spite of this, massive losses were suffered by American automobile manufacturers as consumers turned in very large numbers to foreign cars whose low costs and high gas mileages they preferred even in the face of heavy advertising of American cars. The decline of railroads for passenger travel is manifest in many ways, as the troubled financial history of once great railroading corporations shows. The Pullman Company was the nation's tenth largest firm in 1909; today it is not even in the top 300. The rise of air and motor travel and the decline of railroading were accompanied by a rise in the use of oil and a decline in the use of coal. More recently, the surge in demand for electric power and the shortage of oil have revitalized the coal industry.

Changes in demand and in taste can be sudden and dramatic, but mostly they are gradual, continuous, and less noticeable month by month than decade by decade. As one example, beef consumption per capita has fallen from 92 lbs. in the 1970s to 77 lbs. in the early 1980s, and the trend is continuing. On the average, about two new firms enter the top 100 every year, and as a consequence two others leave. This means a significant change over a decade.

Turnover in the list of leading companies is continuous and revealing. Only two, U.S. Steel and Exxon (Standard Oil of New Jersey), were in the top 10 both in 1910 and in 1982. Consider these giants of 1910, none of them among the largest 250 today: International Mercantile Marine (today United States Lines), United States Cotton Oil, American Hide and Leather, American Ice, Baldwin Locomotive, Cudahy, International Salt, and United Shoe Machinery. They have slipped or disappeared largely because of the relative decline in the demand for their products. Today's giants include automobile, oil, airline, computer, and electric power companies—for the obvious reason that demand for these products is strong.

Are these demand shifts explained by the corporate manipulation of consumers' tastes through advertising, or by more basic changes? Advertising has two major aspects: it seeks to inform consumers about the available products, and it seeks to influence consumers by altering their demands. The first aspect, informative advertising, plays an important part in the efficient operation of any free-market system; the second aspect is one through which firms seek to control the market rather than to be controlled by it.

Clearly, advertising does influence consumers' demand. If GM were to stop advertising, it would surely lose sales to Ford, Chrysler, and foreign imports, but it is hard to believe that the automotive society was conjured up by Madison Avenue. When you are persuaded to "fly the friendly skies of United," your real alternative is hardly a Conestoga wagon, a bicycle, or even a Greyhound bus; more likely you are foregoing American, Eastern, or Northwest Airlines. Careful promotion can influence the success of one rock group over another, but could it sell the waltz to today's teenager? Advertising—taste making—unquestionably plays a role in shaping demand, but so too do more basic human attitudes, psychological needs, and technological opportunities. The beef industry is advertising to stem the tide of consumers turning away from its product but is only slowing the tide's pace, as people pay attention to calories, cholesterol, and price.

Certainly advertising shifts demands among very similar products. It is hard to believe, however, that the American economy or the average American's system of values would be fundamentally changed if there were available one more or one less make of automobile or television set or brand of shoes. A look at those products that have brought basic changes to the economy—and perhaps to our value systems—suggests that these products succeeded *because consumers wanted them*, not because Madison Avenue brainwashed people into buying them. Consider a few major examples.

The automobile transformed American society and is in demand everywhere, even in Communist countries where only informative advertising exists. The Hollywood movie had an enormous influence in shaping our world and in changing some of our values; it was—and still is—eagerly attended throughout the world, whether or not it is accompanied by a ballyhoo of advertising. The jet airplane has shrunk the world: It has allowed major league sports to expand beyond the northeastern and midwestern United States (and those cities that could be reached by an overnight bus or rail jour-

THE MARKET CONTROLS THE FIRM: THE A&P STORY

The Great Atlantic and Pacific Tea Company (A&P), was the world's first grocery chain store. In 1859, A&P opened 100 stores in New York City, and their large-scale purchasing and low-price policies led the company and the concept to prosper. By 1912 A&P was running a national chain of economy stores whose central policy was described as "cash and carry, no deliveries, no credit, no advertising, no telephone."

Although widely copied—Kroger's was formed in 1887 and Safeway in 1915, among many others—A&P was dominant, with over 50 percent of the chain food sales all through the 1920s and into the 1930s. The firm was so dominant in the 1930s that antitrust authorities tried to restrain it, and legislation was introduced to limit its ability to compete so effectively.

Did A&P control the market? Many in and out of the company believed that it did, but events were to show that it did not. Its first big mistake occurred in the early 1930s, when it made the decision to neglect an innovation in marketing—the supermarket. Supermarkets consisted of several departments (meat, produce, and baked goods as well as dry groceries) under one roof and relied on self-service. A&P was a *grocery* chain and used clerks. Scale efficiencies and lower labor costs enabled the supermarkets to operate much more economically than traditional clerk-operated chain grocery stores. "King Kullen the Price Wrecker" opened the first supermarket in 1930 and, aided by the depression, was extremely successful. Supermarkets spread rapidly. A&P believed that supermarkets were a passing fad, and it refused to go along. Part of this was its feeling of loyalty to its clerks, who would have had a difficult time finding new jobs during the depression.

But A&P's policy, whatever the motivation, meant higher labor costs and higher prices than its supermarket competitors. In 1937 John Hartford, the company president, belatedly and reluctantly decided that A&P should enter the supermarket business seriously. By then, however, A&P had lost more than half its market share.

Though A&P never regained the 50 percent market share it had in the early 1930s, its profit levels and rates rebounded as the depression ended and A&P supermarkets were opened. By the early 1950s, it had secured roughly 33 percent of the chain grocery market. Although less dominant than in its heyday, it was still the leading chain.

The second crisis of A&P's existence was the opening in the 1950s and 1960s of suburban shopping malls. A&P resisted this trend because traditional company policy had been against signing long-term leases for store locations. Long-term leases were, however, necessary to secure stores in suburban malls. Company policy clashed with market necessity, and the latter won. By the time A&P realized its mistake, the prime locations had been taken by the company's competitors.

A&P had believed that it was big and powerful enough to continue attracting customers without moving to giant stores in high-rent suburban shopping malls. In later years, as gasoline costs rose and large numbers of women entered the work force, the demand for one-stop shopping grew. When other stores increased brand coverage and started stocking nonfood items, A&P's shelves in its smaller stores were already full. Between 1953 and 1971, A&P's gross sales stayed roughly constant at between $5 and $6 billion—but its market share slid from 30 percent to 12 percent. By 1972 it was losing money, and over the decade of the 1970s its losses continued. Late in the 1970s, the question was not whether A&P was too powerful, but rather whether it would even survive.

As the 1980s began, A&P was once again rebuilding—by closing many of its too-small, badly located stores and by employing new marketing techniques copied from its competitors. Today it has less than 10 percent of a market it once dominated and is fighting to survive. It is too early to tell if it will make it.

Does the firm control the market? A&P thought so, and found out that it was wrong.

ney); it has made the international conference a commonplace; and it has made European, Hawaiian, and Caribbean vacations a reality for many. For better or worse, the birth control pill has revolutionized many aspects of behavior in spite of the fact that it has never been advertised in the mass media. Television has changed the activities of children (and adults) in fundamental ways. Among others, it has created national rather than regional markets in dozens of commodities.

The new products that have significantly influenced the allocation of resources and the pattern of society, such as those mentioned above, have succeeded because consumers wanted them; most of those that failed did so because they were not wanted—at least not at prices that would cover their costs of production. The box on page 323 deals with a case study of a firm that found out the hard way just how much control the market can assert.

The evidence suggests that the allocation of resources in the American economy owes more to the tastes and values of consumers than it does to corporate advertising and related activities.

Who Controls the Government?

Is government subservient to big business? Lobbying is a legal, large-scale activity employed by many groups. Big business has its influence, but so do farmers, labor unions, and small business.

Cases of corrupt behavior have been documented at all levels of government; it does not follow, however, that government is subservient to the corporations and that decision making by the former is *dominated* by the wishes of the latter. It is easy to assert that "everyone knows that the oil lobby dominates Congress," but such assertions do not resolve empirical questions. Lobbying and influence may well help to explain why for years the United States imposed quotas on foreign oil imports, but lobbying by the oil companies did not prevent a delay of the Alaska pipeline for many years, the reduction in special tax relief, restrictions imposed on offshore oil drilling, or the passage of a windfall profits tax. Relaxation of many antipollution restrictions came because of the oil

shortages of the 1970s, not political pressure. Government contracts bolster the aerospace industry, yet Lockheed's deep financial trouble in the 1970s came in part as a result of government decisions. Tobacco companies have seen government agencies first publicize the hazards of their principal product and then restrict their advertising. Airlines finally lost their decades-long battle to prevent the introduction of the cheap transatlantic air fares and have now lost virtually all regulatory bolstering of fare structures and limitation of competition on routes.

These examples show that while business often succeeds in attempts to protect its commercial interests through political activity, it does so within limits. Where the truth lies between the extremes of "no influence" and "no limits" is a subject of current research. Yet it does seem safe to say that, first, corporations have a lot of political influence and, second, there are some serious constraints on the ability of corporations to exert political influence over all levels of American government.

Neglect of the Public Interest?

One aspect of the Galbraithian critique has found a receptive public: the apparent disregard by large corporations of the adverse effects of productive activities on the environment. The problems of pollution, which we will discuss in Chapter 24, arise from the activities of both small and large corporations and the activities of government units and citizens. Do such polluting activities represent irresponsible behavior by corporations that can be changed by such things as Campaign GM (an effort to make General Motors responsible), or does their correction require direct policy action in the form of rules, regulations, penalties, and tax incentives?

Consumerism is a movement that asserts a conflict between the interests of firms and the public interest. Consumerists hold that the conflict should be removed by pressuring firms to be motivated by the public interest rather than by their stockholders' desires for maximum profits.

Consumerists believe, for example, that GM's directors must be made to recognize that automobiles pollute and cause accidents, and that GM's resources should be invested in the development and installation of safety and antipollution devices. This, they argue, is proper use of GM's funds, even if GM's stockholders do not see it that way and even if automobile purchasers do not want to pay for the extra safety and antipollution devices.

What are the main arguments *for* this view? First, only the company can know the potentially adverse effects of its actions. Second, by virtue of holding a corporate charter, the corporation assumes the responsibility to protect the general welfare while pursuing private profits.

What are the main arguments *against* the consumerist view? Managers of companies have neither the knowledge nor the ability to represent the general public interest; they are largely selected, judged, and promoted according to their ability to run a profit-oriented enterprise, and the assumption that they are especially competent to decide broader *public* questions is unjustified. Moral, as distinct from economic, decisions—such as whether or not to make or use nerve gas, to make or use internal combustion engines, to manufacture or smoke cigarettes, and to manufacture or utilize DDT or aerosol sprays—cannot properly be delegated to corporations or their executives. Some are individual decisions; others require either the expertise or the authority of a public regulatory agency. Whoever makes decisions on behalf of the public must be potentially responsible to the public.

Those opposing the consumerist view hold that most required changes in corporate behavior should be accomplished not by exhorting business leaders to behave responsibly, nor by placing consumer representatives on the corporation's board of directors, but by regulations or incentives that force or induce the desired corporate behavior. Let corporations pursue their profits—subject to public laws. For example, Congress can require that all cars have seat belts, or have airbags, or have antipollution valves, or meet specific standards of emission levels. Another alternative is to open the way for lawsuits that would either enjoin certain behavior or force corporations to pay for the damages their products cause.

The controversy over policy alternatives is current and important. Much of the credit for the dialogue belongs to Galbraith and Nader. Important policy issues are at stake—whether and how to change the behavior of corporations. The same issues arise whether corporations are primarily responding to market signals or are impervious to them. If the public does not approve the results of corporate behavior, it will want to control the behavior.

WHO CONTROLS THE MODERN FIRM?: ALTERNATIVE MAXIMIZING THEORIES

Galbraith's is not the only modern criticism of the theory of firm behavior. Most other critics, however, accept (what Galbraith denies) that industries face market demand curves that the firms can influence only slightly. The critics then go on to suggest that firms will behave in ways different from those suggested by profit maximizing. In effect, these theories view firms as maximizers—of something other than profits.

Corporations play a dominant role in much of American industry, and large corporations have dominant market shares in many industries. But who or what *is* the corporation? In some corporations, a small group or family provided most of the original capital, and the firm grew with little or no sale of equities to the public. Modern American examples are the Ford Motor Company, which until 1956 was wholly owned by the Ford family; the Great Atlantic and Pacific Tea Company, which until recently was controlled by the Hartford family; E. I. du Pont de Nemours and Company (du Pont family); and the Aluminum Company of America (Mellon family). At the other extreme, the giant American Telephone and Telegraph Company is owned by more than 3 million shareholders, no one of whom owns as much as 1 percent of the 700 million outstanding shares.

Between these extremes lie the majority of corporations. The characteristic pattern of corporate ownership is that tens of thousands or hundreds of thousands of shareholders own minute fractions of the total, while dominant groups (often including other corporations) hold from 3 percent to 20 percent of the voting stock.

In major areas of the business world, the days of the single proprietor who is both owner and manager of a company are gone forever. Diversification of ownership is a major characteristic of the modern corporation. Does it matter? Traditional profit-maximizing theory answers no. The two hypotheses considered next suggest that the answer is yes.

The Hypothesis of Minority Control

It is quite possible for the owners of a minority of the stock to control a majority of the shares that are voted and thus to exercise effective control over the decisions of the corporation.

This possibility arises because not all shares are actually voted. Each share of common stock has one vote in a corporation. Shares must be voted at the annual meeting of stockholders, either in person or by assigning a **proxy** to someone attending. Any individual or group controlling 51 percent of the stock clearly controls a majority of the votes. But suppose one group owns 30 percent of the stock, with the remaining 70 percent distributed so widely that few of the dispersed group even bother to vote; in this event, 30 percent may be the overwhelming majority of the shares *actually voted*. In general, a very small fraction (sometimes as little as 5 percent) of the shares may exercise dominant influence at meetings of stockholders.

The hypothesis of minority control is that a well-organized minority often controls the destiny of the corporation against the wishes of the majority.

Dispersed ownership and minority control are well established in the corporate sector. But the hypothesis requires more than that a minority control the voting shares; it requires that stockholders be able to exert a significant influence on the firm's behavior *and* that the controlling minority have interests and motives different from the holders of the majority of the firm's stock. If all stockholders are mainly interested in having the firm maximize its profits, then it does not matter, as far as market behavior is concerned, which set of stockholders actually influences the firm's policy. There is no accepted evidence to show that controlling groups of stockholders generally seek objectives different from those sought by the holders of the majority of the firm's stock. Of course, disagreements between stockholder groups sometimes arise. A colorful phenomenon in corporation history is the **proxy fight,** in which competing factions of stockholders (or management) attempt to collect the voting rights of the dispersed and generally disinterested stockholders.

The Hypothesis of the Separation of Ownership from Control

A different consequence of diversified ownership was suggested in the 1930s by A. A. Berle and Gardiner Means. They hypothesized that, because of diversified ownership and the difficulty of assembling stockholders or gathering proxies, the managers rather than the stockholders or the directors exercise effective control over the corporation.

The hypothesis of the separation of ownership from control is that managerial control occurs and leads to different behavior than would stockholder control.

In the modern corporation, the stockholders elect directors, who appoint managers. Directors are supposed to represent stockholders' interests and to determine broad policies that the managers will carry out. In order to conduct the complicated business of running a large firm, a full-time professional management group must be given broad powers of decision. Although managerial decisions can be reviewed from time to time, they cannot be supervised in detail. In fact the links are typically weak enough that top management often does truly control the destiny of the corporation over long periods of time.

As long as directors have confidence in the managerial group, they accept and ratify their proposals, and stockholders elect and re-elect directors who are proposed to them. If the managerial group behaves badly, it may later be removed and replaced—but this is a disruptive and drastic action, and it is infrequently employed.

Within wide limits, then, effective control of the corporation's activities resides with the managers, who need not even be stockholders. Although the managers are legally employed by the stockholders, they remain largely unaffected by them. Indeed, the management group characteristically asks for, and typically gets, the proxies of a large enough number of stockholders to elect directors who will reappoint it—and thus it perpetuates itself in office.

Professors Berle and Means made a pioneering study of the ownership of the 200 largest nonfinancial corporations in 1929. They showed that for the majority of these corporations no dominant ownership group could be identified and that managers appeared to be in a position to control corporation decisions. What is the significance of this?

The hypothesis of the separation of ownership from control requires not only that the managers be able to exert effective control over business decisions but that they wish to act differently from the way the stockholders and directors wish to act. If the managers want to maximize the firm's profits—either because it is in their own interests to do so or because they are legally compelled or voluntarily choose to reflect the stockholders' interest—then it does not matter that they have effective control over decisions.

The Berle and Means finding is important only if the managers wish to pursue different goals than owners. Consider then theories that take the separation of ownership and control as their starting point and proceed on the assumption that managers are motivated by desires other than to maximize the profits of the firm.

DO FIRMS MAXIMIZE PROFITS?

Doubts about whether firms maximize profits have led to the development of several alternative theories, considered in the following pages. A differ-

ent line of attack on profit maximization—that firms are unable to maximize profits—is discussed in the box on page 328.

The Sales Maximization Hypothesis

The theory that firms seek to maximize not their profits but their sales revenue was first advanced by Professor William Baumol. Firms, it is assumed, wish to be as large as possible. Faced with a choice between profits and sales, they would choose to increase sales rather than profits.

This theory begins with the separation of management and ownership. In the giant corporation, the managers need to make some minimum level of profits to keep the shareholders satisfied; after that they are free to seek growth unhampered by profit considerations. This is a sensible policy on the part of management, the argument runs, because salary, power, and prestige all rise with the size of a firm as much as with its profits. Generally the manager of a large, normally profitable corporation will earn a salary considerably higher than that earned by the manager of a small but highly profitable corporation.

The sales maximization hypothesis says that managers of firms seek to maximize their sales revenue, subject to a profit constraint.

Sales maximization subject to a profit constraint leads to the prediction that firms will sacrifice some profits by setting price below, and output above, their profit-maximizing levels. See Figure 19-1.

Organization Theory

According to profit-maximizing theory, firms constantly scan available alternatives and choose the most profitable ones. A common criticism of this theory is that behavior is influenced seriously by the organizational structure of the firm. **Organization theory** argues that in big firms decisions are made after much discussion by groups and committees and that the structure of the process affects the substance of the decisions.

NON-MAXIMIZATION DUE TO IGNORANCE

A frequent but misguided line of criticism holds that firms are unable to maximize profits because they cannot equate marginal cost with marginal revenue. This criticism is based on the observation that many accounting practices are not set up to provide managers with marginal information. Indeed, most managers have never even heard of the concepts of marginal cost and marginal revenue. Thus, these critics conclude, firms cannot be maximizing profits because they cannot be using the necessary marginal concepts.

The constructs of the theory of the firm are merely tools employed by economists to predict the consequences of certain behavior patterns. They are not meant to describe how firms reach decisions. Economic theorists use the mathematical concepts of marginal cost and marginal revenue to discover what will happen as long as, by one means or another—by guess, hunch, clairvoyance, luck, or good judgment—firms ap-

proximately succeed in maximizing profits. The predictions of the theory are thus independent of the thought processes by which the managers of firms actually reach their decisions.

A famous analogy concerns the determination of how safe it may be for a driver to pass a truck on a two-lane road. The analyst must consider a complex equation relating the automobile's speed, the truck's speed, the car's ability to accelerate, the possibility of an oncoming car (and its speed and distance), weather conditions, and so on. But the driver, unlike the analyst, need not solve a mathematical equation to make his or her decision. Yet if the driver and analyst are competent, both will reach the same decision.

What is at issue, then, is not whether firms calculate and equate marginal magnitudes. The question is whether or not they regularly engage in behavior that tends to choose the most profitable of the available alternatives.

The central prediction of organization theory is that different decisions will result from different kinds of organizations, even when all else is unchanged.

One proposition that follows from this theory is that large and diffuse organizations find it necessary to develop standard operating procedures to help them in making decisions. These decision rules arise as compromises among competing points of view and, once adopted, are changed only reluctantly. An important prediction following from this hypothesis is that the compromises will persist for long periods of time despite changes in conditions affecting the firm. Even if a particular compromise were the profit-maximizing strategy in the first place, it would not remain so when conditions changed. Thus profits will not usually be maximized.

Another prediction is that decision by compro-

mise will lead firms to adopt conservative policies that avoid large risks. Smaller firms not faced with the necessity of compromising competing views will take bigger risks than larger firms.

Organization theorists have suggested an alternative to profit maximization that they call **satisficing.** Satisficing theory was first suggested by Professor Herbert Simon of Carnegie-Mellon University, who in 1978 was awarded the Nobel Prize in economics for his work on firm behavior. Speaking of his theory, he wrote, "We must expect the firm's goals to be not maximizing profits but attaining a certain level or rate of profit, holding a certain share of the market or a certain level of sales."

According to the satisficing hypothesis, firms will strive to achieve certain target levels of profits, but having achieved them, they will not strive to improve their profit position further. This means

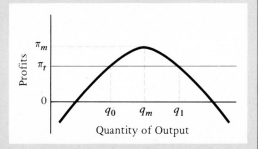

FIGURE 19-1
Output of the Firm Under Profit Maximizing, Sales Maximizing, and Satisficing

The "best" level of output depends on the motivation of the firm. The dark black curve shows the level of profits associated with each level of output. A profit-maximizing firm produces output q_m. A sales-maximizing firm, with a minimum profit constraint of π_t, produces the output q_1. A satisficing firm, with a target level of profits of π_t is willing to produce any output between q_0 and q_1. Thus satisficing allows a range of outputs on either side of the profit-maximizing level while sales maximizing results in a higher output than does profit maximizing.

that the firm could produce any one of a range of outputs that yield at least the target level of profits rather than the unique output that maximizes profits. This too is illustrated in Figure 19-1.

Full-Cost Pricing

As we noted in Chapter 16, most American firms are price setters: They must quote a price for their products rather than accept a price set on some impersonal competitive market. Profit-maximizing theory, literally interpreted, requires that these firms change their prices in response to every change in demand and costs that they experience. Yet as we have noted, that much price flexibility is not observed. In the short run, prices of manufactured goods are sticky.

A *non*-profit-maximizing explanation of fixed markups and sticky prices was advanced by Hall and Hitch in the 1930s, following a series of de-

tailed case studies of actual pricing decisions made in and around Oxford, England. They offered the following explanation of firms' behavior, known as the full-cost hypothesis:

Firms, instead of equating marginal revenue with marginal cost, set price equal to average total cost at capacity output, plus a conventional markup.

The **markup** may be either so much per unit or a percentage of average costs. Price having been set, sales are determined by what can be sold at that price.

Full-cost pricing leads a firm to alter its prices only when its average costs change substantially (as a result of such events as a new union contract or a sharp change in the prices of key raw materials), and it may occasionally change its markup. However, its short-run pricing behavior is rather conventional and is *cost* rather than *demand* determined. Those supporting this view believe that the prevalence of conventional full-cost practices shows that prices are typically not at their profit-maximizing level. They also hold that the prevalence of full-cost pricing shows that firms are creatures of custom rather than profit maximizers.

Modern supporters of profit-maximizing theory accept the full-cost evidence but argue that it reveals the more subtle maximizing behavior of oligopolists, as we saw in Chapter 16. (See pages 264–266.) As they see it, if saucer-shaped cost curves, fluctuating demands, and the costliness of price changes are considered, it is more profitable for firms to keep prices steady and vary output than to change prices with every change in demand. Indeed, they argue (along lines explored in the box on page 330) that firms cannot afford to depart from behavior that approximates profit maximization.

These economists argue that full-cost price theorists have confused the administrative procedure by which prices are set from day to day with the underlying pricing strategy. They point to the fact that many demand changes *do* lead to price changes. While for long periods prices are held constant (and given constant average costs, therefore so are markups), firms frequently reduce mark-

HOW FAR CAN CORPORATIONS DEPART FROM PROFIT-MAXIMIZING BEHAVIOR?

Many of the criticisms of modern microeconomic theory assume that firms seek to do things other than maximize their profits. If the present management elects not to maximize its profits, this implies that some other management could make more money by operating the firm. A major restraint on existing managements is the threat of a stockholder revolt or a takeover bid. As we shall see in Chapter 22, the maximum amount one can afford to pay for any asset depends on how much it is expected to earn. If I can make an asset produce more than you, I can rationally outbid you for it.

A management that fails to come close to achieving the profit potential of the assets it controls becomes a natural target for acquisition by a firm that specializes in taking over inefficiently run firms. The management of the acquiring firm makes a **tender offer** (or **takeover bid,** as it is sometimes called) to the stockholders of the target firm, offering them what amounts to a premium for their shares, a premium it can pay because it expects to increase the firm's profits. Managers who wish to avoid takeover bids cannot let the profits of their firm slip far from the profit-maximizing level—because their unrealized profits provide the incentives for takeovers.

Some, though by no means all of the so-called conglomerate firms, have specialized in this kind of takeover. In the last two decades the example par excellence of this has been International Telephone and Telegraph, which acquired (among other companies) Avis Car Rental, Continental Baking, Sheraton Hotels, Canteen Food Service, and Hartford Life Insurance. In each case it substantially increased the operating profits of the acquired company after the takeover.

The pressure of the threat of takeovers must be regarded as limiting the discretion of corporate management to pursue goals other than profit maximization.

ups by discounting prices when demand falls sharply or permanently and increase markups to take advantages of shortages when they seem likely to persist.

Evolutionary Theories

The modern evolutionary theories advanced by such economists as Richard Nelson and Sidney Winter of Yale University build on the earlier theories of satisficing and full-cost pricing. Nelson and Winter argue that firms do not—indeed, could not—behave as profit maximizing predicts. They accept that firms desire profits and even strive for profits; what they deny is that firms seek to *maximize* profits.

Evolutionary theorists have gathered much evidence to show that tradition seems to be paramount in planning. The basic effort at the early stages of planning is directed, they argue, toward the problem of performing reasonably well in established markets and maintaining established market shares. They quote evidence to show that suggestions in preliminary planning documents to do something entirely new are usually weeded out in the reviewing process. They believe that most firms spend very little effort on *planning* to enter entirely new markets, and still less on direct efforts to leave or even reduce their share in long-established markets. These attitudes were illustrated by one executive who—even though his firm was faced with obviously changing circumstances—reported that "We have been producing on the basis of these raw materials for more than 50 years with success, and we have made it a policy to continue to do so."

The evolutionary theory of the firm draws many analogies with the biological theory of evolution. Here are two of the most important.

The genes. In biological theory, behavior patterns are transmitted over time by genes. Rules of behavior fulfill the same function in the evolutionary theory of the firm. In Sidney Winter's words

That a great deal of firm decision behavior is routinized . . . is a "stylized fact" about the realities of firm decision process. Routinized . . . decision procedures . . . cover decision situations from pricing practices in retail stores to such "strategic" decisions as advertising or R and D effort, or the question of whether or not to invest abroad.

Winter talks of firms "remembering by doing" according to repetitive routines. He adds that government policymakers tend to have unrealistic expectations about firms' flexibility and responsiveness to changes in market incentives. These expectations arise from the maximizing model, whose fatal flaw, Winter alleges, is to underestimate the importance and difficulty "of the task of merely continuing the routine performance, i.e., of preventing undesired deviations."

The mutations. In the theory of biological evolution, mutations are the vehicle of change. In the evolutionary theory of the firm, this role is played by innovations. Some innovations are similar to those discussed in Chapter 13, the introduction of new products and new production techniques. However, a further important class of innovations in evolutionary theory is the introduction of new rules of behavior. Sometimes innovations are thrust on firms; at other times firms consciously plan for and create innovations.

According to maximizing theory, innovations are the result of incentives—the "carrot" of new profit opportunities. In evolutionary theory, the firm is much more of a satisficer, and it usually innovates only under the incentive of the "stick" either of unacceptably low profits or some form of external prodding. Firms change routines when they get into trouble, not when they see a chance to improve an already satisfactory performance. For example, in the growing markets of the 1960s

many firms continued all sorts of wasteful practices that they shed fairly easily when their profits were threatened in the more difficult 1970s and early 1980s.

The Significance of Non-Maximizing Theories

An impressive array of evidence can be gathered in apparent support of various non-maximizing theories. What are the implications if they are accepted as being better theories of the behavior of the economy than profit maximization?

If non-maximizing theories are correct, the economic system does not perform with the delicate precision that follows from profit maximization. But the system described by evolutionary theory does function. Firms sell more when demand goes up and less when it goes down. They also alter their prices and their input mixes when hit with the "stick" of sufficiently large changes in relative input prices.

Evolutionary and other non-maximizing theories do not upset the major conclusion about the price system: that it produces a coordinated response from decentralized decision makers to changes in tastes and costs. But profit-oriented non-maximizing firms will also exhibit a great deal of inertia. They will not respond quickly and precisely to small changes in market signals from either the private sector or government policy. Neither are they likely to make radical changes in their behavior even when the profit incentives to do so are large.

Non-maximizing models imply sensitivity of the price system to large but not to small changes in signals caused by changes in demand, costs, or public policy.

As a result, non-maximizing theories may be regarded as potential modifications of the theory developed earlier rather than as fundamental rejections of its major conclusions.

Profits, however, are unmistakably a potent force in the life—and death—of firms. The resilience of profit-maximizing theory and its ability to predict how the economy will react to some major changes (such as the recent dramatic increases in energy prices) suggests that firms are at least strongly motivated by the pursuit of profits and that, other things being equal, they prefer more profits to less profits.

If profit-maximizing theory should eventually give way to some more organizationally dominated theory, the new theory will still be a profit-oriented theory. The search for profits and the avoidance of losses drive the economy even when firms do not turn out to be continual profit maximizers.

SUMMARY

1. A sweeping attack on the traditional theory of the behavior of the firm is made by Galbraith, along with Nader and others. He argues that large corporations manipulate markets, tastes, and governments instead of responding to market and governmental pressures. While there is evidence about the undoubted size and influence of large corporations, there is also much evidence of market influence on corporate behavior.

2. In recent years, serious concern has developed over whether corporations should represent the interests of their owners and managers or whether they should be responsible to a broader public interest. Consumerists argue for the latter point of view; others prefer to rely on markets and government control to protect the public interest.

3. The widespread ownership of the modern corporation leads to the question, who really controls the modern corporation? Attempts to answer this question have led to alternative theories that firms maximize something other than profits. Two important hypotheses have been advanced.

a. A minority group of stockholders often controls the corporation against the wishes of the majority. The fact of minority control is widely accepted, but there is little evidence to suggest that the minority usually coerce the majority.

b. Because of the widespread ownership of the cor-

poration, stockholders cannot exert effective control over the managers; thus the latter have the real control of the organization and operate it for their advantage rather than that of their stockholders. This hypothesis has some serious, but by no means universal, support.

4. These and other hypotheses suggest that firms may seek to maximize something other than profits. One standard alternative is Professor Baumol's hypothesis of sales maximization: firms seek to be as large as possible (judged by sales revenue), subject to the constraint that they achieve a minimum rate of profit.

5. An alternative set of hypotheses denies that firms maximize profits in either the local or the global sense of maximization.

a. Organization theorists see firms as insensitive to short-term fluctuations in market signals. Their reason lies in the decision-making structure of large organizations, which must rely on routines and rules of thumb rather than on fresh calculations of profitabilities as each new situation presents itself.

b. The full-cost hypothesis states that firms determine price by adding a customary—and infrequently changed—markup to full costs. This also makes their pricing behavior relatively insensitive to short-term fluctuations in demand.

c. Evolutionary theorists build on full-cost and organizational theories. They see the firm as a profit-oriented entity in a world of imperfect information, making small, profit-oriented changes from its present situation but being more resistant to large, "structural" changes. Resources are still reallocated by evolutionary firms as demand and costs shift but usually more in response to the "stick" of threatened losses than the "carrot" of possible extra profits.

6. Under both maximizing and non-maximizing theories, profits are an important driving force in the economy, and changes in demand and costs cause changes in profits, which cause firms to reallocate resources. The speed and precision, but not the general direction of the reallocations, are what is different between maximizing and non-maximizing theories.

TOPICS FOR REVIEW

The New Industrial State
The long-run sensitivity of firms to market pressures
Consumerism
Alternate maximizing theories
Ownership, management, and control of corporate decisions
Sales maximization
Non-maximizing theories
Full-cost pricing
Satisficing
Evolutionary theories

DISCUSSION QUESTIONS

1. In 1976 the automobile manufacturers introduced their 1977 models. GM and American Motors (AMC) put major emphasis on smaller, more economical cars, and Ford and Chrysler stayed with their 1976 model sizes. Read the following news headlines (which appear in chronological order) and then discuss the light they shed on the hypothesis that firms control the market.
   a. "GM's 1977 Line Runs Ahead of the Pack. The big question: Do people want small cars?"
   b. "Ford, Chrysler, beam; AMC in trouble on sales."
   c. "GM's Fuel-Saving Chevette: Right Car at the Wrong Time."
   d. "Price Cuts and Rebates Lift Sales of Small AMC and GM Cars."
   e. "GM Confirms Plans to Drop the Subcompact Vega."
   What do these further events reveal about the same hypothesis?:
   f. "In 1979 auto firms sold all the small cars they could produce. But they were left with sizable unsold inventories of large cars, and as a result they are preparing to alter their production mix in favor of small cars."
   g. "By 1981, all American car makers were in trouble, as Japanese imports grew to over 25 percent of the U.S. market."
2. "Because automobile companies were interested only in profits, they would not produce the safer, less polluting, but more expensive cars that the public really wanted. Legislation was necessary, therefore, to force producers to meet consumer needs." Discuss.

3. Assume that each of the following assertions is factually correct. Taken together, what would they tell you about the prediction that big business is increasing its control of the U.S. economy?
   a. The share of total manufacturing assets owned by the 200 largest corporations has been rising steadily for the last 25 years.
   b. The number of new firms begun every year has grown steadily for the last 25 years.
   c. The share of manufacturing in total production has been decreasing for 40 years.
   d. Profits as a percent of national income are no higher now than half a century ago.
4. "Our economy, like an engine, must have fuel to operate. And the fuel our economy runs on is profit. Profits keep it going—and growing. But there is strong evidence that the economy's fuel supply is running low. Profits of U.S. corporations today are about 5 percent on sales—less than the 1965 rate.

   "We Americans have become accustomed to a quality of life that can survive only through profits. For profits not only create jobs and goods, they furnish essential tax revenues. Federal, state, and local taxes finance the countless programs that our citizens demand—from paving the roads on which we drive to building our country's defense forces . . . to helping millions of Americans who need some form of assistance."

   Comment on this excerpt from an Allied Chemical Corporation advertisement.
5. "The business of the businessman is to run his business so as to make profits. If he does so, he will serve the public interest better than if he tries to decide what is good for society. He is neither elected nor appointed to that task." Discuss.
6. "Our list prices are really set by our accounting department: they add a fixed markup to their best estimates of fully accounted cost and send these to the operating divisions. Managers of these divisions may not change those prices without permission of the Board of Directors, which is seldom given. Operating divisions may, however, provide special discounts if necessary to stay competitive." Does this testimony by the president of a leading manufacturing company support the full-cost pricing hypothesis?
7. The leading automobile tire manufacturers (Goodyear, Firestone, etc.) sell original equipment (OE) tires to automobile manufacturers at a price below the average total cost of all the tires they make and sell. This happens year after year. Is this consistent with profit-maximizing behavior in the short run? In the long run? If it is not consistent, what does it show? Do OE tires compete with replacement tires?

PART FIVE
FACTOR PRICING
AND THE DISTRIBUTION
OF INCOME

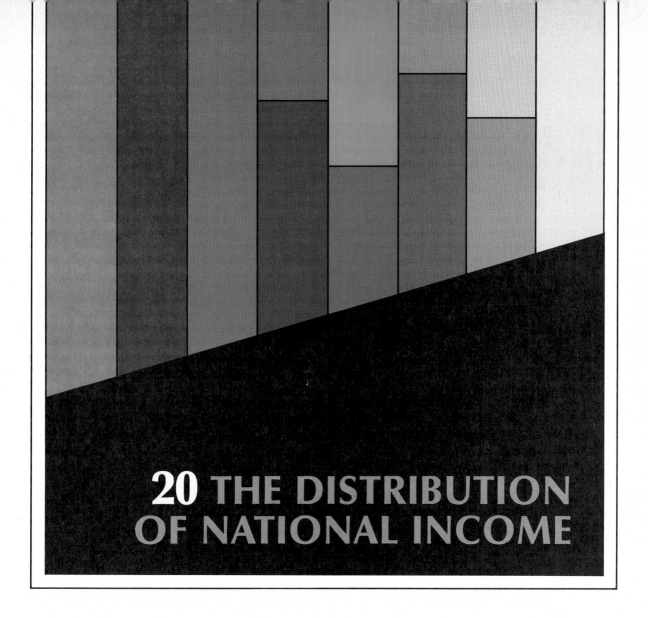

20 THE DISTRIBUTION OF NATIONAL INCOME

Problems of Distribution

Are the poor getting poorer and the rich richer as Karl Marx thought they would? Are the rich becoming relatively poorer and the poor relatively richer as Alfred Marshall hoped they would? Is the distribution of income affected by social changes such as the increased participation of women in the labor force, or by changes in public policy toward poverty? Should we reject the view held by Pareto that inequality of income is a social constant deter-

mined by forces that are possibly beyond human understanding and probably beyond human influence?

The founders of classical economics, Adam Smith and David Ricardo, were concerned with the distribution of income among what were then the three great social classes: workers, capitalists, and landowners. To deal with this question they defined three factors of production: labor, capital, and land. The return to each of these factors was the income of each of the three classes in society.

TABLE 20–1 **THE FUNCTIONAL DISTRIBUTION OF NATIONAL INCOME IN THE UNITED STATES, 1981**

Type of income	Billions of dollars	Percentage of total
Employee compensation	$2,354	75.1
Corporate profits	191	8.1
Proprietors' income	125	5.3
Interest	236	10.0
Rental income	34	1.5
Total	$2,354	100.0

Source: Survey of Current Business, December 1982.

Total income is classified here according to the nature of the factor service that earned the income. While these data show that employee compensation is more than three-quarters of national income, they do not show that workers and their families receive only that fraction of national income. Many households will have income in more than one category listed in the table.

Smith and Ricardo were interested in what determined the income of each group relative to the total national income, and in how a nation's economic growth affected this income distribution. Their theories predicted that as society progressed landlords would become relatively better off and capitalists would become relatively worse off. Karl Marx provided different answers to the same questions: He concluded that as growth occurred capitalists would become relatively better off and workers relatively worse off (at least until the whole capitalist system collapsed).

These and similar nineteenth century debates focused on the distribution of total income among the major factors of production, now called the **functional distribution of income.** Table 20-1 shows data for the functional distribution of income in the United States in 1981. Although functional distribution categories (wages, rent, profits) pervade current statistics, much of the attention of non-Marxist economists has shifted to another way of looking at differences in incomes.

Around the beginning of the present century, Pareto studied what is now called the **size distribution of income,** the distribution of income

TABLE 20–2 **INCOMES OF AMERICAN FAMILIES,[a] 1981**

Income class (thousands of dollars)	Percentage of families
Less than 10.0	17.3
10.0 to 17.4	20.1
17.5 to 24.9	18.5
25.0 to 36.9	24.1
37.0 or more	20.0

[a] The census definition of a family is two or more persons related by blood, marriage, or adoption and residing together.
Source: Current Population Reports, Series P-60, No. 134.

Although median family income in 1981 was $22,400, many received much less than this comfortable level of income and some a great deal more.

TABLE 20–3 **INEQUALITY IN FAMILY INCOME DISTRIBUTION, 1981**

Family income rank	Percentage share of aggregate income
Lowest fifth	5.0
Second fifth	11.3
Middle fifth	17.4
Fourth fifth	24.4
Highest fifth	41.9
	100.0
Top 5 percent	15.6

Source: Current Population Reports, Series P-60, No. 134.

While far from showing overall equality, income distribution is relatively equal for the middle 60 percent of the distribution. If the income distribution were perfectly equal, each fifth of the families would receive 20 percent of aggregate income. These data are plotted in Figure 20-1.

among different households without reference to the social class to which they belonged. He discovered that inequality in income distribution was great in all countries and, more surprising, that the degree of inequality was quite similar from one country to another. Tables 20-2 and 20-3 show that even in the United States in 1981 there were many

FIGURE 20-1
A Lorenz Curve of Family Income in the United States

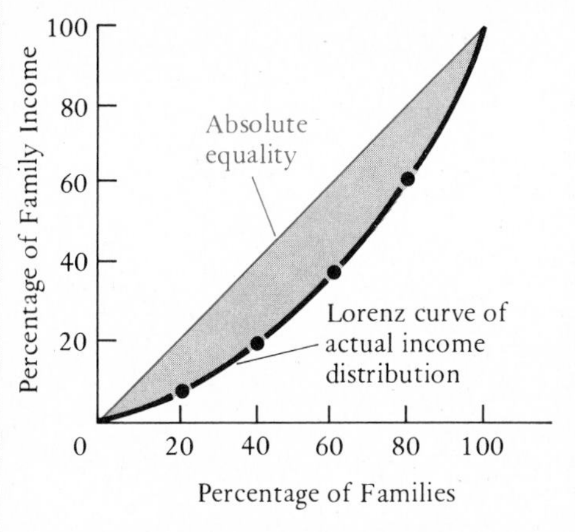

The size of the shaded area between the Lorenz curve and the diagonal is a measure of the inequality of income distribution. If there were complete income equality, the bottom 20 percent of income receivers would receive 20 percent of the income, and so forth, and the Lorenz curve would be the diagonal line. Because the lower 20 percent receive only 5 percent of the income, the actual curve lies below the diagonal. The lower curve shows actual American data. The extent to which it bends away from the straight line indicates the amount of inequality in the distribution of income.

families with very low incomes and there was much inequality in the distribution of income.

Inequality in the distribution of income is shown graphically in Figure 20-1. This curve of income distribution, called a **Lorenz curve,** shows how much of total income is accounted for by given proportions of the nation's families. For example, in 1981 the bottom 20 percent of all U.S. families earned only 5.0 percent of all income earned. The farther the curve bends away from the diagonal, the more unequal is the distribution of income. The present distribution of income is virtually unchanged from what it was 20 years ago.

There are good reasons why much of the atten-

tion of modern economists is devoted to the size distribution rather than the functional distribution of income. After all, some capitalists (such as the owners of small retail stores) are in the lower part of the income scale, while some wage earners (such as skilled athletes) are at the upper end of the income scale. Moreover, if someone is poor, it matters little whether that person is a landowner or a worker. Today many who want to decrease inequality focus on influences such as race, sex, age, education, occupation, and region of residence.

We shall look closely at the poverty problem in Chapter 23. In order to understand this and other problems concerning the distribution of income, we must first study how the income of households is determined and what forces cause it to change.

It is tempting to give superficial explanations of differences in income with remarks like, "People are paid what they are worth." But the economist must ask, Worth what to whom? What gives a particular man his value? His wife, his mother-in-law, and his employer may all respond differently. Sometimes people say, "People earn according to their ability." But incomes are distributed much more unequally than any *measured* index of ability, be it IQ, physical strength, or typing skill. In what sense is Tom Watson five times as able a golfer as Curtis Strange? His average score is only 1 percent better, yet he earns five times as much.

If answers couched in terms of worth and ability are easily refuted, so are answers such as, "It's all a matter of luck" or "It's just the system." We want to discover whether the theories of economics provide explanations of the distribution of income that are more satisfactory than the shallow ones mentioned above.

The Theory of Distribution

Every element of income has, in a purely arithmetical sense, two components: the quantity of the income-earning service that is provided and the price per unit paid for it. The amount a worker earns in wages depends on the number of hours worked and the hourly wage received. The amount

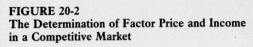

FIGURE 20-2
The Determination of Factor Price and Income in a Competitive Market

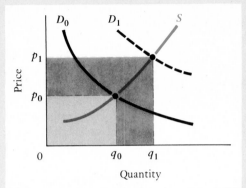

Demand and supply for factors determine prices and quantities of factors in competitive factor markets. With demand and supply curves D_0 and S, the price of the factor will be p_0 and the quantity employed q_0. The total income earned by the factor is the lighter shaded area. A shift in demand from D_0 to D_1 raises equilibrium price and quantity to p_1 and q_1. The income earned by the factor rises by the darker shaded area.

factors will be becoming relatively more expensive, some relatively cheaper. We shall use the phrase *rise in price* to mean a rise in relative price, and the phrase *fall in price* to mean a fall in relative price. (See pages 77–78 for fuller discussion.)

In this chapter we consider competitive markets. Price theory states that the competitive market price of any commodity or factor is determined by demand and supply. The competitive market determination of the equilibrium price and quantity—and thus the money income—of a factor of production is illustrated in Figure 20-2. Look again at Figure 5-8, page 76, to see why this analysis is familiar.

To go further we need to understand what determines the demand for factors and their supply. This will give us some insight into how equilibrium is determined when factors are bought and sold competitively. Then in Chapter 21 we shall look at how labor unions, employers' associations, and other labor market institutions may introduce monopoly-like elements into labor markets.

a group of workers (say, union members) earns depends on how many of them there are and how much each earns. The amount of dividends a stockholder receives depends on the number of shares of stock he or she owns and the dividends that each share pays.

Because factor prices are one of two elements that determine factor incomes, a theory of factor prices is essential to a theory of distribution.

The theory of factor prices is just a special case of the theory of price; any factor's price depends upon its supply and the demand for it.

As with the theory of product prices studied in Chapter 5, the theory of distribution is concerned with *relative* prices. One factor becomes "more expensive" when its price rises relative to that of other factors. In an inflationary world most prices will be rising, but not at the same rate. So some

THE DEMAND FOR FACTORS

A firm requires labor, raw materials, machines, and other factors of production, not for their own sake, but in order to produce the goods and services that it sells.

The demand for any factor of production depends on the existence of a demand for the goods that it helps to make; it is described as a **derived demand.**

Examples of derived demand are easy to find. The demand for computer programmers and technicians is growing as we use more and more electronic computers. The demand for carpenters and building materials rises or falls with the level of house building. Anything that increases the demand for new housing—population growth, lower interest rates on mortgages, and so on—will increase the demand for the factors required to build houses.

Typically one factor will be used in making

many commodities. Steel is used in dozens of industries, as are the services of carpenters.

The total demand for a factor will be the sum of the demands for it in every activity in which it is used.

The Downward Slope of the Demand Curve

The demand curve for a factor of production shows how the quantity demanded of that factor will vary as its price varies, the prices of all other factors remaining constant. Although demand curves for factors generally slope downward, they do so for somewhat different reasons than do demand curves for commodities.

What would happen to quantity demanded if there were a rise in the price of a factor? Because demand is a derived demand, the effect must be traced to the commodities that the factor is used to make. One effect is related to the link between a factor's price and the price of the good or service it helps to produce. Consider for example a rise in the wages of carpenters, which increases the cost of producing houses. The rise in cost shifts the supply curve of houses upward. This leads to a rise in the price of houses and to a decrease in the number of houses sold. If fewer houses can be sold fewer will be built and lesser quantities of factors will be needed. Thus there will be a decrease in the quantity demanded of carpenters used to produce houses.

The second effect relates to substitution among factors: When the price of a factor goes up, relatively cheaper factors will be substituted for the factor whose price has risen. For example, if carpenters' wages rise relative to those of factory workers, some prefabricated door and window frames made by factory workers will be used in place of on-the-job carpenters. This is simply the principle of substitution in operation.

Demand curves for factors slope downward because of (1) the effect of factor price changes on the prices of the commodities the factor makes and (2) the substitution of relatively cheaper for relatively more expensive factors.

The Nature of Factor Demand: The Marginal Productivity Theory of Distribution

Because demand for factors is a derived demand, its nature can be derived from the conditions for firms seeking to maximize profits, which were discussed in Chapter 14. Just as it is true that all profit-maximizing firms, whether they are selling under conditions of perfect competition, monopolistic competition, oligopoly, or monopoly, produce to the point at which marginal cost equals marginal revenue, so it is true that all profit-maximizing firms will hire units of the variable factor up to the point at which the last unit of any variable factor employed adds as much to revenue as it does to cost. Thus it is merely an implication of profit-maximizing behavior that firms will hire units of a variable factor up to the point where the marginal cost of the factor (i.e., the addition to the total cost resulting from the employment of one more unit) equals the marginal revenue produced by the factor.

Because we use the term *marginal revenue* to denote the change in revenue resulting when the rate of product sales is increased by one unit, we shall use another term **marginal revenue product (MRP)**, to refer to the change in revenue caused by the sale of the product contributed by *an additional unit of the variable factor*. [28] The relevance of *MRP* in determining the worth of a particular factor of production is illustrated in the box on page 342. We may now state more concisely the equilibrium condition stated above:

| The marginal cost of the variable factor | = | The marginal revenue product of that factor | [1] |

If the firm is unable to influence the price of the variable factor by buying more or less of it (i.e., if the firm is a price taker when *buying* factors), then the marginal cost of the factor is merely its price. The cost, for example, of adding an extra ton of coal is the price that must be paid per ton of coal purchased. In these circumstances we may state

WHAT IS A PERSON WORTH? THE ECONOMICS OF SUPERSTAR SALARIES

Joe Namath, an aging but flamboyant quarterback with injured knees, was paid $450,000—then a salary that was far higher than any other in pro football—to play for the New York Jets in 1976, a season in which they won only three of their fourteen games (for the second year in a row). At the end of the dismal season, the Jets owners gladly accepted the resignation of the club's coach but wanted Broadway Joe to play again in 1977 at the same salary. Sportscasters and fans agreed that the team played better and had more chance of winning with their second-string quarterback, who was paid less than one-tenth of Namath's salary. Yet the Jets continued to want to play—and pay—Joe Namath. Was this sound economics?

It was. The principal products the Jets sell are football tickets and television rights to their games. Despite their poor won-lost record, the Jets were in those days a major drawing card not only in New York but throughout the country. Joe Namath was a main reason for this, remembered as the David who in 1969 led the Jets of the scorned American Football League to victory over the mighty National Football League Champion Baltimore Colts, quarterbacked by John Unitas. Eight years later thousands of extra fans paid to see the Jets because of Namath. On the road during 1976, the Jets attracted roughly 10,000 more fans per game (in the same stadiums) than did the Buffalo Bills with 1976's reigning superstar, O. J. Simpson. For the season the Jets were estimated to have earned about $240,000 in their share of extra ticket sales for seven games away from home—just because of Namath. At home Namath was credited with attracting more than 10,000 extra fans per game, and this was worth at least another $350,000 in ticket sales to the football club. Add in the additional value in television rights, and Joe was plainly a bargain: his *MRP* was more than his wage. When Namath left the Jets, attendance fell.

Before the 1979 baseball season, Pete Rose *at age 37* ("over the hill" for an athlete) signed a four-year contract at $800,000 per year, the highest baseball salary ever paid up to that time. His new employers expected (and have not been disappointed) that the fans who appreciated the acquisition of "Charlie Hustle" would pay to see him play. If they did it would not matter whether he got 200 hits or batted .300.

Arnold Palmer made golf prizes swell and earnings of professional golfers soar by a magnetic personality that made golf a major spectator sport and brought national television coverage. Walter Cronkite, Barbara Walters, and other "personality" newspeople made television's news anchor positions a source of wealth to those lucky enough to catch on.

Notice that it is not the direct product produced that is responsible for high salaries. It is not yards gained or birdies scored that made Namath and Palmer rich, nor is it interviews conducted or hours on the air that led to Barbara Walters' million-dollar salary. It is tickets sold, or advertising sold, that converts the physical feats of these people into marginal revenue product.

Both owners and players understand all this these days. New York Yankee owner George Steinbrenner put it succinctly: "You measure a ballplayer's value by how many fannies he puts in the seats." An econometric study by Professor Paul Sommers showed that the marginal revenue products of the 14 top-paid baseball players were even greater than their seemingly enormous salaries. Recognition of the concept of high *MRPs* led professional football players in 1982 to strike in an attempt to get salaries determined contractually as a percent of gross receipts.

Will the extraordinary skills of Russian gymnasts or Japanese volleyball players one day make athletes in those sports worth their weight in gold? That will depend on some entrepreneur's ability to generate a market for their product. Whatever happened to Mark Spitz and Eric Heiden?

the condition of Equation [1] in this form:

$$w = MRP \qquad [2]$$

where w is the price of the factor.

A profit-maximizing firm that is a price taker in factor markets hires a factor up to the point at which its price equals its marginal revenue product.

This is an equilibrium condition for a profit-maximizing firm that does not influence the price of a factor by buying more or less of it. It is sometimes called the **marginal productivity theory of distribution** because it says that, in equilibrium, factors of production will receive a price equal to the value of output that is added by the hiring of an additional (marginal) unit of the factor. This comes about by firms adjusting the quantity of the variable factor they hire at the established market price.

This important yet frequently misunderstood proposition means that, under the circumstances specified, all units of a factor will be paid a price equal to the marginal revenue product of the factor. It applies in long-run equilibrium to all factors because in the long run all factors are variable. Two misconceptions about marginal productivity theory are discussed in the box on page 344.

What Determines
the Elasticity of Factor Demands?

The greater the change in quantity of a factor demanded for a given change in its price, the greater is the elasticity of demand for the factor. What considerations play a role in determining elasticity?

The Demand for
the Commodities That Use the Factor

Other things being equal, elasticity of demand for a factor will be larger the more elastic is the demand for the commodity that the factor helps to make. If an increase in the price of the commodity causes a large fall in the quantity demanded (i.e., the demand for the commodity is very elastic),

there will be a large decrease in the quantity of factors needed to produce it. But if the increase in the price of the commodity causes only a small fall in its quantity demanded (i.e., the demand for the commodity is inelastic), there will be only a small decrease in the quantity of the factors now required.

The Importance of the Factor
in Total Costs of Production

The elasticity of demand for a factor will be greater the larger is the fraction of total costs that are payments to the factor.[1] Suppose that wages are 50 percent of the costs of producing a good while raw materials account for 10 percent. A 10 percent rise in the price of labor would raise the cost of producing the commodity by 5 percent (10 percent of 50 percent), but a 10 percent rise in the price of raw materials would raise the cost of the commodity by only 1 percent (10 percent of 10 percent). Thus a 10 percent increase in labor's price would cause a larger increase in the cost of the commodity than a 10 percent rise in the price of raw materials. The larger the increase in cost, the larger the increase in the commodity's price— and hence the larger the decrease in the quantity demanded of the commodity and the factors used to make it.

Substitution of One Factor for Another

Obviously, the greater the ease with which one factor can be substituted for another in response to changes in relative factor prices, the greater is the elasticity of demand for those factors. The ease

---

[1] This is necessarily true when there is only one variable factor of production. When there are many variable factors, we must also consider the ease of substitution. For example, copper tubing may be a small part of building costs, but if aluminum or steel tubing are nearly perfect substitutes, the demand for copper tubing may be quite elastic. In contrast, the demand for tubing of some kind may be quite inelastic. The text statement is another example of something that is correct *ceteris paribus*: For a given degree of substitutability among factors, the demand for any one factor will be more elastic the larger the proportion of total costs that are payments to that factor.

IMPORTANT MISCONCEPTIONS
ABOUT MARGINAL PRODUCTIVITY THEORY

In certain quarters *marginal productivity theory* is almost a dirty word, for it seems to say that each factor, including labor, is paid exactly the value of what it produces. The theory has been criticized on the grounds that it is inhumane and that it falsely implies that the market leads to factor prices that, however low they might be, are "just." Both criticisms rest on misconceptions of what the theory says and implies.

Is Marginal Productivity Theory Inhumane?

Marginal productivity theory does not take into account the differences between human services and other services. Thus the theory is sometimes called inhumane because it treats human labor as it treats a ton of coal or a wagonload of fertilizer. Coal, fertilizer, and human labor are of course different, but each is purchased in making products.

The marginal productivity theory is only a theory of the *demand* for a factor. It predicts only what profit-maximizing employers would like to buy. It predicts that desired purchases of a factor depend on the price of the factor, the technical conditions of production, and the demand for the product made by the factor. *Supply* conditions undoubtedly differ between human and nonhuman factors, but these differences are accommodated within the theory of distribution, as we shall see. No evidence has been gathered to indicate that it is necessary to have separate theories of the demand for human and nonhuman factors of production.

Does the Theory Define a Just Distribution of Income?

In a world of perfectly competitive factor markets, the theory predicts that in equilibrium all factors receive payment equal to the values of their marginal products. Some eminent economists in the past spoke as if this led to a just distribution because factors were rewarded according to the value of their own contributions to the national product. "From each according to his ability; to each according to his own contribution" might have been the slogan for this group. One of its most famous exponents was the American economist John Bates Clark (1847–1938). Many critics of the low levels of wages that then prevailed reacted passionately to a theory that was claimed to justify them.

It is not necessary here to enter into normative questions of what constitutes a just distribution of income. It is, however, worth getting the facts straight. According to the marginal productivity theory, each worker does not receive the value of what he or she personally contributes to production. The worker receives instead the value of what one more worker would add to production if that worker were taken on while all other factors were held constant. If one million similar workers are employed, then each of the one million will receive a wage equal to the extra product that would have been contributed by the millionth laborer if he or she had been hired while capital and all other factors remained unchanged. Whether such a distribution of the national product is or is not "just" may be debated. The marginal productivity theory does not, however, contribute to that debate; it does *not* say that each unit of a factor receives as income the value of its own contribution to production. Indeed, where many factors cooperate in production, it is generally impossible to divide total production into the amounts contributed by each unit of each factor of production.

It is possible both to hold that marginal productivity tends to determine how people get paid and to believe that government policies that change the distribution of income are desirable. Many economists hold both positions.

of substitution depends on the substitutes available and technical conditions of production. A contractor in Anaheim, California, may normally use Anaheim laborers. But should they demand higher wages, the contractor might well be able to bring workers from nearby Azusa or Cucamonga at only the additional cost of daily transportation. It is well known that a bushel of wheat can be produced by combining land either with a lot of labor and a little capital or with a little labor and a lot of capital, and that manufactured goods can be made either by capital-intensive or by labor-intensive techniques. In other cases short-run substitutions are not simple to make. For example, recent rises in the price of electricity have not led quickly to massive substitutions of other fuels.

While it is easy to think of barriers to substitution, they can be exaggerated. Even in the short run it is possible to vary factor proportions in surprising ways. For example, in automobile manufacture and in building construction, glass and steel can be substituted for each other simply by varying the dimensions of the windows. Grain in the form of gasohol can substitute for oil as automobile fuel.

Nor are such direct (if dramatic) short-run substitutions the end of the story. In the long run a factory that has a particular technique embodied in its equipment (and thus cannot easily vary factor proportions in the short run) can be replaced. Plant and equipment are continually being replaced, and more or less capital-intensive methods can be adopted in new plants in response to changes in factor prices. Similarly, engines that use less gasoline per mile (or that use a cheaper fuel) will surely be developed if the price of gasoline remains high.

THE SUPPLY OF FACTORS

Two important economic questions concern the supplies of factors: First, to what extent do economic forces determine the total supply of a factor to the whole economy? Second, to what extent do such forces determine the supply available to a particular industry that wants to purchase only a part of the total supply?

The Total Supply of Factors

It might seem plausible to assume that the total supplies of factors available to the economy are fixed and not subject to economic influences. After all, there is an absolute maximum to the world's land area; there is an upper limit to the number of workers; there is only so much sand and gravel, coal, oil, copper, and iron ore in the earth. In none of these cases, however, are we near the upper limits. The *effective* supplies of land, labor, and natural resources are thus not fixed in any meaningful sense. What, then, causes variations in the supply of a factor of production available to the *whole economy?*

The Total Supply of Labor

The total supply of labor means the total number of hours of work that the population is willing to supply. This quantity, which is often called the **supply of effort,** is a function of the size of the population, the proportion of the population willing to work, and the number of hours worked by each individual.

There are many obvious determinants of the supply of effort, such as the rewards for working, the age at which people enter the labor force and retire from it, and the length of the conventional work week. There are also many less obvious ones. For one example, social trends, such as the women's liberation movement, can cause major changes in labor force participation. For another, the whole pattern of tax rates, unemployment insurance, and welfare payments affects the relative advantages of working and not working. What is debated is not whether these things affect working, but how large their impact is. These matters have been the subject of a great deal of research. As discussed more fully in the box on page 347, the evidence shows some but relatively small adverse effects of taxes and welfare benefits on the supply of effort. While for a significant—and much noticed—number of persons, welfare and unemployment compensation have become substitutes for available work, most persons who can find work, find it worthwhile to do so for their sense of participation in society as well as for the extra income.

The Total Supply of Arable Land

If the term *land* is used to refer to the total area of dry land, then the total supply of land in a country will be almost completely fixed. It was nineteenth century practice (following Ricardo) to define land as the *original and inexhaustible powers of the soil*. But dust bowls were a phenomenon unknown to Ricardo, who also did not know that the deserts of North Africa were once fertile plains. Clearly the supply of fertile land is not inexhaustible; considerable care and effort is required to sustain the productive power of land. If the return to land is low, its fertility may be destroyed within a short time. Moreover, scarcity and high prices may make it worthwhile to increase the supply of arable land by irrigation and other forms of reclamation.

The Total Supply of Natural Resources

People worry—sometimes when it is too late—about exhausting natural resources. The great iron ore deposits of the Mesabi Range were exhausted in 1965, and America's known supplies of oil and gas had shrunk by 1982 to less than an 11-year supply.[2]

The problem of actual exhaustion of natural resources does not arise as often as one might think. There is frequently a large undiscovered or unexploited quantity of a given resource or of an adequate substitute. The exhaustion of high-grade iron ore reserves in the United States did not end steel production—partly as a result of the discovery of ways to use low-grade iron ores once thought worthless and partly because new supplies in Labrador and the Caribbean have been developed.

[2] It should not be inferred that supplies of oil and gas will be exhausted by 1993. The known supply was reported to be at most 20 years in every year from 1920 to 1950; in other words, each year as much was discovered as was used. What *is* new in recent years is that discovery has lagged behind production, and thus the number of years of known supply has been shrinking.

Emerging shortages may lead to their own corrections. As long as oil remains sufficiently valuable, it will pay to find more of it. As oil becomes scarce, its price will rise. A sufficient increase in the price of oil would make it economically worthwhile to process the vast quantities of previously unexploited shale oil. Consumers will feel the scarcity in terms of higher prices, and this will lead them to use less oil; this in turn will decrease the rate of exhaustion of known reserves.

Ultimately, of course, there is an upper limit, and resources can be totally exhausted; worse, they can be contaminated or otherwise despoiled so as to render them useless long before they have been consumed.

The Total Supply of Capital

Capital is a man-made factor of production, and its supply is in no sense fixed. The supply of capital in a country consists of the stock of existing machines, plant, equipment, and so on. The stock is diminished by the amount that wears out each year and is increased by the production of new capital goods. On balance the trend has been for the capital stock to grow over the decades.

The Supply of Factors to Particular Uses

Plainly it is easier for any one user to acquire more of a scarce factor of production than it is for all users to do so simultaneously. One use or user can bid resources away from another use or user even though the total supply is fixed. Most factors have many uses; a given piece of land can be used to grow any one of several crops, or it can be subdivided for a housing development. A computer programmer in Detroit can work in a variety of automobile plants, or in a dozen other industries, or even in the physics laboratories at Wayne State University. A lathe can be used to make many different products and requires no adaptation when it is turned from one use to another.

The total supply must be allocated among all the different uses to which it can possibly be put.

TAXES, WELFARE, AND THE SUPPLY OF EFFORT

Many believe that today's high income taxes tend to reduce the supply of effort by lowering the work incentive. They say that it is not worthwhile to work because of the crushing tax burdens they have to shoulder. Yet such objective evidence as exists suggests that high taxes do not always reduce the supply of effort. To the extent that they do, the aggregate effect may be small.

There is a good theoretical basis for a small aggregate effect. A tax cut sets up two opposing forces, and the final effect on the amount of work done by people depends on the relative strengths of each. An example will suggest why. Take Barry Bluecollar, who has a job on an assembly line. He typically takes 5 hours a week off and so works only 35 hours with a take-home pay of $8.50 an hour or $297.50 per week. Now suppose there is a tax cut so that his take-home pay rises to $10 an hour. He might elect to work a little more since every hour he works now nets him $10 instead of $8.50. Say his average weekly hours rise to 37 hours. Then he will raise his take-home pay by $72.50 to $370. Economists call the tendency to work more because the reward for an hour's work has risen the *substitution effect.* However, Bluecollar might elect to work a little less since with the rise in hourly take-home pay, he can have more income *and* get more leisure. Suppose he elects to take off an extra 3 hours a week. His take-home pay is now $320 a week (32 hours at $10), compared to the $297.50 before the tax cut. Now he has 3 more hours of leisure a week *and* $22.50 more income. Economists call the tendency to work less because it is possible to have more income *and* more leisure, the *income effect.*

If the substitution effect dominates, people respond to a tax cut by working more. If the income effect dominates, they work less. Either result is theoretically possible. So a tax cut may raise or lower the amount of work people want to do. A good deal of research has shown that while some people may work fewer hours in response to rising taxes, others feel poorer and thus work more to maintain their after-tax incomes. The most recent research suggests at most a small net disincentive up to a level of marginal tax rates of 50 percent, such as exists today in the United States.

At tax rates of 75 percent or more, important distortions may occur. In Britain, where marginal tax rates used to rise to 85 percent at moderate levels of income, a "brain drain" occurred in many professional, scientific, and managerial occupations. Low salaries combined with very high tax rates on "extra" earnings to produce dramatic evidence that workers can "vote with their feet" against high taxes on earnings. Such mobility was made easier by the existence of jobs in other English-speaking countries.

One reason why the possible adverse effect on the supply of effort is not larger is that there are other responses to high taxes. Citizens may vote for politicians who promise to reduce taxes; or they may simply not pay income taxes. Tax avoidance, including outright cheating, may become common and even socially acceptable. The rapid growth of barter and the so-called underground economy—possibly accounting for as much as a quarter of all transactions—are almost surely a response to high tax rates.

Do welfare payments and other aids to the poor make them less willing to take jobs? Some significant disincentives to working have been found, but they do not seem to have a major effect when the financial aids are structured so as to leave those who can work with some incentive to do so. Many of those receiving payments are unable to work. But there is no doubt that some welfare rules actually discourage work by making welfare recipients turn over much or all of any income they might earn. If a family's welfare payment of, say, $500 per month is decreased dollar for dollar by any earnings, this amounts to a 100 percent tax on the first $500 of earnings per month. The person who can earn $400 by part-time work would have no economic incentive to do so. In recent years most welfare schemes have recognized this problem and allowed persons on welfare to keep a good fraction of any extra money.

If the factor's owners are concerned only with making as much money as they can, they will move their factor to that use at which it earns the most money. Such a movement out of one use and into another would continue until the marginal earnings of units of the factor in all of its various possible uses were the same. Because owners of factors are known to take things other than money into account—such as risk, convenience, and a good climate—it is not sufficient to consider only monetary incentives; we must consider the sum of monetary and nonmonetary rewards.

The Hypothesis of Equal Net Advantage

The **hypothesis of equal net advantage** says that owners of factors will choose that use of their factors that produces the greatest net advantage to themselves. (Net advantage includes both monetary and nonmonetary rewards.)

This hypothesis plays the same role in the theory of distribution as the assumption that firms seek to maximize profits plays in the theory of production. It leads to the prediction that the units of each kind of factor of production will be allocated among various uses in such a way that their owners receive the same net return in every use.

Non-monetary advantages have a big role to play in explaining differences in levels of pay in different occupations and jobs. But since they are quite stable over time they do not diminish the importance of monetary advantages. Variations in monetary advantages tend to lead to changes in *net* advantage, and thus they play a big role in reallocating resources.

A change in the relative rate of pay of a factor between two uses will tend to change the net advantages of the uses. It will lead to a shift of some units of that factor to the use whose rate of pay has increased.

This prediction implies a rising supply curve for a factor in any particular use. When the price of a factor rises, more of it will be supplied. Such a supply curve (as all supply curves) can *shift* in response to changes in other variables. One of the variables that can shift the supply curve is a change in size of nonmonetary benefits.

Factor Mobility

When considering the supply of a factor to a particular use, the most important concept is **factor mobility.** The term is used in the sense of shiftability in use. The more mobile a factor is, the greater is the elasticity of supply. A factor that shifts easily between uses in response to small changes in incentives is said to be highly mobile, and it will be in very elastic supply in any one of its uses because small increases in the price offered will attract a large flow of the factor from other uses. A factor that does not shift easily from one use to another, even in response to large changes in remuneration, is said to be highly immobile, and it will be in very inelastic supply in any one of its uses because even a large increase in the price offered will attract only a small inflow from other uses.

Mobility of land. Land, which is physically the least mobile of factors, is one of the most mobile in an economic sense. Consider agricultural land. Within a year at most, one crop can be harvested and a totally different crop planted. A farm on the outskirts of a growing city can be sold for subdivision and development on short notice.

Once land is built on, as urban land usually is, its mobility is much reduced. A site on which a hotel has been built can be converted into an office building site, but it takes a large differential in the value of land use to make it worthwhile because the hotel must be torn down.

Although land is highly mobile among alternative uses, it is completely immobile as far as location is concerned. There is only so much land within a given distance of the center of any city, and no increase in the price paid can induce further land to locate within that distance. This locational immobility has important consequences, including high prices for desirable locations and the tendency to build tall buildings that economize on the use of land where it is very scarce, as in the centers of large cities.

Mobility of capital. While some kinds of capital equipment—lathes, trucks, and computers, for example—can be readily shifted among uses, many others are comparatively unshiftable. A great deal of machinery is utterly specific: once built, it must either be used for the purpose for which it was designed or else not used at all. (It is the immobility of much fixed capital equipment that makes the exit of firms from declining industries a slow and difficult process.)

In the long run, capital is highly mobile. When capital goods wear out, firms might simply replace them with identical goods. But the firm has many other options: It may buy a newly designed machine to produce the same goods, it may buy machines to produce totally different goods, or it may spend its resources in other ways. Such decisions lead to changes in the long-run allocation of a country's stock of capital among various uses.

Labor mobility. Labor is unique as a factor of production in that the supply of the service requires the physical presence of the owner of the source of the service. Absentee landlords can obtain income from land located in remote parts of the world while continuing to live in the place of their choice. Investment can be shifted from iron mines in northern Minnesota to mines in Labrador while the owners of the capital commute between New York and the French Riviera. But when a worker employed by a firm in Pittsburgh decides to supply labor service to a firm in Chicago, the worker must physically travel to Chicago. This is all quite obvious, but it has an important consequence.

Because of the need for physical presence, nonmonetary considerations are much more important in the allocation of labor than in the allocation of other factors of production.

People may be either satisfied with or frustrated by the kind of work they do, where they do it, those they do it with, and the social status of their occupations. Since these considerations influence their decisions about what they will do with their labor services, they will not move every time they can earn a higher wage.

Nevertheless, according to the hypothesis of equal net advantage, occupational and job movement will occur when there are changes in the wage structure. The mobility that does occur depends

on many forces. For example, it is not difficult for a secretary to shift from one company to another or to take a job in New York City instead of in Jersey City, but it can be difficult for a secretary to become an editor or a fashion model in a short period of time. There are three considerations here: ability, training, and inclination. Lack of any one will stratify some people and make certain kinds of mobility difficult for them.

An important key to labor mobility is time. The longer the time interval the easier it is to change occupations.

Some barriers may seem insurmountable for a person once his or her training has been completed. It is not easy, and it may be impossible, for a farmer to become a surgeon or a truck driver to become a professional athlete, even if the relative wage rates change greatly. But the children of farmers, doctors, lawyers, and athletes, when they are deciding how much education or training to obtain, are not nearly as limited in their choices as their parents, who have completed their education and are settled in their occupations.

Thus it is important to recognize that the labor force as a whole is more mobile than individual members of it. At one end of the age distribution people enter the labor force from school; at the other end they leave it via retirement or death. The turnover due to these causes is about 3 or 4 percent per year. Over a period of 20 years, a totally different occupational distribution could appear merely by redirecting new entrants to jobs other than the ones left vacant by workers leaving the labor force, without a single individual ever changing jobs. The role of education in adapting people to available jobs is very great. In a society in which education is provided to all, it is possible to achieve large increases in the supply of any desired labor skill within a decade or so.

THE PRICE OF FACTORS IN COMPETITIVE MARKETS

We have now developed theories of both the demand for and the supply of factors of production. These theories predict a downward-sloping demand curve and an upward-sloping supply curve. This is all that is needed for a theory of factor pricing in competitive markets. If factor prices are free to vary, prices and quantities employed will tend toward the point at which quantity supplied equals quantity demanded. Furthermore, shifts in either the demand for or the supply of factors will have the same effects on prices, quantities, and factor incomes as are predicted by standard price theory.

The theory of factor prices is absolutely general. If one is concerned with labor, one should interpret factor prices to mean wages; if one is thinking about land, factor prices should be interpreted to mean land rents, and so on.

In dealing with factor prices, just as in dealing with product prices, it is sometimes essential to distinguish between *real* and *money* factor prices. For example the money wage rate of a worker gives the number of dollars per hour paid to the worker, while the real wage rate is the money wage rate relative to the general price level. If the price level is constant, changes in the money and real wage rates are the same. If the price level is rising, a rise in money wages becomes an increase in real wages only when wages rise more than the price level. The amount of the increase in *real* wages is the difference between the increase in money wages and the increase in the price level. For example, if prices rise by 6 percent and money wages by 8 percent, real wages rise by 2 percent.

In general the theory of factor prices is based upon real factor prices. We shall follow usual practice and mean *real* factor prices unless we specifically distinguish real and money factor prices.

Factor Price Differentials

Prices of different units of factors such as labor or land vary. Consider the prices of a number of closely related factors such as different kinds of labor. If all these factors were identical and if all benefits were monetary, then all their prices would tend toward the same level. Factors would tend to move from low-priced occupations to high-priced ones. The quantities supplied would diminish in

occupations in which prices were low, and the resulting shortage would tend to force prices up; the quantities of factors supplied would increase in occupations in which prices were high, and the resulting surplus would force factor prices down. The movement would continue until there were no further incentives to transfer—that is, until factor prices were equalized. Factor price differentials are commonly seen and may be divided into two distinct types.

Dynamic Differentials

Some factor price differentials reflect a temporary state of disequilibrium. These are self-eliminating and are called **dynamic differentials**. They could equally well be called *disequilibrium differentials*. They are brought about by circumstances such as the growth of one industry and the decline of another. Such differentials themselves lead to reallocations of factors, and these reallocations will in turn act to eliminate the differentials.

Consider the effect on factor prices of a rise in the demand for air transport and a decline in the demand for railroading. The theory predicts an increase in airlines' (derived) demand for factors and a decrease in the railroad industry's (derived) demand for factors. Relative factor prices are thus predicted to go up in the airline industry and down in railroading. The differential in factor prices will itself foster a net movement of factors from the railroad industry to the airline industry, and this movement will cause the dynamic price differentials to lessen and eventually disappear. How long this process takes will depend on how easily factors move from one industry to the other—that is, on the extent of factor mobility.

Equilibrium Differentials

Some factor price differentials may persist in equilibrium without generating forces that eliminate them. These **equilibrium differentials** are related to differences in the factors themselves (e.g., land of different fertilities or labor of different abilities), to differences in the cost of acquiring skills, and to different nonmonetary advantages of different factor employments.

It is usual to pay academic research workers less than they could earn in the world of commerce and industry because there are substantial nonmonetary advantages attached to the former. If labor were paid the same in both employments, many people would try to move out of industry and into academic employment. Excess demand for labor in industry and excess supply in universities would then cause industrial wages to rise relative to academic ones until the movement of labor stopped.

Equilibrium differentials may also be caused by differences in skills. People will not make the investment of time and money to acquire scarce skills, even if they are able to do so, unless the differentials in wages remain large enough to repay the costs incurred in acquiring these skills.

The two kinds of differentials are closely linked to factor mobility and the hypothesis of equal net advantage. Dynamic differentials lead to, and are eroded by, factor movements; equilibrium differentials are explained in part by different nonmonetary benefits, in part by lack of mobility, and in part by the cost of acquiring specific skills. Dynamic differentials tend to disappear over time; equilibrium differentials persist indefinitely.

Transfer Earnings and Economic Rent

The amount that a factor must earn in its present use to prevent it from transferring to another use is called its **transfer earnings.** Any excess that it earns over this amount is called its **economic rent.** The distinction is critical in predicting the effects of changes in earnings on the movement of factors.

The concept of economic rent, a surplus over transfer earnings, is analogous to the notion of economic profit as a surplus over opportunity cost.

Origins of the Concept of Economic Rent

The present concept of economic rent arose out of a policy controversy. In the early nineteenth century there was a public debate about the high prices of wheat in England. The high price was causing great hardship because bread was a primary source of food. Some argued that "corn" (in England the generic term for all grains) had a high price because landlords were charging very high rents to tenant farmers. In order to meet these land rents, the prices that farmers charged for their corn also had to be raised to a high level. In short it was argued that the price of corn was high because the rents of agricultural land were high. Those who held this view advocated restricting the power of the landlords and somehow forcing them to behave more reasonably.

David Ricardo held that the situation was exactly the reverse. The price of corn was high, he said, because there was a shortage of corn caused by the Napoleonic wars. Because corn had a high price, it was profitable to produce it and there was keen competition among farmers to obtain land on which to grow corn. This competition in turn forced up the rents of corn land. If the price of corn were to fall so that corn growing became less profitable, then the demand for land would fall and the price paid for the use of land (i.e., its rent) would also fall. Ricardo advocated removing the tariff so that imported corn could come into the country, thereby increasing the supply and bringing down both the price of corn and that of the land on which it was grown.

Stated formally, the essentials of Ricardo's argument were these: Land was regarded as having only one use, the growing of corn. The supply of land was regarded as unchangeable—that is, in perfectly inelastic supply. Nothing had to be paid to prevent land from transferring to a use other than growing corn because it had no other use. No self-respecting landowner would leave land idle as long as he could obtain some return, no matter how small, by renting it out. Therefore, all the payment to land—that is, rent—was a surplus over and above what was necessary to keep it in its present use. Given a fixed supply of land, the price depended on the demand for land, which was *derived* from the demand for corn. Rent, the term for the payment for the use of land, thus became the term for a surplus payment to a factor over and above what was necessary to keep it in its present use.

The Modern View of Economic Rent

Later two facts were realized. First, land itself often had alternative uses, and from the point of view of any one use, part of the payment made to land would necessarily have to be paid to keep it in its present use. Second, factors of production other than land also often earn a surplus over and above what is necessary to keep them in their present use. Television stars and great athletes, for example, are in short and fairly fixed supply, and their potential earnings in other occupations are often quite moderate. But because there is a huge demand for their services as television stars or athletes, they may receive payments greatly in excess of what is needed to keep them from transferring to other occupations.

Thus it appears that all factors of production are pretty much the same; part of the payment made to them is a payment necessary to keep them from transferring to other uses, and part is a surplus over and above what is necessary to keep them in their present use. This surplus is now called *economic rent* whether the factor is land or labor or a piece of capital equipment.

The Division of Factor Earnings Between Rents and Transfer Earnings

In most cases the actual earnings of a factor of production will be a composite of transfer earnings and economic rent. It is possible, however, to imagine cases in which all earnings are either transfer earnings or economic rent. The possibilities are illustrated in Figure 20-3. When the supply curve is perfectly inelastic (vertical), the whole of the payment is an economic rent: even a price barely above zero would not lead suppliers to decrease the quantity supplied. After all, some price is better than none. The price actually paid allocates the fixed supply to those most willing to pay for it. When the supply curve is perfectly elastic (horizontal), the whole of the price paid is a transfer earning: if the purchasing industry does not pay this price, it will not obtain any quantity of the factor.

The more usual situation is that of a gradually

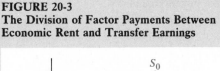

FIGURE 20-3
The Division of Factor Payments Between Economic Rent and Transfer Earnings

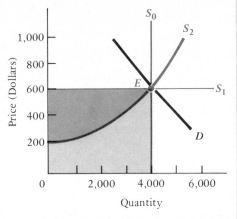

The division of total factor payments between economic rent and transfer earnings depends on the shape of the supply curve. A single demand curve is shown with three different supply curves. In each case the competitive equilibrium price is $600, and 4,000 units of the factor are hired. The total payment ($2.4 million) is represented by the entire shaded area.

When the supply curve is vertical (the line S_0), the whole payment is economic rent because a decrease in price would not lead any unit of the factor to move elsewhere.

When the supply curve is horizontal (the line S_1), the whole payment is transfer earnings because even a small decrease in price offered would lead all units of the factor to move elsewhere.

When the supply curve rises to the right (the curve S_2), part of the payment is rent and part is transfer earnings. As shown by the height of the supply curve, at a price of $600 the 4,000th unit of the factor is just receiving transfer earnings, but the 2,000th unit (for example) is earning well above its transfer earnings. The aggregate of economic rents is shown by the dark shaded area, and the aggregate of transfer earnings by the light shaded area.

rising supply curve. In this case a rise in the price serves the allocative function of attracting more units of the factor into the employment, but the same rise in the factor's price provides an extra economic rent to all units of the factor already employed. We know it is an economic rent because the owners of these units were willing to supply them at the original price.

This is quite a general result. If a factor becomes scarce in any or all of its uses, its price will rise. This will serve the allocative function of attracting additional units, but it will also give an economic rent to all units of the factor already in that employment, whose transfer earnings were already being covered.

Using Wage Increases to Increase the Quantity of a Factor Supplied

The relative size of transfer earnings and economic rents has policy implications. Consider one. If the government wants more physicists, should it subsidize physicists' salaries? As we have seen, such a policy may well have an effect on supply. It will persuade some students uncertain about whether to become engineers or physicists to become physicists. Whether it is an efficient use of the money will depend on the slope of the supply curve. Clearly, however, raising all physicists' salaries may mean that a great deal of money will have to be spent on extra payments to those who are already physicists. These payments will be economic rents, for existing physicists have demonstrated that they are prepared to be physicists at their old salaries. If these rents are a large part of the total subsidy, an alternative policy may produce more physicists per dollar. One such alternative is to subsidize scholarships, and fellowships for students who will train to become physicists. The National Science Foundation and the Atomic Energy Commission did precisely this. The effect of such subsidies is to shift the supply curve of physicists to the right.

If the supply curve is quite inelastic, an increase in the quantity supplied may be achieved more easily and at less cost by policies designed to shift the supply curve to the right than by the policy of raising price and moving up the original supply curve. See Figure 20-4.

Precisely this issue was encountered in the discussion of the draft versus the volunteer army in Chapter 7. The "premium" earned by willing soldiers under the volunteer army is an economic rent.

What Questions Does the Theory Answer?

Consider again the questions discussed in the early paragraphs of this chapter. The theory of distribution we have here developed concentrates on the pricing of factors in many of the markets of the economy. We certainly can reject the view that the size distribution of income is beyond understanding, or beyond influence. We know that when something improves the productivity of a factor,

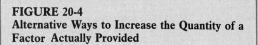

FIGURE 20-4
Alternative Ways to Increase the Quantity of a Factor Actually Provided

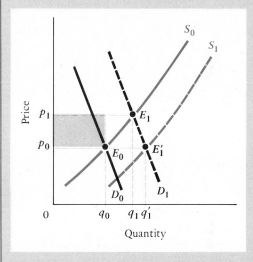

A subsidy that shifts the supply curve may achieve an increase in quantity actually provided without giving economic rents to those previously employed. With demand and supply curves D_0 and S_0 the factor market is in equilibrium at E_0. An increase in demand to D_1 would signal the need for an increase in quantity. One way to achieve it would be to let price rise from p_0 to p_1; this would lead to equilibrium at E_1. Such a price rise would give substantial rents to those already employed, as shown by the shaded area. An alternative policy in response to the demand shift would be to provide subsidies to new entrants and thus shift the supply curve to S_1. This leads to equilibrium at E_1' with no increase in price above p_0. It provides the additional quantity $q_0 q_1'$ without increasing the payments to the q_0 units already employed.

the factor's price will tend to increase. We know that factor mobility and immobility play an important role in the supply of factors to particular uses and thus to the pay of factors in those uses. We know how and why factor price differentials arise. We know that some differentials persist as equilibrium differentials and that others are the signals that lead to their own erosion.

In other words, we can offer a large part of the explanation of why some people earn large salaries and incomes and others do not. Thus this theory has a great deal to say about the *size distribution* of income. It is also well understood today that government policies of taxation and expenditure can affect the distribution of income. Income inequality diminished in the United States as a result of systematic attention to problems of poverty, discrimination, and immobility of labor.

While the theory worked out in this chapter answers many questions, it leaves others unanswered. It emphasizes the determination of both factor and product prices in millions of individual markets. But market economies are complex, and it is not easy to go from what happens in one market to what happens in the whole economy. Yet this is precisely what must be done if we wish to answer questions such as, "What is the effect of labor unions on the distribution of income?" As a result this market-oriented theory of distribution contributes little to the broad questions about functional distribution of income considered by Marx and raised before him by Ricardo and Smith, questions such as the distribution of income among labor (wages), capital (interest and profits), and land (rent).

To see why our theory may not be of much help, suppose we wish to know how much, if at all, a growth in labor unions' influence leads to an increase in labor's share of total income. To answer this question we would need to be able to discover not only what would happen in each individual market of the economy but also to aggregate to find the overall result. Clearly we are a long way from being able to do all this with our present state of knowledge.

One reason that questions concerning the overall functional distribution of income are difficult, and perhaps impossible, to answer is that the broad categories such as "labor" are themselves highly diverse: a theoretical physicist, a baseball superstar, and a bus driver all receive labor income. It makes sense to talk about laws governing distribution into three main factor shares if labor, capital, and land are each relatively homogeneous and each subject to a common set of influences not operating on the other two factors. In fact, however, there may well be as much difference between two different types of labor as between one kind of labor and one kind of machine. Thus there is no more reason to expect that there should be simple laws governing the overall functional distribution of income between land, labor, and capital than to expect that there should be simple laws governing the overall distribution of income between blondes and brunettes or Methodists and Baptists.

SUMMARY

1. The functional distribution of income refers to the shares of total national income going to each of the major factors of production. It focuses on sources of income. The size distribution of income refers to the shares of total national income going to various groups of households. It focuses only on the size of income, not its source.

2. The income of a factor of production can be broken into two elements: (a) the price paid per unit of the factor and (b) the quantity of the factor sold. The determination of factor prices and quantities is an application of the same price theory used to determine product prices and quantities.

3. The demand for any factor is *derived* from the commodities the factor is used to make. Factor demand curves slope downward because a change in a factor's price will affect the cost of production (and thus product price, quantity produced, and the need for factors) and because of the ability to substitute cheaper for more expensive factors.

4. A profit-maximizing firm will hire units of any variable factor until the last unit hired adds as much to costs as it does to revenue. If buyers of factors are price takers in factor markets, the addition to cost will be the price of a unit of a factor. From this comes the important condition that in competitive equilibrium the price of a factor will equal its marginal revenue product. This is the marginal productivity theory of distribution.

5. The elasticity of factor demand will tend to be greater (a) the greater is the elasticity of demand of the products it makes, (b) the greater is the proportion of the total cost of production accounted for by the factor, and (c) the easier it is to substitute one factor for another.

6. The total effective supplies of most factors are variable over time and respond to some degree to economic influences. The supply of a factor to particular uses tends to be much more elastic than the total supply of the factor.

7. The hypothesis of equal net advantage is a theory of the allocation of the total supply of factors to particular uses. Owners of factors will choose the use that produces the greatest net advantage, allowing for monetary and nonmonetary advantages of a particular employment.

8. Factor mobility (shiftability in use) is important. Land is mobile between uses but cannot change its geographical location. Capital equipment is durable, but firms regularly replace discarded or worn out machinery with totally different machines and so change the composition of the nation's capital stock gradually but steadily. Labor mobility is greatly affected by nonmonetary considerations. The longer the period of time allowed to elapse, the more mobile is the labor force.

9. In competitive factor markets, prices are determined by demand and supply, but factor price differentials occur. Dynamic differentials in the earnings of different units of factors of production serve as signals of a disequilibrium and induce factor movements that eventually remove the differentials. Equilibrium differentials reflect differences among units of factors as well as nonmonetary benefits of different jobs; they can persist indefinitely.

10. Payments to a factor consist of both transfer earnings and economic rents. Transfer earnings are what must be paid to a factor to prevent it from transferring to another use. Economic rent is the difference between a factor's transfer earnings and its actual earnings. Whenever the supply curve is upward-sloping, part of the factor's earnings is transfer earnings and part is rent.

11. The existence of rents in a factor's price has a potentially important policy implication: If supply is inelastic, raising the factor's price may be a relatively expensive way to induce increases in the quantity of the factor supplied.

12. The theory of distribution developed in this chapter has a great deal to say about the size distribution of income, but it has little to say about changes in the broad functional distribution of income among labor, land, and capital.

TOPICS FOR REVIEW

Factor demand as a derived demand
Marginal revenue product
The marginal productivity theory of distribution ($w = MRP$)
Factor mobility
The hypothesis of equal net advantage
Dynamic and equilibrium differentials in factor prices
Transfer earnings and economic rent

DISCUSSION QUESTIONS

1. Other things being equal, how would you expect each of the following to affect the size distribution of after-tax income? Do any of them lead to clear predictions about the functional distribution of income?
   a. An increase in unemployment
   b. Rapid population growth in an already crowded city
   c. An increase in food prices relative to other prices
   d. An increase in social security benefits and taxes
2. Consider the effects on the overall level of income inequality in the United States of each of the following.
   a. Labor force participation of women increases sharply due to many women shifting from work in the home to full-time paid jobs

b. Increasing use by California agricultural producers of Mexican farm workers who are in the United States illegally

c. Increasing numbers of minority group members studying law and medicine

3. The demands listed below have been increasing rapidly in recent years. What derived demands would you predict have risen very sharply? Where will the extra factors of production demanded be drawn from?

a. The demand for home computers

b. The demand for medical services

c. The demand for international and interregional travel

4. When Football Coach Jackie Sherrill signed a contract with Texas A&M for a reported $287,000 a year, it evoked widespread comments:

a. A University of Arizona journalism professor: "It's completely out of line."

b. A University of Michigan mathematician: "A sad sidelight on American society."

c. A University of Wisconsin agriculture professor: "Outrageous. If that were to happen in Madison, there would be a faculty revolt."

d. The general secretary of the American Association of University Professors: "It raises serious questions about the way resources are being allocated."

Discuss these reactions.

5. To what extent do the same principles help to explain

a. Why horse racer Robert Sangster paid $4.25 million for an untested yearling son of Nijinsky II.

b. Why baseball magnate George Steinbrenner signed a 10-year contract with star outfielder Dave Winfield that amounts to about $22 million over Winfield's playing career?

Are there important *differences* in the market for horses and for baseball players?

6. Overall participation in the labor force has remained at about the same proportion of the total population for the last 20 years, but its composition has changed substantially. Among the features of the labor force over this period are

a. Virtually all married men between 25 and 45 years of age have participated in the labor force in each year.

b. The labor force participation of women aged 40 and over has risen sharply.

c. The participation of men over 55 has dropped.

d. The participation of both men and women under 25 has declined.

Hypothesize about the social and economic changes that might explain these conditions. How do they relate to the theory of distribution?

7. What, if anything, do each of the following have to do with factor mobility?

a. A newspaper advertisement by the New Jersey Development Council: "Open your new plant in the Garden State. Our sizable labor force of skilled and unskilled workers is a major benefit for any employer. New Jersey workers are experienced, easy to find, easy to train. And just as important for your profit picture, they like it in New Jersey and don't move away."

b. Trailways Bus Company offered one-way bus tickets to anywhere in the United States at half price to anyone in Detroit who had been unemployed for six months or more. Hundreds of people brought these "opportunity fare" tickets.

c. Rising housing prices in the sun belt and falling prices in the Midwest.

8. Comment on each of the following. In what way are the two subject to the same economic analysis?

a. A recent study showed that after taking full account of differences in education, age, hours worked per week, weeks worked per year, and so forth professionally trained people earned approximately 15 percent less if they worked in universities than if they worked in government service.

b. "Unquestionably, ballet dancers are among the most grossly underpaid professionals in America. I refer here not to that handful of megastars who command huge salaries, but to the anonymous dancers who constitute the corps and soloist ranks of our major companies."

9. Distinguish between economic rent and transfer earnings in each of the following payments for factor services.

a. The $200 per month a landlord receives for the use of an apartment leased to students

b. The salary of the president of the United States

c. The $800,000 annual salary of a football player who says, "I'd play for nothing if I had to, I love this game."

d. The salary of a window cleaner who says, "It's dangerous, dirty work, but it beats driving a truck."

10. Which of the following are dynamic and which equilibrium differentials in factor prices?

a. The differences in earnings of football coaches and wrestling coaches

b. A "bonus for signing on" offered by a construction company seeking carpenters in a tight labor market

c. Differences in monthly rentals charged for three-bedroom houses in different parts of the same metropolitan area

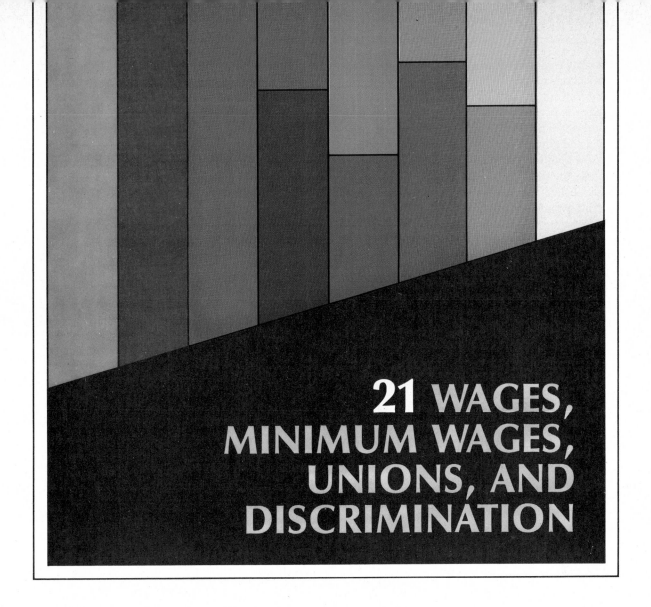

21 WAGES, MINIMUM WAGES, UNIONS, AND DISCRIMINATION

Why do steel workers get the same pay for the same work, no matter where they work in the United States? Why do carpenters get different wages in different locations? Why do railroad employees, who work in a declining industry, get higher rates of pay than equally skilled workers in many expanding industries? How does a worker in a plant employing 5,000 people "ask for a raise"? How does a worker let her employer know that she would be glad to trade so many cents per hour in wages for a better medical insurance scheme? Why do strikes occur?

The competitive theory of factor price determination, the subject of the preceding chapter, yields many useful and confirmed predictions about factor prices, factor movements, and the distribution of income. Indeed, for the pricing of many non-human factors, there is little need to modify the competitive model. Much of what is observed about labor markets is also consistent with the theory. But not all of it is.

Labor is in many ways the exceptional factor of production. The forces that govern working conditions and pay are critically important to workers and their families. When employees and employers negotiate the price to be paid to the factor of production called labor, they are negotiating about something that is vital to most households. It is not surprising that people are sometimes prepared to fight over such negotiations. Considerations other than material advantage enter the relationship between employer and employee, for it is a relationship between people who look for loyalty, fairness, appreciation, and justice along with paychecks and productivity and who, if they believe these are denied them, can often respond with aggression, malice, and hatred.

Labor unions, employers' associations, and the institutions and customs that influence collective bargaining are features of the real world. They have developed in response to the exceptional conditions that govern the bargaining between free people about the terms on which one will work for another. These institutions are important because they influence wages and working conditions. They also affect the levels of employment and unemployment in many industries.

Because labor markets are characteristically imperfectly competitive, and sometimes monopolistic, the theory of factor price determination must be extended somewhat before it can be applied to the full range of problems concerning the determination of wages.

THEORETICAL MODELS OF WAGE DETERMINATION[1]

In a labor market, firms are the buyers and workers, either individually or through a labor union, are the sellers. Noncompetitive elements can enter

[1] Remember that, unless otherwise specified, we are dealing with real wages—that is, wages relative to the price level.

on either or both sides of the market. The outcome of the wage bargain will be affected by the market situation.

Two extreme but relevant cases are, first, the one in which there are so many employers that no one of them can influence the wage rate by varying its own demand for labor and, second, the one in which there is a single purchaser of labor, either a single firm or an association of several firms operating as a single unit in the labor market. In the former case, labor is said to be purchased under competitive conditions; in the latter case, under monopsonistic conditions. **Monopsony** means a single buyer; it is the equivalent, on the purchasing side, of a monopoly (a single seller). What is the effect of introducing a union into each of these extreme situations?

A Union in a Competitive Labor Market

Where there are many employers and many unorganized workers there is a competitive factor market of the kind discussed in the previous chapter. Under competitive conditions the wage rate and level of employment are set by supply and demand. This is shown in Figure 21-1.

Suppose a union enters such a market and sets a wage for the industry above the competitive level. By so doing it is establishing a minimum wage below which no one will be allowed to work. This changes the supply curve of labor. The industry can hire as many units of labor as are prepared to work at the union wage, but the union will not let the wage rate fall. Thus the industry (and each firm) faces a supply curve that is horizontal at the level of the union wage up to a quantity of labor willing to work at that wage. This too is shown in Figure 21-1. The intersection of this new supply curve and the demand curve establishes a wage rate and level of employment that differ from the competitive equilibrium.

The major effects of a union's setting a wage above the competitive level are (1) to raise the wage rates of those who remain employed; (2) to lower the actual

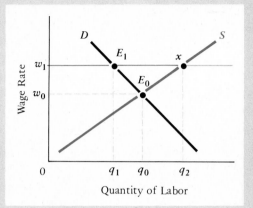

FIGURE 21-1
Union Wage Setting Above the Competitive Level

Quantity of Labor

A union can raise the wages of those who continue to be employed in a competitive labor market at the expense of the level of employment. The competitive equilibrium is at E_0, the wage is w_0, and employment is q_0. If a union enters this market and sets a wage of w_1, a new equilibrium will be established at E_1. The supply curve has become w_1xS. At the new wage, w_1, there will be q_2 workers who would like to work, but the industry only wishes to hire q_1. Employment will be q_1. The decrease in employment due to the wage increase over the competitive level is q_1q_0 and the level of unemployment is q_1q_2.

This figure can also be used to illustrate the effect of government's imposing a minimum wage of w_1 on the market. The q_1 workers who remain employed benefit by the wage increase. The q_1q_0 workers who lose their jobs in this industry suffer to the extent that they fail to find new jobs at a wage of w_0 or more.

amount of employment in the industry; and (3) to create a group of workers who would like to obtain jobs in the industry but cannot.

Ample evidence confirms these theoretical predictions. The unemployment that results presents a problem for the union if it seeks to represent *all* the employees in the industry or occupation. A conflict of interest has been created between employed and unemployed union members. Pressure

to cut the wage rate may develop among the unemployed, but the union must resist this pressure if the higher wage is to be maintained.

The loss of employment opportunities in the affected industry may well be permanent, and the unemployment may be quite long lasting. Often the actions of unions will force up the wages of those whose wages would be high in any case. This means that some displaced workers will have difficulty finding jobs that are equivalent in pay, particularly when their skills are not readily transferable to other jobs. For this reason the union jobs are likely to be prized, and many of the displaced may prefer to wait for openings caused by death or retirement rather than seek employment in other occupations.

A Monopsonistic Labor Market Without a Union

Consider a labor market in which there are many unorganized workers but only a small number of firms. For simplicity imagine a case in which the firms form an employers' hiring association in order to act as a single unit so that there is a monopsony in the labor market.

The employers' association realizes that, faced with a rising supply curve for labor, it can pick a wage rate and take the quantity of labor offered, or it can pick the quantity of labor to hire and pay the wage rate required to bring forth that quantity of labor. While the employers' association can offer any wage rate that it chooses—the laborers must either work at that rate or find a different job—the wage rate chosen will affect the profitability of its operations. For any given quantity that the monopsonist wishes to purchase, the labor supply curve shows the price per unit that it must offer; to the monopsonist, this is the *average cost curve* of labor. In deciding how much labor to hire, however, the monopsonist will be interested in *marginal cost* because it is aware that it can bid up the wage against its own interest.

Whenever the supply curve of labor slopes upward, the marginal cost of employing extra units

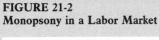

**FIGURE 21-2
Monopsony in a Labor Market**

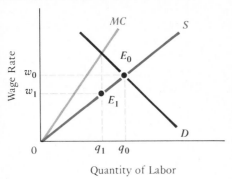

Quantity of Labor

A monopsonist lowers both the wage rate and employment below their competitive levels. D and S
are the competitive demand and supply curves. In
competition equilibrium is at E_0, the wage rate is w_0,
and the quantity of labor hired is q_0. The marginal
cost of labor (MC) to the monopsonist is above the
average cost. The monopsonistic firm will maximize
profits at E_1. It will hire only q_1 units of labor. At q_1
the marginal cost of the last worker is just equal to
the value to the firm of that worker's output, as shown
by the demand curve. The wage that must be paid to
get q_1 workers is only w_1.

will exceed the average cost.[2] It exceeds the wage
paid (the average cost) because the increased wage
rate necessary to attract an extra worker must be
paid to everyone already employed. [29] The
profit-maximizing monopsonist will hire labor up
to the point where the marginal cost just equals the
amount it is willing to pay for an additional unit
of labor. That amount is determined by the marginal revenue product of labor and is shown by the
demand curve. This is illustrated in Figure 21-2.

[2] If, for example, 100 units of labor are employed at $2 per
hour, then total cost is $200 per hour and average cost per hour
is $2. If 101 units are employed and the wage rate is driven up
to $2.01, then total labor cost becomes $203.01 an hour. Although average cost is only $2.01, the total cost has been in-
creased by $3.01 as a result of hiring one more laborer. Thus
the marginal cost of the extra unit of labor is $3.01.

Monopsonistic conditions in a factor market will result
in a lower level of employment and a lower wage rate
than would rule when the factor is purchased under
competitive conditions.

The common sense of this result is that the
monopsonistic firm is aware that by trying to purchase more of the factor it is driving up the price
against itself. It will therefore stop short of the
point that is reached when the factor is purchased
by many different firms, no one of which can exert
an influence on the wage rate.

A Union in a Monopsonistic Market

What if a wage-setting union enters a monopsonistic market and sets a wage below which labor will
not work? There will then be no point in the employer's reducing the quantity demanded in the
hope of driving down the wage rate, nor will there
be any point in holding off hiring for fear of driving
the wage up. Here, just as in the case of a wage-
setting union in a competitive market, the union
presents the employer with a horizontal supply
curve (up to the maximum number who will accept
work at the union wage). The union raises wages
above the monopsony level. This result is demonstrated in Figure 21-3.

Because the union turns the firm into a price taker in
the labor market, it can prevent the exercise of the
firm's monopsony power and raise both wages and
employment to the competitive levels.

The union may not be content merely to neu-
tralize the monopsonist's power. It may choose to
raise wages further. If it does, the argument will
be exactly the same as that surrounding Figure 21-
1. If the wage is raised above the competitive level,
the employer will no longer wish to hire all the
labor offered at that wage. The actual amount of
employment will fall, and unemployment will develop. This too is shown in Figure 21-3. Notice,
however, that the union can raise wages substantially above their competitive level before employment falls to a level as low as it was in the pre-
union monopsonistic situation.

FIGURE 21-3
A Wage-Setting Union Enters a Monopsonistic Labor Market

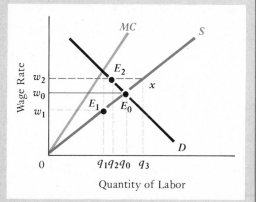

By presenting a monopsonistic employer with a fixed wage, the union can raise both wages and employment over the monopsonistic level. The monopsony position before the union enters is at E_1 (from Figure 21-2), with a wage rate of w_1 and q_1 workers hired. A union now enters and sets the wage at w_0. The supply curve of labor becomes $w_0 E_0 S$, and wages and employment rise to their competitive levels of w_0 and q_0 without creating a pool of unemployed workers. If the wage is raised further, say to w_2, the supply curve will become $w_2 x S$ and the quantity of employment will fall below the competitive level to q_2 while a pool of unsuccessful job applicants of $q_2 q_3$ will develop.

This figure can also be used to illustrate the effect of the government's imposing a minimum wage of w_0 or w_2 on a monopsonistic labor market.

MINIMUM WAGES AS A MATTER OF LAW[3]

When unions set wages for their members, they are in effect setting a minimum wage. Governments can cause similar effects by legislating specific minimum wages. It is worth digressing to discuss government minimum wages before taking a closer look at unions.

[3] This section may be omitted without loss of continuity.

In the United States the federal minimum wage was $3.35 per hour in 1983. It covered about 80 percent of the labor force. For a very large fraction of all employment covered by the law, this minimum wage is below the actual market wage. When this is true the minimum wage is said to be not binding. But many workers are in occupations or industries where the free-market wage rate would be below the legal minimum, and there the minimum wage is said to be binding, or effective.

Minimum wages are accepted in American life but are controversial among economists. To the extent that they are effective, they raise the wages of employed workers. But, as our analysis in Chapter 7 indicated, an effective floor price (which is what a minimum wage is) may well lead to a market surplus—in this case, unemployment. Thus minimum wages will benefit some groups while hurting others. The effects of minimum wages have been studied extensively.[4] The problem is more complicated than the analysis of Chapter 7 would suggest both because not all labor markets are competitive and because minimum wage laws do not cover all employment. Moreover some groups in the labor force, especially youth and minorities, are affected very much more adversely than the average worker.

Employment Effects on a Comprehensive Minimum Wage

Suppose first that minimum wage laws apply equally to all occupations. The occupations and industries in which minimum wages are effective will be the lowest-paying in the country; they usually involve unskilled or at best semiskilled labor. In most of them the workers are not members of unions. Thus the market structures in which effective minimum wages apply are likely to include both those in which competitive conditions pertain and those in which employers exercise monopsony power. The employment effects of minimum wages are different in the two cases.

[4] A recent comprehensive survey is Charles Brown, Curtis Gilroy, and Andrew Kohen, "The Effect of the Minimum Wage on Employment and Unemployment" *Journal of Economic Literature* (June 1982), pp. 487–528.

Effective Minimum Wages in a Competitive Labor Market

The employment effects of an effective minimum wage are unambiguous when the labor market is competitive. By raising the wage facing employers, minimum wage legislation leads to a reduction in the quantity of labor demanded and an increase in the quantity supplied. As a result the actual level of employment falls, and a surplus of labor (i.e., unemployment) is generated. This situation is exactly analogous to the one that arises when a union succeeds in setting a wage above the competitive equilibrium wage, as illustrated in Figure 21-1. The excess supply of labor at the minimum wage also creates incentives for people to evade the law by working below the legal minimum wage.

In a competitive labor market, when evaluating the effect of a minimum wage, the benefits of the wage increase to workers who remain employed should be weighed against the cost to workers who become unemployed.

The adverse effects of minimum wages fall most heavily on those with least education and training. It is this group—which includes many teenagers, women, and blacks—that will have fewer job opportunities as the wage rate rises. Many of them would have found jobs at lower wages. Furthermore this is not merely a one-time loss of jobs. Much skill acquisition occurs on the job. In a free market, employees in occupations in which such on-the-job training occurs "pay" for their education by receiving low wages in the initial stages of their employment. Minimum wage legislation makes this much more difficult. Instead of being able to "apprentice" in jobs that will lead to productive careers, many teenagers or blacks or women become trapped in low-skill, short-term employment that has frequent and prolonged periods of unemployment.

Effective Minimum Wages in a Monopsonistic Labor Market

This case is exactly analogous to the one in which a union facing a monopsonistic employer succeeds in setting a wage above that which the employer would otherwise pay, as shown in Figure 21-3. By effectively flattening out the labor supply curve, the minimum wage law can simultaneously increase wages and employment. Of course, if the minimum wage is raised above the competitive wage, employment will start to fall again, as in the union case. When set at the competitive wage, the minimum wage can protect the worker against monopsony power and lead to increases in employment.

It is theoretically possible that in an economy with both competitive and monopsonistic sectors, an effective minimum wage might raise employment enough in monopsonistic sectors to offset loss of employment in other sectors. The empirical evidence in the United States, however, is overwhelmingly that minimum wages do decrease employment.[5]

A Noncomprehensive Minimum Wage

Suppose a minimum wage covers only 80 percent of all jobs and that applying the minimum wage to the covered jobs does cause some unemployment in that sector. The workers displaced can move to the uncovered sector. If they do, they will shift the supply curve in the uncovered sector to the right. This will lead to lower wages and increased employment in the uncovered sector. See Figure 21-4. As a general rule the increase in employment in the uncovered sector will not be large enough to offset the decrease in the covered sector.[6]

The Overall Effect of Minimum Wage Laws

A great deal of empirical work has been done on the actual effect of minimum wages on employment. Minimum wages cause unemployment, par-

---

[5] Their effect on *measured* unemployment is less clear because many of those squeezed out—for instance, teenagers—simply withdraw from or never join the labor force.

[6] Only if the demand curve in the uncovered sector is horizontal (infinitely elastic), or if the supply curve is vertical (completely inelastic), will every displaced worker from the covered sector find employment. But these are not realistic possibilities.

ticularly among youths aged 16 to 19: it is estimated that the rate of youth employment is
decreased from 1 percent to 3 percent for every 10
percent increase in minimum wages. For young
adults (aged 20 to 24) the employment effect is also
adverse but smaller in size. Other differences too
have been documented. Blacks suffer more loss of
employment due to minimum wages than whites,
and females are more disadvantaged than males.
Many of the adverse employment effects are borne
largely by those who are least skilled, least experienced, and perhaps most intended to be the beneficiaries of minimum wage policies. In Canada
several provinces responded to this kind of evidence by allowing lower minimum wages for young
or inexperienced workers and for workers demonstrably in a "learning period."[7] No exceptions
on those bases are permitted in the United States
under current law, although President Reagan has
talked about the need for a "youth wage."

The adverse employment effect is, however,
only one element in deciding whether, overall, minimum wages are beneficial or harmful. It is clear
that minimum wage laws raise the incomes of many
workers at the very lowest levels of pay. Some of
those who benefit most are members of groups that
are chronically poor, whom the government is anxious to aid by income redistribution. But it is not
only the lowest paid who gain. Because union wage
structures maintain differentials between skill
classes, an increase in minimum wages also raises
wages in a large number of occupations that are
already above the minimum. Indeed it may raise
the whole wage structure.

Thus there are gainers and losers from minimum
wage laws, and individuals or groups may be expected to evaluate minimum wages differently.
Considering aggregate earnings, labor union members as a whole are gainers, as are both white and
black adult males. Black and white females and
teenagers are net losers because the loss of earnings
due to less employment is larger than the gains due

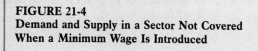

FIGURE 21-4
Demand and Supply in a Sector Not Covered When a Minimum Wage Is Introduced

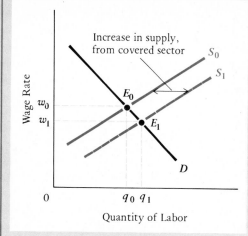

**Increased supply in uncovered sectors will lower
wages there and lead to some increase in employment.** Start from E_0, with wage rate w_0 and employment in this sector of q_0. The imposition of a minimum
wage on other sectors displaces workers who seek jobs
in the uncovered sector. This shifts the supply curve
from S_0 to S_1 and leads to a new equilibrium at E_1.
The new wage w_1 is lower than w_0, and employment
has increased by q_0q_1.

---

to higher wage rates. Of course there are gainers
and losers within each group. The losers are the
ones without jobs, the gainers those who receive
higher wages than they otherwise would.

Given this mixed result, what explains the widespread, almost uncritical belief in using increased
minimum wages to alleviate poverty and redistribute income from the rich to the poor? Much of the
explanation, we believe, rests on neglect of adverse
employment effects.

Organized labor finds minimum wages beneficial
to most of its employed members, and labor unions
have been consistently in favor of both increasing
the level of minimum wages and expanding coverage. No equally powerful political force opposes
them since those who do not find jobs because of
the minimum wage laws are unlikely to identify
these laws as the cause of their unemployment.

---

[7] It may be objected that such exceptions are discriminatory.
But, as we saw on page 250, labeling something "discriminatory" does not necessarily mean that it is bad. Here the question
arises as to whether it is better to be employed at a lower wage
or unemployed at a higher one.

THE VOCABULARY OF AMERICAN UNIONISM

Kinds of Unions

Unions today have two different principles of organization: the craft (or trade) union and the industrial union. In the **craft union** workers with a common set of skills are joined in a common association, no matter where or for whom they work. The craft principle of organization was and is the hallmark of the American Federation of Labor (AFL). The **industrial union** is organized along industry lines: All workers in a given plant or industry are collected into a single union. This is the pattern developed by the member unions of the Congress of Industrial Organizations (CIO). Among the prominent industrial unions are the United Automobile Workers and the United Steelworkers.

The two principles of unionism conflict. Should a carpenter employed in the steel industry be represented by the carpenters' union or the steelworkers' union? Disputes over which union shall have the right to *organize* (i.e., bring into their union) a particular group of workers are known as **jurisdictional disputes.** They have led to prolonged, bitter, and bloody battles of union against union, and they played an important role in American labor history until the merger of the AFL and CIO in 1955.

The important level for most of the economic functions of the union is the national level. The national officers do the bargaining, set the policies, and set the tone. Individual workers, however, belong to a local to which they pay dues (a part of which goes to the national). There are about 200 national unions, which have over 75,000 locals. The local for a craft union is geographical—the Chicago chapter of the carpenters, say. The local for an industrial union is a plant or a company—the Ford local of the United Automobile Workers, for example.

The **federation** is a loose organization of national unions. Before 1955 the AFL and CIO were two separate organizations; today there is one federation, the AFL–CIO. The federation serves an important role not in individual labor markets but as a voice of organized labor. Its function in recent years has been largely a public relations and political one; it has thrown its support behind certain candidates, its representatives have testified before Congress, appeared on *Meet the Press,* and so on.

Kinds of Bargaining Arrangements

In an **open shop** a union represents its members but does not have exclusive bargaining jurisdiction for all workers in the shop. Membership in the union is not necessary to get or to keep a job.

Unions vehemently oppose such an arrangement, and economic theory explains why. If, on the one hand, the employer yields to union demands and raises wages, the nonmembers ("free riders") get the benefits of the union without paying dues or sharing the risks or responsibilities. If, on the other hand, the firm chooses to fight the union, it can run its plants with the nonunion employees, thereby weakening the power of the union in the fight.

If the union succeeds in raising wages above their competitive level, there will be an excess supply of labor (see Figure 21-1). With an open shop, there is nothing to prevent unemployed nonunion workers from accepting a wage below the union one and so undermining the union's power to maintain high wages.

If all members of an occupation must join the union in order to get a job, the union can prevent its members from accepting less than the union wage and so have the power to maintain high wages in spite of the existence of excess supply. This arrangement is called a closed shop. In a **closed shop** only union members may be employed, and the union controls its membership as it sees fit. Employers traditionally regard this as an unwarranted limitation of their right to choose their employees. Since passage of the Taft-Hartley Act in 1948, its use has been virtually prohibited in the United States.

The **union shop** is a compromise between a closed shop and an open shop. It is the most common union arrangement in the United States today. In a union shop a firm may hire anyone it chooses at the union wage, but every employee must join the union within a specified period. This leaves employers free to hire whomever they wish but gives the union the power to enforce its union wages because workers are prevented from accepting employment at lower wages.

Weapons of Conflict

The **strike,** the union's ultimate weapon, is the concerted refusal to work by the members of the union. It is the strike or the threat of a strike that backs up the union's demands in the bargaining process. Workers on strike are, of course, off the payroll, so many unions set aside a portion of the dues collected to have a fund for paying striking workers.

Picket lines are made up of striking workers who parade before the entrance to their plant or firm. Other union members will not, by time-honored convention, "cross" a picket line. Thus, if bricklayers strike against a construction firm, carpenters will not work on the project, although they themselves may have no grievance against the firm, nor will any teamster deliver supplies to a picketed site. Pickets represent an enormous increase in the bargaining power of a small union. (Much of the bitterness against jurisdictional disputes arises from the fact that an employer may be unable to settle with either union without facing a picket line from the other union.)

A **labor boycott** is an organized attempt to persuade customers to refrain from purchasing the goods or services of a firm or industry whose employees are on strike. The boycotts organized by Cesar Chavez's United Farm Workers Union against grapes, lettuce, and most recently bananas are prominent examples.

The **lockout** is the employer's equivalent of the strike. By closing the plant the employer locks out the workers until such a time as the dispute is settled. **Strikebreakers** (scabs) are workers brought in by management to operate the plant while the union is on strike. A **blacklist** is an employer's list of workers who have been fired for playing a role in union affairs that was regarded by the employer as undesirable. Other employers are not supposed to give jobs to blacklisted workers.

While many economists are critical of minimum wages, as a practical matter the minimum wage is likely to remain. It is one of the hard-won labor gains dating back to President Roosevelt's New Deal, and it has great symbolic significance for labor.

THE NATURE AND EVOLUTION OF MODERN LABOR UNIONS

Labor-Market Institutions

No one bothers to define unions any more, perhaps because everyone knows what they are, or perhaps because a union is so many things: a social club, an educational instrument, a political club, one more source of withholding money from a worker's pay, a bargaining agent for an individual worker, and, to some, a way of life. For the purposes of our discussion of labor markets, a **union** (or **trade union** or **labor union**) is an association of individual workers that speaks for them in negotiations with their employers. Unions negotiate—"collectively bargain"—with employers, either individually or in groups. American unionism has developed not only its own institutions but also something of a specialized vocabulary, some of which is presented in the box on pages 364–365.

Employers' associations are groups of employers who band together for a number of purposes, one of which may be to agree on a common policy in labor negotiations. Today formal employers' associations that appoint official bargaining representatives exist on a local level in many industries, including the hotel, restaurant, newspaper printing, and construction industries. There are regional or national associations in the garment manufacturing, hosiery, textile, coal mining, and furniture manufacturing industries, among others.

At least as important as formal associations are informal ones in which the several firms in an industry follow the lead set by a key firm. The industrywide pattern characterizes many manufacturing industries today. The automobile industry, for example, achieves nationwide agreement with its workers without the formal apparatus of an employers' association.

The process by which unions and employers (or their representatives) arrive at and enforce their agreements is known as **collective bargaining.** This process has an important difference from the theoretical models with which we began this chapter. There we assumed that the union set the wage and the employer decided how much labor to hire. In collective bargaining the wage is negotiated. In terms of Figure 21-3 it may be that the employer wants the wage to be w_1 and the union wants w_2. Depending on each side's market power and their bargaining strength, the final agreed wage may be anywhere in between. In collective bargaining there is always a substantial range over which an agreement can be reached, and in particular cases the actual result will depend on the goals and strengths of the two bargaining parties and on the skill of their negotiators.

When representatives of the United Automobile Workers sat down with representatives of the General Motors Company in 1982 to discuss wages, contributions to pension funds, number and length of holidays, and employment security, they were engaged in what has been termed *mature collective bargaining*. At the end of the negotiations the newspaper and television coverage showed the smiling representatives shaking hands. Each of the approximately 400,000 workers in the GM plants then knew the conditions under which he or she would work for the next three years.

Unionism today is both stable and accepted. It was not always so. Within the lifetime of many of today's members, unions were fighting for their lives and union organizers and members were risking theirs. In the 1930s the labor movement evoked the loyalties and passions of people as a great liberal cause in ways that seem quite extraordinary today. Indeed unions today often appear as conservative (even reactionary) groups of hard hats. Why the change and how did it come about?

The Urge to Organize

Trade unionism had its origin in the pitifully low standard of living of the average nineteenth century

FACTORY LIFE IN THE UNITED STATES, 1903

Stories of the workers' very real suffering during the Industrial Revolution and the years that followed could fill many volumes, but an example will at least illustrate some of the horrors that lay behind the drive for change and reform. (The quotation comes from *Poverty*, by Robert Hunter, published in 1904.)

In the worst days of cotton-milling in England the conditions were hardly worse than those now existing in the South. Children—the tiniest and frailest—of five and six years of age rise in the morning and, like old men and women, go to the mills to do their day's labor; and when they return home, they wearily fling themselves on their beds, too tired to take off their clothes. Many children work all night—"in the maddening racket of the machinery, in an atmosphere insanitary and clouded with humidity and lint." It will be long before I forget the face of a little boy of six years, with his hands stretched forward to rearrange a bit of machinery, his pallid face and spare form showing already the physical effects of labor. This child, six years of age, was working twelve hours a day in a country which has established in many industries an eight-hour day for men. The twelve-hour day is almost universal in the South, and about twenty-five thousand children are now employed on twelve-hour shifts in the mills of the various Southern states. The wages of one of these children, however large, could not compensate the child for the injury this monstrous and unnatural labor does him; but the pay which the child receives is not enough, in many instances, even to feed him properly. If the children fall ill, they are docked for loss of time. . . . The mill-hands confess that they hate the mills, and no one will wonder at it. A vagrant who had worked in a textile mill for sixteen years once said to a friend of mine: "I done that [and he made a motion with his hand] for sixteen years. At last I was sick for two or three days with a fever, and when I crawled out, I made up my mind that I would rather go to hell than go back to the mill."

worker and his family. Much of the explanation for the low standard of living throughout the world lay in the small size of the national output relative to the population. Even in the wealthiest countries an equal division of national wealth among all families in 1850 would have left each one in poverty by our present standards.

Poverty had existed for centuries. It was accentuated, however, by the twin processes of urbanization and industrialization. The farmer who was moderately content working the land usually became restive and discontented when the family moved into a grimy, smoky nineteenth century city, lived in a crowded, unsanitary tenement, and took jobs in a sweatshop or a factory. The box provides a vivid picture of factory conditions at the turn of the present century. The focus of resentment was usually the employer.

The employer set the wages, and the wages were low. The boss was often arbitrary and seldom sympathetic. And the boss was usually conspicuously better off than his employees. Unhappy workers had, of course, the right of all free people to quit their job—and starve. If they grumbled or protested, they could be fired—and worse, blacklisted, which meant no one else would hire them.

Out of these conditions and other grievances of working men and women came the full range of radical political movements. Out of the same conditions also came a pragmatic American form of collective action called **bread-and-butter unionism,** whose goals were higher wages and better working conditions rather than social and political reform.

The early industrial organizer saw that 10 or 100 employees acting together had more influence than one acting alone and dreamed of the day when all would stand solid against the employer. (The word *solidarity* occurs often in the literature and songs of the labor movement.) The union was the organization that would provide a basis for confronting the monopsony power of employers with the collective power of the workers. But it was easier to see solidarity as a solution than it was to achieve it. Organizations of workers would hurt the employer, and employers did not sit by idly; they too knew that in union there was strength. "Agitators" who tried to organize other workers were fired and blacklisted; in some cases they were beaten and killed.

Requirements of a Successful Union

In order to realize the ambition of creating some effective power over the labor market, a union had to gain control of the supply of labor and have the financial resources necessary to outlast the employer in a struggle for strength. There was no right to organize. The union had to force an employer to negotiate with it, and few employers did so willingly. Unions started in a small way among highly skilled workers and spread slowly.

There are good theoretical reasons that help explain why the union movement showed its first real power among small groups of relatively skilled workers. First, it was easier to control the supply of skilled workers than unskilled ones. Organize the unskilled, and the employer could find replacements for them. But skilled workers—the coopers (barrelmakers), the bootmakers, the shipwrights— were another matter. There were few of them, and by controlling the conditions of apprenticeship, they controlled the access to their trade. The original craft unions were, in effect, closed shops: One had to belong to the union to hold a job in the craft, and the union set the rules of admission.

Second, a union of a relatively few highly skilled specialists could attack the employers where they were vulnerable. Because a particular skilled occupation may be close to indispensible in an industrial process, other factors cannot easily be substituted for it. Because labor in a particular skilled occupation is likely to account for a relatively low proportion of total costs, the effect on the employer's overall costs of giving in to a small group's demand for a wage increase is much less than the effect of giving in to an equivalent demand from the numerous unskilled workers.

In other words, both the difficulty of substituting other factors for skilled labor and a relatively small contribution to total costs combined to create an inelastic demand. This gave the unions of skilled workers an advantage in fighting the employer not enjoyed by other groups of workers. In the early days unions needed every advantage they could get since anti-unionism was for some employers a matter of principle, a crusade, and a way of life.

Even where unions gained a foothold in a strategic trade, they had their ups and downs. When employment was full and business booming, the cost of being fired for joining a union was not so great because there were other jobs. However, during periods of depression and unemployment the risks were greater. An individual worker knew that if he or she caused trouble, unemployed members of the trade would be there to take the job. Solidarity could yield to hunger. Membership in trade unions showed a clear cyclical pattern, rising in good times and falling in bad.

The Historical Development of American Unions

The Beginnings: Before 1933

The American Federation of Labor, founded in 1886 by Samuel Gompers, a cigar maker from England, was totally committed to organizing the skilled trades, to pursuing bread-and-butter issues, and to restricting labor supply. It is no coincidence that Gompers, himself an immigrant, led the AFL in vigorous opposition to further immigration: restriction of supply was the key to preserving union power.

Because it was impossible to control supply, the prospects for unionization were bleak for the unskilled. Their hope lay in political reform, in socialism, in cooperatives, or in revolution. The Knights of Labor, organized in 1869, sought one big union for all workers. At its peak in 1886 it had 700,000 members. But the political climate was hostile, and the Knights collapsed in 1887 for many reasons, including some unsuccessful strikes of unskilled workers. The depression of 1887 finished this ambitious venture in political rather than bread-and-butter unionism.

The AFL avoided noble causes and continued its steady growth among the skilled until the end of World War I. In 1900 it had just over half a million members (2 percent of the labor force), and by 1920 it had 5 million members, 10 percent of the labor force. By 1922, in the face of depression and the strong anti-labor attitude of government and business alike, union membership had declined to 8 percent, and by 1933, after a decade of gradual decline, to about 6 percent of the labor force.

The New Deal: 1933–1945

The dramatic effect of the New Deal on union membership is seen in Figure 21-5. What happened? First, the monstrousness of the Great Depression created a climate of public opinion openly hostile to big business and tolerant of even violent responses of labor over this period. Second, the Wagner Act (1935) guaranteed the *right* of workers to organize and to elect, by secret ballot, an exclusive bargaining agent by majority vote of the employees. And third, the unskilled were organized in industrial unions. The Wagner Act provided the means to control the supply of even unskilled labor.

The unions won—first by force and even violence, finally by law—the recognition that was required to permit workers through unions to articulate their grievances and to bargain to relieve them.

After World War II

The New Deal period and its legislation were unmistakably pro-labor. By the end of World War II attitudes had changed for several reasons, including an increasing number and the changing character of strikes. The jurisdictional strikes between rival AFL and CIO unions were less comprehensible to public and employer alike than the strikes designed to compel employers to deal with unions. An unprecedented wave of strikes in 1946

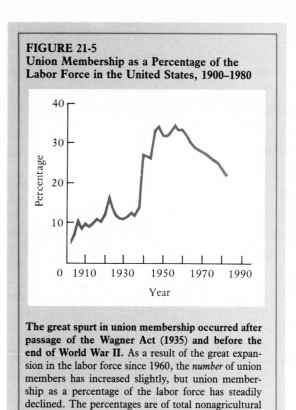

FIGURE 21-5
Union Membership as a Percentage of the Labor Force in the United States, 1900–1980

The great spurt in union membership occurred after passage of the Wagner Act (1935) and before the end of World War II. As a result of the great expansion in the labor force since 1960, the *number* of union members has increased slightly, but union membership as a percentage of the labor force has steadily declined. The percentages are of total nonagricultural employment.

led to the loss of over 100 million worker days (about 1 percent of estimated working time), more than four times the loss of any previous year.

Congress passed the Taft-Hartley Act in 1948, despite all-out labor opposition. Among its many provisions, unfair labor practices on the part of unions as well as management were defined and prohibited, use of the closed shop was limited, and strikes that "imperiled the national health and safety" were subject to an 80-day cooling off period. The most controversial feature of the act was the encouragement it gave to states to pass **right-to-work laws.** These laws permit the open shop—the right to work without belonging to a union.

Since 1950 union membership has continued to grow in absolute numbers to over 22 million, but despite that growth the percentage of the labor force in unions has declined steadily. Part of the reason is continued employer opposition; part is the absence of employment growth in traditionally unionized industries and in industries with large concentrations of employees. The biggest question mark is the future of unionism among employees in white-collar, professional, and service fields. Some observers believe that if inflation continues for very long, it will accelerate a trend toward unionization in these traditionally unorganized occupations.

The main development in the nature of unionization over the last three decades has been the stabilizing of union-management relations in industry after industry. Strikes still occur, and always will, for they are a key part of the poker game of collective bargaining. The number and duration of strikes today are relatively minor compared with those of the 1930s and late 1940s. It has been more than 20 years since strikes resulted in the loss of even one-half of 1 percent of all working time, and typically the work time lost amounts to only two- or three-tenths of 1 percent. Particular strikes—for example, among teamsters, teachers, police officers, or even professional athletes—can cause real disruption in peoples' daily lives and arouse public opinion. The strikes that do occur, however, are directed overwhelmingly toward specific issues and negotiations rather than recognition or jurisdiction, and the violence and passions of a generation ago are largely gone. Labor unions are now part of the establishment.

METHODS AND OBJECTIVES OF THE MODERN UNION

Union constitutions are extremely democratic documents. All members have one vote, officers are elected by the vote of the membership, the rights of individual workers are fully protected, and so on. In practice, however, the relation between the members of a union and its national officers is closer to that of the relationship between stockholders and managers of a giant corporation than to that of the American people and their govern-

ment. Unions tend toward one-party democracy in most cases. Union leaders are highly paid professionals whose business is to run the union, while the main business of union members is to earn a living on the job. The union members' indifference is understandable; they are paying dues that permit the union to pay generous salaries to union leaders to look out for the rank and file's interests—and as long as the leadership "delivers," all goes well. But delivers what and to whom?

Restricting Supply to Increase Wages

At the beginning of this chapter we saw that if a union raises the wage above the competitive level, it will create a pool of people eager to work at the going wage rate but unable to find employment. An alternative is to determine the quantity of labor supplied and let the wage be determined on the open market. This is illustrated in Figure 21-6. The union can restrict entry into the occupation by methods such as lengthening apprenticeship periods and restricting openings for trainees. Such tactics make it more difficult and more expensive to enter the occupation.

Under these restrictive conditions, the quantity supplied is reduced at any given wage rate and the supply curve of labor shifts to the left. This has the effect of raising wages without anyone's ever having to negotiate a rate above what would naturally emerge from the free operation of the competitive market. Furthermore there is no pool of unemployed wanting to work at the new higher wage but unable to find employment. Thus there is no wage-reducing pressure from unemployed persons who are trained for the occupation but are unable to find jobs.

The choice unions may face between the tactics of wage setting and supply restriction will be affected by the relative ease of enforcing one or the other kind of arrangement and the public acceptability of its tactics. Limiting entry is much easier where a specific, hard-to-acquire set of skills is not only required but is perceived by the public to demand certification. In this respect unions are no

FIGURE 21-6
Raising Wages by Restricting Entry

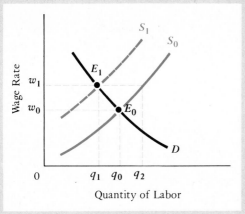

By restricting entry into an occupation, a union can shift the supply curve and raise wages. A competitive industry would be in equilibrium at E_0. When the supply curve shifts to S_1, the wage rises to w_1 and employment falls to q_1. Compare this to the strategy of simply imposing the wage w_1. In each case q_1 workers obtain employment at q_1. By shifting the supply curve, no pool of unsuccessful job applicants is created. When a wage of w_1 is imposed without shifting the supply curve from S_0, $q_1 q_2$ workers are unable to find jobs.

otherwise would be *because* the barriers to entry into the profession prevent increases in the number of those admitted to medical practice. Most investigators have concluded that restrictions on entering medicine are much greater than they need be to protect the public and that earnings are substantially higher as a result.

Lawyers, by contrast, have been less successful in limiting entry into their profession. The major law schools admit only a small portion of the qualified applicants, and they have not expanded sufficiently to keep pace with the sharply increased demand for admission. But new law schools, often of lower quality than the older ones, have sprung up to serve the growing excess demand. (While it is very expensive to establish a new medical school, it is relatively cheap to establish a law school.) The new law schools have proven financially beneficial to the institutions or individuals who organized them. Their graduates have, for the most part, gained access to the profession, often with the aid of "cram schools" that prepare them for the bar exams.

Lawyers, faced with an inability to limit competition by limiting entry into the profession, have turned to "wage setting"—having their state bar associations prescribe and enforce minimum fees for services such as drawing a will, probating an estate, and representing a client in court. They have also tried to label advertising and other forms of competition for clients as unethical. As the theory predicts, many lawyers are underemployed in the sense that they have fewer clients than they could comfortably handle. In contrast, doctors have typically been overworked.

Restriction of supply will tend to raise wages without creating unemployment. Raising wages without restricting supply will lead to unemployment.

Competing Goals

Wages Versus Fringe Benefits

Indirect or **fringe benefits**—such as company contributions to union pension and welfare funds,

different than professional groups, who may treat unions with utter disdain. Consider the professions of medicine and law. Since professional standards were long regarded as necessary to protect the public from incompetent practitioners, doctors and lawyers found it publicly acceptable to try and limit supply by attempting to limit entry into their profession.

Doctors were in short supply—and doctors' incomes became the highest of any profession—because of barriers to entry, including the difficulties of getting into an approved medical school, the high cost of creating new medical schools, long years of low-paid internship and residency, and various certification rules. Whatever the need for high standards of entry into medical practice, there is no doubt that doctors' earnings are higher than they sick leave, and vacation pay, as well as required payments toward social security and unemployment compensation insurance—are estimated to make up almost a third of the total compensation of industrial workers. Why do unions and employers not simply agree to a wage and let it go at that? Why should the average employed automobile worker have earned $19,800 in wages in 1980 but cost the company $31,700?

Fringe benefits appeal to employees in part because they are not subject to income taxes. Pension funds and medical benefits let employees provide for their future and that of their families more cheaply than they could by purchasing private insurance, and their benefits often protect them even when they lose their jobs. A package of fringe benefits that includes job security and unemployment benefits along with wage increases also appeals to union leaders trying to hold together unions because it provides at least something for everyone.

There may also be advantages to employers in giving indirect or fringe benefits. One advantage is that some forms of fringe benefits, such as pension funds, tend to bind the worker more closely to the company, thereby decreasing the turnover rate among employees. If employees stand to lose part of their benefits by changing jobs, they will not be so ready to move.

Wages Versus Employment

A union that sets wages above the competitive level is making a choice of higher wages for some and unemployment for others. Should the union strive to maximize the earnings of the group that remains employed? If it does, some of its members will lose their jobs and the union's membership will decline. Should it instead maximize the welfare of its present members? Or should it seek to expand employment opportunities (perhaps by a low-wage policy) so that the union membership grows?

Different unions decide these questions differently. The United Mine Workers Union employed a high-wage, shrinking-employment strategy for decades, and both employment and union membership declined. The longshoremen's union has achieved high wages but chooses to ration the available jobs among its members rather than reduce its membership. It thus spreads the underemployment around. In the garment trades the demand for labor is relatively elastic, and the major unions have traditionally accepted lower wages than they could have attained in order to protect the employment of their members.

The recession of the early 1980s combined with the growing competition to American manufactured goods from foreign competition led to a new recognition among major American industrial unions that high wages and high levels of layoffs and unemployment of their members often went hand in hand. Not only did major unions in automobiles, steel, rubber, smelting, airlines, and many others accept wage increases less than increases in the cost of living, many also accepted "givebacks" by reopening old contracts and agreeing to significant reductions in wages and other benefits under existing contracts. They did so in order to prevent further plant closings and to encourage the rehiring of unemployed union workers.

Wages versus employment poses a long-term problem as well as a short-term problem brought on by the recession. Unionization and rising wages in fruit picking have led to mechanization and a drop in the demand for labor. In the auto industry the high wage policy of the United Automobile Workers has encouraged the major manufacturers to increase automation. There would be 100,000 fewer jobs in the auto industry in 1983 than 10 years before even if production were back to old levels.

The fundamental dilemma of choosing between high wages and high employment is splitting many unions and dividing the American labor movement. Only 52 percent of the auto workers at GM approved a contract containing wage concessions by the union despite the intense lobbying for the contract by the union's leaders. Not all unions are going the same way. While steel, auto, and many others are trying to preserve jobs, the electrical workers are resolutely refusing to do so, and employment in this field is shrinking.

Wages Versus Job Security

Until the 1980s people who were in their teens during the Great Depression dominated the leadership of American unions. Not surprisingly, they had a strong defensive attitude toward their jobs. They lived through a period when unemployment was above 20 percent of the total labor force and nearer 50 percent in many of the hardest hit areas. They saw people grow up, marry, and raise children on relief or part-time work.

In a period of heavy unemployment, the installation of a labor-saving machine in a factory is likely to mean unemployment for those whose jobs are lost by the change. It is little wonder that new machines were opposed bitterly and that job-saving restrictive practices were adhered to with tenacity.

The heritage of this fear survived in featherbedding practices such as the standby musician at the television studio and the meticulous division of tasks in the building trades. But in the long run, mechanization increases productivity, and consequently the wages and profits that are earned. After World War II the attitude of many unions slowly changed from one of resisting technological change to one of collaborating with it and trying to reduce some of its costs to individuals who are adversely affected.

The return of higher unemployment rates in recent years has again heightened union interest in job security but in more constructive ways. Elimination of some restrictive practices that raised labor costs have been accepted by unions in return for company agreement to pass on savings in lower product prices and to delay planned layoffs. The biggest change in attitude (compared with the past) is that the current generation of leaders see the increased mechanization of Japanese, Korean, and German firms rather than their own employers as the principal threat to union workers' jobs. Many

of today's labor leaders seem prepared to help their American employers improve their international competitiveness.

LABOR-MARKET INSTITUTIONS AND THE PERSISTENCE OF INVOLUNTARY UNEMPLOYMENT

Labor unions and the various institutions and practices that have developed in collective bargaining have long been known to make a difference in the way in which particular markets function. Recently a major and important debate has developed among economists about whether—and if so, how—these institutions and practices affect the overall ability of the economy to cope with unemployment. We are now in a position to look at this question.

The Absence of Unemployment in Competitive Labor Markets

In the traditional or neo-classical theory of competitive wage determination, the wage rate adjusts to equate the demand and supply of labor. This is the sort of standard supply and demand analysis that is now familiar, and it is shown by the thicker curves in Figure 21-1.

If the wage rate is free to vary, the competitive wage rate will equate demand and supply and "clear the market." At this wage rate there is no involuntary unemployment.

It is true (as the supply curve shows) that there are more potential workers than those employed at the competitive wage, but extra workers are *voluntarily* employed—they do not choose to work at the competitive wage rate.

It follows that persistent involuntary unemployment can occur in this world only if the real wage is held above its competitive equilibrium level. If, for example, the wage is w_1 in Figure 21-1, there will be q_1q_2 units of labor involuntarily unemployed: they would like to work at the going wage rate, but there is no demand for their services. The remedy for involuntary unemployment in the neo-classical world is thus obvious: *reduce the real wage rate*. There can be no involuntary unemployment at the competitive equilibrium wage.

Market Theories of Unemployment

How then could economists explain the act of un-employment? Plainly either labor unions or mon-opsony, or both together, could lead to unemploy-ment. For example, a wage-setting union could raise the wage rate above the market clearing level and accept the unemployment of some of its mem-bers. Similarly monopsony could lower the level of employment below the competitive level, as was shown in Figure 21-2.

Classical economists readily accepted that either monopsony or monopoly might lead to unemploy-ment. Thus they did not deny the existence of unemployment. *What they could not accept was that unemployment could persist in competitive markets.* Yet the evidence, accumulated in recession after reces-sion, showed that it did occur, and any doubts about its persistence were shattered during the dec-ade of the 1930s.

Nonmarket Theories of Unemployment

The Great Depression triggered a major interest in understanding the problem of persistent unem-ployment. For a long time economists were satis-fied with the explanation offered by early Keyne-sian economists: workers would fail to appreciate the link between wages and unemployment and would in a variety of ways resist a downward move-ment in their money wage rate. Thus, when the real wage rate was too high, competitive forces would not reduce it by forcing money wages down because workers would stubbornly resist such a fall. Similarly, in some markets a government min-imum money wage—of the kind labor leaders per-suaded governments to establish—would prevent wages falling to the market-clearing wage.

Recently economists have sought alternative ex-planations of persistent unemployment by re-examining the determination of wages in terms of labor-market institutions. As a result, a new set of theories has arisen. These theories question whether forces exist in actual markets that cause wages to fluctuate in order quickly to equate the current demands for, and supplies of, labor. If they do not, then there is reason for supply and demand *not* to be equated for extended periods of time.

These theories start with the observation that labor markets are not auction markets in which prices always respond to excess demand or excess supply. When unemployed workers are looking for jobs, they do not knock on employers' doors offer-ing to work at lower wages than are being paid to existing workers—instead they answer want ads and hope to get the jobs offered but are often disappointed. Nor do employers, seeing an excess of applicants for the few jobs available, go to their existing workers and reduce their wages until there is no one looking for a job; instead they pick and choose until they fill their needs and then hang out a sign saying "no help wanted."

Are these familiar observations understandable? The explanation, in the newer theories, rests on the advantages to both workers and employers of relatively long-term, stable employment relation-ships. Workers want job security even in the face of fluctuating demand. Employers want a work force that understands the firm's organization, pro-duction, and marketing plans. Under these circum-stances both parties care about things other than the wage rate, and wages become somewhat insen-sitive to fluctuating current economic conditions. Wages are in effect regular payments to workers over an extended employment relation rather than a device for fine tuning the supply and demand for labor. Given this situation the tendency is for em-ployers to "smooth" the income of employees by paying a steady money wage, letting profits fluc-tuate to absorb the effects of temporary increases and decreases in demand for the firm's product.

Many labor-market institutions work to achieve these results. For one example fringe benefits pro-viding pensions, health care, and other benefits tend to bind workers to particular employers. For another the fact that pay tends to rise with years of service to the employer binds the employee to the company, while seniority rules for layoffs bind the employer to the long-term worker. Precisely such rules have become the norm in collective bargaining agreements.

These things tend to be the adhesive that leads to long-term employment despite the fact that the marginal product of workers rises rapidly as they gain experience, reaches a peak, and then falls off as their age advances. Under gradually rising wages, experienced workers tend to get less than the value of their marginal product at earlier ages and more as they near retirement. But over the long pull they are paid, on average, the value of their marginal product, just as the theory predicts they should. Between rising wages with age and dismissal in recessions in ascending order of seniority, employers and employees are held to each other, allowing payment of a more or less steady wage in the face of fluctuating economic circumstances.

In many American markets the wage rate does not fluctuate so as to clear the market in the short run. When wage rates are insulated from short-term fluctuations in demand, much of the market clearing that does occur is through fluctuations in the volume of employment rather than in the wage.[8]

As we shall see, these labor-market phenomena have important implications for dealing with pockets of unemployment as well as with the overall level of unemployment in the economy.

DISCRIMINATION IN LABOR MARKETS

The first major labor discrimination law suit was settled in 1973 when AT&T paid $15 million in back pay and an additional $23 million a year in raises to women and minority males against whom

---

[8] Of course, wages and employment do respond to major or permanent shocks to a market or industry.

it had allegedly discriminated in job assignments, pay, and promotions. Since then, such suits and settlements have become commonplace. In 1982 Northwest Airlines was ordered to pay $52.5 million to nearly 3,500 stewardesses who were judged to have been less well paid than men performing similar duties, and United Airlines was ordered to reinstate 1,800 female flight attendants who lost their jobs when they married in the 1960s. Coal companies have paid fines for denying women access to high-paying underground jobs. The construction industry has agreed to quotas for black workers to remedy the past exclusion of blacks from a variety of occupations. Sears, Roebuck & Company has been charged with discrimination against women, blacks, and Hispanics. Such suits or settlements focus on what many had long suspected—that discrimination by race and by sex have often occurred in the American job market.

The economic effects of discrimination against minorities and women take many forms. Discrimination does not wholly explain, but it surely contributes to, higher unemployment rates (fact: black unemployment rates are more than twice white unemployment rates) and to lower rates of pay (fact: female hourly earnings are 25 percent below male hourly earnings). Both lower wages and greater unemployment lead to lower incomes for the workers involved.

They may also lead to different attitudes toward the workplace and toward society. Discrimination affects not only the workers discriminated against but their children, whose aspirations and willingness to undertake the education or training required to "succeed" may be adversely affected. Indeed it may change the definition given to success. The costs of all this are borne by the groups discriminated against but also by society as a whole.

The problems of racial discrimination and sex discrimination are different from each other, and so is the nature of the policies required to eliminate them. With respect to the economics of discrimination, there are similarities as well as differences. It is helpful to look first at how either kind of discrimination produces its effects.

A Model of the Effects of Discrimination

We begin by building a simplified picture of a world without discrimination and then introduce discrimination. While this reverses the contemporary problem (reducing or eliminating discrimination), it provides insight into the effects of discrimination. We are concerned here with discrimination between two sets of workers who are in every sense equally qualified. Our discussion is phrased in terms of black versus white, but it applies equally to female versus male, alien versus citizen, Catholic versus Protestant, or any other prejudicial basis for dividing workers.

Suppose there are two groups of equal size in a society. One is white; the other is black. Except for color, the groups are the same—each has the same proportion who are educated to various levels, each has identical distributions of talent, and so on. Suppose also that there are two occupations. Occupation E (for elite) requires people of above average education and skills, and occupation O (ordinary) can use anyone, but if wages in the two occupations are the same, employers in occupation O will prefer to hire the above average worker. There is no racial discrimination; everyone is color-blind. The nonmonetary advantages of the two occupations are equal.

The competitive theory of distribution suggests that the wages in E occupations will be bid up slightly above those in O occupations in order that the E jobs attract the workers of above average skills. Whites and blacks of above average skill will flock to E jobs while the others, white and black alike, will have no choice but to seek O jobs. Because skills are equally distributed, each occupation will have half whites and half blacks.

Now we introduce discrimination in its most extreme form. All E occupations are hereafter open only to whites; all O occupations are open to either whites or blacks. The immediate effect is to reduce by 50 percent the supply of job applicants for E occupations (they must be *both* white and above average) and, potentially, to increase by 50 percent the supply of applicants for O jobs (this group includes all blacks and the below average whites).

Wage Level Effects

Suppose, first, that there are no barriers to mobility of labor, that everyone seeks the best job he or she is eligible for, and that wage rates are free to vary so as to equate supply and demand. The analysis is shown in Figure 21-7. Wages rise sharply in E occupations and fall in O occupations. The take-home pay of those in O occupations falls, and while the O group still includes both whites and blacks, it is now approximately two-thirds black.

Discrimination, by changing supply, can decrease the wages and incomes of a group that is discriminated against.

In the longer run further changes may occur. Notice that total employment in E industries falls. Employers may find ways to utilize slightly below average labor and thus lure the best qualified white workers out of O occupations. While this will raise O wages slightly, it will also make them increasingly "black occupations." An important long-run effect may be that blacks will learn that it no longer pays to acquire above average skills since they are forced by discrimination to work in jobs that do not use them. Yet if they never acquire the skills, they will be locked into the O occupations even if the discriminatory policy is reversed. And their children may conclude that education is for whites only.

Employment Effects

For a number of reasons, labor market discrimination may have adverse employment effects that are even more important than effects on wage levels. Labor is not perfectly mobile, wages are not perfectly flexible downward, and not everyone who is denied employment in an E occupation for which he or she is trained and qualified will be willing to take a "demeaning" O job.

If wages do not fall to the market-clearing level

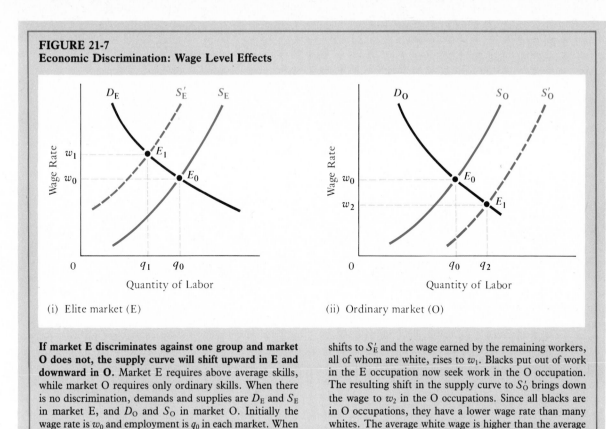

FIGURE 21-7
Economic Discrimination: Wage Level Effects

(i) Elite market (E)

(ii) Ordinary market (O)

If market E discriminates against one group and market O does not, the supply curve will shift upward in E and downward in O. Market E requires above average skills, while market O requires only ordinary skills. When there is no discrimination, demands and supplies are D_E and S_E in market E, and D_O and S_O in market O. Initially the wage rate is w_0 and employment is q_0 in each market. When all blacks are barred from E occupations, the supply curve shifts to S_E' and the wage earned by the remaining workers, all of whom are white, rises to w_1. Blacks put out of work in the E occupation now seek work in the O occupation. The resulting shift in the supply curve to S_O' brings down the wage to w_2 in the O occupations. Since all blacks are in O occupations, they have a lower wage rate than many whites. The average white wage is higher than the average black wage.

(say, because of minimum wage laws), the increase in supply of labor to O occupations will cause excess supply and result in unemployment of labor in O occupations. Since, in our model, blacks dominate these occupations, blacks will bear the brunt of the extra unemployment. This is illustrated in Figure 21-8(i). A similar result will occur if labor is not fully mobile between occupations, say because many of the O occupation jobs are in parts of the country to which the workers discriminated against are unable or unwilling to move. See Figure 21-8(ii). Potential O workers who cannot move to where jobs are available become unemployed or withdraw from the labor force.

A different mechanism can produce the identical result if those persons who lose their E jobs as a result of discrimination withdraw from the labor force. They may do just this if they have the skill and training to do the more respectable and more rewarding E jobs. Indeed it may be less demeaning to accept unemployment compensation or even welfare than to accept the only jobs that the discriminatory society offers them.

In the long term these unemployment effects may be increased by sociological and economic forces. Children of those discriminated against may well take as role models those who have made a life outside the labor force. Technological changes in the economy tend to decrease the demand for less skilled labor of the kind required in O occu-

FIGURE 21-8
Economic Discrimination: Employment Effects

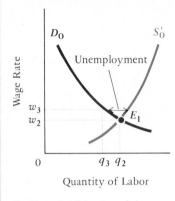 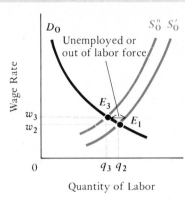 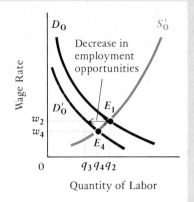

(i) Wage rigidities (or minimum wage)

(ii) Immobile labor (or withdrawal from labor force)

(iii) Declining demand

Increasing supply and/or decreasing demand in occupations in which those discriminated against are the major sources of labor can increase unemployment. In each part of the diagram the curves D_O and S_O' are those from Figure 21-7(ii); they show the market for O workers after the discriminatory policies are put into effect. Equilibrium is at E_1. In each case the wage w_2 would clear the market and provide employment of q_2.

(i) If the wage rate cannot fall below w_3, perhaps because of a minimum wage law, employment will fall to q_3 and unemployment will occur in the amount shown by the black arrow.

(ii) If some of the potential workers in O occupations

are unable or unwilling to take employment in O jobs, the supply curve will not be S_O' but S_O''. Equilibrium will be at E_3. While O wages will rise somewhat to w_3, employment will be only q_3 and a number of workers, shown by the black arrow, will not be employed. Whether they are recorded as "unemployed" or as having withdrawn from the labor force will depend on the official definitions.

(iii) If demand is declining in O occupations over time, say from D_O to D_O', either wages and employment will fall to the new equilibrium E_4 with w_4 and q_4 or wages will be maintained but employment will fall to q_3. The black arrow illustrates the latter case, where the fall in employment is q_3q_2.

pations, which become increasingly oversupplied. This possibility is sketched in Figure 21-8(iii).

All these theoretical possibilities have their counterparts in the real world. We shall discuss them briefly with respect to both black-white and female-male differences in the United States.

Black-White Differentials in Labor Markets

The differences in employment and pay rates for blacks and for whites are dramatic and easily measured. By 1980, after more than two decades of

vigorous equal employment activity, the median black family had earnings of $12,800, only 60 percent as high as those of the median white family. This figure reflected fewer jobs, lower-paying jobs, and more frequent part-time employment. Unemployment among blacks normally runs at more than twice the level for whites—roughly 13 percent to 6 percent in relatively good times—and in sharp recessions the ratio increases. Among blacks 16 to 19 years old the official unemployment rate was over 50 percent in 1982, while a rate adjusted to include those who have given up looking for work after repeated turndowns was over 60 percent!

We are talking here about averages. Of course there are some blacks who do as well as or better than their white counterparts in employment opportunities and in pay. But this is true of too few to raise the average black to the economic position of the average white.

Even employed blacks are often disadvantaged. Blacks tend to have less seniority than whites of similar ages, often because of past discrimination. The seniority they do have tends to be in the less skilled, lower-paid job categories. Blacks as a group have poorer health, shorter life expectancy, and shorter working lives.

All these characteristics contribute to lower economic status, but not all of them necessarily represent racial discrimination. Many of the disadvantages remain even when there is equal pay for equal work. Whites and blacks have, on average, different educational backgrounds and different sorts of professional or vocational training. Since these too affect employment opportunities and actual pay rates within occupations, is it not possible that they, rather than discrimination, account for the differentials?

To answer this question it is necessary to note that discrimination might be present not only directly (e.g., refusing to hire blacks because they are black) but also indirectly (e.g., refusing to hire blacks because they are not well trained, when training has been denied them because they are black).

Direct discrimination has decreased over the last 30 years. Direct employment discrimination against black athletes ended in that period, and federal laws have resulted in equal pay for equal work in many industrial jobs. But blatant discrimination undoubtedly survives in some occupations, and a preference for whites still exists in many others. Minorities account for 26 percent of the total work force but only 5 percent of managerial positions.

Indirect discrimination is harder to measure. If racial and sexual prejudice and discrimination vanished from the world today, its effects would be felt for generations. A black man whose grandfather and father were illiterate farm workers be-cause they were denied a decent education even after they were freed from slavery is unlikely to have had the opportunity or motivation to get much education himself. For one thing, he will have been needed on the farm to help feed the family. More important, he may have been raised in a culture that failed to see in education either the path to economic opportunity or a desirable end in itself. Even when employers are prepared to treat all applicants equally, blacks are often less skilled in hearing about, applying for, and interviewing for many good jobs.

The Persistence of Black Unemployment

The 1950s and 1960s saw a direct attack on blacks' labor market disabilities as part of a larger federal commitment to affirmative action to reverse the effects of discrimination.

Despite expenditures under the Comprehensive Employment Training Act (CETA) and other federal programs (now running at more than $12 billion per year), employment of blacks has not increased relative to employment of whites. There are a number of well-identified but not easily corrected reasons for this continuing problem. Special training programs do not have much effect on those unused to learning or without basic learning skills. Reinforcing this situation is the steady decline in employment opportunities in the unskilled and semiskilled jobs traditionally open to those with limited education. This decline reflects both increased automation in such heavy industries as automobiles and steel and the rising importance of service industries (as compared with manufacturing).

A further cause is the lesser geographic mobility of poor blacks as many available jobs have tended to move from the central cities to the suburbs and from the older population centers of the North to the sun belt. Among additional reasons are rising minimum wages, which reduce employment opportunities in some unskilled occupations, and some disdain on the part of modern blacks for the lowest-paying jobs as being beneath the dignity of people who wish to be treated equally. Finally, it seems unmistakable that the greater labor force participation of women and the deferral of retirement among older workers have increased the competition for jobs. Unfortunately, blacks have often been losers in that competition.

Female-Male Differentials in Labor Markets

Women have fared somewhat better under affirmative action than have blacks. Traditionally denied employment in many "male" occupations, adult women in the last three decades have increased their labor force participation from 34 percent in 1953 to more than 53 percent in 1983. (This is still short of the 78 percent participation rate of adult males.) Moreover, the female unemployment rate in 1983 was approximately the same as the rate for males. Women have steadily increased their participation in "higher status" occupations, including managerial, sales, scientific, and technical jobs. For one example women in 1966 accounted for 13.6 percent of the "professional" labor force; by 1980 that had risen to 34 percent. They have thus done much better than blacks in getting and keeping jobs.

But getting jobs is not the whole story. It has long been clear that women and men make and are offered different occupational choices, that proportionately fewer women than men reach higher-paying jobs in the occupations in which both work, and that those who do, do so more slowly. As a result average earned income of females in the labor force is well below that of males of similar ages. A number of careful studies have established that in the 1970s labor market earnings were approximately 25 percent lower for employed women than for employed men of the same age and race.

To what extent do these differences reflect discrimination against women and to what extent such other sex-linked characteristics as the voluntary choice of different lifetime patterns of labor force participation? The statistics show that, on average, women have fewer years of education, training, and work experience than men of the same age. The average working female is less mobile occupationally and geographically than her male counterpart. At least some of these facts reflect voluntary choice; for example, many women decide to withdraw from the labor force, or to work only part-time, in order to have and raise children.

The extent of direct discrimination in an occupation may be measured by taking groups with similar characteristics and comparing their employment and pay status. For example, comparing starting salaries in college teaching of new Ph.D.s from the same graduate schools in a given subject and a given class of institutional employment, Professors Frank Stafford and George Johnson found the average pay of females was about 6 percent below that of males (with allowance for differences in age and prior experience). They attributed this part of a larger male-female pay differential to direct discrimination.

Women have also suffered indirect discrimination. They have been refused admission or discouraged from seeking entry into certain occupations; for example, they have traditionally been pushed into nursing rather than medicine, social work rather than law, and secretarial rather than managerial training programs. Similarly, there is ample evidence that many women in dual career marriages are under substantial pressure to put their husband's job needs first. Girls raised in a culture in which their education seems less important than that of their brothers, or where they are raised to think of themselves as potential homemakers and are urged to prepare themselves to attract and serve a husband, are less likely to acquire the skills or the opportunities for many high-paying forms of employment that are wholly within their capabilities.

Discrimination against women in job opportunities is being eliminated much more quickly than discrimination against racial minorities; the effect of Women's Liberation on attitudes—male as well as female—has been very great in a very short time. Moreover, women—especially white women—have relatively quickly closed the educational gap that led to indirect discrimination. Between 1971 and

1982 the fraction of earned doctorates awarded to women rose from 14 to 28 percent and nearly half of the new graduate enrollments were women, so this upward trend is likely to continue. In 1981, 17 percent of first professional degrees (law, medicine, etc.) were awarded to women—compared to 6.5 percent 10 years earlier. Current enrollments in these professional schools are roughly 30 percent women. These trends reflect affirmative action on the part of schools, changed attitudes on the part of women, and wider employment prospects for women than even 10 years before.

What accounts for the greater success in eliminating the economic impact of sex discrimination than that of racial discrimination? The economic and educational backgrounds of males and females of the same generation have been much more nearly equal than between blacks and whites of either sex. Moreover, cultural and motivational barriers to women can apparently be changed in a single generation, while such a change may take longer for blacks. It is perhaps also true that sex prejudices in the labor market are less deeply ingrained than racial prejudices. Yet the continuing pay disadvantages of women in the labor force are likely to persist as long as women are less mobile and choose to interrupt their work during child-rearing years.

Who Loses from Discrimination?

Obviously, the victims lose as a result of labor market discrimination. To the extent that they are denied employment or receive lower pay than they otherwise would, minorities and women are punished for their race or sex. But it would be a mistake to think that they are the only losers. Society loses too because of the efficiency losses that discrimination causes, and in other ways.

Efficiency losses arise for several reasons. If women or blacks are not given equal pay with white males for equal work, the labor force will not be allocated so as to get the most out of society's resources. When people are kept from doing the jobs at which they are most productive and must instead produce goods or services that society values less, the total value of goods and services produced is reduced. And when prejudice increases unemployment, it reduces the nation's total output.

The gainers from discrimination are those who earn the higher pay that comes from limiting supply in their occupations, those who get the jobs that blacks and women would otherwise have held, and the bigots who gain pleasure from not having to work with "them" or to consume services provided by "them." But if the total output of society is less, the net losses will have to be borne by the society as a whole.

Beyond the efficiency losses that discrimination imposes on society are further economic and social costs. Increased welfare or unemployment payments may be required, and the costs of enforcing antidiscrimination laws must be paid. The costs of discrimination also include increased crime, hostility, and violence. These things are all by-products of unemployment, poverty, and frustration. Discrimination, if not attacked and rolled back, has one more cost, perhaps the most important: a sense of shame in a society that does not do what is necessary to eliminate the barriers to equal treatment.

SUMMARY

1. A wage-setting union entering a competitive market can raise wages, but only at the cost of reducing employment and creating a pool of unsatisfied former workers who would like to work at the going wage but are unable to gain employment.

2. A wage-setting union entering a monopsonistic market may increase both employment and wages over some range. If, however, it sets the wage above the competitive level, it too will create a pool of unsatisfied workers who are unable to get the jobs they want at the going wage.

3. Unions setting wages above the competitive level are not unlike governments setting minimum wages. The overall effects of minimum wages in the United States have now been extensively studied. It is clear that such minimum wages raise the incomes of many employees, but they have adverse employment effects on many of those with the very lowest levels of skills.

4. Labor markets have developed a wide variety of institutions, including labor unions and employers' associations. Such institutions greatly affect the nature of wage determination.

5. American unionism developed first in the skilled trades, along craft lines, where it was possible to control supply and prevent nonunion members from undercutting union wages. Widespread organization of the unskilled did not occur until after the legal right to organize was established by the Wagner Act in 1935. The emergence of mature collective bargaining is a relatively recent development in the stormy and sometimes bloody history of American labor unions.

6. Unions must decide on their goals. There is a basic conflict between the goals of raising wages by restricting supply (thereby reducing the union's employed membership) and preserving employment opportunities for members and potential members. Other trade-offs concern wages and job security, and wages and fringe benefits.

7. The various labor-market institutions studied lead to labor markets that operate very differently from the competitive labor market of neo-classical economics in which wage rate fluctuations equated demand and supply and quickly eliminated involuntary unemployment. Involuntary unemployment may persist not only because of monopsony and monopoly but also because of government policies and labor-market practices that arise because employers and workers each value relatively long-term, stable employment relationships. Much of the market clearing in labor markets that occurs in the face of fluctuations in demand takes the form of fluctuations in employment rather than fluctuations in wage rates.

8. Discrimination by race and by sex has played a role in labor markets, as it has in other aspects of American life. Direct discrimination can affect wages and employment opportunities by limiting the supply in the best-paying occupations and increasing it in less attractive occupations. Economic theory leads to the predictions that groups subject to discrimination will earn lower wages and/or suffer higher levels of unemployment than their counterparts who do not suffer discrimination. These predictions are borne out in the labor force experiences of blacks (and other minorities) and women.

9. Precisely how much of the wage and employment differentials between whites and blacks and males and females is due to discrimination is a matter of continuing research. Indirect discrimination has had an effect through limiting the opportunities for education and training available to those subject to discrimination and through lowering people's aspirations in their choices of training and of careers.

10. Affirmative action programs over the past two decades have been more successful in reversing the effects of discrimination against women than against blacks.

11. Discrimination imposes costs on the victims of discrimination. In addition it leads to inefficiency and loss of output and is costly in other ways.

TOPICS FOR REVIEW

Monopsony power
Union power
Effects of minimum wages
Collective bargaining
Goals of unions
Possible causes of involuntary unemployment
Economic discrimination
Wage effects and employment effects of economic discrimination
Direct and indirect discrimination

DISCUSSION QUESTIONS

1. American unions have traditionally supported laws
   a. Restricting immigration
   b. Expelling illegal aliens
   c. Raising the minimum wage and extending its coverage
   Do these positions benefit or hurt (1) the American consumer, (2) American workers as a whole, and (3) unionized workers with seniority in their jobs?

2. A union that has bargaining rights in two plants of the same company in different states almost always insists on "equal pay for equal work" in the two plants. It does not always insist on equal pay for men and women in the same jobs. Can you see any economic reasons for such a distinction?

3. During 1982 the United Auto Workers accepted lower rates of pay for its members working for Chrysler than the same categories of workers received from Ford and General Motors. This violated the UAW's traditional policy of a single wage rate schedule nation-wide. Suggest why its traditional policy existed but why it might have changed its policy in 1982.

4. "The labor of a human being is not a commodity or article of commerce," the Clayton Act states. The context of this statement was a provision that gave labor unions some measure of exemption from antitrust action. Why should wage fixing not be in violation of the antitrust laws when price fixing is?

5. Why were craft unions more successful than industrial unions in the late nineteenth century in the United States? What happened to change this in the 1930s?

6. Interpret the following statements or practices in terms of the subject matter of this chapter.
   a. A requirement that every passenger train carry a fireman though there may be nothing for him to do
   b. A requirement that one must pass an English language proficiency test to be a carpenter in New York City
   c. A statement by an official of a textile workers union in Massachusetts: "Until we have organized the southern textile industry, we will be unable to earn a decent wage in New England."
   d. An official of the United Steel Workers' Union: "Things are getting rough in our locals because the youngsters have different views about wages than the old-timers."

7. Each of the following headlines appeared in 1982. Explain each one and speculate on whether it might (or might not) have appeared in 1952.
   a. "Lifetime employment—a key union goal"
   b. "American labor—from fighting cartels to fighting competition"
   c. "GM and UAW agree to tie car prices to wage concessions"
   d. "Fringe benefits loom large in key bargains"

8. "The great increase in the number of women entering the labor force for the first time means that relatively more women than men earn beginning salaries. It is therefore not evidence of discrimination that the average wage earned by females is less than that earned by males." Discuss.

9. The American Cyanamid Corporation once had a policy of removing women of child-bearing age from, or not hiring them for, jobs that expose them to lead or other substances that could damage a fetus. Is this sex discrimination? Whether it is or not, debate whether this sort of protective hiring rule is something the government should require, encourage, or prohibit.

10. "One can judge the presence or absence of discrimination by looking at the proportion of the population in different occupations." Does such information help? Does it suffice? Consider each of the following examples. Relative to their numbers in the total population, there are
    a. Too many blacks and too few Jews among professional athletes
    b. Too few male secretaries
    c. Too few female judges

11. Could economic discrimination persist in a competitive labor market? Consider the argument that in a world of employers prejudiced against blacks, any firm that violated the taboo and hired blacks would reduce costs, make profits, and be able to take business from its prejudiced competitors.

12. "Of nearly 40 million working women, 40 percent are in traditionally female occupations—secretaries, nurses, cashiers, waitresses, elementary school teachers, beauticians, maids, and sales clerks, for example. While this may result from past sex stereotyping, the notion that only a women can do these jobs may also benefit women by preserving employment opportunities for them, given the high unemployment rates among black males and teenage males." Discuss this argument.

22 INTEREST AND THE RETURN ON CAPITAL

The interest rate is the price paid for the use of money. Since that money is often invested in capital goods, interest can be thought of as part of the payment for use of capital goods. When interest is paid for the use of capital, it becomes part of the income of those who own the capital goods—that is, capitalists. The interest rate and interest income play roles in the allocation of resources and the distribution of income analogous to wage rates and labor income, but there are important differences.

Firms are willing to invest in capital goods only if the capital is "productive" in the sense of permitting production that repays all of the costs of the capital goods, including the cost of tying up money in capital goods. We shall first explore the nature of the return on productive capital and then the way that this return helps determine the rate of interest.

Capital, Capitalists, and Capitalism

The use of capital goods in production leads to a series of interrelated but often confusing terms. It is worth getting them sorted out at the start.

We have defined capital goods as man-made aids to further production. The two most essential characteristics of capital goods are first, that they are produced inputs into further production rather than things found in nature, and second, that they tend to be durable, lasting for many periods of production. Because of their produced nature, they use scarce resources and thus have an opportunity cost. Because of their durability it is necessary to distinguish two different prices of capital goods. First is the price paid to *acquire* the capital good, called its purchase price or the value of the asset at the time of purchase. Second is the price paid to *use* the capital good for a period of time. This may be thought of as the rental price of the capital good. Both the value of a capital good and its rental price will concern us in the first part of this chapter, and (as you may well suspect) the two prices are related to each other.

A **capitalist** is simply one who owns capital goods. The role played by the capitalist in different economic philosophies often have ideological overtones. For example to many Marxists the capitalist is a villain; to many socialists the capitalist is at best a dispensable drone; while to many conservatives the capitalist is the hero who steers the economy through the risky channels that lead to ever higher living standards. Ideology aside, if there is capital, someone must own it. Capital may be predominantly in private hands (in which case the economy is sometimes described as **capitalistic**), or it may be entirely owned by the state, in which case the economy will be described as socialistic or communistic. In virtually all economies, some capital is owned privately and some publicly.

No matter who owns the capital goods, they are indispensable in the productive process. A primitive society in which there are no capital goods—no spear, no lever, no stone for grinding grain, no jug for carrying water—has never occurred in recorded human history.

Capital, being made by human beings, uses resources in its manufacture. Capital goods, like other valuable products, are scarce in the sense that most producers would like to have more of them than they have if the price were zero. Any economic system interested in maximizing production will want to allocate scarce capital to its most productive uses. One effective way of doing this is to assign a rental price to capital that is meant to reflect its opportunity cost and to allow firms to use more capital only if the capital earns enough to cover this price. Actually charging producers for use of capital, while not necessary, serves such important functions that it is hard to eliminate it without serious consequences.

Early Communist rulers thought differently. Payments for use of capital were officially barred during the years following the Russian Revolution of 1917 on the ground that a communistic society should purge itself of this reminder of capitalism. But prices are such an efficient allocative device that today all Communist states use them for allocating scarce capital among competing uses. Furthermore, their planners give a good deal of attention to setting the correct price for capital.

If capital is privately owned and a price charged for its use, the payments go to the capitalists and become their incomes. In Communist countries capital is owned by the state, and payments for its use go to the state rather than to private capitalists. The desirability of private versus public ownership of the *means of production* (the term often used in Socialist and Communist literature to describe capital) is still debated hotly.

Our concern in this chapter is with capital, particularly in the context of a market economy. But much of what is discussed applies to the use of capital goods in any economy. What is it that makes capital indispensable in any modern economy, and what rental price fosters its efficient use? What determines whether a particular capital good should be manufactured and what price should it be sold for?

The Productivity of Capital

In what sense is capital productive? To be productive it must lead to higher output than would be possible without it. Productive effort goes first into the manufacture of capital goods. The capital goods are then used to make consumers' goods. The use of capital renders production processes roundabout. Instead of making what is wanted directly, producers engage in the indirect process of first making capital goods that are then used to make consumer goods.

In many cases production is very roundabout indeed. For example, a worker may be employed in a factory that makes machines that are used in mining coal; the coal may be burned by a power plant to make electricity; the electricity may provide power for a factory that makes machine tools; the tools may be used to make a tractor; the tractor may be used by a potato farmer to help in the production of potatoes, which are the final good that may ultimately be eaten by consumers. This kind of indirect production is worthwhile when the farmer, using a tractor, can produce more potatoes than could be produced by applying all the factors of production involved in the chain directly to the production of potatoes (using only such tools as were provided by nature). In fact, the roundabout capital-using method of production very often leads to more output than the direct method. The difference between the flows of output that would result from the two methods is called the **productivity of capital.**

The extra output, however, is not achieved without cost, usually in the form of the reduction of current consumption.

A decision to increase the amount of capital available usually entails a present sacrifice and a future gain.

The present sacrifice occurs because resources are diverted from producing consumption goods to producing capital goods. The future gain occurs because in the long run production will be higher with the new capital than without it (even after allowing for maintenance and replacement of capital goods). The extension of this concept to human capital is discussed in the box.

The Rate of Return on Capital

When capital is productive, its use necessarily yields a return in excess of the amounts required to cover the costs associated with all other factors of production. This return is merely a measure of the productivity of capital. How is this measure determined? Take the receipts from the sale of the goods produced by a firm and subtract the appropriate costs for purchased goods and materials, for labor, for land, and for the manager's own contributed talents. Subtract also an allowance for the taxes the firm will have to pay, and what is left may be called the **gross return to capital.**

It is convenient to divide gross return into four components.

1. **Depreciation** is an allowance for the decrease in the value of a capital good as a result of using it in production.
2. The **pure return on capital** is the amount that capital could earn in a riskless investment in equilibrium.
3. The **risk premium** compensates the owners for the actual risks of the enterprise.
4. **Economic profit** is the residual after all other deductions have been made from the gross return. It may be positive, negative, or zero.

The productivity of capital—also called the *net return on capital*—is its gross return minus the depreciation.

There is an important difference between the first three components, all of which are elements of opportunity cost, and the fourth component. In a market economy positive and negative economic profits are a signal that resources should be reallocated because earnings exceed opportunity costs in some lines of production and fall short of them in other lines. Profits, defined in this way, are thus a phenomenon of disequilibrium. In equi-

HUMAN CAPITAL

While capital goods are usually discussed in terms of tangible assets such as buildings or machines, the notion of a capital asset as something that produces an increase in the stream of future output suggests another sort of capital good. Consider a high school graduate who has enough schooling to get and keep a job. Instead of taking a job, however, she elects to go to college, and possibly to graduate or professional school. During her college career, her contribution to society's current output is small (only a summer job perhaps), but because of her education, her lifetime contribution to production may be substantially larger than it would have been had she taken a job after high school.

The choice of whether to take a job now or to continue one's education has all the basic elements of an investment decision, and it is useful to regard the student as making an investment to acquire capital. Because the capital is embodied in a person—in terms of greater skills, knowledge, and the like—rather than in a machine, this is known as acquiring **human capital**. Major elements of human capital are health and education of all sorts. An extended education program requires, for example, that resources be withdrawn from the production of goods for current consumption; the resources include materials in the school, the services of the teachers, and the time and talents of the pupils. The education is productive if the difference between the value of the lifetime output of the trained worker and the lifetime output of the untrained one exceeds the value of the resources—teachers, buildings, and so on—used up in training her. If so, education increases the value of total production of the economy.

The payoff to education as an investment in human capital has been studied extensively, and many investigators have concluded that investment in higher education pays, in the sense just defined. Of course, education also has other payoffs; it may be valued for cultural or social reasons, and it may bestow benefits or costs on individuals other than those who are educated. But the fact that it may be more than a capital investment does not prevent it from being an investment. The same is true of a painting by Rembrandt.

librium profits will be zero and the return to capital will be equal to the opportunity cost of capital.

In order to study the return to capital in its simplest form, we consider an economy that is in equilibrium with respect to the allocation of existing factors of production among all their possible uses. Thus economic profits are zero in every productive activity. This does not mean that the owners of capital get nothing; it means rather that the gross return to capital includes only the first three elements listed above. To simplify further at the outset, we assume that there is no risk in this economy. Consequently the gross return to capital does not include a risk premium.

In these circumstances the net return to capital is all pure return (item 2 on the previous list), while the gross return is pure return plus depreciation (items 1 and 2). What determines the size of the pure return on capital? Why is it high in some time periods and low in others? What causes it to change?

In discussing such questions, it is usual to deal with a rate of return *per dollar* of capital. This concept requires placing a money value on a unit of capital (the "price of capital goods") and a money value on the stream of earnings resulting from the productivity of capital. If we let X stand for the annual value of the net return on a unit of capital and P for the price of a unit of capital, the ratio X/P may be defined as the **rate of return** on capital. As a preliminary to understanding the determinants of the rate of return on capital, we must define two key concepts: marginal efficiency of capital and present value.

The Marginal Efficiency of Capital

It is convenient to think of society as having a quantity of capital that can be measured in physical units. The term **capital stock** refers to this total quantity of capital.[1] As with any other factor of production, there is an average and a marginal product of capital. The marginal product of capital is the contribution to output of the last unit of capital added to a fixed quantity of other factors.

Marginal product is a physical measure, an amount of output per unit of capital. To obtain a value measure we value the output and the capital at their market prices and express one as a ratio of the other. This gives the monetary return on the marginal dollar's worth of capital and it is called the **marginal efficiency of capital (MEC)**. A schedule that relates this to the size of the capital stock is called the **marginal efficiency of capital schedule.** The MEC schedule is constructed on the assumptions that the society's population is fixed and that technology is unchanging. These assumptions are made in order to focus on changes in the quantity of capital, other things remaining equal. As more and more capital is accumulated, with unchanging technical knowledge and population, the ratio of capital to labor increases. This is called **capital deepening.** To see why it occurs, consider the difference between a single firm and the whole economy.

When a single firm wants to expand output, it can buy another piece of land, build a factory identical to the one it now has, and hire new labor to operate the new plant. In this way the firm can replicate what it already has. Since each worker in

the new factory can be given the same amount of capital to work with as each worker in the old factory, output per worker and per unit of capital can remain unchanged as output rises. Increasing the quantity of capital without changing the proportions of factors used is called **capital widening.**

For the economy as a whole, capital widening is possible only as long as there are unemployed quantities of labor and other factors of production. Additional workers, for example, must be drawn from somewhere. In a fully employed economy, what one small firm can do the whole economy cannot do. If the size of the capital stock is to increase while the total labor force remains constant, the amount of capital per worker must increase. Capital deepening must occur.

What is the effect of capital deepening on the marginal efficiency of capital? Because capital is subject to diminishing returns, as are all factors of production, the amount of output per unit of capital will fall as capital deepening occurs. Each unit of capital has, as it were, fewer units of labor to work with than previously. As more and more capital deepening occurs, the marginal return to capital declines. The MEC schedule when plotted graphically is thus downward-sloping (see Figure 22-1).

A Recapitulation of Terminology

The theory of capital can seem quite bewildering at first encounter because there are so many terms that mean almost the same thing. Let us review the standard terminology. The *productivity* of capital is usually measured as an amount per dollar's worth of capital, which makes it a *rate of return on capital.* This rate may be calculated as an average over all capital, in which case it is called the *average efficiency of capital* (or *average rate of return*); or it may be calculated on the last unit of capital, in which case it is called the *marginal efficiency of capital* (or *marginal rate of return*). The MEC schedule relates the rate of return on the marginal unit of capital to the total capital stock. It shows that as the total stock grows the marginal return on each additional unit declines.

---

[1] The idea of capital stock being measured by a single number is a simplification. Society's stock of capital goods is made up of factories, machines, bridges, roads, and other man-made aids to further production. For expository purposes, it is useful to assume that all these can be reduced to some common unit and summed to obtain a measure of the society's *physical* stock of capital.

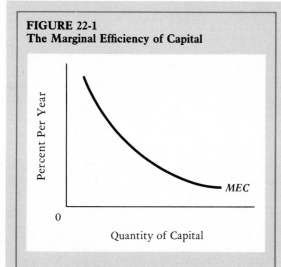

FIGURE 22-1
The Marginal Efficiency of Capital

MEC

Percent Per Year

0

Quantity of Capital

The *MEC* schedule shows the relation between the size of the capital stock and the rate of return on the marginal unit of capital. The *MEC* schedule slopes downward because of the hypothesis of diminishing returns applied to capital. Each successive unit of capital adds less to output than each previous unit. Thus the curve, which relates the value of the additional output of each additional dollar's worth of capital added to the capital stock, is downward-sloping.

The Present Value of Future Returns

Productive capital usually takes the form of producing a stream of output extending into the future that, as it is sold, yields a stream of gross returns to the firm. How are the purchase and rental prices of capital related to the productivity of capital? To know what price a firm would be willing to pay for a piece of capital, we must be able to put a present value on the stream of gross returns that the capital will yield to the firm.

We assume first that the price level is constant; later we consider the effects of inflation.

The value of a single future payment. How much would you be prepared to pay *now* to acquire the right to receive $100 in cash in one year's time? Say the interest rate on savings accounts is 5 percent. One way to answer this question is to ask how much would you have to deposit in a savings

bank now in order to have $100 a year from now? It would surely not be profitable for you to pay more than such an amount.

The question and answer of the previous paragraph can be reduced to the question, how much money *now* is equivalent to $100 in one year's time if the interest rate is 5 percent? Letting X stand for this unknown amount, we can write $X(1.05) = \$100$. Thus $X = \$100/1.05 = \$95.24$, which tells us that the value today of $100 next year is $95.24 if the interest rate is 5 percent. That sum is said to be the present value of $100 next year. In general, the term **present value** (***PV***) refers to the value now of a payment, or payments, to be made in the future.

The particular numerical value depends on the interest rate used to "discount" (i.e., reduce to its present value) the $100 to be received one year hence. If the interest rate is 7 percent, the present value of the $100 receivable next year is $100/1.07 = \$93.46$. In general, the present value of X dollars one year hence at an interest rate of i per year is

$$PV = \frac{X}{(1 + i)}$$

(Note that in this expression a rate of interest of 5 percent is written $i = .05$, so that $1 + i$ is 1.05.)

One hundred dollars two years hence has a present value (at an interest rate of 5 percent) of

$$\frac{\$100.00}{(1.05)(1.05)} = \$90.70$$

because $90.70 put in a savings bank now would be worth $100 in two years. In general, we may write, for the present value of X dollars after t years at i percent,

$$PV = \frac{X}{(1 + i)^t}$$

The present value of a given sum will be smaller the further away the payment date is and the higher the rate of interest.

The value of an infinite stream of payments. So much for a single sum payable in the future; now consider the present value of a stream of income. An **annuity** is a given sum of money paid at regular intervals for a specified length of time. We here consider an *infinite annuity,* one that continues indefinitely. At first its value might seem very high since over time the total received grows without reaching any limit. Consideration of the previous section suggests, however, that payments that are far in the future will not be valued highly. To find the present value of $100 a year, payable forever, we need only ask how much money would have to be invested now at an interest rate of i percent per year to obtain $100 each year. This is simply $i \times X = \$100$, where i is the interest rate and X the sum required. This tells us that the present value of an infinite annuity of $100 is

$$PV = \frac{\$100}{i}$$

If the interest rate were 10 percent ($i = 0.10$), present value would be $1,000 which is another way of saying that $1,000 invested at 10 percent would yield $100 per year, forever. Notice that PV here, as above, is negatively related to the rate of interest.

The higher the interest rate, the less the present value of any streams of payments that occur in the future.

If you can buy an asset at its present value, the investment will yield neither gain nor loss. For example, if you buy an annuity conferring the right to receive $100 a year forever for $1,000, and borrow the money to buy the asset at an interest rate of 10 percent, annual receipts ($100) and interest payments ($100) will be exactly offsetting.

The Value of an Asset

Many assets are valued only because of the streams of income they are expected to produce.[2] The value of any such asset will tend to be equal to the present

value of the income stream produced. This is often called the **capitalized value** of the asset producing the income stream.

Every expected income stream can be reduced to a present value. In the previous section we considered finding the present values of amounts at specific future dates and of infinite streams of income. All actual streams of income can be treated as the sum or difference of such streams and amounts; thus the present value of *any* stream of future payments can be computed.[3] As a result the capitalized value of an asset can always be computed.

What then determines the market price of any existing asset that will produce a stream of output over time? The asset might be a piece of land, a machine, a contract for a baseball player's services, or an apartment house. The asset produces a stream of output, and market conditions will determine the price of this output. This allows us to convert the stream of output into an equivalent stream of money. The value of this stream of money is the value of the asset to whoever purchases it. But we know how to calculate the present value of a stream of money, and this is what people will be willing to pay for it.

If the capitalized value of a machine (or other capital asset) is greater than the purchase price of such machines, it will pay firms to buy additional machines. As they do, given diminishing productivity, the capitalized value of additional machines will fall. Eventually it will fall to the level of the purchase price of the machines.

The equilibrium market price of an asset will be equal to the capitalized value of the asset. This is equal to the present value of the stream of returns associated with it.

---

[2] Assets can yield utilities in forms other than income streams. A painting, a house, and valuable jewelry are cases in point. They may be regarded as yielding a stream of utilities each of which could be given a monetary value.

[3] For example, receiving $100 per year for three years can be considered either as the present value of $100 next year plus the *PV* of $100 two years hence plus the *PV* of $100 three years hence, or as the *difference* between the *PV* of $100 received each year from now to infinity and the *PV* of $100 received from year four to infinity, or as the present value an annuity of $100 for 3 years. There are standard actuarial tables that make calculation of present value very easy.

A THEORY OF INTEREST RATE DETERMINATION

Interest rates play a major role, as we have seen, in determining the return to capital and the value of capital assets. But what determines the rate of interest? Given the concepts just discussed, we can develop a theory that relates *MEC* for the economy as a whole to the rate of interest. It is helpful to begin with the behavior of an individual firm.

The Demand for Additional Capital by a Firm

Suppose that for $8,000 a firm can purchase a machine that yields net returns of $1,000 a year into the indefinite future. Also suppose that the firm can borrow (and lend) money at an interest rate of 10 percent. The present value of the stream of returns produced by the machine is $1,000/0.10 = $10,000; the present value of $8,000 now is of course $8,000. Clearly the firm can make money by purchasing the machine.

Another way to see this is to suppose that the firm has only two uses for its money: to buy the machine or to lend out the $8,000 at 10 percent interest. It will pay to buy the machine, for the firm can do so and earn $1,000 per year net, while if it lends the $8,000 at 10 percent, it will earn only $800 per year.

It pays to purchase a capital good whenever its *MEC* is greater than the interest rate that could be earned on the money invested in it.[4]

The firm will go on investing in new capital equipment as long as its rate of return, the *MEC*, exceeds the opportunity cost of capital, *i*. *MEC* declines as the firm's capital stock rises, and the firm will reach equilibrium with respect to its capital stock when *MEC* is equal to *i*.

The Economy As a Whole

Assume for the moment that the interest rate is free to vary and that the only demand to borrow money is from firms seeking funds to invest in new capital equipment. The whole economy has an *MEC* schedule showing how the return on the marginal dollar of new capital declines as the capital stock grows. This *MEC* schedule represents the market demand curve for capital (since each firm will wish to acquire capital until $MEC = i$).

A Fixed Stock of Capital

Since the existing stock of capital can be changed only very slowly, we may take the stock as fixed over short-term periods. This stock will have an *MEC* that determines the amount that can be made by investing in a bit more capital. If the rate of interest were lower than this, there would be a rush to borrow money for profitable investment and the rate would be bid up. When the capital stock, technical knowledge—and hence the *MEC*—are given, the interest rate will tend to equal the *MEC* in equilibrium. This is illustrated in Figure 22-2.

A Growing Stock of Capital

Over time, firms and households save and invest in new capital equipment, causing the capital stock to grow. This is shown in Figure 22-2 by a rightward shifting of the vertical line indicating the given capital stock. This has the effect of reducing both the marginal efficiency of capital and the equilibrium interest rate. In an economy with static technology and fixed supplies of land and labor, capital accumulation will tend to lower the marginal efficiency of capital and the rate of interest.

The growth of technical knowledge provides new productive uses for capital. This tends to push

---

[4] In this chapter we assume that the rate of interest reflects the opportunity cost of capital to the firm. We saw on page 178 that this may not always be the case. When the market rate of interest and the firm's own opportunity cost of capital diverge, the *MEC* must be equated to the latter, not the former.

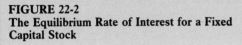

FIGURE 22-2
The Equilibrium Rate of Interest for a Fixed Capital Stock

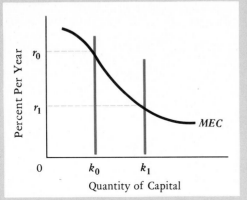

The rate of interest tends toward the *MEC*. When the economy has a stock of capital of k_0, the rate of interest will tend toward r_0. If the stock of capital grows k_1, the interest rate will tend to fall to r_1. Alternatively, k_0 and k_1 could be the capital stock in two otherwise similar economies. The interest rate would be higher in the economy where capital was scarce than in the economy where capital was plentiful.

the *MEC* schedule outward and *ceteris paribus* will raise *MEC* and the rate of interest.

The accumulation of capital tends to lower the interest rate and the marginal efficiency of capital. The growth of technical knowledge tends to raise both rates.[5]

The Pure and the Market Rates of Interest

The above discussion refers to what is called the **pure rate of interest.** This is the rate of interest that would rule in equilibrium in a riskless economy when all lending and borrowing is to provide funds for investing in productive capital. The discussion allows us to isolate the influences that the size of the capital stock and the efficiency of capital exert on the interest rate.

[5] Graphs illustrating the two effects will be found in Chapter 38.

The actual interest rate ruling at any moment of time is called the **market rate of interest.** This rate will be influenced by the pure rate, but it will diverge from the pure rate because it is influenced by additional forces that do not influence the pure rate.

Some Further Determinants of the Market Rate of Interest

Other Demands for Money to Borrow

Households borrow money to buy goods on time and to buy houses and financial assets such as stocks and bonds. State and local governments borrow to build highways and schools. The federal government borrows to finance part of its expenditures. Each of these is a major component of the aggregate demand for funds to borrow.

Government Control of Interest Rates

Not only is the government a borrower of funds, it also affects the supply of funds available for lending. (We shall see how it does this when we study monetary policy in Chapter 35.) Governments commonly influence the rate of interest for purposes of public policy.

Bank Administration of Interest Rates

The rate of interest does not fluctuate in response to every minor fluctuation in demand and supply. As a result, the interest rate is not always determined in such a way as to equate i with *MEC*. Banks, for example, consider many factors when they fix the rate of interest that they charge on loans. They are reluctant to change these rates every time changes occur in the demand for money to borrow. If there is an excess demand for loanable funds (perhaps because the *MEC* is much greater than the interest rate), banks, rather than raise the interest rate, will often ration the available supply of funds among their customers. In doing this they follow such criteria as the borrower's credit rating, how long the banker has known the borrower, and the amount of business the borrower does. This is called **credit rationing.** It is commonly found in lending institutions in most Western countries. When the market rate of interest is below the pure return on capital, money will appear "tight"—hard to borrow—to the typical business person.

Expectations About Business Conditions

In discussing the willingness of firms to borrow money and invest it in capital goods, we have stressed the relation between the rate of interest and the marginal efficiency of capital. Even though capital is physically productive in the sense that more can be produced with it than without it, no one will wish to invest in new equipment if there is no demand for the products produced by the capital goods. In times of severe business depression, the demand to borrow and invest money may fall to very low levels as a result of a declining demand by households for consumption goods.

Market expectations are incorporated in the marginal efficiency framework by recognizing that the efficiency of capital is measured in terms of the *values* (not the quantities) of goods it produces and that these values depend on people's willingness to buy the goods. The *MEC* schedule is quite elastic in a fully employed economy; thus a small reduction in the rate of interest will lead to a large increase in investment in new capital. When a depression develops however, and the output of existing capital cannot be sold, it might not be worth borrowing money for new investment even at very low rates of interest. In either case expectations about future events matter.

The Rate of Inflation

An inflation means that the purchasing power of money is falling. When this occurs, it becomes very important to distinguish between the real rate and the money rate of interest. The **money rate of interest** is measured simply in dollars paid. If you pay me $8 interest for a $100 dollar loan for one year, the money rate is 8 percent.

The real rate of interest concerns the ratio of the purchasing power of the money returned to the purchasing power of the money borrowed, and it may be different from the money rate. The **real rate of interest** is the *difference* between the money rate of interest and the rate of change of the price level.

Consider further my $100 loan to you at 8 percent. The real rate that I earn depends on what happens to the overall level of prices in the economy. If the price level remains constant over the year, then the real rate that I earn will also be 8 percent. This is because I can buy 8 percent more real goods and services with the $108 that you repay me than with $100 that I lent you. However, if the price level were to rise by 8 percent, the real rate would be zero because the $108 you repay me will buy the same quantity of real goods as did the $100 I gave up. If I were unlucky enough to have lent money at 8 percent in a year in which prices rose by 10 percent, the real rate would be minus 2 percent.

If lenders and borrowers are concerned with the real costs measured in terms of purchasing power, the money rate of interest will be set at the real rate they require *plus* an amount to cover any *expected* rate of inflation. Consider a one-year loan that is meant to earn a real return to the lender of 5 percent. If the expected rate of inflation is zero, the money rate set for the loan will also be 5 percent. However, if a 10 percent inflation is expected, the money rate will have to be set at 15 percent.

To provide a given expected real rate of interest, the money rate will have to be set at the desired real rate of interest plus the expected annual rate of inflation.

The Significance of Multiple Influences

Because the market rate of interest is influenced by many factors other than the demand to borrow money for new investment, the market rate can diverge from the pure rate set by the *MEC*. If the market rate is well below the *MEC*, there will be a heavy desire to borrow and invest in new capital; the stock of capital will then grow, and the *MEC* will begin to fall toward the market rate of interest.

However, if the market rate is held above the *MEC*, there will be little or no desire to borrow to invest in new capital. Capital may not even be replaced as it wears out. As the capital stock shrinks, the *MEC* will rise toward the market rate of interest.

In general there is a tendency for the interest rate and the marginal efficiency of capital to be drawn toward each other.

Since the stock of capital (and thus the *MEC*) can change only slowly, most of the short-term adjustment is done by the interest rate. If, however, the interest rate were fixed, the *MEC* would change to adjust to it. One way or the other, there is a tendency for the two rates to come together.

A Complication: Many Rates of Interest

In the real world there are many different rates of interest. Speaking in terms of a single rate can be a valid simplification for many purposes because the whole set of rates *tends* to move upward or downward together. Concentrating on one "typical" rate as "the" rate of interest in such cases is quite acceptable. For some purposes, however, it is important to take into account the multiplicity of interest rates.

At the same time that you receive an interest rate of 6 percent or 7 percent on deposits at a savings and loan association, you may have to pay 11 percent or 12 percent to borrow from that savings and loan assocation to buy a house. Interest rates on consumer installment credit of 16 percent and 20 percent are observed. A small firm pays a higher interest rate on funds it borrows from banks than does a giant corporation. Different government bonds pay different rates of interest, depending on the length of the period for which the bond runs. Corporate bonds tend to pay higher interest than government bonds, and there is much variation among bonds of different companies. Considering the extreme mobility of money, why do such differences exist? Why do funds not flow between different uses to eliminate these differences? The

answer is that money does flow quite rapidly between alternative assets in response to disequilibrium interest differentials, but differences persist because quoted interest rates are composites of many things. Many of them lead to equilibrium differentials of the kinds discussed in Chapter 20.

Differences in risk. Corporate bonds generally have higher interest rates than U.S. government bonds because they carry a greater degree of risk. At one point in 1970, bonds of Ling-Temco-Vought (LTV) were selling at a price that made their "interest rate" more than 50 percent per year at the same time that some U.S. government bonds were yielding only 8 percent. Why? Investors were sure of the ability of the U.S. government to pay both the interest and the principal on its bonds, but they were less sure about LTV, which was having financial difficulties in 1970. Much of the high interest rate on LTV bonds was a risk premium. By 1976 the effective rate of interest on LTV bonds had declined to about 12 percent. Clearly investors had become much happier with LTV's financial position and were no longer demanding the enormous risk premium that they required in 1970.

Secured loans, where the borrower pledges an asset as collateral, tend to have lower interest rates than unsecured loans, other things being equal. Loans secured by houses (mortgages) tend to have lower interest rates than loans secured by automobiles, in part because it is harder to run away with a house than with a car and in part because a car can depreciate much more rapidly and unpredictably than a house.

Differences in duration. The *term* (duration) of a loan may likewise affect its price. The same bank will usually pay a higher rate of interest on a certificate of deposit that cannot be redeemed at the bank (without penalty) for at least one year than on a straight savings account, which can be withdrawn in a matter of minutes. Yet many savers prefer savings accounts because they want to be able to withdraw their money on short notice. Except when interest rates are thought to be temporarily abnormally high, borrowers are usually willing to pay more for long-term loans than for short-term loans because they are certain of having use of the money for a longer period. Lenders usually require a higher rate of interest the longer the time before the borrower must repay. Other things being equal, the shorter the term of a loan, the lower the interest rates.

Differences in costs of administering credit. There is great variation in the cost of different kinds of credit transactions. It is almost as cheap (in actual dollars) for a bank to lend United Airlines $1 million that the airline agrees to pay back with interest after one year as it is for the same bank to lend you $4,000 to buy a new car on an installment loan that you agree to pay back over two years in 24 equal installments.

The loan to you requires many more bookkeeping entries than the loan to the airline. In addition, it is easier, and therefore less costly, to check United Airlines' credit rating than it is to check yours. The difference in the cost *per dollar* of each loan is considerable. The bank may very well make less profit per dollar on a $4,000 loan at 20 percent per year than on a $1 million loan at 10 percent per year. In general, the bigger the loan and the fewer the payments, the less the cost per dollar of servicing the loan. Why then do banks and finance companies usually insist that you repay a loan in frequent installments? They worry that if you do not pay regularly, you will not have the money when the loan comes due.

In the market for borrowed funds there will be a structure of interest rates for credit transactions of different kinds.

Individual rates will be set that take into account such factors as risk premiums, duration of loan, and costs of administration. Nevertheless, it is useful and usual to talk about movements of interest rate structures up and down as changes in "the" interest rate. This simplification is most useful when the entire structure of rates moves up or down together so that changes in a single typical rate can capture changes in all rates.

SOURCES OF FUNDS FOR INVESTMENT

So far in this chapter we have considered financing investment only with borrowed money. But loans are just one of several sources of finance available to firms for new investment. Most firms use several sources; a profit-maximizing firm that is free to do so will obtain funds from each source until the marginal cost of the last dollar obtained from each is the same.[6] (Otherwise the firm could reduce costs by shifting from higher-cost sources of funds to lower-cost sources.) The analysis of the first part of the chapter can now be generalized. When the *MEC* exceeds the cost of obtaining funds for new investment, firms will try to raise funds not only by borrowing but by tapping their other main sources of funds. When the *MEC* is less than the opportunity cost of capital, the demand for new investment funds from all sources will be low or nonexistent.

Financing the Modern Corporation

The most important ways in which firms obtain funds for new investment are (1) offering shares, stocks, or equities (as they are variously called) for private or public sale; (2) borrowing by the sale of bonds; (3) borrowing from banks; and (4) reinvesting the firm's profits.

The money that a firm raises for carrying on its business is sometimes called its **money capital** as distinct from its **real capital,** the physical assets that constitute plant, equipment, and inventories. Money capital may be broken down into **equity capital,** provided by the owners, and **debt,** which consists of the funds borrowed from persons who are not owners of the firm.

The use of the term *capital* to refer to both an amount of money and a quantity of goods can be

---

[6] If a firm could get all the funds it wished from each source at constant marginal costs, it would use only the cheapest source. But firms usually face rising marginal costs of funds from each source, and thus they typically obtain funds from many sources.

confusing, but it is usually clear from the context whether a sum of money or a stock of equipment is being referred to. The two uses are not independent of each other, for much of the money capital raised by a firm will be used to purchase the capital goods that the firm requires for production.

Stocks and Stockholders

The owners of the firm are its **stockholders**—persons who have put up money to purchase shares in the firm. They make their money available to the firm and risk losing it in return for a share in the firm's profits. Stocks in a firm often proliferate into a bewildering number of types. Basically, however, there is common stock and preferred stock.

Common stock usually carries voting rights and has only a residual claim on profits. After all other claims have been met, the remaining profits, if any, belong to the common stockholders. There is no legal limit to the profits that may be earned by the company and therefore no limit to potential dividends that may be paid out to common stockholders. Firms are not obliged by law to pay out any fixed portion of their profits as dividends, and in fact the practice among corporations as to the pay-out ratio varies enormously. Firms sometimes pay out a large fraction and hold back only enough to meet contingencies; at other times they pay small or no dividends in order to reinvest retained funds in the enterprise.

The basic difference between **preferred stock** and common stock is that preferred stock carries with it a right to a preference over common stock to any profits that may be available after other obligations have been met. If profits are earned, the corporation is obliged to pay a dividend to preferred stockholders, but there is a stated maximum to the rate of dividends that will be paid per dollar originally invested.

Bonds and Bondholders

Bondholders are creditors, not owners, of the firm. They have loaned money to the firm in return for

a **bond,** which is a promise to pay a stated sum of money each year by way of interest on the loan and to repay the loan at a stated time in the future (say 10, 20, or 30 years hence). This promise to pay is a legal obligation on the firm's part whether or not profits have been made. If these payments cannot be met, the bondholders can force the firm into bankruptcy. Should this happen, the bondholders have a claim on the firm's assets prior to that of the stockholders. Only when the bondholders and all other creditors have been repaid in full can the stockholders attempt to recover anything for themselves.

A major disadvantage to the corporation of raising capital through the sale of bonds is that interest payments must be met whether or not there are profits. Many a firm that would have survived a temporary crisis had all its capital been share capital has been forced into bankruptcy because it could not meet its contractual obligations to pay interest to its bondholders.

Loans from Financial Institutions

Much of a firm's short-term and some of its long-term monetary needs are met through bank loans. This is true of giant corporations as well as of small businesses. Indeed, making commercial and industrial loans is one of the major activities of the banking system (which we shall discuss in Chapter 33). Banks, however, limit the amounts they are willing to lend companies, typically to specified fractions of the companies' total financial needs.

Many small businesses that are not well established cannot sell stocks to the public, nor can they raise all the funds they require from banks. Such companies often seek funds from other financial institutions such as insurance companies and small loan companies, usually at higher rates of interest. Several government agencies, such as the Small Business Administration, have been established to help them get access to funds at "reasonable" rates. Generally, term (i.e., short-term) borrowing tends to be expensive. Firms prefer to raise money capital in other ways for long-term purposes.

Reinvested Profits

Another important source of funds for the established firm is the reinvesting, or plowing back, of the firm's own profits. One of the easiest ways for the firm to raise money is to retain some of its own profits rather than pay them out as dividends. Reinvestment has become an extremely important source of funds in modern times; over $50 billion per year is plowed back into U.S. firms. The shareholder who does not wish his or her profits to be reinvested can do very little about it except to sell the stock and invest in a company with a policy of paying out a larger fraction of its dividends.

Securities Markets (Stock Markets)

When a household buys shares newly issued by a company, it hands over money to the company and becomes one of its owners. The household cannot get its money back from the company except in the unlikely event that the company is liquidated. If the household wishes to get its money back, it can only persuade someone else to buy its shares in the company.

Similarly, when a household buys a bond from a company, it cannot get its money back from the company before a specified date. If I bought a 2004 bond in 1984, the bond will be redeemed by the company (i.e., the loan will be paid back) only in 2004. If I wish to get my money back sooner, all I can do is sell the bond.

An organized market where stocks and bonds are bought and sold is a **stock market** or a **securities market.** Such markets include not only the well-known New York Stock Exchange and the American Stock Exchange but also the whole network of "over-the-counter" markets handled by brokers and specialists. The selling of existing shares on the stock market indicates that the company's existing ownership is being transferred; it does not indicate that the company is raising new money from the public.

Securities markets are important because by providing for the ready transfer of corporate securities they make it possible for individuals to invest without committing themselves for long periods.

Because of the existence of securities markets, people are willing to put their savings in securities that are not themselves directly or quickly redeemable. For example, if I want to invest in a particular stock or bond that pays an attractive yield, I may do so even though I know that I will want to withdraw my money after only a year. Given a securities market, I can be confident that I can sell the stock or bond a year from now.

But while securities markets provide for the quick sale of stocks and bonds, they do not guarantee that the securities will sell at the same price at which they were bought. The price at any time is the price that equates the demand and supply for a particular security, and rapid fluctuations in stock prices are common.

Prices on the Stock Market

Figure 22-3 shows the wide swings in a well-known index of stock market prices. In January 1977 the Dow Jones index showed the average price of leading U.S. industrial stocks to be well above the figure for mid 1975. People who bought a representative selection of industrial stocks in 1975 and held them to January 1977 saw the average value of their holdings rise by about 25 percent (and of course they earned dividends as well).

After that prices fell. By March 1978 the index was well below what it had been in January 1977. Investors who bought stocks in 1975 and held them until 1978 first saw the paper value of their stocks rise by one-fourth and then saw these gains quickly disappear. Those who had bought stocks near the top of the market saw their value cut by over 25 percent within 14 months. There followed two years of relatively stable prices, but then prices began to rise, although not without fluctuations. By the spring of 1983 the index passed the 1200 mark, up 50 percent from the level of the previous three years. The investor who bought in April 1980 and sold in April 1983 made a handsome profit.

What causes such rapid gains and losses, and what do they have to do with the kind of invest-

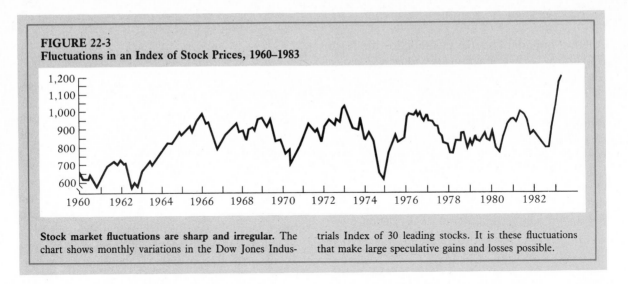

FIGURE 22-3
Fluctuations in an Index of Stock Prices, 1960–1983

Stock market fluctuations are sharp and irregular. The chart shows monthly variations in the Dow Jones Indus- trials Index of 30 leading stocks. It is these fluctuations that make large speculative gains and losses possible.

ment we have been talking about in this chapter? When investors buy a company's stock, they are buying rights to shares in the stream of dividends to be paid out by that company. They are also buying something they can sell in the future at a gain or loss. The value of that stock depends on two things: first, what people expect the stream of future dividend payments to be and, second, what capital gain or loss people expect to realize when the stock is sold.

Both things make dealing in stocks an inherently risky operation. Will the company in which you are investing pay more or less dividends over future years? Will the company's value rise or fall so that you can sell your share in it for more or less than what you bought it for? While dividend policies of most established companies tend to be fairly stable, stock prices are subject to wide speculative swings.

Speculative Swings

Expectations about future stock prices are important. They can be based on such factors as present earnings, careful estimates of future earnings, or the vague feeling that stock prices will be rising or falling.

In major stock market booms, people begin to expect rising stock prices and hurry to buy while stocks are cheap. This action bids up the prices of shares and creates the capital gains that justify the original expectations. This is the phenomenon of *self-realizing expectations*. Everyone gets rich on paper in the sense that the market value of their holdings rises. Money making now looks easy to others, they also rush in to buy, and new purchases push up prices still further. At this stage, attention to current earnings all but ceases. If a stock can yield, say, a 50 percent capital gain in one year, it does not matter much if the current earnings represent only a small percentage yield on the purchase price of the stocks. Everyone is "making money," so more people become attracted by the get-rich-quick opportunities. Their attempts to buy bid up prices still further. This causes current earnings to represent an ever-diminishing percentage yield on the current price of the stocks.

Capital gains are so attractive that investors may buy stocks on margin—that is, borrow money to buy them, using the stocks themselves as security for the loans. In doing this, many investors may be borrowing money at a rate of interest considerably in excess of the rate of yield on current dividends. If $50,000 is borrowed at 10 percent (interest, $5,000 per year) to buy stocks yielding a current dividend return of only 4 percent (dividend, $2,000 per year), never mind, says the investor's logic, the stocks can be sold in a year or so for a handsome capital gain that will more than repay the $3,000 of interest not covered by dividends. Some people have the luck or good judgment to sell out near the top of the market, and they actually make money. Others wait eagerly for ever greater capital gains, and in the meantime they get richer and richer—on paper.

Eventually something breaks the period of unrestrained optimism. Some investors may begin to worry about the very high prices of stocks in relation not only to current yields but to possible future yields even when generous allowances for growth are made. Or it may be that the prices of stocks become depressed slightly when a sufficiently large number of persons try to sell out in order to realize their capital gains. As they offer their securities on the market, they cannot find purchasers without some fall in prices. Even a modest price fall may be sufficient to persuade others that it is time to sell. But every share that is sold must be bought by someone. A wave of sellers may not find new buyers at existing prices, and prices will come down. Panic selling may now occur.

A household that borrowed $50,000 to buy stocks near the top of the market may find the paper value of its holdings sliding below $50,000. How will it repay its loan? Even if it does not worry about the loan, its broker will. The household may sell now before it loses too much, or its broker may "sell the customer out" to liquidate the loan before it is too late. All this brings prices tumbling down and provides another example of self-realizing expectations. If enough people think prices are going to come down, their attempt to sell out at the present high prices will itself create the fall in prices the expectations of which caused selling.

This is a very simple and stylized description of a typical speculative cycle, yet it describes the basic elements of market booms and busts that have recurred throughout stock market history. It happened in the Jay Cooke panic of 1873 and in the Grover Cleveland panic of 1893. What was possibly the biggest boom of all began in the mid 1920s and ended on Black Tuesday, October 29, 1929. The collapse was dramatic: The average price of 50 leading stocks in November 1929 was about 50 percent below the September peak. Nor did it stop there. For three long years, stock prices continued to decline until the average value of stock sold on the New York Stock Exchange had fallen from its 1929 high of $89.10 a share to $17.35 a share by late 1933.

Are these booms and busts only ghosts from a lurid and reckless past? Until 1969 many would have said that the modern investor was too sophisticated for it ever to happen again. But look again at Figure 22-3. The Dow Jones index of the prices of leading industrial stocks tumbled by 30 percent between December 1968 and April 1970—in just over a year. The market then recovered, and by January 1973 prices had reached an all-time high. This "boom" was followed by an even bigger "bust": In the two-year period prices fell to less than 60 percent of their January 1973 values. A sustained decline in prices from January 1977 to March 1978 took about 25 percent off of the value of stocks in the Dow Jones index. Between June 1982 and June 1983, the index rose by 50 percent. By the time you read this, you will know what we do not: whether prices rose from this level, stayed stable, or fell.

Stock Markets: Investment Marketplaces or Gambling Casinos?

Stock markets fulfill many important functions. It is doubtful that the great aggregations of capital needed to finance modern firms could be raised under a private ownership system without them. There is no doubt, however, that they also provide an unfortunate attraction for many naive investors whose get-rich-quick dreams are more often than not destroyed by the fall in prices that follows the occasional booms they help to create.

To some extent public policy has sought to curb the excesses of stock market speculation through supervision of security issues. This is handled by the Securities and Exchange Commission, which was set up in 1934. It seeks, among other things, to prevent both fraudulent or misleading information and trading by "insiders" (those in a company with confidential information). Moreover, the government can limit the ability of speculators to trade on margin.

All in all, the stock market is both a real marketplace and a place to gamble. As in all gambling situations, those who are less well informed and less clever than the average tend to be losers in the long term.

SUMMARY

1. Capital goods are man-made aids to production; they include machines, buildings, trucks, and human capital. When production with capital is more efficient than production without it (even when full allowance is made for the resources needed to produce and maintain the capital goods), capital is said to be *productive*.

2. The gross return to capital is the excess of a firm's revenue over the amount payable to factors of production other than capital, and after allowance for taxes. The net return is the gross return minus depreciation. This can be divided into a pure return on capital, a risk premium, and economic profits.

3. The marginal efficiency of capital schedule is downward-sloping because there are diminishing returns as more capital is added to fixed quantities of other resources with constant technical knowledge.

4. A piece of capital equipment is valued because it promises an expected stream of future income to its owners. The value of this capital equipment is the present value of the stream of gross returns it is expected to produce. A single payment of X after t years has a present value of $X/(1 + i)^t$. A stream of returns of X dollars per year forever has a present value of X/i.

5. A profit-maximizing firm will invest in a machine whenever the present value of the future stream of expected gross returns—the capitalized value of the machine—exceeds the purchase price of the machine or (what is the same thing) whenever the rate of return on the capital exceeds the rate of interest that correctly reflects the opportunity cost of capital to the firm. At equilibrium the firm will purchase capital equipment until the marginal rate of return is equal to the rate of interest.

6. The amount of investment that firms wish to undertake will depend on the relation between the market rate of interest and the *MEC*.

7. The society as a whole will tend to acquire capital stock as long as the *MEC* is greater than the opportunity cost of money invested in capital, i. If there is competition among borrowers and lenders of money, the rate of interest will tend toward the *MEC*.

8. There are important influences on the market rate of interest other than those connected with the productivity of capital: (a) expectations about price level changes, (b) expectations about the future state of the economy, (c) demands for funds to borrow for purposes other than investment in capital goods, (d) government control of interest rates as a tool of monetary policy, and (e) bank administration of interest rates.

9. At any moment in time there is a whole structure of interest rates. Individual rates depend on the riskiness, duration, and liquidity of a loan and also on the cost to the lender of processing the loan and collecting payments of interest and principal.

10. Corporations can raise money in four main ways: by selling shares in the firm; by selling bonds; by borrowing from banks or other financial institutions; and by reinvesting (or plowing back) their own profits.

11. Securities (stock) markets allow firms to raise new capital from the sale of newly issued securities and allow the holders of existing securities to sell their securities to other investors.

12. Prices on the stock market tend to reflect the public's expectations both of firms' future earnings and of future changes in prices (for whatever reason). This necessarily puts a strong speculative dimension into security prices and large speculative swings do occur. Such swings are accentuated by the phenomenon of self-realizing expectations.

TOPICS FOR REVIEW

The productivity of capital

The marginal efficiency of capital and the *MEC* schedule

The gross return, the net return, and the pure return on capital

The present value of future returns and the capitalized value of assets

The negative relationship between interest rates and the prices of assets

Reasons for the multiplicity of market interest rates

Equity capital and debt

Functions of securities markets

Self-realizing expectations

DISCUSSION QUESTIONS

1. The Atlas Company has calculated that it has the following opportunities to invest:
   a. $20,000 to make a critical replacement of an inadequate machine, with an estimated rate of return of 50 percent
   b. $100,000 in an additional machine, with an estimated return of 10 percent
   c. $50,000 for plant expansion, with a return of 25 percent
   How much would the company probably be willing to invest at an interest rate of 20 percent? of 8 percent?

2. Each of the following is sometimes described as an "investment" in everyday usage. Which represent investments in capital in the economist's sense?
   a. building of the Aswan Dam by the government of Egypt
   b. acquisition of a law degree at Harvard
   c. purchase of a newly discovered Picasso painting. (Does it matter to your answer if the purchaser is the Metropolitan Museum or a private collector?)
   d. purchase by one company of the stock or assets of another company

3. The future profits of Skeeter, Inc., a going concern, are estimated at $100,000 annually for the indefinite future. What is the present value of the business at interest rates of 5 percent, 10 percent, and 25 percent? What factors will determine the appropriate rate of capitalization to use for a prospective buyer of Skeeter, Inc.?

4. Irving Fisher (1867–1947), a distinguished Yale economist, said the durability of capital goods and consumer goods was affected by the rate of interest. Assume that the more durable a house, the higher is its present cost of construction. Would you expect rising interest rates to lead to more or less durable houses being built? Would you expect rising interest rates to foster or discourage sales of mobile homes?

5. How might each of the following affect the pure rate of return on capital? How might they affect the market rate of interest?
   a. a major innovation in a specific industry
   b. an increase in the rate of inflation
   c. a wave of corporate bankruptcies
   d. a substantial increase in economic activity due to renewed confidence in the business outlook

6. Suppose you are offered, free of charge, one of each of the following pairs of assets. What considerations would determine your choice?
   a. a perpetuity that pays $20,000 a year forever; an annuity that pays $100,000 a year for only five years
   b. owning an oil-drilling company that earned $100,000 after corporate taxes last year; owning a bond that paid $100,000 interest last year
   c. owning a municipal bond that provides for a tax-free interest payment of $1,000 per year; owning a U.S. government bond that provides a taxable interest payment of $1,500 per year

7. Many stores, including the large mail-order chains, sell for cash or credit at the same prices. If you do not pay your bill completely within 30 days (and you are encouraged to make partial payments) a service charge of 1.5 percent per month of the unpaid balance is added to the bill. What circumstances make it desirable
   a. to pay cash
   b. to pay the bill within the next month
   c. to pay in "easy monthly installments"
   Explain whether unpaid bills by customers represent a capital investment by the firm. Is the 1.5 percent per month paid by customers on their unpaid bills a pure return on the money that the firm has tied up?

8. Update Figure 22-3 on the Dow Jones Industrials Index. Looking at data in the *Economic Report of the President* (or the *Survey of Current Business*), can you "explain" the changes that have occurred in the years since 1983? What data did you look at in attempting to explain what happened? What other data, not in the president's report, might have been useful?

23 POVERTY, INEQUALITY, AND MOBILITY

National income divided by the total population is the average income for all Americans. Some individuals and groups get much more than the average, and others get much less. Distribution theory attempts to explain, among other things, why this happens.

Possibly the most discussed aspect of distribution concerns the proportion of national income that goes to the very poor. Who are they? Why are they poor? What can—or should—we do about it?

Poverty and the means used to alleviate it play a very large part in political debates. President Lyndon Johnson's so-called War on Poverty began an enormous investment in programs to aid the poor. Was the investment affordable? Did the war succeed? Those issues are as intensely debated today as they were two decades ago. The Reagan administration sharply cut back on those programs and evoked a new and bitter debate. We discuss the problems of poverty in the first part of this chapter. In the last part we examine the relevance of the theory of distribution for understanding income differences.

THE DISTRIBUTION OF INCOME BETWEEN RICH AND POOR: THE PROBLEM OF POVERTY

There are a number of reasons for the variations in what different individuals can earn. People differ in the talents they possess and the factors of production that they own; consequently both the quantity of factor services they can sell and the price they can receive will vary. Some factor owners are in a position to respond quickly to, and thus to take advantage of, changing opportunities. Others are immobile and will suffer when events leave them in markets where no one wants what they have to sell. To what extent do such reasons account for the continuing presence of poverty in the United States?

The Concept of Poverty

One possible definition of poverty is to be poorer than most of your fellow citizens. There will, of course, always be 10 percent of the population that is poorer than the other 90 percent. If poverty is regarded as a matter of low relative income, it is here to stay, for we inescapably have the (relatively) poor among us.

Clearly poverty must mean more than low relative income. Some minimum family income standard is required to define the **poverty level** below which a family is said to be poor. Such a standard specifies a dollar amount based on estimates of need and the cost of living. In 1981 the American poverty level was defined by the Department of Commerce as $9,288 per year for a nonfarm family of four.

The concept of poverty reflects the expectations and aspirations of society as a whole—and of the poor themselves—as to what constitutes an acceptable minimum standard of living. Less than 100 years ago, poverty would have been defined as the lack of the minimum amounts of food, shelter, and clothing needed to sustain life. Once this condition faced (or threatened) a large portion of the world's urban and rural masses. Total output was so low that all but a privileged minority lived at or near this level, and any flood or famine or crop failure plunged thousands into starvation. Poverty in this sense is still present in the world, even in the United States. Starvation, hunger, and malnutrition are suffered by millions of individual Americans, and some Americans born in 1984 will starve to death.

Yet in most advanced industrial countries, as in the United States, output has risen until the average family enjoys a high material standard of living, and the provision of *subsistence requirements* of food, shelter, and clothing is a major problem for only a small number of families. If this is so—if mere subsistence does not define the poverty level—what does it mean to say (as the Department of Commerce did in 1981) that over 30 million Americans lived in poverty?

Consider the income of a member of a family just at the poverty level. Income of $9,288 for a family of four is $2,322 per person. This will not seem like a great deal to most of you, but it is above the per capita income of three-quarters of the world's population. This should not lead anyone to minimize poverty problems; the black American living in Harlem and working as a porter at LaGuardia airport needs more clothes, transportation, and other basics than an Indonesian peasant. Visit the slums of any American city and you will not lightly dismiss poverty.

While $9,288 for a family of four buys enough food, shelter, and clothing to get by, it is only about 40 percent of the average (median) income of American families. What it does not provide is enough money for the necessities and also for the full range of commodities that 90 percent of us take for granted, such as having a refrigerator, hot water, a television set that works, and attending an occasional movie. Many of the poor are understandably bitter and resentful that they and their children are outsiders looking in on the comfortable way of life shown in ads and on television. "I'd like, just once," one of them said to a *Newsweek* interviewer, "to buy Christmas presents the children want instead of the presents they need."

The Extent of Poverty

The extent of poverty may be measured either by the number and percentage of persons in households having incomes below this level or by measuring the **poverty gap**: the number of dollars per year required to raise everyone's income to this level. In 1981 over 30 million persons (14 percent of the population) were classified as poor, and the poverty gap was approximately $30 billion.

These figures are themselves controversial. Critics such as Stanford University economist Martin Anderson and the University of Virginia's Edgar Browning argue that they neglect such extras as illegal income, unreported income, and noncash benefits such as food stamps and subsidized housing. An accurate measure, they say, might count those really in poverty as only 7 million and lower the poverty gap to somewhere between $8 to $10 billion. Others, such as Wisconsin's Robert Haveman, agree that it is appropriate to add such benefits but say that adjustment, if done accurately, would still show at least 6 percent—13 million people—living in poverty.

The historical trend. Whatever the deficiencies of these numbers as absolutes, they are useful for tracing changes in the magnitude of the poverty problem. In 1933 President Franklin D. Roosevelt spoke of a third of a nation as being in poverty. By 1959 the official definitions placed 22 percent of the nation below the poverty line. Figure 23-1 charts the course of poverty in American since that date. The steady downward trend from 22 percent to just over 12 percent in the decade from 1959 to 1969 is impressive, but since then there is no visible downward trend. Indeed the upturn since 1978 is a major source of concern: by 1981 the poverty percentage had risen to 14 percent.

While the failure to continue a downward trend in the percentage of Americans in poverty during the late 1970s and 1980s is disappointing for those

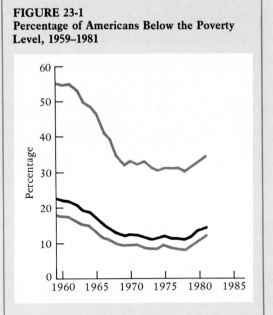

FIGURE 23-1
Percentage of Americans Below the Poverty Level, 1959–1981

Poverty declined sharply during the 1960s but declined much less during the 1970s and was rising at the end of the decade. The poverty level is adjusted annually to incorporate changes in the Consumer Price Index. For 1981 a nonfarm family of four with an income below $9,288 was considered poor. The frequency of poverty is much higher for blacks than for whites, and there is no suggestion in the chart that this condition is likely to change soon.

who would like to eradicate poverty, the long-term trend has been impressive. It was largely the result of a century of rapid economic growth that doubled average living standards every generation. But today, even after this century of rapid growth, the poor are still with us.

Future trends? Many economists believe future progress in reducing poverty will require more than a resumption of rapid economic growth because much of the remaining poverty would not be eradicated by such growth. For the poverty problem is no longer rooted in low *average* productivity but in the fact that particular groups have been left behind in the general rise of living standards. For the most part the easy gains have already been made.

This conclusion—that if we rely only on growth of average income the poor will be with us a century hence—is strongly supported by recent research. The University of Wisconsin, Institute for Research on Poverty found that most of the sharp decreases in the poverty rate between 1965 and 1980 were due to transfer payments to the poor such as food stamps and welfare payments and to increases in social security benefits, not to the 40 percent increase in *average* real income that occurred over this period.

Recent experience suggests that government programs of income redistribution are much more important than economic growth in achieving further reductions in American poverty.

The apparent fact that today's poverty is due to some groups being left behind is hardly a consolation to the hard-core poor. Indeed it adds to the gall that they remain poor in an increasingly affluent society.

Who Are the Poor?

There are poor among people of all ages, races, and educational levels, among the working as well as the unemployed and the retired. Yet some groups have very much higher incidences of poverty than others. Figure 23-1 shows this is true of blacks. Table 23-1 shows that poverty is also particularly high among those under 18 years of age (particularly if they are black), those unemployed or not in the labor force, and those with limited education.

The data in Table 23-2 permit us to look at the problem somewhat differently. Instead of focusing on the prevalence of poverty among certain subgroups in the population, we look at those who are poor and describe some of their characteristics. A great many of the poor are employed, many are aged, and many did not complete high school. Many are members of small families. These data may help dispose of two superficial caricatures:

TABLE 23-1 THE INCIDENCE OF POVERTY AMONG AMERICAN FAMILIES, 1981

Characteristic	Percentage of population who fall below the poverty line
All families	11
Race	
White	9
Black	31
Spanish origin	24
Youth and race	
Children under 18 years	
of age and living in families	20
White	15
Black and other	44
Employment status of family head	
Employed (including armed forces)	6
Unemployed	25
Not in the labor force	23
Education of family heads over 24 years of age	
Elementary school only	21
1–3 years high school	18
4 years of high school	10
Some college	4

Source: U.S. Department of Commerce, Bureau of the Census, *Current Population Reports,* Series P-60, Nos. 133,134.

Race, employment status, education, and age all affect the likelihood of poverty. The percentages show the fraction of families in the designated class whose incomes fall below the poverty level. Thus, while only 4 percent of family heads with some college education were below the poverty level, 44 percent of nonwhite children living in families were so classified. (These data do not include persons living outside of families; they count families, not persons. The percentage of persons below the poverty line in 1981 was 14 percent.)

One is the slothful father faking a disability because he is too lazy to do an honest day's work; the other is the family with so many children that an ordinarily decent wage is spread so thin that the whole household is reduced to poverty. Of course indi-

TABLE 23–2 **SELECTED CHARACTERISTICS OF AMERICAN FAMILIES BELOW POVERTY LEVEL, 1981**

Characteristic	White (percentage)	Black (percentage)
Employment status of family head		
Employed (including armed services)	45	29
Unemployed	11	12
Not in labor force	44	59
	100	100
Age of head		
Under 25 years	12	13
25–44 years	51	51
45–64 years	24	24
65 years and over	13	12
	100	100
Education of family heads over 24 years of age		
Elementary school or none	31	31
1–3 years high school	21	30
4 years of high school	33	30
Some college	15	9
	100	100
Size of family		
2 or 3 persons	58	49
4 or 5 persons	32	33
6 or more	10	18
	100	100

Source: U.S. Department of Commerce, Bureau of the Census, *Current Population Reports*, Series P-60, No. 134.

Employment status, age, education, and size of family all affect the likelihood of poverty. Many of those below the poverty level are working poor; they are found in all age groups and in small families as well as large. Over half those in poverty are in families whose head did not finish high school.

vidual households that come close to these extremes exist, but most poor households do not.

Causes of Poverty

The causes of poverty are various. The fact that many of the poor are over age 65 shows that age

and illness force people out of the labor market. Other important groups suffering poverty include the rural poor, who strive in vain to earn a decent living from marginal or submarginal farmlands; the urban working poor, who simply lack the skills to command a wage high enough to support themselves and their families above the poverty level; the immobile poor, who are trapped by age and outdated skills in areas and occupations where the demand for their services is declining faster than their number; and, most important, the minority poor—blacks, Indians, Puerto Ricans, Chicanos, Chinese—who constitute only one-eighth of the population but are almost one-third of the poor and who often suffer the additional barriers of discrimination.

There is no single answer to the question: What causes poverty in the midst of plenty? It is partly a result of mental and physical handicaps, partly of low motivation, and partly of the raw deal that fate gives to some. Partly it is a result of current and past prejudice. Partly it is a result of unwillingness or inability to invest in the kind of human capital that does pay off in the long run. Partly it is a result of the market's valuing the particular abilities that an individual does have at such a low price that, even in good health and with full-time employment, the income that can be earned leaves that person below the poverty line. The box provides a few profiles of individuals in poverty in the 1980s.

The extent of poverty is also affected greatly by the performance of the economy. A recession, with its increase in unemployment, pushes additional millions into poverty. (The recession of 1980–1982 did this to at least 5 million people.) Inflation continually erodes the resources of those on fixed incomes, and the recent rapid inflation has far outstripped increases in welfare payments and the earnings of many families at or near the poverty level.

The Persistently Poor

Fluctuations in the number classified as poor as a result of swings in the economy highlight the important distinction between the *occasionally poor*

PROFILES OF POVERTY

Each of the following newspaper sketches concerns a person or family living below the poverty level. Only the names are fictitious.

■ A 34-year-old mother of four children ranging in age from 5 to 15 waited in the Nassau County, N.Y., Social Services building recently for recertification for welfare.

Divorced last year from her husband, who "lived at home on and off," Glenda Rodriguez has been on welfare for 10 years. She is entitled to $450 a month in welfare grants; of that, $271 goes for rent and $67 for heating. She works as a part-time waitress whenever she can and earns $60 in a good week.

For every $60 she earns, however, her welfare grant is reduced by $40.

"Right now, I don't know how I'll make it the next two days until Friday," she said. "I owe the oil company $400—money I haven't been able to pay. We're not starving, but my kids get a little tired of eating eggs and franks.

"I'm working and I'm trying to give my children a little better life, rather than being completely on assistance," she said, "but I'm not getting any place. I'm in the hole each month."

■ Eddie Mason, 19 years old, drank cheap wine and smoked marijuana recently in an abandoned building on Jones Street in St. Louis's slums as he told a visitor, "I've been to the employment office and they've got jobs there only in the suburbs, and I don't have a car. It wouldn't be worth my time to pay bus fare, taxes, lunch, and stuff for a job way out in the suburbs that pays $3.35 an hour."

Mr. Mason lives with his mother and admits to just enough petty thievery "to stay alive."

■ The slightly built woman, holding two small children by the hand, walked into the cafeteria near the Welfare Office, where she had been waiting all morning, and gazed at the menu posted on the wall.

The warmth and smell of the food set the children to clamoring: "Mamma, I want . . . " and "Mamma, can I have . . . ?" She hushed the children and looked at the prices: tuna salad, $1.65; two eggs, $.96, with ham or bacon, $1.42; deli sandwich, $1.65; hamburger, $.85; cheeseburger, $1.00.

Checking her purse she bought two frankfurters at $.60 each, two containers of milk at $.33 each, and, for herself, a cup of coffee, $.32.

"I don't know what I'm going to do if I'm not approved for welfare," she told the visitor at the table where she was drinking her coffee and wiping sauerkraut from her children's clothes. She said she lived in Freeport with her sick husband, an unemployed carpenter.

"Things have been bad in the past," she said, "what with the high cost of everything—food, rent, clothing. But it's never been like this. We've never had to ask for help before."

■ The old man is sitting at the bus stop, "just resting." He's very old, but he's not slow witted. He's hunched a little forward, hands cupped on the top of the cane that he holds between his knees.

He wants to talk, and in a little time he covers a lot of ground. Private Julius Goldman in World War I, master sergeant in World War II, and 1929 and the depression in between. Kids, inflation, retirement, a dead wife, more inflation. The way it is and the way it was.

He is a pet food devotee. Heat it; it tastes like hash.

and the *persistently poor*. It is much easier to withstand six months (or even several years) of poverty due to a bout of unemployment or illness than it is to be permanently poor. For the latter condition erodes hope and warps one's entire outlook on life. While perhaps one-third of those officially classified as being in poverty at any time are only temporarily poor, half of the rest are virtually permanently poor, according to a recent study by the University of Michigan Survey Research Center.

The study defines the persistently poor as those who have been in poverty for *nine consecutive years*. They are the hard-core poor; they will not be rescued by an upswing in the economy, by another decade of economic growth, or even by somewhat bigger welfare payments and less inflation. A shocking statistic from the Michigan study is that more than three-quarters of the persistently poor are black. Blacks represent 11 percent of the total population, 31 percent of those below the poverty level, and 77 percent of the persistently poor.

Black Poverty

The incidence of persistent poverty among blacks is particularly acute.

This results from two related circumstances. First, blacks have many of the characteristics associated with poverty: many of them farm in the rural South or live in areas of the North where jobs are disappearing; a disproportionate number are less well educated than the average American; working blacks have the bad luck to be heavily concentrated in industries with declining demands for labor; and their health has often been seriously impaired by malnutrition or untreated diseases. The second factor is discrimination, whose effects were discussed in Chapter 21.

The two factors interact with and reinforce each other. Whatever the combination of reasons, and despite attempts to deal with them as a matter of public policy, a gap in incomes exists and does not show signs of diminishing. In 1970 the average black family's income was 64 percent of the average white family's income. In 1980 it was 58 percent of that income.

Should We Wage War on Poverty?

Eliminating poverty is easier than eliminating air pollution or cancer, for which cures are as yet unknown. For an amount estimated at about $30 billion per year in 1982 dollars, every family now below the poverty level could be given a sufficient income supplement to bring it to that level. Congress could, in other words, close the poverty gap. Although $30 billion is a lot of money, it is less than 20 percent of the national defense budget, and it represents only about 1 1/2 percent of the total income earned in the nation.

Surprisingly perhaps, a good deal of the debate about attacking poverty does not concern whether we can afford it or how best to do it, but whether we *ought* to do it.

The Case Against an All-Out War on Poverty

Everyone concedes that there are poor people who deserve to be helped. President Reagan referred to the most deserving as the "truly needy." They are those who despite their best efforts have not been able to escape the ravages of illness, blindness, desertion, age, or obsolescence. There are as well the helpless children of the poor, who should not be made to suffer endlessly for the failings or misfortunes of their parents. But there are also the "undeserving poor," those who could work but will not as long as someone else will support them and their families.

Disincentive effects. Not only is it unnecessary and perhaps immoral to support such people, the argument says, but their number will grow rapidly if we choose to adopt more generous programs for relieving existing poverty. Even if we could afford to eliminate poverty, the attempt to do so would be self-defeating. For, the argument continues, it would destroy the incentives of those now supporting themselves just above the level at which the government would support them. They would stop working and end up on welfare as quickly as others were raised above the poverty level.

These critics point to the decline in the work ethic that accompanies increased welfare payments, unemployment compensation, and the issuance of food stamps. There is some factual basis for this argument. Today many gladly accept unemployment compensation, welfare payments, and free goods and services—and indeed expect them, as a matter not of charity but of basic rights. Almost every program has had its scandals, and all too many people can identify others who are relying on public assistance when in fact they could support themselves.

A second disincentive effect is on the beneficiaries of government welfare payments: Children who grow up knowing they have a welfare safety net under them may not develop the attitudes or gain the skills needed to climb above the level of the net. This effect may be particularly noticeable in those who, because of the limitations of their abilities, could never in any case hope to climb far above that level.

A third possible disincentive effect relates to those who will be asked to pay the extra taxes that must be levied if welfare spending increases. As more people go on welfare, fewer will be left to pay the taxes, so tax rates must rise. If, in response, taxpayers work less, the total amount of income available for redistribution will shrink.

The important question is whether such effects are merely occasional horror stories or whether they are frequent and quantitatively significant. Opponents of an all-out attack on poverty believe that these magnitudes are, and will be proven to be, very large.

Opportunity costs. Some maintain that we cannot afford to eliminate poverty, given all the competing uses of public money. They contend that welfare spending is already at cripplingly high levels.

Advocates of the view that total government spending is already too large often argue that there are few other items over which so much discretion may be exercised. On the one hand, less could no

doubt be spent on such items as defense or schools. Many believe, however, that significant cuts in these items are either impractical or undesirable. On the other hand, a genuine option does exist with welfare expenditures. One of the few realistic hopes of keeping government spending under control, so goes this view, lies in holding a tight rein on the expansion of transfer payments and in particular eliminating payments to the dishonest, the lazy, and the relatively well off, who are receiving payments without real need.

The Case for an All-Out Attack on Poverty

The war on poverty has its supporters as well as its opponents. Welfare cheaters, supporters agree, should be identified, exposed, and eliminated from welfare rolls wherever possible. But the abuses should not be allowed to confuse the issue. It was one thing to put up with poverty when we had no alternative; it is another to do so when we are rich enough to spend billions on cosmetics, sports, and other frills—to say nothing of space exploration, foreign "diplomacy," and an immense nuclear arsenal.

The shame of poverty, the argument says, is not that of the victim but of the society that lets it continue. One great advance of modern civilization has been to lift the stigma from those who are less able and less fortunate. It is to our credit that we have replaced the poorhouse with programs of social insurance as a matter of right, not charity. To let a few cheaters plus some unsupported fears about destruction of the will to work be the excuse for not "coming to peace with poverty" is, they say, a real immorality in modern society.

Of course any scheme that reduces welfare payments by $.65 or $.75 for every dollar that the recipient earns means a 65 percent or 75 percent tax on earnings and may well provide a short-term disincentive to work. But this is the fault of the scheme, not of the people who are only responding rationally to it. Schemes that reduce this marginal disincentive feature can be designed. Moreover, the supporters argue, the theoretical possibility of disincentive effects is far from an empirical reality.

Most people who can support themselves and their families willingly do so.

Resolving the Debate?

Choosing whether to expand or to contract poverty programs depends in part on value judgments of what is good and right and worth doing, and in part on positive factual assessments of what can be done and how much it will cost. Positive economic research can help to narrow the range of these uncertainties, even if it cannot dictate what we should finally do. Today a great deal of research is devoted to studying the effects of welfare expenditure on incentives. But such research will not quickly resolve the debate. To see why, consider a recent study by the University of Wisconsin, Institute for Research on Poverty, which estimated that all government transfer programs—including among others social security, unemployment insurance, medicaid, and all welfare payments—had the effect of reducing the labor force by 4.8 percent. If an extra 4.8 percent of the labor force found productive work, a big dent could be made in the problem of poverty. If, however, there is already unemployment in a slack economy, an increase in labor supply of 4.8 percent might lead mostly to increases in the number and percent unemployed and not solve many of the problems of the poor.

The Traditional Nature of Poverty Programs

The two underlying assumptions in the development of existing programs were, first, that the able-bodied should work and, second, that heads of households should support their families whenever possible.

The traditional strategy for dealing with poverty was to provide job opportunities for all who are able to work and income-support programs for those not holding jobs.

One part of such programs provided social insurance, related to work, for temporary unemployment and for retirement. A second part provided monetary assistance and in-kind assistance to those poor who are unable to work for reasons of age, health, or family status.

Providing more and better employment opportunities. Families with an employed member have very much less chance of being below the poverty level than those without one. Thus providing job opportunities for the unemployed and for those not even looking for work is of major importance. But providing work is not a guarantee that families will escape poverty. About 40 percent of all poor families have a full-time working head; for these *working poor,* the problem is usually the lack of skills that command a wage that will allow them to rise above the poverty level rather than an absence of demand for the skills they have. Programs of education, training, and retraining are designed to lessen these causes of poverty by providing better job opportunities. Such programs have proven both expensive and limited in the number of persons they can reach. Educational opportunities for the children of the poor may free them from inheriting poverty, but such progress is measured from generation to generation, not from year to year.

Social insurance. Table 23-3 shows the major income-support programs that existed in 1980. The first prong of traditional antipoverty protection was social insurance. In 1980 such programs added up to nearly $200 billion dollars. The Social Security Act (first passed in 1935) provides Old Age and Survivors Disability Insurance (OASDI) to millions of Americans who are old and to the widows and orphans of eligible workers. Medicare provides medical expenses for those receiving OASDI benefits, and unemployment insurance is paid to those covered workers who lose their jobs. The expenditures keep millions off the poverty roles and for many others reduce the size of the poverty gap, but it should be noted that none of them is primarily a *poverty* program. Middle income and wealthy individuals also share in such benefits.

Successive increases in eligibility for coverage and in the size of benefits, including increases to match rises in the cost of living, make social in-

TABLE 23–3 MAJOR INCOME-SUPPORT PROGRAMS, 1980

Program	Expenditures (Billions of Dollars)
Social Insurance	**194.3**
Cash benefits	
Social Security (OASDI)	117.1
Unemployment Insurance	18.0
Workmen's Compensation	11.1
Other	13.1
In-kind Benefits	
Medicare	35.0
Income Assistance (Welfare)	**63.3**
Cash Benefits	
Aid to Families with Dependent Children (AFDC)	11.3
Supplementary Security Income (SSI)	8.2
Other	5.0
In-kind Benefits	
Medicaid	24.6
Food Stamps	8.7
Housing Assistance	5.5
Total	**257.6**

Source: University of Wisconsin, Institute for Research on Poverty.

In 1980 the income-support programs cost $258 billion, about 10 percent of GNP. The table shows the range and size of programs in 1980, before the Reagan administration. Note that nearly three-quarters of the programs are not welfare—that is, they are not need-related—but rather are categorical entitlements to the aged, unemployed, and others regardless of their other sources of income. Only about one-quarter of the total were welfare programs targeted to the poor. AFDC and food stamps, the most publicized programs, are a relatively small part of the total cost of income-support programs. OASDI, medicare, and medicaid—"social security"—represent more than two-thirds of the total.

surance an increasingly effective preventative or antidote to poverty for the majority of Americans. But they also have created a funding crisis in social security, which is discussed in the box on pages 412–413.

Income assistance (welfare). The second prong of traditional antipoverty protection was limited to those who fall into categories for which need is presumed. The poorest of the poor are those who have never worked or for whom employment is not the answer. So-called income assistance programs are designed to identify categories of the poor who cannot use labor market participation to avoid poverty, either directly by way of earnings or indirectly by way of employment-related social insurance. In 1980 these programs cost $63 billion. The largest single item is medicaid, free medical care to the poor. Also important are the aids to nearly 5 million aged, blind, and disabled persons under the Supplemental Security Income (SSI) program, the aid to 11 million families with dependent children (AFDC), and food stamps and housing assistance. All of these programs have certain common characteristics. They are administered by the states, which share some of the costs with the federal government. States individually determine both eligibility and levels of payment. Eligibility is limited to demonstrated cases of need; maximum payments under each of these programs are reduced when the family has other income.

The Size and Accomplishments of the War on Poverty Before Reagan

Public expenditures for income-support programs in 1980 totaled $258 billion. That is such a large figure that it is hard to relate to it. It came to about $1,000 for every person in the country and represented about 10 percent of GNP (gross national product) and about 30 percent of all government spending for that year. Moreover, such spending had shown great growth in a generation. In 1950 public expenditure for these purposes was 2 percent of GNP and 14 percent of government spending.

This growth reflected several developments. First, rising affluence in post-World War II America raised the level of what was defined to be a minimum adequate standard of living and also made it possible to provide benefits to those who did not achieve these levels by their own efforts. Second, some programs, especially social security programs, grew automatically when more and more eligible people reached retirement ages. Third,

THE CRISIS IN SOCIAL SECURITY

Late in the 1970s the American public gradually discovered what insiders had long known; unless major changes were made, the social security system was going to run out of money. It was calculated that by 1982 the system's funds would be exhausted and 36 million beneficiaries would not get their July 3, 1983, checks. Such payments represent, on average, 60 percent of the total income of the recipients. Almost all of those 36 million people are voters, and Congress and the president could no longer ignore the problem. How did all this happen? What was the solution? Will it happen again?

The Short-Run Crisis

From its inception in 1935, social security was never "actuarially sound." While it was considered politically necessary to "sell" social security as merely social insurance, social security has always been a set of entitlements (benefits) and also a set of (loosely linked) taxes imposed on workers and employers. People and firms pay in via a payroll tax whatever amount Congress legislates. This amount was a maximum of $30 per worker per year each by the employee and by the employer in 1935. By 1968 the maximum was $344. In 1983 it was $2,400. While some individuals never get their contributions back, most beneficiaries eventually collect far more than they (and their employers) paid in. The average person retiring in 1980 had an actuarial claim to about $50,000. That person will with-draw $125,000 during retirement. Since this average excess of benefits over contributions on behalf of retirees has been true for every cohort of beneficiaries, you should not be surprised to hear that social security is actuarially "unsound."

The theory has always been that this year's workers would pay in enough for this year's beneficiaries, but not for their own retirement. In the 1940s there were lots of workers and few eligible retirees, so reserves accumulated, even with very modest taxes per worker. As time passed more and more people reached age 65 and began drawing benefits. Eventually the reserves stopped growing and were drawn down. By 1983 the benefits payable exceeded tax receipts by $25 billion, and there were no more reserves. Hence the crisis.

The crisis was purely financial and finite—about $150 billion to $200 billion in uncovered deficits over the period 1983–1990. From 1990 to 2015 the baby-boom generation of the 1950s and 1960s [you students!] will be fully at work and would, even under the old rates of social security taxes, be paying in more than enough to meet annual costs. The interim deficits could, of course, be met by the government diverting about $25 billion a year of other revenues into social security.

How did the short-run crisis occur? How did the system suddenly run out of reserves? The short answer is that Congress from 1939 until 1976 found it politically attractive to in-

benefits under many existing programs were deliberately increased and some of the benefits were indexed to the cost of living. Fourth, a series of expensive new programs were introduced, of which medicare, medicaid, and food stamps were the most important.

As we have noted many of these programs provide substantial transfer payments to persons who are not poor. Moreover, not all of the money aimed at the poor actually reached them due to administrative costs, graft, and even corruption. As one cynic said, "There is money in poverty."

crease the benefits payable without increasing the tax rates enough to compensate. Ths has had several related aspects: (1) a shift from thinking of old age benefits as a poverty-insurance *supplement* to other sources of income for the retired, to thinking of it as the *primary source* of a decent and comfortable retirement income. Over the years Congress has steadily changed the formula to raise the benefits. (2) Since 1972 the benefits have been indexed to the cost of living, thus causing them to rise unexpectedly rapidly. (3) The eligibility for social security has been expanded until there is virtually universal coverage. (4) The benefits available to each covered worker have been sharply increased: Dependents and survivors were added in 1939, disabled workers were added in 1950, and medical coverage (Medicare) was added in 1965.

These things, combined with ever greater longevity, let the deficits grow and reserves vanish.

Solving the short-term crisis. The solution has long been obvious but politically difficult: raise taxes or reduce benefits, or both. Finally, as reserves ran out a bipartisan commission was established to take the president and Congress off the hook. Its recommendations were adopted in 1983. They include accelerated social security tax increases, delay of scheduled cost-of-living adjustments, and making some social security benefits taxable income to the recipients. They also compel some young workers not now covered to join the system, thus increasing pay-ins over the critical years to 1990.

These and related changes will generate the funds needed to cover the current annual deficits and assure the stability of the present levels of benefits well into the next century.

The Long-Run Problem

While the baby-boom generation of the 1950s and 1960s will bail out the system in 1990, what happens when this generation retires in 2015 to 2035? Recent declines in birth rates mean there will be ever fewer workers to support ever more retirees.

In 1945 there were 42 workers supporting each retiree. By 1965 the number was 5, and by 1982 the number was 3.2. By 2030 it will be down to 2. *Every working couple will have to provide funds to support not only itself and its children, but one retired person as well.* Given generous benefits, this implies a heavy tax, maybe two or three times as high as the present 7 percent level. If this burden of too many retired depending too heavily on too few workers is unacceptable, there are only a few options. One is to change retirement ages to keep people working longer. The commission report recommends gradually changing eligibility from age 65 to age 67. Another option is to reduce benefits paid to retirees, encouraging them to rely more on their own savings. The alternative is to tax workers more or to find some other way to subsidize those who are not producing. The choice will be a key issue of the early years of the twenty-first century.

But the fact is, the expenditures did have a highly significant effect on the poverty problem. Table 23-4 shows how, since 1965, money and in-kind transfers have reduced the number of people living below the poverty level. Additionally these same programs reduced the poverty gap of those

below the poverty level. If these figures are reliable, the war on poverty achieved large benefits to go with its large costs. Whether the benefits justified the costs is inherently a matter of individual values, and for the nation, a political decision. The election of Ronald Reagan was widely perceived as a man-

TABLE 23–4 **EFFECTIVENESS OF GOVERN-
MENT INCOME ASSISTANCE
PROGRAMS, 1965–1980**

	Percent of population below poverty level, measured by		
	Income excluding all transfers (market income)	Census money income	Adjusted income
1965	21.3	15.6	12.1
1970	18.8	12.6	9.3
1976	21.0	11.8	6.7
1980	21.9	13.0	6.1

Source: University of Wisconsin, Institute for Research on Poverty.

The reduction of the incidence of poverty between 1965 and 1980 was largely due to government income-assistance programs. Market income includes no government transfers and thus provides a benchmark for evaluating the effect of transfers. Based only upon market income the percent falling below the poverty line fluctuated but did not decrease. Census money income adds social security and other known *cash* transfers from government to market income. These additions to household income decrease the numbers of those living below the poverty line. Census money income shows a small downward trend in the poverty population. "Adjusted income" adds in-kind transfers, and underreported income to census money income and subtracts taxes paid. It thus seeks to measure the total resources available to meet basic needs. By this measure government programs in the war on poverty had a big effect in reducing the number living below the poverty level.

date to stop the growth and roll back the size of the whole set of government programs designed to provide income support and eliminate poverty by government transfer payments.

Poverty and the Reagan Administration

When Ronald Reagan assumed the presidency in 1981, he had already gone on record with a radically different view of the poverty problem. The Reagan administration adopted a view of the causes and solutions for the poverty problem different from those that had been in effect for decades. What were the essential differences?

Reliance on Growth Rather Than Income Transfers

Traditional antipoverty policy was heavily dependent upon the use of income transfers to the poor. The Reagan policies rejected this approach in principle, believing instead that the main cure for poverty lay in economic recovery and the growth of the private sector. As President Reagan put it, "Our aim is to increase national wealth so all will have more, not just redistribute what we already have, which is just a sharing of scarcity."

Given this frame of mind, any measure that fostered economic recovery or growth, even if in the short run worsening the plight of the poor, would in the longer run lead to reductions in poverty. This reliance on growth instead of redistribution also reflected a disbelief in the historical effectiveness of transfers, as was stated concisely by Budget Director David Stockman in 1982: "All the programs that were created out of Washington in the 1960s had almost nothing to do with the progress that was made in reducing poverty. The real war was waged by the private sector . . . with economic growth of 4, 5, 6 percent a year and with massive increases in jobs and employment."

If this controversial view is correct—and it is surely in conflict with the statistics presented in Table 23-4—it would make sense, even to those in poverty, to *reduce* the programs of income transfer if by so doing economic recovery would be fostered. Established income-support programs became a target of Reaganomics. The general economic philosophy of the administration was that decreasing the federal government's domestic expenditures was a key to economic recovery. What better way to reduce government expenditures than to cut expensive welfare programs that had not (in any case) contributed to progress! Many of these programs were the cornerstones of the traditional antipoverty strategy. The administration sharply cut funds for food stamps, AFDC, and Medicaid in the hope that the resulting economic recovery and reduced inflation would ameliorate the lot of the poor. Nearly 20 percent of the recipients of welfare lost some or all of their benefits. Whether or not in the long run this strategy will work, in the short run it has unmistakably increased rather than alleviated poverty.

Hard-Core Poverty

The Reagan administration recognized, as had prior administrations, that not all of the poor could be rescued by economic growth, even in the long run. The hard-core poor, or "truly needy," would always require help. Here too changes in philosophy became apparent. A major change was the belief that welfare and other transfers should be designed simply to assure a minimum standard of living, not to close the poverty gap. Edwin Dale of the Office of Management and Budget put it succinctly: "The policy decision is that welfare is a safety-net and not an income supplement program."

What this meant was that persons whose income from other sources raised them above the threshold level of the safety net were to be cut off from eligibility for welfare, medicaid, and food stamps. The first dollars earned above the threshold level caused major losses of benefits. The intent was to eliminate those who were not truly needy, including the welfare cheaters. But a side effect was to penalize all the working poor who were above the safety net but below the poverty level. This policy had the undesired effect of creating disincentives to continued work and discouraging some of those without work from finding or accepting it.

Who Should Deal with Poverty?

Until the Great Depression and the New Deal of Franklin Roosevelt, poverty had been thought of as a family problem to be suffered through with such help as private charity might provide. Roosevelt changed all that, arguing that it was a *national* scandal that one-third of the nation was ill-housed, ill-clothed, and ill-fed. Forty years later,

public programs had made the amelioration of poverty a major policy concern of local, state, and federal governments. The trend, indeed, was increasingly to make poverty a *federal* government concern, and former President Carter proposed "federalizing welfare" as the most significant possible way to provide needed economic aid to beleaguered state and local governments.

President Reagan called for an abrupt reversal of these trends. He urged increased private giving to fill any gap left by the reduction in government programs and, more importantly, he called for a return to state and local governments of the responsibility for aid to the poor.

The Impact of the Reagan Approach

It is too early (in 1983 as this is written) to assess definitively the success or failure of the Reagan administration's changed approach. But some facts are clear. The number of people living in the United States below the poverty level increased sharply between 1980 and 1983. Part of this had relatively little to do with policy, since the poverty rate always rises when the economy suffers from a recession and the severe unemployment that accompany it.[1] A better test will occur once the recovery which began in 1983 has run its course. Reagan supporters argue also that the administration's policies were always designed to work not as a quick fix but as a gradual middle- and long-run solution. In this view the real test of President Reagan's policies will have to be judged from the perspective of 1988, not 1983 or 1984.

Most economists believe that the rise in the number of those classified as living in poverty was due to more than rising unemployment during the recession and that there is little hope that growth will eventually provide an antidote to the extra poverty created by decreases in the income-support programs. Moreover, the shift from income-support to safety-net strategy seems likely to have sig-

---

[1] Of course the severity of the recession may itself have reflected a policy decision of the administration that was willing to endure a deep recession to deal with the rapid inflation. This matter is discussed in Part Nine.

nificantly increased the potential disincentive effects to working.

The highly regarded Center for the Study of Welfare Policies of the University of Chicago found that the Reagan policies all but eliminated the economic incentive to work of the working poor. Since 40 percent of all the poor were working, the possibility of increasing the number of people who did not find it economically worthwhile to work was very substantial. It is too soon to know how many people actually reduced their work effort in order to re-establish their eligibility for food stamps, medicaid, and other forms of welfare.

Future Directions of Policy Toward Poverty

Poverty has not been eliminated. The fact that the poor are both numerous and politically aware assures that the debate about philosophy and policy will continue for many years to come.

The debate is now vigorous. The case for federal control rests upon defining poverty as a national problem and on the fact that there are great differences in the ability or willingness of state and local governments to cope with the problem. The poor are not distributed evenly throughout the United States—42 percent live in the South, many of the rest in northern urban slums. Much of the state and local tax base is generated in political jurisdictions in which poverty is not a major problem. Thus the tax burden of fighting poverty locally falls very unevenly. Differences in ability and willingness to pay lead to great differences in programs. For example, in 1979 a woman with no income and three dependent children in Newark, New Jersey, who was eligible for aid could receive $4,488 per year; in Biloxi, Mississippi, she would get at most $1,440. While each amount is below the poverty line, the difference in the realized levels of poverty is enormous—and it is not explained by differences in the cost of living.

The case against federalization rests on the advantages of pluralism and local control. There are great differences in costs of living and in local standards of what constitute an adequate minimum standard of living; such differences cannot easily be taken into account (as a political matter) by federal bureaucrats or by Congress. Yet to provide equal welfare payments in Newark and Biloxi would also be unjust.

Part of the debate concerns one's view of whose problem poverty is. If poverty of any part of the population is viewed as a national problem and its elimination as a national goal, there is little reason to believe a decentralized system or a reliance on voluntarism will succeed in accomplishing anything approximating a uniform set of policies. If, on the other hand, the tolerable level ought to be one of local option, then a uniform national policy will seem intrusive as well as inefficient. If poverty is merely a personal problem, then its amelioration should fall to individual effort, or to family, friends, and neighbors.

Much of the debate about poverty is at the normative level. Should poverty and its elimination be a compelling national concern? Should policies distinguish between the deserving and the undeserving poor? Should relief attempt to bring the poor to a decent standard of living or merely to a subsistence standard?

There are of course important positive questions as well: Which policies work best? Is there a conflict between short-run amelioration and long-run solution owing to incentive and disincentive effects? If so, how long are the lags before the present group of poor will be better off? These and other questions will occupy many economists for many years.

THE RELEVANCE OF DISTRIBUTION THEORY

A large part of the problem of poverty is due to the pricing of the labor services that people have to offer. Factor pricing, and hence the distribution of income, is a by-product of the market-allocation system. This allocation helps to determine both the quantities of the various goods and services that are produced and the methods by which they are produced.

Does the theory of distribution studied in this part satisfactorily explain the allocation process in our economy? For the answer to be yes, it is necessary to give affirmative answers to two more basic questions. First, do market conditions of demand and supply play important roles in determining factor earnings? Second, do factors move in response to changes in factor earnings?

Some would answer no to each question. They argue that prices of products and factors bear little relation to market conditions because prices and wages are administered by oligopolies and giant unions. Such administered prices and wages are sticky downward and tend to rise annually at a bit more than the general rate of inflation. Products with above average price increases are produced by firms with above average market power, and the most powerful unions get the biggest wage increases. Entry barriers in industry and mobility barriers for factors of production, the argument continues, prevent significant movements of resources in response to product and factor price differentials that exist or develop. Thus, they argue, the theory of distribution we have studied is irrelevant to the real world.

Some of the views expressed in the previous paragraph are closely related to those discussed on pages 319–325. In the following sections of this chapter, we examine whether market forces do in fact play the roles predicted by the theories of competition and monopoly in determining factor prices and the allocation of resources.

Do Market Conditions Determine Factor Earnings?

Factors Other Than Labor

Many, if not all, nonhuman factors are sold on competitive markets. The theory predicts that changes in the earnings of these factors will be associated with changes in market conditions. Overwhelmingly the evidence supports this prediction of the theory, as shown by the examples that follow.

The market theory of factor pricing provides a good explanation of raw material prices and hence of the incomes earned by their producers. The prices of plywood, tin, rubber, cotton, and hundreds of other materials fluctuate daily in response to changes in their demand and supply. The responses of factor markets to the many shortages that seemed to characterize the American economy in the 1970s provide dramatic confirmation. When the price of agricultural commodities shot up following a grain shortage, farm income soared. When oil became scarce, prices rose and oil producers and owners of oil properties found their profits and incomes rising rapidly. Not only did the relative prices of oil products rise, so also did the relative prices of commodities, such as chemical fertilizers and air travel, that make use of petroleum products. When oil became abundant in the early 1980s, these trends were reversed.

Land in the heart of growing cities provides another example. Such land is clearly fixed in supply, and values rise steadily in response to increasing demand for it.[2] Very high land values even make it worthwhile to destroy durable buildings in order to convert the land to more productive uses. Several of New York's old and once favorite hotels have been pulled down, to be replaced by high-rise office buildings. The skyscraper is a monument to the high value of urban land. In many smaller cities the change from shopping downtown to shopping in outlying shopping centers has lessened the demand for land downtown and influenced relative land prices. The increase in the price of land on the periphery of every growing city is a visible example of the workings of the market.

Similar results occur in markets that are far from being perfectly competitive. In 1979 the price of power in virtually all forms rose sharply in response to the extra energy shortage caused by the change in government in Iran. Oligopolists producing key metals such as zinc, molybdenum, steel, and aluminum have not hesitated to increase prices as their costs of production rose or when demand outran

[2] A friend is fond of saying, "Nobody buys land any more; its price is much too high because everybody wants it."

their production. Further examples can be found in almost every issue of the *New York Times* and the *Wall Street Journal,* but the point should now be clear:

The prices and earnings of nonhuman factors are successfully predicted by market theories of factor pricing.

Labor

When we apply the theory to labor, we encounter two important sets of complications. First, labor being the human factor of production, nonmonetary considerations loom large in its incentive patterns, and thus market fluctuations may have less effect. Second, the competitive and noncompetitive elements of labor markets occur in different proportions from market to market. These complications make it harder to answer the question, Do market conditions determine factor earnings? Monopolistic elements and nonmonetary rewards, both difficult to measure, must be carefully specified if the theory that labor earnings respond to market forces is to be confirmed. Nevertheless there is a mass of evidence to go on.

Market fluctuations in demand and supply. Do earnings respond to normal fluctuations of demand and supply as the theory predicts? The evidence shows that they often do. The competitive theory predicts that a decline in the demand for a product will cause a decline in the derived demand for the factors that make the product and thus a decline in their owners' incomes. A rise in the demand for a product will have the opposite effect. Cases come easily to mind.

With the advent of the automobile, many skilled carriage makers saw the demand for their services decline rapidly. Earnings fell, and many older workers found that they had been earning substantial economic rents for their scarce but highly specific skills. They suffered large income cuts when they moved to other industries. Workers who acquired skills wanted in the newly expanding automotive industry found the demands for their services and their incomes rising rapidly.

More recently there has been a large increase in the earnings of first class professional athletes in most sports. In part this has been caused by rising demand due to expansion in the number of major league teams. In part it has resulted from increased revenues to the teams and leagues from televising sports, which has increased the marginal revenue product of the athletes. And in part it has been the result of athletes' acquiring the right to offer their services to more than one employer, thereby reducing the ability of employers to hold down wages by acting as monopsonists.

Doctors as a group have also gained from an increase in demand for their services. With the rise in real incomes in the twentieth century, the typical household has spent an increasing proportion of its income on medical services. The resulting rise in demand has greatly increased the incomes of physicians relative to the incomes of many other groups in the society.

College professors are an example of a group that gained as a result of changes in labor markets during the 1960s but fell back in the 1970s. The relative earnings of a college professor were much higher by 1970 than they had been 20 years earlier as a result of the baby boom population's reaching college age and thus creating an enormous demand for college teachers. Demand increased much faster than the supply for a long while. In response to the higher incomes, however, many more college graduates went on to get advanced degrees, and a rising proportion stayed on to teach and do research in universities.

By 1970 supply had caught up to demand and salaries stabilized. Supply continued to grow faster than the demand for teachers and relative salaries began to fall. The relative downward pressure on college professors' salaries continued throughout the 1970s and shows no sign of abating.

Another group that has been suffering the chill winds of the consequences of factor price determination on competitive markets is college graduates. During the 1970s the earnings of college graduates fell relative to other workers as employment opportunities dropped sharply, especially for new graduates. The downturn is explained by slackening demand due to changes in industrial structure (e.g., substituting sophisticated computers for college-trained persons) and continued growth of supply.

Wage changes induced by market conditions have little to do with abstract notions of justice or merit. If you have some literary talent, why can you make a lot of money writing copy for an advertising agency on Madison Avenue but very little money writing poems? It is not because an economic dictator or group of philosophers has decided that advertising is more valuable than poetry. It is because in the American economy there is a large demand for advertising and only a tiny demand for poetry.

Effects of monopoly elements in labor markets.
A strong union—one able to bargain effectively and to restrict entry of labor into the field—can cause wages to rise well above the competitive level. Highly skilled plasterers, plumbers, and electricians have all managed to restrict entry into their trades and as a result maintain wages well above their transfer earnings. Many similar cases have been documented. Unions can and do succeed in raising wages and incomes when they operate in small sections of the whole economy. The high earnings attract others to enter the occupation or industry, and the privileged position can be maintained only if entry can be effectively restricted.

Not only can monopoly elements raise incomes above their competitive levels, they can also prevent wages from falling in response to decreases in demand. Of course, if the demand disappears more or less overnight, there is nothing any union can do to maintain incomes. But the story may be different when, as is more usually the case, demand shrinks slowly but steadily.

Consider coal mining in the years just after World War II. From 1945 to 1965 the production of coal declined as oil, gas, and electricity were steadily substituted for it. The coal that was produced was used largely by electric utilities, and it was mined by ever more capital-using and labor-saving techniques. Both these forces led employment to shrink steadily.

What would competitive theory predict about wages? Coal mining was plainly a declining labor market from 1945 until 1965; competitive theory would predict relatively low wages and low incomes, followed by exit of the most mobile coal miners under this forceful disincentive, and hard times for those who decide to stick it out. Precisely this happened in Canada. Average wages, which in 1945 had been 36 percent above those in manufacturing, fell steadily until in 1965 there were 8 percent below those in manufacturing. Employment declined to 35 percent of its previous level, and those who remained in coal mining saw their relative incomes fall.

In the United States, however, this was *not* the pattern. Faced with a similar decline in production, relative wages actually rose in coal mining, from 18 percent above manufacturing in 1945 to 34 percent above it in 1965. Employment did fall—indeed by 1965 employment was only 30 percent of the 1945 level. Unemployed coal miners contributed to the generally depressed conditions in Appalachia. But those who kept jobs did relatively well.

What happened was that a powerful union, the United Mine Workers, prevented wages from falling. By raising wages despite falling demand, the union actually accelerated the decline in employment. Economic theory suggests that lower wages *or* declining employment opportunities (or both) will serve to decrease labor earnings and trigger movements of factors out of the industry. The lower employment that accompanied the "high wage" policy of the United Mine Workers Union discouraged the young from waiting for jobs in the industry. As workers left the industry because of retirement, ill health, or death, they were not replaced.

Since 1965 the demand for coal miners has rebounded as the demand for coal to produce electricity has surged. As a result both in the United States and in Canada—as theory predicts—employment rose sharply *and* wages in coal mining shot up relative to those of all industry. Consequently labor earnings in coal mining rose sharply.

All the above examples support the general proposition:

Earnings of labor respond to significant changes in market conditions.

Do Factors Move in Response to Changes in Earnings?

The theory of factor supply says that factors will move among uses, industries, and places, taking both monetary and nonmonetary rewards into account. They will move in such a way as to equalize the net advantages to the owners of factors. Because there are impediments to the mobility of factors, there may be lags in the response of factors to changes in relative prices, but in due course adjustments will occur. We now ask, Does the world behave in the way the theory predicts?

Factors Other Than Labor

The most casual observation reveals that the allocative system works pretty much as described by the theory with respect to land, materials, and capital goods.

Land is transferred from one crop to another in response to changes in the relative profitabilities of the crops. Land on the edge of town is transferred from rural to urban uses as soon as it can earn substantially more as a building site than as a cornfield. Materials and capital goods move from use to use in response to changes in relative earnings to those uses.

This is hardly surprising. Nonmonetary benefits do not loom large for factors other than labor, and the theories of both competition and monopoly predict that quantities supplied will respond to increases in earnings generated by increased demand.

In the case of nonhuman factors, there is strong evidence that factors move in response to earnings differentials.

Labor

Labor mobility can occur in many dimensions. Labor can move among occupations, industries, skill categories, and regions. These categories are not exclusive; to change occupation from a farm laborer to a steelworker, for example, a person will also have to change industries and probably towns.

Response to changes in demand. The mobility of labor is as well documented as it is impressive. When wages on the West Coast soared during World War II, workers flocked there to take lucrative jobs in the rapidly expanding aircraft and shipbuilding industries. When new oil fields were discovered in Alaska and northern Canada, high wages attracted welders, riveters, and the many other types of labor that the oil fields required. During the period 1950–1970 black workers migrated steadily from South to North in search of jobs. Since 1970, and especially since 1975, this flow has slowed and stopped; indeed, it has been reversed as the movement of industry to the sun belt has created new jobs in the South.[3]

Overall, major reallocations of labor have occurred. The fraction of the labor force in agriculture declined from 23 percent in 1930 to about 3 percent in 1980.

In the non-agriculture labor force, the changes have been equally dramatic. Heavy industry—manufacturing, mining, construction, and the like—decreased from over 50 percent in 1930 to less than 30 percent by 1980, and the decline continues. What has increased are trade, government service, finance and—especially—service employment. The rise in service employment has been especially dramatic since 1970. Over the 1970s there was a net increase of 19 million jobs in the United States, 87 percent of which were in the service sector. Meanwhile traditional blue-color production jobs were decreasing in number. This process of deindustrialization is discussed in the box.

Labor is highly mobile in response to changes in demand from decade to decade.

---

[3] During the 1960s it was often argued that the northward migration of the unemployed was motivated not by job opportunities but by the more generous welfare benefits offered in northern states and cities. The reversal of the labor flow, despite the continuing differential in welfare benefits, is taken by a recent Department of Commerce study as conclusive refutation of that argument.

DEINDUSTRIALIZATION: FROM BIG STEEL TO BIG MAC

The growth of employment in services and retail trade over the last decades has been dramatic. Employment in these two sectors has risen three times faster than total employment and sixteen times faster than employment in the goods-producing sector, with the growth concentrated in three areas: eating and drinking places, health services, and business services. *Total employment in manufacturing of durable goods today (under 11 million persons) is less than the increase in employment in services over the last two decades.*

This is in one sense good news, for without these new job opportunities overall unemployment would have been far worse. But the substitution of service employment and production for industrial employment and production is not an unmixed blessing to the American economy. High levels of productivity and the opportunities for growth in productivity have fueled high standards of living and the growth of the economy. But productivity is lower in service industries, and the opportunities for growth are much more limited than in goods-producing industries. The possibilities for substituting capital for labor are much less in making and serving hamburgers than in producing metal and metal products.

The nature of employment has also changed as a result of the changing composition of output. There is more part-time work and more contact with the public. The role of women in the work force has increased, and women are concentrated in the sectors of greatest expansion in job opportunities. In many industrial areas where men have been laid off by the steel mills and auto factories, their wives and daughters have found jobs in restaurants and offices while the men search in vain. The fact that in these areas many women are working while many men are not, reflects an important change in the American economy—and in American society—over the last decade.

Does it matter to the economy if one kind of worker (e.g., service workers) increasingly replaces another kind (e.g., heavy industrial workers)? It is a change that worries many labor leaders and industrialists. Service jobs usually pay less than jobs in manufacturing, particularly in such basic manufacturing industries as steel, automobiles, glass, and rubber. A typical steel worker earns $9 to $10 per hour, a McDonald's kitchen worker less than $4 per hour. Because of this differential, service jobs generally make a smaller contribution to national income than do manufacturing jobs. Moreover the levels of productivity and the opportunities for improvement tend to be smaller in many service industries.

The Reagan administration has advocated a program designed to restore America's economic might by cutting income and business taxes to encourage investment, by increasing military spending to boost vital segments of the economy, and by reducing the burden of government on goods-producing industries through reductions in bureaucratic regulations. Will the strategy work?

There are reasons for doubt. Reindustrialization policies are largely aimed at rejuvenating the manufacturing sector of the economy. If the policies succeed in making American manufacturers once again competitive in world markets, rising demand for American industrial production will fuel an industrial revival. Many observers believe that is a very big task, one that would require a major effort to achieve.

An alternative strategy would be to foster new, high-productivity service industries, such as those utilizing high technology. This strategy would not promise to reemploy the unemployed steel and auto workers but it could readily provide jobs for their sons and daughters that are more rewarding and more satisfying than slinging hash or delivering pizza.

Barriers to labor mobility. There are, of course, barriers to labor mobility. Unions, pension funds, and other institutions can and do inhibit labor mobility substantially. By influencing supplies of labor in various markets, they exert considerable influence on labor earnings. It is easier to move from one occupation to another within one industry when there is a single industrial union than it is when each occupation in the industry is organized in its own craft union. It is easier to move between two industries in the same occupation when both are organized by craft unions than it is when each has its own industrial union.

Although various barriers to the entry of labor exist in particular markets, few seem able to withstand for long the pressures of severe excess demand. Prejudice against females, for example, did not hold up under the excess demand for labor during World War II. Once millions of men had been absorbed by the armed forces, occupations traditionally closed to women suddenly opened up. Employers, with profits at stake, quickly decided they would rather have Rosie for a riveter than no riveter at all. This occurred without the benefit of social pressures arising out of concern for discrimination against women. Once the excess demand had disappeared after the war, however, many of the old prejudices reasserted themselves—and barriers were not again lowered until they were directly assaulted.

The effect of excess supply. Excess supply also tends eventually to generate out-migration of labor. Yet it may not occur quickly enough to prevent substantially depressed conditions. Consider regional mobility. On the one hand, the regional distribution of population has been shifting toward the sun belt and other centers of rapid economic growth in the United States; on the other hand, depressed Appalachian areas have remained regions of excess labor supply for over 25 years, since coal mines in Pennsylvania and West Virginia began to shut down.

Although it is relatively easy to get *some* out-migration, it is difficult to get large-scale transfers in a short period of time. When demand falls rapidly, pockets of poverty tend to develop. In Appalachia labor has been leaving yet poverty has increased. The reason for this is that the rate of exit has been slower than the rate of decline of the economic opportunities in the area. Indeed the exit itself causes further decline: when a family migrates, both the supply of labor and the demand for labor decline. This is because all the locally provided goods and services that the family consumed before they migrated now suffer a reduction in demand.

Such lagging mobility creates a cruel policy dilemma. On the one hand, it is desirable to ease the poverty of those who cannot move; on the other, policies designed to do just that reduce the incentives to move to areas with available jobs.

Labor mobility: summary. The theories of competitive and monopolistic factor markets go a long way in explaining what we see and in predicting many of the consequences of changes in market conditions on labor mobility and the consequences of barriers to mobility on the welfare of those trapped by immobility.

Of course not all behavior is neatly explained by the theory. For example, despite the recent decline in academic salaries and job opportunities, many more students today persist in getting Ph.D.s in fields such as history and English than can reasonably expect to find jobs that will require or utilize their training. Economists can speculate about such behavior—for example, by saying that for many students, graduate education is a consumption good as well as an investment in human capital or that the nonmonetary advantages of an academic position are large enough to be worth the gamble of finding a job. But such hypotheses go beyond elementary economics. At this stage we have to be satisfied with a theory that explains much, but not all, behavior.

SUMMARY

1. The concept of poverty involves both relative and absolute levels of income and reflects the aspirations of society as well as the income needed for subsistence alone. Today roughly 14 percent of all Americans are classified as living in poverty. Since the aggregate poverty gap is small relative to national income, the possibility exists of eradicating poverty in the United States.

2. Economic growth, though it has led to a reduction of poverty, will by itself never eliminate it, for many of those in need do not share directly in the fruits of growth.

3. The incidence of poverty is much greater among some groups than among others, particularly those who are not employed and who are relatively uneducated. But there are many poor among the working, and poverty is appreciable in all ages and among those who have had considerable education.

4. Poverty is particularly acute among such minority groups as blacks. This reflects in part the minority group's lower average stock of human capital—especially education and training—and in part the discrimination that has prevented utilizing more fully the skills and talents that the group's members have. Recent years have seen no significant decrease in the relative income disadvantage of blacks relative to whites.

5. The desirability of pursuing antipoverty policies is a matter of fierce current debate. Some people believe that it is possible and desirable to make further major reductions in poverty now. They place particular importance on income supplements to the poor regardless of why they are poor. Others believe that further attacks on poverty are undesirable both because of the burdens such government expenditures place on the economy and because of the disincentive effects generated by welfare programs.

6. The antipoverty policies that developed between the 1930s and 1980 included antidiscrimination laws that seek to expand employment opportunities for blacks and other minority groups; retraining programs intended to match people with available jobs; social insurance that helps the ablebodied to meet the risks of unemployment and retirement; and categorical assistance designed to serve those unable to care for themselves. Most economists believe these policies did greatly reduce poverty in the United States.

7. The Reagan administration advocated and partially adopted policies that represented a sharp break with the trend of the previous half century. The underpinning of the Reagan policy was to seek economic growth by reducing government spending even if that meant decreasing income transfers to the poor. For the very poor the notion of an income supplement was to be replaced by a safety net to protect only the truly needy. Moreover the philosophic approach of the Reagan administration was increasingly to return poverty programs to state and local control and to private charity. These controversial policies have yet to be fully implemented, and their long-run effect is not yet known. In the short run they have increased the incidence of poverty.

8. Market conditions excercise a powerful influence on factor earnings. This is most evident for nonhuman factors such as raw materials and land. For labor the influence of nonmonetary factors is greater because the owners of labor must accompany their labor services to work. Nevertheless market forces exert powerful influences on earnings of labor.

9. There is much evidence of the movement of factors in response to changes in earnings. Factor mobility is typically greater for nonhuman factors than it is for labor. Even where impediments to mobility exist, factors (including labor) tend to move in response to persistent differences in earnings or employment opportunities.

TOPICS FOR REVIEW

Poverty and the poverty gap
Correlates of poverty
Occasional poverty and persistent poverty
Possible disincentive effects of alleviating poverty
Social insurance versus income assistance
Alternative policies toward poverty

DISCUSSION QUESTIONS

1. In what ways are the problems of poverty in the United States likely to be different from the problems of poverty in an underdeveloped poor country, such as Bangladesh? In what ways are they easier to solve in one place than in the other?

2. The official poverty level used in the United States is based only on money income. It does not take into account food stamps or subsidized housing. It does not consider the assets of the family. It does not consider whether families with low incomes have wealthy relatives. Do these omissions lead to an exaggerated view of the poverty problem? Should the poverty line rise if average income of the American people rises, with no increase in the prices of individual items of consumption?

3. Suppose that your objectives are (first) to eradicate poverty and (second) to reduce unemployment. Evaluate the probable effectiveness of each of the following in meeting each objective.
   a. increasing welfare payments
   b. increased aid to education
   c. creating a program of public works to hire the poor
   d. ending employment discrimination against blacks

4. A proposed program of rental allowances to the poor has been attacked in Congress as giving money to slumlords instead of to the poor and thereby worsening the distribution of income. Evaluate this position. Argue the case for and against assistance that is tied to a particular kind of expenditure rather than giving the money to the poor to spend as they think best.

5. Comment on each of the following headlines in terms of the matters discussed in this chapter:
   a. "Working poor are victims of Reaganomics"
   b. "On welfare or working: poor is poor"
   c. "Few States seek to ease effects of cuts for poor"
   d. "Economic recovery decreases number on welfare"
   e. "War on poverty is difficult to call off"

6. Is the Empire State Building immobile? Is the Empire State Building more mobile among uses than the use of the land it sits on? How about the uses of the pyramids of Egypt? What resources can you think of that are immobile over a time span as long as 25 years? In general, are a factor's earnings likely to be greater or smaller if its mobility is relatively low?

7. The supply of regular New York taxicabs is rigidly controlled by a licensing system that keeps the number of cabs well below what it would be in a free-market situation. A "medallion" issued for a nominal fee by the city confers the right to operate a cab. The medallion, however, is freely salable; in 1980 its price was $68,000. What forces determine the price of a medallion? Evaluate the effect on the price of the medallion of
   a. an increase in average incomes of New Yorkers
   b. increased operation of "gypsy cabs" (cabs without medallions)
   c. increases in parking lot fees and parking violation fines in New York
   d. a new law that bans private passenger autos from midtown during business hours
   e. doubling the number of medallions

8. Suppose that you had been on the margin about whether to buy a medallion and become a licensed cab operator in 1980. A 50 percent increase in taxi fares was then authorized. How, if at all, would this affect your decision? Toronto uses a similar scheme, but the price of a medallion there is only about one-half as much as it is in New York. What might account for this difference?

9. It has been estimated that it costs employers $20,000 to move an executive from one city to another. Is this a barrier to labor mobility? Despite the cost some 200,000 executives move (at company expense) every year. Is this consistent with the theory of distribution? Executives involved in the moves were asked whether they liked having to move; 69 percent said they did not, yet 78 percent said they could have remained in their old jobs if they had so chosen. Are these replies consistent with one another and with the theory of distribution?

PART SIX

THE MARKET ECONOMY: PROBLEMS AND POLICIES

24 MICROECONOMIC POLICY I: BENEFITS AND COSTS OF GOVERNMENT INTERVENTION IN THE MARKET ECONOMY

There are two caricatures of the American economy. One pictures the United States as the last stronghold of free enterprise, with millions of Americans in a mad and brutal race for the almighty dollar. In the other, American business people, workers, and farmers are seen strangling slowly in a web of red tape spun by the spider of government regulation. Neither is realistic.

Many aspects of economic life in the United States, perhaps more than in most other countries,

are determined by the operation of a free-market system. In the United States, private preferences, expressed through private markets and influencing private profit-seeking enterprises, determine much of what is produced, how it is produced, and the incomes of productive factors.

But even casual observation makes it clear that public policies and public decisions play a very large role. Not only do laws restrict what people and firms may do, but taxes and subsidies influence their choices. Much public expenditure is not market determined, and this leads to a distribution of national product very different from what would exist in a system that relied entirely on private markets. The United States is in fact a mixed economy.

The general case for some reliance on free markets is that allowing decentralized decision making is more efficient in a number of identifiable ways than having all economic decisions made and consciously coordinated by a centralized planning body. This is a lesson that the governments of the USSR and the countries of Eastern Europe have learned the hard way.

The general case for some public intervention is that almost no one wants to let the market decide everything about our economic affairs. Most people's moral and practical sense argues for some state intervention to mitigate the disastrous results that the market deals out to some. Most people believe that there are areas where the market does not function well and where state intervention can improve or replace its functioning for the general social good. For such reasons there is no known economy where the people have opted for complete *laissez faire* and against any kind of government intervention.

Thus the operative choice is not between an unhampered free-market economy or a fully centralized command economy. It is instead the choice of what mix between markets and government intervention best suits a people's hopes and needs. Although all economies are mixed, the mixture varies greatly among economies and over time. Whether the existing mixture is wrong—and if so, in which direction—is debated sharply today in the United States. One reason for the mixture (and the debate) relates to what an unkind critic called the economists' two great insights: markets work, and markets fail. A second reason is what the critic might call the political scientists' great insights: government intervention can work, and it can fail. In this chapter we discuss the role of the government in economic markets. Why is it there at all? What does it do well, and what badly? Do we need more or less government intervention?

MARKET SUCCESS

Any economy consists of thousands upon thousands of individual markets. There are markets for agricultural goods, for manufactured goods, and for consumers' services; there are markets for semi-manufactured goods, such as steel and pig iron, which are outputs of some industries and inputs of others; there are markets for raw materials such as iron ore, trees, bauxite, and copper; there are markets for land and for thousands of different types of labor; there are markets in which money is borrowed and in which securities are sold.

An economy is not a series of markets functioning in isolation but an interlocking system in which an occurrence in one market will affect many others.

How Markets Coordinate

Any change, such as an increase in demand for beef, requires many further changes and adjustments. Should production of beef change? If so, by how much and in what manner? Someone or something must decide what is to be produced, how, and by whom, and what is to be consumed and by whom.

Coordination in a Market Economy

The essential characteristic of the market system is that its coordination occurs in an unplanned, decentralized way. Millions of people make millions of independent decisions concerning production and consumption every day. Most of these decisions are not motivated by a desire to contribute to the social good or to make the whole economy work well but by fairly immediate considerations of personal or group self-interest. The price system coordinates these decentralized decisions, making the whole system fit together and respond to the wishes of the individuals who compose it.

The basic insight into how this system works is that decentralized, private decision makers, acting in their own interests, respond to such signals as the prices of what they buy and sell. Economists have long emphasized price as the signaling agent. When a commodity such as oil becomes scarce, its free-market price rises. Firms and households that use it are led to economize on it and to look for alternatives. Firms that produce it are led to produce more of it. How the price system gets these decisions made has been examined at several places in this book (for example, with respect to carrots and brussels sprouts in Chapter 4, agriculture in Chapter 8, and ball-point pens in Chapter 17). When a shortage occurs in a market, price rises and windfall profits develop; when a glut occurs, price falls and windfall losses develop. These are *signals*, for all to see, that arise from the overall conditions of total supply and demand.

The Role of Windfall Profits and Losses

Although the free-market economy is often described as the *price system*, the basic engine that drives the adaptation of the economy is what are generally called windfall profits and losses.[1] A **windfall profit** is a change in earnings of a firm that arises out of unanticipated changes in market conditions. Windfall profits are *disequilibrium* phenomena.

A rise in demand or a fall in production costs creates windfall profits for that commodity's producers, while a fall in demand or a rise in production costs creates windfall losses. Windfall profits signal that there are too few resources devoted to that industry. In search of these profits, more resources will enter the industry, increasing output and driving down price, until windfall profits are driven to zero. Windfall losses signal the reverse. Resources leave the industry until those left behind are no longer suffering losses.

The importance of windfall profits is that they set in motion forces that tend to move the economy toward a new equilibrium.

---

[1] Frequently we will use the phrase windfall *profits* to include, as negative profits, windfall *losses*. In economic theory windfall profits are sometimes described as *quasi-rents*.

Individual households and firms respond to common signals according to their own best interests. There is nothing planned or intentionally coordinated about their actions, yet when (say) a shortage causes price to rise, individual buyers begin to reduce the quantities they demand and individual firms begin to increase the quantities they supply. As a result the shortage will begin to lessen. As it does, price begins to come back down, and windfall profits are reduced. These signals in turn are seen and responded to by firms and households. Eventually, when the shortage has been eliminated, there will be no windfall profits to attract further increases in supply. The chain of adjustments to the original shortage is completed.

People sometimes speak of windfall profits and losses as "undeserved." And so they are! They result from changes over which the beneficiaries have no control. But that does not mean they should be eliminated by government action. If the government taxed away *all* windfall profits and replaced by subsidy *all* windfall losses, it would effectively destroy the market economy by removing its driving force.

Because the economy is continuously adjusting to shocks, a snapshot of the economy at any given moment reveals substantial positive windfall profits in some industries and substantial windfall losses in others. A similar snapshot at another moment will also reveal windfall profits and losses, but their locations will be different.

The *unplanned* price system, like an *invisible hand* (Adam Smith's famous phrase), coordinates the responses of individual decision makers who seek only their own self-interests. Because they respond to signals that reflect market conditions, their responses are coordinated without any conscious planning of who may or must do what.

Who Responds?

Notice that in the sequence of signal-response-signal-response no one had to foresee at the outset the final price and quantity. Nor did any government agency have to specify who would increase production and who would decrease consumption.

Some firms responded to the signals for "more output" by increasing production, and they kept on increasing production until the signals got weaker and weaker and finally disappeared. Some buyers withdrew from the market when they thought prices were too high, and perhaps they re-entered gradually, when they wanted to, as prices became "more reasonable." Households and firms responding to market signals, not government bureaucrats issuing orders, "decided" who would increase production and who would limit consumption. No one was forced to do something against his or her best judgment. Voluntary responses collectively produced the end result.

Consider an example. Suppose that 10,000 families from neighboring areas decide that at existing prices they all want to move into single-family houses in the hills of Berkeley, California, overlooking San Francisco Bay. However, that beautiful residential area is already heavily populated. There are at most (say) 1,000 vacant houses or building sites. Obviously, not all of the present and potential residents can live there. Which ones will be able to do so, and which ones will be disappointed?

The market system makes the allocation in the following way. The first impact of the great increase in demand would be a sharp rise in the asking prices of houses in the Berkeley hills. This would persuade some Berkeley residents, who previously had not intended to move, to sell their houses and move to other areas. The same rises in price would discourage many who had hoped to move into the Berkeley hills. The rising prices will also lead some owners of vacant lots to sell or develop them.

One way or the other—by reducing quantity demanded and by encouraging an increase in quantity supplied—the market will make the allocation. Of the 10,000 families who originally wanted to move in, 3,000 may end up living there, while 2,500 old residents move away and 500 of the vacant houses or lots become occupied. Which 3,000 moved in? Those who valued it the most. Which 2,500 moved out? Those who valued the extra money more than the privilege of staying in Berkeley. The market has sorted them out without anyone's having to issue orders ("you go, you stay")

and without the need for a court or a board to hear appeals from those who object to the orders.

Of course it is not *necessary* to rely on the market system to achieve coordination. Had prices not been free to rise, some other system for allocating supply would have been needed. Suppose prices had been frozen by law in order to "keep Berkeley housing within the reach of the ordinary family." There would have been dozens of applicants for any house that became available. The sellers would then have had great power to decide to whom to sell (and thus whom to turn down). They might have exercised their prejudices, or they might have found ways to get a secret payoff.

Alternatively, the Berkeley City Council might set up a Berkeley Authorized Waiting List (BAWL) to determine the order in which people would be permitted to become residents. This would give some public official the duty (or perhaps the privilege) of judging the relative worthiness of potential Berkeleyites and ranking them accordingly. It would also provide opportunities for bribery of those with allocative authority.

The Limited Information Required in Market Coordination

Another important characteristic of the market economy is that it functions with very limited information. As Professor Thomas Schelling put it:

The dairy farmer doesn't need to know how many people eat butter and how far away they are, how many other people raise cows, how many babies drink milk, or whether more money is spent on beer or milk. What he needs to know is the prices of different feeds, the characteristics of different cows, the different prices . . . for milk . . . , the relative cost of hired labor and electrical machinery, and what his net earnings might be if he sold his cows and raised pigs instead.

By responding to such limited information as the costs and prices of what he buys and sells, the dairy farmer helps to make the whole economy fit together, producing more or less what people want and providing it more or less where and when they want it.

It is, of course, an enormous advantage that all

the producers and consumers of a country can collectively make the system operate without any one of them, much less all of them, having to understand how it works. (Such a lack of knowledge becomes a disadvantage when people assess schemes for interfering with or replacing market allocation.)

Coordination Does Not Require Perfect Competition

To say that the price system coordinates is not to imply that it leads to results such as those that perfect competition would produce. It coordinates responses even to prices "rigged" by monopolistic producers or altered by government controls. The signal-response process occurs in a price system even when the "wrong" signals are sent.

When an international cartel of uranium producers decided to reduce production and raise price, they created a current shortage (and a fear of worse future shortages) among those electric utilities that depend on uranium to fuel nuclear power plants. The price of uranium shot up from under $10 per pound to over $40 in less than a year. This enormous price rise greatly increased efforts among producers outside the cartel to find more uranium and to increase their existing production by mining poorer grade ores previously considered too expensive to mine.

The increases in production from these actions slowly began to ease the shortage. On the demand side, high prices and short supplies led some utilities to cancel planned nuclear plants and to delay the construction of others. Such actions implied a long-run substitution of oil or coal for uranium. (Only the fact that the OPEC cartel had also sharply raised the price of oil prevented an even more rapid reversal of the previous trend from oil to nuclear-powered generators.) With the prices of both uranium and oil quadrupling, the demand for coal increased sharply, and its price and production rose. Thus the market mechanism generated adjustments to the relative prices of different fuels, even though some prices were set by cartels rather than by the free-market forces of supply and de-

mand. It also set in motion reactions that place limits on the power of the cartel.

The Case for the Market System

In explaining and defending free-market economies, economists have used two very different approaches. One of these may be characterized as the formal defense. It is based upon showing that a free-market economy consisting of nothing but perfectly competitive industries would lead to an optimal allocation of resources. The case was suggested in Chapter 14, pages 230–233.

The other defense, which may be characterized as informal, or even as intuitive, is at least as old as Adam Smith. It is based on variations and implications of the theme that the market system is an effective coordinator of decentralized decision making. The case is intuitive in the sense that it is not laid out in equations leading to some mathematical, maximizing result. But it does follow from some hard reasoning, and it has been subjected to some searching intellectual probing. What is the nature of this defense of the free market?

The Best Coordinator

Defenders of the market economy argue that compared with the alternatives, the decentralized market system is more flexible and leaves more scope for adaptation at any moment in time and for quicker adjustment to change over time.

If, for example, a scarcity of oil raises its price, one household can elect to leave its heating up high and economize on its driving, while another may wish to do the reverse, and a third may instead give up air conditioning. This flexibility is surely preferable to forcing the same pattern on everyone, say by rationing heating oil and gasoline, regulating permitted temperatures, and limiting air conditioning to days when the temperature exceeds 80° F.

Furthermore, as conditions change over time, prices change, and so decentralized decision makers can react continuously. In contrast government quotas, allocations, and rationing schemes are much more difficult to adjust. The great value of the market is its providing automatic signals *as a situation develops,* so that all of the changes consequent on some major economic change do not have to be anticipated and allowed for by a body of central planners. Millions of adaptations to millions of changes in tens of thousands of markets are required every year, and it would be a Herculean task to anticipate these and plan for them all.

Stimulus to Innovation and Growth

Major changes in resource availabilities will surely occur in all economies over the next decades. New products, new inputs, and new techniques will have to be devised if we are to cope with those vast changes. In a market economy individuals risk their time and money in the hope of earning profits. Almost every possibility tends to be explored by someone. While many fail, some succeed. New products and processes appear continually; others disappear. Some are passing fads or have little impact; often, however, they become items of major significance. The market system works by trial and error to sort them out. The market system allocates resources to what prove to be successful innovations.

In contrast, more centralized systems have to guess which are going to be productive innovations or wanted products. Planned growth may achieve wonders by permitting a massive effort in a chosen direction, but central planners may also guess wrong and put far too many eggs in the wrong basket or reject as unpromising something that will turn out to be vital.

Prices Tend Toward the Level of Costs

A market system tends to drive prices toward the average total costs of production. When markets are close to competitive this occurs very quickly and completely; but even where there is substantial market power it occurs as new products and new producers respond to the lure of profits and their output drives prices down toward the costs of production.

Whenever private costs to firms reflect social costs to society, there is an advantage in having relative prices reflect relative costs because market choices are then made in the light of social opportunity costs. Firms will not choose methods that use more valuable resources over methods that use less valuable resources. Households will choose commodities that use more valuable resources to produce over commodities that use less valuable ones only when they value the chosen commodities correspondingly more at the margin.

Having relative prices reflect relative costs tends to be efficient in that it encourages both producers and consumers to use the nation's resources to achieve what we have called allocative efficiency.

Self-Correction of Disequilibrium

The economic system is continually thrown out of equilibrium by change. If in this situation the economy does not "pursue" equilibrium, there will be little comfort in saying that if only it reached equilibrium, things would be bright indeed. (We all know someone who would have been a great surgeon if only he or she had gone to medical school.)

An important characteristic of the price system is its ability to set in motion forces that tend to correct disequilibrium.

To review the advantages of the price system in this respect, imagine operating without a market mechanism. Suppose that planning boards make all market decisions. The Board in Control of Women's Clothing hears that pantsuits are all the rage in neighboring countries. It orders a certain proportion of clothing factories to make pantsuits instead of the traditional women's skirt. Conceivably the quantities of pantsuits and skirts produced could be just right, given shoppers' preferences. But what if the board misguessed, producing too many skirts and not enough pantsuits? Long lines would appear at pantsuit counters while mountains of unsold skirts piled up. Once the board saw the lines for pantsuits, it could order a change in quantities produced. Meanwhile, it could store the extra skirts for another season—or ship them to a country with different tastes.

Such a system can correct an initial mistake, but it may prove inefficient in doing so. It may use a lot of resources in planning and administration that could instead be used to produce commodities. Further, many consumers may be greatly inconvenienced if the board is slow to correct its error. In such a system the members of the board may have no incentive to admit and correct a mistake quickly. Indeed, if the authorities do not like pantsuits, the board may get credit for having stopped that craze before it went too far!

In contrast, suppose that in a market system a similar misestimation of the demand for pantsuits and skirts was made by the women's clothing industry. Lines would develop at pantsuit counters, and inventories of skirts would accumulate. Stores would raise pantsuit prices and run skirt sales. Pantsuit manufacturers could earn windfall profits by raising prices and running extra shifts to increase production. Some skirt producers would be motivated to shift production quickly to pantsuits and to make skirts more attractive to buyers by cutting prices. Unlike the planning board, the producers in a market system would be motivated to correct their initial mistakes as quickly as possible. Those slowest to adjust would lose the most money and might even be forced out of business.

Impersonal Decision Making and the Absence of Coercion

Another important part of the case for a market economy is that it tends to decentralize power and thus requires less coercion of individuals than does any other type of economy. Of course, while markets tend to diffuse power, they do not do so completely; for example large firms and large unions clearly do have and do exercise substantial economic power.

While the market power of large corporations and unions is not negligible, it tends to be constrained both by the competition of other large entities and by the emergence of new products and firms. This is the process of *creative destruction* described by Joseph Schumpeter. (See pages 299–300.) In any case, say defenders of the free market,

even such aggregations of private power are far less substantial than government power. Governmental power must be exercised if markets are not allowed to allocate people to jobs and commodities to consumers. Not only will such decisions be regarded as arbitrary by those who do not like them, but the power surely creates major opportunities for bribery, corruption, and allocation according to the tastes of the central administrators. If at the going prices and wages there are not enough apartments or coveted jobs to go around, the bureaucrat can allocate some to those who pay the largest bribe, some to those with religious beliefs, hairstyles, or political views that he likes, and only the rest to those whose names come up on the waiting list.

Qualifications to the Case for the Free Market

The case *for* the market system has a strong intuitive appeal. Many nineteenth century economists advocated a policy of **laissez faire**: government should not interfere with the operation of markets. They did so because they believed the price system actually achieved all of the beneficial results we have just reviewed.

Each of the virtues of market systems that we have examined *may* occur; that does not mean that each *does* occur in every free-market situation. Consider a few counter arguments. The price system coordinates responses, but this system has not proven to be the only possible, or necessarily the best one for regulating an economy. The assertion that it is the *best* coordinator is not one that can be proven, and some disagree. Nor has rapid innovation and growth been limited to free-market economies, as will be seen in Part Eleven.

Moreover, to the extent that the prices and the costs that are closely related are not the prices and costs that lead to allocative efficiency, either because of monopoly elements or because of some other form of "market failure," the adjustments that the self-adjusting market system achieves may not be anywhere near being efficient.

Finally, and to many critics of free-market economies most important, a free-market economy distributes output as well as produces it. There are many very different possible allocations of resources. The actual distribution of income of a freely functioning market system reflects its past as well as current contributions to output. Executives and their children exert more influence on market allocations than do taxi drivers and their children. Even if a market system "succeeds" in allocating resources quickly, impersonally, and efficiently, but distributes income in a way that the majority consider highly unfair or unjust, the members of the society are unlikely to be satisfied with market allocation.

The supporters of laissez faire focused on the virtues that a market system might achieve and neglected or played down its limitations. The more important these limitations are—in other words, the greater the actual or perceived failures of the market system—the greater will be the incentive to reduce the reliance placed upon it.

THE CASE FOR INTERVENTION

The United States does not have a laissez faire economy. What has led a majority of Americans to believe that a pure private enterprise system is not the best of all possible worlds? What has led them to lessen their reliance on the unrestricted workings of the free market and, in many cases, to impose regulations on markets or to substitute collective action for individual action? What leads many Americans today to question whether we have gone far enough—or too far—away from free markets?

Whenever market performance is judged to be faulty, it is the practice to speak of **market failure.** The word *failure* in this context probably conveys the wrong impression.

Market failure does not mean that nothing good has happened, only that the *best attainable outcome* has not been achieved.

As a result of market failure, many people believe it desirable to modify, restructure, complement, or supplement the unrestricted workings of the market. There are several major sources of dissatisfaction with market allocation and distribution, and it is important to understand how they arise. There are two somewhat different senses in which the phrase is used. One is the failure of the market system to achieve efficiency in the allocation of society's resources, the other is its failure to serve social goals other than efficiency, such as a different distribution of income or the preservation of value systems. We shall discuss each.

Externalities As a Source of Inefficiency

Cost, as economists define it, concerns the value of resources used up in the process of production. According to the opportunity cost principle, value is the benefit the resources would produce in their best alternative use. But who decides what resources are used and what is their opportunity cost? When a timber company buys a forest, it perhaps regards the alternative to cutting the trees this year as cutting them next year or five years hence. But citizens in the area may value the forest as a nature sanctuary or a recreation area. The firm values the forest for the trees; the local residents may value the trees for the forest. The two values need not be the same.

These differences in viewpoint lead to the important distinction between private cost and social cost.

Private cost measures the value of the best alternative uses of the resources available to the producer.

As we noted in Chapter 11, private cost is usually measured by the market price of the resources that the firm uses.

Social cost measures the value of the best alternative uses of resources that are available to the whole society.

For some resources the best measure of the social cost may be exactly the same as the private cost: the price set by the market may well reflect the value of the resources in their best alternative use. For other resources, as will soon be clear, social cost may differ sharply from private cost.

Discrepancies between private and social cost lead to market failure from the social point of view. The reason is that efficiency requires that prices cover social cost, but private producers, adjusting to private costs, will neglect those elements of social cost that are not included in private costs. When an element of (social) cost is not part of a private firm's profit and loss calculation, it is *external* to its decision making process.

Discrepancies between social and private cost lead to **externalities,** which are the costs or benefits of a transaction that are incurred or received by members of the society but are not taken into account by the parties to the transaction. They are also called **third-party effects** because parties other than the two primary participants in the transaction (the buyer and the seller) are affected. Externalities arise in many different ways, and they may be beneficial or harmful.

Some externalities are beneficial. When I paint my house, I enhance my neighbors' view and the value of their property. When an Einstein or a Rembrandt give the world a discovery or a work of art whose worth is far in excess of what he is paid to produce it, he confers an external benefit. Educating my children may make them better citizens and thus benefit third parties, even if they do not prove to be latter-day Nightingales or Mozarts.

Private producers will produce too little of commodities that generate beneficial externalities because they bear all of the costs, while others reap part of the benefits.

Other externalities are harmful. We consider several examples immediately below.

Private producers will produce too much of commodities that generate harmful externalities because they bear none of the extra costs suffered by others.

Pollution

A major source of differences between private cost and social cost occurs when firms use resources they do not regard as scarce. This is a characteristic of most examples of pollution. When a paper mill produces pulp for the world's newspapers, more people are affected than its suppliers, employees, and customers. Its water-discharged effluent hurts the fishing boats that ply nearby waters, and its smog makes many resort areas less attractive, thereby reducing the tourist revenues that local motel operators and boat renters can expect. The firm neglects these external effects of its actions because its profits are not affected by them while they are affected by how much paper it produces.

Examples have become all too familiar as a result of the expansion of activities of the Environmental Protection Agency (EPA) in the decades of the 1960s and 1970s and the cutback in its activities under the Reagan administration. Dumping of hazardous wastes, air pollution, and water pollution all may occur both as a result of calculated decisions as to what and how to produce or consume, and as a result of private producers taking risks that prove to inflict injury on others. Even an apparently fortuitous oil blowout or the breakup of a tanker, which is desired by no one, may be caused by a private firm's insufficient avoidance of the risk since it bears only part of the costs.

Common-Property Resources

The world's oceans once teemed with fish, but today a world-wide fish shortage is upon us. There seems to be no doubt that overfishing has caused the problem. How could this happen?

Fish are one example of what is called a **common-property resource.** No one owns the oceans' fish until they are caught. The world's international fishing grounds are common property for all fishermen. If by taking more fish one fisherman reduces the catch of other fishermen, he does not count this as a cost, but it is a cost to society.

Assume, as is true of most fishing grounds, that each additional boat that fishes the area adds less than each previous boat (declining marginal product) and also that each additional boat lowers the catch of each other boat (declining average product). A social planner adding boats to the fishing ground would go on increasing the size of the fleet until the value of the marginal product (the value of the net *addition* to the total catch) just equaled the cost of operating the marginal boat. But the free market will not produce that result. Private fishermen will go on entering the area as long as they can show a profit; that is, as long as the value of *their own catch* at least covers their cost of operation. Thus private boats will be added to the fleet until the value of the *average product* per boat has been driven down to the average cost of operating a fishing boat. Because average product is greater than marginal product when average product is declining, the quantity of resources devoted to the activity will be larger than if the value of the marginal product were driven down to the cost of operating the last boat. The free market thus leads to overexploitation of a common-property resource.

Congestion

Collisions between private planes and commercial airliners are headline news when they occur. They cannot occur unless *both* planes are in the air; this is what creates the externality. Suppose that the probability of a midair plane crash is roughly proportional to the number of planes in the air. Suppose too that I have the choice of flying from Phoenix to Los Angeles in my own plane or on a commercial airliner that has 100 of its 150 seats filled. In choosing to fly by myself, I decide that the slight extra risk to me of a midair collision is more than balanced by the fun or convenience of my own plane.

What I have neglected is the social cost of my action: the increased risk for every other person in the air on my route of flight that results from one more plane in the air. Since I do not consider other travelers' increased risk, my private decision may have been the wrong social decision.

Neglect of Future Consequences of Present Actions

When private producers ignore or undervalue future effects on others, they neglect an externality. A business facing bankruptcy tomorrow may be motivated to cheat on safety standards in order to cut costs today, even if it would hurt the firm's reputation in the long term and impose heavy future costs on others.

A less callous example concerns taking actions without finding out whether there are as-yet-unknown adverse externalities. One dramatic example of the neglect of future effects concerns DDT. In 1948 the Swiss chemist Paul Mueller won the Nobel prize for his discovery of its extraordinary value as a pesticide. Gradually, however, it was confirmed that DDT did more than kill unwanted insects. Once sprayed, the chemical did not break down for years. It entered the food chain and worked its way up from insects to birds and fish, to small mammals, and to larger and larger birds and mammals, including human beings. Arctic penguins, though thousands of miles from any sprayed areas, have measurable amounts of DDT in their bodies. DDT has thinned the egg shells of large birds to the point where breakage threatens many species, among them the peregrine falcon, the osprey, and the eagle. In 1962 Rachel Carson labeled DDT an "elixir of death," and by 1972 its use was banned in the United States.

While unavoidable ignorance of the future can never be described as market failure, unwillingness to determine whether there will be future adverse effects may be a form of market failure.

Externalities, whether adverse or beneficial, make privately efficient market results socially inefficient because they lead to the wrong allocation of resources from the societal point of view.

Market Imperfections and Impediments As a Source of Inefficiency

The efficiency of the price system depends on firms and households receiving and responding to the signals provided by prices, costs, and windfall profits. Forces that seriously change these signals or distort or prevent the required response to them may cause a market to fail to perform efficiently. Consider a few examples.

Moral Hazard, Adverse Selection, and Other Informational Asymmetries

Moral hazard arises when nonsymmetric knowledge leads to socially uneconomic behavior. For example suppose because a person has ample fire insurance he does not take reasonable precautions against fire; or suppose because of the availability of unemployment insurance he refuses to accept a job he would otherwise have taken. In each of these cases the individual has the special knowledge that he can afford to take certain actions that impose unexpected costs on those who provide the insurance, but the insurers cannot identify him as the person taking unintended advantage of the system. The socially valid purpose of insurance is to permit people to share given risks, not to increase the size of the aggregate risk. But in these two examples the behavior described did increase the risk and thus the social cost.

Closely related to moral hazard, though somewhat different, is the problem of **adverse selection.** A person suffering a heart attack may immediately seek to increase his life insurance coverage by purchasing as much additional coverage as possible without medical examination. People taking out insurance almost always know more about themselves as individual insurance risks than do their insurance companies. The company can try to limit the variation in risk by setting up broad categories based on variables, such as age and occupation, over which actuarial risk is known to vary. The rate charged is then different across categories based on the average risk in the category. But there must always be much variability of risk *within* any one category. Those who know they are well above average risk within their category are offered a bargain and will be led to take out more car, health, life, or fire insurance than they otherwise would. Someone who knows she is a low risk pays more than her own risk really warrants and is motivated to take out less insurance than she otherwise would.

What of the person who decides to commit suicide and buys life insurance the day before? This involves such serious adverse selection that most insurance companies guard against it by writing policies that do not pay off for suicide within six months or a year after purchase. If, however, a person with suicidal tendencies and with life insurance is more likely to commit suicide since he knows that his family will be financially secure, the behavior would involve moral hazard and is not easily guarded against.

More generally, any time either party to a transaction is ignorant, or is deceived by claims of the other party, market results will tend to be affected, and such changes may lead to inefficiency. Economically (but not legally) it is but a small step from these consequences of asymmetric knowledge to outright fraud. The arsonist who buys fire insurance before setting his fire or the businessman with fire insurance who decides a fire is preferable to bankruptcy are extreme examples of adverse selection and moral hazard.

Informational asymmetries are involved in many other situations. For example, the apparent over-discounting of the prices of used cars because of the buyer's risk of acquiring a "lemon" is a case of asymmetric information affecting behavior. See the discussion of this problem on pages 150–151.

Principal-Agent Issues

If profits are the spur to efficient performance, it is clear that when a firm's managers choose not to pursue the *firm's* profits they impede the system's workings. A manager or a salesman may incur unnecessary costs because the activities entailing these costs provide perquisites to the employee. On a small scale this occurs whenever a purchasing agent is swayed by the Christmas present a salesman gives him, or when a car renter is swayed to hire a more expensive car by the premium *he* will receive while his employer pays the bill. More serious are cases where managers regularly pursue their own goals or perquisites at the expense of minimizing the costs of production. Most serious yet are outright sellouts of company interests or secrets to other firms in return for personal rewards.

Barriers to Mobility

Another kind of market impediment is factor immobility. If increases in a factor's pay do not lead to increases in supply (for any of the reasons discussed in Chapters 21 and 23), the market will fail to reallocate resources promptly in response to changing demands. Monopoly power creates market imperfections by preventing enough resources from moving in response to the market signals of high profits. In this case, barriers to entry rather than factor immobility frustrate the flow of resources.

Collective Consumption Goods

Certain goods and services, if they provide benefits to anyone, necessarily provide them to a large group of people. Such goods are called **collective consumption goods.** National defense is the prime example of a collective consumption good. An adequate defense establishment protects everyone in the country whether they want it or not, and there is no market where you can buy more of it and your neighbor less. The quantity of national defense provided must be decided collectively. Other examples of collective consumption goods include the beautification of a city, a levee to protect a city from a flood, and a hurricane-warning system. In general, market systems cannot compel payment for a collective consumption good since there is no way to prevent a person from receiving the services of the good if he or she refuses to pay for it. Governments, by virtue of their power to tax, can provide the services and collect from everyone.

Excessive or Prohibitive Transactions Costs

The costs incurred in negotiating and completing a transaction, such as the costs of billing or the bad-debt cost of those who never pay, are examples of **transactions costs.** They are always present to some degree, and they are a necessary cost of doing business. If buyers cannot be made to pay for the product, the producer will not be motivated to provide it. For a private firm to stay in business, it must be able to recover both production and transactions costs. If transactions costs are higher than they need to be because of imperfections in the private market, some products that it is efficient to produce will not be produced, and the market will have failed. Consider an example.

Could a private entrepreneur provide a road system for Los Angeles, paying for it by collecting tolls? The answer is surely no (at least with today's technology). It would be prohibitively expensive, both in money and in delays, to erect and staff a toll booth at every freeway exit. Thus requiring collection of revenues via tolls would impose a prohibitive transactions cost. The users of a road system may be more than willing to pay the full costs of its construction and maintenance, but without an inexpensive way to make them pay, no private firm can produce the road. The government, collecting revenue by means of a gasoline tax, can do what the private market fails to do. (Whether it can do so without making a different mistake—producing more of the product than users are willing to pay for—is discussed below.)

The warning about technology merits an additional comment. Technology changes rapidly. For example, the electronic metering of road use may make the toll booth unnecessary just as the postage meter has made licking stamps unnecessary. Thus what a private market cannot do today, it may be able to do efficiently tomorrow.

Market imperfections may lead to market failure by preventing firms and households from completing transactions that are required for efficient resource allocation or by causing too much or too little consumption or production of particular goods.

The Distribution of Income As a Source of Government Intervention

An important characteristic of a market economy is that it determines a *distribution* of the total income that it generates. People whose services are in heavy demand relative to supply, such as television anchormen and superior football players, earn large incomes, while people whose services are not in heavy demand relative to supply, such as Ph.D.'s in English and high school graduates without work experience, earn very much less and sometimes nothing.

The distribution of income produced by the market can be looked at in equilibrium or in disequilibrium. In equilibrium, in an efficiently operating free-market economy, similar efforts of work or investment by similar people will tend to be similarly rewarded everywhere in the economy. Of course, dissimilar people will be dissimilarly rewarded. In disequilibrium, windfall profits and losses abound, so that similar people making similar efforts are likely to be very dissimilarly rewarded. People in declining industries, areas, and occupations suffer the punishment of windfall losses through no fault of their own. Those in expanding sectors earn the reward of windfall gains through no extra effort of their own. These rewards and punishments of course serve the important function in decentralized decision making of motivating people to adapt. The "advantage" of such a system is that individuals can make their own decisions about how to alter their behavior when market conditions change; the "disadvantage" is that temporary rewards and punishments are dealt out as a result of changes in market conditions that are beyond the control of the individuals affected.

Moreover, even the equilibrium differences may seem unfair. A free-market system rewards certain groups and penalizes others. The workings of the market may be stern, even cruel; consequently society often chooses to intervene, as was discussed in Chapter 23. Should heads of households be forced to bear the full burden of their misfortune if, through no fault of their own, they lose their jobs? Even if they lose their jobs through their own fault, should they and their families have to bear the whole burden, which may include starvation? Should the ill and aged be thrown on the mercy of their families? What if they have no families? Both private charities and a great many government policies are concerned with modifying the distribution of income that results from such things as where

one starts, how able one is, how lucky one is, and how one fares in the free-market world.

Other Bases for Seeking Government Intervention

Just as failure to achieve efficient resource allocation and/or an acceptable distribution of income may lead people to ask government to intervene in the workings of a market economy, so may other things, which may be described as the protection of value systems.

Public Provision May Lead to Different Preferred Goods

Police protection, even justice, might be provided by private market mechanisms. Watchmen, Pinkerton detectives, and bodyguards all provide policelike protection. Privately hired arbitrators, "hired guns," and vigilantes of the Old West represent private ways of obtaining "justice." Yet the members of society may believe that a public police force is *preferable* to a private one and that public justice is *preferable* to justice for hire.

For another example, public schools may be better or worse than private schools, but they are likely to be different, particularly because persons others than parents, teachers, and owners influence their policies. Much of the case for public education rests on the advantages to you of having other people's children educated in a particular kind of environment that is *different* from what a private school would provide. Of course you can debate whether the differences make it better or worse. The market will be said to produce unsatisfactory results by those who believe the public product is better.

Protecting Individuals from the Acts of Others

People can use—even abuse—other people for economic gain in ways that the members of society find offensive. Child labor laws and minimum standards of working conditions are responses to such actions. Yet direct abuse is not the only example of this kind of market failure. In an unhindered free market, the adults in a household would usually decide how much education to buy for their children. Selfish parents might buy no education, while egalitarian parents might buy the same quantity for all their children regardless of their abilities. The members of society may want to interfere in these choices, both to protect the child of the selfish parent and to ensure that some of the scarce educational resources are distributed according to intelligence rather than wealth. All households are forced to provide a minimum of education for their children, and strong inducements are offered—through public universities, scholarships, and other means—for gifted children to consume more education than either they or their parents might voluntarily choose if they had to pay the entire cost themselves.

Paternalism: Protecting Individuals from Themselves

In a significant number of cases, members of society acting through the state seek to protect adult (and presumably responsible) individuals, not against others, but against themselves. Laws prohibiting heroin and other hard drugs and laws prescribing the installation and use of seat belts are intended primarily to protect individuals from their own ignorance or shortsightedness.

Intervention of this kind with the free choices of individuals is called **paternalism.** Whether or not such actions reflect real values of the majority of the society, or whether they simply reflect overbearing governments, there is no doubt that the market will not provide this kind of protection. Buyers do not buy what they do not want, and sellers have no motive to provide it.

The Existence of "Social Obligations"

In a market system if you can pay another person to do things for you, you may do so. If you can persuade someone else to clean your house in return for $25, presumably both parties to the transaction are better off: You would prefer to part with $25 rather than clean the house yourself, and your household help prefers $25 to not cleaning your house. Normally society does not interfere with people's ability to negotiate mutually advantageous contracts.

Most people do not feel this way, however, about activities that are regarded as social obligations. A prime example is military service. At times and places in which military service is compulsory, contracts similar to one between you and your housekeeper could also be negotiated. Some persons faced with the obligation to do military service could no doubt pay enough to persuade others to do their tour of service for them.[2] By exactly the same argument as we used above, we can presume that both parties will be better off if they are allowed to negotiate such a trade. But such contracts are usually prohibited. Why? Because there are values other than those that can be expressed in a market. In times when it is necessary, military service by all healthy males is usually held to be a duty independent of an individual's tastes, wealth, influence, or social position. It is felt that everyone *ought* to do this service, and trades between willing traders are prohibited.

Nor is this the only example. You cannot buy your way out of jury duty, nor legally sell your vote to another, even though in many cases you could find a willing trading partner.

Even if the price system allocated goods and services with complete efficiency, we would not wish to rely solely on the market if members of society have other goals that they wish to serve by the allocation of resources.

RESPONDING TO MARKET FAILURE

While private collective action can sometimes remedy the failures of private individual action (private charities can help the poor; volunteer fire depart-

---

[2] Indeed, during the Civil War a man could avoid the draft by hiring a substitute to serve in his place.

ments can fight fires; insurance companies can guard against adverse selection by more careful classification of clients), by far the most common remedy for market failure is reliance on government intervention.

It is useful to ask several questions about possible government policies designed to correct market failure. First, what tools does the government have? Second, when and how vigorously should the tools be used? Third, under what circumstances is government intervention likely to fail?

The Tools of Microeconomic Policy

The legal power of the government to intervene in the workings of the economy is limited only by the Constitution (as interpreted by the courts) and by the willingness of Congress to pass laws and the executive branch to enforce them. There are numerous ways in which one or another level of government can prevent, alter, complement, or replace the workings of the unrestricted market economy. It is convenient to group these methods into four broad categories:

1. *Public provision.* Goods and services may be publicly provided in addition to or instead of private provision.
2. *Redistribution.* Public expenditures and taxes may be used to provide a distribution of income and output different than that which the private market provides.
3. *Rule making.* Rules and regulations may be adopted to compel, forbid, or specify within acceptable limits the behavior that private decision makers may engage in.
4. *Structuring incentives.* Government may alter market signals to persuade rather than force decision makers to adopt different behavior.

Each of the four methods is frequently used, and each has great capacity to change whatever outcomes the unregulated market would provide. The first two will be discussed in detail in Chapter 25; the remainder of this section concerns the last two, rule making and structuring incentives.

Rule Making

Rules require, limit, or compel certain activities and market actions. It is helpful to distinguish between *proscriptive* and *prescriptive rules*.

Proscriptive Rules

Some regulations are like the Ten Commandments; they tell people and firms what they can and cannot do. Such rules require parents to send their children to school and to have them inoculated against measles and diphtheria. Laws that prohibit gambling and pornography attempt to enforce a particular moral code on the whole society. In Chapter 18 we discussed an important form of policy by prohibition—antitrust policy.

There are many other examples: Children cannot legally be served alcoholic drinks. Prostitution is prohibited in most places, even between a willing buyer and a willing seller. In most states you must buy insurance in case you should do damage with your private motor car. A person who offers goods for sale, including his or her own house, cannot refuse to sell because of a dislike for the customer's color or dress. There are rules against fraudulent advertising and the sale of substandard, adulterated, or poisonous foods.

Such rules only set limits to the decisions that firms and households can make; they do not replace those decisions. But the allowed limits can be changed. An important means of government regulation is to change old rules or add new ones that redefine the boundary between forbidden and permitted behavior.

Prescriptive Rules

Prescriptive rule making substitutes the rule maker's judgment for the firm's or the household's judgment about such things as prices charged, products produced, and methods of production. It tends to restrict private action more than proscriptive regulation does because it replaces private decision making rather than limiting it to an acceptable set of decisions. Regulation of public utilities is an important example of prescriptive regulation (see Chapter 18). But prescriptive regulation goes far beyond the natural monopoly regulation we have discussed.

Federal regulatory commissions have until very recently played the major rule in deciding such matters as who may broadcast and on what frequencies; which airlines may fly which routes; what rates bus lines and pipeline operators may charge for different kinds of services; what prices may be paid for gasoline; how much foreign sugar may be imported into the United States; and how many miles to the gallon the average automobile sold by General Motors in 1985 must deliver. The trend toward deregulation in the 1980s has reduced but not eliminated prescriptive rule making.

Problems with Rule Making

Rule making often appears to be a cheap, simple, and direct way of compelling desirable behavior in the face of market failure. But the simplicity is deceptive. Rules must be enforceable and enforced, and once enforced they must prove effective if they are to achieve the results hoped for by those who made them. These conditions are often difficult and expensive to achieve.

Consider the requirement for the installation of an antipollution device that will meet a certain standard in reducing automobile exhaust emissions. Such a law may be the outcome of congressional debate on pollution control—and having passed the bill, Congress will turn to other things. Yet certain problems must be solved before the rule can achieve its purpose. It may be relatively easy to enforce the law upon manufacturers because they are often few in number. But even with perfect compliance by the manufacturer, the device will not work well unless it is kept in working order by the individual driver. Yet it would be expensive to inspect every vehicle regularly and to force owners to keep the devices at the standard set by law. Even a well-designed rule will work only until those regulated figure out a way to evade its intent while obeying its letter. There will be substantial incentive to find such a loophole, and resources that could be used elsewhere will be devoted to the search—and to counteracting such avoidance or evasion.

Structuring Incentives

Government can change the incentives of households and firms in a great variety of ways. It can fix minimum or maximum prices (as we saw in the discussions of agriculture and rent control in Chapters 7 and 8). It can adjust the tax sytem to offer many exemptions and deductions. Tax deductible mortgage interest and real estate taxes, for example, can make owned housing relatively more attractive than rental housing. Such tax treatment sends the household different signals than those sent by the free market. Scholarships to students to become nurses or teachers may offset barriers to mobility into those occupations. Fines and criminal penalties for violating the rules imposed are another part of the incentive structure.

Internalizing Externalities

An important means of influencing incentives is to change the prices that firms and households pay in such a way as to eliminate externalities. Because externalities are a major source of market failure, much attention has been given to means of inducing decision makers to take them into account. Charging a producing firm for the pollution it causes can motivate the firm to alter its production in a socially desirable way. Procedures that make firms take account of the extra social costs they impose are said to **internalize** the external effects of production. How exactly does this work?

Net social benefit defined. First we need to define terms. The **net private benefit (*NPB*)** of a unit of production is the difference between that unit's contribution to a firm's revenue and its contribution to the firm's cost. In other words, it is the contribution to profit of that unit. If we think of each unit of production as contributing to social welfare (and call that contribution **social benefit**) and to cost (*social cost*, defined on page 434), we can define the difference between social benefit and social cost as **net social benefit (*NSB*)**.

Net social benefit is the key concept in judging efficiency. A unit should be produced if, but only if, its *NSB* is greater than or equal to zero.

To go from *NPB* to *NSB*, we need to add beneficial externalities and subtract adverse externalities. In the following discussion, we consider an adverse externality (such as pollution) so that *NSB* is less than *NPB*.

A graphic example. A private firm responding only to private benefits and costs will produce up to the point at which marginal *NPB* becomes zero. But at that output marginal *NSB*, being less than *NPB*, is necessarily negative: too much has been produced from the social point of view. This market failure can be avoided by the procedure shown in Figure 24-1. Once the firm has been forced to pay for what were previously externalities, the new net private benefit is exactly the same as net social benefit. That is, *NPB* = *NSB*. Thus the firm will be motivated to produce only as long as marginal *NSB* is not negative.

Internalization avoids the market failure caused by externalities.

There are many ways to internalize external costs. Consider two. If the amount of the external cost imposed per unit of output is known, it is possible to impose an **effluent charge,** or pollution tax, that compels the producer to pay a tax on every unit of polluting production. Such a charge might lead the producer to find a way to produce without polluting. Another way to internalize external costs is to give legal standing to private citizens to sue for damages against polluters or to seek court injunctions against polluting activities. The legal action makes it costly for polluters; there will be damage payments if they lose and legal payments win or lose.

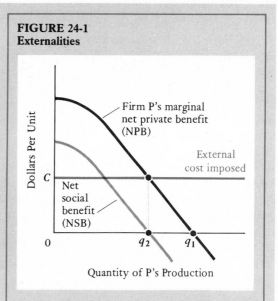

FIGURE 24-1
Externalities

Internalizing an externality can correct market failure. The NPB earned by a private firm, P, is shown by the dark black curve. The firm is motivated to produce all units that make a positive contribution to its profits. Its equilibrium output is q_1 where NPB is zero. This production imposes an external cost of \$C per unit on outsiders, as shown by the colored line. Subtracting this additional social cost from the NPB yields the NSB, the curve shown by the shaded black line. The socially optimal output is q_2, where the NSB just equals zero. At this output NPB is just equal to the external cost imposed on outsiders for each unit of production. At q_2 the outsiders are still having costs inflicted on them by P, but these costs *plus* P's private costs are just equal at the margin to P's profit from production.

Suppose the firm is required to pay an "effluent tax" of \$C per unit. Its NPB now becomes the shaded black line. The externality has been *internalized*, and the profit-maximizing firm is motivated to reduce its output from q_1 to q_2. It does this because any units produced beyond q_2 would now subtract from total profits.

The Costs of Government Intervention

Consider the following argument: (1) The market system is working imperfectly; (2) government has the legal means to improve the situation; (3) therefore the public interest will be served by government intervention.

This appealing argument is deficient because it neglects two important considerations. First, government intervention is costly. For that reason not every market failure is worth correcting; the benefit of the correction must be balanced against the cost of achieving it. Second, government intervention may be imperfect. Just as markets sometimes succeed and sometimes fail, so government intervention sometimes succeeds and sometimes fails. In this section we consider costs of intervention, neglecting government failure; later we consider the added problem imposed by imperfect governmental intervention.

The *benefits* of government intervention are the value of the market failures averted. If pollution imposes external costs of $X, then government action that prevents that amount of pollution will avoid $X of social costs. In other words it provides public benefits of $X.

To evaluate governmental intervention it is necessary to consider the costs of the intervention and compare costs with benefits. In many cases each is large.

Large benefits do not justify government intervention, nor do large costs make it unwise. What matters is the relative size of benefits to costs.

There are several kinds of costs of government intervention. Consider three.

Government Expenditures on Corrective Activities: Internal Costs

When government inspectors visit plants to see whether they are complying with federally imposed standards of health, industrial safety, or environmental protection, they are imposing costs on the American public in the form of the salaries and expenses of the inspectors, among other ways. When regulatory bodies develop rules, hold hearings, write opinions, or have their staff prepare research reports, they are incurring costs. When the antitrust division has 40 lawyers spend 10 years preparing for and engaging in antitrust prosecution of IBM, they are incurring costs. The costs of the judges and clerks and court reporters who hear and transcribe and review the evidence are likewise costs imposed by regulation. All these activities use valuable resources, resources that could have provided very different goods and services.

The aggregate size of federal expenditures for activities that regulate market behavior alone are large indeed: in 1980 they were estimated at about $5 billion. Such costs have grown greatly in the last several decades. They represent one cause of growth in the size of government in the economy. However, they are only the most visible part of the total costs of government regulatory activities.

Costs Imposed on Those Regulated: Direct External Costs

The nature and size of the extra costs borne by firms subject to government intervention are themselves of several kinds, and they vary with the type of regulation. A few examples are worth noting.

Changes in costs of production. Antipollution regulations forced producers not to burn high sulfur coal. As a result, extra fuel costs were imposed on many firms. Such cost increases are directly attributable to regulation.

For 50 years (until the mid 1970s), the prices of automobiles relative to other consumer goods were falling because of continuing technological advances in automobile engineering. Recent federal safety and emission standards have added so much to the cost of producing automobiles that since 1976 Americans have had to adjust to a steadily rising trend in the relative prices of American autos, and automobile workers to the decreases in production that resulted.

Costs of compliance. Government regulation and supervision generate a flood of reporting and related activities that are often summarized in the phrase *red tape*. The number of hours of business time devoted to understanding, reporting, and contesting regulatory provisions is enormous. Affirmative action, occupational safety, and environmental control have greatly increased the size of nonproduction payrolls. The legal costs alone of a major corporation can run into tens of millions of dollars per year. While all of this provides lots of employment for lawyers and economic experts, it is costly because there are other tasks that such professionals could do that would add more to the production of consumer goods and services.

Losses in productivity. Quite apart from the actual expenditures, the regulatory climate may reduce the opportunity or the incentive for experimentation, innovation, and the introduction of new products. Requiring advance government clearance before a new method or product may be introduced (on grounds of potential safety hazards or environmental impact) can eliminate the incentive to develop it. The requirement for advance approval by a regulatory commission before entry is permitted into a regulated industry can discourage potential competitors.

Costs Imposed on Third Parties: Indirect External Costs

It has been estimated that regulatory activities decrease the growth rate of output per person in the United States by about 0.4 percent per year. This much lost growth translates into a big loss in the real living standards that could have been achieved. An extra 0.4 percent growth for 100 years would lead to a 50 percent increase in purchasing power. Such lost purchasing power is an externality of government intervention because the regulators do not take it into account. It may seem paradoxical that government intervention to offset adverse externalities can create new adverse externalities, but it is plain that it can.

Consider an example. Government regulations designed to assure that all new drugs introduced are both effective and safe have the incidental effect of delaying by an average of about nine months the introduction of drugs that are both effective and safe. The benefits of these regulations are related to the unsafe and ineffective drugs kept off the market. But nothing is without cost. Here the cost includes the unavailability for about nine months of all those safe and effective drugs whose introduction was delayed.

The Theory of Government Intervention: Optimal Regulation

Economic principles are useful in making decisions concerning the optimal correction of market failure in a particular case. In order to develop these principles, we shall look at the question of preventing pollution.

There are people who are wholly unconcerned about pollution and regard the current fuss as the troublemaking activities of a pampered generation. There are others who regard every form of pollution as a national scandal and some forms as threatening an imminent crisis of survival. A more balanced view recognizes that "pollution" covers many externalities, ranging from threats to our survival to minor nuisances. Virtually all activity leaves some waste product; to say that all pollution must be removed whatever the cost is to try for the impossible and to ensure a vast commitment of society's scarce resources to many projects that will yield a low social value. But somewhere between trying for the impossible and maintaining a callous indifference to the problem lies a middle ground. Economics helps to define it.

We approach the problem by assuming that government intervention is free from error. Later we shall relax this artificial assumption.

Costless Intervention

We start with the easiest case: Government intervention is costless except for the direct costs imposed by changes in the nature of production. All the government must do is identify the best form of pollution control, determine the right amount of it, and institute the appropriate means of achieving it. How should it proceed?

A first step is to choose the best means of pollution control. Suppose in this case a factory is emitting noxious gases, and it is determined that the best control method is to install filters on the smokestacks.[3]

The next step is to decide how much of the pollution should be eliminated. Suppose the prob-

---

[3] This choice of *means* is not trivial or always easy. Alternatives might include changing the method of production or moving people out of the path of the polluting gases. This first-stage determination among alternative means is of prime importance in achieving the correct solution. A major source of "government failure" is choice of the wrong technique of control.

lem is sulfur dioxide (SO_2) discharge, and that simple recirculation of the gases would reduce the discharge of SO_2 by 50 percent; after that, the cost doubles for each further 10 percent reduction in the remaining SO_2. At most it would be possible to eliminate 99.44 percent of all SO_2, but the cost would be vast. In economic terms the marginal costs of removal rise sharply as the amount of SO_2 eliminated rises from 50 percent to 99.44 percent.

What percentage of the gases should be eliminated? The answer depends on the marginal benefits relative to marginal costs. The marginal benefits of pollution control are the external effects avoided. The optimal amount of prevention will occur where the marginal costs of further prevention equal the marginal benefits. This is illustrated in Figure 24-2.

The optimal amount of pollution prevention will be less than the maximum possible when pollution is costly to prevent. Thus the optimal amount of pollution is not equal to zero.

This important proposition can be generalized: The optimal amount of government intervention to avoid market failure will be lower, the greater are the costs of prevention.

The Effect of Enforcement Costs

Next we add to our consideration the fact that government intervention brings with it enforcement costs—costs to the government, to the firm, and to third parties—of the kinds already discussed. These costs have to be added to the direct costs we have just considered.

Suppose for simplicity that enforcement costs are variable and rise as the level of pollution to be eliminated increases. The marginal costs of enforcement must be added to the marginal direct costs of prevention, thereby shifting upward the marginal costs of prevention. This is shown by the dashed marginal cost curves in Figure 24-2. The addition of such costs will surely decrease the amount of prevention that is optimal. If the costs are large enough, they may even make any prevention uneconomical.

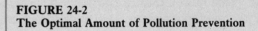

**FIGURE 24-2
The Optimal Amount of Pollution Prevention**

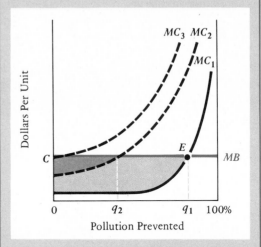

The optimal quantity of pollution prevention occurs where marginal benefits from prevention equal marginal costs of prevention. *MB* represents the marginal benefit achieved by pollution prevention, assumed in this example to be constant at $\$C$ per percentage point. MC_1 represents the marginal costs of preventing pollution; it rises sharply as more and more pollution is eliminated. The optimal level of pollution control is q_1, where $MB = MC_1$. *Notice that not all pollution is eliminated.* For all units up to q_1, marginal benefits from pollution prevention exceed marginal costs. Net benefits are shown by the total shaded area. Any further pollution elimination would add more to costs than to benefits.

If the marginal cost curve shifts upward to MC_2, due, say, to the addition of enforcement costs, the quantity of optimal prevention will decrease to q_2 and the net benefits will be reduced to the darker shaded area. If costs increase to MC_3, the optimal amount of prevention becomes zero.

GOVERNMENT FAILURE

All costs of intervention discussed in the previous section would be present with a government that had perfect foresight in defining goals, an unerring ability to choose the least costly means of achieving them, and intelligent and dedicated officials whose concern was to do those things—and only those things—that achieved the greatest possible efficiency of the economy.

Causes of Government Failure

Government intervention usually falls short of the high standard just described. This is not because bureaucrats are worse than other people, more stupid, more rigid, or more venal. Instead, it is because they are like others, with the usual flaws and virtues. Here are six reasons why government intervention can be *imperfect* (i.e., "fail") in achieving its potential.

Imperfect knowledge or foresight. Regulators may not know enough to set correct standards. For example, natural gas prices may, with the best of intentions, be set too low. The result will be too much quantity demanded and too little quantity supplied, with no automatic correction built in. Or the automobile emission standards prescribed for a particular year may be too demanding, thereby proving unexpectedly expensive to achieve—or too lax, thereby leading to unexpected excessive pollution.

Rigidities. Regulatory rules and allocations are hard to change. Yet technology and economic circumstances change continually. Regulations that at one time protected the public against a natural monopoly may perpetuate an unnecessary monopoly after technological changes have made competition possible. Giving AT&T a monopoly in long-distance communication, and specifying its price structure, made sense when the technology for transmitting messages (use of cable) led to natural monopoly. After a communications satellite had been placed in orbit, there was room for many competitors, but the regulatory commission was not free simply to open up the industry to anyone. Too many people had invested in the telephone industry and accepted limited profits on the expectation of continued regulation.

Inefficient means. Government may fail to choose the least costly means of solving a problem.

It may decree a specific form of antipollution device that proves less effective and more expensive than another. A strict rule that proves all but impossible to enforce may be passed, when a milder one would have achieved higher compliance at lower enforcement cost.

Myopic regulation. Regulation may become too restricted and too narrowly defined because the regulators are forced to specialize. Specialization may lead to expertise in a given area, but the regulators may lack the breadth to relate their area to broader concerns. Officials charged with the responsibility for a healthy *railroad* industry (dating from the time when railroads were the dominant means of transportation) may fail to see that the encouragement of trucking, even at the expense of the railroads, may be necessary for a healthy *transportation* industry.

Political constraints. Political realities may prevent the "right" policy from being adopted, even when it has been clearly identified. This is particularly true in a government such as ours that is based on checks and balances. Suppose a technically perfect tax (or tariff or farm policy) is designed by the experts. It will surely hurt some groups and benefit others. Lobbyists will go to work. The policy is likely to be modified by the cabinet, mutilated by the Senate, rebuilt in a different image by the House, and finally passed by Congress in a form the experts know is inadequate. Although the president may be aware of its flaws, he will sign it into law because it is "better than nothing." This scenario occurs because the political process must respond to political realities. "After all," the official may reason as he yields to the demands of the widget lobby (against his best judgment about the public interest), "if I'm defeated for reelection (or not reappointed), I won't be here to serve the public interest on even more important issues next year." (Next year he will support widgets out of a sense of consistency!)

Decision maker's objectives. Public officials almost always wish to serve the public interest. But they have their careers, their families, and their prejudices as well. This is not unlike the principal-agent problem mentioned as a source of market failure. Public officials' own needs are seldom wholly absent from their consideration of the actions they will take. Similarly, their definition of the public interest is likely to be influenced heavily by their personal views of what policies are best.

A close relationship often exists or develops between the regulators and those they regulate. Many government regulators come from industry and plan to return to it. The broadcasting official who serves five years on the Federal Communications Commission and hopes to become a network vice-president after that term of office may view the networks' case in a not wholly disinterested way. Indeed, regulators may protect an industry in ways that would be quite illegal if done from within the industry.

The Effect of Government Failure on Optimal Intervention

Suppose, for any of the reasons discussed above, the government makes a mistake in regulation. Say the government mistakenly specifies a method of pollution control that is less effective than the best method. This will increase the cost of achieving any given level of prevention. If the government insists on the level of control appropriate to the correct method but requires the incorrect method, it can convert a social gain from control into a social loss. This is illustrated in Figure 24-3.

To generalize from the specific example, it is clear that any form of government failure adds to the costs or decreases the benefits of government intervention. Thus the lower the public's confidence in government's ability to do the right thing, the lower will be its willingness to have government intervention.

Government Intervention in the United States Today

The theoretical principles for determining the optimal amount of intervention that we have just developed are individually accepted by virtually

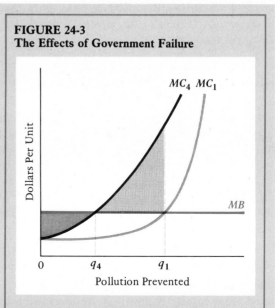

FIGURE 24-3
The Effects of Government Failure

Choice of the wrong method of control will reduce the optimal amount of intervention and may convert the gains from intervention into losses. The *MB* and *MC*$_1$ curves are similiar to those in Figure 24-2. One common form of government failure is to specify the wrong method of intervention. Suppose the government specifies a method of pollution control that leads to the costs shown by *MC*$_4$. This is inefficient because costs at every level of pollution prevention are higher than necessary. Under such a method, the optimal level of prevention falls to q_4 with net benefits shown by the dark shaded area. Government failure reduces the appropriate amount of prevention that is optimal. The government will compound its failure if it insists on the level of prevention q_1 while requiring use of the inefficient method. The cost of every unit of pollution prevented beyond q_4 is in excess of its benefits, as shown by the light shaded area. Indeed the result is worse than no intervention at all (the light shaded area is larger than the dark shaded area). While the best possible government intervention would have produced a net gain, government failure produces a net loss.

everyone. What they add up to, however, is more controversial.

Does government intervene too little or too much in response to market failure? This question reflects one aspect of the ongoing argument about the role of government in the economy. Much of the rhetoric of our concern with ecology urges government intervention against heartless, profit-mad, giant corporations that pervert the environment for their own crass purposes. Such feelings lead to the demand for more—and more stringent—government regulation.

At the same time, the heavy hand of government regulation is seen as contributing greatly to both inflation and recession by burdening private companies with regulations that add to costs and impede innovation and by keeping prices and wages artificially high. Even perfect intervention would be costly, but imperfect intervention makes it much too costly. In this view, the deregulation movement of the 1980s was long overdue.

To what extent can the debate be resolved by economic analysis? Evaluating the costs and the probable effectiveness of government intervention requires a comparison of the unregulated economic system as it is working (not as it might work ideally) with the pattern of government intervention as it is likely to perform (not as it might perform ideally). There is a role for analysis, but it is not likely to resolve all issues.

The Role of Analysis

Economic analysis and measurement can help to eliminate certain misconceptions that cloud and confuse the debate. We have noted one such misconception: the optimal level of pollution (or of any other negative externality) is not, as some urge, zero. Another mistake is to equate market failure with the greed of profit-motivated corporations. Externalities do not require callous, thoughtless, or deliberately deceptive practices of private, profit-seeking firms; they occur whenever the signals to which decision makers respond do not include social as well as private benefits and costs. Such situations are not limited to private firms in a capitalistic system. Cities and nationalized industries pollute just as much as privately owned industries when they are operated in the same way, as they typically are. A third mistake is to think that the profits of a corporation tell something about neglected externalities. It is possible for a

profitable firm (such as Dow Chemical) or an unprofitable one (such as Chrysler) to spend too little on pollution control or on safety, but it is also possible for it to spend too much. The existence of profits provides no clue as to which is the case.

The Role of Ideology

While positive analysis has a role to play, there are several reasons why ideology plays a bigger role in the evaluation process here than in many other areas.

First, measuring the costs of government intervention is difficult, particularly with respect to indirect costs, because some of the trade-offs are inherently uncertain. How important and how unsafe is nuclear power? Does the ban on DDT cause so much malnutrition as to offset the gains in the ecology it brings? What cannot be readily measured can be alleged to be extremely high (or low) by opponents (or supporters) of intervention. The numerous findings by well-known scholars on both sides of each of these subjects has led one economist to the cynical conclusion that "believing is seeing."

Second, classifying the actual pattern of government intervention as successful or not is another matter touched by ideology. Has government safety regulation been (choose one) useful if imperfect, virtually ineffective, or positively perverse? All three views have been expressed and "documented."

A third difficulty arises in defining what constitutes market failure. Does product differentiation represent market success (by giving consumers the variety they want) or failure (by foisting expensive and useless variations on them)?

In the United States in the mid 1980s it seems safe to conclude that confidence in the existing mix of free-market and government regulation is at a relatively low ebb. Not only are specific policy suggestions hotly argued, so is the whole philosophy of intervention. There is as yet no consensus as to what is wrong; the pressures for changes are strong in *both* directions.

SUMMARY

1. The various markets in the economy are coordinated in an unplanned, decentralized way by the price system. Windfall profits play a key role in achieving a coordinated market response. Changes in prices and profits, resulting from emerging scarcities and surpluses, lead decision makers in far-flung markets to make adaptations in response to a change in any one market of the economy. Such responses tend to correct the shortages and surpluses as well as to change the market signals of prices and profits.

2. Important features of free-market coordination include voluntary responses to market signals, the limited information required by any individual, and the fact that coordination will occur under any market structure.

3. There is a widely held "case for the free market" that goes beyond its ability to provide automatic coordination. Many believe its flexibility and adaptability make it the best coordinator and also encourage innovation and growth. The tendency of the market to push relative prices toward the costs of production fosters efficient allocation of resources and self-correction of disequilibrium. Furthermore the market economy tends to be impersonal, to decentralize power, and to require relatively little coercion of individuals.

4. Such alleged virtues of the free market led many nineteenth century economists to believe that government should not interfere in any way with the free-market determination of prices and quantities. There are, however, important qualifications to this case for the free markets, which may be collectively described as market failure.

5. Markets do not always work perfectly. Dissatisfaction with market results often leads to government intervention. We identify four main kinds of reasons: (a) externalities arising from differences between private and social costs and benefits, (b) market imperfections and impediments, (c) dissatisfaction with the free-market distribution of income, and (d) the protection of value systems.

6. Pollution is an example of an externality. An important source of pollution is producers' use of water and air that they do not regard as scarce. Since they do not pay all the costs of using these resources, they are not motivated to avoid the costs. Individual use of common-property resources, congestion, and neglect of future consequences are other sources of externalities.

7. Market imperfections and impediments are anything that prevents the prompt movement of resources in response to market signals; they include informational asymmetries, barriers to mobility, excessive transactions costs, and the existence of collective consumption goods.

8. Changing the distribution of income the free market achieves is one among many values that members of a society may wish to achieve in spite of market forces. These include values placed on public provision for its own sake, on protection of individuals from themselves or from others, and on recognition of social obligations.

9. Microeconomic policy concerns activities of the government that alter the unrestricted workings of the free-market system in order to affect either the allocation of resources among uses or the distribution of income among people. Major tools of microeconomic policy include (a) public provision, (b) redistribution, (c) rule making, and (d) structuring incentives. The first two are the subject of Chapter 25. Both prescriptive and proscriptive rule making occur in a variety of forms. Incentives can be structured in a number of ways including the use of fines, subsidies, taxes, and effluent charges. All are designed to lead private decision makers to internalize externalities or to give weight to nonmarket goals.

10. There are costs as well as benefits of government intervention, and they must be considered in choosing whether, when, and how much intervention is appropriate. Among these costs are the direct costs of government incurred; the costs imposed on those regulated, direct and indirect; and the costs imposed on third parties. These costs are seldom negligible and are often large. In addition to these costs there is the fact that government

intervention may fail; if it does, the costs of intervention may be incurred without the achievable benefits of avoiding market failure being fully realized. The optimal degree of government intervention must consider the magnitude of market failure. It is neither possible nor efficient to correct all market failure; neither is it always efficient to do nothing.

11. An additional deterrent to government intervention is the possibility of "government failure"—that is, imperfect intervention, which may occur in a number of ways. The less effective actual government intervention will be, the lower the optimal level.

12. Just how and where to change the proportions of free-market decision making and government intervention is a subject of continuing economic and political debate. Both analysis and ideology have roles to play.

TOPICS FOR REVIEW

The difference between central planning and market coordination
How the price system coordinates
The role of windfall profits
Differences between private and social valuations
Causes of market failure
Externalities
Internalizing externalities
Net social benefit (*NSB*) and net private benefit (*NPB*)
Benefits and costs of government intervention
Causes of government failure
The optimal amount of pollution

DISCUSSION QUESTIONS

1. Should the free market be allowed to determine the price for the following, or should government intervene? If you distinguish among them, defend your distinctions.
   a. transit fares
   b. heating oil
   c. plastic surgery for victims of fires
   d. garbage collection
   e. postal service to newspapers and magazines
   f. fire protection for churches
   g. ice cream
2. Each of the following activities has known harmful effects: (a) cigarette smoking, (b) driving a car at the national speed limit of 55 mph, (c) private ownership of guns, and (d) drilling for offshore oil. In each case identify whether there is a divergence between social and private costs.
3. Suppose the facts asserted below are true; should they trigger government intervention? If so, what policy alternatives are available?
   a. The Concorde jet is twice as fast, twice as noisy on takeoff and landing, and carries one-third the passengers of jumbo jets.
   b. Hospital costs have been rising at about four times the rate of increase of personal income, and proper treatment of a serious illness has become extraordinarily expensive.
   c. The cost of the average one-family house in Washington, D.C., is now over $160,000, an amount that is out of the reach of most government employees.
   d. Cigarette smoking tends to reduce life expectancy by eight years.
   e. Saccharin in large doses has been found to cause cancer in Canadian mice.
4. Each of the four quotations below is from a careful study of air pollution. Assume each is true. Discuss whether the Clean Air Act ought to be left on the books.
   a. "The air is cleaner today than it was 10 years ago in part because of the Clean Air Act and also because newer plant and equipment use cleaner technology."
   b. "The Clean Air Act may be the most expensive piece of regulatory legislation in history. The most serious costs are opportunity costs reflecting lost production resulting from delays and inefficient production resulting from constraints of scale, operation or location. In addition to opportunity costs, there are administrative and technical costs required to obtain air permits, inflationary impacts on delayed projects and high costs for (control) technology.
   c. "Implementation of air pollution regulations frequently has an adverse impact on economic growth, job formation, and new energy resource development by diverting scarce capital into nonproductive pollution control equipment. This especially hurts small businesses with limited capital resources."
   d. "Ozone, a major air pollutant, is costing the nation losses of $2 billion to $4.5 billion a year in production of corn, wheat, soybeans, and peanuts."
5. Consider the possible beneficial and adverse effects of each of the following forms of government interference.
   a. charging motorists a tax for driving in the downtown

areas of large cities—and using the revenues to provide peripheral parking and shuttle buses

b. prohibiting doctors from purchasing malpractice insurance

c. mandating no-fault auto insurance, in which the car owner's insurance company is responsible for damage to his or her vehicle no matter who causes the accident

d. requiring automobile manufacturers to warrantee the tires on cars they sell instead of (as at present) having the tire manufacturer be the warrantor

6. Consider the following (alleged) facts about pollution control and indicate what, if any, influence they might have on policy determination.

a. In 1982 the cost of meeting federal pollution requirements was $61 per person.

b. More than a third of the world's known oil supplies lie under the ocean floor, and there is no known blowout-proof method of recovery.

c. Sulfur removal requirements and strip mining regulations have led to the tripling of the cost of a ton of coal used in electrical generation.

d. Every million dollars spent on pollution control creates 67 new jobs in the economy.

7. The president of Goodyear Tire and Rubber Company complained that government regulation had imposed $30 million per year in "unproductive costs" on his company. These costs of compliance were broken down:

a. environmental regulation, $17 million

b. occupational safety and health, $7 million

c. motor vehicle safety, $3 million

d. personnel and administration, $3 million

How would one determine whether these costs were "productive" or "unproductive"?

8. During a Pittsburgh air pollution alert a newspaper reporter interviewed a 69-year-old retired steelworker. He said: "I've got a heart condition myself, and I know that when I look out the window and see the air like it was this morning, I've got to stay inside. Yesterday, I tried to drive to the store, and I couldn't see 50 feet ahead of me, it was so thick, so I just came home. I remember that when I was young, we never thought about pollution. Everybody was working, and everybody had money, and the smokestacks were smoking, and the air was dirty, and we were all happy. I think the best air we ever had in Pittsburgh was during the Depression. That's when nobody was working." Comment on this statement in terms of the issues discussed in this chapter.

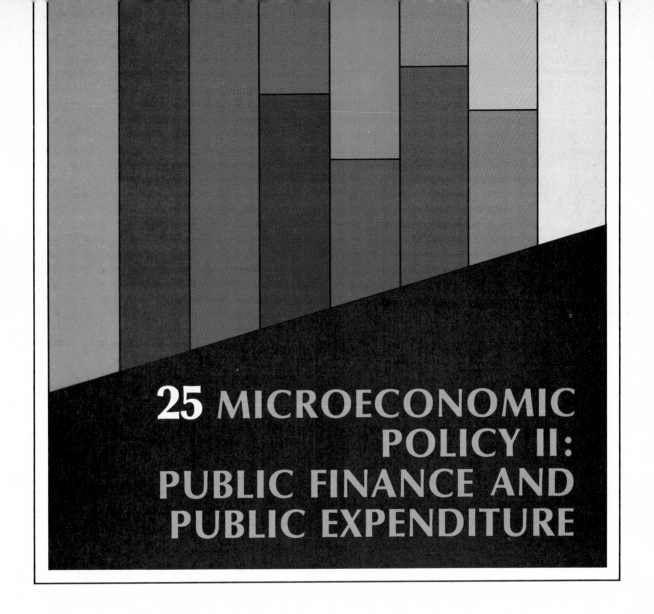

25 MICROECONOMIC POLICY II: PUBLIC FINANCE AND PUBLIC EXPENDITURE

All governments spend money, and they must raise revenue in order to do so. The American federal government is no exception. To do what the Constitution mandates, it must spend and tax. But government spending and government taxation today go far beyond the minimum required to provide such essentials as a system of justice and protection against foreign enemies. Spending and taxing are also key tools of both macroeconomic and microeconomic policy.

In this chapter we look at spending and taxing as tools of microeconomic policy. Government expenditure and government taxation inescapably affect both the allocation of resources and the distribution of income—sometimes intentionally, sometimes not.

There is no simple and sharp functional distinction between expenditure and tax policies. One way to deal with polluted rivers, for example, is by public expenditure to clean them up. An alterna-

TABLE 25–1 GOVERNMENT TAX RECEIPTS, BY SOURCE

Kind of tax	Federal		State		Local		All government	
	Billions of dollars	Percentage	Billions of dollars	Percentage	Billions of dollars	Percentage	Billions of dollars	Percentage
Personal income	217.8	49	32.6	20	4.3	5	254.7	37
Corporate income and related	65.7	15	12.1	8	0.0	0	77.8	11
Social security and related	127.2	28	35.4	22	3.7	4	166.3	24
Subtotal (income and related)	410.7	92	80.1	50	8.0	9	498.8	72
Excise and sales	26.7	6	63.7	40	10.6	13	101.0	15
Property	0.0	0	2.5	1	62.4	74	64.9	9
All others	8.7	2	14.0	9	3.3	4	26.0	4
Total	446.1	100	160.3	100	84.3	100	690.7	100

Source: Facts and Figures on Government Finance, 21st Biennial Edition (New York: Tax Foundation, 1981).

The federal government places major reliance on income taxes; state governments on income, excise and sales taxes and local governments on property taxes. Different levels of government rely on different kinds of taxes. The most important are highlighted by the percentages printed in white. The data are for fiscal 1979.

tive is to use taxes to penalize pollution or to give tax concessions to firms that install pollution-abating devices. Tax concessions that seek to induce market responses are now called **tax expenditures**—that is, sacrifices of revenue by the taxing authorities that are designed to achieve purposes that the government believes are desirable.

In this chapter we are concerned both with the overall impact of public expenditure and taxation on microeconomic decisions and with the deliberate use of these tools for effecting such decisions.

TAXATION AS A TOOL OF MICRO POLICY

There is a bewildering array of taxes, some highly visible (such as sales taxes and income taxes) and others all but invisible to the consumer because they are imposed on raw materials producers or manufacturers at an early stage. People are taxed on what they earn, on what they spend, and on what they own. Firms are taxed as well as house-holds. And taxes are not only numerous, they take a big bite. Aggregate taxes amount to roughly one-third of the total value of goods and services produced in the United States each year. The diversity and yield of various taxes are shown in Table 25-1.

Taxes and the Distribution of Income

A government that taxes the rich and exempts the poor is redistributing income. How much redistribution is achieved by U.S. taxes today?

Progressivity

Rhetoric about income distribution and tax policy often invokes the important but hard to define concepts of "equity" and "equality." Equity—fairness—is a normative concept; what one group thinks is fair may seem outrageous to another. But equality is a straightforward concept—or is it?

To tax people equally might mean several things. It might mean that each person should pay the same tax, which would be very hard on the unemployed worker and very easy on Reggie Jackson. It might mean that each should pay the same proportion of his or her income, say a flat 17 percent, whether rich or poor, living alone or supporting eight children, healthy or suffering from a disease that requires heavy use of expensive drugs. It might mean that each should pay an amount of tax such that everybody's income after taxes is the same—which would remove any incentive to earn above average income. Or it might mean none of these things.

People may not agree on what redistributions are fair, but they can agree on what redistributions actually occur. To get precise measurements of what happens, the distributional effects of taxes are usually discussed using the concept of **progressivity of taxation,** the ratio of taxes to income at different levels of income.

A **proportional tax** takes amounts of money from people in direct proportion to their income.

A **regressive tax** takes a larger percentage of income from people, the lower their income.

A **progressive tax** takes a larger percentage of income from people, the larger their income.

A tax system is said to be progressive if it decreases the inequality of income distribution and to be regressive if it increases the inequality.

It is easier to assess the progressivity or regressivity of particular taxes than of the tax system as a whole.

The Regressivity of Sales, Excise, and Consumption Taxes

If two families each spend the same proportion of their income on a certain commodity that is subject to a sales or an excise tax, the tax will be proportional in its effects on them. If the tax is on a commodity, such as food, that takes a larger proportion of the income of lower-income families, it will be regressive; if it is on a commodity such as jewelry, where the rich spend a larger proportion of their income than the poor, it will be progressive.

Commodities with inelastic demands provide easy sources of revenue. In many countries commodities such as tobacco, alcohol, and gasoline are singled out for very high rates of taxation. But these commodities usually account for a much greater proportion of the expenditure of lower-income than higher-income groups, and taxes on them are thus regressive.

The sales and excise taxes used in the United States today are as a whole regressive.

Two types of consumption taxes have been widely discussed recently. One, called a *value-added tax,* is widely used in Western Europe. It is nothing more than a generalized retail sales tax, collected as goods move through the production and distribution systems rather than at the retail sales stage. It shares the regressivity of the sales tax.

Another consumption tax is an *expenditure tax,* which is levied on the total value of income minus saving. Compared with an income tax it is regressive because the rich save a larger fraction of their income than do the poor.

The Regressivity of Property Taxes

The progressivity of the property tax has been studied extensively. It is well known that the rich live in more expensive houses than the poor, but all that this establishes is that the rich tend to pay more dollars in property tax than do the poor. Because the rich tend to live in different communities than the poor and thus pay taxes at different rates, and because they tend to spend a different proportion of their income for housing, the question of the progressivity or regressivity of the property tax is difficult and controversial. Most studies have shown that the proportion of income spent for housing tends to decrease with income. Many but not all public finance experts believe that the property tax tends to be regressive in its overall effect.

The Progressivity of Personal Income Taxes

The personal tax rate is itself a function of taxable income, and it is useful to distinguish between two different rates. The **average tax rate** paid by

TABLE 25-2 **THE RATE STRUCTURE OF THE FEDERAL INCOME TAX, 1982**

(1) Taxable income after deductions and exemptions	(2) Personal income tax	(3) Average tax rate, percentage (2) ÷ (1)	(4) Marginal tax rate, percentage (tax on extra dollar)
$ 2,400	$ 0	0	0
3,400	0	0	12
6,000	326	5.4	14
10,000	934	9.3	16
15,000	1,828	12.2	19
20,000	2,899	14.5	22
30,000	5,615	18.7	33
50,000	13,305	26.6	44
75,000	25,055	33.4	49
100,000	37,449	37.4	50
150,000	62,449	41.6	50
200,000	87,449	43.7	50
250,000	112,449	45.0	50
1,000,000	487,449	48.7	50
10,000,000	4,987,449	49.9	50

Both marginal and average tax rates rise with income; thus the tax is progressive in structure. These data give the amount of federal tax to be paid at different income levels by a married couple in 1982. The marginal tax rate rises with income and reaches 50 percent at $100,000. However, these rates are based on taxable income, not total income received. Because of a variety of deductions and exemptions, the effective average tax rates on income received are much lower than those shown in column 3.

an individual or by a couple is their income tax divided by total income. The **marginal tax rate** is the amount of tax the taxpayer would pay on an additional dollar of income. Table 25-2 shows the applicable rates on federal income tax in 1982.

In structure, the federal personal income tax is quite progressive because the average rate rises steadily with income. However, because of the special definitions given to net income by the tax laws, the overall effect of the federal income tax is actually less progressive than Table 25-2 suggests. To arrive at taxable income, total income is modified by certain exemptions from income, by capital

gains provisions, and by permitted deductions from gross income.

Despite modifications, the federal income tax is progressive in effect as well as in structure.

The Unknown Progressivity of Corporate Income Tax

The federal corporate income tax is, for practical purposes, a flat-rate tax of 46 percent of profits as defined by the taxing authorities. It is difficult to determine its effects on income distribution, for there is great controversy over the extent to which it is "shifted" to consumers.[1] So far as the tax falls on stockholders, they as a group tend to be wealthier than individuals who do not own stock, and there is thus a tendency toward progressivity. But within the stockholder group, lower-income stockholders bear a disproportionate share of the tax relative to wealthy stockholders. If a dollar were paid out in dividends instead of taxes, rich stockholders would keep a much smaller share than poorer stockholders because of their high marginal personal tax rates.

The Progressivity of the Tax System

To assess the way in which the whole tax system, as distinct from any one tax, affects income distribution is more difficult. One aspect concerns the mix of taxes of different kinds. Federal taxes (chiefly income taxes) tend to be somewhat progressive. State and local authorities rely heavily on property and sales taxes and thus have tax systems that are regressive.

The matter of assessing progressivity is even more complex than this. Is progressivity defined for the individual or for the family? When a couple with two children pays the same tax as a childless couple with the same income, is this proportional or regressive taxation? If the *family* is the relevant unit, it is proportional taxation. If the *person* is the relevant unit, equal tax rates on families of different sizes having the same income would be regres-

---

[1] The question of tax incidence—that is, who really pays a tax imposed on any one group—is discussed later in this chapter.

sive. As it is, a household with children pays less *income* tax than a household without children but with the same income. (This does not mean, as childless people often assume, that the household with children pays less total taxes. For other taxes, such as sales taxes, tend to fall more heavily on large families than on small ones.)

The difficulty of determining progressivity is increased by the fact that income from different sources is taxed at different rates. For example, in the federal individual tax, income from royalties on oil wells is taxed more lightly than income from royalties on books; profits from sales of assets (called *capital gains*) are taxed more lightly than wages and salaries; and some bond interest is tax exempt while most interest income is taxed. To evaluate progressivity one needs to know the way in which different levels of income correlate with different sources of income.

The empirical evidence shows that the combined effect of all U.S. taxes, federal, state, and local, is virtually proportional today for families with incomes between $5,000 and $100,000. For families of very low income, the tax structure is regressive.

Can Progressivity Be Increased?

Taxes can be levied on any of three different monetary magnitudes: on assets, on incomes, and on expenditures. Inheritance taxes and gift taxes are taxes on assets; such taxes do not—and cannot—play a large continuing role in the overall revenue picture. Taxes on incomes are important and can be quite progressive. Taxes on expenditures—especially sales and excise taxes—are related to the dollar value of expenditures, not the incomes of those spending the money; they are known to be regressive.

Many observers have argued that to achieve overall proportionality in the tax structure is in itself a significant accomplishment. Some argue that, given the enormous fraction of national income that is taxed away, more progressivity cannot be achieved since we are already forced to tax heavily average and below-average income persons simply to meet revenue requirements.

Substantial progressivity in income taxes is required merely to achieve proportionality in the overall tax pattern.

Whether or not more progressivity is desirable, is more progressivity possible?

Would Increasing Reliance on Income Taxes Increase Progressivity?

It may seem obvious that, since income taxes are progressive, raising income tax rates would surely increase progressivity. Surprisingly, some conservative economists have argued that this is not the case. While a shift to higher tax rates would raise both the average rate and the marginal rate of tax on incomes, it might or might not raise the total amount of revenue actually collected from income taxes. Whether it did would depend on the incentive effects of tax rates.

A graph that relates the government's income tax revenue yield to the level of tax rates has recently gained attention as the **Laffer curve**, named after economist Arthur Laffer whose views were influential within the Reagan administration. Its essential feature is that tax revenues reach a maximum at some rate of taxation well below 100 percent. The general shape of the Laffer curve is a matter of simple logic: at a zero tax rate, no revenue will be collected. Similarly, at a 100 percent tax rate, revenues would again be zero because no one would bother to earn taxable income just to support the government. For some intermediate rates people will both earn income and pay taxes. Government tax revenues will thus reach an upper limit at some rate of taxation below 100 percent. For rates higher than the rate that produces this maximum, every increase in tax rates will lead to a decrease in tax revenues. (See Figure 25-1.)

Just where this maximum occurs—whether with average tax rates of 40 percent or 80 percent or 95 percent—is an important empirical matter. Laffer and others assert that tax policy has already carried progressiveness too far. They believe that by the 1970s the United States had already increased taxes past the point where higher tax rates yielded more

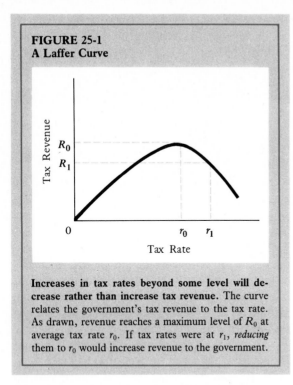

FIGURE 25-1
A Laffer Curve

Increases in tax rates beyond some level will de-crease rather than increase tax revenue. The curve relates the government's tax revenue to the tax rate. As drawn, revenue reaches a maximum level of R_0 at average tax rate r_0. If tax rates were at r_1, *reducing* them to r_0 would increase revenue to the government.

revenue. As a result, they argue, any attempt to increase progressivity by raising income tax rates would be self-defeating. Many others disagree. While they might concede that some countries (such as the United Kingdom) may have reached such a point, they argue that this has happened only because their residents can migrate to countries with lower taxes, such as the United States. They believe that the current U.S. top marginal tax rate of 50 percent and even the top rate of 70 percent that applied in the 1970s are still short of being self-defeating in terms of tax revenue. That is, they believe that Professor Laffer identified a potential rather than an actual problem. The box identifies an early precursor of the Laffer curve.

Increasing Progressivity by Changing the Income Tax Structure

If the government raises income taxes for one group and lowers them for another in a way that leaves the total tax yield constant, the *structure* of

the income tax will have been changed. Much repeated demand for "tax reform" relates to proposed changes in the structure of income taxes. Most economists believe that such changes can be made (whether or not they consider them desirable) and that if they were made, they would increase the progressivity of the total tax system. Here are two important and widely advocated proposals.

The negative income tax (NIT). A tax can be negative if at some level of income the government pays "the taxpayer" instead of the other way around. The so-called **negative income tax** is a policy tool designed to increase progressivity and combat poverty by making taxes negative at very low incomes. Such a tax would extend progressivity to incomes below those where people currently have income tax liability.

There are many versions of NIT proposals; the one described here will illustrate the basic idea. The underlying belief is that a family of four should be allowed a minimum annual income—say, $6,000. The aim is to guarantee this income without eliminating the incentive to become self-supporting. This is done by combining a grant with a tax. At a break-even level—well above the minimum income level guaranteed—the family will neither receive money from the government nor pay any tax. Below this break-even income level the family will be paid by the government (i.e., the family pays a "negative tax"). Above this break-even level it will pay a positive tax. An example based on a grant of $6,000, a break-even level of $12,000, and a marginal tax rate of 50 percent is given in Figure 25-2.[2]

Supporters of the negative income tax believe that it would be a particularly effective tool for reducing poverty. It provides a minimum level of income as a matter of right, not of charity, and it does so without removing the incentive to work of those eligible for payments. Every dollar earned adds to the after-tax income of the family. As a

---

[2] The example is unrealistic in assigning a 50 percent marginal tax at such low levels of income as $12,000. The cost of an NIT would be much higher if it were necessary for political reasons to combine it with a sharply graduated rate structure of the sort shown in Table 25-2.

FIGURE 25-2
The Negative Income Tax

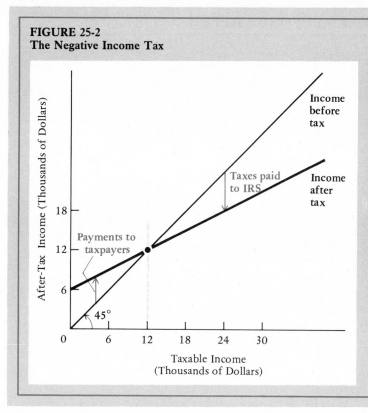

Instead of having a zero income tax up to some level and a positive tax thereafter, there could be a negative tax up to a break-even income and a positive tax above it. The scheme illustrated here combines a notional $6,000 grant to every family, with a 50 percent tax on all income. A family with $12,000 of income breaks even. A family with income below $12,000 is paid by the government. A family with income above $12,000 pays taxes. The heavy black line shows the after-tax income for different levels of taxable income under this particular scheme. The 45° line shows the after-tax income *if* taxes were zero at all levels of income: therefore the vertical distance between it and the heavy black curve shows the payments by or to taxpayers at any level of income under this scheme.

potential replacement for many other relief programs, it promises to avoid the most pressing cases of poverty with much less administrative cost and without the myriad exceptions that are involved in most programs. An incidental advantage is that it removes whatever incentive people might have to migrate to states with better welfare programs, but it does not discourage migration to places where work may be available.

Comprehensive income taxation (CIT). Dr. Joseph Pechman of the Brookings Institution has taken the lead in arguing that it is possible to raise more revenue from the income tax, increase its progressivity, and at the same time *reduce* both average and marginal tax rates! This sounds like magic, but it is a matter of simple arithmetic. The **tax base** is the total amount of taxable income.

Under present definitions taxable income is much less than total income because there are all sorts of deductions and exemptions. If all income were taxed, regardless of source, it would be possible to raise more revenue by applying lower rates to this larger tax base. The idea of **comprehensive income taxation** is to eliminate virtually all the so-called loopholes, the deductions and exemptions that make taxable income less than total income. By eliminating some or all personal deductions, homeowner preferences, special treatment of capital gains, and exemptions for dependents, old age, and blindness, the tax base could be increased by up to 70 percent. It would then be easy to reduce tax *rates* in all income brackets.

Under these schemes it would be possible to achieve substantially more progressivity without increasing anyone's marginal tax rate at all. For

THE LAFFER CURVE 600 YEARS BEFORE LAFFER

In the fourteenth century the Arabic philosopher Ibn Khaldun wrote:

It should be known that at the beginning of the dynasty, taxation yields a large revenue from small assessments. At the end of the dynasty, taxation yields a small revenue from large assessments. . . .

When the dynasty follows the ways of group feeling and (political) superiority, it necessarily has at first a desert attitude. The desert attitude requires kindness, reverence, humility, respect for the property of other people, and disinclination to appropriate it, except in rare instances. Therefore, the individual imposts and assessments, which together constitute the tax revenue, are low. When tax assessments and imposts upon the subjects are low, the latter have the energy and desire to do things. Cultural enterprises grow and increase, because the low taxes bring satisfaction. When cultural enterprises grow, the number of individual imposts and assessments mounts. In consequence, the tax revenue, which is the sum total of (the individual assessments), increases.

When the dynasty continues in power and their rulers follow each other in succession, they become sophisticated. The Bedouin attitude and simplicity lose their significance, and the Bedouin qualities of moderation and restraint disappear.

As a result, the individual imposts and assessments upon the subjects, agricultural laborers, farmers, and all the other taxpayers, increase. Every individual impost and assessment is greatly increased, in order to obtain a higher tax revenue. Customs duties are placed upon articles of commerce. Gradual increases in the amount of assessments succeed each other regularly, in correspondence with the gradual increase in the luxury customs and many needs of the dynasty, and the spending required in connection with them. Eventually, the taxes will weigh heavily upon the subjects and overburden them. Heavy taxes become an obligation and tradition, because the increases took place gradually, and no one knows specifically who increased them or levied them. They lie upon the subjects like an obligation and tradition.

The assessments increase beyond the limits of equity. The result is that the interest of the subjects in cultural enterprises disappears, since when they compare expenditures and taxes with their income and gain and see the little profit they make, they lose all hope. Therefore, many of them refrain from all the activity. The result is that the total tax revenue goes down.

Finally, civilization is destroyed, because the incentive for cultural activity is gone. It is the dynasty that suffers from the situation, because it (is the dynasty that) profits from cultural activity.*

*From the Muqaddimah: An Introduction to History, translated from the Arabic by Franz Rosenthal. Bollingen Series XLIII. Copyright © 1958 and 1967 by Princeton University Press. Reprinted by permission of Princeton University Press.

---

example, imagine a definition of the CIT where comprehensive income is 150 percent of present taxable income. Rates could be left unchanged for high-income taxpayers and greatly reduced for middle- and low-income taxpayers in such amounts as to maintain the same total tax revenue but to increase progressivity.

Alternatively, some rates could be decreased by a little and others by a great deal—as long as the average decrease was one-third. Pechman, considering one specific form of the CIT, concludes:

If unnecessary exclusions, deductions and exemptions were removed from the federal individual income tax, tax rates could be reduced by an average of 22 percent in 1984, while exempting [from any tax whatever] all individuals . . . below the poverty line.

Needless to say, even if everyone's tax *rates* went down under the CIT, not everyone's tax *payments* would do so because the elimination of exclusions, deductions, and exemptions would raise the tax liability of those taxpayers who had utilized them.

What some regard as unfair loopholes may be for others their toehold on economic prosperity.

There are many different versions of the CIT, and they vary in what is included and in the progressivity of the tax rate schedule. Pechman favors using the CIT to increase progressivity. Many supporters of the CIT have precisely the opposite motivation. The least progressive form of the CIT is the so-called *flat-rate plan*, a current version of which would tax all income above $4,000 per family, from any source, at a fixed rate of 17 percent. This would make the personal income tax virtually a proportional tax and would surely make the overall tax system regressive.

Political Barriers to Using Tax Policy to Redistribute Income

While almost everyone agrees our present tax structure is much too complex and in many ways illogical, the calls for fundamental and sweeping tax reform are unlikely to be answered. The purely political barriers to tax reform are formidable. Any single reform is likely to impose large costs on a relatively well-identified group, while the benefits it gives would be more widely diffused.

The 10 people who would each lose a million dollars from a particular tax reform are much more interested in the issue than the 10 million people who would each gain a dollar. The 10, not the 10 million, hire lobbyists and make campaign contributions. Legislators must respond to these pressures if they want long public careers. With *expenditure* programs the political pressures are reversed. The beneficiaries of a program to increase social security payments, provide medical care, or give aid to the cities are much more intensely and immediately involved than the millions of others whose taxes will rise a little bit to pay for it. The 100,000 who would gain a hundred dollars each from a particular expenditure policy are much more likely to be heard than the 10 million whose taxes would rise by a dollar each. (Even when people demand lower taxes, they vote out of office politicians who refuse to provide the services the taxes would make possible.)

Political considerations tend to make redistribution by expenditures more attractive than redistribution by tax reform.

How Much Progressivity Is Desirable?

Suppose increased progressivity could be achieved; would we want it? Many say no.

One obvious objection to tax reform designed to increase progressivity is that not everyone wants more progressivity. A second is that many who do not oppose more progressivity do not want changes that would make it easier for the government to raise more money. Such people fear schemes such as the NIT and the CIT precisely because they do not generate tax revolts. They point to the introduction of "pay as you go" (withholding) taxes in the 1940s. The argument used then to persuade people to accept withholding was that it was more convenient and less painful to have one's employer collect the taxes on income as it was earned than to have to come up with a lump sum on a date such as April 15. But levels of taxation did not remain constant. Opponents of government spending charge that governments discovered they could exploit the system: they kept raising taxes until the original level of pain was suffered all year round.

A third source of opposition to increasing progressivity by means of tax reform is that every aspect of present tax policy was introduced to benefit some group whose members believe they have valid claims to special treatment. Consider some of the "loopholes" that the CIT would reduce or eliminate. Tax deductibility of charitable and educational contributions provide incentives for gifts to churches, universities, and private charities and foundations. Tax-exempt municipal bonds help hard-pressed cities raise money.

Fourth, more progressivity may conflict with what is seen as fair. Much erosion of the tax base has arisen from adjustments made in the name of equity. Special tax treatment of the aged seems fair to many in view of the probable needs by the aged for extensive medical treatment. More favorable tax treatment of families with children than of childless couples seems fair to some on the basis of need, but it seems undesirable to those who think population is already too high.

Finally, the case against tax policy as a means of achieving redistributive goals has some support even among those who favor more redistribution of income from rich to poor. They argue that it is misleading, unnecessary, and poor tactics politically to pay so much attention to *tax* progressivity. After all, how the money is spent is just as important, and often less controversial, than how it is collected. A regressive tax, say a sales tax, may provide funds for increasing welfare payments and thus redistribute income to the poor. Social security taxes are regressive; social security payments are progressive. It is the combined overall effect of the two that is important, and it is easier to get Congress to enact progressive expenditure programs than progressive taxes.

Tax Structure and the Allocation of Resources

The tax system influences the allocation of resources by changing the *relative* prices of different goods and factors and the *relative* profitability of different industries and of different uses of factors of production. These changes in turn affect resource movements.

While it is theoretically possible to design a neutral tax system—one that leaves all relative prices unchanged—actual tax policy, both intentionally and unintentionally, is never neutral. It leads to a different allocation of resources than would occur without it.

Intended Effects

The tax structure is often used deliberately to change incentives and thus to affect resource allocation. Taxing gasoline to discourage energy consumption is one example; effluent charges on polluters are another. And tax provisions may be used as a carrot as well as a stick. One way is to allow the deduction of some expenditures from income before computing the amount of taxes payable, or

to give tax credits for some kinds of expenditures. Every $100 spent by a wealthy family in the 50 percent marginal tax bracket on an item that is tax deductible costs them $50 in after-tax income. Every $100 they spend on items that are not tax deductible costs the full $100 in after-tax income. This encourages them to contribute money and assets to charitable and educational institutions. Interest payments for a mortgage are tax deductible under the U.S. tax code, while payments for rental housing are not deductible. This encourages home ownership by lowering the cost of buying a house relative to the cost of renting one. When corporations are allowed "accelerated depreciation" or "investment credits" on certain investments, it encourages them to make such investments in larger amounts.

Unintended Allocative Effects

Not all of the allocative effects of the tax system are intended. To the extent that high income taxes discourage work, or induce people to spend money on tax avoidance, we are plainly reaping unintended and undesirable by-products of a tax system.

Consider further the tax incentives to home ownership, which were surely intended. An incidental result of providing such incentives through the income tax is that the incentive effect is much less for a poor person than for a rich one. The value of the deduction for interest is much greater to a taxpayer in the 50 percent marginal tax bracket than to someone in the 12 percent bracket. When a bank charges them each 12 percent, the richer taxpayer pays only 6 percent in after-tax dollars, the poorer one 10.6 percent if he or she itemizes deductions. For the many middle- and low-income persons who take the standard deduction, the actual interest rate remains 12 percent. Thus the lower one's income, the less the incentive that is provided to obtain a property stake in the society. This is surely an unintended effect.

The major unresolved question about taxes and allocation is empirical: Just how different is the allocation because of tax policy? Perhaps surprisingly, there is no consensus on this question. The reason is that we are not sure who really pays the taxes that are levied. This is called the problem of **tax incidence.**

Tax Incidence

When a tax is imposed on a firm, does the firm pay the tax, or does it pass it on to the consumer in the form of higher prices? To see why this is a difficult question to answer, consider two examples.

Do Landlords or Tenants Pay the Property Tax?

Landlords characteristically protest that the crushing burden of property taxes makes it impossible for them to earn a reasonable living from renting buildings to tenants who as often as not abuse the property. Tenants are likely to reply that landlords typically shirk their responsibilities for building maintenance and that the whole burden of the tax is passed on to the tenants in the form of higher rents. Both sides cannot be right in alleging that they each bear the entire burden of the tax! They are arguing about the incidence of the property tax.

To examine the incidence, suppose that a city inposes a property tax. Each of the thousands of landlords in the city decides to raise rents by the full amount of the tax. There will be a decline in the quantity of rental accommodation demanded as a result of the price increase. (For one reason, higher rents will induce some renters to economize on space now that it has become more expensive.)

The decline in the quantity demanded without any change in the quantity supplied will cause a surplus of rental accommodations at the higher prices. Landlords will find it difficult to replace tenants who move out, and the typical unit will remain empty longer between tenancies. Prospective tenants will find many alternative sites from which to choose and will become very particular in what they expect from landlords.

Some prospective tenants, seeing vacant apartments, will offer to pay rents below the asking rent.

Some landlords will accept the offer rather than earn nothing from vacant premises. Once some landlords cut rents, others will have to follow suit or find their properties staying unrented for longer periods of time. Eventually rentals will reach a new equilibrium at which the quantity demanded equals the quantity supplied. This equilibrium price for rental housing will be higher than the original pre-tax rent but lower than the rent that passes the entire tax on to the tenants. This argument is shown graphically in Figure 25-3.

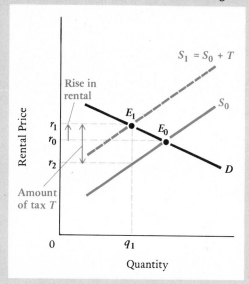

FIGURE 25-3
The Incidence of a Tax on Rental Housing

Since the equilibrium rent rises by less than the amount of the tax, landlords and tenants share the burden. The supply schedule S_0 reflects landlords' willingness to supply apartments at different levels of rents received. When a tax of T is imposed on landlords, the supply curve (in terms of rent paid by the tenant) shifts up by the full amount of the tax to S_1. At any quantity $S_1 = S_0 + T$. Because the demand curve slopes downward, equilibrium shifts from E_0 to E_1 and equilibrium rent rises to r_1. The landlord receives only r_2 net of the property tax. Of the total tax, tenants have paid only $r_0 r_1$ per unit and landlords $r_2 r_0$.

The burden of the property tax is shared by landlords and tenants.

Just how it is shared by the two groups will depend on the elasticity of the demand and supply curves.[3]

Notice that this result does not depend on who writes the check to pay the tax bill. In many European countries, the tenant rather than the landlord is sent the tax bill and pays the tax directly to the city; even in this case, however, the landlord bears part of the burden. As long as the existence of the tax reduces the quantity of rental accommodations demanded below what it otherwise would be, the tax will depress the amount received by landlords. In this way landlords will bear part of its burden.

Notice also that this result emerges even though neither landlords nor tenants realize it. Because rents are changing for all sorts of other reasons, no one will have much idea of what equilibrium rentals would be in the absence of the tax. It does not do much good just to look at what happens immediately after tax rates are changed because, as we have already seen, landlords may begin by raising rents by the full amount of the tax. Although they think they have passed it on, this creates a disequilibrium, and in the final position prices will have risen by less than the full amount of the tax.

Do Taxes on Profits Affect Prices?

Economic theory predicts that a general percentage tax on pure profits will have no effect on price or output, and thus the full incidence of such a tax will fall on producers. To see this quickly suppose that one price-quantity combination gives the firm higher profits (without considering taxes) than any other. If the government imposes a 20 percent profits tax, the firm will have only 80 percent as much profits after tax as it had before; *this will be true for each possible level of output.* The firm may grumble, but it will not be profitable for it to alter its price or output.

Notice that this argument is independent of the tax rate. [30] It applies equally whether the tax rate is 10 percent or 75 percent.

A tax on corporation income. American corporate income taxes are taxes on profits as defined by the tax laws. The definitions make them a tax on a combination of pure profits plus some of the return to the factors of production, "capital," and "risk taking."

Because such a profits tax will reduce the returns to these important factors of production, it can have significant effects on the allocation of resources and on the prices and output of goods. Suppose a risky industry requires, say, a 20 percent return on its capital to make prospective owners willing to take the risk of investing in the industry. Suppose that every firm is earning 30 percent on its investment before taxes. A 50 percent corporate income tax will reduce the return to 15 percent, below the point that makes investment attractive, and resources will leave the industry. Obviously price and output changes will occur. As firms leave the industry, and as supply decreases, prices will rise until the remaining firms can earn a sufficient level of after-tax profits so that they are once again compensated for the risks involved. Thus customers must bear part of the burden of the tax through a price increase.

A tax on profits, as defined by the taxing authorities, will have an effect on prices and outputs and thus will be shared by the consumer.

Because industries differ in degree of risk, the impact of a corporate income tax will be greater on more risky industries than on less risky ones. It will thus affect the allocation of resources among industries.

PUBLIC EXPENDITURE AS A TOOL OF MICRO POLICY

Public expenditure is large and growing. It affects both the distribution of income and the allocation of resources. In recent years, spending by federal,

---

[3] We suggest you draw a series of diagrams with demand and supply curves of different slopes to see how this works. In each case, shift the supply curve up by the same vertical amount—to represent the property tax—and see what proportion of the increase is reflected in the new equilibrium price.

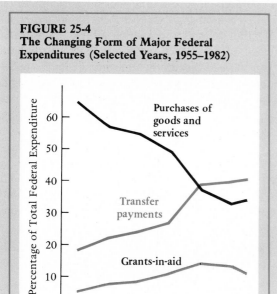

FIGURE 25-4
The Changing Form of Major Federal Expenditures (Selected Years, 1955–1982)

From 1955 until the "tax revolt" of the mid 1970s transfer payments and grants-in-aid grew steadily in importance. In 1955 two-thirds of all federal expenditures were for purchases of goods and services. By 1980 the fraction was only one-third. Transfer payments to persons in the United States and grants-in-aid to state and local governments have increased from less than one-fourth to more than one-half of the total. The Reagan administration has halted the trend. The three categories of expenditure graphed here account for almost 90 percent of total federal expenditures. The largest item not shown on the graph is net interest paid by the government.

ment, 18 percent by state governments, and 28 percent by local governments.

Figure 25-4 shows the changing importance of different types of federal government expenditures. Until 1974 the largest category of federal expenditures was for provision of goods and services that the market fails to provide or is not allowed to provide. Foremost among these (in volume of expenditure) are the defense and defense-related activities of the federal government; expenditures on police services, education, roads, conservation, and urban redevelopment are similar in character.

Although such purchases of goods and services are large (about $257 billion in 1982), they have remained roughly constant in real terms over the last 25 years. They have been overtaken by transfer payments as the largest form of government expenditure. Transfer payments and grants-in-aid steadily increased in importance until the onset of the Reagan administration. Their increase from 1955 to 1980 led to important changes in both the distribution of income and the allocation of resources.

Public Expenditures and Redistribution of Income

The federal government, as Table 25-1 indicates, raises the great bulk of its revenues by income-related taxes. When these federal receipts are transferred back to individuals or to state and local governments, they have a substantial redistributive effect.

Federal Transfer Payments to Individuals

Transfer payments are defined generally as payments to private persons or institutions that do not arise out of current productive activity. (They do not include intergovernment transfers.) Welfare payments are transfers; so, too, are social security payments, pensions, veterans' benefits, fellowships, unemployment insurance, and Medicare payments. Some federal transfers are made to foreigners as part of aid programs. Some transfer payments are private, such as private pensions and charitable contributions by individuals and corporations. Many are made by state and local govern-

state, and local government units in the United States—that is, by the public sector—has amounted to about 38 percent of the nation's expenditures. Defense, international relations, education, and social security are the largest items; collectively they make up half the total. Public welfare, highways, and interest on the public debt add up to another 18 percent of the total. The remainder covers everything else, from police protection and sanitation to general administration of government and space research. About 54 percent of the expenditure is made by the federal governments, often using funds they have received as federal grants-in-aid. The greatest part, which we consider here, is paid by the federal government to individuals. In 1982 they amounted, in the aggregate, to $316 billion. Most of these transfer payments are part of public income-maintenance programs of the kind examined in Chapter 23. The percentage of all personal income received in the form of government transfer payments has increased sharply, from under 5 percent in 1955 to 7 percent in 1965 and more than 14 percent in 1983.

The growth of transfer payments reflected several developments. A major source of growth has been the steadily increasing coverage and level of social security (including Medicaid and Medicare). As was seen in the box on pages 412–413, the exhaustion of the Social Security Administration's reserves signaled that either benefits would have to be curtailed or else large amounts of government general funds would have to be allocated to social security. While the growth of social security has had an important redistributive effect, it has been primarily from younger to older rather than from rich to poor. Because of the attempt to finance much of the cost of social security by payroll taxes, much of the cost has fallen on middle- and lower-middle-income groups.[4]

Other sources of the growth of transfer payments include the War on Poverty of the 1960s and 1970s and the persistent unemployment of the 1970s and early 1980s, which greatly increased unemployment compensation payments.

Transfer payments have undoubtedly had a tendency to redistribute income toward the very poor and away from the middle classes.

Grants-In-Aid as Forms of Redistribution

In addition to the federal government, there are 50 state governments, 3,000 county governments,

8,000 municipalities, and 17,000 townships in the United States. Further, there are about 20,000 districts for schools and another 20,000 for miscellaneous purposes such as sewage. Each of the more than 80,000 governmental units spends public money, and each must get the money to spend. Not all units have equal access to revenue, which necessitates both some division of responsibilities and intergovernmental grants-in-aid.

Grants-in-aid from federal to state and local governments have been among the most rapidly increasing forms of public expenditure. The growth in grants-in-aid is a response to a growing inability of state and local communities to manage their finances. (See Figure 25-5).

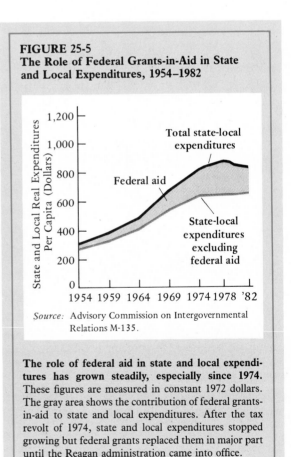

FIGURE 25-5
The Role of Federal Grants-in-Aid in State and Local Expenditures, 1954–1982

Source: Advisory Commission on Intergovernmental Relations M-135.

The role of federal aid in state and local expenditures has grown steadily, especially since 1974. These figures are measured in constant 1972 dollars. The gray area shows the contribution of federal grants-in-aid to state and local expenditures. After the tax revolt of 1974, state and local expenditures stopped growing but federal grants replaced them in major part until the Reagan administration came into office.

[4] The political consequences of this are just emerging. Older Americans, traditionally Republican, are being pulled toward the Democrats, who stand as protectors of social security. Blue collar workers, traditionally Democratic, have supported Republican attempts to decrease the cost to workers of social security programs.

Grants-in-aid are of two general types: categorical and general. At present, 90 percent of all federal grants are **categorical grants-in-aid,** that is, for specific categories of assistance such as highways, education, and welfare payments. Not only are such grants restricted as to use, they usually require some degree of state or local matching. General grants-in-aid without restriction or matching requirements are now called **revenue sharing.**

Many grants-in-aid programs were not designed primarily for redistribution. Do they, incidentally, have a big effect on the distribution of income? Economists are now looking at this question; they do not yet know the answer. Some categorical assistance goes for inequality-reducing welfare payments and other programs of aid to the poor. But grants for highways, hospitals, and research probably tend to increase the inequality of income distribution. Revenue sharing money goes to state and local governments whose uses of the funds vary enormously and therefore have no single pattern of impact.

Rising state and local expenditures of the magnitude shown in Figure 25-5 encountered increased voter resistance during the mid 1970s. The passage in 1978 of Proposition 13 in California was but one of several similar measures designed to limit state and local governments' ability to increase taxes. For a time the federal government made up the losses, but the level of real expenditures per capita peaked in the late 1970s and has now begun to decline. Such expenditures are largely devoted to maintaining essential services rather than to reducing income inequality.

Many public finance specialists believe that grants-in-aid to states tend not to decrease inequality of income distribution and may increase it, while grants to the cities tend to reduce inequality.

The Overall Redistributive Effects of Government Expenditures

Since tax policy tends to be roughly proportional in its effect, the overall progressivity of government policies depends on the progressivity of government expenditures. Here the large and growing role of transfer payments to the poor and the use of many grants-in-aid to the cities (for programs that ultimately help the poor) probably assured that from the mid 1950s until 1980 there was some net redistribution of income from high-income and middle-income groups to the poor. But such redistribution was not very large and probably came to a halt during the Reagan administration.

Changes in the degree of income inequality from decade to decade are extremely small, despite high and growing government expenditures.

The Lorenz curve on page 339 does not look appreciably different than one based on data from 1940.

Why does government expenditure not have a bigger effect on income distribution? One view is that government programs are really less progressive than observers once thought because progressive programs are offset by regressive ones. Another view is that market forces exert steady pressure toward more inequality, which government programs merely offset.

To understand the second view—that one must run hard just to stay even with inequality—imagine that the government today created complete equality in wealth and income. Inevitably market forces would produce inequality by next year, as some people and firms did well because they worked hard and long or were lucky, while others did poorly or failed because they took it easy or were unlucky, as some invested wisely while others squandered their resources on a binge. Most economists agree that there is a limit to how much inequality can be eliminated; there is controversy as to how close we are to that limit. (And beyond that there is controversy as to how close it is desirable to get to "as much equality as possible," both on ethical grounds of justice and economic grounds of incentives.)

Government Expenditure and Resource Allocation

Governments spent nearly one quarter of a trillion dollars in 1982 to provide goods and services. In

THE RISING COST OF HEALTH CARE

Health care is an emotional and provocative issue. Almost everyone would agree that in a wealthy society, such as the United States in the 1980s, some minimum level of health care should be available to all citizens by right. At the same time public outrage continues at the high current cost of medical care. Elementary economic analysis shows that these two events—the right to free medical care and the clamor over its high social cost—are not unrelated.

Explaining the High Cost

Health care has become extremely expensive. Without health insurance, a single major operation can be an enormous financial burden and a prolonged illness will impoverish even the most prudent middle-income household. Why has health care become so costly?

One set of reasons may be the ordinary supply and demand forces that would occur no matter how medical care was provided. This includes the fact that health care is highly labor intensive. The wages of nurses, laboratory technicians, and other medical service personnel have risen substantially relative to their productivity (the number of temperatures taken, beds made, and meals served per employee do not increase much over time). It also reflects the steadily rising quality of medical care. Available knowledge, techniques, equipment, and the training of new physicians all have improved over time. Thus it becomes possible not only to provide quicker, surer cures for common and recurring ailments but to prevent other less common ailments and complications. Moreover the demand for medical care tends to rise due to rising real income. As per capita income rises, people are prepared to consume more and better health. Health has proven to be income-elastic.

A second reason for rising medical costs is that the way medical care is provided or paid for has tended to greatly weaken incentives to economize on its use or to keep costs down. Either free public provision, or comprehensive prepaid (or employer-paid) health insurance is virtually sure to lead to costs rising more rapidly than when the price system allocates resources.

This is an example of moral hazard, discussed in Chapter 24.

Most insurance and publicly provided medical programs have eliminated significant *marginal* charges to the patient for the incremental medical or hospital care consumed. Instead they charge either the patient or the insurance company something closer to the average cost. An individual has no incentive to economize on the quantity or quality of his or her own elective care because doing so will not significantly raise the average cost of total care. Everyone wants the very best care to which the "plan" entitles him or her. In the market system individual patients would choose medical care (as they choose housing and clothing) from a wide variety of price-quality alternative forms of health care.

If patients had to pay their own bills, and if they could make fully informed choices, many might prefer to pay less and not have the best available equipment and doctors in all circumstances. But at zero marginal cost patients will naturally prefer to have the extra benefits of the best possible care, no matter what the extra cost to the insurance company, employer, or state. They will consume "free" hospital and medical services until their marginal utility is zero.

Nor do doctors and hospitals have strong incentive to hold costs down. They can pass along the higher costs of advanced modern techniques to insurers in higher fees, especially if they do not have to worry that those higher fees may cause a reduction in the quantity of their services demanded. They may well reason: Our job is to give the best treatment; let others worry about the costs. Indeed unscrupulous doctors can prescribe unnecessary surgery or other medical care to increase the demand for their services. Of course the insurance companies have to pass on higher claims in the form of higher premiums, and thus they might exercise cost control. But if the government or a giant employer pays most of the bill (as it does for many patients), insurers may not feel too much resistance to rising insurance rates, at least for a long time.

What Is the Right Quantity and Quality of Medical Care?

While everyone agrees that some minimum level of health care should be provided to all who need it, the definition of that minimum is a controversial and arbitrary issue. No doubt our concept of the minimum level of health care has grown over time; accordingly we have had increasing public intervention in the health sector.

The issue provokes more emotion than a discussion of housing or clothing, however. After all, human lives are at stake. True enough, but that does not end the matter. A first response is that much (although of course not all) medical and hospital care is elective and has almost nothing to do with life or death. By way of analogy, to say that no one should starve is not to say that everybody should receive all the free food they can eat. Nonvital attention accounts for a large part of our demand for health care. If it is offered at little or no marginal cost to users, it will be consumed beyond the point where marginal utility is equal to the cost of providing it.

But even where life is at stake, do we really always want the very best? Suppose the extra cost of the very best at all times does pay off in a small increased probability of survival. How much would we pay to have, say, 9 instead of 10 people in 10,000 die from a particular disease? Surely few would want to spend a billion dollars per life saved; we would say that the opportunity cost was too high. Yet doctors in hospitals often make the decision implicitly by ordering the best of everything and then pass the costs on to society as a whole through increased resource allocation to the health sector. The issue is not whether to save lives but the opportunity cost of doing so. Money spent to save lives here is money not available to save lives (or improve the quality of life) elsewhere.

Because the issues are difficult to face, the political process has tended to avoid them. Instead of asking *how much* care we should provide, we have asked *to whom should it be provided* at little or no marginal cost. The president and other key government officials, veterans, members of the armed forces, the very poor (via Medicaid), and the elderly (via Medicare) are heavily subsidized. Much of the clamor of the 1970s was to make similar coverage available to all. But lavish and expensive per capita care may be affordable for the few, not for the many.

Controlling the Cost

Neither providers nor patients have sufficient incentive under present schemes to keep down the costs of medical care. The most obvious solution is to place enough of a marginal charge on users so that they will ask themselves whether this doctor's visit, this extra day in the hospital, this use of the most expensive health monitoring system, is worth the cost to them. Another proposed solution is to ask the government to regulate the quantity, quality, and prices of service provided or the rates insurance companies may charge. The last of these gives insurance companies the motivation to exercise cost control.

If we reject such solutions, then we must live with the costs. The government must either provide the services demanded directly or subsidize others to do so; or it must limit the demand to the quantity available. In countries with national health services, rationing is accomplished in part by long lines at doctors' offices and long waits for hospital admissions and in part by a lower average quality of medical services, which then reduces demand.

In adopting a policy toward health care there are at least three separable decisions: How much care to provide, how to allocate the costs of that care, and how to ration the supply. In the market system, prices do all three. When we elect to have the government intervene—because we do not like the free-market results—someone has to make these decisions.

When the government chooses not to have the price system make these decisions, it must do so in other ways. When the stakes and costs are large, this becomes a major political issue. In recent years budgetary liberals have demanded medical care for all no matter what the costs, and budgetary conservatives, deploring the burden of costs, have urged curtailing them no matter what the effects on health care.

these activities governmental units act like firms, using factors of production to produce outputs. They produce outputs rather than leave them to the free market because the people, acting through their state legislatures, Congress, and city councils, have decided that they should. They are responding to the various sources of dissatisfaction with market outcomes discussed in Chapter 24. In so doing governments are plainly changing the allocation of resources.

From time to time, major new initiatives are undertaken that have the purpose and the effect of a sharp further change in resource allocation.

A central debate of the 1970s concerned the role of government in providing medical care to the population. It is discussed briefly in the box on pages 468–469. A widely debated current issue concerns the appropriate level of expenditure to cope with the deterioration of the country's biggest cities.

Urban Problems

Some of the biggest news stories of the late 1970s concerned the feared bankruptcy of such cities as New York, Philadelphia, and Cleveland. The crisis of the cities is in part a fiscal crisis because of the limited ability of local governments to raise revenues equal to their necessary expenditures. The purely fiscal crisis *could* be solved by financial help to the cities from state and federal governments. As the 1980s began the Reagan administration was, however, decreasing its aid to both cities and states. States, in turn, were decreasing their aid to the cities. The purely fiscal crisis of the cities thus has been worsening. Underlying the fiscal crisis are some "real" problems that inhere in the changing character of the central cities (as distinguished from the suburbs). If urban decline is to be reversed, major changes in the allocation of resources will be required.

The Economics of Urban Decay

The root cause of the changing character of the nation's biggest cities is the change in who lives in them.

The selective flight to the suburbs (and beyond) that has triggered the urban crisis is a function of many circumstances—among them, different preferences of different groups in the population, rising incomes that permit the wealthier to move away, and sometimes prejudice. To understand why more and more families have chosen to trade the traditional advantages of the big city for cleaner neighborhoods, safer streets, and whiter schools, it is helpful to explore the dynamics of suburban migration. Much of it can be understood in economic terms. The scenario that follows suggests some causes of the urban crisis.

The flight of the wealthy. As the relatively wealthier residents of a densely populated city find their incomes rising, they choose to spend extra income on bigger houses, more spacious lots, and tree-lined streets. Very high real estate prices in the central cities make extra space a luxury, but low-cost land exists just outside the central cities. Thus suburban communities begin to be formed. As more upper-income residents move out, the concentration of lower-income residents in the city increases.

The disenchantment of the middle classes. The services required by the poor are of a different type from those sought by the middle class. More money goes to welfare, social work, and police and less to civic symphonies, schools, parks, and amenities. At the same time, the average income per capita that is subject to taxation declines as the relatively wealthy move beyond the reach of city tax authorities. Remaining middle-class residents discover that they are paying more taxes but receiving fewer services of the kind they value. They find the museums closed and the park toilets unclean. Their schools curtail the "frills" in the curriculum, such as interscholastic athletics, foreign languages, and music and art. Life in the city costs more but offers less.

Meanwhile, empty expensive houses tend to be converted to cheaper housing as three or four families move in where one used to live. The housing also deteriorates because it does not pay landlords to maintain it at its former standard. If the poor are black or Chicano, their increasing presence in the schools, the streets, and the parks does not go unnoticed by whites.

Upper–middle-class residents who remain see their tax burdens rising, their neighborhoods becoming more crowded, the older sections of "their" city deteriorating, the racial composition of their schools changing, and the crime rate increasing. Some move into more expensive neighborhoods or send their children to private schools; more and more flee to the suburbs.

Shifting employment opportunities. Many discover that they have added incentive to move as jobs move from the old cities of the Northeast to the Southwest and from central cities to suburbs. During the 1970s more than 3 million people moved out of the Northeast and Midwest, and many of those that remained in these areas moved to the suburbs and away from the central cities. For one example, over the 1970s Detroit's central city population decreased by 317,000 and its suburbs increased by 226,000. Stores and banks follow their customers, first by establishing branches in suburban shopping centers, later by closing central-city locations. Industry, too, moves outward, partly because of the available labor force, partly in response to the interstate highway system and the trucking industry.

The inner city becomes a ghetto. When the jobs go, not all the workers will follow. But the division of who goes and who stays is hardly random. Many poorer inner-city residents, held together by the bonds of race, language, or, indeed, poverty as well as by lack of cars and lack of middle-class aspirations, stay put. Unemployment increases, more families need welfare, housing deteriorates further, clean streets seem less important—and, of course, the tax base continues to shrink.

A reform mayor raises the sales tax or proposes a city income tax and finds that these measures only hasten the exodus. At this stage the city may actually be underpopulated. Existing residents abandon the worst neighborhoods as they deterio-

rate—and move to and begin the downgrading of more expensive housing. The worst slums may become homes for new immigrants from rural areas, Cuba, or Puerto Rico, or they may be abandoned and begin to crumble. Rats, disease, crime, and decay spread.

However bleak this story seems, it comes close to representing the plight of many American cities today. One might attack urban decay by channeling efforts and funds into rebuilding the city itself. Alternatively, one might attack the problems of poverty, unemployment, and prejudice that contribute so heavily to urban deterioration. Cities, without help, can do neither.

The Fiscal Crisis of the Cities

If greater spending on municipal services and urban renewal might halt the decline of the cities, why do cities not solve their problems by more spending? The answer lies in four sets of forces: (1) tax revenues of local governments are relatively unresponsive to growth in average income, (2) the limited ability of cities to borrow, (3) the rapidly rising demand for local government services, and (4) the rising cost per unit of providing these services. Together they contribute to local governments' steadily worsening financial situation and their urgent demand for federal assistance.

Tax revenues. Whether government tax revenues rise as fast as the average income of residents depends on the government's ability to use income taxes. The larger the percentage of income raised by income taxes, the stronger the fiscal position of any government unit will be as income rises. While 92 percent of federal tax receipts and 50 percent of state tax receipts today come from income taxes, only 9 percent of local taxes are so raised.

Local governments cannot readily increase their reliance on income taxes. As the percentage of personal income taken by the federal government has grown, the resistance of taxpayers to higher taxes of any kind has grown—and this is especially true of further taxes on income. Many state and local governments have tried to impose (or increase) income taxes; however, the electoral defeats of officials who advocated these taxes, and the interstate and intercity competition to attract residents and industries by having lower taxes than neighboring jurisdictions, have severely limited the additional revenue that state and local governments have been able to raise in this way.

State and local governments thus rely heavily on property, sales, and excise taxes. Revenues from these taxes rise more slowly than income in the short run, and in the long run they rise only at the same rate as the income levels *of the population in their jurisdictions*. Here is where the selective outward migration of richer taxpayers has hurt so much. In most of the largest cities average real income (and thus per capita tax revenue) is falling because of the movement of higher-income families to the suburbs and the higher unemployment rates in the cities. But the problem for the cities runs deeper. Much of the tax revolt of the 1970s involved mandated *decreases* in existing levels of property taxation.

The limited ability of cities to borrow.

Cities, unlike the federal government, cannot spend more than they raise in taxes, receive as gifts, or borrow, for they cannot print money. In some states, cities are constitutionally limited in their ability to borrow; even where this is not the case, prudence limits what is possible.

While the tax-free status of municipal bond interest has long helped cities to sell bonds, they must still pay the interest when due and repay the principal at maturity. Rising interest rates in the late 1970s made paying the interest an ever-growing drain on cities' current receipts. Furthermore, repaying principal requires a major revenue source when the bonds come due. Depending on how the receipts of the bond issue are used, such a source may or may not be available.

Cities borrow for three reasons: (1) to finance long-term capital investment projects such as schools or hospitals, (2) to smooth out seasonal or cyclical fluctuations in the patterns of expenditures and receipts, and (3) to cover continuing current account deficits. The first two reasons are wholly responsible. The third is irresponsible and unacceptable to bondholders because the revenue to repay the bonds is nowhere provided for. Because of this it cannot long continue.

What happens when a city sells bonds to cover a continuing deficit? As these bonds come due, money will be needed to repay the bondholders, but there will be no current surplus available. The obvious solution is to borrow still more. Then rumors of trouble will start, and they will lead to the downgrading of the city's credit rating. Investors will become unwilling to buy new issues to replace the old ones without sharply higher interest rates. At some point the city effectively loses its ability to borrow even for legitimate purposes.

Demand for government services rises more rapidly than average income.

Local government expenditures have been rising more rapidly than their residents' incomes. An historically important reason is the high income elasticity of demand for city services. As societies become wealthier their residents want more parks, more police protection, more and better public schools and colleges, and more generous treatment of their less fortunate neighbors. This alone, combined with the limited tax sources available, would create budgetary problems for local governments in a period of rising incomes and rising expectations—a fact that many mayors have learned the hard way. Taxpayers increasingly want the social services that governments provide, but they do not want to accept the taxes required to pay for them. Elected officials arouse the public wrath when they fail to provide wanted programs, but they also do so when they provide the services and then raise taxes.

A second and, in the past two decades, much more important reason for a rise in the quantity of local government services demanded, has to do with the changing character of central-city populations and the increased need for local government expenditures associated with these changes. The selective outward migration from the cities to the suburbs has led to ever increasing proportions of low-income groups in the central cities. This in turn has led to more poverty, more crime, and thus to more demand for the welfare and the public services to cope with them.

The rising relative cost of local government services. Government services tend to use much labor of a kind whose productivity has increased much less rapidly than its cost. Thus cost per unit of output has risen. While the national average of output per hour in manufacturing has risen about 50 percent in the last decade, the size of the beat covered by a police officer, the number of students taught by each schoolteacher, and the number of families that can be handled effectively by a social worker have not risen in proportion. Because wage levels tend to rise with national average productivity, the costs of services in sectors where productivity growth is low have soared.

The inevitable crisis. The four forces just described lead inevitably to a crisis. Overall it is estimated that, on average, state and local expenditures have risen at 1.67 times the rate of increase of national income.

Rising quantities and rising unit costs of government services cause local government expenditures to rise more than their revenues.

Eventually the city's reserves will be used up. It must then either reverse the causes of its decline, get help from the outside, or default on its obligations.

The Growing Urban Crisis

Once the interrelated processes of urban decay and movement out of the cities has begun, the city has passed the point of self-help. Only a massive dosage of money will now help. The city recognizes that it can recover its tax base if it can annex suburban areas, but those who have escaped the city's problems will reject the overtures for annexation, and their political influence in the state governments is usually sufficient to prevent forced annexation. The city, unable to solve the problem itself, now tries to persuade the state or federal government to channel funds to it. Substantial funds are required simply to maintain the status quo but must compete with other demands on public budgets.

The rising level of federal contributions to state and local government during the 1970s was a re-

sponse to this problem. That it was not sufficient was made clear by New York City's fiscal crisis of 1975, by the sharply worsening plights of Philadelphia, Chicago, Detroit, and other cities in the 1980s, and by the urgency with which the nation's mayors keep clamoring for more help.

The Reagan administration not only turned a skeptical ear to such pleas but adopted policies that actually decreased outside help to the cities. This partly reflected its philosophic commitment to returning responsibility to local communities, even though they lack the resources to deal with them, and partly reflected the fact that its expenditure cuts fell disproportionately on programs whose beneficiaries tend to be city residents. Cities have responded both by raising taxes and by cutting back further on services such as police, fire, health, street maintenance, highways, sewers, and mass transit systems.

As of the mid 1980s, the plight of the cities has never looked worse.

Is There a Long-Run Solution?

Cities play too vital a role in the nation's political and economic life to let them wither and their millions of inhabitants be overwhelmed by poverty, disease, and crime. Yet what is to be done?

One solution is a more or less permanent subsidization of the cities by taxes levied on those who live elsewhere. A great expansion in unconditional revenue sharing would give revenues to state and local governments on a per capita basis, in effect making residents of wealthy states and rich suburbs pay some part of the costs of areas densely populated by the poor.

An alternative approach favored by many is increasingly to federalize aid to the poor wherever they reside by guaranteeing a minimum family income sufficient to permit escape from slum conditions. Others hope to provide this minimum income not by grants to individuals, categorical or otherwise, but by manipulation of the tax structure—specifically, by introducing a negative income tax.

Mayors of large cities, and many economists who specialize in urban economies, believe that the needed support to the cities is appropriately provided by state and federal governments because the key problems of the cities are those of race, poverty, and unemployment, which are *national* problems. The fact that these problems are most severe among city dwellers does not make them city problems to be ignored by those who live in the suburbs or smaller cities, towns, and villages.

If this argument is accepted, regular and permanent transfers of money to the cities or their residents will be viewed not as charity to an imprudent relative but as a regular part of public attention to persistent national problems. An alternative view regards urban crises as the product primarily of irresponsible city governments, and aid to the cities as a temporary necessity that perhaps has to be given "this time" but not next. The conflict between these views is emerging as a key in the policy debate of the 1980s.

As is usually the case in real debates, there is some truth in both extreme views. New York, for example, greatly compounded its problems by some irresponsible expenditure policies and fiscal maneuvering. But even a more prudent city administration is going to have desperate trouble making ends meet in the 1980s, for the basic problems are still there.

EVALUATING THE ROLE OF GOVERNMENT

Most everyone would agree that the government has some role to play in the economy because of the myriad sources of possible market failure. Yet there is no consensus that the present level and role of government intervention is about right.

One aspect of the contemporary debate—the efficient level of government intervention—was discussed at the end of Chapter 24. There we asked when and to what degree government ought to attempt to modify private market behavior—say, by affecting the way a paper mill discharges its wastes. Other issues arise when government provides goods and services that the private sector does not and will not provide.

Do Benefits of Government Programs Exceed Costs?

The federal government has developed techniques of evaluation designed to provide estimates of benefits and costs in order to determine whether the former exceed the latter. If they do, the program is said to be *cost effective*, and thus to be justified. For some government programs, such as flood control, there are well-defined benefits and costs. It is thus relatively easy to decide whether the project is justified. But consider the evaluation of a program such as the great space adventure of the 1960s—placing a man on the moon before the end of the decade. The budgetary costs were easily defined. At its peak in 1966, the program absorbed (in 1982 dollars) about $19 billion per year. Unmistakably, the project succeeded; it met its stated objective. But was the "giant step for mankind" worth the billions it cost? The benefits certainly included the psychological lift that the moon walks may have given the American people and the substantial advances in technology and knowledge that the space program is known to have spawned. The real costs are those things that the expenditure would have replaced. But what was the alternative? More arms to Vietnam? Massive urban redevelopment? A return of funds to private spenders to use as they saw fit? Most of us will evaluate the worth of the space program very differently, depending on what we see as the alternative uses of the resources involved.

Such questions can never be answered unambiguously. As a result the evaluation of government programs is inherently political and controversial. Economic analysis of benefits and costs is involved, but it does not play the sole or even the dominant role in answering some big questions.

The Balance Between Private and Public Sectors

When the government raises money by taxation and spends it on an activity, it increases the spending of the public sector and decreases that of the private sector. Since the public sector and the private sector spend on different things, the government is changing the allocation of resources. Is that good or bad? How do we know if the country has the right balance between the public and private sectors? Should there be more schools and fewer houses, or more houses and fewer schools?

Because automobiles and houses are sold on the market, consumer demand has a significant influence on the relative prices of these commodities, and (through prices) on the quantities produced and, thence, on the allocation of the nation's resources. This is true for all goods produced and sold on the market. But there is no market that provides relative prices for apartments versus public schools; thus the choice between allowing money to be spent in the private sector and spending it for public goods is a matter to be decided by Congress and other legislative bodies.

John Kenneth Galbraith in a 1958 best seller, *The Affluent Society,* proclaimed the "liberal" message that a correct assignment of marginal utilities would show them to be higher for an extra dollar's worth of expenditure on parks, clean water, and education than for an extra dollar's worth of expenditure on television sets and deodorants. In this view, the political process often fails to translate preferences for public goods into effective action; thus more resources are devoted to the private sector and fewer to the public sector than would be the case if the political mechanism were as effective as the market.

The "conservative" view has a growing number of supporters who agree with Professor James Buchanan that society has already gone beyond the point where the value of the marginal dollar spent by the government is greater than the value of that dollar left in the hands of households or firms that would have spent it had it not been taxed away. Because bureaucrats, the conservatives argue, are spending other people's money, they regard a few million (or billion) dollars here or there as a mere nothing. They have lost all sense of the opportunity cost of public expenditure; thus they tend to spend far beyond the point where marginal benefits equal marginal costs.

This debate is not readily settled on a scientific basis because of the difficulty of measuring benefits when the things produced (e.g., clean air or the preservation of the Everglades) are not readily marketable.

Ultimately the decision will be made politically. From the 1930s to the 1970s the trend was unmistakably toward more and more government intervention. By the mid 1970s the pendulum was swinging the other way. The so-called taxpayers' revolt, symbolized by the passage of Proposition 13 in California and similar measures intended to limit the powers of government to collect taxes, foreshadowed the election of Ronald Reagan in 1980. Deregulation, decreasing domestic expenditures, and decreasing willingness to use governmental spending power to alleviate private distress are each central visible elements of the Reagan administration's policies. Whether this trend will continue for decades or will itself be reversed will be decided at the nation's polling places.

What Is the Role of Government Today?

We have been looking at the role of the government in the market economy throughout the microeconomic part of this book. Now, at the end, let us pause for perspective. One of the most difficult problems for the student of the U.S. economic system is to maintain perspective about the scope of government activity in the market economy. There are literally tens of thousands of laws, regulations, and policies that affect firms and households. Many believe that significant additional deregulation would be possible and beneficial.

But private decision makers still have an enormous amount of discretion about what they do and how they do it. One pitfall is to become so impressed (or obsessed) with the many ways in which government activity impinges on the individual that one fails to see that these only make changes— sometimes large but often small—in market signals in a system that basically leaves individuals free to make their own decisions. In the private sector most individuals choose their occupations, earn their livings, spend their incomes, and live their lives. In this sector firms, too, are formed, choose products, live, grow, and sometimes die.

A different pitfall is to fail to see that some, and perhaps most, of the highly significant amounts paid by the private sector to the government as taxes also buy goods and services that add to the welfare of individuals. By and large the public sector complements the private sector, doing things the private sector would leave undone or do very differently. To recognize this is not to deny that there is often waste, and sometimes worse, in public expenditure policy. Nor does it imply that whatever is, is just what people want. Social policies and social judgments evolve and change.

Yet another pitfall is failing to recognize that the public and private sectors compete in the sense that both make claims on the resources of the economy. Thus government activities are not without opportunity costs, except in those rare circumstances in which they use resources that have no alternative use.

Public policies in operation at any time are not the result of a single master plan that specifies precisely where and how the public sector shall seek to complement, help along, or interfere with the workings of the market mechanism. Rather, as individual problems arise, governments attempt to meet them by passing ameliorative legislation. These laws stay on the books, and some become obsolete and unenforceable. This is true of systems of law in general. As a result it is easy to find outrageous examples of inconsistencies and absurdities in any system. A distinguished professorship at Harvard gives its incumbent the right to graze a cow in Harvard Yard; laws still exist that permit the burning of witches.

Many anomalies exist in our economic policies; for example, laws designed to support the incomes of small farmers have created some agricultural millionaires, and commissions created to assure competition often end up creating and protecting monopolies. Neither individual policies nor whole programs are above criticism.

In a society that elects its policymakers at reg-ular intervals, however, the majority view on the amount and type of government interference that is desirable will have some considerable influence on the interference that actually occurs. This now seems sure to be one of the major political issues of the 1980s. Fundamentally, a free-market system is retained because it is valued for its lack of coercion and its ability to do much of the allocating of society's resources. But we are not mesmerized by it; we feel free to intervene in pursuit of a better world in which to live. We also recognize, however, that some intervention has proven excessive and/or ineffective.

SUMMARY

1. Two of the most powerful tools of microeconomic policy are taxation and public expenditure.

2. While their main purpose is to raise revenue, taxes represent a means of redistributing income. Federal taxes overall are progressive because of their heavy reliance on income taxation; state and local taxes are on balance regressive, particularly because of their heavy reliance on property and sales taxes.

3. The total American tax structure is roughly proportional except for very low-income groups (for whom it is regressive) and very high-income groups (for whom it is mildly progressive). Either a negative income tax or a move in the direction of comprehensive income taxation would increase progressivity. Whether this is feasible politically, or desirable, is a subject of sharp current debate.

4. Evaluating the effects of taxes on resource allocation requires first determining tax incidence—that is, determining who really pays the taxes. For most taxes, the incidence is shared. Excise taxes, for example, affect prices and are thus partially passed on, but part is absorbed by producers. The actual incidence depends on such economic considerations as demand and supply elasticities.

5. A large part of public expenditure is for the

provision of goods and services that private markets fail to provide. Direct and indirect subsidies, transfer payments to individuals, and grants-in-aid to state and local governments are all rising sharply.

6. The major redistributive activities of the federal government take the form of direct transfer payments to individuals and grants-in-aid to state and local governments for economic welfare payments. While the public sector has a tendency to redistribute some income from high-income and middle-income groups to the poor, the change in income inequality from decade to decade has been relatively small.

7. Government expenditure of all kinds has a major effect on the allocation of resources. The government determines how much of our total output is devoted to national defense, education, and highways. It is also influential in areas where private provision of goods and services is common; health care is a notable example.

8. Grants-in-aid to state and local government are a key form of public expenditure policy; they lead to a different allocation of resources than would occur without them. The need for such grants-in-aid is dramatically revealed by the plight of the nation's cities.

9. The urban crisis is in large part a result of the selective migration of residents to the suburbs and out of reach of the urban taxing authorities. Such migration develops a dynamic that feeds itself, and increasingly the central cities have become occupied by the poor, with rising needs and a shrinking tax base. This leads to the urban fiscal crisis, for which state or federal assistance may be the only solution.

10. Evaluating public expenditures involves reaching decisions about absolute merit (do benefits exceed costs?), about the relative merit of public and private expenditures, and about the desirable size of government.

11. The U.S. economy is a mixed economy and a changing one. Each generation faces anew the choice of which activities to leave to the unfettered

market and which to encourage or repress through public policy.

TOPICS FOR REVIEW

Tax expenditures
Progressivity and regressivity of taxes
Tax incidence
Transfer payments to individuals
The uses of grants-in-aid to state and local governments
The sources of urban crises
Choosing between private and public expenditures

DISCUSSION QUESTIONS

1. The American taxpayer is assaulted by dozens of different taxes with different incidence, different progressivity, and different methods of collection. Discuss the case for and against using at most two different kinds of taxes. Discuss the case for and against a single taxing authority that would share the revenue with all levels of government.

2. Under federal tax law certain kinds of income are tax exempt. Two of these are social security benefits and municipal bond interest. For each one, who benefits from the provision? What are its effects on the distribution of income and the allocation of resources? In what sense is this a "tax expenditure"?

3. How might each of the following affect the incidence of a real estate property tax imposed on central city rental property?
   a. The residents of the community are largely blacks who face racial discrimination in neighboring areas.
   b. The city installs a good, cheap rapid-transit system that makes commuting to the suburbs less expensive and more comfortable.
   c. The income tax laws are changed to eliminate the deductibility of property taxes on owner-occupied housing from taxable income for those who itemize deductions.

4. Under the federal tax laws, all state and local income taxes can be deducted from income in computing the federal tax liability. Suppose two local communities each impose a 10 percent tax on personal incomes. Richville is composed of families who earn $100,000 per year or more. Uniontown consists mainly of workers' families who earn about $20,000 per year. Who really pays the taxes in each case? What, if anything, prevents Richville from raising its taxes?

5. Develop the case for and against having the federal government (rather than state and local governments) provide
   a. police protection
   b. teachers' salaries
   c. highways
   d. welfare payments to the poor

6. Classify each of the following programs as "transfer payment," "grant-in-aid," "purchase of goods and services," or "none of the above." Which ones clearly tend to decrease the inequality of income distribution?
   a. payments of wages and family living allowances to soldiers serving overseas
   b. unemployment insurance payments to unemployed workers
   c. payments to states for support of highway construction
   d. a negative income tax
   e. pensions of retired Supreme Court justices
   f. an excess-profits tax on oil companies

7. Medical and health costs were 4.5 percent of GNP in 1950 and over 10 percent in 1982. Is 10 percent necessarily too much? Is it necessarily a sign that we are providing better health care? How might an economist think about what is the right percentage of GNP to devote to medical care?

8. The city of Miami and Dade County have gained about 200,000 new residents from Cuba in just a few years. A city official says "Federal marshals bring in refugees, they bring them to us. We are the only jailer, we are the only public hospital. . . . We shouldn't have to pay the bill."

   In what sense is the problem one that ought to be met by the City of Miami, by Dade County, by Florida, by the federal government? Why is it a *government* problem at all?

9. "I believe the spirit of volunteerism lives in America. We see examples of it on every hand: the community charity drive, the rallying around whenever disaster strikes. The truth is, we've let Government take away many things we once considered were really ours to do voluntarily, out of the goodness of our hearts and a sense of neighborliness. I believe many of you want to do those things again."

   Discuss the probable effects in the 1980s of getting the government out of all activities once covered by private charity. The quotation is from a speech of President Reagan.

10. "Poverty, discrimination, and unemployment are federal, not state and local, problems. If the federal government solved these problems, urban crises would disappear."

    Discuss.

11. If governments tend to step in when markets do not produce satisfactory results, why are not similar functions performed similarly in different countries? Medical care, sport fishing rights, steel production, broadcasting, telephone service, and garbage collection are provided publicly in some Western countries and privately in others. What accounts for the diversity?

PART SEVEN

NATIONAL INCOME AND FISCAL POLICY

26 INFLATION, UNEMPLOYMENT, AND GROWTH: AN INTRODUCTION TO MACROECONOMICS

Inflation, unemployment, recession, and economic growth are now everyday words. Governments worry about how to reduce inflation and unemployment, how to prevent or cure recessions, and how to increase growth. Firms are concerned about how inflation affects their earnings and how to improve productivity; many businesses have good reason to fear recessions. Households are anxious to avoid the unemployment that comes in the wake of recessions and to protect themselves against the hazards of inflation.

WHAT IS MACROECONOMICS?

As we saw in Chapter 4 economics is customarily divided into two main branches, microeconomics and macroeconomics.[1] Each of the concerns mentioned above plays a major role in macroeconomics. But what exactly is macroeconomics?

Macroeconomics studies in broad outline the flow of income in the economy, illustrated in Figure 4-1, while avoiding much of its interesting but confusing detail. As a result macroeconomics deals with **aggregate data** that express broad totals and averages derived from the whole economy. In contrast microeconomics deals with **disaggregate data** that describe the behavior of individual markets, such as those for wheat, coal, or strawberries.

The following examples illustrate the difference between the two branches of economics. Explaining the behavior of automobile prices is a typical microeconomic problem. For decades car prices fell in relation to the prices of most other commodities. Why has the trend reversed over the last decade, with automobiles becoming increasingly expensive relative to other commodities? In microeconomics, we seek to understand the causes and the effects of such changes in relative prices. On the other hand, accounting for the average behavior of all prices is a typical macroeconomic problem. This average is called the *price level* and is measured by a price index. Why does the price level rise slowly in some decades and very rapidly in others? In macroeconomics we are trying to understand the causes and effects of such changes in the price level.

Major Macroeconomic Issues

The economy proceeds in fits and starts rather than in a smooth upward trend. Why did the 1930s see the greatest economic depression in recorded history, with up to a quarter of the labor force in the United States unemployed and massive unemployment in all other major industrial countries? Why were the 25 years following World War II a period of sustained boom with only minor interruptions from modest recessions? Why did the early 1980s see the onset of the worst worldwide recession and slowest recovery since the 1930s?

We live in an inflationary world. Why did the pace of inflation during the 1970s and early 1980s reach levels never before seen in peacetime in most advanced western nations? If Americans and Canadians thought that inflation rates in the range of 10 percent to 12 percent were serious, what was it like to live in Israel, Italy, or Great Britain, where inflation rates were much higher?

Alternating bouts of inflationary boom and deflationary slump have caused many policy headaches in the past. Why were the recessions of the last decade accompanied not only by their familiar companion, high unemployment, but also by an unexpected fellow traveler, rapid inflation? Is the new disease of stagflation—simultaneous high unemployment and rapid inflation—here to stay?

Total and per capita output have risen for several decades in advanced (and in many less advanced) countries. These long-term trends have meant rising living standards for the average person. Does the recent slowdown in world-wide growth rates represent a basic change in underlying trends, or is it just a reflection of the prolonged downturn of the last decade? Can governments do anything to affect growth rates?

KEY MACRO VARIABLES

Employment, total output, and the price level are key variables in macroeconomics. We hear about them on television; politicians give campaign speeches about them; economists theorize about them. To discuss them in a reasoned fashion we must first understand them. How are they defined, why are we concerned about them, and how have they behaved over the past half century?

Labor Force Variables

Employment denotes the number of adult workers (defined in the United States as workers 16 years old and over) who hold full-time jobs.[2] **Unemploy-**

---

[1] The prefixes *macro* and *micro* derive from the Greek words *makros*, for large, and *mikros*, for small.

[2] In January 1983, these figures were amended to include personnel in the military who had previously not been included in measures of the labor force.

ment denotes the number of adult workers who are not employed and are actively searching for a job. The **labor force** is the total of the employed and the unemployed. The **unemployment rate,** usually represented by the symbol U, is unemployment expressed as a percentage of the labor force:

$$U = \frac{\text{unemployed}}{\text{labor force}} \times 100\%$$

Why Unemployment Is a Matter of Concern

The social and political significance of the unemployment rate is enormous. The federal government is blamed when it is high and takes credit when it is low. Few macroeconomic policies are planned without some consideration of how they affect it. No other summary statistic, with the possible exception of the inflation rate, carries such weight as both a formal and an informal concern of policy as does the percentage of the civilian labor force unemployed.

There are two main reasons for worrying about unemployment: it produces economic waste and it causes human suffering. The economic waste is obvious. Human effort is the least durable of economic commodities. If a fully employed economy with a constant labor force has 100 million people willing to work in 1980, their services must either be used in 1980 or wasted. When the services of only 90 million are used because 10 percent of the labor force is unemployed, the potential output of 10 million workers is lost forever. In an economy where there is not enough output to meet everyone's needs, any waste of potential output seems undesirable and large wastes seem tragic.

The human cost of unemployment is also obvious. Severe hardship and misery can be caused by prolonged periods of unemployment. A person's spirit can be broken by a long period of wanting work but being unable to find it. Crime, divorce, and general social unrest usually rise with unemployment. In the not so distant past, only private charity or help from friends and relatives stood between the unemployed and starvation. Today

welfare and unemployment insurance have softened those effects.

When an economic slump is deep and prolonged, however, as in the mid 1970s and again in the early 1980s, people begin to exhaust their unemployment insurance and must fall back on savings, welfare, or charity. In 1976 and again in 1981–1982, many people sank below the poverty level for the first time in their lives. They did so because they had used up their unemployment insurance but were unable to find jobs because of a persistently high unemployment level.

Unemployment: The Historical Experience

Figure 26-1 shows the trends in the civilian labor force, employment, and unemployment since 1929. Despite business booms and slumps, and inflations and deflations, the main trend has clearly been a growth in employment that roughly matches the growth in the labor force. This growth is part of the total economic growth of the economy. Although a long-term growth trend dominates the employment figures, some unemployment is always present. It fluctuates with the ebb and flow of business activity that is often referred to as the **business cycle.** The unemployment *rate* graphed in Figure 26-2 clearly shows the short-term cyclical behavior of unemployment.

Consideration of employment and unemployment suggests another concept, that of *full employment*. Contrary to what you might think, full employment does not mean zero unemployment. There is a constant turnover of individuals in given jobs and a constant change in job opportunities. Older workers retire or die; new members enter the work force and take time to find employment. Some people quit their jobs, while others are fired. These people usually find new jobs, but only after some delay. So at any one time, there will be unemployment due to the normal turnover of labor that exists in any healthy economy. Such unemployment is called **frictional unemployment.**[3]

---

[3] Later in the book we distinguish a particular type of frictional unemployment called *structural* unemployment.

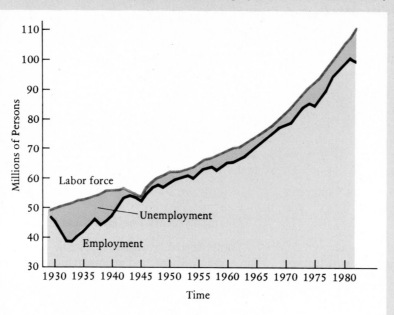

FIGURE 26-1
Civilian Labor Force, Employment, and Unemployment in the United States, 1929–1982

The labor force and employment have grown since the 1930s with only a few interruptions. The size of the American labor force has doubled since 1930, and so has the number of the employed. The fall in the labor force in the early 1940s was in the civilian labor force. The missing workers were in the military. Unemployment, the gap between the labor force and employment, has fluctuated but has not again reached the magnitude suffered in the 1930s.

Source: Economic Reports of the President.

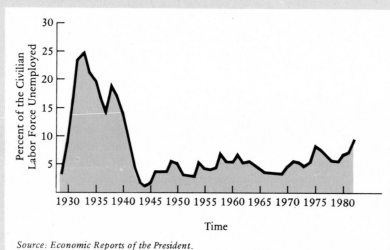

FIGURE 26-2
Percentage of the Civilian Labor Force Unemployed in the United States, 1929–1982

The unemployment rate responds to the cyclical behavior of the economy. Booms are associated with low unemployment, slumps with high unemployment. The Great Depression of the 1930s produced record unemployment figures for an entire decade. During World War II unemployment rates fell to very low levels. Since 1945, however, the unemployment rate has demonstrated a slight upward trend. The recession of the early 1980s produced unemployment rates second only to those of the 1930s; these rates were extremely high by the standards of the post-World War II behavior of the American economy.

Source: Economic Reports of the President.

When we say full employment we mean that the only existing unemployment is frictional. The measured unemployment rate that occurs at full employment is often called the **natural rate of unemployment.** Estimates of the natural rate indicate that it rose substantially throughout the 1970s and has now stabilized or may even be declining. (We shall discuss the reasons for these changes later.)

Output Variables

There are several related measures of the country's total output. The one most commonly used is called the **gross national product (GNP).** Its definition and calculation are discussed in the next chapter; here we simply note that it is designed to measure the total market value of the nation's output.

The GNP may be measured in current dollars. This figure tells us the total value of the nation's output in prices ruling at the moment. It is then called **nominal GNP** or **current dollar GNP,** and changes in it reflect changes both in quantities produced and in market prices.

The GNP may also be measured in constant dollars. In this case, the quantities produced in each year are valued in terms of prices ruling in some base year, such as 1972. It is then called **real GNP** or **constant dollar GNP.** Since prices are held constant in calculating it, real GNP changes only when output quantities change.

Total output and national product both refer to constant dollar GNP, a measure of total output produced. This is given the symbol Y.

To see what is involved in distinguishing real from nominal GNP, consider a very simple economy that produces and consumes only one product: wheat. (The concepts are easier to understand by first using this simple example. We then apply them in more complex and realistic situations.) In the one-product wheat economy, real national product is the number of bushels of wheat produced per year. Table 26-1 shows the problems involved in calculating GNP measures when both prices and quantities change. In the economy illustrated in the table, real GNP fluctuates but nominal GNP rises continuously because inflation hides the ups and downs in wheat output. If you knew only the nominal GNP, you would need to separate its changes into quantity and price changes to see how real output and the price level were behaving individually. This is done by calculating the value of wheat output at constant prices so that all the changes reflect only changes in quantities. This calculation gives us real or constant dollar GNP in the one-product wheat economy.

Realistically, we know that the output of any economy consists of many products, and to obtain real GNP these outputs must be aggregated. The prices from an arbitrary base year are used to value the outputs for each year. These values are then summed to obtain real GNP, which is the GNP

TABLE 26–1 REAL AND NOMINAL GNP IN A ONE-PRODUCT ECONOMY

Year	(1) Price of wheat ($ per bushel)	(2) Output of wheat (millions of bushels)	(3) Nominal GNP (millions of $)	(4) Real GNP (constant [1982] prices)
1982	2.00	10	20	20
1983	2.50	12	30	24
1984	3.00	11	33	22

Changes in nominal GNP reflect changes in both prices and quantities. In this example, output of wheat and hence real GNP rises in the second year but falls in the third. However, nominal GNP rises in both years because the rise in prices in the third year swamps the fall in output.

The fourth column calculates the GNP at constant prices and correctly shows that real output rose from 1982 to 1983 but fell from 1983 to 1984.

TABLE 26–2 GNP IN CURRENT AND CONSTANT DOLLARS

Year	(1) GNP in billions of current dollars	(2) GNP in billions of 1972 dollars	(3) Implicit GNP deflator (1972 = 100)
1935	72	261	27.6
1945	212	580	37.9
1955	400	658	60.8
1965	691	929	74.4
1975	1,549	1,232	125.8
1980	2,633	1,474	178.6
1982	3,058	1,476	207.2

Source: Economic Reports of the President.

Current dollar GNP tells us about the money value of output; constant dollar GNP tells us about changes in physical output. The GNP in current dollars gives the total value of all final output in any year, valued in the selling prices of that year. The GNP in constant dollars gives the total value of all final output in any year, valued in the prices ruling in one particular year, in this case, 1972.

The ratio *GNP in current dollars/GNP in constant dollars* times 100 is the implicit GNP deflator. (It is in effect a price index with current-year quantity weights.)

valued at constant prices. Year-to-year changes in this measure are due solely to quantity changes (since prices are held constant).

As with the wheat economy, each change in nominal GNP can be split into a change due to quantities and a change due to prices. For example, in 1982 nominal GNP in the United States was 157 percent higher than in 1972. This increase is due to a 133 percent increase in prices and a 24 percent rise in real GNP. Table 26-2 gives nominal and real GNP for selected years since 1935.

Why Output Variables
Are a Matter of Concern

Short-run fluctuations in national product give rise to what is called the business cycle. In periods of high activity, often called *booms*, employment is high and unemployment correspondingly low. In periods of low activity, often called *slumps*, employment is low and unemployment correspondingly high. Policymakers care about short-term fluctuations in national income because slumps bring unwanted unemployment and lost output while booms may create strong inflationary pressures.

Long-run trend changes in real national product have generally been upward in the modern era. Thus we refer to them as **economic growth.** With growth, each generation can expect, on the average, to be substantially better off than all preceding generations. The horrors of the early industrial revolution are no longer with us, primarily because economic growth has resulted in more and more output for less and less work over the last century.

Output: The Historical Experience

Figure 26-3(i) shows real GNP produced by the American economy since 1929 while Figure 26-3(ii) shows the annual percentage change in the GNP; that is, the real growth rate. The series in (i) shows two kinds of movement. The major movement is a trend increase in real output that represents the growth of the American economy. Real output quintupled in the half century from 1932 to 1982. A secondary movement in the GNP series is the short-term fluctuations associated with the cyclical behavior of the economy. Overall growth so dominates the GNP series that the cyclical behavior is hardly visible in this figure. Cyclical patterns are more readily apparent in the series for the growth rate, shown in (ii) and in another series called the *GNP gap* considered in the next section.

FIGURE 26-3
United States National Income and Growth, 1929-1982

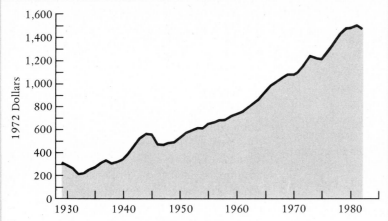

(i) Annual GNP in Constant (1972) Dollars

Constant dollar GNP measures the quantity of total output produced by the nation's economy over the period of a year. National product has risen steadily since the early 1930s, with only a few interruptions. This demonstrates the growth of the American economy. Shorter-term fluctuations are obscured by the long-term growth trend in (i) but are highlighted in (ii), which plots changes in real GNP. In (ii), the short-term fluctuations are more readily apparent, but the long-term upward trend still shows up because the majority of figures are positive.

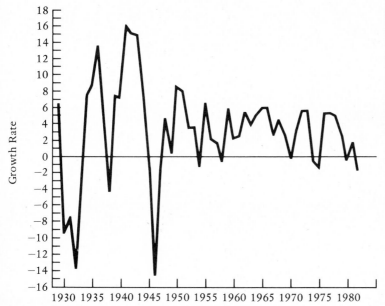

(ii) Annual rate of growth of GNP in constant dollars

Source: Economic Reports of the President.

Potential GNP and the GNP Gap

Actual GNP is what the economy does in fact produce. We have seen that when measured in current dollars it is called *nominal GNP* and when measured in constant dollars it is called *real GNP*.

We now need to add an additional concept. **Potential GNP** or **full-employment GNP** is what the economy would produce *if* its productive resources were fully employed at their normal intensity of use. This assumes that any unemployment of labor is frictional, and that capital—plant and equipment—is being used at its normal capacity levels. Potential GNP can be measured either in current or in constant dollars in the same way as actual GNP. We use the symbol Y^* to denote potential GNP measured in constant dollars.[4]

The **GNP gap** is potential GNP minus actual

[4] The terminology used to refer to potential income is constantly changing. Full-employment income used to be common, but high-employment income is used more often today. To avoid picking one particular term in a world where terminology is not settled, we use the neutral symbol Y^* rather than Y_P, Y_F, or Y_H for potential, full-employment, or high-employment income.

GNP. It measures the market value of goods and services that *could have been* produced if the economy's resources had been fully employed but that actually went unproduced. This is sometimes referred to as the *deadweight loss* of unemployment.

Slumps in business activity are associated with large GNP gaps, booms with small ones. In a major boom the gap can even become negative, indicating that actual GNP exceeds the economy's potential GNP. This situation is often referred to as one of *excess demand*, while *excess supply* refers to a situation where actual GNP is below its potential level.

Actual GNP can exceed potential GNP because potential GNP is defined for a normal rate of utilization of factors of production, and there are many ways in which normal rates of utilization can be exceeded temporarily. Labor may work harder or work longer hours than normal; factories may operate an extra shift or not close for routine repairs and maintenance. While these expedients are only temporary, they are effective in the short run.

Figure 26-4 shows the GNP gap for the American economy over a period of years. The fluctuations in economic activity are apparent from the fluctuations in the size of the gap. The deadweight

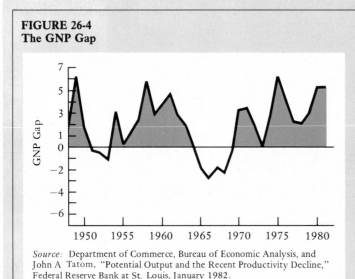

**FIGURE 26-4
The GNP Gap**

The GNP gap measures the difference between the economy's potential output and its actual output; it is expressed here as a percentage of potential output. The cyclical behavior of the economy is clearly apparent from the behavior of the GNP gap from 1955 to 1982. Slumps in economic activity cause large gaps, booms reduce the gap. The shaded area above the zero line represents the deadweight loss from unemployment.

Source: Department of Commerce, Bureau of Economic Analysis, and John A Tatom, "Potential Output and the Recent Productivity Decline," Federal Reserve Bank at St. Louis, January 1982.

loss from unemployment over any time span is indicated by the overall size of the gap over that span; that is, by the shaded area between the curves and the horizontal line indicating full-employment output.

The measurement of potential GNP is not straightforward. Since it cannot be observed directly, the problem is not only one of observation and measurement but also of establishing acceptable definitions for such concepts as "normal levels of utilization" and "full employment capacity." Because Y^* is hard to measure, the GNP gap, given by $(Y^* - Y)$, is correspondingly hard to measure.

The Relation Between Output and Employment

Output and employment, and therefore output and unemployment, are closely related. If more is to be produced, either more workers must be used in production or existing workers must produce more. The first change means a rise in employment; the second means a rise in output per person employed, called a rise in **productivity.** Increases in productivity are a major source of economic growth.[5]

Unemployment is the difference between the labor force and employment. Unemployment can rise either because employment falls or the labor force rises, other things being equal. For example, in recent decades the number of people entering the labor force has exceeded the number leaving the labor force because of retirement and death. The rise in the labor force has often led to increases in unemployment even in periods when total employment is growing.

Changes in productivity and in the labor force dominate the long-term behavior of output and employment. But productivity and the labor force generally change only slowly from year to year, and thus they have little effect on the short-term behavior of the economy. We will assume for the time being that the labor force and productivity are constant. This is a reasonable approximation of reality for purposes of analyzing the short-term behavior

[5] Productivity was discussed at great length in Chapter 13 and will be further discussed in Chapter 38 on economic growth.

of the economy. It also has the important implication that unemployment and output are negatively related while employment and output are positively related.

The Price Level

The **price level** refers to an average of some broad group of prices ruling in the economy. It is measured by an index number of these prices.[6] The three most common price indexes are the Consumer Price Index (CPI), which covers commodities bought by the "typical consumer"; the Producer's Price Index, which covers goods at earlier stages of production; and the GNP deflator, which covers everything produced in the economy. The price level is usually denoted by the symbol P.

We have already discussed (see Chapter 3) the calculation of such base weighted indexes as the CPI. A new kind of index, however, arises from calculations of real and nominal national income: the **implicit GNP deflator.**[7] It is defined as follows:

$$\text{GNP deflator} = \frac{\text{GNP in current dollars}}{\text{GNP in constant dollars}} \times 100\%$$

The GNP deflator is the most comprehensive measure of the price level because it covers all the goods and services produced by the entire economy. The value of the deflator in any particular year, such as 1982, is obtained by valuing 1982 output first at current prices and then at base year (say, 1972) prices. The difference between the two measures must be due to the price changes between the base year and the current year since the quantities are the same.

The data for the one-product wheat economy yield a GNP deflator by dividing the nominal GNP in column 3 of Table 26-1 by the constant price GNP in column 4 and multiplying by 100. This yields values of 100, 125, and 150, respectively.

[6] The construction of index numbers and their strengths and weaknesses were discussed in Chapter 3.

[7] It is called implicit because it is not constructed in the way a normal index is constructed. Instead national income is valued at two different sets of prices and the price index is implied by the ratio of the two national income measures multiplied by 100 percent.

Data for the actual implicit GNP deflator appear in Table 26-2.

Why the Price Level
Is Not a Matter of Concern

By and large, governments do not have policies about the price level per se. No one feels that the price level ruling in the United States in 1776 was intrinsically better or worse than the one ruling in 1976. The level of prices of commodities and factors of production at which the economy's transactions occur is irrelevant to living standards. Our well-being is affected by the adjustments that occur while the price level is changing. Inflation and deflation affect us even if the price level does not

matter. What does matter is the *process of inflation;* that is, what happens while the price level is changing. Whatever the present level of prices, there will be many economic consequences if it rises or falls sharply over the next few years.

Price Levels: The Historical Experience

Figure 26-5 shows the behavior of the American price level for the period 1929–1982. Two facts stand out. The price level changes constantly, although by amounts that vary considerably in different years. Second, and more important, the price level has displayed a distinct upward trend over the period; in only 2 out of the over 50 observations did the price level fall. In 1982 prices

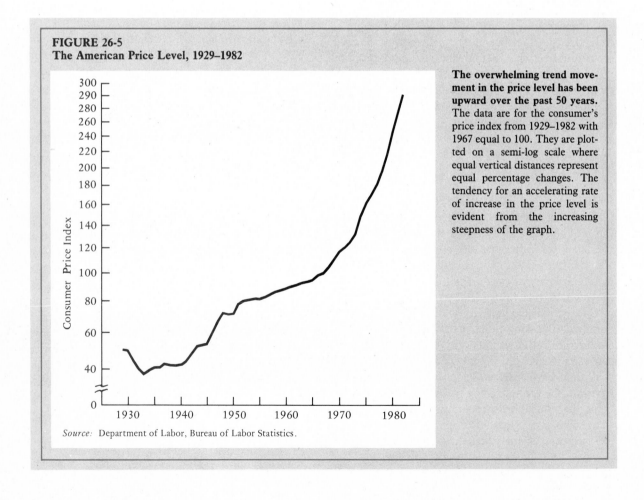

FIGURE 26-5
The American Price Level, 1929–1982

The overwhelming trend movement in the price level has been upward over the past 50 years. The data are for the consumer's price index from 1929–1982 with 1967 equal to 100. They are plotted on a semi-log scale where equal vertical distances represent equal percentage changes. The tendency for an accelerating rate of increase in the price level is evident from the increasing steepness of the graph.

Source: Department of Labor, Bureau of Labor Statistics.

were on average 463 percent higher than in 1929. This, of course, has greatly reduced the value of the currency. At the beginning of 1983 it took $563 to buy what could be bought for $100 in 1929.

Inflation

The rate of inflation is the percentage increase in some price index from one period to another. In the rare event of a drop in the price level, we speak of a deflation.

The formula for measuring the inflation rate is

$$\frac{\text{this period's } P - \text{last period's } P}{\text{last period's } P} \times 100\%$$

If the periods are not a year apart it is common to convert the result to an annual rate. Assume for example that the CPI was 150 last month and 151.5 this month. This yields an inflation rate of 1 percent *per month*. Prices rose by 1 percent during the month. Compounding yields a rate of inflation of just over 12 percent per year. When we say that over the last month prices rose at an annual rate of 12 percent, what we mean is that *if* the rate of increase that actually occurred over the last month persisted for a year, prices would rise by 12 percent over the year. This is the inflation rate that is most commonly quoted in the press when the monthly CPI figures are released. If the figures were as illustrated above, you would read something like "Prices rose 1 percent last month, making the current annual inflation rate 12 percent."

Another common method is to use the latest monthly CPI figure and the CPI for the same month last year. The resulting figure is at an annual rate since the increase in the CPI is being measured over a 12-month period. (The box on page 492 explores the advantages and disadvantages of these and other similar measures.)

Why Inflation Is a Matter of Concern

Whatever the present level of prices, there will be many economic consequences if it rises (or falls) sharply over the course of the next few years. Most of the consequences are associated with changes in what is called the **purchasing power of money**. This term refers to the amount of goods and services that can be purchased with a given amount of money. Inflation, which is a rise in prices, reduces the purchasing power of money.

Some of the effects of inflation can be avoided by adding "escalator" or "indexing" clauses to such things as social security benefits and specific wage and price contracts. Such clauses link the payments made under the terms of the contract to changes in the price level. Escalator clauses are common in labor agreements, in long-term raw material contracts, and in many government procurement agreements.

Even without a formal contract expressed in real terms, it is possible to allow for the effects of an *expected* inflation. Wage and price contracts are major examples. If, say, a 10 percent inflation is expected over the next year, a money wage that rises by 10 percent over that period will preserve the expected purchasing power of wages. Similarly, lending contracts can allow for the loss of purchasing power of money due to an expected inflation. If a 10 percent increase in inflation is expected, a 10 percent increase in the interest rate on any loan will compensate the lender for the loss of purchasing power of the money lent and leave unaltered the expected purchasing power of the amount the borrower has to repay.

Unanticipated inflations are more harmful than are anticipated inflations. Contracts freely entered into when the price level was expected to rise at 10 percent a year will mean hardships for some and unexpected gains for others if the inflation rate accelerates unexpectedly to 15 percent.

If a wage contract specifies wage increases of 10 percent in expectation of a 10 percent inflation, workers lose unexpectedly if inflation turns out to be 15 percent (since the purchasing power of their wage is less than they anticipated when they agreed to the contract). Employers lose if the inflation turns out to be only 5 percent (since the price of what they sell has risen by less than they expected when they agreed to the wage increase). Similarly, if a loan contract specifies a 13 percent interest rate

HOW THE INFLATION RATE IS MEASURED

The Bureau of Labor Statistics calculates the Consumer Price Index every month. When it is announced, the monthly inflation rate makes big news in the press. But just what does it mean when we hear that the inflation rate has soared, or moderated slightly, or even been zero this month?

Such figures almost always refer to the CPI. But because changes in the CPI can be calculated in different ways, we must beware of accepting the figures too uncritically. "The" inflation rate is commonly measured in three different ways, each with its own advantages and shortcomings.

The CPI for This Month over the CPI for the Same Month Last Year

This measure uses the newly announced CPI for this month and the CPI for the same month last year in the equation given in the text. For example, the CPI in July 1982 was 292.2, while it was 274.4 in July 1981. On this measure the July 1982 inflation rate was 6 percent. This measure tells us that the CPI actually did rise 6 percent over these 12 months. The disadvantage of this measure is that it is not sensitive to sudden changes in inflation. Say, for example, that the CPI rose by 2 percent every month of one year and then remained constant for every month of the second year. This measure will give an inflation rate of 12 percent in January of the second year, 11 percent in February, and so on. It will not fall to zero until the *end* of the second year, although for 12 successive months the price level will have been unchanged.

This Month's CPI over Last Month's CPI

As discussed in the text, this method uses this month's CPI and last month's CPI to calculate a monthly inflation rate, and then compounds the result to give an annual rate. What this figure tells us is the percentage change in the CPI that would occur *if* prices rose over the coming year at the rate they have risen over the last month. It has the advantage of immediately reflecting changes in the inflation rate. In the previous example, where the CPI rose in each month of the first year, but remained stable in the second year, the measured rate of inflation would be zero from February of the second year onward. The problem with this measure is that it can be very erratic since the timing of price changes before or after the end of the month will have a big accidental effect on it.

This Year's Average CPI over Last Year's Average CPI

This method adds up monthly CPIs from each year and divides by 12 to get an average CPI for each year. Then the formula in the text is used by dividing the difference between the two figures by last year's figure and multiplying the 100. This is the least erratic of the three figures. Its disadvantage is that variations in the monthly inflation rate within the year are completely suppressed.

There are many different ways of computing "the" inflation rate. Properly understood they all give useful and complementary information. It is often said that you can prove anything you want with figures. Certainly by carefully selecting your figures you can get quite different inflation rates for any one year. But people who understand what each inflation measure does and does not reveal need not be fooled by such selective presentation of data. Figures only lie to those uninformed enough to be unaware of what they do and do not actually say!

in expectation of a 10 percent inflation, lenders lose unexpectedly if inflation turns out to 15 percent (since the purchasing power of the repayment is less than they expected when they agreed to lend the money at only 13 percent). Borrowers lose if inflation is only 5 percent (since the purchasing power of the repayment is greater than they ex-

pected when they agreed to pay 13 percent on the loan).

Inflation: The Historical Experience

Figure 26-6 shows the course of American inflation from 1929 to 1982. Considerable year-to-year

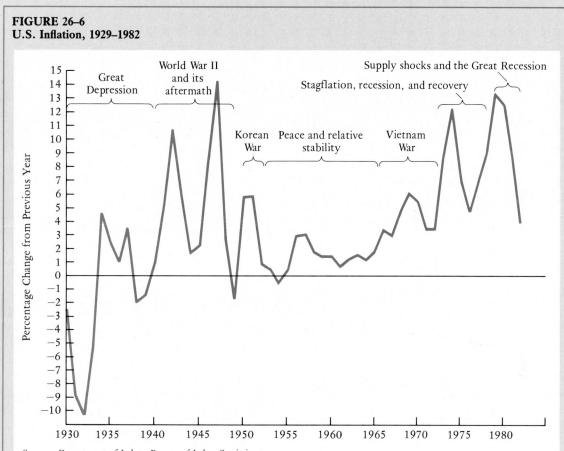

FIGURE 26–6
U.S. Inflation, 1929–1982

Source: Department of Labor, Bureau of Labor Statistics.
Note: The data before 1948 are based on year-to-year changes while those after 1948 are calculated on the basis of December-to December changes in the price level.

The rate of inflation has varied from -10 percent to +14 percent over the period since 1930. Prices fell dramatically during the onset of the Great Depression. They rose sharply during and after World War II and during the Korean War. Although variable, there was no discernible trend in the inflation rate from the end of the Korean War to the mid 1960s. The period starting in the mid 1960s, however, experienced a strong upward trend in the inflation rate, interrupted by short-term fluctuations. In 1982, however, the inflation rate fell to the lowest figure since the early 1970s.

fluctuations are apparent. The general acceleration of the inflation rate from the mid 1960s until the mid 1970s is dramatic. The falloff of the inflation rate in the mid 1970s and again in the early 1980s was a delayed response to the two major recessions.

AGGREGATE DEMAND AND AGGREGATE SUPPLY

Why are the price level, output, and employment what they are today? What causes them to change? The concepts of demand and supply help us to answer these questions.

In Chapter 5 we saw how the interaction of demand and supply can determine prices and quantities for individual commodities. If we had a single demand curve and a single supply curve for the whole economy, we could determine the economy's price level and the quantity of its total output just as we can determine price and quantity for a single product such as potatoes or coal.

This possibility is illustrated in Figure 26-7, which assumes the existence of an aggregate demand curve and an aggregate supply curve for the entire economy. The **aggregate demand curve** (**AD**) shows the relation between the total amount of all output that will be purchased and the price level of that output. The **aggregate supply curve** (**AS**) shows the relation between the total amount of output that will be produced and the price level of that output. This output is measured by constant dollar GNP and is referred to as real national product.

To clarify what is being measured in this diagram, it is instructive to return for a moment to

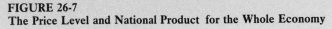

FIGURE 26-7
The Price Level and National Product for the Whole Economy

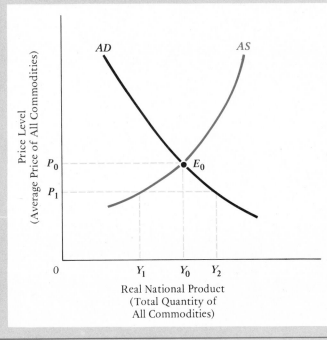

Aggregate demand and aggregate supply determine the price level and national product for the entire economy. Actual output is determined by the intersection of the aggregate demand and aggregate supply curves. Equilibrium is at E_0, with a price level of P_0 and a national product of Y_0. At higher price levels, aggregate supply exceeds aggregate demand; at lower price levels, aggregate demand exceeds aggregate supply. For example, if the price level were P_1, purchasers would wish to buy Y_2 of total output but producers would only be willing to make and sell only Y_1. The resulting shortage would then force prices up from P_1 to P_0.

our simple example of a one-product wheat economy. Here the aggregate-demand and aggregate supply curves depict relations between the price of wheat and the quantity of wheat. Because there is only one product the economy's price level is the price of wheat. The economy's output is the number of bushels of wheat produced. Its real GNP values that output in terms of the prices ruling in some base year.[8]

In a real economy there are, of course, many products and many prices. The principle is, however, the same. Now the vertical axis measures the index of all the economy's prices and the horizontal axis measures its GNP valued in constant dollars.

The aggregate demand curve is negatively sloped indicating that the lower the price level the greater the quantity of output demanded by purchasers. The aggregate supply curve is positively sloped, indicating that the higher the price level the greater the quantity of output produced by sellers.

The intersection of the aggregate demand and aggregate supply curves determines the equilibrium values of the real national product and the price level.

Only at the equilibrium price level is the amount purchasers wish to buy equal to the amount producers wish to sell. At any other price level the amount demanded is not equal to the amount supplied.

The Aggregate Demand Curve

The aggregate demand curve is negatively sloped. This shape indicates that, other things being equal:

The higher the price level the smaller the total quantity demanded, and the lower the price level the larger the total quantity demanded.

Why does it have this slope?

---

[8] Of course multiplying each year's output by a constant wheat price does nothing other than change the scale of measurement. The rate of change between any two years is the same for the output series in column 2 and the real GNP series in column 4 of Table 26-1.

The *AD* Curve and Individual Market Demand Curves

The aggregate demand curve used in macroeconomics slopes downward, as do the individual market demand curves used in microeconomics. But it does so for very different reasons.

Recall that a market demand curve describes what happens when the price of one product changes, with the price of all other products being held constant. What happens along a market demand curve happens, therefore, because the relation among prices is changing; that is, the product in question is getting cheaper or more expensive relative to all other products. The *AD* curve, however, plots aggregate demand against the *price level*. Thus what happens along the *AD* curve depends on the average behavior of all prices, not on the behavior of any individual price. So the forces at work are different from those that explain the market demand curve.

The Slope of the *AD* Curve

Then what does explain the downward slope of the *AD* curve? Although one reason will emerge in Chapter 28 when we discuss what are called *wealth effects*, all the reasons can be explained fully only after we have covered money and interest rates. In the meantime, some readers may decide for now just to take the aggregate demand curve's slope on faith, knowing that it will be more completely explained later. Others who may like a preview of these reasons can have one by studying the box now.

The Aggregate Supply Curve

Figure 26-8 adds potential output to the aggregate demand–aggregate supply diagram. The *potential* level of real output is shown by a *vertical* line. This line indicates that potential output is independent of the price level. It is dependent only on the

THE SHAPE OF THE AGGREGATE DEMAND CURVE

Why the Aggregate Demand Curve Is Not Simply the Sum of Individual Market Demand Curves

In Chapter 5 we studied the demand curves for individual products. It is tempting to think that the properties of the aggregate demand curve arise from the same behavior that gives rise to those "individual" demand curves. Unfortunately, life is not so simple. Let us see why we cannot take such an approach.

The Fallacy of Composition

If we assumed that we could obtain a downward-sloping aggregate demand curve in the same manner that we derived downward-sloping individual market demand curves, we would be committing the fallacy of composition. This is to assume that what is correct for the parts must be correct for the whole.

Consider a simple example of the fallacy. Any art collector can go into the market and add to her private collection of nineteenth century French paintings provided only that she has enough money. But to assume that because any one person can do this, everyone could do so simultaneously is plainly wrong. The stock of nineteenth century French paintings in the world is totally fixed. All of us cannot do what any one of us with enough money can do.

How does the fallacy of composition relate to demand curves?

The Shape of an Individual Demand Curve

An individual demand curve describes a situation in which the price of one commodity, such as cotton shirts, changes with the prices of all other commodities and consumers' money incomes are held constant. The demand curve for the commodity in question is negatively sloped for two reasons. First, as the price of one commodity rises, each consumer's given money income will buy a smaller total amount of goods, so a smaller quantity of the commodity in question will be bought. Second, as the price of one particular commodity rises, consumers buy less of it and more of the now relatively cheaper substitutes.

The first reason has no application to the aggregate demand curve, which relates the total demand for all output to the price level. All prices and total output are changing as we move along the *AD* curve. Since the value of output determines income, there is no reason to expect consumers' money incomes to be constant along this curve.

The second reason does have some, but very limited, applicability to the aggregate demand curve. A rise in the price level entails a rise in all domestic commodity prices. Thus there is no incentive to substitute among domestic commodities. But it does give rise, as we shall see below, to some substitution between domestic and foreign goods.

Why the Aggregate Demand Curve Is Negatively Sloped

Three reasons account for the negative slope of the *AD* curve.

Wealth Effect on Expenditure

A rise in the price level lowers the real value of assets denominated in money terms. As a result, people spend less in order to save more, causing the aggregate demand for the nation's output to fall, other things being equal.

Bank balances, bonds, and many other assets are denominated in terms of money. When the price level rises, the real purchasing power of these assets is reduced. For example if I hold a $1,000 bond and the price level doubles, the amount of commodities I can buy with the money I get back when the bond is redeemed falls by half. Since the bond's real value is halved, the real value of my wealth falls. This may cause me to increase my savings in order to recoup some of my lost wealth; to save more, I must spend less on current consumption.

Substitution of Foreign Goods

A rise in the American price level, other things being equal, reduces foreign demand for American exports and leads Americans to buy foreign imports rather than increasingly expensive American commodities.

When the American price level rises American goods become expensive relative to foreign goods and American residents reduce their purchases of relatively expensive American goods and buy relatively cheap foreign goods instead. Foreign consumers reduce their purchases of the increasingly expensive goods exported from America. Since the aggregate demand curve describes the demand for American goods from all sources, including foreign ones, aggregate demand will fall as the American price level rises.

Interest Rate Effects on Expenditure

A rise in the price level creates a shortage of money, which drives up interest rates. This in turn discourages interest-sensitive expenditures.

The third reason why the aggregate demand curve slopes downward is to be found in the effects of money on interest rates and of interest rates on total demand. The main forces are only suggested here; they will be fully apparent later when the necessary links in the argument have been studied. (The full explanation can be found in Chapter 34, starting on page 656.)

When the price of everything rises, firms and households require larger working balances of money. Firms need to finance enlarged payrolls; households need to cover their increased money expenses between one payday and the next. Many try to borrow the extra working balances that they need. This extra demand for money creates a shortage of money. When money is in short supply, the price you have to pay to borrow it—which is the interest rate—rises. Firms that borrow money to build plants and purchase equipment, and households that borrow money to buy consumer goods, respond to rising interest rates by choosing to spend less on capital goods, housing, automobiles, and other goods. This means a decline in the aggregate quantity demanded of the nation's output.

economy's technology and supply of resources and on the normal utilization rates of those resources, including labor.

Why does the aggregate supply curve not coincide with the vertical line depicting potential output? In Figure 26-4 we saw that *actual* output does, in fact, diverge from potential output.

The upward-sloping aggregate supply curve shows that

changes in the price level are associated with changes in actual output in the short run and thus with changes in the size of the GNP gap.

The aggregate supply curve shows what total ouput all the firms in the economy will decide to produce as all prices change. From now on we will label this curve the **short-run aggregate supply (*SRAS*) curve.**

Figure 26-8 shows the *AD* and the *SRAS* curves intersecting to produce a positive GNP gap. In this case, actual output is below potential output.

The Slope of the *SRAS* Curve

Suppose that firms experience a general increase in the demand for their products. If they are to meet the new demand, they must increase their current production levels. This may require that less efficient standby machines and plants are used, that less efficient marginal workers are employed, and that existing workers are given overtime hours at premium wages. All these means of increasing output imply higher costs of production per unit of output, which is referred to as rising **unit costs.** Since expanding output implies higher unit costs, firms will only produce the extra output if it can be sold at higher prices. What happens when a fall

in demand causes firms to reduce output? There will be cost savings as the least efficient labor is laid off first and the least productive capital is put on standby. In depressed times, firms may also lower their profit margins.

For these reasons the lower output will be associated with somewhat lower unit costs and with lower output prices. It follows that the aggregate supply curve slopes upward. This is because output and unit costs of production (as well as profit margins) are positively associated even when input prices are constant. We refer to this curve as the *short run* aggregate supply curve because input *prices* are held constant along it, and they will surely not remain constant over a long period of time. Even with that restriction, increased output is associated with increased *costs* because it requires the use of more and more costly methods of production.

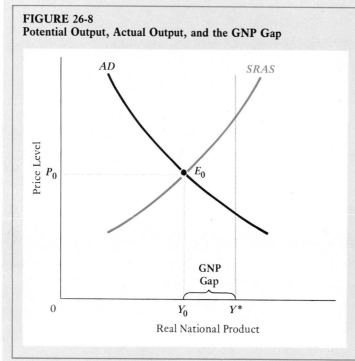

**FIGURE 26-8
Potential Output, Actual Output, and the GNP Gap**

The GNP gap is the difference between potential output and actual output. Potential output is shown by a vertical line because it is not influenced by the price level.

Actual output is determined at Y_0 by the intersection of the aggregate demand (*AD*) and short-run aggregate supply (*SRAS*) curves.

The difference between actual and potential output is the GNP gap.

Changes in Output and Prices

We have seen that the aggregate demand and aggregate supply curves determine national income and the price level. What we really want to know is why income and prices change and how government policy can influence these changes. Here is a simple overview.[9]

Shifts in the Aggregate Curves

What happens to total output and to the price level when one of the aggregate curves shifts? When one shifts, the intersection with the other curve changes. As a result the equilibrium values of real output and the price level also change.

A shift in one aggregate curve leads to changes in the price level and real output.

A shift in the *AD* curve is called an **aggregate demand shock**. A shift in the *SRAS* curve is called an **aggregate supply shock**.[10]

Aggregate Demand Shocks

Figure 26-9 illustrates the effects of an increase in aggregate demand on the price level and real output. The increase could have occurred because of increased investment spending, increased government spending, or greater exports. For now we are not concerned with the source of the boom; we are interested in its implications for the price level and real output. The increase in aggregate demand causes the *AD* curve to shift outward. The new equilibrium thus entails a movement along the *SRAS* curve so that both the price level and the quantity of real output increase.

---

[9] The discussion of movements along and shifts of curves in Chapter 5 could usefully be reviewed at this stage. Recall especially that the phrase "a change in quantity demanded" refers to a *movement along a demand curve*, while the phrase "a change in demand" refers to a *shift of the demand curve*. A similar distinction applies to the supply curve.

[10] What actually happens to Y and P may be influenced by whether or not people see the shock coming. Later we return to this important distinction between unanticipated and anticipated shocks.

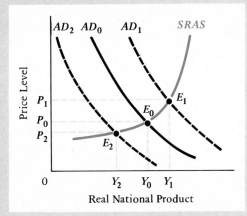

FIGURE 26-9
Aggregate Demand Shocks

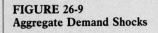

Shifts in *AD* cause the price level and real output to move in the same direction. An increase in aggregate demand causes *AD* to shift from, say, AD_0 to AD_1, and equilibrium to shift from E_0 to E_1. The price level rises from P_0 to P_1, and real output rises from Y_0 to Y_1.

A decrease in aggregate demand causes *AD* to shift from, say, AD_0 to AD_2. The new equilibrium is at E_2, and prices fall to P_2 while real output falls to Y_2.

Figure 26-9 also illustrates that both the price level and the quantity of real output will fall as a result of a reduction in aggregate demand.

Aggregate demand shocks cause the price level and real output to change in the same direction, both rising or both falling together.

Demand-shock inflation. A typical demand shock occurred with the boom that began in 1965. (This boom is of particular interest because it was the transition between the two decades of low inflation rates that followed World War II and the two decades of high inflation rates that governments have had to try hard to bring under control in the 1980s.) In 1965 the buildup of defense spending to finance the accelerating war in Vietnam hit the economy with a severe demand shock. Although there were lapses from full employment, the period was mainly one of excess demand with high output, low unemployment, and rapidly rising prices. The shift in the *AD* curve led to a movement along the *SRAS* curve.

Aggregate Supply Shocks

Figure 26-10 shows the effect of an upward shift in the *SRAS* curve with no change in the *AD* curve: the price level rises and output falls (which implies a larger GNP gap). This combination of events is now called **stagflation**. This rather inelegant word was derived by running together *stagnation* (a colloquial term meaning less than full

employment) and *inflation* (a rise in the price level). Figure 26-10 also shows that a shift of *SRAS* downward will lead to an increase in real output and a decrease in the price level.

Aggregate supply shocks cause the price level and real output to change in opposite directions, one rising and the other falling.

Supply-shock stagflation. The first dramatic stagflation of the modern era began in 1974. One major aspect of that era was that the economy was hit with some severe supply shocks. Serious crop failures combined with the sale of surplus wheat to the U.S.S.R. raised food prices greatly. The policies of the newly aggressive OPEC forced up not only the price of energy but the prices of fertilizer, plastics, synthetic rubber, and dozens of other petroleum-based products. Since many of these are used in the manufacture of yet other commodities, many costs of production rose. The rise in costs led firms to raise their selling prices. Hence the aggregate supply curve shifted upward. The same output would only be supplied at a higher price level. The upward shift in the *SRAS* curve caused a serious stagflation. The economy experienced simultaneously the twin "evils" of falling output and rising prices.

The mid 1970s were the first time in 50 years that the behavior of prices and output resulted largely from a sharply upward-shifting aggregate supply curve. People were used to the behavior of the economy under the impact of demand shocks—where inflation is associated with boom conditions characterized by high and rising output. Consequently its behavior under severe supply shocks—where inflation is associated with slack economic conditions characterized by low and falling output—seemed incomprehensible, even paradoxical. Many commentators who customarily explained observed events in terms of demand-side shocks did not at first appreciate what was happening. Some announced the collapse of conventional macroeconomic theory; others claimed to see a complete change in all economic behavior. Although plausible at the time, such reactions can now be seen as excessive. Once the part played by

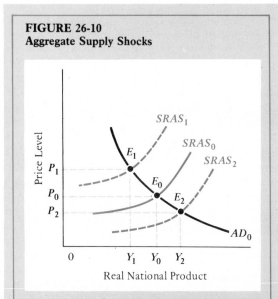

FIGURE 26-10
Aggregate Supply Shocks

Shifts in *SRAS* cause the price level and real output to move in opposite directions. A reduction in aggregate supply causes *SRAS* to shift up and to the left, say, from $SRAS_0$ to $SRAS_1$. Equilibrium then goes from E_0 to E_1. The price level rises to P_1, but real output falls to Y_1.

An increase in aggregate supply causes *SRAS* to shift down and to the right. The new *SRAS* is given by $SRAS_2$, and equilibrium is at E_2. The price level falls to P_2, but real output rises to Y_2.

aggregate supply was understood, the then mysterious events of the mid 1970s became quite understandable, no matter how undesirable.

Supply-side economics. As we saw in Figure 26-10, a downward shift of the *SRAS* curve will lead to a rise in real output and a fall in the price level. To anyone living in economies plagued by stagflation, these conditions, which are just the opposite of stagflation, appear to be ideal. A desire to achieve just this combination was the purpose that lay behind the recently popular "supply-side economics." Supply-siders advocate tax cuts and other incentives to increase supply in order to bring about the desirable outcome of increased output and reduced prices. "Very simple" said the advocates; "easier said than done" replied the critics in a debate we shall take up later.

SUMMARY

1. Macroeconomics examines the behavior of such broad aggregates and averages as the price level, national product, potential GNP, the GNP gap, employment, and unemployment.

2. The dominant theme of the economy is the growth of real output and employment. A secondary theme involves cyclical factors represented by fluctuations in output and employment around the growth trend. In order to study these fluctuations, we focus attention on the GNP gap and the unemployment rate. Unemployment imposes serious costs on the economy.

3. The price level has risen continuously since 1929. The inflation rate measures the rate of change of the price level. Although it fluctuates considerably, it has been consistently positive. Inflation imposes serious costs on the economy.

4. Two major tools of macroeconomics are the aggregate demand and aggregate supply curves. Typically the aggregate demand (*AD*) curve is negatively sloped, indicating that the lower the price level, the higher the demand for the nation's output. Although *potential* output can be taken as independent of the price level, the aggregate supply curve typically slopes upward in the short run. This positively sloped short-run aggregate supply (*SRAS*) curve indicates that the higher the price level the greater will be the output produced.

5. The reasons for the negative slope of the aggregate demand curve will be fully explored in subsequent chapters. The reasons for the positive slope of the short-run aggregate supply curve can, however, be developed now: increases in output entail increases in the costs of producing each unit of output and hence will only be undertaken if output prices rise.

6. Macroeconomic equilibrium occurs at the intersection of the *AD* and *SRAS* curves, thus determining the economy's price level and total ouput. Shifts in the *AD* or *SRAS* curve cause the equilibrium price level and total output.

7. Demand shocks tend to cause output and the price level to change in the same direction so that booms are associated with rising prices and slumps with falling prices. Supply shocks tend to cause output and the price level to change in opposite directions.

TOPICS FOR REVIEW

Employment, unemployment, and the labor force
Gross national product (GNP)
Potential GNP and the GNP gap
The price level and the rate of inflation
Aggregate demand and aggregate supply
The effects of aggregate demand shocks
The effects of aggregate supply shocks

DISCUSSION QUESTIONS

1. Classify as micro or macro (or both) the issues raised in the following newspaper headlines.
   a. "Lettuce crop spoils as strike hits California lettuce producers."

b. "Analysts fear rekindling of inflation as economy recovers toward full employment."

c. "Index of Industrial Production falls by 4 points."

d. "Price of bus rides soars in Centersville as city council withdraws transport subsidy."

e. "A fall in the unemployment rate signals the beginning of the end of the recession in the Detroit area."

f. "Silicon chip technology brings falling prices and growing sales of microcomputers."

g. "Wage settlements in key industries seen by the president to signal the decline of inflationary threats."

h. "Rising costs of imported raw materials cause most Americans manufacturers to raise prices."

2. Explain each of the following by shifts in either (or both) the aggregate demand and aggregate supply curves. (Pay attention to the initial position before the shift(s) occurs.)

a. Output and unemployment rise while prices hold steady.

b. Prices soar but employment and output hold steady.

c. Inflation accelerates even as the recession in business activity deepens.

d. The inflation rate falls, but at the expense of employment.

3. In 1979–1980, the British government greatly reduced income taxes but restored the lost government revenue by raising excise and sales taxes. This led to a short burst of extra inflation and a fall in employment. Explain this in terms of shifts in the aggregate demand and/or supply curves.

4. Indicate whether each of the following events is the cause or the consequence of a shift in aggregate demand or supply. If it is a cause, what do you predict will be the effect on the price level and on real national income?

a. Unemployment increases in 1981–1982 in the United States.

b. OPEC raises oil prices in 1979.

c. OPEC is forced to accept lower oil prices in 1982–1983.

d. In the late 1960s and early 1970s the United States suffered a rapid inflation under conditions of approximately full employment.

e. In country X, income and employment continue to fall while the price level is quite stable.

f. The recovery of the economy of country Y from a severe slump has led to a large increase in income and employment.

g. President Reagan achieves a large increase in defense spending in 1983–1984.

h. Budget deficits soar in the early 1980s as tax revenues fall in the face of the most serious recession since the 1930s.

5. Discuss the various reasons why two truthful people could announce that very different rates of inflation are ruling in the U.S. today.

6. How would unemployment rise at a time when employment was increasing rapidly? Why is unemployment not as serious a matter as it was at the beginning of this century?

7. If you thought the inflation rate was going to be 10 percent next year, why should you be unwilling to lend money at 5 percent interest? Say 5 percent was all you could get and you had money you didn't want to spend for a year. Would you be better just to hold the money? What could you do that would be better than lending your money at 5 percent?

27 THE CONCEPTS OF NATIONAL PRODUCT AND NATIONAL INCOME

The aggregate demand curve shows a relation between the price level and the nation's total ouput. This latter concept is measured by the gross national product (GNP), which is the sum of all the economy's outputs of final products produced over some period, usually a year. The term **final products** excludes all semi-finished products that are further processed and hence used as inputs by other firms. Such semi-finished products are called **intermediate products.** Bread produced by a bak-

ery is a final product, for example, while the flour bought by that bakery is an intermediate product.

The GNP is the nation's total output. As we shall see this total output is equal to its **gross national income.** which is the income claims generated in the process of producing that output. Corresponding to these two concepts are two ways of measuring GNP: the value of what is produced *and* the value of incomes generated by the act of production. Because, however, there are two different ways in which output itself can be measured, there are altogether *three* alternative approaches to measuring GNP. From the production side, the most obvious way is simply to add up the total value of all final goods and services. This is done by calculating expenditure on each of the main components of final output and hence is called *the expenditure approach.* From the production side we can also add up the net contribution to final output of every firm in the economy. This is called the *output approach.* The third approach is to measure the incomes generated by the act of production. This is called the *income approach.*

These three approaches are alternative ways of arriving at the GNP. They give answers that are conceptually identical and that differ in practice only because of errors of measurement. Each approach is of interest, however, because each gives a different and useful breakdown of the GNP.

NATIONAL INCOME ACCOUNTING

National income accounting is the set of rules and techniques for measuring the total flow of output (goods and services) produced and the total flow of incomes generated by this production. How are these measured and what can they tell us?

A standard convention of double-entry bookkeeping is that all value produced must be accounted for by a claim that someone has to that value. Gross national product is the market value of all the production in the economy during one year, while gross national income is the value of all the claims generated by that production. It is a matter of accounting convention that gross national product and gross national income be equal.

Gross national product and gross national income are two different ways of looking at one magnitude: the market value of the nation's output.

Because both concepts have the same total value, the terms *national income* and *national product* are used interchangeably whenever we are interested only in their total value. National product emphasizes the economy's output; national income emphasizes the income generated by producing that

output. In Chapter 26 we spoke of national product to emphasize the quantity-of-output aspect of the aggregate demand and supply diagrams. In theoretical work the total value of output is more often referred to as national income.

What is the value of the different parts of the nation's output that contribute to its GNP? We can look at this question in two ways.

The Expenditure Approach to Measuring Output

The most obvious method is to add up the market values of all the final goods produced in the economy. This is called the *expenditure approach* to measuring GNP because in practice, it is done by adding up the expenditures made to purchase final output.

The total expenditure on final output is called **aggregate expenditure,** and its symbol is boldface **AE.** It is the sum of four broad categories of expenditure: consumption, investment, government, and net exports. Although each of these may be subdivided into finer groupings, the fourfold classification is extremely useful.

Consumption Expenditure

Consumption expenditure covers all goods and services produced and sold to households during the year (with the exception of residential houses, which are counted as investment). It includes services such as haircuts, medical care, and legal advice; nondurable goods such as fresh food and newspapers; and durable goods such as cars, television sets, and air conditioners. This class of expenditure is the output of the economy that is applied directly to satisfying the wants of consumers. We denote it by a boldface symbol **C.**

Investment Expenditure

Investment expenditure covers all final goods and services produced but not used for present consumption. Such goods are called **investment goods.** Investment can be in inventories, in capital goods such as plant and equipment, or in residential housing.

First consider inventories. Virtually all firms hold stocks of their inputs and their own outputs. These stocks are called **inventories.** Inventories of inputs allow production to continue at the desired pace despite short-term fluctuations in the deliveries of inputs bought from other firms. Inventories of outputs allow firms to meet orders despite temporary fluctuations in the rate of output or sales.

Inventories are an important part of the productive process. They require an investment of the firm's money since the firm has paid for but not yet sold the goods. An accumulation of inventories counts as current investment because it represents goods produced but not used for current consumption. A drawing down—often called a *decumulation*—counts as disinvestment because it reduces the stock of goods produced in the past.

Additions to inventories are a part of the economy's final production of investment goods. These are valued in the national income accounts at market value, which includes the wages and other costs the firm incurred in producing the goods and the profit the firm will make when the inventories are sold. Thus, in the case of inventories of a firm's own output, the expenditure approach measures what would have to be spent to purchase them when they are sold rather than what has actually been spent on them at the moment.

Next consider investment in plant and equipment. All production uses capital goods: man-made aids to production such as hand tools, machines, and factory buildings. The economy's total quantity of capital goods is called the **capital stock.** The act of creating new capital goods is an act of investment and is called *investment in fixed capital* or **fixed investment** for short.

The third main category of investment is residential housing. A house is a very durable asset that yields its utility slowly over a long life. For this reason, housing construction is counted as investment expenditure rather than as consumption expenditure. This is done by assuming that the investment is made by the firm that builds the house and that the sale to a user is a mere transfer of ownership that is not a part of national income.

The total investment that occurs in the economy is called **gross investment.** Gross investment is divided into two parts, replacement investment and net investment. Replacement investment, required to maintain the existing capital stock intact, is called the **capital consumption allowance** or simply **depreciation. Net investment** is gross investment minus the capital consumption allowance. Net investment increases the economy's total stock of capital, while replacement investment keeps the existing stock intact by replacing what has been used up.

The investment that is a part of the GNP is gross investment. This is because all investment goods are part of the nation's total output, and their production creates income (and employment) whether the goods produced are a part of net investment or are merely replacement investment. Total investment expenditure is given the bold-faced symbol **I.**

Government Expenditures on Goods and Services

When the government produces goods and services that households want, such as roads and air traffic control, it is obviously adding to the sum total of valuable output in the same way that private firms do when they produce the trucks and airplanes that use the roads and air lanes. Whether other government activities contribute to total output may not seem so clear. Should expenditures by the federal government to send a rocket to Jupiter or to pay a civil servant to file and refile papers from a now defunct department be regarded as contributions to GNP? A lot of people believe that many (or even most) activities "up in Washington" or "down at City Hall" are wasteful if not downright harmful. But most of us also know other people who believe that it is governments, not private firms, that produce many of the important things of life, such as education and pollution control.

National income statisticians do not speculate about which government expenditures are or are not worthwhile. Instead they count all government expenditure that produces goods or services and uses factors of production. Just as the national product includes, without distinction, the output of both gin and Bibles, it also includes the production of bombers and the upkeep of parks, along with the services of internal revenue investigators, CIA agents, and even members of Congress. Actual government expenditure is signified by the symbol **G.**

All government output is valued at cost rather than market value. In many cases there is really no choice. What, for example, is the market value of the Environmental Protection Agency's services or of the services of a court of law? No one knows. But we do know what it costs the government to provide these services, so we value them at their cost of production.

Although valuing at cost is the only possible way to evaluate many government activities, it does have one curious consequence. If, due to a productivity increase, one civil servant now does what two used to do, and the displaced worker shifts to the private sector, the government's contribution to the GNP will register a decline. On the other hand, if two now do what one used to do, the government's contribution will rise. Both of these changes could occur even though what the government actually does is unchanged. This is an inevitable but curious consequence of measuring the value of the government's output by the value of the factors, mainly labor, used to produce it.

There is an important exception to the rule that all government expenditure is included in national income. When a government agency makes welfare payments to a mother of five children whose husband has deserted her, income is transferred to the welfare recipient but the government does not receive, nor does it expect to receive, any marketable services from the deserted mother in return for the welfare payments.[1] The payment itself adds neither to the employment of factors nor to total output.

Government payments to households that are not made in return for the services of factors of production are called *government transfer payments,* or simply **transfer payments.** Such payments do not lead directly to any increase in output, and they are not included in the nation's national income. The major transfer payments arise from social security, unemployment insurance, welfare payments, veterans' pensions, and interest on the national debt (which transfers income from tax payers to holders of government bonds).

Transfer payments are not included in the government expenditure that is part of national income. Thus, when we talk of **government expenditure** or government purchases, and when we use the symbol **G,** we *include* all government expenditure on currently produced goods and services and we *exclude* all government transfer payments.

Net Exports

The fourth main element of aggregate expenditure arises because of foreign trade, a factor that has become increasingly important to the U.S. economy in recent decades. How do imports and exports influence the GNP?

One country's GNP is the total value of final commodities produced in that country. If you spend $9,000 to buy an American car whose synthetic rubber tires are made from Mexican oil, not all of that $9,000 is expenditure on the output of American producers. Because the oil was produced abroad, it is part of the national product of another country. If your cousin spends $6,000 on a Japanese car, only a small part of that value will represent expenditure on American production. Some of it goes for the services of U.S. dealers and U.S. transportation; the rest is the output of Japanese firms and expenditure on Japanese products.

Similarly, when an American firm makes an investment expenditure on an American-produced machine tool made partly with imported raw materials, only part of the expenditure is on American production. The rest is expenditure on the production of the countries supplying the raw materials. The same is also true for government expenditure on such things as roads and dams. Only part of the expenditure is for domestically produced

---

[1] In looking after her children, the mother is performing a useful and valuable function. What she is not doing is producing a commodity that adds to total *marketed* production. The treatment of transfer payment recognizes that fact; it does not imply a value judgment that the mother's activities have zero usefulness, only that they are not sold on the market.

goods and services, some of it for imported materials.

Consumption, investment, and government expenditures all have an import content. To arrive at total expenditure on American products, we subtract the total domestic expenditure on imports, represented by the symbol **M**.

There is a second consideration. If American firms sell goods to German households, the goods are a part of German consumption expenditure but are also a part of U.S. national product. Indeed, all goods and services produced in the United States and sold abroad must be counted as part of American output (they create incomes for the Americans who produce them). To arrive at the total value of expenditure on American national product, we add in the value of American exports, denoted by the symbol **X**.

It is customary to group (**X** – **M**) together and call them **net exports**.

Total Expenditure

Aggregate (or total) expenditure is the sum of these four categories of expenditure.

The expenditure approach measures GNP as the sum of consumption, investment, government expenditure, and net exports.

In symbols we write:

$$\text{GNP} = \text{AE} = C + I + G + (X - M)$$

The value of net exports is usually small in relation to the total value of either **X** or **M**. Thus the correction to national income made to allow for foreign trade will not usually be large. However, a change in either **X** or **M** will cause the national income to change by the same amount as would an equivalent change in **C**, **I**, or **G**.

Figure 27-1(i), page 510, shows American gross national product for 1982 calculated according to the expenditure approach.

The Output Approach

The second way of measuring the nation's GNP is to add up the contributions to final output made by every sector of the economy whether or not that sector is itself producing final outputs. If each firm in the economy produced only final output, there would be no problem. We would just add up the values of all firms' outputs. In reality, however, production of commodities is divided into stages, with particular firms and industries often specializing in the production of intermediate products. For example, one set of firms may mine iron ore; the ore may be sold to another set of firms for manufacturing into steel; the steel may be sold to another set of firms for use in making household tools; and the manufacturer of the tools may sell them to a wholesaler, who sells them to a retailer, who in turn finally sells them to households.

Stages of production, and the consequent inter-firm sales of intermediate products, raise a problem for measuring GNP from production data. If we merely added up the market values of the outputs of all firms, we would obtain a total greatly in excess of the value of output actually available for use. Suppose we took the value of all farmers' outputs of wheat and added to it the value of all flour mills' outputs of flour, plus the value of the outputs of bakeries, plus the value of the sales of bread by all retail shops. The resulting total would be much larger than the value of the final product—bread—produced by the economy. We would have counted the value of the wheat four times, of the flour three times, of the bread produced by the bakery twice, and of the services of the retail shop once.

This is called the problem of double counting. Multiple counting would be a better term, since if we add up the values of all sales, the same output is counted *every time* it is sold from one firm to another. This problem is avoided by using the important concept of value added. Each firm's **value added** is the value of its output *minus* the value of the inputs that it purchases from other firms. Thus a flour mill's value added is the value of its output *minus* the value of the grain it buys from the farmer and the values of any other inputs, such as electricity and fuel oil, that it buys from other firms. The relation between value added and total value of sales is further illustrated in the box.

VALUE ADDED THROUGH STAGES OF PRODUCTION

Because the output of one firm often becomes the input of other firms, the total value of goods sold by all firms greatly exceeds the value of the output of final goods. This general principle is illustrated by a simple example in which firm R starts from scratch and produces goods (raw materials) valued at $100; the firm's value added is $100. Firm I purchases raw materials valued at $100 and produces semi-manufactured goods that it sells for $130. Its value added is $30 because the value of the goods is increased by $30 as a result of the firm's activities. Firm F purchases the semi-manufactured goods for $130, works them into a finished state, and sells them for $180. Firm F's value added is $50. The value of the final goods, $180, is found either by counting only the sales of firm F or by taking the sum of the values added by each firm. This value is much smaller than the $410 that we would obtain if we merely added up the market value of the commodities sold by each firm.

		Transactions between firms at three different stages of production		
	Firm R	Firm I	Firm F	All Firms
A. Purchases from other firms	$ 0	$100	$130	$230 Total interfirm sales
B. Purchases of factors of production (wages, rent, interest, profits)	100	30	50	180 Value added
Total A + B = value of product	$100	$130	$180	$410 Total value of all sales

The output approach measures GNP in terms of the values added by each of the sectors of the economy.

The breakdown of these figures allows us to measure the contribution of each industry to the value of final output whether the industry is itself producing final products, intermediate products, or some mixture of the two. Indeed many industries' products are partly final and partly intermediate. For example, electricity sold to households is a final product while electricity sold to firms and used by them in their own productive processes is an intermediate product.

The Income Approach

Another way of measuring the nation's GNP is to look at the value of total incomes generated in the process of production, which is called the **gross national income.**

The production of the GNP generates income. Labor must be employed, land rented, and capital used.

Because all value produced must be owned by someone, the value of production must equal the value of income claims generated by that production.

The main income claims are shown in Figure 27-1(ii). Wages and salaries, which national income accountants call *compensation to employees*, is by far the largest income share generated. This includes take-home pay, taxes withheld, social security, and pension fund contributions. In total these represent that part of the value of production attributable to labor. Next comes corporate profits, followed by the capital consumption allowance. The latter is part of gross profits but, being that part which is needed to compensate for capital used up in the

THE IDENTITY OF OUTPUT, INCOME, AND EXPENDITURE

In all of national income accounting the basic *overall* aggregate being measured is the total value of output at market prices (either in constant or in current market prices). This can be looked at directly in terms of the output itself, O, or the income it generates, Y, or the expenditure required to purchase it, E. Although the details of each calculation give us independent information, the totals do not, since all three are defined so that they are identical:

$$Y = O = E$$

The reason for the identity of Y and O is that Y does not measure incomes actually paid out during the course of the year but instead measures the income claims generated by producing O. The identity of Y and O then follows from the accounting practice that all output must be matched by claims on that output: what is not wages, interest, and rent becomes either profits or the government's claim through indirect taxes. Between them they must account for all output since someone must own the value that has been produced. Also, goods produced and not sold are valued at market prices, and the difference between their value and their cost of production is counted as profits and recorded as part of profit income even though this will not accrue until the goods are sold.

Now consider the identity between O and E. This follows obviously because E measures the expenditure required to purchase the nation's output, which is of course the same thing as the value of that output. In calculating expenditure national income accountants add up the amounts actually spent to purchase what is sold plus the amount that would have to be spent if inventories were sold; that is, firms are assumed to have purchased the inventories and to have paid the market price for them. This, of course, makes E the same thing as O.

The interest in having all three measures lies not in their identical total but in the breakdown of each. In the case of O, this is by industry, such as electricity generation; in the case of E, it is by type of expenditure, such as consumption; in the case of Y, it is by type of income, such as wages and salaries.

process of production, it is not part of net profits. Smaller items include *income of proprietors* and rental income. The former is mainly the income of farmers, unincorporated businesses, and professionals who either work on their own or form partnerships. The latter includes rents on rented housing and imputed rent for the use of owner-occupied housing.

A final important claim to the value of output arises out of indirect taxes—taxes on the production and sale of goods and services. If, for example, a good's sale value of $10 includes $6 of intermediate goods and $1 of business excise taxes, only $3 is available as income to factors of production. One dollar's worth of market value represents the government's claim on that value. When adding up income claims to get GNP, it is therefore necessary to add in that part of the total market value of output that is the government's claim arising out of its taxes on goods and services.[2]

The income approach measures GNP as indirect taxes plus the sum of the factor incomes generated in the process of producing final output.

The equivalence of the three approaches is discussed in the box.

[2] It is also necessary to subtract government subsidies on goods and services since these allow incomes to *exceed* the market value of output. For example, if a single proprietor produces $20,000 worth of value added over the year and receives a $5,000 subsidy from the government, his income is $25,000. So to get the market value of his output from the income side, we must take his income and *subtract* the government subsidy.

FIGURE 27-1
Two Ways of Accounting for GNP

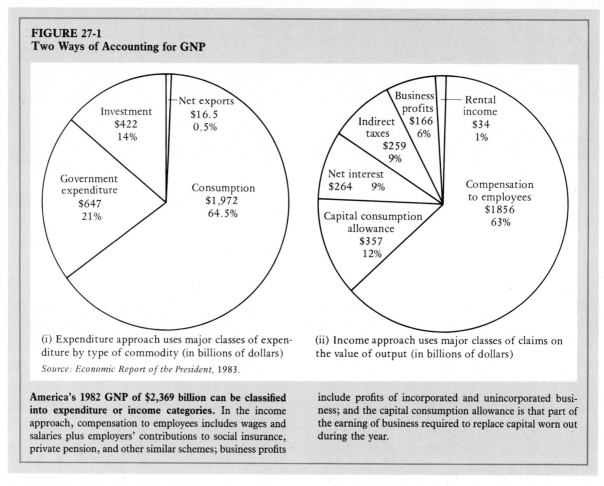

(i) Expenditure approach uses major classes of expenditure by type of commodity (in billions of dollars)

Source: Economic Report of the President, 1983.

(ii) Income approach uses major classes of claims on the value of output (in billions of dollars)

America's 1982 GNP of $2,369 billion can be classified into expenditure or income categories. In the income approach, compensation to employees includes wages and salaries plus employers' contributions to social insurance, private pension, and other similar schemes; business profits include profits of incorporated and unincorporated business; and the capital consumption allowance is that part of the earning of business required to replace capital worn out during the year.

Some Different Income Concepts

Gross national product is the most comprehensive of the several national income concepts. It measures the sum of all values added in the economy, the sum of the market values of final goods produced, and the sum of all claims to the value of that production.

The next most comprehensive measure is **net national product (NNP)**. This is GNP minus the capital consumption allowance. NNP is thus a measure of the net output of the economy after deducting from gross output an amount necessary to maintain intact the existing stock of capital. It is the maximum amount that could be consumed by the private and the government sectors without actually running down the economy's capital stock.

Personal income is income earned by or paid to individuals before allowance for personal income taxes. Some personal income goes for taxes, some for saving, and the rest for consumption. A number of adjustments to NNP are required to arrive at personal income. The most important are (1) subtracting from NNP indirect taxes, which are that part of the market value of output going directly to governments, (2) subtracting from NNP the business earnings retained by corporations, (3) subtracting from NNP the income taxes paid by business, and (4) adding to NNP the government transfer payments to households. The first three represent parts of the value of output not paid to persons; the fourth represents payments to households that households have available to spend or to save even though these payments are not part of GNP.

Disposable income is a measure of the amount of current income that households have to spend and to save. It is calculated as personal income minus personal income taxes.

Disposable income is GNP *minus* any part of it that is not actually paid over to households, *minus* the personal income taxes paid by households, *plus* transfer payments received by households.

The relation among GNP, NNP, personal income, and disposable income is elaborated in Table 27-1.

TABLE 27–1 VARIOUS NATIONAL INCOME MEASURES, 1982 (Billions of Dollars)

A. Gross national product (GNP)	$3,058
Less: Capital consumption allowance	357
B. Net national product (NNP)	2,701
Less:	
1. Retained earnings	80
2. Business taxes (including social security)	513
3. Miscellaneous adjustments	20
Plus:	
4. Transfer payments to individuals	482
C. Personal income	2,570
Less: Personal tax payments	397
D. Disposable income	2,173

Source: Economic Report of the President, 1983.

Each of the four related national income measures focuses on a different aspect of the national output. GNP measures the market value of total output. NNP measures the net value of output after an allowance for maintaining the capital stock. Personal income measures income earned or received by persons before personal income taxes. Disposable income is a measure of after-tax income of persons; it is the amount they have available to spend or to save.

INTERPRETING NATIONAL INCOME MEASURES

The information provided by measures of national income can be extremely useful, but unless carefully interpreted, it can also be seriously misleading, as is further discussed in the box on page 514. Furthermore, each specialized measure—GNP, NNP, personal income, disposable income, and others to be considered shortly—gives different information, so each may be the best statistic for studying a particular range of problems.

Money Values and Real Values

We saw in Chapter 26 that GNP can be valued in current or constant dollars. When valued in current dollars, it tells us nominal GNP. When valued in constant dollars, it tells us real GNP. When studying the effect of inflation on the value of GNP, we need to look at nominal GNP. When studying changes in the economy's quantity of output, we need to look at real GNP.

Total Output and Per Capita Output

The rise in real GNP during this century has had two main causes: first, an increase in the amounts of land, labor, and capital used in production; and second, an increase in output per unit of input. In other words, more inputs have been used, and each input has become more productive. For many purposes, we want to measure total output, for example, to assess a country's potential military strength or to know the total size of its market. For other purposes, such as studying changes in living standards, we require per capita measures, which are obtained by dividing a total measure such as GNP by the relevant population.

There are many useful per capita measures. Dividing GNP by the total population gives a measure of how much GNP there is on average for each person in the economy; this is called **per capita**

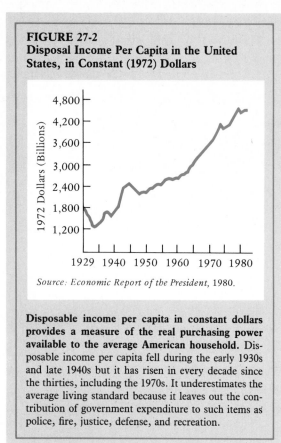

FIGURE 27-2
Disposal Income Per Capita in the United States, in Constant (1972) Dollars

Source: Economic Report of the President, 1980.

Disposable income per capita in constant dollars provides a measure of the real purchasing power available to the average American household. Disposable income per capita fell during the early 1930s and late 1940s but it has risen in every decade since the thirties, including the 1970s. It underestimates the average living standard because it leaves out the contribution of government expenditure to such items as police, fire, justice, defense, and recreation.

GNP. Dividing GNP by the number of persons employed tells us the average output per employed worker. Dividing GNP by the total number of hours worked measures output per hour of labor input. A widely used measure of the purchasing power of the average person is disposable income per capita in constant dollars. This measure is shown in Figure 27-2.

Omissions from Measured National Income

Finally, we come to a series of omissions from the GNP and thus also from the NNP, disposable income, and other measures based mainly on parts of the GNP. The importance of these omissions can be judged only when we know the purpose for which the data are to be used.

Illegal Activities

The GNP does not measure illegal activities even though many of them are ordinary business activities which produce goods and services that are sold on the market and generate factor incomes. The liquor industry during Prohibition in the 1920s was an important example because it accounted for a significant part of the nation's total economic activity. Today the same is true of many forms of illegal gambling, prostitution, and the illicit drug trade. To gain an accurate measure of the *total* demand for factors of production in the economy or of *total* marketable output—whether or not we as individuals approve of particular products—we should include these activities. Because such activities are illicit, however, it would be hard to find out enough to include them even if we wanted to.[3]

The omission of illegal activities is no trivial matter. The drug trade alone is a multi-billion dollar business. No one knows exactly the value of its output, but a typical estimate runs around $30 billion for 1981. This was 1 percent of the entire GNP for that year.

Unreported Activities

An important omission from the measured GNP is the so-called underground economy. The transactions in the underground economy are perfectly legal in themselves. The only illegal thing about them is that they are not reported for income-tax purposes. For example, a neighbor repairs a leak in your roof and takes payment in cash or in kind in order to avoid tax. Because such transactions go unreported, they are unrecorded in the country's GNP.

There are numerous reasons for the growth of the underground economy. Probably the most im-

[3] Some of them do get included because people often report their earnings from illicit activities as part of their earnings from legal activities in order to avoid the fate of Al Capone. Having avoided conviction on many counts, he was finally caught for income tax invasion.

portant reason is to evade income taxes. But the underground economy also allows the evasion of a host of other taxes and regulations. Sales and excise taxes are not paid by the underground economy. Safety regulations, minimum wage laws, antidiscrimination regulations, and social security payments may all be avoided by people operating in that economy. Generally the higher the tax rates and the greater the restrictions arising from rules and regulations, the greater the incentive to evade them all by "going underground." Another reason for this growth is the rising importance of services in the nation's total output. It is much easier for a carpenter or television repairman to pass unnoticed by government authorities than it is for a manufacturing establishment whose presence is highly visible.

Estimates of the value of income earned in the American underground economy run from 5 percent to 15 percent of the American GNP. Since this income is produced by ordinary market activities, its omission is an important source of error in published GNP figures. In other countries the income omitted is much higher. The Italian underground economy, for example, has been estimated at close to 25 percent of that country's total GNP!

Increases in the proportion of GNP that goes unreported may have caused GNP data for the last decade to under-report the actual growth in output and hence living standards. If, for example, *actual* GNP grows by 2 percent, 1 percent of which goes unrecorded, then *measured* GNP will only grow by 1 percent.

Nonmarketed Economic Activities

When a bank teller hires a carpenter to build a bookshelf in his house, the value of the bookshelf enters into the GNP; if the teller or his wife builds the bookshelf, the value of the bookshelf is omitted from the GNP. Such omissions also include, for example, the services of housewives, any do-it-yourself activity, and voluntary work such as canvassing for a political party, helping to run a volunteer day-care center, or leading a boy scout troop.

Does the omission of nonmarketed economic activities matter? Once again, it all depends. If we wish to measure the flow of goods and services through the market sector of the economy, or to account for changes in the opportunities for employment for those households who sell their labor services in the market, most of these omissions are acceptable. If, however, we wish to measure the overall flow of goods and services available to satisfy people's wants, whatever the source of the goods and services, then the omissions are undesirable and potentially serious.

In most advanced industrial economies, the nonmarket sector is relatively small, and it can be ignored even if GNP is used for purposes for which it would be appropriate to include nonmarketed goods and services. The omissions become serious, however, when GNP or disposable income figures are used to compare living standards in very different economies. Generally, the nonmarket sector of the economy is larger in rural than in urban settings and in less developed than in more developed economies. Be a little cautious, then, in interpreting data from a country with a very different climate and culture from our own. When you hear that the per capita GNP of Nigeria is $900 per year, you should not imagine living in Washington, D.C., on that income.

Factors Affecting Human Welfare but Not Included in the Value of Output

Many factors that contribute to human welfare are not included in the GNP. Leisure is one. In fact, although a shorter work week may make people happier, it will tend to reduce measured GNP.

GNP does not allow for the capacity of different goods to provide different satisfactions. A million dollars spent on a bomber or a missile makes the same addition to GNP as a million dollars spent on a school, a stadium, or candy bars—expenditures that may produce very different amounts of consumer satisfaction.

GNP does not measure the quality of life. To the extent that material output is purchased at the

THE SIGNIFICANCE OF ARBITRARY DECISIONS

National income accounting uses many arbitrary decisions. Goods that are finished and held in inventories are valued at market value, thereby anticipating their sale even though the actual sales price may not be known. In the case of a Ford in a dealer's showroom, this practice may be justified because the *value* of this Ford is perhaps virtually the same as that of an identical Ford that has just been sold to a customer. But what is the correct market value of a half-finished house or an unfinished novel? Accountants arbitrarily treat goods in process at cost (rather than at market value) if the goods are being made by business firms. They ignore completely the value of the novel-in-progress. While these decisions are arbitrary, so would any others be. Clearly, practical people must arrive at some compromise between consistent definitions and measurable magnitudes.

The definition of final goods provides further examples. Business investment expenditures are treated as final products, as are all government purchases. Intermediate goods purchased by business for further processing are not treated as final products. Thus, when a firm buys a machine or a truck, the purchase is treated as a final good; when it buys a ton of steel, however, the steel is treated not as a final product but as a raw material that will be used as an input into the firm's production process. (But if the steel sits in inventory, it is regarded as a business investment and thus *is* a final good.)

Such arbitrary decisions surely affect the size of measured GNP. Does it matter? The surprising answer, for many purposes, is no. In any case, it is wrong to believe that just because a statistical measure falls short of perfection (as all statistical measures do) it is useless. Very crude measures will often give estimates to the right order of magnitude, whereas substantial improvements in sophistication may make only second-order improvements in these estimates.

In the third century B.C. for example, the Alexandrian astronomer Eratosthenes measured the angle of the sun at Alexandria at the moment it was directly overhead 500 miles south at Aswan, and he used this angle to calculate the circumference of the earth to within 15 percent of the distance as measured today by the most advanced measuring devices. For the knowledge he wanted—the approximate size of the earth—his measurement was decisive. To launch a modern earth satellite, it would have been disastrously inadequate.

Absolute figures mean something in general terms, although they cannot be taken seriously to the last dollar. In 1982 GNP was measured as $3,058 billion. It is certain that the market value of all production in the United States in that year was not $100 billion, nor was it $10,000 billion. It was not $500 billion, but it might well have been $3,200 billion or $2,900 billion had different measures been defined with different arbitrary decisions built in.

International and intertemporal comparisons, though tricky, may be meaningful when they are based on measures all of which contain roughly the same arbitrary decisions. American per capita GNP is a little less than three times the Spanish and 30 percent higher than the Japanese per capita GNPs. Other measures might differ, but it is unlikely that any measure would reveal that either the Spanish or the Japanese per capita production was higher than the per capita production in the United States. But the statistics also show that per capita GNP was 4 percent higher in the United States than in Sweden, a difference too small to have much meaning. American output grew at 2.8 percent per year for the 30 years following World War II; it is unlikely that another measure of output would have indicated a 6 percent increase. Further, the Japanese output grew at about 9 percent per year over the same period. It is inconceivable that another measure would change the conclusion that Japanese national output rose faster than American national output in recent decades.

expense of overcrowded cities and highways, polluted environments, defaced countrysides, maimed accident victims, longer waits for public services, and a more complex life that entails a frenetic struggle to be happy, GNP measures only part of what contributes to human well-being.

Which Measure Is Best?

There are several distinct income measures. To ask which is *the* best income measure is something like asking which is *the* best carpenter's tool. The answer is that it all depends on the job to be done.

The use of several measures of national income rather than one is common because different measures provide answers to different questions. GNP answers the question, What was the market value of goods and services produced for final demand? NNP answers the question, By how much did the economy's production exceed the amount necessary to replace capital equipment used up? Disposable income answers the question, How much income do consumers have to allocate between spending and saving? In addition, real (constant dollar) measures eliminate purely inflationary changes and allow comparisons of purchasing power over time; per capita measures shift the focus from the nation to the average person.

Which measure is used will depend on the problem at hand. For example, if we wish to predict households' consumption behavior, disposable income is the measure we need. If we wish to account for changes in employment, constant dollar GNP is wanted.

For yet other purposes, such as providing an overall measure of economic welfare, we may need to supplement or modify conventional measures of national income.[4] Even if we do, we are unlikely to discard GNP (and its offspring) entirely in favor

of such a measure. Economists and politicians who are interested in the ebb and flow of economic activity that passes through the market, and in the rise and fall in employment opportunities for factors of production whose services are sold on the market, will continue to use GNP as the measure that comes closest to telling them what they need to know.

SUMMARY

1. National product is the total market value of goods and services produced in the economy during a year. National income is the total of all income claims generated over the same period of time. By virtue of standard accounting conventions, national product and national income have the same value.

2. National output may be calculated either by measuring directly the value of final goods (the expenditure approach), or by calculating the values added by every sector in the economy (the output approach). Both approaches yield the same value, for they are just two ways of accounting for the total value of output. National income, measured by the income approach, provides a third, and equivalent, measure.

3. Using the expenditure approach, GNP = $\mathbf{AE}$ = $\mathbf{C} + \mathbf{I} + \mathbf{G} + (\mathbf{X} - \mathbf{M})$. $\mathbf{C}$ represents consumption expenditures of households and $\mathbf{I}$ represents investment in plant and equipment, residential construction, and inventory accumulation. Gross investment can be split into replacement investment (necessary to keep the stock of capital intact) and net investment (net additions to the stock of capital). $\mathbf{G}$ represents government expenditures except transfer payments. $(\mathbf{X} - \mathbf{M})$ represents the excess of exports over imports; it will be negative if imports exceed exports.

4. The output approach measures the value of the output of final goods and services by taking the sum of the *values added* in the economy. Value added is the market value of the firm's output

---

[4] Concepts that come closer to measuring economic welfare than GNP have been developed. One was worked out by Professors William Nordhaus and James Tobin. It tries to measure consumption of things that provide utility to households rather than total production; it gives value to such nonmarketed activities as leisure and makes subtractions for such "disutilities" as pollution and congestion.

minus the cost of inputs purchased from other firms.

5. The income approach divides total GNP according to who has a claim to the value arising from the production and sale of commodities. Wages, interest, rents, profits, depreciation (called *capital consumption allowance*), and indirect taxes are the major items.

6. Several related but different income measures are used in addition to the GNP. Net national product (NNP) measures total output after deducting the capital consumption allowance. Personal income is income actually earned by households before any allowance for personal taxes. Disposable income gives the amount that is actually available to households to spend or to save.

7. GNP and related measures of national income must be interpreted with regard for their limitations. GNP excludes production resulting from activities that are illegal, take place in the underground economy, or do not pass through markets (such as what is produced by do-it-yourself activities). Moreover, GNP does not measure everything that contributes to human welfare.

8. Notwithstanding its limitations, GNP remains the best measure available for estimating the total economic activity that passes through the markets of our economy and for accounting for changes in the employment opportunities that face households who sell their labor services on the open market.

TOPICS FOR REVIEW

The equality of national product and national income

Output expenditure, and income approaches to measuring national income

Final goods, intermediate goods, and value added

GNP = **AE** = **C** + **I** + **G** + (**X** − **M**)

National income, GNP, NNP, personal income, and disposable income

Major characteristics of GNP

Limitations of GNP as a measure of economic welfare

DISCUSSION QUESTIONS

1. If Canada and the United States were to join together as a single country, what would be the effect on their total GNP (assuming that output in each country is unaffected)? Would any of the components in their GNPs change significantly?

2. "Every time you rent a U-haul, brick in a patio, grow a vegetable, fix your own car, photocopy an article, develop your own film, sew a dress, stew fruit, or raise a child, you are committing a productive act, even though these activities are not reflected in the gross national product." To what extent are each of these things "productive acts"? Are any of them included in GNP? Where they are excluded, does the exclusion matter?

3. What would be the effect on the measured value of America's *real* GNP of (a) the destruction of a thousand homes by flood water; (b) the passage of a constitutional amendment making abortion illegal; (c) a complete cessation of all imports from South Africa; and (d) the outbreak of a new Arab-Israeli war in which American troops became as heavily involved as they were in Vietnam. Speculate on the effects of each of these events on the true well-being of the American people.

4. A Social Security Administration study, using 1972 data, found the "average American housewife's value" to be $4,705. It arrived at this total by adding up the hours she spent cooking, multiplied by a cook's wage; the hours spent with her children, multiplied by a babysitter's wage; and so on. Should the time a parent spends taking children to a concert be included? Are dollar amounts assigned to such activities a satisfactory proxy for market value of production? For what, if any, purposes should such values be excluded from, or included in, national income?

5. Use the endpaper at the back of this book to calculate the percentage increase over the most recent two decades of each of the following magnitudes: (a) GNP in current dollars; (b) GNP in constant dollars; (c) disposable income in constant dollars; and (d) disposable income per capita in constant dollars. Can you account for the relative size of these changes?

6. Consider the effect on measured GNP and on economic well-being of each of the following: (a) a reduction in the standard work week from 40 hours to 30 hours; (b) the hiring of all welfare recipients as government employees; (c) further increases in oil prices that lead to a general inflation; and (d) an increase in the salaries of priests and ministers as a result of the increased contributions of churchgoers.

28 NATIONAL INCOME AND AGGREGATE DEMAND

In Chapter 26 we gave an overview of aggregate demand and aggregate supply. We now begin our more in-depth study of how these forces influence output and prices.

A note on terminology. In Chapter 27, we discovered the identity of total output, total expenditure, and total income: all equal GNP. To refer to all these concepts economists usually employ the generic term **national income.** When we wish to emphasize output we refer to *total* output or to *GNP*. But in our theoretical discussion we normally use the term *national income* to mean both the value of the economy's total output of final goods *and* the value of total incomes generated by the act of producing this output. The same usage also applies to potential income. We use the terms *potential income* and *potential output* to refer to the economy's potential GNP, the real output and income it can generate when all factors are fully employed at their normal rates of utilization.

The Keynesian *SRAS* Curve

For the next two chapters we are going to concentrate on the influence of aggregate demand. Ultimately, we want to know what causes national income and the price level to change at the same time. But because it is easier to deal with things one at a time, we will first look at the forces that determine national income, and hence determine employment and unemployment, when the price level is treated as constant. Then in Chapters 29 and 30 we will see what happens when the price level also varies.

In this chapter we consider an economy whose national income is varying over the range below potential income. Furthermore, we use an extreme version of the *SRAS* curve over that range. This curve is called the **Keynesian short-run aggregate supply curve** after the English economist John Maynard Keynes, who pioneered the study of the behavior of economies under conditions of heavy unemployment. The behavior that gives rise to the Keynesian *SRAS* curve can be described as follows. When real national income is below potential national income, individual firms are operating at less than normal capacity output. Firms respond to cyclical declines in demand by holding their prices constant at the level that would be most profitable if production were at normal capacity. They then respond to demand variations below that capacity by altering output. In other words they will supply whatever they can sell at their existing prices as long as they are producing below their normal capacity. This means that the firms have horizontal supply curves and that their output is *demand determined*. Under these circumstances, the whole economy has a horizontal aggregate supply curve, indicating that any output up to potential output will be supplied at the going price level. The amount that is actually produced is then determined by the position of the aggregate demand

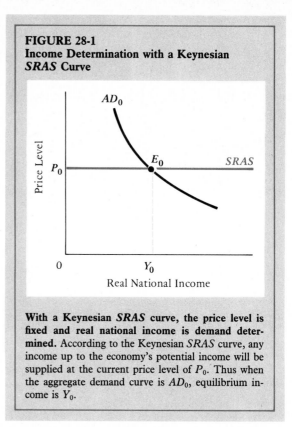

FIGURE 28-1
Income Determination with a Keynesian *SRAS* Curve

With a Keynesian *SRAS* curve, the price level is fixed and real national income is demand determined. According to the Keynesian *SRAS* curve, any income up to the economy's potential income will be supplied at the current price level of P_0. Thus when the aggregate demand curve is AD_0, equilibrium income is Y_0.

curve. Thus we say that real national income is *demand determined*.[1]

If demand rises enough so that firms are trying to squeeze more than normal output out of their plants, their costs will rise and so will their prices. Thus the horizontal Keynesian *SRAS* curve only applies to national incomes below potential income.

Figure 28-1 shows such a Keynesian *SRAS* curve. The curve is horizontal at the current price level of P_0. Under these circumstances, income is determined by the position of the aggregate demand curve. Shifts in *AD* will cause equilibrium income to change.

[1] The evidence is very strong that firms, particularly in the manufacturing sector, do behave like this in the short run. One possible explanation is that changing prices frequently is too costly, so firms set the best possible (profit-maximizing) prices when output is at normal capacity and then do not change prices in the face of normal cyclical fluctuations in demand. This is discussed further in Chapter 16.

With a Keynesian *SRAS* curve the questions of why national income is what it is, and why it changes, boil down to the questions of why aggregate demand is where it is and why it shifts.

In order to see how aggregate demand determines national income on the Keynesian *SRAS* curve, we first need to see why a particular price level is associated with one equilibrium level of national income rather than some other level. Why, for example, is the price level P_0 in Figure 28-1 associated with the equilibrium level of income of Y_0? In other words, why is the *AD* curve where it is rather than somewhere else?

To begin to answer this question we must first look at expenditure and distinguish between desired and actual expenditure.

DESIRED EXPENDITURE

In the last chapter we discussed how national income statisticians measure actual aggregate expenditure, **AE,** and its components: consumption, **C;** investment, **I;** government, **G;** and net exports, **(X − M).**

In this chapter, we are concerned with a different concept. It is variously called *desired, planned,* or *intended expenditure.* Of course, everybody would like to spend virtually unlimited amounts if only they had the money. Desired expenditure does not refer, however, to what people would like to do under imaginary circumstances. It refers instead to what everybody, given the resources at their command, wants to spend.

Everyone with money to spend makes expenditure decisions. Fortunately it is unnecessary for our purpose to look at each of the millions of such individual decisions. Instead it is sufficient to place decision makers in four main groups: domestic households, firms, governments, and foreign purchasers of domestically produced products. Their actual purchases account for the four main categories of expenditure studied in the previous chapter: consumption, investment, government expenditure, and exports. Their desired purchases can also be divided in the same fashion: desired con-

sumption, desired investment, desired government expenditure, and desired exports. Allowing for the fact that some of the commodities desired by each group will have an import content, we subtract import expenditure to obtain total desired expenditure on domestically produced goods and services:

$$AE = C + I + G + (X - M)$$

Earlier we indicated *actual* aggregate expenditure and its components by the boldface letters **AE, C, I, G,** and **(X − M).** Now we use lightface letters to indicate *desired* amounts of expenditure in the same categories.

Desired expenditure need not equal actual expenditure, either totally or in each individual category. For example, firms may not plan to invest in inventory accumulation this year but may unintentionally do so. If they produce goods to meet estimated sales but demand is unexpectedly low, the unsold goods that pile up on their shelves will represent undesired, and unintended, inventory accumulation. In this case actual investment expenditure, **I,** will exceed desired investment expenditure, I.

National income accounts measure *actual expenditures* in each of the four categories: consumption, investment, government purchases, and net exports. National income theory deals with *desired expenditures* in each of these four categories.

To develop a theory of national income, we need to know what determines each of the components of desired aggregate expenditure. We begin by focusing primarily on C, desired consumption expenditure, which is the largest single component of actual aggregate expenditure. Later we shall look in more detail at the determinants of desired I, G, and (X − M).

Desired Consumption and Saving

Households can do one of two things with their disposable income: they can spend it on consumption or they can save it. **Saving** is defined as all income that is not consumed. It follows that households have to make a single decision: how to split their disposable income between consumption and saving.

What determines the amount that households decide to spend on goods and services for consumption and the amount they decide to save? These decisions are summarized in the consumption function and its counterpart, the saving function.

The Consumption Function

The **consumption function** relates the total desired consumption expenditure of all households in the economy to the factors that determine it. It is, as we shall see, one of the central relations in macroeconomics.

Consumption as a Function of Disposable Income

One important force influencing desired consumption expenditure is household disposable income, represented by Y_d. As disposable income

rises, households have more money to spend on consumption—and the evidence is that they do just that. We therefore treat desired consumption expenditure as varying positively with disposable income.

Other forces such as interest rates and inflationary expectations also exert an influence, but we shall neglect them for the moment. The simple theory of consumption focuses on changes in disposable income to explain changes in consumption. We will reserve the term *consumption function* for describing the relationship between consumption and income.

Some consumption expenditure does not depend on national income—this we call the *autonomous* component. The bulk of consumption expenditure, however, varies with national income—this we call the *induced* component. As an example, a schedule relating disposable income to desired consumption expenditure for a hypothetical economy appears in the first two columns of Table 28-1. In this example autonomous consumption expenditure is $100 billion, whereas induced expenditure is 80 percent of disposable income. In what follows we use this

TABLE 28–1 THE CALCULATION OF THE AVERAGE PROPENSITY TO CONSUME (APC) AND THE MARGINAL PROPENSITY TO CONSUME (MPC) (Billions of Dollars)

Disposable income (Y_d)	Desired consumption (C)	$APC = C/Y_d$	ΔY_d (Change in Y_d)	ΔC (Change in C)	$MPC = \Delta C/\Delta Y_d$
$ —	$ 100	—			
100	180	1.800	100	$ 80	0.80
400	420	1.050	300	240	0.80
500	500	1.000	100	80	0.80
1,000	900	0.900	500	400	0.80
2,000	1,700	0.850	1,000	800	0.80
3,000	2,500	0.833	1,000	800	0.80
4,000	3,300	0.825	1,000	800	0.80

The *APC* measures the proportion of disposable income that households desire to spend on consumption; the *MPC* measures the proportion of any *increment* to disposable income that households desire to spend on consumption. The data are hypothetical. The *APC* calculated in the third column exceeds unity below the break-even level of income because consumption exceeds income. Above the break-even level the *APC* is less than unity and declines steadily as income rises.

The last three columns are set between the lines of the first three columns to indicate that they refer to changes in the levels of income and consumption. In this example, the *MPC* calculated in the last column is constant at 0.8 at all levels of Y_d. This indicates that in this illustration $.80 of *every* additional $1 of disposable income is spent on consumption and $.20 is used to increase saving (or decrease dissaving).

hypothetical data to illustrate the various properties of the consumption function.

Average and marginal propensities to consume. To discuss the consumption function concisely, economists use two technical expressions.

The **average propensity to consume (*APC*)** is total consumption expenditure divided by total disposable income. The third column of Table 28-1 shows the APCs calculated from the data in the table.

The **marginal propensity to consume (*MPC*)**

relates the *change* in consumption to the *change* in disposable income that brought it about. *MPC* is the change in disposable income divided into the resulting consumption change: $MPC = \Delta C/\Delta Y_d$ (where the Greek letter Δ, delta, means "a change in"). The last column of Table 28-1 shows the *MPC* calculated from the data in the table. [31]

The slope of the consumption function. Figure 28-2(i) shows a graph of the consumption function plotted from the first two columns of Table 28-1. The figure makes it clear that the consumption

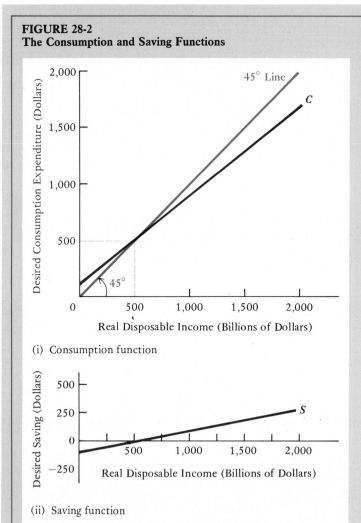

FIGURE 28-2
The Consumption and Saving Functions

(i) Consumption function

(ii) Saving function

Both consumption and saving rise as income rises. This diagram plots the data from Table 28-2. The *C* and *S* lines relate desired consumption expenditure and desired saving to real disposable income. The slopes of the lines are $\Delta C/\Delta Y_d$ and $\Delta S/\Delta Y_d$, which are *MPC* and *MPS* respectively. At the break-even level of income ($500), the consumption line cuts the 45° line and the saving line cuts the horizontal axis. Since saving is all disposable income not spent on consumption ($S = Y_d - C$), the vertical distance between the *C* line and the 45° line in (i) is by definition the height of *S* in (ii). That is, at each level of income, disposable income must be accounted for by the amount consumed plus the amount saved.

function has a slope of $\Delta C/\Delta Y_d$ which is, by definition, the marginal propensity to consume. The upward slope of the consumption function shows that MPC is positive; increases in income lead to increases in expenditure.

Using the concepts of the average and marginal propensities to consume, we can summarize the properties of the short-term consumption function:

1. There is a break-even level of income at which $APC = 1$. Below this level APC is greater than unity; above it APC is less than unity.
2. MPC is greater than zero but less than unity for all levels of income.

The 45° Line

Figure 28-2(i) also contains a second line that will prove useful. It is constructed by connecting all points where desired consumption (measured on the vertical axis) equals disposable income (measured on the horizontal axis). Since both axes are given in the same units, this line has an upward slope of unity, or (what is the same thing) it forms an angle of 45° with both axes. The line is therefore called the **45° line.**

The 45° line makes a handy reference line. In Figure 28-2(i) it helps locate the break-even level of income at which consumption expenditure equals disposable income. Graphically, the consumption function cuts the 45° line at the break-even level of income, in this instance $500. (It is steeper than the consumption function because MPC is less than unity.)

The Saving Function

Households decide how much to consume and how much to save. As we have said, this is a single decision: how to divide disposable income between consumption and saving. It follows that, once we know the dependence of consumption on disposable income, we also automatically know the dependence of saving on disposable income. (This is illustrated in Table 28-2.)

Two saving concepts are exactly parallel to the consumption concepts of APC and MPC. The **average propensity to save (APS)** is the proportion of disposable income that households want to save.

APS is figured by dividing total desired saving by total disposable income: $APS = S/Y_d$. The **marginal propensity to save** (MPS) relates the *change* in total desired saving to the *change* in disposable income that brought it about: $MPS = \Delta S/\Delta Y_d$.

There is a simple relation between the saving and the consumption propensities. APC and APS must sum to unity and so must MPC and MPS. Since income is either spent or saved, it follows both that the fractions of incomes consumed and saved must account for all income ($APC + APS = 1$) and that the fraction of any increment to income consumed and saved must account for all of that increment ($MPC + MPS = 1$). [32]

Calculations from Table 28-2 will allow you to confirm these relations in the case of the example given. MPC is 0.8 and MPS is 0.2 at all levels of income while, for example, at income of $2,000 APC is 0.85 while APS is 0.15.

Figure 28-2(ii) shows the saving schedule given in Table 28-2. At the break-even level of income where desired consumption equals disposable income, desired saving is zero. The slope of the saving line $\Delta S/\Delta Y_d$ is MPS.

TABLE 28–2	**CONSUMPTION AND SAVING SCHEDULES (Billions of Dollars)**	
Disposable income	Desired consumption expenditure	Desired saving
$ 0	$ 100	− $100
100	180	− 80
400	420	− 20
500	500	− 0
1,000	900	+ 100
2,000	1,700	+ 300
3,000	2,500	+ 500
4,000	3,300	+ 700

Saving and consumption account for all household disposable income. The first two columns repeat the data from Table 28-1. The third column is disposable income minus desired consumption. The three columns thus show desired consumption and desired saving at each level of income. Consumption and saving each increase steadily as disposable income rises. In this example, the break-even level of disposable income is $500 million.

Wealth and Consumption

We have seen that disposable income is an important factor influencing the consumption-saving decision. A second important factor is the level of each household's wealth. By a household's **wealth** we mean the sum of all the valuable assets it owns. This will include its car, its house and contents, its money in the bank, the value of its pension fund, and any stocks, bonds, or other investments that it holds.

Households save in order to add to their wealth. Thus, other things being equal, a rise in wealth tends to reduce the incentive to add further to wealth; that is, it reduces the incentive to save. Hence a rise in wealth will cause a larger fraction of disposable income to be spent on consumption and a smaller fraction to be saved. This shifts the consumption function upward, and the saving function downward, as shown in Figure 28-3. A fall in wealth increases the incentives to save in order to restore wealth. This shifts the consump-

FIGURE 28-3
Wealth and the Consumption Function

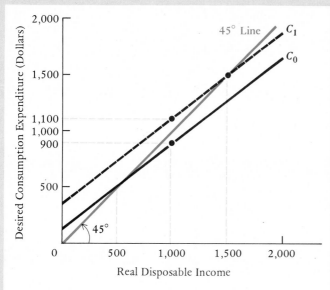

(i) The consumption function shifts up with wealth

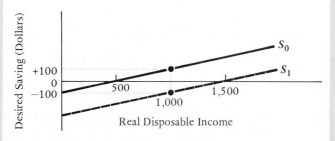

(ii) The saving function shifts down with wealth

Changes in wealth shift consumption as a function of disposable income. In (i), the solid line C_0 reproduces the consumption function from Figure 28-2(i). An increase in the level of wealth raises desired consumption at each level of disposable income, thus shifting the consumption line up. In the figure, the consumption function shifts up by $200 so that, for example, with disposable income of $1,000, desired consumption *rises* from $900 to $1,100. The saving function in (ii) shifts down by $200. Thus, for example, at Y_d of $1,000, saving *falls* from plus $100 to minus $100. As a result of the rise in wealth, the break-even level of income rises to $1,500.

THE LONG-TERM CONSUMPTION FUNCTION

The text deals with what can be called a short-term consumption function. It is suitable for describing how consumption varies from year to year as income varies. It is based on empirical observations of cyclical variations in consumption and income. Figure 28-2 shows a typical short-term consumption function. It is an upward sloping straight line with a positive intercept. With such a function, MPC is constant while APC declines as income rises. [33]

Some empirical studies of the consumption function have used 10-year averages of consumption expenditure and income. When plotted on a graph, one point would relate average consumption in, say, 1900–1909 to average disposable income in that period. The next point would do the same for the next decade; and so on. Ten such points would span a century of observations. The characteristic of such data is that each point averages out the effects of cyclical fluctuations in national income. The series of points thus focuses attention on the long-run reaction of consumption to long-run trend changes in national income.

Such studies suggest that there is a highly stable long-term division of national income between consumption and saving. In other words, the consumption expenditure of American households over the long run tends to be a stable fraction of their disposable income. In technical terms, APC tends to hold constant as income rises in the long run. The figure shows a long-run consumption function that exhibits these properties. [34]

The consumption function in the text is suitable for analyzing the effects of cyclical fluctuations that take only a few years to work themselves out. The consumption function illustrated in this box is suitable for analyzing the effects of long-term growth over a span of several decades.

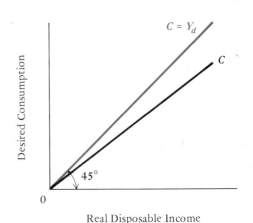

A long-term consumption function

tion function downward, and the saving function upward, as also shown in Figure 28-3.

Individual households experience both expected and unexpected changes in wealth. For example, either planned saving or unplanned bequests will increase wealth. Similarly either planned dissaving or unplanned losses reduce wealth.

Many unexpected changes in wealth cancel out across households and so are unimportant for the macro consumption function. We will see, however, that inflation can be an important source of unexpected changes in wealth that are common to most households.

Planned increases in wealth as a result of past accumulation in wealth can be important for the whole society and can lead to upward shifts in the macro consumption function as wealth accumulates. This effect operates only slowly since wealth accumulates only slowly. In order to focus on short-term issues, the consumption function used in the text does not include the effects of changes in wealth. The box, however, explores the possible effect of wealth on the consumption function over the long term.

National Income and Consumption

We have seen that desired consumption is related to *disposable* income. For a theory of the determination of national income, however, we need to know how consumption is related to *national income*.

The transition from a relation between *consumption and disposable income* to one between *consumption and national income* is readily accomplished since, as we saw above, disposable income and national income are themselves related to each other.

The relation between disposable income and national income. On pages 510 and 511 we saw the adjustments required to derive disposable income from national income. Since transfer payments (the major addition) are smaller than total income taxes (the major subtraction), the net effect is for disposable income to be substantially less than national income. (It was about 89 percent of national income in 1982.)

The general relation between disposable income and national income can be illustrated by assuming that disposable income, Y_d, is a given proportion of national income, Y. The relation, for example, might be that disposable income is 70 percent of national income.

Substituting national income for disposable income in the consumption function. If we know how consumption relates to disposable income and how disposable income relates to national income, it is a routine matter to derive the relation between consumption and national income.

As an example, again assume that disposable income is always 70 percent of national income. Then, whatever the relation between C and Y, we can always substitute $0.7Y$ for Y_d. Thus, if consumption were always 90 percent of Y_d, then C

TABLE 28–3 CONSUMPTION AS A FUNCTION OF DISPOSABLE INCOME AND NATIONAL INCOME (Billions of Dollars)

(1) National income (Y)	(2) Disposable income ($Y_d = 0.7Y$)	(3) Desired consumption ($C = 0.8Y_d$)
100	70	56
1,000	700	560
2,000	1,400	1,120
3,000	2,100	1,680
4,000	2,800	2,240

If desired consumption depends on disposable income, which in turn depends on national income, desired consumption can be written as a function of either income concept. The data are hypothetical. They show deductions of 30 percent of any level of national income to arrive at disposable income. Deductions of 30 percent of Y imply that the remaining 70 percent of Y becomes disposable income. The numbers also show consumption as 80 percent of disposable income.

By relating columns 2 and 3, one sees consumption as a function of disposable income. By relating columns 1 and 3, one sees consumption as a function of national income. In this example, the *APC* out of disposable income is 0.8 while it is 0.56 out of national income. You can check for yourself by dividing any figure in column 3 by the corresponding figures in columns 1 and 2.

would always be 63 percent (70 percent of 90 percent) of Y. **[35]**

This relation is further illustrated in Table 28-3. Since we can write desired consumption as a function of Y as well as of Y_d, we can define marginal and average propensities to consume from Y as well as from Y_d. The new propensities tell us the proportion of total national income that goes to desired consumption (C/Y) and the proportion of any change in national income that goes to a change in desired consumption ($\Delta C/\Delta Y$).

The marginal propensity to consume out of *national income* is equal to the marginal propensity to consume out of *disposable income* multiplied by the fraction of national income that becomes disposable income.

We now have a function showing how desired consumption expenditure varies as national income varies. The relation is defined for real income and real expenditure (i.e., income and expenditure measured in constant dollars). For every given level of real income, measured in terms of purchasing power, households desire to spend some fraction of that purchasing power and to save the rest.

Other Expenditure Categories

Now consider briefly the other major expenditure categories I, G, and (X − M).

Desired Investment Expenditure

Firms plan how much to invest in new capital equipment and in inventories. For the present it is convenient to study how the level of national income adjusts to a fixed level of planned real investment. So we assume that firms plan to make a constant amount of investment in plant and equipment each year and that they plan to hold their inventories constant. (In Chapter 31 we shall drop these assumptions and study the important effects on national income caused by changes in the level of desired investment.)

Desired Government Expenditure

Government expenditures on currently produced goods and services are part of aggregate expenditure on the nation's output. At the outset we take desired and actual real government expenditure as a constant. Governments intend to spend, and succeed in spending, so many billions of dollars on goods and services. We assume that this amount does not change as the circumstances of the economy change. This assumption allows us to see how national income adjusts to a constant level of real government expenditure. (In Chapter 32 we shall drop this assumption and study how national income responds to changes in desired and actual government expenditure.)

Desired Net Exports

American exports depend on spending decisions made by foreign households who purchase U.S. goods and services and therefore may be assumed not to change as a result of changes in U.S. national income. Imports, however, depend on the spending decisions of American households. Since all categories of expenditure have an import content, imports will rise when the other categories of expenditure, C, I, and G, rise. Because consumption rises with income, imports of foreign-produced consumption goods and materials that go into the production of domestically produced consumption goods will also rise with income.

Since exports are unchanged and imports rise as U.S. national income rises, net exports (X − M) are negatively related to income.

The calculation of a net export function appears in Table 28-4.

TABLE 28–4 **A NET EXPORT SCHEDULE**
(Billions of Dollars)

National income (Y)	Exports (X)	Imports (M = 0.1Y)	Net exports
1,000	240	100	140
2,000	240	200	40
2,400	240	240	0
3,000	240	300	−60
4,000	240	400	−160
5,000	240	500	−260

Net exports fall as national income rises. The data are hypothetical. They assume that exports are constant and that imports are 10 percent of national income. Net exports are then positive at low levels of national income and negative at high levels.

The Aggregate Expenditure Function

Total desired expenditure on the nation's output is the sum of desired consumption, investment, government expenditure, and net exports. How do changes in national income affect total desired ex-

TABLE 28–5 **THE AGGREGATE EXPENDITURE FUNCTION** (Billions of Dollars)

(1) National income (Y)	(2) Desired consumption (C = 100 + 0.6Y)	(3) Desired investment (I = 250)	(4) Desired government expenditure (G = 410)	(5) Desired net exports (X − M = 240 − 0.1Y)	(6) Desired aggregate expenditure (AE = C + I + G + [X − M])
$ 100	$ 160	$250	$410	$230	1,050
400	340	250	410	200	1,200
500	400	250	410	190	1,250
1,000	700	250	410	140	1,500
2,000	1,300	250	410	40	2,000
3,000	1,900	250	410	− 60	2,500
4,000	2,500	250	410	− 160	3,000
5,000	3,100	250	410	− 260	3,500

The aggregate expenditure function is the sum of desired consumption, investment, government expenditure, and net exports. Desired aggregate expenditure has an autonomous component that is independent of national income and an induced component that varies positively with national income.

penditure? To answer this question, we need the **aggregate expenditure function,** which relates the level of desired real expenditure to the level of real income. Table 28-5 illustrates how such a function can be calculated, given the consumption function and the levels of desired investment, government expenditure, and net exports at each level of income.[2]

The aggregate expenditure function tells how much domestic governments, domestic firms and households, and foreigners would like to spend on purchasing final domestic output at each level of national income.

Autonomous and Induced Expenditure

Since for the present we are assuming that I, G, and X are constant, C and (X − M) are the components of aggregate expenditure that vary systematically with income. Their variation is enough to make total desired expenditure vary with national income.

[2] The table is based on hypothetical data where consumption is $100 + 0.6Y, imports are 0.1Y, and I, G, and X are constant at values of $250, $410, and $240 respectively. The figures in the table are in billions of dollars.

Components of aggregate expenditure that do not depend on national income are called *autonomous* expenditures. Components that *do* depend on national income are called *induced* expenditures. At this stage of our analysis, I, G, and X are all autonomous, while C and (X − M) are, at least in part, induced. (Recall the discussion on page 25 making the general distinction between autonomous and induced variables.)

The Propensity to Spend out of National Income

Earlier we defined propensities to consume and to save that, together, account for all household disposable income. We now define propensities to spend and not to spend that together account for all national income.

The fraction of any increment to national income that will be spent on domestic production is measured by the change in aggregate expenditure divided by the change in income, and is symbolized by $\Delta AE/\Delta Y$. It is called the economy's **marginal propensity to spend.** The remainder, $1 - \Delta AE/\Delta Y$, is the fraction that is not spent. This is the **mar-**

ginal propensity not to spend.[3] The value of the marginal propensity to spend, which is something greater than zero but less than one, may be indicated by the letter z. This makes the value of the marginal propensity not to spend $1 - z$.

To illustrate, imagine that the economy receives $1 of extra income. If $.60 more is now spent on domestically produced goods, the marginal propensity to spend is 0.6 (i.e., 0.60/1.00), while the marginal propensity not to spend is 0.4 (i.e., 1.00 − 0.60).

DETERMINING EQUILIBRIUM NATIONAL INCOME

Now we can see how equilibrium national income is determined, *given a Keynesian SRAS curve.* To do this we study the **equilibrium conditions,** the conditions that must be fulfilled if national income is to be in equilibrium.

Aggregate Expenditure Equals National Income in Equilibrium

Table 28-6 illustrates the determination of equilibrium national income for a simple hypothetical economy with no taxes or transfer payments. In this case, disposable income is the same as national income.

Suppose that firms are producing a final output of $1,000 and thus national income is $1,000. According to Table 28-6 total desired expenditure, $C + I + G + (X − M)$, is $1,500 at this level of income. If firms persist in producing a current output of only $1,000 in the face of an aggregate desired expenditure of $1,500, one of two things must happen.

One possibility is that households, firms, and governments will be unable to spend the extra $500 that they would like to spend, so lineups of unsa-

tisfied customers will appear. These lineups send a signal to firms that they can increase their sales if they increase their production. When the firms increase production, national income rises. Of course the individual firms were only interested in their own sales and profits, but their joint action has, as its inevitable consequence, an increase in GNP that is, after all, simply the total of everyone's current production (i.e., the total of their values added).

The second possibility is that everyone will spend all that they wanted to spend. But then expenditure will exceed current output, which can only happen when some expenditure plans are fulfilled by purchasing inventories of goods that were produced in the past. In this example, the fulfill-

TABLE 28–6 THE DETERMINATION OF EQUILIBRIUM NATIONAL INCOME (Billions of Dollars)

(1) National income ($Y =$)	(2) Desired aggregate expenditure ($AE = C + I + G + [X − M]$)	
$ 100	1,050	Pressure on income to increase ↓
400	1,200	
500	1,250	
1,000	1,500	
2,000	2,000	Equilibrium income
3,000	2,500	↑
4,000	3,000	Pressure on income to decrease
5,000	3,500	

National income is in equilibrium where aggregate desired expenditure equals national income. The data are taken from Table 28-5. When national income is below its equilibrium level, aggregate desired expenditure exceeds the value of current output. This creates an incentive for firms to increase output and hence for national income to rise. When national income is above its equilibrium level, desired expenditure is less than the value of current output. This creates an incentive for firms to reduce output and hence for national income to fall. Only at the equilibrium level of national income is aggregate desired expenditure exactly equal to the value of the current output.

---

[3] More fully, these terms would be the marginal propensity to spend *on national product* and the marginal propensity not to spend *on national product.* Expenditures on imports are included in the latter.

ment of plans to purchase $1,500 worth of commodities in the face of a current output of only $1,000 must reduce inventories by $500. As long as inventories last, more goods can be sold than are currently being produced. Eventually inventories will run out, but long before this happens firms will increase their output. Extra sales can then be made without a further pulling down of inventories. Once again the consequence of each individual firm's behavior, in search of its own individual profits, is an increase in national income. Thus the final response to an excess of aggregate desired expenditure over current output is a rise in national income toward its equilibrium value.

At any level of national income at which total desired expenditure exceeds total output, there will be pressure for national income to rise.

Next consider the $4,000 level of national income in Table 28-6. At this level, desired expenditure on domestically produced goods is only $3,000. If firms persist in producing $4,000 worth of goods, $1,000 worth must remain unsold. Therefore, inventories must rise. But firms will not allow inventories of unsold goods to rise indefinitely; sooner or later they will reduce the level of output to the level of sales. When they do, national income will fall.

At any level of income for which total desired expenditure falls short of total output, there will be a pressure for national income to fall.

Finally, look at the national income level of $2,000 in the table. At this level, and only at this level, total desired expenditure is exactly equal to national income. Purchasers fulfill their spending plans without causing inventories to change. There is no incentive for firms to alter output. Since total output is the same as national income, national income will remain steady; it is in equilibrium.

The equilibrium level of national income occurs where total desired expenditure equals total output.

A glance at Table 28-6 will show that there is always a tendency for national income to be pushed in the direction of its equilibrium value. Only when

desired aggregate expenditure is equal to total output will national income remain unchanged. This conclusion is quite general and does not depend on the numbers used in the specific example.

A Graphical Determination of Equilibrium

Figure 28-4 shows the determination of the equilibrium level of national income. The *AE* line graphs the aggregate expenditure function. Its slope is the marginal propensity to spend. The 45° line shows the equilibrium condition that desired aggregate expenditure, *AE*, equals national income, *Y*. Any point on this line is a possible equilibrium.

Graphically, equilibrium occurs at the level of income at which the aggregate desired expenditure line intersects the 45° line. This is the level of income where desired expenditure is just equal to total national income and, therefore, is just sufficient to purchase total final output.

We have now explained the equilibrium level of national income that arises at a *given price level*. In the next chapter we will study the forces that cause equilibrium income to change. We shall see that shifts in desired consumption and investment expenditure can cause major swings in national income. We shall also see that changes in government spending and taxation policies can do the same. In later chapters we shall see that not only can these things happen, but they do happen. At that point our theoretical framework will help us to understand many real-world events that we read and hear about.

SUMMARY

1. When the price level is fixed along a horizontal Keynesian *SRAS* curve, equilibrium national income is demand determined.

2. Desired aggregate expenditure includes desired consumption, investment, and government expen-

FIGURE 28-4
Equilibrium National Income

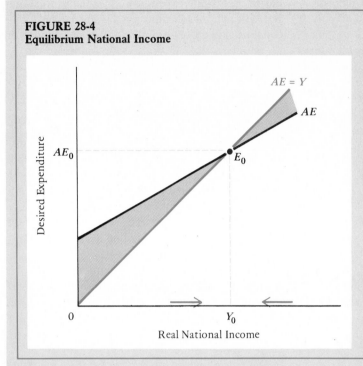

The equilibrium level of national income occurs at *E*, where the aggregate desired expenditure line intersects the 45° line. If real
national income is below Y_0, desired expenditure will exceed national income and produc-
tión will rise. This is shown by the left-hand
arrow. If national income is above Y_0, desired
expenditure will be less than national income
and production will fall. This is shown by the
right-hand arrow in the figure.

diture, plus desired net exports. It is the amount
that decision makers want to spend on purchasing
the national product.

3. A change in disposable income leads to a change
in consumption and saving. The responsiveness of
these changes is measured by the marginal propensity to consume and the marginal propensity to
save, which are both positive and sum to one.

4. A change in wealth leads to a change in the
allocation of disposable income between consumption and saving. The change in consumption is
positively related to the change in wealth while the
change in saving is negatively related to this
change.

5. At the equilibrium level of national income purchasers wish to buy neither more nor less than what
is being produced. At incomes above equilibrium,
desired expenditure falls short of national income

and output will sooner or later be curtailed. At
incomes below equilibrium, desired expenditure
exceeds national income and output will sooner or
later be increased.

6. Graphically equilibrium national income occurs
where the aggregate expenditure curve cuts the 45°
line; that is, where total desired expenditure equals
total output.

TOPICS FOR REVIEW

The consumption function
Average and marginal propensities to consume and save, and
   to spend and not to spend
The 45° line
The aggregate expenditure function
Equilibrium national income at a given price level

DISCUSSION QUESTIONS

1. "The concept of an equilibrium level of national income is useless because the economy is never in equilibrium. If it ever got there, no economist would recognize it anyway." Discuss.

2. Interpret each of the following statements either in terms of the shape of a consumption function or the values of MPC and/or APC.

   a. "Tom Green has lost his job and his family is existing on its past savings."

   b. "The Grimsby household is so rich that they used all the extra income they earned this year to invest in a wildcat oil-drilling venture."

   c. "The widow Harris can barely make ends meet by clipping coupons on the bonds left to her by dear Henry, but she would never dip into her capital."

   d. "We always thought Hammerstein was a miser, but when his wife left him he took to wine, women, and song."

   e. "The inflation has made the Schutzs feel so poor that they are adding an extra $10 a week to their account at the Savings and Loan Society."

3. Can you think of any reasons why an individual's marginal propensity to consume might be higher in the long run than in the short run? Why it might be lower? Is it possible for an individual's average propensity to consume to be greater than unity in the short run? In the long run? Can a country's average propensity to consume be greater than unity in the short run? In the long run?

4. Along the 45° line, what relationship holds between total expenditures and total income? In determining equilibrium graphically, are we restricted to choosing identical vertical and horizontal scales?

5. Explain carefully why national income changes when aggregate desired expenditure does not equal national income. Sketch a scenario that fits the cases of too much and too little desired expenditure. What factors might influence the speed with which national income moves toward its equilibrium level?

6. Explain how a sudden unexpected fall in consumer expenditure would initially cause an increase in investment expenditure by firms.

7. What relationship is suggested by the following 1983 newspaper headline: "Big Three Auto Sales Soar As Recovery Booms"?

29 CHANGES IN NATIONAL INCOME I: THE ROLE OF AGGREGATE DEMAND

In Chapter 28 we investigated the conditions for national income to be in equilibrium. The equilibrium value of national income does not, however, remain unchanged. In this chapter we study why it changes. But before we do this we must make an important distinction which, if not properly understood, can be the source of endless confusion.

Movements Along Curves and Shifts of Curves

Suppose desired expenditure rises. This may be either a response to a change in national income or the result of an increased desire to spend at each level of national income. A change in national income causes a *movement along* the aggregate expenditure function. An increased desire to spend at each level of national income causes a *shift in* the aggregate expenditure function. Figure 29-1 illustrates this important distinction.

CHANGES IN NATIONAL INCOME WITH A FIXED PRICE LEVEL

For the moment we continue with our assumption that the price level is fixed. For any specific aggregate expenditure function there is then a unique level of equilibrium national income. But if the aggregate expenditure function shifts, the existing equilibrium will be disturbed and national income will change. Thus if we wish to find causes of changes in national income, we must look for causes of shifts in the *AE* function.

Shifts in the Aggregate Expenditure Function

The aggregate expenditure function shifts when one of its components shifts; that is, when there is a shift in the desired consumption expenditure of households, in the desired investment expenditure of private firms, in government expenditure, or in exports. Such shifts are called *autonomous* changes in aggregate expenditure.

An Autonomous Increase in Expenditure

What will happen if, say, households permanently increase their levels of consumption spending at each level of disposable income? If the Ford Motor Company increases its rate of annual investment by $25 million in order to meet the threat from imported cars? If the U.S. government increases its defense spending? Or if U.S. grain exports soar? (In dealing with these questions, it is important to remember that we are dealing with continuous flows measured as so much per period of time. An upward shift in the expenditure function means that expenditure rises to and stays at a higher amount.)

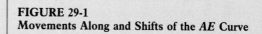

FIGURE 29-1
Movements Along and Shifts of the *AE* Curve

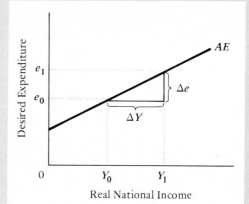

(i) A movement along the *AE* function

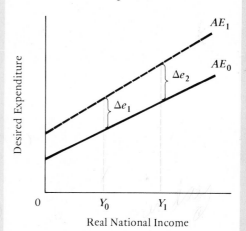

(ii) A shift of the *AE* function

A movement along the aggregate expenditure function occurs in response to a change in income; a shift of the *AE* function indicates a different level of desired expenditure at each level of income. In (i), a change in income of ΔY, from Y_0 to Y_1, changes expenditure by Δe, from e_0 to e_1. In (ii), a shift in the expenditure function from AE_0 to AE_1 raises the amount of expenditure associated with *each* level of income. At Y_0, for example, desired aggregate expenditure is increased by Δe_1; at Y_1, it is increased by Δe_2. (If the shift is a parallel one, then $\Delta e_1 = \Delta e_2$.)

FIGURE 29-2
Shifts in the *AE* Function

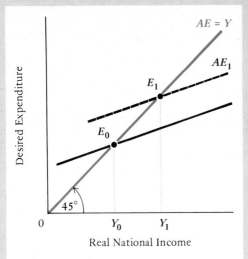

(i) A parallel shift in *AE*

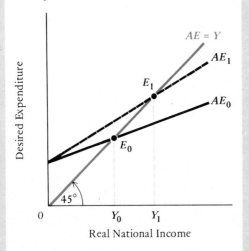

(ii) A change in the slope of *AE*

Upward shifts in the *AE* function increase equilibrium income; downward shifts decrease equilibrium income. In both (i) and (ii), the aggregate expenditure function is initially AE_0, with national income Y_0.

As shown in (i), a parallel upward shift in *AE*, say to AE_1, increases equilibrium income to Y_1. A downward shift in the function from AE_1 to AE_0 lowers equilibrium income from Y_1 to Y_0. In (ii), the marginal propensity to spend out of national income increases, shifting the expenditure function to AE_1. Equilibrium income increases to Y_1. The opposite change, a fall in the propensity to spend out of national income, is shown by a shift of the expenditure function from AE_1 to AE_0 and of equilibrium income from Y_1 to Y_0.

Because any such increase shifts the entire aggregate expenditure function upward, the same analysis applies to all of the changes mentioned above. Two types of shifts in *AE* are illustrated in Figure 29-2. First, if the same addition to expenditure occurs at all levels of income, the *AE* curve shifts parallel to itself as shown in the first part of the figure. Second, if there is a change in the propensity to consume, the slope of the *AE* curve changes, as shown in part (ii) of the figure. (Recall that the slope of the *AE* curve is the marginal propensity to spend out of national income.)

Figure 29-2 shows that all upward shifts in the aggregate expenditure function increase equilibrium national income. Why is this so? After the shift in the *AE* curve, income is no longer in equilibrium at its original level because desired expenditure now exceeds national income. This causes income to rise, which in turn causes a further rise in aggregate expenditure (a movement along the *AE* curve). Since the slope of the *AE* curve is less than one (as we saw in Chapter 28), this induced rise in aggregate expenditure is less than the rise in income that induces it. The rise in income continues until desired expenditure is once again equal to the now higher level of national income. In other words, the response of income to the upward *shift* of the *AE* function induces a movement *along* the new *AE* function until the flow of desired expenditure again equals national income.

An Autonomous Decrease in Expenditure

What will happen to national income if there is a *fall* in consumption, investment, exports, or government spending? What will happen if households permanently decrease their spending at each level of income? If a loss of markets to foreign cars causes the American automobile producers to reduce their investment expenditure permanently? If the American government drastically reduces expenditure on urban renewal? If exports of refrigerators to Mexico fall because of new Mexican import restrictions?

All these changes shift the aggregate expenditure function downward. A constant reduction in ex-

TABLE 29–1 **TAX CHANGES SHIFT THE FUNCTION RELATING CONSUMPTION TO NATIONAL INCOME**

(1) National income (Y)	Disposable income equal to 70 percent of national income		Disposable income equal to 60 percent of national income	
	(2) Disposable income ($Y_d = 0.7Y$)	(3) Consumption ($C = 0.9Y_d$)	(4) Disposable income ($Y_d = 0.6Y$)	(5) Consumption ($C = 0.9Y_d$)
100	70	63	60	54
500	350	315	300	270
1,000	700	630	600	540

The consumption function shifts if the relation between disposable and national income changes. The table is based on simplified hypothetical data where C is always a constant fraction of Y_d and Y_d is always a constant fraction of Y. Initially, $Y_d = 0.7Y$ and $C = 0.9Y_d$. This yields a schedule relating consumption to national income that is given in columns 1 and 3. Income tax rates are then increased so that only 60 percent of national income becomes disposable income. Column 4 now indicates the Y_d that corresponds to each level of Y shown in column 1. With an unchanged propensity to consume out of disposable income of 0.9, consumption is now given by column 5. Columns 1 and 5 give the new schedule relating consumption to national income.

penditure at all levels of income shifts AE parallel to itself. A fall in the propensity to consume out of national income reduces the slope of the AE function. Figures 29-2(i) and 29-2(ii) show that both kinds of shifts cause equilibrium national income to fall.

Income Changes

We have now derived two important general predictions of the elementary theory of national income.

1. A rise in the amount of desired consumption, investment, government, or export expenditure associated with each level of national income will increase equilibrium national income.
2. A fall in the amount of desired consumption, investment, government, or export expenditure associated with each level of national income will lower equilibrium national income.

A Further Application

What would be the effects of a rise in tax rates? Recall that a tax increase shifts the relation between consumption and national income without shifting the relation between consumption and disposable income. Suppose, for example, that the government raises its rates of income tax so as to collect an additional 10 percent of national income in tax revenues. Disposable income falls correspondingly, and so therefore does consumption. If, for example, 90 percent of disposable income is always consumed, desired consumption expenditure will fall by 9 percent (90 percent of 10 percent) of national income. In this case the consumption schedule in Table 29-1 changes from that shown by columns 1 and 3 to that shown by columns 1 and 5. The result of this downward shift of the aggregate expenditure function will be a fall in equilibrium national income, as shown in part (ii) of Figure 29-2.

Not surprisingly, a drop in taxes has the opposite effect on national income. A fall in tax rates means more disposable income and hence more expenditure at each level of national income. This raises the aggregate expenditure function and causes an increase in equilibrium national income, as shown by the upward shift in the aggregate expenditure function in Figure 29-2(ii).

We have now derived two additional predictions of the elementary theory of national income.

3. A rise in tax rates will lower the level of national income.
4. A fall in tax rates will raise the level of national income.

The Multiplier: A Measure of the Magnitude of Changes in Income

We now know the *direction* of the changes in national income that occur in response to various shifts in the aggregate expenditure function. But what about the *magnitude* of these changes?

Economists need an answer to this question to determine the effects of changes in expenditures in both the private and public sectors. During a recession the government often takes measures to stimulate the economy. If these measures have a larger effect than estimated, demand may rise too much and full employment may be reached with demand still rising. This outcome will have an inflationary impact on the economy. If, on the other hand, the government greatly overestimates the effect of its measures, the recession will persist longer than is necessary. In this case there is a danger that the policy will be discredited as ineffective, even though the correct diagnosis is that too little of the right thing was done.

Definition of the Multiplier

From the theory of national income we know that an increase in autonomous expenditure, whatever its source, will cause an increase in national income. The change in autonomous expenditure might come, for example, from an increase in private investment, from new government spending, or from additional exports.[1] The **multiplier** is defined as the change in national income divided by the change in autonomous expenditure that brings it about.

---

[1] For simplicity, we assume that there is no import content to any change in autonomous expenditure, so that the entire change occurs in the demand for domestically produced goods.

The Multiplier: An Intuitive Statement

What will happen to national income if, with unchanged tax rates, the government increases its spending on road construction? Suppose, for example, that this type of spending rises by $1 billion per year. (Since tax rates are unchanged, the government will have to borrow the additional money that it spends on roads.)

Initially the road program will create $1 billion worth of new national income and a corresponding amount of employment for those households and firms on which the money is spent. But this is not the end of the story. The increase in national income of $1 billion will cause an increase in disposable income, which will cause an induced rise in consumption expenditure. Road crews and road contractors, who gain new income directly from the government's road program, will spend some of it on food, clothing, entertainment, cars, television sets, and other consumption commodities. When output expands to meet this demand, employment will increase in all the affected industries. New incomes will then be created for workers and firms in these industries. When they in turn spend their newly earned incomes, output and employment will rise further. More income will be created and more expenditure induced. Indeed, at this stage you could wonder whether the increases in income will ever come to an end. To deal with this concern, we need to consider the multiplier in somewhat more precise terms. This is done below and also in the box, which gives a numerical example akin to the above discussions.

The Multiplier: A Formal Statement

Consider an increase in autonomous expenditure of ΔA, which might be, say, $2 billion per year. Remember that ΔA stands for *any* increase in autonomous expenditure; this could be an increase in investment, government purchases, or in exports. This new autonomous expenditure shifts up the AE function by that amount. National income is no longer in equilibrium at its original level since

THE MULTIPLIER: A NUMERICAL APPROACH

Consider an economy whose marginal propensity to consume out of national income is 0.5. Suppose that autonomous expenditure increases because the government spends an extra $1 million per year on new roads. National income initially rises by $1 million. But that is not the end of it; there is a second round of spending. The factors of production involved directly and indirectly in road building receive an extra $600 thousand as disposable income, and then spend an extra $500 thousand each year on domestically produced goods and services. This $500 thousand generates $300 thousand of new disposable income and $250 thousand of new consumption expenditure (the remaining $50 thousand goes to increased imports and savings), which is a third round of additions to aggregate expenditure.

And so it continues, each successive round of new income generating 50 percent as much in new expenditure. Each additional round of expenditure creates new income and yet another round of expenditure.

The table below carries the process through 10 rounds. Students with sufficient patience (and no faith in mathematics) may compute as many rounds in the process as they wish; they will find that the sum of the rounds of expenditures approaches $2 million, which is twice the initial injection of $1 million. [36] The multiplier is thus 2, given these numerical assumptions about the relations between national income and disposable income and induced expenditure.

	Increases in disposable income	Increases in expenditure
	(thousands of dollars per year)	
Initial increase in government expenditure		$1,000.00
2nd round	$600.00	500.00
3rd round	300.00	250.00
4th round	150.00	125.00
5th round	75.00	62.50
6th round	37.50	31.25
7th round	18.75	15.63
8th round	9.38	7.81
9th round	4.69	3.91
10th round	2.34	1.95
Sum of 1st 10 rounds		1,998.05
All other rounds		1.95
Total		$2,000.00

desired aggregate expenditure now exceeds income. Equilibrium is restored by a *movement along the new AE function*, as shown in Figure 29-3. The figure makes it clear that the multiplier is greater than one.

We refer to this case as the simple multiplier, because it is simplified by our assumption that the price level is fixed.

The simple multiplier identifies the change in equilibrium national income that occurs in response to a change in autonomous expenditure *at a constant price level*.

The Size of the Multiplier

It is now clear that the multiplier is greater than unity. But what does its size depend on? When can we expect it to be large and when can we expect it to be small? The answer is illustrated in Figure 29-4. The figure shows that the size of the multiplier depends on the slope of the AE function; that is, on the marginal propensity to spend.

A high marginal propensity to spend means a steep AE curve. The consumption expenditure induced by the initial increase in income is large,

FIGURE 29-3
The Multiplier with a Constant Price Level

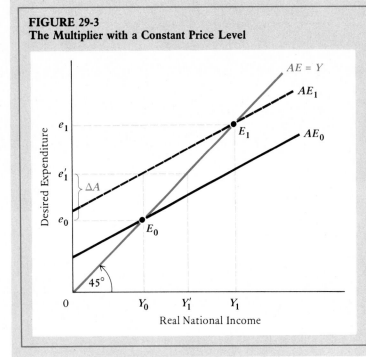

An increase in autonomous expenditure increases national income by a multiple of the initial increase. The initial equilibrium occurs where AE_0 cuts the 45° line, making desired expenditure of e_0 equal to national income of Y_0. An increase in autonomous expenditure of ΔA then shifts the desired expenditure function upward to AE_1. This raises total expenditure to e'_1 and would raise income to Y'_1 if there were no induced new expenditure. But at Y'_1 desired expenditure exceeds income and income rises to Y_1. Here desired expenditure of e_1 equals income of Y_1. The extra income and expenditure of $Y'_1 Y_1$ ($e'_1 e_1$) represents the *induced* increases in expenditure and is the amount by which the final increase in income exceeds the initial increase in autonomous expenditure.

with the result that the final rise in income is correspondingly great. On the other hand a low marginal propensity to spend means a relatively flat *AE* curve. The consumption expenditure induced by the initial increase in income is small. The result is that the final rise in income is not much larger than the initial rise in autonomous expenditure that brought it about.

The larger the marginal propensity to spend, the steeper the aggregate expenditure function and the larger is the multiplier.

The precise value of the multiplier can be derived by using the aggregate expenditure function and the $E = Y$ equilibrium condition. This is done in the box on page 540 for those who wish to see how it can be done. The result is that the multiplier, which we call K, is given by

$$K = \frac{\Delta Y}{\Delta A} = \frac{1}{(1 - z)}$$

where z was defined earlier as the marginal propensity to spend; that is, the slope of the expenditure function. The term $(1 - z)$ stands for the marginal propensity not to spend.[2] For example, if \$.75 of every \$1 of new national income is spent ($z = 0.75$), then \$.25 ($1.00 - 0.75$) is the amount not spent. The value of the multiplier is then calculated as $K = 1/0.25 = 4$.

The simple multiplier can be written as the reciprocal of the marginal propensity not to spend.

From this we see that if $(1 - z)$, the marginal propensity not to spend, is very small, the multiplier will be very large (because extra income induces much extra spending). The largest possible value of $(1 - z)$ is unity, indicating that all extra income is not spent. In this case the multiplier itself has a value of unity, indicating that the increase in

[2] The marginal propensity not to spend $(1 - z)$ is often referred to as the marginal propensity to *withdraw*. Not spending a part of one's income amounts to a *withdrawal* from the circular flow of income described in Figure 4-1.

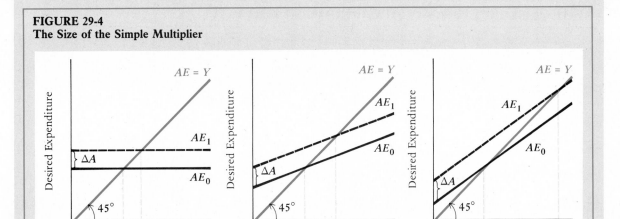

FIGURE 29-4
The Size of the Simple Multiplier

(i)   (ii)   (iii)

The steeper the desired expenditure function, the larger the marginal propensity to spend and the larger the simple multiplier. In (i), (ii), and (iii), initial desired expenditure of E_0 is equal to real national income of Y_0, and this equilibrium is then disturbed by an increase in autonomous expenditure of ΔA.

In (i), the AE function is horizontal, indicating a marginal propensity to spend of zero. The multiplier is then unity. Income rises by only the increment to exogenous expenditure since there is no induced expenditure by those who receive the initial increase in income.

In (ii), the AE curve is upward-sloping but still quite flat. The increase in national income to Y_2 is only slightly greater than the increase in autonomous expenditure that brought it about.

In (iii), the AE function is quite steep. Now the increase in income to Y_3 is much larger than the increase in autonomous expenditure that brought it about. The multiplier is quite large.

income is confined to the initial increase in autonomous expenditure.

VARIATIONS IN THE PRICE LEVEL

The simple multiplier just derived shows how a change in autonomous expenditure causes a change in national income on the assumption that the price level does not change. This works because we have been dealing with the case of a horizontal aggregate supply curve first introduced in Figure 28-1 on page 518. But we do not want to be confined to situations where the price level is constant. We wish additionally to see what happens when the price level rises or falls; that is, we wish to study inflations and deflations. To see what is involved here, we need to take the key step of relating the AE curve to the AD curve.

The Relation Between Aggregate Expenditure and Aggregate Demand

The relation between the AE and the AD curves is shown in Figure 29-5. Because the horizontal axes of both figures measure the same thing, real national income, they can be placed one above the other so that the level of national income on each can be directly compared. Part (i) of the figure

THE MULTIPLIER: AN ALGEBRAIC APPROACH

High school algebra is all that is needed to derive the exact expression for the multiplier. Readers who feel at home with algebra may like to follow this derivation. Others can skip it and rely on the graphical and numerical arguments given in the text.

First we derive the equation for the AE curve. Aggregate expenditure is divided into autonomous expenditure, A, and induced expenditure, N.* So we write

$$AE = N + A \qquad [1]$$

Since N is expenditure that varies with income, we can write

$$N = zY \qquad [2]$$

where z is a positive constant less than unity, the marginal propensity to spend out of national income. Substituting Equation [2] into Equation [1] yields the equation of the AE curve.

$$AE = zY + A \qquad [3]$$

Now we write the equation of the 45° line,

$$AE = Y \qquad [4]$$

* In simple models N is mainly consumption expenditure, but in other models it may include other types of expenditure; all that matters is that there is one class of expenditure, N, that varies with income and another class, A, that does not.

which is the equilibrium condition that aggregate desired expenditure should equal national income. Equations 3 and 4 are two equations with two unknowns, AE and Y. To solve them, we substitute Equation [3] into Equation [4] to obtain

$$Y = zY + A$$

Subtracting zY from both sides yields

$$Y - zY = A$$

Factoring out the Y yields

$$Y(1 - z) = A$$

Dividing through by $1 - z$ yields

$$Y = A/(1 - z).$$

This tells us the equilibrium value of Y in terms of autonomous expenditures, A, and the propensity not to spend (or to withdraw income from the circular flow), $(1 - z)$. The expression $Y = A/(1 - z)$ tells us that if A changes by ΔA, the change in Y, which we call ΔY, will be ΔA divided by $(1 - z)$. We write this

$$\Delta Y = \Delta A/(1 - z)$$

Dividing through by ΔA gives the value of the multiplier, which we designate by K:

$$K = \Delta Y/\Delta A = 1/(1 - z)$$

which is the expression given in the text.

describes the process by which equilibrium income is reached at any given price level. That equilibrium level of income and the given price level are then plotted in part (ii) as a single point on the AD curve.

To understand the relation between these curves it is important to understand the economic processes that lie behind these curves. The AE curve shows, for the given price level, desired aggregate expenditure at every possible level of income. Part (i) of Figure 29-5 shows that at any level of income below the equilibrium level, people are trying to buy more than is produced, while at any level of income above the equilibrium, people are buying less than is produced. Since the $SRAS$ curve is flat, firms will supply all that is demanded at the going price level. Thus, when desired expenditure exceeds current output, real income rises (as firms

FIGURE 29-5
The Relation Between the *AE* and the *AD* Curves

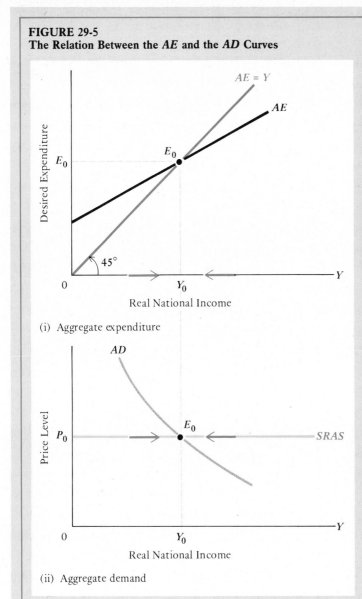

(i) Aggregate expenditure

(ii) Aggregate demand

The *AE* curve determines the equilibrium level of national income; that equilibrium is then plotted against the relevant price level to yield a point on the *AD* curve. In (i), the *AE* curve is drawn for the price level P_0. The forces acting to push income to Y_0 are shown by the arrows. At incomes less than Y_0, the *AE* curve lies above the 45° line, indicating that desired expenditure exceeds income; at incomes above Y_0, *AE* lies below the 45° line, indicating that desired expenditure is less than income. In (ii), the equilibrium income Y_0 is plotted against the price level P_0. The same adjustment of income toward Y_0 occurs in (ii), with the price level constant at P_0. This too is shown by arrows.

produce more), but the price level does not change. When desired expenditure is less than current output, real income falls (as firms produce less), but once again the price level does not change.

The second part of Figure 29-5 shows how the equilibrium income just determined can be plotted against the price level to yield a point on the *AD* curve.

The *AE* curve shows how equilibrium income is reached for a given price level. The *AD* curve plots that equilibrium income against that given price level.

Aggregate Expenditure, National Income, and the Price Level

What does a change in the price level do to desired real expenditure and hence to the *AE* curve? The effects were briefly discussed in Chapter 26: a rise in the price level reduces the level of desired real expenditure. One channel by which a change in the price level influences aggregate expenditure is via its effect on the real value of financial wealth.

Let us see how this works. Much wealth is held in the form of assets with a fixed money value. This is obviously true of money itself—cash and bank deposits—and is also true of many kinds of debt such as treasury bills and bonds. A rise in the price level lowers the purchasing power of these assets and lowers the real value of wealth.

Changes in the real value of financial wealth influence aggregate expenditure in two ways. First, there is a *direct* effect of wealth on consumption expenditure. Second, there is an *indirect* effect on expenditure operating via interest rates. The indirect effect is quantitatively the most important, but it is also much more complex to understand. Consequently we defer detailed study of it until Chapter 34 when we have studied the theory of money and interest rates. For now, we can understand the basic principles underlying the link between the price level and aggregate expenditure by focusing on the direct wealth effect on consumption.

We saw in Figure 28-3 that a fall in the household's wealth shifts the consumption function down. Because households have less wealth, they increase their saving (cut their consumption) so as to get back toward the wealth they wish to have for such purposes as retirement.

A fall in the consumption function shifts the whole aggregate expenditure function downward since for any given level of real income, people now wish to purchase a smaller quantity of goods and services. We already know that a downward shift in the *AE* function reduces equilibrium national income.

A fall in the price level has the opposite effect. The purchasing power of some existing assets is increased. Households, being wealthier in the aggregate, spend more. This shifts the *AE* curve upwards and raises equilibrium national income.

We have now reached an important result.

A rise in the price level lowers equilibrium national income, other things being equal. A fall in the price level raises equilibrium national income, other things being equal.

Deriving the *AD* Curve

Part (i) of Figure 29-6 shows how equilibrium national income changes when there are changes in the price level. The *AE* curve shifts, thus causing a new equilibrium income to be associated with the new price level. Each combination of equilibrium income, and its associated price level, becomes one point on the *AD* curve in part (ii) of the figure. *A movement along the AD curve thus traces out the response of equilibrium income to a change in the price level.*

Since the *AD* curve relates equilibrium national income to the price level, changes in the price level that cause *shifts* in the *AE* curve cause *movements along* the *AD* curve.

Changes in National Income and the *AD* Curve

The analysis conducted earlier in this chapter in terms of the *AE* curve can now be related to the *AD* curve. We have just seen that the *AD* curve plots equilibrium national income as a function of the price level. Thus anything that alters equilibrium national income at a given price level must shift the *AD* curve. This allows us to restate our earlier conclusions as follows.

A rise in the amount of desired consumption, investment, government, or export expenditure associated with each level of national income shifts the *AD* curve

FIGURE 29-6
The Relation Between the *AE* and the *AD* Curves When the Price Level Changes

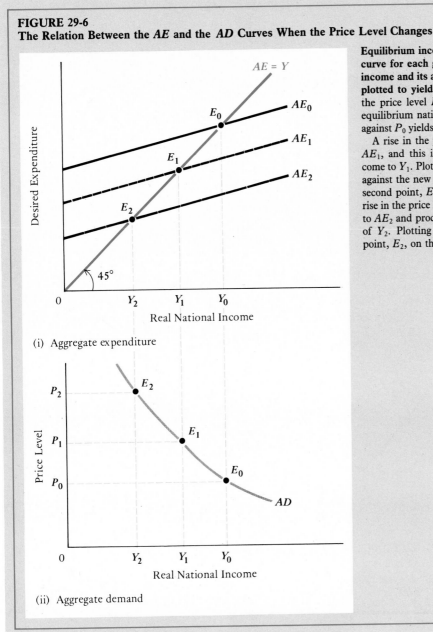

(i) Aggregate expenditure

(ii) Aggregate demand

Equilibrium income is determined by the *AE* curve for each given price level; the level of income and its associated price level are then plotted to yield the *AD* curve. Starting with the price level P_0, the *AE* curve is AE_0 and equilibrium national income is Y_0. Plotting Y_0 against P_0 yields the point E_0 on the *AD* curve.

A rise in the price level to P_1 lowers *AE* to AE_1, and this in turn lowers equilibrium income to Y_1. Plotting the new lower income, Y_1, against the new higher price level, P_1, yields a second point, E_1, on the *AD* curve. A further rise in the price level to P_2 lowers the *AE* curve to AE_2 and produces the lower level of income of Y_2. Plotting P_2 against Y_2 yields another point, E_2, on the *AD* curve.

to the right. A fall in any of these expenditures shifts the *AD* curve to the left.

A rise in tax rates shifts the *AD* curve to the left. A fall in tax rates shifts the *AD* curve to the right.

The simple multiplier measures the magnitude of the change in equilibrium national income when the price level is constant. It follows that the simple multiplier gives the magnitude of the *horizontal*

FIGURE 29-7
The Simple Multiplier and Shifts in *AD*

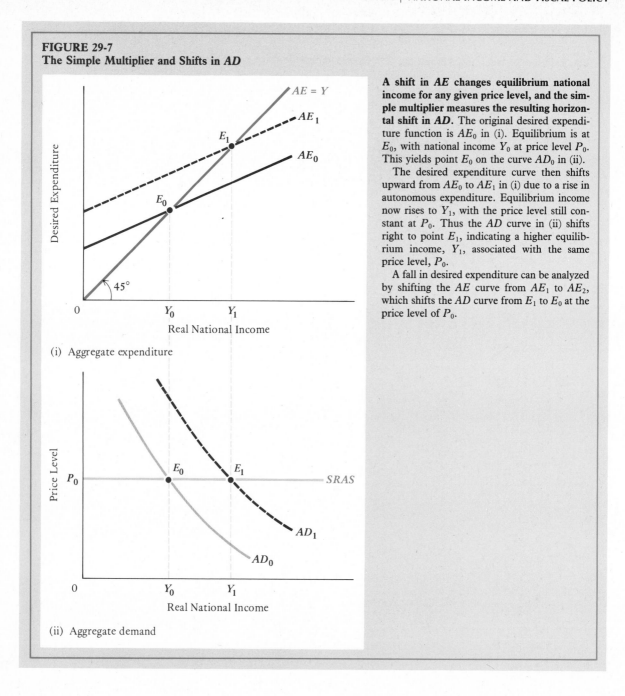

(i) Aggregate expenditure

(ii) Aggregate demand

A shift in *AE* changes equilibrium national income for any given price level, and the simple multiplier measures the resulting horizontal shift in *AD*. The original desired expenditure function is AE_0 in (i). Equilibrium is at E_0, with national income Y_0 at price level P_0. This yields point E_0 on the curve AD_0 in (ii).

The desired expenditure curve then shifts upward from AE_0 to AE_1 in (i) due to a rise in autonomous expenditure. Equilibrium income now rises to Y_1, with the price level still constant at P_0. Thus the AD curve in (ii) shifts right to point E_1, indicating a higher equilibrium income, Y_1, associated with the same price level, P_0.

A fall in desired expenditure can be analyzed by shifting the AE curve from AE_1 to AE_2, which shifts the AD curve from E_1 to E_0 at the price level of P_0.

shift in the *AD* curve in response to a change in autonomous expenditure. This is shown in Figure 29-7.

The simple multiplier determines the horizontal shift in the *AD* curve in response to a change in autonomous expenditure.

If the *SRAS* curve is horizontal, indicating that firms will supply everything that is demanded at the going price level, then the simple multiplier also tells us the change in equilibrium income that will occur in response to a change in autonomous expenditure. But what if the aggregate supply curve is upward-sloping? In this case a rise in national income will cause a rise in the price level. But a rise in the price level (by lowering the real value of household wealth) shifts the *AE* curve downward, which tends to lower national income. The outcome of the conflicting forces is easily seen using aggregate demand and aggregate supply curves.

The Multiplier When the Price Level Varies

Figure 29-8 shows that when the *SRAS* curve is upward-sloping the change in national income caused by a change in autonomous expenditure is no longer equal to the size of the horizontal shift in the *AD* curve. A rightward shift of the *AD* curve causes the price level to rise, which in turn causes the rise in national income to be less than the horizontal shift of the *AD* curve. Part of the expansionary impact of an increase in demand is dissipated in a rise in the price level, and only part is transmitted to a rise in real output.

When the *AS* curve is positively sloped, the multiplier is smaller than the simple multiplier derived for a given price level.

Why is the multiplier smaller when the *SRAS* curve is upward-sloping? The answer lies in the behavior of the *AE* curve. To understand this, it is useful to think of the final change in national income as occurring in two stages as shown in Figure 29-9.

First, with prices constant an increase in autonomous expenditure shifts the *AE* curve up and therefore shifts the *AD* curve to the right. The result is a change in national income given by the simple multiplier. This first stage shows up as a shift up of *AE* in (i) and the *AD* curve in (ii). But this cannot be the final equilibrium position be-

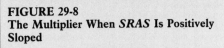

**FIGURE 29-8
The Multiplier When *SRAS* Is Positively Sloped**

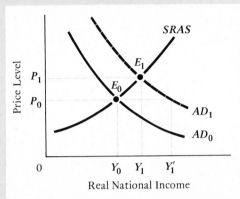

The multiplier effect of a shift in *AD*, when *SRAS* is positively sloped, is less than the simple multiplier. Equilibrium is initially at E_0, with a real national income of Y_0 and a price level of P_0. An increase in autonomous expenditure shifts the aggregate demand curve from AD_0 to AD_1. The new equilibrium is at E_1, with income Y_1 and price level P_1. The change in income Y_0Y_1 is smaller than Y_0Y_1', the change measured by the simple multiplier.

cause firms are unwilling to produce enough to satisfy the extra demand at the existing price level.

Second, we take account of the rise in the price level that occurs due to the upward slope of the *SRAS* curve. As we have seen a rise in the price level via its effect on wealth and consumption leads to a downward shift in the *AE* curve. This second shift in the *AE* curve partially counteracts the initial rise in national income and so reduces the size of the multiplier. The second stage shows up as a *downward shift* of the *AE* curve in (i) and a *movement along* the *AD* curve in (ii).

Which Curves Best Handle Price Level Changes?

We can now see why we must use *AD*–*AS* curves rather than the *AE* curve once the price level can

FIGURE 29-9
The *AE* Curve and the Multiplier When the Price Level Varies

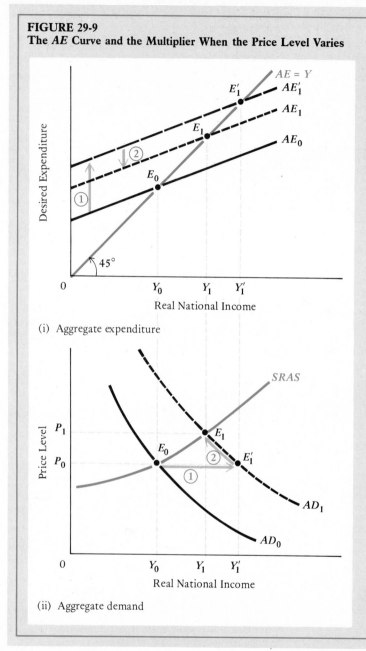

(i) Aggregate expenditure

(ii) Aggregate demand

The autonomous shift in expenditure causes the *AE* curve to shift up, but the rise in the price level causes it to shift part of the way down again. Hence the multiplier effect on *Y* is smaller than when *P* is constant. Originally, equilibrium is at point E_0 in both (i) and (ii), with real national income Y_0 and price level P_0. Aggregate desired expenditure then shifts to AE'_1, taking the aggregate demand curve to AD_1 (arrow ① in both panels). If the price level had remained constant at P_0, the new equilibrium would have been at E'_1 and real income would have risen to Y'_1. The amount $Y_0Y'_1$ is the change called for by the simple multiplier.

Instead, however, the shift in the *AD* curve raises the price level to P_1 because the *SRAS* curve is upward-sloping. The rise in the price level shifts the aggregate expenditure line down to AE_1 in (i) (arrow ②). This is shown as a movement along the *AD* curve in (ii) (arrow ②). The new equilibrium is thus at E_1. The amount Y_0Y_1 is the actual increase in real income, while the amount $Y_1Y'_1$ is the shortfall relative to the simple multiplier due to the rise in the price level.

vary. If all we had was the *AE* curve plus the knowledge that the *AS* curve was upward-sloping, we could not discover the final change in either *P* or *Y*. We would know that the initial rise in autonomous expenditure shifted the *AE* curve upward.

We would also know that the consequent rise in the price level would shift *AE* back downward somewhat. But by how much? Where will the final equilibrium be in relation to the original equilibrium and the equilibrium that would occur if prices had remained constant? We cannot answer these questions unless we know by how much the price level rises. But there is nothing in part (i) of the Figure 29-9 to tell us this. Thus the AE–45° line analysis is not sufficient to deal with situations in which the price level can change. But if we first use the AE curve to derive the AD curve, we can then determine the changes in Y and P by relating the AD and the AS curves.

SUMMARY

1. A movement along the aggregate expenditure curve represents an induced change in expenditure in response to a change in national income. A shift of the aggregate expenditure curve represents a change in the expenditure that is associated with each level of national income.

2. Equilibrium national income is increased by an upward shift in the consumption, investment, government, or export expenditure associated with each level of the national income. National income is decreased by the opposite changes.

3. Equilibrium national income is decreased by an increase in the taxes associated with each level of income and increased by a fall in taxes.

4. The magnitude of the effect on national income of shifts in autonomous expenditure (such as I, G, and X) is given by the multiplier. This is defined as $K = \Delta Y/\Delta A$, where ΔA is the change in autonomous expenditure.

5. The elementary theory of national income gives the value of the simple multiplier as $1/(1 - z)$, where z is the marginal propensity to spend. Thus the larger the propensity to spend, the larger the multiplier. It is a basic prediction of national income theory that the multiplier is greater than unity.

6. The AE curve is drawn for a particular price level. It shows the relation between desired expenditure at each level of income and shows how equilibrium income is achieved. The AD curve plots the equilibrium level of income against the price level.

7. A change in the price level shifts the AE curve and leads to a new level of equilibrium national income. It is shown by a movement along the AD curve to a new equilibrium income and price level.

8. The simple multiplier determines the horizontal shift in the AD curve following from a shift in autonomous expenditure. It determines the actual change in equilibrium real national income *if* the economy is on a horizontal Keynesian aggregate supply curve.

9. When the aggregate supply curve is upward-sloping, part of the effect of the multiplier is dissipated in a rise in prices and only part goes to raise real income. The division of the effects between a change in national income and a change in the price level are easily discovered from aggregate demand and aggregate supply curves.

TOPICS FOR REVIEW

Shifts of and movements along expenditure curves
The effect on national income of changes in the amounts of I, G, and X associated with each level of income
The effect on national income of a change in tax rates
The simple multiplier with a constant price level
The relation between the size of the simple multiplier and the slope of the expenditure schedule
The multiplier when the price level *and* output vary
The relation between the AE and the AD curves
How changes in autonomous expenditure shifts the AE and the AD curves

DISCUSSION QUESTIONS

1. In what direction would each of the following change national income? Which expenditure flows would be affected first? Be sure to distinguish between movements along curves and shifts of curves.
   a. The production and sale of a new nuclear reactor
   b. A decrease in personal income-tax withholding for low-income taxpayers

c. A major reduction in social security payments to the elderly

d. A spurt in consumer spending for video recorders accompanied by a reduction in savings

e. A reduction in spending on foreign travel accompanied by an equivalent increase in saving

f. A large increase in defense expenditure accompanied by an across-the-board tax cut.

2. Predict whether each of the following events will, other things being equal, increase, decrease, or leave unchanged *the size of the multiplier.*

   a. A shift from foreign travel to holidays at home

   b. An expansion of expenditures on highways

   c. Decisions by corporations to pay out a smaller percentage of their earnings in dividends and to increase their bank balances whenever national income falls

   d. Widespread adoption by cities of a city income tax

   e. A large increase in the percentage of disposable income saved by households

3. The president of the Chamber of Commerce of Southeastern Connecticut commented on the effects in his area of a 22-week strike at a shipyard where the lost payroll was $2 million per week: "You don't just figure $2 million a week times 22 weeks, you have to multiply by four or five. That shipyard is the prime source of money in this region. Money comes into the region from Washington and then the shipyard worker's wife takes it to the grocery, and the grocery clerk takes it to the gas station, and so on until it leaves the area in taxes or some other way." Interpret his statement in terms of the analysis of this chapter.

4. Homer Hardcrust, chairman of the Council of Economic Advisors, proposes that because of the current heavy unemployment, government should prepare an austerity program and cut down government expenditures to set an example for private households. Would his policy tend to raise or lower unemployment?

5. A private research agency estimates the GNP gap to be $10 billion and recommends that it be eliminated by an increase in government expenditures of $10 billion. Does the agency's staff understand the multiplier?

6. What would happen to employment and income if, in an attempt to lower American unemployment, Congress passed very large increases in American tariff rates? What would happen if, in the face of a worldwide recession, all countries did the same?

30 CHANGES IN NATIONAL INCOME II: THE ROLE OF AGGREGATE SUPPLY

The aggregate supply curve plays a key role in the behavior of the economy. First, as we saw at the end of Chapter 29, the shape of the *SRAS* curve determines how the impact of aggregate demand shocks is divided between changes in output and changes in the price level. Second, as we saw in Chapter 26, aggregate supply shocks—which *shift* the aggregate supply curve—are themselves a major cause of changes in both output and the price level. In this chapter we analyze the role played by

aggregate supply in more detail. We look both at short-run and at long-run effects.

AGGREGATE SUPPLY IN THE SHORT RUN

In this section we focus attention on the short-run effects of aggregate demand and aggregate supply shocks. To do this we must first examine the shape of the short-run aggregate supply curve in more detail than we did in Chapter 26.

The Shape of the *SRAS* Curve

In Chapter 26 we encountered the upward sloping *SRAS* curve. It relates the quantity of output producers that are willing to sell to the price level, other things being equal. Such an *SRAS* curve is also shown in isolation in Figure 30-1. Notice two things about its shape: it has a positive slope, and the slope increases as output rises.

Positive slope. The most obvious feature of the *SRAS* curve is its positive slope, indicating that, other things being equal, a higher price level is associated with a higher volume or real output.

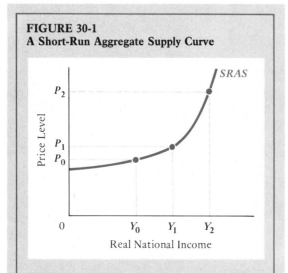

FIGURE 30-1
A Short-Run Aggregate Supply Curve

SRAS **slopes upward and is steeper, the larger is real national income.** The upward slope of *SRAS* shows that, according to the supply decisions of firms, output and the price level will be positively associated. The increasing slope shows that the higher the level of output, the larger the increase in the price level associated with any further increment to output. For example, the change in output in moving from Y_0 to Y_1 is the same as that in moving from Y_1 to Y_2, but the rise in prices, P_0 to P_1, associated with the first increment to output is smaller than the rise, P_1 to P_2, associated with the second increment.

The key to understanding why the *SRAS* curve has a positive slope is knowing what is being held constant as the price level is varied. The prices of *factors of production*, the most important being the wage rate, are what is being held constant. If the prices of everything that firms sell rise, while the prices of everything that firms use to make their products remain constant, production becomes more profitable. Firms are interested in making profits. When production becomes more profitable, they will usually produce more.[1] Thus, when the price level of final output rises while input prices are held constant, firms are motivated to increase their outputs. This increase gives rise to the upward slope of the *SRAS* curve.

The higher the price level the higher the total output that firms are willing to produce and offer for sale, other things being equal.

The "other things being equal" clause is the key to why we have called the upward-sloping relationship a *short-run* aggregate supply curve. Treating wages and other factor prices as constant is only appropriate when the time period under consideration is short. Hence the *SRAS* curve is used only to analyze the effects that occur in the short run. We also call these *impact* effects.

Increasing slope. There is a somewhat less obvious, but in many ways more important, property of a typical *SRAS* curve: its slope *increases* as output rises. It is rather flat to the left of potential output and rather steep to the right. Why? Below potential output, firms will typically have unused capacity—some plant and equipment will be idle. When firms are faced with unused capacity, only a small increase in the price of their output may be needed to induce them to expand production, at least up to normal capacity. (Indeed, firms may be willing to sell more at *existing prices* if only the demand were there. If all firms are in this situation, we will have the horizontal "Keynesian" *SRAS* curve as in Figure 28-1.)

---

[1] Those who have already studied microeconomics can understand this in terms of price-taking firms being faced with higher prices and thus expanding output *along* their marginal cost curves until marginal cost is once again equal to price.

Once output is pushed very far beyond normal capacity, however, unit costs tend to rise quite rapidly. Higher-cost standby capacity may have to be used. Overtime and extra shifts may have to be worked. Both expedients raise the cost of producing a unit of output. Many more costly expedients may also have to be adopted. These higher cost methods will not be used unless the selling price of the output has risen enough to cover them. Furthermore, the more output is expanded beyond normal capacity, the more rapidly unit costs rise and hence the larger the rise in price needed to induce firms to increase output even further.

The increasing slope of the *SRAS* curve in Figure 30-1 is meant to reflect this important *asymmetry:*

Below potential national income, changes in output are accompanied by only *small* changes in the price level. Above potential national income, changes in output are accompanied by *large* changes in the price level.

Why the Shape of *SRAS* Matters When Demand Shocks Hit

How does the asymmetry of the *SRAS* curve, which is reflected in its *increasing* slope, influence the analysis of aggregate demand shocks? At the end of the previous chapter, we saw that the positive slope of the *SRAS* curve reduced the size of the multiplier. (See Figure 29-8). We now examine how the increasing slope of the *SRAS* curve influences how an aggregate demand shock is divided between changes in real output and changes in the price level.

Figure 30-2 contains an *SRAS* curve that highlights the increasing slope by taking on extreme forms at both low and high level of national income. The curve shows three distinct ranges.

Over the *Keynesian range* at the left, where the *SRAS* curve is horizontal, any change in aggregate demand leads to *no* change in prices and, as seen earlier, a response of output equal to that predicted by the simple multiplier.

Next, there is an *intermediate range* along which *SRAS* is positively sloped. In this range a shift in the *AD* curve gives rise to a change in real income

and to a change in the price level. As we saw in Figure 29-9, the change in the price level means that real income will change by less in response to a change in autonomous expenditure than it would if prices were constant.

At the extreme right, the curve shows a range where the *SRAS* curve is vertical. This so-called *Classical range* deals with an economy right up against its capacity constraints; nothing more can be produced, however large the demand. Over this range, any change in aggregate demand leads only to a change in the price level and to *no* change in real national income. The multiplier in this case is zero.

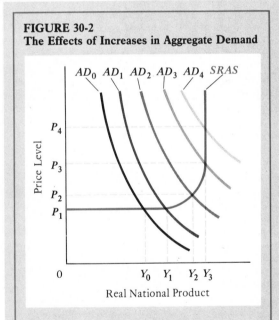

FIGURE 30-2
The Effects of Increases in Aggregate Demand

Increases in aggregate demand may cause an increase in output alone, an increase in both output and prices, or an increase in prices alone, depending on the shape of the *SRAS* curve. An increase in aggregate demand from AD_0 to AD_1 increases total output from Y_0 to Y_1, leaving the price level unchanged at P_1. An increase to AD_2 raises output from Y_1 to Y_2 and raises the price level from P_1 to P_2. An increase to AD_3 brings a smaller increase in output (from Y_2 to Y_3) and a larger increase in the price level (from P_2 to P_3). An increase to AD_4 raises the price level from P_3 to P_4 but leaves output constant at Y_3.

FIGURE 30-3
Aggregate Demand Shocks in the Classical Range

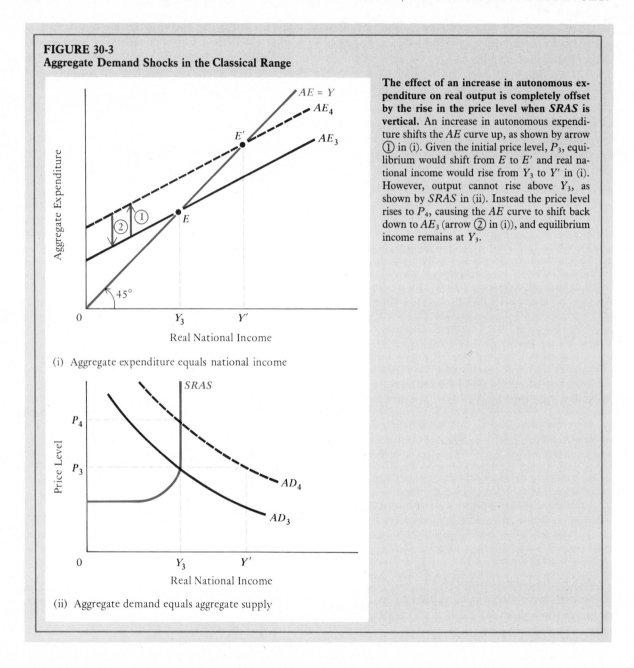

(i) Aggregate expenditure equals national income

(ii) Aggregate demand equals aggregate supply

The effect of an increase in autonomous expenditure on real output is completely offset by the rise in the price level when *SRAS* is vertical. An increase in autonomous expenditure shifts the *AE* curve up, as shown by arrow ① in (i). Given the initial price level, P_3, equilibrium would shift from E to E' and real national income would rise from Y_3 to Y' in (i). However, output cannot rise above Y_3, as shown by *SRAS* in (ii). Instead the price level rises to P_4, causing the *AE* curve to shift back down to AE_3 (arrow ② in (i)), and equilibrium income remains at Y_3.

These three cases illustrate the general proposition that how the effect of any given shift in aggregate demand will be divided between a change in real output and a change in the price level depends on the conditions of aggregate supply. The steeper the *SRAS* curve the greater the price effect and the smaller the output effect.

The slope of the aggregate supply curves implies that at low levels of national income shifts in aggregate demand mainly affect output with only a minor impact on prices while at high levels of national income shifts in aggregate demand mainly affect prices and have only a relatively minor impact on output.

AD shocks and the classical range of SRAS. Let us consider the classical case in more detail, and in so doing look again at the aggregate expenditure curve. An increase in autonomous expenditure shifts the *AE* curve upward, thus raising the amount that would be demanded if the price level remained constant. But a vertical *SRAS* curve means that output cannot be expanded. The extra demand merely forces prices up and as prices rise, the *AE* curve is shifted down once again. The rise in prices continues until the *AE* curve is back where it started. Thus the rise in prices fully offsets the expansionary effect of the original shift, leaving both real aggregate expenditure and equilibrium real income unchanged as a result. This is illustrated in Figure 30-3.

Causes of Shifts in the *SRAS* Curve

Aggregate supply is important not only because the *shape* of the *SRAS* curve determines the effects of shifts in aggregate demand but also because *shifts* in the *SRAS* curve affect the price level and national income.

The *SRAS* curve can shift for many reasons. For example, an increase in the supplies of labor and capital will increase the quantity of output that can be produced. Below we consider two sources of shift that are of particular importance.

A Change in Costs

We have seen that input prices are held constant along the *SRAS* curve. This suggests a very important reason for the *SRAS* curve to shift. If input prices rise, firms will find that the profitability of their current production has been reduced. Their response causes the *SRAS* curve to shift up and to the left.

Using the terminology of Chapter 5, an upward shift in the *SRAS* curve is referred to as a *decrease in supply* because at any given price level, less out-

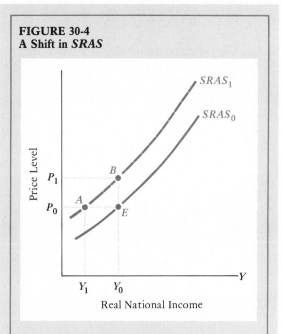

FIGURE 30-4
A Shift in *SRAS*

An increase in costs shifts the *SRAS* curve upward. The initial *SRAS* is shown by the solid curve, $SRAS_0$. An increase in costs shifts it upward to the dashed line, $SRAS_1$.

Because the *SRAS* curve is positively sloped, this upward shift is equivalent to a leftward shift. For example, suppose the price level is initially at P_0 and output is Y_0. Following an increase in costs that reduces profitability, firms could maintain prices and reduce output, thus moving from point E to point A.

They might, instead, maintain output but increase prices, thus moving to point B. In fact, the point to which the firms actually adjust depends, as we have seen, on the *AD* curve. But we know that $SRAS_1$ lies above and to the left of the original curve, $SRAS_0$.

put will be willingly produced. Equivalently, for any given level of output to be willingly produced, an increase in price will be required. This is illustrated in Figure 30-4.

Similarly a fall in input prices causes the *SRAS* curve to shift down and to the right. This is referred to as an *increase in supply.*

A change in costs shifts the *SRAS* curve because any given output will be supplied at a different price level than previously.

An Increase in Productivity

If labor productivity rises, meaning that each worker can produce more, then the costs of producing a unit of output must fall as long as wage rates remain constant. Lower costs generally lead to lower prices. Competing firms cut prices in attempts to raise their market shares, and the net result of such competition is that the fall in costs of production is accompanied by a fall in prices.[2] If the same output is sold at a lower price, this causes a downward shift in the *SRAS* curve. This shift means an *increase in supply*: the same quantity of output is associated with a lower price level while the same price level is associated with a larger quantity of output.

A rise in productivity shifts the *SRAS* curve downward because any given output will be supplied at a lower price level than previously.

Effects of Shifts in the *SRAS* Curve

What happens if the price of imported oil rises, pushing up many firms' production costs? This happened in 1974 and again in 1979–1980, and it may well happen again before the end of the 1980s. What happens if changed conditions in the markets for basic industrial raw materials cause their prices to rise, pushing up many firms' costs of production? We have seen that such events will shift the *SRAS* curve up. What happens if the events of the 1970s are reversed, and the prices of oil or other raw materials fall, lowering the costs of production for many firms and thus shifting the *SRAS* curve down?

We have just seen that a supply shock will cause the *SRAS* curve to shift. This leads to new equilibrium values for the price level and real output. In Chapter 26 we saw that since the new equilibrium represents a *movement along* the *AD* curve, output and the price level change in opposite directions, one rising and the other falling.

[2] Even a monopoly will cut its prices and raise its output when its marginal costs fall. See Chapter 15.

In the short run an upward shift in the *SRAS* curve lowers output and raises the price level, while a downward shift raises output but lowers the price level.

Stagflation. Until about a decade ago, most of the short-term fluctuations in the economy stemmed mainly from demand-side disturbances. As a result, people became accustomed to rising output combined with rising prices, and falling output combined with stable or falling prices. Over the last decade, however, the economy has been buffeted by severe supply-side shocks. Increases in the prices of inputs such as oil, natural gas, and raw materials have raised the price at which output is supplied, thus shifting the *SRAS* curve upward. These increases have made familiar the combination of rising prices and falling output.

AGGREGATE SUPPLY IN THE LONG RUN

The key to understanding the long-run properties of aggregate supply is to see how changes in aggregate demand *induce* shifts in the *SRAS* curve. This means that our studies of impact effects, which were based on a single *SRAS* curve, are not the final word on what happens.

Long-Run Effects of Aggregate Demand Shocks

Up to now when examining aggregate demand shocks we have maintained the other-things-being-equal clause that underlies the short-run aggregate supply curve. This allowed us to concentrate on short-term effects. But what about the longer-term effects?

An Inflationary Shock

What we have learned so far about aggregate supply can help us study inflation in more detail. Assume that the economy starts off in the happy position of full employment and a stable price level,

FIGURE 30-5
Demand-Shock Inflation

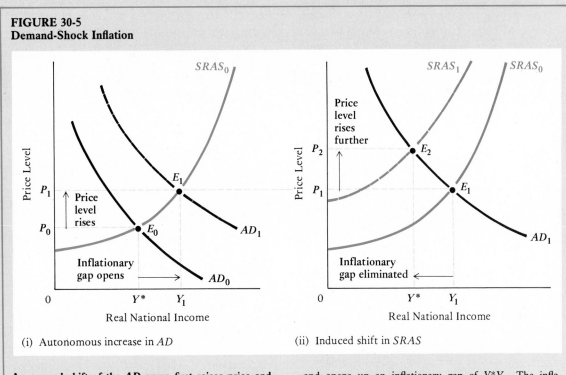

(i) Autonomous increase in *AD*   (ii) Induced shift in *SRAS*

An upward shift of the *AD* curve first raises price and output along the *SRAS* curve and then induces a shift of *SRAS* that further raises prices but lowers output along the *AD* curve. In (i), the economy is in equilibrium at point E_0, with output Y^* and price level P_0. The aggregate demand curve then shifts to AD_1. This moves the equilibrium to E_1, with income of Y_1 and price level P_1, and opens up an inflationary gap of Y^*Y_1. The inflationary gap results in an increase in wages and other input costs, shifting *SRAS* upward, as shown in (ii). As *SRAS* moves upward, income falls and the price level rises along AD_1. Eventually, when the *SRAS* curve has shifted to $SRAS_1$, income is back to Y^*, the inflationary gap has been eliminated, and the price level has risen further to P_2.

as pictured in part (i) of Figure 30-5. A rise in autonomous expenditure, perhaps caused by an investment boom, increases aggregate demand. The immediate effects are that the price level rises and that real income rises above its potential level. This is also shown in part (i) of Figure 30-5.

Firms will now be producing beyond their normal capacity output, so there will be a heavy demand for all factor inputs, including labor. Workers will be demanding wage increases to compensate them for the higher cost of living caused by the increase in the price level. Thus the boom generates a combination of conditions—high profits for firms, heavy demand for labor, and a

desire on the part of labor for wages to catch up with the price rises—that is a recipe for sharp increases in wages. And this sequence is just what past experience of the economy tells us will happen.[3]

Sharp rises in wages mean sharp rises in costs. These, as we have already seen, lead to upward shifts in the *SRAS* curve as firms seek to pass on their increases in input costs by increasing their

[3] Wage contracts often allow for changes in prices that are *expected* to occur during the life of the contract. The role of expectations in causing the *SRAS* curve to shift plays an important role in many macroeconomic debates and will be discussed in detail below.

output prices. For this reason the rise in the price level and real output shown in part (i) of Figure 30-5 is *not* the end of the story. As seen in part (ii) of the figure, the upward shift of the *SRAS* curve causes a further rise in the price level, but this time the price rise is associated with a fall in output. The cost increases and the upward shifts in the *SRAS* curve go on until income returns to its potential level. Only then is there no abnormal demand for labor.

The excess of output above its potential level, Y^*Y, is a negative GNP gap. Often this is called an **inflationary gap** because Y in the range above Y^* tends to be associated with inflation. The process comes to a halt when the inflationary gap has been removed.

This very important demand-shock inflation sequence can be summarized as follows:

1. Starting from full employment, a rise in aggregate demand raises the price level and raises income above its potential level as the economy expands along a given *SRAS* curve.
2. The expansion of output beyond its normal capacity level puts heavy pressure on factor markets; factor prices begin to rise, shifting the *SRAS* curve upward.
3. The shift of the *SRAS* curve causes output to fall along the *AD* curve; this process continues *as long as* actual output exceeds potential output. Therefore, actual output eventually falls back to its potential level. The price level will, however, now be higher than it was after the initial impact of the increased aggregate demand, but inflation will have come to a halt.

The ability to wring more output from the economy than its underlying potential output (point 2) is only a short-term success. Y greater than Y^* sets up inflationary pressures that tend to push national income back to Y^*.

There is a self-adjustment mechanism that brings any inflation caused by a one-time demand shock to an eventual halt by returning output to its potential level and thus removing the inflationary gap.

A continuing inflation. Continuing inflation normally requires that the government frustrate the self-adjustment process just described. It does so by adopting policies that allow the *AD* curve to *shift* upward just as fast as the *SRAS* curve does. In Part Nine, we shall study such policies and raise the question of why such seemingly undesirable pro-inflationary policies are adopted.

Experience of Demand Inflations

We have just seen that demand inflations are associated with national income at or above its potential level. In other words, when too much demand is the cause of the inflation, boom conditions and rising prices go together. The American economy has suffered from such demand-shock inflations many times in the last 40 years.

Demand shocks have been common throughout our history. The business cycle, which we shall study in detail in Chapter 31, is largely due to variations in private-sector investment expenditure, which in turn cause shifts in the aggregate demand curve. Also, major wars have usually been associated with expansionary demand shocks. These occurred during the First and Second World Wars in the first half of the century, during the Korean War in the early 1950s, and during the Vietnam War in the late 1960s and early 1970s. During such wars the government greatly increases its spending on military goods and services. It usually finds it difficult, however, to increase its tax revenue as fast as its spending is increased. As a result, there is usually a large increase in government spending (G) *not* matched by an equivalent fall in disposable income or private consumption expenditures (C). The net effect is for aggregate demand to increase. The result is high output combined with rising prices.

A Deflationary Shock

Let us return to that happy economy with full employment and stable prices. It appears again in part (i) of Figure 30-6, which duplicates part (i) of Figure 30-5. Now assume a *decline* in aggregate

FIGURE 30-6
Demand-Shock Deflation with Flexible Wages

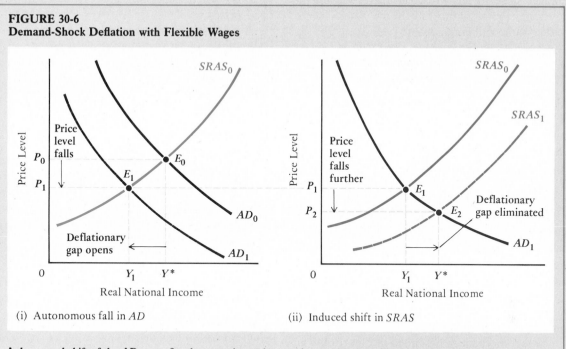

(i) Autonomous fall in *AD*

(ii) Induced shift in *SRAS*

A downward shift of the *AD* curve first lowers price and output along the *SRAS* curve and then induces a (slow) shift of *SRAS* that further lowers prices but raises output along the *AD* curve. In (i), the economy is in equilibrium at E_0, with output Y^* and price level P_0. The aggregate demand curve then shifts to AD_1, moving equilibrium to E_1, with income of Y_1 and price level of P_1, and opens up a GNP (or deflationary) gap of Y_1Y^*.

Part (ii) shows the adjustment back to full employment that would occur from the supply side of the economy if wages were sufficiently flexible downward. The fall in wages would shift *SRAS* downward. Real national income would rise, and the price level would fall further along the *AD* curve. Eventually the curve would reach $SRAS_1$, with equilibrium at E_2. The price level would stabilize at P_2 while income would return to Y^*, eliminating the deflationary gap.

demand, perhaps due to a major reduction in investment expenditure.

The impact of this decline is a fall in output and some downward adjustment of prices, as shown in part (i) of the figure. As output falls, unemployment figures will rise. The difference between potential output and actual output is, as we have already seen, called the GNP gap. When the GNP gap is positive, as in Figure 30-6, it is also sometimes called the **deflationary gap.** This terminology suggests the operation of an automatic adjustment mechanism that would remove the gap by shifts in the *SRAS* curve.

Consider what would happen *if* heavy unemployment caused wage rates to fall sharply. Falling wage rates would lower costs for firms, and competition among them to sell in a depressed market would, once their falling costs gave them scope to do so, lead them to cut prices. This in turn would cause a downward shift in the short-run aggregate supply curve, as shown in part (ii) of Figure 30-6. As a result, the economy would move along its fixed *AD* curve with falling prices and rising output until full employment was restored at potential national income of Y^*. This possible process is illustrated in part (ii) of the figure. We conclude that *if* wages were to fall whenever there was unemployment, the resulting fall in the *SRAS* curve would restore full employment.

Flexible wages that fell when there was unemployment would provide an automatic adjustment mechanism that would push the economy back toward full employment whenever output fell below potential.

We now come to what may be called the *second important asymmetry* of the economy's aggregate supply behavior (the first being the shape of the *SRAS* curve). Boom conditions with severe labor shortages *do* cause wages to rise rapidly, carrying the *SRAS* curve upward with them. But many economists believe, and the recent experience of many economies suggests, that slump conditions with heavy unemployment *do not* cause wages to fall with anything like the corresponding speed. In other words, wages are not very flexible in a downward direction. Unemployment has, at most, a weak and sluggish downward effect on wages. The adjustment mechanism described in Figure 30-6 is, at best, weak and slow-acting.

Notice that the weakness of the automatic adjustment mechanism does not mean that slumps must last indefinitely. All that it means is that speedy recovery back to full employment must be generated mainly from the demand side. If the economy is not to experience a lengthy stagnation, the force leading to recovery must be an upward shift in the *AD* curve rather than a downward drift in the *SRAS* curve.

A second asymmetry of aggregate supply behavior is that the *SRAS* curve shifts upward fairly rapidly when *Y* exceeds *Y** but shifts downward only slowly (if at all) when *Y* falls short of *Y**.

This asymmetry explains two key facts about our economy. First, unemployment *can* persist for quite long periods without causing large decreases in wages and prices (which would, if they did occur, help to remove the unemployment). Second, booms, with labor shortages and production beyond normal capacity, *cannot* persist for long

periods without causing large increases in wages and prices.

To emphasize this asymmetry, the term *GNP gap* (rather than deflationary gap) is used when output is below its capacity level, and the term *inflationary gap* (rather than negative GNP gap) is used when output is above its capacity level.

Downward Inflexibility: The 1930s

The last time that the American price level really fell significantly was at the onset of the Great Depression. At its peak in 1933, unemployment reached 25 percent of the labor force! And it never fell below 15 percent during the rest of the decade. The price level fell dramatically in the three years 1931–1933. After 1933, however, there were no further major reductions, even in the face of a persistent GNP gap. Between 1933 and 1939 the price level sometimes rose and sometimes fell, but its average change over that whole period of depression was a *rise* of just over 0.5 percent per year. (See Figure 26-5).

In short, the economy was operating on the Keynesian portion of its aggregate supply curve, and that curve did not shift down in the face of the persistent excess supply of labor. The main problem facing the economy throughout the decade of the 1930s was a deficiency of aggregate demand. In these circumstances, any policy that increased demand would have helped to alleviate the depression. This was Keynes' great insight.

Students often wonder why economists so frequently look back to the Great Depression. Is it a nostalgia for past times on the part of now-senior economists who grew up in that era? No, it is more than that on two counts. First, evidence is not irrelevant just because it comes from the past. Second, the 1930s constituted the key "experiment" that determined ideas that still are embodied in today's theories. Economists thought they learned two things from this period. First, price levels can be very slow to adjust in a downward direction even in the face of very large GNP gaps. Second, as a consequence, large GNP gaps can persist for quite a long time unless they are removed by stimulus from the demand side of the economy.

The Long-Run Aggregate Supply Curve

Although the downward adjustments of wages may not remove deflationary gaps fast enough to be of practical importance, the *possibility* of automatic adjustments gives rise to a very important concept: the **long-run aggregate supply curve** (**LRAS**). This curve relates the price level to real national income *after wage rates and all other input costs have been fully adjusted to eliminate any unemployment or overall labor shortages.* This is the output that would occur *if* wages were flexible enough in both directions to eliminate any excess demand or excess supply of labor. Full employment would then prevail and output would be at its potential level, Y^*.

So when all input prices are fully adjusted, the aggregate supply curve becomes a vertical line at Y^*, as seen in part (i) of Figure 30-7. This is called the *long-run aggregate supply curve* because it refers to adjustments that take a substantial amount of time. (If a *downward* adjustment is needed, it can take a very long time.)

Along the *LRAS* curve all the prices of *all outputs* and *all inputs* have been fully adjusted to eliminate any excess demands or supplies. Proportionate changes in money wages and the price level (which, by definition, will leave real wages unaltered), will also leave equilibrium employment and output unchanged. The key concept is this: if the price of absolutely everything (including labor), doubles, then nothing real changes. When the price of everything bought *and* sold doubles, neither workers nor firms gain any advantage and hence neither has any incentive to alter their behavior. Output, therefore, is unchanged. The level of output will be what can be produced in the economy when all factors of production, including labor, are utilized at "normal" levels of their capacity.

The vertical long-run AS curve shows that given full adjustment of input prices, potential income, Y^*, is compatible with any price *level*.

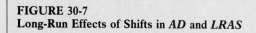

FIGURE 30-7
Long-Run Effects of Shifts in *AD* and *LRAS*

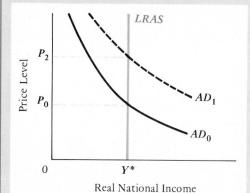

(i) A rise in aggregate demand

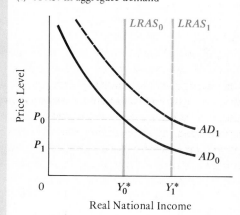

(ii) A rise in long-run aggregate supply

When *LRAS* is vertical, aggregate supply determines *Y* and aggregate demand determines *P*. In (i), a shift in the aggregate demand curve from AD_0 to AD_1 raises the price level from P_0 to P_2 but leaves output unchanged at Y^* in the long run. In (ii), a shift in the long-run aggregate supply curve from $LRAS_0$ to $LRAS_1$ with the aggregate demand curve constant at AD_0 raises output from Y_0^* to Y_1^*, but also lowers the price level from P_0 to P_1. If the new output of Y_0^* were to be purchased at the original price level of P_0, it would be necessary for the aggregate demand curve to shift to AD_1 when the aggregate supply shifts to $LRAS_1$.

Equilibrium Output and Price Level in the Long Run

Figure 30-7 shows the equilibrium output and price level determined by the intersection of the *AD* curve and the vertical *LRAS* curve. One important implication is:

With a vertical *LRAS* curve, output is determined solely by conditions of supply, and the role of aggregate demand is simply to determine the price level.

Note in the figure that a shift in the *AD* curve changes only the price level. However, a shift in the *LRAS* curve changes both output and the price level. An outward shift in the *LRAS* curve, for example, increases output, but at the old price level there is not sufficient demand to buy the new output. Either prices must fall so that the new output will be bought with the old *AD* curve, or the *AD* curve itself must shift right so that the new output can be purchased at the original price level.

Of course these are only long-term tendencies. To see the short-term impact of demand and supply shocks, we need to use the short-run aggregate supply curve.[4]

Note the sharp difference between the long-term and short-term results. Aggregate demand shocks only exert an influence on real income in the short term. When national income is already at full employment, it cannot be permanently increased by raising aggregate demand. What is needed is a rightward shift of the *LRAS* curve, and a major source of such shifts is investment. Recall that early Keynesians paid little attention to the long-run effect of investment on aggregate supply. Although not an unreasonable thing to do when analyzing severe deflationary conditions, the neglect is seri-

ous when the economy is operating at full employment.

Supply-Side Economics

An increase in aggregate supply produces a situation that governments in all countries would have welcomed any time in the 1970s and 1980s: rising output combined with *downward* pressure on the price level. This was the promise of supply-side economics that was an important plank in Ronald Reagan's campaign platform in the 1980 presidential elections. Although supply-side economics had many aspects, we are here concerned specifically with the short-term effects of supply-side policies on the price level and on real national income.

A major part of supply-side economics was the provision of tax incentives that were to increase potential national income by increasing the nation's supplies of labor and capital. Incentives were given to firms to increase their investment, thus increasing national productive capacity. Personal taxes were to be cut across the board to give everyone an incentive to work more. It was argued that people already employed would be more inclined to work longer and harder when they were able to keep a larger fraction of their gross earnings for themselves, and people outside of the labor force would be drawn in as a result of the higher after-tax wages. Taxes would be especially cut or exemptions especially raised on higher incomes, so as to increase the incentives for work and risk-taking on the part of the most productive people. These people tend to earn the most already, but they have the disincentives of high tax rates on any additional earnings that they make.

But what about the budget deficits that would result from cuts in tax rates and increases in tax exemptions? No worry, went the argument. The increase in national income will create a larger tax base so that even at the lower tax rates, total tax revenues would be restored. For example, if a 10 percent cut in tax rates were followed by a 10 percent increase in real national income, it would leave tax *revenues* approximately the same.

---

[4] Many of the Classical economists were concerned with the behavior of the economy in long-run equilibrium. For this reason, they were concerned with the vertical *LRAS* curve that occurs at the long-run normal rates of output rather than with the vertical portion of the *SRAS* curve (see Figure 30–2), which occurs when no more output can be squeezed from the economy. The key thing, however, is that in their analysis the *AS* curve was vertical.

FIGURE 30-8
Supply-Side Measures

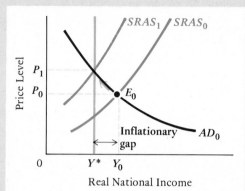

(i)

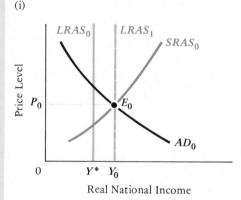

(ii) Supply-side success

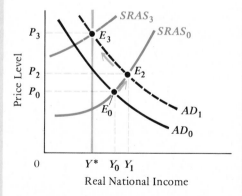

(iii) Supply-side failure

Supply-side measures intended to increase output and reduce inflationary pressures are more likely in the short run to increase inflation. Part (i) shows an economy in short-run equilibrium at E_0 on AD_0 and $SRAS_0$ with income Y_0 and price level P_0. As a result of the inflationary gap of $Y_0 - Y^*$, $SRAS$ will be shifting upward, taking the equilibrium along AD_0, with falling Y and rising P as shown by the arrow. Other things being equal, the inflation will come to a halt at price level P_1 and income Y^* once the short-run aggregate supply curve has reached $SRAS_1$.

Part (ii) shows the economy in the same initial short-run equilibrium as does (i). The curves AD and $SRAS_0$ yield income Y_0 and price level P_0. There is an inflationary gap, with Y_0 exceeding Y^* on $LRAS_0$. Now, however, supply-side measures shift the long-run aggregate supply curve to $LRAS_1$. This makes Y_0 the new level of potential income and removes the inflationary gap. The fall of income and rise in the price level shown in (i) are both prevented.

Part (iii) again shows the economy in the same short-run initial equilibrium but assumes that the demand side effects of the policy measures are fully felt before any alleged supply-side effects come into play. The aggregate demand curve shifts outward to AD_1. This gives a temporary increase in output to Y_1 at the cost of a rise in the price level of P_2. But the inflationary gap is increased to $Y_1 - Y^*$. Now $SRAS$ starts to shift up, taking the equilibrium along AD in the direction shown by the arrow, with falling output and rising prices. If nothing else happens, the inflation will finally come to an end at price level P_3 and output Y^*.

We have seen that starting from an equilibrium situation, an increase in aggregate supply raises output and lowers prices. (The policy was advocated, however, at a time of rapid inflation—the inflation rate in 1979 was close to 10 percent. The effect, therefore, was expected to prevent prices from rising further rather than actually to reduce them.) This possibility is shown in Figure 30-8. An initial inflationary situation shown in (i) is converted into the situation shown in (ii), where output has risen and the inflationary gap removed by a rightward shift in the long-run aggregate supply curve.

Critics had two sorts of doubts. First, many doubted that the tax changes would have the desired effects even in the long run. Economic theory makes no definite prediction about the effects of tax cuts on how much people will work. It might make them work more—because they earn more for each additional hour that they work. But it might make them work less—because the tax cut means that they can, if they wish, have both more disposable income and more leisure. For example, if in response to a 10 percent tax cut they worked 5 percent less, they would have approximately 5 percent more disposable income and 5 percent more leisure.[5] Note that several countries with taxes much higher than those in the United States have also had higher rates of growth of potential income.

The second doubt concerned the demand-side effects of these measures. Whatever the long-term effects on the supply side, economic theory is clear about their short-term effects on the demand side. Cuts in personal tax rates that are intended to be permanent leave households with an increase in their disposable income that they will expect to persist. They will spend more as a result and, as we saw on pages 535–536, this will cause an upward shift in the function relating consumption to disposable income. Also we know that an increase in investment increases aggregate demand. New investment will increase potential output in the long run once the new plants are constructed, the

new equipment installed, extra labor hired, and production commenced. But in the short run the extra expenditure on capital goods creates new incomes for the factors of production that produce these goods, and through the multiplier process, new incomes for others as well.

The short-run or impact effect of new investment is to raise aggregate demand, and the long-run effect is to raise potential output.

Thus, the short-run effects of the proposed Reagan policies may have been on aggregate demand, with the results shown in part (iii) of the figure:

The impact effect of the proposed supply-side measures would have been to increase the inflationary gap, causing the price level to rise more than it otherwise would have done.

There might have been a short-run gain in output as equilibrium moved outward along the SRAS curve before that curve started to move upward. But any lasting effect on output would have depended on the alleged long-run effect of shifting the LRAS curve outward.[6]

What actually transpired during the first years of the Reagan administration bears little resemblance to either what the supply-side proponents or their critics predicted. Output fell and unemployment rose, as the economy suffered a major recession. After responding only slowly at first, inflation then fell dramatically. What is the explanation of this? First, the proposed supply-side measures were never fully implemented so neither the AD or the SRAS curves shifted very much on this

---

[5] This topic is explored in much more detail in Chapter 38.

[6] It is also worth noting that the predictions about the reduction in the budget deficit are less contentious than those about the long-term increase in real national income. If tax rates are held constant, tax revenues are increased by any rise in nominal national income, PY. From the point of view of raising extra revenue, either an increase in P or an increase in Y is effective. For example, tax revenues rise either if 10 percent more people gain work at existing wage rates and hence earn more taxable income, or if wage rates rise by 10 percent so that the same number of people earn 10 percent more income. It follows that if the tax cuts cause an inflation, this will raise money incomes and tax revenues enough to substantially reduce the deficit initially caused by the cut in tax rates.

account. Second, as we shall see in Chapter 35, very restrictive monetary policies were pursued, causing the *AD* curve to shift leftward.

Supply-side economics has left some important legacies. Policy makers are much more alert to the supply-side effects of their policies than many of them used to be. *But the belief that supply-side measures would produce a quick fix, raising output while relieving inflationary pressures, is now discredited—as its critics always said it would be.* The timing of effects is such that measures that do succeed in shifting both aggregate demand and long-run aggregate supply will have their initial effects through a rapid shift in the *AD* curve and their longer-run effects through a gradual shift in the *SRAS* curve.

SUMMARY

1. The short-run aggregate supply (*SRAS*) curve, drawn for given factor prices, is upward-sloping.

2. One asymmetry of aggregate supply is that the slope of the *SRAS* curve increases as the level of output increases. This occurs because when output is low and firms have much unused capacity, output can be increased with little or no rise in prices; but when output is high and capacity constraints are met, further output increases become increasingly costly, and output will only be increased if prices are increased substantially.

3. The steepness of the *SRAS* curve determines how the impact of a shift in the *AD* curve is divided between a change in output and a change in the price level. When the *SRAS* curve is flat, shifts in the *AD* curve mainly affect real national income. When the *SRAS* curve is steep, shifts in the *AD* curve mainly affect the price level.

4. A change in factor costs or in productivity can cause the *SRAS* curve to shift.

5. On impact an aggregate demand shock causes a movement along the *SRAS* curve. But the change in the GNP gap associated with the new equilibrium value of *Y* then causes a change in factor prices and induces a shift of the *SRAS* curve, leading eventually to elimination of the inflationary gap (caused by an increase in aggregate demand) or the GNP gap (caused by a decrease in aggregate demand).

6. A second asymmetry of aggregate supply is that an inflationary gap leads to a fairly rapid wage rise and reduction of *Y* to *Y**, while a deflationary gap leads to only very sluggish wage fall and increase of *Y* to *Y**.

7. In the long run, output is determined by the *LRAS* curve while the only role of the *AD* curve is to determine the price level.

8. Supply-side economics seeks to reduce the inflationary gap and increase output by incentive measures to increase potential output. The long-term effect of supply-side measures on potential output is still debated, but the short-term effect is to increase the inflationary gap by increasing aggregate demand.

TOPICS FOR REVIEW

The factors leading to the positive slope of the *SRAS* curve
The factors leading to the increasing slope of the *SRAS* curve
Impact effects of changes in the *AD* curve
The causes of shifts of the *SRAS* curve
The effects of shifts in the *SRAS* curve
Long-run effects of shifts in the *AD* curve
The fast upward shift of the *SRAS* curve in response to an inflationary gap
The slow downward shift of the *SRAS* curve in response to a GNP (deflationary) gap
Effects of shifts in the *LRAS* curve

DISCUSSION QUESTIONS

1. Following are the combinations of output and price level, given by indexes for GNP and the CPI respectively for some recent years. Plot these and indicate in each case the direction of shift of the *SRAS* or *AD* curves that could have caused them.

	CPI[a]	GNP[b]
1977	182	1370
1978	195	1439
1979	217	1479
1980	247	1474
1981	272	1502
1982	290	1476

[a] 1967 = 100.
[b] Billions of 1972 dollars.

What would you think were the main causes of the shifts? Why might you be uncertain about some of the shifts? What additional information would you require to be able to answer the question?

2. Identify the effects of each of the following events on the *SRAS* curve.

    a. an increase in the price of imported raw materials used in key manufacturing industries

    b. an increase in the price of imported consumption goods such as coffee or bananas

    c. increased restrictions on pollution emissions in an attempt to combat acid rain

    d. projections of increased federal government deficits over the next five years

    e. an improved economic outlook leading to an investment boom

    f. an increased labor force participation rate of key sectors of the population

3. Interpret each of the following news items in terms of *AD* and *SRAS* curves.

    a. "Management representative says union wage demands are irresponsible in the face of current high unemployment rates."

    b. "Administration spokesman says that although the recovery is expected to be vigorous, it will witness only modest reductions in the unemployment rate."

    c. "Inflation fell quickly in 1982 due to 'lucky break' of reduced union strength in the automobile and steel sectors."

    d. "Wage increases have failed to keep up with inflation during the current boom."

    e. "Innovations in microelectronic technology will lead to an increase in both national output and unemployment."

    f. "Reagan's tough stance with public sector unions has vastly improved the inflation outlook over the next few years."

4. Show the effects on the price level and output of income tax cuts that make people work more in an economy currently experiencing an inflationary gap.

5. "Starting from a full employment equilibrium an increase in government spending can produce more output and employment at the cost of a once-and-for-all rise in the price level."

    "Increased spending can never lead to a permanent increase in output above its full employment level."

    Discuss these two statements in terms of short- and long-run aggregate supply curves.

31 BUSINESS CYCLES: THE EBB AND FLOW OF ECONOMIC ACTIVITY

Changing, always changing; this is the dominant characteristic of the GNP for as far back as we have records. The two major components of changes in the GNP that we can see are long-term growth and short-term fluctuations. Long-term growth (which is studied in Chapters 38 and 44) appears in the upward trend in potential GNP. Short-term fluctuations are seen in oscillations of actual GNP around the level set by potential GNP. Such oscillations are caused by changes in aggregate demand and aggregate supply. They lead to changes in what is actually produced, which in turn cause variations in the amount of employment and unemployment. They also affect living standards since the goods and services available to the economy for all purposes, including consumption and investment, vary as total output varies.

What is called the **business cycle** refers to the continuous ebb and flow of business activity that is reflected in statistical series for GNP, industrial production, and employment and unemployment. The business cycle is the subject of the present chapter.

The Historical Record

Figure 31-1 shows the year-to-year changes in real GNP over the nearly 40 years since the end of World War II, while Figure 31-2 gives a much longer perspective. Continual oscillations in the GNP are apparent.

The short-term behavior of the economy cannot, however, be fully caught by a single statistic, even one as important as GNP. Figure 31-3 shows three other important economic series. Each of these, as well as a dozen others that might be studied, tells us something about the general variability of the economy. It is clear that some series vary more than others and that they do not all move exactly together.

The picture suggested by Figures 31-1 to 31-3 is not one of occasional sharp shifts in the aggregate

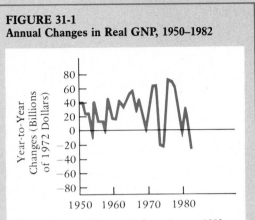

FIGURE 31-1
Annual Changes in Real GNP, 1950–1982

Source: Survey of Current Business, January 1983.

Real national income changes continually from one year to the next. Despite a strong upward trend, shown by the fact that most changes are increases, real national income does not rise steadily year after year. Generally, two or three years of very rapid increase tend to be followed by two or three years of slow increase, or even decline, in GNP.

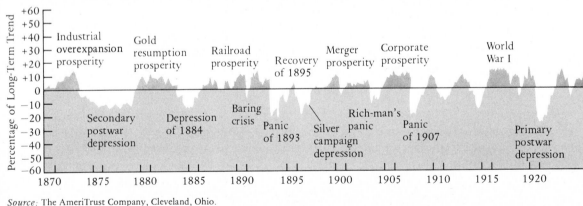

FIGURE 31-2
American Business Activity Since 1870

Source: The AmeriTrust Company, Cleveland, Ohio.

Cyclical ups and downs have dominated the short-term behavior of the U.S. economy at least since 1870. This chart is constructed by selecting one index of general economic activity, fitting a trend line to it, and plotting the deviations of the index from its trend value. It shows clearly the tendency for an economy to fluctuate. Major booms and slumps are unmistakable.

There is no great significance to being above or below the

demand and supply curves. If it were, we would expect national income to show occasional sharp changes followed by long periods of little or no change. Instead the short-term situation is one of continual change at a varying rate.

Evidently there are factors at work causing output to display continual short-term fluctuations around the economy's long-term growth trend.

The fluctuations shown in the figures are far from random. They exhibit a systematic pattern. A year of relatively high growth is likely to occur in conjunction with other years of high growth, with such groups separated by groups of relatively low-growth years. This pattern of a sequence of highs followed by a sequence of lows followed again by another sequence of highs is, of course, the source of the term *cyclical* used to describe economic fluctuations.

The upward and downward movements in economic activity seem to acquire a momentum of their own. After a while, however, such cumulative

movements appear to run their course and generate the seeds of their own reversal. While all cycles are not alike in duration or intensity, each appears to have tendencies toward cumulative movements that eventually reverse themselves. This was true long before governments attempted to intervene to stabilize their economies, and it is true still.

The late Alvin Hansen, a distinguished American authority on business cycles, once reported that there were 17 cycles in the U.S. economy between 1795 and 1937, with an average duration of 8.35 years. A shorter "inventory cycle" of 40 months' duration was also found, as well as longer cycles associated with building booms (15 to 20 years). The Russian economist Kondratieff thought he could identify long waves of 40 to 50 years associated with the introduction of major innovations. Some economists have recently argued that in many Western democracies there exists a political business cycle associated with the pattern of elections.

While the evidence is diverse and varied, as we

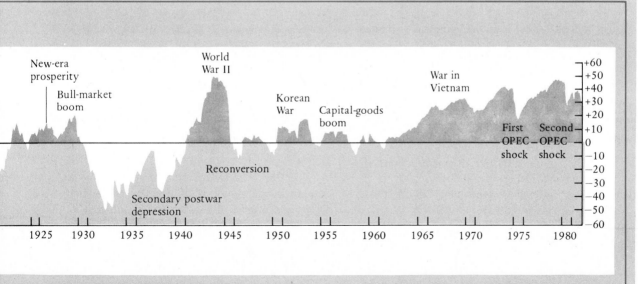

zero line because this line is based on an arbitrary trend. In particular the fact that every year since 1960 has been above the long-term trend does not mean that there has been a continuous boom since 1960. It suggests instead that the

historical trend line is an inadequate description of the average tendency during the recent period. What matter, and what are clearly shown, however, are the continual ups and downs that characterize economic activity.

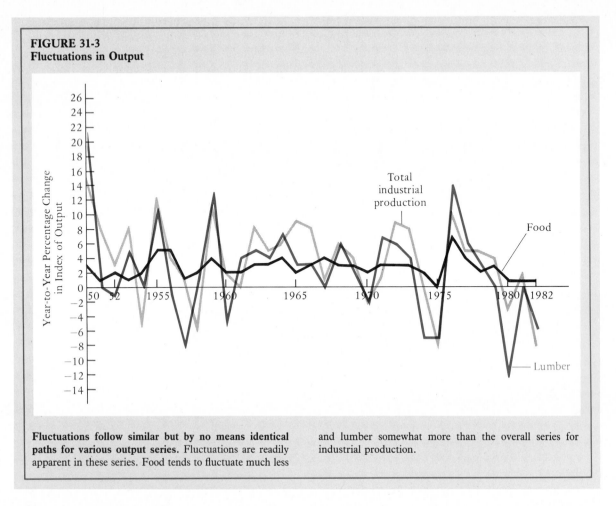

FIGURE 31-3
Fluctuations in Output

Fluctuations follow similar but by no means identical paths for various output series. Fluctuations are readily apparent in these series. Food tends to fluctuate much less and lumber somewhat more than the overall series for industrial production.

have seen, it is nevertheless possible to identify some basic characteristics of the pattern of business cycles:

1. There is a common pattern of variation that more or less pervades all economic series.
2. There are differences among economic series in their particular patterns of fluctuations.
3. There is a substantial difference from cycle to cycle in the length and the size of the swings involved.

The Terminology of Business Fluctuations

Although recurrent fluctuations in economic activity are neither smooth nor regular, a vocabulary

has developed to denote their different stages. Figure 31-4 shows stylized cycles that will serve to illustrate some terms.

Trough. The trough is, simply, the bottom. A trough is characterized by high unemployment of labor and a level of consumer demand that is low in relation to the capacity of industry to produce goods for consumption. There is thus a substantial amount of unused industrial capacity. Business profits will be low; for some individual companies they will be negative. Confidence in the future will be lacking and, as a result, firms will be unwilling to risk making new investments. If a trough is deep enough it may be called a slump or a **depression.**

Expansion or recovery. When something sets off a recovery, the lower turning point of the cycle has been reached. The symptoms of an expansion are many: worn-out machinery will be replaced; employment, income, and consumer spending all begin to rise; expectations become more favorable as a result of increases in production, sales, and profits. Investments that once seemed risky may now be undertaken as the climate of business opinion starts to change from pessimism to optimism. As demand expands, production can be expanded with relative ease merely by re-employing the existing unused capacity and unemployed labor.

Peak. At the peak there is a high degree of utilization of existing capacity; labor shortages may be severe, particularly in key skill categories; and shortages of essential key raw materials may develop. It now becomes difficult to increase output because the supply of unused resources is rapidly disappearing; output can be raised further only by means of investment that increases capacity. Because of such investment expenditure, investment funds will be in short supply. Because such investment takes time, further rises in demand are now met more by increases in prices than by increases in production. As shortages develop in more and more markets, a situation of general excess demand for factors develops. Costs rise but prices rise also, and business remains generally very profitable.

Losses are infrequent because a money profit can be earned simply by holding on to goods whose prices are rising and selling them later at higher prices. Expectations of the future are favorable, and more investment may be made than is justified on the basis of current levels of prices and sales alone.

Recession. When the peak is passed, the economy turns downward. When the GNP falls for two quarters in succession, it is called a **recession.** Demand falls off, and as a result production and employment fall. As employment falls so do households' incomes; falling income causes demand to fall further. Profits drop and more and more firms get into difficulties. New investments that looked profitable on the expectation of continuously rising demand suddenly appear unprofitable. Investment is reduced to a low level. It may not even be worth replacing capital goods as they wear out because unused capacity is increasing steadily.

Turning points. The point at which a recession begins is often called the **upper turning point,**

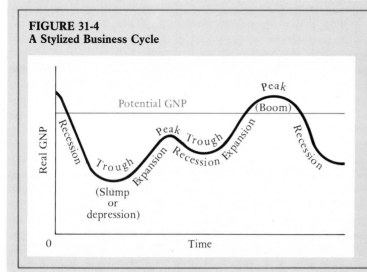

FIGURE 31-4
A Stylized Business Cycle

While the phases of business fluctuations are described by a series of commonly used terms, no two cycles are the same. Starting from a lower turning point, or trough, a cycle goes through a phase of expansion, reaches an upper turning point, or peak, and then enters a period of recession. Cycles differ from one another in the severity of their troughs and peaks and in the speed with which one phase follows another. Severe troughs are called *depressions.*

while the **lower turning point** refers to the point at which a recovery begins.

Explaining Business Cycles

An explanation of the business cycle must answer two questions. (1) What are the factors causing GNP and other key macro variables to *fluctuate?* (2) What are the factors causing those fluctuations to get smoothed or transformed into a *cyclical* pattern? These two questions are taken up in the two main sections that follow.

WHY DO INCOME AND EMPLOYMENT FLUCTUATE?

Figure 31-5 presents an explanation of the fluctuations of GNP in terms of a fluctuating *AD* curve and a stable *SRAS* curve.

There is general agreement that over the course of American economic history, the business cycle has mainly been driven by fluctuations in aggregate demand rather than in aggregate supply. Nevertheless particular cycles can sometimes be explained in part by aggregate supply shocks. Indeed events of the mid 1970s made the citizens of advanced industrial countries acutely aware of supply-side causes.

Aggregate demand shocks are the major historical source of fluctuations in GNP; aggregate supply shocks are a secondary source.

Sources of Aggregate Demand Shocks

To say that cycles are mainly caused by fluctuations in aggregate demand only pushes the need for explanation one stage further back. What are the sources of the continuous disturbances to aggregate demand? The theory of income determination suggests four main candidates—shifts in each of the four main components of aggregate expenditure.

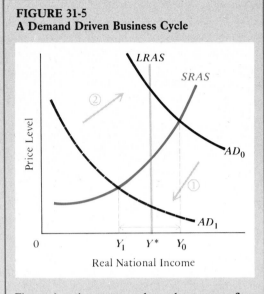

FIGURE 31-5
A Demand Driven Business Cycle

Fluctuations in aggregate demand can cause fluctuations in income and employment. Assume that over the course of the business cycle aggregate demand oscillates regularly. Starting from a high AD_0 and an income at the peak of Y_0, the curve falls continuously, as shown by arrow ①, until it reaches AD_1. Income falls through Y^* and reaches its trough at Y_1.

The AD curve then rises continuously, as shown by arrow ②. Income is taken back through Y^* and reaches Y_0 at the next peak.

Changes in Consumption

Consumption is the largest single component of aggregate expenditure, measuring about two-thirds of the total. When searching for the causes of income changes, we are not concerned with changes in consumption in response to changes in income but instead with shifts in the function relating consumption to income. Such shifts do occur from time to time, and they can have many causes.

Changes in tastes. For example in the late 1970s and early 1980s there was a significant reduction in car purchases. If enough of the money that was to have been spent on automobiles were saved instead, there would be a significant downward shift in the aggregate demand curve. Jobs and incomes would first be lost in the auto industry. The induced reduction in spending by workers no longer earning incomes in that industry would then set up a multiplier effect as cuts in output, income, and spending spread throughout the economy.

Changes in expectations and interest rates. Expectations of future inflation may lead to a burst of spending to buy now while goods are cheap. On the other hand, a wave of uncertainty about the future may lead to a rise in saving and hence a cut in spending. High interest rates can be a powerful incentive to postpone buying durable goods. For example, in 1981 rates of over 20 percent helped to depress the housing and automobile markets.

In an inflationary world like the one we live in today, it is important to distinguish between the real and the nominal rate of interest. The nominal rate of interest concerns the ratio of the *amount* of money repaid to the amount of money borrowed. The real rate of interest concerns the ratio of the *purchasing power* of the money repaid to the *purchasing power* of the money borrowed, and it may be different from the nominal rate. The real rate of interest is the difference between the nominal rate of interest and the rate of change of the price level. It is this real rate that matters for most expenditure decisions. This distinction is further elaborated in the box on page 572.

Both uncertainty and high real interest rates contributed to the recession of 1981–1983 by discouraging consumer spending.

Tax changes. As we saw in Chapter 29, tax changes can also shift the aggregate consumption function. Income tax cuts mean that more *total* income becomes *disposable* income, leading to an increase in consumers' spending. Tax increases have the opposite effect. Tax changes that affect consumption expenditure can occur for at least two important reasons: first because tax rates are changed and second because inflation changes tax yields. In 1975 reductions in income tax rates (plus a rebate on 1974 taxes) added about $20 billion to households' disposable income. In 1974 rapid inflation pushed consumers into higher tax brackets, increasing the yield for personal income taxes. Dis-

posable income fell by about $8 billion as a result of this increase in effective taxes even though there was no change in official tax rates.

All these forces can, and occasionally do, operate to shift the consumption function. When this happens, the aggregate demand curve shifts, and income and employment are disturbed.

Changes in Government Expenditures on Goods and Services

Look again at Figure 31-2. It is obvious that every war in this century has been accompanied by a rapid expansion of economic activity. Wars result in an enormous increase in federal government expenditure as people and materials are shifted from civilian to military uses. This shift is usually reversed in the postwar period. For example, federal government purchases of goods and services (measured in constant dollars at 1972 prices) rose from $27 billion in 1940 to $270 billion in 1944 and then fell to $36 billion by 1947. Changes in government purchases of goods and services during 1941–1946 were the principal cause of changes in GNP during that period.

Such expenditures played a similar though less dramatic role during the Vietnam War, rising from $100 billion in 1965 to $128 billion in 1968 and falling back fairly steadily to reach $96 billion by 1973. The extra Vietnam expenditures, on top of a full-employment civilian economy, helped to open up a large inflationary gap in the late 1960s and early 1970s.

Figure 31-6 shows the changes in real purchases of goods and services by all levels of government and compares these with changes in gross investment. The largest shifts in government expenditure occurred during the initial build up of the Vietnam war in the last half of the 1960s. Since that time there have been some significant demand shocks caused by shifts in G. In seven years since the beginning of the 1970s, the shift in G from one year to the next has exceeded $4 billion (1977 dollars). The figure makes it apparent, however, that the shocks caused by changing government expenditure have been much smaller on average than

REAL AND NOMINAL INTEREST RATES:
AN IMPORTANT DISTINCTION

When an expected inflation occurs, lenders and borrowers can compensate for it by adjusting the nominal rate of interest so as to maintain any desired real rate. If you pay me $8 interest for a $100 loan for one year, the nominal rate is 8 percent. The real rate that I earn, however, depends on what happens to the overall level of prices in the economy.

In the above example, if the price level remains constant over the year, then the real rate that I earn will also be 8 percent. This is because I can buy 8 percent more goods and services with the $108 that you repay me than with $100 that I lent you. However, if the price level were to rise by 8 percent, the real rate would be *zero* because the $108 you repay me will buy the same quantity of goods as did the $100 I gave up. If I were unlucky enough to have lent money at 8 percent in a year in which prices rose by 10 percent, the real rate I would have earned would be *minus* 2 percent.

If lenders and borrowers are concerned with the real costs measured in terms of purchasing power, the nominal rate of interest will be set at the real rate they require plus an amount to cover any expected rate of inflation. Consider a one-year loan that is meant to earn a real return to the lender of 5 percent. If the expected rate of inflation is zero, the nominal rate set for the loan will be 5 percent. However, if a 10 percent inflation is expected, the nominal interest rate will be 15 percent.

To provide a given expected real rate of interest the nominal rate will be set at the desired real rate of interest plus the expected annual rate of inflation.

This point is often overlooked, and as a result people are surprised at the high nominal rates of interest that exist during periods of rapid inflation. For example, when nominal interest rates rose drastically in 1979, many commentators expressed shock at the "unbearably" high rates. Most of them failed to notice that with inflation running at about 12 percent, an interest rate of 15 percent represented a real rate of only 3 percent. Had the Fed given in to the heavy pressure to hold interest rates to the more "reasonable" level of 10 percent, it would have been imposing a negative real rate of interest. Lenders would then have been "rewarded" for lending their money by receiving less purchasing power in interest plus principal than the purchasing power of the principal they parted with initially.

When an inflation is fully expected, the nominal rate can be set to give any desired real rate of interest. Problems arise when policy makers control nominal interest rates. Laws prohibiting "exorbitant" rates of, say, 10 percent or more, may not do much harm when the inflation rate is 1 percent or 2 percent, as it was in the early 1960s. But when the inflation rate is over 10 percent, such laws enforce negative real rates. Not surprisingly many people refuse to lend money on these unfavorable terms. Contracts that would have been freely negotiated by lenders and borrowers to yield a modest positive real rate of interest are prohibited by law. As a result potential borrowers and lenders are both worse off, so everyone loses.

Concern about the burden of borrowing should be directed at the real rather than the nominal rate of interest.

A nominal rate of 8 percent combined with a 2 percent rate of inflation is a much greater real burden on borrowers than a nominal rate of 16 percent combined with a 14 percent rate of inflation.

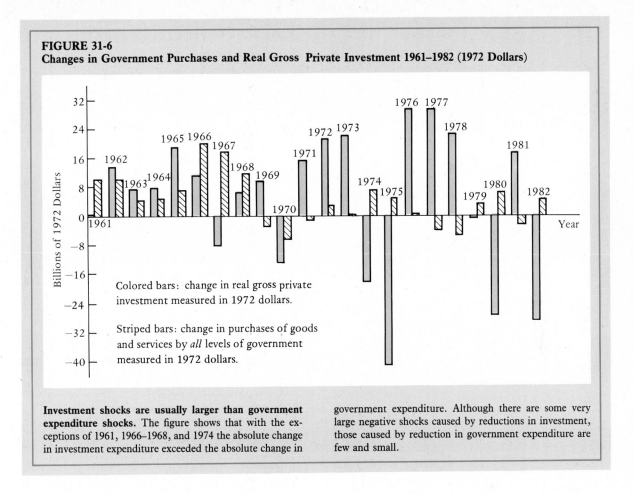

FIGURE 31-6
Changes in Government Purchases and Real Gross Private Investment 1961–1982 (1972 Dollars)

Investment shocks are usually larger than government expenditure shocks. The figure shows that with the exceptions of 1961, 1966–1968, and 1974 the absolute change in investment expenditure exceeded the absolute change in government expenditure. Although there are some very large negative shocks caused by reductions in investment, those caused by reduction in government expenditure are few and small.

the shocks caused by changing private investment expenditure. We return below to a discussion of the important role played by changing investment expenditure.

Changes in Net Exports

A quarter of a century ago, the United States could be studied as if it were a completely closed economy, so unimportant were imports and exports. Today, although trade is still a much smaller part of national income than it is for most other industrialized countries, it is a significant part of American GNP. Exports, for example, which were 5 percent of GNP in 1960, rose to just over 10 percent in the early 1980s. Now a rise in imports,

due say to a preference for foreign over American automobiles or to a fall in exports resulting from a European recession, can have a major impact on American national income and employment.

Shifts in consumption, government spending, and net exports can and sometimes do cause major fluctuations in American national income and employment.

Changes in Investment

Changes in investment expenditure are a major source of economic fluctuations. Consider, for example, the period 1929–1932. In 1929 total investment expenditure of firms and households in the American economy was $16.2 billion at current

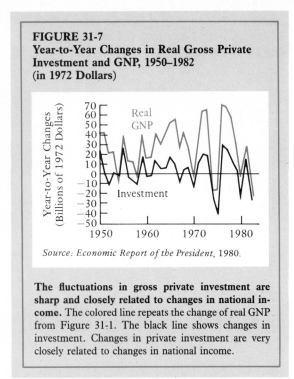

FIGURE 31-7
Year-to-Year Changes in Real Gross Private Investment and GNP, 1950–1982 (in 1972 Dollars)

Source: *Economic Report of the President, 1980.*

The fluctuations in gross private investment are sharp and closely related to changes in national income. The colored line repeats the change of real GNP from Figure 31-1. The black line shows changes in investment. Changes in private investment are very closely related to changes in national income.

prices, almost double the amount of expenditure needed to replace the capital goods that were used up that year in the process of producing a GNP of $103 billion. The American economy in 1929 was thus adding rapidly to its stock of capital equipment. Three years later, in 1932, total investment expenditure was $1 billion. This was less than one-sixth of the amount needed just to keep the stock of capital intact. The American economy in 1932, with its GNP reduced to $58 billion, was rapidly reducing its stock of capital equipment.

As Figure 31-6 shows, investment expenditure is quite volatile. Quite large shocks due to changes in investment expenditure hit the economy frequently. On average the change in investment from one year to the next has been about three times the average change in government expenditure.

Changes in investment are also quite closely correlated with changes in national income, as shown in Figure 31-7. Rising investment tends to be associated with rapidly rising GNP, while falling in-

vestment tends to be associated with slowly rising or falling GNP. This is consistent with the view that investment shocks are a major cause of changes in national income.

Investment expenditures play a key role in most theories of cyclical fluctuations.

Why Does Investment Change?

Figure 31-8 shows the behavior of the three major components of total investment expenditure: inventories, plant and equipment, and residential housing. Changes in investment are one of the prime causes of short-term fluctuations, but we do not have the whole story unless we know why investment fluctuates. In discussing the theory of income determination in Chapters 28 and 29 we talked simply of shifts in investment, not of the underlying causes of such shifts. While each dollar of investment has the same consequences for aggregate demand, different types of investment respond to different sets of causes. Thus it is useful to discuss separately the determinants of the three major types of investment expenditures.

Investment in Inventories

Inventory changes represent only about 5 percent of private investment in a typical year. Their average size is not an adequate measure of their importance. In reality, they are one of the more volatile elements of total investment and therefore contribute in a major way to shifts in investment expenditure.

Studies show that the stock of inventories held tends to rise as production and sales rise. But while the size of inventories is related to the level of sales, the *change* in inventories (which is current investment) is related to the *change* in the level of sales.

A firm may decide, for example, to hold inventories of 10 percent of its sales. Thus, if sales are $100,000, it will wish to hold inventories of $10,000. If sales increase to $110,000, it will want to hold inventories of $11,000. Over the period during which its stock of inventories is being in-

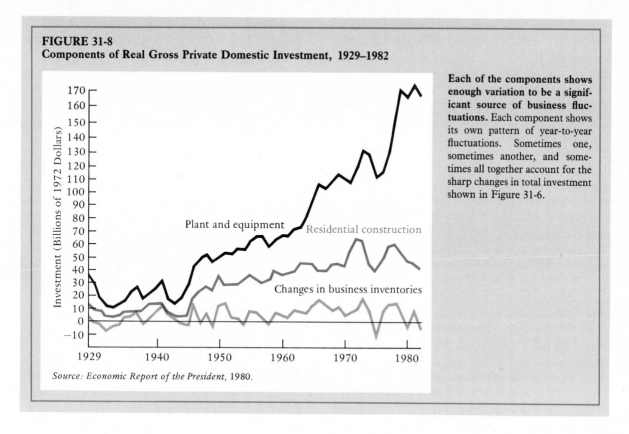

FIGURE 31-8
Components of Real Gross Private Domestic Investment, 1929–1982

Each of the components shows enough variation to be a significant source of business fluctuations. Each component shows its own pattern of year-to-year fluctuations. Sometimes one, sometimes another, and sometimes all together account for the sharp changes in total investment shown in Figure 31-6.

Source: *Economic Report of the President*, 1980.

creased, there will be a total of $1,000 new inventory investment.

The higher the level of production and sales, the larger the desired stock of inventories. Changes in the rate of production and sales cause temporary bouts of investment (or disinvestment) in inventories.

When a firm ties up funds in inventories, those same funds cannot be used eleswhere to earn income. At the very least the money could be lent out at the going rate of interest. Thus the higher the real rate of interest, the higher will be the cost of holding an inventory of a given size. And the higher that rate of interest, the more firms will try to lower their inventory holdings. By causing firms to change the inventory levels that they desire to hold, a change in the rate of interest can lead to a flurry of investment or disinvestment in inventories.

The higher the real rate of interest, the lower the desired stock of inventories. Thus changes in the rate of interest cause temporary bouts of investment (or disinvestment) in inventories.

Investment in Residential Housing Construction

Since 1970 spending on residential construction has varied between one-fifth and one-third of all gross private investment in the United States and between 2.5 percent and 5.5 percent of GNP. Figure 31-8 shows the course of residential investment expenditure in the United States since 1929. Notice the substantial fluctuations from year to year. Because expenditures for housing construction are both large and variable, they exert a major impact on the economy.

Many influences on residential construction are noneconomic and depend on demographic or cultural considerations such as new family formation. But households must not only want to buy houses, they must be able to do so. Periods of high employment and high average family earnings tend to lead to increases in house building, and those of unemployment and falling earnings to decreases in such building.

Almost all houses are purchased with money borrowed on mortgages. Interest on the borrowed money typically accounts for over one-half of the purchaser's annual mortgage payments; the other half is repayment of principal. It is for this reason that sharp variations in interest rates exert a substantial effect on the demand for housing.

The box on page 577 provides an example illustrating the importance of interest rates for housing. This importance was borne out by experiences from 1979 to 1982. During this period mortgage rates rose from less than 11 percent to just over 15 percent and housing starts fell from 1,194 thousand units to a mere 661 thousand in 1982. (Since inflation fell from 1980, the increased nominal interest rates also meant increased real rates.) The construction industry itself and its major suppliers such as the cement and the lumber industries felt the blow of a dramatic fall in demand.

Expenditures for residential construction tend to vary positively with changes in average income and negatively with interest rates.

Investment in Plant and Equipment

Investment in plant and equipment is the largest component of domestic investment. Over half is financed by firms' retained profits (profits *not* paid out to its shareholders). This means that current profits are an important determinant of investment.

A second major determinant is the rate of interest. Much investment is financed by borrowed money. As became abundantly clear in the early 1980s, very high interest rates greatly reduce the volume of investment as more and more firms find their expected profits from investment do not cover the interest on borrowed investment funds.

A third major determinant is *changes* in national income. If there is a rise in aggregate demand that is expected to persist and cannot be met by existing capacity, then investment in new plant and equipment will be needed. Once the new plants have been built and put into operation, however, the rate of new investment will fall.

This further illustrates an important characteristic of investment already encountered in the case of inventories: *if the desired stock of capital goods increases, there will be an investment boom while the new capital is being produced.* But if nothing else changes, and even though business conditions continue to look rosy enough to justify the increased stock of capital, investment in new plant and equipment will cease once the larger capital stock is achieved. This aspect of investment leads to the *accelerator* theory of investment, which requires a closer look.

The Accelerator Theory of Investment

According to the accelerator theory (usually called the **accelerator**), investment is related to the rate of change of national income. When income is increasing, it is necessary to invest in order to increase the capacity to produce consumption goods; when income is falling, it may not even be necessary to replace old capital as it wears out, let alone to invest in new capital.

The main insight which the accelerator theory provides is the emphasis on the role of net investment as a phenomenon of *disequilibrium*—something that occurs when the stock of capital goods differs from what firms and households would like it to be. Net investment will not occur when the desired quantities of inventories, buildings, or equipment has been achieved. Anything that changes the desired quantities can generate investment. The accelerator focuses on one such source of change, changing national income. This gives the accelerator its particular importance in connection with *fluctuations* in national income. As we shall see, it can itself contribute to those fluctuations.

THE COST OF BUYING A HOUSE ON TIME

Few people who buy a house can pay cash. Most purchases are financed by borrowing money on a *mortgage*. A mortgage is a loan to the house purchaser (sometimes of as much as 85 or 90 percent of the purchase price, but 60 to 75 percent is common). In return, the borrower promises to make fixed monthly payments that cover interest on the money borrowed and repay the amount borrowed over some agreed period, commonly 20 years. (The monthly payments often include an amount to cover insurance and taxes, but this is ignored in what follows.) The house itself acts as security for the loan. Loans of this type are said to be *amortized*, which means that fixed payments cover the interest on the principal outstanding *and* repay the principal over a stated period.

Because the loan stretches over a long period, a great deal of the total amount paid by the borrower is interest on the outstanding loan. For example, on a 20-year mortgage for $50,000 at a nominal annual interest rate of 8 percent per year (a monthly rate of 8/12 of 1 percent), a total of $100,375 would be paid in 240 monthly installments of $418.23 each. This is $50,000 to repay the principal of the loan and $50,375 of interest. At a 12 percent nominal annual rate (a monthly rate of 1 percent) the total payments would be $132,130, making $82,130 total interest as well as $50,000 to repay the principal.

The interest on a mortgage is calculated on the amount of the loan still outstanding. After each payment the amount outstanding is reduced so that, with fixed annual payments, most of the total amount paid goes to paying interest in the early years and to repaying principal in later years. It follows that the purchaser's equity in the house builds up slowly at first, then more and more rapidly as the terminal date approaches.

Note in the table that when half the life of the mortgage has passed, only about a quarter of the principal has been repaid. In the first year of the mortgage, $4,965 goes as interest and only $825 to reduce the principal on the loan. In the last year, only $300 is interest and $5790 goes to repay the principal.

BREAKDOWN OF PAYMENTS IN SELECTED YEARS ON A 20-YEAR MORTGAGE FOR $50,000 AT 10 PERCENT (All Figures to the Nearest Dollar)

Year	Payments made over the year	Interest paid over the year	Principal (amount of loan) repaid over the year	Equity (amount of loans repaid over all the years)
1	$5,790	$4,965	$ 825	$ 825
2	5,790	4,875	915	1,745
5	5,790	4,560	1,230	5,100
10	5,790	3,765	2,025	13,490
15	5,790	2,455	3,335	27,290
19	5,790	820	4,970	44,510
20	5,790	300	5,490	50,000

TABLE 31–1 AN ILLUSTRATION OF THE ACCELERATOR THEORY OF INVESTMENT

(1) Year	(2) Annual sales	(3) Change in sales	(4) Required stock of capital, assuming a capital-output ratio of 5/1	(5) Net investment: increase in required capital stock
1	$10	$0	$ 50	$ 0
2	10	0	50	0
3	11	1	55	5
4	13	2	65	10
5	16	3	80	15
6	19	3	95	15
7	22	3	110	15
8	24	2	120	10
9	25	1	125	5
10	25	0	125	0

With a fixed capital-output ratio net investment occurs only when it is necessary to increase the stock of capital in order to change output. Assume that it takes $5 of capital to produce $1 of output per year. In years 1 and 2, there is no need for investment. In year 3, a rise in sales of $1 requires investment of $5 to provide the needed capital stock. In year 4, a further rise of $2 in sales requires an additional investment of $10 to provide the needed capital stock. As columns 3 and 5 show, the amount of net investment is proportional to the *change* in sales. When the increase in sales tapers off in years 7–9, investment declines. When, in year 10, sales no longer increase, net investment falls to zero because the capital stock of year 9 is adequate to provide output for year 10's sales.

How the Accelerator Works: A Numerical Example

To see how the theory works, it is convenient to make the simplifying assumption that there is a particular capital stock needed to produce a given level of an industry's output. (The ratio of the value of capital to the annual value of output is called the **capital-output ratio.**) Given this assumption, suppose that the industry is producing at capacity and the demand for its product increases. If the industry is to produce the higher level of output, its capital stock must increase. This necessitates new investment.

Table 31-1 provides a simple numerical example of the accelerator that, worked through step by step, leads to three conclusions:

1. Rising rather than high levels of sales are needed to call forth net investment.
2. For net investment to remain constant, sales must rise by a constant amount per year.
3. The amount of net investment will be a multiple of the increase in sales because the capital-output ratio is greater than one.[1]

The data in Table 31-1 are for a single industry, but if many industries behave in this way, one would expect aggregate net investment to bear a similar relation to changes in national income. This is what the accelerator theory predicts. [37]

The accelerator theory says nothing directly about replacement investment, but it does have implications for such investment. When sales are constant (no net investment required), replacement investment will be required to maintain the capital stock at the desired level. When sales are increasing from a position of full capacity, both net investment and replacement investment will be required. When sales are falling so that the desired capital

[1] In the example in the table the capital-output ratio is 5. Why should anyone spend $5 on capital stock to get $1 of output? It is not unreasonable to spend $5 to purchase a machine that produces only $1 of output *per year*, provided that the machine will last enough years to repay the $5 plus a reasonable return on this investment.

stock is below the actual capital stock, not only will net investment be zero but there will be a tendency to postpone replacement investment as well until the capital stock falls to the desired levels.

Limitations of the Accelerator

Taken literally, the accelerator posits a rigid response of investment to changes in sales (and thus, aggregatively, to changes in national income). In fact the relation is more subtle than that.

Changes in sales that are thought to be temporary will not necessarily lead to new investment. It is usually possible to increase the level of output for a given capital stock by working overtime or extra shifts. While this solution would be more expensive per unit of output in the long run, it will usually be preferable to making investments in new plant and equipment that would lie idle after a temporary spurt of demand had subsided. Thus expectations about what the required capital stock is may lead to a much less rigid response of investment to income than the accelerator suggests.

A further limitation of the accelerator theory is that it takes a very limited view of what constitutes investment. The fixed capital-output ratio emphasizes investment in what economists call **capital widening,** the investment in additional capacity that uses the same ratio of capital to labor as existing capacity. It does not explain **capital deepening,** which is the increase in the amount of capital per unit of labor that occurs in response to a fall in the rate of interest. Neither does the theory say anything about investments brought about as a result of new processes or new products. Furthermore, it does not allow for the fact that investment in any period is likely to be limited by the capacity of the capital-goods industry.

For these and other reasons, the accelerator does not by itself give anything like a complete explanation of variations in investment in plant and equipment. It should not be surprising that a simple accelerator theory provides a relatively poor overall explanation of changes in investment. Yet accelerator-like influences do exist, and empirical evidence continues to suggest that they play a role in the cyclical variability of investment.

THEORIES OF THE CYCLE

There are several main theories about the cycle. They do not have to be regarded as competing. Indeed each one captures some of the forces that contribute to the cycle. We shall examine three.

Systematic Fluctuations in Private Spending

The most commonly accepted theory looks to systematic fluctuations in aggregate expenditure brought about by systematic alterations in spending behavior as the cause of the cycle. Several influences can cause such alterations.

The Multiplier-Accelerator Mechanism

The combination of the multiplier and the accelerator can make upward or downward movements in the economy cumulative. Imagine that the economy is settled into a depression with heavy unemployment. Then a revival of investment demand occurs. Orders are placed for new plant and equipment, which creates new employment in the capital-goods industries. The newly employed workers spend most of their earnings. This creates new demand for the consumer goods that they buy. A multiplier process is now set up, with new employment and incomes created in the consumer-goods industries.

The spending of the newly created incomes in turn means further increases in demand. At some stage the increased demand for consumer goods will create, through the accelerator process, an increased demand for capital goods. Once existing equipment is fully employed in any industry, extra output will require new capital equipment—and the accelerator theory takes over as the major determinant of investment expenditure. Such investment will increase or at least maintain demand in the capital-goods sector of the economy. So the process goes on, the multiplier-accelerator mechanism continuing to produce a rapid rate of expansion in the economy.

The upper turning point. A very rapid expansion can continue for some time, but it cannot go on forever. Eventually the economy will run into bottlenecks (or ceilings) in terms of certain resources. For example, investment funds may become scarce, and as a result interest rates will rise. Firms now find new investments more expensive than anticipated, and thus some will become unprofitable. Or suppose that what limits the expansion is exhaustion of the reservoir of unemployed labor. Once this has happened, further expansion requires growth of the labor force or growth of labor productivity. The full-employment ceiling guarantees that any sustained rapid growth rate of real income and employment will eventually be slowed.

At this point the accelerator again comes into play. A slowing down in the rate of increase of production leads to a decrease in the investment in new plant and equipment. This decrease causes a drop in employment in the capital-goods industries and, through the multiplier, a fall in consumer demand. Once consumer demand begins to fall, investment in plant and equipment will be reduced to a low level because firms will already have more productive capacity than they can use. Unemployment begins to mount, and the upper turning point has been passed.

The lower turning point. A contraction, too, is eventually brought to an end. Consider the very worst sort of depression imaginable, one in which every postponable expenditure of households, firms, or governments is postponed. Even then aggregate demand will not fall to zero. Figure 28-2 on page 521 shows that as aggregate disposable income falls, households will spend a larger and larger fraction of that falling income. Finally, should income fall to the break-even level, all disposable income will be spent (and none will be saved). Neither does government spending fall in proportion to the fall in government tax revenues. Government expenditures on programs committed

by legislation will continue even if tax revenues sag to low levels. Finally, even investment expenditures, in many ways the most easily postponed component of aggregate expenditure, will not fall to zero. Industries providing basics will still have substantial sales and need replacement investment. Even in the worst depression some new processes and new products appear, and these require new investment.

Taken together, the minimum levels of consumption, investment, and government expenditure will assure a minimum equilibrium level of national income that, although well below the full-employment level, will not be zero. There is a floor below which income will not fall.

Sooner or later, an upturn will begin. If nothing else causes an expansion of business activity, there will eventually be a revival of replacement investment because as existing capital wears out the capital stock will eventually fall below the level required to produce current output. At this stage new machines will be bought to replace those that are worn out.

The rise in the level of activity in the capital-goods industries will cause, by way of the multiplier, a further rise in income. The economy has turned the corner. An expansion, once started, will trigger the sort of cumulative upward movement already discussed.

Other Endogenous Forces

The multiplier-accelerator is one endogenous force contributing to cyclical fluctuations. Two others are inventories and construction.

Inventory cycles. There are, as we have seen, good reasons to suppose that the required size of inventories is related to the level of firms' sales, and sales are related to the level of national income. If firms maintain anything like a rigid inventory-to-sales ratio, this will cause an accelerator-like linkage between investment in inventories and *changes* in national income.

Look back at the fluctuating investment in business inventories shown in Figure 31-7. Many observers believe that these sharp and somewhat periodic fluctuations lead to an "inventory cycle" of roughly 40 months' average duration.

A building cycle? Economists have noted some long-run, wavelike movements of roughly 20 years' duration in the statistics for expenditures on residential construction. These are sometimes referred to as "building cycles." Some economists suggest an accelerator-like explanation that runs from external events to demographic changes, to changes in the demand for housing and other buildings, and thence to changes in construction activity.

A major war, by taking males away from home, tends to retard family formation and thereby tends to depress the demand for private housing. After the conclusion of the war there is typically an increase in marriages and household formation, an increase in the demand for housing, and a boom in the construction industry.

Depending on the capacity of the building industry, the boom may last many years before the desired increases in the stock of buildings of various kinds are achieved, but eventually the demand will taper off and the construction boom will have ended. Then, approximately 20 years after the end of the war that triggered the boom, there is likely to be a further boom in the number of marriages and births as the new generation starts its process of family formation. Wars are not the only source of such population-induced cycles; a severe depression will lead to a similar postponement of family formation.

The evidence concerning construction spending over the past century is thought by many economists to support the theory just outlined, a theory very much like the accelerator, though with changes in demographic factors, rather than changes in income, providing the impetus.

Random Shocks and Long Lags

An alternative theory does not assume cyclical behavior from firms and households in order to generate cycles. It suggests instead that random shifts in expenditure are transformed into systematic cycles of output and employment.

This theory begins with lags. For example, if a fall in the rate of interest makes an investment in a new project profitable, it may take 6 months to plan it, 3 months to let contracts, 6 months before spending builds up to its top rate, and another 24 to complete the project. These lags mean that changes in the rate of interest will cause reactions in investment expenditure that are distributed over quite a long period of time.

These lags have important implications for key macro variables. Although the disturbing influences might be random or erratic, income and employment both follow a cyclical path.

Each major component of aggregate expenditure has sometimes undergone shifts large enough to disturb the economy significantly. The long lags can convert such shifts into cyclical oscillations in national income.

A Policy-Induced Cycle

It has been alleged that government-induced demand shocks have sometimes caused cyclical fluctuations. Government expenditure has not often been the cause of major shocks due to sudden large changes. But government tax policy and government monetary policy have both been shifted enough to cause significant demand shocks. But why should the government administer such potentially disturbing demand shocks? Several reasons have been suggested.

A Political Business Cycle

As early as 1944 the Polish-born Keynesian economist Michael Kalecki warned of a political business cycle. He argued that once governments had learned to manipulate the economy, they would engineer an election-geared business cycle. In preelection periods they would raise spending and cut taxes. The resulting expansionary demand shock would create high employment and good business conditions that would bring voters' support for the government. But the resulting inflationary gap would lead to a rising price level. So, after the election was won, the government would depress demand to remove the inflationary gap and provide some slack for expansion before the next election.

This theory invokes the image of a very cynical government manipulating employment and national income solely because it wants to stay in office. Few people believe that governments deliberately do this all the time, but the temptation to do it some of the time, particularly before elections, may prove irresistible. Indeed, Professor Alan Blinder of Princeton has made a persuasive case that one such politically inspired demand shock was inflicted by the Nixon adminstration just prior to the 1972 elections.

Alternating Policy Goals

A variant of the policy-induced cycle does not require a cynical government and an easily duped electorate. Instead both sides need only be rather shortsighted.

In this theory, when there is a recession and relatively stable prices, the public and the government identify unemployment as the number one economic problem. The government then engineers an expansionary policy shock through some combination of tax cuts and spending increases. This, plus such natural cumulative forces as the multiplier-accelerator, propels the economy back into the boom range. Unemployment is low and income high, but as Y begins to exceed Y^*, the price level begins to rise. It first rises along the stable $SRAS$ curve and then rises further as boom conditions raise factor prices and shift the $SRAS$ curve upward. (See Figure 30–5.)

At this point the unemployment problem is declared cured. Now inflation is seen as the nation's number one economic problem. A contractionary policy shock is then engineered. The natural cumulative forces again take over, reducing aggregate demand and income to low recessionary levels. The inflation subsides but unemployment rises, setting the stage once again for an expansionary shock to cure the unemployment problem.

Many economists have criticized government policy over the last few decades as sometimes causing fluctuations by alternately pushing expansion to cure unemployment and then contraction to cure inflation. We shall see in Chapter 39 that this charge is particularly strong against monetary policy. But whatever the policy used to expand or contract the economy, the charge is that policy makers have sometimes been too shortsighted in alternating their concern between unemployment and inflation.

Misguided Stabilization Policy

In a variant of the previous theory the government tries to hold the economy at potential national income by countering fluctuations in private-sector expenditure with offsetting changes of its own spending and taxes. The government can in principle dampen such cyclical fluctuations by its stabilization policies. But unless it is very sophisticated, bad timing may accentuate rather than dampen fluctuations. We return to this difficulty in a subsequent chapter.

Causes of Business Cycles: A Consensus View?

Economists once argued long and bitterly about which was the best explanation of the recurrent cyclical behavior of the economy.

Today most economists agree that there need not be only one cause or class of causes governing business cycles.

In an economy that has tendencies for both cumulative and self-reversing behavior, any large shock, whether from without or within, can initiate a cyclical swing. Wars are important; so, too, are major technical inventions. A rapid increase in interest rates and a general tightening of credit can cause a sharp decrease in investment. Expectations can be changed by a political campaign or a development in another part of the world. The list of possible initial impulses, autonomous or induced, is long. It is probably true that the characteristic cyclical pattern involves many outside shocks that sometimes initiate, sometimes reinforce, and sometimes dampen the cumulative tendencies that exist within the economy.

Cycles differ also in terms of their internal structure. In some, full employment of labor may be the bottleneck that determines the peak. In others, high interest rates and shortages of investment funds may nip an expansion and turn it into a recession at the same time that the unemployment of labor is still an acute problem. In some cycles the recession phase is short; in others a full-scale period of stagnation sets in. In some cycles the peak phase develops into a severe inflation; in others the pressure of excess demand is hardly felt, and a new recession sets in before the economy has fully recovered from the last trough. Some cycles are of long duration; others are very short. These and other differences occupy the attention of economists concerned with understanding the business cycle.

In this chapter we have suggested reasons why an economy that is subjected to periodic external shocks will tend to generate a continuously changing pattern of fluctuations, as first cumulative and then self-reversing forces come into play. In the next chapter we study how governments seek to influence the cycle and remove some of its extremes through the use of fiscal policy.

SUMMARY

1. The historical record shows that the economy experiences continuous fluctuations. There is a self-reinforcing cumulative process that leads to a cyclical pattern of fluctuations.

2. Economists break down a stylized cycle into four phases: trough, expansion, peak, and recession. These phases have certain characteristic features, although no two real-world cycles are exactly the same.

3. Short-term fluctuations in GNP are usually, though not always, the result of variations in aggregate demand. Overall, these fluctuations show a fairly clear pattern that is described as cyclical.

Despite the overall pattern, the evidence is that the cycles are irregular in amplitude, in timing, in duration, and in the way they affect particular industries and sectors of the economy.

4. Any explanation of the business cycle must explain both *why* income fluctuates and *how* those fluctuations get transformed into cycles.

5. Shifts in consumption, government spending, and net exports can, and sometimes do, cause major fluctuations in American national income and employment.

6. Investment is large enough and volatile enough to be an important cause of fluctuations in aggregate demand. The three principal components of private investment are changes in business inventories, residential construction, and investment in plant and equipment.

7. Changes in business inventories, the smallest of the three major components of investment expenditure, often account for an important fraction of the year-to-year changes in the level of investment. They respond both to changes in the level of production and sales and to the rate of interest.

8. Residential construction, a major component of investment, shows a wavelike motion of its own. House building responds to economic (as well as noneconomic) influences, varying directly with the level of national income and inversely with the rate of interest. The rate of interest is important because interest payments are a large fraction of the mortgage payments that greatly affect a household's ability to purchase a house.

9. Investment in plant and equipment depends on a number of variables. These include innovation, expectations about the future, the level of profits, the rate of interest, and changes in national income.

10. The accelerator theory relates net investment to changes in national income on the assumption of a fixed capital-output ratio. Its central prediction is that rising income is required to maintain a given level of investment. Its central insight is that net investment is a disequilibrium phenomenon that occurs when the actual capital stock is different from the desired capital stock.

11. There are several explanations of the cyclical pattern of economic fluctuations. Among these are (1) that expenditure shifts themselves are systematic; (2) that lags in the system transform random expenditure shifts into systematic cyclical changes in income; and (3) that in part the cycle is either the conscious or accidental result of government policy.

TOPICS FOR REVIEW

Business cycles and economic fluctuations
Phases of the cycle
Cumulative upward and downward movements in economic activity
Causes of economic fluctuations
Components of investment
The accelerator
The interactions of the multiplier and the accelerator
The political business cycle

DISCUSSION QUESTIONS

1. How and in what direction might each of the following shift the function relating consumption expenditure to disposable income?
   a. Introduction of free medical care
   b. A change in attitudes so that we become a nation of conspicuous conservers rather than conspicuous consumers, taking pride in how little we eat or spend for housing, clothing, and so on
   c. Increases in income taxes
   d. News that due to medical advances everyone can count on more years of retirement than ever before
   e. A spreading belief that all-out nuclear war is likely within the next 10 years
   f. Sharp increases in the down payments required on durable goods
2. Suppose the government wished to reduce private investment in order to reduce an inflationary gap. What policies might it adopt? If it wished to do so in such a way as to have a major effect on residential housing and a minor effect on plant and equipment expenditures, which measures might it use?
3. What effect on total investment—and on which categories of investment—would you predict as a result of each of the following?
   a. Widespread endorsement of ZPG (zero population growth) by young couples
   b. A sharp increase in the frequency and duration of strikes in the transportation industries
   c. Forecasts of very low growth rates of real national income over the next five years
   d. Tax reform that eliminated deductions for property taxes in computing taxable personal income
4. Recently, when interest rates rose sharply, home construction fell dramatically but sales of mobile homes increased. How does the rise in the sale of mobile homes relate to the notion that investment responds to the rate of interest?
5. Empirical studies show that as the volume of a firm's sales increases, the size of its inventories of raw materials tends to increase in proportion. It is common for business firms to speak of such inventories in terms of "a 20-day supply of coal" rather than "52,000 tons of coal" or "$280,000 worth of coal." Why should relative size be more important than absolute quantity or dollar value?
6. Which "cause" of business investment is being relied on in each of the following quotes?
   a. An aluminum industry spokesman, justifying a $.50 a pound increase in aluminum prices: "We must have it to build the new capacity we need."
   b. "The two major classes of consumer expenditures most closely related to the onset of a recession are housing and auto expenditures. Buying attitudes toward both markets have eroded seriously during the past year."
   c. Bethlehem Steel, in a newspaper ad: "We need lower taxes not cheaper money or government deficits to help lower barriers to capital formation."
   d. "The Regan administration used a credit crunch to bring on a recession and reduce inflation."
7. Since different series behave differently, does it make sense to talk about a business cycle? Predict the comparative behavior of the following pairs of series in relation to fluctuations in the GNP:
   a. Purchases of food, purchases of consumer durables
   b. Tax receipts, bankruptcies
   c. Unemployment, birth rates
   d. Employment in New York, employment in Michigan
   Check your predictions against the facts for the last decade.
8. The highest interest rates in American history occurred in 1981–1982. The deepest recession since the 1930s occurred in 1982. How might these facts be related?

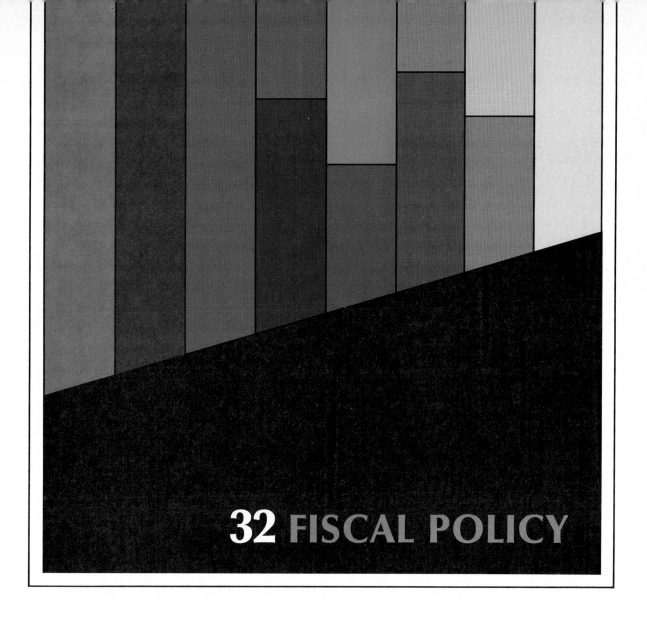

32 FISCAL POLICY

Fiscal policy involves the use of government spending and tax policies to influence aggregate expenditures, thereby shifting the aggregate demand function toward some desired position. Since government expenditure increases aggregate demand and taxation decreases it, the *directions* of the required changes in spending and taxation are easily determined once we know the *direction* of the desired change in the aggregate demand function. But as we shall see, the *timing* and the *magnitude*

of changes in spending and tax policies pose more difficult issues.

Any policy that attempts to stabilize national income at or near a desired level (usually full-employment national income) is called **stabilization policy.** This chapter deals first with the theory of fiscal policy as a tool of stabilization policy and then with the actual experience of using it.

There is no doubt that the government can exert a major influence on aggregate demand and hence on the size of national income. Prime examples of such influence occur during major wars when governments abandon fiscal caution to engage in massive military spending. U.S. federal expenditure during World War II (measured in 1972 dollars) rose from $26 billion, or 7.7 percent of GNP, in 1940 to $268 billion, or 47.3 percent of GNP, in 1944. At the same time the unemployment rate fell from 14.6 percent to 1.2 percent. Economists agree that the increase in government spending caused the fall in unemployment and the associated rise in GNP. Similar experiences occurred during the rearmament of most European countries before, or just following, the outbreak of World War II in 1939.

When used appropriately, fiscal policy can be an important tool for influencing the economy. In the heyday of fiscal policy in the 1940s, 1950s, and 1960s, many economists were convinced that the economy could be adequately regulated just by varying the size of the government's taxes and expenditures. That day is past. Today most economists are aware of the limitations of fiscal policy. There is now much discussion of other tools of stabilization that can complement fiscal policy or possibly replace it.

THE THEORY OF FISCAL POLICY

Fiscal policy is often referred to as the government's budgetary policy, or simply as the budget. Changes in either government spending or tax policies will influence the *budget balance*.

The Budget Balance

The **budget balance** refers to the difference between all government revenue and all government expenditures. In this definition *government expenditure* includes both purchases of currently produced goods and services and transfer payments. Thus the budget balance is the difference between all the money the government takes in as revenue and all the money it pays out, which are called *budget receipts* and *outlays*.

There are three possible relations between these two amounts. If receipts are exactly equal to outlays, the government has a **balanced budget;** if receipts exceed outlays, there is a **budget surplus;** if receipts fall short of outlays, there is a **budget deficit.** If the government raises its outlays without raising taxes, the extra expenditure is said to be *deficit financed.* If the extra outlays are accompanied by an equal increase in tax rates that yields an equal increase in receipts, we speak of a *balanced budget change in spending*.

Financial Implications of Budget Deficits and Surpluses

When the government spends more than it raises, where does the money come from? If the government raises more than it spends, where does the money go? The difference between expenditure and current revenue shows up as changes in the level of the government's debt. When expenditures exceed revenues, the balance must be borrowed from someone; when revenues exceed expenditures, the balance pays off some of the loans made in the past.

A deficit requires an increase in borrowing, for which there are two main sources: the central bank and the private sector.[1] The government borrows money from these sources by selling treasury bills or bonds. A **treasury bill,** or **note,** is a promise to repay a stated amount at some specified date between 90 days and one year from the date of issue. It is sold in return for a smaller amount paid to the government now. The difference between the two sums represents the interest on the loan. A government bond is also a promise to pay a stated sum of money in the future, but in the more distant future than a bill—as much as 25 years from now.

A surplus allows the government to reduce its outstanding debt. Treasury bills and bonds may be redeemed from tax revenue when they fall due, rather than from money raised by selling new bills and bonds.

When the government makes new loans from or repays old loans to the private sector, this action merely shifts funds between the two sectors. When

[1] The major private-sector purchasers of public debt are firms, households, banks, and other financial institutions.

the government "borrows" from the central bank, however, the central bank creates new money. Since the central bank can create as much money as it likes, there is no limit to what the government can "borrow" from the central bank.

The Paradox of Thrift

When a government follows a balanced budget policy, as most governments tried to do during the Great Depression of the 1930s, it must restrict its expenditure during a recession because its tax revenue will necessarily be falling at that time. During a recovery, when its revenue is high and rising, it increases its spending. In other words it rolls with the economy, raising and lowering its spending in step with everyone else.

Not so long ago people generally accepted, and indeed many still fervently believe, that a prudent government should always balance its budget. This argument is based on an analogy with what seems prudent behavior for the individual household. It is a foolish household whose current expenditure consistently exceeds its current revenue so that it goes steadily further into debt. From this commonsense observation some people argue that if avoiding an ever-rising debt is good for the individual, it must also be good for the nation. But the *paradox of thrift* suggests that the analogy between the government and the household may be misleading.

The theory of national income developed in Chapters 28 through 30 predicts that if all spending units in the economy simultaneously try to increase the amount that they save, the combined increase in thriftiness will *reduce* the equilibrium level of income. The contrary case, a general decrease in thriftiness and increase in expenditure, increases national income.[2]

The policy implication of this prediction is that substantial unemployment is correctly combated by encouraging governments, firms, and households to spend more, *not* to save more. In times of unemployment and depression, frugality will only make things worse. This prediction goes directly against the idea that we should tighten our belts when times are tough. The concept that it is not just possible but acceptable to spend one's way out of a depression touches a very sensitive point with people raised with the belief that success is based on hard work and frugality and not on prodigality; as a result, the idea often arouses great emotional hostility.

As is discussed in detail in the box, the implications of the paradox of thrift were not generally understood during the Great Depression of the 1930s. However, by the middle of that decade, many economists had concluded that the government, by going along with the common opinion, was not making the most of its potential to control the economy in a beneficial manner. Why, they asked, should not the government try to stabilize the economy by doing just the opposite of what everyone else was doing—by increasing its demand when private demand was falling and lowering its demand when private demand was rising? At its best this policy could hold aggregate demand constant even though its individual components were fluctuating.

When Milton Friedman said, "We are all Keynesians now," he was referring to (among other things) the general acceptance of the view that the government's budget is much more than just the revenue and expenditure statement of a very large organization. Whether we like it or not, the sheer size of the government's budget inevitably makes it a powerful tool for influencing the economy.

---

[2] The prediction is not in fact a paradox. It is a straightforward implication of the theory of the determination of income. It seems paradoxical to those who expect the way in which a single household should act if it wishes to raise its wealth and its future ability to consume ("save, save, and save some more") to be directly applicable to the economy as a whole. Indeed the expectations that lead to the "paradox" are based on the fallacy of composition, the belief that what is true for the parts is necessarily true for the whole.

Fiscal Policy When Private Expenditure Functions Do Not Shift

A relatively easy problem faces fiscal policy makers when private-sector expenditure functions for consumption, investment, and net exports are given and unchanging. What is needed then is a once-

FISCAL POLICY AND THE GREAT DEPRESSION

Failure to understand the implication of the paradox of thrift led many countries to adopt policies during the Great Depression that were disastrous. Failure to understand the role of built-in stabilizers has also led many observers to conclude, erroneously, that fiscal expansion had been tried in the Great Depression but had failed. Let us see how these two misperceptions are related.

The paradox of thrift in action. In 1932 Franklin Roosevelt was elected president on a platform of fighting the Great Depression with government policies. His actual policies did not, however, lead to an increase in aggregate demand. They were based instead on the notion that in a recession it is necessary to "tighten our belts." In his 1933 inaugural address he urged: "Our great primary task is to put people to work. . . [this task] can be helped by insistence that the Federal, State and local governments act forthwith on the demand that their costs be drastically reduced. . . . There must be a strict supervision of all banking and credits and investment."

Across the Atlantic, King George V told the British House of Commons in 1931, "The present condition of the national finances, in the opinion of His Majesty's Ministers, calls for the imposition of additional taxation, and for the effecting of economies in public expenditure."

As the paradox of thrift shows, these policies tended to worsen, not to cure, the depression.

Interpreting the deficit in the 1930s. The deficits that occurred following Roosevelt's election were not the result of a program of deficit-financed public expenditure. Instead they were the result of built-in stabilizers, mainly the fall in tax yields brought about by the fall in national income as the economy sunk into the Great Depression. President Roosevelt and his advisors did not advocate a program of massive deficit-financed spending to shift the aggregate demand curve well to the right. Instead they hoped that a small amount of government spending plus numerous policies designed to stabilize

prices and to restore confidence would lead to a recovery of private investment expenditure that would substantially shift the aggregate demand curve. To have expected a massive revival of private investment expenditure as a result of the puny increase in aggregate demand instituted by the federal government now seems hopelessly naive.

When we judge Roosevelt's policies from the viewpoint of modern multiplier theory, their failure is no mystery. Indeed Professor E. Cary Brown of MIT, after a careful study, concludes: "Fiscal policy seems to have been an unsuccessful recovery device in the 'thirties—not because it did not work, but because it was not tried." In 1933 the federal government was spending $2 billion for purchases of goods and services, only slightly more than the $1.3 billion it spent in 1929. This was a small drop in a very large bucket—considering that GNP fell from $103 billion in 1929 to $46 billion in 1933! Given the deficits achieved, it would have taken a multiplier of 25 for the American economy to have approached full employment; in fact, the multiplier in the 1930s was closer to 2. Expenditures were wastefully small, not (as many people thought at the time) wastefully large.

Once the massive, war-geared expenditure of the 1940s began, income responded sharply and unemployment evaporated. Government expenditures on goods and services, which had been running at under 15 percent of GNP during the 1930s, jumped to 46 percent by 1944, while unemployment reached the incredible low of 1.2 percent of the civilian labor force.

The performance of the American economy from 1930 to 1945 is quite well explained by modern national income theory. It is clear that the government did not effectively use fiscal measures to stabilize the economy. War cured the depression because war demands made acceptable a level of government expenditure sufficient to remove the deflationary gap. Had the first Roosevelt administration been able to do the same, it might have ended the waste of the depression many years sooner.

and-for-all fiscal change that will remove any existing inflationary or deflationary gap.

Changes in either expenditure or tax rates. The necessary policies were explained in Chapter 29. A reduction in tax rates or an increase in government expenditure shifts the aggregate demand curve to the right, leading to an increase in GNP. An increase in tax rates or a cut in government expenditure will shift the aggregate demand curve to the left, leading to a decrease in GNP.

The key proposition in the theory of fiscal policy follows these results.

Government taxes and expenditure, by shifting the aggregate demand function, can be used to remove inflationary and GNP gaps.

Balanced budget changes in expenditure and tax rates. The changes analyzed so far would move government expenditure and tax rates in opposite directions. Another policy available to the government is to make a balanced budget change in both spending and taxes.

Consider a balanced budget increase in expenditure. Say the government increases personal income-tax rates enough to raise an extra $1 billion that it then uses to purchase goods and services. Aggregate expenditure would remain unchanged if, and only if, the $1 billion that the government takes from the private sector would have been spent by the private sector in any case. If that occurs the government's policy will reduce private expenditure by $1 billion and raise its own spending by $1 billion. Aggregate expenditure, and hence national income and employment, would remain unchanged.

But this is not the usual case. When an extra $1 billion in taxes is taken away from households, they usually reduce their spending on domestically produced goods by less than $1 billion. If the marginal propensity to consume out of disposable income is, say, 0.75, consumption expenditure will fall by only $750 million. If the government spends the entire $1 billion on domestically produced goods, aggregate expenditure will increase by $250 million. In this case the balanced budget increase in government expenditure has an expansionary effect

because it shifts the aggregate expenditure function upward and hence shifts the *AD* curve to the right.

A balanced budget increase in government expenditure will have an expansionary effect on national income, and a balanced budget decrease will have a contractionary effect.

The **balanced budget multiplier** measures these effects. It is the change in income divided by the balanced budget change in government expenditure that brought it about. Thus, if the extra $1 billion of government spending financed by the extra $1 billion of taxes causes national income to rise by $500 million, the balanced budget multiplier is 0.5; if income rises by $1 billion, it is 1.

Now compare the sizes of the multipliers for a balanced budget and a deficit-financed increase in government spending. With a deficit-financed increase in expenditure, there is no increase in taxes and hence no consequent decrease in consumption expenditure to offset the increase in government expenditure. With a balanced budget increase in expenditure, however, the offsetting increase in taxes and decrease in consumption does occur. Thus the balanced budget multiplier is much lower than the multiplier that relates the change in income to a deficit-financed increase in government expenditure with tax rates constant.

Fiscal Policy When Private Expenditure Functions Are Shifting

As we saw in Chapter 31, private expenditure functions are constantly changing. Investment expenditure shifts a great deal with business conditions, and consumption functions sometimes shift upward as the public goes on a spending spree or downward as people become cautious and increase their saving. This makes stabilization policy much more difficult than it would be otherwise if it were possible simply to identify a stable inflationary or GNP gap and then take steps to eliminate it once and for all.

What can the government reasonably expect to achieve by using fiscal policy when private expenditure functions are shifting continually? Fiscal policy might be altered often in an effort to stabilize the economy completely, or it might be altered less frequently as a reaction to gaps that appear to be large and persistent.

Fine Tuning

In the heyday of Keynesian fiscal policy in the 1950s and 1960s, many economists advocated the use of fiscal policy to remove even minor fluctuations in national income around its full-employment level. Fiscal policy was to be altered frequently, and by relatively small amounts, to hold national income almost precisely at its full-employment level. This is called **fine tuning** the economy.

Fiscal fine tuning was never really possible in the United States because of the length of the **decision lag,** the period of time between perceiving a problem and making the desired reaction to it. Many things contribute to the length of this lag. Experts must study the economy and agree among themselves on what fiscal changes are most desirable. They must persuade the president to call for the action they endorse. The president must temper their advice with what he believes to be politically possible as well as desirable. Then Congress must be persuaded to enact the necessary legislation. A majority of the legislators must be convinced to vote for the measure, either because it is in the country's interests or because it would be politically advantageous to do so. The time required for this process can be very long, as much as two or three years.

While the American form of government makes the decision lag rather long, both the British system—used in the rest of the English-speaking world—and the political systems in most European countries make the decision lag very short. In such countries fine tuning has often been tried. Careful assessment of the results shows that its success, if any, has fallen far short of what was hoped. The basic reason lies in the complexity of any economy. Although economists and policy makers can identify broad and persistent trends, they do not have detailed knowledge of what is going on at any moment in time, of all the forces that are operating to cause changes in the immediate future, and of all the short-term effects of small changes in the various government expenditures and tax rates.

Efforts at fine tuning often have done as much to encourage minor fluctuations in the economy as to remove them.

As a result of these experiences, fine tuning is currently out of favor.

The Removal of Persistent Gaps

In addition to more or less continuous fluctuations, the economy occasionally develops severe and persistent inflationary or GNP gaps. For example, an inflationary gap developed in the United States in the late 1960s as Vietnam War expenditures accelerated while two GNP gaps developed in 1974 and in 1981–1983 when America, along with many Western countries, experienced the deepest and longest-lasting depression since the 1930s. Gaps such as these may persist long enough for their major causes to be studied and understood and for fiscal remedies to be carefully planned and executed. Many economists who do not believe in fine tuning do feel that fiscal policy can aid in removing persistent gaps. Others believe that, even with persistent gaps, the risks that fiscal policy will destabilize the economy are still too large. They would have the government abandon any attempt at stabilization policy, instead setting its budget solely in relation to such long-term considerations as the desirable size of the public sector and the need to obtain a satisfactory long-term balance between revenues and expenditures.

A persistent GNP gap. The removal of a GNP gap is illustrated in Figure 32-1. There are three possible ways in which the gap may be removed.

First, wages and other factor prices may eventually be forced down enough to shift the *SRAS* curve down to a level that will reinstate full employment and potential income (but at a new lower equilibrium price level). The evidence is, however, that this drop would take a very long time to happen.

FIGURE 32-1
Removal of a GNP Gap

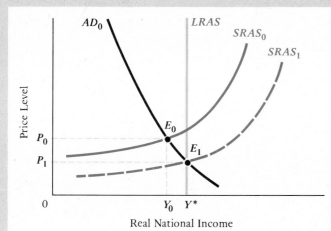

(i) A GNP gap removed by a downward shift in the *SRAS* curve

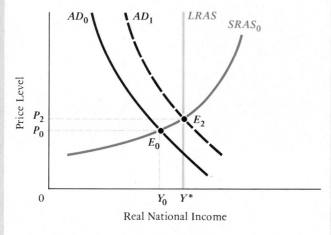

(ii) A GNP gap removed by an upward shift in the *AD* curve

A GNP gap may be removed by a (slow) downward shift of the *SRAS* curve, a natural revival of private-sector demand, or a fiscal policy–induced increase in aggregate demand. Initially equilibrium is at E_0, with national income at Y_0 and the price level at P_0. The GNP gap is Y_0Y^*.

As shown in (i), the gap might be removed by (slow) reductions in wage rates and other input prices until the short-run aggregate supply curve shifted to $SRAS_1$. This shifts equilibrium to E_1, achieving full-employment income, Y^*, and bringing the price level down to P_1.

As shown in (ii), the gap might be removed by a shift of the aggregate demand curve to AD_1, taking income to Y^* and the price level to P_2 (with equilibrium point E_2). This shift in *AD* could occur either because of a natural revival of private-sector expenditure or because of a fiscal policy–induced increase in expenditure.

Second, the natural cyclical forces of the economy could induce a demand-side recovery for the reasons spelled out in Chapter 31. This would cause an upward shift in the *AD* curve, moving the economy back to full employment and potential income. The evidence is that such recoveries do occur. Sometimes they happen quickly; sometimes, however, a recession can be both deep and prolonged.

Third, government expenditure can be increased or taxes cut in an effort to shift the *AD* curve to the right. The advantage of using fiscal policy is that it may substantially shorten the length of what would otherwise be a long recession. The

FIGURE 32-2
Removal of an Inflationary Gap

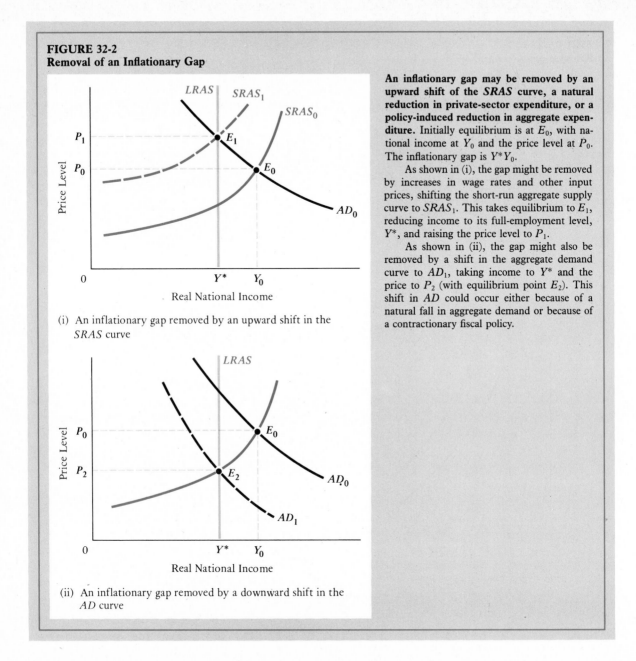

(i) An inflationary gap removed by an upward shift in the SRAS curve

(ii) An inflationary gap removed by a downward shift in the AD curve

An inflationary gap may be removed by an upward shift of the *SRAS* curve, a natural reduction in private-sector expenditure, or a policy-induced reduction in aggregate expenditure. Initially equilibrium is at E_0, with national income at Y_0 and the price level at P_0. The inflationary gap is Y^*Y_0.

As shown in (i), the gap might be removed by increases in wage rates and other input prices, shifting the short-run aggregate supply curve to $SRAS_1$. This takes equilibrium to E_1, reducing income to its full-employment level, Y^*, and raising the price level to P_1.

As shown in (ii), the gap might also be removed by a shift in the aggregate demand curve to AD_1, taking income to Y^* and the price to P_2 (with equilibrium point E_2). This shift in AD could occur either because of a natural fall in aggregate demand or because of a contractionary fiscal policy.

disadvantage is that it may stimulate the economy just before private-sector spending recovers due to natural causes. If it does, the economy may overshoot its potential output, and a serious inflationary gap may open up.

A persistant inflationary gap. Figure 32-2 shows the three ways in which this gap will be removed.

First, wages and other factor prices will be forced upward by the excess demand. This will

shift the *SRAS* curve upward, eventually eliminating the gap, reducing income to its potential
level, and raising the price level even further.

Second, a spontaneous, cyclical reduction in aggregate demand may occur for the reasons outlined
in Chapter 31. This reduction may take income
back to its potential level without the further rise
in the price level associated with the first possibility. But unless this happens quickly, the first possibility will do the job, since we know that an
inflationary gap has a fairly rapid effect in raising
wages and other input prices and thus in shifting
the *SRAS* curve upward.

Third, the government, by raising taxes or cutting spending, may force aggregate demand down
sufficiently to remove the inflationary gap. The
advantage of this approach is that it avoids the
inflationary increase in prices that accompanies the
first method. The disadvantage is that if private
sector expenditures should also fall off, it risks
pushing income below its potential level, inducing
a serious recession and opening up a large GNP
gap.

TOOLS OF FISCAL POLICY

The major fiscal tools can be classified in many
ways; one important classification is based on the
division between automatic and discretionary tools.

Automatic Tools of
Fiscal Policy: Built-In Stabilizers

As a result of factors discussed in Chapter 31, the
aggregate demand and aggregate expenditure functions are continually fluctuating. A stabilization
policy for fine tuning the economy would thus require a policy that was itself ever changing. If such
a conscious fine tuning policy is impossible, must
we throw up our hands and say that nothing can
be done through fiscal policy except in the face of
major and long-lived inflationary or deflationary
gaps?

Fortunately, this is not so. Much of the adjustment of fiscal policy to an ever-changing economic
environment is done automatically by what are
called *built-in stabilizers*. A **built-in stabilizer** is
anything that reduces the marginal propensity to
spend out of national income and hence reduces
the value of the multiplier. Built-in stabilizers thus
lessen the magnitude of the fluctuations in national
income caused by autonomous changes in such expenditures as investment. Furthermore, they do so
without the government's having to react consciously to each change in national income as it
occurs.

The three principal built-in stabilizers are taxes,
government expenditure on goods and services,
and government transfer payments.

Taxes

Direct taxes act as a built-in stabilizer because
they reduce the marginal propensity to consume
out of national income. For example, if there were
no taxes, every change in national income of $1
would cause a change in disposable income of
nearly a dollar.[3] With a marginal propensity to
consume out of disposable income of, say, 0.8,
consumption would change by $.80. With taxes,
however, disposable income changes by less than
$1; hence consumption expenditure will change by
less than $.80 when national income changes by $1
(even though the *MPC* out of disposable income
is still 0.8).

Direct taxes reduce the fluctuations in disposable income associated with a given fluctuation in national
income. Hence, for a given *MPC* out of disposable
income, they reduce the *MPC* out of national income.

This is illustrated in Table 32-1. The lower is the
MPC out of national income, the lower will be the
multiplier (as we saw on pages 537–538). Thus
higher tax rates will reduce the fluctuations in national income associated with autonomous shifts in
expenditure functions.

---

[3] Undistributed profits and other minor items would still
hold disposable income below national income. We ignore these
in the text because taxes are the major source of the discrepancy
between national income and disposable income.

TABLE 32–1 THE EFFECT OF TAX RATES ON THE MARGINAL PROPENSITY TO CONSUME OUT OF NATIONAL INCOME

Marginal rate of tax	Change in national income (millions) ΔY	Change in tax revenue (millions) ΔT	Change in disposable income (millions) ΔY_d	Change in consumption (millions) ΔC	Marginal propensity to consume out of national income $\Delta C/\Delta Y$
0.2	$1,000	$200	$800	$640	0.65
0.4	1,000	400	600	480	0.48

The higher the marginal rate of tax, the lower the marginal propensity to consume out of national income. When national income changes by $1,000, disposable income changes by $800 when the tax rate is 20 percent and by $600 when the tax rate is 40 percent. Although the MPC out of disposable income is 0.8 in both examples, consumption changes by $640 in the first case and by only $480 in the second. Although households' MPC out of their disposable income is unchanged, an increase in tax rates lowers the MPC out of national income on which the size of the muliplier depends.

Tax rates have increased greatly over this century. Although citizens complain about the burden of high taxes—perhaps with good reason—few are aware that high taxes help to stabilize the economy and reduce the large swings in national income and employment that once plagued all industrial economies.

To see the common sense of this, consider the extreme case in which the marginal personal income-tax rate is 100 percent. If there is an autonomous rise of $1 billion in investment expenditure, none of the $1 billion that accrues to households will be disposable income. There are no induced rounds of secondary expenditure; the rise in national income is limited to the initial $1 billion in new investment, and the multiplier is unity. Similarly, a drop in investment expenditure of $1 billion reduces incomes earned in the investment industry by $1 billion and hence reduces government tax revenue by $1 billion. But it does not affect disposable income. Thus there are no secondary rounds of induced contractions in consumption experience to magnify the initial drop in national income caused by the investment decline.

Government Purchases

Government purchases of goods and services tend to be relatively stable in the face of cyclical variations in national income. Much spending is already committed by earlier legislation, so only a small proportion can be varied at the government's discretion from one year to the next. And even this small part is slow to change.

In contrast, private consumption and investment expenditure tend to vary with national income. The consumption function is an expression of the tendency for consumption expenditure to rise and fall as national income rises and falls. And as we saw in Chapter 31, investment expenditure tends to vary with national income; it is high in booms and low in slumps.

The twentieth century rise in the importance of the government's role in the economy may be a mixed blessing. One benefit, however, has been to put a large built-in stabilizer into the economy.

The rise in the relative importance of more stable government expenditure means a fall in the relative importance both of consumption, which varies with income, and of investment, which varies for many systematic and unsystematic reasons.

Government Transfer Payments

Transfer payments act as built-in stabilizers. They tend to stabilize disposable income, and hence consumption expenditure, in the face of fluctuations in national income.

To illustrate this important proposition assume a reduction in autonomous expenditure of $10 billion that, in the absence of transfer payments, would reduce disposable income by $6 billion. With an *MPC* out of disposable income of 0.8, this $6 billion reduction would cause an initial induced fall in consumption expenditure of $4.8 billion. Now assume instead that the fall in national income is accompanied by an increase in transfer payments of $4 billion. Instead of falling by $6 billion, disposable income now falls by only $2 billion. With the *MPC* out of disposable income still at 0.8, the initial induced fall in consumption expenditure is only $1.6 billion instead of $4.8 billion.

Social insurance and welfare services. Welfare payments rise with the unemployment that accompanies falling national income. Many welfare schemes are financed by taxes based on payrolls or earnings, and these taxes yield less when income is low. Thus welfare schemes act to make net additions to disposable income in times of slumps. They also serve as net subtractors in times of boom and full employment, when payments are low and revenues high.

The Old-Age, Survivors, and Disability Insurance program (popularly known as *social security*) is financed by taxes (called *social security premiums*) that are paid jointly by employers and employees. Unemployment insurance is financed by a payroll tax on employers. During recessions these tax collections decrease while payments to the unemployed rise.

Both social security and unemployment insurance support disposable income when national income falls and hold it down when national income rises.

Agricultural support policies. When there is a slump in the economy, there is a general decline in the demand for all goods, including agricultural products. The free-market prices of agricultural goods fall, and government agricultural supports come into play. This means that government transfers, which support agricultural disposable income, will rise as national income falls.

The Origin of Built-In Stabilizers

Most built-in stabilizers are fairly new phenomena. Fifty years ago high marginal tax rates, high and stable government expenditures, farm stabilization policies, and large unemployment and other social security payments were unknown in the United States. Each of these built-in stabilizers was the unforeseen by-product of policies originally adopted for other reasons. The progressive income tax arose out of a concern to make the distribution of income less unequal. Social insurance and agricultural support programs were adopted more because of a concern with the welfare of the individuals and groups involved than with preserving the health of the economy. But unforeseen or not, they work. (Even governments can get lucky.)

The President's Council of Economic Advisers estimated some time ago that with the existing tax system and schedules of unemployment compensation benefits, a decline in GNP automatically produced a reduction in government receipts and an increase in transfer payments that limits the decline in after-tax income to about $.65 for each $1 of reduction of GNP. Thus about a third of any decline is automatically offset by these two stabilizers alone.

The Partial Nature of the Job Done by Built-In Stabilizers

No matter how lucky governments have been in finding built-in stabilizers, these cannot reduce fluctuations to zero. Stabilizers work by producing stabilizing reactions to changes in income. But until income changes, the stabilizer is not even brought into play.

Discretionary Fiscal Policy

Short-term, minor fluctuations that are not removed automatically by built-in stabilizers cannot, given present knowledge and techniques, be removed by consciously fine tuning the economy. We have already seen, however, that larger and more persistent gaps sometimes appear. In these cases there may be time for the government to operate a **discretionary fiscal policy;** that is, to institute changes in taxes and spending that are designed to offset gaps. To do this effectively an administration must periodically make conscious decisions to alter fiscal policy. The Council of Economic Advisers must study current economic trends and predict the probable course of the economy. If the predicted course is unsatisfactory, Congress must be persuaded to enact the necessary legislation.

In considering discretionary fiscal policy, we shall deal with two main questions. First, why is it important that the fiscal change be easily reversible? Second, does it matter whether households and firms regard the government's fiscal changes as temporary or as long-lived?

The Need for Reversibility

To see what is involved in the issue of reversibility, assume that national income is normally at or near its full-employment level. A *temporary* slump in private investment then opens up a large deflationary gap. The gap persists. Eventually the government decides to adopt some combination of tax cuts and spending increases to push the economy back toward full employment. If this policy is successful, private investment can be expected to recover to its pre-slump level. But then if the government does not quickly reverse this policy, an inflationary gap will open up as the combination of rising investment expenditure and continuing fiscal stimulus takes national income into the inflationary range. The process is illustrated in Figure 32-3.

Alternatively, assume that starting from the same situation of approximately full employment, a temporary investment boom opens up an inflationary gap. Rather than let the inflation persist, the government reduces expenditure and raises taxes to remove the gap. Then, when the investment boom is over, investment expenditure will return to its original level. If the government does nothing, a GNP gap will open up and a serious slump may ensue. This too is analyzed in Figure 32-3.

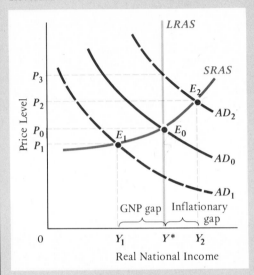

FIGURE 32-3
Effects of Fiscal Policies That Are Not Reversed

Fiscal policies that are initially appropriate may become inappropriate when the private expenditure function shifts. The normal level of the aggregate demand function is assumed to be AD_0, leaving income normally at Y^*.

Suppose a persistent slump in private investment shifts aggregate demand to AD_1, with income Y_1, price level P_1, and the GNP gap indicated by the left brace. The government now cuts taxes and raises expenditure to restore aggregate demand to AD_0. This takes equilibrium to E_0, with national income Y^* and price level P_0. Later, private investment recovers to its original level, and this further raises aggregate demand to AD_2. If the fiscal policy can be quickly reversed the aggregate demand curve can be shifted back to AD_0, restoring full-employment level and price level P_0. If the policy is not quickly reversed the inflationary gap associated with equilibrium at E_2 (the right brace in the figure) will cause wage rates to rise, shifting the SRAS curve upward and eventually raising the price level to P_3.

Now suppose that starting from equilibrium point E_0 a persistent investment boom takes AD_0 to AD_2. In order to stop the price level from rising to the face of the newly opened inflationary gap, the government raises taxes and cuts expenditure, thereby shifting the aggregate demand back to AD_0. Further assume, however, that the investment boom soon comes to a halt so that the aggregate demand curve shifts down to AD_1. Unless the fiscal policy can be rapidly reversed, a GNP gap (indicated by the left brace) will open up and equilibrium income will settle at Y_1.

Fiscal policies designed to remove persistent inflationary or GNP gaps resulting from abnormally high or low levels of private expenditure will destabilize the economy unless the policies can be fairly rapidly reversed once private expenditure returns to its more normal level.

In the American economy, where decision lags for changes in government spending or taxes are measured in years, rapid reversals are not easily accomplished. This fact is a powerful argument against fiscal policy, at least as it is practiced in the United States. Even if the inflationary and GNP gaps persist long enough for fiscal changes to be agreed on and to be made, subsequent rapid changes in private expenditure may require a quick reversal of the fiscal stance—a reversal that cannot easily be made, given the slow political decision-making process that is built into the American constitution.

The Choice Between Changes Seen by Households as "Temporary" and Those Seen as "Long Lasting"

Consider the attempt to remove a persistent inflationary or deflationary gap through changes in tax rates. Such a gap, though persistent, is unlikely to be a permanent feature of the economy. The relevant tax changes should therefore be advocated only for "the duration"; that is, for as long as the administration thinks the gaps would persist without the tax changes.

It might have seemed reasonable at the time, for example, to have expected the inflationary gap of the late 1960s to persist only as long as the Vietnam War. A discretionary fiscal policy designed to remove that gap could then have taken the form, say, of a surcharge on income taxes for a two-year period. For another example, the recession that began in 1974 was fought by "temporary" tax rebates that had to be renewed by Congress every six months—with the clear implication that taxes would return to their "normal" levels when recovery was well under way.

Such tax changes cause changes in household disposable income and, according to the Keynesian theory of the consumption function, would cause changes in consumption expenditure. Consumption expenditure would increase as tax rebates rose in times of GNP gaps and would decrease as tax surcharges rose in times of inflationary gaps. This theory of the effects of short-term tax changes relies on the assumption that household consumption depends on current disposable income.

Permanent-income theories. Many recent theories of the consumption function have emphasized what is called a household's expected **lifetime income,** or **permanent income,** as the major determinant of consumption. The two most important theories of this type are the *life-cycle* and the *permanent-income* hypotheses. The first is associated principally with Franco Modigliani and James Tobin, the second with Milton Friedman. According to such theories, households have expectations about their lifetime incomes and adjust their consumption to those expectations. When temporary fluctuations in income occur, households maintain their long-term consumption plans and use their stocks of wealth as buffers to absorb income fluctuations. Thus, when there is a purely temporary rise in income, households will save all the extra income; when there is a purely temporary fall in income, households will maintain their long-term consumption plans by using up part of their wealth accumulated through past saving.

To the extent that such behavior is at work, it may have serious consequences for short-lived tax changes. A temporary tax rebate raises households' disposable income, but households, recognizing it as temporary, might not revise their expenditure plans and instead save the extra money. Thus the hoped-for increase in aggregate expenditure would not occur. Similarly, a temporary rise in tax rates reduces disposable income, but that may merely cause a drop in saving. Thus total expenditure is again unchanged, and a temporary surcharge fails to reduce the inflationary gap.

If households' consumption expenditure is more closely related to lifetime income than to current income, tax

THE VIETNAM INFLATION AND THE 1968 TAX SURCHARGES: A FISCAL POLICY FAILURE?

We have seen that in 1983 the President's Council of Economic Advisors rejected fiscal policy as a means of removing a GNP gap. An earlier experience suggested to many observers that fiscal policy might be ineffective in removing an inflationary gap.

In the second half of the 1960s the full effects of the 1964 tax cut, discussed in the following box, were just being felt. At the same time, the large increases in military expenditures due to the escalation of the war in Vietnam were also exerting a substantial expansionary effect on the economy. With GNP already at the full-employment level, a large 1967 budget deficit produced a serious inflationary gap in 1968.

By mid 1968 a temporary tax surcharge bill was approved by Congress. This bill raised effective tax rates for a period of about 18 months and produced a substantial budget surplus. The object was to slow inflation by removing the inflationary gap. The restraining effect was disappointingly small; inflation hardly slowed its trend toward ever-higher rates.

The apparent failure of the contractionary budgetary policy of 1968–1969 caused much de-

bate among economists. The general judgment, after long discussions, seems to be that the "failure" of the 1968–1969 tax surcharges to restrain inflation revealed the shortcomings of fine tuning but did not show fiscal policy to be generally impotent in shifting the aggregate demand curve. Numerous factors offset the effects of the surcharge: (1) federal government expenditure rose more than expected; (2) state and local fiscal changes were expansionary; (3) there was an unexpected surge in the demand for automobiles, which caused an upward shift in the consumption function; (4) there was an unexpected increase in investment expenditure; (5) the knowledge that the tax surcharge was temporary may have caused households to make only small downward revisions in their expected permanent incomes and hence only very small reductions in their consumption.* Another factor, understood now but unappreciated then, is that inflationary expectations, once entrenched, are not easily shaken—especially by any measure known to be transitory.

* For further discussion see the appendix to this chapter.

changes that are known to be of short duration may have relatively small effects on current consumptions.[4]

The advantage of having households perceive as permanent any tax cut or tax surcharge conflicts with the need for the reversibility of cuts and surcharges if they are not to destabilize the economy at a later date. This problem further reduces the

[4] The permanent-income theory is not as immediately applicable to fiscal policy as it may seem. This is because fiscal policy seeks to affect *expenditure* (on consumption and investment goods) while permanent-income theories seek to explain the consumption of goods and services—which in the case of durables is spread over the whole life of the durable. This important matter is discussed further in the appendix to this chapter.

effectiveness of changes in tax rates as a stabilizing tool. See the box for further discussion.

Judging the Stance of Fiscal Policy

Governments seek to shift aggregate demand by consciously changing their fiscal policy stance. The *stance* of fiscal policy refers to its expansionary or contractionary effects on the economy. An expansionary fiscal policy increases aggregate demand and thus tends to increase national income; a contractionary fiscal policy reduces aggregate demand and tends to lower national income. In the previous chapter and earlier in this one, we looked separately at taxes, purchases of goods and services, and transfer payments as means of influencing aggregate demand. But people want a summary measure, one number to express the government's effect on the economy. Not surprisingly people tend to zero in on the government's deficit.

To what extent do changes in the deficit from one year to the next indicate changes in the stance of fiscal policy? When the government's current deficit rises, this is widely taken to indicate an expansionary change in fiscal policy. When the deficit falls this is widely taken to indicate a contractionary policy. This argument is based on a comparison of government expenditure and tax revenue. But tax revenue is the result of the interaction of tax rates, which the government does set, and the level of national income, which is influenced by many forces beyond the government's control.

Assume for example that at current tax rates the government takes 20 percent of national income in taxes. With a national income of $3 trillion, tax revenues are $600 billion. Now assume that tax revenues sink to $500 billion, opening up an additional $100 billion budget deficit. This could be the result of a discretionary cut in tax rates so that they now yield only 16 2/3 percent of national income. It could also be the result of a fall in national income itself to $2.5 trillion, with tax rates constant. In the first case it was a conscious change in the government's fiscal policy that caused the fall in tax revenues. In the second case it was a fall in national income not caused by fiscal policy that changed tax revenue.

The above example illustrates that judging changes in the stance of fiscal policy from changes in the government's budget balance can be very misleading. It confuses changes due to flucuations in national income, which are not the result of shifts in fiscal policy, with exogenous changes, which are the result of shifts in fiscal policy.

The major tools of fiscal policy are government expenditure and *tax rates*. The budget deficit or surplus is the relation between government expenditure and *tax revenues*.

The distinction between the two causes of changes in the budget balance is easily seen in what is called the government's **budget surplus function.** This function, which relates the surplus (government revenue minus government expenditure) to national income, is graphed in Figure 32-4(i). Endogenous changes in the government's budget balance due to changes in national income are shown by movements along a given surplus function. Changes in the budget balance due to policy-induced changes in government expenditure or in tax rates are shown by shifts in the surplus function. Such shifts indicate a different budget balance at *each* level of national income.

When measuring changes in the stance of fiscal policy, it is common to calculate changes in the estimated budget balance at some base level of national income. Holding income constant ensures that measured shifts in the budget balance are due to policy-induced movements along the function. The base most commonly used is full-employment national income, and the measure calculated is called the **high-employment surplus (*HES*)**.[5] This is an estimate of government tax revenues minus government expenditures, not as they actually are, but as they would be if potential national income had obtained. In this usage a high-employment budget deficit is a negative full-employment surplus.

Changes in the high-employment surplus are an indicator of changes in the stance of fiscal policy.[6]

---

[5] This used to be called the *full-employment* surplus but as the amount of unemployment associated with potential income crept up, calling so much unemployment *full employment* became increasingly embarrassing. So it was renamed the *high-employment* surplus. But the concept remains the same; an estimate of the difference between budget receipts and expenditures when actual national income equals potential national income.

[6] The high-employment surplus is the simplest adequate measure, and it is vastly superior to the current surplus for estimating year-to-year changes in the stance of fiscal policy. The balanced budget multiplier discussed earlier in this chapter indicates one reason why the budget surplus, even the HES, is not a completely reliable measure of fiscal stimulus. More sophisticated measures exist and are often used in detailed empirical work.

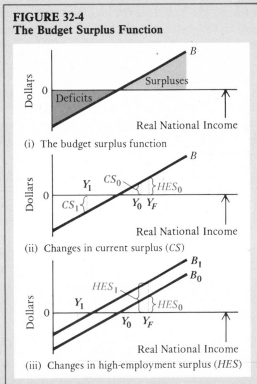

FIGURE 32-4
The Budget Surplus Function

(i) The budget surplus function

(ii) Changes in current surplus (CS)

(iii) Changes in high-employment surplus (HES)

Changes in national income cause changes in the current surplus by moving the economy along its surplus function; changes in the stance of fiscal policy shift the surplus function. The budget surplus function expresses the difference between the government's tax revenues and its expenditures at each level of national income. The curve in (i) shows that deficits are associated with low levels of income and surpluses with high levels of income.

In (ii), a fall in national income from Y_0 to Y_1 causes the budget to go from a current surplus of CS_0 to a current deficit of CS_1, with no change in government expenditure or tax rates—that is, the fiscal policy stance is unchanged. The unchanged fiscal stance is correctly captured by the constant high-employment surplus, HES_0.

In (iii), there is a contractionary change in the stance of fiscal policy: a government expenditure cut and/or a tax rate increase shifts the surplus function from B_0 to B_1. Now there is a larger budget surplus *at each level of national income.* This change is correctly captured by the rise in the high-employment surplus from HES_0 to HES_1. Note that if national income had fallen from Y_0 to Y_1 at the same time that the surplus function shifted from B_0 to B_1, the current balance would have gone from surplus to deficit despite the rise in the full-employment surplus. This illustrates the misleading effects of judging changes in the policy stance from changes in the current surplus.

Figure 32-4 analyzes the use of the high-employment surplus, as well as the errors that can arise from use of the current surplus as an indicator of the stance of fiscal policy.

FISCAL POLICY IN ACTION

We have seen that governments inevitably have a major impact on GNP through their fiscal behavior. The very size of a government's budget guarantees that. The conscious use of the budget to influence GNP that constitutes fiscal policy is, however, by no means inevitable. Fiscal *impact* is unavoidable, but fiscal *policy* is a matter of choice.

The years following World War II were characterized by steady growth of real GNP and, once the post-war inflation had ended, only gradual inflation. As the 1950s wore on, however, economic growth became increasingly sluggish. Unemployment began an upward creep from 2.9 percent in 1953 to 6.7 percent in 1961. Many worried that the combination of general prosperity, rising prices, and rising unemployment represented a new set of structural problems that could not easily be solved by using the existing tools of macroeconomic policy. These fears did not, however, prove justified as the 1960s turned out to be relatively buoyant years. High growth continued, although both inflation and unemployment also increased toward the end of the decade. The box on page 601 highlights a key fiscal episode of the period.

Fiscal Policy Since 1968

Since the late 1960s the American economy has undergone a series of cyclical swings that fiscal policy sometimes aggravated and sometimes resisted. The stance of fiscal policy in each of these years can be judged from the high-employment surpluses shown in Table 32-2.

The Nixon-Ford Years: 1969–1976

After a mild recession in 1970–1971, an inflationary gap emerged once again as the economy

FISCAL DRAG AND THE 1964 TAX CUTS: A FISCAL POLICY SUCCESS

Fiscal drag, first diagnosed in the early 1960s, is the problem of a rising full employment surplus produced by economic growth acting on stable government expenditure and fixed tax rates. (In terms of Figure 32-4, the drag is due to a movement along the budget surplus function as potential income grows.)

Throughout the 1950s potential GNP rose 2 percent to 3 percent per year because of economic growth. Such growth increases aggregate supply. In the figure below it is represented by the shift of $LRAS_0$ and $SRAS_0$ to $LRAS_1$ and $SRAS_1$. But since higher output means higher income earned, aggregate demand was also shifting outward. With both demand and supply increasing, it might seem that maintaining full employment would be no problem. There was a problem, however, and it lay with the tax system.

With tax rates constant, rising national income causes rising tax revenues. These revenues are money that does not become disposable income for households. If the government spent all its extra tax revenue, aggregate demand would not be depressed. Since at the time, however, there was a relatively stable level of government expenditure, rising tax revenues exerted a drag on the growth of aggregate demand by taking income away from households who would have spent it and transferring it to governments who did not. There was thus a growing high-employment surplus.

This is illustrated in the figure, where we start with the curves AD_0, $LRAS_0$, and $SRAS_0$. These yield equilibrium at E_0 and potential income Y_0^*. Economic growth now shifts the supply curves to $LRAS_1$ and $SRAS_1$. As a result of fiscal drag, however, the aggregate demand curve only shifts to AD_1 rather than to AD_2, which would have been required to sustain full employment. A GNP gap of $Y_1Y_2^*$ is thus created.

To prevent the exertion of an ever-stronger depressing effect on national income by a growing high-employment surplus, it is necessary to reduce the surplus periodically either by increasing government spending or by reducing tax rates. This problem arose in the American economy during the 1950s. Economic growth was producing a growing high-employment surplus. As a result each cyclical upswing was weaker than the one before it, and the average level of unemployment over the cycle was creeping upward. By the beginning of the 1960s many economists were calling for a tax cut to remove the drag and restore full employment. Both the Kennedy and Johnson administrations advocated a large cut in tax rates. Their concern was not with cyclical stabilization of the economy but with solving a problem associated with long-term economic growth.

When the 1964 tax cut was enacted, the predicted effects occurred. The tax cuts increased disposable income, causing an increase in consumption expenditure that in turn caused an increase in national income and employment.

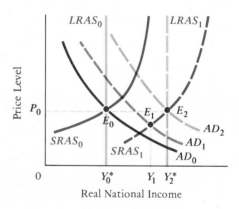

TABLE 32-2 **ACTUAL AND HIGH EMPLOYMENT BUDGET BALANCES FOR THE FEDERAL GOVERNMENT**
(Billions of Dollars)

Year	Actual budget surplus	High-employment budget surplus' HES
1969	8.5	3.0
1970	−12.1	−2.6
1971	−22.0	−9.2
1972	−17.3	−21.5
1973	−5.6	−11.3
1974	−11.5	−0.7
1975	−69.3	−28.4
1976	−53.1	−16.6
1977	−45.9	−20.4
1978	−29.5	−15.9
1979	−16.1	−1.9
1980	−61.4	−17.1
1981	−60.0	4.5
1982P	−147.9	−16.0

Source: *Economic Report of the President*, 1981, and *Monetary Trends* (Federal Reserve Bank of St. Louis).
Note: A minus indicates a deficit, a P preliminary.

Wide swings in the high employment surplus in the 1970s indicate wide swings in the stance of fiscal policy. Because the economy operated at less than full employment during most of the 1970s, actual budget surpluses were less than high employment surpluses in most years. The very large actual deficits in the mid 1970s were mainly an endogenous response to low levels of national income during the recession. Variations in the HES show the variability of the stance of fiscal policy. It was most expansionary in 1972 and 1975 and most contractionary in 1974, 1979, and 1981.

expanded into a major boom in 1971–1972. Fiscal policy contributed substantially to the initial recession and the ensuing boom. Lower taxes and increased expenditures were the rule in the election year of 1972. In a major study of the period, Professor Alan S. Blinder of Princeton University concludes that "fiscal stimulus transformed 1972 from a year of healthy growth into an unsustainable and inflationary boom."

In early 1973 fiscal policy swung from being expansionary to being contractionary. In 1974 there was an even larger change in the stance, and this time it was unplanned. By 1974 the inflation had

become very rapid. During an inflation prices and money incomes rise rapidly. Progressive income-tax rates then yield more and more revenue even though there is no change in the structure of tax rates. This gave rise, as Table 32-2 shows, to a shrinking high-employment deficit, which exerted strong contractionary pressure on the economy. As a result, discretionary changes in fiscal policy were enacted in 1975 to try to offset the severe recession that developed.

The next four years saw a gradual recovery, with the GNP gap narrowing and unemployment falling. At first the policy seemed successful; the inflation rate measured by the CPI fell to 7 percent in 1975 and 4.6 percent in 1976.

The Carter Administration: 1977–1980

The Carter administration continued the policy of fiscal expansion in 1977. Recovery continued, but two worrisome questions remained. First, since the inflation rate did not fall to near zero in the face of the most severe slump since the 1930s, was inflation now a permanent phenomenon? (We shall consider this question in Part Nine.) Second, would the rate accelerate back to double-digit levels when recovery took the economy within striking distance of full employment?

Unfortunately, the second question was answered with a resounding yes. As the recovery proceeded, the inflation rate rose to 9.6 percent in 1978 and 13.3 percent in 1979. By mid 1980 recovery was over and inflation rather than unemployment came to be perceived as the major enemy. The high-employment deficit was first reduced and then turned into a surplus in 1979.

Assessment of this experience is complicated, however, by the fact of a severe OPEC shock in 1979. For the second time in a decade OPEC raised its price by a major amount. The resulting shock working through the economy represented a major upward shift in the aggregate supply curve. Thus all of the inflation at the turn of the decade could not be blamed on demand influences. Instead transitory supply-side shocks were much to blame.

Nonetheless the 1980 *Economic Report of the President* was dominated by concern over inflation.

The control of inflation was stated to be the major goal of macroeconomic policy. Contractionary fiscal and monetary policies were called for to reduce aggregate demand in the hope that this would reduce inflation. In other words an inflationary gap due to too much demand was diagnosed as one cause of the inflation. The Carter administration had little trouble inducing a recession at the beginning of the year. Indeed the experience of the 1970s indicated an impressive ability to manipulate aggregate demand. The stance of fiscal (and monetary) policy was changed several times, sometimes in pursuit of stabilization policy, sometimes for political motives, and sometimes because of automatic effects (e.g., when rapid inflation increased tax yields). Each time, the response was in the direction predicted by economic theory.[7]

The Reagan Administration: 1981–

The Reagan administration inherited a serious inflationary problem and agreed with its predecessor that this was economic and social enemy number one. There was a major shift, however, to almost exclusive emphasis on monetary policy. (We shall study this episode after we have covered monetary policy in Part Eight.)

The Reagan administration disavowed fiscal policy as a device for any short-term manipulation of aggregate demand. Here are some of the reasons why.

1. The administration wished to set budgetary policy with long-run considerations in view and to avoid "fiscal fine tuning." Indeed it rejected fiscal policy as a device for attacking even such a deep and persistent slump as occurred in 1982–1983.

2. The administration wished to bring in cuts in taxes on personal and business incomes to increase long-run incentives to work, save, and invest. Later, its concern over the growing budget deficit caused some of these plans to be abandoned. But fulfilled or not, its long-run tax objectives were not compatible with manipulations of tax rates for purposes of short-term stabilization policy.

3. Caught up with an historically unprecedented

budget deficit in 1982, the administration, committed both to reduce deficits and to raise defense spending, was in no position to tailor its fiscal decisions to the objectives of stabilization policy. Notice from Table 32-2 that although the actual deficits were unprecedented, the high-employment deficit was not. It had been as high or higher several times in the past. The main reason, therefore, for the enormous deficit was the severity of the recession. The GNP gap was much larger than it had ever been in recent history, and the induced budget deficit was correspondingly high. Judged by the measure of the high-employment surplus, the stance of fiscal policy was not unusually expansionary. But the current deficit became the main concern of the administration and its critics. The use of tax cuts as an anti-cyclical device was therefore incompatible with concern over the current deficit.

4. The administration dismissed as unfeasible alterations of government purchases as an effective stabilization measure. The 1983 *Economic Report of the President* gave an explicit rejection of this fiscal stabilization policy:

Direct provision of public works jobs by the government is a politically popular response to cyclical unemployment during recessions. Available evidence suggests, however, the inherent incapability of public works programs to combat cyclical unemployment. (1) Such programs often have their greatest effects on public employment long after an economic recovery has begun. (2) Federal public works expenditures may (merely) alter the timing of public works projects. The expectation of the public works programs may induce state and local governments to delay making outlays during the early stages of downturns in the hope that they will receive Federal funds for projects they have "on the shelf." (3) Insofar as public works outlays are financed by borrowing from the public, interest rates are raised, crowding out some forms of private spending and reducing private employment. (4) Most jobs in countercyclical public works projects are of extremely short duration and are unlikely to provide participants with lasting job skills. (Condensed from pp. 39–41 of the 1983 *Economic Report of the President*.)

These are contentious points, rejected by some economists and accepted by others. Nonetheless

---

[7] Indeed it is noteworthy that all four major downturns of the period can be attributed to explicit fiscal contraction.

this statement constitutes a major rejection of fiscal stabilization policy.

Despite the rejection of discretionary fiscal policy, the automatic stabilizers were still in place. As national income fell and unemployment rose, tax revenues fell and transfer expenditures rose until about one-third of the unprecedentedly large 1982 deficit was induced by the cyclical decline in the economy. Without the stabilizing effect of this induced deficit, both the decline in output and rise in unemployment would have been substantially larger.

The Economics of Budget Deficits

Probably the most commonly known and debated fiscal policy statistic is the size of the federal government's budget deficit. This presents an interesting contrast to the countries of Western Europe, where budget deficits pass almost without notice. The average American has some idea of the size of the federal budget deficit. (If he doesn't know exactly how big it is, he is pretty clear that it is too big.) The average Briton or West German is unlikely to have any idea of the size of the government's budget deficit and no very strong opinion

on whether or not it is too large. Why is our budget deficit so large? Why do Americans worry so much about it? Is it really such a big problem?

Facts About the Deficit

Those who wish to spread dismay, as well as those who do not know any better, often quote figures for the deficit in current dollars. When this is done the mere fact of inflation almost guarantees that current deficits will be vastly larger than deficits of earlier eras. But so are company debts, peoples' incomes, and everything else that is measured in nominal money units. GNP in 1982, for example, was 30 times as large as GNP in 1929 when measured in current dollars. Does this mean that we were 30 times as well off? It does not, since most of the increase was merely due to a change in the price level. Measured in constant dollars GNP in 1982 was four and a half times larger than GNP in 1929. A 4 1/2-fold increase is impressive enough, but it is very different from a 30-fold increase.

As with income, so it is with deficits. To get some perspective on deficits we therefore need to remove the effect of price level changes. To do this Figure 32-5 compares total federal receipts and

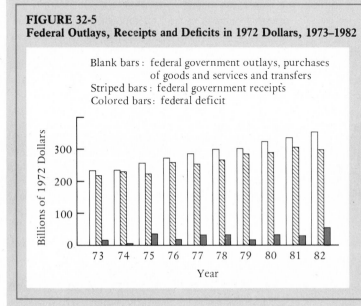

FIGURE 32-5
Federal Outlays, Receipts and Deficits in 1972 Dollars, 1973–1982

Blank bars : federal government outlays, purchases
of goods and services and transfers
Striped bars : federal government receipts
Colored bars : federal deficit

Billions of 1972 Dollars

Real federal outlays and receipts have shown a rising trend. Notice the rising trend in both outlays and receipts, with more variability in receipts than in outlays. The deficit, measured in real terms, has fluctuated substantially over the period. In 1982 it rose to unprecedented heights—over twice the average value of deficits in the previous 10 years and one and a half times the size of 1975's deficit, previously the largest deficit in the period.

spending (on goods and services and transfers) since 1973, measured in 1973 dollars. The trend toward an increase in expenditures and receipts is readily apparent. With expenditures the increase is continual; with revenues there is a little more variation due mainly to fluctuations in national income. Revenues fell, for example, in 1975 and 1982, both recession years. The figure also shows the deficit, again measured in real terms. Before 1982 the deficit was not unusual by historical standards. In 1982, however, the real value of the deficit increased dramatically. Why? First, expenditures continued to grow, possibly a little faster than their historic trend. Second, revenues actually fell instead of growing at their trend value. The latter event was the consequence of the severe slump in economic activity during that year.

What accounts for the steady increases in federal expenditures that Figure 32-5 shows to have occurred in every year since 1979? Figure 32-6 answers this by showing the percentage of the *increase* in government expenditure accounted for by each of the main categories of spending. We see that in the 1970s the biggest contributors to increased government expenditures were income security, health and education, and defense. In the early 1980s defense, income security, and interest on the national debt were the big contributors. The rising contribution of interest reflected both the increase in the national debt and the very high interest rates during the early 1980s. Although income security payments continued to be a major contributor to increasing government spending, its relative contribution fell substantially—from 45 percent in

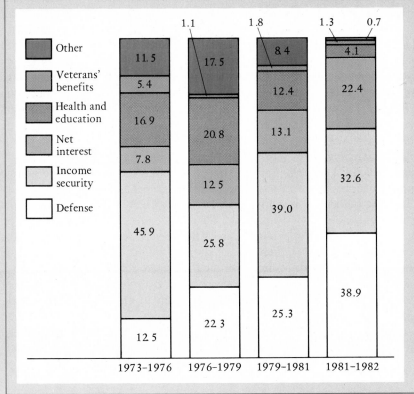

FIGURE 32-6
Contribution of Major Spending Categories to the Increase in Federal Government Spending, 1973–1982

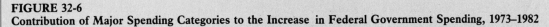

Four categories have contributed most of the federal government's spending increases. The data show for each period the percentage of the *increase* in federal government spending contributed by each category. (Note that the figures do not show the importance of each category in *total* spending but rather the contribution of each to *increased* spending.) The contributions of net interest and defense to the spending increases have been steadily rising, while those of health and education and income maintenance have recently been falling.

1973–1976 to only 32 percent in 1981–1982. Health and education fell most, contributing 16.8 percent of the increase in spending in 1973–1976 and only 4.2 percent of this increase in 1981–1982. Defense, on the other hand, rose the most. It contributed 12.5 percent of the increase in spending in 1973–1976 and fully 38 percent of this increase in 1981–1982.

Why Do We Worry About the Deficit?

People worry about deficits for many reasons. We will look at three major worries, which can be phrased as three questions.

Will the deficit crowd out private investment? We saw that one of the fears expressed by the President's Council of Economic Advisors is that deficit spending may lead to a more or less equivalent reduction in private-sector investment spending. To cover its deficit without creating new money the government must enter the lending market and borrow enough for this purpose. Such borrowing can absorb a significant proportion of private savings. In 1982, for example, the federal deficit was about 80 percent of household savings and fully 20 percent of total private-sector savings by households and firms, respectively. The fear is that the government will acquire funds that would otherwise have been lent to private firms for their own investment purposes. These firms will be "crowded out" of the market by the large government demand, as shown in Figure 32-7.

What happens is that heavy government borrowing drives up the interest rate and the higher interest rate reduces private investment expenditure. This effect is more likely if the economy is close to full employment. When there is a large GNP gap, the rise in income will increase the volume of savings (as households move along their savings functions, as shown in Figure 28-2 on page 521). In this case the new savings generated by the rise in income helps to finance the deficit so that less crowding out of existing private-sector borrowing need occur.

It is worth noting that in so far as a deficit that is financed by the sale of bonds to the public causes crowding out, it cannot cause a demand inflation. Complete crowding out means that for every extra dollar the government borrows and spends, the private sector borrows and lends a dollar less. In this case there is no net increase in aggregate demand, and hence no upward pressure on either the price level or real national income.

If government borrowing to finance its deficit drives up the interest rate some private investment expenditure will be crowded out. This effect is likely to be larger the closer the economy is to full employment.

Will a deficit cause inflation? Neither economic theory nor the available evidence suggests that deficits are sufficient to cause inflation. They may do so under some circumstances but there is no reason to think that they must do so.

Consider an example of an economy in equilibrium in which actual income equals potential income and where, say, 15 percent of national income is saved by households and firms. Further assume that two-thirds of these savings are used by firms for private investment and that one-third is lent to governments to finance their budget deficits. Of course these funds will be used differently, and possibly less productively, by governments than they would have been if they had been lent to, and spent by, private firms. But total demand and hence any demand pressures on the price level are the same whether the savings are spent by the private or by the public sector.

The above is enough to show that the government can borrow and spend indefinitely, just as the private sector can, without necessarily causing an inflation. What is required is that total desired borrowing of the private and of the public sectors not exceed desired savings and that aggregate desired spending not exceed potential output.

The worry with an inflation caused by a permanent deficit is that it may lead to a continuous expansion in the money supply. This case cannot be studied in detail until Chapter 36. In the meantime we merely observe that if a deficit is financed by "borrowing" from the Fed, the money supply will be increased every year by the amount of the

FIGURE 32-7
Crowding Out of Private Investment by Public Borrowing

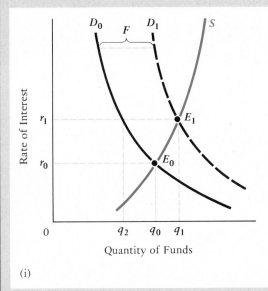

(i)

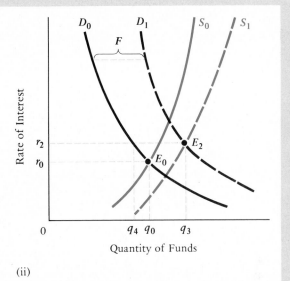

(ii)

Government borrowing may crowd out private-sector borrowing and investing. Part (i) of the figure shows a supply of funds available to be lent, S, that is fairly insensitive to the interest rate. Initially the demand to borrow funds is D_0, giving an equilibrium interest rate of r_0 and a quantity of funds borrowed for all purposes of q_0.

Government spending now increases by F, all of which is borrowed. This shifts the demand for funds to D_1, taking equilibrium to E_1. The interest rate rises to r_1, and the quantity of funds borrowed rises to q_1. But $q_2 q_1$ of these go to the government, so the private sector only borrows q_2,

which is $q_0 q_2$ less than it was able to borrow, and hence invest, before the deficit forced the government into the market.

If, however, the extra government expenditure increases national income, it will raise saving. The savings function will then shift outward, say, from S_0 to S_1 in part (ii) of the figure. Crowding out will then be lessened. At equilibrium E_2 the interest rate rises to r_2, and private borrowing is only $q_0 q_4$ less than before the government entered the market.

deficit. (In effect the Fed *creates* the money to finance the deficit.) No one believes that this is desirable.

Deficits financed by sale of bonds to the public do not need to cause a permanent inflation. Deficits financed by the continual creation of new money will sooner or later cause an inflation.

Will the burden of the debt eventually bankrupt the nation? Internal debts do not bankrupt nations. Since the central bank can create as much new money as the government requires, there is

no need for federal governments to default on their national debts. (The same is not true of state and city governments since they do not have central banks to create new money for them.) The ultimate worry is rather that the debt will get so large that interest on it cannot be financed through current taxation. Then new money will have to be created to service the debt. This will be done by having the central bank create the money needed to do so. As we shall see in Part Nine, continually increasing the money supply is the one sure road to permanent inflation. So the worry is that if the government is

FIGURE 32-8
The Relative Importance of the National Debt

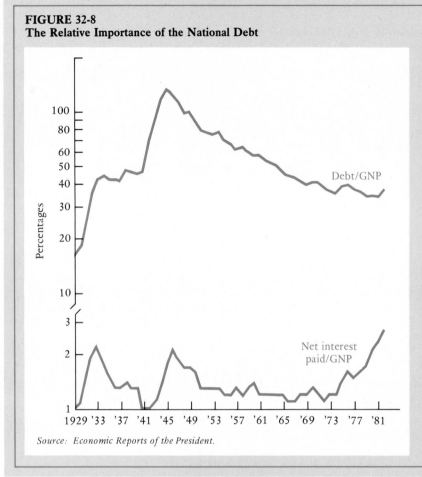

The national debt has not reached alarming proportions in relation to GNP. Stated as a proportion of the country's national income, the national debt rose dramatically during the slide into the Great Depression, 1929–1933, but not much during the heyday of the New Deal, 1933–1941. It rose dramatically again during World War II, slightly during the major slump of 1974–1976, and slightly again in 1982. Net interest payments on the national debt have been a rising proportion of GNP since 1973. The different trends in debt and debt servicing between 1973 and 1981 are accounted for by the rising cost of servicing the debt due to rising interest rates.

Source: *Economic Reports of the President.*

driven to this extreme, the debt will cause a major inflation. A less extreme worry is that the debt will become so large that raising taxes to service it, even if feasible, will put such a crushing burden on people that their will to work will be reduced and their incentive to evade taxes greatly increased.

To see if the burden of interest payments is reaching crushing levels we look at the data in Figure 32-8. The figure shows that interest on the national debt has been rising as a fraction of GNP since 1973. The figures have now exceeded what they were at the end of World War II, when they were high as a result of the very heavy borrowing used to finance that war. The levels are not yet

disturbing. Since the nation was able to handle interest payments of this magnitude during the recovery from World War II, there is no reason to think that it cannot handle them now. But once the war ended, a downward trend was established. Currently the trend is *upward*. Clearly, there is genuine cause for worry here. If the trend continues, interest payments could eventually put an intolerable burden on the government's taxing capacity. Ever bigger deficits would occur and with them even more borrowing. Sooner or later, if not reversed, these developments would force the government to finance its deficit by creating new money, and inflation would return in a serious way.

Although the level of interest payments is not yet a cause for concern, the upward direction of the trend may be. To avoid inflationary consequences it needs to be reversed.

Having said this, it is worth noting that much of this rising trend is due to the rising trend of interest rates that started in the 1970s and was not reversed until 1983. If instead of looking at the flow of interest payments we look at the stock of outstanding debt, we see a somewhat different story.

The size of the debt. The national debt in December 1982 was $1.1 billion, almost $5,000 for every man, woman, and child in the country. Just over 30 percent of the debt was held by the government itself and by Federal Reserve banks.[8] Interest payments on this part of the debt are only bookkeeping transactions. The debt actually held by the private sector is almost $800 billion, or more than $3,400 per person.

The national debt represents money that the federal government has borrowed by selling bonds to households, firms, and financial institutions. In this sense the national debt is owed by all of us to some of us.

We have seen that these "per person" figures, which are often quoted in an attempt to shock the reader, require interpretation. For a government, as for a household, the significance of debt depends on what it represents and on whether the income is available to pay the interest. No one would be shocked, for example, to find that an average American family of four had a mortgage of $50,000 on a $75,000 home.

Consider the actual size of the public debt. The trend of the debt has been steadily upward. But as national income grows, the scale of government activity can be expected to grow. Just to maintain its relative share of GNP, government spending would have to increase at the same rate as GNP. If

a constant proportion of government expenditures was financed by borrowing, government debt would be growing at the same rate as GNP. This suggests that debt statistics should be looked at in the perspective of national income data.

The top line of Figure 32-8 shows the national debt as a proportion of GNP. It shows that the proportion started to fall at the end of World War II and continued to fall until 1981. Only in 1982 was the trend reversed as the debt rose to 37.5 percent of GNP. But that figure is still much less than the more than 100 percent achieved at the postwar peak.

Proposals Concerning the Budget Balance

Whatever one thinks about the current size of the debt no one wants to see government spending and deficits increase in an uncontrolled fashion. Various proposals abound that are designed to keep spending and the debt under control. President Reagan, who has presided over some of the largest deficits in American history, put his support in 1982 behind a constitutional amendment to require the government to balance its budget each year. Let us look at this and other proposals.

An Annually Balanced Budget?

Much current rhetoric of fiscal restraint calls for a balanced budget. Some people would even make an annually balanced budget an object of policy or an obligation enforced by an act of Congress.

The discussion earlier in this chapter suggests that an annually balanced budget would be extremely difficult—perhaps impossible—to achieve. With fixed tax rates, tax revenues fluctuate endogenously as national income fluctuates. We have seen that much government expenditure is fixed by past commitments and that most of the rest is hard to change quickly. Thus an annually balanced budget may be quite unfeasible, particularly with the long decision lags inherent in the American system of government. But suppose an annually balanced budget, or something approaching it, were feasible.

---

[8] Federal Reserve banks buy government bonds in the course of operating monetary policy (see Chapter 35). Government departments can acquire government bonds when they have funds that they do not require for short, or even long, periods of time.

What would its effects be? Would they be desirable?

We saw earlier that a large government sector whose expenditures on goods and services are not very sensitive to the cyclical variations in national income is a major built-in stabilizer. To insist that annual government expenditure be tied to annual tax receipts would be to abandon the present built-in stability provided by the government. Government expenditure would then become a major *destabilizing* force. Tax revenues necessarily rise in booms and fall in slumps; an annually balanced budget would force government expenditure to do the same. Changes in national income would then cause induced changes not only in household consumption expenditure but also in government expenditure. This would greatly increase the economy's marginal propensity to spend and hence increase the value of the multiplier.

An annually balanced budget would accentuate the swings in national income that accompany changes in such autonomous expenditure flows as investment and exports.

A Cyclically Balanced Budget?

Annually balanced budget proposals are aimed at two major problems: first, to avoid the alleged inflationary consequences of chronic budget deficits; second, to prevent stabilization policy from leading to a continual increase in the size of the government sector. How could the growth in the public sector occur? During a slump the government increases expenditures to stimulate the economy, but during a boom the government allows inflation to occur rather than cut expenditure. In the next slump, government expenditure is raised once again. Willingness to follow an expansionary fiscal policy in slumps and reluctance to follow a contractionary policy in booms can lead to a long-term increase in the size of the government sector.

The annually balanced budget would prevent both these occurrences—but at the cost, as we have seen, of destabilizing the economy.

An alternative policy, one that would prevent continual deficits and could inhibit the growth in the size of the government sector, would be to balance the budget over a number of years, say, over a five-year or a seven-year period. This would be more feasible than the annually balanced budget, and it would not make government expenditure a destabilizing force. The policies are illustrated in Figure 32-9.

Although more attractive in principal than the annually balanced budget, a cyclically balanced budget would carry problems of its own. Congress might well spend in excess of revenue in (say) 1987, leaving the next Congress the obligation to spend less than current revenue in 1988 and 1989. Could such an obligation to balance over a period of several years be made binding? It could be made a legal requirement through an act of Congress. But what Congress does, Congress can undo. (This has been the history of attempts to limit the size of the national debt by legal restriction.) A constitutional amendment might only mandate an action that was impossible or manifestly foolish to achieve; the response would surely be a mixture of window dressing and a redefinition of terms that produces a paper balance without any change in the substance of present tax and spending policies.

The problems of achieving a cyclically balanced budget or a budget balanced over any reasonable time span remain unsolved. Clearly, however, the cyclically balanced budget is both more feasible and more desirable than the annually balanced budget.

Yet there is serious doubt that the idea of a balanced budget over any time period is a sensible one. Many economists believe that a superior alternative to insisting on a precise balance is to pay attention to the balance without making a fetish of never adding to the national debt.

The Political Economy of the Debt

Perhaps the national debt has a wider political and sociological significance than does the debt of a mere corporation. Let us consider two views.

The Keynesian View

The Keynesian view of the debt is that within limits it is a trivial matter. Keynesians agree that,

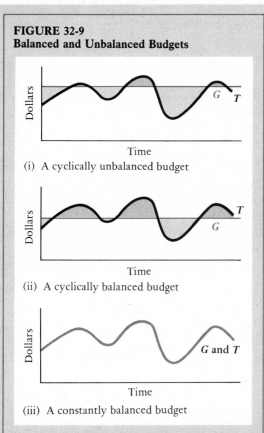

FIGURE 32-9
Balanced and Unbalanced Budgets

(i) A cyclically unbalanced budget

(ii) A cyclically balanced budget

(iii) A constantly balanced budget

An annually (constantly) balanced budget is a destabilizer; a cyclically balanced budget is a stabilizer.
The flow of tax receipts is shown varying over the business cycle while in parts (i) and (ii) government expenditure is shown at a constant rate.

In (i) deficits (dark areas) are common and surpluses (light areas) are rare because the average level of expenditure exceeds the average level of taxes. This policy will tend to stabilize the economy against cyclical fluctuations, but the average fiscal stance of the government is expansionary. This has been the characteristic U.S. budgetary position over the last several decades.

In (ii) government expenditure has been reduced until it is approximately equal to the average level of tax receipts. The budget is now balanced cyclically. The policy still tends to stabilize the economy against cyclical fluctuations because of deficits in slumps and surpluses in booms. But the average fiscal stance is neither strongly expansionary nor strongly contractionary.

In (iii) a balanced budget has been imposed. Deficits have been prevented, but government expenditure now varies over the business cycle, tending to destabilize the economy by accentuating the cyclical swings in aggregate expenditure.

as already discussed, there is an upper limit to the debt. If the debt got so large that it could not be serviced without either putting a crushing burden on taxpayers or forcing the government to *create* new money to service it, there would be serious problems. But most Keynesians think we are still a long way from that point.

The basic points in the Keynesian view are that until the upper limit on the debt is approached (1) the size of the debt is of no great practical importance and (2) the debt should be increased or decreased according to the needs of stabilization policy.

A Non-Keynesian View

An alternative view is based on what has come to be called *fiscal conservatism*. Fiscal conservatives accept many parts of the Keynesian view but maintain that they are irrelevant. The conservatives believe that deficits have important harmful effects that are not recognized by Keynesians.

The main premise of this alternative theory is that governments are not passive agents who do what is necessary to create full employment and maximize social welfare. Instead governments are composed of individuals, such as elected officials, legislators, and civil servants, who, like every one else, seek mainly to maximize their own well-being. And their welfare is best served by government's having a big role and by a satisfied electorate. Thus they tend to favor spending and to resist tax increases. This creates a persistent tendency toward deficits that is quite independent of any consideration of a sound fiscal policy.

In the conservative view the government is an irresponsible body by economists' standards because it seeks to increase its own welfare by creating a large budget deficit. The theory of national income predicts that whenever the economy is at or near full-employment income, the large-deficit policy will be undesirable because it will create an inflationary gap.

The non-Keynesian theory takes a broad historical perspective. It says that in the eighteenth century, spendthrift European rulers habitually spent more than their tax revenues and so created inflationary gaps. The resulting inflations were harmful because they reduced the purchasing power of savings and disrupted trade. By the end of the nineteenth century, the doctrine was well established that a balanced budget is the citizen's only protection against profligate government spending and consequent wild inflation. Thus the balanced budget doctrine was not silly and irrational, as Keynes made it out to be. Instead it was the symbol of the people's victory in a long struggle to control the spendthrift proclivities of the nation's rulers.

The Keynesian revolution swept away that view. Budget deficits became, according to Keynesians, the tool by which benign and enlightened governments sought to ensure full employment. But, say the non-Keynesians, deficit spending let the tiger out of the cage. Released from the nearly century-old constraint of balancing the budget, governments went on a series of wild spending sprees. Inflationary gaps, deflationary gaps, or full employment notwithstanding, governments spent and spent and spent. Deficits accumulated, national debts rose, and inflation became the rule.

Inflation robbed the people of the real value of their savings by lowering the purchasing power of money saved. When governments were finally forced to reduce inflation, they created massive GNP gaps. Today we see the legacy of these disastrous policies: the simultaneous occurrence of high inflation, high unemployment rates, and large budget deficits.[9]

The debate reflects deeply held views about the role of government, the nature and motivation of public officials, and the desirability of stabilization. Keynesians tend to regard government officials as well-meaning and substantial government intervention as essential to an effective and humane society. Fiscal conservatives regard public officials as self-serving and of limited competence and see public intervention, however well motivated, as probably inept and ultimately destabilizing. Both recognize that an interventionist government will play a large

role in economic affairs. Conservatives regard that prospect with concern, Keynesians with relative equanimity.

SUMMARY

1. Fiscal policy uses government expenditure and tax policies to influence the economy by shifting the aggregate demand curve.

2. The paradox of thrift is not a paradox at all. It predicts that severe recessions are combatted by encouraging an increase in spending.

3. When private expenditure functions are fixed, it is a relatively simple matter to increase expenditure, to cut tax rates, or to make a balanced budget increase in expenditure in order to remove a GNP gap (and to make the opposite changes to remove an inflationary gap).

4. Fiscal policy is more difficult when, as is almost always the case, private expenditure functions are continually shifting. Fine tuning, the attempt to hold the aggregate expenditure function virtually constant by offsetting even small fluctuations in private expenditure, has been largely discredited. Many still believe, however, that large and persistent gaps can be offset by fiscal policy.

5. Short-term stabilization by fiscal policy works largely through such automatic stabilizers as tax revenues that vary directly with national income, expenditures on goods and services that do not vary with national income, and transfer payments that vary negatively with national income.

6. Discretionary fiscal policy is sometimes used to attack large and persistent gaps. It must be reversible. Otherwise the economy may overshoot its target once private investment recovers from a temporary slump or falls back from a temporary boom. Tax changes also need to be perceived as relatively long-lived if they are to induce major changes in household spending patterns. (Temporary changes may merely affect the current saving rate and not

---

[9] The pro-Keynesian view can be found in almost any modern textbook on macroeconomics. The view of the fiscal conservatives is well presented in J. M. Buchanan, J. Burton, and R. E. Wayne, *The Consequences of Mr. Keynes* (London: Institute of Economic Affairs, 1978).

expenditure.) This possibility is further discussed in the appendix to this chapter. The need to have tax changes perceived as long-lived conflicts, however, with the need to have fiscal policy easily reversible.

7. Changes in the stance of fiscal policy may be reasonably judged by changes in the high-employment surplus. This is the balance between revenues and expenditures as they would be if full employment prevailed.

8. American national debt and debt service have risen and fallen as a percentage of national income, but they have not shown a long-term trend to grow inexorably.

9. An annually balanced budget would be virtually unfeasible; even if it were possible, it would destabilize the economy. A cyclically balanced budget would act as a stabilizer while also curbing the secular growth of the government sector.

10. Keynesians take a relatively sanguine view of the national debt. As long as it does not grow wildly as a proportion of national income, they view its short-term fluctuations and its long-term upward trend in absolute terms as a stabilizing device. Fiscal conservatives mistrust government and view insistence on a balanced budget as the only effective means of curtailing reckless government spending that wastes scarce resources and feeds the fires of inflation.

TOPICS FOR REVIEW

Fiscal policy
Budget balance, balanced and unbalanced budgets, surpluses and deficits
Fine tuning
Built-in stabilizers
Discretionary fiscal policy
The stance of fiscal policy
The actual budget balance and the high-employment surplus
The Keynesian and the fiscal conservative views of budget deficits

DISCUSSION QUESTIONS

1. On presidential economics:
   a. President Ford in 1975 maintained that his proposed package of a $28 billion cut in federal expenditure and a $28 billion tax cut "as a short-term measure would not affect the economy in any significant way." Does this mean that President Ford believed the balanced budget multiplier was zero? If so, why then might he have proposed the package? If not, what might he have meant?
   b. President Carter in 1977 said, "There will be no new programs implemented under my administration unless we can be sure that the cost of those programs is compatible with my goal of having a *balanced budget* before the end of that term." Does this mean President Carter rejected fiscal policy? What might it mean?
   c. President Regan said in 1983, "I remain committed to the idea that we can reduce budget deficits without increasing the burden on the poor, without weakening our national defense, and without destroying economic incentives by counterproductive tax increases."
   d. Why is it so much easier for presidential candidates to advocate balanced budgets than it is for incumbent presidents to achieve them?
2. A study by the Public Interest Research Group in Michigan (PIRGIM) found that every $1 billion in new federal expenditure produced 55,000 jobs, but $1 billion in state and local expenditure created 100,000 jobs. If the study is correct, would a sound fiscal policy (other considerations aside) dictate more and more grants to state and local governments and less and less federal expenditure? Why or why not?
3. Which of the following would be built-in stabilizers?
   a. Food stamps for the needy
   b. Cost of living escalators on government contracts and pensions
   c. Income taxes
   d. Free college tuition for unemployed workers after six months of unemployment, provided that they are under 30 years old and have had five or more years of full-time work experience since high school
4. When the government subsidizes particular industries or regions rather than industry in general, is this a sure sign of "playing politics" with fiscal policy?
5. In his first inaugural address President Franklin D. Roosevelt expounded the doctrine of "sound finance"— that the government's budget should always be balanced. Government spending, however, rose faster than taxes

could be increased, and deficits resulted. Would the effect of the New Deal on employment have been more or less favorable if Roosevelt had been successful in keeping the budget balanced throughout his first term?

6. The Employment Act of 1946 made no explicit mention of price stability as an objective of national income policy. Why do you suppose this was so? Can fiscal policy affect the price level as well as the level of employment?

7. Consider the typical annual expenditures and revenues of the organizations listed below. Comment on the appropriate debt policy for each, taking into account their respective goals, life spans, and resources.
    a. Family household
    b. Private corporation (differentiate between a rapidly growing and a mature firm)
    c. A village of 5,000 inhabitants
    d. New York City
    e. New York State
    f. The U.S. government
    g. The United Nations

8. If Congress passed a law limiting government borrowing from the public in each year to X percent of the national income in that year, would this tend to stabilize or destabilize the economy? Does it matter how large X is? Would such a law be either necessary or sufficient to assure that the government debt did not become excessive?

9. Between 1973 and 1974 the high-employment surplus went from $11 billion to $1 billion while the actual budget balance went from a deficit of almost $7 billion to a deficit of over $11 billion. What was the change in the stance of fiscal policy? What do you think happened to national income? What do you think might have happened to national income and to the actual budget surplus if the stance of fiscal policy had remained constant?

10. Explain the reasoning that lies behind the following 1983 headline: "White House reduces estimates of U.S. deficit: figures reduced to reflect the greater than expected strength of the recovery."

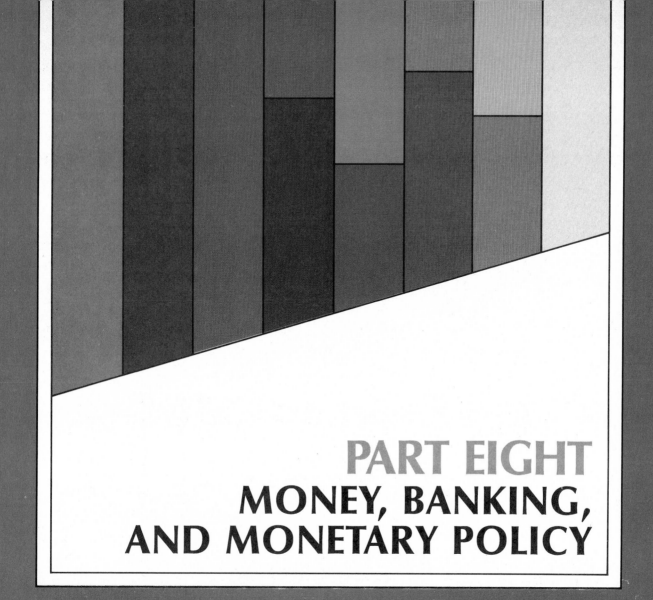

PART EIGHT
MONEY, BANKING,
AND MONETARY POLICY

33 THE NATURE OF MONEY AND MONETARY INSTITUTIONS

What is the significance of money to the economy, and why are economists concerned about it? Indeed, what is money, and how did it come to play its present role?

Most people believe that money is one of the more important things in life and that there is never enough of it. Money gives an *individual* command over goods, but increasing the world's money supply would not change the total quantity of goods available. Economists argue that increasing the world's money supply would not make the average person better off, although it would cause an inflation.

The "Real" and "Monetary" Parts of the Economy

Very early in the history of economics changes in the quantity of money were seen to be associated with changes in the price level. Eighteenth and nineteenth century economists developed the first comprehensive theories of the economy, with money playing a special part in those theories. The economy was conceived of as being divisible into a "real part" and a "monetary part."

The allocation of resources is determined in the real part of the economy by demand and supply. This allocation depends on the structure of *relative* prices. Whether a lot of beef is produced relative to pork depends on the relation between the prices of the two commodities. If the price of beef is higher than the price of pork and both commodities cost about the same to produce, the incentive exists to produce beef rather than pork. This argument depends on the relationship between the prices of the two commodities, not on the money price of either. At prices of $1 a pound for pork and $3 for beef, the *relative* incentive will be the same as it would be at $2 for pork and $6 for beef. As with beef and pork, so with all other commodities: The allocation of resources between different products depends on relative prices.

According to the early economists the price *level* was determined in the monetary part of the economy. An increase in the money supply led to an increase in all money prices. In the beef and pork example, an increase in the total money available might raise the price of pork from $1 to $2 a pound and the price of beef from $3 to $6, but in equilibrium it would leave relative prices unchanged. Hence it would have no effect on the real part of the economy, that is, on the amount of resources allocated to beef and to pork production (or to anything else). If the quantity of money were doubled, the prices of all commodities would double; and money income would also double, so everyone earning an income would be made no better or worse off by the change. Thus, in equilibrium, the real and the monetary parts of the economy were believed to have no effect on each other. The doctrine that the quantity of money influences the level of money prices but has no effect on the real part of the economy is called the doctrine of the **neutrality of money.**

Because early economists believed that the most important questions—How much does the econ-

omy produce? What share of it does each group in the society get?—were answered in the real sector, they spoke of money as a "veil" behind which occurred the real events that affected material well-being. Modern economists still accept the insights of the early economists that relative prices are a major determinant of the real allocation of resources and that the quantity of money has a lot to do with determining the absolute level of prices. They do not, however, always accept the neutrality of money, as we shall see in Chapter 34.

In this chapter we look first at the experience of price level changes—one aspect of the importance of money—and then at the nature of money itself and the operation of the modern institutions that comprise the monetary system of our economy.

The Experience of Price Level Changes

Figure 33-1 shows the course of American producer (or wholesale) prices from 1785 through 1982. Considerable year-to-year fluctuations are apparent. Despite the large fluctuations that occurred during the nineteenth century, the price trend during that period was neither upward nor downward. In contrast so far the twentieth century has also seen large fluctuations *and* a distinct rising trend in the price level.

Although admittedly a long time, even two centuries may still not be enough to give a clear perspective of very long-term price fluctuations. Indeed, nineteenth century price levels were not typical. The experience of the period since 1946 looks much more dramatic and unusual when compared only with the nineteenth century than when considered in longer perspective. For an indication of the longer-term course of price levels we can look across the Atlantic. Figure 33-2 shows the course of the price level in England over *seven* centuries! The figure shows that there was an overall inflationary trend but that it was by no means evenly spread over the centuries.

Modern economists have devoted much effort to identifying and measuring the consequences of inflation. Even the early economists, with their strict division between the economy's real and

FIGURE 33-1
An Index of Producer Prices in the United States, 1785–1979 (1967 = 100)

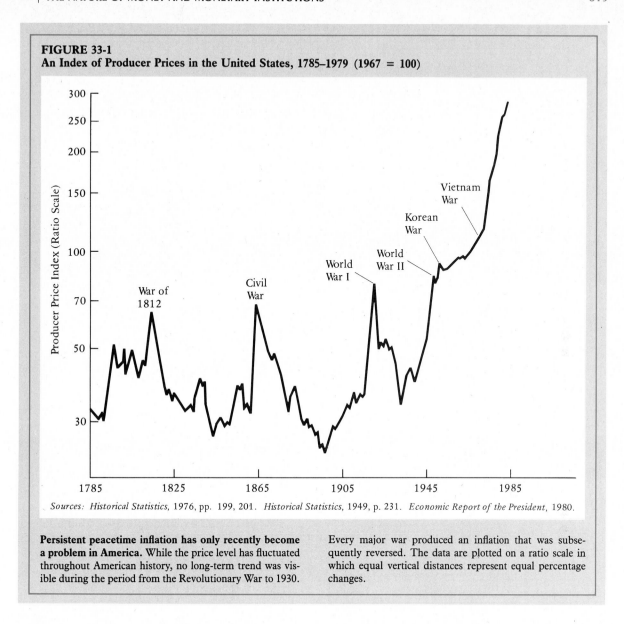

Sources: Historical Statistics, 1976, pp. 199, 201. Historical Statistics, 1949, p. 231. Economic Report of the President, 1980.

Persistent peacetime inflation has only recently become a problem in America. While the price level has fluctuated throughout American history, no long-term trend was visible during the period from the Revolutionary War to 1930. Every major war produced an inflation that was subsequently reversed. The data are plotted on a ratio scale in which equal vertical distances represent equal percentage changes.

monetary sectors, were strongly opposed to rapid inflations or deflations because of the harm that could be done during the transition from one price level to another. Indeed it may take years to move from one equilibrium price level to another, and in the course of the movement many people may be hurt.

THE NATURE OF MONEY

Inflation is a monetary phenomenon in the sense that a rise in the general level of prices is the same thing as a decrease in the purchasing power of money. But what exactly *is* money? There is prob-

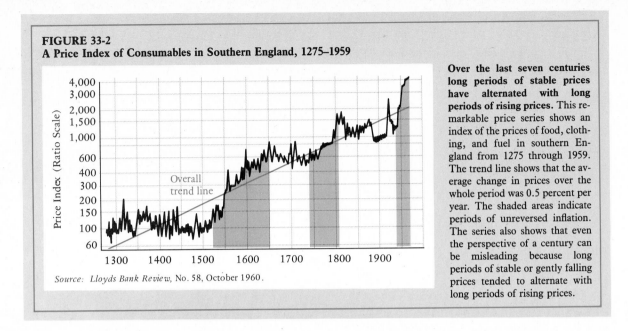

FIGURE 33-2
A Price Index of Consumables in Southern England, 1275–1959

Source: *Lloyds Bank Review*, No. 58, October 1960.

Over the last seven centuries long periods of stable prices have alternated with long periods of rising prices. This remarkable price series shows an index of the prices of food, clothing, and fuel in southern England from 1275 through 1959. The trend line shows that the average change in prices over the whole period was 0.5 percent per year. The shaded areas indicate periods of unreversed inflation. The series also shows that even the perspective of a century can be misleading because long periods of stable or gently falling prices tended to alternate with long periods of rising prices.

ably more folklore and general nonsense believed about money than about any other aspect of the economy. In this section we describe the functions of money and briefly outline the history of money. One purpose of this account is to remove some misconceptions. In addition, the recent revival of interest in a return to the gold standard makes some discussion of early monetary systems relevant.

What is Money?

Traditionally in economics **money** has been defined as any generally accepted medium of exchange—anything that will be accepted by virtually everyone in exchange for goods and services. But in fact:

Money has several different functions. It acts as a medium of exchange, as a store of value, and as a unit of account.

Different kinds of money vary in the degree of efficiency with which they fulfill these functions, and different definitions of money may be required for different purposes.

A Medium of Exchange

An important function of money is to facilitate exchange. Without money the economic system, which is based on specialization and the division of labor, would be impossible, and we would have to return to primitive forms of production and exchange. It is not without justification that money has been called one of the great inventions contributing to human freedom.

If there were no money, goods would have to be exchanged by barter, one good being swapped directly for another. We discussed this cumbersome system in Chapter 4; the major difficulty with barter is that each transaction requires a *double coincidence of wants*. For an exchange to occur between A and B, not only must A have what B wants, but B must have what A wants. If all exchange were restricted to barter, anyone who specialized in producing one commodity would have to spend a great deal of time searching for satisfactory transactions.

The use of money as a generally accepted **medium of exchange** removes these problems. People can sell their output for money and subsequently use the money to buy what they wish from others. The double coincidence of wants is unnecessary when money is used as a medium of exchange. Efficient production demands specialization, and this in turn requires that people satisfy most of their desires by consuming goods produced by others. In any complex economy such exchanges entail the use of some kind of money.

The difficulties of barter force people to become more or less self-sufficient. With money as a medium of exchange, everyone is free to specialize; with specialization, the production of all commodities can be increased.

To serve as an efficient medium of exchange, money must have a number of characteristics: it must be readily acceptable; it must have a high value for its weight (otherwise it would be a nuisance to carry around); it must be divisible because money that comes only in large denominations is useless for transactions having only a small value; and it must not be readily counterfeitable because if money can be easily duplicated by individuals, it will lose its value.

A Store of Value

Money is a handy way to store purchasing power when the price level is relatively stable. With barter, some other good must be taken in exchange; with money, goods may be sold today and money stored until it is needed. This provides a claim on someone else's goods that can be exercised at a future date. The two sides of the transaction can be separated in time with the obvious increase in freedom that this confers.

To be a satisfactory store of value, however, money must have a relatively stable value. When prices are stable, the purchasing power of a given sum of money is also stable. When prices change rapidly, this is not so. For example, rising prices reduce the purchasing power of money. This undermines the usefulness of money as a store of value. An extreme example is discussed in the box.

Although money can serve as a satisfactory store of accumulated purchasing power for a single individual, it cannot do so for the society as a whole.

If a single individual accumulates a pile of dollars, he or she will, when the time comes to spend it, be able to command the current output of some other individual. The whole society cannot do this. If all individuals were to save their money and then retire simultaneously to live on their savings, there would be no current production to purchase and consume. The society's ability to satisfy wants depends on goods and services being available; if some of this want-satisfying capacity is to be stored up for the whole society, goods that are currently producible must be left unconsumed and carried over to future periods.

A Unit of Account

Money may also be used purely for accounting purposes without having a physical existence of its own. For instance, a government store in a truly communist society might say that everyone had so many "dollars" to use each month. Goods could then be assigned prices and each consumer's purchases recorded, the consumer being allowed to buy until the allocated supply of dollars was exhausted. These dollars need have no existence other than as entries in the store's books, yet they would serve as a perfectly satisfactory unit of account. Whether they could also serve as a medium of exchange between individuals depends on whether the store would agree to transfer dollar credits from one customer to another at the customer's request. Banks will transfer dollars credited to demand deposits in this way, and thus a bank deposit can serve as both a unit of account and a medium of exchange. Notice that the use of *dollars* in this context suggests a further sense in which money is a unit of account. People think about values in terms of the monetary unit with which they are familiar.

A further but related function of money is sometimes distinguished: that of a "standard of deferred payments." Payments that are to be made in the future, on account of debts and so on, are reckoned in money. Money is used as a unit of account with the added dimension of time because the account will not be settled until some time in the future.

HYPERINFLATION

Can a sharp inflation continue year after year without triggering an explosive inflation that destroys the value of a currency? The answer appears to be yes—at least some of the time. Inflation rates of 50, 100, and even 200 percent or more a year have occurred year after year and proven manageable as people adjust their contracts to real terms. While there are strains and side effects, the evidence shows such situations to be possible without hyperinflation.

Does this mean that there is no reason to fear that rapiid inflation will turn into hyperinflation? The historical record is not entirely reassuring. There have been a number of so-called hyperinflations where prices began to rise at an ever-accelerating rate until the nation's money ceased to be a satisfactory store of value even for the short period between receipt and expenditure. Consider the index of wholesale prices in Germany during and after World War I:

Date	Wholesale price index (1913 = 1)
Jan 1913	1
Jan 1920	13
Jan 1921	14
Jan 1922	37
July 1922	101
Jan 1923	2,785
July 1923	74,800
Aug 1923	944,000
Sept 1923	23,900,000
Oct 1923	7,096,000,000
15 Nov 1923	750,000,000,000

The index shows that a good purchased with one 100 mark note in July 1923 would have required *ten million* 100 mark notes for its purchase only four months later!

While Germany had experienced substantial inflation during World War I, averaging more than 30 percent per year, the immediate postwar years of 1920 and 1921 gave no sign of an explosive inflation. Indeed during 1920 price stability was experienced. But in 1922 and 1923 the price level exploded. On November 15, 1923, the mark was officially repudiated, its value wholly destroyed. How could this happen?

When an inflation becomes so rapid that people lose confidence in the purchasing power of their currency, they rush to spend it. But people who have goods become increasingly reluctant to accept the rapidly depreciating money in exchange. The rush to spend money accelerates the increase in prices until people finally become unwilling to accept money on any terms. What was once money then ceases to be money.

The price system can then be restored only by repudiation of the old monetary unit and its replacement by a new unit. This destroys the value of monetary savings and of all contracts specified in terms of the old monetary units.

There are approximately a dozen documented hyperinflations in world history, among them the collapse of the *continental* during the American revolution, the *ruble* during the Russian revolution, the *drachma* during and after the German occupation of Greece in World War II, the *pengo* in Hungary during 1945 and 1946, and the Chinese national currency during 1946–1948. Every one of these hyperinflations was accompanied by great increases in the money supply; new money was printed to give governments purchasing power they could not or would not obtain by taxation. And every one occurred in the midst of a major political upheaval in which grave doubts existed about the stability and future of the government itself.

Is hyperinflation likely in the absence of civil war, revolution, or collapse of the government? Most economists think not. And it is clear that inflation rates of 5 or 10 or 20 percent per year—which many Americans find so upsetting—do not mean the inevitable or likely onset of a disastrous hyperinflation, however serious their distributive and social effects may be.

The Origins of Money

The origins of money are lost in antiquity; most primitive tribes known today make some use of it. The ability of money to free prople from the cumbersome necessity of barter must have led to its early use as soon as some generally acceptable commodity appeared.

Metallic Money

All sorts of commodities have been used as money at one time or another, but gold and silver proved to have great advantages. They were precious because their supply was relatively limited, and they were in constant demand by the rich for ornament and decoration. They had the additional advantage that they do not easily wear out. Thus they tended to have a high and stable price. They were easily recognized and generally known to be commodities that, because of their stable price, would be accepted by most people. They were also divisible into extremely small units (gold, to a single grain).

Precious metals thus came to circulate as money and to be used in many transactions. Before the invention of coins it was necessary to carry precious metals around in bulk. When a purchase was to be made, the requisite quantity of the metal would have to be weighed carefully on a scale. A sack of gold and a highly accurate set of scales were the common equipment of the merchant and trader.

Such a system, though better than barter, was cumbersome. Coins eliminated the need to weigh the metal at each transaction. The prince or ruler weighed the metal and made a coin out of it to which he affixed his own seal to guarantee the amount of precious metal it contained. Suppose a coin was certified to contain exactly 1/16 of an ounce of gold. If a commodity was priced at 1/8 of an ounce of gold, two coins could be given over without weighing the gold. This was clearly a great convenience as long as traders knew that they could accept the coin at its "face value." The face value itself was nothing more than a guarantee that a certain weight of metal was contained therein.

Abuses of metallic money. The prince's subjects, however, could not let a good opportunity pass. Someone soon had the idea of clipping a thin slice off the edge of the coin. If he collected a coin stamped as containing half an ounce of gold, he could clip a slice off the edge and pass the coin off as still containing half an ounce of gold. ("Doesn't the stamp prove it?" he would argue.) If he got away with this, he would have made a profit equal to the market value of the clipped metal.

Whenever this practice became common, even the most myopic traders noticed that things were not what they seemed in the coinage world. It became necessary to weigh each coin before accepting it at its face value; out came the scales again, and most of the usefulness of coins was lost. To get around this problem, the idea arose of minting the coins with a rough edge. The absence of the rough edge would immediately be apparent and would indicate that the coin had been clipped. The practice, called milling, survives on some coins as an interesting anachronism to remind us that there were days when the market value of the metal in the coin (if it were melted down) was equal to the face value of the coin.

Debasement of metallic money. Not to be outdone by the cunning of his subjects, the prince was quick to seize the chance of getting something for nothing. Because he was empowered to mint the coins, he was in a very good position to work a *really* profitable fraud. When he found himself with debts that he could not pay and that it was inexpedient to repudiate, he merely used some suitable occasion—a marriage, an anniversary, an alliance—to remint the coinage. The subjects would be ordered to bring their gold coins into the mint to be melted down and coined afresh with a new stamp. The subjects could then go away the proud possessors of one new coin for every old coin that they had brought in. Between the melting down and the recoining, however, the prince had only to toss some inexpensive base metal in with the molten gold to earn a handsome profit. If the coinage were debased by adding, say, one pound of new base metal to every four pounds of old coins, five coins would be made for every four turned in. For every four coins brought in, the prince could return four and have one left for himself as profit. With these coins he could pay his debts.

The result was inflation. The subjects had the same number of coins as before and hence could demand the same quantity of goods. When the prince paid his bills, however, the recipients of the extra coins could be expected to spend some or all of them, and this would represent a net increase in demand. The extra demand would bid up prices. Debasing the coinage thus led to a rise in prices. It was the experience of such inflations that led early economists to propound the *quantity theory of money and prices.* They argued that there was a relation between the average level of prices and the quantity of money in circulation, such that a change in the quantity of money would lead to a change in the price level in the direction. (We shall have more to say about this theory in Chapter 34.)

Gresham's law. The early experience of currency debasement led to a famous economic "law" that has stood the test of time. The hypothesis is that "bad money drives out good." It has come to be known as **Gresham's law** after the Elizabethan financial expert Sir Thomas Gresham, who first explained the workings of the law to Queen Elizabeth I of England.

To see how the law works, assume there are two kinds of gold coins, Royals and Sovereigns. Royals have not been debased—the gold in the coin is actually worth its face value. Sovereigns have been debased to the point that the gold in the coin is worth only 80 percent of its face value. If you possessed one of each type of coin, each with the same face value, and had a bill to pay, what would you do? Clearly, you would pay the bill with the debased Sovereign and keep the undebased Royal. You part with less gold that way. If you wanted to obtain a certain amount of gold bullion by melting down the gold coins (as was frequently done), which coins would you use? Clearly, you would use Royals because you would part with less "face value" that way—for according to face value, five Sovereigns are equal to five Royals, but if you melt them down it takes only four Royals to get the

same amount of gold as is contained in five Sovereigns. The debased coins would thus remain in circulation and the undebased coins would disappear. Whenever people got hold of an undebased coin, they would hold on to it; whenever they got a debased coin, they would pass it on. The example in the box shows that Gresham's Law is as applicable today as it was 400 years ago.

Paper Money

The next important step in the history of money was the evolution of paper currency. Artisans who worked with gold were called goldsmiths. Naturally they kept very secure safes in which to store their gold. Among the public the practice evolved of storing gold with the goldsmith for safekeeping. In return, the goldsmith would give the depositor a receipt promising to hand over the gold on demand. If the depositor wished to make a large purchase, he or she could go to the goldsmith, reclaim the gold, and hand it over to the seller of the goods. Chances were that the seller would not require the gold but would carry it back to the goldsmith for safekeeping.

Clearly, if people knew the goldsmith to be reliable, there was no need to go through the cumbersome and risky business of physically transferring the gold. The buyer need only transfer the goldsmith's receipt to the seller, who would accept it, secure in the knowledge that the goldsmith would pay over the gold whenever it was needed. If the seller wished to buy a good from a third party who also knew the goldsmith to be reliable, this transaction too could be effected by passing the goldsmith's receipt from the buyer to the seller. The convenience of using pieces of paper instead of gold is obvious.

Thus, when it first came into being, paper money was a promise to pay on demand so much gold, the promise being made first by goldsmiths and later by banks. Banks too became known for their vaults ("safes") where the precious gold was stored and protected. As long as the institutions were known to be reliable, their pieces of paper would be "as good as gold." Such paper money

WHERE HAS ALL THE COINAGE GONE?

American tourists traveling in Chile in the 1970s, and other countries with rapid inflation, often wondered aloud why paper currency is used even for transactions as small as the purchase of a newspaper or a pack of matches. Metallic currency in such places is often very scarce and sometimes nonexistent. Similarly, the silver dollar, half-dollar, quarter, and dime have disappeared from circulation in the United States. The reason for these things is a nice example of Gresham's law.

Consider a country that has three different "tokens," each of them legal tender in the amount of $.25. One is a silver quarter with $.10 worth of recoverable silver in it; a second is made of cheaper metals with $.5 worth of recoverable metal in it; the third is a $.25 bill, a brightly colored piece of paper money that says plainly on its face "legal tender for all debts public and private."

If prices are stable and the government produces all three forms of money, there is no reason why they should not all circulate freely and interchangeably. Each is legal tender, and each is worth more as money than as anything else.

However, suppose an inflation starts and prices—including proportionally the prices of silver and other metals—begin to rise sharply. By the time prices have tripled, the silver quarters will have disappeared because the silver in each one is now worth $.30, and people will hoard them or melt them down rather than spend them to buy goods priced at only $.25. While not everyone will do this, coins passing from hand to hand will eventually reach someone who withdraws them from circulation.

What about the coins made of cheaper metal? Since prices have tripled, they now contain metal worth $.15, still less than their face value. Will they too disappear? They will if there is a further inflation of, say, 100 percent. They may even disappear without such a further inflation if people begin to expect one. Suppose people believe there is a reasonable chance that metal prices will soon double again. It will be worth holding on to the coins and using paper money instead. Why spend coins that may in the foreseeable future be more valuable than their face value when you can spend paper that isn't worth anything at all *except* as money?

Thus inflation—and even the expectation of inflation—may make some money "good" and some "bad" in Gresham's sense. If it does, the bad will displace the good.

was *backed* by precious metal and was *convertible* on demand into this metal. When a country's money is convertible into gold, the country is said to be on a *gold standard*.

In nineteenth century America, private banks operating under either federal or state charters commonly issued paper money nominally convertible into gold. **Bank notes** represented banks' promises to pay. In areas such as the American West, where banks were small and were often unreliable in meeting demands for payment in gold, bank notes had a shady reputation. The gold bag and scales persisted in America well into the second half of the nineteenth century, even after paper money became widely accepted in most parts of the country.

Fractionally backed paper money. For most transactions, individuals were content to use paper currency. It was soon discovered that it was not necessary to keep an ounce of gold in the vaults for every claim to an ounce circulating as paper money. It was necessary to keep some gold on hand because, for some transactions, paper would not do. If a man wished to make a purchase from a distant place where his local bank was not known, he might have to convert his paper into gold and ship the gold. Further, he might not have perfect confidence in the bank's ability to honor its pledge to redeem the notes in gold at a future time. His alternative was to exchange his notes for gold and store the gold until he needed it.

For these and other reasons, some holders of notes demanded gold in return for their notes. However, some of the bank's customers received gold in various transactions and stored it in the bank for safekeeping. They accepted promises to pay (i.e., bank notes) in return. At any one time, then, some of the bank's customers would be withdrawing gold, others would be depositing it, and the great majority would be trading in the bank's paper notes without any need or desire to convert them into gold. Thus the bank was able to issue more money redeemable in gold than the amount of gold held in its vaults. This was good business because the money could be profitably invested in interest-earning loans to households and firms.

This discovery was made by the early goldsmiths. From that time to the present, banks have had many more claims to pay outstanding against them than they actually had in reserves available to pay those claims. In such a situation we say that the currency is *fractionally backed* by the reserves.

In the past the major problem of a fractionally backed, convertible currency was that of maintaining its convertibility into the precious metal by which it was backed. The imprudent bank that issued too much paper money found itself unable to redeem its currency in gold when the demand for gold was even slightly higher than usual. This bank would then have to suspend payments, and all holders of its notes would suddenly find them worthless. The prudent bank, which kept a reasonable relation between its note issue and its gold reserve, found that it could meet the normal everyday demand for gold without any trouble.

If the public lost confidence and *en masse* demanded redemption of their currency, the banks would be unable to honor their pledges and the holders of their notes would lose everything. The history of nineteenth and early twentieth century

banking on both sides of the Atlantic is replete with examples of banks ruined by "panics," sudden runs on their gold reserves. When this happened the banks' depositors and the holders of its notes would find themselves holding worthless pieces of paper.

The so-called central bank was a natural outcome of this sort of banking system. Where were the commercial banks to turn when they had good investments but were in temporary need of cash? If they provided loans for the public against reasonable security, why should not some other institution provide loans to them against the same sort of security? Central banks evolved in response to these and other needs.

The development of fiat currencies. As time went on, note issue by private banks became less common and central banks took control of the currency. Central banks in turn became governmental institutions. In time *only* central banks were permitted to issue notes. Originally the central banks issued currency that was fully convertible into gold. In those days gold would be brought to the central bank, which would issue currency in the form of "gold certificates" that asserted the gold was there on demand. The gold supply thus set some upper limit on the amount of currency. But central banks could issue (as bank notes) more currency than they had gold because not all of the currency was presented for payment at any one time. Thus even under a gold standard, central banks had substantial discretionary control over the quantity of currency outstanding.

During the period between World Wars I and II, virtually all the countries of the world abandoned the gold standard: their currencies were no longer convertible into gold. Money that is not convertible by law into anything valuable depends upon its acceptability for its value. Money that is declared by government order (or fiat) to be legal tender for settlement of all debts is called a **fiat money.** Some issues raised by the abandoning of the gold standard are discussed in the box.

SHOULD CURRENCY BE BACKED BY GOLD?

The gold standard imposed an upper limit on the quantity of convertible currency that could be issued. When the United States abandoned the gold standard in 1934, many in Congress feared that the Federal Reserve Bank would issue too much currency, so Congress imposed the requirement that the Fed hold a certain fraction of gold backing (called the *gold cover*) for currency.* If the gold backing had been taken seriously, gold would have placed an upper limit on the quantity of currency. Below that limit the central bank would have had discretionary power. Until this provision was repealed in 1968, the gold supply thus put an apparent upper limit on the quantity of currency that the Fed might issue. But at the time our gold holdings were vastly in excess of the amount required to back all of the currency the public wanted to hold. Thus in practice the theoretical limit placed on currency by gold never became binding. Indeed the removal of the gold cover occurred in 1968 when a shortage of gold for international payments led to the possibility that the requirement for gold backing might become binding. Like the ceiling on the national debt, the gold cover was designed to make people feel better, not to affect policy.

Does it matter that the central bank is not limited to its ability to issue currency? Consider the gold standard again. Gold derived its value because it is scarce relative to the demand for it (the demand being derived from its monetary and its nonmonetary uses). Tying a currency to gold meant that the quantity of money in a country was determined by such chance occurrences

* The gold itself is in government vaults, most of it at Fort Knox, Kentucky, and at the Federal Reserve Bank of New York. The central bank merely held gold certificates asserting that the gold was there.

as the discovery of new gold supplies. This was not without advantages, the most important being that it provided a check on governments' ability to cause inflation. Gold cannot be manufactured at will; paper currency can. There is little doubt that in the past, if the money supply had been purely paper, many governments would have attempted to pay their bills by printing new money rather than by raising taxes. Such increases in the money supply, in periods of full employment, would lead to inflation in the same way that the debasement of metallic currency did. Thus the gold standard provided some check on inflation by making it difficult for the government to change the money supply. Periods of major gold discoveries, however, brought about inflations of their own. In the 1500s, for example, Spanish gold and silver flowed into Europe from the New World, bringing inflation in their wake.

A major problem caused by a reliance on gold is that it is usually desirable to increase the money supply when real national income is increasing. This cannot be done on a gold standard unless, by pure chance, gold is discovered at the same time. The gold standard took discretionary powers over the money supply out of the hands of government. Whether or not one thinks this is a good thing depends on how one thinks governments would use this discretion. In general, a gold standard is probably better than having the currency managed by an ignorant or irresponsible government, but it is worse than having the currency supply adjusted by a well-informed and intelligent one. *Better* and *worse* in this context are judged by the criterion of having a money supply that varies adequately with the needs of the economy but does not vary so as to cause violent inflations or deflations.

Today virtually all currency is fiat money.

Look at any bill in your wallet—it is not convertible into anything. Until recently much American currency bore the statement: "The United States of America Will Pay to the Bearer on Demand Twenty Dollars" (or whatever the currency was worth). The notes were signed by both the secretary of the Treasury and the treasurer. If you took this seriously and demanded $20, you could have handed over a $20 bill and received in return a different but identical $20 bill! Today's Federal Reserve $20 notes simply say, "The United States of America," "Twenty dollars," and "This note is legal tender for all debts, public and private." It is, in other words, fiat money pure and simple.

The meaning of the phrase **legal tender** is that if you are offered something that is legal tender in payment for a debt and you refuse to accept it, the debt is no longer legally collectible.

Not only is our currency fiat money, so is our coinage. Modern coins, unlike their historical ancestors, rarely contain a value of metal equal to their face value; indeed, the value of the metal is characteristically a minute fraction of the value of the coin. In 1966, faced with a shortage of silver for commercial purposes, the United States Treasury removed the silver from the $0.25 piece. Quarters, however, continued to be traded four to the dollar. Modern coins, like modern paper money, are merely tokens.

Why Is Fiat Money Valuable?

Today our paper money and our coinage is valuable because it is generally accepted. Because everyone accepts it as valuable, it *is* valuable; the fact that it can no longer be converted into anything has no effect on its functioning as a medium of exchange.

In the early days of the gold standard, paper money was valuable because everyone believed it was convertible into gold on demand. Experience during periods of crisis, when there was often a temporary suspension of convertibility into gold, and of panic, when there were bank failures, served

to demonstrate that the mere *promise* of convertibility was not sufficient to make money valuable. Gradually the realization grew that neither was convertibility necessary.

Paper money is valuable when it will be accepted in payment for goods and for debts.

Many people are disturbed to learn that present-day paper money is neither backed by, nor convertible into, anything more valuable—that it is nothing but pieces of paper whose value derives from common acceptance and from confidence that it will continue to be accepted in the future. People believe their money should be more substantial than that; after all, what of "dollar diplomacy" and the "bedrock solidity" of the Swiss franc? But money is in fact only pieces of paper. There is no point in pretending otherwise.

If paper money is acceptable, it is a medium of exchange; if its purchasing power remains stable, it is a satisfactory store of value; and if both of these things are true, it will also serve as a satisfactory unit of account.

Modern Money

By the twentieth century private banks had lost the authority to issue money in form of bank notes. Yet they did not lose the power to create money in the form of deposit money.

Deposit Money

Banks' customers frequently deposit coins and paper money with the banks for safekeeping, just as in former times they deposited gold. Such a deposit is recorded as an entry on the customer's account. If the customer wishes to pay a debt, he or she may come to the bank and claim the money in dollars, then pay the money over to another person. This person may then redeposit the money in a bank.

Like the gold transfers, this is a tedious procedure, particularly for large payments. It is more convenient to have the bank transfer claims to this money on deposit. The common "check" is an instruction to the bank to make the transfer. As soon as such transfers became easy and inexpensive, and checks became widely accepted in payment for commodities and debts, the deposits became a form of money called **deposit money.**

When individual A deposits $100 in a bank, his account is credited with $100. This is the bank's promise to pay $100 cash on demand. If A pays B $100 by giving her a check that B then deposits in the same bank, the bank merely reduces A's account by $100 and increases B's by the same amount. Thus the bank still promises to pay on demand the $100 originally deposited, but it now promises to pay it to B rather than to A. What makes all of this so convenient is that B can actually deposit A's check in any bank, and the banks will arrange the transfer of credits.

Checks are in some ways the modern equivalent of old-time bank notes issued by commercial banks. The passing of a bank note from hand to hand transferred ownership of a claim against the bank. A check on a deposit account is similarly an order to the bank to pay the designated recipient, rather than oneself, money credited to the account. Checks, unlike bank notes, do not circulate freely from hand to hand; thus checks themselves are not currency. The balance in the demand deposit *is* money; the check transfers money from one person to another. Because checks are easily drawn and deposited, and because they are relatively safe from theft, they are widely used. In 1983 approximately 50 billion checks were drawn in the United States. During the 1970s the number of checks drawn increased at about 7 percent per year.

Thus, when commercial banks lost the right to issue notes of their own, the form of bank money changed but the substance did not. Today banks have money in their vaults (or on deposit with the central banks) just as they always did. Once it was gold, today it is the legal tender of the times—paper money. It is true today, just as in the past, that most of the bank's customers are content to pay their bills by passing among themselves the bank's promises to pay money on demand. Only a small proportion of the transactions made by the bank's customers is made in cash.

Today, just as in the past, banks can create money by issuing more promises to pay (deposits) than they have money available to pay out.

THE BANKING SYSTEM

There are many types of institutions that make up a modern banking system such as exists in the United States today. At one level one can distinguish between the central bank and the financial intermediaries. The **central bank** is the government owned and operated institution that serves to control the banking system. Through it, the government's monetary policy is conducted. In the United States the central bank is the Federal Reserve System, nicknamed the Fed; we study it in detail in Chapter 35. Financial intermediaries are privately owned institutions that serve the general public. They are called intermediaries because they stand between savers, from whom they accept deposits, and investors, to whom they make loans. In this chapter we focus on an important class of financial intermediaries, the *commercial banks*.

Modern commercial banking systems are of two main types. In one system there is a small number of banks, each with a very large number of branch offices; in the other system there are many independent banks. The banking systems of Britain and Canada are of the first type, with only a few banks accounting for the overwhelming bulk of the business. The American system is of the second type. In 1980 there were approximately 15,000 independent banks, some (such as the Bank of America) with hundreds of branches and others with only a single office. Branch banking in the United States is governed by state law. Interstate branching is not allowed. In some states, such as New York and California, banks are permitted to branch statewide. Illinois and Missouri, among others, are "unit-bank" states and permit no branching. Other states, such as Pennsylvania, permit limited branching into areas near the home office. The functioning of the banking system is, however, essentially the same in all these systems.

The Commercial Banks

The basic unit of the American banking system is the ordinary **commercial bank,** which is a privately owned, profit-seeking institution. All commercial banks have common attributes: They hold deposits for their customers, permit certain deposits to be transferred by check from an individual account to other accounts held in any bank in the country, make loans to households and firms, and invest in government securities.

It is these common features, in particular the holding of demand deposits, that distinguish commercial banks from other financial institutions, each of which may perform some but not all of these functions. Many other institutions such as credit unions, savings and loan associations, and mutual savings banks accept time deposits and grant loans for specific purposes. Finance companies make loans to households for practically any purpose. The post office and Western Union will transfer money; American Express will issue travelers' checks. Credit card companies will extend credit so that purchases can be made on a buy-now, pay-later basis.

Commercial banks differ from one another in many ways. Some are very large (in 1980 the Bank of America had deposits in excess of $86 billion) and others are very small; some are located in big cities, others in small towns; some hold charters from the federal government (national banks), others from state governments (state banks). Nearly 40 percent of the commercial banks, including most of the larger ones, are members of the Federal Reserve System. All national banks must be members, and any state bank may join the system by agreeing to abide by its regulations. However, nonmember banks are indirectly tied into the system since they are invariably *correspondents* of larger member banks. The nonmember banks keep their reserves on deposit with member banks, depend on them for loans when they are pressed for cash, and rely on them for a variety of other services that the Federal Reserve System provides for its members. In practice, then, all commercial banks, members and nonmembers alike, have always come under the effective regulatory influence of the Fed. (New banking legislation passed in March 1980 greatly reduced the difference in regulatory rules applying to member and nonmember banks).

Interbank Activities

Commercial banks have a number of interbank cooperative relationships. These are encouraged by special banking laws because they facilitate the smooth functioning of money and credit markets.

For example, banks often share loans. Even the biggest bank cannot meet all the credit needs of an industrial giant such as General Motors, and often a group of banks will offer a "pool loan," agreeing on common terms and dividing the loan up into manageable segments. On a different scale a small bank, when approached for a loan larger than it can safely handle, will often ask a larger bank to "participate" in the loan.

Another form of interbank cooperation is the bank credit card. VISA and MasterCard are the two most widely used credit cards, and each is operated by a large group of banks.

Probably the most important form of interbank cooperation is check clearing and collection. Bank deposits are an effective medium of exchange only because banks accept each other's checks. If a depositor in bank A writes a check to someone who deposits it in bank B, bank A now owes money to bank B. This, of course, creates a need for the banks to present checks to each other for payment.

There are millions of such transactions in the course of a day, and they result in an enormous sorting and bookkeeping job. Multibank systems make use of a **clearing house** where interbank debts are settled. At the end of the day, all the checks drawn by bank A's customers and deposited in bank B are totaled and set against the total of all the checks drawn by bank B's customers and deposited in bank A. It is necessary only to settle the difference between the two sums. The actual checks are passed through the clearing house back to the bank on which they were drawn. Both banks are then able to adjust the individual accounts by a set of book entries; a flow of cash between banks is necessary only when there is a net transfer of

TABLE 33–1 CONSOLIDATED BALANCE SHEET OF U.S. COMMERCIAL BANKS, DECEMBER 31, 1982
(Billions of Dollars)

Assets		Liabilities	
Reserves (cash assets including deposits with Federal Reserve banks)	$ 200.4	Deposits	
		Demand	$ 376.4
Loans	1,055.5	Savings	296.9
U.S. government securities	132.7	Time	737.0
Other securities	242.2		
Other assets	341.8	Borrowings	278.2
		Other liabilities	148.5
		Capital accounts	135.6
	$1,972.6		$1,972.6

Source: *Federal Reserve Bulletin*, January 1983.

Reserves are only a small fraction of deposit liabilities. If all the banks' customers who held demand deposits tried to withdraw them in cash, the banks could not meet this demand without liquidating $214 billion of other assets. This would be impossible without assistance from the Fed.

cash from the customers of one bank to those of another. For member banks in the United States, much of this clearing function is performed by the Federal Reserve System.

Commercial Banks As Profit-Seeking Institutions

Banks are private firms that start with invested capital and seek to "make money" in the same sense as do firms making neckties or bicycles. (Banks, as we shall see, do not set out to "make money" in the literal sense; nonetheless they do so as a by-product of their attempt to make profits for their owners.)

A commercial bank provides a variety of services to its customers: a safe place to store money; the convenience of demand deposits that can be transferred by personal check; a safe and convenient place to earn a modest but guaranteed return on savings; and often financial advice and estate management services. The bank earns some revenue by charging for these services, but such fees are a small part of the bank's total earnings. The largest part (typically about five-sixths) of a bank's earnings is derived from the bank's ability to invest profitably the funds placed with it.

Principal Assets and Liabilities

Table 33-1 is the combined balance sheet of the commercial banks in the United States. The bulk of a bank's liabilities are deposits that are owed to its depositors. The principal assets of a bank are the *securities* it buys (including government bonds), which pay interest or dividends, and the *loans* it makes to individuals to buy houses, cars, television sets, and securities and to businesses to build factories, buy machines, and finance the purchase of goods and raw materials. A bank loan is a liability to the borrower (who must pay it back) but an asset to the bank. The bank expects not only to have the loan repaid but to receive interest that more than compensates for the paperwork involved and the risk of nonpayment.

Most money deposited with banks is "at work," having been invested in loans or securities. Banks earn money by lending and investing the money left with them so as to earn more than it costs them to attract the deposits. Deposits are the lifeblood of a commercial bank. Without them the bank has nothing to lend or invest except the small amount of its initial capital.

Most bank services are designed to attract or keep deposits. In the case of time deposits a bank pays the depositor an interest rate in the expectation that it can earn more than that by reinvesting the money.[1] In the case of demand deposits banks until 1980 were not permitted to pay interest to their depositors, but they could and did provide free checking, monthly statements, and postage-paid deposit-by-mail envelopes. NOW and ATS accounts and money market mutual funds have created something very much like an interest-paying demand deposit. And new legislation passed in 1980 phases out interest rate limitations over a period of six years.

Competition for Deposits

Competition for deposits is active among banks and between banks and other financial institutions. Savings and loan associations (S & Ls) and mutual savings banks are important competitors of commercial banks for time deposits. These nonbank savings institutions specialize primarily in mortgage lending secured by residential real estate; their rapid postwar growth has reflected the high and growing demand for home financing. Competitive bidding for funds by various kinds of financial institutions was traditionally heavily regulated. But the 1980 banking law provided for the gradual phasing out of such restrictions as maximum interest rates on savings and time deposits. Money-market funds, high-interest CDs, advertising, personal solicitation of accounts, giveaway programs for new deposits to existing accounts, and improved services are all forms of competition for funds. Among the special services are payroll-accounting and pension-accounting schemes for industrial customers. The "lock box" is another kind of service: banks establish locked post office boxes to which retail customers of large companies send their payments. Most gasoline companies have credit card customers remit to a lock box. The bank opens the remittances, deposits them to the company's account, and forwards notices of payment to the company. Among other features, this speeds the receipt of funds to the company and decreases the need to borrow money for working capital. All these services are costly to the bank, but they serve as inducements to customers in order to gain deposits.

Reserves

The Need for Reserves

All bankers would as a matter of convenience and prudence keep *some* cash on hand against their deposits in order to be able to meet depositors' day-to-day requirements for cash. But the reserves required for these needs are far less than 100 percent. Just as the goldsmiths of old discovered that only a fraction of the gold they held was ever withdrawn at any given time, and just as banks discovered that only a fraction of convertible bank notes was actually converted, so, too, have banks discovered that only a fraction of their deposits will be withdrawn in cash at any one time. Most deposits of any individual bank remain on deposit with it; thus an individual bank need only keep fractional reserves against its deposits.

Many of the funds withdrawn by the depositor from one bank do not leave the banking system, even though they leave the bank. Even if Ms. Jones withdraws $5,000 from her bank to buy a new car, the chances are great that the car dealer will deposit the check received from Jones in its own account. Thus the banking system as a whole will simply have transferred its deposit liabilities from one depositor to another and from one bank to another. For this reason, the banking system as a whole can operate with fewer reserves than would be needed by any one bank standing alone. While one bank may be losing reserves, others may be gaining them; the bank experiencing a shortage can borrow from those banks with surplus reserves.[2]

The reserves needed to assure that depositors can withdraw their deposits on demand will be quite small in normal times.

---

[1] Historically, legal ceilings have applied to interest rates that banks could pay on time deposits. These ceilings have been phased out since 1978.

[2] There is an active market, the federal funds market, in which surplus reserves are loaned among banks on a short-term basis.

The psychological effect of a bank's refusing to give a depositor cash can be devastating. Until relatively recent times, such an event—or even the rumor of it—could lead to a "run" on the bank as the bank's depositors rushed to withdraw their money. Faced with such a panic, the bank would have to close until it had borrowed funds or liquidated enough assets to meet the demand or until the demand subsided. But the closing of even one bank often led nervous depositors to demand cash from other banks. Bankers could not instantly turn their loans into cash since the borrowers had the money tied up in such things as buildings. They could not even quickly sell their securities since many of the potential purchasers found their money was tied up in the closed banks. Thus, in a domino effect, once many banks closed, a wave of foreclosures, bankruptcies, and further bank failures would ensue. Moreover, as many banks tried to sell their securities at the same time, the prices of the securities often fell disastrously, and the resulting decline in the value of the banks' assets added to the risk of their insolvency.

To avoid panics reserves must be large enough to meet extraordinary demands for cash.

The need of the commercial banking system for reserves against depositors' panics has been diminished by governmental policies. First, the central bank can provide commercial banks with needed cash either by lending them money or by buying the securities they want to sell. Second, the government provides Federal Deposit Insurance, which guarantees that depositors will get their money back even if a bank fails completely. Such insurance decreases the likelihood of a widespread panic because one bank's failure is much less likely to lead to a run on other banks. Most depositors will not withdraw their money as long as they are *sure* they can get it when they need it.

Actual and Required Reserves

Look again at Table 33-1 and observe that the banking system's cash reserves are just a fraction of its deposits. If the holders of even 60 percent of its demand deposits had demanded cash sometime in January 1983, the commercial banking system would have been unable (without outside help) to meet the demand.

The American banking system is a **fractional reserve system,** with banks holding reserves of much less than 100 percent of their deposits. The size of the reserves reflects not only the judgment of bankers, it also reflects the legal requirements imposed on the banks by the Fed.

A bank's **reserve ratio** is the fraction of its deposits that it holds as reserves either as cash or as deposits with the central bank. Those reserves that the Federal Reserve System requires the bank to hold are called **required reserves.** Any reserves held over and above required reserves are called **excess reserves.** Reserves are required by the Fed both to assure the stability of the banking system and as part of its policy arsenal in attempting to control the money supply, as we shall discuss at the end of this chapter.

THE CREATION AND DESTRUCTION OF DEPOSIT MONEY BY COMMERCIAL BANKS

The fractional reserve system creates the leverage by which privately owned and operated banks and other financial institutions can create new money.

If banks can increase their reserves, they can increase their deposits even more. Since deposits are money, banks can thus increase the money supply.

In a real sense, that is all there is to money creation. Yet the process is worth examining in some detail. We shall limit our attention to commercial banks and their creation of demand deposits.

Some Simplifying Assumptions

To focus on the essential aspects of how banks create money, assume that banks can invest in only one kind of asset, loans, and that there is only one kind of deposit, a demand deposit.

Three other assumptions listed below are provisional; later, when we have developed the basic ideas concerning the bank's creation of money, these assumptions will be relaxed.

Fixed required reserve ratio. It is assumed that all banks have the same required reserve ratio, which does not change. In our numerical illustration we shall assume that the required reserve ratio is 20 percent; that is, that banks must have at least $1 of reserves for every $5 of deposits.

No excess reserves. It is assumed that all banks want to invest any reserves they have in excess of the legally required amount. This implies that they always believe there are safe investments to be made when they have excess reserves.

No cash drain from the banking system. It is assumed that the public holds a fixed amount of currency in circulation. Thus changes in the money supply will take the form of changes in deposit money. If extra money is created, the money will be deposited in a bank; if money is destroyed bank deposits will be decreased.

The Creation of Deposit Money

Suppose that the country is served by many banks. A typical bank's balance sheet is shown in Table 33-2. The Immigrants Bank and Trust Company

TABLE 33–2 THE INITIAL BALANCE SHEET OF THE IMMIGRANTS BANK AND TRUST COMPANY (IB&T CO.) (Thousands of Dollars)

Assets		Liabilities	
Cash and other reserves	$ 200	Deposits	$1,000
Loans	900	Capital	100
	$1,100		$1,100

The IB&T Co. bank has a reserve of 20 percent of its deposit liabilites. The commercial bank earns money by finding profitable investments for much of the money deposited with it. In this balance sheet, loans are its earning assets.

TABLE 33–3 THE BALANCE SHEET OF IB&T CO. AFTER AN IMMIGRANT DEPOSITS $100 (Thousands of Dollars)

Assets		Liabilities	
Cash and other reserves	$ 300	Deposits	$1,100
Loans	900	Capital	100
	$1,200		$1,200

The immigrant's deposit raises deposit liabilities and cash assets by the same amount. Since both cash and deposits rise by $100, the cash reserve ratio, formerly 0.20, now increases to 0.27. The bank has more cash than it needs to provide a 20 percent reserve against its deposit liabilities.

(IB&T Co.) has assets of $200 of reserves, held partly as cash on hand and partly as deposits with the central bank, and $900 of loans outstanding to its customers. Its liabilities are $100 to those who initially contributed capital to start the bank, and $1,000 to current depositors. (All figures are in thousands of dollars.) The bank's ratio of reserves to deposits is 200/1,000 = 0.20, exactly equal to its minimum requirement.

An immigrant arrives in the country and opens an account by depositing $100 with the IB&T Co. This is a wholly new deposit for the bank, and it results in a revised balance sheet (Table 33-3). As a result of the immigrant's new deposit, both cash assets and deposit liabilities have risen by $100. More important, the reserve ratio has increased from 0.20 to 300/1,100 = 0.27. The bank now has excess reserves—with $300 in reserves it could support $1,500 in deposits.

A Single Monopoly Bank

If the IB&T Co. were the only bank in the system, it would know that any loans that it made would eventually give rise to new deposits of an equal amount. It would then be in a position to say to the next business executive who comes in for a loan, "We will lend your firm $400 at the going rate of interest." The bank would do so by adding that amount to the firm's deposit account. Table

TABLE 33-4 **THE MONOPOLY BANK'S BALANCE SHEET AFTER MAKING A $400 LOAN (Thousands of Dollars)**

Assets		Liabilities	
Cash and other reserves	$ 300	Deposits	$1,500
Loans	1,300	Capital	100
	$1,600		$1,600

The loan restores the reserve ratio of 0.20. By increasing its loans by a multiple of its new cash deposit, the bank restores its reserve ratio of 0.20.

33-4 shows what would happen in this case. The new immigrant's deposit initially raised cash assets and deposit liabilities by $100. The new loans created an additional $400 of deposit liabilities. This restored the reserve ratio to its legal minimum (300/1,500 = 0.20), and no further expansion of deposit money is possible. As the bank's customers do business with each other, settling their accounts by checks, the ownership of the deposits will be continually changing. But what matters to the bank is that its total deposits will remain constant.

The extent to which a monopoly bank could increase its loans *and thus its deposits* (which are part of the money supply) depends on the reserve ratio. Because in this case the ratio is 1/5(= 0.20), the bank would be able to expand deposits to five times the original acquisition of money. In general, if the reserve ratio is *r*, a bank can increase its deposits by 1/*r* times any new reserves. As we shall see, this general relationship proves true of a banking system whether or not there is a monopoly bank. [38]

Many Banks

Deposit creation is more complicated in a multibank system than in a single-bank system, but *the end result is exactly the same*. It is more complicated because, when a bank makes a loan, the recipient of the loan may pay the money to someone who deposits it not in the original bank but in another bank. How this works is most easily seen under the extreme assumption that every new borrower immediately withdraws the borrowed funds from the lending bank and pays someone who in turn deposits the money in another bank or banks.

With its present level of deposits at $1,100, the bank needs only $220 of reserves (0.20 × $1,100 = $220), so it can lend the $80 excess that it has on hand. Table 33-5 shows the position after this has been done and after the proceeds of the loan have been withdrawn to be deposited to the account of a customer of another bank. The Immigrants Bank once again has a 20 percent reserve ratio.

So far deposits in the IB&T Co. have increased by only the initial $100 of new immigrant's money with which we started, as shown in Table 33-3. (Of this, $20 is held as a cash reserve against the deposit and $80 has been lent out in the system.) But other banks have received new deposits of $80 as the persons receiving payment from the firm or household who borrowed the $80 from the Immigrants Bank deposited those payments in their own banks. The receiving banks (sometimes called *second-generation banks*) receive new deposits of $80, and when the checks clear, they have new reserves of $80. Because they require an addition to their reserves of only $16 to support the new deposit, they have $64 of excess reserves. They now increase their loans by $64. After this money is spent by the borrowers and has been deposited in other, third-generation banks, the balance sheets of the

TABLE 33-5 **THE IB&T CO. BALANCE SHEET AFTER A NEW LOAN AND CASH DRAIN OF $80**

Assets		Liabilities	
Cash and other reserves	$ 220	Deposits	$1,100
Loans	980	Capital	100
	$1,200		$1,200

The bank lends its surplus cash and suffers a cash drain. The bank keeps $20 as a reserve against the new deposit of $100. It lends $80 to a customer who writes a check to someone who deals with another bank. When the check is cleared, the IB&T Co. has suffered an $80 cash drain, has increased its loans by $80, and has restored its reserve ratio to 0.20.

TABLE 33–6 CHANGES IN THE BALANCE SHEETS OF SECOND-GENERATION BANKS (Thousands of Dollars)

Assets		Liabilities	
Cash and other reserves	+$16	Deposits	+$80
Loans	+ 64		
	+$80		+$80

Second-generation banks receive cash deposits and expand loans. The second-generation banks gain new deposits of $80 as a result of the loan granted by the IB&T Co., which is used to make payments to customers of the second-generation banks. These banks keep 20 percent of the cash they acquire as their reserve against the new deposit, and they can make new loans using the other 80 percent. When the customers who borrowed the money make payments to the customers of third-generation banks, a cash drain occurs.

second-generation banks will have changed, as in Table 33-6.

The third-generation banks now find themselves with $64 of new deposits. Against these they need hold only $12.80 in cash, so they have excess reserves of $51.20 that they can immediately lend out. Thus there begins a long sequence of new deposits, new loans, new deposits, and new loans. The stages are shown in Table 33-7. The series in the table should look familiar, for it is the same convergent process we met when dealing with the multiplier.

The banking system has created new deposits and thus new money, although each banker can honestly say, "All I did was invest my excess reserves. I can do no more than manage wisely the money I receive."

If r is the reserve ratio, the ultimate effect on the deposits of the banking system of a new deposit will be $1/r$ times the new deposit. [39] This is

TABLE 33–7 MANY BANKS, A SINGLE NEW DEPOSIT (Thousands of Dollars)

Bank	New deposits	New loans	Addition to reserves
Immigrants Bank	$100.00	$ 80.00	$ 20.00
Second-generation bank	80.00	64.00	16.00
Third-generation bank	64.00	51.20	12.80
Fourth-generation bank	51.20	40.96	10.24
Fifth-generation bank	40.96	32.77	8.19
Sixth-generation bank	32.77	26.22	6.55
Seventh-generation bank	26.22	20.98	5.24
Eighth-generation bank	20.98	16.78	4.20
Ninth-generation bank	16.78	13.42	3.36
Tenth-generation bank	13.42	10.74	2.68
Total first 10 generations	446.33	357.07	89.26
All remaining generations	53.67	42.93	10.74
Total for banking systems	$500.00	$400.00	$100.00

The banking system as a whole can create deposit money whenever it receives new reserves. The table shows the process of the creation of deposit money on the assumptions that all the loans made by one set of banks end up as deposits in another set of banks (called the *next-generation banks*), that the required reserve ratio (r) is 0.20, and that there are no excess reserves. Although each bank suffers a cash drain whenever it grants a new loan, the system as a whole does not, and the system ends up doing in a series of steps what a monopoly bank would do all at once; that is, it increases deposit money by $1/r$, which in this example is five times the amount of any increase in reserves that it obtains.

exactly the same result reached in the monopoly bank case.[3]

Many Deposits

The two cases discussed above, the monopoly bank and the single new deposit in a many-bank situation, serve this purpose: They show that under either set of opposite extreme assumptions, the result is the same. So it is, too, in intermediate situations where banks suffer some, but less than a total, cash drain to other banks. A far more realistic picture of the process of deposit creation is one in which new deposits (or new withdrawals) tend to accrue simultaneously to all banks, perhaps because of changes in the monetary policy of the government. Say, for example, that the community contains ten banks of equal size and that each received new deposits of $100 in cash. Now each bank is in the position shown in Table 33-3, and each can begin to expand deposits based on the $100 of excess reserves. (Each bank does this by granting loans to customers.)

Because each bank does one-tenth of the total banking business, an average of 90 percent of any newly created deposit will find its way into other banks as the customer pays other people in the community by check. This will represent a cash drain from the lending bank to the other banks. However, 10 percent of each new deposit created by every other bank should find its way into this bank. All banks receive new cash and all begin creating deposits simultaneously; no bank should suffer a significant cash drain to any other bank.

Thus all banks can go on expanding deposits without losing cash to each other; they need only worry about keeping enough cash to satisfy those depositors who will occasionally require cash. The expansion can go on with each bank watching its own ratio of cash reserves to deposits, expanding

deposits as long as the ratio exceeds 1/5 and ceasing when it reaches that figure. The process will come to a halt when each bank has created $400 in additional deposits, so that for each initial $100 cash deposit, there is now $500 in deposits backed by $100 in cash. Now *each* of the banks will have entries in its books similar to those shown in Table 33-4.

The general rule, if there is no cash drain, is that a banking system with a reserve ratio of r can change its deposits by $1/r$ times any change in reserves.

Excess Reserves and Cash Drains

Two of the simplifying assumptions made earlier can now be relaxed.

Excess reserves. If banks do not choose to invest excess reserves, the multiple expansion discussed will not occur. Turn back to Table 33-3. If the Immigrants Bank had been content to hold 27 percent reserves, it might well have done nothing more. Other things being equal, banks will choose to invest excess reserves because of the profit motive. But there may be times when they believe the risk is too great. It is one thing to be offered 12 percent or even 24 percent interest on a loan, but if the borrower defaults on the payment of interest and principal, the bank will be the loser. Similarly, if the bank expects interest rates to rise in the future, it may hold off making loans now so that it will have reserves available to make more profitable loans after the interest rate has risen.

There is nothing automatic about credit expansion; it rests on the decisions of bankers. If banks do not choose to use excess reserves to expand their investments, there will not be an expansion of deposits.

Banks tend to hold larger excess reserves in times of business recession, when there is a low demand for loans and very low interest rates, than they do in periods of boom, when the demand for loans is great and interest rates are high.

The significance of relaxing the assumption of

---

[3] The "multiple expansion of deposits" that has just been worked through applies in reverse to a withdrawal of funds. Deposits of the banking system will fall by a multiple of $1/r$ times any amount withdrawn from the bank and not redeposited at another.

no excess reserves is that it cuts the automatic link between the creation of excess reserves and money creation.

Excess reserves make it *possible* for the banks to expand the money supply, but only if they want to do so.

The money supply is thus at least partially determined by the commercial banks in response to such forces as changes in national income and interest rates. However, the upper limit of deposits is determined by the required reserve ratio and by the reserves available to the banks, both of which are under the control of the central bank.

Cash drain. Suppose firms and households find it convenient to keep a fixed *fraction* of their money holding in cash (say 5 percent) instead of a fixed *amount* of dollars. In that case an extra $100 in money supply will not all stay in the banking system; only $95 will remain on deposit, while the rest will be added to money in circulation. In such a situation any multiple expansion of bank deposits will be accompanied by a cash drain to the public that will reduce the maximum expansion below what it was when the public was content to hold all its new money as bank deposits. Table 33-8 shows the position of a typical bank after a credit expansion of $400 and a cash drain of $20.

The story of deposit creation when there is a cash drain to the public might go like this: Each bank starts creating deposits and suffers no significant cash drain to other banks. But because approximately 5 percent of newly created deposits is withdrawn to be held as cash, each bank suffers a cash drain to the public. The expansion continues, each bank watching its own ratio of cash reserves to deposits, expanding deposits as long as the ratio exceeds 1/5 and ceasing when it reaches that figure. Because the expansion is accompanied by a cash drain, it will come to a halt with a smaller deposit expansion than in the no cash drain case.[4]

THE MONEY SUPPLY

The total stock of money in the economy at any moment is called the **money supply** or the **supply of money.** Economists and financial analysts tend to use a number of different definitions for the money supply, many of which are regularly reported in the *Federal Reserve Bulletin.* Typically the definitions involve the sum of currency in circulation plus some types of deposit liabilities of financial institutions. Definitions vary in terms of what deposits are included. Different definitions come into use or go out of favor as the importance of different types of deposits change. A customer's deposit in a bank can be kept in one of two basic forms, as a demand deposit or as a time deposit.

Demand Deposits

A **demand deposit** means that the customer can withdraw the money on demand (i.e., without giving any notice of intention to withdraw). Demand deposits are transferable by check. Such a check instructs the bank to pay without a delay a stated sum of money to the person to whom the check is made payable. Until very recently banks in the United States were prohibited from paying interest on demand deposits.

TABLE 33–8 **THE MONOPOLY BANK'S BALANCE SHEET AFTER A CREDIT EXPANSION AND AN ACCOMPANYING CASH DRAIN**

Assets		Liabilities	
Cash and reserves	$ 280	Deposits	$1,480
Loans	1,300	Capital	100
	$1,580		$1,580

The maximum possible deposit expansion is reduced by a cash drain. This example differs from that shown in Table 33-4 because, after a new deposit of $100 and a new loan of $400, 5 percent of the newly created money is withdrawn as cash to be held by the public. Cash and deposits each fall by $20 and the reserve ratio falls below 20 percent.

[4] It can be shown algebraically that the percentage of cash drain must be added to the reserve ratio to determine the maximum possible expansion of deposits. [40]

Time Deposits

A **time deposit** is an interest-bearing deposit that is legally withdrawable only after a certain amount of notice, such as 30 days for a passbook account and up to six months on certificates of deposit. Although banks, savings and loan associations, and other savings institutions do not usually enforce this delay, they could legally do so if proposed withdrawals threatened their reserves. Until quite recently it was impossible to pay a bill by writing a check on a time deposit. A depositor wishing to use a time deposit to pay a bill had to withdraw money from a savings (time) account and then either pay the bill in cash or deposit the funds in a demand account and then write a check on the demand account.

The Disappearing Distinction Between Demand and Time Deposits

For decades interest rates on time deposits amounted to only a few percent, and people were content to keep their savings in time deposits and their reserves of cash for ordinary transactions in demand deposits. Then, interest rates available on time deposits and other safe liquid investments grew, and it became more and more expensive (in terms of lost interest) to keep cash in demand deposits, even for a week or two. Starting in the early 1970s, a series of devices were invented that tended to make it easier to convert interest-bearing deposits into demand deposits transferable by check.

One of the first was the **negotiable order of withdrawal (NOW)**, a checklike instruction to the savings institution to transfer funds from the depositor's time deposit to the recipient of the **NOW**. A similar device is the **automatic transfer service (ATS)**, which allows depositors to maintain both a demand and a time deposit at the bank and to make all deposits to the time deposit. The bank automatically transfers funds to the demand deposit as needed to cover checks when they are written. This permits the customer to maintain only a small minimum amount (for example, $200) in the demand deposit account. All the rest earns interest. The ATS comes close to being both a demand deposit

that pays interest and a time deposit that can be transferred by check. Nonbank financial institutions such as brokerage firms now offer **money market mutual funds (MMFs)**, which earn high interest and are checkable—although usually subject to minimum withdrawal restrictions. Growth in MMFs was phenomenal in the early 1980s. They increased *sixteenfold* from the end of 1978 to the end of 1981. Many banks now offer similar instruments called *money market accounts*.

New devices such as NOW, ATS, and money market accounts have all but obliterated the distinction between time and demand deposits.

Definitions of the Money Supply

Different definitions of the money supply include different types of deposits. Narrow definitions include currency plus those deposits that are readily used to finance day-to-day transactions. Broader definitions include other deposits as well.

Prior to 1980, when the distinction between demand and time deposits was quite clear, narrow money was defined simply as the sum of currency plus demand deposits. The growth in ATS, NOW, and money market accounts led, in 1980, to the creation of two measures of narrowly defined money. **M1** as conventionally defined—currency plus demand deposits—became M1A, and a new definition, M1B, was introduced. M1B incorporated M1A plus NOW, ATS, and similar accounts at credit unions and mutual savings banks. In 1982 the Fed stopped publishing a series for M1A (the original M1) and M1B has been renamed M1.

Broader definitions include M2 and M3. **M2** is M1 plus savings and smaller time deposits of all kinds, including money-market fund shares. **M3** is M2 plus large denomination **certificates of deposit (CD)**. CDs are savings deposits, the evidence for which is a slip of paper, or certificate, rather than an entry in the saver's passbook. The most important is the large denomination, negotiable CD, which is designed to attract funds from large businesses. These pay a much higher rate of interest than ordinary savings deposits.

TABLE 33–9 **MONEY SUPPLY IN THE UNITED STATES, 1978 AND 1982 (Billions of Dollars)**

	1978	1982
Currency	97.4	132.6
Demand deposits	257.4	244.6
Other checkable deposits (including NOW and ATS)	8.4	101.3
M1	363.2	478.5
Savings deposits[a]	479.9	400.3
Small time deposits	557.9	949.8
MMFs	7.1	177.5
M2	1,403.9	1,999.1
Large time deposits[b]	225.1	404.6
M3	1,629.0	2,403.7

Source: Economic Report of the President, 1983.
[a] Includes money market account introduced December 1982.
[b] Over $100,000.

There are several widely used measures of the money supply. The traditional, narrow view of the money supply concentrates on currency and demand deposits and checkable substitutes such as NOW and ATS (M1). M2 and M3 add in deposits that serve the store-of-value function and can be readily converted into demand deposits or cash on a dollar-for-dollar basis. The table shows the shifting pattern of deposits, with demand deposits declining in absolute and relative importance and other checkable deposits and MMFs growing sharply.

M1 concentrates on the medium-of-exchange function. The others add in highly liquid assets that serve the temporary store-of-value function and are in practice quickly convertible into a medium of exchange at a known price ($1 on deposit in a savings account is always convertible into a $1 demand deposit or $1 in cash). Table 33-9 shows the principal elements in the money supply and the changes that have occurred since 1978.

Near Money and Money Substitutes

Over the past two centuries what has been accepted by the public as money has expanded from gold and silver coins to include, first, bank notes and then bank deposits subject to transfer by check.

Until recently, most economists would have agreed that money stopped at that point. No such agreement exists today, and an important debate centers on the definition of money appropriate to the present world.

If we concentrate only on the medium-of-exchange function of money, there is little doubt about what is money in America today. Money consists of notes, coins, and deposits subject to transfer by check or checklike instruments. No other asset constitutes a generally accepted medium of exchange; indeed, even notes and checks are not universally accepted—as you will discover if you try to buy a pack of cigarettes with a $1,000 bill (or even a $100 bill in a corner grocery store) or if you try to walk out of a store on a Saturday afternoon with a mink coat after having offered your personal check in exchange. But these exceptions are unimportant.

The problem of deciding what is money arises because cash, which best fulfills the medium-of-exchange function, may provide relatively poor ways to meet the store-of-value function (see Table 33-10). Interest-earning assets will do a better job of meeting this function of money than will currency or demand deposits that earn no interest. At the same time, however, they are less capable of

TABLE 33–10 **THE DOLLAR AS A STORE OF VALUE SINCE 1962**

$1 put aside in	Had the purchasing power 5 years later of	Its average annual loss of value was
1962	$.91	1.6%
1967	.80	4.6%
1972	.69	7.7%
1977	.63	9.7%

The dollar has become an increasingly less satisfactory store of value over the last two decades. The second column shows the purchasing power, measured by the Consumer Price Index, of $1 five years after it was saved (assuming it earned no interest). In order for it to have maintained its real purchasing power, it would have had to earn the annual percentage return shown in the last column. The growth in the required return explains the increasing use of near moneys and money substitutes that (unlike currency and demand deposits) earn interest.

filling the medium-of-exchange function. NOW and ATS accounts provide a better store of value than currency and demand deposits, without too much loss of the medium-of-exchange function. Once it is recognized that there is a trade-off between these functions, it is possible to consider other monetary assets.

Near Money

Assets that fulfill adequately the store-of-value function and are readily converted into a medium of exchange but are not themselves a medium of exchange are sometimes called **near money.** Deposits at a savings and loan association are a characteristic form of near money. When you have a deposit at a savings and loan association, you know exactly how much purchasing power you hold (at today's prices) and, given modern banking practices, you can turn your deposit into a medium of exchange—cash or a checking deposit—at a moment's notice. Additionally, your deposit will earn some interest during the period that you hold it. Why then does not everybody keep their money in such deposits instead of in demand deposits or currency? The answer is that the inconvenience of continually shifting money back and forth may outweigh the interest that can be earned. One week's interest on $100 (at 5 percent per year) is only about $.10, not enough to cover carfare to the bank or the cost of mailing a letter. For money that will be needed soon, it would hardly pay to shift it to a time deposit.

In general, whether it pays to convert cash or demand deposits into interest-earning savings deposits for a given period will depend on the inconvenience and other transaction costs of shifting funds in and out on the amount of interest that can be earned.

There is a wide spectrum of assets in the economy that pay interest and also serve as reasonably satisfactory temporary stores of value. The difference between these assets and savings deposits is that their capital values are not quite as certain as are those of savings deposits. If I elect to store my purchasing power in the form of a treasury bill that matures in 30 days, its price on the market may change between the time I buy it and the time I want to sell it—say 10 days later. If the price changes, I will suffer or enjoy a change in the purchasing power available to me. But because of the short horizon to maturity, the price will not change very much. (After all, the government will pay the bond's face value in a few weeks.) Such a security is thus a reasonably satisfactory short-run store of purchasing power. Indeed any readily salable capital asset whose value does not fluctuate significantly with the rate of interest will satisfactorily fulfill this short-term, store-of-value function.

Money Substitutes

Things that serve as a temporary medium of exchange but are not a store of value are sometimes called **money substitutes.** Credit cards are a prime example. With a credit card many transactions can be made without either cash or a check. The evidence of credit, the credit slip you sign and hand over to the store, is not money because it cannot be used to make further transactions. Furthermore, when your credit card company sends you a bill, you have to use money in (delayed) payment for the original transaction. The credit card serves the short-run function of a medium of exchange by allowing you to make purchases even though you have no cash or bank deposit currently in your possession. But this is only temporary; money remains the final medium of exchange for these transactions when the credit account is settled.

Changing Concepts of What Is Money

What is an acceptable enough medium of exchange to count as money has changed and will continue to change over time. NOW and ATS accounts have broadened the spectrum. New monetary assets (such as certificates of deposit and money-market fund shares) are continuously being developed to serve some, if not all, the functions of money, and they are more or less readily convertible into money. There is no single, timeless definition of what is money and what is only near money or a money substitute. Indeed, as we have seen, our monetary authorities use several different definitions of money, and these definitions change from year to year.

SUMMARY

1. Early economic theory regarded the economy as being divided into a real part and a money part. The real part was concerned with production, the allocation of resources, and the distribution of income—determined only by relative prices. The monetary part merely determined the level of prices at which real transactions took place. This was determined by the quantity of money. Double the quantity of money, and in the new equilibrium all money prices would double but relative prices and the entire real sector would be left unaffected. Modern economists recognize interconnections between the two parts, as will be discussed in Chapter 34.

2. Inflation has been a common but by no means constant state of affairs in world history. Although inflation is widespread in the world today, the rate of inflation varies greatly from country to country.

3. Traditionally in economics, money has referred to any generally accepted medium of exchange. A number of functions of money may, however, be distinguished—the major ones are the medium of exchange, the store of value, and the unit of account.

4. Money arose because of the inconvenience of barter, and it developed in stages from precious metal to metal coinage, to paper money convertible to precious metal, to token coinage and paper money fractionally backed by precious metals, to fiat money, and to deposit money. Societies have shown great sophistication in developing monetary instruments to meet their needs.

5. The banking system in the United States consists of two main elements: commercial banks and the Federal Reserve System, which is the central bank. Each has an important effect on the money supply.

6. American commercial banks are profit-seeking institutions that allow their customers to transfer demand deposits from one bank to another by means of checks. They create and destroy money as a by-product of their commercial operations—by making or liquidating loans and various other investments.

7. Because most customers are content to pay their accounts by check rather than by cash, the banks need not keep anything like a 100 percent reserve against their deposit liabilities. Consequently banks are able to create deposit money. When the banking system receives a new cash deposit, it can create new deposits to some multiple of this amount. The amount of new deposits created depends on the legal minimum reserves the Federal Reserve enforces on the banks, the amount of cash drain to the public, and whether the banks choose to hold excess reserves.

8. There is nothing automatic about the expansion of the money supply when reserves of commercial banks increase. If bankers do not choose to use excess reserves to expand their investments, there will be no expansion. In normal times it is profitable for bankers to keep excess reserves small, but in times of depression they may not find the investment risks worth taking.

9. The money supply—the stock of money in the country at a specific moment—can be defined in various ways. M1 is currency plus demand deposits plus checkable substitutes, the narrowest definition now in use. (M1 was about $475 billion in 1983.) M3, the widest commonly used definition, adds in all time and savings deposits. (M3 was about $2,400 billion in 1983.)

TOPICS FOR REVIEW

Real and monetary parts of the economy
Functions of money

Gresham's law
Fully backed, fractionally backed, and fiat money
The creation and destruction of deposit money
Reserve ratio, required reserves, and excess reserves
Demand and time deposits
The money supply
Near money and money substitutes

DISCUSSION QUESTIONS

1. "For the love of money is the root of all evil" (I Timothy 6:10). If a nation were to become a theocracy and money were made illegal, would you expect the level of national income to be affected? How about the productivity of labor? Might classical economists have answered this question differently than modern ones?

2. Consider each of the following with respect to its potential use as a medium of exchange, a store of value, and a unit of account. Which would you think might be regarded as money? (a) a $100 Federal Reserve note, (b) an American Express credit card, (c) a painting by Picasso, (d) a NOW account, (e) a U.S. Treasury certificate of indebtedness payable in three months, (f) a savings account at a savings and loan association in Las Vegas, Nevada, (g) one share of American Telephone & Telegraph Company stock, (h) a lifetime pass to Pittsburgh Steelers football games.

3. When in 1976 the Austrian government minted a new 1,000 shilling gold coin—worth $59 face value—the one-inch diameter coin came into great demand among jewelers and coin collectors. By law, the number of such coins to be minted each year is limited. Lines of people eager to get the coins formed outside the government mint and local banks.

   "There is exceptional interest in the new coin," said a Viennese banker. "It's a numismatic hit and a financial success." It has disappeared from circulation, however. Explain why.

4. In Canada, American and Canadian coins often circulate side by side, exchanging at their face values, even though notes often are of unequal value. Someone who receives a U.S. coin has the option of spending it at face value or taking it to the bank and converting it to Canadian money at the going rate of exchange. When the rate of exchange was near "par," so that $1 Canadian was within plus or minus $0.03 of $1 U.S., the two monies circulated side by side. When the Canadian dollar fell to $0.80 U.S., predict which money disappeared from circulation according to Gresham's law. Why did a $0.03 differential not produce this result?

5. Some years ago a strike closed all banks in Ireland for several months. What do you think happened to money, near money, and money substitutes during the period?

6. During hyperinflations in several foreign countries after World War II, American cigarettes were sometimes used in place of money. What made them suitable?

7. Take some five-year period during the last 10 years and (using library sources) calculate which of the following was the best store of value over that period: (a) the dollar, (b) the Dow Jones industrial average, (c) a Georgia Power 11¾ percent, '05 bond, (d) gold, (e) silver. How confident are you that the one that was the best store of value over those five years will be the best over the *next* 18 months?

8. If all depositors tried to turn their deposits into cash at once, they would find that there are not sufficient reserves in the system to allow all of them to do this at the same time. Why then do we not still have panicky runs on the banks? Would a 100 percent reserve requirement be safer? What effect would such a reserve requirement have on the banking system's ability to create money? Would it preclude any possibility of a panic?

9. What would be the effect on the money supply of each of the following?
   a. a decline in the public's confidence in the banks
   b. a desire on the part of banks to increase their levels of excess reserves
   c. the monopolizing of the banking system into a single super bank
   d. the increased use of credit cards
   e. allowing banks to pay any level of interest they wish on demand deposits.

34 THE ROLE OF MONEY IN MACROECONOMICS

At one time or another most of us have known the surprise of opening our wallet or purse to discover that we had either more or less money than we thought. There can be as much pleasure in deciding how to spend an unexpected windfall in the first case as there can be pain in deciding what intended expenditure to eliminate in the second case.

What determines how much money people hold in their purses and wallets and how much they keep in the bank? What happens when everyone discovers that they are holding more, or less, money than they believe they need to hold?

These turn out to be key questions for our study of the influence of money on output and prices. The answers will help us to establish links between the money supply and the aggregate expenditure and aggregate demand functions.

Kinds of Assets

At any moment in time households have a given stock of wealth. This wealth is held in many forms. Some of it is money in the bank or in the wallet; some is in short-term securities such as CDs, money market shares, and treasury bills; some is in long-term bonds; and some is in real capital, which may be held directly (in the form of family businesses) or indirectly (in the form of shares that indicate ownership of a corporation's assets).

These ways of holding wealth may be grouped into three main categories: (1) assets that serve as a medium of exchange, that is, paper money, coins, and bank checking deposits; (2) other financial assets, such as bonds earning a fixed rate of interest, that will yield a fixed money value at some future date (called the *maturity date*) and that can usually be sold before maturity for a price that fluctuates on the open market; and (3) claims on real capital (physical objects such as factories and machines).

Money and bonds. To simplify our discussion, it is helpful to regroup wealth into only two categories: money and bonds. By money we mean M1 as defined in Chapter 33; and by bonds we mean everything else. Money therefore includes currency and demand deposits and NOW, ATS, and similar accounts. Bonds include all other interest-earning financial assets *plus* claims in real capital.[1]

The Rate of Interest and the Price of Bonds

A bond is a promise by the issuer to pay a stated sum of money as interest each year and to repay the face value of the bond at some future maturity date, often many years distant. The time until the date is called the **term to maturity** or often simply the **term** of the bond. Some bonds, called perpetuities, pay interest forever and never repay the principal.

The price of any bond reflects the value of the stream of future payments that its owner will receive.

[1] This simplification can take us quite a long way. However, for some problems it is necessary to treat debt and equity as distinct assets so that three categories—money, debt (bonds), and equity stocks—are used.

The relationship between interest rates and bond prices is most easily seen in the case of a perpetuity. Assume that such a bond will pay $100 per year to its holder. The *present value* of this bond depends on how much $100 per year is worth, and this in turn depends on the rate of interest. (The discussion of the concept of present value in Chapter 22, pages 389–390, may profitably be read at this time.)

A bond that will produce a stream of income of $100 a year forever is worth $1,000 at 10 percent interest because $1,000 invested at 10 percent per year will yield $100 interest per year forever. But the same bond is worth $2,000 when the interest rate is 5 percent per year because it takes $2,000 invested at 5 percent per year to yield $100 interest per year. The lower the rate of interest obtainable on the market, the more valuable is a bond paying a fixed amount of interest.

Similar relations apply to bonds that are not perpetuities, though the calculation of present value must allow for the lump-sum repayment of principal at maturity.

In general, the present value of any asset that yields a stream of money over time is negatively related to the interest rate.

This proposition has two important implications: (1) if the rate of interest falls, the value of an asset producing a given income stream will rise; and (2) when the market price of an asset producing a given income is forced up, this is equivalent to a decrease in the rate of interest earned by the asset.

Thus a promise to pay $100 one year from now is worth $92.59 when the interest rate is 8 percent and only $89.29 when the interest rate is 12 percent: $92.59 at 8 percent interest ($92.59 × 1.08) and $89.29 at 12 percent interest ($89.29 × 1.12) are both worth $100 in one year's time.

The present value of bonds that are not perpetuities becomes increasingly dominated by the fixed redemption value as the maturity date approaches. Take an extreme case: The present value of a bond that is redeemable for $1,000 in a week's time will be very close to $1,000 no matter what the interest rate. Thus its value will not change much even if the rate of interest leaps from 5 percent to 10 percent during that week.

The sooner is the maturity date of a bond, the less the bond's value will change with a change in the rate of interest.

For example, a rise in the interest rate from 8 to 12 percent will lower the value of $100 payable in one year's time by 3.6 percent but will lower the value of $100 payable in ten years time by 37.9 percent.[2]

THE SUPPLY OF AND THE DEMAND FOR MONEY

The Supply of Money

The supply of money is a stock: It is so many billions of dollars. (It is *not* a flow of so much per unit of time.) In January 1983 M1 was approximately $480 billion.

We saw in the previous chapter that deposit money is created by the commercial banking system, but only within limits set by their reserves, which are under the control of the Federal Reserve Board. Thus the ultimate control of the money supply is in the Fed's hands. In Chapter 35 we shall look at the degree to which the Fed can in fact control the money supply. In this chapter we shall simplify by assuming that the money supply can be precisely controlled by the Fed.

The Demand for Money

The amount of wealth everyone in the economy wishes to hold in the form of money balances is called the **demand for money.** Because households have only one decision to make on how to divide their given stock of wealth between money and bonds, it follows that if we know the demand for money, we also know the demand for bonds. If with a given level of wealth the demand for money rises, then the demand for bonds must fall: if people wish to hold $1 billion more money, they must wish to hold $1 billion less of bonds. It also follows that if households are in equilibrium with respect to their money holdings, they are in equilibrium with respect to their bond holdings.

What Determines The Demand for Money?

When we say that on January 2, 1983, the demand for money was $480 billion, we mean that on that date everyone wished to hold money balances that totaled $480 billion. But why do firms and households wish to hold money balances at all? There is a cost to holding any money balance. The money could instead be used to purchase bonds; it would then earn more interest.[3]

The opportunity cost of holding any money balance is the extra interest that could have been earned if the money had instead been used to purchase interest earning assets.

Clearly money will be held only when it provides services that are valued at least as highly as the opportunity cost of holding it. The services provided by money balances are, first, to finance purchases and sales; second, to provide a cushion against uncertainty about the timing of cash flows; and third, to provide a hedge against uncertainty over the prices of other financial assets. The desire to hold money to obtain each of these services is

---

[2] The example assumes annual compounding. The first case is calculated from the numbers of the previous example: $(92.58 - 89.29)/92.58$. The 10-year case uses the formula

$$\text{present value} = \text{principal}/(1 + r)^n$$

which gives $46.30 with 8 percent and $28.75 with 12 percent. The percentage fall in value is thus $(46.30 - 28.75)/46.30 = 0.379$.

[3] As we saw in Chapter 33, the definition of M1 was changed in 1982 to include some interest-bearing checkable deposits. This complicates but does not fundamentally alter the analysis of the demand for money. In particular, it means that the opportunity cost of holding those interest-bearing components of M1 is not the *level* of interest rates paid on bonds but the *differential* between that rate and the rate paid on M1 assets. For simplicity, we treat the interest rate on all M1 assets as being zero so that we can identify the *level* of the interest rate on bonds as the opportunity cost of money.

summarized by the so-called transactions, precautionary, and speculative motives for holding money. We now examine each of these motives in detail.

National Income and the Demand for Money: The Transactions Motive

The majority of the transactions that take place in any economy require money. Money passes from households to firms to pay for the goods and services produced by firms; money passes from firms to households to pay for the factor services supplied by households to firms. Money balances that are held to finance such flows are called **transactions balances.**

In an imaginary world, where the receipts and disbursements of households and firms were perfectly synchronized, it would be unnecessary to hold transactions balances. If every time a household spent $10 it received $10 as part payment of its income, no transactions balances would be needed. In the real world, however, receipts and disbursements are not perfectly synchronized.

Consider, for example, the balances held because of wage payments. Assume, for purposes of illustration, that firms pay wages every Friday and that households spend all their wages on the purchase of goods and services, with the expenditure being spread out evenly over the week. Thus on Friday morning firms must hold balances equal to the weekly wage bill; on Friday afternoon households will hold these balances. Over the week, households' balances will be drawn down as a result of purchasing goods and services. Over the same period, the balances held by firms will build up as a result of selling goods and services until, on the following Friday morning, firms will again have amassed balances equal to the wage bill that must be met on that day.

On the average over the week, firms will hold balances equal to half the wage bill, and so will households; thus, in this example, total money balances held will be equal to the total weekly wage bill. Notice that while the money circulates so that each group holds a varying balance over the week, the combined demand for balances summed over the two groups remains constant.

Our argument has been conducted in terms of the wage bill, but a similar analysis holds for all receipts and payments of households and firms. Because their receipts and payments are not perfectly synchronized, they must hold money balances to bridge the gap.

The transactions demand for money arises because of the nonsynchronization of payments and receipts.

What determines the size of the transactions balances to be held? It is clear that in the above example total transactions balances vary with the value of the wage bill. If the wage bill doubles for any reason (e.g., because twice as much labor is hired at the same wage rate or because the same amount of labor is hired at twice the wage rate), the transactions balances held by firms and households on this account will also double. As it is with wages so it is with all other transactions: the size of the balances held is positively related to the value of the transactions.

Next we must ask how the total value of transactions is related to national income. Because of the "double counting" problem first discussed on page 507, the value of all transactions exceeds the value of the economy's final output. When the flour mill buys wheat from the farmer and when the baker buys flour from the mill, both are transactions against which money balances must be held, although only the value added at each stage is part of national income. Typically the total value of transactions tends to be 5 to 10 times as large as the total value of final output, which is national income.

We now make an added assumption that there is a stable, positive relation between transactions and national income: if a rise in aggregate expenditure leads to a rise in national income, it also leads to a rise in the total value of all transactions and hence to an associated rise in the demand for transactions balances. This allows us to relate transactions balances to national income. [41]

The larger the value of national income measured in current prices, the larger the value of transactions balances that will be held.

National Income and the Demand for Money: The Precautionary Motive

Many goods and services are sold on credit. The seller can never be certain when payment for those goods will be made, and the buyer can never be certain of the day of delivery and thus of the day on which payment will fall due. In order to avoid cash crises when receipts are abnormally low and/or disbursements are abnormally high, firms and households carry money balances as a precaution. These are called **precautionary balances.** The larger are such balances, the greater is the degree of protection against running out of money because of temporary fluctuations in cash flows.

How serious this risk is depends on the penalties for being caught without sufficient money balances. A firm is unlikely to be pushed into insolvency, but it may have to incur considerable costs if it is forced to borrow money at high interest rates for short periods in order to meet a temporary cash crisis.

The precautionary motive arises because the firm is uncertain about the *degree* to which payments and receipts will be synchronized.

The protection provided by a given quantity of precautionary balances depends on the volume of payments and receipts. A $100 precautionary balance provides a large cushion for a person whose volume of payments per month is $200, and a very small cushion for a firm whose monthly volume is $10,000. Haphazard fluctuations of the sort that create the need for precautionary balances may be expected to vary directly with the size of the firm's cash flow. To provide the same degree of protection as the value of transactions rises, more money is necessary.[4]

The precautionary motive also causes the demand for money to vary positively with the value of national income measured at current prices.

Wealth and the Demand for Money: The Speculative Motive

Households will have to sell some of their bonds if a temporary excess of payments over receipts exceeds their money holdings. At one extreme, if a household or firm held all its wealth in bonds, it would earn interest on all that wealth, but it would have to sell some bonds the first time its payments exceeded its receipts. At the other extreme, if a household or firm held all its wealth in money, the money would earn no interest, but the household or firm would never have to sell bonds to meet excesses of payments over current receipts. Wealth holders usually do not adopt either extreme position; instead, they hold part of their wealth as money and part as bonds. (Don't forget that "bonds" are here defined to include such interest-earning assets as deposits in savings accounts, certificates of deposit, and treasury bills.)

A household that holds bonds and money runs the risk that an unexpected gap between its receipts and its payments will force it to sell some bonds. But the price of bonds fluctuates from day to day on the open market. A household that may have to sell bonds to meet a need for money takes the risk that the price of bonds may be unexpectedly low at the time it sells them. Of course, if the household is lucky, the price may be unexpectedly high. But because no one knows in advance which way the price will go, firms and households must accept a risk whenever they hold bonds. Many firms and households do not like risk—they are *risk averse.* Hence they hold less bonds and more money than they otherwise would.

The motive that leads firms to hold more money in order to avoid the risks inherent in a fluctuating price of bonds was analyzed first by Keynes. Money balances held for this purpose are called **speculative balances.** The modern analysis of this motive, sketched in the preceding paragraph, is the work of Professor James Tobin of Yale University.[5]

---

[4] Institutional arrangements affect precautionary demands. In the past, for example, a traveler would have carried a substantial precautionary balance in cash, but today a credit card covers most unforeseen expenses that may arise while traveling.

[5] Professor Tobin was awarded the Nobel Prize in Economics in 1981 for his research in monetary economics and the analysis of financial markets.

Firms and households tend to insure against this risk by holding some fraction of their wealth in money and the rest in earning assets. Thus the demand for money varies positively with wealth. For example, Ms. B. O'Reiley might elect to hold 5 percent of her wealth in money and the other 95 percent in bonds. If Ms. O'Reiley's wealth is $50,000, her demand for money will be $2,500. If her wealth increases to $60,000, her demand for money will rise to $3,000. Although an individual's wealth may rise or fall rapidly, the total wealth of a society changes only slowly. For the analysis of short-term fluctuations in national income, the effects of changes in wealth are fairly small, and we shall ignore them for the present. (Over the long term, however, variations in wealth can have a major effect on the demand for money.)

There is a second important aspect of the speculative demand for money. This leads to the extremely important relation discussed in the next section.

The Rate of Interest and the Demand for Money: Speculative and Precautionary Balances

Wealth held in cash earns no interest; hence the reduction in risk involved in holding more money, which was studied in the previous section, also carries a cost in terms of interest earnings foregone.

The speculative motive leads a household or firm to add to its money holdings until the reduction in risk obtained by the last dollar added is just balanced (in the wealth holder's view) by the cost in terms of the interest foregone on that dollar.

Because the cost of holding money balances is the interest that could have been earned if wealth had been held in bonds instead, the demand to hold money will be negatively related to the interest rate. When the rate of interest falls, the cost of holding money falls. This leads to more money being held both for precautionary motives (to reduce risks caused by uncertainty about the flows of payments and receipts) and for speculative motives (to reduce risks associated with fluctuations in the market price of bonds). When the rate of

interest rises, the cost of holding money rises. This leads to less money being held for speculative and precautionary motives.

The demand for money is negatively related to the rate of interest.[6]

Real and Nominal Money Balances: An Important Distinction

In referring to the demand for money, it is important to distinguish real from nominal values. Real values are measured in purchasing power units, nominal values in money units.

First, consider the demand for money in real terms. This means the number of units of purchasing power the public wishes to hold in the form of money balances. In an imaginary one-product, wheat economy, this would be measured by the number of bushels of wheat that could be purchased with the money balances held. In any more complex economy it could be measured in terms of the number of weeks of national income; for example, the demand for money might be equal to one month's national income. Our previous discussion suggests that the demand for money measured in purchasing-power units will be related to the real value of national income, the real value of wealth, and the rate of interest.

Now we may determine the nominal demand for money merely by multiplying real demand by the price level, P. Thus the nominal demand for money varies in proportion to the price level; that is, doubling the price level doubles nominal demand. This is a central tenet of the quantity theory of money, discussed further in the box.

The Total Demand for Money: Recapitulation

Figure 34-1 summarizes the influences of national income, the rate of interest, and the price level, the three variables that account for most of

---

[6] When the price level is changing continuously, it is necessary to distinguish the real from the nominal rate of interest. For now, there is no need to distinguish these two concepts of the interest rate since they are the same when the price level is constant, and they are measured by the market rate of interest.

THE QUANTITY THEORY OF MONEY AND THE VELOCITY OF CIRCULATION

The basic quantity theory of money can be set out formally in terms of the following four equations. Equation [1] states that the demand for money balances depends upon the value of transactions as measured by nominal income, given by the product PY.

$$M_d = kPY \qquad [1]$$

Equation [2] states that the supply of money, M, is set by the central bank at whatever level it desires.

$$M_s = M \qquad [2]$$

Equation [3] states the equilibrium condition at the demand for money must equal its supply

$$M_d = M_s \qquad [3]$$

Substitution produces the basic relation among P, M, and Y, as shown in Equation [4]

$$M = kPY \qquad [4]$$

National income, PY, is proportional to the money supply.

The original form of the Classical quantity theory assumes that k is a constant given by the transactions demand for money and that Y is constant because full employment is maintained. Thus M and P move proportionally. Increases or decreases in the money supply lead to proportional increases or decreases in prices.

Often the quantity theory is presented using the concept of the velocity of circulation, V, instead of the proportion of the money income that people wish to hold in cash, k. The **velocity of circulation** is defined as national income divided by the quantity of money, as given in Equation [5].

$$V = PY/M \qquad [5]$$

Rearranging, the quantity theory can be written in terms of the equation of exchange, Equation [6].

$$MV = PY \qquad [6]$$

Velocity may be interpreted as showing the average amount of "work" done by a unit of money while acting as a medium of exchange for the transactions that produce the country's national income. Thus, if the annual national income is $1,200 billion and the stock of money is $300 billion, then each dollar's worth of money is used on average four times to effect the exchanges required in producing national income.

Fortunately there is a simple relation between k and V. One is the reciprocal of the other, as may be seen immediately by comparing Equations [4] and [6]. Thus it makes no difference whether we choose to work with k or V. Further, if k is assumed to be constant, this implies that V must also be treated as being constant. An example may help to illustrate the interpretation of each. Assume that the stock of money people wish to hold is equal to one-fifth of the value of total transactions. Thus k is 0.2 and V, the reciprocal of k, is 5. This indicates that if the money supply is to be one-fifth of the value of annual transactions, the average unit of money must account for $5 worth of transactions—that is, each dollar must be used on average five times in order to bring about an aggregate value of national income five times as large as the stock of money.

FIGURE 34-1
The Demand for Money as a Function of Interest Rates, Income, and the Price Level

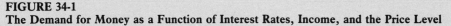

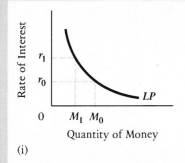
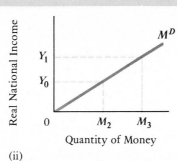
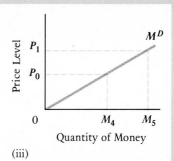

(i)   (ii)   (iii)

The quantity of money demanded varies negatively with the rate of interest and positively with both national income and the price level. In (i), the demand for money is shown varying negatively with the interest rate along the liquidity preference function. When the interest rate rises from r_0 to r_1, households and firms reduce the quantity of money demanded from M_0 to M_1.

In (ii), the demand for money is shown varying posi-

tively with national income. When national income rises from Y_0 to Y_1, households and firms increase the quantity of money demanded from M_2 to M_3.

In (iii), the demand for money is shown varying positively with the price level. When the price level rises from P_0 to P_1, households and firms increase the quantity of money demanded from M_4 to M_5.

the short-term variations in the nominal quantity of money demanded. The function relating money demand to the rate of interest is often called the **liquidity preference (LP) function.** Whichever name is used the relation describes how the quantity of money people wish to hold varies as the rate of interest varies.

MONETARY FORCES AND NATIONAL INCOME

We are now in a position to examine the relationship between monetary forces, on the one hand, and the equilibrium values of national income and the price level, on the other hand. There are two steps in explaining this relationship. The first is a new one: the link between changes in monetary equilibrium and shifts in aggregate demand. The second is familiar from earlier chapters: the effects of shifts in aggregate demand on equilibrium values of national income and the price level.

Monetary Equilibrium and Aggregate Demand: The Transmission Mechanism

Monetary equilibrium occurs when the demand for money equals the supply of money. In Chapter 5 we saw that in a competitive market for some commodity such as carrots, the price will adjust so as to ensure equilibrium. What does the same job with respect to money demand and money supply?

The answer is that the *rate of interest* will change so as to equate the demand for money to its supply. This is shown in Figure 34-2.

The condition for monetary equilibrium is that the rate of interest will be such that everyone is willing to hold the existing supply of money.

But as we saw in Chapter 31, desired investment expenditure is sensitive to changes in the interest rate. Here, then, is a link between monetary factors and real expenditure flows.

The mechanism by which changes in the demand for and the supply of money affects aggregate demand is called the **transmission mechanism.** In the next three sections we study the three stages of the transmission mechanism: first, the link between monetary equilibrium and the interest rate; second, the link between the interest rate and investment expenditure; and third, the link between investment expenditure and aggregate demand.

From Monetary Disturbances to Changes in the Rate of Interest

We saw that firms and households decide how much of their wealth to hold as money and how much to hold as bonds. When a single household or firm finds that it has less money than it wishes to hold, it can sell some bonds and add the proceeds to its money holdings. This transaction simply redistributes given supplies of bonds and money between individuals; it does not change the total supply of either money or bonds.

Now assume that everyone in the economy has an excess demand for money balances. They all try to sell bonds to add to their money balances. But what one person can do, everyone cannot do. At any moment in time, the society's total supplies of money and bonds are fixed; there is just so much money and so many bonds in existence. If everyone tries to sell bonds, there will be no one to buy them. Instead the price of bonds will fall.

We saw earlier that a fall in the price of bonds is the same thing as a rise in the rate of interest. As the interest rate rises, people economize on money balances because the opportunity cost of holding such balances is rising. This is what we saw in Figure 34-1 where the quantity of money demanded falls along the liquidity preference curve in response to a rise in the rate of interest. Eventually the interest rate will rise enough that people will no longer be trying to add to their money balances by selling bonds. At that point there is no longer an excess supply of bonds, and the interest rate will stop rising. The demand for money again equals the supply.

Assume next that firms and households hold larger money balances than they would like. A single household or firm would purchase bonds

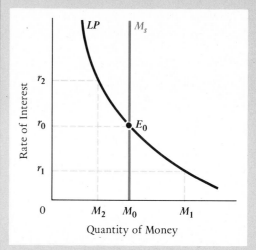

FIGURE 34-2
Monetary Equilibrium and the Rate of Interest

The interest rate rises when there is an excess demand for money and falls when there is an excess supply of money. The fixed quantity of money, M_0, is shown by the completely inelastic supply curve M_s. The demand for money is LP. Equilibrium is at E_0, with a rate of interest of r_0.

If the interest rate is r_1, there will be an excess demand for money of $M_0 M_1$. Bonds will be offered for sale in an attempt to increase money holdings. This will force the rate of interest up to r_0 (the price of bonds falls), at which point the quantity of money demanded is equal to the fixed available quantity of M_0. If the interest rate is r_2, there will be an excess supply of money $M_2 M_0$. Bonds will be demanded in return for excess money balances. This will force the rate of interest down to r_0 (the price of bonds rises), at which point the quantity of money demanded has risen to equal the fixed supply of M_0.

with its excess balances, achieving monetary equilibrium by reducing its money holdings and increasing its bond holdings. But just as in the above example, what one household or firm can do, all cannot do. At any moment in time, the total quantity of bonds is fixed so that everyone cannot simultaneously add to their holdings of bonds. When all households enter the bond market and try to purchase bonds with unwanted money balances, they bid up the price of existing bonds—the interest rate falls. Hence households and firms become willing to hold larger quantities of money; that is, the quantity of money demanded increases along the liquidity preference curve in response to a fall in the rate of interest. The rise in the price of bonds continues until firms and households stop trying to convert bonds into money. In other words, it continues until everyone is content to hold the existing supply of money and bonds.

Now look at this result in terms of the condition for monetary equilibrium. The rate of interest must adjust until people are willing to hold the fixed supply of money. If they want to hold more, their attempts to get it by selling bonds will drive up the interest rate. If they want to hold less, their attempts to buy bonds with their unwanted holdings will drive down the interest rate.

Monetary disturbances, which can arise due to either changes in the demand for or supply of money, cause changes in the interest rate.

From Changes in the Rate of Interest to Shifts in Aggregate Expenditure

The second link in the transmission mechanism is one that relates interest rates to expenditure. We saw in Chapter 31 that investment, which includes expenditure on inventory accumulation, residential construction, and plant and equipment, responds to changes in the rate of interest. Other things being equal, a decrease in the rate of interest makes borrowing cheaper and will set off a bout of new investment expenditure.[7] This negative relation between investment and the rate of interest is called the **marginal efficiency of investment (*MEI*)** function.

The first two links in the transmission mechanism are shown in Figure 34-3. We concentrate for

[7] In Chapter 31 we saw that purchases of durable consumer goods also respond to changes in interest rates. In this chapter we concentrate on investment expenditure, which may be taken to stand for *all interest-sensitive expenditure*.

FIGURE 34-3
The Effects of Changes in the Money Supply on Investment Expenditure

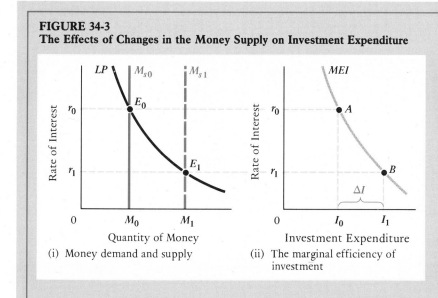

(i) Money demand and supply

(ii) The marginal efficiency of investment

Increases in the money supply reduce the rate of interest and increase desired investment expenditure. The economy is in equilibrium at E_0, with a quantity of money of M_0 (shown by the inelastic money supply curve M_s), an interest rate of r_0, and an investment expenditure of I_0 (point A). The Fed then increases the money supply to M_1 (shown by the money supply curve M_{s1}). This forces the rate of interest down to r_1 and increases investment expenditure by ΔI to I_1 (point B). This is the effect of an expansionary monetary policy.

A contractionary monetary policy reduces the money supply from M_1 to M_0, for instance. This raises interest rates from r_1 to r_0 and lowers investment expenditure by ΔI, from I_1 to I_0.

the moment on changes in the money supply, although the process can also be set in motion by changes in the demand for money. In (i), we see that a change in the money supply causes the rate of interest to change in the opposite direction. In (ii), we see that a change in the interest rate causes the level of investment expenditure to change in the opposite direction. Therefore changes in the money supply cause investment expenditure to change in the same direction.

An increase in the money supply leads to a fall in the interest rate and an increase in investment expenditure. A decrease in the money supply leads to a rise in the interest rate and a decrease in investment expenditure.

From Shifts in Aggregate Expenditure to Shifts in Aggregate Demand

Now we are back on familiar ground. In Chapter 29 we saw that a shift in the aggregate expenditure curve can lead to a shift in the AD curve. This is shown again in Figure 34-4.

Changes in the money supply, by causing changes in investment expenditure and hence shifts in the AE curve, cause the AD curve to shift.

An increase in the money supply causes an increase in investment expenditure and therefore an increase in aggregate demand. A decrease in the money supply causes a decrease in investment expenditure and therefore a decrease in aggregate demand.

The Transmission Mechanism Summarized

The transmission mechanism provides a connection between monetary forces and real expenditure flows. It works from a change in the demand for, or the supply of, money to a change in bond prices and interest rates, to changes in investment expenditure, to a *shift* in the aggregate demand curve.

Aggregate Demand, the Price Level, and National Income

A change in the money supply shifts the aggregate demand curve. If we want to know what it does to real national income and to the price level, we need

FIGURE 34-4
The Effects of Changes in the Money Supply on Aggregate Demand

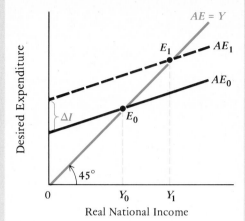

(i) Shift in aggregate expenditure

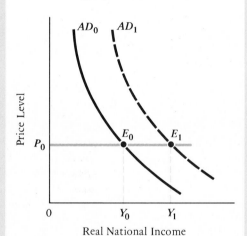

(ii) Shift in aggregate demand

Changes in the money supply cause shifts in the aggregate expenditure and aggregate demand functions. In Figure 34-3 an increase in the money supply increased desired investment expenditure by ΔI. In (i), the aggregate expenditure function shifts up by ΔI (which is the same as ΔI in Figure 34-3), from AE_0 to AE_1. At the fixed price level P_0, equilibrium income rises from Y_0 to Y_1, as shown by the horizontal shift in the aggregate demand curve from AD_0 to AD_1 in (ii).

When the supply of money falls (from M_{s1} to M_{s0} in Figure 34-3), investment falls by ΔI, thereby shifting aggregate expenditure from AE_1 to AE_0. At the fixed price level P_0, this reduces equilibrium income from Y_1 to Y_0.

to know the slope of the aggregate supply curve. This step, which is familiar from earlier chapters, is recalled in Figure 34-5.[8]

The key result is that the increase in equilibrium real income is less than the horizontal shift in the *AD* curve. This is because part of this shift is dissipated by a rise in the price level. If the aggregate demand curve were vertical, the rise in the price level would not diminish the effect on real output; real output would rise by an amount equal to the horizontal shift of the *AD* curve. But because the *AD* curve is negatively sloped, the rise in real output is smaller.

We have seen that the transmission mechanism explains the shift in the *AD* curve caused by a change in the money supply. It also explains the negative slope of the *AD* curve—that is, it explains why equilibrium national income is negatively related to the price level. This is because a rise in the price level raises the money value of transactions and thus leads to an increased demand for money. Provided the Fed holds the nominal money supply constant, there will be an excess demand for money, which brings the transmission mechanism into play. People try to sell bonds to add to their money balances, but collectively all they succeed in doing is forcing up the interest rate. The rise in the interest rate reduces investment expenditure and so reduces equilibrium national income.

In Chapter 26 we gave three reasons why the *AD* curve was negatively sloped. In Chapter 29 we relied on the wealth effect (real balance effect) to explain this negative slope because it was simple and direct. Now that we have developed a theory of money and interest rates, we are able to understand the indirect effect that works through the transmission mechanism. This effect, which could only be alluded to in Chapter 26, is more compli-

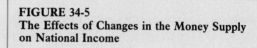

FIGURE 34-5
The Effects of Changes in the Money Supply on National Income

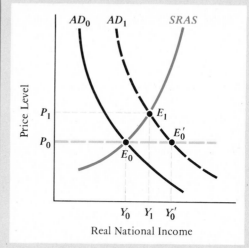

A change in the money supply leads to a change in national income that is smaller than the shift in the *AD* curve. An increase in the money supply causes the *AD* curve to shift to the right, from AD_0 to AD_1. With the price level constant, national income would rise from Y_0 to Y_0'. With the upward-sloping short-run aggregate supply curve, income only rises to Y_1 while the price level rises as well—to P_1.

cated than the direct wealth effect. But it is also much more important because, empirically, the interest rate is the most important linkage between monetary factors and real expenditure flows. The accompanying box is for those who wish to study the reasons for the slope in more detail.

The Monetary Adjustment Mechanism

Let us now examine the mechanism by which an inflationary gap is eliminated. This involves a very important but subtle implication of the theory:

A sufficiently large rise in the price level will eliminate any inflationary gap, *provided the nominal money supply remains constant.*

---

[8] Since the demand for money in general will depend on the level of national income, as shown in Figure 34-1(ii), our analysis at this stage is incomplete. The induced change in equilibrium national income will lead to a shift in the liquidity preference function in Figure 34-2. For simplicity we have assumed in the text that the liquidity preference function does not shift in response to a change in national income. The appendix to this chapter presents a formal analysis in which this effect is allowed for and in which equilibrium levels of the interest rate and national income are determined simultaneously.

THE SLOPE OF THE AGGREGATE DEMAND CURVE

Let us recall what we know about the aggregate demand curve. First, the curve relates the price level to the equilibrium level of real national income. Second, the curve is negatively sloped because the higher the price level, the lower is equilibrium national income. The main reason for this slope is found in the transmission mechanism.

Let us now follow this process in detail. Although the argument contains nothing new, it does require that you follow carefully through several steps. When you have done this you will have understood the critical link between money and the price level. This is no small accomplishment, for you will then understand matters that have confused many policy makers and not a few economists for generations.

We start with an initial position depicted in part (i) of the figure. The liquidity preference schedule is LP_0, and the money supply is given by M_s. Hence equilibrium is at E_0 with the interest rate at r_0. The MEI schedule given in part (ii) shows that, at the rate of interest r_0, desired investment expenditure is I_0. In part (iii) the aggregate expenditure curve AE_0 is drawn for that level of investment (I_0). Equilibrium is at E_0 with a real national income of Y_0. Plotting

Y_0 against the initial price level (P_0) yields the point A on the aggregate demand curve in part (iv).

An increase in the price level to P_1 raises the money value of transactions and increases the quantity of money demanded at each possible value of the interest rate. As a result the liquidity preference function shifts from LP_0 to LP_1. This raises interest rates to r_1 and lowers investment expenditure by ΔI_1 to I_1. The fall in investment causes the AE curve in (iii) to shift down by an equal amount to AE_1. Equilibrium income falls to Y_1. Plotting Y_1 against P_1 produces point B on the AD curve in (iv).

A further increase in the price level to P_2 shifts the liquidity preference function to LP_2, raises the interest rate to r_2, and lowers investment expenditure by ΔI_2 to I_2. The fall in investment shifts the AE curve in (iii) to AE_2, and equilibrium income falls to Y_2. Plotting Y_2 against P_2 produces point C on the AD curve in (iv).

The negative relation between the price level and equilibrium real income shown by the AD curve occurs because, other things being equal, a rise in the price level raises the *demand* for money. Notice the qualification, "other things

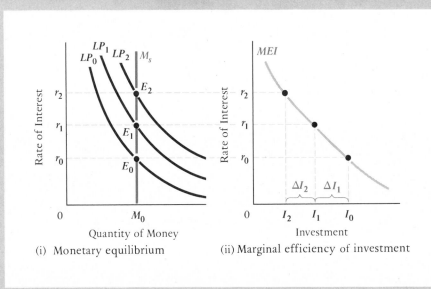

(i) Monetary equilibrium

(ii) Marginal efficiency of investment

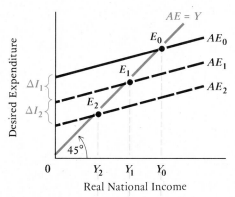

(iii) Equilibrium national income

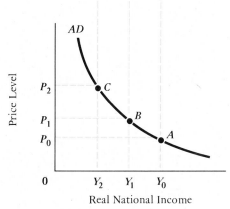

(iv) The aggregate demand curve

Assume that an increase in expenditure has created an inflationary gap so that equilibrium national income exceeds capacity output, as shown in Figure 34-6. This will cause factor prices to rise, shifting the $SRAS$ curve up and taking the price level with it. This raises the money value of transactions, and the resulting increase in the demand for money raises interest rates. Hence at any level of real income, desired real expenditure falls. The fall in real expenditure as the price level rises is shown by a movement upward to the left *along* the AD curve. This reduces the inflationary gap. Eventually, when the price level is high enough, the inflationary gap disappears and the price level stops rising.

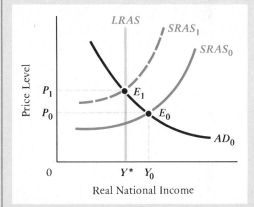

FIGURE 34-6
The Monetary Adjustment Mechanism

A rise in the price level will eliminate an inflationary gap. Equilibrium is at E_0, with income Y_0 and price level P_0. There is an inflationary gap of Y^*Y_0, where Y^* is potential income and hence the national income corresponding to long-run aggregate supply.

The inflationary gap causes wages to rise, shifting the $SRAS$ curve up to $SRAS_1$, and the price level to rise to P_1. The monetary adjustment mechanism (working through a rising demand for money, a falling price of bonds, a rising interest rate, and falling investment) lowers aggregate expenditure, eliminating the inflationary gap and producing equilibrium at E_1 with income at Y^*. The economy moves upward along its AD curve until at price level P_1 aggregate demand equals aggregate supply at full-employment income. The excess aggregate demand has been eliminated.

being equal." It is important for this process that the nominal money *supply* remain constant. The transmission mechanism operates because the demand for money increases when the price level rises while the money supply remains constant. The attempt to add to money balances by selling bonds is what drives the interest rate up and reduces desired expenditure, thereby reducing equilibrium national income. (This argument is conducted in terms of the nominal supply and demand for money. Arguing in terms of the real demand and supply of money leads to identical results.) [42]

This mechanism, described further in Figure 34-6, may be called the *monetary adjustment mechanism*. It works through the transmission mechanism described above.

The monetary adjustment mechanism will eliminate any inflationary gap, provided that the nominal money supply is held constant.

The reason is that the ensuing inflation causes a shortage of money. This shortage will sooner or later cause interest rates to rise enough to eliminate the inflationary gap. Thus inflationary gaps tend to be self-correcting as long as the money supply does not increase. They will cause the price level to increase, but those increases set in motion a chain of events in the markets for financial assets that will eventually remove the inflationary gap.

The self-correcting mechanism is the reason why price levels and the money supply have been linked for so long in economics. Many things can cause the price level to rise for some time. Yet whatever the reason for the rise, unless the money supply is expanded, the price level increase itself sets up forces that will remove any initial inflationary gap and so bring any demand inflation to a halt.

Frustration of the Monetary Adjustment Mechanism

The self-correcting mechanism for removing an inflationary gap can be frustrated indefinitely if the money supply is increased at the same rate that prices are rising. Say that the price level is rising 10 percent a year under the pressure of a large inflationary gap. Demand for money will also be rising at about 10 percent per year. Now suppose that the Fed increases the money supply at 10 percent per year. No excess demand for money will develop, for the extra money needed to meet the rising demand will be forthcoming. The real interest rate will not rise, and the inflationary gap will not be reduced. This process is analyzed in Figure 34-7.

If the money supply increases at the same rate as the price level rises, the real money supply and hence the real interest rate will remain constant, and the monetary adjustment mechanism will be frustrated.

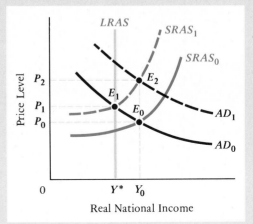

FIGURE 34-7
Frustration of the Monetary Adjustment

An inflationary gap can persist indefinitely if the money supply increases as fast as the price level. Initially the economy is at E_0, with income Y_0 and price level P_0. Since potential income is Y^*, there is an inflationary gap of Y^*Y_0. The price level now rises, which tends to shift the economy upward to the left along any given AD curve, thereby tending to reduce the excess aggregate demand. But the Fed increases the money supply so that the aggregate demand curve shifts outward, thereby tending to increase excess aggregate demand. If the two forces just balance each other, by the time the price level has risen to P_2 the aggregate demand curve will have shifted to AD_1, leaving the inflationary gap unchanged, with equilibrium at E_2.

An inflation is said to be *validated* when the money supply is increased as fast as the price level so that the monetary adjustment mechanism is frustrated. A validated inflation can go on indefinitely, although as we shall see, possibly not at a constant rate.

CONTROVERSIES OVER STABILIZATION POLICY

Stabilization policy aims to avoid the extremes of large GNP gaps and large inflationary gaps by using monetary and fiscal policy to shift the aggregate demand curve. Many controversies surround the use of stabilization policy, and we are now in a position to take a look at some of them. What role have these policies played in the past? What role should be prescribed for them in the future?

Two Sources of Controversy

The economics profession has often been deeply divided over how stabilization policy should be conducted. It is helpful to distinguish between two important controversies that have occupied a central place in policy debates. The first concerns the relative strengths of monetary and fiscal policy. The second concerns the degree of built-in stability in the economy and hence the need to use either policy. The latter is often referred to as the debate about *policy activism*.

In both cases the profession has split into two camps. While it is true that economists who agree on one issue tend to also agree on the other issue, there is no obvious reason why this should be so. The debates involve very different issues, and some economists are in the monetarist camp on one issue and the neo-Keynesian camp on the other.

In this chapter we focus on the debate about the relative strengths of monetary and fiscal policy. The debate on policy activism is taken up in Chapter 39.

The Relative Effectiveness of Monetary and Fiscal Policy

We saw in Chapter 32 that fiscal policy operates *directly* on aggregate expenditure. Monetary policy influences aggregate expenditure only *indirectly* by altering the money supply and interest rates. When the Fed changes the money supply, it shifts the aggregate demand curve via the transmission mechanism, whose effects we have just studied.

We will now see how views about the key behavioral relations translate into views about the relative strengths of monetary and fiscal policies. The effects of either policy depend on the slope of the *SRAS* curve and on how the policy affects the *AD* curve. Whatever the slope of the *SRAS* curve,

it is common to both policies. Hence we focus on what makes the two policies differ: their ability to shift the *AD* curve.

The Strength of Monetary Policy

Suppose that the economy is in equilibrium at less than potential income. Desired aggregate expenditure equals national income and demand for money equal to its supply. The Fed then increases the money supply. Firms and households now hold excess money balances, and they try to buy bonds. This action forces up the price of bonds, which implies a fall in the rate of interest. Desired investment rises along the *MEI* curve. These changes, shown previously in Figure 34-3, are merely part of the transmission mechanism.

The increase in desired investment expenditure shifts the aggregate demand curve rightward, indicating a higher demand for output at each price level. This raises equilibrium national income, as shown in Figures 34-4 and 34-5.

What happens when the Fed decreases the money supply? This creates an excess demand for money because firms and households no longer have the money balances they wish to hold at the existing level of interest rates. In an effort to replenish their inadequate holdings of money, firms and households will seek to sell bonds. But they cannot all succeed in doing this, for their efforts to sell will drive the price of bonds down, causing an increase in the interest rate. The increased interest rate will cause a reduction in investment expenditure. This in turn shifts the aggregate demand curve leftward and lowers equilibrium income.

Monetary policy works through the transmission mechanism to shift the aggregate demand curve and so change equilibrium national income. An increase in the money supply is expansionary, a decrease contractionary.

But how strong is this effect? If, for example, the Fed engineers an immediate 10 percent increase in the money supply, by how much will income rise? As a first step in answering that question, we focus on the shift of the *AD* curve.

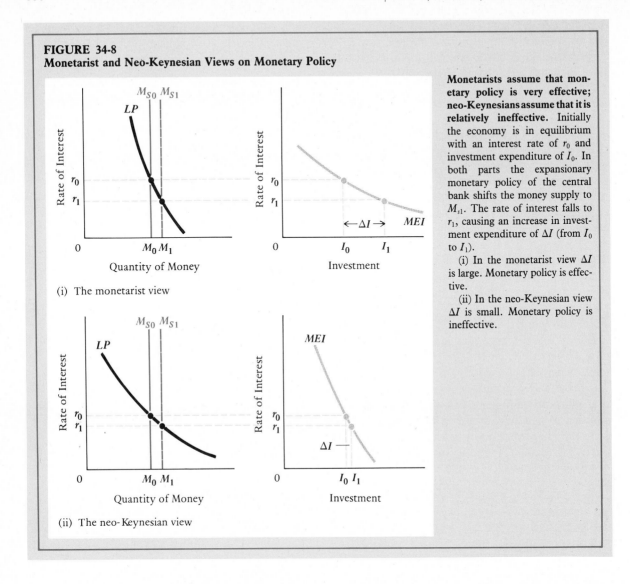

FIGURE 34-8
Monetarist and Neo-Keynesian Views on Monetary Policy

(i) The monetarist view

(ii) The neo-Keynesian view

Monetarists assume that monetary policy is very effective; neo-Keynesians assume that it is relatively ineffective. Initially the economy is in equilibrium with an interest rate of r_0 and investment expenditure of I_0. In both parts the expansionary monetary policy of the central bank shifts the money supply to M_{s1}. The rate of interest falls to r_1, causing an increase in investment expenditure of ΔI (from I_0 to I_1).

(i) In the monetarist view ΔI is large. Monetary policy is effective.

(ii) In the neo-Keynesian view ΔI is small. Monetary policy is ineffective.

The size of the shift in aggregate demand in response to an increase in the money supply depends on the size of the increase in investment expenditure. This in turn depends on two factors.

The first is how much interest rates fall in response to the increase in the money supply. The more interest-sensitive is the demand for money, the less interest rates will have to fall in order to induce firms and households to willingly hold the increase in the money supply.

The second is how much investment expenditure increases in response to the fall in interest rates. The more interest-sensitive is investment expenditure, the more it will increase in response to any given fall in the interest rate.

It follows that the size of the shift in aggregate demand in response to a change in the money supply depends on the shapes of the liquidity preference and marginal efficiency of investment curves. The influences of the shapes of the two curves are shown in Figure 34-8 and may be summarized as follows:

1. The steeper (less interest-sensitive) the *LP* function, the greater the effect a change in the money supply will have on interest rates.
2. The flatter (more interest-sensitive) the *MEI* function, the greater the effect a change in the rate of interest will have on investment expenditure and hence on aggregate demand.

The combination that produces the largest effect on aggregate demand for a given change in the money supply is a steep *LP* function and a flat *MEI* function. This combination is illustrated in 34-8(i). It accords with the monetarist view that monetary policy is relatively effective as a means of influencing the economy. The combination that produces the smallest effect is a flat *LP* function and a steep *MEI* function. This combination is illustrated in 34-8(ii). It accords with the view of some neo-Keynesians that monetary policy is relatively ineffective.

Not surprisingly, much of the controversy about the effectiveness of monetary policy as a means of influencing national income has centered on the shapes of these two functions.

According to the monetarists, changes in the money supply cause large changes in interest rates that in turn cause large changes in expenditure. According to some neo-Keynesians, changes in the money supply cause small changes in interest rates that in turn cause small or negligible changes in expenditure.

The Strength of Fiscal Policy

As with monetary policy, the amount by which a given fiscal stimulus raises national income depends upon both the *AD* curve and the *SRAS* curve. Again, we focus for the moment on the role of the *AD* curve.

We saw in Chapter 32 that the horizontal shift in the *AD* curve due to, say, an increase in government expenditure is given by the multiplier. In the final equilibrium when the price level has adjusted,

however, the change in aggregate demand will depend on the consequent response of interest rates and investment expenditure. Disagreement over these responses cause monetarists and neo-Keynesians to disagree over the potency of fiscal policy. This is illustrated in Figure 34-9.

Consider an increase in government expenditure. It raises national income and creates excess demand for money because it causes a rise in the demand for transactions balances. The interest rate rises until everyone is content to hold the existing stock of money. The rise in the interest rate lowers private investment expenditure. (A parallel analysis applies to a decline in government expenditure.)

The tendency just discussed is called the **crowding out effect.** It may be defined as the offsetting reduction in private investment caused by the rise in interest rates that follows an expansionary fiscal policy. The analysis of Figure 34-9 shows that the crowding out effect is smaller (1) the flatter (more interest-sensitive) the *LP* function, so that increases in the transactions demand for money do not cause large increases in the interest rate, and (2) the steeper the *MEI* function, so that increases in the interest rate do not cause large changes in investment expenditure.[9]

Monetarists believe the crowding out effect is large. An increase in government expenditure will crowd out almost the same amount of private expenditure and thus have only a small net expansionary effect on aggregate demand. Neo-Keynesians believe that the crowding out effect is small, at least when the economy is suffering from a substantial GNP gap, which is when one is likely to wish to use an expansionary fiscal policy. In this case only a small part of any rise in government expenditure will be offset by a fall in private expenditure. Thus there will be a large net increase in aggregate expenditure and hence a large increase in aggregate demand.

The box recasts the debate about the strengths of monetary and fiscal policy using the terminology of the quantity theory of money.

---

[9] We encountered the crowding out effect in Chapter 32. See especially the discussion surrounding Figure 32-7.

FIGURE 34-9
Monetarist and Neo-Keynesian Views on Fiscal Policy

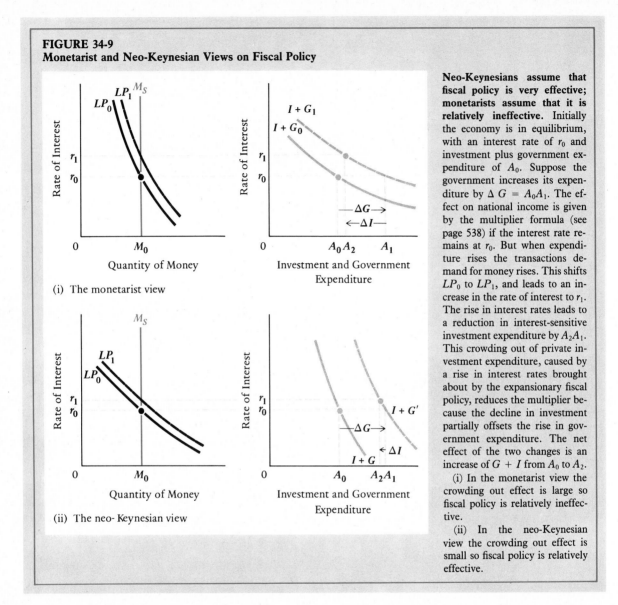

(i) The monetarist view

(ii) The neo- Keynesian view

Neo-Keynesians assume that fiscal policy is very effective; monetarists assume that it is relatively ineffective. Initially the economy is in equilibrium, with an interest rate of r_0 and investment plus government expenditure of A_0. Suppose the government increases its expenditure by $\Delta G = A_0 A_1$. The effect on national income is given by the multiplier formula (see page 538) if the interest rate remains at r_0. But when expenditure rises the transactions demand for money rises. This shifts LP_0 to LP_1, and leads to an increase in the rate of interest to r_1. The rise in interest rates leads to a reduction in interest-sensitive investment expenditure by $A_2 A_1$. This crowding out of private investment expenditure, caused by a rise in interest rates brought about by the expansionary fiscal policy, reduces the multiplier because the decline in investment partially offsets the rise in government expenditure. The net effect of the two changes is an increase of $G + I$ from A_0 to A_2.

(i) In the monetarist view the crowding out effect is large so fiscal policy is relatively ineffective.

(ii) In the neo-Keynesian view the crowding out effect is small so fiscal policy is relatively effective.

According to the monetarists, changes in government expenditure will induce large changes in interest rates that in turn cause large offsetting changes in private investment, leaving only a small net effect on aggregate demand. According to the neo-Keynesians, changes in government expenditure cause only small changes in interest rates that in turn cause small or negligible offsetting changes in investment expenditure.

The Role of the *SRAS* Curve

Neither monetarists nor neo-Keynesians can assess the final effects of monetary or fiscal policy on *real* output and employment without reference to the shape of the *SRAS* curve.

The role of the *SRAS* curve is common to both fiscal and monetary policies: for any given shift in

MONETARY VERSUS FISCAL POLICY: A RESTATEMENT IN TERMS OF THE VELOCITY OF CIRCULATION

The differences between monetarist and neo-Keynesian views about the relative strengths of monetary and fiscal policy can be reinterpreted in terms of differences in views about the behavior of the *velocity of circulation of money balances,* or velocity. This concept was first discussed in the box on page 650.

The starting point is the *equation of exchanges,* $MV = PY$, discussed in the earlier box. The right-hand side is nominal GNP.

We can now discuss the monetarist and neo-Keynesian views about the strengths of monetary and fiscal policies on shifting the AD curve in terms of their ability to alter nominal GNP, with the division of the change in nominal GNP between price and real output determined by the $SRAS$ curve, as discussed later in the text. The equation of exchange focuses on the relationship between the behavior of nominal income and the behavior of velocity. It is important to realize that nothing different is involved here; the analysis in the text can simply be *restated* in terms of velocity.

First consider monetary policy. The monetarist view that changes in the money supply cause a substantial shift in the AD curve means that a change in M will lead to a substantial change in nominal income. This follows their belief that V is relatively stable so that changes in M lead to corresponding changes in PY. The neo-Keynesian view that changes in M cause only small changes in PY follows their view that V will tend to change to offset the change in M. (An increase in M leads to a fall in interest rates, so people wish to hold larger money balances—that is, k rises, which means V falls. Hence M times V does not change by very much.)

Now consider fiscal policy. Monetarists believe that fiscal policy will lead to a small shift in the AD curve. This means that it will have only a small effect on PY. Again this is because they believe that V is relatively stable. With M constant and V stable, PY does not change significantly. Neo-Keynesians believe that fiscal policy causes a substantial shift in the AD curve and hence a large change in PY. Again this follows from their belief that V will change. (An increase in expenditure increases income and the transactions demand for money. This raises interest rates and leads people to economize on money; the reduction in k is an increase in V.)

Monetarists who believe that monetary policy is powerful and fiscal policy is not can be interpreted as believing that velocity is relatively stable. Neo-Keynesians who believe that fiscal policy is powerful and monetary policy is not can be interpreted as believing that velocity is relatively unstable.

the AD curve, the steeper is the $SRAS$ curve, the smaller the increase in national income and the larger the increase in the price level. (This should be familiar from Chapter 30—see Figure 30-2.) However, the mechanism by which the $SRAS$ curve influences the outcome differs between the two policies.

Monetary policy. An increase in the money supply is expansionary because it lowers interest rates. If the expansion causes the price level to rise, the demand for money rises, dampening the fall in interest rates. This means that investment does not rise as much as it would have if the price level had been constant. Therefore equilibrium national income does not rise as much.

In the extreme case of a vertical aggregate supply curve, prices rise so much that the increase in money demand matches the increase in money supply, and interest rates do not fall at all. In this case investment expenditure and national income are unaffected by changes in the money supply. This is shown in Figure 30-3.

Fiscal policy. Following a fiscal-induced expansion, any rise in the price level raises the demand for money even further than the initial rise due to the expansion in national income. This then causes interest rates to rise even further, crowding out more investment expenditure. In the extreme case of a vertical *SRAS* curve, prices and interest rates rise by enough to cause investment expenditure to fall by an amount exactly equal to the rise in government expenditure. This is the case of *complete* crowding out, where national income is not influenced by fiscal policy at all.

The Present State of the Controversy

The controversy about the relative strengths of monetary and fiscal policy is no longer a central source of disagreement among economists. Few economists believe in either extreme view, although the extremes are still studied since they help in understanding the important role played by the shapes of the key behavioral relations.

Indeed although monetarist and neo-Keynesian are convenient labels to give to the extreme views, ideas continue to evolve. Whereas 20 years ago Keynesians gave little place to monetary policy, today most neo-Keynesians accept both monetary and fiscal policy as potent methods of influencing the economy; traditional monetarists are still inclined to downgrade fiscal policy. Disagreements now tend to be focused more on aggregate supply rather than, as in the above controversy, aggregate demand. One new school of thought argues that what matters more is whether policy is expected or unexpected than whether it acts through monetary or fiscal channels. This important distinction is encountered again in Chapter 39.

Policy Debates: A Preview

There is still considerable debate about the relevance of the monetary adjustment mechanism to policy. Monetarists make it the centerpiece of their policy recommendations. They maintain that central banks can and should hold the money supply constant in the face of increases in the price level and that to do so is both necessary and sufficient to control inflation.

Opponents of the monetarist view are divided into several groups. A few say that it is not within the power of central banks to control the money supply over a long time period. (This denies the analysis of the money supply presented in Chapter 33.) Others say that, given the political and economic objectives of anything but a very right-wing government, it is quite unrealistic to expect the Fed to attempt to actually hold the money supply constant for a long time period in the face of an inflation, even though it is able to do so. Still others say that while an inflation can be stopped by the monetary adjustment mechanism, the economic and social costs of doing so are too great.

For example, in the early 1980s Chairman Paul Volcker of the Fed held to his tight monetary, anti-inflationary guns while under pressure from President Reagan to ease up a bit in order to alleviate the costs of the anti-inflationary battle. The Reagan administration, while occasionally in conflict with Volcker, was very tough-minded in its commitment to disinflation, so one can only imagine the pressures the Fed would have felt under some other, less conservative, administration. Whenever there is a serious inflation, the key issue for policy is whether the central bank *should* frustrate the monetary adjustment mechanism and whether the government should find other ways of bringing inflation under control. We shall return to these very important debates in Part Nine.

SUMMARY

1. For simplicity we divide all forms of holding wealth into money, which is a medium of exchange and earns no interest, and bonds, which earn an interest return but can be turned into money only by selling them at a price that is determined on the open market.

2. The price of bonds varies negatively with the rate of interest. A rise in the rate of interest lowers the prices of all bonds. The longer its term to maturity, the greater the change in the price of a bond for a given change in the interest rate.

3. The value of money balances people wish to hold is called the *demand for money*. It is a stock (not a flow), and it is measured as so many billions of dollars.

4. The reasons for holding money balances despite the opportunity cost of bond interest foregone are described by the transactions, precautionary, and speculative motives. They have the effect of making the nominal demand for money vary positively with national income valued in constant dollars, with the price level, and with wealth, and to vary negatively with the rate of interest.

5. When there is an excess demand for money balances, people try to sell bonds. This pushes the price of bonds down and the interest rate up. When there is an excess supply of money balances, people try to buy bonds. This pushes the price of bonds up and the rate of interest down. Monetary equilibrium is established when people are willing to hold the fixed stocks of money and bonds at the current rate of interest.

6. A change in the interest rate causes desired investment to change along the *MEI* function. This shifts the aggregate desired expenditure function and causes equilibrium national income to change. This means that the aggregate demand curve shifts.

7. Points 5 and 6 together describe the transmission mechanism that links money to national income. A decrease in the supply of money tends to reduce aggregate demand. An increase in the supply of money tends to increase it.

8. Other things being equal, each price level is associated with an equilibrium real national income such that desired expenditure equals income and the demand for money equals the supply. Each price level and its corresponding equilibrium real national income gives one point on the aggregate demand curve.

9. The aggregate demand curve is negatively sloped because the higher the price level, the lower equilibrium national income. The explanation lies with the monetary adjustment mechanism: the higher the price level, the higher the demand for money, the higher the rate of interest, the lower the aggregate expenditure function, and thus the lower equilibrium income.

10. The monetary adjustment mechanism that causes the aggregate demand curve to have a negative slope means that a sufficiently large rise in the price level will eliminate any inflationary gap. However, this mechanism can be frustrated if the Fed increases the money supply as fast as the price level is rising.

11. Monetary policy seeks to influence national income by creating a change in monetary equilibrium that will work through the transmission mechanism. The steeper the *LP* curve and the flatter the *MEI* curve, the greater the effect of a given change in the money supply on aggregate demand.

12. Fiscal policy operates to shift the *AD* curve directly, but its effectiveness also depends on its indirect effects on private expenditure via changes in the interest rate. A given change in government expenditure will have larger effects on aggregate demand the flatter the *LP* curve is and the steeper the *MEI* curve is.

13. The appendix to this chapter presents a formal model that integrates the monetary and expenditure sides of the economy.

TOPICS FOR REVIEW

Interest rates and bond prices
Transactions, precautionary, and speculative motives for holding money
The liquidity preference (*LP*) function
Monetary equilibrium
The transmission mechanism

The shape of the aggregate demand function
The monetary adjustment mechanism and its frustration
The strength of monetary and fiscal policy

DISCUSSION QUESTIONS

1. Describing a possible future "cashless society," a public report recently said: "In the cashless society of the future, a customer could insert a plastic card into a machine at a store and the amount of the purchase would be deducted from his 'bank account' in the computer automatically and transferred to the store's account. No cash or checks would ever change hands." What would such an institutional change do to the various motives for holding money balances? What functions would remain for commercial banks and for the central bank if money as we now know it disappeared in this fashion? What benefits and disadvantages can you see in such a scheme?

2. What motives do you think explain the following holdings?
   a. the currency and coins in the cash register of the local supermarket at the start of each working day
   b. the payroll account of the Ford Motor Company in the local bank
   c. certificates of deposit that mature after one's retirement
   d. the holdings of government bonds by private individuals

3. What would be the affects on the economy if Congress were to vote a once-and-for-all universal social dividend of $5,000 paid to every American over the age of 17, to be financed by the creation of new money?

4. What sort of situation might lead a society to have a very flat liquidity preference schedule and a very steep marginal efficiency of investment schedule? Is this a good combination for those who wish to affect the level of income by changing the money supply?

5. One relationship encountered in this chapter and else-

where is the negative one between bond prices and interest rates. Be sure that you can explain just why this occurs. Is this a special feature of bonds, or does it apply to the value of other earning assets as well?

6. Suppose you are sure that the Fed is going to engage in policies that will decrease the money supply sharply starting next month. How might you make speculative profits by purchases or sales of bonds now?

7. In the days of the gold standard the money supply was tied rigidly to the quantity of refined gold. What would be the effects of new discoveries of gold if (1) the economy were in the midst of a severe recession and (2) the economy were producing its full-employment national income?

8. What do you expect to happen to interest rates if the Fed reduces the money supply? What would happen if, starting from a situation of 10 percent rates of inflation and of monetary expansion, the Fed cut the rate of monetary expansion to 5 percent?

9. Trace out the full sequence of events by which the monetary adjustment mechanism would work if, in the face of a constant money supply, workers and firms insisted on actions that raised prices continually at a rate of 10 percent per year. "Sooner or later in this situation something would have to give." What possible things could "give"? What would be the consequence of each "giving"?

10. If the monetary adjustment mechanism is always present in any economy, why did it not prevent the inflations of the 1970s and 1980s?

11. What is the theory of the interest rate that lies behind the following newspaper headline: "Bond prices fall based on investor's fear of U.S. deficit and Volcker's remarks"? The remarks referred to were made by Paul Volcker, Chairman of the Fed, who also stated, "As things now stand, rising private credit demands, in reflection of rising private activity, are beginning to clash with the continuing heavy financing needs of the government." These quotes are from July 1983. Check and see what has actually happened to bond prices over the intervening period. Explain.

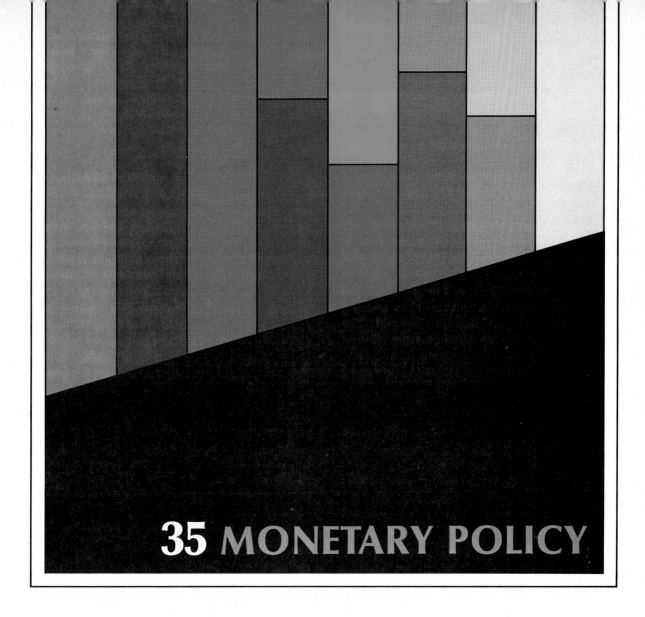

35 MONETARY POLICY

Central banks influence the size of their country's money supply, and in doing so they seek to influence national income and the price level. In this chapter we study how our central bank, the Fed, has influenced the American economy through its monetary policy.

CENTRAL BANKS

All advanced free-market economies have, in addition to commercial banks, a central bank. Many of the world's early central banks were private, profit-making institutions that provided services to ordinary banks. Their importance, however, led to their developing close ties with the government. Central banks soon became instruments of the government, though not all of them were publicly owned. The Bank of England (the "Old Lady of Threadneedle Street"), one of the world's oldest and most famous central banks, began to operate as the central bank of England in the seventeenth century but was not "nationalized" until 1947.

The Federal Reserve System

The central bank of the United States, the *Federal Reserve System,* was organized in 1914. The most important thing about the Fed is this:

In its role as the central bank of the United States, the Federal Reserve System is responsible for the U.S. government's monetary policy.

This is stressed because things are not always as they seem. The organizational structure of the system appears, at first glance, to consist of a number of privately owned banks over which commercial banks rather than the government have control.

The basic elements in the Federal Reserve System are (1) the board of governors; (2) the Federal Advisory Council, which has no real power but whose 12 members advise the board of the views of commercial bankers; (3) the 12 Federal Reserve banks; (4) the Federal Open Market Committee; and (5) the member commercial banks, of which there are more than 5,700.

The board of governors. The board consists of seven members appointed by the president and confirmed by the Senate. Members serve for 14 years. The length of term is important, for it means that each member of the board serves beyond the term of the president making the appointment. Board members are top-level public servants who often, but not inevitably, come from the world of business or banking. In 1980 two of its members, Henry Wallick and Nancy Teeters, were professional economists. The board is responsible to Congress but works closely with the Department of the Treasury. It supervises the entire Federal Reserve System and exercises general policy control over the 12 Reserve banks.

The chairman of the board (Paul A. Volcker in 1983) is in a powerful position to influence the country's monetary policies.

The Reserve banks. Twelve Federal Reserve banks serve the 12 districts into which the country is divided. The banks are located in Boston, New York, Philadelphia, Cleveland, Richmond, Atlanta, Chicago, St. Louis, Minneapolis, Kansas City, Dallas, and San Francisco. Each bank is nominally owned by the member banks in its district. A commercial bank that is a member of the system is required to purchase Reserve bank stock to an amount equal to 3 percent of the member bank's own capital. The commercial banks receive a flat 6 percent dividend on this investment. Each Federal Reserve bank has nine directors: three bankers elected by the member banks; three representatives of business, agriculture, or industry; and three public members appointed by the board of governors.

Although technically privately owned and operated, the Federal Reserve banks are actually operated under guidelines set down by the board of governors in what it deems to be the public interest.

The Federal Reserve banks have a strong tradition of service to the banking community within the policy guidelines laid down by the board of governors. Revenues they have earned in excess of expenses and of fixed minimum profits are turned over to the U.S. Treasury. Most Reserve banks, along with the office of the board of governors, engage in research and publish many bulletins of interest to the financial communities they serve.

The Open Market Committee. The Open Market Committee has 12 members: the 7 members of the board of governors plus 5 presidents of various Reserve banks. This committee determines the open market policy of the system, which deals principally with how many government securities the Reserve banks should buy or sell on the open market. This is the group that determines the country's monetary policy.

Basic Functions of a Central Bank

The similarities in the functions performed and the tools used by the world's central banks are much more important than the differences in their organization. Although our attention is given to the operations of the Federal Reserve System, its basic functions are similar to those of the Bank of England, the Bank of Greece, or the Bank of Canada.

TABLE 35-1 FEDERAL RESERVE BANKS, CONSOLIDATED BALANCE SHEET, JANUARY 30, 1983
(Billions of Dollars)

Assets		Liabilities	
Gold certificates and other cash	$11.1	Federal Reserve Notes outstanding	$143.3
U.S. government securities	138.2	Deposits of member bank reserves	28.0
Loans to commercial banks	1.8	Deposits of U.S. Treasury	3.6
Other assets	16.5	Other liabilities	9.8
		Capital	3.0
	187.7		187.7

Source: *Federal Reserve Bulletin*, February 1983.

The balance sheet of the Fed shows that it serves as banker to the commercial banks and the U.S. Treasury and as issuer of our currency; it also suggests the Fed's role as regulator of money markets and the money supply. The principal liabilities of the Fed are the basis of the money supply. Federal Reserve notes are currency, and the deposits of member banks give commercial banks the reserves they use to create deposit money. The Fed's principal assets, holdings of U.S. government securities, arise from its open market operations designed to regulate the money supply and also from direct purchases from the Treasury.

A central bank serves four main functions: It is a banker for commercial banks, a bank for the government, the controller of the nation's supply of money, and a regulator of financial markets.

The first three functions are reflected in the Fed's balance sheet, shown in Table 35-1.

Banker to Commercial Banks

The central bank accepts deposits from commercial banks and will, on order, transfer them to the account of another bank. In this way the central bank provides each commercial bank with the equivalent of a checking account and with a means of settling debts to other banks. The deposits made by the commercial banks with the central bank appear in Table 35-1. The reserves of the commercial banks deposited with the central bank are *liabilities* of the central bank because it promises to pay them to the commercial banks on demand.

From their very beginnings central banks have acted as "lenders of last resort" to the commercial banking system. Commercial banks with sound investments sometimes find themselves in urgent need of cash to meet the demands of their depositors. If such banks cannot obtain ready cash, they may be forced into insolvency despite their being in a basically sound financial position. Central banks provide temporary assistance to such commercial banks by making short-term loans to them.

Loans made by the Fed to commercial banks are said to be made available through the Fed's "discount window." The rate of interest the Fed charges on such loans is called the **discount rate.** Table 35-1 shows that such loans amounted to 6.4 percent of reserves at the end of January 1983.

Bank for the Government

Governments, too, need to hold their funds in an account into which they can make deposits and on which they can write checks. The U.S. Treasury keeps its checking deposits at the Federal Reserve banks, replenishing them from much larger tax and loan accounts kept at commercial banks. When the government requires more money than it collects in taxes, it too needs to borrow, and it does so by selling securities. Most are sold directly to the public, but when the central bank buys a new government bond on the open market, it is indirectly lending to the government. As of January 1983 the Federal Reserve System held over $140 billion in U.S. government securities.

Controller of the Money Supply

One of the most important functions of a central bank is to control the money supply. From Table 35-1 it is clear that the overwhelming proportion of a central bank's liabilities (its promises to pay) are either Federal Reserve notes or the deposits of commercial banks, which provide reserves for demand deposits owned by households and firms. Later in this chapter we shall study how the Fed seeks to control the money supply.

Regulator of Money Markets

The central bank frequently enters money markets for purposes other than controlling the money supply. For instance, it may, as an arm of the government, attempt to keep interest rates low in periods when the government is increasing its debt to reduce the government's cost of financing a given deficit.

Central banks also assume as a major responsibility support of the country's financial system and prevention of serious disruption by wide-scale panic and the resulting bank failures. Various institutions are in the business of borrowing on a short-term and lending on a long-term basis. Examples include savings and loan associations, which take in short-term deposits from the public and lend on long-term mortgages. Large, unanticipated increases in interest rates tend to squeeze these institutions. The average rate that they earn on their investments rises only slowly as old contracts mature and new ones are made, but they must either pay higher rates to hold on to their deposits or accept wide-scale withdrawals that could easily bring about their insolvency. The Fed can help such institutions by preventing very rapid swings in interest rates. If a shortage of funds is rapidly driving up interest rates, the Fed can sup-

ply funds to the market and thus make the rise in rates more gradual. Indeed it could stop the rise at least for a while if it were willing to provide sufficient funds and accept the consequences of doing so.

Conflicts Among Functions

The several functions of the central bank are not always compatible. When in pursuit of its anti-inflationary policy the Fed reduces the money supply below the current demand for it. This causes interest rates to rise. The resulting squeeze makes life uncomfortable for banks and other financial institutions and makes borrowing expensive for the government. If the Fed chooses to ease those problems, say, by lending money to banks, it is relaxing its tight-money, anti-inflationary policy. The Fed must strive to balance these conflicting objectives. When it wishes to raise interest rates to control the money supply, it should do so by an amount and on such a timetable as to prevent severe financial problems in money markets. Many critics think that the Fed does not always succeed in finding the right balance between its conflicting objectives, periodically causing problems by its monetary mismanagement.

CENTRAL BANKS AND THE MONEY SUPPLY

As we saw in Chapter 34, changes in the money supply lead to shifts in the *AD* curve and to changes in equilibrium national income. We now discuss the various ways in which monetary policy can influence the money supply and so influence national income.

Deposit money is a large part of the money supply, no matter how the supply of money is defined. Demand deposits of commercial banks account for 50 percent of M1, the narrowest definition of money, and roughly 10 percent of M3, the broadest measure in widespread use (see Table 33-10). As we have seen, the ability of commercial banks to create deposit money depends on their reserves. The ability of the central bank to affect the money supply is critically related to its ability to affect the size and adequacy of these reserves. In the following sections we shall discuss four ways in which the central bank affects the money supply.

Open Market Operations

The central bank's most important tool for influencing the supply of money is its **open market operations,** the purchase or sale of government securities on the open market. At the start of 1982 the Federal Reserve held more than $140 billion in government securities. In a typical year the Fed buys and sells $20 to $40 billion worth of government securities on the open market. What is the effect of these purchases and sales?

Purchases on the Open Market

When a Federal Reserve bank buys a bond from a household or firm, it pays for the bond with a check drawn on the central bank and payable to the seller. The seller deposits this check in its own bank. The commercial bank presents the check to the Fed for payment and the central bank makes a book entry, increasing the deposit of the commercial bank at the central bank.

Table 35–2 shows the changes in the balance sheets of the several parties involved in a Federal Reserve bank purchase of $100 in government securities from a household.

The Fed has increased its assets by the value of the security it purchased and increased its liabilities in the form of the deposits of commercial banks. The commercial bank has increased its deposit liabilities and its reserves by the amount of the transaction. Each asset change is matched by a change in liabilities.

After these transactions are completed the commercial banks have excess reserves and are in a position to expand their loans and deposits. The household that sold the bond to the Fed has merely switched assets: Where it used to hold a bond it now holds money. When it sold the bond it re-

TABLE 35–2 BALANCE SHEET CHANGES CAUSED BY AN OPEN MARKET PURCHASE FROM A HOUSEHOLD

Private household	
Assets	Liabilities
Bonds −$100	No change
Deposits + 100	

Commercial banks	
Assets	Liabilities
Reserves (deposits with central bank) +$100	Demand deposits +$100

Central bank	
Assets	Liabilities
Bonds +$100	Deposits of commercial banks +$100

The money supply is increased when the Fed makes an open market purchase from a household. When the Fed buys a $100 bond from a household, the household gains money and gives up a bond. The commercial banks gain a new deposit of $100—and thus new reserves of $100. Commercial banks can now engage in a multiple expansion of deposit money of the sort analyzed in Chapter 33.

ceived a check from the Fed in payment. When the household deposited this check in its own commercial bank account, its bank was placed in the same position as was the bank in Table 33-3 that received the new deposit from the immigrant. It can now expand deposits on the basis of these new cash reserves in the manner that we analyzed in Chapter 33. If the central bank buys many securities in the open market, the entire banking system will gain new reserves.

When the central bank buys securities on the open market, the reserves of the commercial banks are increased. These banks can then expand deposits, thereby increasing the money supply.

Sales on the Open Market

When the central bank sells a $100 security to a household or firm, it receives in return the buyer's check drawn against its own deposit in a commercial bank. The central bank presents the check to the private bank for payment. Payment is made by a book entry that reduces the private bank's deposit at the central bank.

The changes in this case are the opposite of those shown in Table 35-2. The central bank has reduced its assets by the value of the security it sold and reduced its liabilities in the form of the deposits of commercial banks. The household or firm has increased its holdings of securities and reduced its cash on deposit with a commercial bank. The commercial bank has reduced its deposit liability to the household or firm and reduced its reserves (on deposit with the central bank) by the same amount. Each of the asset changes is balanced by a liability change. Indeed everything balances.

But the commercial bank finds that by suffering an equal change in its reserves and deposit liabilities, its ratio of reserves to deposits falls. Consider, for example, a bank with $10 million in deposits backed by $1 million cash in fulfillment of a 10 percent cash reserve ratio. As a result of the Fed's open market sales of $100,000 worth of bonds, the bank loses $100,000 of deposits and reserves. Reserves are now $900,000 while deposits are $9.9 million, making a reserve ratio of only 9.09 percent.

Banks such as the one in the above example whose reserve ratios are driven below the minimum requirement must take immediate steps to restore their reserve ratios. The necessary reduction in deposits can be accomplished by not making new investments when old ones are redeemed (e.g., by not granting new loans when old ones are repaid) or by selling (liquidating) existing investments.

When the central bank sells securities on the open market, the reserves of the commercial banks are decreased. These banks in turn are forced to contract deposits, thereby decreasing the money supply.

But what if the public does not wish to buy the securities the Fed wishes to sell? Can it force the public to do so? The answer is that there is always a price at which the public will buy. The Fed in its open market operations must be prepared to have the price of the securities fall if it insists on suddenly selling a large volume of them. As we have seen, a fall in the price of securities is the same thing as a rise in interest rates, so if the Fed wishes to curtail the money supply by selling bonds, it may well drive up interest rates.

Notice in Table 35-1 that the Fed's holdings of government securities are large relative to the reserves of commercial banks. By selling securities it can contract those reserves very sharply if it chooses. Similarly, by buying securities it can expand them. In its open market operations the central bank has a potent weapon for affecting the size of member bank reserves—and thus for affecting the money supply.

Tools Other Than Open Market Operations

The major tool the Fed uses in conducting monetary policy is its open market operations. But other tools are available and have on occasion been used extensively.

Reserve Requirements

One way that the Fed can control the money supply is by altering the required minimum reserve ratios. Suppose the banking system is loaned-up; that is, it has no excess reserves. If the Fed increases the required reserve ratio (say from 20 percent to 25 percent), the dollar amount of reserves held by the commercial banks will no longer be adequate to support their outstanding deposits. Commercial banks will then be forced to reduce their deposits until they achieve the new, higher required reserve ratio.[1] This decrease in demand

---

[1] They will do this by gradually decreasing their loans and/ or selling some of their securities. In the short term they may borrow from the Fed to give themselves time to meet the increased reserve requirements without disrupting financial markets.

TABLE 35–3(a) **BALANCE SHEET FOR A LOANED-UP BANKING SYSTEM WITH A 20 PERCENT RESERVE RATIO**

Assets		Liabilities	
Reserves	$1,000	Deposits	$5,000
Loans	4,100	Capital	100
	$5,100		$5,100

Increasing the required reserve ratio forces a loaned-up bank to reduce its deposits—and thus decreases the supply of deposit money. The banking system in part (a) has a ratio of reserves to deposits of 0.20. If the Fed now raises the required reserve ratio to 0.25, the reserves of $1,000 will support deposits of only $4,000. As shown in

TABLE 35–3(b) **BALANCE SHEET FOR A LOANED-UP BANKING SYSTEM AFTER A CHANGE IN RESERVE RATIO TO 25 PERCENT**

Assets		Liabilities	
Reserves	$1,000	Deposits	$4,000
Loans	3,100	Capital	100
	$4,100		$4,100

(b) the banking system can reduce its deposits by reducing its loans. A reduction in reserve requirements from 0.25 to 0.20 would permit a banking system in the position of (b) to expand it loans and deposits to those of (a) with no increases in its dollar reserves.

deposits is a decrease in the money supply. The process is illustrated in Table 35-3.

The effect of a reduction in required reserve ratios is also shown in the table. Of course, if banks choose not to increase their loans, they will not need to respond to a decrease in required reserves since those requirements are only minimum requirements. The first effect of a decrease in required reserves is to create excess reserves. In normal times the profit motive will lead most banks to respond by increasing loans and deposits—and thus lead to an increase in the money supply.

Increases in required reserve ratios force banks with no excess reserves to decrease deposits and thus reduce the money supply. Decreases in required reserve ratios permit banks to expand deposits and thus may increase the money supply.

In 1934 the Federal Reserve Board was given authority by Congress to set (within limits) required reserve ratios for both demand and time deposits. The Fed has frequently changed reserve requirements within the allowable limits, and Congress has from time to time changed the limits.

In recent times the use of reserve ratio changes has fallen out of favor. The chief argument against manipulating the reserve ratio is that it is a ponderous weapon for changing excess reserves. Open

market policy can be applied flexibly to achieve the same effects.

The Discount Rate

The *discount rate* is the rate at which the Fed will lend funds to member banks who need to replenish their reserves. (When a bill is discounted it is purchased at a *discount*, i.e., at a price below its redemption value, the difference representing an interest return to the purchaser.) As a matter of policy the Fed discourages long-term borrowing from it by commercial banks, and the reserve banks tend to accommodate requests at their "discount window" only on a short-term basis. Hence the discount rate plays a relatively minor role as a policy weapon.

The importance of the discount rate is as a signal of the Fed's intentions.

During World War II and the postwar period, the discount rate was little used because the Fed was cooperating with the Treasury in an attempt to keep down the interest cost on the federal debt. During the 1960s discount policy re-emerged as a major weapon.

Changes in the discount rate are usually associated with like changes in other interest rates. It is not always clear whether the discount rate follows or leads changes in other interest rates. One reason for the discount rate's following other developments is that open market operations that apply the monetary brakes by selling bonds tend to push up interest rates. To discourage banks from turning to its discount window, the Fed must then raise the discount rate. One reason for the discount rate's leading other rates is that sharp changes in the discount rate often create expectations about the relative abundance or scarcity of funds.

Selective Credit Controls

Monetary policy seeks to make money and credit generally scarce or plentiful, leaving the private sector to cope with the conditions it creates. **Selective credit controls,** on the other hand, allow the Fed to decide where the initial impact of tight or plentiful credit will be felt. Among the selective controls that have sometimes been used during the postwar period are margin requirements, installment-credit control, mortgage control, and maximum interest rates.

These controls can be very powerful. Increasing the down payment required for an installment-plan purchase, for example, can cause a major fall in demand until households accumulate enough money to make the new, larger down payments.

Many selective controls have been used in the United States in the past, and all of them are now in use somewhere in the Western world. In the United States, however, only margin requirements and interest rate ceilings were used in 1983. Installment-credit controls were dropped after World War II and mortgage controls after 1953. Indeed in 1983 interest rate ceilings were also being phased out.

Margin requirements. Stock market speculation can be controlled by the Federal Reserve through its power to regulate the **margin requirement,** which is the fraction of the price of a stock that must be put up by the purchaser. (The balance may be borrowed from the brokerage firm through which the purchaser buys the security.) Since 1960 the margin requirement has varied between 50 percent and 90 percent. Such variations can have a

substantial selective effect on stock market activity that is independent of the general credit picture. Thus, if the Federal Reserve wishes to impose moderate credit restraint generally but is particularly apprehensive about stock market speculation, it may combine a moderate amount of open market selling with a sharp increase in margin requirements.

Interest rate ceilings. Under the provisions of Regulation Q, which are being phased out over a period from 1980 to 1985, banks were restricted in the amount of interest they could pay on certain types of deposits. Most economists opposed these ceilings on the grounds that they interfered with the efficient functioning of financial markets and monetary policy. When interest rates rose in times of tight money, the rates of savings and other deposits subject to such regulations had to stop at their ceilings while other rates went on rising. As the interest differential widened, depositors would withdraw their funds from regulated types of accounts and place them in unregulated types where interest rates were free to rise. Typically this caused a shift of deposits out of commercial banks, whose deposit interest rates were regulated, and into nonbank financial institutions, whose rates were often either unregulated or regulated less stringently. When interest rates fell, savings deposits would flow back into commercial banks. The sudden shifts of funds could put the system under great stress, for under the fractional reserve system, a bank that loses deposits is in a difficult position.

Moral Suasion

If the commercial banking system is prepared to cooperate, the Federal Reserve banks can operate a tight-money policy merely by asking banks to be conservative in granting loans. When the need for restriction is over, the commercial bankers can then be told that it is all right to grant loans and extend deposits up to the legal maximum. The use of "moral suasion" does not depend on pure "jawboning." Member banks depend on the Federal Reserve banks for loans, and in the long term noncooperation with the Fed's "suggestions" can prove costly to a bank.

The Monetary Control Act of 1980

Under the Depository Institutions Deregulation and Monetary Control Act, a number of important changes to the Banking system are being phased in over a five-year period starting in 1980. Since the Fed's use of tools other than open market operations has been limited by the existence of regulations that are now being removed, this act may have important implications for the future conduct of monetary policy. The general purpose of the act is "to facilitate the implementation of monetary policy, to provide for a gradual elimination of all limitations on the rates of interest which are payable on deposits and accounts, and to authorize interest-bearing transactions accounts."

The 1980 act set the same reserve requirements for all banks, large or small and members of the Federal Reserve System or not, thus eliminating the preferential treatment given previously to small banks who faced lower reserve requirements. A bank's reserve requirements were set at 3 percent against its first $25 million in demand deposits (and other accounts subject to direct or indirect transfer by check) and at a ratio to be determined by the Fed (between the limits of 8 percent and 14 percent) on demand deposits in excess of $25 million. The ratio on time deposits is to be set by the Fed between the limits of 3 percent and 9 percent.

The Fed was also given the power to require that all banks hold up to 4 percent additional reserves, provided that "the sole purpose of such requirements is to increase the amount of reserves maintained to a level essential for the conduct of monetary policy." This instrument is copied from one long used by the Bank of England to prevent deposit expansion when commercial banks unexpectedly find themselves with excess reserves at a time when the central bank does not deem monetary expansion desirable.

The act also initiated a phasing out of the interest rate ceilings that, as discussed above, had existed for certain types of deposits. The act will make the banking system much more competitive. It will also free monetary policy from the need to offset distortions caused by such regulations as ceilings on deposit interest rates.

INSTRUMENTS AND OBJECTIVES OF MONETARY POLICY

The Fed conducts monetary policy in order to influence output, unemployment, and inflation. These variables—the ultimate objectives of the Fed's policy—are called **policy variables.** The variables that it controls *directly* in order to achieve these objectives are called its **policy instruments.** Sometimes it is also useful for the Fed to identify variables that are neither policy variables nor policy instruments but that nevertheless play a key role in the execution of monetary policy. These variables are called the central bank's **intermediate targets;** their importance lies in the influence they exert on the policy variables.

Policy Variables

The major policy variable that we shall consider in this chapter is nominal national income. The Fed can seek to remove inflationary and GNP gaps by its monetary policy and thus seek to influence national income. In so doing it also influences employment and, hence, unemployment.

Another major policy variable that is sometimes important is the rate of interest. For a number of reasons the Fed may be concerned about the rate of interest quite separately from any effects that the rate may have on national income. Indeed, as discussed in the box, there is potential conflict between the interest rate and national income as policy variables.

Nominal GNP as a policy variable. Changes in nominal GNP reflect changes both in real GNP and in the price level. In principle the central bank will be concerned about how a given change in nominal GNP is divided between these two components. However, as we saw in Chapter 34, monetary policy operates by influencing aggregate de-

A CONFLICT BETWEEN NATIONAL INCOME AND THE RATE OF INTEREST AS POLICY VARIABLES

There are several reasons why the Fed may wish to focus on the interest rate as a policy variable in its own right. First, the higher the rate of interest, the higher the cost of servicing the national debt. The government thus is obviously concerned to keep the interest rate it pays as low as possible, and the Fed may sometimes wish to assist the government in holding the rate down. Second, the Fed may want to prevent interest rates from changing too rapidly, thereby causing severe financial strain on those who are vulnerable to rapid changes in interest rates. Third, the Fed may be concerned with the American balance of payments. If American interest rates are high relative to those in the rest of the world, there may be an influx of foreign capital to take advantage of the high U.S. rates. If American rates are low relative to those in the rest of the world, there may be a large outflow of capital from the United States to foreign financial centers. Rapid movements of international funds can be upsetting to the economy (as we shall see in Chapter 42). The Fed may thus desire to control U.S. interest rates in order to influence international capital flows.

The Fed cannot set policies with respect to both national income and the interest rate and expect to achieve them both. Assume, for example, that the Fed picks a rate of interest that it wishes to maintain. It must now enter the open market and buy or sell however many bonds are necessary to stabilize the interest rate at its desired level. If the Fed has to buy bonds to stop the rate of interest from rising above its target level, it will be expanding the money supply. If the Fed has to sell bonds to stop the rate of interest from falling below its target level, it will be contracting the money supply. In either case the Fed's policy with respect to the interest rate *determines* what it must do to the money supply. By choosing the rate of interest as the policy variable, the Fed loses control over the money supply—the money supply will rise or fall depending on whether the Fed is acting to prevent the interest rate from falling below or rising above its target value.

What are the consequences of a Fed policy to stabilize, or at least to reduce the fluctuations in, the rate of interest? Normally in the upswing of a business cycle interest rates rise as funds for investment become scarce. The rise in interest rates causes a reduction in all interest-sensitive expenditure, which helps to restrain the boom. However, when the Fed is committed to a policy of holding the rate of interest constant, it must supply all the funds that are demanded at the fixed rate of interest but not supplied by the private sector. The Fed's policy will cause the money supply to expand and will prevent interest rates from rising to restrain investment demand. This will cause the boom to be stronger than it otherwise would have been.

An analogous result occurs in the downswing of a cycle. Normally in a recession the falloff in the demand to borrow money leads to a fall in the rate of interest, which helps to increase all interest-sensitive expenditure and thereby reduce the severity of the recession. However, if the Fed is committed to holding the rate of interest constant, it will have to enter the market and sell bonds to keep their price from rising. This reduces the money supply and prevents interest rates from falling. The policy of stabilizing the rate of interest thus tends to make the downswing more severe than it otherwise would have been.

When the rate of interest is a policy variable, the money supply varies with the business cycle. Cyclical swings in national income are larger than they would be if the Fed controlled the money supply and left interest rates free to vary.

mand, and the most that can be hoped for is to achieve a given *AD* curve.

The analysis in Chapter 34 suggests that in the short-run, the influence of monetary policy will be *divided* between the price level and real output in a manner determined by the slope of the *SRAS* curve. Thus, while the central bank cares about the separate reactions of the price level *and* of real output, there is little it can do in the short run to achieve such goals independently. For any price level response that is achieved, the real output consequence must be accepted. Alternatively, for any real output response that is achieved, the price level consequence must be accepted. The two objectives of influencing *P* and *Y* cannot be pursued independently using monetary policy. For this reason we choose to focus on nominal GNP (*PY*) as the target for monetary policy, at least in the short run.

We have seen that in the long run, when the level of wages is fully adjusted to the price level, the *LRAS* curve is vertical and hence the major impact of monetary policy will be on the price level. Monetary policy is ineffective in influencing long-run real output.

Policy Instruments

Having selected its policy variables and formulated targets for their behavior, the Fed must decide how to achieve these targets. How can the policy variables be made to perform in the way that the Fed wishes? Since the Fed cannot control income or inflation directly, it must employ its policy instruments, which it does control directly, to influence aggregate demand in the desired manner.

The primary method used by the Fed to conduct monetary policy is open market operations.

The Fed may choose between two alternative procedures in conducting its open market operations. It may set the *price* (and hence the interest rate) at which it sells or buys bonds on the open market. In this case the quantity of bonds sold or purchased is determined by market demand. If the Fed wishes to change its policy, it must change the price at which it stands willing to buy and sell bonds. This approach is called **interest rate con-**

trol, and here the interest rate is properly viewed as a policy instrument.

Alternatively, the Fed may choose to set the *quantity* of open market sales or purchases. In this case it is the price of bonds, and hence the interest rate, that is determined by market demand. If the Fed wishes to change its policy, it changes the amount of its open market purchases or sales. (Of course this means that the interest rate at which these transactions are made may also change.) Open market operations change the size of the Fed's monetary liabilities, also called the **monetary base**, given by the sum of currency in circulation plus reserves of the commercial banks.[2] (See Table 35-3.) In this case, where the Fed chooses to set the quantity of its open market operations, it is said to be using **base control**, and the monetary base is properly viewed as the policy instrument.

The central bank cannot expect to be able to control both the interest rate and the monetary base independently. This is because of the liquidity preference function, which relates the quantity of money to the rate of interest.

Intermediate Targets

Major changes in the direction or method of monetary policy are made only infrequently. Decisions regarding the implementation of policy must, however, be made almost daily. Given the values desired for the policy variables and the current state of the economy, is a purchase or a sale in the open market called for? How big a purchase? Or how big a sale? At what interest rate? These questions must be answered continually by the Fed in its day-to-day operations.

While these decisions have to be made frequently, information about the policy variables is available only infrequently. Inflation and unemployment rates are available only on a monthly basis, and then with a considerable lag. National income figures are available even less regularly; they appear on a quarterly basis. Thus the policy-

---

[2] These monetary liabilities, as we saw in Chapter 33, form the *base* on which commercial banks can expand and create deposits.

makers do not know exactly what is happening to the policy variables when they make decisions regarding the setting of their policy instruments.

How, then, does the Fed make decisions? Central banks have typically used other variables, called *intermediate targets*, to guide them when implementing monetary policy in the very short run. To serve as an intermediate target, a variable must satisfy two criteria. First, information about it must be available on a frequent basis, daily if possible. Second, its movements must be closely correlated with those of the policy variable so that changes in it can reasonably be expected to indicate that the policy variable is also changing.

The two most commonly used intermediate targets are the money supply and the interest rate. As we have seen the two are not independent of each other. Hence it is important that the central bank not choose a target for one that is inconsistent with the other. By the same token, since the two are closely related it might appear not to matter much which one is used. We take up this point below.

Table 35-4 illustrates some possible operating regimes for the central bank. If the Fed chooses the interest rate as its intermediate target, it can achieve that target directly by using interest rate control as its instrument. In this case the distinction between intermediate target and policy instrument is superfluous. If the Fed chooses the money supply as its intermediate target, it must achieve its target indirectly by means of either base control or interest rate control.

TABLE 35-4 ASSIGNMENT OF VARIABLES UNDER ALTERNATIVE OPERATING REGIMES OF MONETARY POLICY

Regime	Policy instrument	Intermediate target	Policy variables
1. Monetary targeting: base control	Open market operations; regulate volume of open market sales and purchases	Quantity of money (M1) via money supply process	GNP Inflation Unemployment
2. Monetary targeting: interest rate control	Open market operations; regulate price at which open market sales and purchases are made (i.e., regulate interest rate)	Quantity of money (M1) via liquidity preference	GNP Inflation Unemployment
3. Interest rate targeting	Open market operations; regulate intermediate target directly	Interest rates	GNP Inflation Unemployment

Even with a given set of policy variables, central banks might adopt a variety of operating regimes. The central bank could use either the quantity of money or the interest rate as its intermediate target.

When the central bank opts for monetary targeting, it can influence its target only indirectly. Through its open market operations it can control directly either the size of the monetary base or the level of interest rates. If it controls the monetary base (Regime 1), the quantity of money is influenced via the money supply process while the interest rate is determined via monetary equilibrium as in Figure 34-2. If the central bank controls the interest rate (Regime 2), the influence on the quantity of money op-

erates via the liquidity preference function.

Should the central bank choose to use the interest rate as an intermediate target (Regime 3), it can achieve its target directly by using open market operations to control the interest rate. Although this appears to be a simpler process (and in terms of operation, it is simpler), many economists favor monetary targeting.

Other variables, such as the interest rate and the exchange rate, might also appear as policy variables. The interest rate could then appear as a policy instrument, an intermediate target, or a policy variable, depending on the policy regime.

National income, unemployment, and inflation are all policy variables. The money supply can be an intermediate target or a policy instrument. The interest rate can be a policy target, a policy instrument, or an intermediate target.

Controlling Nominal National Income Through Monetary Policy

When the Fed makes nominal national income its main policy variable, it must work through such policy instruments as the money supply and the rate of interest.

Assume that in pursuit of an expansionary policy the Fed wishes to increase aggregate demand. It will enter the open market and buy bonds. This expands the reserves of the commercial banks and leads to an increase in the money supply, as analyzed in Chapter 33. The increase in the money supply forces the interest rate down and leads to an increase in investment expenditure. As we saw in Chapter 34, this shifts the aggregate demand function rightward, which is the result desired. A contractionary policy is achieved by reversing the process: the Fed sells bonds, thereby reducing the money supply, raising interest rates, and shifting the aggregate demand curve to the left.

But how does the Fed decide whether to buy or sell bonds on the open market? This is the role of the intermediate targets.

The Choice Between the Money Supply and the Rate of Interest As Intermediate Targets

Suppose the Fed takes the level of national income as its policy variable and chooses either the rate of interest or the money supply as its intermediate target. Since the two potential instrumental variables are not independent of each other, it might not seem to matter which the Fed selects.

For example, if the Fed wishes to remove an inflationary gap by forcing interest rates up, it will sell securities and thus drive their prices down. These open market sales will also contract the money supply. Thus it is largely immaterial whether the Fed seeks to force interest rates up or

to contract the money supply; doing one will accomplish the other. Similarly, driving interest rates down by open market purchases of government securities will tend to expand the money supply as the public gains money in return for the securities it sells to the Fed.

Despite the interrelation of these two variables, many economists have argued that the Fed should' use the money supply rather than interest rates as its intermediate target. They maintain that when the money supply is used not only is it much easier for the Fed to assess the trends of the economy, but it is also easier for commentators and key economic decision makers to assess the current stance of the Fed's policy.

The argument proceeds in three steps.

1. In times of business expansion, both interest rates and the money supply will be rising. Interest rates rise because of a heavy demand to borrow money and an increasing shortage of loanable funds. The money supply expands because banks let their excess reserves fall to very low levels in order to meet the pressing demands from their customers for loans.

2. If the Fed seeks to restrain this business expansion because it is threatening to produce a serious inflationary gap, it will wish to *accentuate* the rising trend in interest rates but *reverse* the rising trend in the money supply. This is because a restrictive monetary policy requires the Fed to increase interest rates and reduce (or slow the rate of expansion of) the money supply. By selling bonds on the open market it does both.

3. It is easier to determine whether the Fed's current policy is contradictory, expansionary, or neutral when it is working through the money supply rather than through interest rates. When a typical interest rate rises to 15 percent during an expansion, we may be uncertain how much of this rise is due to the Fed's tightening of monetary policy and how much of it would have happened anyway. Indeed, the more rapid the expansion, the more rapidly will interest rates be rising without assistance from the Fed. But when the rate of increase of the money supply rises above its target range during an expansion, this indicates that monetary policy is accommodating the expansion, *pro-*

vided the demand for money remains a stable function of income and interest rates.

The italicized qualification is important. What we observe is the money supply. Whether or not monetary policy is tight concerns the *relation between* the demand for money and its supply. If the demand for money is shifting, the money supply may provide a misleading intermediate target. Assume, as for example has happened in the past, that the demand for money is shifting to the left, so that less money is demanded at each interest rate and level of income. A declining money supply may then be misread as an indicator of a tight monetary policy. If, however, the demand is falling faster than the supply, then monetary policy may actually be very lax.

In the 1950s and 1960s, the Fed operated with interest rates as its main intermediate target. This led to occasional uncertainty about the stance of monetary policy. For example, in the period 1961–1965 short-term interest rates rose steadily from around 2 percent to over 4 percent, apparently indicating a period of restrictive monetary policy. However, that was also a period of economic recovery, with unemployment falling steadily from the historically high level of 6 percent to 7 percent in 1961 to 4.5 percent in 1965. It was this boom that fueled the rise in interest rates; the rate of growth of the money supply actually increased from 1.8 percent in 1962 to 3.7 percent in 1963 and 4.7 percent in the next two years, indicating that monetary policy was actually accommodating the boom rather than resisting it.

MONETARY POLICY IN ACTION

Having studied the objectives and instruments of monetary policy, we may now consider how monetary policy has actually worked in the period since World War II. Monetary policy is formulated by the Federal Open Market Committee (FOMC), which was described earlier in this chapter. The FOMC generally meets every four weeks; its decisions are embodied in a directive issued to the Federal Reserve Bank of New York. Open market operations are conducted in the New York Fed by the manager of the system's Open Market Account.

The Accord

The use of monetary policy as a tool of stabilization policy in the postwar period began in 1951 with the famous Treasury-Federal Reserve Accord. Under this agreement the Federal Reserve discontinued the practice, which had been carried on throughout World War II, of supporting the prices of treasury securities to facilitate the financing of the war effort. This practice had meant that the Fed held the interest rate down—thereby keeping the cost of servicing the debt low[3]—and that it supplied new money to buy any part of a government debt issue that the public would not buy at the fixed rate of interest. The effect of this policy was that the Fed had no control over the money supply. Indeed the supply expanded rapidly, with serious inflationary consequences, whenever the government demand to borrow was too heavy to be met by private lending at the going rate of interest.

The Shift from Interest Rates to the Money Supply As the Main Intermediate Target

The basic concern of monetary policy since the accord has been the achievement of such policy objectives as full employment and price stability. To make these broader economic objectives operational, however, the FOMC must translate them into the intermediate targets over which the Fed has a direct influence.

Prior to 1970 the operating instructions of the FOMC were generally couched in terms of money-market conditions, that is, short-term interest

[3] During World War II this was a dominant objective of the Fed. Between 1941 and 1945 the federal debt rose from about $50 billion to about $250 billion. This enormous debt offering was kept inexpensive to the Treasury by the Fed's keeping the interest rate on three-month treasury bills at 0.375 percent and on three-to-five year bonds at under 1.5 percent.

rates, borrowing by member banks from the Federal Reserve, and the net excess reserve position of member banks.[4] Some references were made to monetary aggregates, but they were generally confined to statements concerning the desired behavior of bank credit.

In the 1970s monetary aggregates came to play a more prominent role, and the emphasis shifted from intermediate targets that were specified in terms of money-market conditions to those specified as target rates of growth of the money supply. The measure used for this purpose has generally been the narrowly defined money supply, M1, but broader definitions have also been taken into account.[5] The shift to greater emphasis on controlling the money supply on the part of the Federal Reserve reflected the growing influence of the monetarist view within the economics profession.

[4] Net excess reserves are defined as total reserves *minus* legally required reserves *minus* borrowing from the Fed. These are sometimes also called *free reserves*.

[5] As we explained in Chapter 33, the definition of M1 has changed over the years. The Fed now publishes a revised, "shift-adjusted" series that takes account of these changes and allows historical comparisons.

The Use of Monetary Policy Since the Accord

Figure 35-1 shows the behavior of M1, the narrowly defined money supply, and of M2, a broader definition of the money supply. Although the two measures differ sharply in behavior in any given year, two things stand out. First, by either measure, monetary growth has shown sharp, short-period changes—from being quite expansive to being highly restrictive. Second, by either measure, there has been a steady upward trend in the rate of monetary expansion.

The Variability of Monetary Policy

From 1952 to 1967 the inflation rate was relatively low—under 3 percent—but unemployment frequently rose well above what was then regarded as the very high figure of 4 percent. As a result the Fed made national income one of its main target variables with a view to influencing unemployment. The sharp variations in the rate of monetary expansion resulted primarily from the Fed's attempt to use monetary policy to fine tune the economy.

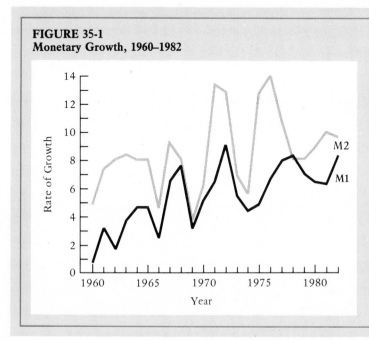

**FIGURE 35-1
Monetary Growth, 1960–1982**

The rate of monetary expansion has shown substantial short-term variability combined with a strong long-term upward trend. The dark black line shows the annual rate of growth of money narrowly defined, M1. The shaded black line shows this same rate for the broader monetary aggregate, M2. Although for any given year fluctuations in the two are not very closely related, both exhibit the same general pattern.

Policy was typically jerky, oscillating from "full ahead" to "hard astern." The recessions of 1954–1955, 1957–1958, 1960–1961, and 1969–1970 were fought with expansionary monetary policies. Then when inflation increased during the later recovery phases, monetary policy typically turned sharply contractionary.

The decade of the 1960s ended with contractionary monetary and fiscal policies. But the restrictive policy was short-lived, and a very expansionary policy was followed over the next three years. The peak rate of monetary expansion in terms of M1 was over 9 percent in 1972. It is clear that both monetary and fiscal policy helped turn the upswing of the early 1970s into an unsustainable boom that ended in an almost unprecedented inflation rate during 1973–1974. This led the Fed once again to reverse direction in 1973. The rate of monetary expansion was steadily reduced until it fell below 5 percent in 1974 and 1975. With the inflation rate running close to 10 percent this represented a very sharp drop in the real money supply. At the same time a severe recession had set in and restrictive monetary restraint certainly helped to accentuate it.

In 1976 and 1977 the Fed pursued a mild expansionary policy. By the end of 1978, however, inflation had once more become a prime concern and mildly contractionary policies were introduced. In mid 1979 the brakes were applied more strongly: the rate of monetary growth was reduced and interest rates were driven to unprecedented levels. By early 1980 it was clear that the policy had worked; a downturn had been induced, and the economy was well into a recession.

Most observers agree that monetary policy was often perverse throughout the 1970s. A series of alternating expansionary and contractionary policies augmented the economy's natural cyclical swings.

Several senior economists have spoken of "this incredible series of self-inflicted wounds." In a detailed study of the mid 1970s, Professor Alan Blinder of Princeton University says that monetary policy in the period "bears eloquent witness to the monetarists' incessant complaint that policy is too variable, too apt to swing from one extreme to another. It is true that whenever monetary policy departed notably from what a fixed rule would have called for, it did so in the wrong direction and made things worse than they need to have been."[6]

The Rising Trend of Monetary Expansion, 1960–1980

As shown in Figure 35-1, fluctuations in monetary expansion have occurred around a rising trend. This rising trend accompanied a similar trend in prices, indicating an unmistakable correlation between the rate of monetary expansion and the rate of inflation. But correlation does not in itself prove causation, and there is some debate about the causes of the American inflation over that period.

Monetarists believe that monetary expansion has been the main cause of inflation in the 1970s and 1980s while others believe that it is mainly a passive reaction to it. Either way there is no doubt that the inflation of the 1970s has been validated by monetary expansion. Most economists believed that there is little chance of reducing inflation to the relatively modest levels of the 1950s and 1960s until the rate of monetary expansion is reduced to the more modest annual rates of those years.

The period 1980–1982 witnessed a concerted effort on the part of the Fed to reduce the rate of monetary expansion, and inflation rates began to respond in late 1982. Whether or not this represents a long-run movement away from the tendency to increasing inflation or just a temporary deviation from that course remains to be seen.

A monetary rule? The dismal record of monetary policy lent force to the monetarists' persistent criticisms of monetary fine tuning. Monetarists argue that (1) monetary policy is a potent force of expansionary and contractionary pressures; (2) monetary policy works with lags that are both long and variable; and (3) the Fed is in fact given to sudden and strong reversals of its policy stance. Consequently monetary policy has a destabilizing effect on the economy, the policy itself accentuating

---

[6] Alan S. Blinder, *Economic Policy and the Great Stagflation* (New York: Academic Press, 1979), p. 201.

CAN MONETARY POLICY BE DESTABILIZING?

In the real world the full effects of monetary policy occur only after quite long time lags. Lags that occur after the decision is made to implement the policy, called *execution lags*, can have important implications for the conduct of monetary policy.

Sources of Execution Lags

1. Open market operations affect the reserves of the chartered banks. The full increase in the money supply occurs only when the banks have granted enough new loans and made enough investments to expand the money supply by the full amount permitted by existing reserve ratios. This process can take quite a long time.

2. The division of all assets into money and bonds was useful for seeing the underlying forces at work in determining the demand for money. In fact, however, there is a whole series of assets—from currency and demand deposits to term deposits, to treasury bills and short-term bonds, to very long-term bonds and equities. When households find themselves with larger money balances than they require, a chain of substitution occurs, with short-term and long-term interest rates falling as households try to hold less money and more interest-earning assets. The change in longer-term interest rates will in turn affect interest-sensitive expenditures. These adjustments along a chain of interest rates can take considerable time to work out.

3. It takes time for new investment plans to be drawn up, approved, and put into effect. It may easily take up to a year before the full increase in investment expenditure builds up in response to a fall in interest rates.

4. The increased investment expenditures will set off a multiplier process that increases national income by some multiple of the initiating increase in investment expenditure. This too takes some time to work out.

Similar considerations apply to contractionary monetary policies that seek to shift the aggregate expenditure function downward. Furthermore, although the end result is fairly predictable, the speed with which the entire expansionary or contractionary process works itself out can vary from time to time in ways that are hard to predict.

Monetary policy is capable of exerting expansionary and contractionary forces on the economy, but it operates with a time lag that is long and unpredictably variable.

Implications of Execution Lags

To see the significance of execution lags for the conduct of monetary policy, assume that the execution lag is 18 months. If on December 1 the Fed decides that the economy needs stimulus, it can be increasing the money supply within days, and by the end of the year a significant increase may be registered.

But because the full effects of this policy take time to work out, the policy may prove to be destabilizing. By the fall of next year a substantial inflationary gap may have developed. The Fed may then call for a contractionary policy, but the full effects of the monetary expansion initiated nine months earlier is just being felt—so an expansionary monetary stimulus is adding to the existing inflationary gap. If the Fed now applies the monetary brakes by contracting the money supply, the full effects of this move will not be felt for another 18 months. By that time a contraction may have already set in because of the natural cyclical forces of the economy. If so, the delayed effects of the monetary policy may turn a minor downturn into a major recession.

The long execution lag of monetary policy makes monetary fine tuning difficult, and it may make it destabilizing.

If the execution lag were known with certainty, it could be built into the Fed's calculations. But the fact that the lag is highly variable makes this nearly impossible. Of course, when a persistent gap has existed and is predicted to continue for a long time, monetary policy may be stabilizing even when its effects occur after a long-time lag.

rather than dampening the economy's natural cyclical swings. This is discussed further in the box.

Monetarists argue from this position that the stability of the economy would be much improved if the Fed stopped trying to stabilize it. What then should the Fed do? Since growth of population and of productivity lead to a rising level of output, the Fed ought to provide the extra money needed to allow the holding of additional transactions, precautionary, and speculative balances as real income and wealth rise over time.

According to the monetarists, the Fed should expand the money supply year in and year out at a constant rate equal to the rate of growth of real income. When the growth rate shows signs of long-term change, the Fed can adjust its rate of monetary expansion. It should not, however, alter this rate with a view to stabilizing the economy against short-term fluctuations.

Theorists have conducted a long debate over this monetarist recommendation. The outcome is that,

at least in many standard models of the economy, cyclical fluctuations can be made smaller with the best fine tuning policy than they are with a constant-rate rule. However:

Experience of the 1970s convinced many that whatever may be true of the best conceivable monetary policy, the Fed's actual policy made cyclical fluctuations much larger than they would have been under a constant-rate rule.

The Reagan-Volcker Monetary Policy, 1981–1982

During the last half of the 1970s the Fed focused on M1 as its intermediate target and formulated monetary policy in terms of target growth rates for the money supply that were reported *in advance* to Congress. In 1980 the Fed reaffirmed its commitment to monetary growth targets and, consistent with the avowed policy of reducing inflation, announced a target range of M1 growth of 3.5 percent

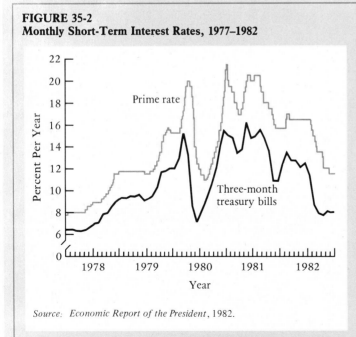

FIGURE 35-2
Monthly Short-Term Interest Rates, 1977–1982

Short-term interest rates were high but variable in the period 1980–1982. Short-term interest rates displayed a gradual upward trend from 1978 through 1980. Tight monetary policy following the Monetary Control Act of 1980 led to sharp interest-rate cycles and high average interest rates.

Source: Economic Report of the President, 1982.

FIGURE 35-3
Nominal and Real Three-Month Treasury Bill Interest Rates, 1955–1982

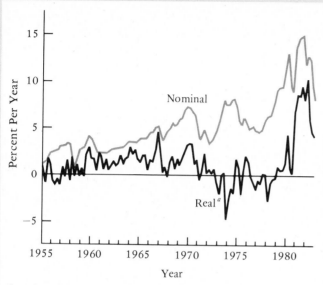

Nominal interest rates rose gradually over the 1960s and 1970s and then rose sharply and irregularly in the 1980s. Real rates fluctuated with no discernable trend until 1980. Until the 1980s the rise in nominal interest rates, as measured by the three-month treasury bill rate, was roughly matched by the increase in the inflation rate, as measured by the percentage annual change in the personal consumption deflator. The real interest rate therefore showed no discernable trend. In the early 1980s, however, real rates also rose sharply, as increases in nominal interest rates outstripped increases in the inflation rate.

[a] Equals nominal yield less actual rate of inflation, defined by personal consumption deflator, over the period to maturity.
Source: Economic Report of the President, 1982.

to 6.5 percent for 1981 and reduced this to 2.5 percent to 5.5 percent for 1982. (The M2 target range was 6 percent to 9 percent for both years.) Actual M1 growth was 6.4 percent in 1981—just within the target range—and 8.5 percent in 1982— well above the target range. Apparently only a fairly moderate monetary slowdown occurred—actual M1 growth had been 7.1 percent in 1979 and 6.6 percent in 1980.

In 1980 the Fed also switched from a regime of interest rate control to a regime of base control. Although this policy requires that interest rates be free to find their own level, many economists did not expect the degree of interest rate volatility shown in Figure 35-2. The sharp rise in interest rates in late 1980 helped choke off the recovery that had just started. The rise in rates in early 1982 fed the downturn and helped make it the most serious recession since the 1930s. Inflation responded dramatically, falling from about 9 percent in 1981 to about 4 percent in 1982, and this led to a significant fall in interest rates over the last half of 1982.

Not only were interest rates variable over this period, the average level of both real and nominal rates was very high, as is shown in Figure 35-3.

These interest rate levels, and the recession they wrought, were more severe than might have been expected from the monetary policy that was planned. What happened to cause the high interest rates and the severe recession in the face of this moderate slowdown in the rate of growth of the money supply?

Changes in money demand. The key to the puzzle lay in the relation between the demand for money and nominal national income. Historically the demand for M1 had been growing about 3 percent slower than nominal income, indicating that the public was gradually economizing on money balances. The Fed projected this past trend and estimated that the demand for money would continue to grow at a rate slower than that of nominal income. The Fed then set a target growth rate for M1 sufficient to allow an increase in nominal income (PY) in excess of the expected rise in the price level (P). This would have allowed some increase, therefore, in real output (Y). But the Fed's projections were mistaken. The demand for money grew only 1 percentage more slowly than nominal income in 1981 and about 5 percent faster than nominal income in 1982. As a result of this unexpected surge in the demand for money, there was a severe money shortage—that is, monetary policy was much tighter than the Fed had expected. This was not because money supply targets were missed but because money demand was underestimated.

How did the Fed react to this change in money demand? In part the Fed's reaction was to raise the level of monetary growth. In late 1981 M1 growth was allowed to run up quite rapidly (reaching an annual rate of 14.5 percent in the third quarter), so that at the end of the year, M1 was well above its target range. But basically the Fed stuck to its monetary targets, and as a result it pursued very restrictive monetary policy. This created a heated controversy in the financial press and caused many critics to openly attack the policies of the Fed and its chairman, Paul Volcker.

In February 1982 the FOMC decided that the rapid increase in M1 in late 1981 was temporary and reaffirmed its money growth targets for 1982. More importantly it planned to achieve those growth *rates* relative to the *target level* of M1, not the *actual level*. The late 1981 run-up in M1 meant that in December 1981 the actual level of M1 was well above the target level. As a result the Fed's announced intentions meant that actual money growth was going to be below the target rate because the *level* of the money supply had to be reduced to compensate for the late 1981 increases

in M1. While the target rate of growth was 4 percent in 1982, meeting that target meant that actual growth relative to the actual December 1981 money stock would be less than 1 percent.

Consequently the Fed slowed down the expansion of reserves in the next few months. By June 1982 M1 was back in its target range. But the serious weakness in the economy and the "room for monetary ease" created by the return of M1 to its target range led to a loosening of monetary policy in the second half of 1982. This, combined with the dramatic fall in the inflation rate, led to a sharp decline in interest rates in late 1982 and early 1983.

Why did the Fed allow this severely contractionary policy to persist so long? One possibility is that the Fed was actually quite happy to have a very contractionary policy. Gradualist policies elsewhere (e.g., in Canada from 1975 to 1980) and previously in the United States had failed to have any marked effect on inflation, and many observers had come to the view that only a sharp contraction would lower expectations and so allow the actual inflation rate to fall.

Another possibility is that having announced its targets for monetary growth, the Fed had to adhere to them in order to maintain its own credibility. Failure to meet the targets, this argument runs, would undermine belief in the Fed's commitment to reducing inflation. Such a loss of confidence would in turn work to make interest rates and the actual inflation rate respond sluggishly to the Fed's policies.

A third possibility is that the ability of the Fed to react to the developments of the 1981–1982 period was hindered by its commitment to targeting on monetary aggregates. Over that period the relationship between those targets and the level of economic activity was subject to many competing forces. Also, the shifts in money demand discussed above were caused by many factors. Some of these shifts occurred in response to regulatory changes that provided new financial opportunities like the NOW accounts and MMFs discussed in Chapter 33. Others occurred in response to financial innovation arising from the explosion in new electronics communication and information technology. These developments made the interpretation of the macroeconomic significance of changes in monetary aggregates very difficult. In the face of such uncertainty, the Fed had to balance the risk of letting monetary aggregates rise too quickly, thus fueling inflation, against the risk of being too contractionary, thus generating too severe a recession.

Recent financial innovation and deregulation has enhanced the efficiency of the U.S. financial system but has severely hampered the operation of monetary policy and in particular wrecked havoc on the role of monetary aggregates as intermediate targets. Information about the growth of the money supply has not provided an accurate indication of the stance of monetary policy because the demand for M1 has been shifting continuously under the impact of these changes. Control of growth in the money supply has not provided precise control of the economy.

It is clear that the performance of monetary policy would have been improved had the monetary targets been revised to offset the *shifts* in money demand. But separating permanent shifts from temporary shifts or just errors in the data is only possible after intensive study. This made the implementation of monetary policy extremely difficult. It has also made economists and central bankers pessimistic not only about the role of monetary rules but also about the usefulness of the money supply as an intermediate target. Indeed explicit targets were temporarily abandoned in late 1982. In February 1983 the Fed announced a new set of targets. But it stated that it was going to focus primarily on its targets for M2 in the expectation that the demand for M2 would prove to be more stable than that for M1 and hence that movements in M2 would prove to be more valuable as a guide to developments in the economy.

Monetary Policy: Some Interim Conclusions

Most economists agree that rapid changes in the money supply have major effects on aggregate demand. They also agree that slowing the rate of monetary expansion is a necessary condition for avoiding rapid inflations. Furthermore, many economists hold that if we knew enough, changes in the money supply could be used to help in the government's efforts to stabilize the economy by avoiding the extremes of large inflationary and deflationary gaps.

There is disagreement, however, on a number of important issues that we summarize here and discuss in more detail in Part Nine.

1. Is control of the money supply a sufficient means of controlling inflation? Some economists answer yes. Others think not and look to causes of inflation in addition to excessive monetary expansion.

2. How strong is the influence of monetary policy on aggregate expenditure? Do small changes in the money supply yield large changes in aggregate expenditure, or are large changes in monetary magnitudes needed to induce desired changes in aggregated expenditure? We discussed this issue in Chapter 34, and we shall return to it in Part Nine.

3. If stabilization policy is to be used, what are the appropriate relative roles of monetary and fiscal policies? At one extreme some economists give monetary policy a relatively minor role as a supplement to fiscal policy; at the other extreme some economists give it the exclusive role, arguing that fiscal policy is effective only to the extent that it causes changes in the money supply.

4. Although the experience of the 1970s convinced many economists that monetary policy had in fact been a serious destabilizer, controversy continues on the conclusion to be drawn from this unhappy experience. Should we give up trying to follow a discretionary monetary stabilization policy and instead adopt a fixed rule of monetary expansion, or should we merely try to do better with discretionary policy next time?

5. With continued financial innovation and shifts in demands for various monetary assets, will any conceivable monetary rule have a stabilizing effect on the economy? In adopting such a rule, won't the Fed then have to continually alter both

the magnitude on which it is targeting and the range of values targeted?

SUMMARY

1. The central bank of the United States is the set of Federal Reserve banks and its board of governors. Although nominally private the Reserve banks in fact belong to a system that functions as a central bank. Effective power is exercised by the board of governors, whose seven members are appointed by the president of the United States for 14-year terms.

2. The Fed (as the Federal Reserve system is called) can affect the reserves of the commercial banking system in many ways. Among other things it can change required reserves, change the rate of interest at which it will lend to commercial banks, and rely on open market operations.

3. The major policy instrument used by the Fed is open market operations. The purchase of bonds on the open market is expansionary because it increases reserves, permitting (but not forcing) a multiple expansion of bank credit. The sale of bonds on the open market reduces bank reserves, forcing a multiple contraction of bank credit on the part of all banks that do not have excess reserves.

4. The ultimate objectives of the Fed's monetary policy are called its *policy variables*. In principle these include real national income and the rate of change of the price level. However, in practice nominal income is often taken to be the policy variable since the Fed cannot expect to be able to influence the composition of changes in nominal income between real growth and inflation. Interest rates are also sometimes taken to be a policy variable.

5. Where the Fed cannot influence its policy variables directly, it must work through policy instruments that it can control and that will in turn influence its policy variables. Intermediate targets are used to guide decisions about policy instru-

ments. The money supply and the interest rate may both be either intermediate targets or policy instruments.

6. National income can also be influenced by open market operations. To reduce national income the Fed sells bonds on the open market, thereby driving up the rate of interest and reducing the reserves. To increase national income the Fed buys bonds on the open market, thereby driving down the rate of interest and increasing the reserves.

7. Since it cannot control both independently, the Fed must choose between the interest rate and the money supply as its intermediate target.

8. The modern use of monetary policy in the United States dates from the 1951 accord between the Treasury and the Fed by which the Fed's main objective ceased to be minimizing the cost of financing the government's debt by controlling interest rates. In the 1950s and 1960s the rate of interest was the main intermediate target through which the Fed sought to influence national income. In the 1970s the emphasis shifted to influencing national income through the money supply.

9. The Fed has sometimes been criticized for alternating too quickly between expansionary and contractionary policy and thereby contributing to cyclical swings in the economy. In the 1960s and 1970s a series of strong and abrupt changes in monetary policy often combined with long execution lags to exert a destabilizing force on the economy.

10. In the early 1980s the Fed underestimated the growth in the demand for money. Meeting its money supply targets thus implied a much tighter monetary policy than was at first intended. Monetary tightness caused high and variable interest rates, leading to a severe recession and eventually to a sharp fall in inflation.

11. It is unclear why the Fed stuck to its tough policy even after it became apparent that it was too severe. Three possible reasons can be offered: (i) disillusioned with the poor performance of gradual monetary restraint, the Fed welcomed the sudden burst of severe monetary stringency it had inadvertently brought about; (ii) having announced monetary targets the Fed was afraid that relaxing them would set up strong inflationary expectations that would upset the economy; and (iii) the strong shifts in money demand may have sufficiently confused everyone so that the severity of the policy was not fully appreciated.

12. It is generally agreed that rapid changes in the money supply and interest rates can have large effects on the economy. There is disagreement, however, on how much monetary policy can and should be used as a device for stabilizing the economy or coping with temporary bouts of rising prices.

TOPICS FOR REVIEW

Functions of a central bank
The discount rate
Open market operations
Policy variables, policy instruments, and intermediate targets
The variability of monetary policy and monetary rules
The appropriateness of monetary targets when money demand is shifting

DISCUSSION QUESTIONS

1. In the study of banking history we often see the term *elastic currency.* For example, to provide an elastic currency was a purpose behind the creation of the Federal Reserve System. What do you think this term might mean, and why might it be emphasized?

2. In the late summer of 1983, a debate raged among critics of the Fed. One group held that monetary policy was too restrictive since high real interest rates were unnecessarily threatening the recovery from the 1982 recession. Another group held that monetary policy was too expansionary since high rates of growth of the money supply portended a rebounding of inflation. Examine the statistics to see what has happened since to interest rates, money supply, inflation, and output, and evaluate the arguments made by the two groups.

3. The Federal Reserve Board runs a facility in Culpeper, Virginia, that costs $1.8 million per year to maintain and to guard against robbery, according to Senator William Proxmire of Wisconsin. Inside this "Culpeper switch," a dugout in the side of a mountain, the government has hidden $4 billion in new currency for the purpose, it says, of "providing a hedge against any nuclear attack that would wipe out the nation's money supply." Comment on the sense of this policy.

4. Describe the chief weapons of monetary policy available to the Federal Reserve and indicate whether, and if so how, they might be used for the following purposes:
   a. to create a mild tightening of bank credit
   b. to signal that the Board of Governors favors a sharp curtailment of bank lending
   c. to permit an expansion of bank credit with existing reserves
   d. to supply banks and the public with a temporary increase of currency for Christmas shopping

5. It is often said that an expansionary monetary policy is like "pushing on a string." What is meant by such a statement? How does this contrast with a contractionary fiscal policy?

6. In what situations might the following pairs of objectives come into conflict?
   a. keeping the cost of government finance low *and* using monetary policy to change aggregate demand
   b. signaling a tighter monetary policy by raising interest rates *and* accommodating the public's desire for money
   c. maintaining stable interest rates *and* controlling inflation

7. In February 1980 *Newsweek* reported that, "In the fight on inflation, the Fed admits it has underestimated the U.S. monetary supply" and quoted a Fed official as saying, "There is no doubt that [monetary] policy has not been as restrained as was intended." Why should underestimating the money supply make monetary policy less anti-inflationary than was intended?

8. "High interest rates portend a serious slump" said *Business Week* in March 1980. Why should this be so? Is there any reason for the sequence of the two news items quoted in questions 7 and 8?

9. Writing in 1979, Nobel Laureate Milton Friedman accused the Fed of following "an unstable monetary policy," arguing that while the Fed "has given lip service to controlling the quantity of money . . . it has given its heart to controlling interest rates." Why might the desire to stabilize interest rates create an "unstable" monetary policy?

PART NINE
ISSUES AND
CONTROVERSIES IN
MACROECONOMICS

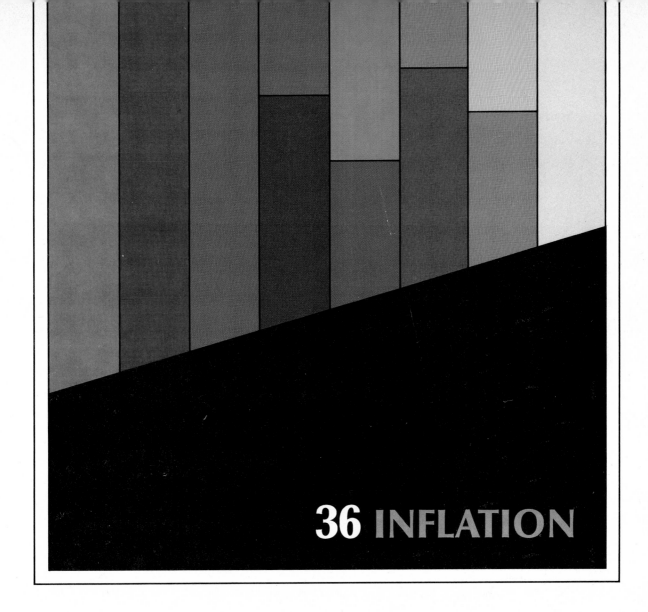

36 INFLATION

If you look again at Figure 26-6 on page 493, you will see that for 20 years following World War II, inflation remained low. The only exceptions were the "bubbles" following World War II and the Korean War. During the last half of the 1960s, however, the inflation rate slowly inched upward. It reached the double-digit range in the mid 1970s. By then inflation had been declared public enemy number one. Even more worrisome, the rate stayed in the 4 percent to 6 percent range during the severe recession of 1974–1975 and then rose again to the double-digit level in the early 1980s.

What were the causes of the inflation? How was the great anti-inflationary war of the late 1970s and early 1980s fought? Can we prevent inflation from skyrocketing into the double-digit range in the future?

MONETARY POLICY AND INFLATION

We start by noting a key distinction:

It is important to distinguish between the forces that cause a once-and-for-all increase in the price level and the forces that can cause a continuing (or sustained) increase.

Failure to make this distinction often leads to much confusion. The distinction and some related terminology are discussed in the box.

In previous chapters we saw that shifts in either the short-run aggregate supply curve or the aggregate demand curve cause a once-and-for-all burst of inflation. In Chapter 34 we encountered the important result that *for any inflation to be sustained it must be accompanied by increases in the money supply.* Thus monetary responses matter. To see how, we begin with an economy in long-run equilibrium: the price level is stable and output is at

its potential, or full-employment, level. The economy is then buffeted by three different types of shocks.

Supply Shocks

Suppose the *SRAS* curve shifts upward. The price level rises and output falls. The rise in the price level shows up as a temporary burst of inflation. What happens next depends upon whether the shock to the *SRAS* curve is an isolated event or is one of a series of recurring shocks. What happens also depends upon whether or not the Fed responds by increasing the money supply. This is referred to as *accommodating* the supply shock.

Isolated Supply Shocks

First suppose that the shift in the *SRAS* curve is an isolated event, say, a once-and-for-all increase in the cost of imported raw materials. How does

INFLATION SEMANTICS

The distinction between once-and-for-all and continuing rises in the price level is important. Some economists have sought to emphasize it by reserving the term *inflation* for a *continuing* or *sustained* rise in the price level while using other terms such as *a rise in the price level* for a *once-and-for-all* increase.

One difficulty with this is that it is counter to ordinary usage, where inflation refers to any rise in the price level. Indeed, using the restricted definition causes real difficulty when communicating with the general public. If we were to use it, we would have to keep saying such things as "only some of the current rise in prices is an inflation, while the rest is merely a rise in the price level," and "we won't know whether or not the current rise in the price level is an inflation or not until we see if it is sustained."

In this book we use the term *inflation* as it is used in everyday speech to mean any rise in the price level. We then describe the key distinction outlined above by referring to *temporary* or *once-and-for-all* bursts of inflation on the one hand and to *continuing* or *sustained* inflations on the other.

No matter of substance turns on the terms that we use to refer to clearly defined concepts. Where we use the terms *sustained* or *continuing* inflation and *temporary* inflation, or their equivalents, others use the terms *inflation* and *a rise in the price level.*

This discussion is important solely because students need to guard against being confused by different usages. Our selection of terms reflects only a desire to keep our language as close as possible to everyday usage.

monetary policy affect the response to such an isolated supply shock?

No monetary accommodation. The upward shift in the *SRAS* curve drives income below its full-employment level, opening up a GNP gap. Pressure now mounts for wages and other factor costs to fall. When they do, the *SRAS* curve shifts downward, causing a return of income to full employment and a fall in the price level. In this case, the period of positive inflation accompanying the original supply shock will be followed by negative inflation (i.e., deflation) until the original long-run equilibrium is re-established. This was shown in Figure 34-6 on page 657. Given that wages and prices fall slowly, the recovery to full employment may take a long time.

Monetary accommodation. Now let us see what happens if the money supply *is* changed in response to the isolated supply shock.

Suppose the Fed reacts to the fall in national income by increasing the money supply. This shifts the *AD* curve upward and causes both the price level and output to *rise*. When the GNP gap has been eliminated, the price level, rather than falling back to its original value, will have risen further. The resulting changes are illustrated in Figure 36-1.

Monetary accommodation of a supply shock causes the initial rise in the price level to be followed by a further rise, resulting in a higher final price level than if the GNP gap were relied on to force wages and prices down.

The monetary authorities might decide to accommodate because relying on wage deflation forces the economy to suffer through an extended slump. Monetary accommodation could return the economy to full employment quickly but at the cost of a once-and-for-all increase in the price level.

A case study. The OPEC oil price shocks of 1974 and 1979 were isolated events. In each case they raised costs and drove the price level up in a single burst of inflation. Canadian policy accommodated the shock; American policy did not. In the United States, real income fell as the economy

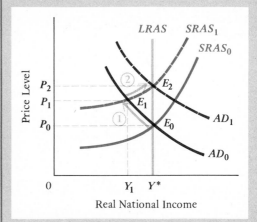

FIGURE 36-1
Monetary Accommodation of a Single Supply Shock

Monetary accommodation of a single supply shock causes costs, the price level, and money supply all to move in the same direction. A supply shock causes the *SRAS* curve to shift upward from $SRAS_0$ to $SRAS_1$, as shown by arrow ①. Equilibrium is established at E_1.

If there is no monetary accommodation, the unemployment would put downward pressure on wages and other costs, causing the *SRAS* curve to shift slowly back to $SRAS_0$. Prices would fall and output would rise until the original equilibrium was restored.

Monetary accommodation shifts the aggregate demand curve upward from AD_0 to AD_1, as shown by arrow ②. This reestablishes full employment equilibrium at E_2 but with a higher price level, P_2.

moved upward along a fixed aggregate demand curve. American unemployment grew steadily through 1974 and reached a peak of 9 percent in May 1975, which was at the time the highest unemployment rate since the 1930s. The inflation rate, which had stayed in the double-digit range throughout 1973–1974, tumbled to about 6 percent in the first quarter of 1975 and stayed in the range of 4 percent to 6 percent throughout the recession.

In Canada the supply shocks were partially accommodated. The money supply was increased sharply in 1974 and 1975. As a result unemployment only rose from 5.3 percent in 1974 to 6.9 percent in 1975. But the inflation rate remained high, hovering at just over 10 percent throughout.

Which policy was better? We take up this question after we have studied *repeated* supply shocks.

Repeated Supply Shocks

Our treatment up to now has assumed that a GNP gap would be associated with *downward* pressure on wages. This implies that labor markets behave much like commodity markets: wages fall when there is excess supply and rise only when there is excess demand.

Now assume, however, that powerful unions are able to raise wages in the absence of excess demand for labor and even in the face of significant excess supply. Large manufacturing firms pass on these higher wages in the form of higher prices. This type of supply shock causes **wage-cost push inflation**: an increase in the price level due to increases in money wages that are not associated with excess demand for labor.

How does monetary policy affect the response to such repeated supply shocks?

No monetary accommodation. First, suppose the Fed does not accommodate these shocks. The initial effect is that a GNP gap opens up (equal to Y_1Y^* in Figure 36-1). If unions continue to negotiate increases in wages, subjecting the economy to further supply shocks, prices will continue to rise and output will continue to fall. Eventually the trade-off between higher wages and unemployment will become obvious to everyone.

Might not really powerful unions continue to force wages up despite this realization? As long as they did so, the GNP gap would go on growing until, finally, unemployment reached 100 percent. Of course this will not happen because long before everyone is unemployed, unions will cease forcing up wages in order to maintain jobs for those who are still employed.

Once the wage-cost push ceases there are two possible scenarios. First, the unions may succeed in holding onto their high wages, although they will not push for further increases. The economy

then comes to rest with a stable price level and a large GNP gap. Second, the persistent unemployment may eventually erode the power of the unions so that wages begin to fall. In this case the supply shock is reversed and the *SRAS* curve shifts downward until full employment is eventually restored.

> Supply shocks caused by wage-cost push have natural correctives in the restraining pressures of rising unemployment on further wage push and in the possible erosion of the power of unions to hold wages above the level that would produce full employment.

Monetary accommodation. Now suppose that the Fed accommodates the shock with an increase in the money supply. (See Figure 36-1.) In the new full-employment equilibrium both money wages and prices have risen. The rise in wages has been offset by a rise in prices. Workers are no better off than they were originally, although those who remained in jobs were better off in the transition after wages had risen (taking equilibrium to E_1 in Figure 36-1) but before the price level had risen (taking equilibrium to E_2 in Figure 36-1).

The stage is now set for the unions to try again. If they succeed in negotiating further increases in money wages, they will hit the economy with another supply shock. If the Fed accommodates the shock, full employment is maintained but at the cost of a further round of inflation. If this process goes on continuously, it can give rise to a continuous wage-cost push inflation. The wage-cost push tends to cause a stagflation with rising prices and falling output. Monetary accommodation tends to reinforce the rise in prices but offset the fall in output. This case is illustrated in Figure 36-2.

Two things are required for wage-cost push inflation to continue. First, powerful unions must press for, and employers must grant, increases in money wages even in the absence of excess demand for labor and goods. Second, governments must accommodate the resulting inflation by increasing the money supply and so prevent the unemployment that would otherwise occur.

Is wage-cost push inflation a real possibility? As far back as the 1940s many Keynesians were

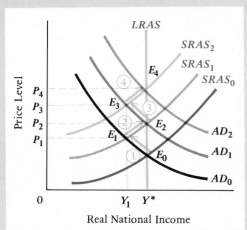

FIGURE 36-2
Monetary Accommodation of a Repeated Supply Shock

Monetary accommodation of a repeated supply shock causes a continuous inflation in the absence of excess demand. The initial equilibrium is at E_0. A supply shock then takes equilibrium to E_1, just as in Figure 36-1. This is the stagflation phase of rising prices and falling output indicated by arrow ①.

The Fed then accommodates the supply shock by increasing the money supply, taking the aggregate demand curve to AD_1 and equilibrium to E_2. This is the expansionary phase of rising prices and rising output indicated by arrow ②.

Repeated supply shock followed by monetary accommodation takes equilibrium to E_3 (arrow ③) and then to E_4 (arrow ④). As long as the supply shocks and the monetary accommodation continue, the inflation continues.

rope where unions are very strong. There is less consensus that it has occurred in the United States—although closer to home, Canada appears to have suffered from something like a wage-cost push inflation in recent years.

Should There Be Monetary Accommodation?

Once started, the spiral of wage-price-wage increases can be halted only if the monetary authorities stop accommodating the shocks. The longer they wait to do so, the more ingrained will be the expectation that they will accommodate. It is argued that this will make wages more resistant to downward pressure arising from unemployment. Hence, the argument runs, it is best never to let the process get started. One way to ensure this is to refuse to accommodate any supply shock whatsoever.

To some people caution dictates that no supply shocks be accommodated lest a wage-price-wage spiral be set up. Others would be willing to risk accommodating obviously isolated shocks in order to avoid the severe, though transitory, recessions that otherwise accompany them.

Demand Shocks

Now assume that the aggregate demand curve shifts rightward. This causes the price level and output to rise, as was shown in Figure 34-5. The shift in the AD curve could have been caused by either an increase in autonomous expenditure or an increase in the money supply.[1]

As with a supply shock, it is important to distinguish between those cases where the FED reacts and those where it does not. With a demand shock, reaction by the Fed is referred to as monetary *validation*. (Note the distinction: response to a *supply* shock is, as we have seen, referred to as monetary *accommodation*.) How does monetary validation affect the reaction to a demand shock?

[1] As we saw in Chapter 34, an increase in the money supply works through the transmission mechanism—excess supply of money, higher price of bonds, lower interest rates, increased investment expenditure—to shift the AD curve rightward.

worried that, once the government was committed to maintaining full employment, much of the discipline of the market would be removed from wage bargains. The scramble of every group trying to get ahead of every other group would lead to a wage-cost push inflation. The commitment to full employment would then lead to accommodating increases in the money supply.

Many economists believe that this process has actually occurred in those countries of Western Eu-

No Monetary Validation

Because output is now above the full-employment level, there is an inflationary gap. Upward pressure will soon cause wages and other costs to rise, shifting the *SRAS* curve upward. As long as the Fed holds the money supply constant the rise in the price level brings the monetary adjustment mechanism into play: the economy moves upward to the left along the fixed *AD* curve. The rise in the price level acts to reduce the inflationary gap. Eventually the gap is eliminated as equilibrium is established at a higher, but stable, price level with income at its potential level. In this case the initial period of positive inflation is followed by further inflation that lasts only until the new equilibrium is reached.

Monetary Validation

Next, suppose that following a demand shock that created an inflationary gap, the Fed frustrated the monetary adjustment mechanism by increasing the money supply when output starts to fall. Two forces are now brought into play. Spurred by the inflationary gap, the wage increases cause the *SRAS* curve to shift upward. Fueled by monetary policy, the *AD* curve shifts upward. As a result, the price level rises but output need not fall. Indeed, if the shift in the *AD* curve exactly offsets the shift in the *SRAS* curve, the inflationary gap will remain constant. This is shown in Figure 36-3.[2]

Validation of a demand shock turns what would have been a transitory inflation into a classic, sustained inflation fueled by monetary expansion.

All subsequent shifts in the *AD* curve that perpetuate the inflationary gap are caused by monetary forces.

[2] Notice that although we distinguish between a single supply shock and a continuing one, we do not make a similar distinction with a demand shock. This is because the accommodation of a single supply shock restores full-employment equilibrium while the validation of a demand shock perpetuates the disequilibrium.

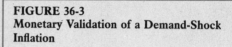

FIGURE 36-3
Monetary Validation of a Demand-Shock Inflation

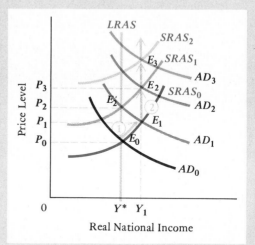

Shifts in the *AD* curve due to increases in the money supply can offset the effects of shifts in the *SRAS* curve due to increases in wages that result from an inflationary gap. The initial equilibrium is at E_0, with full employment income Y^* and price level P_0.

A demand shock shifts the aggregate demand curve to AD_1, raising income along arrow ① to Y_1 and the price level to P_1. With equilibrium at E_1, there is an inflationary gap causing wages to rise and shifting the *SRAS* curve upward. The operation of the monetary adjustment mechanism would entail a movement along AD_1 to a new equilibrium at E_2', where the inflationary gap is eliminated.

However, if the money supply is increased, the *AD* curve is shifted to the right, frustrating the monetary adjustment mechanism. When the *SRAS* curve has reached $SRAS_1$, the money supply is increased sufficiently to take the *AD* curve to AD_2. When the *SRAS* curve reaches $SRAS_2$, *AD* is shifted to AD_3, and so on. This takes the economy on the path indicated by arrow ②, through E_2 and E_3, with a persistent inflationary gap and a continuously rising price level.

Inflation as a monetary phenomenon. Now we can see the sense in which "inflation is a monetary phenomenon." If a rise in prices is to go on continuously it must be accompanied by continuing increases in the money supply. This is true regardless of the shock that set it in motion.

The stronger statement that "inflation is everywhere and always a monetary phenomenon" must rely on the definition of inflation discussed in the box on page 694. We have seen that many forces from both the demand and the supply side can cause the price level to rise. Such "inflations" can continue for some time without monetary expansion although, as we have also seen, the rise in prices must eventually come to a halt unless monetary expansion occurs.

The monetary expansion that allows an inflation to continue can sometimes be a response to some other shock. For example, if wage-cost push were occurring, the Fed might accommodate it in order to avoid the unemployment that would otherwise result. While the monetary expansion is necessary if the inflation is to be sustained, nonetheless the initiating shock is, in this case, a supply shock.

In other cases the monetary expansion may itself be a part of the initiating shock, as when a government budget deficit is financed by printing money. Assume for example that the government increases its expenditure, shifting the aggregate demand curve to create an inflationary gap, and that the new expenditure is financed by selling bonds to the Fed. This, as we have seen, leads to an expansion in the money supply. In this case the deficit provides the required monetary validation for the inflation to continue.

A Recap

We have now reached some important conclusions.

1. Without monetary accommodation supply shocks cause bursts of inflation accompanied by GNP gaps. The gaps are removed if wages fall, restoring potential income at the initial price level.
2. Without monetary validation demand shocks cause temporary bursts of inflation accompanied by inflationary gaps. The gaps are removed as wages rise, restoring potential income at a higher price level.
3. With an appropriate response of the Fed, an inflation initiated by supply or demand shocks can continue indefinitely: an ever-increasing money supply is necessary for an ever-continuing inflation.

SUSTAINED INFLATION

A Decade of Inflation

The great stagflation of 1974–1975 saw inflation reach the double-digit level for the first time in 30 years. Inflation subsequently bottomed out in 1976 at a little less than 5 percent and crept up to 6 percent in 1977 as real output recovered slightly and unemployment fell from 7.7 to 7.1 percent. The recovery continued, with unemployment falling to 6.1 percent in 1978 and 5.8 percent in 1979. Although few economists suggested it at the time, hindsight suggests that 5.8 percent unemployment may have indicated an inflationary gap; the unemployment rate consistent with potential national income may by then have been as high as 6 to 6.5 percent. Certainly the behavior of the inflation rate suggested an inflationary gap; it rose to 9 percent in 1978.

Two disturbing things about the 1970s were the failure of inflation to subside much below 5 percent despite the severe recession in 1974–1975 and the rebounding of inflation to 9 percent as the economy recovered.

In 1979 the second OPEC oil price shock hit. The prices of energy and of such oil-related commodities as fertilizer and plastics soared. Many of these commodities were used as inputs in the production of other goods, so these price increases meant rising production costs. Then as costs rose the prices of all products that used these inputs rose. The annual inflation rate, as measured by the CPI, reached an unprecedented 13.3 percent in 1979 and held at 12.4 percent in 1980.

It was clear from the rebound of inflation at the end of the 1970s that inflation had become entrenched in everyone's mind. Could inflation be tamed? Almost everyone agreed that a recession that was deep and long enough would do the job. But how long and how deep would the recession have to be? This was the key macro policy question

THE PHILLIPS CURVE AND THE SHIFTING *SRAS* CURVE

In the early 1950s Professor A. W. Phillips of the London School of Economics was doing pathbreaking research on the pitfalls of fine tuning well before most of the profession was alerted to the problem. To analyze an economy that was fluctuating around its potential output he included in his model an equation relating the rate of inflation to the difference between actual and potential income, $Y - Y^*$. Some years later he investigated the empirical underpinnings of this equation by studying the relation between the rate of increase of wage costs and the level of unemployment. In 1958 he reported that a stable relation had existed between these two variables for 100 years in the United Kingdom.

employment rates) are associated with rapid *increases* in wages, while GNP gaps (which correspond to high unemployment rates), are associated with slow *decreases* in wages.

The Phillips curve must be sharply distinguished from the *SRAS* curve. The *SRAS* curve indicates the *price level* on the horizontal axis while the Phillips curve indicates the *rate of wage inflation*. Therefore the Phillips curve tells us how fast the *SRAS* curve is shifting when actual income does not equal potential income. This corresponds to the demand component of wage increases discussed in the text.

Only when $Y = Y^*$ (and hence $U = U_N$) is the *SRAS* curve not shifting. When income is at its potential level, Y^*, aggregate demand for

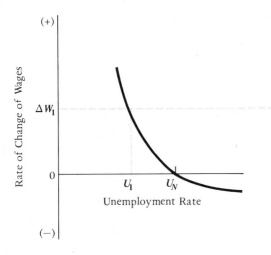 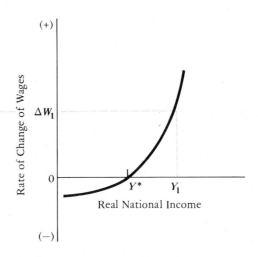

The relation which came to be called the *Phillips curve* is illustrated in the left figure. The curve shows money wages rising when unemployment falls below the natural rate of unemployment, U_N, and falling when unemployment rises above that critical level.

The rate of unemployment is related negatively to national income. Thus the Phillips curve can also be drawn with national income on the horizontal axis, as on the right.

Both figures show the same information: inflationary gaps (which correspond to low un-

labor equals aggregate supply; the only unemployment would thus be frictional unemployment. There would be neither upward nor downward pressure of demand on wages. Thus the Phillips curve cuts the axis at potential income Y^* and at the corresponding level of unemployment U_N.

The Phillips curve was soon famous. It provided a link between national income models and labor markets. This link allowed macro economists to drop the uncomfortable assumption, which they had often been forced to use in in the early 1980s, and it will become the key question again whenever inflation breaks out in the future.

Before we can deal with this question, we must look in greater detail at what is involved in a sustained inflation. We have already stressed the role of monetary expansion in allowing the AD curve to shift up continually. We now focus on the forces that cause the $SRAS$ curve to shift upward.

Wages and Inflation

The $SRAS$ curve shifts upward when costs rise. We concentrate on wages as the most important element of costs. Changing profit margins are not an important part of the process of continuing inflation since, although they can vary, they cannot account for a sustained inflation. Even wide variations from year to year in the profit margin cause only minor differences between wage and price increases.[3]

---

[3] In case this important point is not obvious, here is a numerical example. Suppose that profits initially count for $.20 out of $1 of the market price of goods. If all other costs start to rise by 10 percent per year then the inflation rate could be held to zero *for one year* if profits fall to $.12 out of every $1 and to zero for *the second year* if profits fall to $.032. Such wild variations in the percentage of price accounted for by profits never occur in practice, yet in the face of a 10 percent rise in costs even these can hold the price level constant for only 2 years. Now consider variations in the other direction. If we again start with profits of $.20 of the sales dollar, then a 10 percent inflation in the face of constant costs would require that profits rise to $.30 in the first year and to $.41 in the second year. Such enormous changes in the mark-up over labor and capital costs (from 20/80 = 25 percent, to 30/80 = 37 percent, to 41/80 = 51 percent) never occur, so *sustained* inflations are not caused by increases in profit margins any more than they can be long held in check by decreases in profit margins.

Why Wages Change

Up to now it has been enough to say that an inflationary gap implies excess demand for labor, low unemployment, upward pressure on wages and, hence, an upward-shifting $SRAS$ curve. We now look at three main forces that can cause wages to change at any given level of national income and thus shift the $SRAS$ curve. First, we review the relation between demand forces, as indicated by the inflationary or GNP gap, and wage changes.

Demand Forces

When there is excess demand there will be an inflationary gap. This puts upward pressure on wages, which shifts the $SRAS$ curve upward and causes the price level to rise. When there is excess supply, there will be a GNP gap. This puts downward pressure on wages, which tends to shift the $SRAS$ curve downward. The price level therefore falls. Only when there is neither excess demand nor excess supply is there no demand pressure on wages and hence on prices.[4] An increase in the price level that is due to the pressures of excess demand is called a **demand inflation**.

The natural rate of unemployment. Demand forces can be restated in terms of the concept of the **natural rate of unemployment**. We saw in Chapter 26 that unemployment is not zero at potential income because of substantial amounts of what can be broadly called *frictional unemployment*. The amount of unemployment that exists when national income is at its potential level is often called the *natural rate of unemployment* and symbolized U_N. It corresponds to all unemployment

---

[4] We are simplifying the discussion by ignoring the role of productivity changes. Such changes can alter the relationship between wages and prices.

that is *not due to deficient aggregate demand*. These concepts are discussed in more detail in Chapter 37.

With an inflationary gap, national income exceeds potential income ($Y > Y^*$) and unemployment is less than the natural rate ($U < U_N$). With a GNP gap, national income is less than potential income ($Y < Y^*$) and actual unemployment exceeds the natural rate ($U > U_N$).

When the unemployment rate is below the natural rate, and hence income is above potential, demand forces put upward pressure on wages. When the unemployment rate is above the natural rate, and hence income is below potential, demand forces will put downward pressure on wages.

One way of showing the influence of demand on wages (and hence on the *SRAS* curve) is in the relation called the **Phillips curve,** discussed in the box on pages 700–701.

Expectational Forces

A second force that can influence wages is *expectations*. Suppose for example that both employers and employees expect that a 10 percent inflation will occur next year. Unions will start negotiations from a *base* of a 10 percent increase in money wages, which would hold their real wages constant. Firms will also be inclined to begin bargaining by conceding at least a 10 percent increase in money wages, since they expect that the prices at which they sell their products will rise by 10 percent. *Starting from that base,* unions will then negotiate in an attempt to obtain some desired increase in their real wages. At this point such factors as profits, productivity, and bargaining power become important. The general expectation of an *x* percent inflation creates pressures for wages to rise by *x* percent and hence for the *SRAS* curve to shift upward by *x* percent.

When both labor and management expect inflation, their wage and price setting behavior will tend to cause inflation.

A rise in the price level due to expectations of inflation is called an **expectational inflation.**

Unsystematic Shocks

The third component of wage changes is unsystematic shocks. While such shocks may be very important for once-and-for-all changes in the price level, they are less important for sustained inflations.

A shock effect raises wages but is not associated with either expected inflation or excess demand. For example, an especially strong new union or a weak management may result in an extra 1 percent increase in wages this year. Or a new government policy favorable to management, or one favorable to labor, may tip the wage bargain a bit one way or the other in any one year. All of these are summarized in the third component of wages, shock effects.

The Overall Effect

The overall change in wage costs may be shown as a result of the three basic forces just studied:

percentage increase in money wages	=	demand effect	+	expected inflation rate	+	shock effect

The demand effect is, as we have seen, positive when Y is greater than Y^*, negative when Y is less than Y^*, and zero when Y equals Y^*.

Expectations and Inflation in the Long Run

Look again at Figure 36-3, which represents a continuing inflation. The *SRAS* curve is shifting up due to the inflationary gap and the *AD* curve is shifting up as the inflation is validated by increases in the money supply. What this analysis shows is that, if income is held above potential, the price level will be rising. We know that inflation is positive, but we do not know whether the inflation rate is rising or falling or is constant.

Suppose that initially there are no expectations of inflation. What we have is thus a case of pure demand inflation. In order to maintain the inflationary gap, the upward shift in the *SRAS* curve has to be accompanied by an increase in the money supply such that the *AD* curve shifts up by a like amount.

Eventually people will begin to expect that the monetary validation will continue and hence that prices will continue to rise at roughly the same rate. As these inflationary *expectations* emerge, additional upward pressure will be put on wage increases. In other words, the demand inflation has been augmented by an expectational inflation. The *SRAS* curve will now begin to shift upward more rapidly. In turn, the Fed must increase the rate at which the money supply is growing in order to maintain the level of output constant.

The Acceleration Hypothesis

The response of inflationary expectations to a persistent inflationary or GNP gap leads to **acceleration hypothesis:** When output is held above potential so that an inflationary gap persists, the rate of inflation will tend to accelerate; when output is held below potential so that a GNP gap persists, the rate of inflation will tend to decelerate.

When there is an inflationary gap *and* monetary validation, the continuing inflation will lead to rising inflationary expectations. As we have seen, these expectations will mean rising pressure on wages. The rate at which the *SRAS* curve is shifting up will therefore increase. To maintain the given inflationary gap the Fed will thus have to increase the rate of growth of the money supply so that the upward shifts in the *AD* curve will match those of the *SRAS* curve. As a result, the rate at which the price level is rising will itself be increasing. Of course this will then cause further rises in the expected inflation rate, and so the process continues.

As long as an inflationary gap persists, expectations of inflation will be rising, and this will lead to increases in the actual rate of inflation.

This is discussed further in the box on pages 704–705.

The Natural Rate Hypothesis

Can inflation ever be constant? Or will the demand effect always lead to changing inflationary expectations and hence changing inflation?

The answer is that only when the demand effect is absent, so that all inflation is expectational infla-

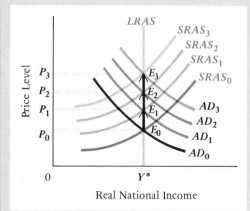

FIGURE 36-4
Steady Inflation and the Natural Rate of Unemployment

When income equals Y^* (and hence unemployment equals U_N) there is no demand effect on wages and steady inflation can proceed at a rate consistent with inflationary expectations. With no demand effect, the *SRAS* curve shifts upward at the expected rate of inflation. If the Fed raises the money supply at the same rate, the upward shift in the *AD* curve will match that of the *SRAS* curve. Output will stay at Y^*, unemployment will be at the natural rate, and inflation will be steady. The steady inflation is shown by the rising price level as equilibrium moves along the arrow from E_1 to E_2 to E_3 in the figure.

tion, can steady inflation persist. When income is at potential so no demand effect is present, there is no pressure on inflation to accelerate or decelerate. As long as the upward shift in the *SRAS* curve, caused by inflationary expectations, is matched by the upward shift in the *AD* curve, caused by growth of the money supply, inflation will remain constant.

This case is illustrated in Figure 36-4. Wages are rising at a rate equal to expected inflation, and the money supply is being increased at the same rate. As a result, the *SRAS* curve and the *AD* curve are shifting up at the same rate. This means that output is not changing and hence that no demand pressures on wages are being created. Wages are simply rising due to expectations of inflation, and these expectations are being fulfilled.

THE PHILLIPS CURVE AND ACCELERATING INFLATION

Professor Phillips was interested in studying the short-run behavior of an economy subjected to cyclical fluctuations (see the box on pages 700–701). Others, however, treated the curve as establishing a long-term trade-off between inflation and unemployment.

To see how this was supposed to work, consider the figure. Let the government fix income at Y_1 (and thus unemployment at U_1) and validate the ensuing wage inflation of ΔW_1 per year. By doing this the government is apparently able to choose a particular combination of inflation and unemployment, with lower levels of unemployment being attained at the cost of higher rates of inflation.

In the text we noted two important influences on wages, demand and expectations. It was gradually understood that the original Phillips curve concerned only the influence of demand and left out inflationary expectations. This proved to be an important and unfortunate omission. As we saw in the text, where there is an inflationary gap expected inflation tends to rise. This in turn creates increased upward pressure on wages. This increase in expected inflation shows up as an upward shift in the Phillips curve drawn in the previous box.

The importance of expectations can be shown by drawing what is called an **expectations augmented Phillips curve**, as in the figures. In both

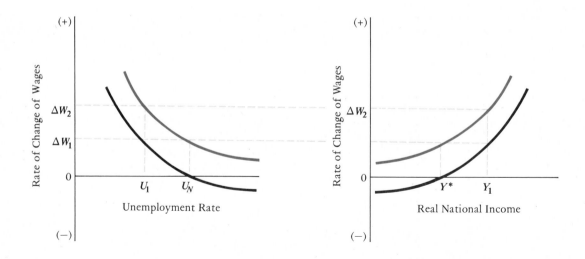

The 1960s was the decade of the Phillips curve trade-off. Curves were fitted to the data for many countries, and governments made decisions about where they wished to be on the trade-off between inflation and unemployment. Then, in the late 1960s, in country after country, the rate of wage and price inflation associated with any given level of unemployment began to rise. Instead of being stable the Phillips curves were shifting upward. The explanation lay primarily in a shifting relation between the pressure of demand and wage increases due to expectations, as discussed in the text.

cases the height of the Phillips curve above the axis at Y^* and at U_n shows the expected inflation rate. This is the amount that wages will rise when there is neither excess demand nor excess supply pressure in labor markets. The actual wage increase is shown by the augmented curve, with the increase in wages exceeding expected inflation when $Y > Y^*$ ($U < U_N$) and falling short of expected inflation when $Y < Y^*$ ($U > U_N$). *The demand component shown by the simple Phillips curve tells us by how much wage changes will deviate from the expected inflation rate.*

Now we can see what was wrong with the

idea of a stable inflation-unemployment trade-off. The Fed picks income Y_1 or unemployment U_1 in the figure. That is fine as long as no inflation is *expected*. But once inflation comes to be expected, people will demand that much just to hold their own. The Phillips curve will shift upward to the position shown in the figure. Now there is inflation ΔW_1 because of expectations and a further increase because of the excess demand.

But this higher rate is above the expected rate. Once that higher rate comes to be expected, the Phillips curve will shift upward once again. *The expectations augmented Phillips curve shows that the actual rate of inflation exceeds the expected rate whenever there is an inflationary gap.* Sooner or later this will cause inflationary expectations to be shifted upward. The inflation rate associated with any given level of Y or U rises over time. This is the theory of accelerating inflation that is further studied in the appendix to this chapter.

Steady inflation with full employment results when the rate of monetary growth, the rate of wage increase, and expected inflation are all consistent.

The inflation is not indicative of any disequilibrium; there is neither excess demand nor excess supply. Output is at its potential level and hence unemployment equals the natural rate. We refer to this situation as an **equilibrium inflation**: all inflation is expectational.

The *natural rate hypothesis* holds that if the rate of monetary growth is fixed, then the economy will converge on a situation such as that depicted in Figure 36-4. The reasons can be understood in terms of the transition from Figure 36-3 to Figure 36-4. In Figure 36-3 the combination of the demand effect and rising expectations meant that the Fed had to *increase continuously the rate of growth of the money supply* to validate the ever-increasing upward shift in the *SRAS* curve. Suppose now that the Fed did not acquiese in this acceleration but instead steadied the rate of monetary growth. Still, as long as the inflationary gap persists, expectations of inflation are rising. Thus the *SRAS* curve will be shifting up at an accelerating rate while the *AD* curve will not; national income will begin to fall toward Y^*, reducing the inflationary gap. Eventually output will stabilize at Y^* and both inflation and inflationary expectations will stabilize at the constant rate of monetary growth.

Most economists now agree with the major thrust of this analysis. Where different theorists disagree is on what determines the expected inflation rate. Neo-Keynesians tend to believe that the expected rate changes only slowly; monetarists tend to believe that it changes quickly in response to current conditions. We shall see that this difference influences the costs that each group foresees in breaking an entrenched inflation.

BREAKING AN ENTRENCHED INFLATION

We begin our story with the continuous, fully validated inflation shown in Figure 36-3 and also shown by arrow 1 in part (i) of Figure 36-5. There is a sustained inflationary gap and a continuously rising price level.[5] Let us suppose that inflation has been occurring for some time and that people expect it to continue; we refer to this as an *entrenched inflation*. Now suppose that the Fed decides to bring the inflation to a halt by ending its policy of monetary validation.

Phase 1 of the anti-inflationary policy consists of slowing the rate of monetary expansion below the rate of inflation. This slows the rate at which the aggregate demand curve is shifting upward. For illustration we take an extreme case: the "cold turkey approach" where the rate of monetary expansion is cut to *zero* so that the upward shift in the aggregate demand curve is suddenly halted.

Under the combined influence of an inflationary gap and expectations of continued inflation, wages continue to rise and the *SRAS* curve thus continues to shift upward. Eventually the gap is removed and income returns to Y^*. If the only influence on wages were current demand, that would be the end

[5] Indeed, according to the acceleration hypothesis, the persistence of the inflationary gap means that the inflation rate should itself be increasing.

of the story. At Y^* there is no inflationary gap and hence no upward *demand* pressure on wages: Wages would stop rising, the *SRAS* curve would be sta-

bilized, and the economy would remain at full employment with a stable price level.

    Governments around the world have many times

FIGURE 36-5
Eliminating an Entrenched Inflation

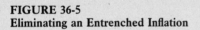

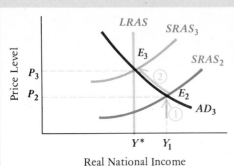

(i) Phase 1 : removing the inflationary gap

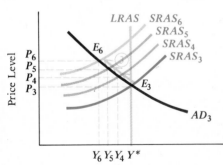

(ii) Phase 2 : stagflation

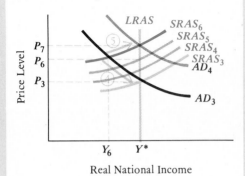

(iii) Phase 3 : recovery

(i) The elimination of an entrenched inflation begins with a demand contraction to remove the inflationary gap. The fully validated inflation shown in Figure 36-3 takes the economy along the path shown by arrow ① in (i). When the curves reach $SRAS_2$ and AD_3, the Fed stops expanding the money supply, thus stabilizing the aggregate demand curve at AD_3. Wages continue to rise, taking the *SRAS* curve upward. The economy moves along arrow ② with income falling and the price level rising. When the *SRAS* curve reaches $SRAS_3$, with income Y^* and price level P_3, the inflationary gap is removed.

(ii) Expectations cause the economy to pass through a stagflationary phase, with falling output and continuing inflation. In (ii) the economy moves along the path shown by arrow ③. The driving force is now the *SRAS* curve, which continues to shift upwards because of inflationary expectations. The GNP gap grows period by period as income falls to Y_4, Y_5, and finally Y_6. The inflation continues but at a diminishing rate as the price level rises to P_4, P_5, and finally P_6. Eventually wages stop rising and the economy reaches equilibrium position E_6. The stagflationary phase is then over.

(iii) After expectations are reversed, recovery takes income to Y^* and the price level is stabilized. Part (iii) shows the recovery phase. There are two possible scenarios. In the first the GNP gap causes wages to fall (slowly), taking the *SRAS* curve back to $SRAS_3$ (slowly). The economy thus retraces the path originally followed in (ii) back to E_3, now shown as arrow ④ in (iii). In the second scenario the Fed increases the money supply sufficiently to shift the AD curve to AD_4. The economy moves along the path shown by arrow ⑤. This restores potential income at the cost of a further temporary burst of inflation that takes the price level to P_7.

wished that things were really that simple. Instead of settling in that happy position of full employment and stable prices, however, the economy tends to overshoot and develop a GNP gap. Why? The reason, as we have already seen, is that wages depend not only on current excess demand but also on inflationary expectations. Various schools of economists differ on why, but they are united in agreeing that in recent history expectations of continuing inflation have been difficult to break. Once inflationary expectations have been established, it may not be an easy matter to get people to revise them downward, even in the face of changed fiscal and monetary policies.

Expectations may cause an inflation to persist after the original causes of the inflation have been removed. At this point what was initially a demand inflation due to an inflationary gap becomes a purely expectational inflation fed by the expectation that it will continue.

We have now entered phase 2, shown in part (ii) of Figure 36-5. Even though the inflationary gap has been eliminated, the expectation of further inflation leads to wage increases. This shifts the *SRAS* curve upward. The price level continues to rise in spite of a growing GNP gap. This is the stagflationary phase.

The growing GNP gap has two effects. First, there is rising unemployment. Thus the demand influence on wages becomes negative. Second, as the recession deepens, people revise their expectations of inflation downward. Eventually, they will have no further expectations of inflation. There will be no further increases in wages and the *SRAS* curve will stop shifting upward. The stagflationary phase is now over. The inflation has come to a halt, but now a large GNP gap exists.

The final phase is the return to full employment. When the economy comes to rest at the end of the stagflation, the situation is exactly the same as when the economy has been hit by an isolated supply shock. (See Figure 36-1.) As we have already seen, the move back to full employment can then be accomplished in either of two ways. First, the GNP gap can be relied on to reduce wages, thus shifting the *SRAS* curve downward to eliminate the effects of the overshooting caused by in-

flationary expectations. Second, the money supply can be increased sufficiently to shift the *AD* curve to a level consistent with full employment.

The trouble with the first approach is that it may take a very long time. The trouble with the second is that expectations of inflation may be rekindled when the Fed increases the money supply. The Fed will then have an unenviable choice. Either it must let another severe recession develop so as to break these new inflationary expectations, or it must validate the inflation in order to reduce unemployment. In this latter case it is back where it started with a validated inflation on its hands.

Controversies

Most economists accept this general scenario for breaking an entrenched inflation. But they still differ on how much time each of these three phases will take.

Neo-Keynesian Views

Phase 1. We saw in Chapter 33 that control of the money supply is not a simple matter. From time to time various extreme antimonetarists have suggested that the Fed could not control the money supply closely and thus could not apply the monetary brakes as simply as we have assumed. But the evidence of the last decade does not support this view. It appears that if a central bank is single-minded enough, it can exert strong control over the money supply and can stop validating an inflation quite quickly.

Phase 2. Neo-Keynesians argue that phase 2 of the process would be long and painful. Two reasons for this are alleged: first, the downward pressure on wages exerted by a GNP gap is small and second, expectations of inflation are slow to change. We consider each in turn.

The first part of their theory involves wage inertia as expounded, for example, by Professor James Tobin of Yale University. Following Keynes, Tobin argues that workers are concerned about their own wages relative to other closely related rates. He adds that wage bargains are made only infrequently: Union wages are rarely negotiated more than once a year, and two- and three-year contracts are common. Since this means that when any particular wage bargain is negotiated many other wages are already set, concern over relative wages is inclined to give inertia to wage bargains.

Furthermore, there is also an asymmetry between raising and lowering relative wages: workers do not mind getting ahead of other closely related groups, but they resist falling behind. Therefore, the wage inertia is mainly on the downside.

The graphical expression of this theory of asymmetric wage behavior is in the shifting of the *SRAS* curve. When national income is above potential, excess demand forces wages upward rapidly—the demand effect on wages is strong. When Y is below Y^*, however, excess supply forces wages downward only slowly—the demand effect on wages is weak. Thus in terms of an immediate reduction of the inflation rate, there is little to be gained from the downward market pressures on wages accompanying a recession.

The second major part of the Keynesian theory argues that expectations of future inflation are based on "backward-looking" comparisons. Its simplest version is the so-called extrapolative theory: People tend to believe that recent past trends will continue, and thus it takes a lot of new evidence to make them think that an inflationary trend is over. The rationale is that unless a deviation from the past trend persists, people dismiss the deviation—say, a fall in the inflation rate—as a transitory change and do not let it influence their long-term wage- and price-setting behavior.

The weak demand forces combined with slowly adjusting expectations mean that phase 2 will take a long time. The stagflation will persist as rising wages carry the *SRAS* curve upward until expectations of further inflation are finally broken.

Phase 3. Keynesians call for a burst of monetary expansion to get the economy back to full employment during the recovery phase. They believe that to rely on a fall in wages to shift the *SRAS* curve downward is to condemn the economy to a very long period of high unemployment. Also, because they feel that these expectations are slow

to change, they doubt that a temporary burst of monetary expansion will rekindle inflationary expectations. Once people come to expect a low or zero inflation rate, it will take more than the experience of a single recovery phase to cause them to revise these expectations.

Monetarist Views

Phase 1. Monetarists see no problem with phase 1. They believe that the Fed can control the money supply within quite a small margin of error.

Phase 2. Monetarists expect phase 2 to be over rapidly. Indeed some say it will never occur at all. Why is this?

First, monetarists deny that significant wage-price inertias exist. New wage bargains are assumed to respond to current market conditions. Thus a large GNP gap with heavy unemployment will lead quickly to new wage settlements well below the expected rate of inflation. The only lag in the adjustment of wages to current demand conditions is caused by the length of wage contracts. Thus it may still take some time for *all* wages to adjust to depressed market conditions.

The second strand to the monetarists' case concerns the response of inflationary expectations. Many monetarists argue that expected inflation will fall rapidly during phase 2. This is because they believe that expectations are "forward-looking." Such expectations are usually called **rational expectations:** People look to the government's current macroeconomic policy when forming their expectations of future inflation; they understand how the economy works and they predict the outcome of the monetary policies currently being followed. In an obvious sense, expectations formed in this way are "forward looking."

Rational expectations are not necessarily always correct; instead, the rational expectations hypothesis assumes that people do not continue to make systematic errors in forming their expectations.[6]

---

[6] Thus, if the system about which they are forming expectations remains stable, their expectations will be correct on average. Any individual's expectations at any moment of time about next year's price level can thus be thought of as the actual price level that will occur next year plus a random error term.

Rational expectations have the effect of speeding up the response to a deflationary demand policy. Instead of being an average of past inflation rates, expected inflation is based on a correct anticipation of the outcome of existing policies.

Once people realize that the Fed has stopped validating the inflation they will, given rational expectations, expect the inflation rate to come to a halt. Thus expected inflation falls quickly to zero, and there is no further upward push to wages from expectations.

The main reason for this happy result is that people believe that the Fed really is going to stick to its restrictive policies. Because of this, they will quickly revise their inflationary expectations downward and their consequent wage- and price-setting behavior will produce a rapid slowdown in the actual inflation rate. But if people are skeptical about the Fed's resolve, they may expect the inflation to continue. They will then increase wages and prices in anticipation of the inflation, and their actions will generate the inflation that they expected.

(Neo-Keynesians argue in response that the general public does not really understand the importance of the money supply to inflation. Sophisticated financial market operators may be monetarists, but most labor leaders and business managers hold different, sometimes crude, theories of inflation. They will tend to extrapolate from past experiences and will not even know what the Fed is doing to the money supply, let alone base their expectations on it.)

Phase 3. Monetarists tend to be skeptical of using a once-and-for-all monetary expansion to help the recovery. They feel that the credibility of the Fed's anti-inflationary policy depends on strict adherence to tight monetary policy and that to relax this policy risks rekindling inflationary expectations. Thus they rely on the automatic recovery that is implicit in waiting for downward shifts in the *SRAS* curve. They do not think this recovery would be as slow as Keynesians think since they believe that demand conditions have a strong effect on wages in both a downward as well as an upward direction.

Additional Anti-Inflationary Policies

Many Neo-Keynesian economists have recommended incomes policies to avoid, or greatly shorten, the stagflationary phase involved in breaking an entrenched inflation. An **incomes policy** represents an attempt by the government to influence directly the setting of wages and prices. There is a wide range of possible measures. The government could simply set voluntary guidelines for wage and price increases—so-called "jaw-boning." The Kennedy administration used such measures in the early 1960s, and they have been frequently considered since. A slightly more "activist" form of incomes policy is consultation on wage and price norms among unions, management, and government. The more centralized a country's wage and price-setting mechanisms the more easily such consultation is accomplished. Hence it is more common in countries of Western Europe than in the United States. An even more activist approach is compulsory controls on wage, price, and profit increases, such as were imposed by the Nixon administration in 1971. A more recent and as yet untried proposal is TIPs (tax-related incomes policies), which introduce penalties or rewards that operate through the tax system to induce desirable wage and price behavior.

Incomes Policies

We can distinguish three main uses of incomes policies: (i) to suppress a demand inflation, (ii) to break an expectational inflation, and (iii) to control a permanent wage-cost push inflation. In the early 1980s the main appeal of incomes policies was for the second use, and we discuss this below. We shall deal with the third in Chapter 39.

Demand inflations. One reason why incomes policies have such a bad reputation throughout the world is that they have often been used, as they were in the United States during Richard Nixon's presidency, in a futile attempt to stop a demand inflation. To see why such an attempt is futile, consider the situation shown at E_1 in Figure 36-3 on page 698. If nothing else is done the inflationary

INCOMES POLICIES AND DEMAND INFLATION

British experience. Several times during the 1950s and 1960s successive British governments tried incomes policies in attempts to control inflation. A large number of empirical studies have credited these attempts with "success" ranging from almost nothing to less than nothing.

Undaunted, the British government drew the conclusion not that incomes policies were ineffective but that they had not been pursued with sufficient severity. In 1972 the British had one of the largest budget deficits in their history, and they allowed the money supply to increase by nearly 25 percent! The result was fully predictable: a rapid inflation. But the government, encouraged by a number of academic economists, clung to its wage-cost push theory that inflation was due solely to union power. The government attempted to suppress the enormous inflationary forces created by its own monetary policies by using direct controls on wages and prices. A head-on battle with the unions was precipitated. Strikes in key industries forced the adoption of a three-day work week and power cuts occurred frequently. In the end an election was called, and the Conservative government was defeated. The new Labor government had little option but to give in to the strikers' demands, and the incomes policy collapsed.

The net effect on controlling inflation was negligible, and the cost in terms of social stress was enormous. But the Labor government failed to control the budget deficit and money supply growth, and in the face of rising inflation it also resorted to an incomes policy. A voluntary scheme to restrain wage increases was instituted in 1974 and was replaced by statutory controls the following year. By 1977 the inflation rate began to fall. Some gave the credit to incomes policies, but this was not an obvious conclusion, since at about this time the Bank of England began to reduce the rate of growth of the money supply.

U.S. experience. The first major use of incomes policies in the United States occurred in 1971 when it was clearly suffering from a demand inflation. The program was implemented in several stages. Phase 1 (which lasted for two months) imposed a complete freeze on virtually all wages and prices in the economy. Phase 2 (fourteen months) attempted to hold wage increases to 5.5 percent per year and price increases to no more than was necessary to cover any increase in costs. Phase 3 (five months) began in mid January 1973. At that time the economy was expanding rapidly and a need was recognized for a more flexible program that would permit substantial changes in relative prices.

When it became apparent that Phase 3 was not restraining inflation, a new freeze was introduced in June 1973 with the announcement that it was to be followed by a further set of Phase 4 controls. During Phase 4 a number of sectors were "decontrolled" as an initial stage of returning to free markets. Phase 4 controls proved ineffective, however, and by April 1974, when the control authority expired, its later phases were acknowledged failures.

Extensive research into the effects of this experiment suggests that the entire costly effort had little or no effect on wages but that it did hold down price inflation by perhaps as much as two percentage points. The restraint on prices was achieved by forcing a narrowing of profit margins. Not surprisingly, once the controls were lifted, profit margins were restored. Thus, the episode had little or no lasting effect on the price level. Furthermore, the restoration of profit margins caused a "post-controls price bubble" that by an extremely unfortunate chance happened to coincide with the beginning of the recession in 1974 and the OPEC oil price shock. The upward push of prices following their decontrol, although temporary, contributed to the Great Stagflation of 1974–1975.

gap will cause the price level to rise to P_2. Wage and price controls could, however, be used to hold the price level at P_1. But once the controls are removed the excess demand will cause prices to rise. Thus:

In the face of an inflationary gap, wage-price controls can postpone an inflation, but once they are removed the price level will rise to the value it would have attained had the controls never been used.

This misguided use of incomes policies is discussed further in the box on page 710.

Expectational inflations. When an entrenched inflation exists, incomes policies provide a possible way of breaking expectations and forcing the inflation rate down faster than might otherwise be expected. Incomes policies could be used in conjunction with a reduction in the rate of growth of the money supply to what is compatible with the target rate of inflation. The hope is that they would reduce the size and duration of the GNP gap and the consequent unemployment until expectations fall.

If successful, incomes policies would eliminate the stagflation phase of the breaking of an entrenched inflation. To see this consider part (ii) of Figure 36-5 on page 706, where the Fed has stopped the AD curve at AD_2 and the $SRAS$ curve has risen to $SRAS_3$. Wage-price controls might eliminate the expectations-induced further shifts of the $SRAS$ curve. Thus the inflation would be eliminated by a *combination* of restrictive demand policy and an incomes policy.

Once the target inflation rate is achieved and *stabilized*, the controls can be removed. If everyone then expects the new rate to persist, expectations will have been broken without the recession required by the use of monetary restraint alone. If such a policy package had been tried, and if it had worked, the recession of the early 1980s, with all its consequent suffering and lost output, would have been avoided.[7]

Supporters of incomes policies contend that they can break an expectational inflation. Opponents disagree, offering several arguments:

Controls are discredited because they did not work under Nixon. But Nixon attempted to use controls alone to repress a *demand* inflation rather than using them in conjunction with restrictive monetary policy to break an expectational inflation.

After the controls are removed, people will expect a resurgence of inflation, and so controls merely postpone inflation. This depends on whether or not the accompanying tight monetary policy of the Fed convinces people that inflation will not break out again.

Controls are unnecessary because even without them the stagflation phase would be short or even non-existent. Monetarists believe that expectations would adjust quickly once the Fed stopped validating. As we shall see below, the experience of 1980–1983 suggests that although the stagflation phase did not last as long as many Neo-Keynesians had predicted, it lasted quite long enough to be very costly.

The controls themselves would do much damage by inhibiting the operation of the price system. This is a valid point whose importance grows the longer the controls last. It is taken up further in the box on page 712.

The Great Policy Experiment of 1981–1983

At the start of the 1980s an explicit policy of monetary restraint was introduced in the United States to eliminate the entrenched inflation inherited from the 1970s. Because this was the first time the Fed had ever tried to halt an entrenched inflation and

---

[7] In the text we have described, for simplicity, a cold turkey monetary policy that requires cold turkey wage-price controls. The rate of monetary expansion is cut suddenly to zero and the controls force wage and price increases immediately to zero. In practice it can be done more slowly. For example the rate of monetary expansion might be cut from 8 to 4 to 0 percent over three years and, at the same time, wage-price controls would be used to force wage and price inflation down from 8 to 4 to 0 percent over the same three years. In that case the aggregate demand curve shifts up at a slower rate each year and the controls force the $SRAS$ curve to shift upward at the same (falling) rate so that a GNP gap does not need to open up while inflation is being reduced.

A VIEW FROM THE OUTSIDE OF THE INSIDE OF UPSIDE DOWN*

On the 18th of October, 1971, I assumed responsibility for the Price Commission in the conduct of Phase II of President Nixon's Wage and Price Control program. . . . I want to relate something about my view of policy-making at the national level. I want to explain why it is inherently a confused sort of occupation and I want to imbue the reader with a healthy skepticism for the ability of central control to solve economic problems.

One of the main reasons why the policy-making process in general and wage and price controls in particular are inherently difficult is because they are attempting to regulate the most sophisticated information system that the world has even seen—namely the North American market economy. . . . The information system is the network formed by free people buying and selling, and the signals are the variations in and the level of wages, prices, interest rates, rents and, unfortunately, taxes.

. . . most of the products and services that we take for granted in our everyday lives can be taken for granted only because there is a functioning price system. A system that, despite its imperfections, delivers just the right quantity of California lettuce to Montana or Alberta, Canada; and decides the relationship between raw log prices in California and the price of furnished lumber in Boston. As we discovered when we tampered with, and effectively suspended, the operation of the price system, we could no longer rely on the system itself and were forced to get more and more involved with what were, before controls, essentially automatic functions.

The problem that policy-makers must cope

with, if they are determined to control the system, is the endless detail that is involved in the operation of the system. To control the system and yet keep it running smoothly, the authorities must intercept all of the signals coming from the system (and there are hundreds of millions), interpret them, appropriately change them (assuming they know how) and retransmit them.

What we at the Price Commission continuously found was that everything is related to everything else and there was, accordingly, no such thing as one intervention. We were drawn inevitably and progressively deeper into the system, and the temptation to limit the necessity for our involvement by arbitrarily changing the system was very great. Herein lies the real danger from centralized control, that is, that an inability to handle the overload of signals, both incoming and outgoing, may produce attempts to simplify the system and hence jeopardize its survival.

The difficulty of taking over the wage-price signalling mechanism is indicated by the fact that during the first three weeks of Phase II there were nearly 400,000 inquiries about the program. In terms of getting down to the nitty gritty, had the Dow Chemical Company and the Commission not agreed to an across the board increase of 2 percent, we would have had to examine nearly 100,000 submissions on different products for that company alone.

. . . Wage and price controls are, by nature, a bureaucratic nightmare. There is no easy way to proceed, no escape from the remorseless tide of detail that is the inevitable consequence of attempting to interrupt the normal current of economic affairs. There is also no escape from the conclusion that detailed regulation breeds a restiveness in those being regulated that eventually must lead either to the collapse of the controls or the adoption of more coercive measures.

* Excerpted from an article of the same title by Jackson Grayson, dean of the School of Business, Southern Methodist University, in M. Walker, ed., *The Illusion of Wage and Price Control*, Vancourver, B.C., The Fraser Institute, 1976.

because it was an unprecedented event for the U.S. economy, no one could be sure what to expect. Neo-Keynesians talked in terms of a phase two, (stagflation) that would last from 5 to 10 years. Monetarists talked of a very short phase two and some rational expectationists doubted there would be any phase two at all. So the stage was set for a fairly strong test of these opposing views.

After some minor policy vacillations the anti-inflation policy was initiated in mid 1981. The unemployment rate rose steadily, reaching 10.9 percent at the beginning of 1983. Inflation fell from 12.4 percent in 1980 to 8.9 percent in 1981 and then tumbled to 3.9 percent in 1982.

By 1983 the policy had succeeded in reducing inflation to a level not seen since the early 1960s but also produced a major recession with all of its attendant costs, including unemployment, lost output, business bankruptcies, and foreclosed mortgages.

The results came out somewhere in between the extremes that had been predicted. The Neo-Keynesians were right in predicting that the anti-inflationary policies would induce a severe recession. But the inflation rate came down much faster than Neo-Keynesians had predicted. Jobs rather than wages quickly became the focus of many contract settlements. Not only were new wage agreements much more moderate in response to the excess supply of labor, a significant number of existing contracts were re-opened and lower wages agreed upon.

Thus, as so often happens with great debates, neither the extreme pessimists nor the extreme optimists were right. The truth lay somewhere in between.

Economists may argue for years why the result turned out the way it did. Neo-Keynesians say that the recession was due to major inertias that, although not as strong as they were first thought, were strong enough to require a large recession to break them. They also argue that the secular weakness of the steel and auto industries, whose strong unions usually provide the backbone of union-induced wage inertias, accounted for the weakness of these inertias during the recession. Monetarists hold that the Fed vacillated too much. This left

people unaware just how resolute the Fed was in its tough monetary stance. As a result, expected inflation did not fall as fast as it would otherwise have done.

Whatever the reasons, there is little doubt that inflation fell faster and the slump was deeper and more prolonged than many had expected.

Indeed the force of the economic slump was strong enough to put serious social strains on the society and to put political and economic strains on the fabric of international co-operation. Many countries were tempted to turn to such politically appealing but economically discredited policies as high tariffs that had caused so much trouble during the 1930s. These issues are discussed in more detail in Part Ten.

SUMMARY

1. Either supply shocks or demand shocks can cause a temporary inflation. For either to lead to sustained inflation, it must be accompanied by a continuing expansion of the money supply so that the *AD* curve is shifting upward.

2. A sustained price inflation will also be accompanied by a closely related growth in wages and other factor costs so that the *SRAS* curve is shifting up.

3. Factors that influence shifts in the *SRAS* can be divided into three main categories: demand, expectations, and shocks.

4. The influence of demand can be expressed in terms of the inflationary and GNP gaps, which relate national income to potential income, or in terms of the difference between the actual and natural rates of unemployment.

5. Expectations of inflation tend to cause wage settlements that preserve the real wage and hence lead to nominal wage increases. They are a major source of inertia and stagflation.

6. It is possible to have a sustained inflation at the capacity level of income (and hence at the natural rate of unemployment). There is no demand pressure on prices, but expectations can cause wages and hence prices to grow at the same rate as the money supply.

7. Stopping an inflation through restrictive monetary policy will lead to a recession that lasts while inflation only gradually falls to a rate consistent with the new lower rate of money growth. The length and depth of the recession will depend on the strength of the downward pressure on wages and on the speed with which inflationary expectations adjust.

8. Incomes policies that try to directly control wage and price increases are also often advocated as measures to reduce inflation. When they have been applied instead of demand restraint, they have proven futile. However, when used along with demand constraint they may be helpful in either speeding up the adjustment of inflationary expectations or temporarily suppressing the role of expectations causing a stagflation.

9. Neo-Keynesians tend to believe that the demand pressures on wages from a GNP gap are weak and that expectations are sluggish to adjust. As a result, they believe that the recession will be deep and prolonged. Monetarists tend to believe that demand pressures from a GNP gap cause wages to respond quickly and that expectations are also fast to adjust. As a result, they believe that the recession will be brief.

10. In the early 1980s a major policy experiment was initiated in an attempt to bring inflation down rapidly. This resulted in a much larger recession than most monetarists predicted but also in a much faster reduction in inflation than most Neo-Keynesians predicted.

TOPICS FOR REVIEW

Temporary and sustained inflations
Monetary accommodation of supply shocks
Monetary validation of demand shocks
Pure demand inflation
Pure expectational inflation
Natural rate of unemployment
Accelerating inflation
Equilibrium inflation
Extrapolative and rational expectations
Incomes policies

DISCUSSION QUESTIONS

1. On what source or sources of inflation do the following statements focus attention?
   a. "The one basic cause of inflation is the government's spending more than it takes in. The cure is a balanced budget."
   b. "Major labor negotiations in steel, autos, and other basic industries will lead to double-digit wage increases and a serious inflationary effect."
   c. "Wage settlements are high. The widespread publicity they are receiving will make it difficult to wind down inflation."
   d. "While the CPI rose by 7 percent last month, most of the increase was in a very few sectors where bottlenecks are developing."

2. Inflations cannot long persist, whatever their initiating causes, unless the inflations are validated by increases in the money supply." Why is this so? Does it not imply that control of inflation is merely a matter of not allowing increases in the money supply to rise faster than the rate of increase of real national income?

3. Look at the rate of increases of the money supply and the CPI over the last three years and decide whether or not the current inflation is being validated.

4. Discuss the following views on the effects of inflation.
   a. "Now the beast [of inflation] is easily visible, a luminescent specter, a killer, a threat to society, public enemy No. 1,"—Robert D. Hersy Jr., 1979.
   b. "Inflation has become the national obsession . . . . the catchall scapegoat for individual and societal economic difficulties, the symptom that diverts attention from the basic maladies."—James Tobin, 1980.

5. What theory or theories of inflation are suggested by each of the following quotations?
   a. "February Producer Prices Up a Sharp 1.5 Percent—Rise in Costs of Energy Largest in 6 Years"—newspaper report, 1979.
   b. "From the point of view of dealing with inflation, this [deficit equal to 4 percent of GNP] was an uncomfort-

ably large deficit for the government of Canada to have at a time when the level of economic activity relative to the economy's demonstrated capacity was as high as it was."—Annual Report of the Governor of the Bank of Canada, 1980.

c. ". . . inflation was the almost inevitable outgrowth of the enormous international stresses during this period. . . . As attempts [to maintain real income growth] were essentially incompatible with the real constraints of the situation, they resulted in higher inflation. . ."—*Economic Review*, 1981.

d. "The nation's spiraling inflation reflects a global depletion of physical resources and therefore cannot be cured by traditional fiscal and monetary tools"—a study issued in 1980 by the Worldwatch Institute.

6. A recent newspaper article on inflation warned, "It is a mistake to think that every higher price is due to inflation." Give some examples of higher prices that have increased the CPI without being a part of a general inflationary process.

7. A recent newspaper discussion of inflation gave the following arguments *for* and *against* reductions in specific taxes.

For:

a. "Cuts in payroll taxes would reduce employment costs, thereby helping to slow down price inflation."

b. "Faster depreciation write-offs would provide greater incentives for new equipment and technology investments, thus boosting productivity."

Against:

c. "Pumping more money and more purchasing power into the economy through a tax cut without cutting federal spending would do little to restrain inflation [indeed it would increase it]."

d. "A better approach would be to achieve a budget surplus and pay off the federal debt."

Match each of the above statements with the following theoretical category that best describes it.

(i) Shift the aggregate demand curve to the right.

(ii) Shift the aggregate supply curve downward.

(iii) Shift the aggregate demand curve to the left.

(iv) Shift the long-run aggregate supply curve outward to the right.

8. William Nordhaus of Yale University recently described inflation as an "inertial process like people standing up at a football game. When some people jump up to see better, other people can't see unless they stand up, too. When everybody is up, people as a group can't see as well as they did when they were all sitting; in fact, they probably see worse and are more uncomfortable. But the problem is how to get them all to sit down together." What view of inflation is Professor Nordhaus embracing?

9. In an article on the harmful effects of inflation, a reporter wrote, "with the rise in mortgage interest rates to 10 percent heaven only knows the price of what was once idealized as "the $100,000 house." At the time the inflation rate was 9 percent. Did the 10 percent interest rate represent a heavy burden of inflation on the new home owner? What do you think the mortgage interest rate would have been if the inflation rate had been zero? What would have been a heavier real burden on the purchaser of a new house?

10. "On the Rise, A New Breed of Debtors," a recent newspaper article suggested that because of the ravages of inflation many people were going into debt to make ends meet. What would be a rational debt policy—to borrow or to lend—if you thought the rate of inflation was going to be at least as high as the current rate of interest? Does your answer suggest possible reasons for the "rise in the new breed of debtors" other than an inability to make ends meet?

11. Consider the factors at work which might give rise to the following (often conflicting) newspaper headlines from early 1983:

a. "The Money Bulge Isn't Inflationary."

b. "Why Continued Success Is Likely in Effort to Tame Inflation."

c. "Drop in Oil Prices, Interest Rates, and Inflation Could Mean Stronger Recovery."

d. "Broker Says Inflation May Be Under Control for Years."

e. "Economists Optimistic on Inflation Outlook."

f. "Though Consensus Sees Mild Inflation Ahead, Some Signs Suggest a Returning Price Spiral."

g. "Inflation Still Alive and Influencing Policy."

37 EMPLOYMENT AND UNEMPLOYMENT

In the early 1980s worldwide unemployment rose to very high levels. Not only was the overall level of unemployment wastefully large, the structure of unemployment was extremely varied. At the beginning of 1983 the unemployment rate in the United States was about 47 percent among black males aged 16 to 19 and "only" 8 percent among white women over 19. At the time the most serious pockets of localized unemployment seemed to be among the many unskilled residents of the decaying inner cores of large industrial cities.

Many social policies designed to alleviate the short-term economic consequences of unemployment have been instituted since the 1930s. Their success may be counted as a real triumph of economic policy. But the longer-term effects of current high unemployment rates in terms of the disillusioned who have given up trying to make it within the system and who sow the seeds of future social unrest should be a matter of serious concern to the haves as well as to the have-nots.

In the 1970s the control of inflation emerged as a major social problem in many Western industrial nations. To cure inflation governments induced the worldwide recession of the early 1980s. Was the resulting unemployment worth it? Can unemployment be reduced in the last half of the 1980s as easily as it was induced in the early 1980s? When inflation in the United States fell drastically in 1982 and reached quite low levels—in the 4 percent to 6 percent range—by mid 1983, most Americans echoed the view expressed in February 1983 by the President's Council of Economic Advisors that "unemployment is the most serious economic problem now facing the United States."

KINDS OF UNEMPLOYMENT

It is helpful to identify a number of kinds of unemployment. Keynes distinguished between voluntary and involuntary unemployment. *Voluntary* unemployment occurs when there is a job available but the unemployed person is not willing to accept it at the going wage rate. *Involuntary* unemployment occurs when a person is willing to accept a job at the going wage rate but cannot find a job.

Until now we have distinguished only two types of involuntary unemployment: *deficient-demand* unemployment, which is unemployment due to a GNP gap, and *frictional* unemployment, which we defined as unemployment that exists when national income is at its potential level and hence there is neither a GNP gap nor an inflationary gap.

For our more detailed study we will now distinguish further between two types of frictional unemployment. For bouts of relatively short-term unemployment, we retain the term *frictional* unemployment. For longer-term bouts we introduce the term *structural* unemployment. We also discuss an additional type, *real wage* unemployment.

Frictional Unemployment

In its more restricted usage frictional unemployment refers to the normal turnover of labor. Older workers leave the labor force and young people enter it, although these new workers do not usually fill the jobs vacated by those who leave. Of course people leave jobs for reasons other than retirement. Some people quit jobs because they are dissatisfied with the working conditions. Others are dismissed. Whatever the reason, they must search for new jobs, which takes time. This turnover gives rise·to a pool of persons who are "frictionally" unemployed while in the course of looking for jobs.

Frictional unemployment would occur even if the structure of jobs in terms of skills, industries, occupations, and location was static and the labor force was fully adjusted to it.

Normal turnover of labor will always produce a pool of persons who are frictionally unemployed. Either they will be between jobs or will be looking for their first job.

Some frictional unemployment is involuntary: no acceptable job in the person's occupational and skill category has yet been located. Often, however, it is voluntary. The unemployed person is aware of available jobs but is searching for better options. Voluntary frictional unemployment is often called **search unemployment.**

The existence of search unemployment shows that the distinction between voluntary and involuntary unemployment is not as clear as it might seem at first sight. How, for example, should we classify an unemployed woman who refuses to accept a job at a lower skill level than the one for which she feels she is qualified? What if she turns down a job for which she is trained because she hopes to get a higher wage offer for a similar job from another employer?

In one sense people in search unemployment are voluntarily unemployed because they could find some job; in another sense they are involuntarily unemployed because they have not yet succeeded in finding the job for which they feel they are suited at a rate of pay that they believe exists. Workers do not have perfect knowledge of all available jobs and rates of pay, and they may be able to gain information only by searching the market. Faced with this uncertainty, it may be sensible to refuse a first job offer, for the offer may prove to be a poor one in light of further market information. How long it will pay to remain in search unemployment depends on the economic costs of being unemployed.

It is socially desirable for there to be sufficient search unemployment to give unemployed people time to find an available job that uses their skills.

Too much search—for example, holding off while being supported by others in the hope of locating a job better than that for which one is really suited—is an economic waste. Thus search unemployment is a gray area: some is useful, some wasteful.

Structural Unemployment

Structural adjustments of the economy can cause unemployment. When the pattern of demand for goods changes, the demand for labor changes; if labor has not adjusted to these changes, structural unemployment occurs. **Structural unemployment** may be defined as unemployment caused by a mismatch between the structure of the labor force—in terms of skills, occupations, industries, or geographic location—and the structure of the demand for labor. In the United States today, structural unemployment exists, for example, in parts of New England, in the automobile industry, and in many of the older foundry and mill towns in the upper Midwest.

Structural unemployment arises when the composition of the demand for labor does not match the composition of the available supply.

Natural causes. Economic growth can cause structural unemployment. As growth proceeds, the mix of required inputs changes, as do the proportions in which final goods are demanded. These changes require considerable economic re-adjustment. Structural unemployment occurs when such re-adjustments are slow enough that severe pockets of unemployment develop in areas, industries, and occupations in which the demand for factors of production is falling faster than the supply.

Changes that accompany economic growth shift the structure of the demand for labor. Demand rises in such expanding areas as the sun belt states and falls in such contracting areas as the midwestern steel- and car-producing centers. Demand rises for workers with certain skills, such as computer programming and electronics engineering, and falls for workers with other skills, such as stenography and bookkeeping. Demand rises, say, for airline pilots and short-order cooks, and falls for auto assembly line workers and crew members on transatlantic passenger liners. To meet changing demands the structure of the labor force must change. Some existing workers can be retrained while new entrants can acquire fresh skills.

Policy causes. Government policies can influence such changes. Often policies that discourage movement among regions, industries, and occupations also raise structural unemployment. Policies that prevent firms from replacing human labor with machines may protect employment in the short term. If, however, such policies lead to the decline of an industry because it cannot compete effectively with innovative foreign competitors, serious structural unemployment can result.

One further cause of structural unemployment is the persistence of a disequilibrium structure of relative wages. Typical causes of such a structure are minimum wages, union agreements that narrow wage differentials, nationally negotiated wage structures that take no account of local market conditions, and equal pay laws where employers do not perceive that the groups concerned all contribute equally to the profitability of the enterprise. Such policies cause particular groups to lose employment because their relative wages are too high.

For example an elderly person may be prepared to work for $70 a week as a caretaker of an apartment. Further, the owner may believe that this person is capable of doing what is needed. But suppose the minimum wage is $120 a week. If there were no minimum wage, the elderly person would get the job. But because of the minimum wage, the owner has to pay almost twice as much as she needs to and therefore hires someone else who can provide her with more services than she needs. She reasons that since she has to pay more, she might as well get something for it.

The same considerations apply to an inexperienced worker just out of school who would accept $75 a week for a first job. A potential employer is willing to pay this wage, but the minimum wage is $120. Once again the employer hires someone else who is overqualified for the job.

Much empirical research supports the conclusion that imposed wage structures like minimum wages tend to transfer employment from those whose relative wages are raised by the intervention to those whose relative wages are lowered. But do imposed wages affect overall employment? That is a much more difficult question. If such policies lead to an increase in the average wage paid, they may contribute to what we will call real wage unemployment, which we study below.

The Distinction Between Frictional and Structural Unemployment

As with many distinctions, the one between structural and frictional unemployment becomes blurred at the margin. In a sense structural unemployment is really long-term frictional unemployment. For illustration consider a change that requires labor to re-allocate from one sector to another. If the re-allocation occurs quickly, we call the unemployment frictional; if the re-allocation occurs slowly, we call the unemployment structural.

The major characteristic of both frictional and structural unemployment is that there is a job available—that is, an unfilled vacancy—for each unemployed person.

In the case of pure frictional unemployment the job vacancy and the searcher are matched. The only problem is that the searcher has not yet located the vacancy. In the case of structural unemployment, the job vacancy and the searcher are mismatched in one or more relevant characteristics such as occupation, industry, location, or skill requirements.

Deficient-Demand Unemployment

Unemployment that occurs because of insufficient total demand for all the output that could be produced by a fully employed labor force is called **deficient-demand unemployment**. It is the unemployment that exists because there is a GNP gap. As a result there are not enough jobs available for all unemployed persons. When deficient-demand unemployment is zero, there is some job available for every person unemployed. In this situation unemployment persists either for structural reasons (the vacancies and the unemployed are mismatched) or frictional reasons (normal labor turnover).

National income theory seeks to explain the causes of, and cures for, unemployment in excess of frictional and structural unemployment. *Full employment* does not mean zero unemployment; it means that all unemployment is frictional or structural.

National income theory seeks to explain the deficient-demand unemployment associated with variations in the nation's total output. The measurement of deficient-demand, frictional, and structural unemployment is discussed further in the box on page 720.

Real Wage Unemployment

Unemployment due to too high a real wage is sometimes called **Classical unemployment** because many economists, whom Keynes dubbed the *Classical economists*, believed that unemployment in the 1930s was caused by a real wage that was too high. The remedy they suggested for unemployment was to reduce wages. Keynesians won that battle, and there is now general agreement that the unemploy-

STRUCTURAL AND FRICTIONAL UNEMPLOYMENT

One useful measure of the total of frictional plus structural unemployment is the percentage of the labor force unemployed when the number of unfilled job vacancies is equal to the number of persons seeking jobs. When these two are equal, there is a job opening for every person seeking a job. Any unemployment that remains must be either frictional or structural.

This measure is illustrated in the figure, which plots the number of unfilled vacancies (v) against the number of unemployed (u). The 45° line is the locus of points where $u = v$. On that line there is some job available to match every unemployed person, so there is no deficient-demand unemployment. The uv curve shows the relationship between unemployment and vacancies that is suggested by empirical evidence. In an economy with the relation uv_1, zero deficient-demand unemployment occurs at the point x with frictional plus structural unemployment given by the amount a measured on either axis.

When a boom occurs employers seek to hire more workers, so more vacancies open up. Since there are more jobs available, the unemployed spend less time searching before finding an acceptable job. Thus the pool of unemployed falls.

A boom therefore takes the economy to some point such as y, where there are more vacancies than unemployed. A slump takes the economy to some point such as z, where there are fewer vacancies than unemployed.

A change in structural plus frictional unemployment shifts the uv curve. For example, if people lose their jobs in New England while more jobs are created in southern California there may be a rise in the number of unemployed (in New England) and a rise in the number of unfilled job vacancies (in southern California). Hence both u and v increase. In the diagram a shift to uv_2 indicates a rise in frictional plus structural unemployment from a to b.

In most countries where reliable vacancy data is available the uv relation shifted outward in the late 1960s and early 1970s. This indicated a rise in structural plus frictional unemployment.

Deficient-Demand Unemployment

We can measure deficient-demand unemployment as total unemployment minus estimated frictional plus structural unemployment. Graphically it is actual unemployment minus the unemployment where the uv relation cuts the 45° line. If the economy is at point z, this measure is ac in the figure.

Real Wage Unemployment

Unemployment due to excessive increases in the real wage will show up in the figure approximately as a movement along the existing uv curve, say from point x to w', rather than as a shift of that curve. There will be a large rise in unemployment and a small fall in vacancies (which would otherwise have resulted from the normal turnover of labor in the now-closed plants). A general rise in the real product wage can lead to a general rise in unemployment that looks like deficient-demand unemployment because there is a rise in unemployment with no corresponding rise in unfilled vacancies.

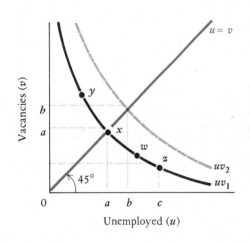

ment of the 1930s was caused by deficient aggregate demand rather than excessive real wages.

Because the battles of the 1930s aroused such emotions, many modern Keynesians have refused to believe that *any* unemployment could be caused by real wages being too high. There is a growing concern, however, that some current unemployment in Western Europe and elsewhere may be traced to excessive real wage levels. The issue is by no means settled. Because of the emotionally loaded nature of the phrase *Classical unemployment,* the term **real wage unemployment,** defined as unemployment due to the existing level of real wages, is the preferred term.

So far we have used the term *real wage* to mean the purchasing power of money wages. This is measured by deflating the money wage by the Consumer Price Index. In this section we are concerned with the real cost to the employer of hiring a worker. We call this the **real product wage.** The nominal cost to the employer includes the pre-tax wage rate, any extra benefits such as pension plan contributions, and any government payroll taxes such as employers' contributions to OASI. The real cost is the nominal cost divided by the output price.

Too high a real wage can affect employment through forces operating both in the short run and in the long run. Consider the short run first. When technological change is embodied in plant and equipment, at any moment in time an industry will have an array of plants, ranging from those that can do little more than cover their variable costs to those that make a handsome return over variable costs. A rise in the real product wage of 10 percent will mean that some plants can no longer cover their variable costs and so will close down. If, for example, a plant had wages of $.70 and other variable costs of $.25 for every $1 of sales, production would be worthwhile since $.05 of every $1 of sales would be available as a return on already invested capital. If the product wage rose so that $.77 for every $1 of sales was paid in wages, then the plant would be shut down, since it would not even be covering its variable costs. The plant's employees would then lose their jobs. This same analysis applies to the economy as a whole.

An economy-wide rise in real product wages, other things being equal, means that some plants and firms will no longer be able to cover their variable costs and will shut down. When they do, the unemployment rate will rise.

Now consider the long run, when there is much more scope for flexibility in the design of production techniques and in the matching of labor demand with the prevailing real product wage. The flexibility arises because much capital is what is called *putty-clay.* At the design stage, more or less capital can be spread over the labor force, thus varying the capital-labor ratio. But once production techniques are designed, factor ratios are embodied in the equipment and cannot be significantly varied. For example a highly automated or quite simple textile plant can be designed and the capital-labor ratio therefore varied over a wide range on the drawing board. Once an automated plant is built, however, this ratio cannot be varied greatly by varying the amount of labor applied to the now-fixed quantity of capital. You cannot productively combine a great deal more labor with automated machinery to make the process less capital-intensive. Neither can you cut in half the labor force that tends a given amount of non-automated machinery in order to make the process much more capital-intensive.

When the real wage is too high across the whole economy, there will be a structural mismatch between the labor force and the capital stock which shows up as unemployment: when the capital stock is working at full capacity there is still unemployed labor. This structural mismatch may persist for a considerable period of time, as is discussed further in the box on page 722.

Indeed it will continue until one of two things happen. Unemployment may force down the real wage until it pays firms to employ all of the existing labor. Alternatively, new technologies may be invented that make profitable use of the unemployed labor in spite of its high real product wage.

Too high a real wage can be the cause of much unemployment. Whether or not this is so in practice is an unsettled empirical issue.

INVESTMENT AND THE PERSISTENCE OF REAL WAGE UNEMPLOYMENT

Real wage unemployment arises when the real product wage is so high as to cause existing capital equipment to be unprofitable, leading to closure of plants and even dissolution of firms. At the same time, investment in new, more capital-intensive plant and equipment will be undertaken.

That a rise in the real product wage would lead to more capital-intensive methods of production (i.e., a substitution of capital for labor) is a direct consequence of the principle of substitution discussed in Chapter 13.

When plants that are too labor-intensive are being replaced by plants that are more capital-intensive, we would expect unemployment to develop. But this may be a transitional phase. Would not more of these capital-intensive plants be built until all of the available labor force is put to work?

The answer depends on whether or not the real product wage is too high to encourage sufficient investment. Two general cases need to be distinguished. First, the real product wage may be so high that no new plants built with existing technology are profitable. Then old plants that cannot cover variable costs will be closed down, no new plants will be built, and an alleviation of the unemployment (assuming the real wage is not lowered) must await the very long run when technologies that are profitable at existing input prices are invented. Second, newly built capital-intensive plants may be profitable at existing prices, in which case some will be built. During the transition while older, more labor-intensive plants are being scrapped and new capital-intensive ones are being built, unemploy-

ment may develop. If the profitability of investment diminishes at the margin as the capital stock grows, then new construction will stop when further units of capital are not sufficiently profitable. Whether or not this happens before the whole labor force is put back to work depends on the real wage (and capital costs) and on the speed with which returns to investment decline at the margin as the capital stock grows. Since these are both empirical matters on which we currently have insufficient evidence, either answer is possible.

Whether or not real wage unemployment is a serious problem is a matter of current dispute. *But the answer is a matter of major importance.* Advocates of the real wage explanation argue that, for example, British real wages were some 10 percent to 15 percent too high in 1982, and, as a result, significant amounts of capital were being scrapped. They also point out that the first sign of such a national disaster is a rise in recorded labor productivity. Since the least efficient plants are scrapped first, the average output per head of those remaining in employment will rise steadily. But such a rise in productivity would be less the first glimmerings of an economic sunrise than the first winds of an economic hurricane.

The evidence of serious real wage unemployment seems stronger for Europe than for the United States. Some observers, however, looking at the shift in manufacturing jobs from the United States to such lower-wage countries as Japan and Taiwan, fear that real wage unemployment may be an emerging problem in the United States as well.

EXPERIENCE OF UNEMPLOYMENT

Measured and Nonmeasured Unemployment

The number of unemployed persons is estimated from the Current Population Survey conducted each month by the Bureau of the Census. Persons who are currently without a job but who say they have actively searched for one during the sample period are recorded as unemployed. The total number of estimated unemployed is then expressed as a percentage of the labor force (employed plus unemployed) to obtain the figure for percentage unemployment.

The measured figure for unemployment may overstate or understate the number of people who are involuntarily unemployed.

On the one hand, the measured figure overstates unemployment by including people who are not involuntarily unemployed. For example, unemployment compensation provides protection against genuine hardship, but it also induces some to stay out of work and collect unemployment benefits for as long as they last. Such people have in fact voluntarily withdrawn from the labor force but they are usually included in the ranks of the unemployed because, for fear of losing their benefits, they may tell the person who surveys them that they are actively looking for a job.

On the other hand, the measured figure understates involuntary unemployment by omitting some people who would accept a job if one were available but who did not actively look for one in the sample week. For example, if a person has not found a job by the time unemployment benefits are exhausted, he or she may become discouraged and stop seeking work. Such people have voluntarily withdrawn from the labor force and will not be recorded as unemployed. They are, however, truly unemployed in the sense that they would willingly accept a job if one were available.

Those who are in this category are referred to as **discouraged workers.** The Bureau of Labor Statistics estimated that at the beginning of 1983 there were nearly 2 million discouraged workers in the United States. These people had voluntarily withdrawn from the labor market because they believe they cannot find a job under current conditions.

In addition there is part-time unemployment. If some workers are working 6 hours a day instead of 8 hours because there is insufficient demand for the product they manufacture, then that group is suffering 25 percent unemployment even though no individual is reported as unemployed. Twenty-five percent of the potential manpower is going unused. Involuntary part-time work is a major source of unemployment of labor resources not reflected in the overall unemployment figures reported in the press. For example, the Bureau of Labor Statistics (BLS) estimated that, at the beginning of 1983, there were 2 million workers on involuntary short time. If they were working only three-quarters time on average, then their unemployment was equivalent to 500,000 workers being out of jobs full time.

The Overall Unemployment Rate

Figure 26-2 (see page 484) shows the behavior of the unemployment rate since the end of World War II. Until 1970 the rate fluctuated cyclically but showed no clear rising or falling trend. During the 1950s the average rate was 4.5 percent and during the 1960s it was 4.8 percent—not a significant difference.[1] From 1970, however, the cyclical fluctuations appeared to be superimposed on a rising trend. From 1970 to 1983 the *low* figure of 4.9 percent unemployment was above the *average* of 4.7 percent for the previous two decades. This low figure was achieved during the boom of 1972–1973, but the subsequent recession caused the figure to rise to 8.5 percent in 1975. Then after a steady fall to 5.8 percent in 1979 the unemployment figure again began to rise. As 1983 began, it was very close to 11 percent, the highest unemployment figure since the Great Depression of the 1930s.

---

[1] Yearly figures in this section are based on annual averages of unemployment.

The level of unemployment that persists when all deficient-demand unemployment is removed has risen in recent years.

Just how much deficient-demand unemployment remains when the overall rate is, say, 8.0 percent is a matter of current debate. Some observers think it is no more than 0.5 percent at most, others think it may be as much as 1.5 percent. Expressed as percentage points, these figures may not seem very big, but a reduction of one percentage point in the unemployment rate means that about one million more people have jobs. It is important to settle the issue of how much deficient-demand unemployment exists. To apply the cure of raising aggregate demand when there is no deficient-demand unemployment would add greatly to inflationary pressure while doing little to reduce unemployment.

The Relative Importance of the Various Kinds of Unemployment

At the beginning of 1983 there were just over 12 million unemployed in the United States, or nearly 11 percent of the labor force. According to the most widely accepted estimates, deficient-demand unemployment accounted for about half this unemployment and frictional, structural, and real-wage unemployment combined accounted for the remainder.

The deficient-demand unemployment will be largely eliminated with recovery from the slump. But what of the 6 or 7 million unemployed who remain? To study them further we look at some of the characteristics of the unemployed. Figure 37-1 gives some idea of the current duration of the spells of unemployment.[2] Data are given for 1982, a year of severe recession, and for 1978, the last year when national income came close to potential income.

[2] The figures are based on the Current Population Survey, which asks currently unemployed individuals how long they have been out of work. Notice that this gives us the duration of *currently uncompleted* bouts of unemployment. It gives different and shorter figures than the duration of *completed bouts* of unemployment, which is obtained by asking people who have just found a job how long they were out of work.

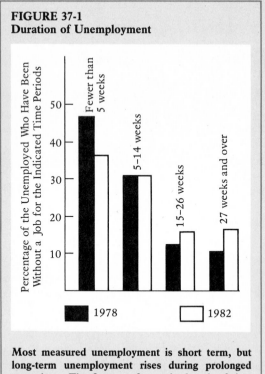

**FIGURE 37-1
Duration of Unemployment**

Most measured unemployment is short term, but long-term unemployment rises during prolonged recessions. The figures refer to the length of time people who are currently unemployed have been out of a job. By far the greatest number are those who have been out of work fewer than 5 weeks. But in 1982, at the trough of a very serious recession, fully 16.6 percent of the unemployed had been out of a job for more than 6 months.

The unemployed in 1978 experienced mainly frictional and structural unemployment, and thus the differences between 1978 and 1982 can be assumed to be due mainly to the addition of deficient-demand unemployment.

The bulk of reported unemployment is apparently short term. In 1977 fully 77 percent of the unemployed had been out of work for 14 weeks or less. Really long-term unemployment, more than half a year, accounted for only 10 percent of the unemployed in 1978 but 16.6 percent in 1982. Thus the potentially soul-destroying bouts of prolonged periods without a job are confined to a relatively small part of the labor force but a part that rises significantly in recessions. Commenting

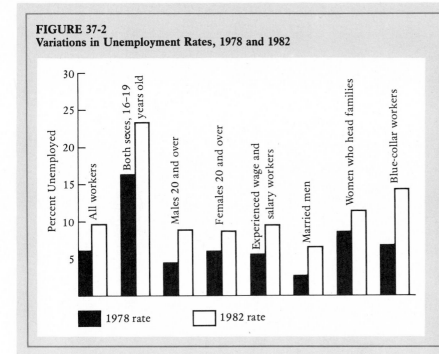

FIGURE 37-2
Variations in Unemployment Rates, 1978 and 1982

Percent Unemployed

All workers
Both sexes, 16–19 years old
Males 20 and over
Females 20 and over
Experienced wage and salary workers
Married men
Women who head families
Blue-collar workers

■ 1978 rate   □ 1982 rate

Unemployment was very un-evenly divided among sex and skill groups in 1978 and again in 1982. In 1978 and 1982 overall unemployment rates of 6.1 per-cent and 9.7 percent respectively concealed large variations in the unemployment rates of different groups. The recession of 1982 led to a rise in unemployment rates among all groups. Unemploy-ment among married men, who typically have very favorable em-ployment experiences, increased 2 1/2-fold from 2.8 percent to 6.5 percent. Unemployment among youth reached close to one in four in 1982. It was also at the very high figure of 16.4 percent in 1978, a year that had no sig-nificant GNP gap.

on these figures, the President's Council of Eco-nomic Advisors in 1983 said

. . . even during recessions, most people who become unemployed either find jobs or leave the labor force relatively quickly. . . . The incidence of long-term un-employment is very sensitive to cyclical conditions, which suggests that it will diminish as the economy recovers. Even after a recovery is well underway, how-ever, a sizable fraction of total unemployment will in-volve protracted joblessness. The needs of the long-term unemployed deserve special recognition in the designing of policies to attack structural unemployment.

Figures 37-2 and 37-3 document some of the inequalities in unemployment rates. Males and fe-males, the young and the experienced have very different unemployment experiences, as Figure 37-2 shows. Even more dramatic are the differences between white and nonwhites, as shown in Figure 37-3. By far the lowest unemployment rates in booms and slumps are recorded by white males 20 years of age and over. By far the highest rates occur for nonwhite females under 20 years of age.

Why Has Frictional Plus Structural Unemployment Risen Over the Last 15 Years?

Structural unemployment can increase because ei-ther the pace of change accelerates or the pace of adjustment to change slows down. An increase in the rate of growth, for example, speeds up the rate of creation of new jobs for which there may be little or no current supply of trained workers. New regulations that make it harder for workers in a given occupation to take new jobs in other states will also increase the degree of mismatch between jobs and available workers.

Demographic changes. Because people usually try several jobs before settling into one for a longer period of time, young and inexperienced workers have higher unemployment rates than experienced workers. Over the last 15 years the proportion of inexperienced workers in the labor force rose sig-nificantly as the baby boom generation of the 1950s entered the labor force along with an unprece-

FIGURE 37-3
Unemployment by Age, Sex, and Race

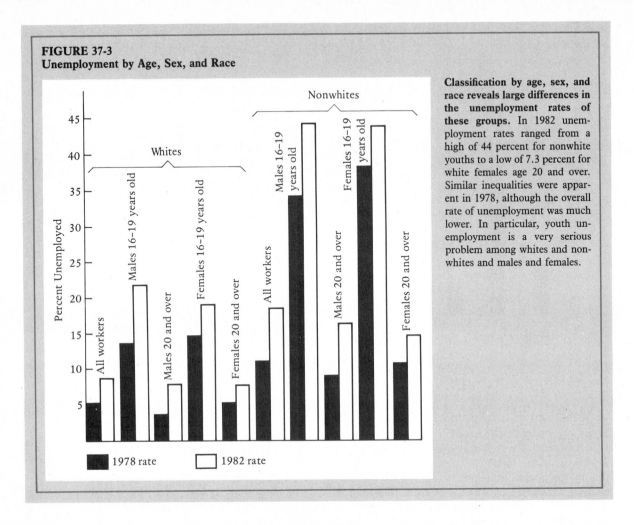

Classification by age, sex, and race reveals large differences in the unemployment rates of these groups. In 1982 unemployment rates ranged from a high of 44 percent for nonwhite youths to a low of 7.3 percent for white females age 20 and over. Similar inequalities were apparent in 1978, although the overall rate of unemployment was much lower. In particular, youth unemployment is a very serious problem among whites and nonwhites and males and females.

dented number of women who elected to work outside the home. It is estimated that these demographic changes added nearly a percentage point to frictional and structural unemployment. Since birthrates were low in the 1960s and a further increase in the percentage of females entering the labor force is unlikely, there may be some demographically induced fall in this type of unemployment over the next decade.

Another significant change is the large increase in the number of households with more than one income earner. In 1962 only 36 percent of white females 20 years and older were in the labor force; in 1972 the figure was 43 percent; by 1982 it had

jumped to 52 percent. (Black females have always had a higher "participation rate" in the labor force. During that 20-year period their rate rose only from 50 percent to 56 percent.) When both husband and wife work, it is possible for one to support both while the other looks for "a really good job" rather than accepting the first job offer that comes his or her way.

Wage and price rigidity. Research such as that done recently by Professor Phillip Cagan of Columbia University suggests that the speed with which wages and prices adjust to changing market conditions has slowed over the years. Anything that slows the speed of adjustment to the economy's ever-changing conditions will create a larger pool of structural unemployment.

Social insurance programs. Minimum wage laws help those who keep their jobs as their wages are forced up. They hurt those who lose their jobs. They may also have a longer-term effect. Employers are discouraged from hiring young people at low wages while providing on-the-job training. During a period of training, employees acquire marketable skills that allow them subsequently to command a higher wage. By discouraging such practices, minimum wage laws create a pool of people without skills who alternate between low-paid jobs and bouts of unemployment, thus raising the number of people who are in structural or frictional unemployment at any one time.

Increasing structural change. The amount of resource re-allocation across industries and areas seems to have increased over the last two decades. In part this is the result of the increasing integration of the U.S. economy with that of the rest of the world. Most observers feel that on balance this integration has been beneficial. But one less fortunate consequence is that changes in demand or supply conditions anywhere in the world requiring adjustments throughout the world's trading sectors increasingly affect the United States.

Internationally one of the most significant demand changes for the United States was the emergence of the Eastern bloc countries as major food importers. The failure of their system of collective agriculture to meet domestic demand led them to become large importers of grain. To pay for these imports, they had to become major exporters of other commodities such as natural gas.

A further demand change was the input price shocks that have buffeted the world over the last 15 years: two enormous oil price increases in the 1970s with a steady downward slide in the early 1980s and an increase of over 200 percent in average basic materials prices in the early 1970s. Such changes have shifted competitive advantages in industrial production, leading to growth in some areas and countries and decline in others.

Changing prices have also caused changes in quantities demanded. The high cost of gas and oil led to a shift to small cars, an enormous investment program to retool U.S. industry, and major car imports from Japan and Germany that cut heavily into the demand for American cars and for their major inputs such as steel. The results have been all too evident in the unemployment figures. At the beginning of 1983, when the overall unemployment rate was just below 11 percent, unemployment was nearly 25 percent in the auto industry and nearly 30 percent in primary metals. Some of these workers will be recalled as output recovers, but many will have to find jobs in other industries and areas where new skills may be required. Rising oil prices also led to a shift to natural gas for home heating, a large demand for insulation, and alterations in typical designs of new houses.

A further factor on the cost side is the increased use of robots in factories and computer-based processes in offices. These changes have eliminated many assembly line and clerical jobs and forced their former holders to look elsewhere for new jobs.

Another major set of forces leading to structural change arise from the shifting pattern of demand. As a result of rising income and changing social patterns, people spend a higher proportion of their income on services than they used to—and a correspondingly smaller proportion on manufactured goods. Restaurant meals and day-care facilities for children are two services with rising demands. As we observed on page 421, the *increase* in employment in the fast food industry during the 1970s exceeded the total combined employment in the automobile and steel industries!

The increasing pace of change over the last 15 years has contributed greatly to a rising volume of structural unemployment.

UNEMPLOYMENT POLICIES

Unemployment can never be reduced to zero. Frictional unemployment is inevitable; some structural unemployment must exist as the pattern of the demand for labor changes faster than the supply of labor can adapt to it, and some deficient-demand unemployment will exist at average levels of business activity. All kinds of unemployment have costs in terms of the output that could have been produced by the unemployed workers. Yet reducing unemployment is also costly. For example, retraining and re-allocation schemes designed to reduce structural unemployment uses scarce resources.

It would be neither possible nor desirable to reduce unemployment to zero. The causes of unemployment could never be removed completely, and reducing the amount of unemployment stemming from those causes is a costly process.

Unemployment insurance is one method of helping people live with unemployment. Certainly unemployment insurance has reduced significantly the human costs of the bouts of unemployment that are inevitable in a changing society. Nothing, however, is without cost. While unemployment insurance alleviates the suffering caused by some kinds of unemployment, it can itself contribute to unemployment for, as we have observed, it encourages voluntary and search unemployment.

Supporters of unemployment insurance emphasize its benefits. Critics emphasize its costs. As with any policy, a rational assessment of the value of unemployment insurance requires a balancing of its undoubted benefits against its undoubted costs. Most Americans seem convinced that, when this calculation is made, the benefits greatly exceed the costs.

Deficient-Demand Unemployment

We do not need to say much more about this type of unemployment since its control is the subject of stabilization policy, which we have studied in several earlier chapters. A major recession that occurs due to natural causes can be countered by monetary and fiscal policy to reduce deficient-demand unemployment.

The 1970s and 1980s saw a new situation: policy-induced, deficient-demand unemployment. This occurred when the government induced a recession in order to combat inflation. Deficient-demand unemployment is viewed by many as the price of reducing inflation. If this is so, then the only way to reduce unemployment is to find ways of first reducing inflation so that policymakers will then be willing to raise aggregate demand.

Real Wage Unemployment

If this type of unemployment is a major problem, its cure is not an easy matter. Basically what is required is a fall in the real product wage combined with measures to increase aggregate demand so as to create enough total employment. But the cure is slow and requires enough time to build the new labor-using capital. The steps might be as follows.

1. The real product wage would be cut substantially, possibly by some form of incomes policy or "social contract."
2. Since wages enter into disposable income and disposable income determines consumer demand, the cut in wages will tend to reduce aggregate demand and hence reduce equilibrium national income. This deflationary force will then be countered by expansionary fiscal and monetary policy that will create sufficient aggregate demand to restore full employment.

If real wage unemployment is a serious problem, then attacking unemployment by increasing aggregate demand may cause the economy to hit capital constraints when there is still a substantial amount of unemployed labor. Further demand increases would then become inflationary long before unemployment fell to levels that would be regarded as satisfactory by historical standards.

Frictional Unemployment

The turnover that causes frictional unemployment is an inevitable part of the functioning of the economy. Insofar as it is caused by ignorance, increasing the knowledge of workers about market opportunities may help. But such measures have a cost, and that cost has to be balanced against the benefits.

Some frictional unemployment is an inevitable part of the learning process. One reason that there is a high turnover rate, and hence high frictional unemployment, is that new entrants have to try jobs to see if they are suitable. They will typically try more than one job before settling into one that most satisfies, or least dissatisfies, them.

Structural Unemployment

The re-allocation of labor among occupations, industries, skill categories, and regions that gives rise to structural unemployment is an inevitable part of growth. There are two basic approaches to reducing structural unemployment: first, try to arrest the changes that accompany growth and, second, accept the changes and try to speed up the adjustments. Throughout history labor and management have advocated, and governments have tried, both approaches.

Resisting change. Since the beginning of the Industrial Revolution workers have often resisted the introduction of new techniques to replace the older techniques at which they were skilled. This is understandable. A new technique will destroy the value of the knowledge and experience of workers skilled in the displaced techniques. Older workers may not even get a chance to start over with the new technique. Employers may prefer to hire younger persons who will learn the new skills faster than older workers, who are set in their ways of thinking. From society's point of view new techniques are beneficial because they are a major source of economic growth. From the point of view of the workers they displace, new techniques can be an unmitigated disaster.

The introduction of new technology is resisted in two main ways. The first involves union-management agreements to continue to employ people who would otherwise lose their jobs because of the new innovation. The second is to support a declining industry with public funds. If the market would support an output of X but subsidies are used to support an output of $2X$, then jobs are provided for, say, half the industry's labor force who would otherwise become unemployed and have to find jobs elsewhere. Both these policies are attractive to the people who would otherwise be-

come unemployed. It may be a long time before they can find another job and, when they do, their skills may not turn out to be highly valued in their new occupations.

In the long term, however, such policies are not viable. On the one hand, agreements to hire unneeded workers raise costs and can hasten the decline of an industry threatened by competitive products. On the other hand, an industry that is declining due to economic change becomes an increasingly large burden on the public purse as economic forces become less and less favorable to its success. Sooner or later, public support is withdrawn and an often precipitous decline then ensues.

In assessing these remedies for structural unemployment, it is important to realize that, although they are not viable in the long run for the economy, they may be the best alternatives for the affected workers during their lifetimes.

There is often a genuine conflict between those threatened by structural unemployment, whose interests lie in preserving their jobs, and the general public, whose interest is served by economic growth, which is the engine of rising living standards.

Aiding change. Another policy to deal with structural change is to accept the decline of industries and the destruction of specific jobs that go with it and to try to reduce the cost of adjustment for those affected. Retraining and relocation grants make movement easier and reduce structural unemployment without inhibiting economic change and growth. Retraining programs exist in the United States but have met with mixed success at best. Relocation grants are used in some other countries (Sweden, for example) but have never been adopted in the United States.

By the early 1980s the Reagan administration had accepted the existence of a serious problem of structural unemployment. In the 1983 *Economic Report of the President* the administration's plan for dealing with it was announced. Here are its main points.

1. The Job Training Partnership Act (JTPA) of 1982 established a partnership among the government, private industry, and vocational training

schools for federally financed training programs. These schemes were aimed at youth, low-skilled and chronically unemployed adults, and skilled workers in declining industries and regions. Although federally financed, the program was to be administered at the state and local levels.

2. The administration proposed a summertime differential minimum wage for people below the age of 22. The wage, which was proposed at 75 percent of the full minimum wage, was intended as an encouragement for firms to hire people just out of school, or on their summer vacation, to provide them with job experience.

3. Since 1979 the government had given significant tax credits on wages paid by firms to hire youths, welfare recipients, Vietnam veterans, and other disadvantaged groups. For a variety of reasons this program had induced only a limited response from firms. In 1982 the program was supplemented by a much larger tax relief for hiring disadvantaged youths aged 16 and 17 over the summer. This tax relief reduced the cost to the employer of such workers to $.50 per hour.

The administration has clearly recognized the existence of a severe problem of structural unemployment and has accepted a responsibility to alleviate it. The program does, however, raise a number of questions. Is it sufficiently broad-based? Is the funding adequate? Will the state and local governments pursue the measures with sufficient vigor? Whether the present measures will have any significant effect on structural unemployment thus remains to be seen.

SUMMARY

1. Unemployment may be voluntary or involuntary. Involuntary unemployment is a serious social concern both because it causes economic waste due to lost output and because it is a source of human suffering.

2. There are several kinds of unemployment: (a) frictional unemployment, which is due to the time taken to move from job to job as a result of normal labor turnover and includes search unemployment, caused by the need to discover the state of the labor market by searching for alternative employment opportunities; (b) structural unemployment, which is caused by the need to re-allocate resources among occupations, regions, and industries as the structure of demands and supplies changes; (c) deficient-demand unemployment, which is caused by too low a level of aggregate demand; and (d) real wage unemployment, which is caused by too high a real product wage.

3. Measured unemployment figures may overestimate or underestimate the actual number of unemployed, for they may include some who are voluntarily unemployed and omit discouraged workers who have left the labor force.

4. The level of unemployment that persists when deficient demand is removed—the total of frictional and structural unemployment—has risen in recent years. It is argued that this is due to demographic changes in the work force, increasing wage and price rigidity in the economy, increasing generosity of unemployment compensation and other social insurance programs, and increasing structural change in the economy.

5. Unemployment insurance helps to alleviate the human suffering associated with inevitable unemment. It also increases unemployment by encouraging voluntary and search unemployment.

6. Unemployment can be reduced by raising aggregate demand, by making it easier to move between jobs, by slowing down the rate of change in the economy, and by raising the cost of staying unemployed. However, it is neither possible nor desirable to reduce unemployment to zero.

TOPICS FOR REVIEW

Voluntary and involuntary unemployment
Deficient-demand unemployment
Frictional unemployment
Structural unemployment

Search unemployment

Real wage unemployment

The effects of demographic and structural changes on unemployment

DISCUSSION QUESTIONS

1. Interpret the following newspaper headlines in terms of types of unemployment
   a. Recession hits local factory, 2,000 laid off.
   b. "A job? I've given up trying," says mother of three.
   c. "We closed down because we could not stand the competition from Taiwan," says local manager.
   d. "When they raised the minimum wage I just could not afford to keep all of these retired policemen on my payroll as security guards," says local shopping center owner.
   e. Slack demand puts local foundry on short time.
   f. "Of course I could take a job as a dishwasher but I'm trying to find something that makes use of my high school training," says local teenager in our survey of the unemployed.
   g. Where have all the jobs gone? They have gone to the sun belt.

h. "Thank God for the minimum wage. Without it, I couldn't earn enough to feed the kids," says single father of four.
   i. Retraining main challenge in increased use of robots.
   j. Modernization may cut U.S. textile workers.
   k. Uneven upturn: signs of recovery hit Louisville, but not all feel its effect, as joblessness stays high.

2. Read the latest *Economic Report of the President* and discover what current policy is with respect to structural unemployment.

3. What differences in approach to unemployment are suggested by these facts: (a) Britain has spent billions on subsidizing firms that would otherwise have gone out of business in order to protect the jobs of the employees; (b) Sweden has pioneered in spending large sums to retrain and relocate displaced workers.

4. In the late 1960s and early 1970s many countries observed an increase in the number who were unemployed when the total number of unemployed was just equal to the number of unfilled vacancies. What factors might have accounted for this shift in the unemployed-vacancy relation?

5. Discuss the following views: (a) "American workers should resist automation, which is destroying their jobs" says a labor leader; (b) "Given the fierce foreign competition, its a case of automate or die" says an industrialist.

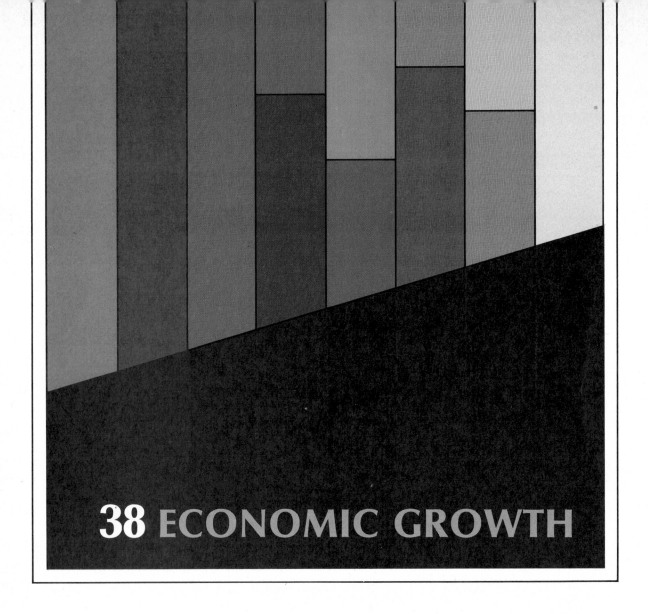

38 ECONOMIC GROWTH

We have seen how national income can be influenced by changes in aggregate demand and in structural unemployment. By far the most potent means of raising national income in the long term, however, is *economic growth*; that is, the increase in potential income due to changes in factor supplies—labor and capital—or in the productivity of factors—output per unit of factor input.

CAUSES OF INCREASES IN REAL NATIONAL INCOME

Popular debate is bedeviled by confusion about the various causes of change in national income. Monetarists sometimes accuse neo-Keynesians of believing that governments can spend their way into

FIGURE 38-1
Ways of Increasing National Income

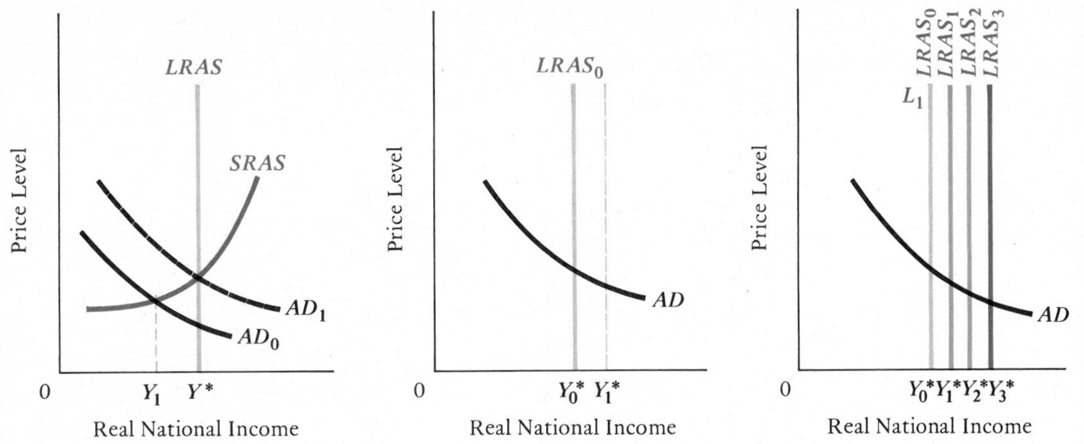

(i) Removing deficient demand unemployment

(ii) Reducing structural unemployment

(iii) Continual economic growth

A once-and-for-all increase in national income can be obtained by raising aggregate demand to remove a GNP gap or by shifting the **LRAS** curve by cutting structural unemployment. **Continued increases in national income are possible by shifting the LRAS curve through continued economic growth.** In (i) there is a GNP gap of $Y_1 Y^*$ at the initial equilibrium position of E_0. An increase in aggregate demand from AD_0 to AD_1 takes equilibrium to E_1, achieving a once-and-for-all change in national income from Y_1 to Y^*.

In (ii) potential output rises from Y_0^* to Y_1^* due to measures that reduce structural unemployment. The **LRAS** curve shifts because those who were formerly unemployed due to having the wrong skills or being in the wrong place are now available for employment.

In (iii) increases in factor supplies and productivity lead to increases in potential income. This *continually* shifts the long-run aggregate supply curve outward. In successive periods it moves from $LRAS_0$ to $LRAS_3$, taking potential income from Y_0^* to Y_1^* to Y_2^* to Y_3^* and so on, as long as growth continues.

a rising national income. Neo-Keynesians sometimes accuse monetarists of wasting national income by their tight money policies. But what actually causes national income to change?

Figure 38-1 illustrates some of the most important possibilities. If there is a GNP gap, raising aggregate demand will yield a once-for-all increase in national income. But once potential income is achieved, further increases in aggregate demand yield only transitory increases in real income but lasting increases in the price level.

Measures that reduce structural unemployment can also increase the employed labor force and thus increase potential income. The increase in income resulting from this change might not be very large. There would, however, be social gain resulting from the reduction in unemployment, especially the long-term unemployment that occurs when people are trapped in declining areas, industries, or occupations.

Over the long haul, however, what really raises national income is economic growth. The removal of a serious GNP gap might raise national income by 10 percent while the elimination of all structural unemployment might raise it by somewhat less. But a modest growth rate of 3 percent per year raises national income by 10 percent in 3 years and *doubles* it in about 24 years.

Over any long period of time economic growth rather than variations in aggregate demand or in structural unemployment exerts the major effect on real national income.

The Short- and Long-Run Effect of Investment on National Income

The theory of income determination that we studied in Part Seven is a short-run theory. It takes potential income as constant and concentrates on the effect of investment expenditure on aggregate demand. This short-term viewpoint is the focus of Figure 38-1(i).

Short-run national income theory concentrates on the effects of investment on aggregate demand and thus on variations of actual national income around a given potential income.

In the long run, by adding to the nation's capital stock, investment raises potential income. This effect is shown by the continuing outward shift of the *LRAS* curve in Figure 38-1(iii).

The theory of economic growth is a long-run theory. It ignores short-run fluctuations of actual national income around potential income and concentrates on the effects of investment in raising potential income.

The contrast between the short- and long-run aspects of investment is worth re-emphasizing. In the short run, any activity that puts income into people's hands will raise aggregate demand. Thus the short-run effect on national income is the same whether a firm invests in digging holes and refilling them or in building a new factory. In terms of growth, however, we are concerned only with that part of investment that adds to a nation's productive capacity.

This point is important because much of what is classified as investment in the national income accounts and what does add to aggregate demand is really consumption expenditure. Assume, for example, that a firm discards an adequate but dingy office building and "invests" in a lavish new head office building with superior facilities for its staff. This will count as investment in the national income data, and the expenditure will add to aggregate demand. In terms of growth, however, it is (at least in part) really disguised consumption for the firm's staff and not investment that will increase the productivity of its labor force.

Similar observations are true of public-sector expenditure. Any expenditure will add to aggregate demand and raise national income if there are unemployed resources. But only some expenditure adds to the growth of full-employment income. Indeed, public investment expenditure that shores up an industry that would otherwise be declining in order to create employment may have an anti-growth effect. Such expenditure may prevent the re-allocation of resources in response to shifts both in the pattern of world demand and in the country's comparative advantage. Thus in the long run the country's capacity to produce commodities that are demanded on open markets may be diminished.

The Short- and Long-Run Effect of Saving on National Income

The short-run effects of an increase in saving are to reduce aggregate demand. If, for example, households elect to save more, this means they spend less. The resulting downward shift in the consumption function lowers aggregate demand and thus lowers equilibrium national income.

In the longer term, however, higher savings are necessary for higher investment. Savings both by firms and households provide the funds out of which investment is financed. Firms usually re-invest their own savings while the savings of households pass to firms, either directly through the purchase of stocks and bonds or indirectly through financial intermediaries. If full employment is more or less maintained in the long run, then the volume of investment will be strongly influenced by the volume of savings. The higher the savings, the higher the investment—and the higher the investment, the greater the rate of growth due to the accumulation of more and better capital equipment.

In the long run there is no paradox of thrift; societies with high savings rates have high investment rates and, other things being equal, high growth rates.

The Cumulative Nature of Growth

Growth is a much more powerful method of raising living standards than removing either GNP gaps or structural unemployment (or for that matter redistributing income) *because it can go on and on indefinitely.* For example, a growth rate of 2 percent per year may seem insignificant, but if it continues for a century, it will lead to a more than sevenfold increase in real national income!

The cumulative effect of small annual growth rates is large.

To appreciate the cumulative effect of what seems like very small differences in growth rates, examine Table 38-1. Notice that when one country grows faster than another, the gap in their respective standards widens progressively. If countries A and B start from the same level of income, and if country A grows at 3 percent per year while country B grows at 2 percent per year, A's income per capita will be twice B's in 72 years. You may not think it matters much whether the economy grows at 2 percent or 3 percent per year, but your children and grandchildren will! (A helpful approximation device is the "rule of 72." Divide any growth rate into 72 and the resulting number approximates the number of years it will take for income to double.) [43]

To dramatize the powerful long-run effects of differences in growth rates, we included in early editions of this text a table showing students of the 1960s that, if the then current growth trends continued, America would not long remain the world's

TABLE 38–1 THE CUMULATIVE EFFECT OF GROWTH

Year	Percentage rate of growth per year				
	1%	2%	3%	5%	7%
0	100	100	100	100	100
10	111	122	135	165	201
30	135	182	246	448	817
50	165	272	448	1,218	3,312
70	201	406	817	3,312	13,429
100	272	739	2,009	14,841	109,660

Small differences in growth rates make enormous differences in levels of potential national income over a few decades. Assume that potential national income is 100 in year zero. At a rate of growth of 3 percent, it will be 135 in 10 years, 448 after 50 years, and over 2,000 in a century. Compound interest is a powerful force!

richest nation, for Sweden, Canada, Japan, and many others were growing at a much faster rate. Many readers of that era rejected the notion as a textbook gimmick; deep down they knew that the material standard of living of the United States was and would remain the highest the world had ever known. Such a table is no longer even interesting, for by 1980 several industrial countries, including Sweden, had indeed passed the United States in terms of per capita national income and several more were within 10 percent of the U.S. level. In addition Kuwait and several other oil producers reported higher average incomes. Japan's experience is discussed in the box on page 736.

THEORIES OF ECONOMIC GROWTH

In theoretical discussions of growth it is useful to have an indicator of the ability of an economy to convert its resources into goods and services. One widely used indicator is output per hour of labor, often called simply *productivity.* Obviously, productivity depends not only on labor input but also on the amount and kind of machinery used, the raw

A CASE STUDY OF RAPID GROWTH: JAPAN, 1953–1973

The real national income of Japan was 5.4 times as large in 1973 as it was in 1953. Japan's economic growth rate was more than double the average rate in 10 North American and European countries and greatly exceeded the rate in any of them. What accounted for the extraordinarily rapid growth of Japan's economy? To answer that question, two economists, Edward F. Denison and William K. Chung, analyzed and measured the sources of economic growth in Japan over two decades and compared the results with those for 10 Western countries. They also measured the difference between levels of output per worker in the United States and Japan in 1970 and identified its sources and magnitude. The results were published in 1976.*

They found that no single factor was responsible for Japan's high postwar growth rate. Rather, the Japanese economy benefited from several major sources of growth: an increase in quantity of labor, an increase in quantity of capital, improved technology in production, and economies of scale. Japan gained more in each of these respects than did any of the 10 other countries studied. In addition, Japan had the greatest reallocation of labor from agriculture to

*Edward F. Denison and William K. Chung, *How Japan's Economy Grew So Fast: The Sources of Postwar Expansion* (Washington, D.C.: Brookings, 1976).

industry of all the countries studied except Italy. Since productivity is generally higher in industry than in agriculture, a shift of this kind raises average productivity and thereby contributes to growth even without an increase in output per person in either sector.

The overall growth record of Japan was high partly because of a low initial *level* of productivity. It is easier to improve from a low base than a high one. At the end of the period productivity was still more than 40 percent lower in Japan than in the United States, even after eliminating the effects of differences between the countries in working hours, in composition and allocation of the labor force, in amounts of capital and land, in size of markets, and in the cyclical positions of the two economies. There was thus an obvious potential for still further Japanese growth relative to the United States.

Can Japan's growth rate be sustained? The authors stressed the probability of the growth rate declining as the various ways of securing fast growth by "catching up" are successively exhausted. Nevertheless, they considered a fairly high rate of long-term growth in Japan— between 5 and 8 percent per year—likely for the rest of this century. (This prediction proved accurate for the 1970s.) By the year 2000 Japan may well be enjoying the highest standard of living of any industrialized country in the world.

materials available, and so on. The focus of this measure is explained by the special emphasis that human beings place on human labor.[1]

Economists today recognize that many different factors may contribute to—or impede—economic growth. Although our present knowledge of the

[1] The discussion of productivity on pages 203–204 of Chapter 13 is relevant here. It should be read now and treated as part of this chapter. (Indeed the whole section on the very long-run, pages 203–210, could be read now with profit.)

relative importance of these factors is far from complete, modern economists look at the problems of growth more optimistically than did the Classical économists of a century or more ago. Of particular importance is the nature and source of the investment opportunities that when utilized lead to growth. The differences between the Classical and contemporary points of view can best be understood by considering a revealing though extreme case.

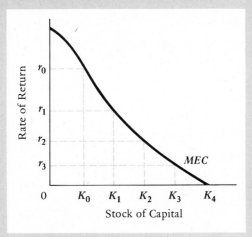

FIGURE 38-2
The Marginal Efficiency of Capital Schedule

A declining *MEC* schedule shows that successive increases to the capital stock bring smaller and smaller increases in output and thus a declining rate of return. A fixed *MEC* schedule can represent the theory of growth in an economy with some unutilized investment opportunities but no learning. Increases in investment that increase the capital stock from K_0 to K_1 to . . . K_4 lower the rate of return from r_0 to r_1 to . . . zero. Because the productivity of successive units of capital decreases, the capital-output ratio rises.

Growth in a World Without Learning

Suppose that there is a known and fixed stock of projects that might be undertaken. Suppose also that nothing ever happens to increase either the supply of such projects or knowledge about them. Whenever the opportunity is ripe, some of the investment opportunities are utilized, thereby increasing the stock of capital goods and depleting the reservoir of unutilized investment opportunities. Of course, the most productive opportunities will be used first.

Such a view of investment opportunities can be represented by a fixed marginal efficiency of capital schedule of the kind also met in Chapter 22. Such a schedule is graphed in Figure 38-2. It relates the

stock of capital to the productivity of an additional unit of capital. The productivity of a unit of capital is calculated by dividing the annual value of the additional output resulting from an extra unit of capital by the value of that unit of capital. Thus, for example, a marginal efficiency of capital of 0.2 means that $1 of new capital adds $.20 per year to the stream of output. The downward slope of the *MEC* schedule indicates that with knowledge constant increases in the stock of capital bring smaller and smaller increases in output per unit of capital. That is, the rate of return on successive units of capital declines. This shape is a consequence of the law of diminishing returns.[2] If, with land, labor, and knowledge constant, more and more capital is used, the net amount added by successive increments will diminish and may eventually reach zero. Given this schedule, as capital is accumulated in a state of constant knowledge, the society will move down its *MEC* schedule.

In such a "nonlearning" world, where new investment opportunities do not appear, growth occurs only so long as there are unutilized opportunities to use capital effectively to increase output. Growth in a nonlearning world is a transitory phenomenon that occurs as long as the society has a backlog of unutilized investment opportunities.

So far we have discussed the *marginal* efficiency of capital. The *average* efficiency of capital refers to the average amount produced in the whole economy per unit of capital employed. It is common in discussions of the theory of growth to talk in terms of the *capital-output ratio*, which is the reciprocal of output per unit of capital. In a world without learning, the capital-output ratio is increasing.

In a world without learning the growth in the capital stock will have two important consequences:

1. Successive increases in capital accumulation will be less and less productive, and the capital-output ratio will be increasing.
2. The marginal efficiency of new capital will be decreasing and will eventually be pushed to zero as the backlog of investment opportunities is used up.

[2] This hypothesis was discussed on pages 188–189.

FIGURE 38-3
Shifting Investment Opportunities: Three Cases

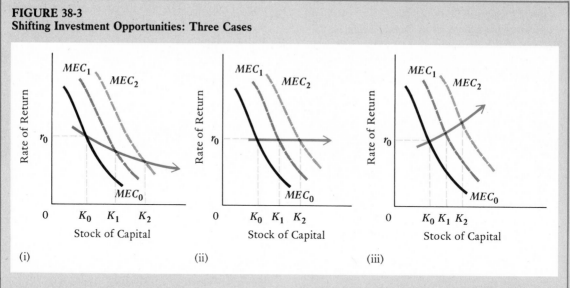

When both knowledge and the capital stock grow, the actual marginal efficiency of capital depends on their relative rates of growth. In each case the economy at period 0 has the MEC_0 curve, a capital stock of K_0, and a rate of return of r_0. In period 1 the curve shifts to MEC_1 and there is investment to increase the stock of capital to K_1. In period 2 the curve shifts to MEC_2 and there is new investment that increases the capital stock to K_2. It is the relative size of the shift of the MEC curve and the additions

of the capital stock that are important.

In (i) investment occurs more rapidly than increases in investment opportunities and the rate of return falls along the black curve. In (ii) investment occurs at exactly the same rate as investment opportunities and the rate of return is constant. In (iii) investment occurs less rapidly than increases in investment opportunities and the rate of return rises.

Growth with Learning

The steady depletion of growth opportunities in the previous case resulted from the fact that new investment opportunities were never discovered or created. However, if investment opportunities are created as well as used up with the passage of time, the MEC schedule will shift outward over time and the effects of increasing the capital stock may be different. This is illustrated in Figure 38-3. Such outward shifts can be regarded as the consequences of "learning" either about investment opportunities or about the techniques that create such opportunities. When learning occurs, what matters is how rapidly the MEC schedule shifts relative to the amount of capital investment being under-

taken. Three possibilities are shown in Figure 38-3.

Gradual Reduction in Investment Opportunities: The Classical View

If, as in Figure 38-3(i), investment opportunities are created but at a slower rate than they are used up, there will be a tendency toward a falling rate of return and an increasing ratio of capital to output. The predictions in this case are the same as those given above (in color) for the world without learning: too slow, rather than no, discovery of new investment opportunities.

This figure illustrates the theory of growth held by most early economists. They saw the economic problem as one of fixed land, a rising population, and a gradual exhaustion of investment opportunities. These conditions, they believed, would ultimately force the economy into a static condition with no growth, very high capital-output ratios, and the marginal return on additional units of capital forced down toward zero.

Constant or Rising Investment Opportunities: The Contemporary View

The pessimism of the Classical economists came from their failure to anticipate the possibility of really rapid innovation—of technological progress that could push investment opportunities outward as rapidly or more rapidly than they were used up, as shown in parts (ii) and (iii) of Figure 38-3.

In a world with rapid innovation

1. Successive increases in capital accumulation may prove highly productive, and the capital-output ratio may be constant or decreasing.
2. Despite large amounts of capital accumulation, the marginal efficiency of new capital may remain constant or even increase as new investment opportunities are created.

The historical record suggests that outward shifts in investment opportunities over time have led to the reality of sustained growth. Evidently modern economies have been successful in generating new investment opportunities at least as rapidly as old ones were used up. Modern economists devote more attention to understanding the *shifts* in the *MEC* schedule over time and less to its shape under a nonlearning situation.

A Contemporary View of Growth

The Classical economists had a relatively simple theory of growth because they viewed a single mechanism—capital accumulation—as decisively important. Contemporary theorists begin by recognizing a number of factors that influence growth, no one of which is necessarily dominant.

Quantity of Capital per Worker

Human beings have always been tool users. It is still true that more and more tools tend to lead to more and more output. As long as a society has unexploited investment opportunities, productive capacity can be increased by increasing the stock of capital. The effect on output per worker of "mere" capital accumulation is so noticeable that it was once regarded as virtually the sole source of growth.

But if capital accumulation were the only source of growth, it would lead to movement down the *MEC* schedule and to a rising capital-output ratio and a falling rate of return on capital. The evidence does not support these predictions. The facts suggest that investment opportunities have expanded as rapidly as investments in capital goods, roughly along the pattern of Figure 38-3(ii). While capital accumulation has taken place and has accounted for much observed growth, it cannot have been the only source of growth.

Quality of Capital

New knowledge and inventions can contribute markedly to the growth of potential national income, even without capital accumulation. In order to see this assume that the proportion of the society's resources devoted to the production of capital goods is just sufficient to replace capital as it wears out. Thus, if the old capital were merely replaced in the same form, the capital stock would be constant and there would be no increase in the capacity to produce. But if there is a growth of knowledge so that as old equipment wears out it is replaced by different, more productive equipment, national income will be growing.

Increases in productive capacity that are intrinsic to the form of capital goods in use are called **embodied technical change.** The historical importance of embodied technical change is clearly visible: the assembly line and automation transformed much of manufacturing, the airplane revolutionized transportation, and electronic devices now dominate the communications industries. These innovations plus less well-known but no less profound ones—for example, improvements in the strength of metals, the productivity of seeds, and the techniques for recovering basic raw materials from the ground—create new investment opportunities.

Less visible but nonetheless important changes occur through **disembodied technical change.** These concern innovations in the organization of production that are not embodied in the form of the capital goods or raw materials used. One example is improved techniques of managerial control.

Most innovations involve both embodied and disembodied changes: new processes require new machines, which make yet newer processes economical. Computerization promises many such changes in the years ahead. One of them, which many regard with a mixture of awe and apprehension, is a cashless society in which banks become parts of vast information networks that receive one's pay, pay one's bills, and invest one's savings. But whatever the form of innovation, the nature of the goods and services consumed and the way they are made changes continually as innovations occur. Major innovations of the past century have resulted from the development of the telephone, the linotype, the automobile, the airplane, plastics, the assembly line, coaxial cable, xerography, computers, transistors, and silicon chips. It is hard for us to imagine life without them.

The Quality of Labor

The "quality" of labor—or what is often called *human capital*—has several aspects. One involves improvements in the health and longevity of the population. Of course, these are desired as ends in themselves, yet they have consequences for both the size of the labor force and its productivity. There is no doubt that they have increased productivity per worker-hour by cutting down on illness, accidents, and absenteeism. At the same time the extension of the normal life span with no comparable increase in the working life span has cre-

ated a larger group of nonworking aged that exercises a claim on total output. Whether health improvements alone have increased output per capita in the United States is not clear.

A second aspect of the quality of human capital concerns technical training, from learning to operate a machine to learning how to be a scientist. Training is clearly required to invent, operate, manage, and repair complex machines. More subtly, there are often believed to be general social advantages to an educated population. It has been shown that productivity improves with literacy and that, in general, the longer a person has been educated, the more adaptable he or she is to new and changing challenges—and thus, in the long run, the more productive. But education may also increase feelings of alienation in a society that is thought to be arbitrary or unjust.

The Quantity of Labor

The size of a country's population and the extent of its participation in the labor force are important in and of themselves, not merely because they affect the quantity of a factor of production. For this reason, it is less common to speak of the quantity of people available for work as a source of, or detriment to, growth than it is to speak of the quantity of capital or iron ore in the same way. But clearly, for any given state of knowledge and supplies of other factors of production, the size of the population can affect the level of output per capita. Every child born has both a mouth and a pair of hands; over a lifetime, each person will be both a consumer and a producer. Thus, on average, it is meaningful to speak of overpopulated or underpopulated economies, depending on whether the contribution to production of additional people would raise or lower the level of per capita income.

Because population size is related to income per capita, it is possible to define a theoretical concept, *optimal population*, that maximizes income per capita.

Many countries have had, or do have, conscious population policies. America in the nineteenth century sought immigrants, as did Australia until very recently. Germany under Hitler paid bonuses for the birth of additional Aryan children and otherwise offered incentives to create Germans. Greece in the 1950s and 1960s tried to stem emigration to Western Europe. All are examples of countries that believed they had insufficient population, though the motives were not in every case purely economic. In contrast, many underdeveloped countries of South America, Africa, and Asia desire to limit population growth.

Structural Change

Changes in the economy's structure can cause large fluctuations in its growth rate. For example, a decline in such low-productivity sectors as agriculture and an expansion in such high-productivity sectors as manufacturing will temporarily boost the measured aggregate growth rate as labor moves from the declining to the expanding sectors.

On the other hand, when one type of energy (say, solar) supplants another type (say, oil), much existing capital stock specifically geared to the original energy source may become too costly to operate and will be scrapped. New capital geared to the new energy source will be built. During the transition, investment expenditure is high, thus stimulating aggregate demand. But there is little if any expansion in the economy's output capacity because the old capital goods have been scrapped. Gross investment is high, but net investment is low since the capital expenditure *transforms* the capital stock but does not *increase* it. Similarly, anything (such as new pollution control laws) will affect investment expenditure but will not lead to growth in capacity. (The reduction in pollution may nonetheless be socially desirable.)

A rise in the international price of *imported* energy will also lower productivity. Although the same volume of goods can be produced with a given input of labor, a smaller portion of the output's value now accrues as income to domestic workers and firms because more must be used to pay for the energy imports. The higher priced imported energy input means that domestic *value added* falls, and with it GNP per worker. This shows up in the

statistics as a decline in productivity and a temporary fall in growth rates.

These are some of the many factors that were operative in the 1970s and early 1980s. They worked to depress growth rates for some considerable period of time. But they are not permanent factors. When the structural adjustments are complete, their depressing effects will pass.

Institutional Considerations

Almost all aspects of a country's institutions can foster or deter the efficient use of a society's natural and human resources. Social and religious habits, legal institutions, and traditional patterns of national and international trade are all important. So too is the political climate. In Chapter 44 many of these institutions will be discussed as potential barriers to development.

Is There a Most Important Source of Growth?

The modern theory of growth tends to reject a dominant source of growth and to recognize that several different influences singly and in interaction affect the growth rate.

Among the major contributors to rapid economic growth are a capital stock that is steadily growing and improving in quality, a healthy and well-educated labor force, and a rate of population growth that is small enough to permit per capita growth in capital.

These factors are more likely to be utilized effectively in some institutional settings than in others.

A complete theory of growth would do more than list a series of influences all of which affect the growth rate. It would include assessments of (1) their relative importance, (2) the trade-offs involved in having more of one beneficial influence and less of another, and (3) the interactions among the various influences. This poses a formidable empirical challenge to research that is just beginning to be accepted.

While much remains to be learned, an important tentative conclusion of such scholars as E. F. Denison and Robert Solow is that *improvements* in *quality* of capital, human as well as physical, have played a larger role than increases in the *quantity* of capital in the economic growth of the United States since 1900. Whether quality rather than quantity of capital is also the more important source of growth for countries with very different cultural patterns, more acute population problems, or more limited natural resources is a matter of continuing research.

COSTS AND BENEFITS OF GROWTH

In the remainder of this chapter, we shall outline some more general considerations concerning economic growth. We start by looking at the benefits and then the costs of growth. The two boxes outline the popular arguments on both sides of the growth debate.

Benefits of Growth

Growth in Living Standards

A country whose per capita output grows at 3 percent per year doubles its living standards about every 24 years.

A primary reason for desiring growth is to raise general living standards.

The extreme importance of economic growth in raising income can be illustrated by comparing the real income of a father with the real income of the son who follows in his father's footsteps. If the son neither rises nor falls in the relative income scale compared with his father, his share of the country's national income will be the same as his father's. If the son is 30 years younger than his father, he can expect to have a real income nearly twice as large as the one his father enjoyed when his father was the same age. These figures assume that the father and son live in a country such as the United States where the growth rate has been 2 or 3 percent per year. If they live in Japan, where growth has been going on at a rate of about 8 percent per year, the

son's income will be about 10 times as large as his father's.

For those who share in it, growth is a powerful weapon against poverty. A family earning $7,500 today can expect an income of $11,000 within 10 years (in constant dollars) if it just shares in a 4 percent growth rate. The transformation of the lifestyle of blue-collar workers in America as well as in Germany and Japan in a generation provides a notable example of the escape from poverty that growth makes possible.

Of course, not everyone benefits equally from growth. Many of the poorest are not even in the labor force and thus are least likely to share in the higher wages that, along with profits, are the primary means by which the gains from growth are distributed. For this reason, even in a growing economy redistribution policies will be needed if poverty is to be averted.

Growth and Income Redistribution

Economic growth makes many kinds of redistributions easier to achieve. For example, a rapid growth rate makes it much more feasible politically to alleviate poverty. If existing income is to be redistributed, someone's standard of living will actually have to be lowered. However, when there is economic growth, and when the increment in income is redistributed (through government intervention), it is possible to reduce income inequalities without actually having to lower anyone's income. It is much easier for a rapidly growing economy to be generous toward its less fortunate citizens—or neighbors—than it is for a static economy.

Growth and Life Style

A family often finds that a big increase in its income can lead to a major change in the pattern of its consumption—that extra money buys important amenities of life. In the same way, the members of society as a whole may change their consumption patterns as their average income rises. Not only do markets in a country that is growing rapidly make it profitable to produce more cars,

AN OPEN LETTER TO THE ORDINARY CITIZEN FROM A SUPPORTER OF THE GROWTH-IS-GOOD SCHOOL

Dear Ordinary Citizen:

You live in the world's first civilization that is devoted principally to satisfying *your* needs rather than those of a privileged minority. Past civilizations have always been based on leisure and high consumption for a tiny upper class, a reasonable living standard for a small middle class, and hard work with little more than subsistence consumption for the great mass of people. In the past, the average person saw little of the civilized and civilizing products of the economy, except when he or she was toiling to produce them.

The continuing Industrial Revolution is based on mass-produced goods for you, the ordinary citizen. It ushered in a period of sustained economic growth that has raised consumption standards of ordinary citizens to levels previously reserved throughout history for a tiny privileged minority. Reflect on a few examples: travel, live and recorded music, art, good food, inexpensive books, universal literacy, and a genuine chance to be educated. Most important, there is leisure to provide time and energy to enjoy these and thousands of other products of the modern industrial economy.

Would any ordinary family seriously doubt the benefits of growth and prefer to go back to the world of 150 or 500 years ago in its same relative social and economic position? Surely, the answer is no. But we cannot say the same for those with incomes in the top 1 percent or 2 percent of the income distribution. Economic growth has destroyed much of their privileged consumption position: they must now vie with the masses when visiting the world's beauty spots and be annoyed, while lounging on the terrace of a palatial mansion, by the sound of charter flights carrying ordinary people to inexpensive holidays in far places. The rich resent their loss of exclusive rights to luxury consumption. Some complain bitterly, and it is not surprising that they find their intellectual apologists.

Whether they know it or not, the antigrowth economists—such as Harvard's Ken Galbraith, Cambridge's Joan Robinson, and the LSE's Ed Mishan—are not the social revolutionaries they think they are. They are counterrevolutionaries who would set back the clock of material progress for the ordinary person. They say that growth has produced pollution and wasteful consumption of all kinds of frivolous products that add nothing to human happiness. But the democratic solution to pollution is not to go back to where so few people consume luxuries that pollution is trivial; it is to accept pollution as part of a transitional phase connected with the ushering in of mass consumption, to keep the mass consumption, and to learn to control the pollution it tends to create.

It is only through further growth that the average citizen can enjoy consumption standards (of travel, culture, medical and health care, etc.) now available to people in the top 25 percent of the income distribution—which includes the intellectuals who earn large royalties from the books they write denouncing growth. If you think that extra income confers little real benefit, just ask those in that top 25 percent to trade incomes with the average citizen. Or see how hard *they* struggle to reduce their income taxes.

Ordinary citizens, do not be deceived by disguised elitist doctrines. Remember that the very rich and the elite have much to gain by stopping growth—and even more by rolling it back—but you have everything to gain by letting it go forward.

Onward!

A. Growthman

but the government is led to produce more high-ways and to provide more recreational areas for its newly affluent (and mobile) citizens. At yet a later stage, a concern about litter, pollution, and ugliness may become important, and their correction may then begin to account for a significant fraction of GNP. Such "amenities" usually become matters of social concern only when growth has assured the provision of the basic requirements for food, cloth-ing, and housing of a substantial majority of the population.

National Defense and Prestige

When one country is competing with another for power or prestige, rates of growth are impor-tant. If our national income is growing at 2 percent, say, while the other country's is growing at 5 per-cent, the other country will only have to wait for our relative strength to dwindle. Moreover, the faster its productivity is growing, the easier a coun-try will find it to bear the expenses of an arms race or a program of foreign aid.

More subtly, growth has become part of the currency of international prestige. Countries that are engaged in persuading other countries of the might or right of their economic and political sys-tems point to their rapid rates of growth as evi-dence of their achievements.

Costs of Growth

The benefits discussed above suggest that growth is a great blessing. It is surely true that, *ceteris paribus*, most people would regard a fast rate of growth as preferable to a slow one, but other things are seldom equal.

Social and Personal Costs of Growth

Industrialization can cause deterioration of the environment. Unspoiled landscapes give way to highways, factories, and billboards; air and water become polluted; and in some cases unique and priceless relics of earlier ages—from flora and fauna to ancient ruins—disappear. Urbanization tends to move people away from the simpler life of farms and small towns and into the crowded slum-ridden and often darkly evil life of the urban ghetto. Those remaining behind in the rural areas find that rural life, too, has changed. Larger-scale farming, the decline of population, and the migration of chil-dren from the farm to the city all have their costs. The stepped-up tempo of life brings joys to some but tragedy to others. Accidents, ulcers, crime rates, suicides, divorces, and murder all tend to be higher in periods of rapid change and in more developed societies.

When an economy is growing, it is also chang-ing. Innovation leaves obsolete machines in its wake, and it also leaves partially obsolete people. No matter how well trained you are at age 25, in another 25 years your skills may well be partially obsolete. Some will find that their skills have be-come completely outdated and unneeded. A rapid rate of growth requires rapid adjustments, which can cause much upset and misery to the individuals affected. The decline in the number of unskilled jobs makes the lot of untrained workers much more difficult. When they lose jobs, they may well fail to find others—particularly if they are over 50.

It is often argued that costs of this kind are a small price to pay for the great benefits that growth can bring. Even if that is true in the aggregate (which is a matter of debate), these personal costs are very unevenly borne. Indeed, many of those for whom growth is most costly (in terms of jobs) share least in the fruits of growth. Yet it is also a mistake to see only the costs—to yearn for the good old days while enjoying higher living standards that growth alone has made possible.

The Opportunity Cost of Growth

In a world of scarcity, almost nothing is free. Growth requires heavy investments of resources in capital goods as well as in activities such as edu-cation. Often these investments yield no *immediate* return in terms of goods and services for consump-tion; thus they imply sacrifices by the current gen-eration of consumers.

AN OPEN LETTER TO THE ORDINARY CITIZEN FROM A SUPPORTER OF THE GROWTH-IS-BAD SCHOOL

Dear Ordinary Citizen:

You live in a world that is being despoiled by a mindless search for ever higher levels of material consumption at the cost of all other values. Once upon a time, men and women knew how to enjoy creative work and to derive satisfaction from simple activities undertaken in scarce, and hence highly valued, lesiure time. Today the ordinary worker is a mindless cog in an assembly line that turns out ever more goods that the advertisers must work overtime to persuade the worker to consume.

Statisticians and politicians count the increasing flow of material output as a triumph of modern civilization. Consider not the flow of output in general, but the individual products that it contains. You arise from your electric-blanketed bed, clean your teeth with an electric toothbrush, open with an electric can opener a can of the sad remnants of a once-proud orange, you eat your bread baked from super-refined and chemically refortified flour, and you climb into your car to sit in vast traffic jams on exhaust-polluted highways. And so it goes, with endless consumption of high-technology products that give you no more real satisfaction than the simple, cheaply produced equivalent products used by your great-grandfathers: soft woolly blankets, natural bristle toothbrushes, real oranges, old-fashioned and coarse but healthy bread, and public transport that moved on uncongested roads and gave its passengers time to chat with their neighbors, to read, or just to daydream.

Television commercials tell you that by consuming more you are happier. But happiness lies not in increasing consumption but in increasing the ratio of *satisfaction of wants* to *total wants*. Since the more you consume the more the advertisers persuade you that you want to consume, you are almost certainly less happy than the average citizen in a small town in 1900 whom we can visualize sitting on the family porch, sipping a cool beer or a lemonade, and enjoying the antics of the children as they play with scooters made out of old crates and jump rope with pieces of old clothesline.

Today the landscape is dotted with endless factories producing the plastic trivia of the modern industrial society. They drown you in a cloud of noise, air, and water pollution. The countryside is despoiled by strip mines, petroleum refineries, acid rain, and dangerous nuclear power stations producing energy that is devoured insatiably by modern factories and motor vehicles.

Worse, our precious heritage of natural resources is being fast used up. Spaceship earth flies, captainless, in its senseless orgy of self-consuming consumption.

Now is the time to stop this madness. We must stabilize production, reduce pollution, conserve our natural resources, and seek justice through a more equitable distribution of existing total income.

A long time ago Malthus taught us that if we do not limit population voluntarily, nature will do it for us in a cruel and savage manner. Today the same is true of output: if we do not halt its growth voluntarily, the halt will be imposed on us by a disastrous increase in pollution and a rapid exhaustion of natural resources.

Citizens, awake! Shake off the worship of growth, learn to enjoy the bounty that is yours already, and reject the endless, self-defeating search for increased happiness through ever-increasing consumption.

Upward!

A. Nongrowthman

Growth, which promises more goods tomorrow, is achieved by consuming fewer goods today. For the economy as a whole this is the primary cost of growth.

An example will suggest the magnitude of this cost. Suppose the fictitious economy of USSA has full employment and is experiencing growth at the rate of 2 percent per year. Its citizens consume 85 percent of the GNP and invest 15 percent. The people of USSA know that if they are willing to decrease immediately their consumption to 77 percent, they will produce more capital and thus shift at once to a 3 percent growth rate. The new rate can be maintained as long as they keep saving and investing 23 percent of the national income. Should they do it?

TABLE 38–2 THE OPPORTUNITY COST OF GROWTH

In year	(A) Level of consumption at 2% growth rate	(B) Level of consumption at 3% growth rate	(C) Cumulative gain (loss) in consumption
0	85.0	77.0	(8.0)
1	86.7	79.3	(15.4)
2	88.5	81.8	(22.1)
3	90.3	84.2	(28.2)
4	92.1	86.8	(33.5)
5	93.9	89.5	(37.9)
6	95.8	92.9	(40.8)
7	97.8	95.0	(43.6)
8	99.7	97.9	(45.4)
9	101.8	100.9	(46.3)
10	103.8	103.9	(46.2)
15	114.7	120.8	(28.6)
20	126.8	140.3	19.6
30	154.9	189.4	251.0
40	189.2	255.6	745.9

Transferring resources from consumption to investment goods lowers current income but raises future income. The example assumes that income in year zero is 100, and that consumption of 85 percent of national income is possible with a 2 percent growth rate. It is further assumed that to achieve a 3 percent growth rate, consumption must fall to 77 percent of income. A shift from (A) to (B) decreases consumption for 10 years but increases it thereafter. The cumulative effect on consumption is shown in (C); the gains eventually become large.

Table 38-2 illustrates the choice in terms of time paths of consumption. How expensive is the "invest now, consume later" strategy? On the assumed figures, it take 10 years for the actual amount of consumption to catch up to what it would have been had no reallocation been made. In the intervening 10 years a good deal of consumption was lost, and the cumulative losses in consumption must be made up before society can really be said to have broken even. It takes an additional 9 years before total consumption over the whole period is as large as it would have been if the economy had remained on the 2 percent path. [44]

A policy of sacrificing present living standards for a gain that does not begin to be reaped for a generation is hardly likely to appeal to any but the altruistic or the very young. The question of how much of its living standards one generation is prepared to sacrifice for its heirs (who are in any case likely to be richer) is troublesome. As one critic put it, Why should we sacrifice for them? What have they ever done for us?

Many governments, particularly those seeking a larger role in world affairs, have chosen to force the diversion of resourses from consumption to investment. The Germans under Hitler, the Russians under Stalin, and the Chinese under Mao Tsetung adopted four-year and five-year plans that did just this. Many less-developed countries are using such plans today. Such resource shifts are particularly important when actual growth rates are very small (say, less than 1 percent), for without some current sacrifice there is little or no prospect of real growth in the lifetimes of today's citizens. The very lowest growth rates are frequently encountered in the very poorest countries. This creates a cruel dilemma, discussed in Chapter 44 as the vicious circle of poverty.

Growth As a Goal of Policy: Do the Benefits Justify the Costs?

Suppose that the members of a society want to increase their output of goods by 10 percent in one year. There are many ways they can do this.

1. They may be able to find idle and unutilized resources and put them to work.
2. They may be able to schedule extra shifts and overtime labor.
3. They may, by exhortation or by an appropriate incentive system, induce people to work much harder.
4. They may (if they have time) increase the supply of machines and factories.
5. They may utilize new techniques that permit them to get more output from the same inputs.

In the short run, the first three approaches seem the more promising; in fact, when nations face such crises as wars, these devices are used to achieve rapid increases in output. But the gains to be achieved by utilizing unemployed resources, extending the hours of use of employed ones, or "working harder" are limited. Eventually they will be used up. When there are no longer unutilized resources or underutilized capacity, further increases in output become more difficult to achieve.

In the long term, it is the last two approaches that bring the sustained increases in living standards that have eliminated the 14-hour day and the six-day work week and made possible both leisure and high material standards of living.

But do the already developed countries need yet more growth? Most people think they do. Poverty is now a solvable problem in the United States as a direct result of its enhanced average living standards. Clearly, people in the top quarter of the present income distribution have more opportunities for leisure, travel, culture, fine wines, and gracious living than have persons with much lower incomes. Most of those now in the bottom half of the income distribution would like these opportunities too. Only growth can give it to them.

Today, many countries that have not yet—or have only newly—undergone sustained periods of economic growth in modern times are urgently seeking to copy those that have in order to obtain the benefits of growth.

Most nations and most people today wish to pursue the goal of growth for the benefits it brings, despite its costs.

How seriously the costs are taken depends in part on how many of the benefits of growth have already been achieved. With mounting population problems, the poor countries are increasingly preoccupied with creating growth. With mounting awareness of pollution, the rich countries are devoting ever more resources to overcoming the problems caused by growth—at the same time that they are understandably reluctant to give up further growth.

Indeed, a similar conflict can often be seen within the same country at one time: a relatively poor community fights to acquire a new paper mill for the employment and income it will create; another, relatively affluent community deplores the ruin of its beaches and its air by an existing mill.

Are There Limits to Growth?

Those opposed to growth argue that sustained growth for another century is undesirable; some even argue that it is impossible. Of course all terrestrial things have an ultimate limit. Astronomers predict that the solar system itself will die as the sun burns out in another 6 billion or so years. To be of practical concern a limit must be within some reasonable planning horizon. Best-selling books of the 1970s by Jay Forrester [*World Dynamics* (1973)] and D.H. Meadows et al. [*The Limits to Growth* (1974)] predicted the imminence of a growth-induced doomsday. Living standards were predicted to reach a peak about the year 2000 and then, in the words of Professor Nordhaus, a leading critic of these models, to "descend inexorably to the level of Neanderthal man." What can be said about this debate?

The Uncontroversial Fact of Increasing Pressure on Natural Resources

The years since World War II have seen a rapid acceleration in the consumption of the world's resources, particularly fossil fuels and basic minerals. World population has increased from under 2.5 billion to over 4 billion in that period, and this alone has increased the demand for all the world's resources. But the single fact of population growth greatly understates the pressure on resources.

Calculations by Professor Nathan Keyfitz of Harvard and others focus on the resources used by those who can claim a life-style of the level enjoyed by 90 percent of American families. This so-called middle class, which today includes about one-sixth of the world's population, consumes 15 to 30 times as much oil per capita and, overall, at least 5 times as much of the earth's scarce resources per capita as do the other "poor" five-sixths of the population.

The world's poor are not, however, content to remain forever poor. Whether they live in the USSR, Brazil, Korea, or Kenya, they have let their governments understand that they expect policies that generate enough growth to give *them* the higher consumption levels that all of *us* take for granted. This upward aspiration is being fulfilled to a degree. The growth of the middle class has been nearly 4 percent per year—twice the rate of population growth—over the postwar period. The number of persons realizing middle-class living standards is estimated to have increased from 200 million to 700 million between 1950 and 1980.

This growth is a major factor in the recently recognized or projected shortages of natural resources: the increases in demand of the last three decades have outstripped discovery of new supplies and caused crises in energy and mineral supplies as well as food shortages. Yet the 4 percent growth rate of the middle class, which is too fast for present resources, is too slow for the aspirations of the billions who live in underdeveloped countries and see the fruits of development all around them. Thus the pressure on world resources of energy, minerals, and food is likely to accelerate even if population growth is reduced.

Another way to look at the problem of resource pressure is to note that present technology and resources could not possibly support the present population of the world at the standard of living of today's average American family. The demand for oil would increase fivefold to tenfold. Since these calculations (most unrealistically) assume no population growth anywhere in the world and no growth in living standards for the richest sixth of the world's population, it is evident that resources are insufficient.

SUMMARY

1. National income can increase as a result of a reduction in the GNP gap, a reduction in structural unemployment, or growth in the level of potential national income.

2. Investment that has short-term effects on national income through aggregate demand also has long-term effects through growth in potential national income. Such growth is frequently measured using rates of change of potential real national income per person or per hour of labor employed.

3. Savings reduces aggregate demand and therefore reduces national income in the short run, but in the long run savings finance the investment that leads to growth in potential income.

4. The cumulative effects of even small differences in growth rates become large over periods of a decade or more.

5. Understanding growth involves understanding both the utilization of existing investment opportunities and the process of creating new investment opportunities. The source of economic growth was once thought to be almost entirely capital accumulation and the utilization of a backlog of unexploited investment opportunities. Today most economists recognize that many investment opportunities can be created, and much attention is given to the sources of outward shifts in the *MEC* schedule through both embodied and disembodied technical change.

6. The most important benefit of growth lies in its contribution to the long-run struggle to raise living standards and escape poverty. Growth also makes more manageable the policies that would redistribute income among people. Economic growth can likewise play an important role in a country's national defense or in its struggle for international prestige.

7. Growth, while often beneficial, is never costless. The opportunity cost of growth is the diversion of resources from current consumption to capital formation. For some individuals who are left behind in a rapidly changing world the costs are higher and more personal. The optimal rate of growth involves balancing benefits and costs. Most people do not wish to forego the benefits growth can bring, but neither do they wish to maximize growth at any cost.

8. In addition to mere increases in quantity of capital per person, any list of factors affecting growth includes the extent of innovation, the quality of human capital, the size of the working population, and the whole institutional setting.

9. The critical importance of increasing knowledge and new technology in sustaining growth is highlighted by the great drain on existing natural resources of the explosive growth of the last two or three decades. Without continuing new knowledge, the present needs and aspirations of the world's population cannot come anywhere even close to being met.

TOPICS FOR REVIEW

The short- and long-run effects of saving and investment
The cumulative nature of growth
Factors affecting growth
Effects of capital accumulation with and without new knowledge
Embodied and disembodied technical change
Benefits and costs of growth
Limits to growth

DISCUSSION QUESTIONS

1. We usually study and measure economic growth in macroeconomic terms. But in a market economy who makes the decisions that lead to growth? What kind of decisions and what kind of actions cause growth to occur? How might a detailed study of individual markets be relevant to understanding economic growth?

2. Why is rising productivity a more significant contributing factor for economic growth than simply increasing the quantity of productive resources? Define *productivity*. List all the factors that increase the productivity of labor and the productivity of capital. Comment on the differences and similarities of the two lists.

3. *Family Weekly* recently listed (among others) the following "inventions that have changed our lives": microwave ovens, digital clocks, bank credit cards, freeze-dried coffee, tape cassettes, climate-controlled shopping malls, automatic toll collectors, soft contact lenses, tubeless tires, and electronic word processors.

   Which of them would you hate to do without? Which, if any, will have a major impact on life in the twenty-first century? If there are any that you believe will not, does that mean they are frivolous and unimportant?

4. The Overseas Development Council, in 1977, introduced "a new measure of economic development based on the physical quality of life." Its index, called PQLI, gives one-third weight to each of the following three indicators: literacy, life expectancy, and infant mortality. While countries such as the United States and the Netherlands rank very high on either the PQLI or on an index of per capita real national income, some relatively poor countries, such as Sri Lanka, rank much higher on the PQLI index than much richer countries such as Algeria and Kuwait. Discuss the merits or deficiencies of this measure.

5. "The case for economic growth is that it gives man greater control over his environment, and consequently increases his freedom." Explain why you agree or disagree with this statement by Nobel laureate W. Arthur Lewis.

6. Growth in income per capita is a necessary condition for a rising standard of living in a country. Is it also a *sufficient* condition for making everyone better off? Why may not everyone benefit from economic growth?

7. GNP in real terms in the United States doubled between 1959 and 1980. Over this period the annual percentage rate of increase in GNP in constant dollars was 3.5 percent per year. Evaluate this measure of growth with respect to how well it reflects changes in (a) the material well-being of the average resident of the United States and (b) the nation's capacity to produce goods and services. In each case suggest what additional information you would like to know.

8. You discover that a particular economy has achieved a rapid increase in the size of its capital stock over several decades with no appreciable change in the rate of return to capital. What, if anything, can you conclude about its rate of innovation? Its rate of growth?

9. Consider a developed economy that decides to achieve a zero rate of growth for the future. What implications would such a "stationary state" have for the processes of production and consumption?

10. Suppose solar energy becomes the dominant form of energy in the twenty-first century. What changes will this make in the comparative advantages and growth rates of Africa and Northern Europe?

11. Discuss the following headlines from the *New York Times* and the *Wall Street Journal* in terms of the sources, costs and benefits of growth:

   a. "Stress Addiction: 'Life in the Fast Lanes' May Have its Benefits."

   b. "Education: An Expert Urges Multiple Reforms."

   c. "Industrial Radiation Risk Higher Than Thought."

   d. "Developments in the Field of Management Design Are Looking Ahead."

   e. "Ford Urged by Federal Safety Officials to Recall Several Hundred Thousand of Its 1981–1982 Front Drive Vehicles Because of Alleged Fire hazards."

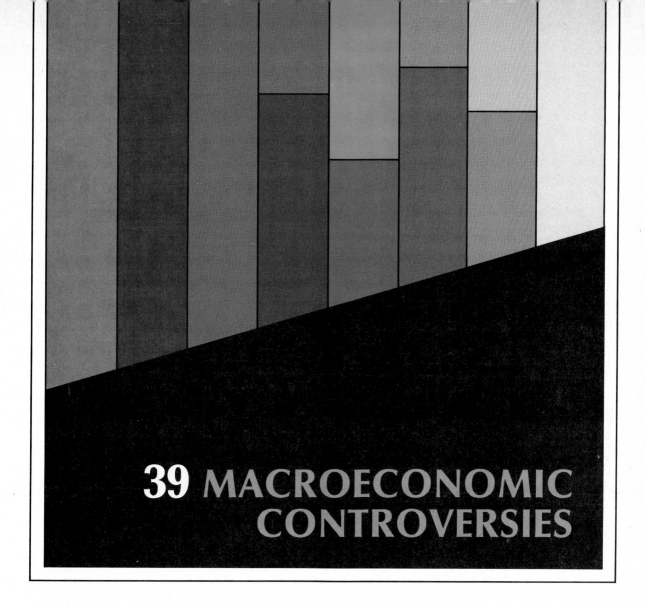

39 MACROECONOMIC CONTROVERSIES

How well do markets work? Can government improve market performance?

In various guises, these two questions are the basics of most disagreements over economic policy. We shall see that different answers to these questions imply big differences in macroeconomic policy prescriptions.

Alternative Views

Macroeconomics is mainly concerned with the behavior of three important variables: employment (and unemployment), the price level, and the rate of economic growth. Macroeconomic policy suggests goals for each: full employment, stable prices,

SOME MYTHS ABOUT THE COSTS OF INFLATION

Popular opinion has it that inflation makes everyone worse off by reducing the purchasing power of working people's incomes. Accordingly over most of the last 15 years inflation was perceived by most people as public enemy number one. Inflation was thought to be eroding our living standards and adding in many ways to life's uncertainties. Yet real per capita disposable income rose through most of the 1970s.

Of course different people have different inflationary experience. If you asked someone living on a fixed income about inflation, he or she would be right in saying that it was hurting very much. But what of the typical wage earner or the typical recipient of social security, which is fully indexed? Clearly the social security recipient is not worse off. Indeed, there are reasons for believing that those who live on incomes that are fully tied to the CPI actually benefit from inflation. (Being a fixed weighted index, the CPI makes no allowance for the quantity adjustments that people make when relative prices change.)

What about the wage earner? The fact is that over the decades money wages have risen faster than money prices, so workers are better off. Why then are so many ordinary working people's perceptions so far wide of the facts? We do not know, but here are some interesting possibilities.

1. It is possible that people confuse the messenger with the message. For example, the rise in OPEC prices in 1979 meant that to pay for the same amount of oil imports, more goods and services had to be exported and hence fewer goods and services were available for home consumption. This meant that domestic living standards had to fall. The mechanism that brought this fall about was a faster rise in prices than in incomes. But the rise in prices was only the means by which the inevitable fall in real living standards was effected. If the price level had been held constant, the same real fall would have occurred through other means (such as a fall in money wages or a rise in unemployment).

Also, in a stagflation output falls while prices rise. People are inclined to attribute their undoubted decline in living standards to the inflation. But in fact the fall in living standards is due to the "stag" not the "inflation." The fall in output means that fewer goods and services are being produced and hence fewer are available for consumption. Even if the price level had remained constant, the fall in output implies a fall in per capita living standards while it lasts.

2. People may think that they could have this year's money incomes and last year's prices. An inflation raises money prices *and* money incomes; if real output has risen, it will raise the latter more than the former. Many people do not understand the link between their own incomes and prices in general. They welcome their 12 percent rise in money wages but lament the percent increase in prices that makes their real incomes rise by a mere 2 percent. They do not realize that if prices had risen by only 4 percent, their money incomes would have risen by only

and a satisfactory growth rate. The advantages of full employment and a positive growth rate are obvious and not subject to serious dispute. Although most people agree that inflation is harmful, there is much debate about what can really be blamed on it. The box deals further with some of the myths surrounding the issue of the effects of inflation.

Broadly speaking we can identify a non-interventionist and an interventionist view with respect to each of the policy goals just specified. The non-interventionist view says that the unaided market economy can best achieve the goal. The interventionist view says that government policy can improve the economy's performance regarding that goal. Since one can take a non-interventionist or

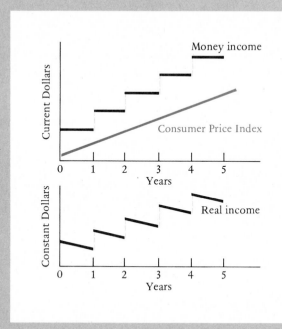

the rate at which money prices increase, so will we reduce the rate at which money incomes increase.

3. Lumpy income increases and continuous price increases may create an erroneous impression of trend reductions in real incomes. Individual money incomes are adjusted discretely, often only once a year, while the CPI rises more or less continuously. When money income is raised annually more than the price level has risen over the year, real income falls week by week but rises year by year, as shown in the figure. The top part shows a typical household's income rising in nominal terms once a year. If the annual rise in money income exceeds the annual rise in prices, real income at any point in one year is higher than it was at the same point in the previous year. But because the price level rises continuously real income falls between points of pay increase, as shown in the lower part. Although the trend of real income is upward and on average people's real incomes rise each year, the short-term comparisons are very different. Comparing each week with the previous week, we find that real income falls (a bit) 51 weeks out of 52 while real incomes rise (a lot) only one week in 52—when the annual wage adjustment occurs. Thus the correct perception that inflation is making one gradually worse off (comparing one week with the next) may lead to the mistaken perception that inflation is ultimately making one worse off (comparing one year with the next).

6 percent, leaving the real income rise unchanged at 2 percent. Thus, when many wage earners deplore the rise in prices, they may be thinking—quite erroneously—that if prices had risen by less this year, they could have preserved the same increase in their money incomes. The fundamental relations in the economy are real relations. Average real incomes can rise only by as much as average per capita output rises. If, with a given real increase in output, we reduce

an interventionist position with respect to each of these three goals, there are six different possible policy combinations.[1]

Consider two extreme policy stances: *conservatives* are non-interventionist on every issue, while

[1] Since each of the three issues breaks up into hundreds of different subissues, there are thousands of different policy stances available on one side or the other of each issue.

interventionists support government intervention at all times. A few people may actually be conservative or interventionist in this sense. Most, however, would find themselves favoring intervention on some issues and opposing it on others. They might still identify themselves as conservative or interventionist because they were more often on one side than the other.

It is popular to identify monetarist with conservative and Neo-Keynesian with interventionist. It is true that many monetarists are on the conservative side while many Neo-Keynesians are on the interventionist side. But it is not always so. It is, for example, quite possible to be Neo-Keynesian in accepting the Keynesian macro model as a reasonable description of the economy's macroeconomic behavior but conservative in believing that the unaided market usually does the best job of allocating resources.

The Conservative View

Conservatives believe that the free-market economy performs quite well on balance. This is because they believe that the economy is inherently stable. While shocks will hit the system, they lead rather quickly, and often painlessly, to the adjustments dictated by the market system. For example, relative prices in booming sectors rise, drawing in resources from declining sectors or regions. As a result, resources (and particularly labor) usually remain fully employed, so there is no need for full-employment policies.

Conservatives hold that macroeconomic performance will be most satisfactory if it is determined solely by the workings of the free market.

Of course, few believe that the market system functions perfectly, thereby ensuring *continuous* full employment. But the view is that the market system works well enough to preclude any constructive role for policy.

In addition, many believe that policy instruments are so crude that their use is often counterproductive. A policy's effects may be so uncertain, with regard to both strength and timing, that it may often impair rather than improve the economy's performance.

In a modern economy some government presence is inevitable. Thus a stance of no intervention is impossible; rather, what is advocated by conservatives is minimal direct intervention in the market system. This involves the government's bearing responsibility for providing a *stable environment* in which the private sector can function.

The Interventionist View

Interventionists believe that the functioning of the free-market economy is often far from satisfactory. Sometimes markets show weak self-regulatory forces and the economy settles into prolonged periods of heavy unemployment. At other times markets tend to "overcorrect," causing the economy to lurch between the extremes of large GNP and large inflationary gaps.

This behavior can be improved, argue the interventionists. Even though interventionist policies may be imperfect, they may be good enough to improve the functioning of the economy with respect to all three main goals of macro policy.

MACROECONOMIC ISSUES

Performance

Everyone agrees that the economy's performance is often less than perfectly satisfactory. Serious unemployment has been a recurring problem. Inflation was a serious problem throughout the 1970s and early 1980s. For nearly two decades now growth rates have been unsatisfactorily low. Conservatives and interventionists differ in diagnosing the causes of these economic ills.

The Business Cycle

We saw in Chapter 26 that cyclical ups and downs can be observed for as far back as records exist. Monetarists and neo-Keynesians have long argued about the causes.

Monetarist views. Monetarists believe that the economy is inherently stable because private-sector expenditure functions are relatively stable. In addition, they believe that shifts in the aggregate

TWO VIEWS ON THE GREAT DEPRESSION

The stock market crash of 1929, and other factors associated with a moderate downswing in business activity during the late 1920s, caused the public to wish to hold more cash and less demand deposits. The banking system could not, however, meet this increased demand for liquidity without help from the Federal Reserve System. (As we saw in Chapter 33, banks are never able to meet from their own reserves a sudden demand to withdraw currency on the part of a large fraction of their depositors. Their reserves are always inadequate to meet such a demand.) The Fed had been set up to provide just such emergency assistance to banks that were basically sound but that were unable to meet sudden demands by depositors to withdraw cash. However, the Fed refused to extend the necessary help, and successive waves of bank failures followed as a direct result. During each wave, hundreds of banks failed, ruining many depositors and thereby worsening an already severe depression. In the last half of 1931, almost 2,000 American banks were forced to suspend operations! One consequence of this was a sharp drop in the money supply; by 1932 the money supply was 35 percent below the level of 1929. To monetarists these facts seem decisive.

While neo-Keynesians accept the argument that the Fed's behavior was perverse, they argue that the cyclical behavior of investment and consumption expenditure was the major cause of the Great Depression. In support of this view, they point out that in Canada and the United Kingdom, where the central bank came to the aid of the banking system, bank failures were trivial during the Great Depression, and as a consequence the money supply did *not* shrink drastically as it did in the United States. Despite these markedly different monetary histories, the behavior of the GNP gap, investment expenditure, and unemployment was very similar in the three countries.

demand curve are mainly due to policy-induced changes in the money supply.[2]

The view that business cycles have mainly monetary causes relies heavily on the evidence advanced by Milton Friedman and Anna Schwartz in their monumental *A Monetary History of the United States, 1867–1960*. They establish a strong correlation between changes in the money supply and changes in the level of business activity. Major recessions have been associated with absolute declines in the money supply and minor recessions with the slowing of the rate of increase in the money supply below its long-term trend.

The correlation between changes in the money supply and changes in the level of business activity is now accepted by virtually all economists. But there is controversy over how this correlation is to be interpreted; do changes in money supply cause changes in the level of aggregate demand and hence of business activity, or vice versa?

Friedman and Schwartz maintain that changes in the money supply cause changes in business activity. They argue, for example, that the severity of the Great Depression was due to a major contraction in the money supply that shifted the aggregate demand curve far to the left. The Great Depression is further discussed in the box.

According to monetarists, fluctuations in the money supply cause fluctuations in national income.

[2] The view that fluctuations often have monetary causes is not new. The English economist R. G. Hawtrey, the Austrian Nobel Laureate F. A. von Hayek, and the Swedish economist Knut Wicksell are prominent among those who have given monetary factors an important role in explaining the turning points in cycles and/or the tendency for expansions and contractions, once begun, to become cumulative and self-reinforcing. Modern monetarists carry on this tradition.

This leads the monetarists to advocate a policy of stabilizing the growth of the money supply. In their view this would avoid policy-induced instability of the aggregate demand curve.

Neo-Keynesian views. The neo-Keynesians' view on cyclical fluctuations in the economy has two parts. First, it emphasizes variations in investment as a cause of business cycles and stresses the nonmonetary causes of such variations.[3]

Neo-Keynesians reject what they regard as the extreme monetarist view that only money matters in explaining cyclical fluctuations. Many neo-Keynesians believe that both monetary and nonmonetary forces are important in explaining the cyclical behavior of the economy. Although they accept serious monetary mismanagement as one potential source of economic fluctuations, they do not believe that it is the only or even the major source of such fluctuations. Thus they deny the monetary interpretation of business cycle history given by Friedman and Schwartz. They believe that most fluctuations in the aggregate demand curve are due to variations in the desire to spend on the part of the private sector and are not induced by government policy.

Neo-Keynesians also believe that the economy lacks strong natural corrective mechanisms that will always force it easily and quickly back to full employment. They believe that while the price level rises fairly quickly to eliminate *inflationary gaps*, the price level does not fall quickly to eliminate *GNP gaps*. Neo-Keynesians stress the asymmetries noted in earlier chapters that imply that prices and wages fall only slowly in response to a GNP gap. As a result, neo-Keynesians believe that GNP gaps can persist for long periods of time unless they are eliminated by an active stabilization policy.

---

[3] Like the monetarists, the neo-Keynesians are modern advocates of views that have a long history. The great Austrian (and later American) economist Joseph Schumpeter stressed such explanations early in the present century. The Swedish economist Wicksell and the German Speithoff both stressed this aspect of economic fluctuations before the emergence of the Keynesian school of thought.

The second part of the neo-Keynesians' view on cyclical fluctuations is that they accept the correlation between changes in the money supply and changes in the level of economic activity but that their explanation reverses the causality suggested by the monetarists: the neo-Keynesians argue that changes in the level of economic activity tend to cause changes in the money supply. They offer several reasons for this, but only the most important need be mentioned.

Neo-Keynesians point out that from 1945 to the early 1970s most central banks, including the Fed, tended to stabilize interest rates as the target variable of monetary policy. To do this they had to increase the money supply during upswings in the business cycle and decrease it during downswings. The central bank followed this monetary policy when an expansion got under way because the demand for money tended to increase, and if there was no increase in the money supply, interest rates would rise. The central bank might prevent this rise in interest rates by buying bonds offered for sale at current prices, but in so doing it would increase banks' reserves and thereby inject new money into the economy. Similarly, in a cyclical contraction interest rates would tend to fall unless the central bank stepped in and sold bonds to keep interest rates up. Generally it did so, thereby decreasing the money supply. This behavior created the positive correlation on which the monetarists rely.

According to neo-Keynesians, fluctuations in national income are often caused by fluctuations in expenditure decisions. Further, they believe that fluctuations in national income cause fluctuations in the money supply.

Nevertheless most neo-Keynesians also agree that policy-induced changes in the money supply can cause national income to change.

The Price Level

As we saw in Chapter 36, sustained inflation requires a sustained expansion of the money supply.

Motives for such excessive monetary expansions

have varied from time to time and place to place. Sometimes central banks have rapidly increased the money supply in an effort to end a recession. Then when the economy expanded due to its own natural recuperative forces, the increased money supply allowed a significant inflation during the boom phase of the cycle. At other times central banks have tried to hold interest rates well below their free-market levels. To do this they buy bonds to hold bond prices up. We have seen that these open market operations increase the money supply and so fuel an inflation. At still other times central banks have helped governments finance large budget deficits by buying up the new public debt. These open market operations monetize the new debt and provide what is popularly known as *printing press finance*. The steady increase in the money supply fuels a continuous inflation.

Monetarist views. Many monetarists hold that inflation is everywhere and always a monetary phenomenon. They thus focus on changes in the money supply as the key source of shifts in the *AD* curve. Many also believe that supply shocks that cause *some* prices to rise do not lead to inflation because, unless the money supply is also raised, some other prices will have to fall.

According to monetarists all inflations are caused by excessive monetary expansion and would not occur without it.

Neo-Keynesian views. Neo-Keynesians accept that a sustained rise in prices cannot occur unless it is accompanied by continued increases in the money supply. To this extent they agree with the monetarists.

Neo-Keynesians also emphasize, however, that temporary bursts of inflation can be caused by shifts in the aggregate demand curve brought about by increases in private- or public-sector expenditure functions (consumption, investment, exports, and government expenditure). If such inflations are not validated by monetary expansion, they are brought to a halt by the monetary adjustment mechanism. Even when not validated they can, however, persist for sufficient periods of time to

worry policymakers and governments concerned about the next election.

Neo-Keynesians also accept the importance of supply-shock inflations. Again, they accept that such inflations cannot go on indefinitely unless accommodated by monetary expansion. But they can go on long enough to be a matter of serious policy concern. Indeed, they can present the central bank with agonizing choices: whether to accommodate the shocks (thereby accepting a bout of inflation to avoid the unemployment) or not to accommodate (thereby accepting a period of unemployment to reduce inflation).

Many Neo-Keynesians also take seriously the possibility of wage-cost push inflation that we studied in Chapter 36. This type of inflation, if it exists, makes full employment incompatible with a stable price level. Again the central bank is faced with the agonizing choice of whether or not to accommodate.

Growth

Conservative views. Conservatives, and indeed most monetarists, feel that in a stable environment free from government interference growth will take care of itself. Large firms will spend much on research and development. Where they fail, or where they suppress inventions to protect monopoly positions, the genius of backyard inventors will come up with new ideas and will develop new companies to challenge the positions of the established giants. Left to itself the economy will prosper as it has in the past, provided only that inquiring scientific spirit and the profit motive are not suppressed.

Interventionist views. Interventionists, and indeed most neo-Keynesians, are less certain than are conservatives about the ability of market forces to produce growth. While recognizing the importance of invention and innovation, they fear the dead hand of monopoly and conservative business practices that choose security over risk taking. Therefore, the state needs at the very least to give a nudge here or there to help the growth process along.

The Role of Policy

The conservative and the interventionist diagnoses of the economy's ills lead, not surprisingly, to very different prescriptions about the appropriate role of economic policy.

Conservative Prescriptions

It is not necessary to distinguish conservative policies with respect to full employment and stable prices. This is because they believe that both goals will be achieved by the same basic policy: provision of a stable environment for the free-market system to operate.

Full employment and stable prices: providing a stable environment.   Creating a stable environment, as the conservatives advocate, may be easier said than done. We focus on the prescriptions for establishing stable fiscal and monetary policies.

One major problem to keep in mind is that macro variables are interrelated. The stability of one may imply the instability of another. In such cases, a choice must be made. How much instability of one aggregate can we tolerate to secure stability in another related aggregate?

Assume for example that people are so worried about budget deficits that the government decides to adopt the goal of stability in the budget balance as part of the stable environment. Whatever the budget balance, the target says that it should be the same from year to year.

This "stability" would require great *instability* in tax and expenditure policy. As we saw in Chapter 32, although governments can set tax *rates*, they cannot directly determine tax *revenues*. Tax revenues depend on the interaction between tax rates and the level of national income. With given tax rates, tax revenues change with the ebb and flow of the business cycle. A stable budget balance would require that the government raise tax rates and cut expenditure in slumps and lower tax rates and raise expenditures in booms.

Not only does this squander the budget's potential to act as a stabilizer but great instability of the fiscal environment is caused by continual changes in tax rates and expenditure levels. A stable fiscal environment requires substantial stability in government expenditures and tax rates. Stability is needed so that the private sector can make plans for the future within a climate of known patterns of tax liabilities and government demand. This in turn requires that the budget deficit vary cyclically, showing its largest deficits in slumps and its largest surpluses in booms.

The target budget balance must be some average over a period long enough to cover a typical cycle. Stability from year to year should be found in tax rates and expenditure programs, *not* in the size of the budget balance.

Advocates of a stable monetary environment are actually advocating stable inflation. Whether a *zero* rate is feasible or not is discussed in the box. The Fed is urged to set a target rate of increase in the money supply and hold it. To establish the target, the Fed estimates the rate at which the demand for money would be growing if actual income equaled potential income and the price level were stable. As a first approximation this can be taken to be the rate at which potential income itself is growing.[4] This then becomes the target rate of growth of the money supply. The key proposition is that the money supply should be changing gradually along a stable path that is independent of short-term variations in the demand for money caused by cyclical changes in national income. This is referred to as a *k* **percent rule.**

Will the *k* percent rule really provide monetary stability? The answer is: "Not necessarily."

Assuring a stable rate of monetary growth does not assure a stable monetary environment: Monetary shortages and surpluses depend on the relation between the supply and the demand for money.

---

[4] Such a rule assumes that members of the public wish to keep their money holdings in a fixed proportion to their real income. If other demand patterns are established—that is, if desired money holdings change as a proportion of real income as income rises—then the Fed can alter its monetary target appropriately.

IS A ZERO INFLATION RATE A FEASIBLE POLICY GOAL?

The 1950s were characterized by what would be regarded today as satisfactory price stability. But prices were not exactly steady. The inflation rate varied between 0.5 percent and 3 percent. Despite what appeared to most observers to be a slowly growing average GNP gap throughout this period, the inflation rate never reached zero in any year. Between 1955 and 1961 there were only two years when the rate was below 1 percent: 1955 (0.4 percent) and 1961 (0.7 percent).

This creeping inflation worried observers at the time. An inflation, even a gradual one in the face of an obvious GNP gap, seemed hard to understand.

The explanation in modern theory would be likely to come from the supply side: the combination of rising prices and GNP gaps usually suggests a supply-shock inflation. The explanation that satisfied many observers at the time was the so-called **structural rigidity theory** of inflation, which was indeed a supply-shock explanation.

This theory assumes that resources do not move quickly from one use to another and that it is easy to increase money wages and prices but hard to decrease them. Given these conditions, when patterns of demand and costs change due to such forces as economic growth, real adjustments occur very slowly. Shortages appear in potentially expanding sectors and prices rise because the slow movement of resources prevents these sectors from expanding rapidly enough. Factors of production remain in contracting sectors on part-time employment or go unemployed because mobility is low in the economy. Wages and prices are slow to move downward so there are few significant wage and price reductions in these contracting sectors.

Thus the mere process of adjustment in an economy with structural rigidities causes inflation to occur: Prices in the expanding sectors rise; prices in the contracting sectors stay about the same; on average, therefore, the price level rises.

The inflation of the late 1950s and early 1960s was very mild and the debate on its causes was inconclusive. However, this was the first suggestion of a force that later became a plaguing policy problem: inflations originating in shifts in the aggregate supply curve.

Although the structural rigidity theory cannot be a major part of the explanation of the very high inflation rates of the 1970s and early 1980s, it suggests that a zero inflation rate may not be an achievable target. If there is anything in the structural rigidity theory, then the minimum inflation rate compatible with a changing economy may be 1 percent to 2 percent rather than zero.

The k percent rule looks after supply, but what about demand?

Problems for the k percent rule arise when the demand for money shifts. For example, payment of interest on checking deposits increases the demand for M1. In this event, if the Fed adheres to a k percent rule, there will be an excess demand for money and interest rates will rise. Thus contractionary pressure will be put on the economy.

Should the Fed commit itself to a specific k percent rule or merely work toward unannounced and possibly variable targets? The pre-announced rule makes it easier to evaluate how well the Fed is doing its job. It also helps to prevent the Fed from succumbing to the temptation to fine tune the economy.

One disadvantage of the pre-announced rule is that it sets up speculative behavior. If, for example, when weekly money supply figures are announced there is too much money, speculators know that the Fed will sell more bonds in the future to mop up the surplus. This will depress the price of bonds. Speculators are thus induced to sell bonds, hoping to rebuy them at bargain prices once the Fed acts.

Stable pre-announced M1 targets can introduce instability into interest-rate behavior.

A second disadvantage of such a rule is that the Fed, in order to preserve its credibility, may fail to take discretionary action that would otherwise be appropriate. For example, after an entrenched inflation is broken, the economy may come to rest with substantial unemployment and a stable price level. (See Figure 36-5.) There is then a case for a once-and-for-all discretionary expansion in the money supply to get the economy back to full employment. The k percent rule precludes this, condemning the economy to a slump.

Despite these problems conservatives believe the k percent rule is superior to any known alternative. Some would agree that in principle the Fed could improve the economy's performance by occasional bouts of discretionary monetary policy to offset such things as, say, major shifts in the demand for money. But they also believe that once given any discretion the Fed would abuse it in an attempt to fine tune the economy. The resulting instability would, they believe, be much more than any instability resulting from the application of a k percent rule in an environment subject to some change.

Long-term growth. Conservatives want to let growth take care of itself. They argue that governments cannot improve the workings of free markets and that their interventions can interfere with market efficiency. Thus they push for reducing the current level of government intervention.

Given the large web of government rules, regulations, and perverse tax incentives that has grown up over many years, the conservatives' agenda for reducing government intervention is usually a long one. Such an agenda was adopted by so-called supply siders during the later 1970s and early 1980s. Supply-side economics may or may not turn out to be a mere fad but the conservative view that growth is best encouraged by reducing the present degree of government intervention will no doubt always find numerous supporters. Some further characteristics of supply-side economics are mentioned in the accompanying box.

The agenda includes eliminating the following policies.

Supporting declining industries. This policy causes resources that could be more productively employed elsewhere to leave the industry more slowly. Most economists agree that such policies are costly, harmful to growth, and in the end self-defeating.

Encouraging monopolies and discouraging competition. Most economists tend to oppose such policies, although there is disagreement over how much competition is desirable in certain industries. For example, conservatives tend to support complete deregulation of fare and route setting by airlines, while interventionists tend to worry that cutthroat competition may reduce airline quality and safety.

Taxing income rather than consumption. Consider a woman in the 40 percent tax bracket who earns an extra $1,000 and pays $400 income tax. If she spends her after-tax income she will be able to buy $600 worth of goods. If she saves the money she will be able to buy a $600 bond. If the bond pays, say, a 4 percent real return, she will earn $24 interest per year. But a 40 percent tax must then be paid on the interest earnings, leaving only a $14.40 annual income. This is a 2.4 percent after-tax return on the bond and *a 1.44 percent after-tax return on the original $100 income.* Conservatives allege that this "double taxing" of saving is a serious disincentive to saving. They argue for taxes on consumption, not on income, so that any income that is saved would be untaxed. A tax would be levied only when the interest earned on the savings was actually spent on consumption.

High rates of income tax. Conservatives allege that high taxes discourage work. But the effect of high taxes may actually be to make people work either more or less hard. Theory is silent on which is more likely, and no hard evidence has yet shown that lowering current tax rates will make people work harder.

SUPPLY-SIDE ECONOMICS

Since the end of the 1970s, a new cry has been frequently heard in popular discussion and in serious debate: supply-side economics. Supply-side economics is not new. Indeed it's what Adam Smith's *Wealth of Nations* was all about. In its modern version, like many general but catchy terms, it sometimes means all things to all people. For example:

1. In explaining inflation and stagflation, it means an emphasis on the aggregate supply curve. As we have seen at length, "supply-side shocks" are now a major part of most explanations of what happened in the 1970s.
2. In control of inflation, it means an emphasis on pushing the aggregate supply curve outward rather than reining the aggregate demand curve inward. This proposition concerns short-run stabilization policy.
3. In concern over living standards, it means an emphasis on pushing the aggregate supply curve out to the right rather than on manipulating aggregate demand. The motto here might be, "It is more important to increase full-employment national income than to try to reduce the temporary deviations from it that the market economy produces." This proposition concerns long-run growth policy.

Point 1 is a diagnosis of our past ills. Points 2 and 3 are policy prescriptions to improve things in the future. Both require pushing the aggregate supply curve outward in the manner shown in Figure 38-1(i) on page 733. The key idea is to provide the appropriate incentives for the private sector to do the job. How might this be done? Many of the measures advocated have been discussed elsewhere in this book. Four of the most important are: (1) to encourage saving, (2) to encourage labor force participation and mobility, (3) to encourage risk taking, and (4) to channel effort into productive activities instead of tax avoidance (by simplifying the tax system).

The number of possible proposals is myriad. They all have the intended effect of increasing full-employment income by increasing the supplies of capital or of labor or by increasing the rate of technical change.

There is little doubt that many current policies and practices do have the alleged output restricting effects, so that some changes in policy would do some of the things alleged by supply-side economics. If even a small increase in the growth rate of full-employment income could be achieved, the long-term effects on living standards would be enormous. (See Table 38-1 on page 735.) Thus objective 3 is viable. Increasing the growth rate of full employment *will* raise living standards.

The second objective, however, is more debatable. It would, for example, be an enormous achievement to raise the growth rate by half a percentage point—and a generation or two down the line the effect on the *level* of income would be large. But two years down the line it is only 1 percent more full-employment output. In the face of an inflationary gap of, say, 10 percent, increasing aggregate supply by 1 percent is not going to do much to the inflation rate. Even the conservative economist Herbert Stein of the *American Enterprise Institute*, who could be expected to be sympathetic to many supply-side measures, warned in early 1980:

> Despite the tone of much of the current argument, the propositions of supply-side economics are not matters of ideology or principle. They are matters of arithmetic. So far one must say that the arithmetic of any of the "newer" propositions is highly doubtful. Supply-side economics may yet prove to be the irritant which, like the grain of sand in the oyster shell, produces a pearl of new economic wisdom. But up to this point the pearl has not appeared.*

Whether or not its potential for controlling inflation is overstated, there is no doubt that supply effects are important, and that supply-side economics in one form or another is here to stay.

* *The AEI Economist*, April 1980, published by *American Enterprise Institute*.

"Double taxation" of business profits, first as income of firms and second as income of households when paid out as dividends. This and other policies that reduce business profits and hence discourage the return to investing in equities, are alleged to discourage households from saving and investing in businesses that are the mainspring of economic growth.

All these policies are alleged to reduce the rate of growth below what it would otherwise be. Problems arise in assessing the existence and importance of the alleged harmful effects of each policy and also, since the government needs revenue, in finding alternative revenue sources that will have less harmful effects than the ones being criticized.

Interventionist Prescriptions

Interventionists call for different policies for each of the three policy goals. So we must consider the interventionist prescriptions for full employment, price stability, and growth. At the same time we give their reasons for rejecting the conservative case.

Full employment. Interventionists call for discretionary fiscal and monetary policies to offset significant inflationary and GNP gaps. Some of the major problems associated with discretionary stabilization policy have been discussed in earlier chapters. The issues in the debate that is popularly known as "rules versus discretion" are discussed further in the box.

A stable price level. In Chapter 36 we discussed the breaking of an entrenched inflation. Here we consider how a low inflation rate might be maintained once it is achieved.

Some interventionists, particularly a group called *post-Keynesians,* believe that the *k* percent rule may not be enough to achieve full employment and stable prices simultaneously. This is because they accept the wage-cost-push theory of inflation discussed in Chapter 36.

Post-Keynesians call for incomes policies to restrain the wage-cost push and so make full employment compatible with stable prices. They be-

lieve that such policies should become permanent features of the economic landscape.

Wage-price controls might work as *temporary* measures to break inflationary inertias (see Chapter 36, pages 709–711), but as permanent features they would introduce all of the inefficiencies and rigidities that were briefly alluded to in the box on page 712.

More permanent incomes policies might be of two types. The first type, commonly used in Europe in the past decades but now out of favor, is often called a *social contract.* Here labor, management, and the government consult annually and agree on target wage changes. These are calculated to be non-inflationary, given the government's projections for the future and its planned economic policies. Such a scheme is most easily initiated in a centralized economy such as West Germany's, where a few giant firms and unions exert enormous power, or in a country such as Britain, where the party in power during much of the period had strong official links with the labor unions.

The other main type of incomes policy is called **tax-related incomes policy,** or as it is often called, **TIPS.** These provide tax incentives for management and labor to conform to government-established wage and price guidelines. For example increases in wages and prices in excess of the guidelines would be heavily taxed. TIPs have not yet been tried, although they have been strongly advocated by some American economists.

TIPs would rely on tax incentives to secure voluntary conformity with the wage and price guidelines whereas wages and price controls try to impose conformity by law.

Advocates of TIPs argue that their great advantage is in leaving decisions on wages and prices in the hands of labor and management while seeking only to influence behavior by altering the incentive system. Critics, however, argue that they would prove to be an administrative nightmare.

Growth

Policies for intervention to increase growth rates are of two sorts. Some policies seek to alter the

RULES VERSUS DISCRETION

Three of the main issues involved in the rules versus discretion debate are discussed in this box.

Lags. Those hostile to discretionary policy emphasize the long and variable lags of both fiscal and monetary policy. Monetary policy can be put into effect quickly, but it takes 6 to 18 months for the full effects of a change in interest rates to be felt in terms of altered private-sector expenditures. It takes a long time to put fiscal policy into effect since both expenditure and tax changes must be passed by an often slow-moving Congress. Once the changes are made, however, their effects spread quickly through the economy. Conservatives feel that these lags destroy the presumption that discretionary full-employment policy will usually be stabilizing. Interventionists feel that although the lags are serious, discretionary policies can be effective in reducing deep and long-lasting GNP gaps. Few interventionists, however, now call for fine tuning.

A stable climate for planning. Supporters of rules emphasize the need for a stable climate for firms and households to plan for the future. They argue that continual changes in tax rates and the money supply designed to stabilize the economy are destabilizing because they create a climate of uncertainty that makes long-term planning difficult. Supporters of discretionary

policy argue that they only want discretion exercised when the occasional serious recession develops and that large fluctuations in income and employment can be as upsetting to long-term planning as are the occasional changes in tax rates and expenditures required by stabilization policy.

Do we know enough? Discretionary stabilization policy requires that we forecast what the state of the economy will be in the absence of that policy. Generally, actual information is available only with a lag. Policymakers know approximately what GNP was last quarter and what unemployment was last month. (The first preliminary figures for many economic variables can be subject to substantial errors. Often these estimates are revised several times over subsequent months and even years.) On the basis of these data, projections of future behavior of the economy must be made and policy set. Supporters of discretionary policy accept that errors in projections may be large in relation to the GNP gaps created by minor recessions but believe that the errors are small in relation to major recessions. They argue that for major recessions policymakers will be in no doubt about the existence of a large GNP gap and of the need for some significant stimulus, even though its precise amount cannot be precisily determined.

general economic climate in a way favorable to growth. They typically include subsidization or favorable tax treatment for research and development, for purchase of plant and equipment, and for other profit-earning activities. Measures to lower interest rates temporarily or permanently are urged by some as favorable to investment and growth. Most interventionists support these general measures.

Some also support more specific intervention,

usually in the form of what is called *picking* and *backing winners* in one way or another. Advocates of this view, such as Professor Lester Thurow of M.I.T., want governments to pick the industries, usually new ones, that have potential for future success and then to back them with subsidies, government contracts, research funds, and all of the other encouragements at the government's command.

Opponents argue that picking winners requires

foresight and that there is no reason to expect the government to have better foresight than private investors. Indeed, since political considerations inevitably get in the way, the government may be less successful than the market in picking "winners." If so, channeling funds through the government rather than through the private sector may hurt rather than help growth rates. Many economists are skeptical of the government's ability to spot and then back the potential winners.

RATIONAL EXPECTATIONS AND THE MICRO FOUNDATIONS OF MACROECONOMICS[5]

For many years Keynesian economics seemed successful both in explaining the overall behavior of the economy and in suggesting policies for controlling inflation and unemployment. As long as it appeared to work, few were interested in *how*. During the late 1960s and the 1970s, however, control of the economy by means of traditional fiscal and monetary policies seemed to become more difficult. This raised concerns about the foundations of Keynesian theory. The main question was: What behavior in the individual markets for goods and factors of production is implied by the Keynesian aggregate relationships? This question concerns what are called the *micro foundations*, or *micro underpinnings*, of macro models.

While these concerns about the Keynesian model were surfacing, the monetarist model seemed to provide an alternative for understanding the macro behavior of the economy and for prescribing appropriate policies. This elicited a debate about the merits of the two models, a debate that still rages today. Micro foundations are at the heart of the debate between monetarism and neo-Keynesianism. The issues are important; because they are at the frontier of modern research, they are also difficult. The analysis depends on material that is treated in detail in microeconomic courses. At this

stage, therefore, we can only discuss the issues in broad outline.

Monetarist Micro Foundations

There is no single set of accepted monetarist micro foundations. Most monetarists, however, view markets as competitive.[6] One important characteristic of competitive markets is that prices and wages are flexible; they adjust to establish equilibrium at all times. When a competitive market is in equilibrium at all times. When a competitive market is in equilibrium (see Chapter 5), the market is said to have *cleared*. This means that every purchaser has been able to buy all he or she wishes to buy at the going price and every seller has been able to sell all he or she wishes to sell at that price.[7] When each and every market is in equilibrium, there is full employment of all resources. The prices that clear markets are called **market clearing prices**.

According to the monetarists there exist strong forces which ensure that departures from full-employment equilibrium are quickly rectified. That is, as we saw above, monetarists believe that the *automatic adjustment mechanism* works quite efficiently. We now consider two particular monetarist views.

Traditional Monetarism

The monetarist school of thought that evolved in the 1960s was led by Professor Milton Friedman of the University of Chicago. Economists of that school, called traditional monetarists, hold that the economy, when left to its own, tends to stabilize at the full-emloyment level. They also hold that, historically, monetary policies have been very erratic.

---

[5] This section may be omitted without loss of continuity.

[6] They realize, of course, that perfect competition does not exist everywhere in the economy, but they believe that the forces of competition are strong—strong enough so that analysis based on the theory of perfect competition will be close to the real behavior of the economy.

[7] Competitive markets clear only at the equilibrium price. At any other price there are either unsatisfied purchasers (excess demand) or unsatisfied sellers (excess supply).

We saw in Chapter 34 that monetarists believe that monetary policy exerts a powerful influence on the economy, so they reach the following conlusion:

Traditional monetarists believe that fluctuations in the money supply are a major source of fluctuations in output and the price level.

Although monetary policy has strong effects, it operates with a long and variable lag. According to Friedman and his followers, these long and variable lags not only doom monetary policy to failure but make it counterproductive as well. In their view monetary policy has actually served to destabilize the economy in the past. For Freidman and his followers, the best course for monetary policy is, as already noted earlier in the chapter, to set the rate of increase of the money supply at some given value and hold it there. We referred to this as the *k percent rule.*

New Classical Monetarism

The *new Classical monetarists* follow Professors Robert Lucas and Thomas Sargeant in holding that temporary departures from full employment occur mainly because people make mistakes. As we shall see, this result is based on the proposition derived from microeconomics that individual supply and demand behavior depends only on the structure of relative prices.

To follow their argument, let us start by assuming that each of the economy's markets is in equilibrium; there is full employment, prices are stable, and the actual and expected rates of inflation are zero. Now let the government increase the money supply by, say, 5 percent. People find themselves with unwanted money balances, which they seek to spend.[8] For simplicity, assume that this leads to an increase in desired expenditure on all commodities: the demand for each commodity shifts to the

right and all prices, being competitively determined, rise. Individual decision makers see their selling prices go up and mistakenly interpret this increase as a rise in their own relative price. This is because they expect the overall rate of inflation to be zero. Firms will produce more and workers will work more; both groups think they are getting an increased *relative* price for what they sell. Thus total output and employment rise.

When both groups eventually realize that their own relative prices are in fact unchanged, output and employment fall back to their initial levels. The extra output and employment occurred only while people are being fooled. When they realized that all prices had risen by 5 percent, they reverted to their initial behavior. The only difference is that now the price level has risen by 5 percent, leaving relative prices unchanged.

According to the new Classical theory, deviations from full employment occur only because people make mistakes that cause markets to clear at more or less than full-employment output. People are not prevented from selling as many commodities or as much labor as they wish; the contraction or expansion in output is voluntary.

New Classical monetarists focus on the role of changes in relative prices in signalling appropriate information in a world where tastes and technology are constantly changing. They hold that fluctuations in the money supply will lead to increased fluctuations in all prices. This makes it hard for households and firms to distinguish changes in relative prices, to which they do wish to respond, from changes in the price level, to which they do not wish to respond. Such confusion, created by fluctuations in the money supply, thus leads to mistakes in supply and demand decisions.

This discussion highlights the importance for firms and households of distinguishing the causes of any price changes. Consider, for example, what happens if there is an unexpected and unperceived increase in the money supply. This will lead to an increase in most, if not all, prices above what most agents had expected. Most firms perceive this as an increase in the relative price of their own output

---

[8] In fact, most monetarists also accept the theory of the transmission mechanism discussed in Chapter 34 where the excess money balances are used to buy financial assets, thus driving down interest rates and stimulating expenditure *indirectly*. However most monetarists tend to stress the relative importance of the *direct* expenditure effects created by excess money balances.

and hence increase their level of production above what it normally would have been. Consequently, national income rises above the full-employment level. A similar argument shows that an unanticipated and unperceived decrease in the money supply would cause output to fall below its full-employment level.

The Lucas aggregate supply curve.

The behavior described above gives rise to the **Lucas aggregate supply curve.**

The Lucas aggregate supply curve posits that national output will vary positively with the ratio of the actual to the expected price level.

This is often also referred to as the *surpises only* supply curve since it implies that only changes in the price level which are unexpected (surprises) will give rise to fluctuations in aggregate supply.

To see this, consider what happens if there is again an increase in the money supply, but this time suppose that it has been widely expected in advance by firms and households. Again, prices will rise. Most firms will now take this to mean only that the *observed* change in the price of their own output has roughly matched the *expected* change in the average of all other prices. Hence they will not interpret it as a rise in the relative price of their own output and will maintain their production level at its normal level. National income will not rise above potential despite the rise in the general price level.

According to the new Classical theory, expected changes in the price level do not lead to fluctuations in aggregate supply.

New Classical policy views.

New Classical monetarists support the *k* percent rule, just as do the traditional monetarists. They believe that firms and households make better decisions when monetary and fiscal policies are stable than when they are highly variable. They believe that active interventionist policies designed to stabilize the economy make it harder for people to interpret the signals generated by the price system and so lead them to make more errors in forming their expec-

tations. This then increases rather than reduces the fluctuations of output around its full-employment level and increases rather than reduces the fluctuations of unemployment around the natural rate.

According to the new Classical economists, active use of monetary policy in an attempt to stabilize the economy will lead to confusion about relative and absolute prices, causing people to make mistakes in their output and purchasing decisions and therfore increasing aggregate output fluctuations.

In turn, this conclusion depends upon the particular view adopted by the new Classical monetarists about how people form predictions or expectations, a subject that has recently become an important part of macroeconomic debates.

The Theory of Rational Expectations

The new Classical model is augmented by the theory of *rational expectations*. People look to the government's current macroeconomic policy to form their expectations of future inflation. They understand how the economy works, and they form their expectations rationally by predicting the outcome of the policies now being followed. People learn fairly quickly from their mistakes; while random errors occur, systematic and persistent errors do not. In an obvious sense, such expectations are *forward looking*.

According to the theory of rational expectations, people do not make persistent, systematic errors in predicting the overall inflation rate; they may, however, make unsystematic errors.

The policy invariance proposition.

Rational expectations, combined with the Lucas aggregate supply curve, gives rise to the new Classical *policy invariance*, or policy neutrality, result:

Systematic attempts to use monetary policy to stabilize the economy will lead to systematic changes in the price level but will not influence the behavior of output.

Thus, according to the new Classicists, monetary policy can do harm—by creating confusion about the source of price changes—but cannot do good except by random chance. Thus, even in the face of major recessions, laissez-faire is the best stabilization policy conceivable.

Let us review how this follows from combining the monetarist micro foundations with the theory of rational expectations.

1. According to the monetarists' micro foundations, deviations from full employment occur only because of errors in predicting the price level (which cause workers and firms to mistake changes in the price level for changes in relative prices).
2. According to the theory of rational expectations, errors in predicting the price level are only random.
3. It follows from (1) and (2) that there is no room for active government policy to stabilize the economy. The causes of fluctuations are random.[9] It is in the nature of random fluctuations that they cannot be foreseen and offset. Thus there is no room for stabilization policy to reduce the fluctuations in the economy by offsetting the disturbances that emanate from the private sector.

Not all monetarists accept the theory of rational expectations. For those who do, however, the contrast with the neo-Keynesians is extreme.

The most extreme monetarist attack on stabilization policy has two parts. The first is a model of an economy where deviations from full employment occur only because of errors. The second is a theory of people's expectations that predicts that persistent systematic errors—and hence systematic deviations from full employment—will not occur.

Monetarist Conclusions

The two monetarist schools obviously do not agree with each other on everything. Both agree, however, that monetary policy should not be used actively to stabilize the economy. This is for two reasons: (1) fluctuations in the money supply are the major source of fluctuations in output and inflation, and (2) there is no long-term trade-off between inflation and national income.[10]

Most economists accept the view that monetary forces are very important in influencing inflation and unemployment, but many do not agree that monetary forces are the *most* important force. Most economists also agree that inflation will tend to accelerate if income is held permanently above its full-employment level.

One aspect of the monetarist model that is particularly controversial is the belief in downward flexibility of prices, which leads to the prediction that as long as national income is below its full-employment level the price level would *fall* at an ever-accelerating rate. Neo-Keynesians say that the observed downward inflexibility of the price level refutes this view. They reject the prediction that the main cause of GNP gaps is *voluntary* reductions in employment and output due to errors in reading the signals provided by the price system. Most neo-Keynesians do not believe that output deviates from its potential level only because workers and firms make mistakes.

Neo-Keynesian Micro Foundations

The neo-Keynesian micro foundations emphasize the non-competitive nature of the economy: most firms are seen as setting their own prices rather than accepting those set on competitive markets. Their per unit output costs tend to be fairly constant, and they set prices by adding a relatively inflexible markup to their costs.[11] They then sell

---

[9] Although because of long lags, macro variables may display cyclical fluctuations, as discussed in Chapter 31.

[10] Recall that any attempt to hold income above its full-employment level will lead not to a constant rate of inflation but to a continuously accelerating inflation. This is just a restatement of the *acceleration* hypothesis and the *natural rate* hypothesis developed in detail in Chapter 36 and its appendix.

[11] Complete cyclical inflexibility of markup is not necessary. What matters is that firms do not adjust prices continually and as a result are willing to sell further units at the same price. This much price inflexibility need not imply an absence of profit maximization. Instead it may follow from profit maximization when it is costly to alter prices. This is discussed further in Chapter 16.

what they can at the going price. Cyclical fluctuations in aggregate demand cause cyclical fluctuations in the demand for each firm's products, which in turn cause individual firms to make cyclical variations in *output and employment* rather than in *price*.

While in the monetarist model fluctuations in aggregate demand have their impact mainly on prices, in the neo-Keynesian model their main impact is on output and employment.

A similar argument holds for labor markets in the neo-Keynesian model. Wages respond to the price level and productivity but are relatively insensitive to short-term cyclical fluctuations in demand. (This is discussed in detail in Chapter 21).

This short-term wage inflexibility can stem from rational behavior on the part of workers. If wage rates adjust to clear labor markets, wages will vary over the cycle. *All* workers will then bear the uncertainty associated with the cyclical movements in wages. However, if wages are set in response to long-term considerations but do not vary cyclically so as to clear labor markets, cyclical fluctuations in demand will cause employment to fluctuate. Since most layoffs and rehires are based on seniority, employment fluctuations are all borne by the 10 percent or 20 percent of workers who are least senior. The majority of workers will then have little uncertainty in the face of cyclical fluctuations in demand, all the uncertainty having been placed on the *minority* with low seniority. Thus contracts that fix wages over the cycle and allow employment to vary may be preferable to the majority of workers compared to contracts that allow wages to vary in order to clear the labor market continually and thus prevent unemployment.

In neo-Keynesian macroeconomics, the economy does not have a unique short-term equilibrium. Because firms would like to sell more and some workers would be willing to work more at current prices, fluctuations in aggregate demand cause output and employment to fluctuate in the short term.

The neo-Keynesian macro model allows for systematic disturbances that can cause prolonged deflationary or GNP gaps.

According to the neo-Keynesians, stabilization policy can then be used to offset at least those gaps that are large and persistent.

Such policies seek to alter aggregate demand using both fiscal and monetary tools.

Differences Between the Two Models

There are many differences in the micro behavior that underlies models. Probably the most important relates to the distinction between voluntary and involuntary unemployment.

In the monetarist model all unemployment and output below capacity is voluntary. Workers decide to be unemployed, and firms decide to produce less than capacity output as a result of errors they make in predicting the general price level (and therefore the relative price of what they sell). So if surveyed, the millions of unemployed around the world in the early 1980s would have said that they could have had a job at the going wage but they refused to accept it because, given their expectations about inflation, the expected real wage was too low.

In the Neo-Keynesian model, prices and wages do not fluctuate to clear markets. Unemployment and production below capacity are involuntary in the sense that unemployed workers would like jobs at the going wage rate but cannot find them, and firms would like to sell more at going prices but customers are not forthcoming.[12] So if surveyed, the millions of unemployed around the world in the early 1980s would have said that they would have accepted a job at the going wage rate but that none were available.

Major current debate centers around these two prototype models and some of their subtler offshoots. Issues such as what determines the degree of wage and price flexibility in the economy, the conditions under which it can be expected that people can form accurate expectations and act on them, and the potential for destabilizing the economy by pursuing an active stabilization policy are

---

[12] Of course, one could still argue that this unemployment is voluntary because the workers had earlier voluntarily agreed to the contracts.

at the forefront of modern research. Views on how the economy behaves both at the micro and macro level will be influenced by the progress of the debate. So will views on the place of fiscal and monetary policy as possible ways to eliminate inflationary or GNP gaps.

CONCLUSION

The Progress of Economics

In this chapter we have discussed a number of current controversies about the behavior of the economy and the evidence now available that relates to them. General acceptance of the view that the validity of economic theories should be tested by confronting their predictions with the mass of all available evidence is fairly new in economics. At this point you might reread the quotation from Lord William Beveridge given on page xxxiii. The controversy that Beveridge describes was the one that followed the 1936 publication of Keynes' *The General Theory of Employment, Interest and Money.* Keynes' work gave rise to the macroeconomic theory discussed in Part Seven and used so often in subsequent sections of this text. The relation of various aspects of macroeconomic theory to evidence has been raised at many points in this book: You might reflect on how very different this approach to the problem of accepting or rejecting theories is from the approach described by Beveridge.

Since 1936 great progress has been made in economics in relating theory to evidence. This progress has been reflected in the superior ability of governments to achieve their policy objectives. The financial aspects of World War II were far better handled than those of World War I. When President Roosevelt tried to reduce unemployment in the 1930s, his efforts were greatly hampered by the failure even of economists to realize the critical importance of budget deficits in raising aggregate demand and in injecting newly created money into the economy. When the Vietnam War forced the government to adopt expansive fiscal and monetary policies, economists had no trouble in predicting the outcome: more involvement abroad was obtained at the cost of heavy inflationary pressure at home.

Theories are generally tested in such important policy areas as the running of wars, the curing of major depressions, and coping with inflations, even if all their specific predictions are not. In some sense, then, economic theories have always been subjected to empirical tests. When they were wildly at variance with the facts, the ensuing disaster could not but be noticed, and the theories were discarded or amended in the light of what was learned. Our current inability to avoid the twin problems of inflation and unemployment is a case in point—and it is leading to intensive new research.

The advances of economics in the last 50 years reflect economists' changed attitudes toward empirical observations. Today economists are much less likely to dismiss theories just because they do not like them and to refuse to abandon theories just because they do like them. Economists are more likely to try to base their theories as much as possible on empirical observation and to accept empirical relevance as the ultimate arbiter of the value of theories. As human beings, we may be anguished at the upsetting of a pet theory; as scientists, we should try to train ourselves to take pleasure in it because of the new knowledge gained thereby. It has been said that one of the great tragedies of science is the continual slaying of beautiful theories by ugly facts. It must always be remembered that when theory and fact come into conflict, it is theory, not fact, that must give way.

SUMMARY

1. Macroeconomic performance is judged in terms of the behavior of many variables. The key variables are (a) output, employment, and unemployment, (b) the rate of change of the price level, and (c) long-term growth.

2. Views about the role of policy in improving macroeconomic performance range between two extremes. The *conservative* view is that there is only a very minimum role for policy; macroeconomic performance will be most satisfactory when the market system is allowed to function as freely as possible. The *interventionist* view is that active use of policy will improve macroeconomic performance. It is common to identify monetarists with conservatives and Keynesians with interventionists.

3. Monetarists believe that because the economy is inherently stable the goal of damping the business cycle is best achieved by avoiding fluctuations in policy, especially monetary policy. Hence they advocate a k percent rule. Keynesians believe that the economy is inherently unstable in that expenditure functions shift regularly and the economy's self-corrective mechanisms are weak. Hence they believe in an active role for both monetary and fiscal policy to stabilize the business cycle.

4. Monetarists believe that inflation is everywhere and always a monetary phenomenon and so advocate the same conservative policies to avoid price instability as they advocated to minimize policy-induced cycles in output. They also argue that in order to control inflation, the long-term growth rate of the money supply must not be too high. Neo-Keynesians accept the view that monetary expansion is necessary for inflation to persist in the long term, but they take seriously the role of other factors in causing short-term but substantial inflation. Hence they believe in an active role for policy in offsetting these factors in the short term.

5. Conservatives believe that long-term growth will be maximized when the incentives provided by the profit motive are strongest. Interventionists see a need for special government programs to channel resources into research and development and other investment expenditures designed to raise potential output.

6. Conservatives see a role for policy in terms of providing a stable environment for individual de-

cision makers. This involves maintaining a consistent set of "fiscal rules of the game" in terms of expenditure and tax rates and providing a steady but gradual growth in the money supply.

7. Interventionists have specific prescriptions for each policy variable. They advocate active use of discretionary monetary and fiscal policy to stabilize output and employment. Despite imperfections caused by lags and incomplete knowledge, they believe such policies are helpful. Similar policies can be combined with incomes policies to stabilize the fluctuations in the price level that arise from various sources and are subject to an upward bias. They also support policies to promote growth through subsidization, tax favors, and more specific intervention.

8. Monetarists view markets as competitive and hence believe that departures from full-employment equilibrium are quickly rectified. As a result, they believe that fluctuations in aggregate demand lead primarily to fluctuations in the price level rather than in the level of output. They believe that the best course for monetary policy is to follow a k percent rule. For traditional monetarists, this is because they believe that long and variable lags in the effect of monetary policy means that an interventionist monetary policy would destabilize output.

9. Now Classical monetarists believe that departures from full-employment output occur only when people make mistakes in predicting the price level. When combined with the theory of rational expectations, this leads to the policy invariance proposition. As a result new Classical monetarists support the k percent rule because they believe an interventionist monetary policy will not be effective in stabilizing output.

10. Neo-Keynesians emphasize the non-competitive nature of the economy. As a result they believe that fluctuations in aggregate demand lead primarily to fluctuations in output rather than in the price level. In this view, an interventionist stabilization policy can be effective in stabilizing fluctuations in output.

TOPICS FOR REVIEW

Conservatives and interventionists
Monetarists and neo-Keynesians
Macroeconomic performance
Setting a stable environment
The *k* percent rule
Fine tuning
Rational expectations
Lucus aggregate supply curve
Policy invariance proposition

DISCUSSION QUESTIONS

1. To what extent is today's unemployment a serious social problem? If people could vote to choose between 10 percent unemployment combined with zero inflation and 2 percent unemployment combined with 10 percent inflation, which alternative do you think would win? Which groups might prefer the first alternative and which groups the second?

2. It is often argued that the true unemployment figure for the United States is much higher than the officially reported figure. What are possible sources of "hidden unemployment"? On the other side, are there reasons for expecting some exaggeration of the number of people reported as unemployed? Would the relative strength of these opposing forces change over the course of the business cycle? What would you expect if a short recession turned into a long and deep depression?

3. In its 1979 Report the Joint Economic Committee of the Congress urged the administration to fight inflation and combat unemployment by encouraging private sector saving and investment. How might expanded saving and in-

vestment help to reduce inflation and/or combat unemployment?

4. Neo-Keynesian and Nobel Laureate Paul Samuelson recently quoted a "conservative economist friend" as saying in mid 1980, "If you're contriving a teensy-weensy recession for us, please don't bother. It won't do the job. What's needed is a believable declaration that Washington will countenance *whatever* degree of unemployment is needed to bring us back on the path to price stability, and a demonstrated willingness to *stick* to that resolution no matter how politically unpopular the short-run joblessness, production cutbacks, and dips in profit might be." Discuss the "conservative friend's" view of inflation. Does experience since 1980 suggest that his advice was followed? If so, what was the consequence?

5. In 1979 in Britain, the newly elected conservative government of Prime Minister Margaret Thatcher embraced the monetarist view of inflation and decided to follow the advice of Professor Samuelson's "conservative friend" quoted in the previous question. Check unemployment and inflation rates and money supply figures in Britain since 1977 to see if she stuck to the advice and if the inflation rate did moderate. How did Mrs. Thatcher's policies compare to those adopted by the Reagan administration in 1980?

6. A recent ad in the *New York Times* had this to say about inflation. "First [our politicians] blamed wage increases and price hikes for inflation. Then when 'voluntary guidelines' were established, the blame shifted to OPEC oil prices. Both explanations were wrong. Government policy is responsible for inflation—paying for deficit spending by 'creating money out of thin air.'" What theories of inflation are rejected and accepted by the writers of this ad?

7. At a time when the U.S. unemployment rate stood at close to 8 percent, the press reported, "Skilled labor shortage plagues many firms—newspaper ads often draw few qualified workers; wages over time are up." What type of unemployment does this suggest to be important?

PART TEN
INTERNATIONAL TRADE
AND FINANCE

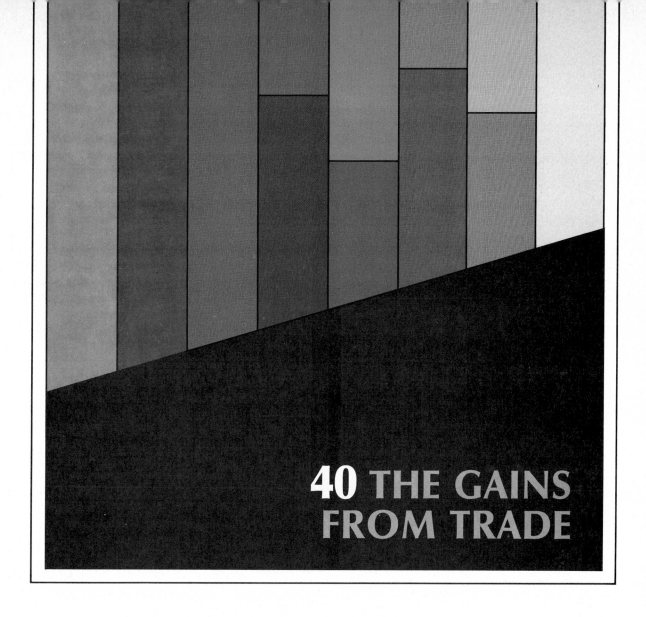

40 THE GAINS FROM TRADE

Americans buy Volkswagens, Germans take holidays in Italy, Italians buy spices from Tanzania, Africans import oil from Kuwait, Arabs buy Japanese cameras, and the Japanese depend heavily on American soybeans as a source of food. *International trade* refers to exchanges of goods and services that take place across international boundaries. This trade gives rise to a number of characteristic problems.

In this chapter we explore the fundamental question of what is gained by international trade. In Chapter 41 we shall deal with the pros and cons of interfering with the free flow of such trade. Chapter 42 will consider the problems caused by different countries' using different currencies. Finally Chapter 43 will be devoted to a brief study of the international monetary systems under which the international exchange of goods and movements of capital have functioned in the twentieth century.

The founders of modern economics were intimately concerned with foreign trade problems. The great eighteenth century British philosopher and economist David Hume, one of the first to work out the theory of the price system as a control mechanism, developed his concepts mainly in terms of prices in foreign trade. Adam Smith and David Ricardo, the two British economists who developed in full the classical theory of the functioning of the economy, were greatly concerned with trade problems. Smith in his *Wealth of Nations* (1776) attacked government restriction of trade. He was personally responsible for many reforms in the control of trade. Ricardo in 1817 developed the basic theory of the gains from trade that is studied in this chapter. The repeal of the Corn Laws—tariffs on the importation of grains into England—and the transformation of Britain during the nineteenth century from a country of high tariffs to one of complete free trade were to a significant extent the result of agitation by economists whose theories of the gains from trade led them to condemn all tariffs.

Interpersonal, Interregional, and International Trade

The advantages realized as a result of trade are usually called the **gains from trade.** The source of such gains is most easily visualized by considering the differences between a world with trade and a world without it. Although politicians often regard foreign trade differently from domestic trade, economists from Adam Smith on have argued that the causes and consequences of international trade are simply an extension of the principles governing domestic trade. What is the advantage of trade among individuals, among groups, among regions, or among countries?

Consider trade among individuals. If there were no such trade, each person would have to be self-sufficient; each would have to produce all the food, clothing, shelter, medical services, entertainment, and luxuries that he or she consumed. Although a world of individual self-sufficiency is wildly unreal, it does not take much imagination to realize that living standards would be very low in such a world.

Trade between individuals allows people to specialize in those activities they can do well and to buy from others the goods and services they cannot easily produce. A bad carpenter who is a good doctor can specialize in medicine, providing a physician's services not only for his or her own family but also for, say, an excellent carpenter without the training or the ability to practice medicine. Thus trade and specialization are intimately connected. Without trade everyone must be self-sufficient. With trade everyone can specialize in what he or she does well and satisfy other needs by trading.

The same principles apply to regions. Without interregional trade each region is forced to be self-sufficient. With such trade, plains regions can specialize in growing grain, mountain regions in mining and lumbering, and regions with abundant power in manufacturing. Cool regions can produce wheat and other crops that thrive in temperate climates, and hot regions can grow such tropical crops as bananas, sugar, and coffee.

To generalize, the living standards of the inhabitants of all regions will be higher when each region specializes in producing the commodities in which it has some natural or acquired advantage and obtains other products by trade, than when all regions seek to be self-sufficient.

The same principle applies to nations. A national boundary does not usually define an area that is naturally self-sufficient. Nations, like regions or persons, can gain from specialization and the international trade that must accompany it. Specialization means that in any given region or country, more of the goods in which production is specialized are produced than residents wish to consume, while for other goods that residents desire, little or no domestic production is available.

International trade is necessary to achieve the gains that international specialization makes possible.

This preliminary discussion suggests one important possible gain from trade.

With trade, each individual, region, or nation is able to concentrate on producing goods and services in which it produces efficiently while trading to obtain goods and services that it does not efficiently produce itself.

Because specialization and trade go hand in hand—there is no motivation to achieve the gains from specialization without being able to trade the goods produced for goods desired—the term *gains from trade* is used to embrace both.

SOURCES OF THE GAINS FROM TRADE

Gains from trade have two main sources. First, at given levels of productive efficiency, total output is larger if everyone specializes in producing what he or she is best at. Second, since large-scale production tends to be more productive than small-scale production (that is, it has a higher output per unit of labor and capital used), it pays countries to specialize in order to reap the economies of large-scale production. This second source is more important for smaller countries such as those of Europe than for very large countries such as the United States or the USSR. We will start by discussing the first source. While it is convenient to use an example involving only two countries and two products, the underlying principles extend to situations involving many products and many countries.

The Gains from Specialization

Concentrating on the gains from specialization, we assume for the moment that each region can produce goods at certain levels of productivity independent of the scale of production. In these circumstances, what is the gain from regional specialization?

A Special Case: Absolute Advantage

The gains from trade are clear when there is a simple situation involving absolute advantage. **Absolute advantage** concerns the quantities of a single product that can be produced using the same quantity of resources in two different regions. *One region is said to have an absolute advantage over another in the production of commodity X when an equal quantity of resources can produce more X in the first region than in the second.*

TABLE 40-1 GAINS FROM SPECIALIZATION WITH ABSOLUTE ADVANTAGE

	One unit of resources can produce	
	Wheat (bushels)	Cloth (yards)
America	10	6
England	5	10

Changes resulting from the transfer of one unit of American resources into wheat production and one unit of British resources into cloth production

	Wheat (bushels)	Cloth (yards)
America	+ 10	− 6
England	− 5	+ 10
World	+ 5	+ 4

When there is a reciprocal absolute advantage, specialization makes it possible to produce more of both commodities. The top half of the table shows the production of wheat and cloth that can be achieved in each country by using one unit of resources. The lower half shows the changes in production caused by moving one unit of resources out of cloth and into wheat production in America and moving one unit of resources in the opposite direction in England. There is an increase in world production of 5 bushels of wheat and 4 yards of cloth; worldwide, there are gains from specialization. Of course the more resources are transferred into wheat production in America and cloth production in England, the larger the gains will be.

Suppose region *A* has an absolute advantage over *B* in one commodity, while region *B* has an absolute advantage over *A* in another. This is a case of reciprocal absolute advantage: each country has an absolute advantage in some commodity. In such a situation the total production of both regions can be increased (relative to a situation of self-sufficiency) if each specializes in the commodity in which it has the absolute advantage.

Table 40-1 provides a simple example. Assume that, with a given quantity of resources, America can produce 10 bushels of wheat or 6 yards of cloth, while England (with the same quantity of resources) can produce 5 bushels of wheat or 10 yards of cloth. Suppose at first that America and England are both self-sufficient, each producing wheat and cloth for home markets. Now assume that trade is opened between the two countries and that America moves resources out of producing cloth and into producing wheat while England moves resources out of wheat and into cloth. The gains and losses are summarized in the lower half of Table 40-1. Total world production of both wheat and cloth increases when this reallocation of production takes place; there is more wheat *and* more cloth for the same use of resources.

The potential gains from *specialization* make possible gains from *trade*. England is producing more cloth and America more wheat than when they were self-sufficient. America is producing more wheat and less cloth than American consumers wish to buy, and England is producing more cloth and less wheat than English consumers wish to buy. If consumers in both countries are to get cloth and wheat in the desired proportions, America must export wheat to England and import cloth from England.

A First General Statement: Comparative Advantage

When one country has an absolute advantage over the other in a commodity, the gains from trade are clear. If each country produces a commodity that it produces more efficiently than the other, world production will be higher than if each country tries to be self-sufficient. But what if America can produce both wheat and cloth more efficiently than England? In essence this was David Ricardo's question, posed over 160 years ago. His answer underlies the theory of comparative advantage that is still accepted by economists as a valid statement of the potential gains from trade.

To start with assume that American efficiency increases above the levels recorded in the previous example, so that a unit of American resources can produce either 100 bushels of wheat or 60 yards of cloth. English efficiency remains unchanged (see Table 40-2). Evidently America, which is better at producing both wheat and cloth than is England,

TABLE 40–2 GAINS FROM SPECIALIZATION WITH COMPARATIVE ADVANTAGE

	One unit of resources can produce	
	Wheat (bushels)	Cloth (yards)
America	100	60
England	5	10

Changes resulting from the transfer of one-tenth of one unit of American resources into wheat production and one unit of British resources into cloth production

	Wheat (bushels)	Cloth (yards)
America	+ 10	− 6
England	− 5	+ 10
World	+ 5	+ 4

When there is comparative advantage, specialization makes it possible to produce more of both commodities. The productivity of English resources is left unchanged from Table 40-1; that of American resources is increased tenfold. England no longer has an absolute advantage in producing either commodity. Total production of both commodities can nonetheless be increased by specialization. Moving one-tenth of one unit of American resources out of cloth and into wheat and moving one unit of resources in the opposite direction in England causes world production of wheat to rise by 5 bushels and cloth by 4 yards. Reciprocal absolute advantage is not necessary for gains from trade.

has nothing to gain by trading with such an inefficient foreign country! But it *does* have something to gain, as shown in Table 40-2. Even though America is 10 times as efficient as in the situation of Table 40-1, it is still possible to increase world production of both wheat and cloth by having America produce more wheat and less cloth, and England produce more cloth and less wheat.

There is still a gain from specialization. Although America has an absolute advantage over England in the production of both wheat and cloth, its margin of advantage differs in the two commodities. America can produce 20 times as much wheat as England by using the same quantity of resources, but only 6 times as much cloth. America is said to have a *comparative advantage* in the production of wheat and a comparative disadvantage in the production of cloth. (This statement implies another: England has a comparative disadvantage in the production of wheat, in which she is 20 times less efficient than America, and a comparative advantage in the production of cloth, in which she is only 6 times less efficient.)

A key proposition in the theory of international trade is this:

The gains from specialization and trade depend on the pattern of comparative, not absolute, advantage.

Comparing Tables 40-1 and 40-2 refutes the notion that the absolute *levels* of efficiency of two areas determine the gains from specialization. The key is that the margin of advantage one area has over the other must differ between commodities. As long as this margin differs, total world production can be increased when each area specializes in the production of that commodity in which it has a comparative advantage.

Comparative advantage is necessary as well as sufficient for gains from trade. This is illustrated in Table 40-3, showing America with an absolute advantage in both commodities and neither country with a comparative advantage over the other in the production of either commodity. America is 10 times as efficient as England in the production of wheat and in the production of cloth. Now there is no way to increase the production of both wheat and cloth by reallocating resources within America and within England. The lower half of the table provides one example of a resource shift which illustrates this. Absolute advantage without comparative advantage does not lead to gains from trade.

A Second General Statement: Opportunity Costs

Much of the previous argument has used the concept of a unit of resources. The assumption is that units of resources can be equated across countries, so that statements such as "America can produce 10 times as much wheat with the same quantity of resources as England" are meaningful. Measurement of the real resource cost of producing commodities poses many difficulties. If, for example, England uses land, labor, and capital in proportions different from those used in America, it may not be clear which country gets more output "per unit of resource input." Fortunately the proposition about the gains from trade can be restated without reference to absolute advantage.

To do this go back to the examples of Tables 40-1 and 40-2. Calculate the opportunity cost of wheat and cloth in the two countries. When resources are assumed to be fully employed, the only way to produce more of one commodity is to reallocate resources and produce less of the other commodity. Table 40-1 shows that a unit of resources

TABLE 40–3 ABSENCE OF GAINS FROM SPECIALIZATION WHERE THERE IS NO COMPARATIVE ADVANTAGE

	One unit of resources can produce	
	Wheat (bushels)	Cloth (yards)
America	100	60
England	10	6

Changes resulting from the transfer of one unit of American resources into wheat production and 10 units of British resources into cloth production

	Wheat (bushels)	Cloth (yards)
America	+ 100	− 60
England	− 100	+ 60
World	0	0

Where there is no comparative advantage, no reallocation of resources within each country can increase the production of both commodities. In this example America has the same absolute advantage over England in each commodity (tenfold). There is no comparative advantage, and world production cannot be increased by reallocating resources in both countries. Therefore specialization does not increase total output.

TABLE 40–4 **THE OPPORTUNITY COST OF ONE UNIT OF WHEAT AND ONE UNIT OF CLOTH IN AMERICA AND ENGLAND**

	Wheat	Cloth
America	0.6 yards cloth	1.67 bushels wheat
England	2.0 yards cloth	0.50 bushels wheat

Comparative advantages can always be expressed in terms of opportunity costs that differ between countries. These opportunity costs can be obtained from Table 40-1 or Table 40-2. The English opportunity cost of one unit of wheat is obtained by dividing the cloth output of one unit of English resources by the wheat output. The result shows that 2 yards of cloth must be sacrificed for every extra unit of wheat produced by transferring English resources out of cloth production and into wheat. The other three cost figures are obtained in a similar manner.

in America can produce 10 bushels of wheat *or* 6 yards of cloth. From this it follows that the opportunity cost of producing one unit of wheat is 0.6 units of cloth while the opportunity cost of producing one unit of cloth is 1.67 units of wheat. These data are summarized in Table 40-4. The table also shows that in England the opportunity cost of one unit of wheat is two units of cloth foregone, while the opportunity cost of a unit of cloth is 0.50 units of wheat. Table 40-2 also gives rise to the opportunity costs in Table 40-4.

The sacrifice of cloth involved in producing wheat is much lower in America than it is in England. World wheat production can be increased if America rather than England produces it. Looking at cloth production we can see that the loss of wheat involved in producing one unit of cloth is lower in England than in America. England is a lower (opportunity) cost producer of cloth than is America. World cloth production can be increased if England rather than America produces it. This situation is shown in Table 40-5.

The gains from trade arise from differing opportunity costs in the two countries.

The gains from trade are further illustrated in the box on pages 782–783.

The conclusions about the gains from trade

TABLE 40–5 **GAINS FROM SPECIALIZATION WHEN OPPORTUNITY COSTS DIFFER**

Changes resulting from each country's producing one more unit of a commodity in which it has the lower opportunity cost		
	Wheat (bushels)	Cloth (yards)
America	+1.0	−0.6
England	−0.5	+1.0
World	+0.5	+0.4

Whenever opportunity costs differ between countries, specialization can increase the production of both commodities. These calculations show that there are gains from specialization given the opportunity costs of Table 40-4. To produce one more bushel of wheat, America must sacrifice 0.6 yards of cloth. To produce one more yard of cloth, England must sacrifice 0.5 bushels of wheat. Making both changes raises world production of both wheat and cloth.

drawn from the hypothetical example of two countries and two commodities may be generalized:

1. Country *A* has a **comparative advantage** over country *B* in producing a commodity when the opportunity cost (in terms of some other commodity) of production in country *A* is lower. This implies, however, that it has a comparative disadvantage in the other commodity.

2. Opportunity costs depend on the relative costs of producing two commodities, not on absolute costs. (Notice that the data in both Tables 40-1 and 40-2 give rise to the opportunity costs in Table 40-4.)

3. When opportunity costs are the same in all countries, there is no comparative advantage and no possibility of gains from specialization and trade. (You can prove this for yourself by calculating the opportunity costs implied by the data in Table 40-3.)

4. When opportunity costs differ in any two countries, and both countries are producing both commodities, it is always possible to increase production of both commodities by a suitable reallocation of resources within each country. (This proposition is illustrated in Table 40-5.)

The Gains from Large-Scale Production

So far we have assumed that unit costs are the same whatever the scale of output. In this case there are gains from specialization and trade as long as there are interregional differences in opportunity costs. If costs vary with the level of output, *additional* sources of gain are possible.

Economies of Scale[1]

Generally real production costs, measured in terms of resources used, fall as the scale of output increases. The larger the scale of operations the more efficiently large-scale machinery can be used and the more a detailed division of tasks among workers is possible. Smaller countries such as Canada, France, and Israel whose domestic markets are not large enough to exploit economies of scale would find it prohibitively expensive to become self-sufficient. They would have to produce a little bit of everything at very high cost.

Trade allows smaller countries to specialize and produce a few commodities at high enough levels of output to reap the available economies of scale.

Bigger countries such as the United States and the USSR have markets large enough to allow the production of most items at home at a scale of output great enough to obtain the available economies of scale. For them the gains from trade arise mainly from specializing in commodities in which they have a comparative advantage.

Learning by Doing

The discussion so far has assumed that costs varied only with the level of output. They may also vary with the length of time a product has been produced.

Early economists placed great importance on a factor that we call learning by doing. They believed that as regions specialized in particular tasks, work-ers and managers would become more efficient in performing them. As people acquire expertise, or know-how, costs tend to fall. Much modern empirical work suggests that this effect really does happen. If it occurs in our example, output of cloth per worker will rise in England as England becomes more specialized in that commodity, and the same will happen to output of wheat per worker in America. This is, of course, a gain over and above that which occurs when costs are constant.

HOW THE GAINS OF TRADE ARE DIVIDED AMONG NATIONS: THE TERMS OF TRADE

So far we have seen that world production can be increased when countries specialize in the production of the commodities in which they have a comparative advantage and then trade with one another. How will these gains from specialization and trade be shared between countries? The division of the gain depends on the terms at which trade takes place. The **terms of trade** are defined as the quantity of domestic goods that must be exported to get a unit of imported goods.

The terms of trade reflect the opportunity cost of imports measured in terms of exports.

In the example of Table 40-4, the American domestic opportunity cost of one unit of cloth is 1.67 bushels of wheat. If Americans can obtain cloth by international trade at terms of trade more favorable than 1.67 bushels of wheat, they will gain by doing so. Suppose that international prices are such that 1 yard of cloth exchanges for (i.e., is equal in value to) 1 bushel of wheat. At those prices, Americans can obtain cloth at a lower wheat opportunity cost by trade rather than by domestic production. Therefore the terms of trade favor selling wheat and buying cloth on international markets.

Similarly, in the example of Table 40-4, English consumers gain when they can obtain wheat abroad at any terms of trade more favorable than 2 yards of cloth per bushel of wheat, which is the English

[1] These are discussed in detail in Chapter 13. The Classic discussion of this effect is quoted in the box on page 47. This is worth reading now, even if you have not yet studied microeconomics.

A GRAPHIC REPRESENTATION OF THE GAINS FROM TRADE

Suppose America has a comparative advantage in wheat and England a comparative advantage in cloth. Initially each country is self-sufficient. Each country will be operating at a point (such as E and e in the diagrams) on its own production—and consumption—possibility curve (the heavy black line). The production possibility curves are straight lines because the opportunity cost of one commodity in terms of the other is assumed to be the same, no matter what the current levels of output of each commodity. America's curve (AB) is steeper than England's curve (CD) because America's opportunity cost of producing cloth (measured in terms of units of wheat foregone) is higher than England's. America has a comparative *advantage* in wheat and a comparative *disadvantage* in cloth.

Suppose America were offered the chance of obtaining cloth by trade at the English opportunity cost. It would pay America to produce nothing but wheat and then acquire cloth at the English opportunity cost. This would allow America to attain some point on AC', which is drawn through A (America's fully specialized output of wheat) parallel to CD. Clearly consumption opportunities have increased: America could now reach a point such as E_1 that was unobtainable without trade. In such circumstances America would gain by trade and England would break even.

Suppose England were offered the chance of obtaining wheat at the American opportunity cost in terms of cloth sacrificed. It would pay England to produce nothing but cloth and to trade along DA' (drawn parallel to AB) to reach a higher point, say e_1, than was obtainable when wheat had to be produced at the English opportunity cost. In such circumstances England would gain by trade, and America would break even.

But this means there is a range of "prices" of cloth in terms of wheat—lower than America's high opportunity cost and higher than England's low opportunity cost—at which each country gains. Represent one such relative price by the slope of the line $AT (= DT)$. If America produces only wheat and England only cloth, and they are willing to trade at this relative price, their consumption possibilities with trade will be shown by the lines AT and DT. America can go to some point such as E_2 that gives it more wheat and more cloth than the self-suffi-

domestic opportunity cost. If the terms of trade are 1 bushel of wheat for 1 yard of cloth, the terms of trade favor English traders' buying wheat and selling cloth on international markets. Here both England and America gain from trade: each can obtain the commodity in which it has a comparative disadvantage at a lower opportunity cost through international trade than through domestic production.

Because actual international trade involves many countries and many commodities, the actual terms of trade is computed as an index number:

$$\text{Index of terms of trade} = \frac{\text{Index of import prices}}{\text{Index of export prices}} \times 100$$

A fall in the index is referred to as a *favorable* change in a country's terms of trade. A favorable change means that less has to be exported to pay for a unit of imports than previously. For example, when America's import price index rises from 100 to 120 while its export price index rises from 100 to 125, the terms of trade index falls from 100 to 96. At the new terms of trade 96 units of exports will buy what formerly required 100 units to buy. An increase in the index of the terms of trade, called an *unfavorable* change, means the country must export more to pay for its now relatively more expensive imports. For example, the sharp rise in oil prices during the 1970s led to large unfavorable shifts in the terms of trade of the oil-importing countries, including the United States.

ciency point E, while England can go to some point such as e_2 that gives it more wheat and more cloth than the self-sufficiency point e. Thus the central generalization of the theory of the gains from trade is graphically illustrated: trade allows each country to have more of each commodity than it otherwise would if each country were self-sufficient.

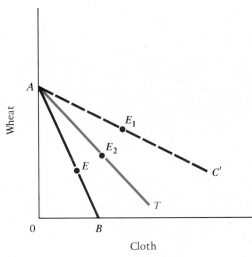

(i) America's consumption possibilities

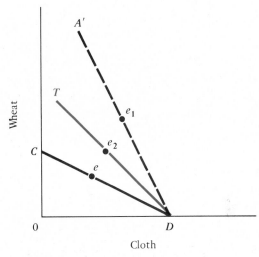

(ii) England's consumption possibilities

SUMMARY

1. The causes of the gains from trade between any two entities—individuals, regions, or nations—are the same.

2. One country (or region or individual) has an absolute advantage over another country (or region or individual) in the production of a commodity when, with the same input of resources in each country, it can produce more of the commodity than can the other.

3. In a situation of absolute advantage, total production of both commodities will be raised if each country specializes in the production of the com-

modity in which it has the absolute advantage. However, the gains from trade do not require absolute advantage on the part of each country, only comparative advantage.

4. Comparative advantage is the relative advantage one country enjoys over another in various commodities. If, for example, America is 10 times as efficient as is England in producing commodity X and 12 times as efficient in producing commodity Y, America has a comparative advantage over England in Y (its margin of advantage over England is larger in Y than it is in X). There are three other ways of saying the same thing: (a) America has a comparative disadvantage in X; (b) England has a comparative advantage in X; (c) England has a comparative disadvantage in Y.

5. World production of all commodities can be increased if each country transfers resources into the production of the commodities in which it has a comparative advantage.

6. The gains from trade result from different opportunity costs in different countries, which in turn lead to differences in comparative advantage.

7. The theory of the gains from trade may be stated thus: Trade allows all countries to obtain the goods in which they do not have a comparative advantage at a lower opportunity cost (in terms of units sacrificed of the commodities in which they do have a comparative advantage) than they would have to accept if they were to produce all commodities for themselves. This allows all countries to have more of all commodities than they could have if they made themselves self-sufficient.

8. As well as gaining the advantages of specialization arising from comparative advantage, a nation that engages in trade and specialization may realize the benefits of the economies of large-scale production and of learning by doing.

9. The terms of trade refer to the quantity of imported goods that can be obtained per unit of goods exported. They show the opportunity cost of obtaining goods by trade. The terms of trade determine how the gains from trade are shared. They are measured by an index number showing the ratio of import prices to export prices.

TOPICS FOR REVIEW

Interpersonal, interregional, and international specialization
Absolute advantage and comparative advantage
The gains from trade: specialization and large-scale production
Opportunity cost and comparative advantage
Terms of trade

DISCUSSION QUESTIONS

1. Adam Smith saw a close connection between the wealth of a nation and its willingness "freely to engage" in foreign trade. What is the connection?

2. Suppose that the following situation exists. Assume no tariffs, no intervention by the government, and that labor is the only factor of production.

Country	Labor cost of producing one unit of	
	Artichokes	Bikinis
Inland	$20	$40
Outland	$20	$X

Let X take different values—say $10, $20, $40, and $60. In each case in what direction will trade have to flow in order for the gains from trade to be exploited?

3. Suppose the United States had an absolute advantage in all manufactured products. Should it then ever import any manufactured products?

4. Suppose, after 1865, the United States had become two separate countries with no trade between them. What predictions would you make about the standard of living compared with what it is today? Does the fact that Canada, the United States, and Mexico are separate countries lead to a lower standard of living in the three countries than if they were united into a new country called Northica?

5. Studies of U.S. trade patterns have shown that very high wage sectors of industry are among the largest and fastest growing export sectors. Does this contradict the principle of comparative advantage?

6. Saudi Arabia has a comparative advantage over West Germany in producing oil. In what, if anything, does it have a comparative disadvantage? When Saudi Arabia lowers the price of oil, does it change the gains from trade? What does it change?

7. Predict what each of the following will do to the terms of trade of the importing country and the exporting country, other things being equal.
   a. A blight destroys a good part of the coffee beans produced in the world.
   b. The Japanese cut the price of the steel they sell to the United States.
   c. Competition among the maritime nations of the world leads prices of ocean transport to fall relative to the prices of the commodities transported.
   d. A general inflation of 10 percent occurs around the world.
   e. Violation of OPEC output quotas leads to a sharp fall in the price of oil.

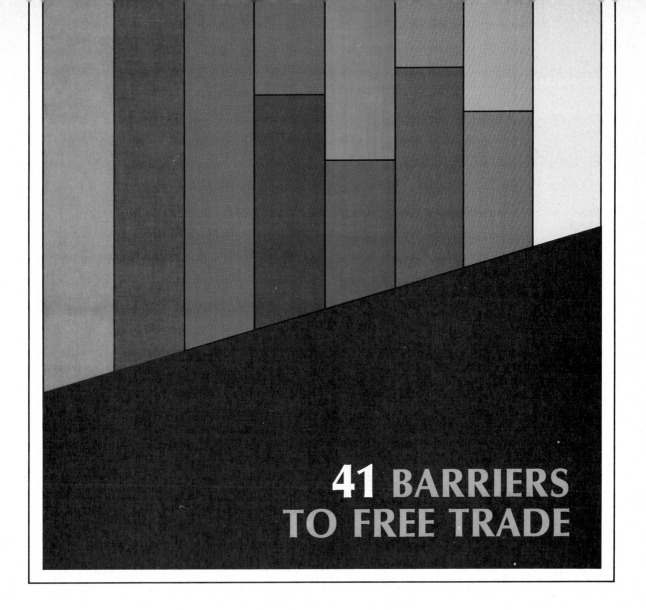

41 BARRIERS TO FREE TRADE

Conducting business in a foreign country is always difficult. Differences in language, in local laws and customs, and in currency all complicate transactions. Our concern in this chapter is not, however, with these difficulties but with the policies by which governments intentionally erect barriers to the free flow of goods and services among nations. Use of such restrictions on international trade is called **commercial policy**.

THE THEORY OF COMMERCIAL POLICY

Today debates over commercial policy are as heated as they were 200 years ago when the theory of the gains from trade was still being worked out. Should a country permit the free flow of international trade, or should it seek to protect its local producers from foreign competition at least to some extent? **Protectionism** refers to the protection of domestic industries from foreign competition. Such protection may be achieved either by *tariffs,* which raise the price of foreign goods, or by such *nontariff barriers* as quotas on imports and subsidies on exports that make importing difficult or impossible. **Free trade** is a situation in which protectionism is not practiced.

The Case for Free Trade

The case for free trade is based on the analysis presented in Chapter 40. We saw that when opportunity costs differ among countries, some degree of specialization will occur, and the trade that results will raise world standards of living. Free trade allows all countries to specialize in producing commodities in which they have a comparative advantage. They can then produce (and consume) more of all commodities than would be possible if specialization had not taken place.

Free trade allows the maximization of world production. It also makes it *possible* for every household in the world to consume more goods than it could without free trade.

This does not necessarily mean that everyone *will* be better off with free trade than without it. Protectionism could give some people a large enough share of a smaller world output so that they will benefit. If we ask whether it is *possible* for free trade to be advantageous to everyone, the answer is "yes." But if we ask whether free trade is in fact *always* mutually advantageous to everyone, the answer is "not necessarily so."

There is abundant evidence that significant differences in opportunity costs exist and that there are large potential gains from trade because of these differences. There is also ample evidence that trade occurs and that no nation tries to be self-sufficient or refuses to sell to foreigners the items it produces cheaply and well.

The case for free trade is thus powerful. What needs explanation is not the extent of trade but the fact that trade is not wholly free. Tariffs and non-tariff barriers to trade continue to exist two centuries after Adam Smith and David Ricardo stated the case for free trade. Do these interferences exist merely because policymakers are ignorant of the principles of comparative advantage, or are there sound reasons (overlooked in the case for free trade) for a nation's enacting protectionist policies? Is there a valid case for protectionism? If so, how does one find the balance between the advantages of more or less trade? Before addressing these questions, let us examine the methods used in protectionist policy.

Methods of Protectionism

Essentially a country can reduce its imports of some good in three ways. (1) The country may place a tax on imported commodites, called a **tariff.** Such a tax shifts the supply curve of the foreign import upward because it adds to the price charged by the foreign producer. (2) The country may impose an **import quota** that limits the quantity of a commodity that may be shipped into the country in a given period. Below the quota there is no change in supply, but once the quota has been reached, the supply curve effectively becomes a vertical line, indicating that no more can be imported whatever the price. (3) The country may adopt domestic policies that reduce its demand for the imported commodity. For example, it may require potential importers to obtain a special license or restrict the ability of its citizens to use their funds to purchase the foreign exchange needed to pay for the commodity. Such steps shift the demand curve for the import to the left.

Figure 41-1 illustrates the three methods of restricting trade. Although each method has somewhat different effects, they all achieve a reduction in the quantity of imports. In what follows we shall concentrate on tariffs, which are probably the single most important tool of trade restriction.

Tariffs come in two main forms: **specific tariffs,** which are so much money per unit of the product, and **ad valorem** tariffs, which are a percentage of the price of the product. These tariffs have two

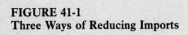

FIGURE 41-1
Three Ways of Reducing Imports

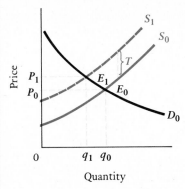
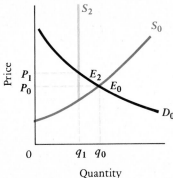
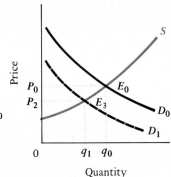
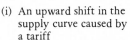

(i) An upward shift in the supply curve caused by a tariff

(ii) A shift in the supply curve caused by a quota

(iii) A shift in the demand curve caused by nontariff barriers

The government can decrease the quantity of imports below the free-market level by policies that either shift the demand curve or the supply curve to the left or that simply regulate the quantity of imports permitted. In each diagram D_0 and S_0 represent the free-market demand and supply for some imported goods, with p_0 and q_0 the equilibrium price and quantity. If the government wishes to achieve a smaller quantity of imports, say q_1, it may do so in various ways.

In (i) it imposes a tariff of T per unit. This shifts the supply curve vertically by the amount of the tariff to S_1 and achieves a new equilibrium at E_1.

In (ii) it imposes an import quota, q_1, as the maximum quantity permitted to enter. This in effect changes the supply curve to the heavy line S_2 and leads to equilibrium at E_2.

In (iii) it causes demand to shift leftward to D_1 by such policies as limiting importers' rights to purchase the commodity or the foreign exchange needed to pay for it. In this case a new equilibrium occurs at E_3. In all three parts the equilibrium quantity imported is reduced to q_1.

different and opposing purposes: to raise *revenue* and to provide *protection*. Protection is more common: to raise the price of imported goods in order to discourage imports by offsetting (to some extent at least) a cost advantage that foreign producers have over the domestic producers of a particular product. The protective function of a tariff conflicts with the revenue function because a tariff will not yield much revenue if it is actually effective in reducing imports. This chapter concentrates on the protective function of tariffs.

To see when and how tariffs work, consider three different commodities that Americans might import—coal, coffee, and steel. We shall make certain simplifying assumptions, shown in Table 41-1, about the price of the commodity in the United States compared with the costs of production in a foreign country plus shipment to the United States.

There is potential demand for the importation of any commodity that can be delivered to a country at a cost lower than the cost at which it can be produced domestically. At any time there is a wide array of potentially importable commodities, some with large cost savings, some with moderate savings, and some with no advantage at all. (In the example, both coffee and steel would be candidates for importation.) In a world of free trade these commodities would face no tariffs. A country

TABLE 41–1 DIFFERENT PROTECTIVE EFFECTS OF TARIFFS

Commodity	U.S. price if all production is domestic	Delivered cost of import	Percentage tariff needed to exclude	Delivered cost of imports in U.S. with 20% tariff
Coal (ton)	$ 30	$ 35	none	$42.00
Coffee (lb)	15	2	650	2.40
Steel (ton)	115	100	15	120.00

Commodities whose delivered cost to the United States is below the price of domestically produced commodities are potential imports; tariffs change the effective delivered costs of imports. In the example foreign producers have a comparative advantage at current prices in both coffee and steel production but not in coal. To make all importation uneconomic would require a tariff of at least 15 percent on steel and 650 percent on coffee. A 20 percent tariff would exclude steel but not coffee; however, it would raise coffee prices. A tariff would not affect coal because coal imports are effectively excluded without a tariff. These data are hypothetical.

would import all those commodities that it could buy from abroad at a delivered price lower than the cost of producing them at home.

Suppose the United States wishes to protect its home industries from foreign competition. It does not need a tariff on coal; it does need (at the assumed prices and costs) a tariff in excess of 15 percent on steel and a tariff of more than 650 percent on coffee.

Now suppose that a country imposes a 20 percent tariff on all imports. This does not prohibit trade, but by making imported goods more expensive, it limits those items that can be imported profitably. Any foreign good that enjoys a cost advantage of less than 20 percent is now effectively prohibited. This is the case of steel in the example. A 20 percent tariff thus provides protection to domestic industries that produce at a cost disadvantage of up to 20 percent. Imported goods that enjoy cost advantages in excess of 20 percent (such as coffee) will still be in demand, but they will not be as big a bargain as previously. Because their price will be higher, a smaller quantity will be demanded than if there were no tariff.

The Case for Protectionism

Two kinds of arguments for protection are commonly offered. The first concerns national objectives other than output; the second concerns the desire to increase domestic national income possibly at the expense of world national income.

Objectives Other than Maximizing Output

It is quite possible to accept the proposition that the value of production is higher with free trade and yet rationally oppose free trade because of a concern with policy objectives other than maximizing real national income. For example, comparative advantage might dictate that a country should specialize in producing a narrow range of commodities. The government might decide, however, that there are distinct social advantages to encouraging a more diverse economy. Citizens would be given a wider range of occupations, and the social and psychological advantages of diversification would more than compensate for a reduction in living standards by, say, 5 percent below what they could be with complete specialization of production according to comparative advantage.

Specializing in the production of one or two commodities, although dictated by comparative advantage, may involve risks that a country does not wish to take. One such risk is that technological advances may render its basic product obsolete. The quartz crystal badly damaged the Swiss watch industry in just this way; between 1974 and 1979 Switzerland's share of the world market in watches dropped from 40 percent to 30 percent, and 30,000 jobs were lost.

Another risk is cyclical fluctuations in the prices of basic commodities, which may face depressed prices for years at a time and then enjoy periods of very high prices. The national income of a country specializing in the production of such commodities will be subject to wide fluctuations. Even though the average income level over a long period might be higher if specialization in the production of a few basic commodities were allowed, the serious social problems associated with a widely fluctuating national income may make the government decide to sacrifice some income in order to reduce fluctuations. The government might use protectionist policies to encourage the expansion of several less cyclically sensitive industries.

Yet another reason for protectionism is the desire to maintain national traditions. For example, many Canadians are passionately concerned with maintaining an identity separate from that of the United States and believe that a tariff helps them to do this. They would be prepared, if necessary, to tolerate a 5 percent or 10 percent differential in living standards in order to maintain this independence.

The most frequently cited noneconomic reason for protectionism concerns national defense. It has traditionally been argued, for example, that the United States needs an experienced merchant marine in case of war and that this industry should be fostered by protectionist policies even though it is less efficient than the foreign competition. Another example is the perceived need for protection of the petroleum industry in order to ensure self-sufficiency in energy.

Although most people would agree that, other things being equal, they would prefer more income to less, economists cannot pronounce as irrational a nation that chooses to sacrifice some income in order to achieve other goals. Economists can do three things when faced with such reasons for imposing tariffs. First, they can try to see if the proposed tariff really does achieve the ends suggested. Second, they can calculate the cost of the tariff in terms of lowered living standards. Third, they can check policy alternatives to see if there are other means of achieving the stated goal at lower cost in terms of lost output.

Protectionism As a Means to Higher National Living Standards

Infant industries. The most important argument for protectionism as a means of raising living standards concerns economies of scale. It is usually called the **infant industry argument.** If an industry has large economies of scale, costs and prices will be high when the industry is small but will fall as the industry grows. In such industries the country first in the field has a tremendous advantage. A newly developing country may find that in the early stages of development its industries are unable to compete with established foreign rivals. A tariff (or import quota) may protect these industries from foreign competition while they grow up. When they are large enough, they will be able to produce as cheaply as foreign rivals and thus be able to compete without protection.[1]

Learning by doing. The theory of the gains from trade takes the production possibility curve as given. As we saw in Chapter 40, additional sources of gain are available due to *learning by doing,* a factor that Classical economists emphasized greatly.

Learning by doing suggests that the existing pattern of comparative advantage need not be taken as immutable. If a country can learn enough by producing commodities in which it currently is at a comparative disadvantage, it may gain in the long run by specializing in those commodities and *developing a comparative advantage* in them as the learning process lowers their costs.

Protecting a domestic industry from foreign competition may give it the time to learn to be efficient and its labor force the time to acquire

---

[1] Such a policy will take business away from foreign rivals. Hence, in the first instance it will increase the developing country's income at the expense of other countries. Once the resources in the other countries are reallocated to other uses, however, world output may rise in response to the development of these new centers of production.

necessary skills. If so, it may pay the government to protect the industry while the learning occurs.

The difficulty with basing tariff policies on these considerations is that the industries that will succeed in the long run must be identified. All too often the protected infant grows up to be a weak sister requiring permanent tariff protection for its continued existence. Or the learning proceeds at a slower rate than is occurring in similar industries in other countries that provide no protection from the chill winds of international competition. In these instances the anticipated comparative advantage never materializes.

The terms of trade. The OPEC countries provide a significant fraction of the world's supply of petroleum. By restricting their output they can and did raise the price of their oil relative to the prices of other traded goods. This turned the terms of trade in their favor: for every barrel of oil exported they were able to obtain a larger quantity of imports. By the same token, of course, it turned the terms of trade against the oil-importing countries, including the United States: for every unit of their goods exported they were able to import fewer barrels of oil.

Now consider a country that provides a large fraction of the total demand for some product that it imports. By restricting its demand for that product through tariffs it can force the price of that product down. This turns the terms of trade in its favor because it can now get more imports per unit of exports.

Trade restrictions can be used to turn the terms of trade in favor of countries that produce a large fraction of the world's supply of some commodity. It can also be used to turn the terms of trade in favor of countries that constitute a large fraction of the world demand for some commodity that they import.

Both of these techniques merely redistribute a given world output. They can, however, be effective methods of raising the living standards of some countries at the expense of others.

To protect against predatory actions by foreign producers. Tariffs may be used to prevent foreign industries from gaining an unfair advantage over domestic industries by use of predatory practices that will harm domestic industries but yield no long-term benefit to domestic consumers. A common form is *dumping*. The circumstances under which dumping provides a valid argument for tariffs are considered in detail later in this chapter.

How Much Protectionism?

So far we have seen that there is a strong case for allowing free trade in order to realize the gains from trade and that there are also reasons for departing from completely free trade.

It is not necessary to choose between free trade on the one hand and absolute protectionism on the other. A country can have some trade and some protectionism, too.

Free Trade Versus No Trade

It would undoubtedly be possible to grow coffee beans in American greenhouses and to synthesize all the oil we require in our factories (as Germany did during the Second World War). But the cost in terms of other commodities foregone would be huge, for artificial means of production require lavish inputs of factors of production. It would likewise be possible for a tropical country, currently producing foodstuffs, to set up industries to produce all the manufactured products that it consumes. But for a small country without natural advantages in industrial production, the cost in terms of resources used could be enormous. It is thus clear that there is a large gain to all countries in having specialization and trade. The real output and consumption of all countries would be very much lower if each had to produce domestically all the goods it consumed.

There are significant gains from trading for commodities in which a country has a large comparative disadvantage. Careful empirical measurement might put an actual numerical value on the amount of the gains, but certainly production and consumption in the world, and in each major trading country, are higher with trade than they would be with no trade.

In an all-or-nothing choice, virtually all countries would choose free trade over no trade.

A Little More Trade
Versus a Little Less Trade

Today we have trade among nations, but that trade is not perfectly free. Table 41-2 shows the levels of tariffs on selected commodities in force today.

Would we be better off if today's barriers to trade were reduced or increased a little bit? This question shifts the focus of our discussion considerably, for it is quite a jump from the proposition that "Free trade is better than no trade" to the proposition that "A little less trade restriction than we have at present is better than a little more." Yet most arguments about commercial policy involve the latter sort of proposition, not the former. "Should American workers be given *some* increased protection against Japanese imports?" is the question debated today, not "Should Japan be totally excluded from the American market?"

Most actual policy disagreements concern the relative merits of free trade versus controlled trade with tariffs on the order of, say, 5 percent, 10 percent, or 15 percent. Such tariffs would not cut out importation to the United States of bananas, coffee, diamonds, bauxite, or any other commodity in whose production we would be really inefficient.

As a rule, tariffs are seldom advocated to protect industries that are extremely inefficient compared with foreign industries; they are usually advocated to protect industries that can very nearly compete, but not quite. Most attempts to measure changes in national income resulting from the imposition of *modest* rates of tariff have suggested that rather small losses are involved.

To see why this is so, compare the effects of a 20 percent uniform ad valorem tariff with those of free trade. Tariffs of 20 percent will protect industries that are up to 20 percent less efficient than foreign competitors. If the costs of the various tariff-protected industries were spread out evenly,

TABLE 41–2 TARIFFS ON SELECTED COMMODITY GROUPS (Ad Valorem Rates), 1981

Commodity	United States	European Economic Community	Japan
Weighted average of all manufactured items	4.4	5.5	3.6
Fruits, vegetables	1.7	3.4	14.5
Tea, coffee, and spices	5.3	1.8	34.1
Paper, paperboard	0.3	4.0	1.4
Textiles	15.9	9.0	8.0
Transport vehicles	2.5	6.2	2.1
Tobacco	13.0	0.0	54.3
Petroleum and coal products	0.0	6.3	1.4
Oil and natural gas	4.0	0.0	0.0
All commodities (trade weighted)	3.2	3.7	5.4

Source: Post-Tokyo Round tariff rates, courtesy Special Trade Representitives Office, U.S. government.

The United States is a low-tariff country overall, yet tariffs on selected items are plainly designed to be protective of important domestic industries. These tariffs, the lowest in history, result from the GATT Tokyo Round negotiations: they began to take effect in 1981. Notice the U.S. use of tariffs for protection on textiles and tobacco. In Japan the high tariffs on tobacco, tea, coffee, and spices are for revenue since Japan does not produce these commodities.

some would be 20 percent less efficient than their foreign competitors and others only 1 percent less efficient. Their average inefficiency would be about half the tariff rate, so they would be on average about 10 percent less efficient than their foreign competitors.

Suppose that as a result of tariffs, approximately 10 percent of a country's resources are allocated to industries different from the ones to which they would be allocated if there were no tariffs. This means that about 10 percent of a country's resources would be working in certain industries only because of tariff protection. If the average protected industry is 10 percent less efficient than its foreign rival, approximately 10 percent of a country's resources are producing about 10 percent less efficiently than they would be if there were no tariffs. This causes a reduction in national income on the order of 1 percent as a result of tariff protection.[2]

Suppose the economic costs of existing tariffs are 1 percent of our national income. Is the sacrifice of national income implied by existing tariffs large or small? As a percentage it seems small, yet in 1983 prices it was $35 billion *per year* in the United States. That amount every year forever could buy a lot of hospitals, schools, medical research, solar energy research—or even imported oil.

Dynamic considerations. Some may be tempted to conclude that the seemingly small economic costs of protectionism make it worthwhile to give in to the clamor to provide more protection for America's hard-pressed industries. Before rushing to that conclusion, however, some long-run political and economic considerations need to be considered. The world prosperity of recent decades has been built largely on a rising volume of relatively free international trade. There are real doubts that such prosperity could be restored if the volume of trade were to shrink steadily because of growing trade barriers. Yet the pressure to use trade restrictions in troubled times is very strong. If countries give in and begin to raise barriers moderately when the initial economic costs are not large, so strong are the political forces involved that there is no telling where the process, once begun, will end.

In today's world a country's products must stand up to international competition if they are to survive. Protection, by conferring a national monopoly, reduces the incentive for industries to fight to hold their own internationally. If any one country adopts high tariffs unilaterally, its domestic industries will become less competitive. Secure in their home market because of the tariff wall, they are likely to become less and less competitive in the international market. Sooner or later, however, as the gap between domestic and foreign industries widens, *any* tariff wall will provide less protection. Eventually the domestic industries will succumb to the foreign competition. Meanwhile domestic living standards will fall relative to foreign ones as an increasing productivity gap opens between domestic tariff-protected industries and foreign, internationally oriented ones.

Fallacious Trade Policy Arguments

We have seen that there are gains from a high volume of international trade and specialization. We have also seen that there can be valid arguments for a moderate degree of protectionism. There are also many claims that do not advance the debate. Fallacious arguments are heard on both sides, and they color much of the popular discussion. These arguments have been around for a long time, but their survival does not make them true. We will examine them now to see where their fallacies lie.

Fallacious Free Trade Arguments

Free trade always benefits all countries. This is not necessarily so. The potential gains from trade might be offset by costs such as unemployment or economic instability or by the interference with policy objectives other than maximizing national income. These factors may render some interference desirable.[3]

Infant industries never abandon their tariff protection. It is argued that granting protection to infant industries is a mistake because these industries seldom admit to growing up and will cling to their protection even when fully grown. But infant industry tariffs are a mistake *only* if these industries never grow up. In this case permanent tariff protection would be required to protect a weak industry never able to compete on an equal

---

[2] The above rough calculation is meant only to give some intuitive understanding of why the many careful measures of the cost of moderate tariffs commonly lead to figures closer to 1 than to 10 percent of the levying country's national income.

[3] To see how sensitive the gains from trade are to other considerations, suppose that totally free trade led to an allocation of resources that was 1 percent more efficient than an allocation resulting from 20 percent tariffs but led simultaneously to an average level of unemployment 1.2 percent higher. In this case, free trade would bring losses rather than gains.

footing in the international market. But if the industries do grow up and achieve the expected scale economies, the fact that like any special interest group they cling to their tariff protection is not a sufficient reason for denying protection to genuine infant industries. When economies of scale are realized, the real costs of production are reduced and resources are freed for other uses. Whether or not the tariff or other trade barriers remain, a cost saving has been effected by the scale economies.

Fallacious Protectionist Arguments

The exploitation doctrine. According to this view one trading partner *must* always reap a gain at the other's expense. But the principle of comparative advantage shows that it is possible for both parties to gain from trade and thus refutes the exploitation doctrine of trade. When opportunity cost ratios differ in two countries, specialization and the accompanying trade make it possible to produce more of all commodities and thus make it possible for both parties to get more goods as a result of trade than they could get in its absence.

Keep the money at home. This argument says, If I buy a foreign good, I have the good and the foreigner has the money, whereas if I buy the same good locally, I have the good and our country has the money, too. Abraham Lincoln is said to have made this argument, and it is still heard today. It assumes that domestic money actually goes abroad physically when imports are purchased and that trade flows only in one direction.

The argument is based on a misconception. When American importers purchase Italian-made goods, they do not send dollars abroad. They (or their financial agents) buy Italian lire (or claims on them) and use them to pay the Italian manufacturers. They purchase the lire on the foreign exchange market by giving up dollars to someone who wishes to use them for expenditure *in the United States.* Even if the money did go abroad physically—that is, if an Italian firm accepted a shipload of dollars—it would be because that firm (or someone to whom it could sell the dollars) wanted them to spend in the only country where they are legal tender, the United States.

Dollars ultimately do no one any good except as purchasing power. It would be miraculous if green pieces of paper could be exported in return for real goods; after all, the Fed has the power to create as much new money as it wishes. It is only because the green paper can buy American commodities and assets that others want it.

Protection against low-wage foreign labor. Surely, the argument says, the products of low-wage countries will drive out products from the market, and the high U.S. standard of living will be dragged down to that of their poor trading partners. Arguments of this sort have swayed many voters through the years.

As a prelude to considering them, stop and think what the argument would imply if taken out of the international context and put into a local one, where the same principles govern the gains from trade. Is it really impossible for a rich person to gain from trading with a poor person? Would the local millionaire be better off if she did all her own typing, gardening, and cooking? No one believes that a rich person cannot gain from trading with those who are less rich. Why then must a rich group of people lose from trading with a poor group? "Well," you say, "the poor group will price their goods too cheaply." Does anyone believe that consumers lose from buying in a discount house or a supermarket just because the prices are lower there than at the old-fashioned corner store? Consumers gain when they can buy the same goods at a lower price. If the Koreans pay low wages and sell their goods cheaply, *Korean* labor may suffer, but we will gain because we obtain their goods at a low cost in terms of the goods that we must export in return. The cheaper our imports are, the better off we are in terms of the goods and services available for domestic consumption.

Stated in more formal terms, the gains from trade depend on comparative, not absolute, advantages. World production is higher when any two areas, say the United States and Japan, specialize in the production of the goods for which they have a comparative advantage than when they both try to be self-sufficient.

Might it not be possible, however, that Japan

will undersell the United States in all lines of production and thus appropriate all, or more than all, the gains for itself, leaving the United States no better off, or even worse off, than if it had no trade with Japan? The answer is no. The reason for this depends on the behavior of exchange rates, which we shall study in Chapter 41. As we shall see there, equality of demand and supply on foreign exchange market ensures that trade flows in both directions.

Imports can be obtained only by spending the currency of the country that makes the imports. Claims to this currency can be obtained only by exporting goods and services or by borrowing. Thus, lending and borrowing aside, imports must equal exports. All trade must be in two directions; we can buy only if we can also sell.

In the long run trade cannot hurt a country by causing it to import without exporting.

Trade then always provides scope for international specialization, with each country producing and exporting those goods for which it has a comparative advantage and importing those goods for which it does not.

Exports raise national income, imports lower it. Exports add to aggregate demand; imports subtract from it. Thus, other things being equal, exports tend to increase national income and imports to reduce it. Surely then, it is desirable to encourage exports and discourage imports. This is an appealing argument, but it is incorrect.

Exports raise national income by adding to the value of domestic output, but they do not add to the value of domestic consumption. In fact, exports are goods produced at home and consumed abroad, while imports are goods produced abroad and consumed at home. The standard of living in a country depends on the goods and services available for *consumption*, not on what is produced.

If exports were really good and imports really bad, then a fully employed economy that managed to increase exports without a corresponding increase in imports ought to be better off. Such a change, however, would result in a reduction in current standards of living because when more

goods are sent abroad and no more are brought in from abroad, the total goods available for domestic consumption must fall.

What happens when a country achieves a surplus of exports over imports for a considerable period of time? It will accumulate claims to foreign exchange for which there are three possible uses: to add to foreign exchange reserves, to buy foreign goods, and to make investments abroad. Consider each of them.

1. Some foreign exchange reserves are required for the smooth functioning of the international payments system, as we shall see in Chapters 42 and 43. But the accumulation of reserves over and above those required serves no purpose. Permanent excess reserves represent claims on foreign output that are never used.

2. British pounds and Indian rupees cannot be eaten, smoked, drunk, or worn. But they can be spent to buy British and Indian goods that can be eaten, smoked, drunk, or worn. When such goods are imported and consumed, they add to the U.S. living standards. Indeed the main purpose of foreign trade is to take advantage of international specialization: trade allows more consumption than would be possible if all goods were produced at home. From this point of view the purpose of exporting is to allow the importation of goods that can be produced more cheaply abroad than at home.

3. An excess of exports over imports may be used to purchase foreign assets. Such foreign investments add to living standards only when the interest and profits earned on them are used to buy imports or when the investment is liquidated. The essence of any investment is to permit the investor to earn profits or interest that can then be used to buy goods. Foreign investments permit the later purchase of foreign goods.

The living standards of a country depend on the goods and services consumed in that country. The importance of exports is that they permit imports to be made. This two-way international exchange is valuable because more goods can be imported than could be obtained if the same goods were produced at home.

Protectionism creates domestic jobs and reduces unemployment. It is sometimes said that an economy with substantial unemployment, such as that of the United States in the 1930s or in the 1980s, provides an exception to the case for freer trade. Suppose that tariffs or import quotas cut the imports of Japanese cars, Korean textiles, Italian shoes, and French wine. Surely, the argument maintains, this will create more employment for Detroit auto workers, Georgia textile workers, Massachusetts shoe factories, and California farm workers. The answer is that it will—initially. But the Japanese, Koreans, Italians, and French can buy from America only if they earn American dollars by selling goods in America. The decline in their sales of autos, textiles, shoes, and wine will decrease their purchases of American machinery, aircraft, grain, and vacations in America. Jobs will be lost in our export industries and gained in those industries that formerly faced competition from imports. The likely long-term effect is that overall unemployment will not be reduced but merely redistributed among industries.

Industries and unions that compete with imports favor protectionism while those with large exports favor more trade. Most economists are highly skeptical about the government's ability to reduce overall unemployment by protectionism.

Subsidizing exports increases employment. Export industries do not necessarily favor free trade; they may argue instead that the government should subsidize them. This argument is closely related to the last point, though it is made by different groups. Assume that there is a rise in exports without a corresponding rise in imports, perhaps because the government pays producers a subsidy on every unit exported. According to the theory of the multiplier, this rise in exports will increase income and employment. Surely in times of unemployment this is to be regarded as a good thing.

Two points may be made about such a policy. In the first place the goods being produced by the newly employed workers in the export sector are not available for domestic consumption and so do not directly raise domestic standards of living. Surely it would be better if, instead of subsidizing exports, the government subsidized the production of goods for the home market so that all goods produced—not just those produced in response to increased incomes—would contribute to a rise in domestic living standards. Or, if there is objection to the government's subsidizing private firms, the government could create new employment by building more roads, schools, and research laboratories. Consequently, income and employment would go up, but there would be something more tangible to show for it in the first instance than the smoke of ships disappearing over the horizon bearing the subsidized exports to foreign markets.

The second point to be made concerns the foreign effects of a policy that fosters exports and discourages imports in a situation of general world unemployment. Although the policy raises domestic employment, it will have the reverse effect abroad, where it creates unemployment. The foreign countries will suffer a rise in their unemployment because their exports will fall and their imports rise. Not surprisingly, they may be expected to retaliate; as we will see, this has been the historical experience. If all countries try a policy of expanding exports and discouraging imports, the net effect is likely to be a large drop in the volume of international trade without much change in the level of employment in any one country.

Arguments About Barriers to Trade: A Final Word

While there are cases in which a restrictive policy has been pursued following a rational assessment of the approximate cost, it is hard to avoid the conclusion that, more often than not, such policies are pursued for flimsy objectives or on fallicious grounds, with little idea of the actual costs involved. The very high tariffs in the United States during the 1920s and 1930s are a conspicuous example. The current clamor for the government to do something about the competition from Japan, Korea, and other countries of the East may well be another.

TRADE POLICY IN THE WORLD TODAY

Tariffs in the United States

Figure 41-2 shows how tariffs have been used in U.S. history. The government of the United States has often paid less attention to economists's arguments for freer trade than to the protests of producers who would be hurt by tariff reductions. Part of the reason was the relative unimportance of trade to the American economy; even today only about 7 percent of the economy's output is exported.[4]

In contrast, trade is extremely important to the economies of many countries. Sweden, Great Britain, and Canada all export between 20 and 25 percent of their GNP. The loss of their foreign

[4] Trade is more important in the United States today than it was half a century ago, in the heyday of prohibitive tariffs. In 1929 exports were less than 5 percent of GNP.

trade would have a devastating effect on their standards of living. America would also suffer from the loss of its foreign trade, but to a lesser degree.

Although foreign trade is not a large *fraction* of American national income, it is very important to particular industries. Large quantities of certain materials—petroleum, bauxite, coffee beans, iron ore, lumber, and newsprint—are imported. The loss of any of these supplies would cause serious difficulties in some industries, and some would cause major disruptions in the whole economy—as we have learned from even the temporary interruptions in oil supplies.

The existence of certain domestic industries—such as those producing steel, television sets, clothing, and automobiles—has been severely threatened by foreign competition. This is one indication that even if the existence of foreign trade is not vital to the country as a whole, it does affect particular sectors in important ways. Whether the country as a whole has an interest in protecting

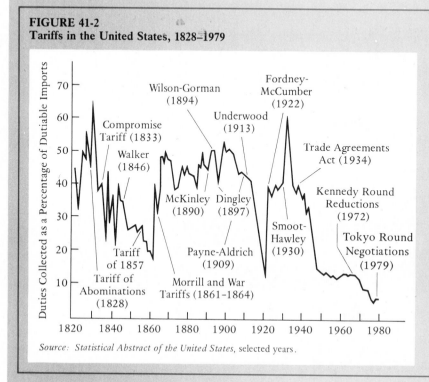

FIGURE 41-2
Tariffs in the United States, 1828–1979

U.S. tariffs have been lower in the post-World War II period than in any other period of comparable length in American history. Throughout its history the United States has alternated between being a high-tariff country and being a modest-tariff country. The average rate of tariff has been lower since World War II than ever before. The rate fell below 10 percent in 1971, and it may be expected to fall below the current 6 percent level when the ongoing Tokyo Round tariff reductions take full effect in the mid 1980s.

Source: Statistical Abstract of the United States, selected years.

such industries is often debated. Yet it is a matter of undeniable political reality that both labor and management representatives of these industries will lobby vigorously for protection. They are often heeded.

Even in areas where foreign trade is not critically important to the U.S. economy, our imports are the exports of other countries. In some cases they are essential to those other countries. For example, nearly two-thirds of Canada's trade is with the United States. Exports to the United States account for about one-sixth of Canadian GNP. A change in U.S. commercial policy that caused only a small ripple in the U.S. economy could cause a tidal wave of economic difficulty in Canada. In contrast, although Canada is the United States' most important export market, these exports only account for 1.5 percent of American GNP.

Foreign countries are both critical of and sensitive to changes in U.S. policy because those changes often have a vital effect on them. They fear that because some of these changes do not have a similarly vital effect on the United States, they may sometimes be carried out without due consideration of their effect on others. It is unpleasant to be in the position of having your welfare affected by decisions that do not matter much one way or the other to the person who makes them. (Americans learned this lesson in the 1970s when OPEC embargoed oil shipments to the United States.) Table 41-3 shows the importance of trade with the United States to the economies of some other countries.

Foreign trade contributes substantially to the standards of living of many countries. Even the United States, with its low dependence on trade, would have its living standard significantly lowered if it refused to participate in the gains from trade among nations.

Nontariff Barriers

While the United States is generally a low-tariff country, many nontariff barriers are in force here at the present time to protect particular domestic industries that have recently been losing ground to foreign competition. Some of these restrictions

TABLE 41–3 PERCENTAGES OF TRADE WITH THE UNITED STATES, 1981

Country	Percentage of exports to United States	Percentage of imports from United States
Canada	64	67
Mexico	60	67
Nigeria	46	9
Venezuela	27	47
Japan	26	18
Ghana	26	14
Brazil	22	17
United Kingdom	12	12
Australia	11	23
Italy	7	7
Germany	7	8
Sweden	6	8
France	5	8
USSR	1	7

Source: IMF, Direction of Trade Yearbook, 1982.

For many countries trade with the United States is a very large part of their total exports, imports, or both. Not surprisingly, the United States is the major trading partner of Canada and Mexico. But the United States as a market for exports or a source of imports is also vitally important to such distant countries as Venezuela, Brazil, Japan, Nigeria, Australia, and Iran.

have been negotiated, the U.S. government putting pressure on the other country to limit "voluntarily" its exports to the United States. Others have been imposed unilaterally. Let us consider one example of each.

Negotiated Import Restrictions in Textiles

In the late 1950s the American textile and clothing industries saw their market shares badly eroded by a rising volume of trade from Hong Kong, Korea, the Philippines, and other developing nations. In response to a United States initiative, a series of international meetings was held in 1961 that reached agreements providing for the limitation of imports into the United States in the interest of what was called orderly marketing. In this way maximum annual quotas were agreed to by each exporting textile-producing country for a 20-year

IMPORT RESTRICTIONS ON JAPANESE CARS: TARIFFS OR QUOTAS

In the early 1980s imports of Japanese cars seriously threatened the automobile industries of the United States, Canada, and Western Europe. While continuing to espouse relatively free trade as a long-term policy, the American government argued that the domestic industry needed short-term protection. This protection was to tide it over the period of transition it faced as smaller cars became the typical American household's vehicle. Once the enormous investment needed to transform the American auto industry had been made and new American models had gained acceptance, free trade could be restored and the American industry asked to stand up to the chill winds of foreign competition.

But how should the temporary protection be achieved? Politically, quotas mutually agreed upon by the two governments seemed the easiest route. An agreement was reached severely limiting the number of Japanese cars to be imported. (A similar agreement was reached between the Canadian and the Japanese governments.)

What does theory predict to be the economic difference between quotas and tariffs? In both cases imports are restricted and the resulting scarcity supports a higher market price. With a tariff the extra market value is appropriated by the government of the importing country—in this case the U.S. government. With a quota the extra market value accrues to the goods' suppliers—in this case the Japanese car makers and their U.S. retailers.

This result is illustrated in the figure. We assume that the U.S. market provides a small enough part of total Japanese car sales to leave the Japanese willing to supply at their fixed list price all the cars that are demanded in the United States. This is the price p_0 in both parts of the figure. Given the American demand curve for Japanese cars, D, there are q_0 cars sold before restrictions are imposed.

In (i) the United States places a tariff of T per unit on Japanese cars raising their U.S. price to p_1 and lowering sales to q_1. Suppliers' revenue is shown by the light shaded area. U.S. government tariff revenue is shown by the dark shaded area.

In (ii) a quota of q_1 is imposed, making the supply curve vertical at q_1. The market clearing price is p_1 and the suppliers' revenue is the whole shaded area (p_1 times q_1).

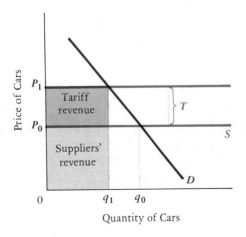

(i) Tariff of T Dollars Per Car

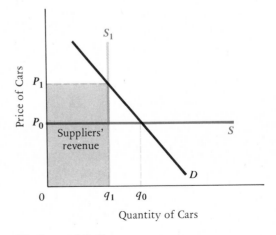

(ii) Quota of Q_1 Cars

The shortage of Japanese cars drives up their price, creating a substantial margin over costs. Under a tariff, the U. S. government captures the margin. Under a quota policy, however, the margin accrues to the Japanese manufacturers. Although this is a simplified picture, it catches the essence of what actually happened. First, while American manufacturers were keeping prices as low as possible and sometimes offering rebates on slow-selling models, Japanese cars were listed at healthy profit margins. Second, while it was always possible for the buyer of an American car to negotiate a good discount off the list price, Japanese cars usually sold for their full list price. Third, Japanese manufacturers tended to satisfy fully the demand for their more expensive cars, which have larger profit margins, and to restrict exports to the United States of the less expensive cars with lower profit margins. This change in the "product mix" of Japanese cars exported to the United States raised the average profit per car exported.

There was nothing immoral or even surprising about these developments. They are the natural responses of sellers whose markets are restricted by quotas. Indeed they were fully predictable in advance by economic theory.

period. Starting in 1981 many of these agreements were renegotiated, generally leading to more restrictive policies.

Similar orderly marketing agreements have been accepted by foreign countries with respect to footwear in 1977, color television sets in 1977, and citizens band radio sets in 1978. Lobbyists for many other industries have urged similar agreements for their products. One of the most recent agreements, which limits Japanese car exports to the United States is considered in the box.

Why, one may ask, would a country such as Korea agree voluntarily to limit its profitable exports to the United States when it needs the revenue and foreign exchange that its exports earn? The answer, one may surmise, is that the United States is so needed and valued an ally that its "requests" have the weight of veiled threats. In any case, the State Department has proven to be quite persistent and persuasive once it has set out to negotiate an agreement.

Unilaterally Imposed Trigger Prices and Antidumping Rules in Steel

The American steel industry has suffered badly from competition from Japan, which (it is charged) is selling steel in the United States at lower prices than it is selling steel at home. This is called **dumping**, and it is a form of price discrimination of the kind studied in the theory of monopoly (see Chapter 15). The steel industry has asked the United States government for help, and it has received it. To understand the issues, we need to understand a bit more about dumping.

Possible motives for dumping. Japanese producers dump steel in the United States because it is profitable for them to do so. There are several reasons why it might pay them to sell more cheaply here than at home.[5]

1. It may be a sensible long-term strategy because of economies of large-scale production and the fact that the Japanese home market is permanently too small to support an industry of efficient size. In such circumstances, to have an efficient industry requires an export market; but to achieve that market, a low-price policy may be required. By selling cheaply abroad, the country can generate sufficient demand to justify an efficient-size industry. Dumping in this case benefits both its domestic and its foreign customers by making it possible to produce output at the lowest possible cost per unit.

2. It may be a sensible middle-term strategy to provide a market for efficiently produced steel for a period—say 5 or 10 years—until Japanese manufacturers will be able to absorb the entire output of Japanese production. In this scenario, home sales would gradually replace export sales. Dumping permits an efficient-size industry now, without

[5] The theory of price discrimination, studied in microeconomics, shows that when elasticity of demand differs in two markets, it pays to charge different prices in each market. Here we are concerned about why Japan may wish to sell in the U.S. market at all, given the distance it must ship and the competition it faces from American producers.

waiting for Japanese demand to grow.

3. It may be a sensible cyclical strategy, providing a market for output in periods when Japanese demand is low, and thereby utilizing the capacity required to meet maximum Japanese demands in periods of boom and expansion. In this scenario, sales in the export market are simply sporadic "white sales" that permit Japanese production to continue on an even level over the cycle.

4. It may be a predatory strategy designed to destroy the foreign industry. In this scenario, after foreign plants have shut down and the foreign industry's work force has dispersed, prices can be raised to exploit the foreigner's new dependence on imports.

Effects on the buying country. Suppose America is the "beneficiary" of dumped Japanese steel, that is, steel sold at less than the Japanese home price and (let us suppose) below the average cost of production in the United States. If such sales continue, they will either eliminate the U.S. industry or force it to become competitive by becoming more efficient. However unfair this may sound to American steel makers, it will benefit American steel buyers for as long as they are able to buy cheaper steel. Cheaper steel will lead to less expensive buildings, refrigerators, nails, and all other products that use steel.

No matter what the Japanese producers' motives, the American steel industry and the United Steelworkers of America will want the U.S. government to stop this, for it threatens profits and their jobs.

Suppose the government chooses to look beyond the political pressures of the moment and to do what is best for the national interest. Here it matters which of the four motivations explains the dumping. If the Japanese are prepared to supply cheap steel on a permanent basis, it would surely benefit Americans to buy Japanese steel and use American resources to produce something in which we have a comparative advantage. This is the case for doing nothing to protect the domestic steel industry and instead helping it to become more efficient or encouraging an orderly shift of its workers and resources into other industries. However, if cheap Japanese steel would destroy the American

industry without replacing the need for it—that is, for any of the last three listed reasons—then sufficient protection to preserve a viable industry may be required. This is the valid case for protectionism.[6]

The problem for policy is to diagnose what is happening and to adopt rules that will preserve needed industries without depriving American buyers of cheaper sources of supply. Currently there is controversy about what is really happening in Japanese steel production; many economists are not persuaded that protection is required to preserve American national interests.

Antidumping provisions and trigger prices. Under current American law, any American producer or the government itself can file suit before the U.S. International Trade Commission, alleging that a foreign producer is dumping. It need not show *harm*, only that the American price is below the foreign producer's home price. Congress has given the commission the power to impose quotas or tariffs on the dumping country when such an allegation is found to be true.

In 1977 the United States announced a series of **trigger prices** for imported steel products. If a foreign producer were to sell below one of those prices, the United States would initiate antidumping proceedings. The trigger prices were set at a level designed to be no lower than the *average total cost* of production and shipment of the Japanese steel industry. In March 1980 the trigger price mechanism was temporarily suspended; it was reintroduced in 1981 with trigger prices raised by 12 percent. Other measures to monitor sudden surges in steel imports were also introduced at that time.

Two features of the trigger-price system now in effect make it highly protectionist. First, the setting of trigger prices at the level of *average total costs* places them above the marginal costs of an industry subject to decreasing costs. This assures that much price discrimination that may be mutually beneficial to Japanese producers and Amer-

---

[6] The fact that three of the four motives listed lead to the protectionist position does not mean that they are three times as likely to apply as the other motive.

ican buyers will be challenged. Second, *any* price discrimination is classified as dumping and thus subject to penalties. Thus the trigger prices become in effect minimum prices below which no foreign producer can risk selling. Thus the provisions inhibit foreign competition and serve as nontariff barriers to trade, both where dumping is beneficial to American interests and where it is not.

Overall Importance of Nontariff Barriers in the United States

American trade policy, all things considered, remains relatively unprotectionist. But in selected industries—textiles and steel among them—the combined effect of nontariff and tariff barriers is significant. Many economists who have seen American policy become less and less protectionist over the last 50 years are concerned that protectionism will spread via nontariff barriers as American policymakers, unable to find a short-run solution to pockets of unemployment, prove unable to resist the protectionist views of the lobbyists for industries hurt by foreign competition.

International Agreements Concerning Trade and Tariffs

In the past any country could impose any desired set of tariffs on its imports. But when one country increases its tariffs, the action may trigger retaliatory changes by its trading partners. Just as an arms race can escalate, so can a tariff war; precisely this happened during the 1920s and early 1930s. Extended negotiations may then be required to undo the damage.

The General Agreement on Tariffs and Trade (GATT)

One of the most notable achievements of the post-World War II world in retreating from the high-water mark of protectionism achieved in the 1930s was the General Agreement on Tariffs and Trade (GATT). Under this agreement, GATT countries meet periodically to negotiate bilaterally on mutually advantageous cuts in tariffs. They

agree in advance that any tariff cuts negotiated in this way will be extended to all member countries. Significant tariff reductions have been effected by the member countries.

The two most recent rounds of GATT agreements have each reduced tariffs by about one-third. The Kennedy Round negotiations were completed in 1967, and new rates were phased in over a five-year period ending in 1972. The recent Tokyo Round negotiations began in 1975 and were completed in 1979. The reductions began to take effect in 1981.

Ironically, as that new round of reductions began, pressure was mounting in many countries to protect jobs at home through trade restrictions. GATT itself came under attack. The worldwide recession that began in late 1981 was undoubtedly the main cause of this pressure. In addition, protectionist pressure in many countries was also created by the decline in the international competitiveness of traditional sectors or industries due to sharp changes in terms of trade. At a November 1982 meeting, the GATT countries recognized—and resolved to overcome—the threat to the system represented by the emerging clamor for increased protectionism, but they failed to achieve any explicit agreements to prevent tariff increases. The disaster of total breakdown may have been avoided, but the result was still a stalemate. Thus many observers feared that the prospects for continued movement toward free trade were dim.

Although GATT has produced enormous reductions in *tariffs*, the results are a bit misleading in terms of the freedom of trade because of the growing use of nontariff barriers. Perhaps the most important feature of the Tokyo Round was the agreement, for the first time, on steps to limit the growth of nontariff barriers. It is still too early to tell whether these efforts will prove as successful as have the tariff reductions.

Regional Common Markets

A common market is an agreement among a group of countries to eliminate barriers to free trade among themselves and to present a common trading front to the rest of the world. The most important example is the so-called European Common Market. In 1957 the Treaty of Rome brought together France, Germany, Italy, Holland, Belgium, and Luxembourg in the European Economic Community (EEC). The original six were joined in 1973 by the United Kingdom, the Republic of Ireland, and Denmark; Greece entered in the early 1980s.

The EEC is dedicated to bringing about free trade, complete mobility of factors of production, and the eventual harmonization of fiscal and monetary policies among the member countries. All tariffs for manufactured goods have been eliminated and much freedom of movement of labor and capital achieved. Movement toward the harmonization of economic and social policies and creation of a common monetary system seem now, however, to be stalled.

Other common markets have been formed, such as the Central American Common Market and the East African Community, but none has yet achieved the success of the EEC, and some have collapsed.

SUMMARY

1. The case for free trade is that world output of all commodities can be higher under free trade than when protectionism restricts regional specialization.

2. Free trade among nations may be restricted intentionally by protectionist policies in the form of tariffs, import quotas, restrictions on the purchase of foreign exchange, and in other ways.

3. Protection can be urged as a means to ends other than maximizing world living standards. Examples of such ends are to produce a diversified economy, to reduce fluctuations in national income, to retain distinctive national traditions, and to improve national defense.

4. Protection can also be urged on the grounds that it may lead to higher living standards for the protectionist country than would a policy of free trade. Such a result might come about through exploiting a monopoly position or by allowing in-

experienced or uneconomically small industries to become efficient enough to compete with foreign industries.

5. Virtually everyone would agree that free trade should be chosen if the only choice were between free trade and *no* trade. However, most real choices facing nations today are not about free trade versus no trade; rather they are about *a little more* trade (caused, say, by a slight lowering of tariffs) versus *a little less* trade (caused, say, by a slight raising of tariffs). Here the choice is not so obvious as that between free trade and no trade. The potential gains from small reductions in barriers to trade must be balanced against other objectives and other effects.

6. Some fallacious free trade arguments are that (a) because it is possible for free trade to be beneficial, free trade will in fact always be beneficial; and (b) because infant industries seldom admit to growing up and thus try to retain their protection indefinitely, the whole country necessarily loses by protecting its infant industries.

7. Some fallacious protection arguments are that (a) mutually advantageous trade is impossible because one trader's gain must always be the other's loss; (b) buying abroad sends our money abroad, while buying at home keeps our money at home; (c) our high-paid workers must be protected against the competition from low-paid foreign workers; (d) imports are to be discouraged because they lower national income and cause unemployment; and (e) subsidizing imports increases employment.

8. Trade is vitally important in the national incomes of many countries. It is relatively less important to the United States. Nonetheless trade is vital to particular American industries, and few economists doubt that American living standards would be lowered significantly if America tried to make itself fully self-sufficient.

9. Although America today has very low tariffs, its recent tendency to institute nontariff barriers either by negotiation (as in textiles) or by unilateral policies causes concern that the 50-year trend to ever freer trade is being reversed.

10. International agreements and negotiations have succeeded in lowering trade barriers from the very high levels of 50 years ago. In 1934 the United States took the lead in negotiating reciprocal trade treaties containing most-favored-nation clauses. After World War II the GATT began a series of multinational rounds of tariff reduction that have greatly lowered tariffs and, more recently, nontariff barriers as well. Nevertheless the recent clamor for protection in many trading nations threatens the free-trade trend GATT has fostered. Regional common markets, such as the EEC, have created substantial free trade areas.

TOPICS FOR REVIEW

Free trade and protectionism
Tariff and nontariff barriers to trade
The case for some protectionism
The case for free trade versus no trade
Fallacious arguments for free trade
Fallacious arguments for protectionism
Dumping
General Agreement on Tariffs and Trade (GATT)

DISCUSSION QUESTIONS

1. Suppose America had imposed prohibitive tariffs on all imported cars over the last three decades. How do you think this would have affected (a) the U.S. automobile industry, (b) the American public, and (c) the kinds of cars produced by U.S. manufacturers?

2. Lobbyists for many industries argue that their products are essential to national defense and therefore require protection. Suppose that supplies of a certain commodity are indeed essential in wartime. How does restricting imports solve the problem? Are there alternatives to import restrictions? If so, how might the alternatives be evaluated?

3. Import quotas are often used instead of tariffs. What real difference (if any) is there between quotas and tariffs? Explain why lobbyists for some American industries (cheese, sugar, shoes) support import quotas, while lobbyists for others (pizza manufacturers, soft drink manufacturers, retail stores) oppose them. Would you expect labor unions to support or oppose quotas?

4. Listed below are some recent average duties paid in the United States, by commodity classes.

Coffee	0%	Raw wool	15%
Whisky	9	Clothing	25
Iron ore and scrap	0	Television sets	5
		Chemicals	9
Natural rubber	0	Newsprints	0

What economic and political reasons can you see for duties on some commodities being well above the average rate (7 percent) of duty charged and for others being zero?

5. "The only pro-tariff argument that is likely to be valid for the whole world taken as an economic unit (rather than for a particular nation at a particular time) is the infant industry argument." Explain why you agree or disagree with this statement.

6. The United States has greatly reduced tariffs since Congress passed trade legislation authorizing the president to negotiate tariff concessions with foreign countries. Why might Congress find it desirable to give the president this authority rather than reserve the authority to itself?

7. When France increased tariff restrictions on foreign poultry, seriously hurting American chicken exporters, the United States reversed tariff reductions that had been made on brandy. Does this kind of "trade war" make any sense?

8. "A commodity that does not face foreign competition, either because of trade barriers or because of transport costs, is going to cost domestic buyers too much in the long term." Is this ever true? Is it always true?

9. "One of the dangers of temporary restrictions on imports to deal with some transitory problem is that the restrictions can easily become permanent and the problems long term." Check this view against the recent history of the temporary import quotas first placed on Japanese cars in 1982.

10. "An issue of *American Heritage* [reminds us] that Karl Marx was a firm, even fervent, free trader. (When he was the London correspondent for Horace Greeley's *New York Tribune*, Marx—the wicked communist—advocated free trade while Greeley—the avid capitalist—exposed protectionism.)" Reflect on what factors might have caused Marx and Greeley, given their political persuasions, to hold these views (as reported in the July 26, 1983, issue of the *Wall Street Journal*).

11. Classical economists favored free trade among nations as a means of interlocking their economies so they could not afford to fight each other. President Reagan has opposed interlocking the economies of the Eastern and Western block on the grounds that this gives too much power of blockage to the Eastern countries. Discuss the "political economy" of these two opposing views.

42 FOREIGN EXCHANGE, EXCHANGE RATES, AND THE BALANCE OF PAYMENTS

The value of the dollar is of great concern to many people. It interests the Japanese firm wanting to build a factory in Illinois, the American wanting to buy a French government bond, a German exporter sending automobiles to the United States, and an American hoping to sell computers in Saudi Arabia. It also matters to American tourists cashing their dollar travelers checks in London, Athens, or Bangkok. In this chapter we are concerned with what it means to speak of the "price of the dollar" and what causes that price to change. The discussion will bring together material on three topics studied elsewhere in this book: the theory of supply and demand (Chapter 5), the nature of money (Chapter 33), and the process of international trade (Chapter 40).

The Nature of Foreign Exchange Transactions

We have seen that money, which consists of any accepted medium of exchange, is vital in any sophisticated economy that relies on specialization and exchange. Yet money as we know it is a *national* matter, one closely controlled by the national governments. Money in the United States is the dollar, money in the United Kingdom is pounds sterling, money in Japan is the yen, and money in Germany is the mark.

Each country has its own monetary system, and all governments regulate the size of the money supply within their own countries. If you live in Sweden, you will earn krona and spend krona; if you run a business in Austria, you will borrow schillings and meet your payroll with schillings. The currency of one country is generally acceptable within the bounds of that country, but it will not usually be accepted by households and firms in another country. The Stockholm bus company will accept krona but not Austrian schillings for your fare. The Austrian worker will not take Swedish krona for wages but will accept schillings.

When American producers sell their products, they require payment in dollars. They must meet their wage bills, pay for their raw materials, and reinvest or distribute their profits. If they sell their goods to American purchasers, there will be no problem; the firms will be paid dollars for their output. However, if American producers sell their goods to Indian importers, either the Indians must exchange their rupees to acquire dollars to pay for the goods or the U.S. producers must accept rupees—and they will accept rupees only if they know that they can exchange the rupees for the dollars that they require. The same holds true for producers in all countries; they must eventually receive payment for the goods that they sell in terms of the currency of their own country.

In general, trade between nations can occur only if it is possible to exchange the currency of one nation for that of another.

International payments that require the exchange of one national currency for another can be made in a bewildering variety of ways, but in essence they involve the exchange of currencies between people who have one currency and require another. Suppose that an American firm wishes to acquire £3,000 for some purpose (£ is the symbol for the British pound sterling). The firm can go to its bank or to some other seller of foreign currency and buy a check that will be accepted in the United Kingdom as £3,000. How many *dollars* the firm must pay to purchase this check will depend on the price of pounds in terms of dollars.

The exchange of one currency for another is part of the process of foreign exchange. The term **foreign exchange** refers to the actual foreign currency or various claims on it, such as bank deposits or promises to pay, that are traded for each other. The **exchange rate** is the price at which purchases and sales of foreign currency or claims on it take place; it is the amount of home currency that must be paid in order to obtain one unit of the foreign currency. For example, if one must give up two dollars to get one pound sterling, the exchange rate is 2.[1]

A rise in the exchange rate (i.e., a rise in the price of foreign exchange) is a **depreciation** of the home currency. *Foreign currencies have become more expensive; therefore the relative value of the home currency has fallen.* A fall in the exchange rate (i.e., a fall in the price of foreign exchange) is an **appreciation** of the home currency. *Foreign currencies have become cheaper; therefore the relative value of home currency has risen.* For example, when the dollar price of sterling rises from $2.00 to $2.50 (in other words the sterling price of the dollar falls from £0.50 to £0.40), the dollar has *depreciated* and the pound has *appreciated*.

Let us see how foreign exchange transactions are carried out. Suppose that an American firm wishes to purchase a British sports car to sell in the United States. The British firm that made the car demands payment in pounds sterling. If the car is priced at £3,000, the American firm will go to its bank, purchase a check for £3,000, and send the check to the British seller. Let us suppose this requires that the firm pay $5,000.[2] (In other words the exchange rate in this transaction is £1.00 =

---

[1] This expresses the relative values of the two currencies in terms of the dollar price of one pound sterling. Equivalently, one could consider the pound sterling price of one dollar which in this example is £0.50.

[2] Banks charge a small commission for making currency exchanges, buy we shall ignore this and assume that parties can exchange moneys back and forth at the going exchange rate.

TABLE 42–1 CHANGES IN THE BALANCE SHEETS OF TWO BANKS AS A RESULT OF INTERNATIONAL PAYMENTS

U.K bank			U.S. bank		
Assets	Liabilities		Assets	Liabilities	
No change	(1) Deposits of car exporter	+£3,000	No change	(1) Deposits of car importer	−$5,000
	(2) Deposits of refrigerator importer	−£3,000		(2) Deposits of refrigerator exporter	+$5,000
	Net change	0		Net change	0

International transactions involve a transfer of deposit liabilities among banks. The table records two separate international transactions at an exchange rate of $1 = £0.60: (1) an American purchase of a British car for £3,000 (= $5,000), and (2) a British purchase of American refrigerators for $5,000 (= £3,000). The American's import of a car reduces deposit liabilities to U.S. citizens and increases deposit liabilities to British citizens. The Britisher's import of refrigerators does the opposite. When a series of transactions are equal in value, there is only a transfer of deposit liabilities among individuals within a country. The American refrigerator manufacturer received (in effect) the dollars the American car purchaser gave up to get a British-made car.

$1.67, or $1.00 = £0.60.) The British firm deposits the check in its bank.

Now assume that in the same period of time a British wholesale firm purchases 10 American refrigerators to sell in Britain. If the refrigerators are priced at $500 each, the American seller will have to be paid $5,000. To make this payment the British importing firm goes to its bank and writes a check on its account for £3,000 and receives a check drawn on a U.S. bank for $5,000. The check is sent to America and deposited in an American bank. The effects of these transactions are shown in Table 42-1.

The two transactions cancel each other out, and there is no net change in international liabilities. No money need pass between British and American banks to effect the transactions; each bank merely increases the deposit of one domestic customer and lowers the deposit of another. Indeed, as long as the flow of payments between the two countries is equal (Americans pay as much to British residents as British residents pay to Americans), all payments can be managed as in the above examples, and there will be no need for a net payment from British banks to American banks.

All these calculations involve comparing magnitudes measured in different currencies. These comparisons are done using the exchange rate. We now turn to an analysis of how such exchange rates are determined.

THE THEORY OF EXCHANGE RATES IN A COMPETITIVE FOREIGN EXCHANGE MARKET

For simplicity we shall consider an example involving trade between the United States and the United Kingdom and the determination of the exchange rate between their two currencies, dollars and sterling. The two-country example simplifies things, but the principles apply to all foreign transactions. Thus sterling stands for foreign exchange in general and the dollar price of sterling stands for the foreign exchange rate in general.

We can relate our example to the demand and supply analysis of Chapter 5. To do so, we need only to recognize that *in the market for pounds sterling* the American firm that wants pounds is a demander of pounds and the British firm that is selling pounds to buy dollars is a supplier of pounds. We can also look at the *same* transaction in the market for dollars: The American firm is a supplier of dollars, and the British firm is a demander of dollars.

TWO WAYS OF LOOKING AT THE EXCHANGE OF DOLLARS FOR POUNDS STERLING

In a world of only two currencies, dollars and pounds, there is only one foreign exchange market, but it can be looked at in two ways: (i) as a market for dollars and (ii) as a market for pounds. The two figures show the alternative perspectives.

In (i) dollars are bought and sold. The price of the purchases is quoted as so many pounds sterling for each dollar. Consider point *a* on the demand curve $D_\$$. This price-quantity pair shows that when each dollar costs £0.52, buyers will purchase $90 million. Point *E* shows that if the price falls to £0.50, buyers will purchase $100 million. Points *a* and *E* are simply points on the demand curve $D_\$$ for dollars. Such a demand curve can shift, say to the curve labeled $D_\$'$, along which more dollars are demanded at each price. Such a shift might be caused by an increase in interest rates offered by American banks. Point *b* is on the new demand curve.

At point *a* buyers who willing to pay £0.52 per dollar to acquire $90 million were prepared to give up £46.8 million to do so ($90 \times 0.52 = 46.8$). They were prepared to supply pounds. The price of pounds in terms of dollars is the reciprocal of the price of dollars in

terms of pounds. That is, when $1.00 = £0.52, £1.00 = $1.92. (This is the same as saying that if the price of hamburgers in terms of dollars is $.50, the price of a dollar is 2.0 hamburgers.)

In (ii), where the supply and demand for *pounds* is measured in dollars, point *a* appears as the willingness to supply £46.8 million at a price per pound of $1.92. It is the *same* point *a* as in (ii); it is the opposite side of the same willingness to give up pounds to acquire dollars. Point *a* is on the demand curve for dollars ($D_\$$) *and* on the supply curve of pounds ($S_£$).

Point *E* in (ii) is the other view of point *E* in (i); it too is on the supply curve of pounds, $S_£$. Similarly, when the demand curve for dollars shifts to $D_\$'$, this is the same as the supply curve of pounds shifting from $S_£$ to $S_£'$. Satisfy yourself that point *b* is the same in both diagrams.

Because both (i) and (ii) show exactly the same information, we can use either one or convert from one to another. This will seem less confusing if you remember that every time you buy (demand) something, you give up (supply) something else. When a farmer swaps a chicken for your axe, does the farmer acquire an axe or lose a chicken? The answer, of course, is both.

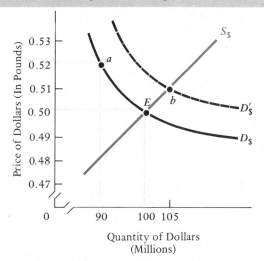

(i) Market for dollars

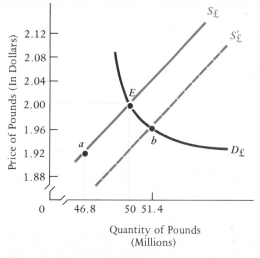

(ii) Market for pounds sterling

Because one currency is traded for another on the foreign exchange market, it follows that to desire (demand) dollars implies a willingness to offer (supply) pounds, while an offer (supply) of dollars implies a desire (demand) for pounds.

When £1.00 = $1.667, a British importer who offers to buy $5.00 with pounds must be offering to sell £3.00. Similarly, an American importer who offers to sell $5.00 for pounds must be offering to buy £3.00. For this reason a theory of the exchange rate between dollars and pounds can deal either with the demand for and the supply of dollars or with the demand for and the supply of pounds sterling; both need not be considered. We shall concentrate on the demand, supply, and price of dollars (quoted in pounds). The parallel between this and the supply, demand, and price of pounds (quoted in dollars) is explored in the box on page 807.

The Demand for Dollars

Sources of Demand for Dollars

American exports. One important source of demand for dollars in foreign exchange markets is someone who does not own dollars but wishes to use his or her own currency to buy American-made goods and services. The British importer of refrigerators was such a purchaser; an Austrian couple planning to vacation in the United States is another; the Soviet government seeking to buy American wheat is a third. All are sources of demand for dollars arising out of international trade. Each potential buyer wants to sell its own currency and buy dollars for the purpose of purchasing American exports.

Long-term capital flows. A second source of a demand for dollars comes from foreigners who wish to purchase American assets. In 1979 a German firm purchased 29 percent of the assets of A&P. This transaction required the purchase of dollars for marks. Billions of "petrodollars" are being invested in American securities and real estate by the oil-rich countries and their residents.

In order to buy American assets, holders of foreign currencies must first buy dollars on foreign exchange markets. Such transactions are called *long-term capital movements or flows.*

Short-term capital flows. When interest rates in the United States soared in the early 1980s, floods of "foreign money" came to the United States to buy short-term treasury bills and notes, certificates of deposit, and so on. The buyers of these securities were seeking a high return on their liquid assets. But first these buyers had to convert their lire, guilder, marks, and francs into dollars. When people sell financial assets in one country for foreign exchange that they then use to buy short-term financial assets in another country, the transactions are called *short-term capital movements or flows.*

A medium of exchange. One other type of transaction may be noted. Certain currencies, the most important of them the American dollar, have come to be accepted by nations, banks, and ordinary people as an international medium of exchange: these currencies are readily acceptable among buyers and sellers who might be less willing to trade with each other using less well-known kinds of money. Thus a Norwegian exporter of smoked fish to a Turkish wholesaler may quote prices in dollars and expect payment in dollars. Most of the oil sold by the OPEC countries must be paid for in dollars, whether the purchasing firm or government is in France, Chad, or India. The French purchaser of oil must first convert francs to dollars, then pay the dollars to Saudi Arabia. There is therefore a demand for currencies that act as an international medium of exchange. Some of the trading in the U.S. dollar exists to provide a medium of exchange quite independent of the flow of American imports or exports.

Reserve currency. Firms, banks, and governments often accumulate and hold currency reserves just as individuals maintain savings accounts. The government of Nigeria, for example, has foreign exchange reserves. It may decide to increase its holdings of dollars and reduce its holdings of pounds; if so, it will be a demander of dollars (and a supplier of pounds) on foreign exchange markets.

The Aggregate Demand for Dollars

The demand for the dollar by holders of foreign currencies is the sum of the demands for it for each of the purposes discussed above—for purchases of American exports, for long-term capital acquisitions, for short-term capital acquisitions, and for purchases of the dollar to use in other transactions or to add to reserve holdings as a reserve currency.

Furthermore, since people, firms, and governments in all countries purchase goods from and invest in many other countries, the demand for any one currency will be the aggregate demand of business, individuals, and governments in a number of different countries. Thus the total demand for dollars, for example, may represent Germans offering marks, British offering pounds, Greeks offering drachmas, and so on. The demand for any one currency comes from many sources, and the supply of that currency comes from many holders of that currency, including banks, individuals, and businesses in many different countries. For simplicity, however, we continue with our two-country example with only Britain and the United States.

The Shape of the Demand Curve for Dollars

The demand for dollars in terms of pounds is represented by a downward-sloping curve such as that shown in Figure 42-1. This figure plots the price of dollars (measured in pounds) on the vertical axis and the quantity of dollars on the horizontal axis. Moving down the vertical scale, the dollar becomes cheaper (i.e., it is worth fewer pounds); its value is depreciating on the foreign exchange market. Moving up the scale the dollar becomes more expensive; it is appreciating on the market.[3]

Why does the demand curve for dollars slope downward? Consider the demand derived from

---

[3] Since we have chosen to work with the demand and supply of dollars, the vertical axis measures the pound sterling price of dollars which is the inverse of the exchange rate.

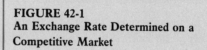

FIGURE 42-1
An Exchange Rate Determined on a Competitive Market

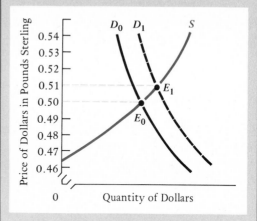

The equilibrium exchange rate equates demand and supply on the foreign exchange market. The quantity of dollars demanded is originally equal to the quantity supplied at a price of £0.50 per dollar (or £1 = $2.00). If the demand for dollars rises to D_1 the equilibrium exchange rate will change to £0.51 per dollar—that is, the dollar appreciates in value and the pound depreciates.

purchases of American exports. If the dollar depreciates in value the sterling price of American exports will fall. The British will buy more of the cheaper U.S. goods and will require more dollars for this purpose. The quantity of dollars demanded will rise. In the opposite case, when the dollar rises in value, the price of American exports rises in terms of foreign currency. The British will buy fewer U.S. goods and thus demand fewer U.S. dollars. Similar considerations affect other sources of demand for dollars. When the dollar is cheaper, American assets or securities become attractive purchases, and the quantity purchased will rise. As it does, the quantity of dollars demanded to pay for the purchases will increase.

The demand curve for dollars on the foreign exchange market is downward-sloping when plotted against the sterling price of dollars.

The Supply of Dollars

Because of the symmetrical nature of foreign exchange markets, the sources of supply of dollars are merely the opposite side of the demand for pounds. (Recall that the *supply* of dollars seeking pounds is the same as the *demand* for pounds by holders of dollars.) Who wants to sell dollars? Americans seeking to purchase foreign goods and services or assets will be supplying dollars and purchasing foreign exchange for the purpose. Holders of American securities may, in response to some international event, decide to sell their American holdings and shift into foreign assets. If they do, they will try to sell dollars—that is, they will be supplying dollars to the foreign exchange market. Similarly, a country with large dollar reserves of foreign exchange may decide the dollar is "weak" and try to sell dollars in order to buy another currency.

Once again, from many sources and for many purposes, people will be wishing to give up dollars and acquire other currencies. For simplicity, we continue with our two-country (Britain and America) example.

What about the shape of the supply curve of dollars? When the dollar depreciates, the effective price of British exports to the United States rises. It takes more dollars to buy the same British good, so Americans will buy fewer of the now more expensive British goods. The amount of dollars being offered in exchange for pounds sterling in order to pay for British exports (American imports) will fall.[4]

In the opposite case, when the dollar appreciates, British exports to the United States become cheaper, more are sold, and more dollars are spent on them. Thus more dollars will be offered in exchange for pounds in order to obtain the foreign exchange needed to pay for the extra imports. Pre-

cisely the same argument used for commodities applies to purchases and sales of assets.

The supply curve of dollars on the foreign exchange market is upward-sloping when plotted against the sterling price of dollars.

Equilibrium Exchange Rates in a Competitive Market

Consider a rate of exchange that is set on a freely competitive market. Like any competitive price, this rate fluctuates according to the conditions of demand and supply.

Assume that the current price of dollars is so low (say, £0.48 in Figure 42-1) that the quantity of dollars demanded exceeds the quantity supplied. Dollars will be in scarce supply, some people who require dollars to make payments to America will be unable to obtain them, and the price of dollars will be bid up. The value of the dollar vis-à-vis the pound will appreciate. As the price of the dollar rises, the sterling price of U.S. exports to the United Kingdom rises and the quantity of U.S. dollars demanded to buy British goods decreases. However, as the dollar price of imports from the United Kingdom falls, a larger quantity will be purchased and the quantity of U.S. dollars supplied will rise. Thus a rise in the price of the dollar reduces the quantity demanded and increases the quantity supplied. Where the two curves intersect, quantity demanded equals quantity supplied—and the exchange rate is in equilibrium.

What happens when the price of dollars is above its equilibrium value? The quantity of dollars demanded will be less than the quantity supplied. With the dollar in excess supply, some people who wish to convert dollars into pounds will be unable to do so. The price of dollars will fall, fewer dollars will be supplied, more will be demanded, and an equilibrium will be reestablished.

A foreign exchange market is like other competitive markets in that the forces of demand and supply tend to lead to an equilibrium price in which quantity demanded equals quantity supplied.

---

[4] As long as the elasticity of demand for imports is greater than one, the fall in the volume of imports will swamp the rise in price and hence fewer dollars will be spent on them. This elasticity condition is related to a famous, long-standing issue in international economics. In what follows, we adopt the standard case of the condition's being met. In a more general form, it is called the *Marshall-Lerner condition* after two famous economists who first studied the problem.

Changes in Exchange Rates

What causes exchange rates to vary? The simplest answer to this question is, changes in demand or supply in the foreign exchange market. Anything that shifts the demand curve for dollars to the right or the supply curve for dollars to the left increases the equilibrium exchange rate and thus tends to lead to the appreciation of the dollar. Anything that shifts the demand curve for dollars to the left or the supply curve for dollars to the right decreases the equilibrium exchange rate and tends to lead to the depreciation of the dollar. This is nothing more than a restatement of the laws of supply and demand, applied now to the market for foreign currencies.

But what causes the shifts in demand and supply that lead to changes in exchange rates? There are many causes, some of them transitory and some persistent; we shall mention several of the most important ones.

A Rise in the Domestic Price of Exports

Suppose the dollar price of American electronic equipment rises. What this will do to the demand for dollars depends on the foreign elasticity of demand for the American product. If the demand is elastic, perhaps because other countries supply the same product in world markets, the total amount spent will decrease and thus fewer dollars will be demanded. That is, the demand curve for dollars will shift to the left and the dollar will depreciate. If the demand is inelastic—say because America is uniquely able to supply the product for which there are no close substitutes—more will be spent, the demand for dollars to pay the bigger bill will shift the demand curve to the right, and the dollar will appreciate.

A Rise in the Foreign Price of Imports

Consider the effects of a large rise in the price at which some important import is supplied. Assume that the sterling price of Scotch whisky increases sharply. Assume also that American drinkers have an elastic demand for Scotch, so they end up spending fewer pounds for Scotch whisky than

they did before. Hence, they must supply fewer dollars to the foreign exchange market. The supply curve of dollars shifts to the left, and the price of the dollar tends to rise.

Changes in the Overall Price Levels

Suppose that instead of a change in the price of a specific export, such as electronic calculators, there is a change in all prices due to inflation. What matters here is the change in our price level relative to the price levels of our trading partners. (In our two-country example, "the United Kingdom" stands for the rest of the world.)

An equal percentage change in the price level in both countries. Suppose there is a 10 percent inflation in both the United States and the United Kingdom. In this case, the sterling prices of British goods and the dollar prices of U.S. goods both rise by 10 percent. At the existing exchange rate the dollar prices of British goods and the sterling prices of American goods will each rise by 10 percent. Thus the relative prices of imports and domestically produced goods will be unchanged in both countries. There is now no reason to expect a change in either country's demand for imports at the original exchange rate, so the inflations in the two countries leave the equilibrium exchange rate unchanged.

This argument forms the basis of what is called the *purchasing power parity* theory of exchange rates, a theory we shall study below.

A change in the price level of only one country. What will happen if there is inflation in the United States while the price level remains stable in the United Kingdom? The dollar price of U.S. goods will rise, and American goods will become more expensive in the United Kingdom. This will cause the quantity of American exports, and therefore the quantity of dollars demanded by British importers in order to pay for American goods, to diminish.

At the same time, British exports to America will have an unchanged dollar price while the price of American goods sold at home will have been increased by the inflation. Thus British goods will be more attractive compared with American goods (because they have become *relatively* cheaper), and more British goods will be bought in America. At any exchange rate the quantity of dollars supplied in order to purchase pounds will be increased.

An American inflation unmatched in the United Kingdom causes the demand curve for dollars to shift to the left and the supply curve of dollars to shift to the right. As a result the equilibrium price of dollars must fall; there is a depreciation in the value of the dollar relative to that of the pound.

Inflation at unequal rates. The two foregoing examples are of course just limiting cases of a more general situation in which each country can experience price level changes at home. The arguments can readily be extended when one realizes that it is the *relative* size of the changes in prices in two countries that determines whether home goods or foreign goods look more or less attractive. If country A's inflation rate is higher than country B's, country A's exports are becoming relatively expensive in B's markets, while imports from country B are becoming relatively cheap in A's markets. This will shift the demand curve for A's currency to the left and the supply curve to the right. Each change causes the price of A's currency to fall.

If the price level of one country is rising relative to that of another country, the equilibrium value of its currency will be falling relative to that of the second country.

Capital Movements

Major capital flows can exert strong influences on exchange rates. For example, an increased desire to invest in British assets will shift rightward the supply of dollars and depreciate the value of the dollar.

A movement of investment funds has the effect of appreciating the currency of the capital-importing country and depreciating the currency of the capital-exporting country.

This statement is true for all capital movements, short term or long term. Since the motives that lead to large capital movements are likely to be different in the short and long terms, it is worth considering each.

Short-term capital movements. A major motive for short-term capital flows is a change in interest rates. International traders hold transactions balances just as domestic traders do. These balances are often lent out on short-term loan rather than being left idle. Naturally the holders of these balances will tend to lend them, other things being equal, in those markets where interest rates are highest. Thus if one major country's short-term rate of interest rises above the rates in most other countries, there will tend to be a large inflow of short-term capital into that country to take advantage of the high rate, and this will tend to appreciate the currency. If these short-term interest rates should fall, there will most likely be a sudden shift away from that country as a source of transactions balances, and its currency will tend to depreciate.

A second motive for short-term capital movements is speculation about a country's exchange rate. If foreigners expect the dollar to appreciate, they will rush to buy assets that pay off in dollars; if they expect the dollar to depreciate, they will be reluctant to buy or hold American securities.

Long-term capital movements. Such movements are largely influenced by long-term expectations about another country's profit opportunities and the long-run value of its currency. A British investor would be more willing to purchase an American factory if it expected that the dollar profits would buy more pound sterling in future years than the profits from investment in a British factory. This could happen if the American firm earned greater profits than the British firm, with exchange rates unchanged. It could also happen if the profits were the same but the investor expected the dollar to appreciate relative to the pound.

Capital movements: summary. Anything that leads to an inflow of capital—relatively high interest rates, high earnings expectations, or expectations of appreciation—increases the demand for the dollar and tends to appreciate its value. Anything that leads to an outflow of capital—relatively low interest rates, low earnings expectations, or expectations of depreciation—decreases the demand for the dollar and tends to depreciate its value.

Structural Changes

An economy can undergo structural changes that alter the equilibrium exchange rate. *Structural change* is an omnibus term for a change in cost structures, the invention of new products, or anything else that affects the pattern of comparative advantage. For example, when a country's products do not improve as rapidly as those of some other country, consumers' demand (at fixed prices) shifts slowly away from the first country's products and toward those of its foreign competitors. This causes a slow depreciation in the first country's currency because the demand for its currency is shifting slowly leftward.

Many people believe that U.S. manufacturing today is suffering just such an adverse structural change, its exports of everything from textiles to automobiles being slowly displaced in third countries by exports from countries such as Korea, Germany, and Japan. This decreases the demand for dollars. The same forces lead domestic American households to turn ever more toward foreign-made goods, thereby increasing the supply of dollars. Each of these changes tends to depreciate the value of the dollar.

Loss of Confidence in the Dollar as a Reserve Currency

In the period since 1944 many nations, banks, and even private firms have come to hold dollars as a major part of their foreign exchange reserves. In 1970 more than $500 billion was held for that purpose. If for any reason these holders come to believe that the dollar will depreciate in world markets, they may decide that it would be shrewd to shift some of their dollar holdings to sterling, marks, or even gold. This happened during the 1970s. When there are large dollar holdings, attempts to "get out of dollars" in a hurry can lead

to large rightward shifts of the supply curve and rapid depreciation of the dollar.

THE BALANCE OF PAYMENTS

The Nature of Balance-of-Payments Accounts

In order to know what is happening to the course of international trade, governments keep track of the *transactions* among countries. The record of such transactions is made in the **balance-of-payments accounts.** Each transaction, such as a shipment of exports or the arrival of imported goods, is classified according to the payments or receipts that would typically arise from it.

Any transaction that would to lead to a payment to other nations is classified as a debit ($-$) item because it uses foreign exchange. American imports and outflows of American capital to purchase foreign assets are debit items. (An export of capital is really an *import* of the foreign assets purchased.) Any transaction that would to lead to a payment by foreigners to the United States or its residents is classified as a credit ($+$) item because it earns foreign exchange. American exports and capital flows into the United States are credit items.

Consider some examples. When a British importer buys an American washing machine to sell in the United Kingdom, this appears as a credit in the U.S. balance of payments because it earns foreign exchange. However, when an American shipping firm insures with Lloyds of London a cargo destined for Alexandria, Egypt, this represents a debit in the U.S. balance of payments because when the insurance premium is paid, the shipping firm will have to pay Lloyds in sterling. This transaction uses foreign exchange. Of course a credit item to one country is a debit item to the other, and vice versa; thus the washing machine transaction is a debit and the insurance transaction a credit in the British balance of payments.[5]

---

[5] As we shall see, there is nothing *inherently* good about "credits" or bad about "debits."

An important thing to notice about the record of international transactions is that the balance of payments refers to actual transactions, not desired transactions. We have seen that at some exchange rate between dollars and pounds it is quite possible for holders of sterling to want to purchase more dollars in exchange for pounds than holders of dollars want to sell in exchange for pounds. In this situation quantity demanded exceeds quantity supplied. But it is not possible for sterling holders to buy more dollars than dollar holders will sell; every dollar that is bought must have been sold by someone, and every dollar that is sold must have been bought by someone.

Because the amount of dollars actually bought must equal the amount of dollars actually sold, the balance of payments always balances.

Although the total number of dollars bought on the foreign exchange market must equal the total number sold, this is not true of purchases and sales for each specific purpose or within particular categories. For example, more dollars may well be sold for the purpose of obtaining foreign currency to import foreign cars than are bought for the purpose of buying American cars for export to other countries. In such a case, the United States has a balance-of-payments deficit on the "car account": the value of U.S. imports of foreign cars exceeds the value of U.S. exports of American cars. Usually we are not interested in the balance of payments for single commodities, but for larger classes of transactions.

Major Categories in the Balance-of-Payments Accounts

Table 42-2 presents the U.S. balance-of-payments account for 1982.

Current Account

The balance of payments on *current account* includes all payments made because of current purchases of goods and services. There is no automatic reason why current account payments should balance (any more than the automobile account

TABLE 42–2 U.S. BALANCE-OF-PAYMENTS, 1981
(Billions of Dollars)

Current account	
Exports	+ 356.1
Imports	– 345.0
Trade balance[a]	+ 11.1
Government grants and other transfers	– 6.6
Balance on current account	+ 4.5
Capital account	
Net change in U.S. investments abroad (increase –, decrease +)	– 23.3
Net change in foreign investments in U.S. (increase +, decrease –)	+ 23.4
Balance on capital account	0.1
Balance on capital plus current accounts	4.6
Official financing	
Changes in liabilities to foreign official agencies (increase +, decrease –)	– 1.3
Use of official reserves (increase –, decrease +)	– 3.3
Balance on official account	– 4.6
Overall balance of payments	Always zero[b]

[a] We do not distinguish here between visible and invisible items. See footnote 6 on page 815.
[b] In balance-of-payments accounts there is a "statistical discrepancy" item that results from the inability to measure accurately some items. For example, many capital transactions are not recorded.

The overall balance of payments always balances, but the individual components do not have to. The principal categories of greatest interest are shown in color. In this example the country shows a positive (surplus) trade balance (exports exceed imports) and a smaller positive (surplus) balance on current account. There is a negative (deficit) balance on capital account because capital exports exceeded capital imports. The capital *plus* current account surplus is what is commonly referred to as the *balance of payments*. It is exactly matched by the balance in the official accounts.

should). It is quite possible that more dollars were sold in order to purchase imports than were bought in order to allow foreigners to purchase our exports. If so, the dollars must have come from somewhere, and the excess of sales over purchases on current account must be exactly matched by an excess of purchases over sales on the capital and official financing accounts.

The main item in the current account is the so-called **balance of trade** (or the trade balance), the difference between the dollar value of exports and imports in a given year. Note that the balance of trade concerns only the *difference* between exports and imports, not the volume of trade. Thus one could have a $30 billion excess of exports over imports on a volume of exports of $300 billion or on a volume of $50 billion. In either case the same pressure on the exchange rate would be exerted. But the effect of foreign trade on the nation's economy would be very different because such things as the gains from trade depend on the volume, not the balance, of trade.

The gains from trade depend on the volume of trade, not the balance of trade. The effect on foreign exchange markets depends on the balance of trade, not the volume of trade.

The trade balance is sometimes divided further into visible and invisible trade balances.[6] **Visibles** are goods—all those things such as cars, pulpwood, aluminum, coffee, and iron ore that can be seen and touched when they cross international borders. **Invisibles** are services—all those things that cannot be seen or touched, such as insurance, freight haulage, and tourist expenditures. Another invisible item is the payment of interest and dividends on loans and investments made by Americans in foreign countries. Interest and dividends on foreign loans and investments provide foreign exchange and are entered as credit items on the balance of payments.

The most important items in the current account

not included in exports or imports are government current transactions. Among them are military expenditures in foreign lands and so-called unilateral transfers (gifts, pensions, etc.) to persons living abroad.

Capital Account

The *capital account* records transactions related to international movements of financial capital. It may seem odd that while the export of a good is a credit item, the export of capital is a debit item. To see that there is no contradiction in this treatment of goods versus capital, consider the export of American capital for investment in a British bond. The capital transaction involves the purchase, and hence the *import*, of a British bond, and this has the same effect on the balance of payments as the purchase, and hence the import, of a British good. Both items involve payments to foreigners and use foreign exchange. They are thus debit items in the American balance of payments.

As we have seen, an important distinction is often made between short-term and long-term capital movements. The distinction is important to the capital account because short-term capital movements tend to be much more volatile than long-term ones. Thus they are more likely to cause sudden sharp changes in the capital-account balance and in exchange rates.

Why do international capital movements occur? Allowing for risk and other such factors, investors will seek to invest where the return is highest. Just as within one country capital moves from industry to industry in search of its most productive uses, so capital tends to move from country to country in search of the highest rates of return. Such capital movements mean that the households and firms of one country are making investments in another country.

Official Financing

The final section in the balance-of-payments account represents transactions in the *official reserves* held by the government. It shows how the balance on the remainder of the accounts was financed.

[6] Terminology is not standardized and the term *balance of trade* is sometimes reserved for the balance on goods alone. When the balance of trade is used, as it is in the text, for the balance on goods *and* services, the term *balance on merchandise account* is used for the balance on the goods account alone.

Here there are two main items: changes in liquid liabilities to foreign official agencies and changes in official reserve assets. The first represents the change in liquid claims on official reserves held by foreign central banks. When the United States has a deficit on the rest of the accounts, foreign monetary authorities accumulate these claims. They may then hold on to them or they may demand payment in official reserve assets. To the extent that they hold on to them (as part of *their* foreign exchange reserves), they are lending to the United States and allowing us to use this loan to finance the deficit on the rest of the accounts.

When holders of dollar claims against the United States present them for payment, there is a loss of official reserve assets. Payment may be made in gold, in foreign exchange (our claims on other convertible currencies), or in other accepted media of official international payments (such as SDRs), which we will encounter in Chapter 43.[7]

The Relation Among Current, Capital, and Official Accounts

The relation among the three divisions of accounts follows from the fact that their sum must be zero.

A deficit on current plus capital accounts must be matched by a net surplus on the official financing accounts—which entails the government's borrowing abroad or decreasing its exchange reserves. A surplus on current plus capital accounts implies a deficit on the official financing accounts. Similarly, deficits on current account can be offset by surpluses on capital account, and vice versa.

To illustrate these relationships, consider a situation in which the value of American exports exceeds the value of American imports. This involves a surplus on the balance of trade, which was the characteristic situation in the years following World War II. In such a situation foreigners will not be

able to obtain all the dollars they demand from Americans wishing to buy foreign goods. Thus the excess of exports over imports can only be paid for if foreigners obtain dollars from other sources.

There are several possibilities. First, U.S. dollars may be provided by American investors eager to obtain foreign currency so that they can buy foreign stocks and bonds. In this case the trade surplus is balanced by a deficit on capital account. Second, the U.S. government, rather than its firms or citizens, may have lent money to foreign governments to finance their purchases of American-produced goods or services. This too is a capital account deficit. Third, the U.S. government may have given away money as aid to other countries. Such gifts allow those countries to purchase more from the United States than they sell to us. This is a unilateral transfer; it appears as a debit in the current account. Fourth, foreign governments may have reduced their holdings of U.S. dollars or gold by selling them to persons who wish to buy U.S. goods, accepting their own domestic currency in exchange. This appears in the official financing accounts. One way or another, the trade surplus can occur only when someone else provides the dollars needed to pay for the excess American exports.

Balance-of-Payments Deficits and Surpluses

Meaning of the Concepts

We have already noted that when all the uses to which foreign currency is put and all the sources from which it came are added up, the two amounts are necessarily equal, and thus the overall accounts of all international payments necessarily balance.

Yet it is common to speak of a country as having a balance-of-payments deficit or surplus. What does this mean? These terms usually refer to the balance of the account *excluding* changes in official financing. A **balance-of-payments surplus** means that the government is reducing its liquid liabilities to foreign governments or else adding to its holdings of official reserves in such forms as gold and

---

[7] If exchange rates were entirely free to fluctuate and were not managed at all, there would be no "official" settlements, for any imbalance in the current plus capital accounts would cause the exchange rate to vary to eliminate the deficit or surplus (see page 810). But official settlements remain important in a world of managed flexible exchange rates.

foreign exchange. A **balance-of-payments deficit** means that the government is adding to its liquid liabilities to foreign governments or else reducing its stocks of official reserves.

The statement, for example, that America had a balance-of-payments surplus of $4.6 billion in 1982 means that the U.S. official reserves (net of claims that foreign governments held against these reserves) rose by $4.6 billion because all other transactions were in surplus by that amount.

A balance-of-payments deficit means that the reserves of the government are being reduced; a surplus means that reserves are rising.

Consequences of Deficits and Surpluses

The very term balance-of-payments *deficit* sounds bad while balance-of-payments *surplus* sounds good. Indeed people often assume that a payments surplus is to be welcomed while a payments deficit is to be avoided. But why should this be so?

A balance-of-payments deficit means that in the aggregate debit items exceed credit items. Nothing is implied about this being beneficial or harmful. For example, an investment by an American firm in foreign countries that will yield future profits for American owners is a debit item that will contribute to a balance-of-payments deficit, yet there is nothing necessarily bad about the investment. On the opposite side the transfer of ownership of American firms to foreigners is a credit item that will contribute to a balance-of-payments surplus, but such loss of control over American firms is not necessarily desirable. Views about surpluses and deficits are further explored in the box on page 818.

There is nothing inherently good about a balance-of-payments surplus or inherently bad about a balance-of-payments deficit.

When a balance-of-payments deficit is caused by something considered undesirable (such as heavy dependence on Mideast oil), it may be that the government will seek a way to decrease such imports. When the same deficit is caused by something considered desirable (such as contributions

to our allies and underdeveloped nations to foster their economic development), the government may be willing to draw down its reserves for the purpose.

Whether desirable or undesirable, permanent deficits on the balance-of-payments accounts cannot be maintained, for the official reserves that are needed to finance such deficits are sure to be exhausted.

It might seem that a permanent surplus could be tolerated, but this is not the case either. If we have a permanent balance-of-payments surplus, some of our trading partners must have a permanent deficit. Unless we are prepared to give them the money, or allow them to increase their debts to us without limit, that too must be ended.

In the long term, when the balance of payments on current plus capital accounts is out of balance in either direction, something must be done. One approach is to maintain the exchange rate and adopt policies to shift the demand and supply curves to the point where the balance of payments is approximately zero. The government can do this through import or export restrictions, changes in interest rates, or a variety of other methods.

Another way is to allow exchange rates to change. Suppose the United States has a balance-of-payments surplus with respect to the United Kingdom. Holders of sterling are trying to make payments in dollars than holders of dollars wish to make in sterling. If exchange rates are free to vary, the dollar will appreciate and the pound depreciate until the balance of payments is in equilibrium.

If exchange rates are completely free to vary, balance-of-payments deficits and surpluses will be eliminated through exchange rate adjustments.

In today's world, while no country need have a balance-of-payments problem, many still have them. As long as governments intervene in foreign exchange markets, there will be balance-of-payments deficits and surpluses. Surpluses will occur whenever the currency is held below its equilibrium level. Persistent deficits will cause persistent loss of reserves; they are evidence that the government is trying to resist longer-term trends.

THE VOLUME OF TRADE, THE BALANCE OF TRADE, AND THE NEW MERCANTILISM

Media commentators, political figures, and much of the general public often judge the national balance of payments as they would the accounts of a single firm. Just as a firm is supposed to show a profit, the nation is supposed to secure a balance-of-payments surplus, with the benefits derived from international trade measured by the size of that surplus.

This view is closely related to the exploitation doctrine of international trade. Since one country's surplus is another country's deficit, one country's gain, judged by its surplus, must be another country's loss, judged by its deficit.

In holding such views today, people are echoing an ancient economic doctrine called *mercantilism*. The mercantilists were a group of economists who preceded Adam Smith. They judged the success of trade by the size of the trade balance. In many cases this doctrine made sense in terms of their objective, which was to use international trade as a means of building up the political and military power of the state rather than raising the living standards of its citizens. A balance-of-payments surplus allowed the nation (then and now) to acquire foreign exchange reserves. (In those days the reserves took the form of gold. Today they are a mixture of gold and claims on the currencies of other countries.) These reserves could then be used to pay armies, composed partly of foreign mercenaries; to purchase weapons from abroad; and generally to finance colonial adventures.

People who advocate this view in modern times are called *neo-mercantilists*. Insofar as their object is to increase the power of the state, they are choosing means that could achieve their ends. Insofar as they are drawing an analogy between what is a sensible objective for a business interested in its own material welfare and what is a sensible objective for a society interest in the material welfare of its citizens, their views are erroneous, for the analogy is false.

If we take the view that the object of economic activity is to promote the welfare and living standards of ordinary citizens, rather than the power of governments, then the mercantilist focus on the balance of trade makes no sense. The law of comparative advantage shows that average living standards are maximized by having individuals, regions, and countries specialize in the things they can produce comparatively best and then trading to obtain the things they can produce comparatively worst. The more specialization, the more trade.

On this view the gains from trade are to be judged by the volume of trade. A situation in which there is a *large volume* of trade but where each country has a *zero balance* of trade can thus be regarded as quite satisfactory.

To the business interested in private profit and to the government interested in the power of the state, it is the balance of payments that matters. To the person interested in the welfare of ordinary citizens, it is the volume of payments that matters.

But there is one great difference between this kind of balance-of-payments problem and that under fixed exchange rates. The government always has an available solution to its balance-of-payments problem: it can stop intervening in the market and let the exchange rate find its equilibrium level. This will not only end its balance-of-payments problem, it will end its loss of foreign exchange reserves.

But most countries find this is not as attractive an option as it first appears. In the absence of intervention the exchange rate may either fall—thus fueling domestic inflation—or rise—thus reducing foreign demand for domestic goods and causing unemployment. Thus domestic policy objectives must, at least in the short run, be weighed against the balance-of-payments problem.

In a world of more or less flexible exchange rates such as has existed since 1972, there are more important problems than the balance of payments—issues such as the extent of trade, the pattern of trade, and the desirability of letting foreigners purchase one's assets.

SUMMARY

1. International trade can occur only when it is possible to exchange the currency of one country for that of another. The exchange rate between two currencies is the amount of one currency that must be paid in order to obtain one unit of another currency. Where more than two currencies are involved, there will be an exchange rate between each pair of currencies.

2. The determination of exchange rates in the free market is simply an application of the laws of supply and demand studied in Chapter 5; the item being bought and sold is a nation's currency.

3. The demand for dollars arises from American exports of goods and services, long-term and short-term capital flows into the United States, and the desire of foreign banks, firms, and governments to use American dollars as an international medium of exchange or as part of their reserves.

4. The supply of dollars to purchase foreign currencies arises from American imports of goods and services, capital flows from the United States, and the desire of holders of dollars to decrease the size of their holdings.

5. A depreciation of the dollar lowers the foreign price of American exports and increases the quantity of dollars demanded; at the same time, it raises the dollar price of imports from abroad and thus lowers the quantity of dollars supplied to buy foreign exchange to be used to purchase foreign goods. Thus the demand curve for dollars is downward-sloping and the supply curve of dollars is upward-sloping when the quantities demanded and supplied are plotted against the price of dollars measured in terms of a foreign currency.

6. A currency will tend to appreciate on foreign exchange markets if there is a shift to the right of the demand curve or a shift to the left of the supply curve for its currency. Shifts in the opposite directions will tend to depreciate the currency. Such shifts are caused by such things as the prices of imports and exports, the rates of inflation in different countries, capital movements, structural changes, expectations about future trends in earnings and exchange rates, and the level of confidence in the currency as a source of reserves.

7. Actual transactions among the firms, households, and governments of various countries are kept track of and reported in the balance-of-payments accounts. In these accounts, any transaction that uses foreign exchange is recorded as a debit item and any transaction that produces foreign exchange is recorded as a credit item. If all transactions are recorded, the sum of all credit items necessarily equals the sum of all debit items since the foreign exchange that is bought must also have been sold.

8. Major categories in the balance-of-payments account are the balance of trade (exports minus imports), current account, capital account, and official financing. The so-called balance of payments is the balance of the current plus capital accounts; that is, it excludes the transactions on official account.

9. There is nothing inherently good or bad about deficits or surpluses. Persistent deficits or surpluses cannot be sustained because the former will eventually exhaust a country's foreign exchange reserves and the latter will do the same to a trading partner's reserves.

10. Balance-of-payment surpluses or deficits can be managed by the government's use of its foreign exchange reserves to buy or sell its currency, by policies that shift the demand and supply for the currency, or by allowing the exchange rate to seek its own level.

TOPICS FOR REVIEW

Foreign exchange and exchange rates
Appreciation, depreciation, revaluation, and devaluation
Sources of the demand for and supply of foreign exchange
Effects of capital flows on equilibrium exchange rates
The effects on exchange rates of inflation, interest rates, and expectations about exchange rates
The balance of trade and the balance of payments
Current and capital account
Official financing items
The balance of trade and the volume of trade

DISCUSSION QUESTIONS

1. What is the probable effect of each of the following on the exchange rate of a country, other things being equal?
   a. The quantity of oil imports is greatly reduced, but the value of imported oil is higher due to price increases.
   b. The country's inflation rate falls well below that of its trading partners.
   c. Rising labor costs of the country's manufacturers lead to a worsening ability to compete in world markets.
   d. The government greatly expands its gifts of food and machinery to underdeveloped countries.
   e. A major recession occurs with rising unemployment.
   f. The central bank raises interest rates sharply.
   g. More domestic oil is discovered and developed.
2. The president of the Federal Reserve Bank of New York said recently, "Inflation is the enemy in maintaining international trade." What might he have had in mind? Compare the behavior of fixed versus fluctuating exchange rates in a world:
   a. with no inflation but short-run fluctuations in prices

   b. with a substantial but similar degree of inflation everywhere in the world
   c. with sharply varying degrees of inflation
3. In recent years money wages have risen substantially faster in Canada than in the United States. Many Canadians have expressed the fear that their rapidly rising costs will price them out of U.S. markets. Did this fear make sense when the Canadian exchange rate was fixed relative to the American dollar? Does it make sense today when exchange rates are free to vary on the open market?
4. Indicate whether each of the following transactions increases the demand for dollars or the supply of dollars (or neither) on foreign exchange markets.
   a. IBM moves $10 million from bank accounts in the United States to banks in Paris to expand operations there.
   b. The U.S. government extends a grant of $3 million to the government of Peru, which Peru uses to buy farm machinery from a Chicago firm.
   c. Canadian investors, responding to higher profits of U.S. rather than Canadian corporations, buy stocks through the New York Stock Exchange.
   d. U.S. oil companies build a pipeline across Canada to transport Alaskan oil to the United States.
   e. Lower interest rates in New York than in London encourage British firms to borrow in the New York money market, converting the proceeds into pounds sterling for use at home.
   Do these transactions affect the balance of payments, exchange rates, or both?
5. "The necessity of the government to stabilize the balance of payments through the settlement account is a relic of the past. It was a by-product of the adherence to a policy of fixed exchange rates." Do you agree?
6. "If a country solves its balance-of-payments problems, it will have solved its foreign trade problems." Discuss.
7. Outline the reasoning behind the following summer 1983 newspaper headline: "Sterling Tumbles as British Interest Rates Weaken."
8. Explain the links between the following two sentences taken from a July 1983 newspaper story: "U.S. dollar hits 7½ year high" and "This happened in response to Friday's unexpected increase in M1."

43 INTERNATIONAL MONETARY SYSTEMS

The nations of the world have tried several different systems of international monetary management. No system has been fully satisfactory, and periods of crisis have alternated with periods of stability. Often changes in the system were introduced following a crisis. The gold standard, the Bretton Woods system, the International Monetary Fund, the Smithsonian Agreements, the European snake, the Jamaica Agreement—all are part of the history of international monetary systems in the twentieth century.

The century began with a system of fixed exchange rates under the gold standard. This system suffered periodic crises in the post-World War I years but did not collapse until the onset of the Great Depression. The 1930s were a period of experimentation with flexible, market-determined exchange rates. This experimentation ended with World War II, when governments fixed exchange rates and managed international payments with the main policy objective of waging war.

In 1944 an era of fixed exchange rates in peacetime was again instituted, this time by international agreement at a conference in Bretton Woods, New Hampshire. The Bretton Woods system lasted for over a quarter of a century, but its shortcomings and the periods of crisis it induced finally prevailed over its advantages and the periods of stability it afforded. After several attempts were made to patch it up in the 1970s, the system finally broke down and was gradually abandoned as countries turned one by one to market determined, flexible exchange rates.

The International Monetary Fund (also called the IMF and the Fund) was created to manage the Bretton Woods system. Under its original charter, the Fund had several tasks. It tried to ensure that countries kept their exchange rates fixed in the short run. It was supposed to consult with countries wishing to alter their exchange rates to make sure that the change was really needed to remove a persistent payments disequilibrium and that a single devaluation did not set off a self-canceling round of competitive devaluations. It also made loans—out of funds subscribed by member nations—to governments to support their exchange rates in the face of temporary payments deficits. The Bretton Woods system has been abandoned but the Fund survives, although its tasks have changed. For example, the Jamaica Agreement of 1976 amended the IMF charter to ratify the adoption of floating exchange rates and de-emphasize gold as a basis for the international payments system.

Even though the issues involved in international payments systems are understood by only a small number of international traders, bankers, financiers, and economists, the workings of these systems greatly affect the general public and its standard of living. In this chapter we review the principal systems and indicate when and why they ran into trouble.

FIXED AND FLEXIBLE EXCHANGE RATES

Among all the principal payments systems two extremes can be distinguished. The first is a system in which exchange rates are fixed at pre-announced "par" values that are changed only when the existing rate can no longer be defended. The gold standard was such a system, as was the Bretton Woods system. (These two systems and their declines are discussed in the appendix to this chapter.) The second is a system of freely fluctuating rates determined by market demand and supply in the absence of government intervention. Some countries have occasionally come close to this system, first in the 1930s and then since 1971.

Between these two extremes, a third, intermediate system, called a *managed* or *dirty float*, is found. In this system the central bank seeks to have some stabilizing influence on the exchange rate but does not try to fix it at a publicly announced par value. This system is really a combination of the other two. We study the two extreme cases of fully fixed and freely fluctuating rates for two reasons. First, understanding them is a prerequisite to understanding the managed float. Second, many economists and policymakers advocate returning to one or the other system at this time.

Characteristics of a Fixed Exchange Rate System

In a system of **fixed** or **pegged exchange rates,** each country's central bank intervenes in the foreign exchange market to prevent that country's exchange rate from going outside a narrow band on either side of its "par value."

This system presents one immediate difficulty: there is one less exchange rate to be determined than there are countries. In a two-country world containing only Japan and the United States, for example, if the bank of Japan fixes the exchange rate at 286 yen to the dollar, the Fed cannot fix a different rate making the dollar worth, say, 325 yen. Under the Bretton Woods system, all foreign countries fixed their exchange rate against the dollar. The Fed accepted these exchange rates and was the only central bank in the world that did not have to intervene to support a particular value of its currency.

Having picked a fixed exchange rate for their

currency against, say, the dollar, each foreign central bank must then manage matters so that the chosen rate can actually be maintained. It must be prepared to offset imbalances in demand and supply by government sales or purchases of foreign exchange. In the face of short-term fluctuations in market demand and supply, each bank can maintain its fixed exchange rate by entering the market and buying and selling as required to stabilize the price.

To do this the central bank has to hold reserves of acceptable foreign exchange. When there is an abnormally high supply of its country's currency on the market, the bank keeps the currency from falling in value by selling foreign exchange and buying up domestic currency. This depletes its reserves of foreign exchange. When there is an abnormally low supply of its country's currency on the foreign exchange market, the bank prevents the currency's appreciating in value by selling domestic currency in return for foreign exchange. This augments its stocks of foreign exchange.

As long as the central bank is trying to maintain an exchange rate that *equates demand and supply on average,* the policy can be successful. Sometimes the bank will be buying and other times selling, but its reserves will fluctuate around a constant average level.

If, however, there is a permanent shift in demand for or supply of a nation's currency on the foreign exchange market, the long-term equilibrium rate will move away from the pegged rate. It will then be very difficult to maintain the pegged rate. For example, if there is a major inflation in France while prices are stable in the United States, the equilibrium value of the franc will fall. In a free market the franc would depreciate and the dollar appreciate. But a fixed exchange rate is not a free-market rate. If the Bank of France persists in trying to maintain the original exchange rate, it will have to meet the excess demand for dollars by selling from its reserves of dollars. This policy can persist only as long as it has reserves that it is willing to spend to maintain its artificially high price of francs. The bank cannot do this indefinitely. Sooner or later the reserves that it has, and those that it can borrow, will be exhausted.

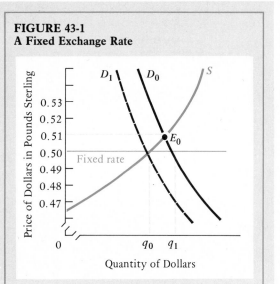

FIGURE 43-1
A Fixed Exchange Rate

When an exchange rate is fixed at other than the equilibrium rate, either excess demand or excess supply will persist. Suppose demand and supply curves of dollars in the absence of government controls are D_0 and S; equilibrium is at E_0, with a price of £0.51 per dollar. The equilibrium price of the pound is $1.96. Now the British authorities peg the price of the pound at $2.00; that is, they fix the price of the dollar at £0.50. They have overvalued the pound and overvalued the dollar. As a result there is an excess of dollars demanded over dollars supplied of q_0. To maintain the fixed rate it is necessary to shift either the demand curve or the supply curve (or both) so that the two intersect at the fixed rate. For example, demand might be shifted to D_1 by the British government's limiting imports. If the curves are not shifted, the fixed rate will have to be supported by the British government's supplying dollars in the amount of q_0q_1 per period out of its reserves.

The management of a fixed rate is illustrated in Figure 43-1. The example used is the maintenance by the Bank of England of a fixed exchange rate between pound sterling and the U.S. dollar.

When the fixed rate is not near the free-market equilibrium rate, controls of various sorts may be introduced in an attempt to shift the demand curve for foreign exchange so that it intersects the supply curve at a rate close to the controlled rate. This is usually done by restricting imports of goods and services or by restricting the export of capital. If the central bank cannot shift demand and supply in order to keep the equilibrium rate approximately as high as the fixed rate, they will have no alternative but to devalue their currency.

Problems with Fixed Exchange Rates

Three problems typically arise in a system of fixed exchange rates: (1) providing sufficient reserves, (2) adjusting to long-term trends, and (3) dealing with speculative crises.

Reserves to Accommodate Short-Term Fluctuations

Reserves are needed to accommodate short-term balance-of-payments fluctuations arising from the current and the capital accounts. On current account, normal trade is subject to many short-term variations, some systematic and some random. This means that even if the value of imports does equal the value of exports taken on average over several years, there may be considerable imbalances over shorter periods.

On a free market, fluctuations in current and capital account payments would cause the exchange rate to fluctuate. To prevent such fluctuations when rates are fixed, the monetary authorities buy and sell foreign exchange as required. These operations require the authorities to hold reserves of foreign exchange. If they run out of reserves, they cannot maintain the pegged rate.

As explained in the appendix, the Bretton Woods system had difficulty providing sufficient reserves. This was because the ultimate reserve was gold and there was not enough of it. As a result the world's central banks held much of their reserves in U.S. dollars and British pound sterling. Currencies that are widely held for this purpose are called **reserve currencies**. This system worked well enough as long as these reserve currencies had a stable value. However, in the mid 1960s fear of an impending devaluation of sterling arose, and in the early 1970s a similar fear arose regarding the

U.S. dollar. In both cases the fears were well founded: sterling was devalued in late 1967, and the dollar was devalued in 1971 and again in 1973.

The devaluation of a reserve currency reduces the value of the reserves of that currency held by the world's central banks. Fear that a devaluation will occur destroys the acceptability of a currency as a means of holding reserves. This is discussed further in the box.

The problem of providing reserves, although serious, should not be insurmountable in any future system of fixed rates. After all, a balanced portfolio composed of some holdings of all currencies could be held as reserves. This would reduce the risks from holding reserves. For whenever one currency falls in value against a second currency, the second currency rises in value against the first.

Adjusting to Long-Term Disequilibria

With fixed exchange rates, long-term disequilibria can be expected to develop because of lasting shifts in the demands for and supplies of foreign exchange. There are three important reasons for these shifts. First, different trading countries have different rates of inflation. Chapter 42 explained how these varying rates produce changes in the equilibrium rates of exchange and, if the rate is fixed, also produce excess supply or excess demand in each country's foreign exchange market. Second, changes in the demands for and supplies of imports and exports are associated with long-term economic growth. Because the economies of different countries grow at different rates, their demands for imports and their supplies of exports can be expected to shift at different rates. Third, structural changes, such as major new innovations or a change in the price of oil, cause major changes in imports and exports.

The associated shifts in demand and supply on the foreign exchange market imply that, even starting from a current account equilibrium with imports equal to exports at a given rate of exchange, there is no reason to believe that equilibrium will exist at the same rate of exchange 5 or 10 years later.

PROBLEMS FOR NATIONS WHOSE CURRENCY IS HELD AS A RESERVE

Under the Bretton Woods system the supply of gold was augmented by reserves of the key currencies, the U.S. dollar, and the British pound sterling. Because the need for reserves expanded much more rapidly than the gold stock after the World War II, the system required nations to hold an increasing fraction of reserves in national currencies, first sterling and then dollars.

While it is prestigious to have one's currency held as a reserve currency—and even advantageous as long as other countries are willing to increase their holdings of one's paper money without making claims on current output—there are both disadvantages and hazards for the country whose currency is involved.

Such a country is placed under great pressure not to devalue its currency. If it does devalue, owing to a severe balance-of-payments deficit, all countries holding that currency will find the value of their reserves diminished. If it tries to avoid devaluation, the fear that it may be unable to do so will in any case impair the usefulness of the currency as a reserve because other countries will become reluctant to hold it. The result may well be that the domestic policy of the country whose currency is the reserve becomes unduly subservient to the overriding need to maintain its exchange rate and its gold reserves.

The Loss of Confidence in the Dollar as a Reserve Currency

In the 1950s and 1960s America ran frequent deficits on the sum of current and capital accounts. This resulted largely from American loans, investments, and contributions to other nations who were rebuilding their economies after World War II. As long as other nations were willing to accumulate dollar holdings, this caused no problem; indeed the buildup of dollars in foreign exchange reserves provided the growth in reserves that was needed to finance the steadily growing volume of world trade. But a declining fraction of gold backing for the dollar slowly eroded confidence in it as a reserve currency.

The effect of the dollar devaluations of the early 1970s. The devaluation of the dollar in 1971 (7.9 percent) and 1973 (11 percent) automatically reduced the value of the exchange reserves of everyone holding dollars. Had everyone believed that these were just isolated adjustments, they might well have licked their wounds and gone on as before. But no fundamental changes arose either in American policy or in international financial arrangements. Thus many believed that the past devaluations were but preludes to inevitable future devaluations.

Fear of further devaluations not only made holders of dollars reluctant to increase their dollar holdings but actually led many prudent holders to want to decrease reliance on such a shaky reserve. As people tried to get rid of dollars, the exchange rate began to slide. Between 1970 and 1973 the dollar declined 22 percent against the yen and 30 percent against the mark. From 1973 to early 1980 it dropped an additional 23 percent against the yen and 31 percent against the mark. The decreasing value of the dollar reduced the adequacy of most countries' dollar reserves and threatened their financial stability.

Attempts to flee from the dollar. While one country (or one bank) can readily reduce its holdings of dollars by buying gold or other currencies, the whole world cannot do so unless alternative sources of international reserves are available. One cause of the startling rise in the price of gold in 1979–1980 from $250 to over $900 an ounce was the attempt of many holders of dollars to flee to gold. Such attempted flights from the dollar will end only if the causes of the decline in demand for dollars are eliminated, or if an adequate alternative international reserve is created to replace it. As noted later in the text, the return to stable prices in the United States has restored some faith in the dollar, and use of the SDR has grown. But few observers are complacent enough to believe that these developments provide a long-run solution.

The rate of exchange that will lead to a balance-of-payments equilibrium will tend to change over time; over a decade the change can be substantial.

Governments may react to long-term disequilibria in at least three ways.

1. The exchange rate can be changed whenever it is clear that a balance-of-payments deficit or surplus is the result of a long-term shift in demands and supplies in the foreign exchange market and not the result of some transient factor.

2. Domestic price levels can be allowed to change in an attempt to make the present fixed exchange rates become the equilibrium rates. To restore equilibrium, countries with overvalued currencies need to have deflations and countries with undervalued currencies need to have inflations. But changes in domestic price levels have all sorts of domestic repercussions. Deflations are difficult and costly to accomplish (e.g., reductions in aggregate demand intended to lower the price level are likely to raise unemployment), and often the explicit goal of government policy is to avoid inflation. One might expect governments to be more willing to change exchange rates—which can be done by a stroke of a pen—than to try to change their price levels.

3. Restrictions can be imposed on trade and foreign payments. Imports and foreign spending by tourists and governments can be restricted, and the export of capital can be slowed or even stopped. Surplus countries are often quick to criticize such restrictions on international trade and payments. But as long as exchange rates are fixed and price levels prove difficult to manipulate, the deficit countries have little option but to restrict the quantity of foreign exchange their residents are permitted to obtain in order to equate it to the quantity available.

Since restrictions on trade and foreign payments are undesirable in our modern world economy, characterized by large-scale international trade and foreign investment, and since deflations of the price level are difficult and costly to bring about, most countries will want to preserve the possibility of making occasional changes in their exchange rates even if fixed rates are the main rule of the day.

The operation of fixed exchanges and the problems they entail are illustrated by the Bretton Woods system. A detailed discussion of its performance and its demise is contained in the appendix to this chapter. Here we note that although most countries defended their exchange rates in the face of crises, there were still major rounds of exchange rate adjustments. Because exchange rates did have to be changed from time to time, the system of fixed rates under the Bretton Woods agreement was called an **adjustable peg system**.

Handling Speculative Crises

When enough people begin to doubt the government's ability to maintain the current exchange rate, speculative crises develop. The most important reason for such crises is that, over time, equilibrium exchange rates get further and further away from any given set of fixed rates. When the disequilibrium becomes obvious to everyone, traders and speculators come to believe that a realignment of rates is due. At such a time, there is a rush to buy currencies expected to be revalued and a rush to sell currencies expected to be devalued. Even if the authorities take drastic steps to remove the payments deficit, there may be doubt that these measures will work before the exchange reserves are exhausted. Speculative flows of funds can reach very large proportions, and it may be impossible to avoid changing the exchange rate under such pressure.

Under an adjustable peg system, speculators have an easy opportunity to make large profits since everyone knows which way an exchange rate will be changed if it is to be changed at all.

As the equilibrium value of a country's currency changes, possibly under the impact of a high rate of inflation, it becomes obvious to everyone that the central bank is having more and more difficulty holding the pegged rate. So when a crisis arises, speculators sell the country's currency. If it is devalued, they can buy it back at a lower price and earn a profit. If it is not devalued they can buy it back at the price at which they sold it and lose only the commission costs on the deal. This asymmetry, with speculators having a chance to make large profits by risking only a small loss, was what eventually undid the Bretton Woods system. As trade became more unsettled, as differences in inflation rates became greater, and as exchange reserves became smaller, more frequent adjustments in the pegged rates were necessary. Seeing these adjustments coming, speculators sold currencies under pressure to be devalued and bought currencies under pressure to be revalued. The resulting massive movements of speculative funds destabilized the system and were a major cause of its abandonment in the early 1970s.

Could anything be done to reduce the problem of speculative crises in some future adjustable peg system? Probably not. Speculative crises are one of the most intractable problems of any adjustable peg system. The impact of such crises might be reduced if governments had more adequate reserves. When a speculative crisis precedes an exchange rate adjustment, however, more adequate reserves may simply mean that speculators will make larger profits. They will be able to sell more of the currency about to be devalued and to buy the currency about to be revalued before the monetary authorities are forced to act.

During the Bretton Woods period, governments tended to resist changing their exchange rates until they had no alternative. This made the situation so obvious that speculators could hardly lose, and their actions set off the final crises that forced exchange rate readjustments. If changes could be made more frequently and before they became inevitable, the number of speculative crises might diminish, and the system of fixed exchange rates might appear more viable. Such changes, however, would remove the day-to-day certainty associated with this system that was one of its chief advantages. Moreover, a surprise change might lead to suspicion that a devaluation was made to gain a competitive advantage for a country's exports rather than to remove a fundamental disequilibrium. After all, governments are not supposed to devalue under an adjustable peg system until it is *clear* that they are faced with a fundamental disequilibrium. If this is clear to them, it is also likely to be clear to ordinary traders and speculators.

Flexible Exchange Rates

Under a system of flexible exchange rates, demand and supply determines the rates without any government intervention. Such rates are called free, or **flexible** or **floating exchange rates.** Since the foreign exchange market always clears, the government can turn its attention to domestic problems of inflation and unemployment, leaving the balance of payments to take care of itself—at least so went the theory before flexible rates were introduced.

For reasons that we shall analyze later in this chapter, this optimistic picture did not materialize when the world went over to flexible exchange rates. Free-market fluctuations in rates were far greater—and hence potentially more upsetting to the performance of national economies and to the flow of international trade—than many economists had anticipated. As a result, central banks have felt the need to intervene quite frequently, and extensively, to stabilize exchange rates.

Managed Floats

The difference between the present system and Bretton Woods is that central banks no longer publicly announce par values for exchange rates that they are committed in advance to defend even at heavy cost. Central banks are thus free to adjust their exchange rate targets as circumstances change. Sometimes they leave the rate completely free to fluctuate, and at other times they interfere actively to alter the exchange rate from its free-market value. Such a system is called a **managed float** or a **dirty float.**

Some countries have opted for what is called a *currency block* by pegging their exchange rates against each other and then indulging in a joint float against the outside world. The best-known currency block is the European **snake.** Under this arrangement the countries of the EEC, with the exception of the United Kingdom, maintain fixed rates among their own currencies but allow them to float as a block against the dollar. Many other countries maintain stable values for their currencies in terms of *one* of the three major trading currencies (the U.S. dollar, the British pound sterling, and the French franc). Their rates then fluctuate against the other two major currencies.

To manage exchange rates, central banks must hold foreign exchange reserves. One major form in which reserves are held is U.S. dollars; another, and one that is growing in size, is the **special drawing rights** (**SDRs**) held with the IMF. First introduced in 1969, SDRs were designed to provide a supplement to existing reserve assets. A Special Drawing Account was set up and was kept separate from all other operations of the Fund. Each member country of the Fund was assigned an SDR quota that was guaranteed in terms of a fixed gold value. Each country could use its quota to acquire an equivalent amount of convertible currencies from other participants. SDRs could be used without prior consultation with the Fund but only to cope with balance-of-payments difficulties. SDR allocations have grown from about $10 billion in 1970 to over $40 billion in 1982.

What Determines the Exchange Rate in a Floating-Rate System?

One of the most surprising results to supporters of floating exchange rates has been the degree of volatility of exchange rates. Why have they been so volatile?

The trend value of exchange rates is approximately determined by their **purchasing power parity** (**PPP**) value. The PPP exchange rate is the one that holds constant the relative price levels in two countries *when measured in a common currency.* For example, assume that the U.S. price level rises by 20 percent while the German price level rises by only 5 percent over the same period. The PPP value of the German mark then appreciates by approximately 15 percent. This would mean that in Germany the prices of all goods (both German-produced goods and imported American goods) would rise by 5 percent measured in German marks, while in the United States the prices of all goods (both American-produced goods and imports from Germany) would rise by 20 percent measured in U.S. dollars. Basically, the PPP rate adjusts so

that the relative price of the two nations' goods (measured in either currency) is unchanged because the change in the relative values of two currencies compensates exactly for differences in national inflation rates. If the actual exchange rate equals the PPP rate, the competitive positions of producers in the two countries will be unchanged. Firms located in countries with high inflation rates will still be able to sell their output on international markets since the exchange rate adjusts to offset the effect of the higher domestic prices.

Figure 43-2 shows that the exchange rate between dollars and sterling has followed the PPP rate over the long run. But notice also how large the fluctuations are around the PPP rate. During the Bretton Woods period of fixed exchange rates the advocates of floating rates argued that speculators would stabilize the actual rates within a narrow band around the PPP rates. The argument was that since everyone knew the normal value was the PPP rate, deviations would quickly be removed by speculators seeking a profit when the rate returned to its PPP level. To illustrate, suppose the current PPP rate is $2.00 = £1.00 and that the actual rate then falls to $1.90 = £1.00. Speculators would rush to buy pounds at $1.90 each, expecting to sell them for $2.00 when the rate returns to its PPP level. This very action would raise the demand for sterling and help push its value back toward $2.00.

Such speculative behavior would stabilize the exchange rate near its PPP value if speculators could be sure that the deviations would be small and short-lived. But in practice the swings around the PPP rate have been wide and have lasted for long periods. Thus, if sterling fell to $1.90, speculators would know that it could go as low as $1.60 and stay there for quite a while before returning to $2.00. In that case it might be worth speculating on a price of $1.80 next week rather than a price of $2.00 in some indefinite future.

The wide swings in exchange rates that have occurred shows that speculative buying and selling cannot be relied on to hold exchange rates very close to their PPP values continuously.

But why have these wide fluctuations occurred? There are many reasons, and one of the most im-

FIGURE 43-2
Actual and PPP Exchange Rate, U.S. Dollar and Pound Sterling, 1972–1983

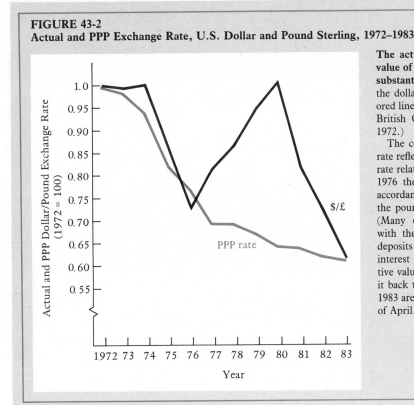

The actual exchange rate follows the trend value of the PPP exchange rate but fluctuates substantially around it. The black line shows the dollar/pound exchange rate while the colored line shows the ratio of the U.S. CPI to the British CPI. (Both series are set to 1.00 in 1972.)

The continual decline of the PPP exchange rate reflects United Kingdom's higher inflation rate relative to that of the United States. Until 1976 the relative value of the pound fell in accordance with the PPP rate, but after 1976 the pound appreciated sharply through 1980. (Many observers associate this appreciation with the onset of production from large oil deposits in the North Sea and with very high interest rates in 1979–1980.) In 1980 the relative value of the pound began to fall, bringing it back toward its PPP value. (The figures for 1983 are those for the exchange rate at the end of April.)

portant is associated with international differences in interest rates.

Exchange Rate Overshooting

Suppose that the Fed forces American interest rates above those ruling in other major financial centers. A rush to lend money out at the profitable rates found in the United States will lead to an appreciation of the dollar.

This process will stop only when the rise in value of the dollar on foreign exchange markets is large enough that investors expect it subsequently to fall in value. This expected future fall then just offsets the interest premium from lending funds in U.S. dollars.

To illustrate, assume that interest rates are 4 percentage points higher in New York than in London due to a very restrictive monetary policy in the United States. Investors believe the PPP rate is $2.00 = £1.00 but, as they rush to buy dollars to take advantage of the higher U. S. interest rates they drive the rate to, say, $1.80 = £1.00. (Since £1.00 now buys fewer dollars, sterling has depreciated and since it takes fewer dollars to buy £1.00, the dollar has appreciated.) They do not believe this rate will be sustained and instead expect the dollar to lose value at 4 percent per year. Now foreign investors are indifferent between lending money in New York and doing so in London. The extra 4 percent of interest they earn in New York per year is exactly offset by the 4 percent they expect to lose when they turn their money back into their own currency.

Any policy that raises domestic interest rates above world levels will cause the external value of the domestic currency to appreciate enough to create an expected future depreciation sufficient to offset the interest differential.

BEGGAR-MY-NEIGHBOR POLICIES PAST AND PRESENT

The onset of the Great Depression of the 1930s brought an end to the long-standing stability of the gold standard and ushered in a period of experimentation in exchange regimes. Experiments were tried with both fixed and fluctuating rates.

But the overriding feature of the decade was that considerations of massive unemployment came to dominate economic policies in virtually every country, and all devices, including exchange rate manipulations, seemed fair game for dealing with them. Many of the policies adopted at this time were acts of desperation that would have made long-term sense only if other countries had not also been in crisis. Governments tended not to consider the long-term effects on trade, or on their trading partners, of the policies they adopted, hoping to gain short-term advantages before their policies provoked the inevitable reaction from others.

The use of devaluations to ease domestic unemployment rested on a simple and superficially plausible line of analysis: if a country has unemployed workers at home, why not substitute home production for imports and thus give jobs to one's citizens instead of to foreigners? One way to do this is to urge, say, Americans to "buy American." Another, probably more effective, way is to lower the prices of domestic goods relative to those of imports. The devaluation of one's currency does this by making foreign goods that much more expensive. (A 10 percent devaluation, other than equal, means that it will take 10 percent more domestic money to buy the same imports; this is equivalent to a 10 percent rise in the prices of all foreign goods.)

Of course, if this policy works other countries will find *their* exports falling and unemployment rising as a consequence. Because such policies attempt to solve one country's problems by inflicting them on others, they are called **beggar-my-neighbor policies** and are described as attempts to "export one's unemployment."

In a situation of inadequate world demand, a beggar-my-neighbor policy on the part of one country can work only in the unlikely event that other countries do not try to protect themselves. A situation in which all countries devalue their currencies in an attempt to gain a competitive advantage over one another is called a situation of **competitive devaluations.**

This is what happened during the 1930s. One country would devalue its currency in an attempt to reduce its imports and stimulate exports. But because other countries were suffering from the same kinds of problems of unemployment, they did not sit idly by. Retaliation was swift, and devaluation followed devaluation. But the simultaneous attempt of all countries to cut imports without suffering a comparable cut in exports is bound to be self-defeating.

If the Fed is trying to achieve some long-run monetary target without causing too much short-term unemployment, these capital flows can be very disturbing. A central bank that is seeking to meet a monetary target must put up with some large fluctuations in the exchange rate. In particular, if a restrictive monetary policy is needed to hold the money supply on target, the resulting high interest rates may lead to a large overshooting of the external value of the currency above its PPP rate. This may put export- and import-competing industries under temporary but very severe pressure from foreign competition.

The other side of this coin is that the high value

When unemployment is due to insufficient world aggregate demand, it cannot be cured by measures designed to redistribute among nations the fixed and inadequate total of demand.

These policies, along with other restrictive trade policies such as import duties, export subsidies, quotas, and prohibitions, led to a declining volume of world trade and brought no relief from the worldwide depression. Moreover, they contributed to a loss of faith in the economic system and in the ability of either economists or politicians to cope with economic crises.

To avoid a recurrence of the beggar-my-neighbor policies of the 1930s, trading nations designed some important institutions. The International Monetary Fund (IMF) was supposed to reduce the chances of competitive devaluations, and the General Agreement on Tariffs and Trade (GATT) was to reduce the chances of competitive increases in tariffs and other trade restrictions. These institutions worked well for over 30 years.

In 1980 the U.S. embarked on tight monetary policy, driving up U.S. interest rates. Just as expansionary monetary policy in the face of world recession tended to "export unemployment" by leading to a depreciation of the home currency and reducing the demand for foreign goods, tight monetary policy in the face of the world inflation tends to "export inflation" by leading to an appreciation of the home currency

and raising the demand for foreign goods. As noted in the text, most foreign governments resisted this by also adopting tight monetary policy. This led the world into the serious recession of 1981–1983.

Under the extreme pressures of this difficult economic situation, beggar-my-neighbor pressures surfaced, and many governments found them hard to resist politically. American voters in November 1982 showed very strong support for advocates of increased tariffs to protect hard-pressed import-competing industries in America. Many countries negotiated unofficial quotas restricting the importation of Japanese cars. European agricultural protectionism nearly wrecked the GATT negotiations in December 1982. Earlier in the year Sweden initiated what appeared to be a beggar-my-neighbor devaluation of the kroner. Less developed countries sought covert ways of protecting their own infant industries and complained, with some justice, that the developed nations paid lip service to, rather than really acting on, the slogan of "trade not aid." It was clear that great pressure was being put on the whole post-war fabric designed to encourage trade and discourage beggar-my-neighbor policies. The longer the recession, the more alarming are the pressures. Only time will tell how much damage has been done to this carefully constructed fabric of post-war international cooperation.

of the U.S. dollar creates inflationary pressure in other countries. U.S. goods become much more expensive abroad, thus putting upward pressure on foreign prices and wages. Authorities in those countries are faced with the uncomfortable choice of accepting this increased inflation or raising their own interest rates and thus maintaining their exchange rates in terms of the U.S. dollar. In the early 1980s many foreign central banks chose this latter option, and the tight U.S. monetary policies were quickly imitated in other countries. This combined monetary contraction contributed to the severity of the world recession as discussed further in the box.

CURRENT PROBLEMS

The shift from fixed rates to a system of managed flexible rates has not ended the recurring crises which continue for several reasons.

The Lack of an Alternative to the Dollar As a Reserve Currency

Governments operating dirty floats need reserves, just as do governments operating adjustable pegs. The search for an adequate supply of reserves has continued unabated since the demise of the Bretton Woods system. In January 1976 agreement was reached for a 30 percent average increase in the quotas of funds that member countries must provide to the IMF and from which the IMF can make loans to countries wishing to support their exchange rates. But the increase in quotas has done no more than keep up with the growth in the volume of world trade. SDRs have grown in importance, but they have certainly not provided a substitute for the enormous role of the dollar. The commitment to lower inflation initiated by the Reagan administration in 1980 has restored some confidence in the dollar as a reserve asset. But overall these developments have not been seen as long-term solutions to the reserve problem.

While it is possible that some other national currencies will take over the reserve currency role played by the dollar, this is not likely. First, such a replacement would require a massive shift in reserves from dollars to the new currency. Unless this were carefully managed, it would result in a sharp depreciation of the dollar that would hurt the United States and all other holders of dollars. Second, no other country is likely to accept for its currency the role of major international reserve. As we saw in the box on page 825, the reserve currency role results in major problems and limits the scope of domestic policy action. The American experience has not gone unnoticed.

Why does the world not turn to an international paper reserve system based on SDRs or some similar creation? Such a solution has much support from academic economists, who see an appropriate international institution managing the supply of international currency to accommodate growth and to avoid inflation.

Critics of such a system—among them most of the world's central bankers—distrust the concept of an international paper currency, pointing out that few countries have managed their own money supplies effectively. However difficult the task of the Fed may be, the task of a World Reserve Bank would be more difficult. Further, private acceptance and use of the SDR has been virtually nonexistent, indicating the enormous difficulties inherent in creating a new currency.

Some who are skeptical of an international paper monetary standard have urged a return to the gold standard. This approach has critical disadvantages. In fact the IMF and the U.S. government have at various times taken the lead in the attempt to "demonetize" gold completely.

For the moment at least, the world cannot agree on an international monetary reserve. Until it does there will be crises whenever there is a desire to shift from one to another of the multiple sources of reserves: dollars, gold, SDRs, marks, francs, and yen. The speculative opportunities inherent in such a system remain large, as evidenced by the recent behavior of the price of gold shown in Figure 43-3.

The Impact of OPEC

The most serious recent event affecting the future payments system—and indeed the whole of international economic relations—was the tenfold increase in the price of oil by the OPEC cartel. These price rises generated an unprecedented imbalance in the international economic system in the form of a massive payments surplus for the oil producers and a corresponding deficit for the oil-importing countries. The excess purchasing power in the hands of oil producers has come to be called **petrodollars.** The cumulative stock of petrodollars may well exceed $500 billion. Petrodollars cause several different kinds of problems, some of them short term, others long term in nature.

FIGURE 43-3
The Price of Gold

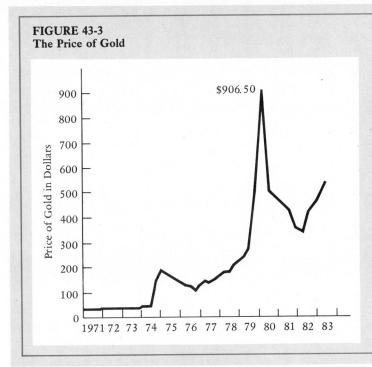

Gold soared in value and proved highly volatile after convertibility of the dollar was suspended in 1973. The two devaluations of the dollar under the gold exchange standard in the early 1970s are barely visible. The course of gold speculation is seen in the subsequent experience. Gold does not exhibit the sort of price stability desired in an international source of reserve assets.

Short-term problems of industrialized countries. Most petrodollars will eventually be used for the purchase of consumption goods and services or investment goods from industrialized countries. In time these countries will thus find their exports to the oil producers rising. But the oil-producing countries could not spend their oil revenues on goods and services as fast as they were earned in the late 1970s.[1] Nor could the industrialized oil-consuming countries produce the goods and services at the rate necessary for all the oil revenues to be spent without creating enormous inflationary pressures.[2]

Thus, in the short term the OPEC countries had

---

[1] There is a limit to the speed with which any country can absorb foreign goods, and many oil-producing countries were at that limit. Ships sometimes wait months to unload for want of dock capacity, unloaded goods sometimes sit in wharfside stockpiles for months—even years—for want of transportation capacity, and so on.

[2] Production of the goods produces factor incomes and thus adds to domestic demand, while export of the goods removes them from domestic markets and thus reduces domestic supplies.

excess dollars. They also had an understandable desire to earn a return on those funds. One way was to invest their surplus revenues in the advanced industrialized nations, thereby returning on capital account the purchasing power extracted from the current accounts of the oil-importing nations. This situation creates many serious problems. One of the most important concerns the havoc brought to foreign exchange markets when surplus oil funds are invested in liquid assets and switched between currencies in response to changes in interest rates and expected capital gains arising from possible exchange rate alterations. This problem is further discussed below.

Surplus petrodollars can also be used speculatively, and many observers believe that a good part of the wild rise and sudden fall in gold prices in 1979–1980 was due to just such a use of petrodollars.

Short-term problems of the underdeveloped countries. Consider a country such as Kenya, for which the OPEC price increase turned a small trade surplus into a massive deficit overnight. The country was unable to generate revenues quickly enough to pay its oil bill, yet it could sharply decrease its use of oil only at the cost of a great slowdown in its domestic economy.

The IMF stepped in with loan arrangements to help such countries most severely affected by the rising oil prices, the repayments of maturing loans were deferred, and the OPEC nations established a fund for short-term loans to such countries. Thus the purely short-term problems can be, and have been, solved through international cooperation and recognition of the need for accommodation on the part of creditor nations.

Many oil exporting countries also borrowed heavily on the expectation of rising oil prices. By early 1983, however, OPEC had lowered its price, and further price cuts appeared possible. Many international loans appear to be threatened, including those made by large private banks to LDCs such as Mexico, which is heavily dependent on oil exports for repayment. The risk of a major default hangs over the system, and the IMF again finds itself facing the likelihood of helping with rescheduling and otherwise organizing repayments of large international loans.

The Challenge for the 1980s

The 1970s witnessed the replacement of a system of managed fixed exchange rates by a system of managed flexible exchange rates. The problems of the latter may have been revealed by the events of the decade, but they cannot be said to have been solved. Officials understand the need both to develop an adequate reserve unit not tied to any national currency and to devise workable guidelines for managing flexible rates.

An International Reserve Currency

Many economists believe that a controlled international money supply based on SDRs and constantly expanded to keep pace with the volume of world trade is the best answer to the reserve prob-

lem. But an international paper currency, like a national currency, cannot work until there is confidence in it. The turmoil of the last two decades has done nothing to create the climate of confidence required for the complete demonetization of gold and the reduction of the role of the dollar as the international medium of exchange. Flawed though either gold or the dollar is as a reserve, each seems better (at this date) to many of the world's bankers than SDRs or similar "pieces of paper."

The Management of Exchange Rates

The managed aspect of managed floating rates poses several potential problems for the international monetary system. They include the possibilities of mutually inconsistent exchange rate stabilization policies, competitive exchange rate depreciation, and instability of exchange rates in the face of speculative pressures. To help avoid these problems the IMF has issued guidelines for exchange rate management. The guidelines emphasize that exchange rate policy is a matter for international consultation and surveillance by the IMF and that intervention practices by individual central banks should be based on three principles: (1) exchange authorities should prevent sudden and disproportionate short-term movements in exchange rates and ensure an orderly adjustment of exchange rates to longer-term pressures; (2) in consultation with the IMF, countries should establish a target zone for the medium-term values of their exchange rates and keep the actual rate within that target zone; and (3) countries should recognize that exchange rate management involves joint responsibilities and is not just the responsibility of the individual country in question.

The experiences of the 1970s have underlined one of the most important problems of managed floating rates not yet solved: coping with the massive volume of short-term funds that can be switched very rapidly between financial centers. Short-term capital flows forced the abandonment of exchange rates that had been agreed on in 1971 and have often caused violent fluctuations in floating rates since then. Severe "currency misalignments" have arisen and persisted, rendering uncompetitive on world markets the export- and import-competing sectors in countries with overvalued currencies while creating enormous profit opportunities in countries with undervalued currencies. Capital flows often prevent the quick return of exchange rates to their PPP values.

Various attempts have been made to limit such capital flows. Italy has adopted a two-tier foreign exchange market, with one price for foreign exchange to finance current account transactions and another price (and another set of controls) for foreign exchange to finance capital movements. Germany has used direct controls on overseas borrowing. There has also been a considerable extension of arrangements under which central banks in surplus countries lend the funds they are accumulating back to central banks in deficit countries. Through such arrangements the ability of banks to maintain stable exchange rates in the face of short-term speculative flights of capital are enhanced.

The major problem in managing speculative flows is to identify them accurately. Experience suggests that exchange rate management can smooth out temporary fluctuations but cannot resist underlying trends in equilibrium rates caused by relative inflation rates, structural changes, and persistent nonspeculative capital flows. In day-to-day management it is not always easy to distinguish among them.

The Need for Cooperation

One of the most impressive aspects of the international payments history of the last 30 years has been the steady rise of effective international cooperation. When the gold standard collapsed and the Great Depression overwhelmed the countries of the world, "every nation for itself" was the rule of the day. Rising tariffs, competitive exchange rate devaluations, and all forms of beggar-my-neighbor policies abounded.

After World War II the countries of the world cooperated in bringing the Bretton Woods system and the IMF into being. The system itself was far

from perfect, and it finally broke down as a result of its own internal contradictions. But the international cooperation that was necessary to set up the system survived the collapse of the system itself. The joint cooperative actions of central banks allowed them to weather speculative crises in the 1970s that would have forced them to devalue their currencies in the 1950s.

Thus the collapse of Bretton Woods did not plunge the world into the same chaos that followed the breakdown of the gold standard. The world was also better able to cope with the terrible strains caused by the sharp rise in oil prices in the 1970s. Of course enormous oil-related problems remain, and they are matters for continuing international dialogue.

Whatever the problems of the future, the world has a better chance of solving them—or even just learning to live with them—when its countries cooperate through the IMF and other international organizations than when each country seeks its own selfish solution without concern for the interests of others.

One of the most disturbing consequences of the Great Recession of 1982–1983 was the severe straining of the carefully constructed fabric of international cooperation as we saw in Chapter 41. There we saw that many countries flirted with beggar-my-neighbor policies of trade restriction and competitive devaluations under the stress of falling domestic national income and rising unemployment rates. Only time will tell whether this activity is just an aberration that will pass with the end of the recession or the beginning of a new trend away from the international economic cooperation that has served the world so well from 1945 to 1980.

SUMMARY

1. Various systems of international monetary arrangements have been tried. All involve aspects of two extreme systems—fixed exchange rates and flexible exchange rates.

2. Under fixed or pegged exchange rates, the central bank intervenes in the foreign exchange market to maintain the exchange rate at or near a preannounced "par value." To do this the central bank must hold sufficient stocks of foreign exchange reserves. Reserves have historically been held in the form of gold or reserve currencies, particularly the dollar. The SDR is a relatively new international paper money meant to provide additional international reserves linked neither to gold nor to the U.S. dollar.

3. Any adjustable peg system must face three major problems: (1) providing sufficient international reserves, (2) adjusting to long-term trends in receipts and payments, and (3) handling periodic speculative crises.

4. Under a system of flexible exchange rates, the exchange rate is market determined by supply and demand without any government intervention.

5. Since their adoption in the mid 1970s, flexible exchange rates have fluctuated substantially. As a result central banks have often intervened to stabilize the fluctuations. Thus the present system is best described as one of managed, or dirty, floating.

6. Fluctuations in exchange rates can be understood as fluctuations around a trend value that is determined by the purchasing power parity (PPP) rate. The PPP rate adjusts in response to differences in national inflation rates.

7. Current problems include the need to find an adequate reserve not tied to a national currency, to accommodate both the short-term and the longerterm impact of OPEC, and to develop rules for managing flexible exchange rates. A continuing commitment to international cooperation will help the world cope with these problems.

TOPICS FOR REVIEW

Fixed and flexible exchange rates
Managed floats
The Bretton Woods system

Exchange rate overshooting
Petrodollars

DISCUSSION QUESTIONS

1. What role in international payments does or did gold play under (a) the gold standard, (b) the adjustable peg Bretton Woods system, and (c) the present system? In 1974 *Barron's* had an editorial headed, "Monetary Reform and Gold: You Can't Have One Without the Other." Does the gold price experience of the 1970s bear out this editorial opinion?

2. "The price of gold soared as much as $50 an ounce on European bullion markets today. Dealers attributed it to fears that the president's economic policy might touch off more worldwide inflation. The dollar and the pound both declined sharply against the mark and the franc in busy trading on foreign exchange markets."

   This quotation from the *New York Times* was made during the administration of one of the following presidents. Guess which one, and explain your answer.

William H. Taft	1909–1913
Franklin D. Roosevelt	1933–1945
Harry S. Truman	1945–1953
John F. Kennedy	1961–1963
Jimmy Carter	1977–1981

3. Might a person who regards inflation as the number one economic danger favor a return to the pre-1914 gold standard? Would you predict non-inflationary results if in order to restore the gold standard, the price of gold had to be set at $1,600 per ounce, either all at once or gradually?

4. The dollar is no longer convertible into gold because of a change in U.S. policy. Does this lack of conversion make the dollar any less useful as an international medium of exchange?

5. Are Americans benefited or hurt when the dollar is the standard form of international reserves?

6. "Under a flexible exchange rate system no country need suffer unemployment, for if its prices are low enough there will be more than enough demand to keep its factories and farms fully occupied." The evidence suggests that flexible rates have not generally eliminated unemployment. Can you explain why? Can changing exchange rates ever cure unemployment?

7. The OPEC oil price increase has caused grave problems in international payments and increased the need for IMF loans. Why has not market adjustment of exchange rates solved the problem?

PART ELEVEN

ECONOMIC GROWTH
AND
COMPARATIVE SYSTEMS

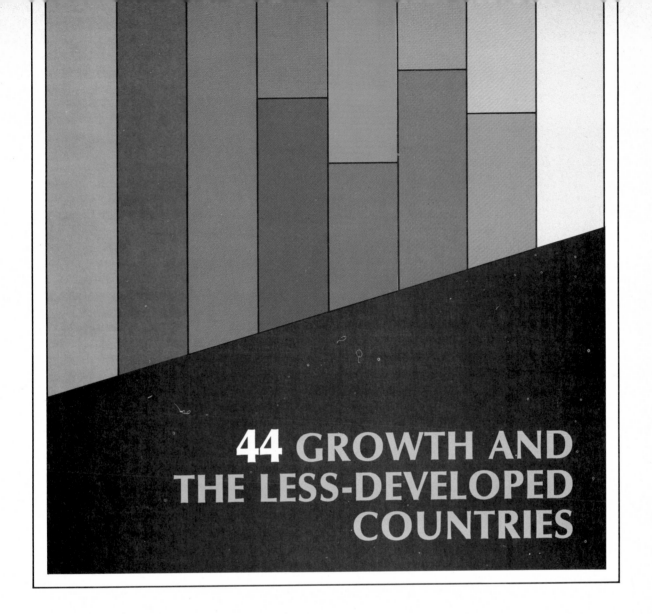

44 GROWTH AND THE LESS-DEVELOPED COUNTRIES

It is only about 10,000 years since human beings became food *producers* rather than food *gatherers*. It is only within the last few centuries that a significant proportion of the world's population could look forward to anything but a hard struggle to wrest a subsistence from a reluctant nature. The concept of leisure combined with high consumption standards as a right to be enjoyed by all is new in human history.

THE UNEVEN PATTERN OF DEVELOPMENT

Table 44-1 repays careful study. It shows how few people have made the transition from poverty to relative comfort. There are more than 4.5 billion people alive today, but the wealthy parts of the world—where people work no more than 40 or 50

TABLE 44–1 INCOME AND POPULATION DIFFERENCES AMONG GROUPS OF COUNTRIES, 1981

Classification (based on GNP per capita in 1976 U.S. dollars)	Number of countries (1)	GNP (billions) (2)	Population (millions) (3)	GNP per capita (4)	Percentage of the world's GNP (5)	Percentage of the world's population (6)	Growth rate[a] (7)
I Less than $400	28	$ 316	1,110	$ 285	3.2	38.2	1.4
II $401–1,000	26	310	517	601	3.2	17.8	4.4
III $1,001–3,000	29	955	466	2,050	9.4	16.0	4.9
IV $3,001–10,000	24	3,094	392	7,894	31.6	13.5	3.8
V More than $10,000	15	5,109	424	12,051	52.2	14.5	4.5

Source: International Financial Statistics Yearbook, 1982; Handbook of Economic Statistics, 1982.
[a]Average annual percentage rate of growth of real GNP per capita, 1975–1981.

Over half of the world's population lives in poverty; many of the very poorest are in countries that have the lowest growth rates and thus fall ever farther behind. The unequal distribution of the world's income is shown in columns 5 and 6. Groups I–II, which have over 50 percent of the world's population, earn less than 10 percent of world income. Groups IV–V, with 28 percent of the world's population, earn over 80 percent of world income. Column 7 shows that the poorest countries are not closing the gap in income between rich and poor countries.

hours per week, enjoy substantial leisure, and have a level of consumption at or above *half* of that attained by the citizens of the United States—contain only about 15 percent of the world's population. Many of the rest struggle for subsistence. Many exist on a level at or below that enjoyed by peasants in ancient Egypt or Babylon.

Data of the sort shown in Table 44-1 cannot be accurate down to the last $100.[1] Nevertheless, the *development gap*—the discrepancy between the standards of living in countries at either end of the distribution—is real and large.

There are many different ways to look at the inequality of income distribution among the world's population. One is shown in Figure 44-1, which plots the Lorenz curve of the world's income distribution. The more the curve bends away from the straight line, the greater is the inequality in income distribution. To give perspective on the great disparity in income among countries, the middle line shows the Lorenz curve of income distribution among people in the United States. It is much closer to equality than the world distribution.

Another way of looking at inequality is to look at the geographic distribution of income per capita, as shown in Figure 44-2. Recent political discussions of income distribution have distinguished between richer and poorer nations as "North" versus "South." The map reveals why.

The Consequences of Underdevelopment

The human consequences of very low income levels can be severe. Someone studying the effect of rainfall variations would find that for a rich country such as the United States, the variations would be reflected in farm output and farm income: for each inch of rainfall below some critical amount, farm output and income would vary in a regular way. In poor countries such as India, var-

[1] There are many problems in comparing national incomes across countries. For example, home-grown food is vitally important to living standards in underdeveloped countries, but it is excluded—or at best imperfectly included—in the national income statistics of most countries. So is the contribution of a moderate climate. But nevertheless the data in the table do reflect enormous real differences in living standards that no statistical discrepancies can hide.

iations in rainfall are reflected in the death rate. Indeed, many live so close to subsistence that slight fluctuations in the food supply bring death by starvation to large numbers. Other less dramatic characteristics of poverty include inadequate diet, poor health, short life expectancy, illiteracy, and—very importantly—an attitude of helpless resignation to the caprice of nature.

These facts make the problems of economic growth very much more pressing in poor countries than in rich ones. Reformers in underdeveloped countries—often called **less-developed countries (LDCs)**—feel a sense of urgency not felt by their counterparts in rich countries. Many now living at the bare subsistence level can look forward to improvements in their lot only if their country experiences an immediate and rapid rate of economic growth. Yet, as the first row of Table 44-1 shows, the development gap for the very poorest countries has been widening. As will be seen, this is a problem of both output and population. It is also an international political problem.

Incentives for Development

Obviously underdevelopment is nothing new.[2] Concern with it as a remediable condition, however, is recent; it has become a compelling policy issue only within the present century. Probably the dominant reason for this newfound concern has been the extraordinary success of planned programs of "crash" development, of which the Soviet experience is the most remarkable and the Chinese the most recent (see Chapter 45). Leaders in other countries ask, If they can do it, why not us?

Demonstration effects should not be underestimated. It has been said that the real secret of the atomic bomb was that it *could* be made, not how. Much the same is true of economic development. In the last 35 years there have been many examples

---

[2] The terminology of development is often confusing. *Underdeveloped, less developed,* and *developing* do not mean the same thing in ordinary English, yet each has been used to describe the same phenomenon. For the most part we shall refer to the underdeveloped countries as the *less-developed countries,* the LDCs for short. Some of them are making progress, that is, developing; others are not.

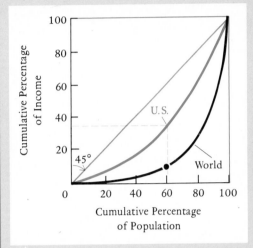

FIGURE 44-1
Lorenz Curves Showing Inequalities Among the Nations of the World and Within the United States

There is much less inequality in the distribution of income within the United States than among all the nations of the world. In a Lorenz curve a wholly equal distribution of income is represented by the 45° line: 20 percent of the population would have 20 percent of the income, 50 percent of the population would have 50 percent of the income, and so on. The very unequal distribution of world income is shown by the black curve. For example, 60 percent of the world's population live in countries that earn only 10 percent of the world's income, as shown by the black dot.

Contrast this with the distribution of income within the United States: the poorest 60 percent of the American population earn 36 percent of the nation's income. This is not equality, but it is much less unequal than the differences between rich and poor countries.

of rapid and more or less planned economic development. In a world that each year is made smaller by communication and transportation improvements, these developments are visible to all. It is bad enough to be poor, but to be poor when others are escaping poverty is intolerable. Suddenly people see that it is possible to achieve better lives for themselves and their children.

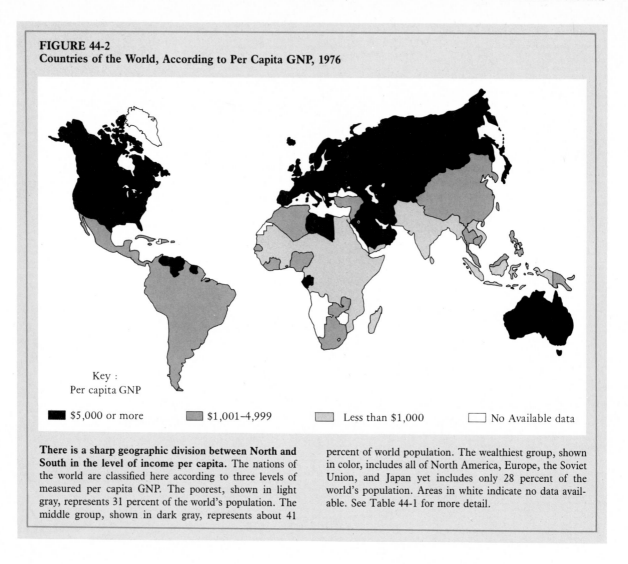

FIGURE 44-2
Countries of the World, According to Per Capita GNP, 1976

Key :
Per capita GNP

■ $5,000 or more   ▦ $1,001–4,999   ▢ Less than $1,000   ☐ No Available data

There is a sharp geographic division between North and South in the level of income per capita. The nations of the world are classified here according to three levels of measured per capita GNP. The poorest, shown in light gray, represents 31 percent of the world's population. The middle group, shown in dark gray, represents about 41 percent of world population. The wealthiest group, shown in color, includes all of North America, Europe, the Soviet Union, and Japan yet includes only 28 percent of the world's population. Areas in white indicate no data available. See Table 44-1 for more detail.

A second push toward development has come from the developed countries, with their policies to aid less-developed countries. We shall discuss such programs and their motivation later.

A third pressure for development results from the emergence of a relatively cohesive bloc of LDCs within the United Nations. The bloc is attempting to utilize its political bargaining power to achieve economic ends.

Both from within and without the LDCs the passive acceptance of underdeveloped status has ended. LDCs want to achieve major increases in living standards within a generation.

What are the causes of underdevelopment, and how may they be overcome?

BARRIERS TO ECONOMIC DEVELOPMENT

When income per head is taken as an index of the level of economic development, a country develops when its aggregate income grows faster than its population. However, there are many impediments to such growth.

Population Growth

Today many LDCs have more national income than before, but they also have more mouths to feed. Thus, their standard of living is no higher than it was a hundred or even a thousand years ago. The average Burmese and the rural Ghanaian are as hungry today as their great-grandparents were. The growth problem faced by underdeveloped countries is how to get off the treadmill and onto the escalator. Will modest gains in the capital stock eventually add up to enough to produce sustained growth? Not necessarily; it is the amount of output *per person* that determines whether living standards will rise. There is all too often a losing race between output and population.

Population growth is a central problem of economic development. If population expands as quickly as national income, per capita income will not increase. When population expands rapidly, a country may by great effort raise the quantity of capital only to find that a corresponding rise in

population has occurred, so that the net effect of its "growth policy" is that a larger population is now maintained at the original low standard of living. Much of the problem of the very poorest countries is due to population growth. They have made appreciable gains in income, but most of the gains have been eaten up (literally) by the increasing population. Table 44-2 shows this.

The population problem has led economists to talk about the *critical minimum effort* that is required not merely to increase capital but to increase it fast enough so that the increase in output outraces the increase in population. The problem arises because population size is not independent of the level of income. When population control is left to nature, nature solves it in a cruel way. Population increases until many are forced to live at a subsistence level; further population growth is halted by famine, pestilence, and plague. This grim situation was perceived early in the history of economics by Thomas Malthus.

In some ways, the population problem is more severe today than it was even a generation ago because advances in medicine and in public health have brought sharp and sudden decreases in death rates. It is ironic that much of the compassion

TABLE 44–2 **THE RELATION OF POPULATION GROWTH TO PER CAPITA GNP, 1975–1981**
(Percentages)

	Classification of countries (GNP per capita, 1976 U.S. dollars)		Average annual rate of growth of			Population growth as a percentage of real GNP growth
Group[a]	Average income level	Percentage of population	Real GNP	Population	Real GNP per capita	
I–II	less than $1,000	56.0	2.8	2.4	2.9	85
III–IV	$1,001–10,000	29.5	5.4	2.1	4.3	38
V	More than $10,000	14.5	3.1	0.8	4.5	25

Source: Calculated from sources in Table 44-1.
[a] Groups from Table 44-1.

Growth in per capita real income depends on the difference between growth rates of real national income and population. The very poorest countries have *both* a relatively low growth rate of income and a relatively high growth rate of population. The middle group shows rising living standards despite large population growth by virtue of a high growth rate of income. The wealthiest countries owe much of their growth in living standards to a low rate of population increase.

shown by wealthier nations for the poor and un-derprivileged people of the world has traditionally taken the form of improving their health, thereby doing little to avert their poverty. We praise the medical missionaries who brought modern medicine to the tropics, but the elimination of malaria has doubled population growth in Sri Lanka. Cholera, once a killer, is now largely under control. No one argues against controlling disease, but other steps must also be taken if the child who survives the infectious illnesses of infancy is not to die of starvation in early adulthood.

Figure 44-3 illustrates actual and projected world population growth. The population problem is not limited to underdeveloped countries, but about seven-eighths of the expected growth in the world's population is in Africa, Asia, and Latin America, those areas where underdevelopment is the rule rather than the exception.

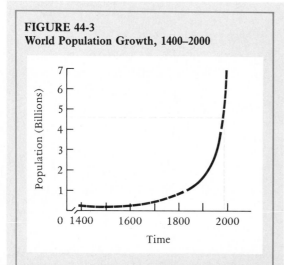

FIGURE 44-3
World Population Growth, 1400–2000

The current growth in the world's population is explosive. The solid line reflects present measurements. The dashed line involves projections from observed trends. It took about 50,000 years from the emergence of modern human beings for the world's population to reach 1 billion. It took 100 years to add a second billion, 30 years to add the third billion, and 15 years to add the fourth billion. If present trends continue, the 1975 population of 4 billion will double by 2005.

Natural Resources

A country with ample fertile land and a large supply of easily developed resources will find growth in income easier to achieve than one poorly endowed with such resources. Kuwait has an income per capita above that of the United States because by accident it sits on top of the world's greatest known oil field. Oil is transforming living standards in Kuwait. But a lack of oil proved a devastating setback to many LDCs when the OPEC cartel increased oil prices tenfold during the 1970s. Without oil their development efforts would be halted, but to buy oil took so much scarce foreign exchange that it threatened to cripple their attempts to import needed capital goods. (This is taken up in more detail later in the chapter.)

The amount of resources available for production is at least in part subject to control. In fact, a nation's supplies of land and natural resources are often readily expandable in their effective use, if not in their total quantity. Badly fragmented land holdings may result from a dowry or inheritance system. When farm land is divided into very small parcels, it may be much more difficult to achieve the advantages of modern agriculture than it is when the land is available in huge tracts for large-scale farming.

Lands left idle because of a lack of irrigations or spoiled by excessive irrigation or lack of crop rotations are well-known examples of barriers to development. Ignorance is another. The nations of the Middle East sat through recorded history alongside the Dead Sea without realizing that it was a substantial source of potash. Not until after World War I were these resources utilized; now they provide Israel with raw materials for its rapidly growing fertilizer and chemical industries.

Inefficiency in the Use of Resources

Low levels of income and slower than necessary growth rates may result from the inefficient use of resources as well as the lack of key resources.

It is useful to distinguish between two kinds of inefficiency. An hour of labor would be used inefficiently, for example, if a worker, even though working at top efficiency, were engaged in making a product that no one wanted. Using society's resources to make the wrong products is an example of **allocative inefficiency.**

In terms of the production possibility boundary encountered in Chapter 1, allocative inefficiency represents operation at the wrong place on the boundary. Allocative inefficiency will occur if the signals to which people respond are distorted—both monopoly and tariffs are commonly cited sources of distortions—or if market imperfections prevent resources from moving to their best uses.

A second kind of inefficiency has come to be called X-inefficiency, following Professor Harvey Leibenstein. **X-inefficiency** arises whenever resources are used in such a way that even if they are making the right product, they are doing so less productively than is possible. One example would be workers too hungry or too unmotivated to concentrate on their tasks.

The distinction between allocative inefficiency and X-inefficiency is illustrated in Figure 44-4. All economies suffer from X-inefficiency because all are to some extent captives of their customs, their institutions, and their histories. But LDCs may be particularly vulnerable because of such factors as illiteracy, poor health, and lack of skills. They may also have cultural attitudes that give greater weight to friendship, loyalty, and tradition than to productivity. However admirable those qualities may be, they may not promote the most efficient use of resources.

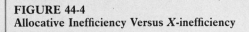

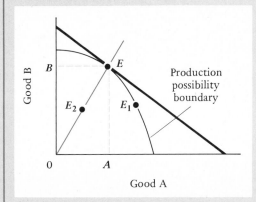

Allocative inefficiency places the society at an inappropriate point on its production possibility boundary, while X-inefficiency places the society inside this boundary. The thinner black curve represents a society's production possibilities between two goods, A and B. The slope of the thicker black line represents the opportunity cost of good B in terms of good A. The efficient output of A and B is represented at point E. E_1 is inefficient in the allocative sense: society is operating on its production possibility boundary but producing too much A and too little B for the given opportunity cost. In contrast, at E_2 the proportions of B and A are the same as at E, but the society is operating inside its boundary. This is X-inefficiency.

Inadequate Human Resources

A well-developed entrepreneurial class, motivated and trained to organize resources for efficient production, is often missing in underdeveloped countries. Its absence may be a heritage of a colonial system that gave the local population no opportunity to develop; it may result from the fact that managerial positions are awarded on the basis of family status or political patronage; it may reflect the presence of economic or cultural attitudes that do not favor acquisition of wealth by organizing

productive activities; or it may simply be due to the nonexistence of the quantity or quality of education or training that is required.

Poor health is likewise a source of inadequate human resources. When the labor force is healthy less time is lost and more effective effort is expended. The economic analysis of medical advances is a young field, however, and there is a great deal to be learned about the size of the drag of poor health on the growth of an economy.

Institutional and Cultural Barriers

The progress of economic development is reflected in the increasing flow of goods and services from a nation's farms and factories to its households. Yet the ability to sustain and expand these flows depends on many aspects of economic and social organization.

Infrastructure

Certain key supporting services—sometimes called the **infrastructure**—such as a transportation and communications network, are necessary to efficient commerce. Roads, bridges, railroads, and harbors are needed to transport people, materials, and finished goods. The most dramatic confirmation of their importance comes in wartime, when belligerents always place high priority on destroying each other's transportation facilities.

Reasonable phone and postal services, water supply, and sanitation are essential to economic development. The absence, whatever the reason, of a dependable infrastructure can impose severe barriers to economic development.

Financial Institutions

The lack of an adequate and trusted system of financial institutions is often a barrier to development. Because investment has a key role in growth, banks are needed to help overcome the shortage of funds for investment. It may take as much as $10 of capital to increase full-employment national income by $1 per year. If this is so, it will take $70 *billion* of capital to raise average income per year by $100 in a country of 70 million—such as Mexico in 1983.

One source of funds for investment is the savings of households and firms. When banks and banking do not function well and smoothly, the link between private saving and investment may be broken and the problem of finding funds for investment greatly intensified.

Many people in LDCs do not trust banks, sometimes with good reason, more often without. Either they do not maintain deposits or they panic periodically, drawing them out and seeking security for their money in mattresses, in gold, or in real estate. The tendency to flee from money is made stronger when, as in recent years, a sharp inflation threatens

the value of money holdings. When this happens, increases in savings do not become available for investment in productive capacity. When banks cannot count on their deposits being left in the banking system, they cannot engage in the kind of long-term loans needed to finance investments.

Developing countries must not only create banking institutions, they must create enough stability and reliability that people will trust their savings to those who wish to invest.

Cultural, Social, and Religious Barriers

Traditions and habitual ways of doing business vary among societies, and not all are equally conducive to productivity. Max Weber argued that the "Protestant ethic" encourages the acquisition of wealth and is consequently more likely to encourage growth than is an ethic that directs activity away from the economic sphere.

Often in the LDCs personal considerations of family, of past favors, or of traditional friendship or enmity are more important than market signals in explaining behavior. One may find a too-small firm struggling to survive against a larger rival and learn that the owner prefers to remain small rather than expand because expansion would require use of nonfamily capital or leadership. To avoid paying too harsh a competitive price for built-in inefficiency, the firms' owners may then spend half their energies in an attempt to influence the government to prevent larger firms from being formed or to try to secure restrictions on the sale of output—and they may well succeed. Such behavior is very likely to inhibit economic growth.

In an environment where people believe that it is more important who your father is than what you do, it may take a generation to persuade employers to change their attitudes and another generation to persuade workers that times have changed. Structuring incentives is a widely used form of policy action in market-oriented economies, but this policy may be harder to effect in a personalistic society than in a market economy. If people habitually bribe the tax collector rather than pay taxes, they will not be likely to respond to policies that are supposed to work by raising or lowering taxes. All that will change is the size of the bribe.

In a society in which children are expected to stay in their fathers' occupations, it is more difficult for the labor force to change its characteristics and to adapt to the requirements of growth than in a society where upward mobility is itself a goal.

There is lively current debate on how much to make of the significance of differing cultural attitudes. Some believe that traditional and cultural considerations dominate peasant societies to the exclusion of economic responses; others suggest that any resulting inefficiency may be relatively small.

If it is true that social, religious, or legal patterns make growth more difficult, this need not mean that they are undesirable. Instead it means that the benefits of these patterns must now be weighed against the costs, of which the effect on growth is one. When people derive satisfaction from a religion whose beliefs inhibit growth, when they value a society in which every man owns his own land and is more nearly self-sufficient than in another society, they may be quite willing to pay a price in terms of growth opportunities foregone.

Whether a society's customs reflect cherished values or only such things as residual influences of a colonial history or an oligarchical political structure is important to the policymakers who must decide whether the cost in terms of efficiency should be paid. In any case, cultural attitudes are not easily changed.

The Challenge to Development Policy

The many barriers to economic development—population growth, lack of natural and human resources, inefficient use of resources, and institutional and cultural restraints—singly or in combination can keep a country poor.

Economic development policy involves identifying the particular barriers to the level and kind of development desired and then devising policies to overcome them. Planners can seek funds for in-vestment, and they can attempt to identify cultural, legal, social, and psychological barriers to growth. They can undertake the programs of education, legal reform, resource development, negotiation of trade treaties, or actual investment that smooth the way to more rapid growth.

All this is more easily said than done. Further, as the dozens of "development missions" sent out by the World Bank and other international, national, and private agencies have discovered, the problems and strategies vary greatly from country to country. Economic development as a field of expertise is in its infancy. However, there are common basic choices that all developing countries must face, and there are many alternative development strategies that may be pursued.

SOME BASIC CHOICES

How Much Government Control?

How much government control over the economy is necessary and desirable? Practically every shade of opinion from "The only way to grow is to get the government's dead hand out of everything" to "The only way to grow is to get a fully planned, centrally controlled economy" has been seriously advocated. The extreme views are easily refuted by historical evidence. Many economies have grown with very little government assistance; Great Britain in the industrial revolution, Holland during the heyday of its colonial period, Singapore and Hong Kong during modern times are all examples. Others, such as the Soviet Union and Austria, have sustained growth with a high degree of centralized control. In other countries there is almost every conceivable mix of government and private initiative in the growth process. Many possible combinations of state and private initiative have been used successfully. On the question of what will prove the best mix at a particular time and in a particular place, there is likely to be much disagreement.

The Case for Planning

Active government intervention in the management of a country's economy often rests on the real or alleged failure of market forces to produce satisfactory results. The major appeal of such intervention is that it is expected to accelerate the pace of economic development.

Any barriers to development may be lowered by enlightened actions of the government. Consider, for example, how the central authorities might seek to ease a shortage of investment funds. In a fully employed free-market economy, investment is influenced by the quantity of savings households and firms make, and thus the division of resources between consumption and saving is one determinant of the rate of growth.

When living standards are low, people have urgent uses for their current income. When savings decisions are left to individual determination, savings tend to be low, and this is an impediment to investment and growth. In a variety of ways, governments can intervene and force people to save more than they otherwise would. Compulsory saving has been one of the main aims of most development plans of centralized governments such as those of the USSR and China.

The goal of such plans is to raise savings and thus lower current consumption below what it would be in an unplanned economy. While forced savings plans are largely associated with totalitarian regimes, a frequent subject of planning in less centrally controlled societies is increasing the savings rate through tax incentives and monetary policies. The object is the same: to increase investment in order to increase growth, and thus to make future generations better off.

Central governments of an authoritarian sort can be particularly effective in overcoming some of the sources of X-inefficiency. A dictatorship may suppress social and even religious institutions that are barriers to growth, and it may hold on to power until a new generation grows up that did not know and does not value the old institutions. It is much more difficult for a democratic government, which must command popular support at each election, to do currently unpopular things in the interests of long-term growth. Whether the gains in growth that an authoritarian government can achieve are worth the political and social costs is, of course, an important value judgment.

The Case for Laissez Faire

Most people would agree that government must play an important part in any development program and especially in programs concerning education, transportation, and communication. But what of the sectors usually left to private enterprise in advanced capitalist countries?

The advocates of laissez faire in these sectors place great emphasis on human drive, initiative, and inventiveness. Once the infrastructure has been established, they argue, an army of entrepreneurs will do vastly more to develop the economy than will an army of civil servants. The market will provide the opportunities and direct their efforts, and individuals will act energetically within it once their self-interest is understood. People who seem irretrievably lethargic and unenterprising when held down by lack of incentives will show amazing bursts of energy when given sufficient self-interest in economic activity.

Furthermore, the argument goes, individual capitalists are far less wasteful of the country's capital than civil servants. A bureaucrat investing capital that is not his own (raised perhaps from the peasants by a state marketing board that buys cheap and sells dear) may choose to enhance his own prestige at the public's expense by spending too much money on cars, offices, and secretaries and too little on truly productive activities. Even if the bureaucrat is genuinely interested in the country's well-being, the incentive structure of a bureaucracy does not encourage creative risk taking. If his ventures fail, his head will likely roll; if they succeed, he will receive no profits—and his superior may get the medal.

What Sorts of Education?

Most studies of underdeveloped countries suggest that undereducation is a barrier to development and often urge increased expenditures on education. This poses a choice: whether to spend educational funds on erasing illiteracy and increasing the level of mass education or on training a small cadre of scientific and technical specialists. The problem is serious because education is expensive and does not pay off quickly.

To improve basic education requires a large investment in school building and in teacher training. This investment will result in a visible change in the level of education only after 10 or more years, and it will not do much for productivity even over that time span.

The opportunity cost of basic education expenditures always seems high. Yet it is essential to make them because the gains will be critical to economic development a generation later.

A great many developing countries have put a large fraction of their educational resources into training a small number of highly educated men and women—often by sending them abroad for advanced study—because the tangible results of a few hundred doctors or engineers or Ph.D.s are relatively more visible than the results from raising the school-leaving age by a year or two, say, from age 10 to age 12. It is not yet clear whether this policy pays off, but it is clear that it has some drawbacks.

Many of this educated elite are recruited from the privileged classes on the basis of family position, not merit; many regard their education as the passport to a new aristocracy rather than as a mandate to serve their fellow citizens; and an appreciable fraction emigrate to countries where their newly acquired skills bring higher pay than they do at home. Of those who return home, many seek the security of a government job, which they may utilize to advance their own status in what is sometimes a self-serving and unproductive bureaucracy.

What Population Policy?

The race between population and income has been a dominant feature of many underdeveloped countries. There are only two possible ways for a country to win this race. One is to make such a massive push that it achieves a growth rate well in excess of the rate of population growth. The other is to control population growth. The problem *can* be solved by restricting population growth. This is not a matter of serious debate, though the means of restricting it are, for there are considerations of religion, custom, and education involved.

The consequences of different population policies are large. Sweden and Venezuela have similar death rates. Yet the birthrate in Sweden is 12 per thousand, and in Venezuela it is 42 per thousand. These variations in birthrates have economic consequences. In Venezuela the net increase of population per year is 33 per thousand (3.3 percent), but it is only 3 per thousand (0.3 percent) in Sweden. If each country were to achieve an overall rate of growth of production of 3 percent per year, Sweden's living standards would be increasing by 2.7 percent per year while Venezuela's would be falling by 0.3 percent per year. In 1977 Sweden's income per capita ($8,400) was three times as high as Venezuela's ($2,600)—and Venezuela is the wealthiest country in South and Central America. The gap will widen rapidly if present population trends continue.

A government can pursue a policy of population control in many ways, although all operate in some fashion to reduce the birthrate. As life expectancy grows and the death rate falls, even a constant birthrate means a rising growth rate of population.

Population control can take the form of public education programs designed to alter attitudes toward family size and to encourage the avoidance of unplanned, or at least involuntary, pregnancies. At the other extreme are massive programs of compulsory sterilization such as Prime Minister Indira Gandhi adopted in India in the mid 1970s. Between these extremes are many other possibilities, most of which use various economic and legal incentives or penalties to encourage a lower birthrate. Customs can be changed to raise the average marriage age and hence lower the birthrate. Prohibition of child labor and the establishment of compulsory education alters the costs and benefits of having children and reduces desired family size. Changing the role of women and providing career alternatives outside of the home can also lower the birthrate.

If this estimate is roughly accurate, then population policy offers an extremely high return on spending to promote per capita growth in LDCs.

University of Maine Professor Johannes Overbeck reported recently that a comprehensive family planning program—involving the provision of a broad selection of birth control techniques, a broad range of social services, and accelerated research to develop more effective and cheaper contraceptives—would have an annual cost of $1 per capita in a typical LDC. Excluding mainland China this amounts to around $2 billion per year for all LDCs combined, a relatively modest sum compared with the over $500 billion currently spent annually on armaments. If this estimate is roughly accurate, then population policy offers an extremely high return on spending to promote per capita growth in LDCs.

Different countries have adopted very different positions with respect to population. Kenya, with a birthrate of 50 per thousand, until very recently rejected any serious national policy of population control. Mexico, with nearly as high a birthrate in the early 1970s, began to dispense free contraceptives and family planning information and has seen its annual rate of population growth drop from 3.2 percent to 2.5 percent in less than five years.

The Chinese—today a quarter of the world's population—have reduced their rate of population increase from more than 3 percent to 1.2 percent in the last 25 years by promoting later marriages and exhorting parents to value daughters as well as sons and thus to be content with fewer children. In 1980 China began more aggressive steps in an announced attempt to achieve zero population growth by the year 2000. It has introduced new regulations to limit families to one or at most two children. Those that comply will receive bonuses and preferential treatment in housing and education for their offspring. (Housing space will be allocated to all families as though they had two children.) Families that do not comply with the policy will have their salaries decreased and will be promoted more slowly.

Aggressive population control policies do not always work. Indira Gandhi's compulsory male sterilization program succeeded in the short run—at its peak nearly 1 million vasectomies per month were being performed—but failed in the longer run because a political storm of opposition toppled her government. Consequently, population control became politically unpopular in India.

Positive economics cannot decide whether population control is desirable, but it can describe the consequences of any choice. Economic development is much easier to achieve with population control than without it.

How to Acquire Capital?

A country can raise funds for investment in three distinct ways: from the savings (voluntary or forced) of its domestic households and firms, by loans or investment from abroad, and by contributions from foreigners.

Capital from Domestic Saving: The Vicious Circle of Poverty

If capital is to be created at home by a country's own efforts, resources must be diverted from the production of goods for current consumption. This means a cut in present living standards. If living standards are already at or near the subsistence level, such a diversion will be difficult. At best, it will be possible to reallocate only a small proportion of resources to the production of capital goods.

Such a situation is often described as *the vicious circle of poverty:* because a country has little capital per head, it is poor; because it is poor, it can devote only a few resources to creating new capital rather than to producing goods for immediate consumption; because little new capital can be produced, capital per head remains low, and the country remains poor.

The vicious circle can be made to seem an absolute constraint on growth rates. Of course it is not; if it were, we would all still be at the level of Neanderthal man. The grain of truth in the vicious circle argument is that some surplus must be available somewhere in the society to allow saving and investment. In a poor society with an even distribution of income, where nearly everyone is at the subsistence level, saving may be very difficult. But this is not the common experience. Usually there will be at least a small middle class that can save and invest if opportunities for the profitable use of funds arise. Also in most poor societies today the average household is usually above the physical subsistence level. Even the poorest households will find that they can sacrifice some present living standards for a future gain. After all, presented with a profitable opportunity, villagers in Ghana planted cocoa plants at the turn of the century even though there was a seven-year growing period before any return could be expected!

The last example points to an important fact: in underdeveloped countries one resource that is often *not* scarce is labor hours. Profitable home or village investment that requires mainly labor inputs may be made with relatively little sacrifice in current living standards. However, this is not the kind of investment that will appeal to planners mesmerized by large, spectacular, and symbolic investments such as dams, nuclear power stations, and steel mills.

Imported Capital

Another way of accumulating the capital needed for growth is to borrow it from abroad. When a poor country, A, borrows from a rich country, B, it can use the borrowed funds to purchase capital goods produced in B. Country A thus accumulates capital and needs to cut its current output of consumption goods only to pay interest on its loans. As the new capital begins to add to current production, it becomes easier to pay the interest on the loan and also to repay the principal out of the increase in output. In this way income can be raised immediately and the major sacrifice postponed until later, when part of the increased income that might have been used to raise domestic consumption is instead used to pay off the loan. This method has the great advantage of giving a poor country an initial increase in capital goods far greater than it could possibly have created by diverting its own resources from consumption industries.

However, many countries, developed or undeveloped, are suspicious of foreign capital. They fear that foreign investors will gain control over their industries or their government. The extent of foreign control depends on the form that foreign capital takes. When foreigners buy bonds in domestic companies, they do not own or control anything; when they buy common stocks, they own part or all of a company, but their control over mangement may be small. If a foreign company (perhaps a multinational corporation) establishes a plant and imports its own managers and technicians, it will have much more control. Finally, if foreign firms subsidize an LDC government in return for permission to produce, they may feel justified in exacting political commitments.

Whether foreign ownership of one's industries carries political disadvantages sufficiently large to outweigh the economic gains is a subject of debate. In Canada, for example, there is serious political opposition to having a large part of Canadian industry owned by U.S. nationals. Many other countries actively seek more foreign investment than they are getting.

The economic choices are quite clear:

Accumulating a given amount of capital through domestic saving requires greater current sacrifice but later pays a higher return. Foreign financing requires small present sacrifices but involves holding down living standards later in order to make the interest payments to foreign investors.

The choice between the two alternatives raises an important intergenerational question: to what extent should the sacrifices required to pay for growth be met now rather than 10 years from now? One suspects that, political considerations aside, most people would prefer to postpone the cost by using borrowed capital.

Reliance on foreign borrowing has literally exploded in the past few years. But not all foreign capital has gone to provide for increased capital accumulation. Some problems related to foreign borrowing are discussed at the end of the chapter.

"AID," "TRADE," OR "RESTITUTION"

The motivations behind international giving have become the subject of debate. Do developed nations give aid for humanitarian reasons, because it serves their political objectives, or because it is economically self-serving? Obviously all three motives can play a role, but which one dominates? Should LDCs demand aid, accept it gratefully, or reject it?

LDCs more or less chronically lack capital and lack wealth. Typically they have large and mounting foreign debts as a result of past borrowing. In these circumstances, one might think that foreign aid, whether from a single country or from an international forum, would be eagerly sought and gratefully received. This is not always so; there is some significant resistance to accepting aid.

The slogan "Trade, not aid" reflected political opposition to U.S. economic aid in certain recipient countries in the 1950s. Yugoslavia turned down much aid proffered by the Soviets after 1948, and China accepted no foreign aid after 1960. In 1975 Colombia made the decision to forego further U.S. aid on the grounds that it bred an unhealthy economic dependency.

The primary explanation of this attitude lies in a country's noneconomic goals. It may suspect the motives of the givers and fear that hidden strings may be attached to the offer. Independent countries prize their independence and want to avoid either the fact or the appearance of being satellites. Pride—a desire to be beholden to no one—is also a factor.

One response was to do without aid, no matter how badly it was needed. Another, increasingly the pattern in the 1970s, was to reject "aid" but to demand "wealth transfers," not as a matter of charity but as a matter of "restitution" or redress for past sins by colonial powers against their former colonies. The obvious problem of asserting such claims against noncolonial powers such as the United States and the USSR has been no deterrent. There is a generalized sense that the inhabitants of the "North" exploited the nations of the "South" in past centuries and that present generations should redress the balance. The paradoxical aspect of this is that while "restitution, not charity" makes LDCs willing to accept aid, precisely that claim decreases the willingness of developed countries to offer it.

What *are* the motives of givers of aid? The Scandinavian Nobel Prize winning economist Gunnar Myrdal has argued that humanitarian considerations have played a large role. The evidence for the existence of humanitarian motives is in part the success of voluntary appeals in developed countries for food, funds, and clothes for persons in stricken areas of the world. As per capita incomes have risen in the Western world, so have contributions, private as well as public. It is the policy of the governments of most of the so-called Western democracies to devote some resources to alleviating poverty throughout the world.

Professor Edward S. Mason, among others, has argued that such aid can best be understood by looking to political and security motives. He points to the substantial U.S. congressional preference for military assistance over economic assistance, the denial of aid to countries such as Sri Lanka that traded with Communist countries, the fostering of Tito's Yugoslavia *because* of its anti-Soviet stand—all of which reveal a strong political motive. Many critics of OPEC think its contributions are designed to quiet opposition among LDCs to the oil price hikes that have proved so profitable to the oil producers and so painful to oil users. LDCs and developed countries alike.

Should motives and attitudes, either of givers or of receivers, matter? After all, it is economically beneficial to receive aid when you are poor. Economists cannot say that fears, aspirations, pride, and "face" are either foolish or unworthy; they can only note that they do have their cost.

Contributed Capital

From the viewpoint of the receiving country, contributed capital might seem ideal. It has the advantage of enabling the country to shift to more rapid growth without either sacrificing consumption now or having to repay later. Investment funds for development are being received today by underdeveloped countries from the governments of the developed countries acting both unilaterally (as in the U.S. Agency for International Development and a similar Soviet program) and through international agencies such as the World Bank, the Export-Import Bank, and the OPEC Fund established in January 1980.

Contributed capital has played a significant role in post-World War II economic development. For example, American foreign aid expenditures in the decade after the war were $90 billion, and even today they amount to more than $3 billion per year. That $3 billion is more than 1 percent of the GNP of the 2 billion people who live in the most underdeveloped nations of the world. The OPEC Fund started with an initial capital of $4 billion and is expected to grow rapidly.

The Soviet Union has given substantial aid to less-developed countries. Russian aid to China in the 1950s was essential to that country's development of heavy industry. In addition to funds, the USSR transported capital in the form of more than 150 complete plants and sent thousands of technicians and specialists to China to help plan, build, and run factories. China today is itself a significant donor to a few ideologically sympathetic countries, including Tanzania and Albania. Some of the issues involved in the relations between LDCs and the more developed nations are further discussed in the box.

ALTERNATIVE DEVELOPMENT STRATEGIES

In the search for development, individual LDCs have a number of policy options. The choice of options is in part a matter of what the planners believe will work and in part a question of the nature of the society that will be created once development has occurred.

The noneconomic aspects of the choice of a development strategy may be illustrated by the Greek government's explicit decision in the mid 1960s to change the direction of its growth. At that time Greece was achieving rapid growth in income per capita largely because of a booming tourist trade and the emigration of many young Greeks to West Germany to work in factories there. The emigrants had been earning incomes in Greece that were substantially below the Greek average, and their remittances home to their families increased both domestic income and foreign exchange reserves. Although it was helpful to the Greek rate of growth to continue to rely on tourism and emigration as bulwarks of the economy, this policy threatened an image of life that visualized "Greece for the Greeks." Even at the prospect of some loss in growth, Greek planners recommended the restriction of emigration, the moderation of the size of the tourist role in the economy, and the development of new industry for the Greek economy.

There may also be economic reasons for choosing a different pattern of growth than the free market would provide. An important role of planning is to direct growth in a different direction, one that the planners guess will have the greatest chance of long-run success.

Unplanned growth will usually tend to exploit the country's present comparative advantages; planners may choose a pattern of growth that involves trying to change the country's future comparative advantages.

One reason that planners seek to effect such a change is their belief that they can evaluate the future more accurately than the countless individuals whose decisions determine market prices. A country need not passively accept its current comparative advantages. Many skills can be acquired, and fostering an apparently uneconomic domestic industry may, by changing the characteristics of the labor force, develop a comparative advantage in that line of production.

The Japanese had no visible comparable advantage in any industrial skill when Commodore Matthew Perry opened that feudal country to Western influence in 1854, but they became a major industrial power by the end of the century. Their continuing gains relative to the United States in fields such as steel, automobile manufacture, and communications do not need to be called to anyone's attention today. Soviet planners in the 1920s and 1930s chose to create an industrial economy out of a predominantly agricultural one and succeeded in vastly changing the mix between agriculture and industry in a single generation (see Chapter 45).

These illustrations suggest why the big choice may be which development strategy to adopt. Governments must choose between agricultural and industrial emphases; between different kinds of industrial development; and between more or less reliance on foreign trade. Several possibilities have been widely advocated, and each has been tried. None is without difficulties.

Agricultural Development

Everyone needs food. An LDC may choose to devote a major portion of its resources to stimulating agricultural production, say, by mechanizing farms, irrigating land, and utilizing new seeds and fertilizers. If successful, the country will stave off starvation for its current population, and it may even develop an excess over current needs and so have a crop available for export. A food surplus can earn foreign exchange to buy needed imports.

Among the attractions of the agricultural strategy are that it does not require a great deal of technical training or hard-to-acquire know-how, nor does it place the country in direct competition with highly industrial countries.

India, Pakistan, Taiwan, and other Asian countries have achieved dramatic increases in food production by the application of new technology—and new seed—to agricultural production. Increases of up to 50 percent have been achieved in grain production, and it has been estimated that with adequate supplies of water, pesticides, fertilizers, and modern equipment, production could be doubled or even tripled. This has been labeled the *green revolution.*

The possibilities of achieving such dramatic gains in agricultural output may seem almost irresistible at first glance, yet many economists think they should be resisted—and that they point to a series of problems.

One problem is that a vast amount of resources is required to irrigate land and mechanize production, and these resources used alternatively could provide industrial development and industrial employment opportunities. Thus there is a clear opportunity cost. Critics of the agricultural strategy argue that the search for a generation free from starvation will provide at best only a temporary solution because population will surely expand to meet the food supply. Instead, they argue, underdeveloped countries should start at once to reduce their dependence on agriculture. Let someone else grow the food; industrialization should not be delayed.

A second problem with the agricultural strategy is that the great increases in world production of wheat, rice, and other agricultural commodities that the green revolution makes possible could depress their prices and not lead to increased earnings from exports. What one agricultural country can do, so can others, and there may well be a glut on world markets. This is the heart of the argument of the distinguished Latin American economist Raúl Prebisch. He maintains that underdeveloped countries, overspecialized in the production of agricultural commodities, are sure to suffer steadily worsening terms of trade relative to manufacturing outputs. Prebisch believes that current market prices fail to anticipate fully this worsening in the terms of trade for agriculture and thus that planners should intervene and shift the country out of what is sure to be a long-run overreliance on agriculture.

A third problem has arisen (most acutely in India and Pakistan) where increasing agricultural output has been accompanied by decreasing labor requirements in agricultural production without a compensating increase in employment opportunities elsewhere. Millions of tenant farmers—and their bullocks—have been evicted from their tenant holdings by owners who are buying tractors to replace them. Many have found no other work.

A final danger of the agricultural strategy is that once a program of agricultural subsidization is put into place, it creates a serious potential dilemma. Continuation of high prices for producers and low prices for consumers creates a substantial, perhaps eventually an impossible, drain on the government's finances. Lowering the subsidy to producers risks a rural revolution. Eliminating the subsidy to consumers risks an urban revolution. The government finds itself with an untenable policy but with no room for maneuver.

Specialization in a Few Commodities

Many LDCs have at present unexploited resources such as copper, uranium, or opportunities for tourism. The principle of comparative advantage provides the traditional case for the desirability of relying on such resources. By specializing in producing those products in which it has the greatest comparative advantage, the country can achieve the most rapid growth in the short run. To neglect these opportunities will result in a lower standard of living than would result from specialization accompanied by increased international trade.

These are cogent reasons in favor of *some* specialization. But specialization involves risks, and the risks may be worth reducing even at the loss of some income. Specialization here, as with agriculture, makes the economy highly vulnerable to cyclical fluctuations in world demand and supply. A recession in developed countries decreases overseas travel and creates problems for an LDC that has relied on tourism for foreign exchange.

The problem is not only cyclical. When technological or taste changes render a product partially or wholly obsolete, a country can face a major calamity for generations. Just as individual firms and regions may become overspecialized, so too may countries.

Import Substitution Industrialization

During the Great Depression the collapse in world agricultural prices caused the value of the exports of agricultural countries to decline drastically relative to the prices of goods those countries imported. During World War II many countries found that the manufactured goods they wished to import were simply unavailable. In each of those situations dependence on foreign trade for necessities did not seem wholly attractive. More recently, the rising prices of fuel and other imports have created enormous balance-of-payments problems for many LDCs. Such countries must either reduce imports or increase exports, or resort to foreign borrowing.

Much of the industrialization by LDCs in the 1950s and 1960s was directed toward **import substitution industry** (**ISI**), which is producing at home goods that were previously imported. It is often necessary both to subsidize the home industry and to restrict imports to allow the ISI time to develop.

A study of import substitution industries in seven countries found that the effective rate of protection or subsidy varied from 25 to more than 200 percent.

The ISI strategy has many problems. It fosters *inefficient* industries, and in the long run countries do not get rich by being inefficient. It aggravates inequalities in income distribution by raising the prices of manufactured goods relative to agricultural goods and by favoring profits over wages.

Industrialization for Export

Most development economists believe that industrialization ought to be encouraged only in areas where the country can develop a reliable and efficient industry that can compete in world markets.

Obviously, if Tanzania or Peru could quickly develop steel, shipbuilding, and manufacturing industries that operated as efficiently as those of Japan or West Germany, they too might share in the rapid economic growth enjoyed by those industrial countries. Indeed, if a decade or two (or even three) of protection and subsidization could give infant industries time to mature and become efficient, the price might be worth paying. After all, Japan and Russia were underdeveloped countries within living memory.

A major problem with this strategy is making up the initial productivity gap. India may create a steel industry and have its productivity increase year by year, but it must do more: it must catch up to the steel industries of other countries in order to compete in world markets. The catch-up problem is a race against a moving target. Suppose you must improve by 50 percent to achieve the present level of a competitor who is improving at r percent per year. If you want to catch up in 10 years, you must improve at $r + 4$ percent per year. [45] If r is 6 percent, you must achieve 10 percent. To achieve 7 percent or 8 percent may be admirable, but you will lose the race just the same.

Industrialization for export often means devoting resources for a long period to education, training, development of an infrastructure, and overcoming the various cultural and social barriers to efficient production. While this is hard, it is not impossible. Indeed, there have been some spectacular success stories: Brazil, Korea, Hong Kong, and Taiwan are charter members in a new category, "newly industrializing countries," that are providing vigorous competition in manufactured goods in world markets. Their success has led to a further (and bitterly resented) problem for the industrialization strategy. When an LDC succeeds, it is likely to find the developed countries trying to protect *their* home industries from the new competition.

LDCs sometimes pursue certain lines of production on a subsidized basis either for prestige purposes or because of a confusion between cause and effect. Because most wealthy nations have a steel industry, the leaders of many underdeveloped nations regard their countries as primitive until they develop a domestic steel industry. Because several LDCs have succeeded in producing consumer durables, many others assume that they should try to do so. However, if a country has a serious comparative disadvantage in steel or in making consumer durables, fostering such industries will make that country poor.

Commodity Price Stabilization Agreements

When all or most producers of a commodity can agree on price and output levels, they can achieve monopoly profits not available in competitive markets. Many LDCs are heavily committed to the production and export of one or more basic commodities such as bananas, bauxite, cocoa, coffee, copper, cotton, iron ore, jute, manganese, meat, oil, phosphates, rubber, sugar, tea, tropical timber, and tin. Why not get together and create an effective cartel that gives producers the enormous profits that are potentially available? This has been tried many times in history; until OPEC, it has always failed. Yet everyone knows that OPEC's success transformed a handful of formerly poor LDCs into the wealthiest of nations.[3]

OPEC's success was substantial, but has proven hard to sustain. Exporters of other commodities have had difficulty achieving even this limited success because the special conditions of demand and supply that apply to oil do not apply equally to most other primary commodities. In the case of oil there are few large producing countries, supply is quite inelastic outside those countries, demand is relatively inelastic in the short and middle run, and the largest producers are Arab nations that find discipline in political and religious unity and in a common hatred of Israel. Perhaps equally important, the largest producer—Saudi Arabia—was often prepared to put up with a good deal of cheating by its partners.

Wheat, coffee, cocoa, tin, rubber, and copper have all been suggested as potential targets for similar joint marketing strategies, but none has the

---

[3] This has added to the terminological confusion. It was once fashionable to speak of a nonaligned *third world* as another term for LDCs, the first two "worlds" being the developed capitalist and developed socialist countries. Now some commentators divide the LDCs into a richer (oil-producing) *third world* and a still poor *fourth world*.

right combination of attributes, and only copper has supply and demand situations that are remotely similar to those of oil. But the inability to utilize "commodity power" more widely through cartelization has not led to its total abandonment, as we will see in the final section of this chapter.

A New International Economic Order (NIEO)?

In May 1974 the General Assembly of the United Nations adopted (over the objections of the developed countries) a Declaration on the Establishment of a New International Economic Order. This represented an attempt on the part of LDCs to utilize collective *political* power to achieve a larger share of the world's goods.[4]

NIEO had its origin in the emergence within the United Nations of a political bloc of LDCs that goes back at least to 1964. These nations, economically weak but numerous, were targets of the struggle between the United States and the USSR for allegiance. They agreed to remain "nonaligned" with either of the two major power groups.

In their many international meetings since 1974, the LDCs have presented dozens of specific demands and proposals covering trade, unilateral and multinational aid, investment, and technology transfers from developed to underdeveloped countries. For instance the NIEO Integrated Programs for Commodities was designed to "raise and stabilize" the prices of 18 products by creating a "common fund" to which both producers and consumers would contribute. But to expect consuming countries to contribute to a fund whose purpose is to permit producers to restrict sales and raise prices sounds like a triumph of hope over reason, and as might have been expected, nothing more substantial than talk has resulted.

Newly industrializing LDCs have also sought preferential tariff and nontariff barriers. It is all

[4] An excellent introduction to this development is Rachel McCulloch's *Economic and Political Issues in the NIEO* (International Institute for Economic Research, 1979). Professor McCulloch's analysis is heavily relied on here.

right, the argument said, for the United States to limit textile imports, but the LDCs should be given preference over developed countries in fighting for shares of the full quota. Most major industrialized nations, including the United States, have granted some such treatment, but the effects have been relatively smaller than the LDCs expected.

LDCs were major borrowers in international markets well before the OPEC price increases. Requests made by the LDCs at various United Nations Conferences on Trade and Development (known, like super bowl games, by Roman numerals, e.g., UNCTAD IV) ranged from debt cancellation and a moratorium on payments for a few years to milder suggestions for case-by-case renegotiation of scheduling and interest payments. Not surprisingly, the general proposals were rejected by developed nations—and were even opposed by some borrowers, who feared that if debts were canceled, their future ability to borrow would be diminished.

The NIEO proposals are aimed basically at wealth transfers instead of wealth creations; they are concerned with a more equal distribution of existing wealth rather than economic development. Thus far the accomplishments of NIEO demands have been small.

Why has the talk proven unpersuasive? The main answer is that the political and economic threats made by the LDCs against the developed countries are no longer regarded as substantial. NIEO's future rests on persuasion rather than coercion of the developed countries. Here the very stridency that unified the "South" in their demands has brought forth a unified resistance on the part of the "North."

From an economic point of view NIEO has two major flaws. First, it focuses too much on redistribution and too little on seeking real growth in world output. Second, it puts its faith in bureaucratic allocations of wealth, trade, and natural resources rather than in market mechanisms. Nothing in the world's experience to date suggests that this will increase total world output.

SOME CONTROVERSIAL UNRESOLVED ISSUES

The economics of development, like most fields of economics, is in a state of change. The view presented in this chapter is perhaps the mainline view of economists in developed economies such as our own. Problems look different when viewed from the inside out, and they look different from the perspective of socialist nations than they do from our sort of market-oriented economy.

Yet even within the group of Western economists studying development there are important current controversies.

The Pace of Development

Reformers in underdeveloped countries often think in terms of transforming their economies within a generation or two. The sense of urgency is quite understandable, but unless it is tempered by some sense of historical perspective, totally unreasonable aspirations may develop—only to be dashed all too predictably.

Many underdeveloped countries are probably in a stage of development analogous to that of medieval England, having not yet achieved anything like the commercial sophistication of the Elizabethan era. It took 600 years for England to develop from the medieval stage to its present one. Such a change would be easier now, for much of the needed technology can be imported rather than invented. But what is the proper pace? To effect a similar growth within 50 or 100 years would require a tremendous achievement of the kind accomplished by America, Japan, and a handful of other countries; to aspire to do it in 20 or 30 years may be to court disaster—or to invite an extraordinary repressive political regime.

The View of Population Policy

The view presented in this chapter of population growth as a formidable barrier to development is neo-Malthusian and constitutes much of current conventional wisdom on underdevelopment.

This view allows no place for the enjoyment value of children by their parents. Critics point out that the psychic value of children should be included as a part of the living standards of their parents. They also point out that in rural societies even quite young children are a productive resource because of the work they can do; and fully grown children provide old-age security for their parents in societies where state help for the aged is negligible.

The neo-Malthusian theory is also criticized for assuming that people breed blindly, as animals do. Critics point out that traditional methods of limiting family size have been known and practiced since the dawn of history. Thus they argue that large families in rural societies are a matter of choice. The population explosion came not through any change in "breeding habits" but as a result of medical advances that greatly extended life expectancy (which surely must be counted as a direct welfare gain for those affected). Critics argue that once an urban society has developed, family size will be reduced voluntarily. This was certainly the experience of Western industrial countries; why, critics ask, should it not be the experience of the developing countries?

The Cost of Creating Capital

Is it true LDCs must suffer if they wish to grow? A recent criticism of this conventional wisdom questions the alleged heavy opportunity cost of creating domestic capital. Production of consumption and capital goods are substitutes only when factor supplies are constant. But, critics say, the development of a market economy will lead people to substitute work for leisure.

For example, the arrival of Europeans with new goods to trade led the North American Indians to collect furs and other commodities needed for exchange. Until they were decimated by later generations of land-hungry settlers, the Indians' standard of living rose steadily with no immediate sacrifice. They created the capital needed for their production—weapons and means of transport—in their abundant leisure time. Thus their consumption began to rise immediately.

This too, the argument says, could happen in

underdeveloped countries if market transactions were allowed to evolve naturally. The spread of a market economy would lead people to give up leisure in order to produce the goods needed to buy the goods that private traders are introducing from the outside world. In this view it is the pattern of development chosen, rather than development itself, that imposes the need for heavy sacrifices.

Debt and the LDCs: A Crisis?

The 1980s witnessed a skyrocketing of the external debt of many LDCs and of the payments required to service this debt. Some commentators felt that this problem had reached crisis proportions and called for drastic measures to deal with it. Others felt that the growth in debt was no more than the appropriate response to changing conditions and that the "problem" was nothing to worry about.

While the growth in debt in the early 1980s was extreme, the trend to increased debt actually started in the early 1970s when OPEC raised the world price of oil. This created huge surpluses in the OPEC countries and, as a result, a large increase in the deposits of the banks where the OPEC funds ultimately ended up. In turn, these banks found themselves with excess liquidity and were anxious to make loans. They found willing customers in many LDCs whose external accounts had suddenly been forced into deficit by the sharp rise in the cost of their oil imports.

Many LDCs were heavily dependent on imported oil and were unable to reduce their imports significantly. (Their demand for oil was *inelastic*, at least in the short run.) The fact that they had to pay more for oil imports meant that less of the value of output produced was available as income to the domestic residents. This caused large current account deficits and thus added substantially to their need for foreign borrowing. This of course represented a desirable *recycling* of the OPEC surpluses, but it also gradually contributed to the external debt of many LDCs.

The extent of the debt is staggering. Total third world debt in 1983 was more than $750 billion, of which $300 billion alone was owed by Latin American countries. Some countries—including Argentina, Chile, Colombia, and Venezuela—have debt-service obligations that in 1983 exceeded the whole of their expected export earnings.

Why has external debt grown? Growth in external debt results when the country's total spending (including consumption, investment, and government expenditure plus interest payments on outstanding debt) exceeds net income received. This indicates a current account deficit, which is just another way of stating that there is a need for foreign borrowing.

Is the need to borrow indicative of a serious problem? There are three possible answers to this question. First, borrowing to pay for the increased costs of oil imports is all right as a stopgap measure until the economy has adjusted by reducing its oil-import requirements. But a continued use of borrowing to pay for oil imports eventually spells disaster. Second, borrowing to pay for successful new investment means that the economy's capacity to produce will be expanding and the increased foreign debt obligations will not represent an increased burden on the citizens of the LDCs. Third, borrowing to finance wasteful government expenditure or lavish consumption splurges means that the increased debt quickly becomes a real burden.

While many people were becoming increasingly aware of the growing debt of the LDCs in the 1970s, most felt that the borrowing was justified by large ongoing investment projects and by the financing needs for short-run adjustment to higher energy prices. Four recent developments have altered this perception.

First, the doubling of the price of oil in 1979 pushed many LDCs into a larger deficit position and seriously set back the progress they were making in adjusting to the 1972 OPEC price hikes. Their borrowing was increased sharply, and their debt rose to a point where their ability to pay was seriously questioned.

Second, recessions in major industrialized countries caused a sharp curtailment in the demand for the exports of the LDCs. Lower income levels in the rich nations meant that less was spent on all goods, including the exports of the LDCs. (In addition, the emerging unemployment problems in those nations led to increasing pressure for protectionist trade policies that, when adopted, further hurt the LDCs.) This caused further increases in LDC debt.

Third, the combination of entrenched inflation and tight monetary policies created very high interest rates (in both real and nominal terms) so that the debt the LDCs had accumulated required larger debt-servicing payments. Often these payments could not be financed out of current income and so were met by further borrowing.

Fourth, it has become apparent that the borrowing of many LDCs was in fact used to finance wasteful excesses and that the policies pursued by these countries were not contributing to their ability eventually to repay the loans. Many, in fact, have come close to defaulting. Brazil unilaterally suspended payments in 1982. Poland has rescheduled its payments and likely will never totally repay. Mexico is now a poor credit risk, for its oil-based wealth has suddenly fallen dramatically with the fall in the world price of oil and the excesses of some of its earlier policies have become more apparent.

The *causes* of the debt explosion seem reasonably well understood. The question remains, Is it a *crisis*?

First, it appears that many of the problems giving rise to the explosion in debt were temporary. Oil prices did not stay at their high 1979–1980 levels, and many LDCs have since reduced their dependence on oil. World recovery and reduced interests rates were on the horizon in 1983. If those trends continue, most observers 10 years from now will point to the debt explosion of the 1980–1982 period as an indication of the ability of the market system to cope with fluctuations in the economic environment.

But the fact is, the LDCs remain vulnerable to a recurrence of these or similar events. And major financial institutions remain vulnerable to the possibility of a default by a major LDC borrower. Several American banks apparently made unwise decisions to lend too much money to specific countries rather than spreading their loans around to many different LDCs. Loans to just three countries—Brazil, Mexico, and Venezuela—by three major banks (Citibank, Chase Manhatten, and Manufacturer's Hanover) amount to almost double the *net worth* of the banks involved. Clearly a default by one of those countries would have major repercussions on those banks and hence on the stability of financial markets.

The financial system *could* collapse, but this is unlikely if proper policies are pursued. Even with a major default, the system as a whole is financially sound. The collapse of one bank might cause others to face a *liquidity* shortage. That is, they may not have enough cash assets to be able to meet the demands for withdrawals of *all* their depositors, even though they have enough total assets. But here, in its lender-of-last-resort function, the government could step in. The IMF has over $45 billion in gold that it could draw on to aid the financially troubled LDCs, and the Fed is available to act as a lender-of-last-resort to the banking system. There is no reason for the entire system to collapse, although there is plenty of room for debate about who is to bear the costs imposed by any default.

SUMMARY

1. Sustained economic development is relatively recent in history and has been highly uneven. About one-fourth of the world's population still exists at a level of bare subsistence, and nearly three-fourths are poor by American standards. The gap between rich and poor is very large and is keenly felt.

2. The pressure for economic development comes in part from the LDCs. The transformation in less than half a century of Soviet Russia from a backward peasant economy to a major industrial power has had a powerful demonstration effect on the quest for economic development. Moreover, as the LDCs have become a cohesive political bloc within the United Nations, they have come to demand economic assistance in their development efforts.

3. Much of the effective push toward more rapid development of the third world has come from the efforts of the World Bank and the development agencies of the developed countries.

4. There are many impediments to economic development; merely to want economic growth and development is not enough to assure it. Population growth, resource limitations, and the inefficient use of resources are among the formidable barriers to economic development in particular underdeveloped countries. So too are a series of institutional and cultural barriers that make economic growth more difficult.

5. A series of basic (and controversial) choices face LDCs as they contemplate development. How much should they intervene in the economy, and how much should they rely on the free market? History has demonstrated that growth is possible with almost any conceivable mixture of free-market and central control. Centralized planning can change both the pace of economic development and its direction; it can also prove highly wasteful and destroy individual initiative.

6. Educational policy, while vitally important to the long-run rate of economic development, yields its benefits only in the future. Consequently, the improvement of basic education is sometimes bypassed in the search for more immediate results.

7. A population policy is an important and volatile issue in most LDCs. The race between output and population is a critical aspect of development efforts in many countries. Different countries have chosen very different attitudes toward limiting population growth.

8. Acquiring capital for development is invariably a major concern in development. One source is domestic savings, but here the vicious circle of poverty may arise: a country that is poor because it has little capital cannot readily forego consumption to accumulate capital because it is poor. Importing capital rather than using domestic savings permits heavy investment during the early years of development, with much smaller sacrifices of cur-

rent living standards. But imported capital is available only when the underdeveloped country has opportunities that are attractive to foreign investors. Much foreign capital for underdeveloped countries in the last three decades has been in the form of contributions by foreign governments and international institutions.

9. Selecting a development strategy involves a number of difficult choices. A country need not simply accept its current comparative advantages; there are reasons for not pushing specialization according to current comparative advantage too far, including the risks of fluctuations or declines in the demand for one's principal product and the overdependence on foreign trade. There may also be noneconomic reasons for preferring a different pattern of development. All considerations must be tempered by knowledge of what will in the end be likely to work.

10. Much current debate about development concerns a choice among (a) agricultural development, (b) exploitation of natural resources, (c) development of import substitution industries, and (d) development of an industrial capacity that will create new export industries. None of these strategies is without problems and risks.

11. Collective rather than individual development efforts became more common in the 1970s. OPEC's success renewed interest in commodity price stabilization cartels but without notable success. A political initiative calling for a New International Economic Order (NIEO) seems to have achieved little more than discussion over this period.

12. The major thrust of NIEO has been for wealth transfers from developed to less-developed countries (as opposed to wealth creation). Of its major proposals, only the granting of some preference to LDC manufacturers has occurred.

13. The view of economic development presented in this chapter is subject to criticism for neglecting to discuss—or misconceiving—important problems. One is the perhaps unrealistic haste that underlies most development efforts. A second is the overemphasis on population growth as a barrier to development. A third is an exaggeration of the opportunity cost of creating capital. Economic development is today a field in ferment.

TOPICS FOR REVIEW

The gap between LDCs and developed economies
Barriers to development
Infrastructure
The role of planning in development
Alternative development strategies
Wealth creation versus wealth transfers

DISCUSSION QUESTIONS

1. Each of the following is a headline from a recent story in the *New York Times*. Relate them to the problem of economic development.
   a. Africa: Ferment for a Better Life
   b. Black Africa: Economies on the Brink of Collapse Because of OPEC
   c. Hungary Reforming Economy to Attract Tourists
   d. Goodyear to Build Plant in Congo for $16 Million
   e. Algeria's 4-Year Plan Stresses Industrial Growth
   f. India: Giant Hobbled by Erratic Rainfall
   g. Foreign Banks to Finance New Guinea Copper Mine
   h. Not All Benefit by Green Revolution
   i. OPEC Nations Provide Loans to Underdeveloped Nations to Pay for Oil Imports
2. If you were a member of a U.S. foreign aid team assigned to study needed development projects for a poor recipient country, to which of the following would you be likely to give relatively high priority, and why?
   a. birth control clinics
   b. a national airline
   c. taxes on imported luxuries
   d. better roads
   e. modernization of farming techniques
   f. training in engineering and business management
   g. primary education
   h. scholarships to students to receive medical and legal training abroad.
3. China requires 5 million tons more grain each year just to keep up with its annual population growth of 17 million people. This is about five times Canada's wheat supply at present. What policy choices do these facts pose for the Chinese government? How should it resolve those choices?

4. "This natural inequality of the two powers of population and of production in the earth . . . form the great difficulty that to me appears insurmountable in the way to perfectability of society. All other arguments are of slight and subordinate consideration in comparison of this. I see no way by which man can escape from the weight of this law which pervades all animated nature. No fancied equality, no agrarian regulations in their utmost extent, could remove the pressure of it even for a single century" (T.R. Malthus, *Population: The First Essay,* Chapter 1, page 6).
   Discuss Malthus's "insurmountable difficulty" in view of the history of the past 100 years.
5. To what extent does the vicious circle of poverty apply to poor families living in developed countries? Consider carefully, for example, the similarities and differences facing a poor black family living in Arkansas and one living in Ghana, where per capita income is less than $400 per year. Did it apply to immigrants who arrived on the New York docks with $10 in their pockets?
6. How might each of the following affect a country's economic development?
   a. a tradition that a man's land be divided equally among all his children
   b. a very unequal distribution of national income
   c. specialization in a commodity in which it has a virtual world monopoly
   d. a decision to be entirely self-sufficient
7. The president of Venezuela said recently: "The decision of OPEC members to raise petroleum prices should be applauded by all third world countries. It represents the irrevocable decision to dignify the terms of trade, to revalue raw materials and other basic products of the third world." Which underdeveloped countries might be expected to have agreed? Which to have disagreed?
8. "High Coffee Prices Bring Hope to Impoverished Latin American Peasants" reads the headline. Mexico, Kenya and Burundi, among other underdeveloped countries, have the right combination of soil and climate to increase greatly their coffee production. Discuss the benefits and risks to them if they pursue coffee production as a major avenue of their development.
9. Discuss the reasoning behind the policies indicated by the following newspaper headlines (all appeared in the summer of 1983):
   a. "Mexico Proposes to Restructure $20 Billion Debt."
   b. "Ecuador Is Allowed to Delay Payment of $200 Million."
   c. "Philippines Propose a 34% Cut Next Year in Its Capital Spending."
   d. "Zimbabwe's Fourth Budget Cuts Spending and Extends Income Tax to More Blacks."

45 COMPARATIVE ECONOMIC SYSTEMS: THE ECONOMIES OF CHINA AND THE USSR

Economics is concerned with the basic questions, What is produced? How is it produced? How is the product distributed? So far we have examined these questions in the context of a free-market economy in which private firms and households interact in markets with some assistance and interference from the government. We have studied this kind of economy for several reasons. First, this is the kind of economy *we* live in. Second, it is the economic environment in which the serious study of economics was born and has grown.

Today, however, over one and a quarter billion people, about a third of the world's population, live in the Soviet Union and China, countries that explicitly reject our kind of economic system. At least another third of the world's population live in countries whose economies have not yet developed to the point where the model of either the free-market or the managed economy fits closely.

Can the same theories and measures be applied to economies quite different from the free-market economy? So far as economics describes the ways in which people respond to incentives and mobilize scarce means to given ends, the same economic principles are applicable under a variety of assumptions about ends, means, or incentive systems.

All economies face scarcity, and all must decide how to allocate scarce goods; most face problems of inflation, unemployment, balance-of-payments deficits, and unsatisfactory rates of growth.

DIFFERENT ECONOMIC SYSTEMS

It is common to speak of the economic systems of *capitalism, socialism,* and *communism* as if they were the only three paths to basic economic decisions. But this is at best a simplification and at worst a confusion. There are *dozens* of economic systems in existence today, not three. Just as there are many differences among the institutions of the United States, the United Kingdom, Germany, Sweden, Japan, France, Greece, and Brazil, so are there differences among the institutions of China, the Soviet Union, Poland, Bulgaria, Cuba, Czechoslovakia, and Yugoslavia. Countries are dissimilar in many respects: in who owns resources, in who makes decisions, in the role of governmental planning, in the nature of the incentives offered to people, and in the way that the economy performs.

Ownership of Resources

Who owns a nation's farms and factories, its coal mines and forests? Who owns its railroads and airways? Who owns its streams and golf courses? Who owns its houses and hotels?

The answers differ in different countries. One characteristic of the capitalist system is that the basic raw materials, the productive assets of the society, and the final goods are predominantly privately owned by individuals singly or in groups. By this standard the United States is predominantly a capitalist economy, although many of its resources are in fact publicly rather than privately held. In the United States there is some public

ownership of power, housing, and utilities as well as of many local transit systems. Although a few observers see evidence of creeping or galloping socialism in such projects as the Tennessee Valley Authority (TVA), most agree that in the United States the pattern of ownership is predominantly private.

In contrast, socialism envisions a society in which the ownership of all productive assets is public. Today there are no completely Communist or Socialist societies. In the Soviet Union, virtually all factories are state-owned and an attempt has been made to collectivize all farms, but though the Soviets officially designate their economy as Socialist, there are three sectors of that economy—agriculture, retail trade, and housing—where some private ownership exists. If the USSR is not a pure Socialist economy, it is sufficiently near the public ownership end of the spectrum to distinguish it from the United States near the private ownership end.

Other countries fall between them on the spectrum. Great Britain has six times in this century elected Labor governments that have been officially committed to socialism to the point of nationalizing key industries: railroads, steel, coal, gas, electricity, atomic power, postal services, telephones, telegraphs, airlines, and some trucking. Figure 45-1 shows the division of fixed investment between public and private sectors in 11 countries.

With respect to the ownership of resources—and virtually every other dimension of an economy—three basic points are worth remembering.

1. Every real economy is "mixed" rather than pure.
2. Among countries the mixture differs in ways that are appreciable and significant.
3. Over time the mixture changes.

The Decision Process (Coordinating Principles)

In Chapter 4 we distinguished between two kinds of systems: a *market system,* in which decisions are made impersonally and in a decentralized way by the interaction of individuals in markets, and a

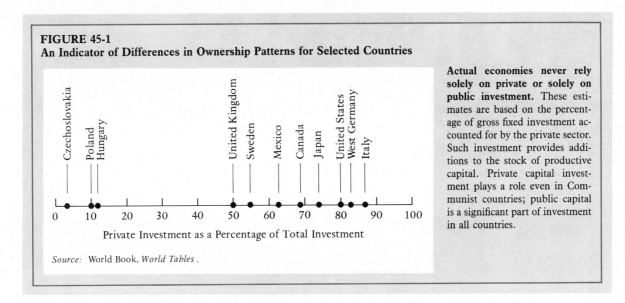

FIGURE 45-1
An Indicator of Differences in Ownership Patterns for Selected Countries

Private Investment as a Percentage of Total Investment

Actual economies never rely solely on private or solely on public investment. These estimates are based on the percentage of gross fixed investment accounted for by the private sector. Such investment provides additions to the stock of productive capital. Private capital investment plays a role even in Communist countries; public capital is a significant part of investment in all countries.

Source: World Book, *World Tables* .

command system, in which centralized decision makers decide what is to be done and issue appropriate commands to achieve the desired results.

Again no country offers an example of either system working alone, but it is true that some economies—those of the United States, France, and Yugoslavia, for example—rely much more heavily on market decisions than do the economies of East Germany, the Soviet Union, and Poland. Yet even in the United States the command principle has substantial sway: minimum wages, many aspects of agricultural policy, rent controls, antipollution regulations, and Supreme Court rulings ordering such things as the equal economic treatment of people and the breakup of particular monopolies are a few obvious examples. More subtle examples concern public expenditures and taxes that in effect transfer command of some resources from private individuals to public officials. (The extent of government interference with market forces was discussed in Chapters 24 and 25.)

In the planned economies of the Eastern bloc, where plans, quotas and directives are important aspects of the decision-making system, there is substantial command at work. But markets are used too. At the retail level, for example, people can spend their incomes with substantial discretion on a wide variety of goods.

Table 45-1, though it suppresses many subtle distinctions, focuses on important tendencies in certain twentieth century economies by a simple classification according to ownership and decision patterns. Later in this chapter we shall examine more closely the economic systems of China and the USSR, both of which are considered Communist societies. The table suggests at once that they differ significantly from each other as well as from the United States.

Much economic behavior depends more on the decision pattern than on the ownership pattern. Thus in the United Kingdom, while a large number of key industries are publicly owned, their contol is vested in semi-autonomous boards over which Parliament exerts very little control. By and large, the boards try to make their enterprises profitable, and to the extent that they succeed, their behavior will be similar to that of profit-seeking privately owned firms.

In contrast, firms in Hitler's Germany were under a high degree of state control, even though technically they were privately owned. An attempt to predict their behavior using the profit-maximiz-

TABLE 45–1 COMPARATIVE ECONOMIC SYSTEMS: OWNERSHIP AND DECISION PATTERNS

Decision pattern	Ownership pattern	
	Predominantly private	Predominantly public
Substantially decentralized with use of market	United States	Yugoslavia
Predominantly centralized with use of command principle	Nazi Germany	USSR

Each of these combinations of private and public ownership and centralized and decentralized control has occurred in practice. This table is a simplification that highlights differences among economic systems. It would be an interesting exercise to use a grid that gives several, rather than just two, gradations for each variable and then attempt to place current and past economies in the appropriate cells.

ing model would not have been successful because the central decision makers guiding their actions were concerned with goals quite different from profit maximization.

Whose Values?

In the market and command systems, different groups make the relevant decisions. It follows that different people's judgments will determine those decisions.

In a capitalist market economy, dollars "vote." The demands of consumers for goods exert a major influence on the nature of the goods produced. Traditionally this is called consumer sovereignty, but it should be noted both that the rich consumer has more say than the poor one and that firms retain a great deal of control over what is and is not produced. Mixed economies often use public policies to modify the decisions that would emerge from the uses of private purchasing power, but they are best regarded as supplementing rather than challenging the principle of consumer and producer sovereignty.

Early Marxists attacked the notion of a market-oriented value system. One of the great slogans of the utopian Marxists was "From each according to his ability, to each according to his need." Such a slogan does not eliminate the allocational problem: in a world in which desires for goods and services exceed the capacity to produce them, someone has to judge who needs what and then take steps to provide it.

In general, in command systems some group must decide what is to be produced and who is to get it. Because no one has yet devised a scheme by which everyone would automatically give according to his or her ability and in which everyone's needs would be clear to all, tough decisions have to be made. Whoever makes the decisions might do so on the basis of majority preferences, with each person having one vote regardless of his or her share of the income. (Cooperatives operate on this principle, each *member* having one vote; the contrast with a corporation, where each *share* has one vote, is marked.) Alternatively, each decision maker might decide on the basis of his or her own preferences (autocracy) or those of a particular group. Or the decision maker might decide on the basis of what he or she thinks is "good for the people."

Different systems are likely to reflect the values of different groups. Planned systems reflect the values of the government somewhat more strongly than do market systems.

Incentive Systems

Psychologists know that people (and most other living creatures) respond to reward and punishment. Incentives may be of two main kinds—the carrot or the stick—and of almost infinite varieties. Direct monetary rewards, in the form of wages or profits or bribes, are well understood. Indirect monetary rewards, such as special housing, vacations, or subsidized education, are not always as readily identified, but they can be effective. Nonmonetary "carrots" include praise, medals, certificates, and applause. Fines, prison terms, and other penalties are used to punish aberrant behavior in all societies; in some societies coercion and fear provide even stronger motivation.

Capitalist market economies place major reliance on monetary incentives. Monetary incentives to the individual in a Socialist society are not very different from those in a capitalist economy. Differential earnings for different occupations are used in Socialist economies, and piece rates are common. Gifts and bonuses of housing, cars, and other sought-after goods or privileges are used and valued. Large accumulations of assets are not permitted, but the importance of this is in dispute. There are no millionaires in the Soviet Union, but the desire for power is perhaps as important as the desire for wealth in both Capitalist and Socialist societies.

The big difference in incentive systems lies in whether those responsible for production respond to what it is *profitable* to produce or whether they respond to what they are directed to produce.

In the first case, profits can provide their own reward in terms of bonuses, salaries, dividends, and perhaps the funds to permit growth and the accumulation of power. In the second case, it is necessary to provide incentives to managers and workers to achieve the assigned quotas.

Ends and Means

Many, perhaps most people in Western societies value the *means* of the free market and democratic processes even more highly than they value the *ends* of high and rising living standards. Most Americans distrust the agglomeration of central power and the loss of democratic institutions that accompany communism or any other form of centrally administered command economy. Many believe that there is no need to choose between means and ends because they feel that the free market and democracy produce better results than do alternative systems in terms of both means and ends.

Few Americans would decide to go over to the Soviet system, even *if* it could be *proved* that the Soviet system was certain to produce a higher growth rate than the American free-market system. In the 1930s it was believed that fascist dictatorships were more efficient than democracies. Mussolini, it was said, "made the Italian trains run on time." It is debatable that the belief was correct, but most people accepted it. Yet few Americans advocated that America become a fascist dictatorship.

In many less-developed countries, ordinary people often put more importance on the ends, higher living standards, than on the means of achieving them. They may regard a change of means per se as unimportant. The choice between a centralized and a decentralized economy may seem to be simply one of which group will exploit them—government officials or powerful monopoly interests. If a highly planned economy offers them a good change of a 4 percent growth rate while a democratically oriented market society offers 2 percent, they may well choose the planned society. To warn them that in so choosing they may throw away their freedom is likely to evoke the reply, What has freedom meant to us in the past but the freedom to be hungry and exploited?

THE ECONOMY OF CHINA

The People's Republic of China, often called Red China by the Western press, dates from 1949, when the Chinese Communists defeated the Nationalist forces of General Chiang Kai-Shek. The Republic has sought to adopt an economic system patterned along Soviet lines and embodying both Marxist principles of ownership and control of resources and a Stalinist strategy of rapid industrialization managed by a highly centralized, command-type economy. As it has evolved, however, the Chinese economy today is much less of a command economy than the Soviet economy, with greater use of market incentives and decentralized decision making. It is, of course, still a highly planned Socialist economy very different from the economy of the United States.

The economic system in China today did not develop smoothly and gradually over the three decades since the Nationalist defeat. Rather it is the product of many political and ideological struggles within the government. Although purely ideological issues have played a role in the development of the economic system, there is little doubt that economic performance has been a major factor. Thus economic setbacks have tended to be followed by political upheavals and reforms of the economic system.

The 1983 government of Deng Xiaoping reflects the emerging dominance since 1976 (when Mao died and the Gang of Four was overthrown) of the pragmatists (sometimes described as the right wing) over the ideologues (described as the left wing). The Chinese government, with a billion mouths to feed, is evidently no longer willing to encourage ideologically pure, but productively inefficient, methods.

There are many underlying economic reasons why the Chinese pattern has developed along lines different from those of the Soviet economy. Perhaps most important is that the vast majority of the population is rural and depends on agriculture for its existence. While 30 percent of Americans and 39 percent of Soviets live in rural areas, over 80 percent of Chinese do so. As agriculture prospers or suffers, Chinese well-being changes. Drought, crop failure, or mismanagement of agricultural production lead to large-scale poverty. A second difference is that this huge country is even now lacking an integrated system of communication and transportation. This makes centralized planning and operation much less effective than it would otherwise be and has inevitably led to substantial decentralization in the planning process.

Finally, China in 1949 was a truly underdeveloped country surrounded by major industrialized nations—most notably the Soviet Union and Japan—that were also historic enemies. In 1949 most of the population lived near the subsistence level and used primitive tools and methods of production.

The Development of the Chinese Socialist Economy

When the Communists finally took power in 1949 they inherited a war-ravaged economy in total disarray as the result of World War II, the lengthy revolution, and the officious and corrupt administration of the displaced Chinese Nationalist government. The Communists, although not numerous, promised to be a unifying force and more honest than the notorious Nationalists.

1949–1958: The First Decade

The initial economic moves were along classical Marxist-Leninist lines. As Chou En-lai, later to be premier, put it, "The present of the Soviet Union is the future of China." The properties of the displaced Nationalist government, of its supporters, and of foreign capitalists were confiscated and nationalized. Large landholdings were broken up and distributed in small plots to peasants. The central government took firm control of the economy as well as of the political system.

By 1953 a first five-year plan was introduced, with Soviet guidance and massive Soviet economic assistance. It was Russian in orientation, emphasizing development of heavy industry through forced saving designed to limit consumption and generate high levels of investment. The Russians actually moved whole factories from the Soviet Union to China.

This first plan neglected agriculture. Encouraged by the favorable harvest of 1955, however, the plan was to begin the collectivization of agriculture. When agriculture did poorly in 1956, the plans were postponed until 1958, when output was once again at a satisfactory level.

1958–1960: The Great Leap Forward

By the end of the first five-year plan the failure to achieve most of the plan's targets, and especially the lack of success in agriculture, led to a major internal split. Out of this Mao Tse-Tung emerged as the new leader. Mao believed that Communist ideology, not capitalist incentives, would provide the means to the economic development of China's sleeping giant.

Mao also believed China's large underemployed population to be its greatest asset. He thought that what was necessary and sufficient for economic growth was to mobilize it. Only 2.5 percent of the labor force worked in industry at the time of the revolution, and the Great Leap Forward was to be founded on a massive mobilization of labor for industrial as well as agricultural development.

Labor was brought to the newly created factories in the urban areas and encouragement given to establishing small labor-using industries in the rural areas. Initially this campaign involved the creation of millions of backyard workshops and furnaces used to smelt steel in workers' and peasants' spare time. However, these small-scale steel mills were soon abandoned as a serious waste of resources. A more important and lasting part of the campaign was the development in rural areas of small-scale factories that produced goods such as the fertilizer and machinery needed in those areas. These plants, scattered about rural China, employed as many as 20 million people. Tens of millions of peasants were also engaged during the slack agricultural season in thousands of irrigation projects designed to increase agricultural productivity.

A major feature of the Great Leap Forward was a tremendous increase in the size of the collective unit of production in agriculture. The 740,000 cooperatives, originally set up in the collectivization that occurred between 1956 and 1958, were reorganized into 24,000 communes averaging 5,000 households each, with communal ownership and organization. The communes were more than agricultural producing units. They represented a tight-knit form of both government and economic management that were involved in everything from crafts to the militia to education. By providing collective child care they freed 90 million women for productive activity outside the home. These communes provided the focus for a substantial regional decentralization of planning and control organized around provincial governments.

The Great Leap Forward was a massive economic failure. By the end of 1960 agricultural output had dropped 20 percent below its 1957 level. Among the causes of this failure were the bitter resistance of peasants to the communes, bad weather, and a political rift with the Soviet Union that led to an abrupt withdrawal of Soviet advisers and economic aid. Perhaps, too, the proposed changes were too massive to be adopted so suddenly, particularly since there was no trained, efficient government bureaucracy to implement new orders in the face of traditional ways. In any event Mao was ousted and a more pragmatic, less ideological faction, with Liu Shaoqi as its dominant figure took over.

1961–1965: The Period of "Readjustment, Consolidation, and Repair"

The pragmatists shifted the emphasis from mobilizing workers to increasing productivity in agriculture. They did so in part by allowing commune members to develop private plots and sell the output in farm markets and in part by having the industrial sector greatly alter its focus so that production of fertilizers and farm machinery could be increased. Within three years agricultural output returned to the levels achieved in the years preceding the Great Leap Forward. Some modest private incentives were also introduced within the industrialized sector.

1966–1975: The Cultural Revolution

With the aid of revolutionary youth, Mao regained power in 1966 in a massive political coup and purged the government of its moderate pragmatists. In the name of ideological purity, education was denounced and scientists and technicians banished to rural labor. On the economic front, all traces of capitalist influence were eliminated: private plots were confiscated, rural markets closed, and material incentive plans for industrial workers eliminated. The political and personal repressions of this period of Chinese history have only recently been exposed.

The program was another economic disaster. The levels of industrial and agricultural output began to decline almost immediately. In 1968 real GNP was well below its level during the first year of the Cultural Revolution. Mao therefore gave greater power to the more moderate Chou En-lai. Chou did a remarkable job, by reinstating experienced administrators and increasing imports of vitally needed machinery and equipment among other things. He proposed a long-run strategy called the *Four Modernizations* for the gradual, simultaneous development of agriculture and industry. However, his death in January 1976 and the emergence of the Gang of Four, Mao's ultra-left-wing colleagues, led to an abrupt reversal and a return of the uncompromising ideology of the Cultural Revolution.

After 1976: Post-Mao China

Mao's death in 1976 and the arrest of the Gang of Four brought to power a new government whose dominant figures were Hua Goufing and Deng Xiaoping. This government still rules China today, with Deng now the dominant personality.

The economy has since had its ups and downs and internal struggles have continued. But there has been an end to the abrupt reversals of policy that characterized the two preceding decades. The pragmatists have gradually moved back toward Chou's objectives, with increased reliance on material incentives in both agriculture and industry, improvements in technology, increased foreign trade, and encouragement of foreign investment in China.

At the 1979 session of the National Peoples' Congress, an ongoing plan for gradual re-adjustment was extended for another five years. Among the key elements in the plan were (1) allowing private plots and production in agriculture for up to 15 percent of total land use; (2) providing bo-

nuses and other incentives to increase output in both agriculture and industry; (3) shifting away from the industrialization-at-all-costs strategy toward a more balanced growth strategy with greater emphasis both on light industry and on consumption; and (4) greatly expanding foreign trade, thus replacing an ideological commitment to self-sufficiency in order to give China access to the gains from international trade.

Agriculture in the Chinese Economy

For the 80 percent of the Chinese population still living in rural areas, agriculture is their source of livelihood and indeed survival. In 1982 per capita income was under $200 per year.

An individual household typically owns its own house but not the land on which it sits or the land it cultivates. Households are members of a production team. Each team contains an average of about 33 families, or 160 persons. The team is the primary unit of production, of ownership, and of income distribution. The *team* owns the land it cultivates (about 50 acres) and the machinery and draft animals that are its capital. Teams are organized into brigades that produce goods and services such as road building, repair shops, and schools. Brigades are organized into communes that provide greater needs like irrigation, banking and credit, high schools, and a militia. Today in sharp contrast to the primary role played by the communes during the Maoist period, the team is the key economic unit. Indeed, communes are being replaced by townships as the local unit of government administration.

The team is given production targets, or quotas. Prices for agricultural inputs and for quota outputs are set by the central government. If the team exceeds its output quotas, it may sell the extra output on farm markets at any price it can get. Similarly, the output from private plots may be sold in rural markets. It is estimated that at least a third of farm income is earned from above-quota or private plot production.

Team income is distributed to individual households by formula. In their work for the collective, peasants are awarded *work points* either on the basis of the hours worked, with different work points awarded for different tasks, or on the basis of the quantity and quality of output produced. The value of each work point is determined annually by dividing the net income of the commune by the total number of work points awarded to its members. During the year, all peasants and their family members are given a grain ration on a per capita basis. At the end of the year, the value of their grain ration is deducted from the value of their work points. They receive cash for any surplus work points they have after this deduction is made and owe a debt to the commune if they end up with a negative balance.

Recently a new alternative to work points, called the *contract responsibility system*, has been gaining popularity. Under this system a group of households, a single household, or even an individual peasant enters into a contract with the team to use a fixed amount of the team's land and machinery to produce a fixed amount of output. Anything produced above that amount is generally shared by the producer and the team. The relative amounts shared vary throughout rural China, but in some cases the producers can keep everything produced above the agreed amount of output. As of mid 1982 the contract responsibility system had spread to more than 90 percent of the communes in China. This new system, which reflects a further decentralization of the incentive system, motivates producers to exceed the output contracted for.

Allowing the team to keep the revenues from extra output has proven a powerful incentive to increased productivity. Teams are encouraged to invest in machinery, fertilizer, and other means of increasing productivity. The central government can increase or decrease the incentive to do so by varying the prices it charges for the inputs. Industries run as sidelines by people primarily working on farms continue to be an important feature of rural life, but their nature has shifted. They no longer smelt steel as in Mao's time but produce simpler goods such as leather products and textiles. Such sideline activities today account for about 15 percent of rural income.

The various agricultural units—teams, brigades, and communes—are run by elected representatives who are awarded work points for the time they put in. They are not bosses or managers in the Western sense but carry supervisory authority for as long as they are elected. The program is too young for us to determine whether or not a permanent managerial class will emerge, but the signs point in that direction, with Communist party membership and loyalty to the party major criteria for success.

One important freedom that is absent in China is labor mobility. Workers must stay in their village or township unless given permission to leave. Consequently there is often substantial underutilization of labor but no labor mobility in response.

Organization of Industry

China's industrial base is of two main types: state and cooperative owned-and-managed. In general, most modern capital-intensive industry is in the state sector; more traditional, small-scale, labor-intensive industry is in the cooperative sector. However, the distinction is not so much dependent on the current function of an enterprise as on its historical origins. During China's socialization process, major industrial enterprises were immediately taken over by the state, while craftsmen and artisans were organized into producer cooperatives. As the political climate varied, the cooperatives' freedom to form, to expand, and to capitalize also varied. They are currently being encouraged both because of the emphasis on light industry and worker participation and because being labor-intensive they can better absorb China's unemployed than can the capital-intensive state industries.

There is also a small but growing urban business sector. Private entrepreneurs are permitted, and by late 1981 there were over 1 million of them, mostly involved in tailoring and similar enterprises. Their capital is largely human, with perhaps a sewing machine or two. Such enterprises may receive permission to employ up to five people if the owners can demonstrate that they will do so in "non-exploitative ways." (This is characteristic of the ever-present mixture of Communist ideology and increasing emphasis on market incentives.)

State-Owned Enterprises

The most closely planned and controlled activities are in the state-owned enterprises. According to regulations each enterprise is given detailed instructions about quantity, quality, and variety of output as well as targets for permissible amounts of inputs, including capital. This implies expected levels of productivity. Output and input prices are also set by the state. Thus there are "profit" quotas for each enterprise. Basic wages are also set by the state. There are eight basic grades, depending on difficulty of job, working environment, and the individual's skills.

These regulations overstate the degree of central control actually practiced, even in the state enterprises. More and more state enterprises have been given permission to sell any outputs they produce above their assigned targets and to keep a share of the profits they earn from these above-target sales. They may invest any retained earnings and keep the first two years' return from such investment. They may also brand their products and advertise to create a market for their above-target production. They may even apply for permission to sell above-quota outputs in export markets. Within limits an enterprise's management committee may alter the methods of production. Its worker-management group may recruit, hire, and (recently and to a limited degree) fire workers. Bonuses may be paid to individual workers from the enterprise's retained earnings. Workers' total compensation consists of their basic wages, bonuses paid to the workshop by the state for cost reduction and innovation, and a series of welfare benefits. Perhaps as much as 50 percent of total compensation comes as supplements to the basic wages.

Because these experiments have led to increased output, they have been extended. Some Western observers even believe that they will soon become the norm for all of China's state-owned industry. However, these arrangements fall far short of total free-market enterprise. The basic decisions about major investments and about what to produce in what quantities and varieties are still left to the state. Also the prices of outputs and raw materials and the basic wage levels—all of which are set by the state—substantially limit the discretion of the local enterprise managers. Moreover, prices are often quite arbitrary, reflecting relative prices that were appropriate decades earlier or the values of central planners.

Cooperative and Individual Enterprises

Cooperatives and individual enterprises are much more nearly free-market units than are state enterprises. While some of their products are controlled in the sense that output is sold only to the state and at prices set by the state, more and more products are being considered "out of plan" and left uncontrolled. Enterprises producing such products do have to pay state-controlled input prices and must pay taxes (including a share of profits) to the state. They are limited in what, and where, they may purchase. They also depend on the state for credit and for funds for major capital investments. Every time such enterprises are given additional discretion, they are exhorted to remain faithful to Socialist ideals and methods.

Consumption Decisions

Perhaps the most visible change in the Chinese economic system in the post-Mao years has been the greater scope given to consumption and to consumption choices. While Western tourists—especially in Shanghai and Peking—comment on the rampant Westernization, with everything from Coca-Cola to Frisbees to electronic games in evidence, the bulk of the Chinese continue to live at very low levels of income, with consumption patterns to match. But the Stalinist philosophy of sacrificing everything for industrial growth has given way to a substantially more consumer-oriented economy, which benefits the present generation. State control of the amount and nature of consumption occurs through its control of income distribution, prices, and ration tickets.

A primary tool of income distribution has been the state-controlled relationship of wages and bonuses to prices of consumer goods. By keeping certain prices low and allowing wages to rise, the central government has created a significant amount of discretionary income for consumers. Furthermore, the opportunity to earn, and keep, incentive pay and bonuses has gradually increased. This has meant refraining from high taxation of marginal income and limiting the share of total national income devoted to new investment. (How much this will hurt long-run economic growth is currently a hotly debated issue.) Additionally, by raising farm prices relative to industrial prices, the government has increased the ability of the large, relatively poorer rural population to earn incomes above the subsistence level.

The prices of consumer goods that are not set in the free market are deliberately controlled. "Essentials" are priced at or below the cost of production. These goods are characteristically rationed, with ration tickets issued to households according to their size and the age of their members, the type of work the members engage in, and the region of residence.

The combination of subsidized consumption of necessities and rationed availability is taken to be an ideological triumph of the Chinese system. Everyday necessities—coal is an example—are priced at something like average total cost, and the objective is to produce a quantity sufficient to meet the demand at the controlled prices. Secondary needs are priced well above cost, with the exact markup determined by the central government's desire to encourage or limit consumption. Some of these secondary-need commodities—such as wristwatches, bicycles, and toothpaste—are rationed by means of waiting lists for the limited available supplies. They tend, however, to be more readily available in large cities than in rural areas. Consequently below-market clearing prices are being charged at least in some areas of the country.

The fact that both food and industrial products are available to some degree in private markets limits the state's ability to control consumption decisions by setting the structure of official prices. Of course it can control consumption indirectly by limiting the production of individual commodities and by reducing the amount of discretionary income households have. But substantial consumer choice is presently being encouraged and is being exercised. The increased opportunity for consumption has reinforced the incentive to earn extra income. There are worthwhile things to work for and to buy.

Economic Reform

The Need for Reform: The Legacy of Mao

The Maoist period accomplished many things, some good and some bad for the health of the economy. Some of its more harmful consequences are listed below. Some are harmful practices introduced by Mao that have persisted. Others represent the long-lasting effects of now-discontinued policies that must still be lived with.

1. A highly centralized planning system put great power into a few hands, leaving few effective methods for challenging or even modifying decisions.

2. The growth policy, which was adapted from the early Russian model, was based on high rates of capital accumulation and a concentration on heavy industry. This has tended to foster an attitude of growth for its own sake.

3. The so-called "iron-rice-bowl" policy means that a worker receives tenure on his first day of work. Under this sytem it is virtually impossible to fire anyone.

4. Managers of state enterprises have been controlled too closely by central directives and given too little scope, or incentive, to exercise initiative on their own.

5. Pricing policies are extremely inefficient in a number of ways. First, capital is often provided freely to enterprises and usually does not have to be repaid. As a result, fixed capital is inefficiently utilized, and many firms carry excessive invento-

ries. Second, in common with most Socialist states, Chinese pricing policies put great emphasis on price stability. As a result, many relative prices bear no relation to current costs of production or to current scarcities. So even when producers are allowed some profit incentive, the incentives tend to encourage them to produce the wrong commodities. Third, the shortages caused by disequilibrium relative prices are countered by rationing schemes that themselves impose added costs and reduce consumer satisfaction. Fourth, food prices are kept very low. This often transfers income from rural to urban areas and greatly diminishes the incentives for increased agricultural production. Also, when prices are held well below costs of production, an ever-growing burden of agricultural subsidies becomes a serious drain on the state budget. To keep the system threatens to absorb an unreasonable amount of public funds. To abandon it threatens to cause unrest among the urban working class.[1]

The Reform Movement

To attack some of these problems, reforms have either been introduced or proposed. We have already seen that many reforms—such as increased incentives, less emphasis on heavy industry, and some relaxation of total job security—are already in effect. In the opinion of many economists, however, the reforms that are the most important, but unfortunately the least likely, are changes in pricing policies to move prices of outputs and inputs closer to efficient, market-clearing levels. Without major price reform, most of the other reform measures will be ineffective or, still worse, result in further misallocations of resources.

---

[1] Extreme cases of this problem are found in such Socialist economies as Poland and such mixed economies as Ghana and Kenya. In many cases where such an agricultural policy is in place, the associated problems have threatened the very structure of the society. In Ghana and Poland reform movements have been defeated by their inability to cope with these problems. Many observers feel that Kenya's democracy may soon founder on the horns of this same self-imposed, urban-rural dilemma. China is not as far along the road of food subsidy problems, but unless something is done, the problem will grow over the decades.

Performance of the Chinese Economy

Growth

In the first 30 years after the revolution, the Chinese economy has grown at an average rate of nearly 6 percent per year and in per capita terms at about 3.6 percent per year. These are impressive growth rates by Western standards, but the comparison may be misleading. China started from an incredibly low base. After decades of occupation, war, and civil unrest, virtually any kind of peacetime economy would have shown growth. In every five-year period except that of the Great Leap Forward, income grew, as did both industrial and agricultural output.

China's growth has been smaller than that of Japan, Korea, Hong Kong, and Singapore but above that of many other Asian countries such as India, Burma, and Indonesia. The pattern of growth has been uneven; it has tended to be higher in the pragmatic, relatively market-oriented periods and lower in the Maoist, culturally oriented ones. It has tended, at least until very recently, to be greater in industry than in agriculture, despite the critical need for—and the great emphasis on—agricultural output.

In 1982–1983 growth rates were below the long-term trend indicated by the preceding three decades, but considerable progress was being made in restoring balance among the sectors of the economy. This should remove one of the major inhibitions to sustained future growth: bottlenecks that have resulted from the unbalanced growth strategies of the past. How much of the credit belongs to the increased use of market incentives, how much to the increased role of foreign trade, how much to the relative political stability, and how much to other factors is a matter for current debate.

Population Control

As the rise in per capita income suggests, China has had some recent success in limiting its population growth. Everything from posters that proclaim "An only child is a happy child" to much more repressive measures have been used. But overpopulation continues to be a problem. Officially there is no unemployment. Every person of working age is assigned to a job, whether in a factory or farm or elsewhere, or is classified as "waiting for employment assignment." But underemployment in rural areas is evident. It is kept from becoming urban unemployment by restrictions that prevent people from leaving their villages. (These restrictions on freedom of movement in order to achieve a "satisfactory" allocation of resources are typical of planned economies.) Urban unemployment is also largely concealed in the cooperative and small-business sectors.

Living Standards

When living standards are considered, especially in Socialist countries, it is important to consider the contribution of nonwage as well as wage income. For 23 years, from 1957 to 1979, rural real wages in China seem to have changed little. Standards of living seem at the same time to have risen through increased literacy, availability of such public services as libraries and schooling, growth of income security at all stages of life, and a spectacular increase in life expectancy. (Life expectancy in rural areas rose from about 40 years in 1950 to over 60 years in 1980. Of all the countries or regions in the world with China's approximate per capita income, only Sri Lanka and the State of Kerala in India appear to have achieved as high a life expectancy.)

Similar remarks apply to urban areas. Here, however, there is in addition the great increase in female labor force participation rates, which has meant that the average household has more workers and hence more income.

Income Distribution

A study by the World Bank suggests that the percentage of real income received by the poorest two-fifths of the income distribution is no higher in China than in Thailand, India, or Indonesia. This is the result of many factors, but one of the most important is the absolute control exercised over internal migration. This has permitted the emergence of large income differentials between rural and urban areas that in a free society would have caused a large shift of population into the cities and towns.

Prognosis for the Future

It is too early to know the degree to which the recent changes in economic management have started China onto a successful path of long-term economic development. On the one hand, it is easy to find in the recent Chinese experience evidence to support the proposition that economic incentives, individual discretion, and foreign trade have proven more productive than mass enthusiasm, self-reliance, the class struggle, and a tightly controlled command economy—all aspects of Maoist doctrine. On the other hand, Chinese communism has often succeeded in tapping the vast potential energy and enthusiasm of the masses.

Has the Chinese experience proven that Maoist-Marxist philosophy is in error in assuming that ideology is more important than material incentives? Many observers feel that it would be premature to answer "yes" to this question. That philosophy is directed primarily to goals other than material well-being, goals that include achieving a classless society with a more equal distribution of income, income security, and guaranteed employment. China under Mao and still to a degree under Deng is pursuing non-economic goals even if they conflict with maximum economic growth. Which goals to pursue, and with what intensity, are always important social choices. At the moment China is leaning toward the material, but there are many in China who believe this is wrong. A leading American student of China believes that latent Maoists are very numerous and may well return to power within the decade. China's future—economic, political, and cultural—will change sharply if they do.

A final word of caution: the Chinese economy has been changing so rapidly and information about it is so hard to get and to verify that any written account is almost certain to be partially obsolete by the time it is published.

THE ECONOMY OF THE SOVIET UNION

The modern *economic* history of the Soviet Union is usually taken to have begun in 1928, 11 years after the Bolshevik revolution. At the time of World War I, Russia was a large and in most ways backward country with an enormous, poor, largely ignorant and illiterate peasantry, who were to prove as sullenly hostile to their new Bolshevik rulers as they had been to the czars. Backward and poor though Russia was, by 1917 industrialization had been under way for three decades; the nucleus of heavy industry and of an industrial labor force already existed.

During its first decade of existence, the new regime hung on by its teeth, contending with recurring famines, internal power struggles, and invasion by the Western powers. By the late 1920s Joseph Stalin had emerged as an effective strong man ready to undertake the economic task of lifting Russia from an underdeveloped giant to a major industrial power. Whatever the costs—and they have been enormous—the economic rise of the Soviet Union in five decades is a major achievement.

Stalin's economic policy had three strategies.

1. To consolidate management over all economic resources in such a way that they would respond surely and quickly to the needs of the regime.
2. To constrict consumption to an absolute minimum so that the maximum possible rate of capital accumulation, and thus growth, could be achieved.
3. To channel growth into the areas of heavy industrial development required for a major military power.

Neither the sacrifices imposed on the people as consumers nor the Herculean efforts asked of them as producers were borne without complaint or opposition. Stalin is perhaps best remembered for his "terrors," dramatized by the purges in which thousands were exiled or killed. Whatever its primary purposes, this regime of terror had the two effects of enforcing centralized power and providing a powerful set of incentives to carry out the orders of the regime.

The famous five-year plans began the rapid industrial development that was to transform the Soviet Union into a major military power by World War II and a major world power in the postwar period. The tenth five-year plan, covering the period 1976–1980, was only the second to put major emphasis on production of consumer goods, perhaps most notably food.

Ownership

With certain limited exceptions the central government—the state—owns all land, all natural resources, all capital goods, all business enterprises, and most urban housing.

In the industrial sector, state ownership is virtually complete; in the retail fields, state stores make up about two-thirds of the total sales, with the bulk of the remainder accounted for by rural cooperatives. A small amount of farm produce is sold in free "farmers' markets." Most rural housing, and perhaps a third of urban housing, is privately owned (and officially restricted to personal use). The rest is publicly owned.

About a third of all agricultural production comes from farms (called *sovkhos*) that are owned, run, and managed by the state. Another half of all production comes from collective farms that, while nominally cooperatives into which peasants were once forced, are in fact so closely controlled by the state that their differences from the sovkhos are minor. The remainder of the total agricultural output is produced on privately owned farms and by members of collective farms on garden plots they are allowed to cultivate in their spare time.

Private enterprise is profitable where it is permitted—in agriculture and in personal services of various kinds from psychiatric counseling to carpentry. The official figures probably underestimate the private sector by ignoring the illegal black market in privately produced goods and services.

The black market is a response by households (who are permitted to own savings deposits and personal possessions) to the restricted supply of officially available goods. They are glad to buy goods and services from others, who in turn are glad to earn extra money by producing them.

The Organization of Production

In the industrial sector of the Soviet economy, production is predominantly organized around individual plants that are managed by a "director" (appointed by the government with the approval of the local Communist party group). Directors may appear omnipotent to the workers, but their orders with respect to how and what to produce and how and when to replace equipment or expand operations are handed down from higher up in the planning hierarchy. Directors are in fact more bureaucrats than entrepreneurs.

Production decisions are made in a highly organized pyramidal bureaucracy. The overall planning agency, the USSR GOSPLAN, develops broad plans that are translated into orders for regional GOSPLANs, which in turn hand down directives to particular ministries. Ministries may be either at the industry level or in control of a particular resource. Ministries' instructions ultimately take the form of orders to individual plant managers, who then do their best to carry them out.

The industrial firm's targets include quotas with respect to total output and output of individual commodities. The wages a firm can offer are fixed by the government, and there is no open market on which the firm's manager can acquire scarce commodities. Within limits, workers are free to choose any job they are offered, and labor mobility is not really restricted—except that workers on collective farms have not been allowed to leave them at will. Despite rather large occupational wage differences, labor mobility has tended to be low.

Industry is governed by the many rules of a command economy. Directives cover many aspects

of a firm's operations, though of course they cannot cover all contigencies. *Within* the guidelines of the plan as it is sent down to the given firm, the firm is instructed and encouraged to be efficient and, where possible, to make "above-plan profits."[2] Planned profits go to the state; part of above-plan profits may be retained in the firm and used for the benefit of the employees. Thus there is some scope for maneuver, but the constraints are much tighter than those that face a typical American firm. A Soviet enterprise cannot usually experiment with new products or new methods of production without first securing permission. Indeed, because there is such emphasis on meeting or exceeding plan quotas, *quantity* of output becomes more compelling than cost savings or quality.

Western observers—and Soviet observers, too—have often noted that many microeconomic inefficiencies result from the command principle. Among them are excessive stockpiles of some commodities, shortages of others, and poor quality of many goods. Similar inefficiencies have been shown to exist in many American governmental activities, such as military procurement, where centralized command systems are in use. This suggests that inefficiencies of these kinds are inherent in highly centralized systems in which incentives are given in terms of fulfilling output quotas rather than earning profits.

Despite inefficiencies the Soviet system clearly works. It has produced a growing flow of armaments, goods, machines, and space vehicles. Soviet industry has proven adequate to the major demands placed on it; its inefficiencies have been serious but not crippling.

One of the sharpest critics of the inefficiencies of overcentralization and rigid control structure is a Soviet professor, E. Liberman. Some Socialist countries, such as Yugoslavia, have responded to his criticisms more than the USSR, but there is currently within the Soviet Union a great debate

---

[2] Because prices are specified by the state and are spelled out in the directive, the firm can earn above-plan profits only by exceeding output quotas. Many critics both outside and inside the system have noticed an overconcentration on physical output—on technological rather than economic efficiency.

on this very issue, and there have been a growing number of reforms aimed at decentralization over the last two decades.

A major problem of planned economies concerns innovation. Soviet managers have little incentive to innovate by experimenting with new products or new ways of producing old products. As long as the Soviet Union is catching up to the capitalist countries, it can copy capitalist products and techniques. It is not so clear that a planned economy left on its own could produce as rapid a rate of innovation as is generated by a profit-oriented, free-enterprise economy where decision making is effectively decentralized. One of the severest critics of the stultifying effects on invention and innovation exerted by a highly centralized economy has been the distinguished Soviet physicist and Nobel Prize winner A. K. Sakharov. (Since 1980 Sakharov has been banned from Moscow as a result of his too persistent criticisms.)

Agricultural production (which in 1928 absorbed 80 percent of the Soviet labor force and today absorbs about 25 percent) is almost as centralized as manufacturing. The results have been much less successful than those in the industrial sector. The collective farms were designed to provide cheap and adequate food supplies but the compulsion required to bring unwilling individual peasants into the collective farms did not generate cooperative responses. Many observers believe that the lack of incentives and rewards is responsible. Meeting quotas of steel wins bonuses, medals, praise—and pay raises—for the steelworkers; meeting grain quotas is likely to lead to even higher quotas for the next period.

Collective farmers do not receive wages; rather, they share in the income of the farm. But the government's policy, designed to keep food prices down by keeping farm prices low, has kept farm income low, too. In any case, low morale and the inability of farm labor to find other jobs have not led to high productivity, and agricultural production has been a chronic trouble spot in the Soviet economy.

Probably the biggest single failure of the Soviet system is its agricultural policy. Communist theorists, who were mainly urban in their origin and experience, sought to make collective farms resemble factories and regarded peasants as if they were assembly line workers. But the world over a farmer's job is tougher than that of an assembly line worker. Farming is not a 9-to-5 job, nor can it run on a five-day week. All the evidence suggests that the constant, backbreaking toil required of farmers is only provided efficiently when the fruits of that toil accrue to the farmers themselves. Whenever Eastern bloc countries have allowed peasants to own their land and to keep much of the proceeds of the crops they sell and have made the necessary agricultural equipment available, food output has risen dramatically. Whenever, as in the Soviet Union, the peasants do not own their land and cannot keep much of the return from marketing their crops, production languishes because peasants are not motivated to apply the necessary effort.

The Distribution of Goods and Household Incentives

Both the nature and quantity of the goods to be produced are specified by the central planners. Those for consumers are placed in the state-owned shops or in cooperatives, to be sold at government-specified prices that include an important "turnover tax" (see the box on page 879).

Households are free to spend their incomes on these goods. Individual choice rather than "command" is at work, but even here the function of a market is restricted. For instance, if too many consumers want a particular item, supplies will run out, but no price rise signals the higher demand to producers. The shortage is not an effective signal because producers are not motivated to respond to it. As a result there is no assurance that production will be increased. There is no automatic feedback indicating what consumers want, and would buy, that has any effect on the goods and services actually produced.

The use of the market, rather than direct allocation, in the distribution of consumer goods is explained by the need to avoid the impossible administrative burden of deciding who gets what, rather than by a philosophic desire to let consumers

PLANNING IN THE SOVIET UNION

Five-year plans. Five-year plans are, roughly, blueprints for later detailed implementation. They contain no orders to individual plants and no detailed quotas of goods to be produced, but they do prescribe both the level of aggregate income that is to be achieved and the *structure* of the economy by major sectors and industries.

Every five-year plan has included decisions about how drastically to curtail consumption in order to release resources for investment. Each has also decided how much effort is to be devoted to developing educational and technical resources that will be needed in the future. Decisions are also required about such matters as the form capital investment should take, and the state-controlled banking system lends only to those enterprises whose expansion the planners want to encourage.

One-year plans. Planning details are spelled out in the one-year plans. They are extremely complex exercises that work out the myriad microeconomic implications of certain broad objectives. The one-year plans translate the objectives of the five-year plans into detail sufficient to enable individual plants (or farms) to meet them and to ensure that the required supplies of needed resources are made available.

There is obviously an enormous coordinating job here. Tentative plans are sent to lower bureaucratic levels for comments and suggestions before being issued as final orders. Actual quotas are to some degree negotiated between the directors at the operating levels, who want to hold down the quotas expected of them, and the higher-level planners, who must achieve apparent miracles to satisfy overall growth objectives.

Prices in the Planning Process

Factor pricing. For internal productive use, "prices" of commodities or resources are designed to measure the scarcity value of the resources, compared to alternative uses. If the efficient use of resources is to occur, the charge for using, say, the services of a carpenter anywhere should reflect the value of his or her marginal product elsewhere.

But the state may wish to pay carpenters a higher wage than this, either because it has embarked on a program of income redistribution in which carpenters are to be favored or because the state wishes to denote carpentry as a "prestige" occupation. To avoid productive inefficiency, the planners assign *two* wage rates for carpenters. One is charged as a cost of production; the other (which may be higher or lower) is actually paid out to carpenters and becomes the source of their income.

With one important exception, this dual treatment of factor prices has long been part of the Soviet planning procedure. The exception concerns the cost of capital. Because "interest" is traditionally a payment to private owners of capital in capitalist societies, interest rates were odious to Marx and to early Marxist planners. Soviet planners were reluctant to assign a real scarcity-value interest rate to funds allocated for investment until a series of studies showed that investment allocation was among the least efficient aspects of Soviet planning. Today a number very much like an interest rate is used to measure the cost of capital.

Consumer prices and the turnover tax. Consumer prices are made up of two parts: the full cost of the good produced, using the correct internal accounting prices for factors, plus the **turnover tax.** This is an excise tax, which varies tremendously from commodity to commodity.

The size of the turnover tax is determined by the planners' idea of what goods people should be encouraged or discouraged to consume. In part this is a means for redistributing income; goods consumed by low-income groups may have very low turnover taxes.

Revenue from the turnover tax is used by the state for new investment. By changing the turnover tax, the planners can affect the relative size of consumption and investment. By varying the tax rate on different commodities, the state affects the relative sacrifice in consumption among different kinds of consumers.

be sovereign. There is a difference between consumer sovereignty, which allows consumer choices to help determine *what is produced,* and consumer freedom to choose from among goods of *predetermined* quantity, quality, and price.

Until recent years Soviet planners were reluctant to respond to such clear consumer signals as shortages of particular goods. The consumer riots in Poland in December 1970 seem to have changed this. After that Soviet planners began to take account of shortages and surpluses of particular consumer goods at existing prices in setting new production targets. To the extent that this occurs, consumer sovereignty has been introduced into the system. Recently there has been increased pressure for, and some experimentation with, a two-phase system. This would allow planners to decide what proportion of the nation's resources to devote to the production of consumer goods. It would also allow consumers, through a decentralized market-type decision mechanism, to exert an influence on how those resources are allocated among various lines of production.

Household incomes come from the state principally in the form of wages and salaries. "To each according to his need" was the Marxist ideal, but in the Soviet Union scientists, engineers, ballet dancers, and athletes apparently need more than do laborers and teachers. Wage *differentials* are in fact very much larger than in the United States; skilled workers characteristically earn three hundred percent more than unskilled workers (in contrast to 50 percent more in the United States).

But wages are not the only determinant of the distribution of income. Many goods and services such as medical care, higher education, and old-age pensions are provided free to those who qualify. State housing is provided at low cost. Large families receive special money allowances and special housing. Thus standards of living in the Soviet Union are considerably less unequal than wage differentials suggest. In contrast to the United States, there are fewer extreme incomes at either end but a somewhat greater spread in the incomes of the middle and upper middle income groups.

Income distribution in the USSR is very much

a matter of conscious policy decisions. Through wages, allownances, free and subsidized goods, and the turnover tax (which is like a sales tax but varies from product to product), the party hierarchy can effectively impose *their* views as to the appropriate pattern of output and distribution of income.

Sources of Investment Funds

The tax revenues of the Soviet state are an important source of state revenues. In addition the central bank (GOSBANK) can expand the money supply and absorb any government deficit it is asked to absorb. If it prints too much money, it will, of course, create an inflationary gap. With such a gap, there will be longer lines, more shortages, and more grumbling. These results can be avoided only by raising prices—by letting the inflation occur. Another aspect of the money supply is the ability of firms to borrow in order to expand. GOSBANK lends only to those enterprises whose expansion the planners want to encourage. It thus becomes a further device for implementing planners' objectives.

Unlike most Western central banks, GOSBANK is a monopoly commercial bank with thousands of branches. Since the central bank controls the commercial banking system completely, it does not use any of the indirect tools such as open market operations used by Western central banks.

Comparative Performance: The United States Versus the Soviet Union

In judging the performance of an economy, there are many different criteria and many different ways of viewing it. Moreover, comparing the actual performances of only two economies can be misleading. For example, during the last 40 years the Soviet Union has experienced twice as great a growth rate as the United States. But before concluding that this demonstrates a growth advantage of communism over capitalism, the even higher growth rates achieved in West Germany and Japan—capitalist countries—should be noted. With this warning in mind, we shall compare elements of the economic performances of the United States and the Soviet Union.

The Standard of Living in the 1980s

Most national income acountants and students of the Soviet economy judge the level of real purchasing power per capita in the Soviet Union to be about 50 percent of that in the United States. This kind of statistic is difficult to interpret. Clearly most Americans would feel very poor if their present incomes were cut in half. But American real incomes a generation ago were half what they are today, and at that time the United States was the richest nation in history. The perceived adequacy of one's income depends on what everyone else's income is and on past and future expectations. The Soviet citizens' standard of living is so much higher than it was even a decade ago, and is rising so rapidly, that it probably seems comfortable to them.

Nevertheless it is clear that Soviet citizens are poorer than their American counterparts. Not only is housing worse and clothing in shorter supply and less elegant, but the average citizen has to work more hours to earn the cost of a pair of shoes or an evening dinner. A small sedan in 1983 cost about twice the annual salary of the average Muscovite, and even at that price there was a three-year wait for delivery. Not surprisingly, the Soviet worker buys less, works longer hours, and has shorter vacations.

Notice, however, that these comparisons reflect in good part *our* social values. An observer might note that the Soviet citizen can see better chess, better gymnastics, and better soccer than an American counterpart—and can see them more cheaply. Yet another observer might note that Soviet citizens need not worry about their ability to provide medical and dental care for their families, the possibility of unemployment due to a severe economic slump, or providing for their retirement or the support of their dependents after their own death. A comprehensive set of welfare programs covers all these contingencies for all Soviet citizens.

Growth

From 1928 to 1970 the Soviet Union achieved an overall rate of growth of more than 4.5 percent per year notwithstanding some major disasters, particularly the famines of the 1930s and the devastating impact of World War II. During the 1960s the Soviet rate of growth was twice the U.S. rate. In more recent times, however, the growth rate has declined (although it is still higher than the U.S. rate). Recent growth experience is shown in Table 45-2.

As we noted, this remarkable growth record has not been costless. It was achieved by sacrificing current consumption for investment that led to greater production in the future. The relative prosperity of today's Soviet citizens is owed to their parents' forced forbearance. To sustain this growth rate for another generation, present-day citizens may well have to continue to forego many of the

TABLE 45–2 **ESTIMATES OF GROWTH OF GNP IN THE USSR, BY SECTOR OF ORIGIN**

	Average annual rate of growth (percent)			
	1966–1970	1971–1975	1976–1978	1979–1981
Agriculture	4.2	2.1	4.4	3.6
Industry	6.3	5.9	3.8	2.5
Construction	5.5	5.3	2.6	1.7
Transportation	7.5	6.6	4.3	3.3
Communications	8.9	7.2	6.1	5.4
Trade	6.4	4.8	3.7	2.6
Services	4.2	3.4	3.0	2.9
Total GNP	5.3	3.7	3.7	1.3

Source: CIA, Research Aid, *Soviet Economy: Performance of 1976–1977 and Outlook for 1978;* Directorate of Intelligence, *Handbook of Economic Statistics,* 1982.

The rate of growth in virtually all major sectors of the Soviet economy slowed in the 1970s. Growth rates vary significantly from sector to sector, with agriculture showing the poorest growth performance. Although growth rates have fallen, they are still above those of the United States.

comforts available to Americans. There is little general enthusiasm for such policies, and the regime has eased the restrictions on the consumer sector even at the cost of its growth rate. But the Soviet economy has demonstrated how an underdeveloped country can develop in one lifetime, if it will pay the price and if it has the unexploited resources on which to base an expansion.

Economic Stability

If growth has been the great triumph of the Soviet experience, economic stability has been a small one. A highly planned economy, if it is insulated from the outside world, need have no deficient-demand unemployment, no unintended inflation or deflation, and no cyclical phenomena. If it must engage heavily in foreign trade, it is not so easily insulated. In this regard the Soviet Union during its period of rapid growth was fortunate. It was a large country with ample and varied natural resources (like the United States), and it did not have to rely heavily on foreign trade. Moreover, much of what it did need was provided from within the Soviet system by the satellite countries of Eastern Europe.

The failure of Soviet agriculture to increase output sufficiently to keep pace with demand has led to increasingly large imports of foodstuffs from the West. Imports of high technology products, a field in which the Soviet Union has not kept pace with the West, have also been increased to meet a growing demand. As a result the Soviets have been faced with an increased need to earn foreign exchange to pay for these imports.

Although unemployment due to deficient aggregate demand need not and does not occur in the Soviet system, frictional and structural unemployment can occur. The state's ability to control the movement of people away from the farms (through a system of work permits and internal passports) has led to much disguised unemployment in the agricultural sector. There is little doubt that if people had been free to move from the farms, they would have moved in great numbers to the cities

in search of the excitement and higher living standards there, and they would have moved at a faster rate than industry could have absorbed them. In a market economy, this would have led to substantial urban overcrowding and unemployment and would have served to depress the wages of those who were successful in finding work. The Soviet policy has been to hold these people on the farms where they are underemployed and to allow them to move to the cities only as fast as they could be absorbed into jobs there.

Again a potential clash of values can be seen. Western observers are inclined to stress what to them is the severe loss of personal freedom, while Soviet observers tend to emphasize the gains to the economy of an orderly relocation of labor. In particular, they see the advantages to urban workers of not having their wages depressed by the unemployed migrants from the farm and the advantage to the farm dwellers in being detained on the farm, where they can be fed and housed at lower cost and in greater comfort until jobs are available in the city.

The Soviets have had less success in controlling inflation than in controlling unemployment. Like the princes discussed in Chapter 33, they found increasing the money supply too easy a way to finance public expenditures, particularly during the war. The high wartime expenditures resulted in a dangerously inflationary piling up of private money balances. But the response of a command economy can be quick and sure, if harsh. When monetary reform came, the state confiscated the bulk of private monetary balances and repudiated some of the public debt that workers had accepted in lieu of part of their wages. Thus workers who thought they had been saving found they really had been taxed.

This was the Soviet response to a problem that existed in all belligerent countries at the end of World War II. Wartime savings and deferred consumption created an enormous backlog of demand. After the war, this demand for goods was far in excess of the supply.

The Soviet response was to destroy the backlog

of purchasing power by monetary reform; the Western answer was to allow people to try to exercise it and accept the inevitable inflation. This reduced the real value of accumulated purchasing power to a level commensurate with the goods actually available for purchase. Both systems achieved the same end of reducing the real value of purchasing power to what was available. To Western eyes, the Soviet solution (confiscation) seems harsh and autocratic; to Soviet eyes, the Western solution (inflation) seems arbitrary and highly inequitable.

Shortcomings of the Soviet Economic Experience

In at least three major ways, a Soviet type of economy compares unfavorably to a Western market economy. First, it is accompanied by what most observers agree to be far more numerous and more serious microeconomic inefficiencies. Many small interdependent decisions have to be made that are difficult or impossible to make quickly, consistently, and efficiently, given a centralized decision hierarchy. The shortages, gluts, misshipments, and shortfalls of key quotas that have annoyed Soviet industry and plagued Soviet agriculture are neither surprising nor wholly avoidable. They are periodically denounced as the "planning errors" of a previous regime. Such errors, however, are apparently a cost of choosing to replace an automatic mechanism (whose implicit values the planners have rejected) by a deliberate mechanism that permits the planners to introduce their own values. In recent years, some pressure has developed within Soviet-type economies to retreat from complete planning and to allow market or marketlike mechanisms to do more of the allocating.

A second deficiency has been in the detailed planning process itself, which makes enormous demands on time and energy. When labor was abundant, and when alternative uses of those with the planners' skills were not numerous, this "transactions cost" of planning was perhaps not serious. Increasingly, however, the Soviet bureaucracy has been absorbing a large quantity of the energies of valuable, highly trained men and women in plan formation and implementation. The Soviets have come to recognize this as a real cost. The major surge of interest in techniques of mathematical programming, input-output analysis, and simulation reflects an official effort to substitute capital for high-priced labor in the "production function of planning." They hope both to save resources and to avoid some microeconomic inefficiencies and mistakes.

A third deficiency is that the goods and services produced reflect planners' preferences rather than those of citizens. This is true not only where a deliberate decision is made to reject consumer sovereignty for national purposes, but also generally, for there is no effective market mechanism by which consumers can signal their preferences. Not every family wants the same size apartment, but when the decision as to what proportion of its income it will spend on housing is taken away from the family and it is allocated space according to family size and occupation, there is no way that family *preferences* will play a role.

Source and Costs of the Achievements

A planned command economy has certain advantages over a market-oriented economy: the leaders can set up whatever priorities they wish, and they can then use the full power of the state to give effect to them. In such economies, the power of the state has been used to achieve forced saving to permit capital formation and rapid growth. It has also been used to prevent widespread unemployment. It may well be that the Soviet growth record could not have been achieved had it depended on popular or majority support, for it is by no means clear that the growth benefited the Soviet population of the 1930s and 1940s.

This rapid growth has had costs—costs not only in current consumption foregone but also the costs of coercing individuals, of their loss of freedom, and of substituting centralized for individual judgments. Because these costs cannot readily be measured, the question of whether the benefits justify the costs involves a judgment. Most citizens of Western countries are content to have foregone both the benefits and the costs; contemporary Russians may feel they have been justified. Not surprisingly, different people and different governments in the rest of the world come down on different sides.

Politically the present government is in many ways a monstrous and terrible tyranny—as Aleksandr Solzhenitsyn has emphasized. It is not necessary to assume, however, that this degree of tyranny *must* accompany any command economy. After all, the tradition of political tyranny in Russia stretches well back into the time of the czars. Other command economies have had regimes less repressive than that of the USSR. However, command economies must by their very nature be more authoritarian than free-market economies. An important and unsettled question concerns the minimum repression of individual freedom that is consistent with a highly centralized planned economy of the Soviet type.

COMPARATIVE SYSTEMS: A FINAL WORD

Perhaps the most important empirical observation about different types of economies is that a wide variety of economic systems seem able to coexist and are successful.

No economic system seems to do everything better than any major competing system; indeed, each has its strengths and weaknesses relative to alternative systems. To talk of "better" and "worse" in this context may itself be misleading: different economic systems imply different choices between current and future consumption, between individual or collective choices, between degrees of freedom or coercion, and between stability and growth.

The economic institutions of a society reflect in part its values, but they also reflect habits and

traditions, experiments and inertia. These institutions change with time in given countries and vary at a given time among countries. In the variety of experience economists hope to find many clues as to which instruments best achieve which ends.

In the contemporary experience, it looks as if the command principle makes the management of certain macro policies much easier than it is in a market system, but it also appears that it is less well suited than the market to handling micro allocations. While a command system can achieve great sacrifices in the short run, the growth evidence suggests no simple conclusion, for many countries with very different economic systems have achieved rapid growth. It is clear that markets are less personal than bureaucrats, and this makes them more acceptable to many people because they are less arbitrary and less subject to autocratic abuse.

SUMMARY

1. Actual economies can differ from one another in a great variety of ways, and such capsule characterizations as *capitalism*, *socialism*, and *communism* represent simplifications of complex matters.

2. Among the important dimensions in which economies can differ from one another are (a) the pattern of ownership of goods and resources; (b) the nature of the decision process used, with a particularly important distinction concerning "command" versus "market" decision mechanisms; (c) whose values control the economy and how these values are articulated; (d) the nature of the incentive systems used; and (e) the relative concern about ends and means.

3. The building of the Socialist economy of the Peoples Republic of China (often called Red China) began after the victory of the the Communists over the Nationalists in 1949. The first decade saw Russian-style planning with emphasis on heavy indus-

try and neglect of agriculture. The Great Leap Forward in 1958–1960 was a failure of doctrinaire Socialist views, which included the collectivization of agriculture. From 1961–1965 the pragmatists were in power and introduced reforms relying on market incentives and decentralization of economic power. From 1966–1975 there was another doctrinaire experiment, called the Cultural Revolution. This produced economic chaos by its rejection of all market values as well as scholarship, learning, and technological innovation. Since 1976 the pragmatists have once more been in power and less centralized control is the rule of the day.

4. Agriculture and related activities occupies 80 percent of the Chinese population. Collectivization has proven a failure, as it has throughout the Communist world. Chinese pragmatists are therefore trying to give more scope to the private profit motive to influence agricultural decisions.

5. Industry is partly state owned and controlled and partly left to individual initiative. Again the propagandists are introducing more decentralization of decision making in industry.

6. The performance of the Chinese economy has been mixed but (a) population control now seems to be finally a matter of serious policy attention and (b) although real wages have not risen much, standards of living—as measured by such factors as absence of famine, greatly increased life expectancy, free medical and hospital care for all, universal old-age security, and a relatively stable price level—have risen significantly under the Communist government.

7. The Chinese economy is characterized by many inefficiencies that various reforms are trying to remedy. By far the most serious are the inefficiencies caused by policies with respect to prices: prices of capital are often too low, prices of many consumer goods are too stable over the long run, disequilibrium prices sometimes require rationing and allocative controls, and prices of food products are often below costs of production and hence require large subsidies to producers.

8. Central planning plays a major role in the Soviet economy. Long-term goals are given structure by a series of five-year plans, which in turn are implemented by highly detailed one-year plans. Most of the key decisions are made centrally by the various GOSPLANs, but prices are used both for internal accounting and to affect the distribution of goods and incomes.

9. A comparison of relative performance between the United States and the Soviet Union reveals that the United States has higher levels of real output per capita but a much less impressive recent growth record. The Soviet Union has suffered less than the United States from unemployment but has not avoided inflationary pressures. Microeconomic inefficiencies have been numerous in the Soviet experience, and agriculture has proven to be a serious, chronic problem.

10. A major difference has been the use of coercion by the state. This has permitted the Soviet economy to achieve certain objectives, including extremely rapid capital formation, monetary reform, and the orderly mobility of labor from farm to city. To most Westerners, the costs in the form of coercion, loss of freedom, and the substitution of centralized for individual judgments seem to have been high. Most Russians today probably believe them to have been justified.

11. A wide variety of different economic systems seems able to coexist and to show successes. No economic system seems to do all things better than any major competing system; indeed, each has its strengths and weaknesses relative to alternative systems.

TOPICS FOR REVIEW

Free-market and command economies
Alternative ownership and decision patterns
Central planning
Decentralized Socialist economies
Effects of Communist pricing policies

DISCUSSION QUESTIONS

1. In an economic report to the 25th Communist Party Congress in 1976, Soviet Prime Minister Aleksei Kosygin said that the crisis of capitalism was marked by inflation and unemployment, in contrast to the Soviet Union's full employment and stable retail prices. How do the Soviet Union and China avoid the problems of inflation and unemployment? In doing so, do they encounter problems not faced by capitalist countries?

2. According to the mayor of Moscow, that city could never have a crisis of the kind that plagues New York and other American cities. "In my country the city government owns and operates not only schools, hospitals, and other non-profit enterprises but also such profitable enterprises as all the restaurants, stores, movie theaters, bakeries, food processing factories, manufacturers of consumer goods, construction companies, and trucks in the city." These activities generate 80 percent of the revenues needed to run the city. The rest of the revenue is raised by taxes collected by the central government and paid to the city. Is a socialist country uniquely able to avoid or solve the problems of its biggest cities? Compare the things the U.S. government might do to help New York meet its deficit with those done for Moscow.

3. Capital is used in the heavy industries of both the United States and the Soviet Union, and in roughly equal amounts. In what sense is the United States capitalist and Russia socialist? Who supplies the capital in a Communist economy?

4. Russian consumers, believing they will get an inferior product for their money, tend to avoid purchasing television sets and other products produced at the end of the planning period, when factories are rushing to fulfill their output targets. By the same token, American consumers are more reluctant to purchase a car produced either at the beginning or at the end of the model year. Thus it seems that concerns about quality exist in both economies. Are these concerns generated by similar or by different factors? Discuss.

5. During World War II, the U.S. government (a) rationed steel, aluminum, and copper; (b) put price controls on most goods and services but rationed only meat, sugar, and gasoline; (c) used the draft to raise armed forces of 11 million but deferred workers in key industries; (d) purchased about half of the goods and services comprising the GNP; and (e) increased income taxes and introduced an excess profits tax.

Would you classify the United States as a command economy at that time? Explain. Can you see reasons for each of the five measures outlined above, given the economic goals of the time?

6. How might the economies of the United States, the Soviet Union, and China attempt to achieve each of the following results? Which system would be likely to do it most easily?

   a. achieve full employment
   b. redistribute income from rich to poor
   c. choose the appropriate mix between tractor production and residential construction
   d. determine the relative pay of carpenters and school teachers
   e. avoid a shortage or surplus of men's shirts
   f. increase the rate of saving

7. "What the world of economics needs is an end to ideology and *isms*. If there is a best system of economic organization, it will prove its superiority in its superior ability to solve economic problems." Do you agree with this statement? Would you expect that if the world survives for another 100 years, a single form of economic system would be found superior to all others? Why or why not?

8. What problems might be in store for the policy indicated by the following news story: "Moscow Will Try Again to Widen Powers of Factory Managers."

9. What might be the implications of the following news story from the summer of 1983: "Barely 14 months after the first trench was dug in the hinterland of Siberia, welders have secured the last length of pipe along the 2,780 mile route that will carry natural gas westward to the Soviet frontier and onward to the homes and factories of Western Europe."

APPENDIXES

MORE ON
FUNCTIONAL RELATIONS
APPENDIX TO CHAPTER 2

The idea of relations among variables is one of the basic notions behind all science. Such relations can be expressed as functional relations.

FUNCTIONAL RELATIONS: THE GENERAL EXPRESSION OF RELATIONS AMONG VARIABLES

Consider two examples, one from a natural science and one from economics. The gravitational attraction of two bodies depends on their mass and on the distance separating them, attraction increasing with size and diminishing with distance; the amount of a commodity that people would like to buy depends on (among other things) the price of the commodity, purchases increasing as price falls. When mathematicians wish to say that one variable depends on another, they say that one variable is a function of the other. [46] Thus gravitational at-

---

[1] Reference numbers in color refer to Mathematical Notes, which begin on page 954.

traction is a function of the mass of the two bodies concerned and the distance between them, and the quantity of a product demanded is a function of the price of the product.

One of the virtues of mathematics is that it permits the concise expression of ideas that would otherwise require long, drawn-out verbal statements. There are two steps in giving compact symbolic expression to functional relations. First, each variable is given a symbol. Second, a symbol is designated to express the idea of one variable's dependence on another. Thus, if G equals gravitational attraction, M equals the mass of two bodies, and d equals the distance between the two bodies, we may write

$$G = f(M, d)$$

where f is read "is a function of" and means "depends on." The whole equation defines a hypothesis and is read "gravitational attraction is a function of the mass of the two bodies concerned and the distance between them." The same hypothesis can be written as

$$G = G(M, d)$$

This is read in exactly the same way and means the same thing as the previous expression. Instead of using f to represent "a function of," the left-hand symbol, G, is repeated.[2]

The hypothesis about desired purchases and price can be written

$$q = f(p)$$

or

$$q = q(p)$$

where q stands for the quantity people wish to purchase of some commodity and p is the price of the commodity. The expression says that the quantity of some commodity that people desire to purchase is a function of its price. The alternative way

---

[2] Any convenient symbol may be used on the right-hand side before the parenthesis to mean "a function of." The repetition of the left-hand symbol may be convenient in reminding us of what is a function of what.

of writing this merely uses different letters to stand for the same functional relation between p and q.

FUNCTIONAL FORMS: PRECISE RELATIONS AMONG VARIABLES

The expression $Y = Y(X)$ merely states that the variables Y and X are related; it says nothing about the form that this relation takes. Usually the hypothesis to be expressed says more than that. Does Y increase as X increases? Does Y decrease as X increases? Or is the relation more complicated? Take a very simple example, where Y is the length of a board in feet, and X is the length of the same board in yards. Quite clearly, $Y = Y(X)$. Further, in this case the exact form of the function is known, for length in feet (Y) is merely three times the length in yards (X), so we may write $Y = 3X$.

This relation is a definitional one, for the length of something measured in feet is defined to be three times its length measured in yards. It is nonetheless useful to have a way of writing relationships that are definitionally true. The expression $Y = 3X$ specifies the exact form of the relation between Y and X and provides a rule whereby, if we have the value of one, we can calculate the value of the other.

Now consider a second example: Let C stand for consumption expenditure, the total amount spent on purchasing goods and services by all American households during a year. Let Y_d stand for the total amount of income that these households had available to spend during the year. We might state the hypothesis that

$$C = f(Y_d)$$

and, even more specifically,

$$C = 0.8Y_d$$

The first expression gives the hypothesis that the total consumption expenditure of households depends on their income. The second expression says, more specifically, that total consumption expenditure is 80 percent of the total available for spending. The second equation expresses a very specific hypothesis about the relation between two observable magnitudes. There is no reason why it *must* be true; it may be consistent or inconsistent with the facts. This is a matter for testing. However, the equation is a concise statement of a particular hypothesis.

Thus the general view that there is a relation between Y and X is denoted by $Y = f(X)$, whereas any precise relation may be expressed by a particular equation such as $Y = 2X$, $Y = 4X^2$, or $Y = X + 2X^2 + 0.5X^3$.

If Y increases as X increases (e.g., $Y = 10 + 2X$), we say that Y is an *increasing function* of X, or that Y and X *vary positively* with each other. If Y decreases as X increases (e.g., $Y = 10 - 2X$), we say that Y is a *decreasing function of X* or that Y and X *vary negatively* with each other.

Y varying negatively with X merely means that Y changes in the opposite direction from X.

ERROR TERMS IN ECONOMIC HYPOTHESES

Expressing hypotheses in the form of functions is misleading in one respect. When we say that the world behaves so that $Y = f(X)$, we do not expect that knowing X will tell us *exactly* what Y will be, but only that it will tell us what Y will be *within some margin of error*.

This error in predicting Y from a knowledge of X arises for two quite distinct reasons. First, there may be other variables that also affect Y. When, for example, we say that the demand for butter is a function of the price of butter, $D_b = f(p_b)$, we know that other factors will also influence this demand. A change in the price of margarine will certainly affect the demand for butter, even though the price of butter does not change. Thus, we do not expect to find a perfect relation between D_b and p_b that will allow us to predict D_b exactly from a knowledge of p_b. Second, variables can never be measured exactly. Even if X is the only cause of

Y, measurements will give various Ys corresponding to the same X. In the case of the demand for butter, errors of measurement might not be large. In other cases, errors might be substantial—as, for example, in the case of a relation between the total consumption expenditure of all American households and their total income. The measurements of consumption and income may be subject to quite wide margins of error, and various values of consumption associated with the same measured value of income may be observed, not because consumption is varying independently of income but because the error of measurement is varying from period to period.

When we say Y is a function of X, we appear to say Y is completely determined by X. Instead of the deterministic formulation

$$Y = f(X)$$

it would be more accurate to write

$$Y = f(X, \epsilon)$$

where ϵ, the Greek letter epsilon, represents an **error term**.[3] Such a term indicates that the observed value of Y will differ from the value predicted by the functional relation between Y and X. Divergences will occur both because of observational errors and because of neglected variables. While economists always mean this, they usually do not say so.

The deterministic formulation is a simplification; an error term is really present in all assumed and observed functional relations.

This is true, by the way, not only for economics and other subjects dealing with human behavior, but for physics, chemistry, geology, and all other sciences. The old-time dichotomy between "exact" and "inexact" sciences is now abandoned; all theories and all measurements are subject to error.

---

[3] The relationship with the error term in it is frequently written $Y = f(X) + \epsilon$.

GRAPHING
IN ECONOMICS
APPENDIX TO CHAPTER 3

The popular saying "The facts speak for themselves" is almost always wrong when there are many facts. Theories are needed to explain how facts are linked together, and summary measures are needed to assist in sorting out what it is that facts show in relation to theories. The simplest means of providing compact summaries of a large number of observations is through the use of tables and graphs. Graphs play important roles in eco-

nomics by representing geometrically both observed data and economic theories.

USE OF GRAPHS
IN ECONOMIC ANALYSIS

Because the surface of a piece of paper is two-dimensional, a graph may readily be used to rep-

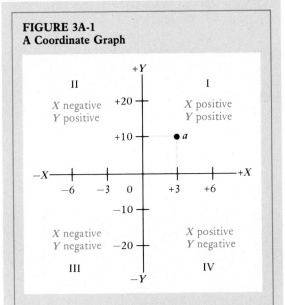

FIGURE 3A-1
A Coordinate Graph

The axes divide the total space into four quadrants according to the signs of the variables. In the upper right-hand quadrant, both *X* and *Y* are greater than zero; this is usually called the *positive quadrant*. Point *a* has *coordinates* $Y = 10$ and $X = 3$ in the coordinate graph. These coordinates *define* point *a*.

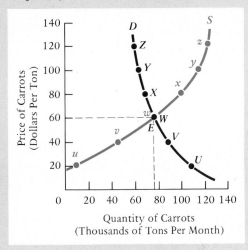

FIGURE 3A-2
Two Different Relationships Between the Price of Carrots and the Quantity of Carrots, Shown Graphically

A two-dimensional graph can show how two variables are related. The two variables, the price of carrots and their quantity, are here shown in two different relationships. The downward-sloping black curve is a demand curve; the upward-sloping colored curve is a supply curve. The intersection of the two curves at point *E* shows the only value of the variables that satisfies both the relationship shown in the demand curve and that shown in the supply curve.

resent pictorially the interrelation between two variables. Flip through this book and you will see dozens of examples. Figure 3A-1 shows generally how a coordinate grid can permit the representation of any two measurable variables.[1]

REPRESENTING THEORIES ON GRAPHS

Figure 3A-2 shows a simple two-variable graph, which will be analyzed in detail in Chapter 5. (In-

deed, the figure is a somewhat simplified version of the one that appears on page 74 as Figure 5-7.) For now it is sufficient to notice that the graph permits us to show the relationship between two variables, the *price* of carrots on the vertical axis and the *quantity* of carrots per month on the horizontal axis.[2] The curve actually shows two different relationships. The dark black downward-sloping curve labeled *D* (which we will call a *demand curve*) shows the relationship between the price of carrots

[1] Economics is very often concerned only with the positive values of variables, and in such cases the graph is confined to the upper right-hand (or "positive") quadrant. Whenever either or both variables take on a negative value, one or more of the other quadrants must be included.

[2] The choice of which variable to put on which axis is discussed in footnote 3 on page 92, and in [8] on page 92.

FIGURE 3A-3
The Theory That Price Is Determined by the Intersection of Supply and Demand Curves, Shown Graphically

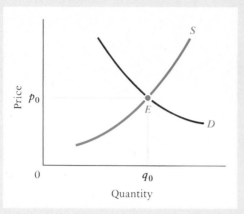

Graphs can illustrate relationships between theoretical variables as well as between specific quantities. Here, in contrast to Figure 3A-2, price and quantity are shown as general variables. The demand curve illustrates an unspecified *negative* relationship between price and quantity, the supply curve an unspecified *positive* relationship between the same two variables. Point E where they cross is the unique point at which both relationships are satisfied. A theory stipulating that both D and S must be satisfied simultaneously leads to the conclusion that price will be p_0 and quantity q_0.

and the quantity of carrots buyers wish to purchase. The dark colored upward-sloping curve labeled S (which we will call a *supply curve*) shows the relationship between the price of carrots and the quantity of carrots producers wish to sell.

Suppose now that we have a theory that says, "Price will tend to the level at which the quantity buyers wish to purchase equals the quantity producers wish to sell." This theory is illustrated in Figure 3A-2, and the conclusion is reached that the price will be $60, for that is the only price at which the two quantities are equal. Do not be concerned about the argument now, for it will be considered in detail in Chapter 5. But notice that the theory

has been displayed using a simple, two-dimensional graph.

Figure 3A-3 is very much like Figure 3A-2 but with one difference. It generalizes from the specific example of carrots to an unspecified commodity and focuses on the intersection of the two curves rather than on specific numerical values. Figure 3A-3 too illustrates the theory that says, "Price will tend to the level at which the quantity buyers wish to purchase equals the quantity producers wish to sell." Now, however, that quantity is labeled q_0 and the resulting price p_0, rather than being given numerical values.

STRAIGHT LINES AND THE SLOPES OF STRAIGHT LINES

Figure 3A-4 illustrates a variety of straight lines. They differ according to their slopes. **Slope** is defined as the ratio of the vertical change to the corresponding horizontal change as one moves to the right.

The symbol Δ is used to indicate a change in variable. Thus ΔX means the value of the change in X, and ΔY means the value of the change in Y. The ratio $\Delta Y / \Delta X$ is the slope of a straight line. Where both increase, the ratio is positive and the line is upward-sloping, as in (i). Where ΔY decreases as ΔX increases, the ratio is negative and the line is downward-sloping, as in (ii). Where ΔY does not change (iii), the line is horizontal and the slope is zero. Where ΔX is zero (iv), the line is vertical, and the slope is often said to be infinite although the ratio $\Delta Y / \Delta X$ is indeterminate. [47]

Slope is a quantitative measure, not merely a qualitative one. For example, in Figure 3A-5 two upward-sloping straight lines have different slopes. The black one has a slope of 2, $\left(\dfrac{\Delta Y}{\Delta X} = 2 \right)$, the colored one has a slope of 1/2, $\left(\dfrac{\Delta Y}{\Delta X} = 0.5 \right)$.

FIGURE 3A-4
Four Straight Lines with Different Slopes

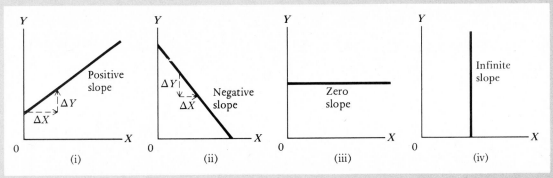

The slope of a straight line is constant but can vary from one line to another. The direction of slope of a straight line is characterized by the signs of the ratio $\Delta Y / \Delta X$. In (i) that ratio is positive because Y increases as X increases; in (ii) the ratio is negative because Y decreases as X increases; in (iii) it is zero because Y does not change as X increases; in (iv) it is said to be infinite because X does not change.

FIGURE 3A-5
Two Straight Lines with Different Slopes

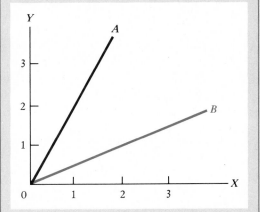

Slope is a quantitative measure. Both lines have positive slopes and thus are similar to Figure 3A-4 (i). But the black curve A is steeper (i.e., has a greater slope) than the colored curve B. For each 1-unit change in X, curve A increases its Y value by 2 units, whereas curve B increases its Y value by only 1/2 unit. The ratio $\Delta Y / \Delta X$ is 2 for curve A and 1/2 for curve B.

CURVED LINES AND THEIR SLOPES

Figure 3A-6 shows four curved lines. The line in (i) is plainly upward-sloping, and in (ii) downward-sloping. The other two shift from one to the other, as the labels indicate. Unlike straight lines, whose slope is the same at every point on the line, the slope of a curve changes. The slope of a curve must be measured at a particular point and is defined as the slope of a straight line that just touches (is *tangent* to) the straight line at that point. This is illustrated in Figure 3A-7. The slope at point A is measured by the slope of the tangent line a. The slope at point B is measured by the slope of the tangent line b.

GRAPHING OBSERVATIONS

A coordinate space such as shown in Figure 3A-1 can be used to graph the observed values of two

FIGURE 3A-6
Four Curved Lines

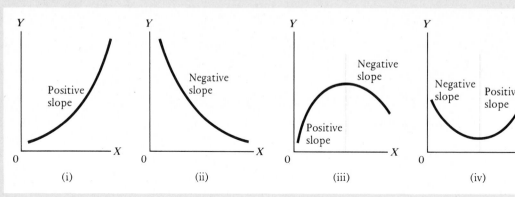

The slope of a curved line is not constant and may change direction. The curves shown in (i) and (ii) have slopes that change in size but not direction, whereas those in (iii) and (iv) change in both size and direction. Unlike that of a straight line, the slope of a curved line cannot be defined by a single number because it changes as the value of X changes.

FIGURE 3A-7
Defining the Slope of a Curve

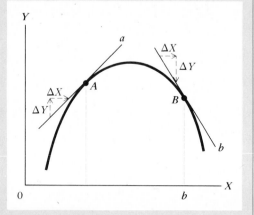

The slope of a curve at any point on that curve is defined by the slope of the straight line that is tangent to the curve at that point. The slope of the curve at point A is defined by the slope of the line a, which is tangent to the curve at that point. The slope of the curve at point B is defined by the slope of the line b.

variables as well as the theoretical relationships between them. For example, the black curve in Figure 3A-2 labeled D might have arisen as a free-hand line drawn to generalize actual observations of the points labeled U, V, W, X, Y, Z. While that graph was not constructed from actual observations, many graphs are. Two of the most important kinds are called *scatter diagrams* and *time series graphs*.

THE SCATTER DIAGRAM

The scatter diagram provides a method of graphing any number of *paired* observations made on two variables. In Chapter 3, data for family income and taxes paid for a sample of 212 American families were studied. To show these data on a scatter diagram, income was measured on the horizontal axis and taxes paid on the vertical axis. Any point in the diagram represents a particular family's income combined with the tax payment of that family. Thus each family for which there are observations can be represented on the diagram by a dot, the coordinates of which indicate the family's income and the amount of taxes it paid in 1979.

The scatter diagram is useful because if there is a simple relation between the two variables, it will be apparent to the eye once the data are plotted. The scatter diagram on page 39, for example, made it apparent that more taxes tend to be paid as income rises. It also made it apparent that the relation between taxes and income is approximately linear. A rising straight line fits the data reasonably well between about $10,000 and $40,000 of income. Above $40,000 and below $10,000, that line provides less resemblance to the data. But since more than two-thirds of the families sampled had incomes in the $10,000 to $40,000 range, the straight line provides a pretty good description of the basic relationship for middle income families.

The diagram also gives some idea of the strength of the relation: If income were the only determinant of taxes paid, all of the dots would cluster closely around a line or a smooth curve; as it is, the points are somewhat scattered and particular incomes are often represented by several households, each with different amounts of taxes paid.

The data used in this example are **cross-sectional data.** The incomes and taxes paid of different households are compared over a single period of time—the year 1979.

Scatter diagrams may also be drawn of a number of observations taken on two variables at successive periods of time. Thus, if one wanted to know whether there was any simple relation between personal income and personal consumption in the United States between 1950 and 1982, data would be collected for the levels of personal income and expenditure per capita in each year from 1950 to 1982, as is done in Table 3A-1. This information could be plotted on a scatter diagram, with income on the X axis and consumption on the Y axis, to discover any systematic relation between the two variables. The data are plotted in Figure 3A-8, and they do indeed suggest a systematic linear relation.

TABLE 3A-1 INCOME AND CONSUMPTION, 1950–1982 (1972 Dollars)

Year	Disposable personal income per capita	Personal consumption expenditures per capita
1950	$2,392	$2,224
1951	2,415	2,214
1952	2,441	2,230
1953	2,501	2,277
1954	2,483	2,278
1955	2,582	2,384
1956	2,653	2,410
1957	2,660	2,416
1958	2,645	2,400
1959	2,709	2,487
1960	2,709	2,501
1961	2,742	2,511
1962	2,813	2,583
1963	2,865	2,644
1964	3,026	2,751
1965	3,171	2,868
1966	3,290	2,979
1967	3,389	3,032
1968	3,493	3,160
1969	3,564	3,245
1970	3,665	3,277
1971	3,752	3,355
1972	3,860	3,511
1973	4,080	3,623
1974	4,009	3,566
1975	4,051	3,609
1976	4,158	3,774
1977	4,280	3,924
1978	4,441	4,057
1979	4,512	4,121
1980	4,472	4,087
1981	4,538	4,123
1982	4,544	4,125

Source: *Economic Report of the President*, 1983.

In this exercise a scatter diagram of observations taken over successive periods of time has been used. Such data are called **time-series data,** and plotting them on a scatter diagram involves no new technique. When cross-sectional data are plotted, each point gives the values of two variables for a particular unit (say, a family); when time-series

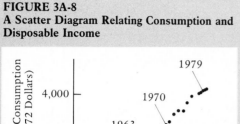

FIGURE 3A-8
A Scatter Diagram Relating Consumption and Disposable Income

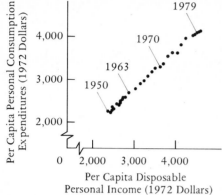

This scatter diagram shows paired values of two variables. The data of Table 3A-1 are plotted here. Each dot shows the values of per capita personal consumption and per capita disposable personal income for a given year. A close, positive, linear relationship between the two variables is established. Note that in this diagram the axes are shown with a break in them to indicate that not all the values of the variables between $2,000 and zero are given. Since no *observations* occurred in those ranges, it was unnecessary to provide space for them.

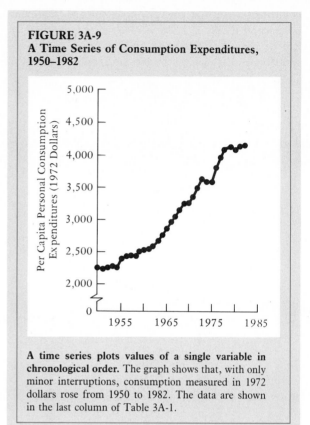

FIGURE 3A-9
A Time Series of Consumption Expenditures, 1950–1982

A time series plots values of a single variable in chronological order. The graph shows that, with only minor interruptions, consumption measured in 1972 dollars rose from 1950 to 1982. The data are shown in the last column of Table 3A-1.

data are plotted, each point tells the values of two variables for a particular year.

TIME-SERIES GRAPHS

Instead of studying the relation between income and consumption suggested in the previous paragraph, a study of the pattern of the changes in either one of these variables over time could be made. In Figure 3A-9 this information is shown for consumption. In the figure, time is one variable, consumption expenditure the other. But time is a very special variable: The order in which successive events happen is important. The year 1965 followed 1964; they were not two independent and

unrelated years. (In contrast, two randomly selected households are independent and unrelated.) For this reason it is customary to draw in the line segments connecting the successive points, as has been done in Figure 3A-9.

A chart such as this figure is called a *time-series graph* or, more simply, a time series. This kind of graph makes it easy to see if the variable being considered has varied in a systematic way over the years or if its behavior has been more or less erratic.

RATIO (LOGARITHMIC) SCALES

The graphs above have all used axes that plotted numbers on a natural arithmetic scale, with distances between two values shown by the size of

TABLE 3A-2 TWO SERIES

Time period	Series A	Series B
0	$10	$ 10
1	18	20
2	26	40
3	34	80
4	42	160

Series A shows constant absolute growth ($8 per period) but declining percentage growth. Series B shows constant percentage growth (100 percent per period) but rising absolute growth.

numerical difference. If *proportionate* rather than absolute changes in variables are important, it is more revealing to use a ratio scale rather than a natural scale. On a **natural scale,** the distance between numbers is proportionate to the absolute difference between those numbers. Thus 200 is placed halfway between 100 and 300. On a **ratio scale** the distance between numbers is proportionate to the absolute difference between their logarithms. Equal distances anywhere on a ratio scale represent equal percentage changes rather than equal absolute changes. On a ratio scale the distance between 100 and 200 is the same as the distance between 200 and 400, between 1,000 and 2,000, and between any two numbers that stand in the ratio 1:2 to each other. For obvious reasons a ratio scale is also called a **logarithmic scale.**

Table 3A-2 shows two series, one growing at a constant absolute amount of eight units per period and the other growing at a constant rate of 100 percent per period. In Figure 3A-10 the series are plotted first on a natural scale, then on a ratio scale. The natural scale makes it easy for the eye to judge absolute variations, and the logarithmic scale makes it easy for the eye to judge proportionate variations.[3]

---

[3] Graphs with a ratio scale on one axis and a natural scale on the other are frequently encountered in economics. In the cases just illustrated there is a ratio scale on the vertical axis and a natural scale on the horizontal (or time) axis. Such graphs are often called *semi-log* graphs. In scientific work graphs with ratio scales on both axes are frequently encountered. Such graphs are often referred to as *double-log* graphs.

FIGURE 3A-10
The Difference Between Natural and Ratio Scales

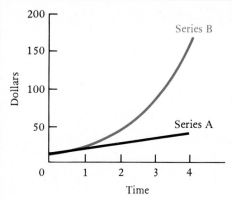

(i) A natural scale

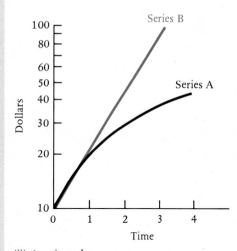

(ii) A ratio scale

On a natural scale, equal distances represent equal amounts; on a ratio scale, equal vertical distances represent equal percentage changes. The two series in Table 3A-2 are plotted in each chart. Series A, which grows at a constant absolute amount, produces a straight line on a natural scale but a downward-bending curve on a ratio scale because the same absolute growth decreases percentage growth. Series B, which grows at a rising absolute rate but a constant percentage rate, is upward-bending on a natural scale but is a straight line on a ratio scale.

GRAPHING THREE VARIABLES IN TWO DIMENSIONS

Often we want to show graphically more than two dimensions. For example, a topographic map seeks to show latitude, longitude, and altitude on a two-dimensional page. This is done by using contour lines, as is shown in Figure 3A-11. Now let us

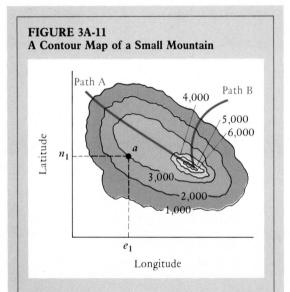

**FIGURE 3A-11
A Contour Map of a Small Mountain**

A contour map shows three variables in two-dimensional space. This is a familiar kind of three-variable graph, with latitude and longitude shown on the axes and altitude on the contour lines. The contour line labeled 1,000 connects all locations with an altitude of 1,000 feet, that labeled 2,000 connects those with an altitude of 2,000 feet, and so forth. Point a, for example, has a latitude n_1, a longitude e_1, and an altitude of 3,000 feet. Where the lines are closely bunched, they represent a steep ascent; where they are far apart, a gradual one. Clearly Path A is a gentler climb from 3,000 to 4,000 feet on this mountain than Path B.

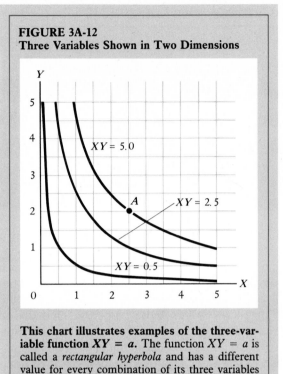

**FIGURE 3A-12
Three Variables Shown in Two Dimensions**

This chart illustrates examples of the three-variable function $XY = a$. The function $XY = a$ is called a *rectangular hyperbola* and has a different value for every combination of its three variables X, Y, and a. The figure shows three members of the family. For example, the point A represents $Y = 2$, $X = 2.5$, and $a = 5.0$.

consider the function $XY = a$, where X, Y, and a are all variables. Now look at Figure 3A-12, which plots this function for three different values of a. The variables X and Y are represented on the two axes. The variable a is represented by the labels on the curves. Several examples of this kind of procedure occur throughout the book. (See, for example, the discussion of indifference curves in Chapter 9 and isoquants in the appendix to Chapter 13.)

ELASTICITY: A FORMAL ANALYSIS
APPENDIX TO CHAPTER 6

The verbal definition of elasticity used in the text may be written symbolically in the following form:

$$\eta = \frac{\Delta q}{\Delta p} \times \frac{\text{average } p}{\text{average } q}$$

where the averages are over the arc of the demand curve being considered. This is called **arc elasticity,** and it measures the average responsiveness of quantity to price over an interval of the demand curve.

Most theoretical treatments use a different but related concept called **point elasticity.** This is the responsiveness of quantity to price at a particular point on the demand curve. The precise definition of point elasticity uses the concept of a derivative, which is drawn from differential calculus.

In this appendix we first study an approximation to point elasticity that uses high school algebra. Then we will replace this approximate definition with the exact definition.

Before proceeding, we should notice one further change. In the chapter text we multiplied all our calculations of demand elasticities by -1, thereby defining elasticity of demand as a positive number. In theoretical work it is more convenient to retain the concept's natural sign. Thus normal demand curves will have negative signs, and statements about "more" or "less" elastic must be understood to refer to the absolute, not the algebraic value of demand elasticity.

The following symbols will be used throughout.

$\eta \equiv$ elasticity of demand
$\eta_s \equiv$ elasticity of supply
$q \equiv$ the original quantity
$\Delta q \equiv$ the change in quantity
$p \equiv$ the original price
$\Delta p \equiv$ the change in price

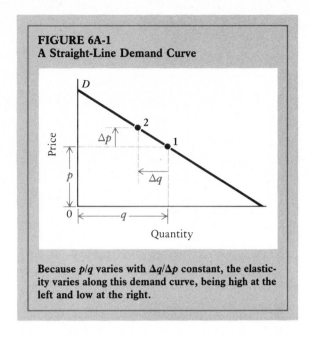

FIGURE 6A-1
A Straight-Line Demand Curve

Because p/q varies with $\Delta q/\Delta p$ constant, the elasticity varies along this demand curve, being high at the left and low at the right.

POINT ELASTICITY ACCORDING TO THE APPROXIMATE DEFINITION

Point elasticity measures elasticity at some point (p,q). In the approximate definition, however, the responsiveness is measured over a small range starting from that point. For example, in Figure 6A-1 the elasticity at point 1 can be measured by the responsiveness of quantity demanded to a change in price that takes price and quantity from point 1 to point 2. The algebraic formula for this elasticity concept is

$$\eta = \frac{\Delta q}{\Delta p} \times \frac{p}{q} \qquad [1]$$

This is similar to the definition of arc elasticity used in the text except that since elasticity is being measured at a point, the p and q corresponding to that point are used (rather than the average p and q over an arc of the curve).

Equation [1] splits elasticity into two parts: $\Delta q/\Delta p$, the ratio of the change in quantity to the change in price, which is related to the *slope* of the demand curve, and p/q, which is related to the *point* on the curve at which the measurement is made.

Figure 6A-1 shows a straight-line demand curve. To measure the elasticity at point 1, take p and q at that point and then consider a price change, say, to point 2, and measure Δp and Δq as indicated. The slope of the straight line joining points 1 and 2 is $\Delta p/\Delta q$. The term in Equation [1] is $\Delta q/\Delta p$, which is the reciprocal of $\Delta p/\Delta q$. Therefore the first term in the elasticity formula is the reciprocal of the slope of the straight line joining the two price-quantity positions under consideration.

Although point elasticity of demand refers to a point (p,q) on the demand curve, the first term in Equation [1] still refers to changes over an arc of the curve. This is the part of the formula that involves approximation and, as we shall see, it has some unsatisfactory results. Nonetheless some interesting results can be derived using this formula as long as we confine ourselves to straight-line demand and supply curves.

1. The elasticity of a downward-sloping straight-line demand curve varies from zero at the quantity axis to infinity (∞) at the price axis. First notice that a straight line has a constant slope, so the ratio $\Delta p/\Delta q$ is the same everywhere on the line. Therefore its reciprocal, $\Delta q/\Delta p$, must also be constant. The changes in η can now be inferred by inspecting the ratio p/q. Where the line cuts the quantity axis, price is zero, so the ratio p/q is zero; thus $\eta = 0$. Moving up the line, p rises and q falls, so the ratio p/q rises; thus elasticity rises. Approaching the top of the line, q approaches zero, so the ratio becomes very large. Thus elasticity increases without limit as the price axis is approached.

2. Where there are two straight-line demand curves of the same slope, the one farther from the origin is less elastic at each price than the one closer to the origin. Figure 6A-2 shows two parallel straight-line demand curves. Pick any price, say, p_0, and compare the elasticities of the two curves at that price. Since the curves are parallel, the ratio $\Delta q/\Delta p$ is the same on both curves. Since elasticities at the same price are being compared on both curves, p is the same, and the only factor left to vary is q. On the curve farther from the origin, quantity is larger (i.e., $q_1 > q_0$) and hence p_0/q_1 is smaller than p_0/q_0; thus η is smaller.

It follows from theorem 2 that parallel shifts of a straight-line demand curve lower elasticity (at each price) when the line shifts outward and raise elasticity when the line shifts inward.

3. The elasticities of two intersecting straight-line demand curves can be compared at the point of intersection merely by comparing slopes, the steeper curve being the less elastic. In Figure 6A-3 there are two intersecting curves. At any point of intersection, p and q are common to both curves and hence the ratio p/q is the same. Therefore η varies only with $\Delta p/\Delta q$. On the steeper curve, $\Delta q/\Delta p$ is smaller than on the flatter curve, so elasticity is lower.

4. If the slope of a straight-line demand curve changes while the price intercept remains constant, elasticity at any given price is unchanged. This is an interesting case for at least two reasons. First, when more customers having similar tastes to those already in the market enter the market, the demand curve pivots outward in this way. Second, when more firms enter a market that is shared proportionally among all firms, each firm's demand curve shifts inward in this way.

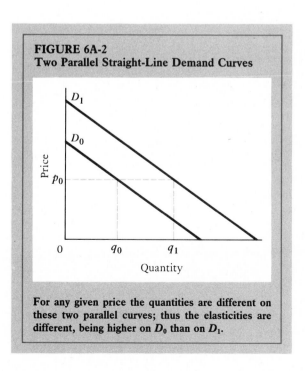

FIGURE 6A-2
Two Parallel Straight-Line Demand Curves

For any given price the quantities are different on these two parallel curves; thus the elasticities are different, being higher on D_0 than on D_1.

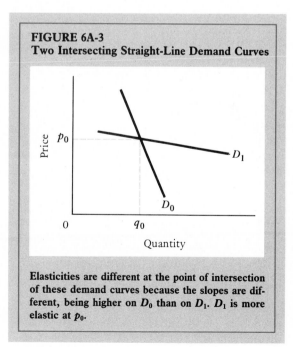

FIGURE 6A-3
Two Intersecting Straight-Line Demand Curves

Elasticities are different at the point of intersection of these demand curves because the slopes are different, being higher on D_0 than on D_1. D_1 is more elastic at p_0.

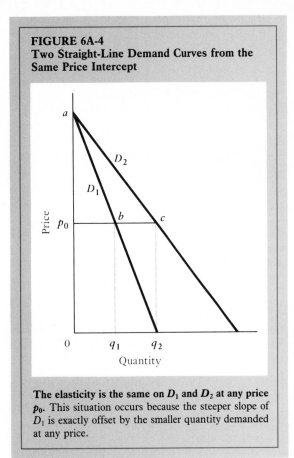

FIGURE 6A-4
Two Straight-Line Demand Curves from the Same Price Intercept

The elasticity is the same on D_1 and D_2 at any price p_0. This situation occurs because the steeper slope of D_1 is exactly offset by the smaller quantity demanded at any price.

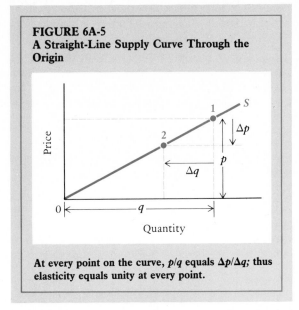

FIGURE 6A-5
A Straight-Line Supply Curve Through the Origin

At every point on the curve, p/q equals $\Delta p/\Delta q$; thus elasticity equals unity at every point.

Consider, in Figure 6A-4, the elasticity at point b on demand curve D_1 and at point c on demand curve D_2. We shall focus on the two triangles abp_0 on D_1 and acp_0 on D_2, formed by the two straight-line demand curves emanating from point a and by the price p_0.

The price p_0 is the line segment $0p_0$. The quantities q_1 and q_2 are the line segments p_0b and p_0c, respectively. The slope of D_1 is $\dfrac{\Delta p}{\Delta q} = \dfrac{ap_0}{p_0b}$ and the slope of D_2 is $\dfrac{\Delta p}{\Delta q} = \dfrac{ap_0}{p_0c}$

Now from Equation [1], we can represent the elasticities of D_1 and D_2 at the points b and c respectively as

$$\eta \text{ at point } b = \frac{p_0b}{ap_0} \times \frac{0p_0}{p_0b} = \frac{0p_0}{ap_0}$$

$$\eta \text{ at point } c = \frac{p_0c}{ap_0} \times \frac{0p_0}{p_0c} = \frac{0p_0}{ap_0}$$

The two are the same. The reason is that the distance corresponding to the quantity demanded at p_0 appears in both the numerator and denominator and thus cancels out.

Put differently, if the straight-line demand curve D_1 is twice as steep as D_2, it has half the quantity demanded at p_0. Therefore in the expression

$$\eta = \frac{\Delta q}{q} \times \frac{p}{\Delta p}$$

the steeper slope (a smaller Δq for the same Δp) is exactly offset by the smaller quantity demanded (a smaller q for the same p).

5. *Any straight-line supply curve through the origin has an elasticity of one.* Such a supply curve is shown in Figure 6A-5. Consider the two triangles with the sides p, q, and the S curve, and Δp, Δq, and the S curve. Clearly these are similar triangles. Therefore, the ratios of their sides are equal; that is,

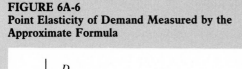

FIGURE 6A-6
Point Elasticity of Demand Measured by the Approximate Formula

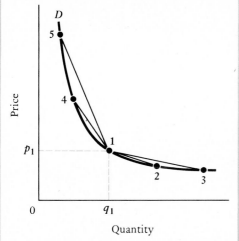

When the approximation of Equation 1 is used, many elasticities are measured from point 1 because the slope of the chord between 1 and every other point on the curve varies.

ratio $\Delta q / \Delta p$—and thus η—will vary according to the size and the direction of the price change.

Theorem 6 yields a result that is very inconvenient and is avoided by use of a different definition of point elasticity.

POINT ELASTICITY ACCORDING TO THE PRECISE DEFINITION

To measure the elasticity at a point exactly, it is necessary to know the reaction of quantity to a change in price *at that point*, not over a range of the curve.

The reaction of quantity to price change at a point is called dq/dp, and this is defined to be the reciprocal of the slope of the straight line tangent to the demand curve at the point in question. In Figure 6A-7 the elasticity of demand at point 1 is

$$\frac{p}{q} = \frac{\Delta p}{\Delta q} \qquad [2]$$

Elasticity of supply is defined as

$$\eta_s = \frac{\Delta q}{\Delta p} \times \frac{p}{q}$$

which, by substitution from Equation [2], gives

$$\eta_s = \frac{q}{p} \times \frac{p}{q} \equiv 1$$

6. *The elasticity measured from any point* p, q, *according to Equation [1] above, is in general dependent on the direction and magnitude of the change in price and quantity.* Except for a straight line (for which the slope does not change), the ratio $\Delta q / \Delta p$ will not be the same at different points on a curve. Figure 6A-6 shows a demand curve that is not a straight line. To measure the elasticity from point 1, the

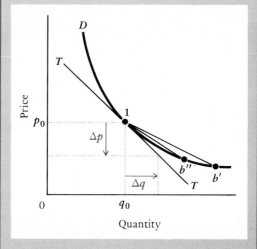

FIGURE 6A-7
Point Elasticity of Demand Measured by the Exact Formula

When the exact definition $\eta = \dfrac{dq}{dp} \times \dfrac{p}{q}$ is used, only one elasticity is measured from point 1 because there is only one tangent to the demand curve at that point.

the ratio p/q (as it has been in all previous measures), now multiplied by the ratio of $\Delta q/\Delta p$ measured along the straight line, T, tangent to the curve at 1, that is, by dq/dp.

Thus the exact definition of point elasticity is

$$\eta = \frac{dq}{dp} \times \frac{p}{q} \qquad [3]$$

The ratio dq/dp, as defined, is in fact the differential calculus concept of the *derivative* of quantity with respect to price.

This definition of point elasticity is the one nor-mally used in economic theory. Equation [1] is mathematically only an approximation to this expression. It is obvious from Figure 6A-7 that arc elasticity will come closer to point elasticity the smaller the price change used to calculate the arc elasticity. The $\Delta q/\Delta p$ in Equation [1] is the reciprocal of the slope of the chord connecting the two points being compared. As the chord becomes shorter, its slope gets closer to that of the tangent T. (Compare the chords connecting point 1 to b' and b'' in Figure 6A-7). Thus the error in using Equation [1] as an approximation to Equation [3] tends to diminish as the size of Δp diminishes.

BALANCE SHEETS, INCOME STATEMENTS, AND COSTS OF PRODUCTION: TWO VIEWS
APPENDIX TO CHAPTER 11

Accounting is a major branch of study in and of itself. Many students of economics will want to study accounting at some stage in their careers. It is not our intention to give a short course in accounting in this appendix, but rather to acquaint you with the kinds of summary statements that are used by both economists and accountants. **Balance sheets** report the picture of a firm *at a moment in time*. They balance in the sense that they show the assets (or valuable things) owned by the firm on

one side and the claims against those assets on the other side. **Income statements** refer to a *period of time* (e.g., a year) and report in summary fashion the flows of resources through the firm in the course of its operations. Balance sheets thus measure a stock; income statements measure a flow.

To illustrate what balance sheets and income statements are, the same example will be treated from two points of view: that of the accountant and that of the economist.

TABLE 11A–1 MAYKBY LEAF COMPANY,
BALANCE SHEET, DECEMBER 31, 1983

Assets		Liabilities and equity	
Cash in bank	$ 10,000	Owed to suppliers	$ 10,000
Plant and equipment	160,000	Bank loan	80,000
Raw materials and supplies	30,000	Equity	110,000
Total assets	$200,000	Total liabilities and equity	$200,000

AN EXAMPLE

Late in 1983, James Maykby, the second vice-president of Acme Artificial Flower Corporation (at a salary of $50,000 per year), decided he would go into business for himself. He quit his job and organized the Maykby Leaf Company. He purchased suitable plant and equipment for $160,000 and acquired some raw materials and supplies. By December 31, 1983, he was in a position to start manufacturing. The funds for his enterprise were $80,000 raised as a bank loan on the factory (on which he is obligated to pay interest of $10,000 per year) and $110,000 of his own funds, which had previously been invested in common stocks. He also owed $10,000 to certain firms that had provided him with supplies.

Maykby, who is a trained accountant, drew up a statement of his company's position as of December 31, 1983 (see Table 11A-1).

Maykby showed this balance sheet to his brother-in-law, an economist, and was very pleased and surprised[1] to find that he agreed that this was a fair and accurate statement of the position of the company as it prepared to start operation.

During 1984, the company had a busy year hiring factors, producing and selling goods, and so on. The following points summarize these activities of the 12-month period.

1. The firm hired labor and purchased additional raw materials in the amount of $115,000, of which it still owed $20,000 at the end of the year.[2]
2. The firm manufactured artificial leaves and flowers whose sale value was $200,000. At year's end it had sold all of these, and still had on hand $30,000 worth of raw materials.
3. The firm paid off the $10,000 owed to suppliers at the beginning of the year.
4. At the very end of 1984, the company purchased a new machine for $10,000 and paid cash for it.
5. The company paid the bank $10,000 interest on the loan.
6. Maykby paid himself $20,000 "instead of salary."

AN ACCOUNTANT'S BALANCE SHEET AND INCOME STATEMENT

Taking account of all these things and also recognizing that he had depreciation on his plant and equipment,[3] Maykby spent New Year's Day 1985 preparing three financial reports (see Tables 11A-2, 11A-3, and 11A-4).

These accounts reflect the operations of the firm as described above. The bookkeeping procedure by which these various activities are made to yield both the year-end balance sheet and the income statement need not concern you at this time, but you should notice several things.

---

[1] He usually finds that he and his brother-in-law disagree about everything.

[2] In this example, all purchased and hired factors are treated in a single category.

[3] The tax people told him he could charge 15 percent of the cost of his equipment as depreciation during 1984, and he decided to use this amount in his own books as well. No depreciation was charged on the new machine.

TABLE 11A–2 MAYKBY LEAF COMPANY,
ACCOUNTANT'S BALANCE SHEET, DECEMBER 31, 1984

Assets		Liabilities and equity	
Cash in bank	$ 65,000	Owed to suppliers of factors	$ 20,000
(See Exhibit 1)		(See Exhibit 4)	
Plant and equipment	146,000	Bank loan	80,000
(See Exhibit 2)		Equity	141,000
Raw materials and supplies	30,000	(See Exhibit 5)	
(See Exhibit 3)		Total liabilities and equity	$241,000
Total assets	$241,000		

TABLE 11A–3 MAYKBY LEAF COMPANY,
EXHIBITS TO BALANCE SHEET OF DECEMBER 31, 1984

Exhibit 1. Cash

Balance, January 1, 1984	$ 10,000	
+ Deposits		
Proceeds of sales of goods	200,000	$210,000
– Payments		
Payments to suppliers (1984 bills)	10,000	
Payments for labor and additional raw materials	95,000	
Salary of Mr. Maykby	20,000	
Purchase of new machine	10,000	
Interest payment to bank	10,000	– 145,000
Balance, December 31, 1984		65,000

Exhibit 2. Plant and Equipment

Balance, January 1, 1984	$160,000	
+ New machine purchased	10,000	170,000
– Depreciation charged		– 24,000
Balance, December 31, 1984		146,000

Exhibit 3. Raw Materials and Supplies

On hand January 1, 1984	$ 30,000	
Purchases in 1984	115,000	145,000
Used for production during 1984		– 115,000
On hand December 31, 1984		30,000

Exhibit 4. .Owed to Suppliers

Balance, January 1, 1984	$ 10,000	
New purchases, 1984	115,000	125,000
Paid on old accounts	10,000	
Paid on new accounts	95,000	– 105,000
Balance, December 31, 1984		$ 20,000

Exhibit 5. Equity

Original investment	$110,000
+ Income earned during year	31,000
(See income statement)	
Balance, December 31, 1984	$141,000

TABLE 11A–4 **MAYKBY LEAF COMPANY, ACCOUNTANT'S INCOME STATEMENT FOR THE YEAR 1984**

Sales		$200,000
Costs of operation		
Hired services and raw materials used	$115,000	
Depreciation	24,000	
Mr. Maykby	20,000	
Interest	10,000	− 169,000
Profit		$ 31,000

First, note that some transactions affect the balance sheet but do not enter into the current income statement. Examples of these are the purchase of a machine, which is an exchange of assets—cash for plant and equipment—and which will be entered as a cost in the income statements of some future periods as depreciation is charged; and the payment of past debts, which entered the income statements in the period in which the things purchased were used in production.[4]

Second, note that the net profit from operations increased the owner's equity, since it was not "paid out" to him. A loss would have decreased his equity.

Third, note that the income statement, covering a year's operation, provides a link between the opening balance sheet (the assets and the claims against assets at the beginning of the year) and the closing balance sheet.

Fourth, note that every change in a balance sheet between two dates can be accounted for by events that occurred during the year. (See the exhibits to the balance sheet, Table 11A-3.)

After studying these records, Maykby feels that it has been a good year. The company has money in the bank, it has shown a profit, and it was able to sell the goods it produced. He is bothered, however, by the fact that he and his wife have felt

---

[4] Beginning students often have difficulty with the distinction between *cash* flows and *income* flows. If you do, analyze item by item the entries in Exhibit 1 in Table 11A-3 and in Table 11A-4, the income statement.

poorer than in the past years. Probably the cost of living has gone up!

AN ECONOMIST'S BALANCE SHEET AND INCOME STATEMENT

When Maykby's brother-in-law reviews the December 31, 1984 balance sheet and the 1984 income statement, he criticizes them in three respects. He says:

1. Maykby should have charged the company $50,000 for his services, since that is what he could have earned outside.
2. Maykby should have charged the company for the use of the $110,000 of his funds. He computes that had Maykby left these funds in the stock market he would have earned $11,000 in dividends and capital gains.
3. Maykby's depreciation figure is arbitrary. The plant and equipment purchased for $160,000 a year ago now has a *market value* of only $124,000. (Assume he is correct about this fact.)

The brother-in-law prepared three *revised* statements (See Tables 11A-5, 11A-6, and the exhibit, Table 11A-7.)

It is not hard for Maykby to understand the difference between the accounting profit of $31,000

TABLE 11A–5 **MAYKBY LEAF COMPANY, ECONOMIST'S INCOME STATEMENT FOR THE YEAR 1984**

Sales		$200,000
Cost of operations		
Hired services and raw materials	$115,000	
Depreciation[a]	36,000	
Interest to bank[b]	10,000	
Imputed cost of capital	11,000	
Services of Maykby	50,000	− 222,000
Loss		$(22,000)

[a] Market value on January 1 less market value on December 31.
[b] Because the bank loan is secured by the factory, its opportunity cost seems to the economist as properly measured by the interest payment.

TABLE 11A–6 MAYKBY LEAF COMPANY, ECONOMIST'S BALANCE SHEET, DECEMBER 31, 1984

Assets		Liabilities and equity	
Cash	$ 65,000	Owed to suppliers	$ 20,000
Plant and equipment	134,000	Bank loan	80,000
Raw materials, etc.	30,000	Equity (see Exhibit)	129,000
	$229,000		$229,000

TABLE 11A–7 EXHIBIT TO BALANCE SHEET, DECEMBER 31, 1984: EQUITY TO MR. MAYKBY

Original investment		$110,000
New investment by Mr. Maykby		
Salary not collected	$30,000	
Return on capital not collected	11,000	41,000
		151,000
Less loss from operations		22,000
Equity		$129,000

and the reported economist's loss of $22,000. The difference of $53,000 is made up as follows:

Extra salary	$30,000
Imputed cost of capital	11,000
Extra depreciation	12,000
	$53,000

What Maykby does *not* understand is in what sense he *lost* $22,000 during the year. To explain this, his brother-in-law prepared the report shown in Table 11A–8.

Although Maykby spent the afternoon muttering to himself and telling his wife that his brother-in-law was not only totally lacking in any business sense but unpleasant as well, he was observed that evening at the public library asking the librarian whether there was a good "teach-yourself" book on economics. (We do not know her answer.)

The next day, Maykby suggested to the economist that they work out together the expected economic profits for next year. "After all," he said, "dwelling on what might have been doesn't really help decide whether I should continue the Leaf Company next year." The economist agreed. Because of expected sales increases, they concluded, the prospects were good enough to continue for at least another year. They dipped deep in the bowl of New Year's cheer to toast those stalwart pillars of society, the independent business person and the economist.

TABLE 11A–8 MAYKBY'S SITUATION BEFORE AND AFTER

	(1) As second vice-president of Acme Flower Company	(2) As owner-manager of Maykby Leaf Company	Difference (2) − (1)
Salary paid	$ 50,000	$ 20,000	− $30,000
Earnings on capital, invested in stocks	11,000	0	− 11,000
Assets owned	110,000 (stocks)	129,000 (equity in Maykby Leaf Co.)	+ 19,000
Net change			− $22,000

Summary

1. The balance sheet reports the assets and the claims against those assets at a moment in time. Balance sheets always balance because the equity of the owners is *by definition* the amount of the assets less the claims of the creditors of the company.

2. How large the "total assets" figure is depends on the valuations placed on them, and these can differ. The valuation problem arises over and over again—in the matter of inventories, patents, properties, and so forth, owned.

3. To avoid arbitrary, misleading, and even deliberately deceptive manipulation of accounts, accountants have developed certain normal and usual procedures of valuation. These may not in all cases reflect the economist's definition of the value of the resources.

4. The income statement reports the revenues and the costs that arise from the firm's use of inputs to produce outputs. It always covers a specified period of time. It also crucially involves the valuation problem: What is the value of the inputs used and outputs produced? Here again there are conventional accounting principles that may or may not be satisfactory for purposes of economic analysis.

5. The income statement of a firm may be important for several different purposes, and different principles of valuation may be required. For determining its income tax liability, the firm must use the valuations specified as permissible by the tax authorities. For determining its comparative performance compared with other companies, or to itself in other periods, it must use a consistent set of procedures, whatever the principle that governs them. For determining whether it has made the best use of the resources under its control, it must use valuations based on the alternative use of these resources. The economist's concept of opportunity cost is designed to do this job.

6. In general, it is the principles of valuation used and not the form of these statements that are important and decisive in interpreting the operations of the firm. Students of the firm who use reported financial data as an aid to their analysis must be prepared to examine in detail whether the principles of valuation used are appropriate for their purpose and to adjust, correct, or recompute in cases where they are not appropriate.

ISOQUANTS:
AN ALTERNATIVE ANALYSIS
OF THE LONG-RUN
PRODUCTION DECISION
APPENDIX TO CHAPTER 13

The production function gives the relation between the factor inputs that the firm uses and the output that it obtains. In the long run, the firm can choose among many different combinations of inputs that will yield it the same output. The production function and the choices open to the firm can be given a graphical representation using the concept of an isoquant.

A SINGLE ISOQUANT

Table 13A-1 illustrates by hypothetical example those combinations of two inputs (labor and capital) that will each serve to produce a given quantity of output. The data from Table 13A-1 are plotted in Figure 13A-1. A smooth curve is drawn through

TABLE 13A–1 ALTERNATIVE METHODS OF PRODUCING SIX UNITS OF OUTPUT: POINTS ON AN ISOQUANT

Method	K	L	ΔK	ΔL	Rate of substitution $\Delta K/\Delta L$
a.	18	2			
			−6	1	−6.0
b.	12	3			
			−3	1	−3.0
c.	9	4			
			−3	2	−1.5
d.	6	6			
			−2	3	−0.67
e.	4	9			
			−1	3	−0.33
f.	3	12			
			−1	6	−0.17
g.	2	18			

An isoquant describes the firm's alternative methods for producing a given output. The table lists some of the methods indicated by a production function as being available to produce six units of output. The first combination uses a great deal of capital (K) and very little labor (L). As we move down the table, labor is substituted for capital in such a way as to keep output constant. Finally, at the bottom, most of the capital has been replaced by labor. The rate of substitution between the two factors is calculated in the last three columns of the table. Note that as we move down the table, the absolute value of the rate of substitution declines.

the points to indicate that there are additional ways, not listed in the table, of producing six units.

This curve is called an **isoquant.** It shows the whole set of technologically efficient possibilities for producing a given level of output—six units in this example. This is an example of graphing a three-variable function in two dimensions. It is analogous to the contour line on a map that shows all points of equal altitude and to an indifference curve that shows all combinations of commodities that yield an equal utility.

As we move from one point on an isoquant to another, we are *substituting one factor for another* while holding output constant. If we move from point b to point c, we are substituting one unit of labor for three units of capital. The marginal rate of substitution measures the rate at which one factor is substituted for another with output held constant. Graphically, the marginal rate of substitution is measured by the slope of the isoquant at a par-

ticular point. Table 13A-1 shows the calculation of some rates of substitution between various points of the isoquant. [48]

The marginal rate of substitution is related to the marginal products of the factors of production. To see how, consider an example. Assume that at the present level of inputs of labor and capital the marginal product of a unit of labor is two units of output while the marginal product of capital is one unit of output. If the firm reduces its use of capital and increases its use of labor to keep output constant, it needs to add only one-half unit of labor for one unit of capital given up. If, at another point

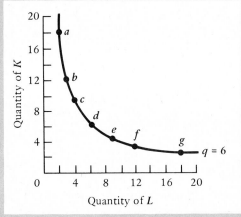

FIGURE 13A-1
An Isoquant for Output of Six Units★

Isoquants are downward-sloping and convex. The downward slope reflects the requirement of technological efficiency. A method that uses more of one factor must use less of the other factor if it is to be technologically efficient. The convex shape of the isoquant reflects a diminishing marginal rate of substitution. Starting from point a, which uses relatively little labor and much capital, and moving to point b, 1 additional unit of labor can substitute for 6 units of capital (while holding production constant). But from b to c, 1 unit of labor substitutes for only 3 units of capital. The geometrical expression of this is that moving along the isoquant to the right, the slope of the isoquant becomes flatter.

★The lettered points are plotted from the data in Table 13A-1.

on the isoquant with more labor and less capital, the marginal products are two for capital and one for labor, then the firm will have to add two units of labor for every unit of capital it gives up. The general proposition is

The marginal rate of substitution is equal to the ratio of the marginal products of the two factors of production.

Isoquants satisfy two important conditions: They are downward-sloping and they are convex viewed from the origin. What is the economic meaning of each of these conditions?

The downward slope indicates that each factor input has a positive marginal product. If the input of one factor is reduced and that of the other is held constant, output will be reduced. Thus, if one input is decreased, production can only be held constant if the other factor input is increased. The marginal rate of substitution has a negative value: Increases in one factor must be balanced by decreases in the other factor if output is to be held constant.

To understand convexity, consider what happens as the firm moves along the isoquant of Figure 13A-1 downward and to the right. Labor is being added and capital reduced to keep output constant. If labor is added in increments of exactly one unit, how much capital may be dispensed with each time? The key to the answer is that both factors are assumed to be subject to the law of diminishing returns. Thus the gain in output associated with each additional unit of labor added is *diminishing* while the loss of output associated with each additional unit of capital foregone is *increasing*. It therefore takes ever-smaller reductions in capital to compensate for equal increases in labor. This implies that the isoquant is convex viewed from the origin.

AN ISOQUANT MAP

The isoquant of Figure 13A-1 referred to six units of output. There is another isoquant for seven

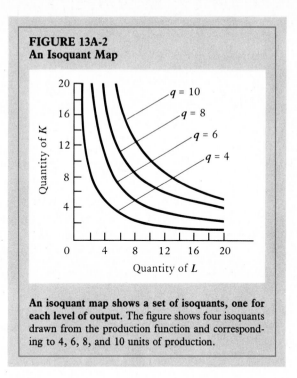

FIGURE 13A-2
An Isoquant Map

An isoquant map shows a set of isoquants, one for each level of output. The figure shows four isoquants drawn from the production function and corresponding to 4, 6, 8, and 10 units of production.

units, another for 7,000 units, and a different one for every rate of output. Each isoquant refers to a specific output and connects alternative combinations of factors that are technologically efficient methods of achieving that output. If we plot a representative set of these isoquants on a single graph, we get an **isoquant map** like that in Figure 13A-2. The higher the level of output along a particular isoquant, the further away from the origin it will be.

ISOQUANTS AND THE CONDITIONS FOR COST MINIMIZATION

Finding the efficient way of producing any output requires finding the least-cost factor combination. To find this combination when both factors are variable, factor prices need to be known. Suppose, to continue the example, that capital is priced at

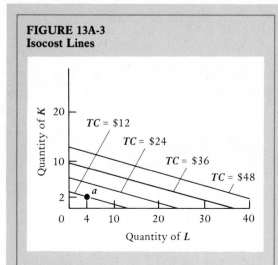

FIGURE 13A-3
Isocost Lines

Each isocost line shows alternative factor combinations that can be purchased for a given outlay. The graph shows the four isocost lines that result when labor costs $1 a unit and capital $4 a unit and expenditure is held constant at $12, $24, $36, and $48 respectively. The line labeled *TC* = $12 represents all combinations of the two factors that the firm could buy for $12. Point *a* represents 2 units of *K* and 4 units of *L*.

$4 per unit and labor at $1. In Chapter 9 a budget line was used to show the alternative combinations of goods a household could buy; here an **isocost line** is used to show alternative combinations of factors a firm can buy for a given outlay. Four different isocost lines appear in Figure 13A-3. The slope of each reflects *relative* factor prices, just as the slope of the budget line in Chapter 9 represented relative product prices. For given factor prices a series of parallel isocost lines will reflect the alternative levels of expenditure on factor purchases that are open to the firm. The higher the level of expenditure, the farther the isocost line is from the origin.

In Figure 13A-4 the isoquant and isocost maps are brought together. The economically most efficient method of production must be a point on an isoquant that just touches (i.e., is tangent to) an isocost line. If the isoquant cuts the isocost line, it is possible to move along the isoquant and reach a lower level of cost. Only at a point of tangency is a movement in either direction along the isoquant a movement to a higher cost level. The lowest attainable cost of producing six units is $24. This cost level can be achieved only by operating at *A*, the point where the $24 isocost line is tangent to the six-unit isoquant. The lowest average cost of producing six units is thus $24/6 = $4 per unit of output.

The least-cost position is given graphically by the tangency point between the isoquant and the isocost lines.

Notice that point *A* in Figure 13A-4 indicates not only the lowest level of cost for six units of output but also the highest level of output for $24 of cost. Thus, we find the same solution if we set out *either* to minimize the cost of producing six units of output *or* to maximize the output that can be obtained for $24. One problem is said to be the "dual" of the other.

The slope of the isocost line is given by the ratio of the prices of the two factors of production. The slope of the isoquant is given by the ratio of their marginal products. When the firm reaches its least-cost position, it has equated the price ratio (which is given to it by the market prices) with the ratio of the marginal products (which it can adjust by varying the proportions in which it hires the factors). In symbols,

$$\frac{MP_L}{MP_K} = \frac{p_L}{p_K}$$

This is equivalent to Equation [2] on page 198. We have now derived this result by use of the isoquant analysis of the firm's decisions. [49]

ISOQUANTS AND THE PRINCIPLE OF SUBSTITUTION

Suppose that with technology unchanged—that is, with the isoquant map fixed—the price of one factor changes. Suppose that with the price of capital

FIGURE 13A-4
The Determination of the Least-Cost Method of Output

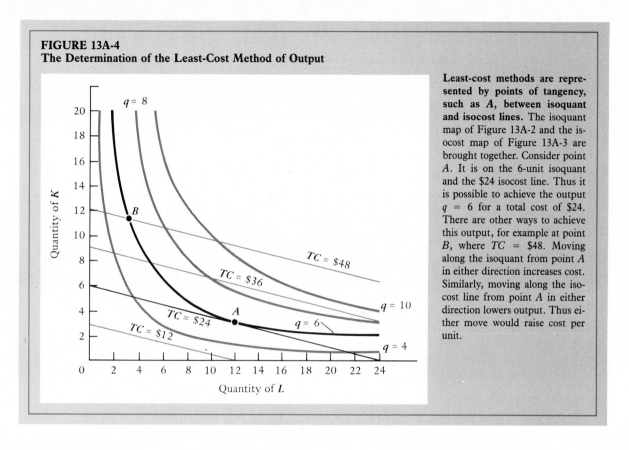

Least-cost methods are represented by points of tangency, such as *A*, between isoquant and isocost lines. The isoquant map of Figure 13A-2 and the isocost map of Figure 13A-3 are brought together. Consider point *A*. It is on the 6-unit isoquant and the $24 isocost line. Thus it is possible to achieve the output *q* = 6 for a total cost of $24. There are other ways to achieve this output, for example at point *B*, where *TC* = $48. Moving along the isoquant from point *A* in either direction increases cost. Similarly, moving along the isocost line from point *A* in either direction lowers output. Thus either move would raise cost per unit.

unchanged at $4 per unit, the price of labor rises from $1 to $4 per unit. Originally, the efficient factor combination for producing 6 units was 12 units of labor and 3 units of capital. It cost $24. To produce that same output in the same way would now cost $60 at the new factor prices. Figure 13A-5 shows why that is not efficient: The slope of the isocost line has changed, which makes it efficient to substitute the now relatively cheaper capital for the relatively more expensive labor.

This illustrates the principle of substitution:

Changes in relative factor prices will cause a partial replacement of factors that have become relatively more expensive by factors that have become relatively cheaper.

Of course, substitution of capital for labor cannot fully offset the effects of a rise in cost of labor, as Figure 13A-5(i) shows. Consider the output attainable for $24. In the figure, there are two isocost lines representing $24 of outlay—at the old and new price of labor. The new isocost line for $24 lies everywhere inside the old one (except where no labor is used). The isocost line must therefore be tangent to a lower isoquant. This means that if production is to be held constant, higher costs must be accepted—but because of substitution it is not necessary to accept costs as high as would accompany an unchanged factor proportion. In the example, six units can be produced for $48 rather than the $60 that would have been required if no change in factor proportions had been made.

FIGURE 13A-5
The Effects of a Change in Factor Prices on Costs and Factor Proportions

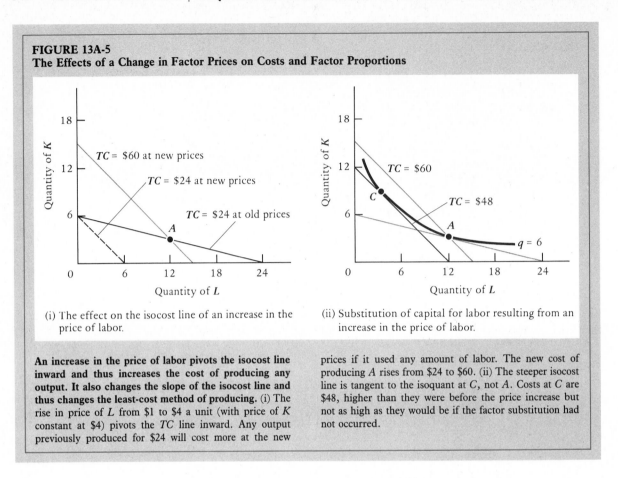

(i) The effect on the isocost line of an increase in the price of labor.

(ii) Substitution of capital for labor resulting from an increase in the price of labor.

An increase in the price of labor pivots the isocost line inward and thus increases the cost of producing any output. It also changes the slope of the isocost line and thus changes the least-cost method of producing. (i) The rise in price of L from $1 to $4 a unit (with price of K constant at $4) pivots the TC line inward. Any output previously produced for $24 will cost more at the new prices if it used any amount of labor. The new cost of producing A rises from $24 to $60. (ii) The steeper isocost line is tangent to the isoquant at C, not A. Costs at C are $48, higher than they were before the price increase but not as high as they would be if the factor substitution had not occurred.

This leads to the predictions that

A rise in the price of one factor with all other factor prices constant will (1) shift upward the cost curves of commodities that use that factor and (2) lead to a substitution of factors that are now relatively cheaper for the factor whose price has risen.

Both these predictions were stated in Chapter 13; now they have been derived formally using the isoquant technique.

MORE ON LONG-RUN COMPETITIVE EQUILIBRIUM
APPENDIX TO CHAPTER 14

In Chapter 14 we showed how the forces of entry and exit in a competitive industry forced firms to an equilibrium position with zero profits. Here we consider further implications of this process and some complications of long-run equilibrium.

LONG-RUN EQUILIBRIUM IMPLIES MINIMUM ATTAINABLE COSTS

A competitive industry will not be in long-run equilibrium as long as any firm can increase its profits by changing its output or its method of production. A firm might change its profits by (1) increasing or decreasing output from an existing plant, (2) opening or closing additional identical plants, or (3) changing the size of the plants it operates.

We saw in Chapter 14 that if a firm is to be in long-run equilibrium, condition (1) implies that price, p, equals short-run marginal cost ($SRMC$) and that (2) implies that price equals short-run average total cost ($SRATC$). These two conditions were met by firms in the position of Figure 14-7(ii), page 225.

The additional condition (3) means that each existing firm must be producing at the lowest point on its long-run average cost curve. Taken together, these conditions mean that all firms in the industry should be in the position illustrated in Figure 14A-1.

To see why this is so, we shall assume that it is not the case and show how firms may increase their profits. (If they can increase their profits, they were not originally in long-run equilibrium.) Figure 14A-2 shows two firms that have $SRMC = SRATC =$ price. Each of these firms can, however, increase its profits by discarding its present plant when it wears out and building a plant of different size. The smaller firm should increase its plant size, thereby lowering its average total costs. The larger firm should build a smaller plant, thereby lowering

its ATC. Since each firm is a price taker, each of these changes will increase the firm's profits.

The only way in which a price-taking firm can be in long-run equilibrium with respect to its size is by producing at the minimum point on its $LRATC$ curve.

Each firm must be producing at minimum $LRATC$ (at a point such as q^* in Figure 14A-2). Since for an industry to be in long-run equilibrium each firm must be in long-run equilibrium, it follows that in long-run competitive equilibrium all firms in the industry will be selling at a price equal to minimum $LRATC$.

In long-run competitive equilibrium, the firm's cost is the lowest attainable cost, given the limits of known technology and factor prices.

LONG-RUN RESPONSES TO CHANGES IN DEMAND

Suppose a competitive industry is in long-run equilibrium, as shown in Figure 14A-1. Now suppose that the demand for the product increases. Price will rise to equate demand with the industry's short-run supply. Each firm will expand output until its short-run marginal cost once again equals price. Each firm will earn profits as a result of the rise in price, and the profits will induce new firms to enter the industry. This shifts the short-run supply curve to the right and forces down the price. Entry continues until all firms are once again just covering average total costs. To recapitulate: The short-run effects of the rise in demand are a rise in price and output; the long-run effect is new entry, which leads to a further rise in output and a fall in price. This process is illustrated in Figure 14A-3.

Now consider a fall in demand. The industry starts with firms in long-run equilibrium, as shown in Figure 14A-1, and the market demand curve shifts left and price falls. The ultimate sequence is the reverse of the sequence found when demand increases. It may also be illustrated in Figure 14A-3, but the process is likely to be different, for exit and entry are not symmetrical in the real world.

How does exit occur when demand declines?

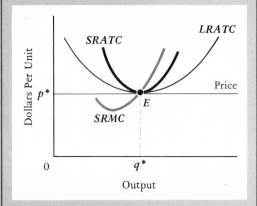

FIGURE 14A-1
The Equilibrium of a Firm When the Industry Is in Long-Run Equilibrium

In long-run competitive equilibrium, the firm is operating at the minimum point on its *LRATC* curve. In long-run equilibrium, each firm must be (1) maximizing short-run profits, $SRMC = p$; (2) earning profits of zero on its existing plant, $SRATC = p$; and (3) unable to increase its profits by altering the size of plant. These three conditions can only be met when the firm is at E, the minimum point on its $LRATC$ curve, with price p^* and output q^*.

FIGURE 14A-2
Short-Run Versus Long-Run Equilibrium of a Competitive Firm

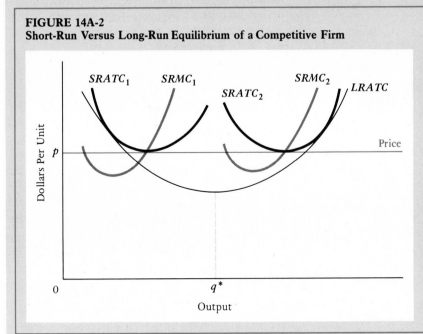

A competitive firm that is not at the minimum point on its *LRATC* curve cannot be in long-run equilibrium. Suppose two firms have identical *LRATC* curves but one firm has too small a plant, with costs *SRATC*₁, while the other firm has too large a plant, with costs of *SRATC*₂. Both firms are in short-run equilibrium at price $p = SRMC = SRATC$, but neither is in long-run equilibrium. Firm 1 can increase its profits by building a larger plant (thereby moving downward to the right along its *LRATC* curve). Firm 2 can increase is profits by building a smaller plant (thereby moving downward to the left along its *LRATC* curve).

There are two possible scenarios. First, suppose the decline in demand forces price below *ATC* but leaves it above *AVC*. Firms are then in the position shown in Figure 14-7(i), page 225. The firms can cover their variable costs and earn some return on their capital, so they remain in production for as long as their existing plant and equipment lasts. But it is not worth replacing capital as it wears out. Exit will occur as old capital wears out and is not placed. As firms exit, the short-run supply curve shifts left and market price rises. This continues until the remaining firms in the industry can cover their total costs. At this point it will pay to replace capital as it wears out, and the decline in the size of the industry will be brought to a halt. In this case the adjustment may take a very long time, for the industry shrinks in size only as existing plant and equipment wears out.

The second scenario occurs when the decline in demand is so large that price is forced below the level of *AVC*. In this case firms cannot even cover their variable costs, and some will shut down immediately. Thus the reduction in capital devoted to production in the industry occurs rapidly because some existing capacity is scrapped or sold for other uses. Once sufficient capital has been withdrawn so that price rises to a level that allows the remaining firms to cover their *AVC*, the rapid withdrawal of capital will cease. Further exit occurs more slowly, as described above.

THE LONG-RUN INDUSTRY SUPPLY CURVE

Adjustments to long-run changes in demand do not necessarily leave the *level* of long-run costs unchanged, as was assumed in Figure 14A-3. The response of costs to such long-run changes in required equilibrium output is shown by the **long-run industry supply curve** (*LRS*). This curve shows the relation between equilibrium price and the output firms will be willing to supply after all desired entry or exit has occurred.

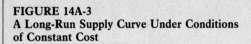

FIGURE 14A-3
A Long-Run Supply Curve Under Conditions of Constant Cost

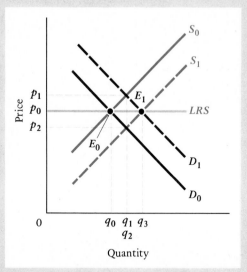

The long-run supply curve connects equilibrium points after demand-induced shifts occur in the supply curve. The initial equilibrium point is E_0. A shift in demand from D_0 to D_1 first raises the price to p_1 as industry output expands along the short-run supply curve to q_1. Firms will be earning profits and entry will thus occur. This induces a shift in the short-run supply curve from S_0 to S_1, and price falls; but output increases to q_3. The long-run supply curve is LRS. In the case illustrated the increase in supply is just sufficient to keep the price at p_0. Thus output has been increased "at constant cost" in the long run.

A decrease in demand from D_1 to D_0, starting from E_1, first lowers price to p_2. Firms that were previously breaking even will earn losses. Eventually, in response, exit will occur. This induces a leftward shift in the supply curve from S_1 to S_0, and price rises again to p_0, where the remaining firms break even. Output has been reduced "at constant cost" in the long run.

The long-run supply curve connects positions of long-run equilibrium after all demand-induced changes have occurred.

When induced changes in factor prices are considered, it is possible for LRS to rise, to fall, or to remain constant. Figure 14A-3 illustrated the case of constant costs; Figures 14A-4 and 14A-5 illustrate the case of a rise and the case of a fall in long-run costs, respectively.

Constant Costs (Constant *LRS*)

The long-run supply curve in Figure 14A-3 is horizontal. This indicates that the industry, given time, will adjust its size to provide whatever quantity may be demanded at a constant price. Such conditions may obtain if factor prices do not change as the output of the whole industry expands or contracts. An industry with a horizontal long-run supply curve is said to be a **constant-cost industry**.

Increasing Long-Run Costs (Increasing *LRS*)

Short-run cost curves rise because of the existence of fixed factors and the law of diminishing returns to variable factors. A different explanation must apply in the long run, since there are no fixed factors.

When an industry expands its output, it needs more inputs. The increase in demand for these inputs may bid up their prices. Such growth-induced changes in prices may be expected whenever rapid growth occurs. The reason for this is that a large industry demands large quantities of certain key materials and certain kinds of skilled labor. As the industry grows larger and larger, these become increasingly scarce. For instance, growth of the airline industry increases the demand of airlines for aluminum, jet fuel, and skilled mechanics, none of which is in perfectly elastic supply. Increasing scarcity of these inputs will tend to raise their price, and this in turn will raise the cost of providing air transport.

If costs rise with increasing levels of industry output, so too will the price at which the producers are willing to supply the market. The common sense of this result is that if firms were just covering their costs before the increase in demand, the price they receive will have to rise enough to cover any increases in factor prices they must pay.

To see more specifically why this result occurs,

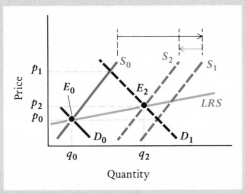

FIGURE 14A-4
A Rising Long-Run Supply Curve

If growth in industry size increases factor prices, the *LRS* will be upward-sloping. Suppose an industry is in equilibrium at E_0. Then demand increases from D_0 to D_1. In the short run price will rise to p_1. In the long run this increases the number of firms, thereby shifting the supply curve from S_0 to S_1 (as shown by the black arrow). This is the supply curve that would pertain to an expanded number of firms if input prices did not change. But the increase in industry production bids up the prices of factors used, thereby shifting the supply curve leftward from S_1 to S_2 (as shown by the colored arrow). Equilibrium E_2 is at price p_2. Price has risen from p_0 to p_2 because firms must recover the costs imposed by the higher input prices.

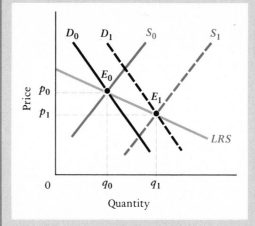

FIGURE 14A-5
A Declining Long-Run Supply Curve

If growth in industry size reduces factor prices, the *LRS* will be downward-sloping. From an original equilibrium at E_0, an increase in demand to D_1 leads to an increase in supply to S_1 and a new equilibrium at E_1. Price p_1 is below the original price p_0 because lower factor prices allow firms to cover their total costs at the lower price.

remember that an increase in the price of inputs will shift the marginal cost (and average cost) curves of all firms upward. This shift in the marginal cost curves of all firms shifts the industry short-run supply curve to the left.

The effect on *LRS* of growth in industry output may be thought of for analytic purposes as occurring in two stages: an increase in the number of firms with no increase in factor prices and an induced increase in factor prices. Figure 14A-4 shows how these two stages lead to an upward-sloping *LRS* curve.

In reality the two stages occur simultaneously. For instance, in recent years the very rapid increase in the demand for electric power in the United States has led to a large increase in the number of

electric generating plants. This in turn has led to sharp increases in the demand for inputs—and hence to increases in their price. This development has been particularly marked with the prices of coal and oil, the key fuels in electricity generation. As one commentator has said, "talk of the energy crisis is mood music for higher fuel prices." Higher fuel prices in turn lead to higher prices of the things the fuel is used to make.

Rising *LRS*—**rising supply price,** as it is sometimes called—is often a characteristic of sharp and rapid growth. A competitive industry with rising long-run supply prices is often called a **rising-cost industry.**

Decreasing Long-Run Costs (Decreasing *LRS*)?

So far we have suggested that the long-run supply curve may be constant or rising. Could it ever decline, thereby indicating that higher outputs were associated with lower prices in long-run equilibrium?

It is tempting to answer yes because of the opportunities of more efficient scales of operation using greater mechanization and more effective specialization of labor. But this answer would not be correct for perfectly competitive industries because each firm in long-run equilibrium must already be at the lowest point on its *LRATC* curve. If a firm could lower its costs by building a larger, more mechanized plant, it would be profitable to do so without waiting for an increase in demand. Since any single firm can sell all it wishes at the going market price, it will be profitable to expand the scale of its operations as long as its *LRATC* is falling.

There is a reason, however, why the long-run supply curve might slope downward: the expansion of an industry might lead to a fall in the prices of some of its inputs. If this occurs, the firms will find their cost curves shifting downward as they expand their outputs.

As an illustration of how the expansion of one industry could cause the prices of some of its inputs to fall, consider the early stages of the growth of the automobile industry. As the output of automobiles increased, the industry's demand for tires grew greatly. This, as suggested earlier, would have increased the demand for rubber and tended to raise its price, but it also provided the opportunity for Goodyear, Firestone, and other tire manufacturers to build large modern plants and reap the benefits of increasing returns in tire production. At first these economies were large enough to offset any factor price increases, and tire prices charged to manufacturers of automobiles fell. Thus automobile costs fell because of lower prices of an important input.

To see the effect of a fall in input prices caused by the expansion of an industry, suppose that the demand for the industry's product increases. Price and profits will rise and new entry will occur as a result. But when expansion of the industry has gone far enough to bring price back to its initial level, cost curves will be lower than they were

initially because of the fall in input prices. Firms will thus still be earning profits. A further expansion will then occur until price falls to the level of the minimum points on each firm's new, lower *LRATC* curve. (This case is illustrated in Figure 14A-5.) An industry that has a declining long-run supply curve is often called a **falling-cost industry**.

THE EXISTENCE OF LONG-RUN COMPETITIVE EQUILIBRIUM

The greatest limitation on the usefulness of the model of perfect competition is that it may not be a suitable yardstick for evaluating real-world markets because it may be that perfect competition cannot exist in some circumstances that commonly occur in the real world.

The Problem Caused by Declining Costs

A necessary condition for a long-run competitive equilibrium to exist is that any economies of scale that are available to a firm should be exhausted at a level of output that is small relative to the whole industry's output. We have seen that a competitive firm will never be in equilibrium on the falling part of its *LRATC*—if price is given and costs can be reduced by expanding scale, profits can also be increased by doing so. Thus firms will grow in size at least until all scale economies are exhausted. Provided the output that yields the minimum *LRATC* for each firm is small relative to the industry's total output, there will be a large number of firms in the industry and the industry will remain competitive. If, however, reaching the minimum *LRATC* leads to a small number of very large firms, they are likely to have significant market power. If so, they will cease to be price takers and perfect competition will cease to exist.

In an industry with declining costs, the market may be too small relative to technology to be compatible with perfect competition. Indeed, if scale economies exist over such a large range that one firm's *LRATC* would still be falling if it served the entire market, a single firm may come to monopolize the market. This is what the classical economists called the case of *natural* monopoly; it is considered in Chapter 18.

The Problem of Constant Costs

Constant long-run costs also create problems for the competitive theory. Only if the firm's *LRATC* curve is U-shaped will there be a determinate size of the firm in a competitive industry. To see why, assume instead that *LRATC* falls to a minimum at some level of output and then remains constant for all larger outputs. All firms would have to be at least the minimum size, but they could be just that size or much larger since price would equal *LRATC* for any output above the minimum efficient size. In other words, there would then be no unique size for the firm. Are there reasons to believe the curve may not be U-shaped?

U-shaped plant curves. There are very good reasons why the *LRATC* curve for a single-plant firm may be expected to be U-shaped. A great deal of modern technology results in lower average costs for large, automated factories compared with smaller factories in which few workers use relatively unsophisticated capital equipment. As a single plant becomes too large, however, costs may rise because of the sheer difficulty of planning for, and controlling the behavior of, a vast integrated operation. Thus we have no problem accounting for a U-shaped cost curve for the *plant*.

U-shaped firm cost curve. What of the U-shaped cost curve for the *firm*? A declining portion will occur for the same reason that the *LRATC* for one plant declines when the firm is so small that it operates only one plant. Now, however, let the firm be operating one plant at the output where its *LRATC* is a minimum. Call that output q^*. What if the firm decides to double its output to $2q^*$? If it tries to build a vast plant with twice the output of the optimal size plant, the firm's average total cost of production may rise (because the vast plant has higher costs than a plant of the optimal size). But the firm has the option of *replicating* its first plant in a physically separate location. If the firm obtains a second parcel of land, builds an identical second plant, staffs it identically, and allows its production to be managed independently, there seems no reason why the second plant's minimum *LRATC* should be different from that of the first plant. *Because the firm can replicate plants and have them managed independently, there seems no reason why any firm faced with constant factor prices should not face constant LRATCs at least for multiples of the output for which one plant achieves the lowest plant LRATC.*

In the modern theory of perfect competition, a U-shaped *firm* cost curve is merely *assumed*. Without it—although a competitive equilibrium may exist for an arbitrary number of firms—there is nothing to determine the equilibrium size of the firm and hence the number of firms in the industry.

THE PERMANENT-INCOME HYPOTHESIS AND THE LIFE-CYCLE HYPOTHESIS

APPENDIX TO CHAPTER 32

In the Keynesian theory of the consumption function, current consumption expenditure is related to current income—either current disposable income or current national income. Recent attempts to reconcile the apparently conflicting empirical data on short-term and long-term consumption behavior have produced a series of theories that relate consumption to some longer-term concept of income than the income that the household is currently earning.

The two most influential theories of this type are the **permanent-income hypothesis (PIH)**, developed by Professor Friedman, and the **life-cycle hypothesis (LCH)**, developed by Professors Modigliani and Ando and the late Professor Brumberg. Although there are many significant differences between these theories, their similarities are more important than their differences, and they may be looked at together when studying their major characteristics. In doing this it is important to ask: What variables do these theories seek to explain? What assumptions do the theories make?

What are the major implications of these assumptions? How do the theories reconcile the apparently conflicting empirical evidence? And what implications do they have for the overall behavior of the economy?

VARIABLES

Three important variables need to be considered: consumption, saving, and income. Keynesian-type theories seek to explain the amounts that households spend on purchasing goods and services for consumption. This concept is called *consumption expenditure*. Permanent-income theories seek to explain the actual flows of consumption of the services that are provided by the commodities that households buy. This concept is called *actual consumption*.[1] With services and nondurable goods, expenditure and actual consumption occur more or less at the same time and the distinction between the two concepts is not important. The consumption of a haircut, for example, occurs at the time it is purchased, and an orange or a package of corn flakes is consumed very soon after it is purchased. Thus, if we knew purchases of such goods and services at some time, say last year, we would also know last year's consumption of those goods and services. But this is not the case with durable consumer goods. A screwdriver is purchased at one point in time, but it yields up its services over a long time, possibly as long as the purchaser's lifetime. The same is true of a house and a watch and, over a shorter period of time, of a car and a dress. For such products, if we know purchases last year, we do not necessarily know last year's consumption of the services that the products yielded.

Thus one important characteristic of durable goods is that *expenditure* to purchase them is not necessarily synchronized with consumption of the stream of services that the goods provide. If in 1985

Mr. Smith buys a car for $8,000, runs it for six years, and then discards it as worn out, his expenditure on automobiles is $8,000 in 1985 and zero for the next five years. His consumption of the services of automobiles, however, is spread out at an average annual rate of $1,333 for six years. If everyone followed Mr. Smith's example by buying a new car in 1985 and replacing it in 1991, the automobile industry would undergo wild booms in 1985 and 1991 with five intervening years of slump even through the actual consumption of automobiles would be spread more or less evenly over time. This example is extreme, but it illustrates the possibilities, where consumers' durables are concerned, of quite different time paths of *consumption expenditure*, which is the subject of Keynesian theories of the consumption function, and *actual consumption*, which is the subject of permanent-income type theories.

Now consider saving. The change in emphasis from consumption expenditure to actual consumption implies a change in the definition of saving. Saving is no longer income minus consumption expenditure; it is now income minus the value of actual consumption. When Mr. Smith spent $8,000 on his car in 1985 but used only $1,333 worth of its services in that year, he was actually consuming $1,333 and saving $6,667. The purchase of a consumers' durable is thus counted as saving and only the value of its services actually consumed is counted as consumption.

So much for consumption and saving. The third important variable in this type of theory is the income variable. Instead of using current income, the theories use a concept of long-term income. The precise definition varies from one theory to another, but basically it is related to the household's expected income stream over a fairly long planning period. In the LCH it is the income that the household expects to earn over its lifetime.[2] Every household is assumed to have a view of its expected lifetime earnings. This is not as unreasonable as it might seem. Students training to be

---

[1] Because Keynes' followers did not always distinguish carefully between the concepts of consumption expenditure and actual consumption, the word *consumption* is often used in both contexts. We follow this normal practice, but where there is any possible ambiguity in the term we will refer to *consumption expenditure* and *actual consumption*.

[2] In the PIH the household has an infinite time horizon and the relevant permanent-income concept is the amount the household could consume forever without increasing or decreasing its present stock of wealth.

FIGURE 32A-1
Current Income and Permanent Income

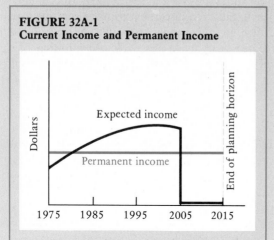

Expected current income may vary greatly over a lifetime, but expected permanent income is defined to be the constant annual equivalent. The graph shows a hypothetical expected income stream from work for a household whose planning horizon was 40 years from 1975. The current income rises to a peak, then falls slowly for a while, and finally falls sharply on retirement. The corresponding permanent income is the amount the household could consume at a steady rate over its lifetime by borrowing early against future earnings (as do most newly married couples), then repaying past debts, and finally saving for retirement when income is at its peak without either incurring debt or accumulating new wealth to be passed on to future generations.

doctors have a very different view of expected lifetime income than those training to become high school teachers. Both expected income streams—for a doctor and for a high school teacher—will be very different from that expected by an assembly line worker or a professional athlete. One possible lifetime income stream is illustrated in Figure 32A-1.

The household's expected lifetime income is then converted into a single figure for *annual **permanent income.*** In the life-cycle hypothesis this permanent income is the maximum amount the household could spend on consumption each year without accumulating debts *that are passed on to future generations.* If a household were to consume

a constant amount equal to its permanent income each year, it would add to its debts in years when current income was less than permanent income and reduce its debt or increase its assets in years when its current income exceeded its permanent income; however, over its lifetime it would just break even, leaving neither accumulated assets nor debts to its heirs. If the interest rate were zero, permanent income would be just the sum of all expected incomes divided by the number of expected years of life. With a positive interest rate, permanent income will diverge somewhat from this amount because of the costs of borrowing and the extra income that can be earned by investing savings.

ASSUMPTION

The basic assumption of this type of theory, whether PIH or LCH, is that the household's actual consumption is related to its permanent rather than to its current income. Two households that have the same permanent income (and are similar in other relevant characteristics) will have similiar consumption patterns even though their current incomes behave very differently.

IMPLICATIONS

The major implication of these theories is that changes in a household's current income will affect its actual consumption only so far as they affect its permanent income. Consider two income changes that could occur to a household with a permanent income of $10,000 per year and an expected lifetime of 30 or more years. In the first, suppose the household receives an unexpected extra income of $2,000 *for this year only.* The increase in the household's permanent income is thus very small. If the rate of interest were zero, the household could consume an extra $66.66 per year for the rest of its expected lifespan; with a positive rate of interest, the extra annual consumption would be more because money not spent this year could be invested and would earn interest.[3] In the second case, the household gets a totally unforeseen increase of $2,000 a year for the rest of its life. In this event the household's permanent income has risen by $2,000 because the household can actually consume $2,000 more every year without accumulating new debts. Although in both cases current income rises $2,000, the effect on permanent income is very different in the two cases.

Keynesian theory assumes that *consumption expenditure* is related to current income and therefore predicts the same change in this year's consumption expenditure in each of the above cases. Permanent-income theories relate *actual consumption* to permanent income and therefore predict very different changes in actual consumption in each case. In the first case there would be only a small increase in actual annual consumption; in the second there would be a large increase.

In permanent-income theories, any change in current income that is thought to be temporary will have only a small effect on permanent income and hence on actual consumption.

Implications for the Behavior of the Economy

According to the permanent-income and the life-cycle hypotheses, actual consumption is not much affected by temporary changes in income. Does this mean that aggregate expenditure, $C + I + G + (X - M)$, is not much affected? *Not necessarily.* Consider what happens when households get a temporary increase in their incomes. If actual consumption is not greatly affected by this, then households must be saving most of this increase. But from the point of view of these theories, households save when they buy a durable good just as much as when they buy a financial asset such as a stock or a bond. In both cases actual current consumption is not changed.

Thus spending a temporary increase in income

on bonds or on new cars is consistent with both the PIH and the LCH. But it makes a great deal of difference to the short-run behavior of the economy which is done. If households buy stocks and bonds, aggregate expenditure on currently produced final goods will not rise when income rises temporarily;[4] if households buy automobiles or any other durable consumer good, aggregate expenditure on currently produced final goods will rise when income rises temporarily. Thus the PIH and the LCH leave unsettled the question that is critical in determining the size of the multiplier: What is the reaction of household *expenditures* on currently produced goods and services, particularly durables, to short-term, temporary changes in income?

The PIH and LCH theories leave unanswered the critical question of the ability of short-term changes in fiscal policy to remove inflationary and deflationary gaps.

Assume, for example, that a serious deflationary gap emerges and that the government attempts to stimulate a recovery by giving tax rebates and by cutting tax rates—both on an announced temporary basis. This will raise households' current disposable incomes by the amount of the tax cuts, but it will raise their permanent incomes by only a small amount. According to the PIH, the flow of actual current consumption should not rise much. Yet it is quite consistent with the PIH that households should spend their tax savings on durable consumer goods, the consumption of which can be spread over many years. In this case, even though actual consumption this year would not respond much to the tax cuts, expenditure would respond a great deal. Since current output and employment depends on expenditure rather than on actual consumption, the tax cut would be effective in stimulating the economy. However, it is also consistent with the PIH that households spend only a small part of their tax savings on consumption goods and seek to invest the rest in bonds and other financial assets. In this case the tax cuts may have only a

---

[3] If the rate of interest were 7 percent, the household could invest the $2,000, consume an extra $161 a year, and just have nothing left at the end of 30 years.

[4] Except for any indirect effect through changes in interest rates.

small stimulating effect on the economy. It is important to note that the PIH and the LCH do *not* predict unambiguously that changes in taxes that are announced to be only short-lived will be ineffective in removing inflationary or deflationary gaps.

A Reconciliation of the Data

The PIH and the LCH are able to reconcile the observation that the *MPC* appears to be equal to the *APC* in long-period data while it is less than the *APC* in short-period and cross-sectional data.[5] They do this by relating changes in observed income to changes in permanent income.

Long-term time-series data using decade-by-decade averages remove the effects of temporary fluctuations in income. The observed changes in *Y* mainly represent permanent increases in real income because of economic growth. Long-term time-series studies will thus tend to measure accurately the propensity to consume out of permanent income.

Now consider short-term data. A study covering 10 or 15 years at the most and using annual observations of *C* and *Y* will use an income series dominated by temporary changes caused by cyclical fluctuations. When a household loses employment because of a business recession, it does not expect to remain unemployed forever; neither does it ex-

pect the extra income that it earns from heavy overtime work during a period of peak demand to persist. It may therefore be assumed that households expect these cyclical changes in current income to be temporary and that they will thus have little effect on permanent income. Since consumption is assumed to depend on permanent income, it follows that the observed relation between consumption and cyclical changes in income will tend to be smaller than the relation shown by the long-term time-series data. What this shows, then, is the lack of relation between changes in consumption and temporary changes in income, not a lack of relation between changes in consumption and changes in permanent income.

A similar analysis shows that cross-section studies are strongly influenced by the behavior of households whose incomes have temporarily departed from their permanent levels. Thus cross-section studies should be expected to yield a much lower observed marginal propensity to consume than that yielded by long-term time-series studies.

CONCLUSION

While permanent-income type theories succeed in reconciling various empirical observations of consumption functions, they leave ambiguous the multiplier effects of temporary increases in income. They are consistent with a constancy in both the *MPC* and the *APC* when *permanent income* changes. They also suggest a high degree of stability of the actual flow of consumption in the face of temporary fluctuations in current income. This is consistent with an *APC* out of *current income* that varies inversely with current income, falling as income rises and rising as income falls.

---

[5] The short-run and long-run time-series data are described in Chapter 28 (see especially page 524). Cross-section data are for a number of households at one point in time, and they show for that point in time how household consumption varies with household income. The data yield a consumption function similar to that obtained from short-term time-series data but with an even lower *MPC*.

MONEY IN THE NATIONAL INCOME MODEL
APPENDIX TO CHAPTER 34

We have studied the interaction between money, interest rates, and national income in terms of the apparatus in Figures 34-3, 34-4, and 34-5. A loose end in that model can best be seen by considering the impact of a change in the money supply. This leads to a fall in interest rates as shown in Figure 34-3(ii), to increases in expenditure as shown in Figure 34-3(ii), and to increased national income as shown in Figure 34-4. But increased national income in turn leads to an increased need for transactions balances. This increased demand for money must then be added to the liquidity preference schedule in Figure 34-3. How is the increase in demand satisfied? Does accounting for it radically alter the conclusions of the analysis of Chapter 34?

The answer to the last question is no. This appendix provides a model that integrates monetary and expenditure factors and shows how they jointly determine the interest rate and the level of national income. The approach is that first suggested by the British economist Sir John Hicks (awarded the Nobel Prize in economics in 1972) in his famous review of Keynes' *General Theory*, "Mr. Keynes and the Classics: A Suggested Interpretation." This approach involves identifying the relationship between income and interest rates that is imposed first by goods market equilibrium and then by money market equilibrium. We then bring the two together to determine the one combination of real national income and interest rate that satisfies both equilibrium conditions simultaneously. Finally we use the model to examine monetary and fiscal policy.

THE INTEREST RATE AND AGGREGATE EXPENDITURE: THE *IS* CURVE

As we saw in going from Figure 34-3(ii) to Figure 34-4(i), a fall in the rate of interest is associated with a rise in the level of real national income due to increased investment expenditures. Figure 34A-1 depicts this relationship between interest rates and national income as the negatively sloped *IS* curve. The negative relationship is derived for *given* values of the other variables influencing the aggregate expenditure function of Figure 34-4(i). The *IS* curve shows the combinations of national income and the rate of interest for which aggregate expenditure just equals total production in the economy.

For given settings of the relationships underlying the aggregate expenditure function, the condition of goods market equilibrium—income equals aggregate expenditure—means that the level of national income will vary negatively with the interest rate.

Fiscal Policy

Increases in the level of government expenditure raise the total level of aggregate expenditure *for any given interest rate;* as Figure 32-1 shows, this in turn leads to a multiplier effect on national income. In terms of the present model, an increase in govern-

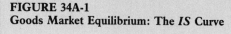

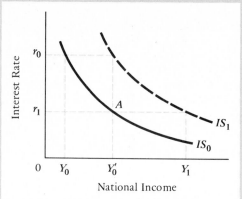

FIGURE 34A-1
Goods Market Equilibrium: The *IS* Curve

The locus of combinations of national income and the interest rate for which aggregate expenditure equals output is called the *IS* curve. The *IS* curve slopes downward to the right, indicating that a fall in the interest rate from r_0 to r_1 leads, via increased investment, to an increased level of national income from Y_0 to Y_0'. Expansionary fiscal policy creates excess demand for output and causes the *IS* curve to shift right to IS_1; from an initial position at A, the interest rate must rise to r_0, or national income must rise to Y_2, or some combination of both along IS_1 must occur.

ment expenditure causes the *IS* curve to shift upward to the right, as shown in Figure 34A-1. Combinations of national income and the interest rate that were on the original *IS* curve and hence were initially positions of equilibrium in the goods market are now positions of excess demand due to the increase in autonomous government demand. Hence output must rise to satisfy the increased demand (in the process leading to the now familiar multiplier effect), or interest rates must rise to reduce investment demand, or as IS_1 in Figure 34A-1 shows, some combinations of both.[1]

[1] A reduction in taxes, by altering the relationship between national income and disposable income, would also lead to a rightward shift in the *IS* curve.

Expansionary fiscal policy causes the *IS* curve to shift upward and to the right, creating a new locus of points for which aggregate expenditure equals national income.

By similar reasoning, cuts in government spending or tax increases shift the *IS* curve down to the left. [50]

LIQUIDITY PREFERENCE AND NATIONAL INCOME: THE *LM* CURVE

When the money supply is held constant, if the demand for and the supply of money are to be equal, the *total* demand for money arising from the transactions, speculative, and precautionary motives must also be constant. As we have seen, the demand for money can be expected to vary positively with the level of national income and negatively with the rate of interest. Hence if there is to be monetary equilibrium with a given money supply, any increase in national income must be accompanied by an increase in the interest rate so as to keep total money demand constant. This is depicted by the positively sloped *LM* curve in Figure 34A-2. The *LM* curve shows the combinations of national income and the rate of interest for which total money demand is constant at the level of a given money supply.

For a given money supply, the condition of monetary market equilibrium means that the level of national income will vary directly with the interest rate.

Monetary Policy

An increase in the supply of money resulting from an open market purchase by the central bank causes the *LM* curve to shift downward to the right, as in Figure 34A-2. The combinations of national income and interest rate that were on the original *LM* curve and hence that were initially positions of monetary equilibrium now correspond

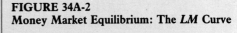

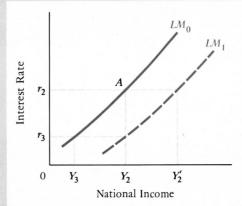

FIGURE 34A-2
Money Market Equilibrium: The *LM* Curve

The locus of combinations of national income and the interest rate for which total money demand equals a given money supply is called the *LM* curve. The *LM* curve slopes upward to the right, indicating that a fall in the rate of interest from r_2 to r_3, which causes the demand for money to rise, must be accompanied by a fall in income, say from Y_2 to Y_3, in order to keep money demand equal to the constant money supply. An open market purchase creates an excess supply of money and causes the *LM* curve to shift right to LM_1; from an initial position at A, the interest rate must fall to r_3, or national income must rise to Y_2', or some combination of both along LM_1 must occur.

to excess supply due to the increase in the supply of money. To reestablish equilibrium, the demand for money must increase to match the larger money supply; hence national income must rise, or the interest rate must fall, or as LM_1 in Figure 34A-2 shows, some combination of both.

An increase in the money supply causes the *LM* curve to shift downward to the right, creating a new locus of points for which total money demand equals the money supply.

By similar reasoning, a decrease in the money supply causes the *LM* curve to shift upward to the left. [51]

MACROECONOMIC EQUILIBRIUM: DETERMINATION OF NATIONAL INCOME AND THE INTEREST RATE

The model is shown in Figure 34A-3. The intersection of the two curves indicates the only combination of national income and the rate of interest for which aggregate expenditure equals national income *and* the demand for money is equal to the supply.

The intersection of the *IS* and *LM* curves gives the equilibrium levels of national income and the rate of interest in a model that combines both expenditure and monetary influences.

Figure 34A-3 shows the effects of particular shifts in the *IS and LM* curves. This analysis leads to four general predictions.

1. A rightward shift of the *IS* curve raises national income and the rate of interest.
2. A leftward shift of the *IS* curve lowers national income and the rate of interest.
3. A rightward shift of the *LM* curve raises national income and lowers the rate of interest.
4. A leftward shift of the *LM* curve lowers national income and raises the rate of interest.

The Effects of Fiscal and Monetary Policy

Given our analysis of the effects of government expenditure on the *IS* curve and the effects of the money supply on the *LM* curve, we can summarize the analysis in our four basic predictions about the effects of monetary and fiscal policy.

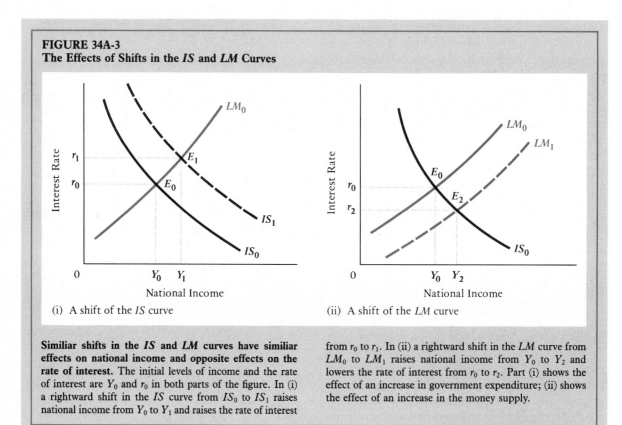

FIGURE 34A-3
The Effects of Shifts in the *IS* and *LM* Curves

(i) A shift of the *IS* curve

(ii) A shift of the *LM* curve

Similiar shifts in the *IS* and *LM* curves have similiar effects on national income and opposite effects on the rate of interest. The initial levels of income and the rate of interest are Y_0 and r_0 in both parts of the figure. In (i) a rightward shift in the *IS* curve from IS_0 to IS_1 raises national income from Y_0 to Y_1 and raises the rate of interest from r_0 to r_1. In (ii) a rightward shift in the *LM* curve from LM_0 to LM_1 raises national income from Y_0 to Y_2 and lowers the rate of interest from r_0 to r_2. Part (i) shows the effect of an increase in government expenditure; (ii) shows the effect of an increase in the money supply.

1. An increase in *G* raises national income and raises the rate of interest.
2. An increase in the money supply raises national income and lowers the rate of interest.
3. A decrease in *G* lowers national income and lowers the rate of interest.
4. A decrease in the money supply lowers national income and raises the rate of interest.

These results represent what may be called the *neo-Keynesian synthesis,* in which both monetary and fiscal policies have an effect on national income and interest rates. [52]

THE PRICE LEVEL AND AGGREGATE DEMAND

So far we have treated the price level as given and presumed that all changes in national income were changes in *real* output. Consider now what would happen to the analysis if the price level were allowed to vary.

Changes in the Price Level

As Figure 34-6 shows, an increase in the price level leads to an increase in liquidity preference. In order for money market equilibrium to be preserved, the interest rate must rise (as Figure 34-6), or the level of income must fall, or, since either leads to a reduction in money demand, some combination of both must occur—that is, the *LM* curve must shift upward to the left.

A fall in the price level reduces liquidity preference and the *LM* curve shifts down and to the right.

Increases in the price level cause the *LM* curve to shift upward to the left; decreases in the price level cause the *LM* curve to shift downward to the right.

But from the previous section we know that the effect in the first case is to reduce national income while the effect in the second case is to increase national income. This is illustrated in Figure 34A-4.

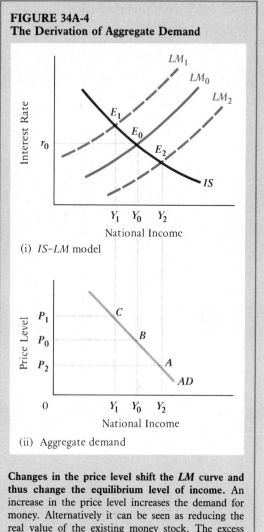

FIGURE 34A-4
The Derivation of Aggregate Demand

(i) *IS–LM* model

(ii) Aggregate demand

Changes in the price level shift the *LM* curve and thus change the equilibrium level of income. An increase in the price level increases the demand for money. Alternatively it can be seen as reducing the real value of the existing money stock. The excess demand for money leads to a leftward shift of the LM_0 curve to LM_1 and a fall in national income. A fall in the price level creates an excess supply of money and a rightward shift of the LM_0 curve to LM_2. The price level and national income are inversely related, as shown by the *AD* curve in (ii).

Equilibrium in the money and goods markets combined implies that the price level and national income are negatively related, as summarized in the downward-sloping aggregate demand curve.

The relationship summarized in the aggregate demand curve is a straightforward extension of the transmission mechanism running from liquidity preference to the rate of interest to aggregate expenditure.

Shifts in the Aggregate Demand Curve

The *AD* curve was derived on the basis of a given money supply and given relationships underlying the *IS* curve; it is a straightforward exercise to demonstrate that fiscal and monetary policies, by influencing the *IS* and *LM* curves, cause the *AD* curve to shift. [53] The mechanism by which monetary and fiscal policy cause the shift in *AD* is illustrated in Figure 34-4.

An increase in the money supply means that the *LM* curve corresponding to any particular price level shifts downward to the right. Hence that price level now corresponds to a higher level of real national income; that is, the aggregate demand curve shifts to the right as a result of an increase in the money supply.

An increase in government expenditure causes the *IS* curve to shift upward to the right as before; it now intersects any given *LM* curve at a higher level of national income. Again, any given price level now corresponds to a larger real national income; that is, the aggregate demand curve shifts to the right as a result of an increase in government expenditure.

SUSTAINED INFLATION AND THE PHILLIPS CURVE
APPENDIX TO CHAPTER 36

In this appendix we use the *Phillips curve*, introduced in the box on pages 700–701, to analyze sustained inflations.

THE PRICE PHILLIPS CURVE

The Phillips curve shown in the box described a relationship between the rate of change of *wages* and the state of demand, as measured by the level of national income. As we saw, changes in wages

cause the *SRAS* curve to shift, giving rise to changes in the price level. These two steps are commonly combined to produce a new curve relating the rate of change of the *price level* and the level of national income. Such a curve, often referred to as a *price Phillips curve,* is shown in Figure 36A-1.

The conditions under which it is possible to derive a price Phillips curve from the original relation between wages and national income are fairly

FIGURE 36A-1
A Price Phillips Curve

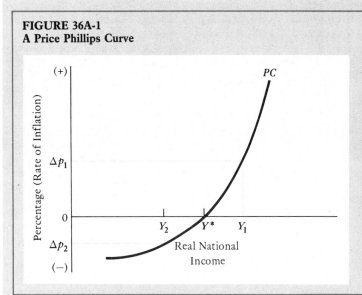

The Price Phillips curve shows the positive relationship between the level of national income and rate of increase in *the price level*. An increase in national income leads to an increase in the rate of change of wages and, other things being equal, to an increase in the rate of increase of prices. A fall in income leads to a decrease in the rate of change of wages and, other things being equal, to a decrease in the rate of decrease of prices.

With zero core inflation and output at its capacity level, Y^*, inflation is zero as shown. When output is above Y^* at, say, Y_1, inflation is positive at Δp_1. When output is below Y^* at, say, Y_2, inflation is negative at Δp_2.

complicated.[1] But the curve is commonly used, and we shall focus on it in this appendix. (We shall henceforth refer to the price Phillips curve simply as the Phillips curve.) The key simplification is that once the level of income has been determined—by the intersection of the *SRAS* and *AD* curves, as before—the rate of inflation can be read *directly* off the Phillips curve.

Notice that the Phillips curve in Figure 36A-1 has the *rate of change of prices* on the vertical axis. The aggregate supply curve that appears so frequently in the text has *the level of prices* on the vertical axis. Since both curves have real national income on the horizontal axis they are easily confused. They must therefore be carefully distinguished.

THE COMPONENTS OF INFLATION

Recall the three influences that cause the *SRAS* curve to shift upward and hence the price level to

[1] For example, at any given level of income the relationship between the rate of change of wages given by the figure in the box and the rate of change of prices given by Figure 36A-1 depends on what is assumed about how fast the Fed is causing the *AD* curve to shift.

rise: demand, expectations, and shocks. We encountered these on page 702. In this appendix we continue to use the terms *demand* and *shock* but introduce the term *core inflation* as a generalization of the term *expectations* used in the text. The rate of increase of prices can now be written as the sum of the three components:

$$\Delta p = C + DE + SE$$

where Δp is the annual percentage rate of changes of prices (i.e., the rate of inflation); C refers to core inflation; DE to demand effect; and SE to shock effect. We now look at these components one at a time.

Demand Inflation

Demand inflation refers to the influence on the price level of inflationary and GNP gaps. We have seen that an inflationary gap involves upward pressure on wages and hence on the price level while a GNP gap involves downward pressure. This is shown in Figure 36A-1 by the vertical distance between the Phillips curve and the horizontal axis.

The Phillips curve in Figure 36A-1 is merely a novel way of expressing relations we have used many times before. (It is important to remember, however, that Figure 36A-1 does not tell the whole story of inflation; it only describes the effects of *demand*.) These relations include the following:

1. There is neither upward nor downward pressure of demand on the price level when national income is at its potential level. Graphically the Phillips curve cuts the axis at Y^*.
2. When there is an inflationary gap, wages and other costs will rise. As we have seen, this shifts the *SRAS* curve upward and causes the price level to rise. The inflation continues as long as the gap persists. Graphically the Phillips curve lies above the axis where Y exceeds Y^*.
3. When there is a GNP gap, wages and other costs will fall. This shifts the *SRAS* curve downward and causes the price level to fall. The deflation continues as long as the gap persists. Graphically the Phillips curve lies below the axis when Y is less than Y^*.
4. The speed of the upward adjustment of the price level in the face of an inflationary gap exceeds the speed of the downward adjustment in the face of a GNP gap. Graphically the Phillips curve gets steeper the further to the right one moves along it. [54]

Core Inflation

The demand component cannot be the whole explanation of inflation since, if it were, inflation would only occur if national income exceeded Y^* and inflation could be quickly removed by forcing income back to Y^*. This prediction is emphatically rejected by the recent experiences of the United States and other Western economies. To explain what we observe about inflation we add the concept of core inflation. Core inflation refers to the underlying trend of inflation and it is referred to by several different names: *core* inflation, *expectational* inflation, *inertial* inflation, or the *underlying rate* of inflation.

In the text we singled out expectations as a main influence on the price level in addition to demand. But we also saw that how expectations are formed is a major source of controversy among economists.

The controversy actually runs deeper than that; some question whether it is explicit expectations about the future or inertia based on past experience that really dominates wage settlements. For example, past experience may matter if recent wage increases have failed to keep up with price increases; in such circumstances current wage settlements may have a "catch-up" component.

For these and other reasons, we use the general term *core inflation* to describe those persistent effects that do not depend on current demand conditions. These include expectations and other elements that stem from both forward- and backward-looking behavior. Some elements may change quickly, others only slowly. Their total influence at any point in time is summarized in the term *core inflation*.

Core inflation operates on the *SRAS* curve through the effects of wages and other costs.[2] Core inflation may also be related to *expected future changes* in wage and capital costs since firms who plan to change prices only infrequently must set prices on the basis of their expected costs over their planning period. If that is the case, to make our concept of core inflation operative we need a theory of how firms form their expectations of the future movement of costs. Some of the theories on how the expectations that determine the core inflation rate are formed were discussed in the text, and they are taken up again in Chapter 39.

Graphically the core inflation rate is added to the demand effect by shifting the Phillips curve upward by the amount of the core rate. This gives rise to a *core-augmented Phillips curve* or more commonly an *expectations-augmented Phillips curve*, as shown in Figure 36A-2. At any given level of income, the height of the core-augmented Phillips curve is given by the sum of the demand effect and the core rate of inflation. For example, at $Y = Y^*$, when demand inflation is zero, the height of the Phillips curve is given by the core rate. At any other level of income the rate of inflation differs from the demand effect by an amount equal to the core rate.

---

[2] As we saw in the text, some variations in net profit margins can and do occur. These cause price inflation to diverge temporarily from cost inflation and are included in shock inflation.

FIGURE 36A-2
Core Inflation and the Short-Run Phillips Curve

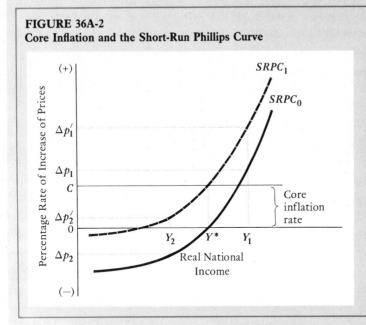

Core inflation shifts the price Phillips curve, and so changes the rate of inflation that corresponds to any given level of national income. The curve $SRPC_0$, which reproduces the Phillips curve from Figure 36A-1, corresponds to a zero core inflation rate. When core inflation rises to, say, C, the Phillips curve shifts up to $SRPC_1$. The rate of inflation at Y^* rises from 0 to C. At Y_1, which is greater than Y^*, inflation rises from Δp_1 to $\Delta p_1'$. At Y_2, which is less than Y^*, inflation was initially negative at Δp_2 but now becomes positive at $\Delta p_2'$.

The short-run Phillips curve.

Because the Phillips curve shifts upward or downward as the core rate of inflation rises or falls, it is called a **short-run Phillips curve (*SRPC*)** when it is drawn at any particular height above Y^* (that is, for any given level of core inflation).

The short-run Phillips curve is drawn for a given rate of core inflation.

Shock Inflation

Shock inflation refers to once-and-for-all changes that give a temporary upward or downward jolt to the price level. These included changes in indirect taxes, changes in profit margins, changes in import prices, and all kinds of other factors often referred to as *supply shocks*. Shock inflation includes everything that is not included under demand and core inflation.

Summary

Putting all of this together, the current inflation rate depends on the influence of (i) demand as indicated by the inflationary or GNP gap, *demand inflation;* (ii) expected increase in costs, *core inflation;* and (iii) a series of exogenous forces coming mainly from the supply side, *shock inflation.* These three components of inflation may be illustrated both numerically and graphically.

For a numerical example, assume that in the absence of any demand pressures, prices would rise by 10 percent because firms expect underlying costs to rise by 10 percent; that this price rise is moderated by 1 percentage point because costs only rise by 9 percent due to heavy unemployment; and that the price rise is augmented by 3 percentage points because large increases in indirect taxes force prices up. The final inflation is 12 percent, made up of 10 percent core inflation minus 1 percent demand inflation plus 3 percent shock inflation.

Graphically, the components of inflation are illustrated in Figure 36A-3 for two cases with a common positive core inflation component. The curve labeled *SRPC* is the Phillips curve shifted up by the core inflation rate. Its height above the axis at Y^* thus indicates core inflation. Points along

FIGURE 36A-3
The Components of Inflation Illustrated

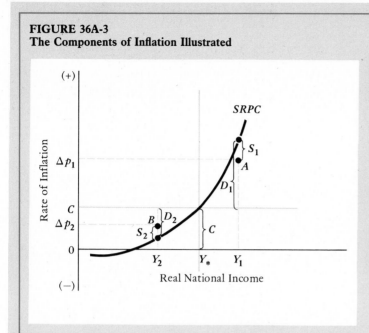

The inflation rate can be separated into three components: core inflation, demand inflation, and shock inflation. In the figure the Phillips curve is drawn for a given core rate of inflation and hence is labeled as a short-run Phillips curve. The given core rate, C, is shown by the height of the horizontal colored line.

Point A indicates a national income of Y_1 combined with an inflation rate of Δp_1. This rate is composed of the following: a core rate, C; a positive demand component, D_1 (determined by the shape of $SRPC$); and a negative shock component, S_1.

Point B indicates a national income of Y_2 combined with an inflation rate of Δp_2. This rate is composed of the following: core inflation is once again given by C; the demand component, D_2, which is now negative (since income, Y_2, is less than Y^*); and a positive shock component, S_2.

$SRPC$ where Y does not equal Y^* indicate how much the pressures of excess or deficient demand cause inflation to deviate from the core rate. Finally the amount by which actual inflation lies above or below the $SRPC$ shows the amount by which shocks cause the actual inflation rate to deviate from the sum of the core and the demand effects.

EXPECTATIONS AND CHANGES IN INFLATION

Originally the Phillips curve of Figure 36A-1 was thought to provide the whole explanation of inflation. When it was realized that the short-run Phillips curve shifted upward or downward, the concept of core inflation was added to explain this. Changes in the core rate shifts in the short-run Phillips curve. As a result we have the following conclusion.

There is a family of short-run Phillips curves, one for each core rate of inflation.

This is illustrated in Figure 36A-4. Let us now see what governs changes in the core rate and hence shifts in the $SRPC$.

Look at point Z on $SRPC_1$ in Figure 36A-5, which is reproduced $SRPC_1$ from Figure 36A-4 and corresponds to a core inflation rate of C_1. At Z shock inflation is zero and demand inflation is positive (since $Y_1 > Y^*$) so the actual inflation rate is above the core rate of C_1. Sooner or later this excess will come to be expected, the core rate will then rise, and the $SRPC$ will shift upward. *As long as national income is held above Y^*, the actual inflation rate will exceed the core rate and as a result sooner or later the core rate will rise. This means that the short-run Phillips curve will sooner or later shift upward, as indicated by the arrow above point Z.*

Now look at point W in Figure 36A-5 where again core inflation is C_1 and shock inflation is zero. At W demand inflation is negative (since $Y_2 < Y^*$) so the actual inflation rate is below the core rate of C_1. Sooner or later this difference will influence expectations and the core rate will fall. *As long as national income is held below Y^*, the actual inflation*

FIGURE 36A-4
A Family of Short-Run Phillips Curves

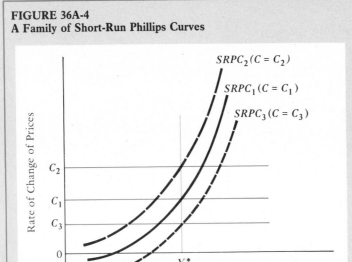

There is a separate short-run Phillips curve for each core rate of inflation. The Phillips curve of Figure 36A-3, shown here as $SRPC_1$, relates national income to inflation on the assumption that core inflation is C_1. The actual rate of inflation depends on both the core rate and the level of national income (as well as on shock inflation, assumed here to be zero).

For each possible core rate of inflation there is a short-run Phillips that lies above the axis at $Y = Y^*$ by the particular core rate to which it relates. If the core rate were C_2, greater than C_1, then the $SRPC$ would lie above $SRPC_1$, as shown by $SRPC_2$. If the core rate were C_3, less than C_1, then the $SRPC$ would lie below $SRPC_1$, as shown by $SRPC_3$.

FIGURE 36A-5
Shifts in the Short-Run Phillips Curve

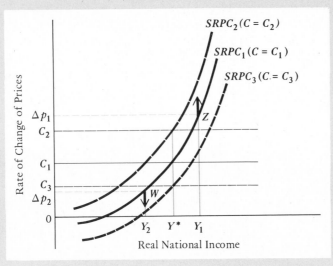

Changes in the core rate of inflation, which arise when actual inflation differs from the core rate, cause the short-run Phillips curve to shift. With a core inflation rate of C_1, the short-run Phillips curve is $SRPC_1$, reproduced from Figure 36A-4.

If income is maintained at Y_1, greater than Y^*, actual inflation will be Δp_1, greater than the core rate, as indicated by point Z. Eventually this excess of the actual inflation rate over the core rate will cause the core rate to rise, from C_1, say, to C_2, shifting the short-run Phillips curve to $SRPC_2$, as indicated by the arrow above point Z.

If income is maintained at Y_2, less than Y^*, actual inflation will be Δp_2, less than the core rate, as indicated by point W. Eventually the shortfall of actual inflation below the core rate will cause the core rate to fall below C_1, say, to C_3, causing the short-run Phillips curve to shift down to $SRPC_3$, as indicated by the arrow below W.

rate will be less than the core rate and sooner or later the core rate will fall. This means that sooner or later the short-run Phillips curve will begin to shift downward, as indicated by the arrow below W.

So we have a basic prediction of the theory:

A persistent inflationary gap will sooner or later cause the inflation rate to accelerate, while a persistent GNP gap will sooner or later cause the inflation rate to decelerate.

This of course is the acceleration hypothesis that we have already encountered in the text. Let us now examine it in more detail.

Accelerating Inflation

Consider an economy with a core inflation of C_1 that has just experienced an increase in aggregate demand so that output is above Y^* as at point Z in Figure 36A-5. There is an inflationary gap with a positive inflation rate; the $SRAS$ curve will be shifting upward while monetary validation by the Fed is shifting the AD curve upward. (It may be worth reiterating what is happening here: Core inflation produces the rise in prices that results from firms' expectations about the long-run trend in costs; the demand component produces the addition to inflation due to what are thought to be transitory demand factors; shock inflation is still treated as zero.)

Is this situation sustainable? Only if the Phillips curve remains stable. If the short-run Phillips curve stayed put, policymakers could conclude that they had achieved a pretty good trade-off. They would have gained a permanent increase in output of Y^*Y_1 at the cost of a permanent increase in inflation from C_1 to Δp_1.

But as we have seen, this is not the end of the story. The persistence of a demand inflation will eventually cause the core inflation rate to rise and hence cause the $SRPC$ to shift upward. In turn, this increases the rate at which the $SRAS$ curve is shifting upward. Let us trace this process in detail.

At point Z, prices and costs are rising at Δp_1 per year, and sooner or later firms and workers will stop believing that this increase from the old rate C_1 is a transitory phenomenon. They will come to

expect some of this increase to persist and incorporate it into core inflation. Let us say that, after a passage of time, firms come to expect wages and other costs to rise at the rate C_2 each period. This will produce a core inflation at a rate of C_2 per annum in Figure 36A-5. The short-run Phillips curve now shifts up to $SRPC_2$ in the figure. The rise in the core rate of inflation increases the actual inflation rate corresponding to each possible level of national income. If national income is maintained at Y_1 so that demand inflation remains positive, the actual inflation rate rises above Δp_1.

Now the $SRAS$ curve will be shifting upward more rapidly. If output is to be maintained at Y_1, the Fed will have to increase the rate of monetary expansion. This will cause the AD to shift up more rapidly to match the more rapid upward shift in $SRAS$. This is illustrated in terms of the $SRAS$ and AD curves in Figure 36-3.

The actual inflation rate, Δp_2, is well above the core rate, C_2. Sooner or later this will cause the core rate to rise again, and the short-run Phillips curve will again shift upwad. As long as output is maintained at Y_1 so that demand inflation is positive, this process of growing core inflation will continue.

From this an important conclusion follows:

If the central bank validates any rate of inflation that results from Y being held above Y^*, then the inflation rate itself will accelerate continuously *and* there will also be an acceleration in the rate of monetary expansion required to frustrate the monetary adjustment mechanism.

THE LONG-RUN PHILLIPS CURVE

Is there any level of income in this model that is compatible with a constant actual rate of inflation? The answer is yes, potential income. When income is at Y^*, the demand component of inflation is *zero*, as shown in Figure 36A-1. This means that, still letting shock inflation be zero, actual inflation equals core inflation. Since the core rate is determined by what people expect the inflation rate to be when actual inflation equals core inflation, the actual inflation rate is equal to the expected rate.

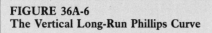

FIGURE 36A-6
The Vertical Long-Run Phillips Curve

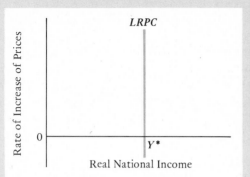

When actual inflation equals expected inflation, there is no trade-off between inflation and unemployment. In long-term equilibrium the actual rate of inflation must remain equal to the expected rate (otherwise expectations would be revised). This can only occur at the full-employment level of income Y^*; that is, along the *LRPC*.

At Y^* there is no demand pressure on the price level; hence the only influence on actual inflation is expected inflation. Any stable rate of inflation (provided it is validated by the appropriate rate of monetary expansion) is compatible with Y^* and its associated natural rate of unemployment.

There are no surprises. No one's plans are upset so no one has any incentive to alter plans as a result of what actually happens to inflation.

Providing the inflation rate is fully validated and shock inflation is zero, any rate of inflation can persist indefinitely as long as income is held at its potential level.

We now define the **long-run Phillips curve** as the relation between *national income* and *stable rates of inflation* that neither accelerate nor decelerate. This occurs when the core and actual inflation rates are equal. On the theory just described the long-run Phillips curve is vertical. This is illustrated in Figure 36A-6.

Maintaining a point on the *LRPC* leads to steady inflation at the core rate. This is illustrated in Figure 36A-7, where we show a situation with a positive core inflation rate and where there is full accommodation by the Fed. In the top panel the intersection of the *SRAS* and *AD* curves determines Y at Y^*. In the bottom panel the Phillips curve shows the rate of inflation. There is no demand effect on inflation so the actual and core inflation rates are equal. As a result the situation is sustainable (as long as the Fed continues to validate the core inflation). The increasing price level in the top panel reflects the positive inflation rate indicated in the bottom panel. Note that in the latter, since the core rate is not changing, the *SRPC* will be stable, which means we are also on the *LRPC*.

We can now state the following general conclusion.

The long-run Phillips curve is vertical at Y^*; only Y^* is compatible with a stable rate of inflation, and any stable rate is, if fully validated, compatible with Y^*.

The Natural Rate of Unemployment

We have talked about variations of Y from Y^*, but for every level of national income there is an associated level of unemployment. Recasting these conclusions in terms of unemployment we have the following: As before, call the unemployment associated with Y^* the natural rate of unemployment. Note that unemployment can be pushed below the natural rate but only at the cost of opening up an inflationary gap. If the government seeks to maintain this lower rate of unemployment the inflation rate will accelerate and will have to be validated by ever increasing rates of monetary expansion.

The lowest rate of unemployment that can be maintained without a tendency for the rate of inflation to accelerate is the natural rate.

Implications for Monetary Policy

The foregoing analysis has three major implications for the understanding and conduct of monetary policy.

First, the interaction among money, inflation,

FIGURE 36A-7
Monetary Accommodation and Steady Inflation

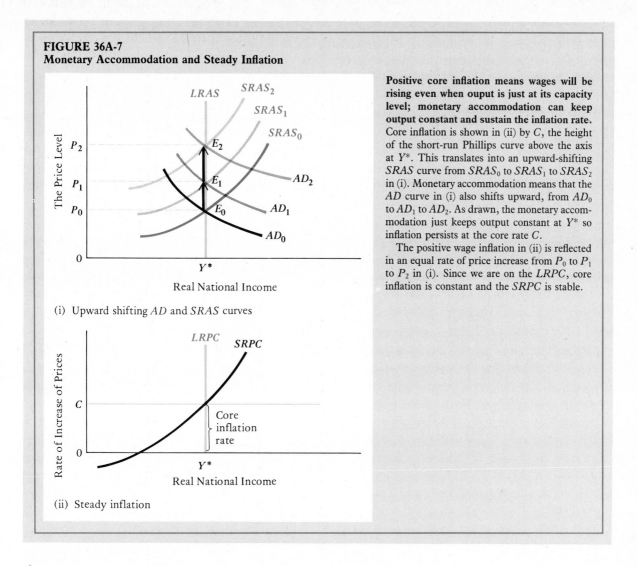

(i) Upward shifting *AD* and *SRAS* curves

(ii) Steady inflation

Positive core inflation means wages will be rising even when ouput is just at its capacity level; monetary accommodation can keep output constant and sustain the inflation rate. Core inflation is shown in (ii) by C, the height of the short-run Phillips curve above the axis at Y^*. This translates into an upward-shifting *SRAS* curve from $SRAS_0$ to $SRAS_1$ to $SRAS_2$ in (i). Monetary accommodation means that the *AD* curve in (i) also shifts upward, from AD_0 to AD_1 to AD_2. As drawn, the monetary accommodation just keeps output constant at Y^* so inflation persists at the core rate C.

The positive wage inflation in (ii) is reflected in an equal rate of price increase from P_0 to P_1 to P_2 in (i). Since we are on the *LRPC*, core inflation is constant and the *SRPC* is stable.

and output is complex. In particular, it depends on how expectations are formulated. Monetary policies may affect expectations differently at different times. Therefore, it would be wrong to expect a simple, mechanical relationship between the money supply and the behavior of output and the price level.

Second, differences between the expected rate of inflation and the rate that is being validated by monetary policy lead to changes in the level of output and in the actual rate of inflation. Hence

changes in the rate of monetary expansion can have powerful though not entirely predictable effects on the economy.

Third, in the long run GNP will move to the level indicated by the long-run aggregate supply curve and the long-run Phillips curve. This means that changes in the rate of monetary expansion will cause changes in the level of output only temporarily. In the long-run changes in the rate of monetary expansion have their only influence on the rate of inflation.

Some Extensions

Shock inflation. All of the above analysis has been done on the assumption that shock inflation is zero. In today's world many shocks hit the price level. What we see is a much less regular experience than the simple combination of core plus demand inflation. The inflation rate varies quite substantially from period to period due to the action of the many shocks that impinge on it.

Asymmetrical speeds of reaction. The shape of the Phillips curve means that it is easier to raise the core rate than to lower it. The change in the core rate from period to period depends on the discrepancy between the actual rate and the core rate. The steepness of the short-run Phillips curve above Y^* means that it is easy to create a substantial gap between the actual rate and the core rate by increasing the inflationary gap. This will tend to drag up the core rate fairly quickly. The flatness of the short-run Phillips curve below Y^* means that only a small discrepancy between the actual and the core rates can be created by even a large output gap. Therefore the core rate can be depressed only slowly by creating output gaps.

It is an important prediction of this theory that the core rate of inflation can accelerate fairly quickly but will decelerate only slowly.

Summary

We now summarize the key points of this theory and indicate where there is substantial agreement and where there is controversy with competing theories.

1. *The inflation rate of prices must follow the trend inflation rate of costs quite closely.* There is little disagreement over this relation, which defines the core, or underlying, rate of inflation. Notice, however, that it is just a matter of simple arithmetic that the major determinant of price inflation is cost inflation. This says nothing about causes. Costs could be rising because of the pressure of excess demand in factor markets or because of the exercise of arbitrary power on the part of unions.

2. *The core inflation rate changes very slowly.* There is a substantial disagreement over this point, for some economists believe the core rate can change quite rapidly. This key controversy underlies many differences in policy recommendations.

3. *The influence of demand on inflation is asymmetrical.* Inflationary gaps cause inflation to rise well above the core rate while output gaps force the actual rate only slightly below the core rate. The evidence for this asymmetry is extremely strong, although some economists deny it.

4. *Shocks caused by such influences as changes in indirect taxes, agricultural crop failures, or increases in import prices temporarily affect the inflation rate.* Economists do not always agree on this point and, at the time of the first OPEC oil-price shocks in 1974, some said that if oil-related prices rose, other prices would fall, keeping the price level constant. As a result of the evidence of the OPEC shocks, most economists now agree that supply shocks affect the price level, causing temporary deviations in the rate of inflation from what it would otherwise be. Another example of a clear supply-shock inflation was the rise in the price level that occurred in Britain in 1979–1980 after income taxes were cut and value-added taxes raised by the new Conservative government.

5. *Demand-induced rises in the inflation rate yield only temporary increases in national income.* Any departure of national income from Y^* sets in motion forces that cause a return to Y^*. Output in excess of Y^* causes an inflation that sets in motion the monetary adjustment mechanism. Frustration of the monetary adjustment mechanism by monetary expansion can sustain output above Y^* but only if the rate of income of wages, prices, and money is continually accelerating.

THE GOLD STANDARD AND THE BRETTON WOODS SYSTEM
APPENDIX TO CHAPTER 43

Two episodes with fixed exchange rates were experienced in the twentieth century. Each ultimately ended in failure. The gold standard, whose origins are as old as currency itself, was used until the late 1920s and early 1930s. The Bretton Woods system, which was the only payments system ever to be designed and established by conscious action, was born out of World War II and collapsed a little less than 30 years later. Their histories are instructive, not the least because many people continue to propose returning to one or the other of these systems. In this appendix we look briefly at the gold standard and in more detail at the Bretton Woods system.

THE GOLD STANDARD

The gold standard was not *designed*. Like the price system, it just happened. It arose out of the general acceptance of gold as the commodity to be used as money. In most countries paper currency was freely convertible into gold at a fixed rate. In 1914 the U.S. dollar was convertible into 0.053 standard ounces of gold, while the British pound sterling was convertible into 0.257 standard ounces. This meant that the pound was worth 4.86 times as much as the dollar in terms of gold, thus making one pound worth U.S. $4.86. (In practice the exchange rate fluctuated within narrow limits set by the cost of shipping gold.)

As long as all countries were on the gold standard, a person in any one country could be sure of being able to make payments to a person in any other country. Someone who was unable to buy or sell claims to the foreign currencies on the foreign exchange market could always convert currency into gold and then ship the gold.

THE GOLD FLOW, PRICE LEVEL MECHANISM

The gold standard was supposed to work to maintain a balance of international payments by forcing adjustments in price levels within individual countries. Consider a country that had a balance-of-payments deficit because the value of what its citizens were importing (i.e., buying) from other countries exceeded the value of what they were exporting (i.e., selling) to other countries. The demand for foreign exchange would exceed the supply on this country's foreign exchange market. Some people who wished to make foreign payments would be unable to obtain foreign exchange. No matter; they would merely convert their domestic currency into gold and ship the gold. Therefore, some people in a surplus country would secure gold in payment for exports. They would deposit this to their credit and accept claims on gold—in terms of convertible paper money or bank deposits—in return. Thus deficit countries would be losing gold while surplus countries would be gaining it.

Under the gold standard, the whole money supply was linked to the supply of gold (see pages 623–625). The international movements of gold

would therefore lead to a fall in the money supply in the deficit country and a rise in the surplus country.[1] If full employment prevails, changes in the domestic money supply will cause changes in domestic price levels. Deficit countries would thus have falling price levels while surplus· countries would have rising price levels. The exports of deficit countries would become relatively cheaper, while those of surplus countries would become relatively more expensive. The resulting changes in quantities bought and sold would move the balance of payments toward an equilibrium position.

ACTUAL EXPERIENCE OF THE GOLD STANDARD

The half century before World War I was the heyday of the gold standard; during this relatively trouble-free period, the automatic mechanism seemed to work well. Subsequent research has suggested, however, that the gold standard succeeded during the period mainly because it was not called on to do much work. Trade flowed between nations in large and rapidly expanding volume, and it is probable that existing exchange rates and price levels were never far from the equilibrium ones. No major trading country found itself with a serious and persistent balance-of-payments deficit, so no major country was called upon to restore equilibrium through a large change in its domestic price level.

Inevitably there were short-run fluctuations, but they were ironed out either by movements of short-run capital in response to changes in interest rates or by changes in national income and employment.

Problems in the 1920s

In the 1920s the gold standard was called on to do a major job. It failed utterly, and it was abandoned. How did this come about? During World

[1] When the person who received gold deposited it in a bank, the bank would be in the position of the Bank in Table 33-3 on page 634, and a multiple expansion of deposit money would ensue.

War I, most belligerent countries had suspended convertibility of currency (i.e., they went off the gold standard). Most countries suffered major inflations, but the degree of inflation differed from country to country. As we have seen, this will lead to changes in the equilibrium exchange rates.

After the war, countries returned to the gold standard (i.e., they restored convertibility of their currencies into gold). For reasons of prestige, many insisted on returning to the prewar rates. This meant that some countries' goods were overpriced and others' underpriced. Large deficits and surpluses in the balance of payments inevitably appeared, and the adjustment mechanism required that price levels should change in each of the countries in order to restore equilibrium. Exchange rates were not adjusted, and price levels changed very slowly. By the onset of the Great Depression, equilibrium price levels had not yet been attained. The financial chaos brought on by the depression destroyed the existing payments system.

Major Disabilities of a Gold Standard

While inflationary policies combined with an overly rigid adherence to pre-World War I exchange rates led to the downfall of the gold standard, one may ask whether an altered gold standard, based on more realistic exchange rates, might not have succeeded. While some modern economists, notably Robert Mundell of Columbia University, think it would, most believe the gold standard suffered from key weaknesses.

Like any other fixed exchange rate system, it required a mechanism for orderly adjustment to changes in the supply and demand for a nation's currency. The price adjustment process worked too slowly and too imperfectly to cope with large and persistent disequilibrium.

Furthermore, gold as the basis for an international money supply suffered several special disadvantages. They included a limited supply that could not be expanded as rapidly as increases in the volume of world trade required, an uneven distribution of existing and potential new gold supplies among the nations of the world, and a large and frequently volatile speculative demand for gold during periods of crisis. These factors could cause large, disruptive variations in the supply of gold available for international monetary purposes.

THE BRETTON WOODS SYSTEM

The one lesson that everyone thought had been learned from the 1930s was that a system of either freely fluctuating exchange rates or fixed rates with easily accomplished devaluations was a sure route to disaster. In order to achieve a system of orderly exchange rates that would facilitate the free flow of trade following World War II, representatives of most of the countries that had participated in the alliance against Germany, Italy, and Japan met at Bretton Woods, New Hampshire, in 1944. The international monetary system they agreed upon was the first and so far the only international payments system consciously designed and then implemented through international governmental cooperation. In the words of Charles Kindleberger of MIT, the Bretton Woods meeting was "the biggest constitution-writing exercise ever to occur in international monetary relations."

The Bretton Woods system had three objectives: to create a set of rules that would maintain fixed exchange rates in the face of short-term fluctuations; to guarantee that changes in exchange rates would occur only in the face of long-term, persistent deficits or surpluses in the balance of payments; and to ensure that when such changes did occur they would not spark a series of competitive devaluations. The basic characteristic of the system was that U.S. dollars held by foreign monetary authorities were made directly convertible into gold at a price fixed by the U.S. government, while foreign governments fixed the prices at which their currencies were convertible into U.S. dollars. It was this characteristic that made the system a **gold exchange standard**: gold was the ultimate reserve, but other currencies were held as reserves because directly or indirectly they could be exchanged for gold.

The rate at which each country's currency was convertible into dollars was pegged. The pegged rate could be changed from time to time in the face of a "fundamental disequilibrium" in the balance of payments. A system with a rate that is pegged against short-term fluctuations but that can be adjusted from time to time is called an adjustable peg system.

In order to maintain the convertibility of their currencies at fixed exchange rates, the monetary authorities of each country had to be ready to buy and sell their currency in foreign exchange markets to offset imbalances in demand and supply at the pegged rates.[2]

In order to be able to support the exchange market by buying domestic currency, the monetary authorities had to have reserves of acceptable foreign exchange to offer in return. In the Bretton Woods system the authorities held reserves of gold and claims on key currencies—mainly the American dollar and the British pound sterling. When a country's currency was in excess supply, its authorities would sell dollars, sterling, or gold. When a country's currency was in excess demand, its authorities would buy dollars or sterling. If they then wished to increase their gold reserves, they would use the dollars to purchase gold from the Fed, thus depleting the U.S. gold stock.

The problem for the United States was to have enough gold to maintain fixed-price convertibility of the dollar into gold as demanded by foreign monetary authorities. The problem for all other countries was to maintain convertibility (on a restricted or unrestricted basis, depending on the country in question) between their currency and the U.S. dollar at a fixed rate of exchange.

Problems of the Adjustable Peg System

Three major problems of the adjustable peg system such as that adopted at Bretton Woods were discussed in the text. Here we see how they actually worked out in the period after World War II.

---

[2] The exchange rates were not quite fixed; they were permitted to vary by 1 percent on either side of their par values. Later the bands of permitted fluctuation were widened to 2.25 percent on either side of par.

Reserves to Accommodate Short-Term Fluctuations

It is generally believed that the average size and frequency of the gaps between demand and supply on the foreign exchange market created when central banks peg their exchange rates will increase as the volume of international payments increases. Since there was a strong upward trend in the volume of overall international payments, there was also a strong upward trend in the demand for foreign exchange reserves.

The ultimate reserve in the Bretton Woods system was gold. The use of gold as a reserve caused two serious problems during the 1960s and early 1970s. First, the world's supply of monetary gold did not grow fast enough to provide adequate reserves for the expanding volume of trade. As a result of the fixed price of gold, rising costs of production, and rising commercial uses, the world's stock of monetary gold during the 1960s was rising at less than 2 percent per year while trade was growing at nearly 10 percent per year. Gold, which had been 66 percent of the total monetary reserves in 1959, was only 40 percent in 1970, and had fallen to 30 percent by 1972. Over this period reserve holdings of dollars and sterling rose sharply. Clearly the gold backing needed to maintain convertibility of these currencies was becoming increasingly inadequate.

Second, the country whose currency is convertible into gold must maintain sufficient reserves to ensure convertibility. During the 1960s the United States lost substantial gold reserves to other countries that had acquired dollar claims through their balance-of-payments surpluses with the United States. By the late 1960s the reduction in U.S. reserves had been sufficiently large to undermine confidence in America's continued ability to maintain dollar convertibility.

Adjusting to Long-Term Disequilibria

The second characteristic problem of a fixed rate system is the adjustment to changing trends in trade. With fixed exchange rates, long-term disequilibria can be expected to develop because of secular shifts in the demands for and supplies of foreign exchange.

These disequilibria did slowly develop. At first they led to a series of speculative crises as people expected a realignment of exchange rates to occur. Finally they led to a series of realignments. These realignments started in 1967, and each occurred amid quite spectacular flows of speculative funds that thoroughly disorganized normal trade and payments.

Speculative Crises

The adjustable peg system often leads to situations in which speculators are presented with one-way bets. In these disequilibria situations, there is an increasing chance of an exchange rate adjustment in one direction, with little or no chance of a movement in the other direction. Speculators then have an opportunity to secure a large potential gain with no corresponding potential for loss. We shall soon see that speculative crises associated with the need to adjust to fundamental disequilibria were the downfall of the system.

COLLAPSE OF THE BRETTON WOODS SYSTEM

The Bretton Woods system worked reasonably well for nearly 20 years. Then it was beset by a series of crises of ever-increasing severity that reflected the system's underlying weaknesses.

Speculation Against the British Pound

Throughout the 1950s and 1960s, the British economy was more inflation prone than the U.S. economy, and the British balance of payments was generally in a less satisfactory state. Holders of sterling thus had reason to worry that the British government might not be able to maintain its pledge to keep sterling convertible into dollars at a fixed rate. When these fears grew strong, there would be speculative rushes to sell sterling before it was devalued. The crises in the 1960s were of this kind. By the mid 1960s it was clear to everyone that the pound was seriously overvalued. Finally,

in 1967 it was devalued in the midst of a serious speculative crisis. Many other countries with balance-of-payments deficits followed, bringing about the first major round of adjustments in the pegged rates since 1949.

Speculation Against the American Dollar

The U.S. dollar was not devalued in 1967. The lower prices of those currencies that were devalued in 1967 plus the increasing Vietnam War expenditures combined to produce a growing deficit in the American balance of payments. This deficit led to the belief that the dollar itself was becoming seriously overvalued. People rushed to buy gold because a devaluation of the U.S. dollar would take the form of raising its gold price. (Under the Bretton Woods system, the dollar was devalued by raising the official price at which the Fed would convert dollars into gold.)

The first break in the Bretton Woods system came when the major trading countries were forced to stop pegging the free-market price of gold. Speculative pressure to buy gold could not be resisted, and the market price was allowed to go free in 1968. From that point there were two prices of gold: one was the official price at which monetary authorities could settle their debts with each other by transferring gold; the other was the free-market price, determined by the forces of private demand and supply independent of any intervention by central banks. The free-market price quickly rose far above the official U.S. price of $35 an ounce. See Figure 43-3.

Once the free-market price of gold was allowed to be determined independently of the official price, speculation against the dollar shifted to those currencies that were clearly undervalued relative to the dollar.[3] The German mark and the Japanese

---

[3] When the free-market price of gold was held the same as the official price, a devaluation of the dollar entailed a rise in the free-market price—and hence profit for all holders of gold. Once the free-market price was left to be determined by the forces of private demand and supply independent of any central bank intervention, there was no reason to believe that a rise in the official price of gold would affect the (much higher) free-market price. Speculators against the dollar then had to hold other currencies whose price was sure to rise against the dollar in the event of the dollar's being devalued.

yen were particularly popular targets, and during periods of crisis billions and billions of dollars flowed into speculative holdings of these currencies. The ability of central banks to maintain pegged exchange rates in the face of such vast flights of funds was in question; on several occasions all exchange markets had to be closed for periods of up to a week.

Devaluation of the Dollar

By 1971 the American authorities had come to the conclusion that the dollar would have to be devalued. This uncovered a problem, inherent in the Bretton Woods system, that had so far gone virtually unnoted. Because the system required each foreign country to fix its exchange rate against the dollar, the American authorities could not independently fix their exchange rate against other currencies.[4]

But when the United States began to inflate rapidly, it became necessary to devalue the U.S. dollar relative to most other currencies. Any other country in this situation would merely unilaterally devalue its currency relative to the U.S. dollar. But the only way that the required U.S. devaluation could be brought about was for all other countries to agree to revalue their currencies relative to the dollar.

Prompted by continuing speculation against the dollar, President Nixon announced the suspension of the gold convertibility of the dollar in August 1971. He also made known the intention of the United States to achieve a de facto devaluation of the dollar by persuading those nations whose balance of payments were in surplus to allow their rates to float upward against the dollar.

By ending the gold convertibility of the dollar, the U.S. government brought the gold exchange standard aspect of the Bretton Woods system officially to an end. The fixed exchange rate aspect of the system lasted a little longer.

[4] If, for example, the British authorities pegged the pound sterling at $2.40, as they did in 1967, then the dollar was pegged at £0.417 and the Fed could not independently decide on another rate. Similar considerations applied to all other currencies.

The immediate response to the announced intention of devaluing the dollar was a speculative run against that currency. The crisis was so severe that for the second time that year foreign exchange markets were closed throughout Europe. When the markets re-opened after a week, several countries allowed their rates to float. The Japanese, however, announced their intention of retaining their existing rate. Despite severe Japanese controls, $4 billion in speculative funds managed to find its way into yen in the last two weeks of August, and the Japanese were forced to abandon their fixed rate policy by allowing the yen to float upward.

After some very hard bargaining, an agreement between the major trading nations was signed at the Smithsonian Institution in Washington, D.C. in December 1971. The main element of the agreement was that all countries consented to a 7.9 percent devaluation of the dollar against their currencies.

The De Facto Dollar Standard

Following the Smithsonian agreements, the world was on a de facto **dollar standard.** This arrangement still had fixed exchange rate features as long as the dollar was regarded as a safe and stable currency. Foreign monetary authorities held their reserves in the form of dollars and settled their international debts with dollars. But the dollar was not convertible into gold or anything else. The ultimate value of the dollar was given not by gold but by the American goods, services, and assets that dollars could be used to purchase.

One major problem with such a dollar system is that the kind of American inflation that upset the Bretton Woods system is no less upsetting to a dollar standard because the real purchasing power value of the world's dollar reserves is eroded by such an inflation.

The Final Breakdown of Fixed Exchange Rates

The Smithsonian agreements did not lead to a new period of international payments stability. This doomed the hope that a de facto dollar standard could provide the basis for an international payments system free of major rounds of crisis and devaluation.

The U.S. inflation continued unchecked, and the U.S. balance of payments never returned to the relatively satisfactory position that had been maintained throughout the 1960s. Within a year of the agreements, speculators began to believe that a further realignment of rates was necessary. In January 1973 heavy speculative movements of capital once again began to occur. In February the United States proposed a further 11 percent devaluation of the dollar. This was to be accomplished by raising the official price of gold to $42.22 an ounce and by not keeping other currencies tied to the dollar at the old rates. Intense speculative activity followed the announcement.

Five member countries of the European Common Market then decided to stabilize their currencies against each other but to let them float together against the dollar. This joint float was called the snake. Norway and Sweden later became associated with this arrangement. The other EEC countries (Ireland, Italy, and the United Kingdom) and Japan announced their intention to allow their currencies to float in value. In June 1972 the Bank of England abandoned the de facto dollar standard with the announcement that it had "temporarily" abandoned its commitment to support sterling at a fixed par value against the U.S. dollar. The events of 1973 led "temporarily" to become "indefinitely."

Fluctuations in exchange rates were severe. By early July the snake currencies had appreciated about 30 percent against the dollar, but by the end of the year they had nearly returned to their February values.

The dollar devaluation formally took effect in October. Most industrialized countries maintained the nominal values of their currencies in terms of gold and SDRs, thereby appreciating them in terms of the U.S. dollar by 11 percent. The devaluation quickly became redundant, for despite attempts to restore fixed rates, the drift to flexible rates had become irresistible by the end of 1973.

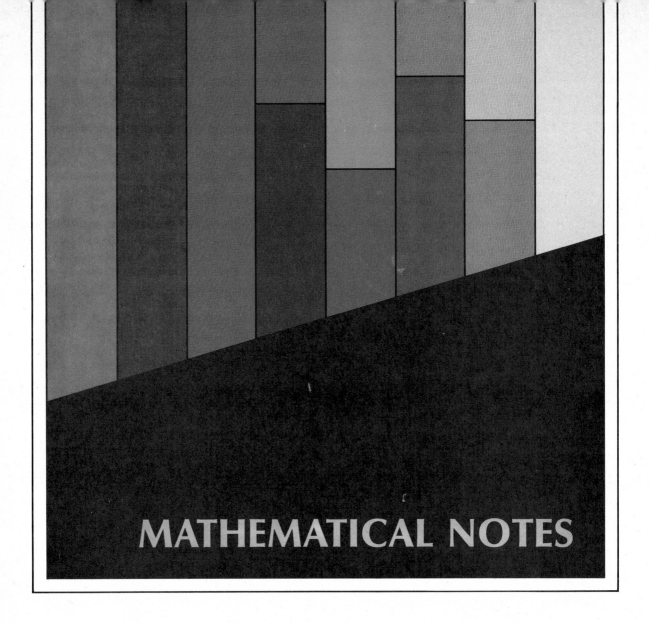

MATHEMATICAL NOTES

1. Calculating the ratio of the cost of purchasing a fixed bundle of commodities in two periods is the same thing as calculating the percentage change in each price and then averaging these by weighting each price by the proportion of total expenditure devoted to the commodity. The following expression illustrates the equivalence of these two procedures for the two-commodity case:

$$\frac{q^A p_1^A + q^B p_1^B}{q^A p_0^A + q^B p_0^B} = \frac{p_1^A}{p_0^A}\left(\frac{q^A p_0^A}{q^A p_0^A + q^B p_0^B}\right)$$
$$+ \frac{p_1^B}{p_0^B}\left(\frac{q^B p_0^B}{q^A p_0^A + q^B p_0^B}\right)$$

The qs are fixed quantity weights while the ps are prices; A and B refer to two commodities; 0 and 1 refer respectively to the base period and some subsequent time period. The expression on the left is the fixed bundle q^A and q^B valued at given year prices divided by its value in base year prices. The first term in the expression on the right gives the ratio of the price of good A in the given and the base year multiplied by the proportion of total expenditure in the base year devoted to good A. The second term does the same for good B. Simple multiplication and division reduces the right-hand expression to the left-hand one.

2. Many variables affect the quantity demanded. Using functional notation, the argument of the next several pages can be anticipated. Let Q^D represent the quantity of a commodity demanded and

$$T,\overline{Y},N,Y^*,p,p_j$$

represent, respectively, tastes, average household income, population, income distribution, its price, and the price of the jth other commodity.

The demand function is

$$Q^D = D(T,\overline{Y},N,Y^*,p,p_j), j = 1, 2, \ldots, n$$

The demand schedule or curve looks at

$$Q^D = q(p) \bigg|_{T,\overline{Y},N,Y^*,p_j}$$

where the notation means that the variables to the right of the vertical line are held constant.

This function is correctly described as the demand function with respect to price, all other variables held constant. This function, often written concisely $q = q(p)$, shifts in response to changes in other variables. Consider average income. If, as is usually hypothesized, $\frac{\partial Q^D}{\partial \overline{Y}} > 0$, then increases in average income shift $q = q(p)$ rightward and decreases in average income shift $q = q(p)$ leftward. Changes in other variables likewise shift this function in the direction implied by the relationship of that variable to the quantity demanded.

3. Quantity demanded is a simple, straightforward, but frequently misunderstood concept in everyday use, but it has a clear mathematical meaning. It refers to the dependent variable in the demand function from note 2 above:

$$Q^D = D(T,\overline{Y},N,Y^*,p,p_j)$$

It takes on a specific value, therefore, whenever a specific value is assigned to each of the independent variables. A change in Q^D occurs whenever the specific value of any independent variable is changed. Q^D could change, for example, from 10,000 tons per month to 20,000 tons per month as a result of a *ceteris paribus* change in any one price, in average income, in the distribution of income, in tastes, or in population. Also it could change as a result of the net effect of changes in all of the independent variables occurring at once. Thus a change in the price of a commodity is a sufficient reason for a change in Q^D but not a necessary reason.

Some textbooks reserve the term *change in quantity demanded* for a movement along a demand curve, that is, a change in Q^D as a result of a change in p. They then use other words for a change in Q^D caused by a change in the other variables in the demand function. This usage gives the single variable Q^D more than one name, and this is potentially confusing.

Our usage, which corresponds to that in all intermediate and advanced treatments, avoids this confusion. We call Q^D *quantity demanded* and refer *any* change in Q^D as a *change in quantity demanded*. In this usage it is correct to say that a movement along a demand curve is a change in quantity demanded. But it is incorrect to say that a change in quantity demanded can occur only because of a movement along a demand curve (since Q^D can change for other reasons, e.g., a *ceteris paribus* change in average houshold income).

4. Continuing the development of note 2, let Q^S represent the quantity of a commodity supplied and

$$G,X,p,p_j,w_i$$

represent, respectively, producers' goals, technology, price, price of the jth other commodity, and costs of the ith factor of production.

The supply function is

$$Q^S = S(G,X,p,p_j,w_i), \; j = 1, 2, \ldots , n$$
$$i = 1, 2, \ldots ,m$$

The supply schedule and supply curve looks at

$$Q^S = s(p) \Big|_{G,X,p_j,w_i}$$

This is the supply function with respect to price, all other variables held constant. This function, often written concisely $q = s(p)$, shifts in response to changes in other variables.

5. Continuing the development of notes 2 through 4, equilibrium occurs where $Q^D = Q^S$. *For specified values of all other variables*, this requires that

$$q(p) = s(p) \tag{1}$$

Equation [1] defines an equilibrium value of p; hence although p is an *independent* variable in each of the supply and demand functions, it is an *endogenous* variable in the economic model that imposes the equilibrium condition expressed in Equation [1]. Price is endogenous because it is assumed to adjust to bring about equality between quantity demanded and quantity supplied. Equilibrium quantity, also an *endogenous variable*, is determined by substituting the equilibrium price into either $q(p)$ or $s(p)$.

Graphically, Equation [1] is satisfied only at the point where demand and supply curves intersect. Thus supply and demand curves are said to determine the equilibrium values of the endogenous variables, price and quantity. A shift in any of the independent variables held constant in the q and s functions will shift the demand or supply curves and lead to different equilibrium values for price and quantity.

6. The definition in the text uses finite changes and is called *arc elasticity*. The parallel definition using derivatives is

$$\eta = \frac{dq}{dp} \times \frac{p}{q}$$

and is called *point elasticity*. Further discussion appears in the Appendix to Chapter 6.

7. The propositions in the text are proven as follows. Letting TR stand for total revenue, we can write:

$$TR = pq$$

$$\frac{dTR}{dp} = q + p\frac{dq}{dp} \tag{1}$$

But from the equation in note 6

$$q\eta = p\frac{dq}{dp} \tag{2}$$

which we can substitute in Equation [1] to obtain

$$\frac{dTR}{dp} = q + q\eta = q(1 + \eta) \tag{3}$$

Because η is a negative number, the sign of Equation [3] is negative if the absolute value of η exceeds unity (demand elastic) and positive if it is less than unity (demand inelastic).

8. The "axis-reversal" arose in the following way. Marshall theorized in terms of "demand price" and "supply price" as the prices that would lead to a given quantity being demanded or supplied. Thus he wrote

$$p^d = D(q) \tag{1}$$

$$p^s = S(q) \tag{2}$$

and the condition of equilibrium as

$$D(q) = S(q) \tag{3}$$

When graphing the behavioral relations [1] and [2], Marshall naturally put the independent variable, q, on the horizontal axis.

Leon Walras, whose formulation of the working of a competitive market has become the accepted one, focused on quantities demanded and supplied *at a given price*. That is

$$q^d = q(p) \tag{4}$$

$$q^s = s(p) \tag{5}$$

and for equilibrium

$$q(p) = s(p) \qquad [6]$$

Walras did not go in for graphic representation. Had he done so he would surely have placed p (his independent variable) on the horizontal axis.

Marshall, among his other influences on later generations of economists, was the great popularizer of graphic analysis in economics. Today we use his graphs, even for Walras' analysis. The "axis-reversal" is thus one of those accidents of history that seem odd to people who did not live through the "perfectly natural" sequence of steps that produced it.

9. The distinction made between an incremental change and a marginal change is the distinction for the function $Y = Y(X)$ between $\dfrac{\Delta Y}{\Delta X}$ and the derivative $\dfrac{dY}{dX}$. The latter is the limit of the former as ΔX approaches zero. Precisely this sort of difference underlies the distinction between arc and point elasticity, and we shall meet it repeatedly—in this chapter in reference to marginal and incremental *utility* and in later chapters with respect to such concepts as marginal and incremental *product*, *cost*, and *revenue*. Where Y is a function of more than one variable—for example, $Y = f(X, Z)$—the marginal relationship between Y and X is the partial derivative $\dfrac{\partial Y}{\partial X}$ rather than the total derivative.

10. The hypothesis of diminishing marginal utility requires that we be able to measure utility of consumption by a function $U = U(X_1, X_2, \ldots, X_n)$ where $X_1, \ldots, X_n$ are quantities of the n goods consumed by a household. It really embodies two utility hypotheses. First, $\dfrac{\partial U}{\partial X_i} > 0$, which says that for some levels of consumption the consumer can get more utility by increasing consumption of the commodity. Second, $\dfrac{\partial^2 U}{\partial X_i^2} < 0$, which says that the marginal utility of additional consumption is declining.

11. The relationship of the slope of the budget line to relative prices can be seen as follows. In the two-commodity example, a change in expenditure (ΔE) is given by the equation

$$\Delta E = \Delta C p_C + \Delta F p_F \qquad [1]$$

Along a budget line, expenditure is constant, that is, $\Delta E = 0$. Thus, along such a line,

$$\Delta C p_C + \Delta F p_F = 0 \qquad [2]$$

whence

$$-\frac{\Delta C}{\Delta F} = \frac{p_F}{p_C} \qquad [3]$$

The ratio, $\Delta C / \Delta F$, is the slope of the budget line. It is negative because, with a fixed budget, to consume more F one must consume less C. In other words, Equation [3] says that the negative of the slope of the budget line is the ratio of the absolute prices (i.e., the relative price). While prices do not show directly in Figure 10-2, they are implicit in the budget line: its slope depends solely on the relative price, while its position, given a fixed money income, depends on the absolute prices of the two goods.

12. Because the slope of the indifference curve is negative, it is the absolute value of the slope that declines as one moves downward to the right along the curve. The algebraic value of course increases. The phrase *diminishing marginal rate of substitution* thus refers to the absolute, not the algebraic, value of the slope.

13. Marginal product as defined in the text is really incremental product. A mathematician would distinguish between this notion and its limit as ΔL approaches zero. Technically, MP measures the rate at which total product is changing as one factor is varied. The marginal product is the partial derivative of the total product with respect to the variable factor. In symbols,

$$MP = \frac{\partial TP}{\partial L}$$

Economists often use the term *marginal product* interchangeably with the term *incremental product*.

14. We have referred specifically both to diminishing *marginal* product and to diminishing *average* product. In most cases, eventually diminishing marginal product implies eventually diminishing average product. This is, however, not necessary, as the following figure shows.

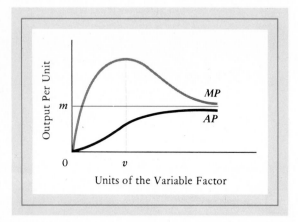

In this case, marginal product diminishes after v units of the variable factor are employed. Because marginal product falls toward, but never quite reaches, a value of m, average product rises continually toward, but never quite reaches, the same value.

15. Let q be the quantity of output and L the quantity of the variable factor. In the short run,

$$TP = q = f(L) \tag{1}$$

We now define

$$AP = \frac{q}{L} = \frac{f(L)}{L} \tag{2}$$

$$MP = \frac{dq}{dL} \tag{3}$$

We are concerned about the relation between these two. Whether average product is rising, at a maximum, or falling is determined by its derivative with respect to L.

$$\frac{d\frac{q}{L}}{dL} = \frac{L\frac{dq}{dL} - q}{L^2} \tag{4}$$

This may be rewritten:

$$\frac{1}{L}\left(\frac{dq}{dL} - \frac{q}{L} \right) = \frac{1}{L}(MP - AP) \tag{5}$$

Clearly, when MP is greater than AP, the expression in Equation [5] is positive and thus AP is rising. When MP is less than AP, AP is falling. When they are equal, AP is at a stationary value.

16. The mathematically correct definition of marginal costs is the rate of change of total cost, with respect to output, q. Thus $MC = dTC/dq$. From the definitions, $TC = TFC + TVC$. Fixed costs are not a function of output. Thus we may write $TC = K + f(q)$, where $f(q)$ is total variable costs and K is a constant. From this, we see that $MC = df(q)/dq$. MC is thus independent of the size of the fixed costs.

17. This point is easily seen if a little algebra is used:

$$AVC = \frac{TVC}{q}$$

but

$$TVC = L \times w$$

and

$$q = AP \times L$$

where L is the quantity of the variable factor used and where w is its cost per unit. Therefore

$$AVC = \frac{L \times w}{AP \times L} = \frac{w}{AP}$$

Since w is a constant, it follows that AVC and AP vary inversely with each other, and when AP is at its maximum value, AVC must be at its minimum value.

18. A little elementary calculus will prove the point:

$$MC = \frac{dTC}{dq} = \frac{dTVC}{dq}$$

$$= \frac{d(L \times w)}{dq}$$

If w does not vary with output

$$MC = \frac{dL}{dq} \times w$$

But $\dfrac{dL}{dq} = \dfrac{1}{MP}$ (see note 15, Equation [3]).

Thus, $MC = \dfrac{w}{MP}$.

Since w is fixed, MC varies inversely with MP. When MP is at its maximum, MC must be at its minimum.

19. For this note and the next two it is helpful first to define some terms. Let

$$\pi_n = TR_n - TC_n$$

where π_n is the profit when n units are sold.

If the firm is maximizing its profits by producing n units, it is necessary that the profits at output q_n are at least as large as the profits at output zero. If the firm is maximizing its profits at output n, then

$$\pi_n \geq \pi_0 \tag{1}$$

The condition says that profits from producing must be greater than profits from not producing. Condition [1] can be rewritten

$$\begin{aligned} TR_n - TVC_n - TFC_n \\ \geq TR_0 - TVC_0 - TFC_0 \end{aligned} \tag{2}$$

But note that by definition

$$TR_0 = 0 \tag{3}$$
$$TVC_0 = 0 \tag{4}$$
$$TFC_n = TFC_0 = K \tag{5}$$

where K is a constant. By substituting Equations [3], [4], and [5] into Condition [2], we get

$$TR_n - TVC_n \geq 0$$

from which we obtain

$$TR_n \geq TVC_n$$

On a per unit basis, it becomes

$$\dfrac{TR_n}{q_n} \geq \dfrac{TVC_n}{q_n} \tag{6}$$

where q_n is the number of units.

Since $TR_n = q_n p_n$, where p_n is the price when n

units are sold, Equation [6] may be rewritten

$$p_n \geq AVC_n$$

This proves rule 1.

20. Using elementary calculus, rule 2 may be proved.

$$\pi_n = TR_n - TC_n$$

each of which is a function of output q. To maximize π it is necessary that

$$\dfrac{d\pi}{dq} = 0 \tag{1}$$

and that

$$\dfrac{d^2\pi}{dq^2} < 0 \tag{2}$$

From the definitions

$$\dfrac{d\pi}{dq} = \dfrac{dTR}{dq} - \dfrac{dTC}{dq} = MR - MC \tag{3}$$

From Equations [1] and [3], a necessary condition of maximum π is $MR - MC = 0$, or $MR = MC$, as is required by rule 2.

21. Not every point where $MR = MC$ is a point of profit maximization. Continuing the equations of the previous footnote,

$$\dfrac{d^2\pi}{dq^2} = \dfrac{dMR}{dq} - \dfrac{dMC}{dq} \tag{4}$$

From Equations [2] and [4], a necessary condition of maximum π is

$$\dfrac{dMR}{dq} - \dfrac{dMC}{dq} < 0$$

which says that the slope of MC must be greater than the slope of MR. Taken with the previous result, it implies that, for q_n to maximize π, $MR_n = MC_n$ at a point where MC cuts MR from below.

22. Marginal revenue is mathematically the rate of change of total revenue with output, dTR/dq. Incremental revenue is $\Delta TR/\Delta q$. But the term *marginal revenue* is loosely used to refer to both concepts.

23. To prove that, for a downward-sloping demand curve, marginal revenue is less than price, let $p = p(q)$. Then

$$TR = p \times q = p(q) \times q$$

$$MR = \frac{dTR}{dq} = q\frac{dp}{dq} + p$$

For a downward-sloping demand curve, dp/dq is negative by definition, and thus MR is less than price for positive values of q.

24. These propositions are easily proved using calculus. Let $p = a - bq$, which is the general equation for a downward-sloping straight line ($b > 0$)

$$TR = pq = aq - bq^2$$

and

$$MR = \frac{dTR}{dq} = a - 2bq$$

25. A monopolist selling in two or more markets will set its marginal cost equal to marginal revenue in each market. Thus, the condition $MC = MR_1 = MR_2$ is a profit-maximizing condition for a monopolist selling in two markets. In general, equal marginal revenues will mean unequal prices, for the ratio of price to marginal revenue is a function of elasticity of demand: the higher the elasticity, the lower the ratio. Thus equal marginal revenues imply a higher price in the market with the less elastic demand curve.

26. This is easily proved. When average variable cost is constant, its derivative is equal to zero.

$$AVC = \frac{TVC}{q} \tag{1}$$

$$\frac{d\frac{TVC}{q}}{dq} = \frac{q\frac{dTVC}{dq} - TVC}{q^2} = 0 \tag{2}$$

Equation [2] implies that $\dfrac{dTVC}{dq} = \dfrac{TVC}{q}$ $\tag{3}$

Remembering that $MC = \dfrac{dTVC}{dq}$, Equation [3] may be written

$$MC = AVC \tag{4}$$

27. Using the expression for MR given in note 23, it can be seen that, at the kink in the demand curve, q and p are unambiguously determined. But dp/dq, the slope of the demand curve, is very different in the upward and downward directions. Thus the level of MR must be different for increases and decreases in price at the same quantity.

28. The marginal revenue produced by the factor involves two elements: first, the additional output that an extra unit of the factor makes possible and second, the change in price of the product that the extra output causes. Let Q be output, R revenue, and L the number of units of labor hired. The contribution to revenue of additional labor is $\dfrac{\partial R}{\partial L}$. This in turn depends on the contribution of the extra labor to output $\dfrac{\partial Q}{\partial L}$ (the marginal product of the factor) and $\partial R/\partial Q$, the firm's marginal revenue from the extra output. Thus

$$\frac{\partial R}{\partial L} = \frac{\partial Q}{\partial L} \cdot \frac{\partial R}{\partial Q}$$

We define the left-hand side as marginal revenue product, MRP. Thus

$$MRP = MP \cdot MR$$

29. The proposition that the marginal labor cost is above the average labor cost when the average is rising is essentially the same proposition proved in math note 15. But let us do it again, using elementary calculus. The quantity of labor depends on the wage rate: $L = f(w)$. The total labor cost is wL. The marginal cost of labor is $d(wL)/dL = w + L(dw/dL)$. This may be rewritten $MC = AC + L(dw/dL)$. As long as the supply curve slopes upward $dw/dL > 0$, therefore $MC > AC$.

30. Let t be the tax rate applied to the profits, π, of the firm. The profits after tax will be $(1 - t)\pi$. If profits are maximized at output q^*, then by definition $\pi(q^*) > \pi(q_i)$ where q_i is any other output. Now multiply each side by $(1 - t)$. Since $(1 - t)$ is positive for any tax rate less than 100 percent, the direction of the inequality does not change. Thus the after-tax profit maximizing output is also q^* for any tax rate less than 100 percent.

31. In the text, we define MPC as an increment ratio. For mathematical treatments it is more convenient to define all marginal concepts as derivatives: $MPC = dC/dY_d$, $MPS = dS/dY_d$, and so on.

32. The basic relation is

$$Y_d = C + S$$

Dividing through by Y_d yields

$$Y_d/Y_d = C/Y_d + S/Y_d$$

or $1 = APC + APS$
Next take the first-difference of the basic relation to yield

$$\Delta Y_d = \Delta C + \Delta S$$

Dividing through by ΔY_d gives

$$\Delta Y_d/\Delta Y_d = \Delta C/\Delta Y_d + \Delta S/\Delta Y_d$$

or $1 = MPC + MPS$

33. The graph shows a linear consumption function $C = a + bY_d$, where $a > 0$ and $0 < b < 1$. $MPC = dC/dY_d = b$. $APC = C/Y_d = (a + bY_d)/Y_d = a/Y_d + b$. This declines as Y_d rises, and clearly $APC \to b$ as $Y_d \to \infty$. The break-even level of income is $C = Y_d$ or $a + bY_d = Y_d$, which solves as $Y_d = a/(1 - b)$.

34. A constant APC necessarily implies the equality of APC and MPC. If $APC = C/Y = k$, a constant, then $C = kY$ and $\Delta C = k\Delta Y$. Thus, $MPC = \Delta C/\Delta Y = k$.

35. This involves using functions of functions. We have $C = C(Y_d)$ and $Y_d = f(Y)$. So by substi-

tution $C = C[f(Y)]$. In the linear expressions used in the text, $C = a + bY_d$ and $Y_d = hY$, so $C = a + bhY$.

36. The total expenditure over all rounds is the sum of an infinite series. Letting A stand for the initiating expenditure and z for the marginal propensity to spend, the change in expenditure is ΔA in the first round, $z\Delta A$ in the second, $z(z\Delta A) = z^2\Delta A$ in the third, and so on. This can be written as

$$\Delta A(1 + z + z^3 + \ldots + z^n)$$

If z is less than 1, the series in brackets converges to $1/(1 - z)$ as n approaches infinity. The change in total expenditure is thus $\Delta A/(1 - z)$. In the example in the box, $z = 0.5$; therefore the change in total expenditure is twice ΔA.

37. The accelerator may be stated as a general macroeconomic theory. Define I_n as the volume of net investment this year and ΔY as the increase in national income from last year to this year. The accelerator theory is the relationship between I_n and ΔY.

Assume that the capital-output ratio is a constant.

$$K/Y = \propto$$

or

$$K = \propto Y$$

If Y changes, K must be changed accordingly:

$$\Delta K = \propto \Delta Y$$

But the change in the capital stock (ΔK) is net investment, so

$$\Delta K = I_n = \propto \Delta Y$$

38. This is easily proven. In equilibrium, the banking system wants sufficient deposits (D) to establish the legal ratio (r) of deposits to reserves (R). This gives $R/D = r$. Any change in D of ΔD has to be accompanied by a change in R of ΔR of sufficient size to restore r. Thus $\Delta R/\Delta D = r$, so that $\Delta D = \Delta R/r$, and $\Delta D/\Delta R = 1/r$.

39. Proof: Let r be the reserve ratio. Let $z = 1 - r$ be the excess reserves per dollar of new deposit. If X dollars are deposited in the system assumed in the text, the successive rounds of new deposits will be X, zX, z^2X, z^3X. . . . The series
$$X + zX + z^2X + z^3X \cdots$$
$$= X[1 + z + z^2 + z^3 + \cdots]$$
has a limit

$$X \frac{1}{1 - z} = X \left[\frac{1}{1 - (1 - r)} \right] = \frac{X}{r}.$$

40. Suppose the public desires to hold a fraction, v, for any new deposits in cash. Now let the banking system receive an initial increase in its reserves of ΔR. It can expand deposits by an amount ΔD. As it does so, the banking system suffers a cash drain to the public of $v\Delta D$. The banking system can only increase deposits to the extent the required reserve ratio, r, makes possible. The maximum deposit expansion can be calculated from

$$r\Delta D = \Delta R - v\Delta D$$
which, collecting terms, can be written

$$(r + v) \Delta D = \Delta R$$
Hence

$$\Delta D = \Delta R/(r + v)$$

41. The argument is simply as follows:

$$M^D = F_1(T), \quad F'_1 > 0$$
$$T = F_2 (Y), \quad F'_2 > 0$$

therefore, $M^D = F_1 (F_2(Y))$
$$= H (Y), H' > 0$$

where H is the function of the function combining F_1 and F_2.

42. Let $L(Y, r)$ give the real demand for money measured in purchasing power units. Let M be the supply of money measured in nominal units and P an index of the price level so that M/P is the real supply of money. Now the equality between the demand for money and the supply of money can be expressed in real terms as

$$L(Y, r) = M/P \qquad [1]$$
or, by multiplying through by P, in nominal terms as

$$PL(Y, r) = M \qquad [2]$$
In Equation [1] a rise in P disturbs equilibrium by lowering M/P, and in Equation [2] it disturbs equilibrium by raising $PL (Y, r)$.

43. The "rule of 72" is an approximation derived from the mathematics of compound interest. Any measure X_t will have the value $X_t = X_0e^{rt}$ after t years at a continuous growth rate of r percent per year. Because $X_1/X_0 = 2$ requires $r \times t = 0.69$, a "rule of 69" would be correct for continuous growth. The "rule of 72" was developed in the context of compound interest, and if interest is compounded only once a year the product of $r \times t$ for X to double is approximately 72.

44. The time taken to break even is a function of the *difference* in growth rates, not their level. Thus, in the example, had 4 percent and 5 percent, or 5 percent and 6 percent, been used, it still would have taken the same number of years. To see this quickly, recognize that we are interested in the ratio of two growth paths: $e^{r1t}/e^{r2t} = e^{(r1 - r2)t}$.

45. The derivation of this result is as follows. Let X be your level and Y your competitor's.

$$X_0 = \frac{2}{3}Y_0 \qquad [1]$$

$$Y_{10} = Y_0e^{10r} \qquad [2]$$

$$X_{10} = X_0e^{10(r + a)} \qquad [3]$$

If $X_{10} = Y_{10}$ then

$$Y_0e^{10r} = X_0e^{10(r + a)} \qquad [4]$$

and

$$\frac{Y_0}{X_0} = \frac{3}{2} = e^{10a} \qquad [5]$$

for which $a = 0.04$.

46. Modern mathematicians distinguish between a correspondence and a function. There is a *correspondence* between Y and X if each value of X is associated with one or more values of Y. Y is a *function* of X if there is one and only one value of Y associated with each value of X. Mathematicians of an older generation described both relations as functional relations and then distinguished between single-valued functions (in modern language, functional relations) and multi-valued functions. In the text we adopt the older, more embracing usage of the term *functional relation*.

47. Since it is impermissible to divide by zero, the ratio $\Delta Y / \Delta X$ cannot be evaluated when $\Delta X = 0$. But the limit of the ratio as ΔX approaches zero can be evaluated, and it is infinity.

$$\lim_{\Delta X \to 0} \frac{\Delta Y}{\Delta X} = \infty$$

48. Strictly speaking, the marginal rate of substitution refers to the slope of the tangent to the isoquant at a particular point while the calculations in Table 13A-1 refer to the average rate of substitution between two distinct points on the isoquant. Assume a production function

$$Q = Q(K, L) \qquad [1]$$

Isoquants are given by the function

$$K = I(L, \overline{Q}) \qquad [2]$$

derived from Equation [1] by expressing K as an explicit function of L and Q. A single isoquant relates to a particular value at which Q is held constant. Define Q_K and Q_L as an alternative, more compact notation for $\partial Q/\partial K$ and $\partial Q/\partial L$, the marginal products of capital and labor. Also, let Q_{KK} and Q_{LL} stand for $\partial^2 Q/\partial L^2$ and $\partial^2 Q/\partial K^2$ respectively. To obtain the slope of the isoquant, totally differentiate Equation [1] to obtain

$$dQ = Q_K dK + Q_L dL$$

Then, since we are moving along a single isoquant, set $dQ = 0$ to obtain

$$\frac{dK}{dL} = -\frac{Q_L}{Q_K} = MRS$$

Diminishing marginal productivity implies Q_{LL}, $Q_{KK} < 0$ and hence, as we move down the isoquant of Figure 13A-1, Q_K is rising and Q_L is falling, so the absolute value of MRS is diminishing. This is called the *hypothesis of a diminishing marginal rate of substitution*.

49. Formally the problem is to maximize $Q = Q(K, L)$ subject to the budget constraint

$$p_K K + p_L L = C$$

To do this, form the Lagrangean

$$Q(K, L) - \lambda(p_K K + p_L L - C)$$

The first-order conditions for finding the saddle point on this function are

$$Q_K - \lambda p_K = 0; \quad Q_K = \lambda p_K \qquad [1]$$

$$Q_L - \lambda p_L = 0; \quad Q_L = \lambda p_L \qquad [2]$$

$$-p_K K - p_L L + C = 0 \qquad [3]$$

Dividing Equation [1] by Equation [2] yields

$$\frac{Q_K}{Q_L} = \frac{p_K}{p_L}$$

that is, the ratio of the marginal products, which is (-1) times the MRS, is equal to the ratio of the prices, which is (-1) times the slope of the isocost line.

50. The equation for the IS curve is given by

$$y = c(y - T) + I(r) + G \qquad [1]$$

where $c'(y - T) > 0$ is the marginal propensity to consume $(c'(y - T) = b)$, $I_r < 0$ is the response of investment to a change in the interest rate, and T is taxes. Substituting $T = T_0 + ty$ into Equation [1], and differentiating, we get

$$w\,dy = -b(dT_0 + y\,dt) + I_r dr + dG \qquad [2]$$

where w is equal to $[1 - b(1 - t)]$, the marginal propensity not to spend. The IS curve is drawn for $dT_0 = dt = dG = 0$. Its slope is therefore

$$\frac{dr}{dy}\bigg|_{IS} = \frac{w}{I_r} < 0 \qquad\qquad [3]$$

The horizontal shift in the IS curve due to a change in any of the exogenous variables (T_0, t, or G) can be calculated from Equation [2] by setting $dr = 0$. For example, a change in G shifts the IS curve by

$$\frac{dy}{dG}\bigg|_{dr=0} = \frac{1}{w} > 0$$

while a change in tax rates causes a shift of

$$\frac{dy}{dt}\bigg|_{dr=0} = \frac{-by}{w} < 0$$

51. The equation for the LM curve is given by

$$M = PL(y, r) \qquad\qquad [1]$$

where $L(y, r)$ represents the demand for real money balances which depends positively on income ($L_y > 0$) and negatively on the interest rate ($L_r < 0$). Differentiating Equation [1] we get

$$dM = L(y, r)DP + PL_y + PL_r dr \qquad\qquad [2]$$

The LM curve is drawn for $dM = dP = 0$. Its slope is therefore

$$\frac{dr}{dy}\bigg|_{LM} = -\frac{L_y}{L_r} > 0 \qquad\qquad [3]$$

The horizontal shift in the LM curve due to a change in the money supply can be calculated from Equation [2] by setting $dr = 0$.

$$\frac{dy}{dM}\bigg|_{dr=0} = \frac{1}{PL_y} > 0 \qquad\qquad [4]$$

52. Equation [2] from each of the two previous math notes can be combined to give two relationships between dy and dr. Solving them simultaneously we can derive the following expressions for the effects of monetary and fiscal policy on national income and interest rates. Restricting our analysis of fiscal policy to the effects of government expenditure (so $dT = dt = 0$), and holding $dP = 0$, these are as follows:

$$\frac{dy}{dM} = \frac{-I_r}{D} > 0 \qquad\qquad \frac{dr}{dM} = \frac{-w}{D} < 0$$

$$\frac{dy}{dG} = \frac{-PL_r}{D} > 0 \qquad\qquad \frac{dr}{dG} = \frac{PL_y}{D} > 0$$

where $D \equiv -(I_r PL_y + wPL_r) > 0$.

53. The aggregate demand curve can be written by solving Equations [1] from each of the math notes 50 and 51 to eliminate the interest rate, thus leaving a relationship between P and y. The relationship between *changes* in P and y can be written

$$Ddy = I_r L(y, P)dP - PL_r dG - I_r dM \qquad\qquad [1]$$

where D is as defined in note 52.

The AD curve is drawn from $dG = dM = 0$, so its slope is given by

$$\frac{dP}{dy}\bigg|_{AD} = \frac{I_r L(y, P)}{D} < 0 \qquad\qquad [2]$$

The horizontal shift in AD can be calculated from Equation [1] by setting $dP = 0$, so that the effects of monetary (dM) and fiscal (dG) policy can be written as follows:

$$\frac{dy}{dM}\bigg|_{dP=0} = \frac{-I_r}{D} > 0$$

$$\frac{dy}{dG}\bigg|_{dP=0} = \frac{-PL_r}{D} > 0$$

which, of course, are as in math note 52.

54. This is expressed in functional notation as

$$DE = f(Y - Y^*)$$

where the restrictions are (i) that $f(0) = 0$ so when $Y = Y^*$ there is no demand effect; and (ii) $f' > 0$ so that as Y rises, the demand effect rises. Together (i) and (ii) imply that $DE > 0$ when $Y > Y^*$ and $DE < 0$ when $Y < Y^*$.

Often, the further restriction is added that $f'' > 0$; that is, that the Phillips curve gets steeper as Y rises.

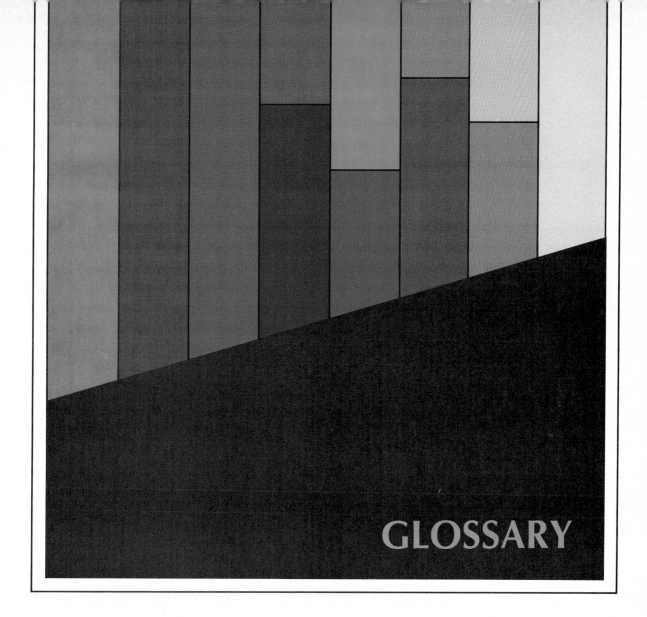

GLOSSARY

absolute advantage One nation has an absolute advantage over another nation in the production of a commodity when the same amount of resources will produce more of the commodity in the one nation than in the other.

absolute cost advantages Existing firms have absolute cost advantages when their average cost curves are significantly lower over their entire range than those of firms that are potential entrants into the industry.

absolute price A price expressed in money terms.

acceleration hypothesis When output is held above potential, the persistent inflationary gap will cause inflation to accelerate; when output is held below potential, the persistent GNP gap will cause inflation to decelerate.

accelerator The theory that relates the level of investment to the rate of change of national income.

actual GNP The gross national product that the economy in fact produces.

administered price A price set by conscious decision of the seller rather than by the impersonal forces of demand and supply.

ad valorem tax See *excise tax*.

adverse selection Self-selection, within a single risk category, of persons of above average risk.

AE In boldface, the term represents actual aggregate expenditure; in lightface, desired aggregate expenditure. See *aggregate expenditure*.

aggregated data Data for very broad totals, such as all investment expenditure in the U.S. economy. Used in contrast to disaggregated data, such as investment by General Motors.

aggregate demand (*AD*) curve A relation between the total amount of all output that will be demanded by purchasers and the price level of that output. It shows the combination of real national income and the price level that makes aggregate desired expenditure equal to national income and the demand for money equal to the supply of money.

aggregate demand shock A shift in the aggregate demand curve.

aggregate expenditure (*AE*) Total expenditure on final output of the economy; $AE = C + I + G + (X - M)$, representing the four major components of aggregate demand, appear in boldface when they are actual expenditures and in ordinary type when they are desired expenditures.

aggregate expenditure (*AE*) function The function that relates aggregate desired expenditure to national income.

aggregate supply (*AS*) curve A relation between the total amount of output that will be produced and the price level of that output.

aggregate supply shock An exogenous shift in the aggregate supply curve.

allocation of resources The distribution of the available factors of production among the various uses to which they might be put.

allocative efficiency An allocation of resources in which price equals marginal cost in all industries and which is thus Pareto-optimal; it is often treated as a goal of economic organization.

allocative inefficiency The absence of allocative efficiency. Some consumers could be made better off by producing a different bundle of goods, without any consumers being made worse off.

annuity A given sum of money paid at stated intervals for a specific period of time, or (in case of an *infinite annuity*) forever.

antitrust laws Laws designed to control monopolistic practices and monopoly power. They include the Sherman Act (1890), the Clayton Act (1914), and the Federal Trade Commission Act (1914).

appreciation A rise in the free market value of domestic currency in terms of foreign currencies.

a-priori Literally, "at a prior time" or "in advance"; knowledge that is prior to actual experience.

arc elasticity Elasticity of demand, for discrete changes in price and quantity. For analytical purposes it is usually defined by the formula

$$\eta = \frac{\Delta q/q}{\Delta p/p}$$

An alternative formula often used where computations are involved is

$$\eta = \frac{(q_2 - q_1)/(q_2 + q_1)}{(p_2 - p_1)/(p_2 + p_1)}$$

automatic transfer service (*ATS*) A savings deposit from which funds are transferred automatically to the depositor's demand deposit to cover checks as they are drawn.

autonomous expenditure In macroeconomics, elements of expenditure that do not vary systematically with other variables such as national income and the interest rate but that are determined by forces outside of the theory. Also called *exogenous expenditure*.

autonomous variables See *exogenous variables*.

average cost (*AC*) See *average total cost*.

average fixed costs (*AFC*) Total fixed costs divided by the number of units of output.

average product (*AP*) Total product divided by the number of units of the variable factor used in its production.

average propensity to consume (*APC*) The proportion of income devoted to consumption: total consumption expenditure divided by income. The income variable may be disposable income, in which case $APC = C/Y_d$, or it may be national income, in which case $APC = C/Y$.

average propensity to save (*APS*) The proportion of income devoted to saving: total saving divided by income. The income variable may be disposable income, in which case $APS = S/Y_d$, or it may be national income, in which case $APS = S/Y$.

average revenue (*AR*) Total revenue divided by quantity. Where a single price prevails, $AR = p$.

average tax rate The ratio of total tax paid to total income earned.

average total cost (*ATC*) Total cost divided by the number of units of output; the sum of average fixed costs and average variable costs. Also called *cost per unit, unit cost, average cost*.

average variable costs (*AVC*) Total variable costs divided by the number of units of output. Also called *direct unit costs, avoidable unit costs*.

balanced budget A situation in which current revenue is exactly equal to current expenditures.

balanced budget multiplier The change in income divided by the tax-financed change in government expenditure that brought it about.

balanced growth policy Simultaneous growth in all sectors of the economy; a growth experience suitable to a closed economy.

balance-of-payments accounts A summary record of a country's transactions that typically involve payments or receipts of foreign exchange.

balance-of-payments deficit A situation in which a country's receipts on current and capital account fall short of its payments (ignoring transactions by monetary authorities).

balance-of-payments surplus A situation in which a country's receipts on current and capital account exceed its payments (ignoring transactions by monetary authorities).

balance of trade The difference between the value of exports and the value of imports of visible items (goods).

balance sheet A report showing a firm's assets and the claims against those assets at a moment in time. Balance sheets always balance because the owners' equity is defined as the amount of the assets less the claims of the creditors.

bank notes Paper money issued by commerical banks.

barriers to entry Legal or other impediments to entry into an industry. Patents, franchises, economies of scale, and established brand preferences may each lead to such barriers.

barter A system in which goods and services are traded directly for other goods and services.

base control A situation in which the Fed chooses to set the quantity of open market transactions.

base year A year or other point in time chosen for comparison purposes in connection with expressing or computing *index numbers* or *constant dollars*. Also called the *base period*.

beggar-my-neighbor policies Policies designed to increase a country's prosperity (especially by reducing its unemployment) at the expense of reducing prosperity in other countries (especially by increasing their unemployment).

blacklist An employer's list of workers who have been fired for union activity.

black market A situation in which goods are sold illegally at prices above a legal maximum price.

bond An evidence of debt carrying a specified amount and schedule of interest payments as well as a date for redemption of the face value of the bond.

bondholders Creditors of the firm, whose evidence of debt is a bond issued by the firm.

boom An extended period of high economic activity around the peak of the business cycle.

boycott A concerted refusal to buy (buyers' boycott) or to sell (producers' or sellers' boycott) a commodity.

bread-and-butter unionism A union movement whose major objectives are wages, hours, and conditions of employment rather than political or social ends.

break-even level of income The level of disposable income where total consumption expenditure equals total disposable income (saving is zero).

budget balance The difference between total government revenue and total government expenditure.

budget deficit The shortfall of current revenue below current expenditure.

budget line (isocost line) A line on a diagram showing all combinations of commodities that a household may obtain if it spends a given amount of money at fixed prices of the commodities.

budget surplus The excess of current revenue over current expenditure.

budget surplus function A function relating the size of the government's budget surplus (revenue minus expenditure) to the level of national income. (Deficits are shown as negative surpluses.)

built-in stabilizer Anything that tends to adjust government revenues and expenditures automatically (i.e., without an ex-

plicit policy decision) so as to reduce inflationary and GNP gaps whenever they develop.

business cycles More or less regular patterns of fluctuations in the level of economic activity.

C In boldface, the term represents actual consumption expenditure; in lightface, desired consumption expenditure.

C + I + G − M Indicates the main components of domestic expenditure on domestically produced commodities.

capacity The level of output that corresponds to the minimum level of short-run average total costs. Also called *plant capacity*.

capital A factor of production defined to include all manmade aids to further production.

capital consumption allowance An estimate of the amount by which the capital stock is depleted through its contribution to current production. Often called *depreciation*.

capital deepening Adding capital to the production process in such a way as to increase the ratio of capital to labor and other factors of production.

capitalist One who owns capital goods.

capitalistic economy An economy in which capital is predominantly owned privately rather than by the state.

capitalized value The value of an asset measured by the present value of the income stream it is expected to produce.

capital-labor ratio A measure of the amount of capital per worker in an economy, it is positively correlated with increases in productivity.

capital-output ratio The ratio of the value of capital to the annual value of output produced by it.

capital stock The aggregate quantity of a society's capital goods.

capital widening Adding capital to the production process in such a way as to leave factor proportions unchanged.

cartel An organization of producers designed to limit or eliminate competition among its members, usually by agreeing to restrict output in an effort to achieve noncompetitive prices.

categorical grants-in-aid Federal grants to state or local governments for specified categories of expenditures such as highways or welfare payments.

ceiling price A maximum permitted price.

central authorities See *government*.

central bank A bank that acts as banker to the commercial banking system and often to the government as well. In the modern world the central bank is usually the sole money issuing authority.

certificate of deposit (CD) A negotiable time deposit carrying a higher interest rate than that paid on ordinary time deposits.

ceteris paribus Literally, "other things being equal"; usually used in economics to indicate that all variables except the ones specified are assumed not to change.

change in demand An increase or decrease in the quantity demanded at each possible price of the commodity, represented by a shift of the whole demand curve.

change in supply An increase or decrease in the quantity supplied at each possible price of the commodity, represented by a shift of the whole supply curve.

civilian labor force The total number of employed, other than persons serving in the armed forces, plus the number of unemployed.

classical unemployment See *real wage unemployment.*

cleared market A market in which buyers have been able to buy all they wish and sellers have been able to sell all they wish at the going price; a competitive market in equilibrium.

clearing house An institution where interbank indebtednesses arising from transfer of checks between banks are computed, offset against each other, and net amounts owing are calculated.

closed shop A bargaining arrangement in which only union members can be employed. Union membership precedes employment.

coefficient of determination (r^2 or R^2) The coefficient showing the fraction of the total variance of the dependent variable that can be associated with the independent variables in the regression equation; r^2 is used for two variables and R^2 for three or more variables.

collective bargaining The whole process by which unions and employers arrive at and enforce agreements.

collective consumption goods Goods or services that, if they provide benefits to anyone, necessarily provide benefits to a large group of people or a community.

collusion An agreement among sellers to set a common price and/or to share a market. Collusion may be overt or secret. It may be explicit or tacit.

command economy An economy in which the decisons of the government exert the major influence over the allocation of resources.

commercial banks Privately owned, profit-seeking institutions that provide a variety of financial services. They accept deposits from customers, which they agree to transfer when ordered by a check, and they make loans and other investments.

commercial policy Restrictions on the free flow of goods and services among nations.

commodities Marketable items produced to satisfy wants. Commodities may be either *goods*, which are tangible, or *services*, which are intangible.

common-property resource A natural resorce that is owned by no one and may be used by anyone.

common stock A form of equity capital usually carrying voting rights and a residual claim to the assets and profits of the firm.

comparative advantage (1) Country A has a comparative advantage over country B in producing a commodity, X, when it can do so at a lesser opportunity cost in terms of other products foregone. (2) As distinguished from absolute advantage: Comparing two countries, A and B, and two commodities, X and Y, country A has a comparative advantage in X when its margin of absolute advantage is greater in X than in Y.

comparative statics Comparative static equilibrium analysis; the derivation of predictions by analyzing the effect of a change in some exogenous variable or parameter on the equilibrium position.

competitive devaluations A round of devaluations of exchange rates by a number of countries, each trying to gain a competitive advantage over the other and each failing to the extent that other countries also devalue.

complement A commodity that tends to be used jointly with the original commodity. Technically, a complement to a commodity is another commodity for which the cross elasticity of demand is nonnegligible and negative.

comprehensive income taxation (CIT) A proposal to expand the tax base from the presently defined concept of taxable income, to include income from most sources and to eliminate most exemptions and deductions. CIT can be defined in many different ways, depending on what is added to taxable income.

concentration ratio The fraction of total market sales (or some other measure of market occupancy) made by a specified number of the industry's largest firms. Four-firm and eight-firm concentrations ratios are the most frequently used.

conglomerate merger See *merger.*

conscious parallel action See *tacit collusion.*

constant-cost industry An industry in which costs of the most efficient size firm remain constant as the entire industry expands or contracts in the long run.

constant dollar GNP Gross national product valued in prices prevailing in some base year; year-to-year changes in constant dollar GNP reflect changes only in quantities produced. Also called *real GNP.*

constant returns A situation in which output increases proportionately with the quantity of inputs as the scale of production is increased.

consumerism A movement that asserts a conflict between the interests of firms and the public interest.

Consumer Price Index (CPI) A measure of the average prices of commodities commonly bought by households; compiled monthly by the Bureau of Labor Statistics.

consumers' durables See *durable good.*

consumers' surplus The difference between the total value consumers place on all units consumed of a commodity and the payment they must make to purchase the same amount of the commodity.

consumption The act of using commodities to satisfy wants.

consumption expenditure In macroeconomics consumption expenditure is household expenditure on all items except housing.

consumption function In general, the term *consumption function* describes the relationship between consumption expenditure and all the factors that determine it. Often used in a more specific sense—to describe the relationship between consumption expenditure and national income.

corporation A form of business organization with a legal existence separate from that of the owners, in which ownership and financial responsibility are divided, limited, and shared among any number of individual and institutional share-holders.

cost (of output) To a producing firm, the value of factors of production used up in producing output.

cost minimization Achieving the lowest attainable cost of producing a specified output. It is an implication of profit maximization that the firm will choose the least costly method available of producing any specific output.

Cournot-Nash equilibrium An equilibrium based on the behavioral assumption that each firm makes its decisions on the assumption that the behavior of all other firms will remain unchanged.

CPI See *Consumer Price Index.*

craft union A union organized according to a specified set of skills or occupations.

credit rationing Rationing of available funds among borrowers in a situation in which there is excess demand for loans at prevailing interest rates.

cross-elasticity of demand (η_x) A measure of the extent to which quantity of a commodity demanded responds to changes in price of a related commodity. Formula:

$$\eta_x = \frac{\text{percentage change in quantity of } x}{\text{percentage change in price of } y}$$

cross-sectional data Data referring to a number of different observations at the same point in time.

crowding-out effect The offsetting reduction in private expenditure caused by the rise in interest rates that follows an expansionary fiscal policy.

current dollar GNP Gross national product valued in prices prevailing at the time of measurement; year-to-year changes in current dollar GNP reflect changes both in quantities produced and in market prices. Also called *nominal GNP.*

debt Amounts owed to one's creditors, including banks and other financial institutions.

decision lag A lapse of time between obtaining relevant information about some problem and reaching a decision on what to do about it.

decreasing returns A situation in which output increases less than in proportion to inputs as the scale of production increases. A firm in this situation, with fixed factor prices, is an *increasing cost* firm.

deficient-demand unemployment Unemployment that is due to insufficient aggregate demand and that can be reduced by measures that raise aggregate demand.

deflationary gap The amount by which the aggregate demand schedule must be increased to achieve full-employment income.

demand There are several distinct but closely related concepts: (1) *quantity demanded;* (2) the whole relationship of the quantity demanded to variables that determine it, such as tastes, household income, distribution of income, population, price of the commodity, and prices of other commodities; (3) the *demand schedule;* (4) the *demand curve.* The phrase increase

(decrease) in demand means a shift of the demand curve to the right (left), indicating an increase (decrease) in the quantity demanded at each possible price.

demand curve The graphic representation of the *demand schedule.*

demand deposit A bank deposit that is withdrawable on demand and transferable by means of a check.

demand for money The total amount of money balances that the public wishes to hold for all purposes.

demand inflation Inflation arising from excess aggregate demand; that is, when national income exceeds potential.

demand schedule The relationship between the quanity demanded of a commodity and its price, *ceteris paribus.*

deposit money Money held by the public in the form of demand deposits with commercial banks.

depreciation (1) The loss in value of an asset over a period of time; includes both physical wear and tear and obsolescence. (2) The amount by which the capital stock is depleted through its contribution to current production. (3) A fall in the free-market value of domestic currency in terms of foreign currencies.

depression A period of very low economic activity with very high unemployment and high excess capacity.

derived demand The demand for a factor of production that results from the demand for products it is used to make.

differentiated products Products sufficiently distinguishable within an industry that the producer of each has some power over its own price; the products of firms in monopolistically competitive industries.

diminishing marginal rate of substitution The hypothesis that the marginal rate of substitution changes systematically as the amounts of two commodities being consumed vary.

direct investment Foreign investment in the form of a takeover or capital investment in a branch plant or subsidiary corporation in which the investor has voting control.

dirty float Although foreign exchange rates are left to be determined on the free market, monetary authorities intervene in this market so as to influence exchange rates, but they are *not* publicly committed to holding their country's exchange rate at any announced "par value." Also called *managed float.*

disaggregated data Detailed data such as investment by General Motors or by automobile manufacturers. Used in contrast to aggregated data, such as total investment by everyone in the economy.

discount rate (1) In banking, the rate at which the central bank is prepared to lend reserves to commercial banks. (2) More generally, the rate of interest used to discount a stream of future payments to arrive at their *present value.*

discouraged workers People who would like to work but have ceased looking for a job, and hence have withdrawn from the labor force, because they believe that no suitable jobs are available.

discretionary fiscal policy Fiscal policy that is a conscious response (not according to any predetermined rule) to each particular state of the economy as it arises.

disembodied technical change Technical change that raises output without the necessity of building new capital to embody the new knowledge.

disequilibrium The absence of equilibrium. The state or condition of a market that exhibits excess demand or excess supply.

disequilibrium price A price at which quantity demanded does not equal quality supplied.

disposable income Y_d The income that households have available for spending and saving.

dividends That part of profits paid out to shareholders of a corporation.

division of labor The breaking up of a task (e.g., making pins) into a number of repetitive operations, each one done by a different worker.

dollar standard (for international payments) International indebtedness between monetary authorities is settled in terms of dollars, which are not necessarily backed by gold or any other ultimate monetary base.

double counting Counting something more than once. For example, adding up the total outputs of all the sectors in the economy so that the value of intermediate goods is counted in the sector that produces them and also when they are purchased as an input by another sector.

draft Compulsory recruitment for military service.

dumping In international trade, the practice of selling a commodity at a lower price in the export market than in the domestic market.

duopoly An industry that contains only two firms.

durable good A good that yields its services only gradually over an extended period of time; often divided into the subcategories *producers' durables* (e.g., machines and equipment) and *consumers' durables* (e.g., cars, appliances).

dynamic (or **disequilibrium**) **differential** A difference in factor prices caused by disequilibrium that will tend to lead to corrective movements of resources. In equilibrium these differentials will be eliminated. Observed because it often takes considerable time for equilibrium to be reached.

economic efficiency (in production) A method of producing some quantity of output is economically efficient when it is the least costly method of producing that output.

economic growth Increases in potential GNP measured in constant dollars.

economic profits or losses (often simply **profits**) The difference in the revenues received from the sale of output and the opportunity cost of the inputs used to make the output. Negative profits are losses.

economic rent That part of the payment to a factor in excess of its *transfer earnings*.

economies of scope Economies achieved by a large firm that is large enough to engage efficiently in multiproduct production, large-scale distribution, advertising, etc.

economy A set of interrelated production and consumption activities.

effluent charge A fee, fine, or tax on a producer for polluting activity, usually on a per unit basis.

elastic demand The situation existing when for a given percentage change in price there is a greater percentage change in quantity demanded; elasticity greater than 1.

elasticity of demand (η) A measure of the responsiveness of quantity of a commodity demanded to a change in market price. Formula:

$$\eta = \frac{\text{percentage change in quantity demanded}}{\text{percentage change in price}}$$

Conventionally expressed as a positive number, it is a pure number ranging from zero to infinity.

elasticity of supply A measure of the responsiveness of the quantity of a commodity supplied to a change in the market price. Formula:

$$\eta_s = \frac{\text{percentage change in quantity supplied}}{\text{percentage change in price}}$$

embodied technical change A technical change that can be utilized only when new capital, embodying the new techniques, is built.

employment The number of workers 16 years of age and older who hold full-time civilian jobs.

endogenous expenditure See *induced expenditure*.

endogenous variables Variables explained within a theory. Also called *induced variables*.

envelope curve Any curve that encloses, by just being tangent to, a series of other curves. In particular, the *envelope cost curve* is the *LRAC* curve; it encloses the *SRAC* curves by being tangent to them but not cutting them.

equilibrium condition A condition that must be fulfilled if some market or sector of the economy is to be in equilibrium.

equilibrium differentials Differences in factor prices that would persist in equilibrium, without any tendency for them to be removed. These differences may be associated with differences in the factors themselves or with the nonmonetary advantages of different employments.

equilibrium inflation The rate of inflation that arises when there is no shock inflation, when output is held at potential so there is no demand inflation, and when there is monetary accommodation of expectational inflation.

equilibrium price The price at which quantity demanded equals quantity supplied.

equity capital Capital provided by the owners of a firm.

error term An expressed or implied variable in a functional relationship to allow (1) omitted variables and (2) errors in measurement.

excess capacity (1) Production at levels below the output at which *ATC* is a minimum. (2) The difference between such actual output and capacity output.

excess capacity theorem The proposition that equilibrium in a monopolistically competitive industry will occur where each firm has excess capacity.

excess demand A situation in which, at the given price,

quantity demanded exceeds quantity supplied. Also called *shortage*.

excess reserves Reserves held by a commercial bank in excess of the legally required minimum.

excess supply A situation in which, at the given price, quantity supplied exceeds quantity demanded. Also called *surplus*.

exchange rate The price in terms of one currency at which another currency, or claims on it, can be bought and sold.

excise tax A tax on the sale of a particular commodity. A *specific tax* is a fixed tax per unit of the taxed commodity. An *ad valorem tax* is a fixed percentage of the value of the commodity.

exemption draft A draft in which specified criteria such as age, occupation, or family status determine who is drafted from among the pool of those who meet the basic requirements (of health, etc.) for military service.

exogenous expenditure See *autonomous expenditure*.

exogenous variables Variables that influence other variables within a theory but that are themselves determined by factors outside the theory. Also called *autonomous variables*.

expectational inflation Inflation that occurs because decision makers raise prices (so as to keep their relative prices constant) in the expectation that the price level is going to rise.

expectations augmented Phillips curve The relationship between output and inflation that arises when the demand and expectations components are combined.

externalities (also called **third-party effects**) Effects, either good or bad, on parties not directly involved in the production or use of a commodity.

factor markets Markets in which households sell the services of the factors of production that they control.

factor mobility The ease with which factors can be transferred between uses.

factors of production Resources used to produce goods and services to satisfy wants. Land, labor, and capital are three frequently used basic categories of factors of production.

falling-cost industry An industry in which the lowest costs attainable by a firm fall as the whole scale of the industry expands.

federation In respect to labor unions, a federation is any loose organization of national unions.

fiat money Paper money or coinage that is neither backed by nor convertible into anything else yet is legal tender.

final output Output not sold to other firms for use as a component used in producing their output.

final products The economy's output of goods and services after all double counting has been eliminated.

fine tuning The attempt to maintain national income closely at its full-employment level by means of frequent changes in fiscal or monetary policy.

firm The unit that makes decisions regarding the employment of factors of production and the production of goods and services.

fiscal drag The tendency for a GNP gap to open up because tax revenues rise faster than government expenditure as full-employment income rises due to economic growth.

fiscal policy The deliberate use of the government's revenue-raising and spending activities in an effort to influence the behavior of such macro variables as the GNP and total employment.

fixed costs Costs that do not change with output. Also sometimes called *overhead cost*.

fixed factors Factors that cannot be increased in the short run.

fixed investment Investment in plant and equipment.

flexible or **floating exchange rate** An exchange rate that is left free to be determined by the forces of demand and supply on the free market with no intervention by the monetary authorities.

floor price A minimum permitted price.

foreign exchange (foreign media of exchange) Actual foreign currency or various claims on it such as bank balances or promises to pay.

45° line In macroeconomics the locus of all points where total desired expenditure equals national income. The line that graphs the equilibrium condition that desired expenditure should equal national income, $AE = Y$.

fractional reserve system In contrast to a 100 percent reserve system, a banking system in which commercial banks are required to keep only a fraction of their deposits in cash or on deposit with the central bank.

freedom of entry and exit The absence of legal or other artificial barriers to entering into production or withdrawing assets from production.

free good A commodity for which the quantity supplied exceeds the quantity demanded at a price of zero. Free goods do not command positive prices in a free-market system.

free-market economy An economy in which the decisions of individual households and firms (as distinct from the government) exert the major influence over the allocation of resources.

free trade A situation in which all commodities can be freely imported and exported without special taxes or restrictions being levied merely because of their status as "imports" or "exports."

frictional unemployment Unemployment caused by the time taken for labor to move from one job to another.

fringe benefits Payments (other than wages) for the benefit of labor. They may include company contributions to pension and welfare funds, sick leave, paid holidays.

full-cost pricing Pricing according to average total cost plus a fixed markup. Usually the costs are standard costs as defined by good accounting practice.

full-employment GNP (Y*) See *potential GNP*.

full-employment national income (Y*) See *potential GNP*.

function Loosely, an expression of a relation between two or more variables. Precisely, Y is a function of the variables X_1, . . . , X_n if for every set of values of the variables X_1, . . . , X_n there is associated a unique value of the variable Y.

functional distribution of income The distribution of income by major factors of production.

G In boldface, the term represents actual government expenditure; in lightface, desired government expenditure.

gains from trade The increased consumption that results from specialization and trade as opposed to a situation of self-sufficiency. It can be applied to persons, regions, or nations.

Giffen good An inferior good for which the negative income effect outweighs the substitution effect and leads to an upward-sloping demand curve.

given year A year or other point in time for which an *index number* measures a change in some variable that has occurred since some earlier point in time *(base period)*. Also called the *given period*.

GNP deflator See *implicit GNP deflator*.

GNP gap Output that could have been produced if the economy were fully employed but that instead goes unproduced; *potential GNP* minus *actual GNP*.

gold exchange standard A monetary system in which some countries' currencies are directly convertible into gold while other countries' currencies are indirectly convertible by being convertible into the gold-backed currencies at a fixed rate. Under the Bretton Woods system only the U.S. dollar was directly convertible into gold.

goods Tangible commodities such as cars or shoes.

government All public officials, agencies, and other organizations belonging to or under the control of state, local, or federal government. Also called *central authorities*.

government expenditure Includes all government expenditure on currently produced goods and services, and does not include government transfer payments.

Gresham's law The theory that "bad," or debased, money drives "good," or undebased, money out of circulation because people will keep the good money and spend the bad money.

gross investment The total value of all investment goods produced in the economy during a stated period of time.

gross national income The sum of all the claims on income generated in the process of producing total output (equal to GNP).

gross national product (GNP) The sum of all values-added in the economy. It is the sum of the values of all final goods produced and, which is the same thing, the sum of all factor incomes earned.

gross return to capital The receipts from the sale of goods produced by a firm less the cost of purchased goods and materials, labor, land, the manager's talents, and taxes.

high-employment surplus (HES) An estimate of government tax revenues less government expenditures as they would be at full-employment national income.

homogeneous product (1) identical products; (2) a product similar enough across an industry that no one firm has any

power over price; (3) the product of a firm in perfect competition.

horizontal merger See *merger*.

household All the people who live under one roof and who make, or are subject to others making for them, joint financial decisions.

human capital The capitalized value of productive investments in persons. Usually refers to investments resulting from expenditures on education, training, and health improvements.

hypothesis of equal net advantage The hypothesis that owners of factors will choose the use of their factors that produces the greatest net advantage to themselves and therefore will move their factors among uses until net advantages are equalized.

hypothesis of diminishing returns The hypothesis that if increasing quantities of a variable factor are applied to a given quantity of fixed factors, the marginal product and average product of the variable factor will eventually decrease. Also called *hypothesis of diminishing returns*, *law of diminishing returns*, *law of variable proportions*.

I In boldface, actual investment expenditure; in lightface, desired investment expenditure.

implicit GNP deflator An index number derived by dividing GNP measured in current dollars by GNP measured in constant dollars and multiplying by 100. It is in effect a price index with current-year quantity weights measuring the average change in price of all the items in the GNP. Also called the *gross national product deflator*.

import quota An amount imposed by a country that limits the quantity of a commodity that may be shipped into the country in a given period.

import substitution industry (ISI) Domestic production for sale in the home market of goods previously imported; usually involves some form of protection or subsidy.

imputed costs The costs of using in production factors already owned by the firm, measured by the earnings they could have received in their best alternative employment.

income-consumption curve A curve showing the relationship for a commodity between quantity demanded and income, *ceteris paribus*.

income-consumption line A line connecting the points of tangency of a set of indifference curves with a series of parallel budget lines, showing how consumption of a good changes as income changes, with relative prices held constant.

income effect The effect on quantity demanded of a change in real income.

income elasticity of demand A measure of the responsiveness of quantity demanded to a change in income. Formula:
$$\eta_Y = \frac{\text{percentage change in quantity demanded}}{\text{percentage change in income}}$$

income statement A financial report showing the revenues and costs that arise from the firm's use of inputs to produce outputs over a specified period of time.

incomes policy Any attempt by the government to influence wage and price formation. The instruments vary from voluntary guidelines at one extreme to legally enforced wage and price controls at the other.

increasing returns A situation in which output increases more than in proportion to inputs as the scale of a firm's production increases. A firm in this situation, with fixed factor prices, is a *decreasing cost* firm.

incremental cost See *marginal cost.*

incremental product See *marginal product.*

incremental revenue See *marginal revenue.*

indexing The automatic increasing of money values as the average level of all prices rises during an inflation.

index numbers Averages that measure changes over time of variables such as the price level and industrial production. They are conventionally expressed as percentages relative to a base period assigned the value 100.

indifference curve A curve showing all combinations of two commodities that give the household equal amounts of satisfaction and among which the household is thus indifferent.

indifference map A set of indifference curves, each indicating a constant level of satisfaction derived by the household concerned and based on a given set of household preferences.

induced expenditure In macroeconomics, elements of expenditure that are explained by variables within the theory, such as national income and interest rates. Also called *endogenous expenditure.*

industrial union A union organized to include all workers in an industry, regardless of skills.

industry A group of firms producing similar products.

inelastic demand The situation in which for a given percentage change in price there is a smaller percentage change in quantity demanded; elasticity less than unity.

infant industry argument for tariffs The argument that new domestic industries with potential economies of scale need to be protected from competition from established low-cost foreign producers so that they can grow large enough to achieve costs as low as those of foreign producers.

inferior goods Goods for which income elasticity is negative.

inflation A rise in the average level of all prices. Sometimes restricted to only prolonged or sustained rises.

inflationary gap The extent to which aggregate desired expenditure exceeds national income at full-employment national income.

infrastructure The basic installations and facilities (expecially transportation and communications systems) on which the growth of a community depends.

injections Income earned by domestic firms that does not arise out of the spending of domestic households and income earned by domestic households that does not arise out of the spending of domestic firms.

innovation The introduction of inventions into methods of production.

inputs Materials and factor services used in the process of production; the services of factors of production plus intermediate products.

interest (i) In microeconomics, the payment for borrowed money; (ii) in macroeconomics, the total income paid for the use of borrowed captial.

interest rate The price paid per dollar borrowed per year. Expressed either as a fraction (e.g., 0.06) or as a percentage (e.g., 6 percent).

intermediate products All goods and services that are used as inputs into a further stage of production.

intermediate targets Variables that the government cannot control directly and does not seek to control ultimately, yet that have an important role in policy.

internalization A process that results in a producer's taking account of a previously external effect.

invention The discovery of something new, such as a new production technique or a new product.

inventories Stocks of raw materials, or of finished goods, held by firms to mitigate the effect of short-term fluctuations in production or sales.

investment expenditure Expenditures on the production of goods not for present consumption.

investment goods Capital goods such as plant and equipment plus inventories; production that is not sold for consumption purposes.

invisibles All those items of foreign trade that are intangible; services as opposed to goods.

isocost line The graphic representation of alternative combinations of factors that a firm can buy for a given outlay.

isoquant A curve showing all technologically efficient factor combinations for producing a specified output; an iso-product curve.

isoquant map A series of isoquants from the same production function, each isoquant relating to a specific level of output.

jurisdictional dispute Dispute between unions over which has the right to organize a group of workers.

k percent rule The proposal that the money supply should be increased at a constant percentage rate year in and year out, irrespective of conditions in the economy.

kinked demand curve A demand curve with a corner, or "kink," at the prevailing price. The curve is more elastic in response to price increases than to price decreases.

labor A factor of production usually defined to include all physical and mental contributions to economic activity provided by people.

labor boycott An organized boycott to persuade customers to refrain from purchasing the products of firm or industry whose employees are on strike.

labor force See *civilian labor force.*

labor union See *union.*

Laffer curve A graph relating the revenue yield of a tax system to the marginal or average tax rate imposed.

laissez faire Literally "let do"; a policy implying the absence of government intervention in a market economy.

land A factor of production usually defined to include all gifts of nature, including raw materials as well as "land" conventionally defined.

law of demand The assertion that demand curves slope downward, indicating an inverse relationship between market price and quantity demanded.

law of diminishing returns See *hypothesis of diminishing returns*.

law of variable proportions See *hypothesis of diminishing returns*.

legal tender Anything that by law must be accepted for the purchase of goods and services or in discharge of a debt, and thus money.

less-developed countries (LDCs) The underdeveloped countries of the world, most of which are in Asia, Africa, and South and Central America. They are also called *undeveloped*, *developing*, and the *South*.

life-cycle hypothesis (LCH) The hypothesis that relates the household's actual consumption to its expected lifetime income rather than, as in early Keynesian theory, to its current income.

lifetime income See *permanent income*.

limited liability The limitation of the financial responsibility of an owner (shareholder) of a corporation to the amount of money he or she has actually made available to the firm by purchasing its shares.

limited partnership Partnership with limited liability for partners not participating in management.

limit price The minimum price at which a new firm can enter a market without incurring a loss; equal to its minimum average cost. Existing lower-cost firms may be able to discourage new entrants by setting the price below this limit.

liquidity The degree of ease and certainty with which an asset can be turned into a given amount of the economy's medium of exchange.

liquidity preference (LP) function The function that relates the demand for money to the rate of interest.

lockout The employer's equivalent of a strike, in which he temporarily closes his plant.

logarithmic scale A scale in which equal proportional changes are shown as equal distances. Thus 1 inch may always represent doubling of a variable, whether from 3 to 6 or 50 to 100. Contrasted with *natural scale*. (Also called *log scale* or *ratio scale*.)

long run The period of time long enough for all inputs to be varied but in which the basic technology of production is unchanged.

long-run aggregate supply curve (LRAS) Total supply that is forthcoming when all wages and prices have adjusted; a vertical line at $Y = Y^*$.

long-run average cost curve (LRAC) The curve relating the least-cost method of producing any output to the level of output. Sometimes called *long-run average total cost (LRATC)*.

long-run industry supply (LRS) curve The curve showing the relation of the quantity supplied to prices with quantities of all factors freely variable, and allowing time for firms to achieve long-run equilibrium.

Lorenz curve A graph showing the extent of departure from equality of income distribution.

lottery draft A draft in which chance selects from an eligible pool those who will be drafted.

lower turning point The bottom point of the business cycle where a contraction turns into an expansion of economic activity.

Lucas aggregate supply curve A curve expressing the hypothesis that GNP varies positively with the ratio of the actual to the expected price level.

M In boldface, the term represents actual imports; in lightface, desired imports.

M1 Currency plus demand deposits plus NOW, ATS, and similar accounts at credit unions and mutual savings banks.

M2 M1 plus savings and smaller time deposits (including money market fund shares).

M3 M2 plus large denominate certificates of deposit (CDs).

macroeconomics The study of the determination of economic aggregates, such as total output, total employment, and the price level.

managed float See *dirty float*.

marginal cost (MC) The increase in total cost resulting from raising the rate of production by 1 unit; mathematically, the rate of change of cost with respect to output. Also called *incremental cost*.

marginal efficiency of capital (MEC) The marginal rate of return on a nation's capital stock. It is the rate of return on one additional dollar of net investment, i.e., an addition of $1 to capital stock.

marginal efficiency of capital schedule A schedule relating *MEC* to the size of the capital stock.

marginal efficiency of investment (MEI) The function that relates the quantity of investment to the rate of interest.

marginal physical product (MPP) See *marginal product*.

marginal product (MP) The increase in quantity of total output that results from using one unit more of a variable factor; mathematically, the rate of change of output with respect to the quantity of the variable factor. Also called *incremental product* or *marginal physical product (MPP)*.

marginal productivity theory of distribution The implication from profit maximization that the use of a factor should be expanded until its marginal revenue product equals its price.

marginal propensity to consume (MPC) The change in consumption divided by the change in income that brought it about; mathematically, the rate of change of consumption with respect to income. The income variable may be disposable income, in which case $MPC = \Delta C / \Delta Y_d$, or it may be national income, in which case $MPC = \Delta C / \Delta Y$.

marginal propensity not to spend The fraction of any increment to national income that is not passed on through new spending, $1 - (\Delta AE/\Delta Y)$.

marginal propensity to save (MPS) The change in saving divided by the change in income that brought it about; mathematically, the rate of change of saving with respect to income. The income variable may either be disposable income, in which case $MPS = \Delta S/\Delta Y_d$, or it may be national income, in which case $MPS = \Delta S/\Delta Y$.

marginal propensity to spend The fraction of any increment to national income that is passed on in terms of new spending by all spending units, $\Delta AE/\Delta Y$.

marginal rate of substitution (MRS) (1) In consumption, the slope of an indifference curve, showing how much more of one commodity must be provided to compensate for the giving up of one unit of another commodity if the level of satisfaction is to be held constant. (2) In production, the slope of an isoquant, showing how much more of one factor of production must be used to compensate for the use of one less unit or another factor of production if production is to be held constant.

marginal revenue (MR) The change in a firm's total revenue arising from the sale of one unit more; mathematically, the rate of change of revenue with respect to output. Also called *incremental revenue*.

marginal revenue product (MRP) The addition of revenue attributable to the last unit of a variable factor. $MRP = MPP \times MR$; mathematically, the rate of change of revenue with respect to quantity of the variable factor.

marginal tax rate The fraction of an additional dollar of income that is paid in taxes.

marginal utility The additional satisfaction obtained by a buyer from consuming one unit more of a good; mathematically, the rate of change of utility with respect to consumption.

margin requirement The fraction of the price of a stock that must be paid in cash, while putting up the stock as security against a loan for the balance.

market A concept with many possible definitions. (1) An area over which buyers and sellers negotiate the exchange of a well-defined commodity. (2) From the point of view of a household, the firms from which it can buy a well-defined product. (3) From the point of view of a firm, the buyers to whom it can sell a well-defined product.

market-clearing prices Prices at which quantity demanded equals quantity supplied so that there are neither unsatisfied buyers nor unsatisfied sellers. The equilibrium price in a perfectly competitive market.

market economy A society in which people specialize in productive activities and meet most of their material wants through exchanges voluntarily agreed upon.

market failure Failure of the unregulated market system to achieve socially optimal results. Its sources include externalities, market impediments and imperfections.

market rate of interest The actual interest rate in effect at a given moment.

market sector That portion of an economy in which commodities are bought and sold and producers must cover their costs from the proceeds of their sales.

market structure Characteristics of market organization likely to affect behavior and performance of firms, such as the number and size of sellers, the extent of knowledge about each other's actions, the degree of freedom of entry, and the degree of product differentiation.

markup The amount added to cost to determine price.

medium of exchange Anything that is generally acceptable in return for goods and services sold.

merger The purchase of either the physical assets or the controlling share ownership of one company by another. In a *horizontal* merger both companies produce the same product; in a *vertical* merger one company is a supplier of the other; if the two are in unrelated industries, it is a *conglomerate* merger.

microeconomic policy Activities of governments designed to alter resource allocation and/or income distribution.

microeconomics The study of the allocation of resources and the distribution of income as they are affected by the workings of the price system and by some government policies.

minimum efficient scale (MES) The smallest size of firm required to achieve the economies of scale in production and/or distribution. Also called *minimum optimal scale (MOS)*.

mixed economy An economy in which some decisions are made by firms and households and some by the government.

monetarists A group of economists who stress monetary causes of cyclical fluctuations and inflations, who believe that an active stabilization policy is not normally required, and who stress the relative efficacy of monetary over fiscal policy.

monetary base The sum of currency in circulation plus reserves of the commercial banks.

monetary equilibrium A situation in which the demand for money equals the supply of money.

monetary policy An attempt to influence the economy by operating on such monetary variables as the quantity of money and the rate of interest.

money Any generally accepted medium of exchange.

money capital The funds used to finance a firm. Money capital includes both equity capital and debt.

money income A household or firm's income in the form of some monetary unit.

money market mutual funds Liquid financial instruments that earn high yields but are subject to minimum transaction restrictions.

money rate of interest A rate of interest expressed in current dollars.

money substitute Something other than money, such as a credit card or a charge account, that permits the holder to purchase goods and services whether or not he or she possesses legal tender at the time.

money supply The total quantity of money existing at a point in time.

monopolistic competition (1) A market structure of an industry in which there are many sellers and freedom of entry but in which each firm has a product somewhat differentiated from the others, giving it some control over its price. (2) More recently, an industry in which more than one firm sells differentiated products.

monopoly A market structure in which the output of an industry is controlled by a single seller or a group of sellers making joint decisions.

monopsony A market situation in which there is a single buyer or a group of buyers making joint decisions. Monopsony and monopsony power are the equivalent on the buying side of monopoly and monopoly power on the selling side.

moral hazard A situation in which market institutions designed to spread risk induce behavior that increases the aggregate risk. Insurance provides many examples.

multiple regression analysis See *regression analysis*.

multiplier The ratio of the change in national income to the change in autonomous expenditure that brought it about.

Nash equilibrium See *Cournot-Nash equilibrium*.

national debt The current volume of outstanding federal government debt.

national income accounting The set of rules and techniques for measuring the total flows of outputs produced and inputs used by the economy.

natural monopoly An industry characterized by economies of scale sufficiently large that one firm can most efficiently supply the entire market demand.

natural rate of unemployment The rate of unemployment (due to frictional and structural causes) consistent with full-employment national income, Y^*. In the Phelps-Friedman theory this is the rate of unemployment at which there is neither upward nor downward pressure on the price level.

natural scale A scale in which equal absolute amounts are represented by equal distances.

near money Liquid assets easily convertible into money without risk of significant loss of value. They can be used as short-term stores of purchasing power but are not themselves media of exchange.

negative income tax (NIT) A tax system in which households with incomes below taxable levels receive payments from the government based on a percentage of the amount by which their income is below the minimum taxable level.

negotiable order of withdrawal (NOW) A checklike device for paying funds in one person's time deposit to another person.

neo-Keynesians Sometimes called *Keynesians*; a group of economists who stress changes in both aggregate expenditure and the money supply as causes of cyclical fluctuations and inflations, who believe that an active government stabilization policy is called for, and who stress the relative efficacy of fiscal policy over monetary policy.

net exports Total exports *minus* total imports $(X - M)$.

net investment Gross investment *minus* replacement investment.

net national product (NNP) Gross national product *minus* a capital consumption allowance.

net private benefit (NPB) The difference between private benefits and private costs.

net social benefit (NSB) The difference between social benefits and social costs. Where private production produces externalities, it is net private benefit *plus* external benefits and *minus* external costs.

neutrality of money The doctrine that the money supply affects only the absolute level of prices and has no effect on relative prices and hence no effect on the allocation of resources or the distribution of income.

nominal GNP See *current dollar GNP*.

nonmarket sector That portion of an economy in which commodities are given away and producers must cover their costs from some source other than the proceeds of sales.

nonprice competition Competition by sellers for sales by means other than price cutting. Advertising, product differentiation, trading stamps, and other promotional devices are examples.

nontariff barriers to trade Restrictions, other than tariffs, that may reduce the flow of international trade.

normal capacity output The level of output that a firm hopes to maintain on average over the business cycle. Typically, somewhat less than full capacity output.

normal goods Goods for which income elasticity is positive.

normal profits A term used by some economists for the imputed returns to capital and risk taking just necessary to keep the owners in the industry. They are included in what the economist, but not the businessman, sees as *total costs*.

normative statement A statement about what ought to be.

NOW See *negotiable order of withdrawal*.

Note See *treasury bill*.

oligopoly A market structure in which a small number of rival firms dominate the industry. The leading firms are aware that they are interdependent.

open market operations The purchase and sale on the open market by the central bank of securities (usually short-term government securities).

open shop A bargaining arrangement whereby a union represents its members but does not have exclusive jurisdiction. Membership in the union is not a condition of getting or keeping a job.

opportunity cost The cost of using resources for a certain purpose, measured by the benefit or revenues given up by not using them in their best alternative use.

organization theory In economics, a set of hypotheses in which the decisions of an organization are a function of its size and form of organization.

outputs The quantities of goods and services produced.

paradox of value The apparent contradiction in the observed fact that some absolute necessities of life are cheap in price while some relatively unimportant luxuries are very expensive.

Pareto-efficiency See *Pareto-optimality*.

Pareto-optimality An allocation of resources in which it is impossible by reallocation to make some consumers better off without simultaneously making others worse off. Also called *Pareto-efficiency*.

partnership A form of business organization with two or more joint owners, each of whom is personally responsible for all of the firm's actions and debts.

paternalism Protection of individuals against themselves.

pegged exchange rate See *fixed exchange rate*.

per capita GNP GNP divided by total populaton. Also called *GNP per person*.

perfect competition A market form in which all firms are price takers and in which there is freedom of entry into and exit from the industry.

permanent income The maximum amount that a household can consume per year into the indefinite future without reducing its wealth. (A number of similar but not identical definitions are in common use.)

permanent-income hypothesis (PIH) The hypothesis that relates actual consumption to permanent income rather than (as in the original Keynesian theory) to current income.

personal income Income earned by individuals before allowance for personal income taxes paid or payable.

petro dollars Money earned by the oil-exporting countries and held by them in short-term, liquid investments.

Phillips curve Originally a relation between the percentage of the labor force unemployed and the rate of change of money wages. It can also be expressed as a relation between the percentage of the labor force employed and the rate of price inflation, or between actual national income as a proportion of potential national income and the rate of price inflation.

picket lines Striking workers parading at the entrances to a plant or firm on strike. A picket line is a symbolic blockade of the entrance.

point elasticity Elasticity calculated at a point, i.e., over an interval where changes in the variables approach zero. The formula for point elasticity of demand is

$$\eta = \frac{dq}{dp} \times \frac{p}{q}$$

The minus sign is often dropped.

point of diminishing average productivity The level of output at which average product reaches a maximum.

point of diminishing marginal productivity The level of output at which marginal product reaches a maximum.

policy instruments The variables that the government can control directly to achieve their policy objectives.

policy variables The variables that the government ultimately seeks to control; the variables in whose behavior it is ultimately interested.

political business cycle Cyclical swings in the economy generated by fiscal and monetary policy for the purpose of winning elections.

portfolio investment Foreign investment in bonds or a minority holding of shares that does not involve legal control. Contrasted with *direct investment*.

positive statement A statement about what is, was, or will be, as opposed to a statement about what ought to be.

potential GNP (Y*) The gross national product the economy could produce if its productive resources were fully employed at their normal intensity of use. Also called *full-employment GNP* or *full-employment national income*.

poverty gap (or **income gap**) The number of dollars required to raise everyone whose income is below the poverty level to that level.

poverty level A measure of the minimum amount of annual income required to avoid poverty.

precautionary balances Money balances held for protection against the uncertainty of the timing of cash flows.

preferred stock A form of equity capital with a preference over common stock to receipt of dividends up to a stated maximum amount; may be voting or nonvoting.

present value (*PV*) The value *now* of a sum payable at a later date or of a stream of income receivable at future dates. *PV* is the discounted value of future payments.

price-consumption line A line connecting the points of tangency between a set of indifference curves and a set of budget lines where one absolute price is fixed and the other varies, money income being held constant.

price discrimination The sale by a single firm of different units of a specific commodity to buyers at two or more different prices for reasons not associated with differences in cost. It may be systematic or unsystematic.

price floor A minimum permitted price.

price index A number that shows the average percentage change that has occurred in some group of prices over some period of time.

price leader A firm that sets a price for its product, and other firms follow it in establishing that price. Price leadership may be of many different kinds, ranging from "barometric" to collusive. The price leader is often, but not always, the dominant firm in an industry.

price level The average level of a group of prices. Changes in the price level are measured by changes in a price index.

price parity The ratio of prices farmers receive for products they sell to the prices they pay for products they buy, compared with some base period; a basic concept in U.S. farm policy.

price taker A firm that acts as if it could alter its rate of production and sales without affecting the market price of its product.

price theory The theory of how prices are determined; competitive price theory concerns the determination of prices in competitive markets by the interaction of demand and supply.

principle of substitution The proposition that the proportions in which various inputs are used will vary as the relative prices of these inputs vary.

private cost The value of the best alternative use of resources used in production as valued by the producer.

private sector That portion of an economy in which principal decisions are made by private units such as households and firms.

producers' cooperative (producers' co-op) An organization of producers of a commodity usually formed to serve as a joint selling organization for the producers and often operated as a cartel.

producers' durables See *durable good*.

producers' surplus The difference between the total amount producers receive for all units sold of a commodity and the aggregate minimum required to produce each successive unit. It is the excess of revenue from sale of the output over total variable costs of producing it. In perfect competition it is shown graphically by the area between the price line and the supply curve.

product differentiation The existence of similar but not identical products sold by a single industry such as the breakfast food and the automobile industries.

production The act of making commodities.

production function A functional relation showing the maximum output that can be produced by each and every combination of inputs.

production possibility boundary A curve on a graph that shows which alternative combinations of commodities can just be obtained if all available productive resources are used. It is the boundary between attainable and unobtainable output combinations.

productive efficiency Production of any output at the lowest attainable cost of producing that output.

productivity Output produced per unit of input; frequently used to refer to *labor productivity,* measured by output per hour worked.

productivity of capital (efficiency of capital) The increase in production resulting from the use of capital, after allowance for the maintenance and replacement of the capital.

product markets Markets in which firms sell their outputs of goods and services.

profit (1) In ordinary usage, the difference between the value of outputs and the value of inputs. (2) In microeconomics, the difference between revenues received from the sale of goods and the value of inputs, which includes the opportunity cost of capital, so that profits are *economic profits*. (3) In macroeconomics, profits exclude interest on borrowed capital but do not exclude the return to owner's capital. Profits in macroeconomics are the sum of the microeconomic concepts of economic profits and the opportunity cost of owner's capital.

progressive tax A tax that takes a larger percentage of income the higher the level of income.

progressivity of taxation The ratio of taxes to income as income increases. If the ratio decreases, the tax is *regressive;* if it remains constant, *proportional;* if it increases, *progressive*.

proportional tax A tax that takes a constant percentage of income at all levels of income and is thus neither progressive nor regressive.

protectionism The partial or complete protection of domestic industries from foreign competition in domestic markets by use of tariffs or such nontariff barriers to trade as import quotas.

proxy A document authorizing the holder to vote one's stock in a corporation.

proxy fight A struggle between competing factions in a corporation to obtain the proxies for a majority of the outstanding shares.

public sector That portion of an economy where production is under control of the central authorities or bodies appointed by them, including all production by governments and nationalized industries.

public utility regulation Regulation of prices and services of industries that have been deemed to be natural monopolies.

purchasing power of money The amount of goods and services that can be purchased with a unit of money. Decreases in the purchasing power of money are measured by increases in a price index.

purchasing power parity (PPP) exchange rate The exchange rate between two currencies that adjusts for relative inflation rates by holding relative prices constant when measured in either country's currency.

pure rate of interest The rate of interest that would rule in equilibrium in a riskless economy where all lending and borrowing is for investment in productive capital.

pure return on capital The amount capital can earn in a riskless investment; hence the transfer earnings of capital in a riskless investment.

quantity actually bought The amount of a commodity that households succeed in purchasing in some time period.

quantity actually sold The amount of a commodity that producers succeed in selling in some time period.

quantity demanded The amount of a commodity that households wish to purchase in some time period. An increase (decrease) in quantity demanded refers to a movement down (up) the demand curve in response to a fall (rise) in price.

quantity exchanged The identical amount of a commodity that households actually purchase and producers actually sell in some time period.

quantity supplied The amount of a commodity producers wish to sell in some time period. An increase (decrease) in quantity supplied refers to a movement up (down) the supply curve in response to a rise (fall) in price.

random sample A sample chosen from a group or population in such a way that every member of the group has an equal chance of being selected.

rate base The total allowable investment to which the rate of return allowed by a regulatory commission is applied.

rate of return The ratio of profits earned by a firm to total investment capital.

rate of return on capital (Sometimes used synonymously with *rate of return*.) Frequently used to refer to a specific capital good; the annual net income produced by a capital good, expressed as a percentage of the price of the good.

rational expectations The theory that people learn quickly from their mistakes, that while random errors may be made, systematic and persistent errors are not made.

ratio scale See **logarithmic scale.**

real capital (or **physical capital**) Physical assets, including plant, equipment, and inventories.

real GNP See *constant dollar GNP.*

real income A household's income expressed in terms of the command over commodities that the money income confers; money income corrected for changes in price levels, thus the purchasing power of money income.

real product wage The nominal cost of labor to the employer—including the pre-tax nominal wage rate, benefits, and payroll taxes—divided by the output price.

real rate of interest A rate of interest expressed in constant dollars. It is the money rate of interest corrected for the change in the purchasing power of money.

real wage unemployment Unemployment caused by too high a real product wage.

recession In general, a downswing in the level of economic activity. The Department of Commerce defines a recession as occurring when real GNP falls for two successive quarters.

regression analysis (sometimes called *correlation analysis*) A quantitative analysis of the systematic interrelationships between two or more variables. *Simple regression* concerns the relation between Y and a single independent variable, X_1; *multiple regression* concerns the relation between Y and more than one independent variable, $X_1, \ldots, X_n$.

regression equation The equation describing the statistically determined best fit between variables in regression analysis.

regressive tax A tax that takes a larger percentage of income at lower levels of income.

relative price The ratio of the price of one good to the price of another good; a ratio of two absolute prices.

replacement investment Investment to replace capital equipment that has depreciated.

required reserves In banking, the minimum amount of reserves a bank must, by law, keep either in currency or in deposits with the central bank.

reserve currencies A currency (such as the U.S. dollar) commonly held by foreign central banks as international reserves.

reserve ratio In banking, the fraction of deposits of the public that a bank holds in reserves.

resource allocation The allocation of an economy's scarce resources among alternative uses.

return to capital The total amount available for payments to owners of capital; the sum of pure returns to capital, risk premiums, and economic profits.

revenue sharing A noncategorical grant-in-aid, in which some of the revenue collected by the federal government is returned to state and local governments for unrestricted expenditure.

right-to-work laws State laws that give an individual the right to work in an organized plant without belonging to the union that is the collective bargaining agent of the workers. These laws prohibit closed or union shops.

rising-cost industry An industry in which the minimum cost attainable by a firm rises as the scale of the industry expands.

rising supply price A rising long-run supply curve, caused by increases in factor prices as output is increased, or by diseconomies of scale.

risk premium The return to capital necessary to compensate owners of capital for the risk of loss of their capital.

sample A small number of items, chosen from a larger group or population, that is intended to be representative of the larger entity.

satisficing A hypothesized objective of firms, in contrast to maximizing behavior, whereby firms set target levels of satisfactory performance (e.g., profits) rather than seek to maximize some objective (e.g., profits).

saving All disposable income that is not consumed.

scarce good A commodity for which the quantity demanded would exceed the quantity supplied at a price of zero.

scatter diagram A graph of statistical observations of paired values of two variables, one measured on the horizontal and the other on the vertical axis. Each point on the coordinate grid represents the values of the variables for a particular unit of observation.

search unemployment Unemployment caused by people continuing to search for a good job rather than accepting the first job they come across when unemployed.

sectors Parts of an economy.

securities market See *stock market.*

selective credit controls Controls on credit imposed through such means as margin requirements, installment buying, and minimum down payments on mortgages.

sellers' preferences Allocation of scarce commodities by decisions of those who sell them.

services Intangible commodities such as haircuts or medical care.

short run The period of time over which the quantity of some inputs cannot, as a practical matter, be varied.

short-run aggregate supply (*SRAS*) curve A relation between the price level of final output and the quantity of output supplied on the assumption that all input prices (including wage rates) are held constant.

short-run equilibrium Generally, equilibrium subject to fixed factors; for a competitive firm, the output at which market price equals marginal cost; for a competitive industry, the price and output at which industry demand equals short-run industry supply and all firms are in short-run equilibrium. Either profits or losses are possible.

short-run supply curve The curve showing the relation of quantity supplied to prices, with one or more fixed factors; the horizontal sum of marginal cost curves (above the level of average variable costs) of all firms in an industry.

single proprietorship A firm consisting of one owner, where the single owner is solely responsible for the firm's actions and debts.

size distribution of income The distribution of income by size class, without regard to source of income.

slope The ratio of the vertical change to the corresponding horizontal change as one moves to the right.

Snake An agreement among 9 of the 10 countries of the European Economic Community (EEC) to fix exchange rates among their own currencies and then let their joint rate float against the dollar. (Britain is the one EEC country not in the snake.)

social benefit The contribution an activity makes to the society's welfare.

social cost (social opportunity cost) The value of the best alternative use of resources available to society, as valued by society.

special drawing rights (SDRs) Established in 1968, the Special Drawing Account of the International Monetary Fund provides additional international reserves for member countries. Subject to certain repayment provisions, members are able to treat SDRs in the same way as their own holdings of international currencies for financing balance-of-payments or deficits.

specialization of labor An organization of production in which individual workers specialize in the production of particular goods or services (and satisfy their wants by trading) rather than produce for themselves everything they consume (and thus be self-sufficient).

specific tax. See *excise tax*.

speculative balances Money balances held as a hedge against the uncertainty of the prices of other financial assets.

stabilization policy Any policy designed to reduce the economy's cyclical fluctuations. Attempts by the government to remove inflationary and deflationary gaps when they appear.

stagflation The coexistence of high rates of unemployment with high, and sometimes rising, rates of inflation.

stockholders The owners of a corporation.

stock market (securities market) An organized market where stocks and bonds are bought and sold.

strike The concerted refusal of the members of a union to work.

strikebreakers Nonunion workers brought in by management to operate the plant while a union is on strike. (Derisively called *scabs* by union members.)

structural rigidity theory The theory that downward inflexibility of money prices means that the adjustment of *relative* prices necessary in any changing economy will cause a rise in the average level of all prices (i.e., an inflation).

structural unemployment Unemployment due to a mismatching between characteristics required by available jobs and characteristics possessed by the unemployed labor.

substitute A commodity that satisfies similar needs or desires as the original commodity; technically, a substitute for a commodity is another commodity for which the cross elasticity of demand is nonnegligible and positive.

substitution effect The change in quantity of a good demanded resulting from a change in its relative price, eliminating the effect on real income of the change in price.

supply There are several distinct but closely related concepts: (1) *quantity supplied;* (2) the whole relationship of the quantity supplied to variables that determine it, such as producers' goals, technology, price of the commodity, prices of other commodities, and prices of factors of production; (3) the *supply schedule;* (4) the *supply curve.* The phrase increase (decrease) in supply means a shift of the supply curve to the right (left), indicating an increase (decrease) in the quantity supplied at each possible price.

supply curve The graphic representation of the *supply schedule*.

supply of effort The total number of hours of work that the population is willing to supply; also called the *total supply of labor*.

supply of money See *money supply*.

supply schedule The relationship between the quantity supplied of a commodity and its price, *ceteris paribus*.

surplus function See *budget surplus function*.

tacit collusion See also *collusion*. The adoption, without explicit agreement, of a common policy by sellers in an industry. Sometimes also called *conscious parallel action*.

takeover bid See *tender offer*.

tariff A tax applied on imports.

tax base The aggregate amount of taxable income.

tax-related income policies (TIPs) Tax incentives for labor and management to encourage them to conform to wage and price guidelines.

tax expenditures The name the Treasury Department gives to exemptions and deductions from taxable income and to tax credits, which amount to subsidies or preferences to tax payers.

tax incidence The location of the ultimate burden of a tax; the identity of the ultimate bearer or bearers of the tax.

technological efficiency (sometimes called *technical efficiency*) A method of production is technologically efficient if the same output cannot be produced with fewer real resources.

tender offer (takeover bid) An offer to buy directly some or all of the outstanding common stock of a corporation from its stockholders at a specified price per share, in an attempt to gain control of the corporation.

term See *term to maturity*.

terms of trade The relation between the average price of a country's exports and the average price of its imports.

term to maturity The period of time from the present to the redemption date of a bond. Often simply the *term* of the bond.

third-party effects See *externalities*.

time deposit An interest-earning bank deposit, legally subject to notice before withdrawal (in practice the notice requirement is not normally enforced) and not transferable by check.

time series A series of observations on the values of a variable at different points in time.

time-series data Data on variables where measurements are made for successive periods (or moments) of time. Contrasted with *cross-sectional data*.

total cost (TC) Fixed costs plus variable costs at a given level of output; the sum of the opportunity costs of the factors used to produce that output.

total product (TP) The total amount produced during some period of time by all the factors of production employed over that time period.

total revenue (TR) The total receipts from the sale of a product; price times quantity.

total utility The total satisfaction resulting from the consumption of a given commodity by a buyer in a period of time.

trade union See *union*.

transactions costs Costs that must be incurred in effecting market transactions (such as negotiation costs, billing costs, and bad debts).

transactions balances Money balances held to finance purchases when purchases and sales are not perfectly synchronized.

transfer earnings That part of the payment to a factor in its present use that is just enough to keep it from transferring to another use.

transfer payment A payment to a private person or institution that does not arise out of current productive activity; typically made by governments, as in welfare payments, but also made by businesses and private individuals in the form of charitable contributions.

transmission mechanism The channels by which a change in the demand or supply of money leads to a shift of the *AD* curve.

treasury bill The characteristic form of short-term government debt. A bill is a promise to pay a certain sum of money at some time in the early future (often one, three, or six months). It carries no interest payment; the lender earns interest because the price at which he or she buys the bill is less than its future redemption value.

trigger prices In U.S. trade policy, prices for imported commodities set by the U.S. government on the basis of average total cost of the low-cost producing nation. A foreign country that sells below a trigger price is subject to proceedings under antidumping laws.

turnover tax An excise tax levied on commodities, commonly used in Socialist countries.

unbalanced growth Different sectors of the economy grow at different rates, which usually implies a changing role of international trade.

undistributed profits Earnings of a firm not distributed as dividends but retained by the firm.

unemployment The number of persons who are not employed and are actively searching for a job.

unemployment rate Unemployment expressed as a percentage of the labor force.

union An association of workers authorized to represent them in bargaining with employers. Also called *trade union* or *labor union*.

union shop A bargaining arrangement in which the employer may hire anyone, but every employee must join the union within a specified period of time (often 60 days).

unit costs Costs per unit of output, equal to total cost divided by total output. Also called *average cost*.

upper turning point The top point of the business cycle where an expansion turns into a contraction of economic activity.

utility The satisfaction that results from the consumption of a commodity.

value added The value of a firm's output *minus* the value of the inputs that it purchases from other firms.

variable A magnitude (such as the price of wheat) that can take on a specific value but whose value will vary among times and places.

variable costs Costs whose total varies directly with changes in output. Also called *direct costs*.

variable factors Factors whose quantity used in production can be varied in the short run.

vertical merger See *merger*.

very long run The period in which even the technological possibilities open to a firm are subject to change.

visibles All those items of foreign trade that are tangible; goods as opposed to services.

wage and price controls Direct government intervention into wage and price formation with legal power to enforce the government's decisions on wages and prices.

wage cost-push inflation Inflation caused by increases in labor costs that are not themselves associated with excess aggregate demand.

wealth A household's wealth is the value of the sum of all the valuable assets it owns minus its liabilities.

windfall profit A change in profits that arises out of an unanticipated change in market conditions such as a sudden increse in demand. Negative windfall profits are sometimes called *windfall losses*.

withdrawals Income earned by households and not passed on to firms in return for goods and services purchased, and income earned by firms and not passed on to households in return for factor services purchased.

X In boldface, the term represents actual exports; in lightface, desired exports.

X − M In boldface, the term represents actual net exports (which is the difference between total exports and total imports); in lightface, the term represents desired net exports.

X-inefficiency When resources are used less productively than is possible so that society is at a point *inside* its production possibility boundary.

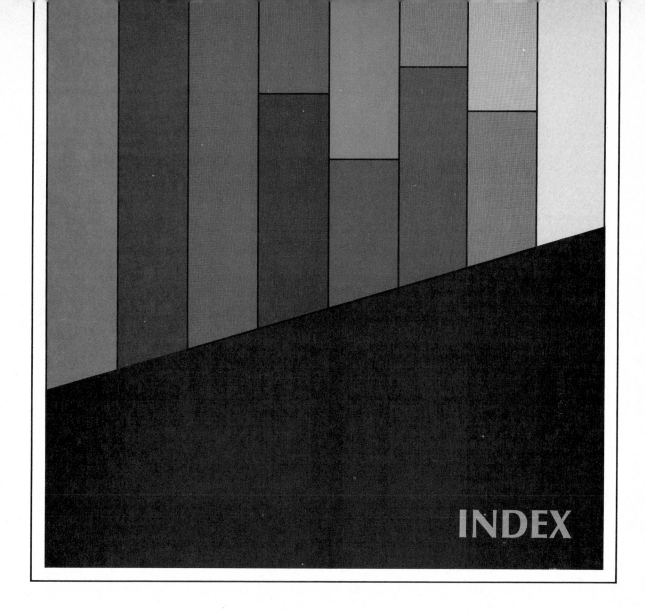

INDEX

COMMON ABBREVIATIONS USED IN TEXT

Greek Letters

Δ	(delta)	change in
Σ	(sigma)	sum of
η	(eta)	elasticity
π	(pi)	profit

Abbreviations

AD	Aggregate Demand
AS	Aggregate Supply
AE	Aggregate Expenditure
ATC	Average Total Cost
AVC	Average Variable Cost
C	Consumption
CPI	Consumer Price Index
D	Demand
E	Equilibrium
Fed	Federal Reserve Board
G	Government Expenditure
GNP	Gross National Product
I	Investment Expenditure
i	rate of interest
LR	Long-run
LRAS	Long-run aggregate supply
M	Imports *or* Money Supply
M1, M2, etc.	Measures of Money Supply
MC	Marginal Cost
MEC	Marginal Efficiency of Capital
MP	Marginal Product
MR	Marginal Revenue
MRP	Marginal Revenue Product
OPEC	Organization of Petroleum Exporting Countries
p	price
P	Price Level
q	Quantity
r	rate of interest, rate of return
S	Supply *or* Saving
SR	Short-run
SRAS	Short-run aggregate supply
T	Tax revenue
TC	Total Cost
TR	Total Revenue
X	Exports
X-M	Net Exports
Y	National Income (generally)
Y^*	Potential Employment National Income
Y_d	Disposable Income